The Outdoor Life
DEER
HUNTER'S
ENCYCLOPEDIA

The Outdoor Life
DEER HUNTER'S ENCYCLOPEDIA

JOHN MADSON
GEORGE H. HAAS
CHUCK ADAMS
DWIGHT SCHUH
LEONARD LEE RUE III

Published by Outdoor Life Books *New York*

Published by

Outdoor Life Books
Times Mirror Magazines, Inc.
380 Madison Avenue
New York, NY 10017

Distributed to the trade by

Stackpole Books
Cameron and Kelker Streets
P.O. Box 1831
Harrisburg, PA 17105

Produced by Soderstrom Publishing Group Inc.
Page designs by Jeff Fitschen

Library of Congress Cataloging-in-Publication Data
Main entry under title:

The Outdoor Life deer hunter's encyclopedia.

Bibliography: p.
Includes index.
1. Deer hunting.   2. Deer.   I. Madson, John.
II. Title: Deer hunter's encyclopedia.
SK301.093   1985   798.2′77357   85-18776
ISBN 0–943822–53–X

Manufactured in the United States of America

TO THE DEER HUNTER

CONTENTS

PART 4

BOWHUNTING TACKLE AND TECHNIQUES **283**

PART 5

HUNTING GEAR **375**

EDITOR'S PREFACE

It was his first deer season at the family's lake cabin. He was 15. In the early light of the first morning, he was told to walk the wooded lakeshore in hopes of driving deer to his dad and other members of the gang.

With a borrowed .30/30, the boy crunched over the thin cover of snow and entered a stand of poplar and balsam that opened into a small clearing. Large deer tracks everywhere! He knelt to touch them. Suddenly, the earth shook with with a heavy, rhythmic pounding. Not 30 feet away, a huge buck with stunted antlers trotted broadside toward the balsams and disappeared. Then came a new pounding sound—that of the boy's heart.

A quicker lad would have shot in time or at least have shouted, "Here he comes, Dad!" But quick or not, anyone in those circumstances could have become the victim of buck fever.

This encyclopedia. If the boy had studied this book before that early morning encounter, he would have been better prepared. In fact, he'd have taken author Chuck Adams's advice and done some preseason scouting. Instead of happening upon large tracks the first morning, he'd have posted himself on stand overlooking those tracks and calmly—maybe not so calmly—waited for the maker of those tracks. Also he'd have heeded author George Haas's advice on practicing with his borrowed rifle before season. And those stunted antlers on the huge body wouldn't have seemed shocking if he'd have known, as author John Madson explains, about the factors that determine antler development. In short, if he'd studied this book, he may well have gotten that buck or at least been deserving of him.

But this book provides much more than advice on getting deer. It covers the whole range of hunting-related topics, including ethics, comfort, field care, first aid, more.

As you can appreciate from the biographies on the next page, this book was written by extraordinary outdoorsmen. John Madson blames the Skunk River in Iowa for forever corrupting him with its hunting and fishing. Somewhere out of that experience John acquired a taste for deer liver, even if it is infested with unsightly liver flukes (harmless to man). Such liver, John advises, should be prepared for frying away from the light of a campfire.

When we were photographing proper rifle-shooting positions, George Haas's son Karl, with "Marine Corps" haircut, served as model. The father's excellent training was evident. No matter the position or sling option, George needed only to announce it, and his son took it up like a firing-range instructor.

Chuck Adams is a hard hunter. Elite in his zeal among hunters, he moved to a new state solely to qualify for its more-generous seasons. To photograph the field-dressing sequence in this book, he waited for a forecast of an overcast day (ideal light for photography). He then set out early and shot a buck behind the ear to ensure that no blood would obscure your view of the deer's body cavity.

Dwight Schuh, too, spends a lot of time hunting. He lamented a bit when the demands of this book made him cancel a long-planned hunting trip. When he advises you on the hazards of following a wounded deer into heavy cover with grizzly tracks all around, you know he's been there.

Lennie Rue has what is likely the world's largest one-man collection of black-and-white wildlife photos. Hundreds appear in this book. In fact, his black-and-whites are so widely distributed that some of the state game agencies complying with our requests for deer photos sent us prints with "Photo by Leonard Lee Rue III" stamped on the back. This man loves his work. He can hardly wait to get up in the morning.

The artists. Most of the deer drawings are by Dr. Charles W. Schwartz, a biologist whose illustrations grace Aldo Leopold's classic *A Sand County Almanac.* Ray Pioch did most of the firearms and gun mechanism drawings. Over the decades, Ray's the artist that magazines such as *Popular Science* have sent to study new engines and power plants prior to illustrating the internal workings. Lloyd Birmingham drew most of the rest, demonstrating a versatility with subjects ranging from people to animals to hardware that is rare among illustrators.

Thanks. There's not space enough to list all the people and agencies that helped our authors. Those providing photos are credited in captions. For help in securing previously published photos, thanks go to Clare Conley, editor of *Outdoor Life;* Craig Boddington, editor of *Petersen's Hunting;* and Dick McCabe, publications director of the Wildlife Management Institute. For help with illustrations beyond the call, thanks go to Dick Dietz of Remington Arms, Dr. Christine Janis of Brown University, and biologist-illustrator Dr. Tony Bubenik. Thanks too to Outdoor Life Books president Jeramy Lanigan and club director Leonard Malleck for planting the seed for this encyclopedia and to John Sill, editor and publisher, for nurturing it.

Neil Soderstrom
Editor and Producer

THE AUTHORS

John Madson

John Madson is best known for his natural history and conservation writing, typically laced with humor. He launches the *Encyclopedia* with parts 1 and 2, "The Deer Family" and "Deer Management." With a degree in wildlife biology, John first wrote for the Iowa Conservation Commission and then worked as a newspaper outdoors writer. He then served for over 20 years as principal writer and assistant director of Winchester-Western's Conservation Department. John has written for the major outdoors magazines as well as *Audubon, Smithsonian,* and *National Geographic.* His books include *Up on the River* (the Upper Mississippi), *Where the Sky Began* (the tallgrass prairie), and *Out Home* (a collection).

George Haas

George H. Haas is a senior editor of *Outdoor Life.* His Part 3, "Firearms and Shooting," covers the gamut from firearms development to today's options in arms, ammo, accessories, and techniques. George started hunting at age nine. His writing and editing began with comic-book western adventure and soon moved into business and management. He was an editor of economics and business for the Textbook Division of McGraw-Hill before joining *Outdoor Life* in 1964. His freelance articles have appeared in *The American Rifleman, National Wildlife,* and *International Wildlife.* As an editor, George most enjoys discovering and guiding talented young writers.

Chuck Adams

Chuck Adams is a widely published and highly prolific hunting writer-photographer, as well as a design consultant to manufacturers of hunting gear. He wrote the vast middle of this book, covering bowhunting tackle, general hunting gear, hunting methods, and procedures after a deer is down. His how-to photos rank among the best in the business. A crack marksman with gun and bow, Chuck has won numerous regional shooting competitions. He has also starred in big-game-hunting videos and is a regular contributor to more than two dozen outdoors magazines. His many books include *The Complete Book of Bowhunting, Bowhunter's Digest,* and *The Complete Guide to Bowhunting Deer.*

Dwight Schuh

Dwight Schuh, a well-known outdoors photojournalist, here provides the *Encyclopedia* parts "Trophy Hunting"; "Safety, Survival, and First Aid"; and "United States and Canadian Deer Surveys." Dwight began reading outdoors magazines as soon as he'd learned to read and decided in high school to become an outdoor writer. He took a B.A. degree in English and journalism, and feels he's earned his M.A. degree in deer hunting. He takes his own photos and does his own photoprocessing. Dwight hunts all types of big game mostly near his home base in the U.S. Northwest. His books include *Modern Outdoor Survival, Bowhunting for Mule Deer,* and *Bugling for Elk.*

Leonard Lee Rue

Leonard Lee Rue III is one of the world's most widely published wildlife photographers. In Part 11, "Deer Watching and Photography," Lennie tells how to get close to deer and capture them on film. His photos have appeared in all leading wildlife and outdoors magazines—over 1,000 photos on covers. He is a columnist for *The American Hunter, Deer and Deer Hunting,* and *Outdoor Photographer.* His nearly two dozen books include *Deer of North America, Complete Guide to Game Animals,* and *How I Photograph Wildlife and Nature.* Lennie is a highly active lecturer. He has also designed photo gear (blinds, vests, camera stocks) for sale by mail from his home in Blairstown, New Jersey.

PART 1
THE DEER FAMILY

BY JOHN MADSON
Drawings by Charles W. Schwartz

Deer are different things to different people.

To the taxonomist—a biologist who classifies living things and gives them scientific names in Latin and Greek—a deer is a ruminating mammal of the great order Artiodactyla and family Cervidae, with cloven hoofs and the bony, annually shed antlers found on most males and even on females of some species. The taxonomist includes moose; caribou; elk; and whitetail, blacktail, and mule deer as members of the North American deer family.

A hunter who's short on taxonomy but long on woods savvy may take the scientist's word that elk, moose, and caribou are deer, but probably has a gut feeling that the only *real* deer are the whitetails, muleys, and blacktails. These are the Big Three—North America's most common large wild animals and the most cherished big game. The deer are also the most bewildering and contradictory American wildlife. They may be incredibly wary or incredibly dumb; they are gentle and timid but capable of violence; they are symbols of the wild but may be pests in suburban gardens. At least one species of the Big Three ranges freely and abundantly in every state; yet, most people have never seen a wild deer and never will. No wild mammals in North America have been studied further and deeper than the whitetails, mule deer, and blacktails—yet parts of their lives are as secret as ever.

The great deer family Cervidae was originally found on every continent except Australia, and in almost every kind of habitat: swamps, open brush country, forest, desert, and tundra. Family members ranged from 40 degrees south latitude to above the Arctic Circle and from sea-level rain forests to alpine slope far above timberline. The family apparently originated in Asia, where fossil remains of deer date from the Lower Oligocene period (30-odd million years ago). In Europe, deer remains go back to the Upper Oligocene (about 26 million years ago). In the Western Hemisphere, deer first appeared during the Lower Miocene period, about 23 million years ago.

As a family, deer are now essentially animals of the world's temperate forests, although a few species are found in the tropics and deserts and others, such as caribou, have gone far into the northern tundras.

From an evolutionary point of view, the deer family is a conservative group not much given to a lot of tinkering and experimentation.

Erwin A. Bauer photo

THE DEER FAMILY TREE

*The common ancestor of all even-toed hoofed mammals was the little **Archaeomeryx**, extinct since the Eocene Epoch. By the end of the Eocene, at least 35 million years ago, the family line of deer had begun to branch. One line led to the goats, sheep, wild cattle, and antelope. Another line became the giraffes and okapis. A third line, which appeared at the beginning of the Oligocene Epoch over 30 million years ago, branched into the pronghorn, the true deer (Cervids), and musk deer, shown lower left. In the long haul of evolution, many spectacular deerlike animals vanished. One was the Sinclairomeryx, extinct for at least 13 million years. The most recent was a large fallow deer that vanished 10,000 years ago—the "Irish elk" with its awesome 9-foot spread of antlers.*

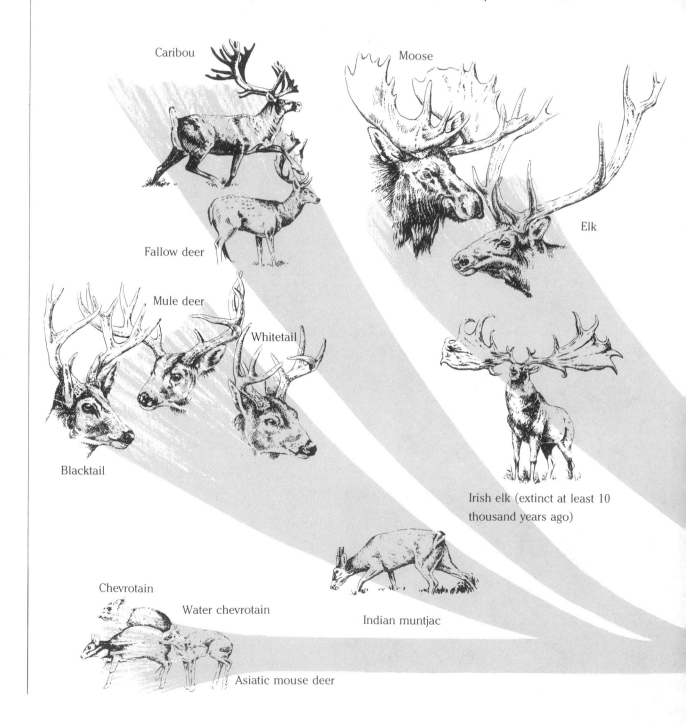

Caribou

Moose

Fallow deer

Elk

Mule deer

Whitetail

Blacktail

Irish elk (extinct at least 10 thousand years ago)

Chevrotain

Water chevrotain

Indian muntjac

Asiatic mouse deer

Order Artiodactyla. Special features separate the entire deer family from other hoofed mammals as clearly as cats differ from dogs. In the first place, all deer belong to the great order Artiodactyla, which means "even-toed," whose members have cloven hoofs divided into two parts. Members of the order Perissodactyla, such as the horse, are "odd-toed" and have undivided hoofs. In North America other artiodactyls include the pronghorn antelope, bison, mountain goat, mountain sheep, musk-ox, and peccary. Some of these chew cud, as do the deer—but none have solid, bony antlers that are grown and shed each year. These antlers separate the deer family from all other hoofed and horned animals.

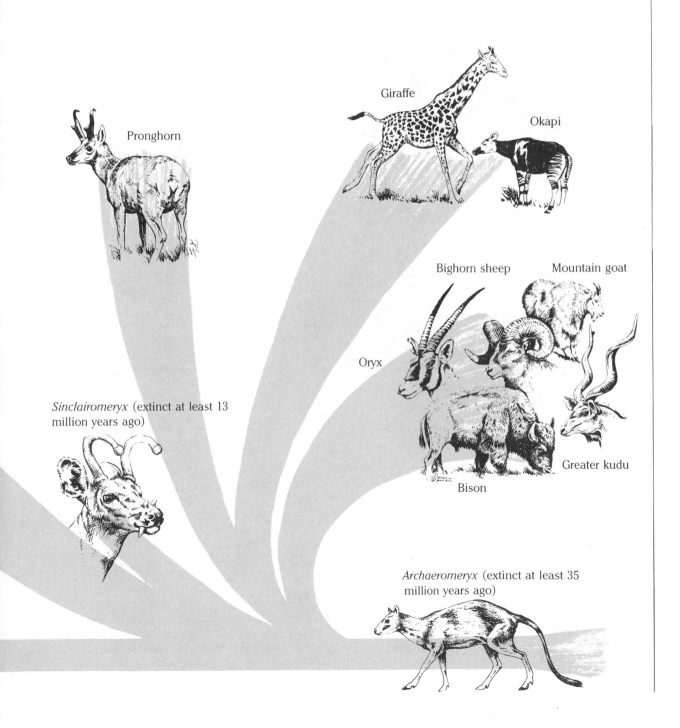

Pronghorn

Giraffe

Okapi

Bighorn sheep

Mountain goat

Oryx

Greater kudu

Bison

Sinclairomeryx (extinct at least 13 million years ago)

Archaeromeryx (extinct at least 35 million years ago)

The American pronghorn, like deer, chews cud and has cloven hoofs. But unlike members of the deer family, it wears horns—permanent parts of the skull covered with tough, horny sheaths. The antlers of deer are true bone, and are grown and shed annually. The pronghorn is not a true antelope, as it is sometimes called but is in a class apart. For although the pronghorn has horns, it sheds the outer sheaths each year. (Irene Vandermolen photo)

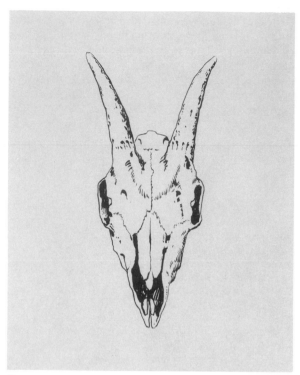

The horn cores of a goat skull are permanent bone parts of the skull itself. Deer antlers are also bone, but are not permanent parts of the skull.

Antlers. Antlers are not "horns" even though hunters who know better may call them that. Horns are permanent bony structures growing from the skull. They are never shed and are covered with tough, keratinous material that is closely related to hair. Mammals such as bighorn sheep and bison never shed their horns, which continue to grow all their lives. But the unique pronghorn sheds the outer sheaths of its horns annually. It is the only horned mammal in the world to do so.

Digestion. Deer are grazers and browsers, like all other cloven-hoofed animals. But unlike the others, most species of deer do not have a gall bladder—the little sac that serves as a reservoir of liver bile. All deer have the four-chambered stomachs found in the true ruminants such as cattle, antelope and giraffes. But hippos, camels, swine and other artiodactyls have only two- and three-chambered stomachs and are not "ruminating." That is, they do not regurgitate their food and chew it as cud.

This trick of cud-chewing is a remarkable eat-now-digest-later adaptation that enables ruminants to pack away large quantities of coarse food and process it later at leisure. No one knows why or how cud-chewing evolved, but it surely developed because it conferred some sort of advantage. As cud-chewers, these animals were simply better adapted to their particular environments.

Full-time herbivores have always been meals-on-the-hoof for the big carnivores. The herbivores' trait of herding may have developed because it served as a defense mechanism, and the same may be true of cud-chewing. A deer, antelope, or sheep can snatch its food where that food is found, wasting no time with such refinements as careful chewing. That's something that can be done at another time and place—quite possibly a much safer time and place. After all, a particular feeding or watering place may be frequented by predators.

A herbivore's digestive system must contend with the special problems of digesting plants—problems that never trouble true carnivores. The meat-eating cougar has a relatively short, simple digestive tract compared to that of his prey, the deer. It's been said that "all flesh is grass," and that is true, for predators depend on their prey to do the basic job of converting plant protein into animal protein.

So how do the herbivores digest plants? A deer snatching a mouthful of browse (such as buds, leaves,

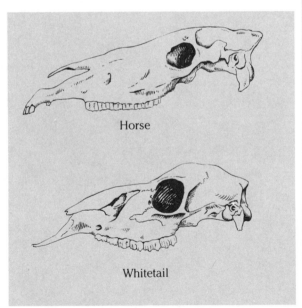

Much of the whitetail's diet is "browse" consisting of buds, leaves, tender stems and twig ends. A deer's muzzle is more pointed than that of a grass-grazing cow's, and so the deer can selectively nip leaves and buds and pick up such small food items as acorns. The drawing shows a deer's "stomach", consisting of 4 specialized chambers: (1) the rumen, (2) reticulum, (3) omasum, and (4) abomasum. (Leonard Lee Rue III photo)

tender shoots and twigs) swallows it with very little chewing. The browse passes into a large chamber, the *rumen,* which is just an enlargement of the esophagus—a sort of storage chamber roughly comparable to the crop of a bird. This is where digestion begins, with microorganisms such as bacteria, yeasts, and protozoa attacking the plant cell walls and beginning to break down the tough cellulose. Seeds and grain pass directly into the second pouch of the digestive system, the *reticulum,* after being chewed and mixed with saliva. Action by microorganisms takes place there, as well.

From the rumen and reticulum all this roughly processed fodder is regurgitated to the mouth and thoroughly chewed. Reswallowed it bypasses the rumen and goes on to another esophageal chamber, the *omasum,* where much of the moisture is squeezed from it. Finally, it passes on to the actual stomach, the *abomasum.* Acid is secreted there; the bacteria and other microorganisms are killed, and the final stages of digestion take place. Much of the digestion, though, has been done by the time those processed plantstuffs get to the stomach—a process achieved less by the deer itself than by the billions of microscopic plants and animals in its digestive tract.

There's no doubt that cud-chewing is a useful trait, and it may be one reason that the hoofed animals that ruminate have done so much better than those that do not. The Perissodactyla, mammals such as horses with undivided hoofs, aren't ruminants and aren't doing nearly as well as the cud-chewers. They were widespread millions of years ago, but two of the five

One of the basic differences between hoofed animals, such as horses and deer, is in the teeth. Deer have no upper front teeth. Horses do.

original groups are now extinct and the surviving three—the tapirs, rhinos, and horses—are greatly reduced in range and numbers. On the other hand, cloven-hoofed artiodactyls that chew cud are still flourishing. Why? They don't appear to have any marked advantage in teeth, brains, legs, or reproductive systems. Maybe it's because they have better designed stomachs that allow thorough plant chewing from safer vantages. At least, that's the one feature that seems to distinguish the small, rather dead-end group of perissodactyls from the large, flourishing group of artiodactyls.

Hoofs. Deer are ungulates, and ungulates are hoofed mammals. A very long time ago, those hoofs were simple claws. But as the ancestral herbivores evolved they became runners, with legs and feet increasingly modified for running at high speed or in a long, tireless lope. It is to the advantage of a hoofed runner to be *digitigrade* (running on its toes) rather than *plantigrade* (running on the flats of its feet). Early hoofed animals did just that, rising up on their toes and modifying ancestral claws into hoofs of two different kinds. In one type, the axis of the foot eventually developed

through the middle toe, resulting in the single hoof of the horse. In the other kind, that axis extended between the third and fourth toes—resulting in cloven-hoofed deer.

And here again, the cloven-hoofed mammals evidently had an edge of some sort, for they include the swiftest of all hoofed mammals as well as the most agile. Of these artiodactyls, the deer family Cervidae is a splendid general compromise of speed, agility, and endurance. None of the deer are the blazing-fast cross-country runners that pronghorns are. The deer can't leap as high or far as some African antelope. And they certainly can't scale a cliff like a mountain goat. But most deer can go all-out through a dense forest better than any pronghorn, leap as high and far as the occasion demands, and outrun any mountain goat or sheep.

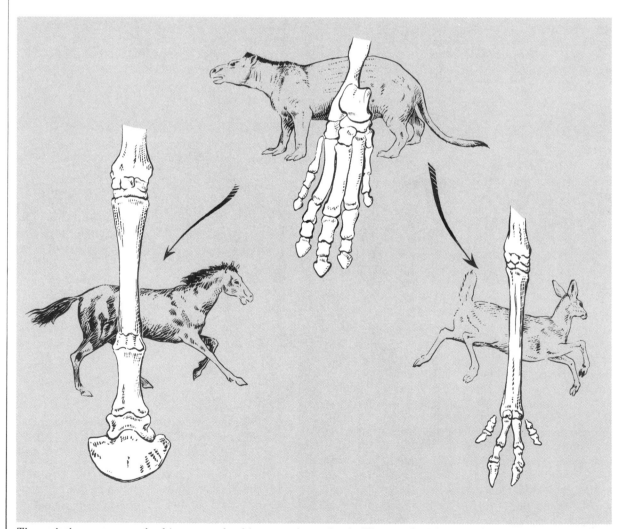

Through the ages, some herbivores evolved into running animals. This resulted from modifications to feet and legs that allowed the animals to run swiftly on their toes. Among the perissodactyls or "odd-toed" mammals such as the horse, this resulted in the development of only the middle toe of each foot (left). In artiodactyls or "even-toed" mammals such as deer, the third and fourth toes became specialized as cloven, or split, hoofs (right).

Hoof prints of common North American animals are often mistaken for one another.

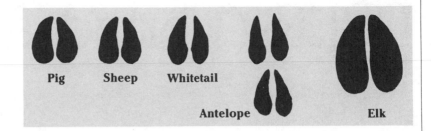

The skeleton of a deer is light but strong, designed through the age-long process of natural selection to be the frame of an agile, graceful, swift-running, and durable animal.

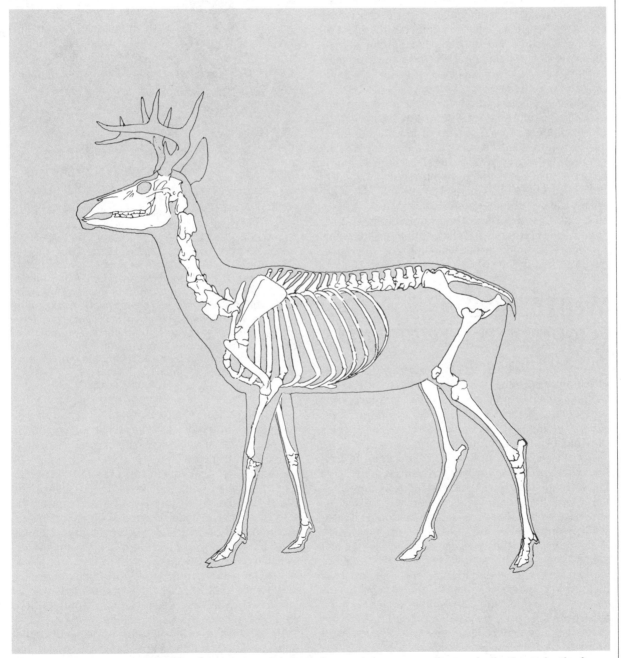

NORTH AMERICAN DEER (Cervidae)

Technically, the family of North American deer includes moose, elk, and caribou, but the family members that most people think of as deer are the whitetail and mule deer (the latter also includes the blacktail subspecies). Not only do these two species include more subspecies than any other North American deer, but they are of the genus *Odocoileus,* which is found only in the Americas.

Moose, caribou, and elk inhabit Europe and Asia as well as North America—known by somewhat different names, of course. In Europe the moose is known as an "elk," the caribou is a reindeer, and the counterpart of the North American elk or wapiti is known as the "red deer." But whitetails and mule deer are native to no other parts of the world. They are strictly natives of the western hemisphere.

At one time there was some question about their genus; early taxonomists placed them in the genus *Dama,* but today both the whitetails and mule deer are classified in the *Odocoileus* genus.

WHITETAILS (*Odocoileus virginianus*)

The whitetail was the deer first seen by Europeans arriving on the Atlantic coast. It was known as the "Virginia deer" from the earliest days and has borne the specific names *virginiana* or *virginianus* ever since. The name even applies to several subspecies of whitetails in South America.

No other species of American big game—in fact, few other species of *any* North American mammal—has as many subspecies and variations as the whitetail. The distinctions among some of these subspecies are so subtle that the hunter is likely to wonder if there really *is* any difference.

Taxonomy, which is the science of classification of living things, is populated by two general groups of workers: the lumpers and the splitters. The former are inclined to combine and simplify groupings of animals wherever possible, while the splitters prefer to establish species, subspecies, and varieties on the basis of finely honed details. Mule deer classification, with only seven subspecies, might be considered to be the result of lumping. But whitetail classification is unquestionably the result of splitting. The whitetails have

North America's most common American deer is named for the large, showy white tail that it often raises and flares when it becomes alarmed. This is usually more prevalent in does than in bucks, and is believed to serve as a visual alarm signal to other deer. The antlers of this galloping buck are typical of the whitetail species in which the tines rise vertically from the main beams. (Leonard Lee Rue III photo)

been divided again and again into a bewildering 30 subspecies—some of which literally require an artist's eye and a Munsell color chart to be seen as distinct subspecies, or races.

Certain island subspecies of whitetails—such as those of Coiba Island, the Florida Keys, Hilton Head Island, and others—are, for all practical purposes, the same as closely related subspecies on the mainland. Isolation, inbreeding, and certain nutritional limitations have produced characteristics that might well vanish if those subspecies were allowed to mix freely. When you get right down to it, the miniature deer of the Florida Keys is essentially an underfed, stunted Florida whitetail that the taxonomic splitters have granted a distinct subspecific rating.

The 30 subspecies of whitetails in North and Central America do show remarkable variations in size and go by many names, but they are whitetails nonetheless. The North American whitetail ranges throughout

WHITETAIL DISTRIBUTION

The whitetail deer is the most widely distributed deer in the New World, with 30 subspecies in North America and Central America alone. Although the ranges of these subspecies often overlap, their boundaries approximate that shown here.

the United States, southern Canada, Mexico and Central America. It is not found in western British Columbia. Nor does it occur through most of California, Nevada, and Utah, western Colorado, northern Arizona, and much of western New Mexico. It does not occur in Baja California.

The whitetail takes its name from the large, showy tail that reaches almost down to the hocks of its hind legs. The tail is bordered with white edges and is pure white on its underside. When alarmed, the deer usually runs with its tail standing straight up—a white banner that may also be "flagged" from side to side.

The size and weight of an adult whitetail varies greatly among some subspecies, ranging from the tiny Key deer of southern Florida to the big deer of the North Woods. Mature bucks wear gracefully curved antlers with tines arising vertically from the pair of main beams that extend slightly backward and then sweep out and forward. These antlers, and that great

white flag of a tail, are unique among North American deer.

In alphabetical order, the following section describes briefly the 30 subspecies of North American whitetails (including Mexico and Central America) and their general ranges.

Acapulco whitetail *(Odocoileus virginianus acapulcensis).* This is the smallest of the Mexican whitetails north of the Isthmus of Tehuantepec. It has shorter hair and a lighter, drabber color than deer of the higher interior plateau region.

Avery Island whitetail *(O. v. mcilhennyi).* The deer that hails from the land of Tabasco Sauce—the Louisiana, Mississippi, and Texas coastal area. It is a large whitetail but averages somewhat smaller than its two neighbors just to the north, the Kansas and Virginia whitetails.

Blackbeard Island whitetail *(O. v. nigribarbis).* This medium-size deer is found on Blackbeard and Sapelo islands off the Georgia coast. Smaller than but similar to the Virginia deer, it has shorter hair, a darker face and ears, and a duller cinnamon color to its winter coat. The beams and tines of its antlers are also more compressed. Tufts of hair on the tarsal glands are less deeply colored than on the nearby Hilton Head whitetail.

Bull Island whitetail *(O. v. taurinsulae).* Found only on Bull Island off the coast of South Carolina, this medium-size whitetail is similar to the Virginia deer

This is a Carmen Mountains whitetail of Big Bend National Park, Texas. (Leonard Lee Rue III photo)

of the mainland but is somewhat smaller and darker, and has distinctly darker facial markings.

Carmen Mountains whitetail *(O. v. carminis).* A small deer of north-central Mexico, it is also found across the Rio Grande in southwest Texas. This whitetail has moderately spreading antlers and a gray and brownish black color to its winter coat.

Chiapas whitetail *(O. v. nelsoni).* This is a small, dark brownish-gray subspecies found in the high mountainous areas of Central America.

Chiriqui whitetail *(O. v. chiriquensis).* A small deer with a coat of snuff brown, it is closely related to the

Nicaragua whitetail. It has short hair and antlers that are short and heavy, usually with three points on each beam.

Coiba Island whitetail *(O. v. rothschildi).* The smallest of the Central American whitetails, it has very short ears. A metatarsal gland is present but difficult to find. This deer has more slender antlers than mainland deer.

Columbian whitetail *(O. v. leucurus).* A large deer of western Oregon and Washington State, it has antlers that curve steeply upward, though usually with a rather

This is a young Coues deer or "fantail," of southern Arizona. (Leonard Lee Rue III photo)

narrow spread. It is a bit smaller than the Northwest whitetail and is now nearly extinct.

Coues whitetail *(O. v. couesi).* A small deer with very large ears, this little "fantail" of the desert Southwest is the second smallest whitetail (after the Florida Key deer). A large buck weighs just 100 pounds.

Dakota whitetail *(O. v. dacotensis).* A very large deer, the Dakota whitetail is thought by some authorities to be the largest of the species. This is the deer of the northern Great Plains and is often found in rough badlands and timbered river "breaks." It has heavy antlers with moderately short tines, and a color somewhat paler than the Northern Woodland or Kansas whitetails.

Florida Coastal whitetail *(O. v. osceola).* This is a medium-size-to-large deer with rather short hair. Somewhat smaller than a typical Virginia deer, it has a narrow skull and paler color.

Florida Key deer *(O. v. clavium).* This deer of the subtropical Keys is similar to the mainland Florida whitetail (listed below) but is much smaller, and the cinnamon-buff to tawny color of its winter coat is duller. An adult Key deer may weigh less than 50 pounds and is undoubtedly the smallest deer in the United States. It formerly ranged through most of the Keys, swimming from one to another, but hurricanes, destruction of habitat, and excessive hunting have nearly wiped it out.

Florida whitetail *(O. v. seminolus).* A large deer of the Florida mainland, this whitetail has rather short

The Florida Key deer is the smallest deer in the United States. This buck was photographed in the rutting season. (Leonard Lee Rue III photo)

This Florida whitetail buck has antlers in velvet, and was photographed in the Okefenokee Swamp, in extreme southern Georgia. (Leonard Lee Rue III photo)

ears and narrowly spreading antlers. Its skull is somewhat narrower than that of the typical Virginia deer.

Hilton Head Island whitetail *(O. v. hiltonensis).* A medium-size deer found only on Hilton Head Island, South Carolina, this whitetail is similar to the Virginia deer. It is smaller and the upper parts of its winter pelage are cinnamon colored, with darkly colored hair tufts on the tarsal glands (the external skin glands on the hocks of its hind legs).

Hunting Island whitetail *(O. v. venatorius).* Of medium size, this deer inhabits only the South Carolina island for which it is named. Its upperparts are usually a paler buff than those of deer on nearby islands or on the mainland. It is smaller than the typical Virginia deer, and has more rugose (wrinkly surfaced) antlers than whitetails on Hilton Head Island.

Kansas whitetail *(O. v. macrourus).* This is a large deer that ranges from southern Minnesota into Louisiana. Its heavy antlers have particularly heavy beams. The beams are especially thick between the burr and snag tine. This subspecies was apparently once more widespread than now. Its skull is similar to northern woodland and Virginia deer but bears heavier cheek teeth. It is generally larger than subspecies to the south—the Texas and Avery Island whitetails.

Mexican Lowland whitetail *(O. v. thomasi).* A small deer, it is usually the most vividly colored of the tropical North American whitetails and has upperparts that are predominantly tawny and cinnamon. Its antlers are usually directed backward and have three tines on each main beam, narrowly spreading.

Mexican Tableland whitetail *(O. v. mexicanus).* This small deer has upperparts colored somewhat cinnamon brown. Its antlers are the longest of any whitetail found in Mexico and Central America, with main beams curved sharply forward and spread rather wide.

Miquihuana whitetail *(O. v. miquihuanensis).* A small deer of central Mexico, it has a grizzled drab coat. It is about the same size as the Coues deer of the Southwest but is darker and has shorter ears.

Nicaragua whitetail *(O. v. truei).* This is a small deer with an inconspicuous metatarsal gland and tuft. The antler main beams are relatively straight and directed backward. Adults may have only simple spikes, or at most two or three points on each antler beam.

Northern Veracruz whitetail *(O. v. veraecrucis).* A small deer colored ochre-tawny, this whitetail has more brightly colored upperparts than many other

subspecies. It is generally found in lowland areas along the Gulf Coast.

Northern Woodland whitetail *(O. v. borealis).* A very large whitetail of northeastern North America, it is possibly the biggest of all the whitetail subspecies. A buck killed in 1977 in Ontario is reported to have weighed 431.2 pounds (196 kilograms) before being dressed, but the weight was not officially verified. The heaviest official weight for a Maine whitetail of this subspecies is 351 pounds dressed (about 440 pounds live weight or roughly 25 percent more than dressed weight).

Antlers of this subspecies are very large and hold the current world record. Though larger, Northern Woodland whitetails closely resemble the Virginia subspecies. The size of the Northern Woodland deer

The northern woodland whitetail is believed by some authorities to be the largest of the whitetail subspecies. In general, whitetail deer tend to be larger in the more northern latitudes, where they are also grayer and paler than their more brightly colored cousins in Central America. (Leonard Lee Rue III photo)

The first whitetail deer to be described by scientists was the Virginia whitetail, from which all New World whitetails took their specific name virginianus. *Before the deer was commonly called the "whitetailed deer," it was often known as the "Virginia deer."*

is similar to that of Kansas and Dakota whitetails, but the cheek teeth of those more western subspecies tend to be somewhat heavier.

Northwest whitetail *(O. v. ochrourus).* This is a large deer with antlers that usually spread wide. It is about the size of the Northern Woodland and Kansas whitetails but is paler in color. Its coloring is most like that of the Dakota whitetail.

Oaxaca whitetail *(O. v. oaxacensis).* A small deer of southern Mexico, this whitetail is colored a grizzled snuff brown. The Oaxaca is smaller than the Mexican Tableland whitetail and lighter in color. Its antlers have a rather narrow spread. It is found in the high mountains in the vicinity of Oaxaca and nearby Cerro San Felipe.

Rain Forest whitetail *(O. v. toltecus).* This small deer of tawny color is found in high mountains of southern Mexico, especially in rain forests facing the Gulf of Mexico. Its antlers have a narrow spread and the main beams are curved sharply forward. The antlers have about four points each.

Sinaloa whitetail *(O. v. sinaloae).* The Sinaloa is a small deer of southwestern Mexico, with antlers that normally bear four points. About as big as the Coues deer of Arizona, its ears are shorter and its color lighter and less grayish. Also, it has a russet tail instead of the fantail's dark brownish color, overlaid with gray.

Texas whitetail *(O. v. texanus).* This deer is found throughout almost all of Texas and extends into northern Mexico. It is Mexico's largest whitetail. Its widely spreading antlers are rather slender, usually with four or five long points. This whitetail is similar to the Coues, or fantail, deer of the Southwest but is larger and somewhat darker in color, and less greyish. A Texas whitetail may carry ten antler points, while a Coues deer's rack seldom bears more than eight.

Virginia whitetail *(O. v. virginianus).* This large, heavy-antlered deer of the Southeast is the "type species" of American whitetails—the first described by early scientists. It differs slightly from neighboring subspecies in average size, shades of its coat, and certain skull measurements. Not quite as big as the Northern Woodland whitetail, it has somewhat lighter molariform teeth than the Kansas whitetail. It closely resembles the Florida Coastal whitetail, though the Virginia whitetail has a heavier, broader skull, on average, and longer, somewhat paler hair.

Yucatan whitetail *(O. v. yucatanensis).* This is a small deer with light, finely grizzled brown upperparts. Its antlers are relatively straight and simply branched, with few tines.

DISTINGUISHING TAILS AND GLANDS

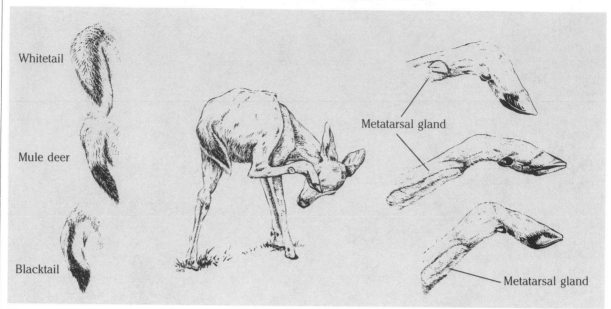

Whitetail

Mule deer

Blacktail

Metatarsal gland

Metatarsal gland

Tails are distinctive among whitetails, mule deer, and blacktails. Also, the metatarsal glands differ greatly in size. Drawing below: Appearing to be discolored tufts of hair on the insides of the hind legs, the whitetail's tarsal glands are the largest of the group—about 3 to 4 inches across, while those of the mule and blacktail deer are only half as large.

WHITETAIL FLARE-UPS

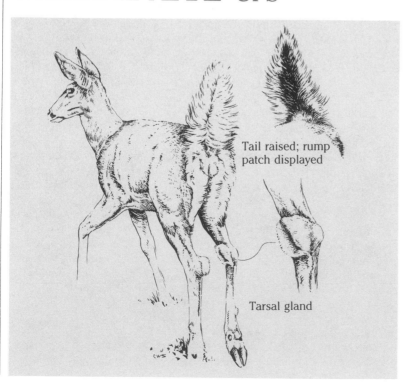

Tail raised; rump patch displayed

Tarsal gland

A stern view of the whitetail's namesake when "flagged" in alarm is uniquely eye-catching.

MULE DEER
(Odocoileus hemionus)

The Rocky Mountain mule deer is the largest of the mule deer subspecies. Named for its long, mule-like ears, this deer's differences from the whitetail are readily apparent. The antlers of the muley are of a "suppressed dichotomy" in which the antlers fork and then refork, rather than arising as single tines from a main beam. The mule deer's tail is short, white and tipped with black, and it is never raised or "flagged" as the deer runs in alarm. (Len Rue Jr. photo)

Mule deer and blacktails belong to the same species, *Odocoileus hemionus,* but have enough differences to warrant different common names. Both are "mule" deer in the sense that they have large, mulelike ears entirely unlike those of the whitetail. Both mule deer and blacktails also have at least some black on their tails, which always have black tips.

In all, the differences between the whitetails and the mule deer and blacktails are significant. They reflect, as the Canadian biologist Ian McTaggart Cowan put it, "two successful experiments in evolution" in North America. Generally speaking, the mule deer and blacktails are blockier, more rugged in appearance, and somewhat less trim than the whitetails—although those are-subjective qualities that depend largely on who is looking at these deer, and the time of year.

The whitetail is basically an eastern deer, more or less adapted to eastern forest conditions. The mule deer and blacktail are western types that evolved in rugged badlands, mountains, and broken brushlands. The running gaits of whitetails and mule deer differ greatly, possibly because of the differences in ancestral ranges. While the whitetails run with a graceful, bounding stride, the mule deer runs in a stiff-legged manner with all four feet striking the ground at once—a style far better adapted to steep, rocky mountainsides.

There are other important differences as well. The whitetail's big, showy white "flag" is usually raised when the deer runs in alarm and usually waves from side to side as well. By comparison, the mule deer's tail is a modest, rope-like thing that may be raised slightly as the animal runs, but never much above horizontal.

The antler structures of healthy mule deer and whitetails are also markedly different. The mule deer's antlers are *dichotomous*; that is, the main beam forks symmetrically rather than giving rise to distinct, individual tines. The whitetail's antlers are a suppressed dichotomy, typically consisting of two main beams from which a number of tines rise more or less vertically. These main beams also curve forward more strongly than the mule deer's. If tree branches can provide the rough analogy, the branching of the mule deer's antlers is like that of a box elder tree whose trunk forks into main limbs that fork and refork. The whitetail's antlers are more like that of a pine whose small limbs grow directly off the main trunk.

Another major difference between the whitetail and mule deer clans is the relative size of the metatarsal glands of their hind legs. Those of mule deer are over two inches long and are entirely surrounded by a tuft of brown hair. In adult whitetails, these glands are rarely more than 1¼ inches in length and are surrounded by whitish hair.

Rocky Mountain mule deer (*Odocoileus hemionus hemionus*). This is the most common and widespread of the mule deer and blacktails. Its range is many times larger than all the other subspecies of *hemionus* combined. In fact, this deer subspecies is more widely distributed than any other subspecies of North American big game except the black bear, even though the mule deer no longer exists in parts of its historic range. It is also the largest of all the deer with black tails. There are records of California bucks weighing 380 pounds hunter-dressed (about 475 pounds live weight).

Differences between the Rocky Mountain mule deer and its close relatives are usually subtle, especially along the boundaries of the various ranges where subspecies *intergrade* (that is, through interbreeding, merge in intermediate forms). Coloring isn't particularly distinctive, although the large white rump patch that completely encircles the base of the tail of the Rocky Mountain deer is fairly characteristic. The real differences lie in certain skull and teeth measurements.

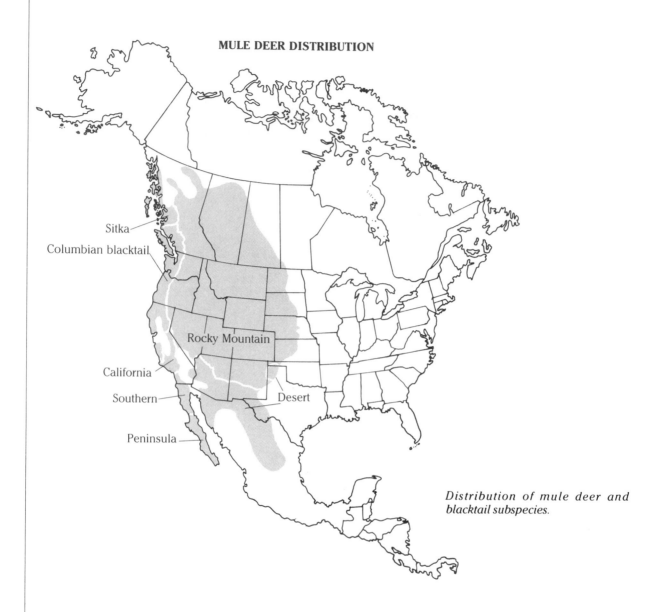

MULE DEER DISTRIBUTION

Distribution of mule deer and blacktail subspecies.

California mule deer *(O. h. californicus).* The summer coat of this deer is much like that of the Rocky Mountain deer, but in winter it has a somewhat paler and more yellow coat. The white rump patch is smaller and not continuous about the base of the tail. Unlike Rocky Mountain deer, California mule deer have a dark stripe down the entire length of their tails in most cases.

The most reliable way to distinguish the California mule deer from its Rocky Mountain cousin is by relative length of the metatarsal glands. The Rocky Mountain deer has glands up to 5 inches long, while the California mule deer glands average about 3½ inches long.

Southern mule deer *(O. h. fuliginatus).* Found in mountains and foothills along the southern California coast and northern portions of Baja California, this is a very dark mule deer. Both its summer and winter pelage are much darker than that of its neighboring relatives.

Peninsula mule deer *(O. h. peninsulae).* Found only in southern Baja California, this pale-colored mule deer's range is now limited to relatively high, rugged, and almost inaccessible areas as a result of excessive hunting pressure. The deer differs from southern mule deer in coloration, the high crown of its skull, and the depression of frontal bones between its eyes.

Desert mule deer *(O. h. crooki).* Inhabiting both the southwestern United States and north-central Mexico, this deer is paler but generally similar in color to the Rocky Mountain deer. It has a smaller rump patch

The blacktail is a member of the mule deer species, but with enough differences so that some scientists think it has nearly evolved into a distinct species of its own. This is the deer of the dense western coastal forests, such as the great Tillamook Burn area of northwestern Oregon. (Leonard Lee Rue III photo)

that is often divided by a dark stripe down the base of the tail. On average it is also smaller than the Rocky Mountain subspecies.

Columbian blacktail deer *(O. h. columbianus).* Generally, this deer inhabits a narrow strip of the Pacific slope in northern California, Oregon, Washington, and British Columbia, although it occurs well inland in parts of northern California. The Columbian black-

tail and the closely related Sitka blacktail differ from the mule deer in enough ways that they are thought to be diverging into an entirely new species.

In general appearance, however, the Columbian deer is similar to the mule deer. On the average it is somewhat smaller and has proportionately shorter ears and a redder summer coat. It does not have a rump patch, and its metatarsal glands are less than 3½ inches long. Metatarsal glands of both the Rocky Mountain and California mule deer are longer.

Sitka blacktail deer *(O. h. sitkensis).* This is the blacktail of the dense coastal forests of southeastern Alaska and northwestern British Columbia. This deer tends to be abundant on coastal islands. It is fairly common along the mainland coast and rare inland. In summer the Sitka deer is less red than the Columbian blacktail, but tends to be redder in the winter coat.

In addition to the above seven subspecies of *hemionus,* four others were once listed as well: the Inyo mule deer, burrow deer, Tiburon Island mule deer, and Cedros Island deer. Those deer types have evidently been found to be identical to the seven subspecies listed above and so have been merged with them.

MOOSE
(Alces alces)

This is is the huge deer of the northerly latitudes, a single species that prefers timbered areas with plenty of water and aquatic vegetation, and trees such as

Largest of the world's deer, the bull moose of the northern latitudes is an awesome beast. The great palmated antlers may span 6 feet and weigh 75 pounds—but as with antlers of all American deer, they are shed annually. (Len Rue Jr. photo)

willows, alder, and poplars. Of the seven circumpolar subspecies of moose, four are North American. Eastern moose *(Alces alces americana)* are found in the northeastern United States and eastern Canada and range westward to the Great Lakes. The northwestern moose *(A. a. andersoni)* live north and west of the Great Lakes to the Pacific coast and up into Yukon Territory. Alaskan moose *(A. a. gigas)* is the largest of the American subspecies and ranges through most of Alaska, over into the western Yukon, and down into northern British Columbia. The Shiras moose *(A. a. shirasi)* ranges down through the Rockies from southern Alberta into northern Utah and Colorado.

The Alaskan moose is the largest living deer in the world and is quite possibly the largest ever. A big Alaskan bull may stand 7½ feet at the shoulder, weigh 1,800 pounds, and wear an enormous rack of palmated antlers that span 6 feet or more. By standing on his hind legs, such an animal can pull down foliage from 12 feet above ground. Moose are strong swimmers and have been known to swim 16 miles.

In spite of their great trophy value and excellent meat, North American moose populations are in generally good shape and not endangered by hunting—thanks to the efficient systems of American and Canadian game management.

CARIBOU
(Rangifer tarandus)

There is only one species of caribou worldwide, but five subspecies occur in North America.

The most southerly is the woodland caribou *(Rangifer tarandus caribou)* found in the forested regions across most of Canada and as far south as northern

Unlike other North American deer, caribou are herding animals. Although barren-ground caribou are usually found in small groups such as this one, the great cow-and-calf gatherings of midsummer may include 80,000 animals. (Len Rue Jr. photo)

Idaho. The barren ground caribou *(R. t. granti)* inhabits much of Alaska and the northern Yukon and summers far north to land's end at the edge of the Arctic Ocean. The Greenland caribou *(R. t. groenlandicus)* is found generally north of the treeline in north-central Canada, west and north of Hudson Bay. Peary caribou *(R. t. pearyi)* live on the arctic islands of northern Canada, while *R. t. eogroenlandicus* is found in a narrow range on the southwestern edge of Greenland.

European reindeer are domesticated barren-ground caribou (although some still range wild in northern

This barren-ground bull caribou, with record-class antlers, may live out his entire life in the North without ever seeing a tree. Bigger and wilder than their reindeer cousins of northern Europe, caribou bulls and cows have antlers. Cow caribou have less impressive antlers than bulls, however. Cow caribou are the only females in the deer family that wear antlers. (Tim Lewis Rue photo)

pounds and are crowned with lofty, spreading antlers, each of which may have seven tines and measure 4 feet or more along the main beam. A unique feature of the elk is the pair of flattened, ivorylike canine teeth in the upper jaw—objects once prized as jewelry by Indians and later by white men.

There is one species of wapiti, with six North American subspecies. The eastern elk *(C. e. canadensis)* once occupied the eastern half of the United States and is now possibly extinct. The Merriam elk *(C. e. merriami)* once occupied parts of Arizona and New Mexico but is now extinct. The Olympic, or Roosevelt, elk *(C. e. roosevelti)* is found in the coastal Northwest. The tule elk *(C. e. nannodes)* lives in central California. The Rocky Mountain elk *(C. e. nelsoni)* is the most common and is found in much of the Rocky Mountain system of the United States and Canada. The Manitoban elk *(C. e. manitobensis)* originally occupied

Scandinavia) and are generally smaller and less rugged than the native Alaskan subspecies.

Alaskan caribou are large, rather awkward-looking deer with thick, hairy muzzles, maned necks, and rather broad, flat hoofs. A large bull stands as high as 5 feet at the shoulder and weighs up to 700 pounds, although the average bull is usually just over 3 feet at the shoulder and 275 pounds or so.

Both cow and bull caribou bear antlers—the only American deer of which both sexes bear antlers—although cow antlers occur far more frequently in the northern herds than those farther south. A cow caribou's antlers are not as impressive as a bull's, but she will carry them until fawning time well past the date when the bull has shed his rack.

A bull caribou's antlers are unique among all deer. They consist of two great, heavy beams bearing many tines (up to a foot long) that are more or less flattened. The brow tine of each beam is a palmate, vertical "shovel" that extends out over the bull's face. An exceptional caribou rack measures over 5 feet along the outer curve of the main beam and has a maximum spread of 4 feet between the antlers.

In its primary range today, the caribou population is at a healthy level. The caribou is an important game species as well as a prime food source for many northern Indians and Eskimos. Its meat, like that of the moose and elk, is excellent.

WAPITI, OR ELK
(Cervus elaphus)

The wapiti is almost universally known as "elk" in North America, where it is second in size only to the moose. Big Rocky Mountain bulls approach 1,000

The Rocky Mountain elk is more properly called "wapiti," since the term "elk" was originally applied to European moose. This elk is a splendid example of the second-largest American deer. Once found from coast to coast, elk are now largely limited to western mountains. (Leonard Lee Rue III photo)

much of the Great Plains in the range generally between the eastern and Rocky Mountain subspecies, but it is now limited to several isolated populations in south-central Manitoba and Saskatchewan.

Of all North American deer, elk probably came closest to being wiped out by the unrestricted hunting of the 18th and 19th centuries. From an estimated 10 million elk before the coming of white men, only 90,000 remained in 1922. Stringent conservation measures were taken to halt the alarming decline, and by the late 1970s the North American population had increased to about 500,000.

DEER OF OTHER LANDS

Deer are not original American livestock. They are of Old World origin, having migrated to North America over the Bering-Chukchi platform—the great land bridge between Asia and North America—over 15 million years ago. Connecting what is now north-eastern Siberia and Alaska, this intercontinental isthmus appeared when so much of the world's water had been locked up in glacial ice that sea level dropped more than 300 feet.

The ancestors of today's North American moose, elk, and caribou crossed the land bridge and found a new home, some arriving less than a million years ago. The genus of American whitetails and mule deer, *Odocoileus,* is believed to have originated in the Old World although it is no longer found there. It was in the Americas that *Odocoileus* flourished and evolved into the distinct species of whitetails and mule deer.

The deer family has its oldest and deepest roots in Asia, however, where some of the world's strangest deer still survive. Today, worldwide, there are 17 genera and 38 species of Cervidae. Only representative examples are profiled on upcoming pages.

ASIAN DEER

Musk deer *(Moschus moschiferus).* Found in central and northeastern Asia from China, Manchuria, Korea, and Sakhalin Island to the Amur region; and through Siberia to western Mongolia, Tibet, Kashmir, Nepal, and Sikkim.

This is a small deer, slightly over 3 feet in length and a bit less than 2 feet high at the shoulder. An adult may weigh up to 25 pounds.

Musk deer are high-country deer and range up to 11,000 feet. They have a heavy coat of long, thick, pithy hair that provides excellent protection against what is a generally harsh environment. The musk deer is one of only two species that never have antlers (the other is the Chinese water deer). Instead, adult males are armed with upper canine teeth that protrude as tusks 3 inches or more. Females also have tusks, but they are much smaller than those of the males. And, unlike most deer, musk deer have gall bladders.

These deer are rarely found in groups. They are shy and timid. That and their rugged habitats has helped save them from extinction. They have been hunted extensively, both for their meat and for the musk that adult males in breeding condition carry in unique abdominal pouches. As much as 28 grams of the brown-

On a musk deer farm in Zhenping County, northwest China, a gamekeeper encourages gregarious behaviors. (New China Photo Co. photo)

Lacking antlers, the strange little musk deer have upper canine teeth that protrude 3 inches or more as tusks in the adult males. The tusks of the does are somewhat smaller. The tusks are strikingly similar to the great stabbing teeth of the extinct saber-tooth tiger's (F. Walther, IUCN/World Wildlife Fund photo)

ish, waxy secretion may be obtained from a single buck. This valuable musk is used in the manufacture of soap and perfume. Both pouch and musk are highly prized by native hunters.

Chinese water deer *(Hydropotes inermis).* As its name implies, this species is usually associated with water. The deer are found in China on islands and shorelines of the Yangtze River and in the tall reeds and rushes of wetlands in Korea. They may also frequent tall grasses on mountainsides and in some cultivated fields.

This is a small deer, standing less than 2 feet at the shoulder and rarely weighing more than 24 pounds. Like the musk deer, it lacks antlers but has large, tusklike canine teeth that extend down from the upper jaws. These tusks may be the basis for the Korean superstition that the bite of the water deer is fatal. But whatever the reason, the Chinese and Koreans in the past did not kill and eat these deer.

Most species of deer normally bear only one or two fawns, but a water deer doe may give birth to as many as seven fawns in a year, even though the doe has but four teats.

Few deer are so adept at concealment and escape as Chinese water deer. Their general coloring of pale rufous yellow blends with rushes and grasses. Also, these deer live in dense cover and rarely gather in groups of any size—and can be almost impossible to see and very difficult to drive or hunt. When finally put out of cover, the little water deer runs in an odd, humpbacked series of leaps.

There are accounts of water deer kept in the paddocks of English parks where there was long, tussocky grass. Visitors might spend hours searching without even glimpsing the deer. Many water deer managed to escape the English parks. They took to the wild and have become local game animals.

Tufted deer *(Elaphodus cephalophus).* This is a single species, found in southern and central China and northern Burma at altitudes up to 8,000 feet. It usually lives near water and was once common in the reed beds bordering the Ningpo and other rivers in eastern China. A large buck may weigh nearly 50

The little tufted deer of China and Burma has protruding canine "tusks," and antlers so small that they may be hidden in the dark bunch of hair that named the deer. (New China Photo Co. photo)

pounds and stand about 2 feet at the shoulder.

The general color of the deer's upper parts is a deep chocolate brown and its coarse, almost spinelike hairs give the animal a shaggy look. The bucks carry antlers that are so small they are sometimes hidden by the tufts of hair that give this deer its common name. Tufted deer of both sexes have long canine teeth curving down from their upper jaws.

These are "barking deer." Both males and females utter sharp, barking calls during the mating season or when they are alarmed by predators.

Pere David's deer *(Elaphurus davidianus).* This large deer of northern China may have originally lived in alluvial plains but is now unknown in the wild. All the known specimens are descendants of a herd kept at the Imperial Hunting Park at Peking.

This deer, which bears little resemblance to any other Old World deer, has been classified by some taxonomists between the American deer and the roe

The Chinese water deer is a small deer, less than 2 feet high at the shoulder. Lacking antlers, the males are equipped with sharp, tusklike canine teeth that are effective weapons during the breeding season.

From its donkey-like tail (left) to the antlers that seem to have been put on backwards, the Père David deer is as unique as it is rare. Unknown to the western world until 1865, it is the last large deer to be "discovered" and described by scientists. Its original home was probably in the swamps and marshes of northern China but it has not existed in the wild state for many years. (Head photo by Jesse Cohen, National Zoological Park, Smithsonian Institution)

deer. It was named after Abbé Armand David, a priest who obtained two skins in 1865 by bribing guards of the imperial herd. The last deer of that herd died in 1920, and the genus *Elaphurus* would probably be extinct today had it not been for the Duke of Bedford. In about 1900, he brought several deer from China to his estate in England, and the surviving worldwide population of about 400 animals is descended from them.

A Pere David's deer stands 4 feet at the shoulder and weighs at least as much as the mule deer or whitetails of North America. It is crowned with distinctive antlers that lack brow tines. Each antler has a single long tine that extends backward and a main beam that points upward—usually with a single fork. The main beam of the antler may measure 32 inches. The deer's tail is exceptionally long and somewhat mulelike, often reaching to the animal's hocks.

The original Pere David's deer probably lived around marshes and wetlands, a type of habitat for which its large, spreading hoofs are well adapted. In parks with lakes, this deer frequently wades and even swims.

INDIA, INDOCHINA, EURASIA

Axis deer *(Cervus axis).* Native to India, Sri Lanka, Nepal, and Sikkim, the axis deer or "chital" has also been introduced to New Guinea, Hawaii, and New Zealand.

There are four species, all of which tend to frequent grasslands or light jungle and seldom penetrate into heavy forest. Most are medium-size deer that stand 3 feet at the shoulder and weigh up to 100 pounds or more, although some species are much smaller. Depending on where it is found, the axis deer is also known as the chital, spotted deer, axishirsch, or axihert. It is the common jungle deer of India. One of the four species of axis deer, the hog deer *(A. por-cinus)*, is native to India and Indochina and has been introduced to Europe, where it is known in Germany as the *Schweinhirsch*. This little deer is famous among hunters for its remarkable courage. When brought to bay by dogs, it may counterattack and has even been known to charge and wound a horse.

The axis, or spotted, deer is marked year-round with small white spots that contrast beautifully with its bay coat. Both adults and fawns have similar markings. The male's antlers are usually rather slender and three-tined, tending to rise (as much as 36 inches) rather than spread outward. The brow tine projects at almost right angles from the main beam. Unlike most species of deer, axis deer may be found in herds of up to 100.

Roe deer *(Capreolus capreolus).* This is an extremely widespread species that occurs throughout Eurasia, except in India and the extreme north. Roe deer inhabit western Europe, western and southern U.S.S.R., Turkey, Iraq, northern Iran, southern Siberia, northern and central China, and Korea. If given any reasonable cover, it can survive well even in parklike areas near densely populated cities and towns.

The roe deer is small and graceful. An adult stands about 26 inches at the shoulder and weighs 60

The graceful little roe deer is the most abundant game deer in Europe. In recent years a half-million of these deer have been taken annually in West Germany alone. Highly adaptable, they are found in all types of habitats—forest, plains, mountains, fields, and meadows—and have largely shifted from their original diet of buds and foliage to domestic crops and produce.

The axis deer, or chital, retains its vividly spotted coat all its life. It has been successfully introduced to western Europe, but proved a disaster in New Zealand where it swiftly overpopulated many areas and required stringent control measures by professional hunters. (Irene Vandermolen photo)

pounds. The bucks have vertical, almost straight antlers that measure 10 to 12 inches over the outer curve. Antlers rarely have more than three tines. Roe deer in Siberia are somewhat larger than those in western Europe. They sometimes stand nearly 3 feet at the shoulder and approach the average weight of larger North American whitetails.

The most abundant game deer of Europe, roe deer were the object of great drive shoots many years ago in Scotland, Germany, and Austria-Hungary. In 1892 over 68,000 roes were shot on various estates in Austria alone. Many of the deer were simply driven by beaters toward waiting guns. With time, though, more attention was given to the sport of stalking roe deer, and in some cases bucks were called to the gun with imitations of the bark of an amorous doe.

Roe deer are the only deer known to have delayed implantation—that is, a long period of dormancy between fertilization of the egg and development of the embryo. The delay may be as long as 4½ months, during which time the fertilized egg rests in the uterus in a state of arrested development. This is rather common among such mammals as bears and weasels, but extremely uncommon among hoofed mammals.

Barking deer *(Muntiacus,* various species). Five species of barking deer are found in a region extending south from southwestern China and Korea to Sumatra,

The little barking deer or "muntjac" has small antlers that may be used in rutting season fights. But in fights, the bucks are more likely to use their long, tusklike upper canine teeth. When excited, these "barking deer" utter a series of short, hard alarm calls similar to the barking of a dog. (Jeanne White/Photo Researchers Inc. photo)

sambar stands as high as 5 feet 4 inches at the shoulders and weighs 600 pounds on the hoof. It has rugged, three-tined antlers measuring 4 feet over the outer curve. Unlike all other antlered deer, sambar bucks in the wild do not always shed their antlers annually. Some may drop their antlers only every third or fourth year.

Almost entirely nocturnal, the sambar often seems to revel in heat. It frequently shelters in hot, stifling valleys and drinks water only once in two or three days. Sambars, like many Old World deer, can be highly vocal at times and have a peculiar trumpetlike call that is sounded during mating season or when predators are nearby. When a hungry tiger is on the prowl through Indian or Ceylonese forests, a chorus of deer calls sometimes follows the big cat's progress: the belling of sambars; the high, single *pow* of a spotted deer; and the short, sharp *grow-ow* of the barking deer. If you are near enough, you may even hear the peculiar moaning, three-noted *pooking* call of a tiger that puts the forest on an alert status.

Barasingha *(Cervus duvaucheli).* This is a large Indian cousin of the sambar that, like most other species

Java, and Borneo and west to Sri Lanka, the Indian peninsula, and Nepal.

These are small deer. Adults average less than 2 feet at the shoulder and weigh about 30 pounds. Antlers of the males are only 5 or 6 inches long, while the brow tine and main beam arise from unusually long, bony, hair-covered pedicels that are as long as the antlers themselves. The buck's upper canine teeth are sharp tusks several inches long and, according to one authority, "the buck knows how to use them." They can seriously injure dogs and other animals.

During the mating season, or when alarmed, the deer utters a barking sound that gives it its more common name. If a predator is nearby, such barking may continue for an hour or more. The deer are also sometimes called "muntjacs."

Sambar *(Cervus unicolor).* This deer ranges from Sumatra to India and is also found in southern and central China, Taiwan, Guam, the Philippines, Bonin Islands, Borneo, and Sri Lanka.

The sambar is distantly related to the red deer of Europe and the elk, or wapiti, of North America. It is a large deer with a rough, shaggy coat, causing one English hunter in India to note that "Compared with the Kashmiri stag, red deer, or wapiti, he looks like an ugly, coarse, underbred brute. . . ." A big Indian

Sambars vary greatly in size and color—from the smaller Philippine sambar that weighs no more than 135 pounds to the big Indian sambar that may weigh over 600 pounds. Indian and Sumatran sambars may be almost plain black, while one of the little Philippine subspecies has a spotted coat as an adult. Sambars are "true deer" of the genus Cervus, *closely related to the red deer of Europe and the elk (wapiti) of North America. (Irene Vandermolen photo)*

of big game in India, has suffered a catastrophic decline because of habitat destruction and almost unlimited hunting. It is a large deer, standing almost 4 feet at the shoulder and weighing up to 400 pounds.

Other Asian relatives of the sambar include the sika deer, thamin, Luzon deer, Thorold deer, and Schomburgk deer.

The barasingha of India has been transplanted into Texas, where over 50 species of exotic ungulates have been introduced. (E. P. Lee/World Wildlife Fund photo)

AFRICA

Only two types of deer have inhabited the African continent within historic times. The fallow deer was once found in North Africa, but no longer. A somewhat smaller type of red deer, the Barbary stag, inhabits pine and cork forests of Algeria and Tunisia, and parts of Morocco. In Africa, no deer ranges south of the Sahara.

EUROPE

Fallow deer *(Dama dama).* Originally a deer of Asia Minor, southern Europe, and apparently North Africa as well, the fallow deer has been transplanted by man to other parts of the world. It is now found in the Baltic region, western Europe, the western Ukraine, Great Britain, and in a few places in the United States.

It is a medium-size deer about as large as a whitetail;

an adult buck stands 3 feet at the shoulder and weighs as much as 200 pounds. In summer, an adult fallow deer has a bright fawn coat with white spots. The winter coat is usually a grayish fawn without spots. The antlers of an adult buck are clearly palmated, but not so much as those of a moose nor as wide-spreading.

Fallow deer are thought to have been introduced to Great Britain by the Romans, and today the deer are common in English deer parks, where they thrive

Fallow deer were once native to Europe, retreating to Asia Minor during the Ice Age. They were reintroduced to northern and western Europe by the Romans, and are now the most widely distributed deer in European parks. With centuries of captivity and selective breeding, fallow deer now occur in many colors—reddish, black, white and "porcelain-colored." (Irene Vandermolen photos)

in semidomesticated herds. In some parts of Scotland they have reverted entirely to the wild. They are excellent game animals in the wild. And even in deer parks where half-tame fallow deer are cropped for venison, they exhibit extraordinary wariness and cunning.

Like most other British game, fallow deer are regularly harvested for sport and for their meat, which some authorities claim to be the most delicious of all venisons.

Red deer *(Cervus elpahus)*. This famous stag of the Scottish highlands and western Europe is the same species as the wapiti, or elk, that inhabits western North America. Probably the most widespread of all deer, the red deer is found in alpine, forest, moorland, and grassland habitats. It ranges from Europe into the Caucasus and central Asia, as well as to western and northern China and the Ussuri region of the U.S.S.R. Red deer are also found in northwestern Tunisia, northeastern Algeria, Corsica, Sardinia, and originally (known as elk) much of the United States. The deer has also been introduced to South America and New Zealand.

This deer is generally regarded as the classic representative of the entire deer family of Cervidae. The red deer is also one of the largest in the family, although British red deer are somewhat smaller than those found in central Europe.

J. G. Millais, author of *British Deer and Their Horns*, tells of shooting a "really fine Highland stag in his prime; weight 16 stone 2 lbs., with a good wide head of ten points and good cups on the top." This weight is about 226 U.S. pounds—hardly in the same class as the 865-pound stag killed in Saxony. In the early 20th century, some red deer stags in the Carpathian Alps reportedly weighed over 500 pounds rough-dressed.

The weight of such alpine stags reflects the enormous range and abundant food available to them. As pointed out by Baille-Grohman, a distinguished English sportsman, these deer were once allowed to "make undisturbed raids upon the rich agricultural valleys . . . the feudal sway exercised by the great territorial magnates permitting the deer to trespass upon the crops with impunity, and thus grow to be the lustiest of their race." Such *carte blanche* treatment diminished with the end of feudalism, and this may be the factor in the general decline of the size of European stags. At least, the careful records kept of the weights of German red deer show a marked decrease in the past two centuries.

Here an old forester is winter-feeding a group of red deer near Mariazell in eastern Austria. Long managed as game animals in Europe, red deer are the classic representatives of the deer family to most Europeans. (Austrian Press and Information Service photo)

The European red deer is the little brother of the North American elk (wapiti)—same species, but of different voice and generally smaller size. Authorities also describe them in "European" terms. For example, in Scotland, this "red deer stag" is "roaring" during the rutting season and gathering a harem of "hinds." In the Rocky Mountains, a "bull elk," or "wapiti," will "bugle" while gathering his harem of "cows." (Irene Vandermolen photo)

To the nomadic Lapps of northern Scandinavia, the reindeer means meat, milk, hides, and even transportation, for the reindeer are sometimes hitched to sleds in winter. In the 1950s herds of reindeer were introduced into northern Canada in an effort to convert the traditional caribou-hunting Indians into reindeer-herders, but the project failed. (Photo courtesy of Norwegian Information Service)

In addition to Great Britain, European red deer are found in southern Sweden, Germany, Russia, France, Spain, Austria, Hungary, Turkey, and Greece. Until recent times, at least, the Barbary stag was found in Algeria, Tunis, and parts of Morocco, and they ranged south almost to the Sahara Desert.

Some early authorities held that the Caspian red deer, or maral, was "incomparably the finest of the red deer species." Said to average about 4½ feet at the shoulder and weigh as much as 560 pounds ("in exceptional specimens, a good deal more"), this species primarily inhabits Iran and is the biggest of the Old World red deer. The English authority H. A. Bryden noted that the great stags hunted in the Galician Carpathians were not "the ordinary red deer of Europe" but Caspian red deer.

Bryden also described the Kashmir stag, noting that it was often mistakenly called "barasingh" by Indian hunters. This large red deer, which stands as high as 4 feet 4 inches at the shoulder, is native to forests on the north side of the Kashmir Valley in northern India. It ranges in altitudes from 5,000 to 12,000 feet with habitats similar to those of the American elk.

European moose *(Alces alces).* The same species occurs in both Europe and North America. It is called a moose only in North America; in Europe it is referred to as an "elk" or "elch." This moose occurs in northern Europe from Scandinavia and the Baltic region to eastern Siberia, ranging south to the Ukraine, southern Siberia, Mongolia, Manchuria, and the Heilkungkiang region of China. It prefers moist habitats with willows, poplars, and aquatic plants.

Reindeer *(Rangifer tarandus).* This is the same species as our native caribou but is of a strain that appears to be far more easily domesticated. Reindeer are herded as livestock by the Laplanders of northern Scandinavia. Trained to harness, they are capable of drawing loaded sleds for great distances, and their milk, flesh, and hides are of great value to the people who keep them. There is still some hunting of wild reindeer in Norway.

Reindeer were once found in Britain. As late as the 12th century, the Jarls of Orkney frequently crossed over to the mainland to hunt reindeer in the wilds of northern Scotland.

SOUTH AMERICA

Pudu *(Pudu,* two species*).* Pudus are extremely small deer with little spikelike antlers. They lack tusks in the upper jaw and have practically no tail.

There are only two species of pudu and they inhabit South America. The species *pudu* is found through Bolivia and Chile, south almost to the Straits of Magellan. It lives in temperate forests from sea level to lower elevations in the Andes.

The species *mephistophiles* is found through much of Ecuador at elevations up to nearly 10,000 feet. It may be the tiniest deer in the world and is surely the smallest of all American deer. An adult stands only 15 inches at the shoulder and weighs 18 pounds—about the size of a terrier dog.

Tiniest of all American deer, South America's odd little pudu stands less than 6 inches high at birth and as an adult is no larger than a small dog. (Tom McHugh/Photo Researchers Inc. photo)

Brocket deer *(Mazama, ten species).* There are about ten species of brockets, ranging from southern Mexico to Paraguay. They are small deer, closely allied to the pudus, and the largest of the group—the red brocket of Guiana, Brazil, and Paraguay—stands only 27 inches at the shoulder. The smallest, the pygmy brocket, found in central Brazil, is only about 19 inches at the shoulder.

Shy and retiring—which is a pretty good idea for such a little deer in a world of jaguars and giant boas—brockets carry antlers that are little more than simple, unbranched spikes.

The brocket of South America is a secretive little deer, a "brush creeper" living in the densest cover and usually emerging to feed at night. The antlers on this red brocket buck are simple, unbranched spikes. In some species the bucks may shed their antlers irregularly or not at all. (A.W. Amber from National Audubon Society/Photo Researchers Inc. photo)

Pampas deer *(Ozotoceros bezoarcticus).* This is a single species generally found in dry, open grassland from Brazil, Paraguay, and Uruguay to Argentina and northern Patagonia. This small deer stands about 2½ feet at the shoulder. Antlers of the males are usually three-pointed and rarely exceed 14 inches in length. Originally, this deer used tall pampas grass for cover, but increasing settlement, cultivation, and heavy grazing in the region have made tall grasses scarce. As a result, the pampas deer has become the increasingly wary inhabitant of more open country.

The pampas deer of the South American grasslands are among the few deer that have a "family life," with the buck and doe remaining together after the young are born. Also unusual is the odor emitted from the interdigital glands of the buck's feet—a strong garlic smell that can be detected a half-mile away. (H. Jungis/World Wildlife Fund photo)

Andean deer *(Hippocamelus, two species).* There are two species of this deer, located in the Bolivian Andes near La Paz and in the Chilean Andes, Colchagua Province.

Second largest of the South American deer, it is named for the Andes, the South American "Rockies," and is found at elevations up to more than 15,000 feet. It is generally an animal of grassy hillsides and dense forests. Standing as high as 31 inches at the shoulder, a big Andean buck may weigh 140 pounds. The males carry simple antlers that usually branch but once.

Like most other species of South American deer, the Andean deer is gradually disappearing. Both species are classed as endangered.

The Andean deer, or guemals, are mountain deer that have been hard-hit by overhunting and domestic livestock diseases. They have been unable to compete with introduced red deer, fallow deer, and axis deer, and have been displaced in some parts of their original range. (Gerald E. Svendsen photo)

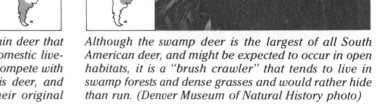

Although the swamp deer is the largest of all South American deer, and might be expected to occur in open habitats, it is a "brush crawler" that tends to live in swamp forests and dense grasses and would rather hide than run. (Denver Museum of Natural History photo)

Swamp deer *(Blastocerus dichotomus)*. This is a single species, found from central Brazil to Paraguay and northern Argentina. Largest of all South American deer, it is a handsome animal about the size of the British red deer, though not as heavy. Standing well over 3 feet at the shoulder, a big buck weighs over 200 pounds.

These deer prefer wet savannas with deep grass cover and wooded islands. Their hoofs can spread wide to facilitate travel over marshy ground, and their antlers are usually doubly forked for a total of four points per beam. They are considered an endangered species.

Whitetail deer *(Odocoileus virginianus)*. Seven subspecies of whitetails (or *venados*) are found in northern South America, down to almost 20 degrees southern latitude; that is, about midway, north to south on the continent. Formerly regarded as a separate species, *cariacou*, they are now recognized as *virginianus*, the same as the North American "type" species. All are small in comparison to most North American subspecies, although most South American whitetails are somewhat larger than those in Central America. The seven species of South American whitetails include:

O. v. cariacou: French Guiana and northeastern Brazil.

O. v. goudotii: the Andes of Colombia and northeast in the Sierra de Merida of western Venezuela.

O. v. gymnotis: savannas of Venezuela, Surinam, and Guiana.

O. v. margaritae: only on the Isla de Margarita off Venezuela.

O. v. peruvianus: Andean mountain slopes in Bolivia and Peru.

O. v. tropicalis: west of the Andes Mountains in Ecuador and Colombia.

O. v. ustus: the Andes Mountains of Ecuador and possibly southern Colombia.

According to Peter Brokx of Ecology and Environment, Inc., Buffalo, New York, these whitetails inhabit each of the principal divisions of northern South America's vast region that includes high and low savannas, high plateaus, mountains, deserts, rain forests, and tropical islands.

Differences between these whitetail subspecies are very minor and show up only in the slight color variations of their winter coats. The largest known *gymnotis* buck is about 67 inches long and weighs 144 pounds —a giant of his breed. Antlers of mature bucks of all these subspecies usually consist of the main beam with a basal snag and two crown tines.

One of the curious differences between these deer and their North American relatives is the total lack of one set of skin glands. North American whitetails have four sets of these external glands: the preorbitals at the inner corners of the eyes, the metatarsals on the outsides of the lower hind legs, the tarsals on the insides of the hind legs at the hocks, and the interdigitals between the toes of all feet. South American whitetails lack the metatarsal glands.

Like other South American deer, these whitetails have undergone a considerable population decline since the 1940s. Much of this is due to expansion of human populations through much of Surinam, Venezuela, Peru, and Brazil, along with a corresponding increase in illegal and indiscriminate hunting.

THE LIVES AND TIMES OF DEER

Of all hoofed animals in North America, only the musk-ox, the pronghorn, and the little peccary of the Southwest really are natives. Moose, elk, caribou, and deer are all North American immigrants—wanderers that began picking their way across the Asian-American land bridge over 15 million years ago.

It was the golden age of mammals, and the ancient plains and forests of North America swarmed with life. But then came intense droughts that wiped out entire suborders of the old-line mammals. In the Pleistocene epoch—the Ice Age—immense ice sheets covered much of the northern world and exterminated many other species. Still, the ancient deer adapted, surviving droughts and the Ice Age, saber-toothed tigers, wolves, and even man, the New Stone Age hunters who also came across the land bridge. These primitive men were master big-game hunters who are now thought to have dealt the final, killing blow to many animal species they found in the New World. Other species survived, however, and these ancestral deer evolved into the large, strong, graceful whitetails and mule deer that differ in many ways from their Old World kin.

When Europeans discovered the New World, they found these two types of deer in markedly different habitats. The whitetails generally held sway over the eastern half of the continent and much of Mexico. The mule deer inhabited those parts of the plains that would later be called (in a masterful piece of mis-naming) "the Great American Desert." They were also

The mule deer has always been a deer of the western deserts, plains, forests, and mountains. Its classic home range is along the Rocky Mountain chain where it may summer in the high country and winter in the foothills and high plains. The mule deer is more typically of dry, high, and open ranges than either its whitetail or blacktail relatives. (Len Rue Jr. photo)

found in high mountains and low, in badlands, river breaks, and the forests of the Pacific coast. Like the elk, mule deer on the Great Plains were nearly wiped out by early hunting. But modern game management systems have brought them back in most areas, and they have regained much of their lost ground. They have not, however, gone any farther east than the traditional limits of their historic range. On the other hand, and for reasons not well understood, whitetail deer have shown a strong tendency toward westward movement. Amazingly adaptable, they're now at home along timbered stream courses far west of what was once thought to be their typical range. And although some diehard cowboys regard the whitetail as an odd sort of bug, not worthy of the name "deer," it looks as if these dude deer are at home on the range—and intend to stay.

SIZES

Whitetails and mule deer are not as big as the average hunter thinks they are. The back of an adult whitetail is seldom higher than the belt buckle of an average man, and the belly of even a big deer may be only 20 inches above the ground. The little Florida Key deer isn't much taller than a collie.

Deer vary greatly in form and proportion, ranging from the slim, long-legged "ridge runners" to short-legged, heavy bodied "swamp deer." Some hunters swear they can tell the favored habitat of a particular deer just by looking at the animal. But in most cases these are just normal variations of the sort you'd find in a group of people. They have little to do with the particular area where the deer was shot.

As we've already seen, the big northern whitetails—especially the Northern Woodland and the Dakota—are the largest of the whitetail tribe. An average three-and-a-half-year-old New Hampshire buck may weigh 192 pounds by the first week in November, and 200-pound-plus bucks don't raise many eyebrows in most northern deer states. One lot of whitetail does from Ohio averaged nearly 138 pounds, and a group of western New York does weighed in at a 133-pound average.

As far as we know, the heaviest whitetail buck on record is a giant from Michigan. It had a hunter-dressed weight (head and hide still on, but innards removed and blood drained) of 354 pounds and an estimated live weight of 425. A New York buck shot in the Adirondacks in 1890 weighed about 400 pounds and stood 4 feet, 3 inches at the withers. It measured 9 feet, 7 inches from nose to tail tip. Maine's largest buck was one weighing 351 pounds dressed, and there

Northern whitetail bucks in prime condition can run big and heavy-antlered, but are generally less bulky and wide-antlered than mule deer. (Irene Vandermolen photo)

The Rocky Mountain muley buck is likely to be somewhat stockier and heavier than a whitetail of comparable age and condition. (Len Rue Jr. photo)

is a report of a Minnesota whitetail buck killed in 1926 that supposedly went 402 pounds, hunter-dressed. In recent times, an enormous whitetail killed in 1977 by bowhunter John Annett near London, Ontario, has not been rivaled, so far as we know. "In the round" with all its plumbing still in place, that buck weighed in at 196 kilos on a set of new, government inspected Toledo balance beam scales. That converts to 431.2 pounds live weight, but unfortunately Annett had skinned and gutted the huge buck before conservation officials inspected it.

Big mule deer tend to run larger than whitetails, although there's a lot of argument around a lot of hot stoves on that one. There isn't a great deal of difference between the extreme weights of the two species, perhaps, but the difference becomes apparent when the subspecies of both deer are considered, because at least half the subspecies of whitetails tend to be small. Figuring in 50-pound bucks, such as those from the Florida Keys or Coiba Island, pulls the average whitetail weight far below that of mule deer. Even on an individual basis, mule deer may have the edge. There is an authentic record of a California mule deer in Modoc County that weighed 380 pounds dressed, or about 475 live weight, and of a mule deer of British Columbia that went about the same.

The writer once asked the late Wendell Bever, then Game Chief for the South Dakota Game, Fish, and Parks Department, how to recognize a really big mule deer buck.

"Well," said Bever thoughtfully, "If you happen to see a bunch of muleys and wonder why on earth an elk is in there with them, *that* is a big mule deer!" He

was quite serious, too. There's that much difference between a record buck and the average run. But whitetail or muley, such individuals are giants of their breed and no more typical of deer than a sumo wrestler is of the average man.

COATS AND COLORS

In most of their United States range, whitetails and mule deer have distinct summer and winter coats.

A typical Rocky Mountain mule deer wears a winter coat that is generally grayish-brown, although there's considerable variation in the hue. Also, the mule deer's coat may actually become somewhat bleached by weather. The summer coat is a distinct reddish-brown, but tends to be somewhat yellower than that of the whitetail. Any color differences by sex are minor, although bucks are usually darker and more strongly marked about their faces.

Whitetails in summer are said to be "in the red" and have a reddish-tan, warm-weather coat that is worn for about three months. The rest of the time they have a heavy, grayish-tan winter coat. The deer are then "in the blue." Seasonal colors of the two coats differ less in southern whitetails, and coloring of coats is usually paler in the plains deer. The most richly colored (and darkest) whitetail is the big Northern Woodland species.

Summer coats of both mule and whitetail deer are composed of scanty, solid hairs with little underhair—a summer suit of no bulk. This coat is worn for about three months. But while it may be cool enough, it

Abnormal coloration sometimes occurs in deer—especially whitetails that have been more subject to controlled breeding and management than the other subspecies. This "pinto" whitetail doe is a mutant whose chances of survival in the wild are less than those of normal deer. (Leonard Lee Rue III photo)

Summer deer hair (left) is thin, solid, and relatively short. Winter hair (center) is coarser, hollow, somewhat kinky, and almost twice as long as the summer hair, and is sometimes underlain with a soft wooly undercoat (right). (Leonard Lee Rue III photo)

offers little protection against insects; so blackflies, mosquitos, and midges can torment deer during the warm months.

By September on most ranges, summer pelage has been entirely replaced by the winter coat. Here, the hairs are about 2 inches long, hollow, and of large diameter. There is an undercoat of soft hair curling loosely next to the skin. The insulating effect of this winter coat is remarkable, and a deer in its full winter dress can bed down in snow for hours without any

The heavy, hollow hairs of a deer's winter coat provide superb insulation. Well-fed deer bedded in deep snow usually appear to be perfectly comfortable. The packed snow beneath them may show little evidence of thawing, and falling snow may cover their thick coats without melting. (Leonard Lee Rue III photo)

appreciable thawing of the snow beneath. However, these hollow, large-diameter hairs of the "blue coat" result in a poorer grade of buckskin (from man's point of view, not the deer's). It's said that Indians have long preferred summer buckskin for the best quality leather, because it has smaller hair follicles and finer grain.

The spring shedding of the whitetail's winter coat begins earliest in the southern ranges. This may be early March in North Carolina. It does not begin until June in Maine. Deer start to put on their winter coats at about the same time, north and south, but finish the job earlier in the north. Both mule deer and whitetails are usually in "full blue" by September or early October in their northerly ranges, and much later in southerly parts of the U.S. The little whitetails of Mexico and Central America, because of the slight seasonal variations in temperature, have molting schedules that are far less clear-cut.

In both summer and winter, the whitetail has a white belly, a white patch on the throat, a white chin marked with a black spot on each side, and white around the eyes, inside the ears, and inside each leg. Its classic trademark, of course, is that great white tail that waves like a flag and may be 14 inches long. It is usually the last thing a stunned hunter sees as the deer vanishes into a jack pine thicket.

As noted earlier, the mule deer's tail is a rather undistinguished little rope that the deer doesn't raise when running (or rather, hopping) from danger. In all seasons, the mule deer has a white chin patch, white lower throat and belly, and a characteristic rump patch that is entirely lacking in the whitetail species.

ANTLERS: THE CROWNING GLORY

What makes a deer a deer instead of something else is the crown of antlers that a buck (and sometimes a doe) wears on its brow.

The annual shedding of antlers seems a wasteful process, because the bony material is a concentrated deposit of salts and minerals drawn from the deer's food. When you consider the amount of food and energy necessary to build a pair of moose antlers, which may span 6 feet and weigh 90 pounds with the skull, only to be cast aside after the breeding season, it's reason to wonder if old Mother Nature is really that wise after all. But antlers are part of her design, and she never really wastes anything.

Dropped antlers don't last long on the forest floor; they are rich stores of mineral salts that are relished by other creatures. Rats, mice, squirrels, and porcupines gnaw them, while wind, sun, and rain bleach and soften them. So antlers again become part of the soil, and even the mighty antlers of moose soon vanish. Ernest Thompson Seton quotes an old Nova Scotian woodsman: "Last winter I found a set of antlers dropped a short time before, and this fall being in the same locality, I had the curiosity to see what had become of the horns. After a good deal of search, at last I found a piece of bone from next the skull about the size of a goose egg, and about the same shape. On examining the surroundings, I soon discovered that

This is a calendar of antler growth for a typical northern whitetail. Periods of antler development vary somewhat with climate and region. Tropical deer have no rigid antler schedule and may develop antlers at any time of year.

August

Mid to late September

July

ANTLER DEVELOPMENT IN THE WHITETAIL DEER

January

June

May

Early spring

The discarded antlers of all deer are rich stores of salts and minerals that are relished by rodents. These whitetail antlers, still attached to the hairy skull (bottom right) of a dead buck, are being chewed up and recycled by the late buck's rodent neighbors. (Leonard Lee Rue III photo)

the squirrels and porcupines had regular roads to the horn, from which they had many a fine meal. This is why it is that although thousands of sets of horns have been dropped in past years, there are so few found."

Antlers provide an essential visual stimulus for social interaction among deer. Massive, many-tined antlers are almost always worn by the strongest and most vigorous bucks. Socially, as well as physically, a yearling forkhorn can never compete with a seven-year-old buck that seems to have a rocking chair on his head. The young buck knows it, the old buck knows it, and the doe knows it. The mere sight of big antlers alone may not be all that awesome to a younger buck, but big, heavy antlers and big, heavy bucks usually come as a set—and the youngsters recognize muscle when they see it. Let that old buck lose his huge rack, though, and he can be dominated by lesser bucks that still wear antlers—puny as those antlers might be. No matter, because the rut is over by then, anyway.

A heavy rack of antlers—with a heavy, mature buck behind them—is a means of achieving dominance over other mature bucks and helps assure that the does are mated with the strongest, most vigorous males.

Antlers may serve other purposes, as well. While an antler is developing, it may have a thermoregulatory effect. It's been theorized that the "velvet" (a membrane covering developing antlers) may help dissipate body heat through the myriad blood vessels that lie close to its surface—a welcome feature to an animal that lacks sweat glands. Some biologists speculate that deer antlers have evolved as cooling organs that are annually renewed. But if there is anything to this, why are they lacking in does? Most experts believe that antlers really evolved as social adaptations geared to reproductive success.

Blood vessels in the soft, velvet membrane also transport building materials to the developing antler. An antler in velvet is tender, sensitive, and easily injured, and will bleed freely if the velvet is cut. Bucks favor and protect their budding antlers, and an injury at this stage will cause a permanent deformity on the mature antler.

Antler growth is launched by the pituitary gland, and that gland is stimulated by strengthening, lengthening spring daylight. Male hormones don't start this growth, because in April the buck's testicles are still shrunken and inactive.

Naturalist Leonard Lee Rue III explains the effects

A deer's antlers begin as "buds" arising from pedicels on the frontal bones of the skull. A rich supply of minerals and salts are fed into the growing antlers through blood vessels in the soft, velvety membrane that sheaths each emerging antler. (Leonard Lee Rue III photo)

of light on antler growth in his *Deer of North America* as follows:

> The start of antler growth is a response to photoperiodism. With the winter solstice in December, the number of daylight hours gradually increases. At the base of the deer's brain is a tiny endocrine gland, the pituitary. The activity of this gland is lowest in January and February. The animal's eye functions rather like a photoelectric cell, transmitting messages about light received. As the hours of daylight increase, the eye is exposed to more light, and this stimulates the pituitary. The gland becomes activated in March and April, producing a somatotropic hormone that governs body, bone, and tissue growth. It is this hormone that starts the antlers growing. Although a deer can live if its pituitary gland is removed, it cannot grow antlers even though the pedicels are formed.

> . . . at the University of British Columbia, Ian McTaggart Cowan subjected mule deer to twelve daily hours of light and twelve daily hours of darkness the year round. These bucks were unable to shed their antlers and grow new ones. Other bucks, kept in continuous light, grew and lost three sets of antlers in two years.

As antlers reach their maximum size in September, an increasing charge of male hormone testosterone somehow ripens them and *halts* their growth, causing the blood supply to the antlers to be cut off and the velvet to dry and slough away. This dried velvet is quickly rubbed and torn away as the buck shadowboxes with trees and brush. Rubbing is probably not a response to itchy antlers, as some hunters believe.

So long as the buck's blood is charged with testosterone during the rutting season, he will keep his antlers. But as the hormone ebbs in the late winter, bone between the base of the antler and the pedicel of the skull is resorbed, and the antler simply falls off. If a buck with growing antlers is castrated, the antlers will not mature due to the lack of testosterone and are never shed. However, such "green" antlers don't last long, because they freeze in winter and then break off bit by bit. If the fawn buck is castrated, antlers never develop; if a buck is castrated early in the fall, antlers are promptly shed.

A doe's lack of antlers is not due to missing male hormones but to certain female hormones that inhibit antler growth. In some does these inhibiting hormones are scanty enough to permit growth of antlers. But, since the doe has no testosterone, antlers seldom mature and are usually small and velvet-covered. (There are some cases of does with well-formed, pol-

By late summer, the antler growth of this whitetail buck (left) still in velvet is nearly complete. It's an easy time of year for the buck, with little to do but eat, loaf, and nurse those tender antlers. The right-hand photo shows the same buck as in the previous photo after the antler "velvet" sloughed away in ragged strips. The gleaming new antlers may vary in color from off white to deep brown. The darker color is likely caused by dried blood. (John Goerg, NY Dept. of Environmental Conservation photos)

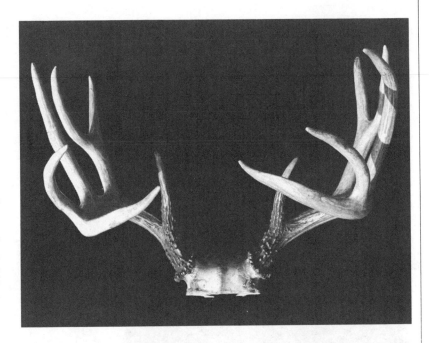

Although whitetail and mule deer antlers are usually markedly different, there can be some confusion. This whitetail rack has nontypical forked tines on each main beam— a mule deer characteristic. On the other hand, some blacktails wear racks that may be almost indistinguishable from those of a whitetail's. (Leonard Lee Rue III photo)

ished antlers.) Most antlered does are capable of bearing fawns.

The color of a mature antler varies from polished white to deep, rich brown. Perhaps, as some believe, this is due to the types of shrubs and trees on which the bucks rub their young antlers; or maybe dried blood is the principal source of color.

Antlers are usually symmetrical, though they can become deformed during devlopment. Antler deformity may result from an injury to the growing antler, or the deformity may be linked in some way to body injury. In one large group of western deer, only a tiny percentage of uninjured bucks had antler deformities. On the other hand, nearly three-fourths of those with deformed antlers had old and conspicuous body injuries. In the great majority of cases the body injury and antler deformity were on opposite sides. Years ago, the naturalist-writer-hunter Archibald Rutledge held the personal opinion that his South Carolina deer generally carried racks that seemed more symmetrical than those of larger Northern Woodland deer he had seen, but he didn't advance any theories on the subject.

Deer sometimes have near-perfect duplications of one or both antlers located close to the normal antler bases, or an abnormal third antler may grow between the normal antlers. One whitetail had an elevated plaque an inch high on his nasal bones, and this may have been a rudimentary antler. Any of the membrane bones on top of the deer's skull may grow antlers, but the tendency to antler growth is much stronger on the frontals than in the areas in front of and behind these bones. Antlers actually grow from an area of specialized brow skin. When this skin was removed from

Antlers may be deformed by injury to either to the "green" antler or to some part of the deer's body. This buck suffered a deformed right antler because of an injury to the left side of his body. (Photo courtesy of Leonard Lee Rue III)

Whitetail antlers come in a variety of configurations. Some, such as this fine 8-point (eastern count) buck's, rise high above the head. (Leonard Lee Rue III photo)

Antlers on some bucks, such as this superb 10-point whitetail spread low and wide making quiet navigation through heavy brush a challenge.(Irene Vandermolen)

one buck, no antler appeared in that area during the growing season, although antlers did develop the following year.

Antler size is less a reflection of age than it is of the buck's general well-being. Among Michigan whitetails in the Upper Peninsula—a region not noted for abundant deer foods—an average 1½-year-old buck may have an average of only 2.8 antler points. On the rich farm soils of southern Michigan, bucks of the same age have averaged 5.8 points. This, by the way, is "eastern count," which includes all points on both antlers. "Western count" includes only one antler, usually the left one.

Dietary calcium is probably the most important factor determining antler size. It's thought that calcium obtained from food in late winter and early spring is deposited in the skeleton and that growing antlers draw bone salts and minerals from these skeletal stores. If this is so, there is a vital link between soil quality and winter food, and the size of next fall's antlers.

Up to a point, deer antlers do grow larger with age, and are usually at their finest when the buck is about

Some physiological imbalance caused this New Jersey buck to develop freak antlers that included 7 main beams and 13 points. Abnormalities in antlers are caused by injury, a physiological or hormonal imbalance of some kind, or heredity. This grotesque rack is probably the result of a hormonal imbalance. (Photo courtesy of Leonard Lee Rue III)

five years old. But the number of antler tines is *not* a reliable indicator of age. A whitetail shot in Texas had 78 antler points, but it's doubtful that even a Texas deer could be 78 years old. The most reliable age indicator in deer is the teeth, which show progressive wear and thus reveal fairly accurately a deer's year class.

Antlers usually begin declining in size and quality after the buck's eighth birthday. As he grows old, his antlers become irregular in size, shape, and symmetry, and the antlers of a 12-year-old deer may be twisted snags that show little resemblance to the regal rack of his prime.

The fully matured antler is solid, polished bone—often beautifully stained in shades of walnut, cream, and ivory. Tines are sometimes so sharp they are painful to touch with a firm pressure. The buck is fully conscious of the rack he carries. He becomes an arrogant, swaggering bully, that is swollen-necked and red of eye—a splendid fighting machine designed for jousts of autumn. But when those antlers are shed naturally, or if they are sawed off, he becomes docile, shy, and retiring, a meek shadow of his old warlike self.

And so the antler cycle has ended and begun, and the salts that built a buck's proud rack may return years later to adorn his great-grandsons.

As a buck enters old age, his antlers are no longer the heavy-beamed, many-tined, symmetrical weapons of his prime. They may be deformed, or may never shed their velvet at all. Or, as with this venerable old muley, the antlers keep much of their maximum spread but develop fewer points. (Leonard Lee Rue III photo)

These five sets of whitetail antlers came from the same buck on successive years, showing the tendency of antlers to retain the same basic conformation from year to year. Also this conclusively illustrates that you can't estimate a buck's age simply by counting the tines. (John Goerg, NY Dept. of Environmental Conservation photo)

THE RUTTING MOON

The bucks, so shy and retiring all spring and summer, are on the prod.

In the world of deer, autumn is the reason for antlers, and antlers mean the winning of does. Sparring sessions with bushes and small trees have helped swell the bucks' necks as much as 10 inches, and the antlers have become polished tines of hard, sharp bone. The fever of the rut is upon them, and the bucks range in search of does.

When a pair of mature breeding bucks meet, the landscape rings with conflict. The stags gauge each other, hair bristling down the crests of their swollen necks, and join battle with a crash of antlers that can be heard for great distances. Unlike rams that repeatedly charge and clash, bucks fence with their antlers and try to break through the other's guard. Heads down, antlers meshed, eyes rolling and bulging with effort, they strain in a mighty test of endurance. For as long as two hours, they may not break apart; their necks swell and their hoofs tear up the sod in this contest of strength that may even end in death.

It's most doubtful that the bucks really "intend" to inflict serious injury. More likely, it's simply a match to determine who's boss. A typical fight doesn't end in serious injury to either combatant; the vanquished buck seems to suffer a *sense* of defeat rather than disabling injury, and retires from the field leaving it— and possibly the doe that was the cause of it all—to the victor.

But when weapons as potentially dangerous as those antlers are involved, anything can happen. One buck may unexpectedly break through the other's guard with a single deadly thrust, goring or even disemboweling his foe. The freshly tanned hide of one five-year-old buck showed signs of 47 wounds that had at least penetrated his skin.

During this powerful jousting, antlers may be sprung slightly by the strain and in that way become inextricably locked. This sometimes ends with the neck of one buck being broken, and the eventual starvation of the other buck. Interlocked antlers are not common, but may not be as rare as is often thought.

When a pair of antler-locked bucks is found alive, they can often be freed by sawing off an antler or two. But this is risky business, because one or both of the freed bucks may charge the man who unlocked them. One game warden who has had two narrow escapes after sawing off antlers refused to do so again unless he was backed up by a capable gunner.

The venting of a buck's rutting madness is not always reserved to other bucks. Captive bucks have killed unresponsive does that weren't ready to breed. One such buck, in a fury of frustration, killed three

Bucks commonly "fight" trees in the rutting season. These furious attacks on imaginary rivals help vent the buck's aggressive energy—a sort of release valve between actual encounters with rivals. This may also function as a sort of training regimen for bouts with other bucks. (Leonard Lee Rue III photo)

Fresh "buck rubs" are reliable sign that a rutting buck isn't far away. The victims are usually small, whippy saplings such as these alders. But bigger bucks often take on bigger growth. (Leonard Lee Rue III photo)

Early in the breeding season, while a buck is still heavy and strong, the strenuous exercise of fighting trees and brush can greatly thicken a buck's neck. By the end of the rut, he will probably look thin and worn. (Irene Vandermolen photo)

Like buck-rubbed saplings, a "scrape" is a sure sign of a rutting buck in the area. Buck scrapes are pawed in a sort of nervous frenzy, often beneath overhanging tree limbs or branches that may be hooked with antlers or nipped with teeth. (Leonard Lee Rue III photo)

Occasionally a buck will defecate or urinate in a scrape, as if to establish a scent post. This scrape was pawed by a whitetail buck that had been eating grass. Bucks rarely return to "rubs" but may revisit their scrapes. (Leonard Lee Rue III photo)

Head raised, neck extended, and ears nearly flattened against his neck, this whitetail buck is assuming a posture of extreme aggression. (Leonard Lee Rue III photo)

penned does in one night. The blood on his antlers, neck, and head attested to the ferocity of his attack. That captive buck, however, may have become demented by confinement. It certainly wasn't "normal" behavior. Most bucks don't make such brutal assaults, and this behavior may not become apparent until a buck is three or four years old.

Many hunters believe the rut is triggered by the first few frosty nights of autumn, but temperature has little to do with it. Again, it is a matter of photoperiodism, of light intensity. Waning light, not freezing temperatures, is what really sets the rutting season.

The peak of the rutting season in the north woods comes around mid-November. In New York State, breeding may be as early as September 22 and as late as February 22. Southern deer usually breed later. Some Central and South American whitetails may have no clear-cut breeding season at all, and may breed throughout the year. The breeding peak for Arizona whitetails is between mid-January and mid-February. However, if any of these deer are moved from one geographic area to another, they usually adjust to the different seasonal light intensities and adapt their breeding season to the new place within a few years.

Mule deer in northeastern California usually enter

A subordinate, but aggressive, whitetail (left) approaches a dominant one. Bucks of unequal size and age, and young bucks like the mule deer at right are more likely to joust and spar than have an all-out fight. (Left photo by Leonard Lee Rue III; right by Irene Vandermolen)

The most serious battles occur between big dominant bucks. These heavy-antlered muleys are staging a battle royal for the doe standing in the background. (Tom W. Hall photo)

The headlong clashes of two big, dominant bucks may cause their heavy antlers to spring and interlock under tension. In this no-win mortal combat, death often results from a broken neck for the losing buck and starvation for the "winner." Note the strands of barbed wire laced across the chest of the loser. (Wisconsin Dept. of Natural Resources photo)

their most intensive breeding condition in mid-November or early December and continue some breeding into early January. In Middle Park, Colorado, the peak of the mule deer breeding is from mid-November into mid-December, while the desert mule deer around Prescott, Arizona, have shown a relatively short breeding peak that extends from late December into early January. Far to the north, in Alberta, Canada, the mating period of mule deer may begin as early as late October and ends by mid-November—the time when many of the mule deer in the United States are just beginning.

Most of this mating, by the way, occurs at night. Bucks may still be sexually active at dawn, but their ardor is evidently cooled by the arrival of full daylight. That isn't particularly surprising, considering the fact that deer tend to be more cautious and restrained during the day. This seems particularly true of whitetails, which are generally more secretive and retiring than muleys.

Unlike elk, whitetails and mule deer do not form harems. They practice a serial polygamy in which a buck must find a doe, determine if she is in or near estrus, and then actively court her before mating.

During this courtship it is to the muley buck's advantage to avoid advertising its presence, in order to attract as little competition as possible. On the other hand, if the doe "plays the field," she helps improve the gene pool because she promotes intense male competition that usually results in her mating with the strongest and most vigorous buck. To do this the doe must roam more than usual, make more noise than usual, and have a rather conspicuous estrus. Yet, once the buck has been attracted, he must try his best to keep the doe quiet, secluded, and to himself. The buck is likely to approach a doe with great courtesy, head low and eyes averted (it's impolite to stare), and makes every effort to avoid spooking her.

A mature, rutting mule deer buck at close quarters must be an awesome sight to a doe that weighs only half as much. So how can the buck assure a doe that there is no need for alarm? Some biologists think the buck appeals to the mother in her. All mule deer, even newborn fawns, have distinct facial markings. In the adults these markings are much stronger in bucks than does, and a mature mule deer buck has a sort of super baby face. As a buck slowly approaches a doe from the rear, neck outstretched and head low, the buck may utter a soft, deep version of a fawn's distress call.

The doe, then, is aware of a very large and somewhat baby-faced deer, crooning what might be construed as masculine baby talk. So, in spite of those heavy shoulders, thick neck, and regal spread of gleaming antlers, she remains unafraid. It's hard for us to avoid the anthropomorphic conclusion that the doe probably thinks the big bruiser is cute!

The rutting buck almost always initiates the mating.

Depending largely on their keen sense of smell, rutting bucks are constantly in search of sexually active does. This whitetail buck is hot on the trail of a doe, following her like a hound in pursuit of a rabbit. (Leonard Lee Rue III photo)

And since the doe may not be receptive for as many as ten days after the buck enters the rut, she often uses every coy trick in the book to elude him—running, hiding, and mingling with other deer. Does seldom meet the violent fate that they might in captivity, because they have room to escape, if necessary. But a buck may hound a doe almost beyond her endurance for a week or two. Or the doe may be tracked by two or more males, usually with the largest buck leading and the smaller ones not far behind. Seven whitetail bucks were once shot on the trail of a single doe, all in the space of a quarter hour. If smaller bucks keep their places in such a passion parade, there is no trouble. But if they catch up with number one, or if another large buck cuts the doe's trail and meets that leading buck, there'll likely be a slam-bang battle.

As a doe enters her estrus or "heat" period, she becomes less shy and finally allows the buck to catch her. The mating itself is often a violent affair, and the buck may drive the doe to her knees. She is actually in full heat for only a day or two at a time, and if she is not successfully bred she may enter another heat period about 28 days later. A single doe can have as many as three heat cycles in a single season, ranging from late September to late November. Near the end of his breeding season, the buck has usually spent most of his earlier passion. Mule deer does still in heat tease the now indifferent bucks in an effort to rekindle their ardor.

COURTING BEHAVIORS

It is to the advantage of the species that a mule deer doe advertise her presence in breeding season and attract as many suitors as possible so that she may be bred by the most vigorous, dominant buck in the area. It's to the buck's advantage to keep the whole affair as secret as possible in order to minimize competition—although this splendid 5-pointer appears able to handle most rivals. (Irene Vandermolen photo)

Odor, as well as behavior, will tell a mule deer buck if a doe is ready for breeding. Below left: Until she is, a doe may do her best to get away from a buck—while he does his best to stay with her until she is receptive. Photo right: As he rubs his hind legs together, this big mule deer buck carefully urinates on the tarsal glands on the insides of his hocks. Urine combining with pheromones emitted by these glands intensify the odor that's an important part of deer communication. Such "rub-urination" is a dominance display of mule deer bucks. (Irene Vandermolen photos)

Among either whitetails or muleys, smelling tarsal glands is an accepted way of saying "hello" and finding out how things are going. (Leonard Lee Rue III photo)

Breeding season ended, the tired buck casts down his weapons. As the bone between pedicel and antler is resorbed, both antlers may drop at about the same time or one may be shed several days before the other. (Leonard Lee Rue III photo)

Deer antlers grow from body pedicels of the skull, which are clearly revealed when the buck loses his crowning glory. (Leonard Lee Rue III photo)

The rut saps the bucks because of the fighting, extensive traveling, and neglect of proper eating. Bucks may lose almost a fourth of their weight in only nine weeks.

The breeding season finally ends in late December and January when bucks lose their antlers. Then, in northern ranges, the unarmed bucks and their pregnant does may herd up in the winter deer yards (feeding areas) of the northern woods or the high valleys of the western mountains. There they will endure the bleak, deadly winter that can doom a sizable portion of some northern deer herds. Only the bucks fought during the rutting season. But from December to April all deer in the north, bucks, does, and fawns alike, begin the most desperate battle of their year.

THE HUNGER MOONS

In spring, summer, and early fall the deer may have roamed widely over forests, mountainsides, meadows, and fields, fattening themselves on a hundred varieties of food. Shelter was of little real concern; food was plentiful and energy demands easily met.

But deer shrink from the raw, cold winds of early winter. They begin leaving the hardwood uplands and high-country ranges to seek the protection of cedar swamps, dense stands of conifers, the sunbathed south slopes of ridges, and farmland valleys. Throughout the entire north the strongest winter drive of both whitetails and mule deer is to escape the worst of the cold. And in doing that, they often maroon themselves in winter ranges that can hardly support them. Of the northern whitetail's total range, only about 10 percent may be used in winter—something like a human family deserting all other rooms in the house to huddle around the furnace.

Once they're yarded up, they often die rather than leave. The late Ilo Bartlett, a veteran Michigan deer biologist, once broke a snowshoe trail from an over-browsed cedar swamp to a nearby area that was completely untouched. He even baited the trail with succulent white cedar to lure the deer to the new feeding ground. But as soon as the trail bait ran out, the deer returned to the overbrowsed area to resume starving. Deer have been moved from such a yard to plentiful food supplies three miles away, only to return to the original yard. Other deer have starved in a cedar swamp that was split by a railroad, refusing to cross

the right-of-way to the rich food supplies on the other side.

Deer seem able to sense the coming of bad weather, and in Michigan the whitetails may begin drifting into the cedar swamps up to 24 hours before a storm strikes. In any case, they are usually "yarded up" when the snow is from 12 to 18 inches deep and stay in their winter cover from late December to early April.

Once in a deer yard, a whitetail herd will not leave as long as there is any significant amount of snow on the ground. They cannot and will not travel in heavy snow. When snow deepens to 20 inches, widespread foraging diminishes. A deer may fight through as much as 30 inches of snow for short distances to reach food—usually working from tree to tree where the snow is not so deep—but there is little movement off the trails when the snow is deeper than 30 inches. In the hilly country of the northeastern United States, deer tend to avoid north slopes and congregate on south-facing slopes where the sun's intensity may be twice that of level land. On one south ridge in western New York, 700 deer were seen in an area less than 3 miles long and ½ mile wide.

Mule deer country is often high country, and even though good winter foods may be available the deer are unable to get to them if the snow is too deep—which is the rule rather than the exception in most mountainous ranges. When there is as much as 17 inches of snow, mule deer are likely to be on the move to lower elevations. But that may not help much. The ridges and hillsides most likely to have the least snow, or no snow at all, are those receiving the most sun. Because that is true in summer as well, such places

Whitetail deer are not herd animals in the way that caribou are, but northern winters usually force them to "yard" together in areas that hold the best available winter cover and food supplies. These deer in Wisconsin's Nicolet National Forest have made it through to March, but the severest tests are probably still ahead. (U.S. Forest Service photo)

Deep snow presents a deadly serious problem to deer. It makes for hard going, draining precious energy and greatly limiting a deer's ability to forage for food. (Leonard Lee Rue III photo)

High-country mule deer may not be bothered much by the first light snows of the season. But as snow depth builds up to 20 inches, burying low forage and making movement more difficult, they begin drifting down-mountain. (Leonard Lee Rue III photo)

Down from the mountain, groups of mule deer forage on sagebrush flats and bullbrush draws of the high plains—often ending up at ranch haystacks. (Leonard Lee Rue III photo)

usually have scanty vegetation. North-facing slopes have better vegetation, on the other hand, but the snow is deeper and, because it is less likely to thaw and crust, simply stays too soft for deer travel. The level areas of valley floors and "parks" may not be of any great help either. Here there is just enough sun to thaw and crust, but not enough to melt away all the snow to vegetation. A Catch 22 situation if ever there was one. In Middle Park, Colorado, it has been estimated that because of snow tenable winter range for mule deer is less than one percent of the total summer range.

In a heavy northern snowstorm, whitetails and mule deer may shelter beneath branches of dense conifers for as long as three days. Some deer may bed near each other, although there is no evidence that they ever really huddle to share body heat. And at 20 or 30 degrees below zero, few deer remain bedded. They must exercise to prevent chilling in the cruel air and this adds to their food requirements.

Trails in a deer yard are usually opened and packed within 48 hours after a storm, but as travel becomes more difficult fewer trails are kept open. In northern yards whitetails seldom go over a quarter mile from shelter to feed, although trails up to a mile long have been seen.

Whitetails and mule deer alike are least active during periods of high winds and low temperatures, on warm days with breaking snow crusts, and in deep snow after storms. But after January thaws create strong snow crusts, there may be a sharp change in deer activity. Then they can travel above the ground on crusted snow, enabling them to get previously out-of-reach browse or to roam to hardwood cover where food is more plentiful. The deer swiftly strip foliage from bowed and broken snow-laden cedars, and regularly eat twigs below porcupine cuttings in hemlocks.

Deer compete viciously for food. And when winter's vise tightens, fawns feel the pinch first. They are not only less able to reach high browse but are often bullied by older deer. Bucks dominate does. Does dominate fawns, even their own. Larger deer drive the smaller ones away from food with their hoofs. There's no family love now; the deer all have the same need. If a fawn grows too weak to follow its mother through deep snow, the doe will promptly abandon it. Of winter-killed mule deer in Oregon's Murderers' Creek Basin over a series of years, as much as 92 percent were fawns and yearlings. Although those young deer may have gone into the winter in top condition, they were simply unable to handle the deadly combination of deep snow, extreme cold, and the overwhelming

Winter takes its heaviest toll of fawns and yearlings. This starving whitetail fawn may not live through the night. (Leonard Lee Rue III photo)

For these whitetails, the cedar swamp in which they sought food and shelter proved to be their dying place. (Michigan Dept. of Natural Resources photo)

competition of bigger, stronger adults.

While northern whitetails and mule deer are enduring their winter siege, southern deer are having troubles of their own. Even in Florida's subtropical Everglades, there is an annual deer loss that closely corresponds to that of the North. When late fall rains raise the water level in the 'Glades, deer are often forced to yard on hammocks and higher ground. As the average water depth approaches 2 feet (similar in depth to northern snows), deer trapped on high ground begin eating themselves "out of house and home." Parasites and disease sap the weakened deer, and many die of pneumonia induced by malnutrition. During such winter high-water periods, the Everglades deer herds may be cut 30 percent. Fawns, yearlings, and does suffer the highest death rate, just as they do in Montana or Michigan.

On the Edwards Plateau of central Texas, and in many parts of Arizona and New Mexico as well, the deadliest season may be summer when drought and competition with grazing livestock for food team up to kill deer wholesale. Thousands of deer die during winter storms as well. On some heavily grazed Texas ranches, the deer are in such pathetic condition that few bucks develop antlers large enough to become legal game. Only half the does may bear fawns.

When a well-fed northern deer yards up in early winter, it literally has handfuls of fat within its body. It is still somewhat on the lean side, even in prime condition. But there is fat around the kidneys and a spot of it on the heart; fat is larded over the saddle and hips, outside the ribs, and on the brisket. The marrow of the long leg bones is rich, creamy white, and waxen with fat content.

Through the harsh, lean times of late winter, these reserves are exhausted. Fat over the rump vanishes first, then that stored between the hide and the body goes and the deer's skin begins to hang loosely. Fat in the body cavity vanishes, and in the deer's last days fat is absorbed from bone marrow. This makes the marrow cranberry red and gelatinous.

During the short days of a severe northern winter, deer totter along the skein of trails in their yards, through copses of spruce low on the mountainsides, or in bull-brush draws above sagebrush flats that are choked with wind-packed snow. Their coats roughen, hip bones show, and great hollows appear in their flanks. Eyes become dull, jaws appear swollen and "mumpy," and the deer stand with backs bowed and humped in their final weakness. Body reserves are gone, and so is food. Still the winter drags on, and late spring snows may block the deer from dispersing to the unbrowsed higher ground. And so the deer starve and die—two in this thicket, twenty in this deer yard, a hundred in the that county. Tens of thousands may die in a single state, and the toll can reach nearly two million nationally in one severe winter.

Under harsh conditions, malnutrition may appear after the deer have spent only six weeks on winter range, and it strikes the fawns first. By mid-March extreme malnutrition is apparent, and this slow starvation, with its attendant pneumonia, is the main cause of death during the rest of March and April.

A severe northern winter may kill half of the fawns born the previous spring. Fawns that do survive may never grow as large as they might have if they'd had enough food their first winter. Pregnant does—drained by malnutrition—may resorb their embryos and fail to give birth in the spring. Such embryo resorption, rather than abortion, is the way a deer usually eliminates a dead fetus. But in some cases a dead fetus becomes mummified and permanently sterilizes the doe.

Even if the fetal fawns survive to be born—and the does make terrible demands on their own bodies to enable unborn fawns to live—their mothers may be so weakened by spring that their milk supply fails and the newborn fawns die of starvation.

FAWNING

There are always winters, and most are cruel. But there are springs as well, with soft times and new life. In early June the northland is lush and green again, with browse, tender grasses, and forbs (herbs other than grasses) that rebuild the herds' strength. Heavy winter coats are shed, the deer are in the red, and the next generation has begun to replace losses suffered in the Hunger Moons.

Perhaps the doe chooses a special place for her fawning, and maybe not. No one is really sure. She needs solitude, though, and will always drift away from other deer to find it, avoiding all company for about two weeks while she gives birth and attends her small fawn.

Mule deer does usually seek nurseries on the edges of open glades or meadows. As it happens, these are almost ideal hiding places for the dappled fawns. They blend well with the half-sun, half-shadow of such edges. It's doubtful the doe has any special appreciation of this, or that she deliberately selects the cover that best matches her fawn's coat—even though it often works out that way. But the place will be relatively secure, and it will be isolated.

Whitetail fawns are born wherever the doe happens to be at the time, and young fawns have been found near creeks and bogs, where blackflies and mosquitos were thick enough to drive a man from the area. Newborn fawns have also been seen in snow when there were snow-free areas nearby. (Well, animals make mistakes too.) One biologist told of a "maternity center" for local deer—a quiet woodlot with mature conifers, deciduous trees, and a substantial understory

FAWNS

This could be three generations of whitetails, with a tiny fawn only 5 minutes old and a yearling buck that may be the doe's fawn from the previous spring. (Leonard Lee Rue III photo)

A fawn is one of the most appealing of all wildlife babies. It is also one of the best protected, with little or no odor, a spotted coat that breaks up its outline, and the ability to remain motionless for many hours. (Leonard Lee Rue III photo)

Unlike many mammals, deer fawns are not helpless at birth. They are born with eyes open and a full coat of hair, and they do not seem to need any special sheltering by their mothers. Barely dry, this new-born whitetail fawn is trying to stand. (Leonard Lee Rue III photo)

Twin deer fawns are quite common, especially with older does. But unlike these little whitetails, fawn twins are not usually found bedded together. (Gerald S. Ratliff, West Virginia Dept. of Commerce photo)

At two months of age, these mule deer twins still have some spots but are capable of following their mother wherever she goes. (Leonard Lee Rue III photo)

of foliage. That spot was also preferred by cows for calving. But, if there is such a thing as a favored whitetail nursery, it may be under a fallen treetop.

The gestation periods of the mule deer and whitetail are about 200 days. Single fawns are the rule for a doe's first fawning, when she is one and a half years old. In both species of deer, an older doe in good condition usually bears twin fawns, or even triplets. One Texas whitetail bore four sets of triplet fawns in the first five years of her life. Quadruplet fawns are rare, and one of the four is usually much smaller than the others. It often dies at birth or soon after. Among northern whitetails, male fawns average about 7½ pounds at birth, and females are usually about 2 pounds lighter, averaging 5 pounds, 11 ounces.

Deer can be enormously productive on good range. One New York whitetail dropped 33 fawns in 15 years, and even at the age of 17 she bore twins. In only five years, a Missouri whitetail had 25 direct descendants. Such fertility, however, is wholly dependent on having energy sources in excess of those needed for a doe's mere survival. Reduce either quality or quantity of those sources below the needs of normal reproduction and it will show up in lowered sex functions and fawn crops.

The actual birth may be rather prolonged and difficult in some cases, although there is good reason to believe that it is usually rapid and almost bloodless. Stillborn fawns or does dying at fawning time are almost unknown. From the time a fawn's head emerges, only a few seconds may pass before it is fully born. The umbilical cord is usually broken as the doe stands after parturition. The doe starts licking the fawn im-

mediately after its birth, and the fawn begins breathing within a few minutes.

A twin whitetail fawn has been seen born eight minutes after his brother. Such twin fawns, by the way, are rarely hidden together. The doe may hide them hundreds of feet apart, which apparently causes the doe no inconvenience or confusion.

Both mule deer and whitetail newborn fawns have tawny red coats with rows of white spots and flecks down back and sides. At birth the tiny hoofs are shod with yellowish pads that darken in color within a few minutes. The fawn gains strength and awareness with astonishing speed. One fawn only 30 minutes old cocked its ears at the sound of a car passing 75 yards away. A two-hour-old fawn will begin nursing if the doe is lying down, and by the time it is a half-day old the fawn can easily nurse while the doe is standing. Fawns less than four days old offer little resistance when handled by humans, but from four days on they fight human handling with increasing strength and determination.

A fawn nurses for several minutes at two- or three-hour intervals, and after feeding lies down and flattens out as much as possible. Deer milk is very rich, with about twice the solids of Jersey cow milk and nearly three times as much fat and protein. It is highly concentrated, but not much is available at one feeding. So fawns suckle for short periods at frequent intervals. Older fawns often nurse roughly, and sometimes even strike the does impatiently with their forefeet. The doe may take a dim view of this and strike back, evoking a bleat of painful surprise from her spanked offspring.

The life of the small fawn is a summer idyll that consists largely of resting, brushing away bugs, and waiting for the next meal. The doe stays with her fawn at night (or alternates between twins) but in daytime

By five months, a whitetail fawn has lost its spots and is a perfect miniature image of its mother. (Leonard Lee Rue III photo)

she wanders off to eat and drink, returning often to nurse her young. She has not lost her fawn, as some well-meaning wildlife kidnappers persuade themselves to believe. In one study of a hundred captive whitetail does, not one ever abandoned her fawns.

As a doe with young fawns feeds some distance away from them, she may often look up and stop chewing, ears pricked forward in the direction of her hidden fawns. She draws no more attention than she must. In rain the fawn may stand under the doe, but she apparently leaves her fawns pretty much alone regardless of foul weather, and never babies them.

The buck takes no part in any of this family life, paying no attention to either mate or offspring in spite of the fact that a fawn may sometimes be seen "hero worshiping" a big buck—following him, imitating him, or just staring at him in what might pass for amazement.

The young fawn's bright bay coat, broken by several hundred perfectly white spots, is almost perfect camouflage against the sun-dappled floor of a thicket. But the fawn's best defense is complete immobility and instinctive obedience to its mother's "commands" to stay put and lie quietly.

At birth the fawn's hearing is acute, and the slightest sound will cause a half-day-old fawn to snuggle close to the ground. Even a newborn fawn may drop to the ground instantly, seek the coolest, darkest place, and put its nose in the dirt when startled by a passing fly. An older fawn will not jump up from hiding until a man is only 2 or 3 feet away and will duck, sidestep, and outrun you even though it's had no previous experience with humans.

Fawns are quiet little creatures and almost never utter a sound unless they are caught, molested, or lost. Then they have a call somewhat like very young calves. Twin fawns in thickets sometimes "talk" to each other in tones that may be mistaken for the soft calls of catbirds.

It's often said that young fawns have no detectable scent and cannot be smelled by predators. Perhaps. One biologist's spaniel could easily trail adult deer by scent, but passed many times within 5 feet of week-old fawns without detecting them. But this scentless period—if it really does exist—must be brief. For deer have an instinctive urge to leave odor in their tracks. At about a month the tarsal leg glands are functioning, and the fawn's odorless babyhood is over.

Fawns nurse heavily for nearly two months and may be completely weaned at three and one-half months. When only a few weeks old, they begin to nip at grass tips and tender browse, and by the time they are a month old they can eat whole shelled corn, acorns, and seedy fruits. Growth is rapid in summer and fall; some little bucks reach dressed weights of 75 pounds when only six months old. Arizona whitetails may gain nearly one-third of a pound each day, doubling their weight in the first two weeks and quadrupling it in a little over a month. Full weight and physical stature of northern whitetails are attained at about five years.

Few things in nature are as downright appealing as a young fawn, honey colored and speckled with snowflakes, that is lying "helpless" in a woodlot or overgrown fenceline. Many people find the fawns irresistible, and easily convince themselves that such fawns are pathetic little orphans crying for adoption. They are rarely orphaned and are never lost by their mothers. And, although they are easily tamed and adapt readily to people, they never really lose the wild streak that makes a deer a deer.

Since deer are protected game species under law in every state, they may be legally brought into private possession only during the open hunting season. So keeping a fawn is unlawful unless it's done under special permit. Game wardens don't relish the job of confiscating a pet fawn from a family that has learned to love it, but the job must be done—for the family's own good, if nothing else.

There was a feature in a national magazine years ago that included a remarkably appealing picture of a broken-hearted little girl and her pet fawn, soon to be separated by a cruel New Jersey statute. The story sarcastically referred to the child's "dangerous fawn" and scoffed at wildlife officials' claims that the lovely little creature could ever be dangerous.

But no common species of wild animal can be more

The dog-deer relationship isn't always one of fear and violence. This whitetail fawn has been befriended by the family collie—a friendship that will probably be broken by the deer. (Leonard Lee Rue III photo)

Object lesson: Never interfere with a big buck's love life. Canadian photographers Dennis Schmidt and the late Tom W. Hall were stalking a herd of six mule deer does and one dominant buck in the Okanagan Valley of British Columbia when the big buck became annoyed with the

invasion of his privacy and turned on the two men. He treed them both, and then angrily circled Schmidt's tree for 2½ hours, as shown. Before the buck finally left, he had whacked off all lower branches on this tree as high as his antlers would reach. (Tom W. Hall photo)

dangerous than a buck deer that has lost its fear of man but retains its natural responses to the Rutting Moon. Beautiful as young fawns, grown bucks may vent their autumnal rages on the same people who bottle-fed them. For example:

A whitetail buck named "Jimmy" had been reared by a Michigan farm wife and had the run of the farmyard as a docile and favored pet. One fall when Jimmy was a mature buck, the farmer penned the buck near his beagles to accustom them to the scent of deer and dull their desire to chase deer instead of rabbits. This farmer was a powerful Irishman who weighed over 200 pounds and was a rough-and-tumble woodsman known for his ability to cope with barroom lumberjacks. But he couldn't cope with Jimmy.

One day during rutting season, the farmer was in the pen when Jimmy charged without warning. The farmer was sent sprawling across the pen into a snowdrift. Jimmy then tried to gore him, but the farmer grabbed the buck's antlers and held it off by sheer strength. Two men nearby heard the farmer's yells and

came on the run, arming themselves on the way with a pick handle and a length of 2×4 studding. They managed to beat off the attacking buck and get the farmer to his feet. They slipped through the pen door just as Jimmy charged a second time and the entire pen trembled as he struck the door.

Knowing that it was rutting season, the farmer tried to temper Jimmy's fury by confining a doe (also illegally obtained) with him. The maddened buck promptly killed her. The buck attacked a second doe and injured her badly before she could be rescued. The farmer then decided to give Jimmy some of his own medicine and put a young spike buck in the pen. The farmer reasoned that the younger animal could drive his small, sharp antlers under the guard of Jimmy's big rack, teaching Jimmy a lesson. It didn't work that way. Jimmy struck first, easily going in below the spike buck's guard and disemboweling him. So a large buck with a massive rack was put into the pen with Jimmy. This buck was also swiftly killed.

In just a few days the "pet" deer had attacked a

man, killed three other deer, and severely wounded a fourth. To quench Jimmy's fire, the farmer sawed off his antlers. That did it; almost overnight the buck became docile again.

In another case, Harold Clemens, now a marine biologist in California, had a similar adventure. His first job out of college was at a midwestern game farm where he did everything from repairing pheasant pens to building fences. The game farm included a high-fenced enclosure of several acres where several whitetail deer were kept. All were deer that had been found as fawns by farmers and later confiscated by game wardens; all were thoroughly tame and would follow the game farm workers like pet dogs. One was a four-year-old buck named—What else?—"Buck." Buck was a beautiful animal and, like the other deer in the pen, quite tame.

One early October day, Clemens was doing some repair work on the lean-to where the deer were usually shed. "I heard a noise behind me and looked around," he remembers. "There was Buck, in full antler, head down and pawing the ground a few feet away from me. I said 'Buck, get out of here!' and made a move to shoo him away. It didn't scare him a bit.

Head slightly lowered, ears nearly flattened against his neck, this buck is showing extreme aggression. Normally there is nothing to fear from a wild deer, which will never attack a human. But a captive "pet" buck, with no restraining fear of man, can be as dangerous as he is agile and powerful. (Leonard Lee Rue III photo)

"So I picked up a 5-foot length of 2×4 and pushed his antlers with it. That didn't have any effect, either. He just moved in a bit closer. So I raised that heavy 2×4 and struck him hard on the antlers.

"That suprised him, all right. It pleased him, too. He raised his head a bit and looked at me, and I could almost hear him saying: 'Hey! Wonderful! Just the fight I've been looking for!'

"As he started to lunge forward, I was already on my way up onto the roof of that lean-to, and barely in time. It took two other men to distract him so that I could get to the gate."

There are many such reports of pet deer, both bucks and does, attacking humans. In many cases, tragedy has resulted. Does will rear and strike with those incredibly sharp hoofs—flashing attacks that few humans can avoid. Bucks also strike, but prefer to attack with their sharp antler tines, which they can drive home with over 200 pounds of bone and muscle.

Today's darling fawn can be tomorrow's devil buck or doe. Leave that fawn where it belongs—in the woods.

FOODS AND FEEDING

Both mule deer and whitetails are primarily browsing animals, wandering through woods and brushland randomly nipping off small leaves, twigs, and buds. Whitetails may graze lightly on summer grasses for a change in diet, but grass is not a major item on their menu. On the other hand, grasses often have a major role in the year-round diet of mule deer.

It might be easier to list plants that deer do not eat, rather than to go through the whole roster of foods. Well over 600 species of plants are eaten by whitetail deer. In order of preference, whitetails like sprout growth of trees and shrubs; seedlings of trees and shrubs; weeds; and grasses.

In the north, white cedar, yew, and ground hemlock are important. The two species of northern aspen are major foods in areas famous for high deer populations—Pennsylvania, Wisconsin, Michigan, and Minnesota. Blueberries and maples are important in many states. In southern forests, greenbriers are heavily browsed by whitetails, as are black gum, flowering dogwood, sweet leaf, maples, white oak, and sumac. In Texas, sumac is one of the most important deer foods, and plum and sassafras are also eagerly browsed. In the western states, whitetails may turn to bearberry, buckbrush, chokecherry, dogwood, and poplar.

Whitetails may dote on shelled corn, and in March as many as a hundred of them have been seen around wire corncribs nibbling at ears of corn through the mesh. In deep winter starving deer will eat domestic

FEEDING

Lacking incisor teeth in the front of the upper jaw, a deer is unable to "bite" off stems as it browses. Instead, it uses its lower canine teeth to press the stem against the tough dental pad of the upper jaw and then tears the stem away. (Leonard Lee Rue III photo)

Oak trees may produce acorns in only one year out of three, but in a good "nut year" a big white oak may drop 8,000 nuts. Easily eaten and rich in carbohydrates, they are a favorite autumn and winter deer food. (Leonard Lee Rue III photo)

Not many possibilities are overlooked by feeding deer. This whitetail doe has found a bed of succulent water plants. (Photo is by Leonard Lee Rue III)

Whitetails may paw through snow to forage acorns from the forest floor and are often joined there by flocks of wild turkeys. (Leonard Lee Rue III photo)

hay and other foods offered by man. But they always prefer browse species to domestic feeds and would rather have poor quality meadow hay than alfalfa. Even starving deer eat only the tenderest parts of alfalfa, leaving the stems and tough portions.

There's a point of contention here: Some authorities disagree over the importance of northern aspen or "popple" as winter food for deer. Some say it's a staple; others claim it is a starvation food. Both factions may be right, depending on the herd and its location. Deer seem to prefer some foods simply because they taste good and overbrowse these to the exclusion of nourishing foods that are less palatable.

Until recent times aspen was a minor deer food in Michigan. The whitetails there didn't seem to care much for it and preferred other foods. But after heavy cutting of the aspens by industry, there was an increased availability of aspen sprouts and suckers and (winter-cut) browse. Deer began to develop a taste for it and took advantage of the new food supply. Aspen then became one of the most important winter foods in Michigan, and the salvation of many winter herds.

In any whitetail range where oaks occur, acorns are a popular late summer food. Poison ivy is also a favorite, as are some mushrooms. White puffballs on stumps in Maine are highly prized by whitetails there. One northern game manager finds beds of morel mushrooms for his own use by simply watching feeding deer.

Deer have even been seen fishing! They may strike at trout or suckers in shallow streams, disabling fish up to 14 inches long and swallowing them headfirst while the fish are still alive. There have also been re-

Whitetails like apple orchards. (Nick Drahos, NY Dept. of Environmental Conservation photo)

Various mammal droppings are clockwise from upper left: deer pellets when feeding on browse, rabbit pellets, porcupine pellets, deer droppings when feeding on grass. (Leonard Lee Rue III photo)

Some of the commonest items in the Rocky Mountain mule deer's diet are plains plants, such as big sagebrush, antelope bitterbrush, and western wheatgrass. These wintering muleys will probably do well if the range has not been overgrazed by cattle or scourged by severe blizzards. (Leonard Lee Rue III photo)

ports of deer robbing strings of freshly caught trout from fishermen's camps. In fact, deer may eat almost anything out of curiosity, even leather belts.

But of all the foods of the northern farm country, the whitetail seems to like apples best. No proper deer will miss a chance to browse apple twigs, eat fruit on the tree, or as windfall. In eastern Maine 175 young orchard trees were browsed and destroyed in one night by six deer. Such hungry deer can raise hob with crops if good wild foods are scarce. Some backwoods farmers in northern Michigan, literally ruined by hungry deer, quit farming in despair. Deer may nip cornsilks, crop sprouts of many kinds, and eat entire gardens in one night. In Spearfish, South Dakota, during the deer boom of the mid-1950s, it was nearly impossible to keep a garden near the edge of town.

There is an enormous range in deer foods simply because the animals themselves have such an enormous range—literally from subarctic regions to the tropics. In many northern and mountain situations, mule deer summer at higher elevations, then drift down-mountain in late fall and winter to valleys and basins. The summer range of the Rocky Mountain mule deer, for example, is a duke's mixture of aspen woodlands, coniferous forest, open mountain "parks," and often even the alpine tundra of meadows well above timberline. Their winter ranges may be even more widely varied: shrub/grass communities, northern desert scrub, broad sagebrush flats, juniper-pinyon

pygmy forest, or even farmland. One food list of the Rocky Mountain mule deer included at least 788 kinds of plants, of which about 481 were forbs; 202 species of shrubs and trees; 84 kinds of grasses, sedges and rushes; and 18 kinds of "lower plants."

In the many food habit studies of Rocky Mountain mule deer, the browse species mentioned most often were snowberry, big sagebrush, rose, black chokecherry, antelope bitterbrush, quaking aspen, willow, and Saskatoon serviceberry. Of grasses, the most commonly cited were bluegrass, wheatgrass, chess, sedge, and fescue. The forbs that often appear in mule deer food lists are buckwheat, aster, lupine, phlox,

California mule deer have browsed this lone manzanita plant growing in a dense stand of chamise. These are typical plants of the community known as "chaparral," which lies between grassland and forest in the "Mediterranean climate" of California. (Leonard Lee Rue III photo)

Good blacktail foods are shown clockwise from upper left: acorns of blue oak, valley oak acorns, coast black oak, and interior live oak. (Leonard Lee Rue III photo)

beardtongue, fleabane, sagebrush, and cinquefoil. Like their whitetail cousins, mule deer will eat mushrooms whenever they can, and this is especially true in some high southwestern mountains where many kinds of fungi are abundant.

In spring as cheatgrass begins to appear on the wintering ranges, mule deer may gorge themselves on the succulent new growth. This sharp transition from the coarse, woody, winter diet can have a diarrhetic effect. The cheatgrass then becomes a last meal of the condemned, because the new grass may cause "scours" that weaken the starving deer even more and kill it on the threshold of summer.

Adult deer need a little over 2 pounds of food per 100 pounds of body weight each day to maintain fair condition in winter. In Michigan, an average of 5 pounds of cut browse each day was needed by yarded deer—about ¾ bushel of twigs, buds, and cedar foliage. Taking everything into account, a normal northern whitetail adult needs well over a ton of food each year.

A chemical analysis of deer food indicates its value only in a general way. For example, white cedar, probably the best northern browse species for whitetail deer, actually has less protein than either balsam or jack pine neither of which is favored by deer. However, a deer prefers the white cedar and may be able to compensate for this protein deficit in more palatable foods by making its own protein! In a number of penned deer, stomach contents showed a protein increase from one and a half to three times the crude protein in the food, suggesting that synthesis makes it possible for some deer to survive on protein-deficient foods. The only element that appears to occur fairly regularly in the preferred deer foods is calcium.

For ages, deer have visited natural "licks," where they eat or lick earth and rock to satisfy subtle but important needs in their diets. Such licks may be muddy places around mineral springs, certain rocky outcroppings, or the brackish pools where does eat mud during the nursing period. Modern "licks" may be salt blocks in feedlots, or even spots along hilly roads where deer are attracted by salt spread on the road to melt ice.

Hunters usually call natural sites "salt licks" and let it go at that. But it was found that, in natural game licks in the Canadian Rockies, common salt probably wasn't the most essential ingredient. Deer and other big game might have actually sought such trace elements as copper and manganese, which were always present at natural licks.

If deer have raw salt available, they seem to use it most heavily in spring and early summer. In southern Ohio salt blocks were used only by does, and only during summer. By the way, it took the Ohio deer about two months to learn about salt blocks; at first they knocked over the blocks and ate the soil beneath them. Missouri deer suddenly began using salt licks in about mid-March and continued to eat considerable quantities of salt through April and May.

Sodium is as important to mule deer as whitetails. Where forage is deficient in this element, as in parts of the Rockies, mule deer get their sodium from salt blocks set out for livestock, natural licks, or brackish water.

Deer can't digest crude fiber well, but do so better than rabbits. They can also use sugars and starches better than rabbits.

A deer's stomach sometimes contains "hair balls" or *trichobezoars*—spheres of densely matted hair

White cedar, or arbor vitae, is one of the northern whitetail's favorite foods. (Irene Vandermolen photo)

Livestock salt blocks can be attractive to deer, and may be most heavily used in early spring. However, heavily salted patches of raw earth may be just as attractive. (Leonard Lee Rue III photo)

Hairballs, or trichobezoars, are sometimes found in the stomach (abomasum) of deer. Made of hair swallowed during grooming, along with some minerals, saliva, and vegetation, they rarely pose any real problem. (T. P. Kistner photo)

covered with a thin, leathery veneer. These hair balls may be 2 or 3 inches in diameter and are formed from hair swallowed by the deer as it licks itself.

Deer stomachs may also contain calcium stones built up in concentric layers like hailstones. These *calculi,* or stomach stones, may result from the irritation of the secreting organ—something like gallstones in humans, except that deer do not have gall bladders. One stomach stone found in the skeleton of a young Virginia whitetail was 2 inches long and contained a pecan nut.

"Madstones," or bezoars, as stomach stones formed from hairballs or calcium were sometimes called, were royal treasures back in the days when there were lots of kings and lots of people wanting to poison them. Among other things, bezoars were supposed to detect poison and even neutralize it. Until very recently, some people swore that the things would cure rabies. In Texas, a bezoar stone was sold for $250 in 1879, and as late as 1933 a Tennessee newspaper ran a classified ad offering one for sale.

As to gall bladders, few herbivores have them, while all carnivorous mammals except whales have these small sacs attached to their livers. Why?

Liver bile is of value in digesting certain fats. Meat-eating mammals do not eat regularly, but when they gorge themselves they need a large supply of bile. So their gall bladders store a ready supply. These reservoirs of liver bile also eliminate the need for a constant flow of bile that would otherwise be largely wasted.

But deer and most other vegetarians eat regularly and almost constantly; with this steady diet and a steady need for bile, there is no reason for a bile reservoir. One exception is the American bison. Its gall bladder was of use to the animal and to the mountain men, who used its gall to season raw buffalo liver, eaten as an appetizer while waiting for roast hump ribs and *boudins* (broiled small intestines).

ACTIONS AND REACTIONS

Traditionally, hunters have regarded the mule deer as less intelligent than the whitetail. It's the muley that has a reputation for bouncing off up the hillside in that odd, pogo-stick way, and then stopping on the skyline to look back at danger—often within fair rifle range.

There's no doubt of this; mule deer did it in the old days, and they still do it—but more often before or after the hunting season than during it. In most parts of his range Old Big Ears isn't the country cousin that he once was. Intensified hunting pressure and constantly improving access to even his remote ranges

A big mule deer buck bedded down in sagebrush is almost invisible. Almost—but not quite. A whitetail buck wouldn't be caught dead in such a situation. Mule deer often are. (Irene Vandermolen photo)

have given him "street smarts" that compare with his whitetail cousin's. Actually, the North American mule deer is as good a survivor as any and is really no smarter or tougher than he ever was—he's just better educated now.

Compared to a whitetail deer, the typical muley tends to be a showier and noisier deer that is not as likely to hide from predators. As Canadian biologist Valerius Geist points out, mule deer fawns call often and noisily. Adult mule deer readily move into the open during daylight and can be easily seen. They have large scent glands on their hind legs and between their toes and have a habit of urinating copiously on their hocks—withal, a noisy, smelly, easy-to-see large animal. Normally, that is. Put the hunting pressure on, and mule deer are almost as ready to go under cover as whitetails.

Most of the whitetails known today (vs. the whitetails of the days before North America was settled, which we know little about) are shy, retiring, but curious animals that are usually most active at dawn, early morning, and dusk. In areas of heavy human activity, their dawn and dusk tendencies become more marked.

No big game animal tolerates people as well as the whitetail deer. They are commonly found in suburbs of large cities and may ravage town gardens like outsized rabbits. They aren't bothered much by man's doings and thrive in heavily settled farm regions.

Their success around people is due to their genius for staying out of sight. Seldom bold or obvious, whitetails prefer to pussyfoot through the woods when humans approach or to simply hide. Huge bucks may lie doggo until almost stepped upon. A remarkable number of these deer can exist almost undetected in

a small patch of woods and fields, and you may learn of their presence only by damage to gardens, over-browsing of favorite food shrubs, tracks in new snow, or by the rare privilege of finding a newborn fawn.

All in all, the whitetail deer tends to have a low threshold of excitement in contrast to the mule deer's somewhat higher threshold. It follows, then, that the whitetail is more easily excited, shy, nervous, and inclined to take as much advantage of cover as possible. The mule deer is relatively calm, tolerant of disturbance, often found in the open, and is probably more easily tamed.

In fact, the whitetail is famous for its intricate strategies of avoidance and escape—sneaking, skulking, backtracking, going into water to cast scent, crossing other deer trails to confuse pursuit, and often employing systems of well-known trails (known to the deer, that is) of swift and efficient escape. Any of these traits *may* be exhibited by mule deer as well, but on the average mule deer aren't the postgraduates in sneaky behavior their whitetail cousins are. The late Jack O'Connor, longtime gun editor of *Outdoor Life*,

Whitetails love to lurk in thickets and dense "shinnery" from which they can watch open woodlands and fields beyond. Binoculars are invaluable for spotting such deer. From a distance, carefully look inside the edges of open land where the undergrowth is the thickest. (Irene Vandermolen photo)

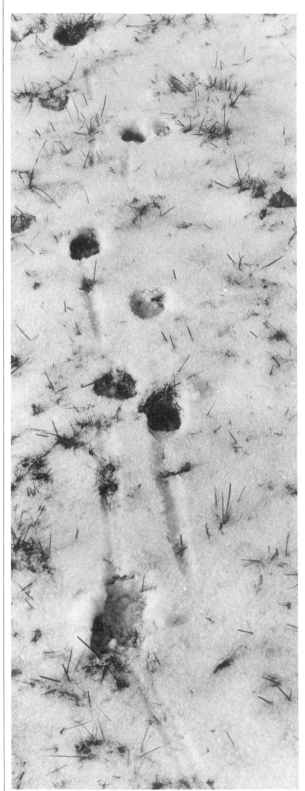

When snow is less than a half-inch deep, "drag" tracks are usually made by the bucks. In deeper snow, of course, all deer will show these drag marks. (Leonard Lee Rue III photo)

knew North American big game from a hunter's viewpoint as few men ever can—and always said flatly that the whitetail deer was the smartest hunted animal on this continent.

The behavioral differences in the two species of deer may have resulted from the differences in typical ranges. Mule deer, after all, have generally evolved in open lands where creatures show a stronger herding habit than in dense forests and edges. Muleys, elk, pronghorns, and bison are all herd species; whitetails and moose are not. More often than not, herd species tend to find security in numbers that the loners never know.

The mule deer's behavior when alarmed may also be attributable to his more open home ranges. A muley's first defense usually consists of putting *distance* between himself and danger—although he often stops to look back while well within rifle range.

By contrast, the whitetail's first defense is putting some *cover* between itself and danger. A whitetail caught in the open will typically dive into the nearest heavy cover, run a short distance, and circle to watch his back trail. If surprised in the woods, the whitetail usually tears out of sight and then sneaks off to one side to watch for pursuit.

There is another factor, too. Mule deer are much stronger travelers than whitetails. Almost all mule deer migrate to some extent in fall and spring, and some may descend as much as 8,000 feet from summer range and migrate up to 100 miles. Whitetails tend to be homebodies. Although some populations may show slight migratory shifts of 20 miles or more, it's not unusual for a whitetail to live out its life in little more than a square mile of range.

Because the mule deer habitually covers so much more ground than its cousin, it does not seem likely that a muley ever really learns country as well as a whitetail does. That is nothing against the mule deer because *no* creature knows its home ground better than a mature whitetail. This is pure speculation, but if a mule deer seems to do something that's particularly stupid, as well as fatal, the mistake may have been made because the deer just didn't know its territory well enough.

Both species of deer, however, share the ability to run fast, hard, and fancy through some rather rough landscape and thick cover. The "stotting" of a mule deer—that incomparable pogo-stick bounding that is found in no other animal in North America—is superbly adapted to steep, rough, rocky landscapes. A mule deer bounding up a mountainside—its four feet seemingly shod with powerful springs—is more than a match for any pursuing danger except a rifle bullet. And even to an expert rifleman, hitting a stotting mule deer is a very iffy thing.

Mule deer do trot and even run in the usual ways, of course, but that stotting is typically an alarm re-

One of the strangest of all deer gaits is the odd "stotting" in which mule deer bounce along as if shod on springs. (Dave Daughtry, Arizona Game and Fish Dept. photo)

An ordinary fence is easily cleared by a strong deer in good health. (Philip K. White, U. S. Fish and Wildlife Service photo)

Or, for some inexplicable reason of its own, a deer may choose to just crawl under a fence that it could have jumped over. (Leonard Lee Rue III photo)

All North American deer are strong swimmers, especially in their winter coats of hollow, buoyant hair. (Len Rue Jr. photo)

At full speed, a whitetail buck levels out in a fast gallop. Such hard-running deer do not always raise their "flags." (Leonard Lee Rue III photo)

A big whitetail can leap across a stream 20 feet wide with little apparent effort, as shown here. (Leonard Lee Rue III photo)

sponse and it is one designed for the most rapid possible exit. It also enables the muley to make almost instant changes in direction. Although it may not eat up horizontal distance as fast as a whitetail in a swift dash, it is admirably suited to the steep, rough hillsides that make up so much of the mule deer's home range.

On the other hand, the whitetail runs in an airy gallop interspersed with great bounds. It is a graceful gait that seems effortless and weightless, but which embodies great strength and power. A startled whitetail may canter for two or three paces and then elevate itself in a high leap as if to take a better look at the situation. If really pressed, it may run in a long, low gallop at full speed and never leap at all. In all of these gaits the whitetail usually shows its flag, waving the tail from side to side, but at really high speed the tail may stream straight out behind the flashing deer.

An undisturbed deer rarely moves out of a walk. In trotting, head and tail are both sharply erect. The deer throws out its legs, which Teddy Roosevelt called "a singularly proud and free motion," after bringing the feet well up in an unusually springy step.

The whitetail is a powerful jumper. A frightened Michigan buck leaped from the middle of a township road and cleared the right-of-way fence in a jump estimated at 30 feet. A New York whitetail made a running leap of 29 feet that included clearing a windfall over 7 feet high.

However, some seasoned woodsmen and hunters think that a deer that isn't hard-pressed would rather crawl under an obstacle than leap over it. One whitetail buck being trailed by a hunter crawled under a barbed wire strand only 17 inches above the ground to reach a food patch of poison ivy.

Whitetails have often been clocked at from 20 to 25 mph and are believed able to run that fast for several miles without significant tiring. In a dead gallop, a strong whitetail buck has been timed at 36 mph. Still, it's been said that a deer's endurance is relatively limited, and there are old reports of crack Indian hunters actually running deer down within 6 hours.

The whitetail deer is almost as adept in water as on land, especially when its hollow-haired winter coat adds buoyancy. Deer often feed in shallows and like to romp in water up to 3 feet deep. There are accounts of frightened fawns submerging completely in ponds and creeks, with only their nostrils, foreheads, and eyes showing. Deer may also wander into deep water for long swims, crossing lakes up to 3½ miles wide, and have been seen swimming in the Atlantic 5 miles from Cape Cod.

Mule deer are also excellent swimmers. Columbian and Sitka blacktails frequently swim wide stretches of ocean to reach offshore islands. But, while whitetails often use water and wetland situations to escape danger, mule deer rarely do. They prefer to take their chances on steep and broken terrain.

Under heavy pressure, all deer tend to seek places with the least disturbance. In the whitetail's case, this may be a deep thicket almost under the hunter's nose. But the muley may simply quit that part of the country and find a different mountain.

AILMENTS

Native North American deer and imported domestic livestock share a number of diseases and parasites, and the deer usually come out on the short end. Diseases and parasites long carried by deer aren't seriously destructive to domestic sheep and cattle, but the reverse is far from true—foot-and-mouth disease, Bang's disease, and necrotic stomatitis, to name a few, can be very destructive to deer.

Of these, foot-and-mouth disease (FMD), is probably the worst. Although it's not a particularly deadly disease, this viral plague can infect large numbers of cattle and deer almost overnight. It attacks the mucous membranes of the mouth and the skin around and between the hoofs causing blisters and severe inflammation. The infamous California outbreak of the 1920s was caused by garbage washed ashore from a ship. Scavenging hogs were infected with the virus, and the disease quickly spread to mountain deer. In order to check the spread of FMD, 22,000 deer were slaughtered in 1924. Luckily, outbreaks are fairly rare today and are kept that way by strict quarantine regulations that govern cattle shipping.

Probably the most spectacular of viral diseases in whitetail deer is epizootic hemorrhagic disease (EHD). In 1955 the first known occurrence of this disease killed about 700 whitetails in New Jersey, and later that year the illness struck in Michigan. Later dieoffs of whitetails occurred in the Dakotas, Wyoming, and Alberta, with suspected kills in Nebraska, Missouri, Iowa, and Washington. In 1976 EHD killed thousands of whitetails in Nebraska, Wyoming, Kansas, and the Dakotas, as well as 4,000 pronghorns in Wyoming and another 1,000 whitetails in New Jersey.

The disease takes its name from the countless hemorrhaging lesions that generally involve the lungs, heart, liver, spleen, kidneys, and intestines. It usually strikes in late summer or early autumn and is transmitted by certain insects, such as bloodsucking gnats. Its main occurrence is in whitetail deer. Although both muleys and blacktails are susceptible, no outbreaks have occurred among these species, except where they've been closely associated with whitetails.

"Bluetongue" is a viral disease of domestic sheep that can infect wild deer, particularly in the West, although the susceptibilty of mule deer on their natural ranges is unknown. Pronghorns, however, are highly susceptible to this virus, and in 1977 several thousand died, mainly in Wyoming.

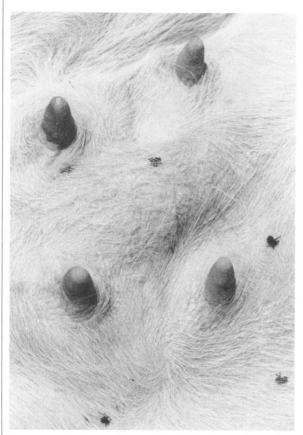

Bloodsucking louse flies or "keds," such as these shown above on a doe's udder, are pests of northern deer. The young adults are winged and probably fly in search of a host but shed their wings once they are established on a deer. Ticks (above right) are common ectoparasites of deer in most regions, especially in parts of the West and South. Some species can transmit such diseases as Colorado tick fever and Rocky Mountain spotted fever to humans—but ticks that do so are usually warm weather types that are seldom found on deer during hunting season. (Leonard Lee Rue III photos)

A relatively common virus-caused disease of deer is the fibroma or papilloma "wart" or skin tumor that can occur on any deer species and on any part of their bodies. These large, ugly warts cannot be transmitted to man and rarely have any serious effect on deer, except when they occur in large numbers about the head and interfere with sight, breathing, or feeding.

Of the bacterial disease of ruminants, brucellosis and anthrax are probably the best known. Brucellosis (Bang's disease) is highly contagious among many animals and does its deadliest damage in the fetal stage, causing abortion during the second half of gestation. It has been found among most ruminants in the United States and Canada, although it appears to be uncommon in whitetails and mule deer. Of 17,000 deer tested for brucellosis in various parts of the United States, only 20 whitetails were considered to be infected. However, the disease is a long-standing problem in bison.

Anthrax occurs in almost every part of the world, and this disease has taken a heavy toll of animals and

human life through the ages. It is probably the plague that Moses predicted would devastate the cattle of the Egyptians. In fact, it is believed that anthrax was introduced to North America from the Valley of the Nile, brought by ships to the Mississippi Delta and spread along the Rio Grande by Spanish explorers. It was already established in Louisiana in the early 1700s and was first seen in deer near the mouth of the Mississippi.

To some degree, the disease can affect all mammals and is highly virulent in most. It can be transmitted to man by various means. For man, prompt diagnosis and early treatment are highly important. Anthrax may have been responsible for wiping out some local populations of bighorn sheep. Although outbreaks among wild North American ruminants are not well documented, it is believed that deer are as susceptible as any hoofed animal.

Whitetail and mule deer are also subject to pneumonias caused by exposure and severe malnutrition. It has been said that few deer really starve to death.

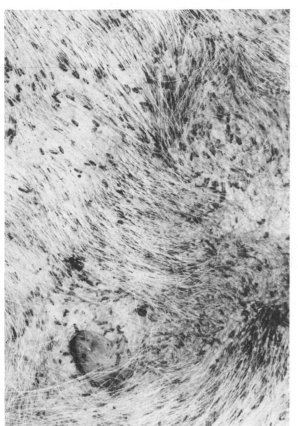 

All deer normally have some external parasites, but such parasites are rarely harmful unless they occur in heavy infestations—and even then they are likely to be an effect, rather than a cause, of poor deer health. Deer on heavily overstocked ranges are likely to suffer most from parasites. Above left, the udder area of a blacktail doe (object in lower left corner is a nipple) is infested with two louse flies, or "keds," and countless lice. In the photo above right, a gaping firearms wound in a deer's neck shows adult lungworms amid the bloody froth. Man is not susceptible (photos by T. P. Kistner)

Instead they actually die of pulmonary infections brought on by malnutrition and lowered resistance. But muleys and whitetails do seem able to cope with the threat of pneumonia and other common diseases if they are well nourished, and few diseases appear to be making major inroads in well-fed herds.

The infectious bacterial disease commonly known as "lumpy jaw" is widespread in the wild and can be contracted by deer when they feed on contaminated food such as poor-quality hay. The mouth region is affected, usually in the lower jaw where large abcesses may form. Lumpy jaw disease can be fatal if the bacterial infection spreads to the brain.

Of the common external parasites, ticks usually infest mule and blacktail deer. This is not as universally true for whitetails, though, for much of their northern range is relatively tick-free. However, some whitetails carry keds or "sheep ticks"—wingless, parasitic flies that resemble ticks. These may be quite common in some parts of the Northeast.

Several species of lungworm infest deer, and up to half the deer in Michigan have been infected. These parasites aren't thought to be as prevalent among western deer, because lungworm larval stages need a degree of warmth and moisture that is lacking in these deer ranges. The rather long, white nematode worms are usually found in the larger air passages of the host deer, and as many as 15,000 larval lungworms may be passed by a single deer in one day. A host deer, by the way, may be the strongest young buck in the herd. Deer can withstand massive infestations with no apparent ill effects, *if* the deer are well nourished and otherwise strong and healthy.

Sheep stomach worms and intestinal roundworms are frequently found in whitetails ranging over sheep pastures. However, deer are not normal hosts for these parasites and tend to pick up only a few.

One problem arising from whitetail overpopulation on livestock range is the shift from normal browsing to cowlike grazing. This leads to the acquisition of livestock parasites that the deer might have avoided had there been sufficient browse. The fact that white-

This whitetail doe is afflicted with fibroma tumors—warty growths caused by a virus. Although unsightly, fibromas do not seem to greatly harm deer unless they occur around the mouth and eyes and interfere with sight and feeding. They cannot be transmitted to man. (Leonard Lee Rue III photo)

tails graze heavily at all may mean they are undernourished, and thus are more susceptible to the ravages of parasites.

Tapeworms commonly occur in the intestinal tracts of deer. Mule and blacktail deer are often hosts to several kinds of tapeworms, although they are not usually detrimental to the deer. But one of these merits special attention because man is an abnormal intermediate host. *Echinococcus granulosus* is a small tapeworm that generally uses a dog as its host, but may also infect man. Both mule deer and Columbian blacktail deer in parts of California and Canada may carry these parasites, although surveys of deer have shown little infestation. Of 2,046 California deer examined over a 25-year period, only 26 were found to be infected with *E. granulosus.*

Deer hunters who relish liver may be appalled to find a deer's liver with several large bloodsucking liver flukes. In some northern forests up to 25 percent of the deer may be infected. Heavy infestations can cause death, particularly in younger animals, but in general deer and fluke coexist with little difficulty. The large American liver fluke *(Fascioloides magna)* uses members of the deer family as its definitive host. Another liver fluke, the sheep liver fluke, is rather widespread in North America but rarely infects deer. Neither of these flukes, by the way, can infect man.

Footworms are common and widespread among mule and blacktail deer and occur in whitetails as well. These slender roundworms are sometimes found coiled along the ligaments or under the skin of the feet near the hoofs. They even occur along the brisket and under the skin in the pelvic region. Infection in California deer is often most acute during winter, and in this season the deer may suffer open lesions and some pain in walking. Generally, though, these footworms are a harmless parasite.

Flies are among the deer's worst enemies. Fly warbles have been found under the hides of deer, and blackflies, horseflies, and mosquitos can make a deer's life almost unbearable. In mountainous regions of New Mexico and Arizona, for example, horseflies reach their maximum concentrations in the last half of June. It has been estimated that female horseflies may feed on mule deer at the rate of 100 per hour for about ten hours each day. In those same regions, the ears of mule deer can be literally packed with blackflies in early morning and late evening.

The spined grubs of some botflies hatch in a deer's nasal passages and pharynx, causing severe irritation and possibly even meningitis, if that irritation extends to the nearby brain tissue. If has been estimated that one type of botfly may infest up to 95 percent of a western deer population. Although bots certainly don't do their hosts any good, they do not cause deer to starve by blocking throat passages. Heavy infestations may be found in starved deer, to be sure, but they also occur in healthy animals.

Until about 1962 the most vicious scourge of all was the southern screwworm fly. This insect, also a serious livestock pest, lays eggs in open wounds and

One of the fringe benefits of being a big mule deer buck is having a built-in back scratcher for itches in those hard-to-get-at places. (Irene Vandermolen photo)

LIVER FLUKES

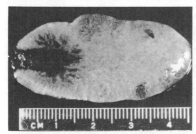

A large, unsightly parasite, the liver fluke (shown actual size) does not usually cause serious harm to the host, although the sight of the cysts and black pigment in an infected liver is unappetizing, to say the least. Because of liver flukes, some old hunters say it's best to slice fresh deer liver in the dark, away from the campfire, before cooking it. They're only half serious, of course—which also means that they're only half fooling. (T. P. Kistner photo)

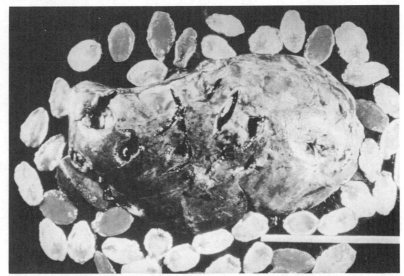

The American liver fluke may be found in livers of deer, moose, and elk across the United States and Canada. However, this fluke and the North American deer evolved together and the deer are well adapted to it. Heavy infestations of flukes as shown removed here, may almost destroy a deer's liver and cause debilitation and death. Immature flukes spend part of their life cycle in snails, and go from there into the water or to aquatic vegetation where they are ingested by deer. The flukes live for several years. Man cannot be infected by the liver stage of these flukes. (T. P. Kistner photo)

BOTFLY LARVAE

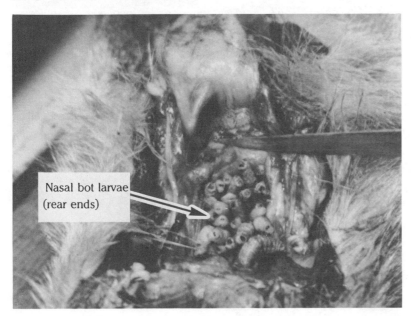

Nasal bot larvae (rear ends)

Throat bots may be found in all three species of North American deer. The adult botfly lays its larvae on the nostrils of deer in summer. These larvae migrate to the lungs and develop there until winter when they move up the deer's windpipe and become attached to pouches in the back part of the throat. They continue to grow there, and in late spring the fully developed larvae pass out the deer's nostrils, burrow into the soil, pupate, and hatch into adult flies during warm weather. It has not been shown that bots are harmful to deer—but it seems doubtful that fawns could run far with their throats distended by 40–80 large bots. The parasites do not infect man. (T. P. Kistner photo)

WORMS

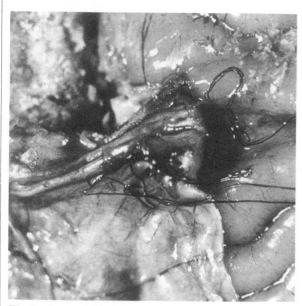

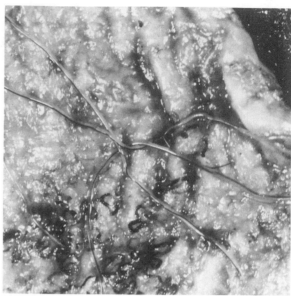

The brainworm (dark strands in photo) of deer is seldom a serious affliction to eastern whitetails, which have evidently developed a tolerance for it, but the parasite can be devastating to all other members of the North American deer family. Brainworm severely limits moose population in the northeastern United States and southeastern Canada and has prevented establishment of elk and blacktails in the Appalachians. Man is not susceptible. (T. P. Kistner photo)

Adults of the legworm (Wehrdikmansia cervipedis) are found on the inside of the skin of the shanks of all three of North American deer. In heavy infections they may be found above the knees and hocks. Hunters won't usually notice the presence of these parasites, but may see them when the legs are cut off deer carcasses that have been hanging overnight with the hides on. Incidentally, these legworms are harmless to deer and man. (T. P. Kistner photo)

The small, pale, fluid-filled bladders are cysts of the abdominal cyst tapeworm (Taenia hydatigena). The cysts develop in the deer's liver and drop into the abdominal cavity as they mature. Man is not susceptible, and its effect on deer is not known. The long, pale, threadlike worms are abdominal worms (Setaria yehi), tending to be most abundant in fawns and weakened older deer. Healthy older deer usually harbor only a few of the worms. They do not appear to seriously harm deer, and man is not susceptible. (T. P. Kistner photo)

The hydatid cyst tapeworm (Echinococcus granulosus) is here shown excised and as it grows on deer liver. It may be found in any species of deer, and particularly in western Canada and Alaska where cycles exist between wolves and moose or caribou. However, there are similar cycles between deer and coyotes or even domestic sheep and sheep dogs. Man is an accidental host when his food is contaminated with tapeworm eggs from dog feces. There is little danger to man in handling infected deer tissues, but dogs should never be allowed to eat deer offal. (T. P. Kistner photo)

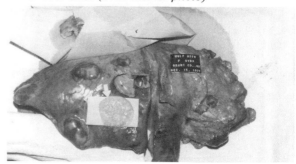

lesions. With a kind of evil genius, the female fly seeks out the navels of fawns, wounds on fighting bucks, scratches on antler velvet, and cuts from thorns and wire. Later, the hatched larvae burrow deeper into the host's flesh. As the larvae feed and grow within the wound, it becomes a great running sore that attracts still more flies. In this way, the slightest wound can be aggravated, and a tiny tick bite can be as lethal as a rifle bullet, but not nearly so quick and merciful. In parts of the South, screwworms completely halted the increase of deer, particularly after mild winters. And they killed up to 80 percent of the annual fawn crop in some areas of Texas.

Fortunately, entomologists located a vulnerable aspect of the screwworm's life cycle: females usually mate only once. Knowing this, entomologists reared millions of screwworm flies in the laboratory and sterilized them with radioactive cobalt. These sterile flies were regularly airdropped over thousands of square miles in the southeast during 1958 and 1959. When the sterile males mated with native females, the female laid eggs that wouldn't hatch and the screwworm population began to collapse. In a few years the southeastern screwworm was virtually eradicated, and a similar program wiped out the pest in the Southwest. Deer responded almost immediately. In Florida the deer population increased over 60 percent during the decade after screwworm eradication had begun.

PREDATORS

Today's whitetail deer have few serious enemies in the wild; most of the big animals that prey on adult deer have either been wiped out or greatly reduced throughout most of the whitetail's range.

Dogs. Although the free-ranging dog has been called the most serious whitetail predator (other than man) in most parts of the deer's midwestern, eastern, and southern ranges today there is some question about this. A number of authorities tend to discount this threat, believing that domestic dogs are usually ineffective deer predators under most conditions.

Other authorities believe that in some cases it's possible that free-ranging dogs can have a significant effect on deer populations. In the mid-1950s dogs were said to have limited the spread of deer into empty deer range in north Georgia, and in southern West Virginia free-running dogs were felt to be a significant barrier to establishing good deer herds. At one time it was believed that the most serious factors limiting southeastern deer were screwworms and dogs. In Ohio, 15 percent of the total dead deer found in one year were thought to have been killed by dogs.

A whitetail's small hoofs give poor traction on smooth ice. This doe was lucky. People found her before predators did. (Leonard Lee Rue III photo)

Man's best friend turned renegade—a feral dog eating a deer. How serious is dog predation on deer? The opinions vary widely. (Leonard Lee Rue III photo)

The truth of the matter probably lies somewhere between the extremes, as is often the case in such longstanding controversies.

The efficiency with which dogs can kill deer depends on the landscape, the condition of the deer involved, and the condition and experience of the dogs. Wild (feral) foxhounds and coonhounds in the Southeast have the potential for being persistent and effective deer predators. With their keen noses and great endurance, they can give even a healthy adult whitetail a great deal of trouble.

While canoeing, one authority once watched a whitetail doe cross a gravel bar and swim a large river in the Ozarks, while hounds bayed down her trail from the ridge above. The deer showed no fear of the canoeists, swimming across the river no more than 30 yards in front of the canoe. The deer appeared extremely tired, with its tongue out and eyes rolling wildly. It had difficulty mounting the steep bank on the far side. The dogs were apparently balked by the river, however, for their baying soon stopped.

East or west, the most serious predation on deer by feral dogs probably occurs in winter. Heavy snow and smooth ice limit a deer's ability to move, making it easy prey for a pack of dogs. In New York State during late January one year, dogs were believed to have killed a thousand snowbound deer. And even if the deer are not caught by dogs in late-winter chases, they cannot afford the loss of energy spent in escaping. Such chases can exhaust the meager reserves that might have brought that deer through a lean winter.

Still, there are many variables in the deer-dog equation. Dogs have been observed chasing deer on the extremely rough ice of a mid-January "ice gorge" on the Mississippi River. In one instance two large dogs were chasing five whitetails down the center of the river over masses of up-ended blocks of floe ice frozen in place by a sudden cold snap. The dogs were big and strong, but were having a very hard time of it, laboring mightily to move through the crazy jumble of ice cakes. The deer bounded easily through this mess, stopping now and then to look back at the frantic dogs. Seen through a powerful spotting scope, the deer weren't even breathing hard. The chase continued for nearly a mile before the weary dogs returned to the mainland and the deer walked casually into the sheltering willows of an island. They were lucky; if that ice had been glass-smooth, they would have lost their footing and become easy prey for the dogs.

In the West and North, dog predation on deer is most serious when deer are concentrated on winter ranges—probably because snow limits their movements and because they are in a somewhat weakened condition as well. In the desperate winter of 1983–84, when starving deer and antelope invaded some cities and towns in western mountain states to browse suburban shrubbery, they were sometimes attacked by free-running dogs. In some cases conservation officers were forced to shoot dogs within the city limits, and a difficult problem became even more difficult.

There's little doubt that free-running dogs can be significant deer predators and harassers at certain times and places. And considering that there may be from 12 to 30 million free-roaming dogs in the United States today, the problem may be far more prevalent than some authorities currently believe.

Coyotes. Coyotes can kill deer of all age classes, although fawns are probably the most vulnerable—especially in poor forage years. But there is disagreement among the experts about the overall effect coyotes have on deer populations. In the Missouri River

Coyotes can and will prey on deer, especially fawns, but a healthy deer herd usually is not threatened significantly by coyotes. (Len Rue Jr. photo)

Breaks, Montana, coyotes may have killed almost all the fawns born in 1975. On Steens Mountain, Oregon, a study in the late 1960s revealed that nearly 80 percent of the fawns were lost in their first nine months of life—and that predation (mostly by coyotes) accounted for 75 percent of those losses. Still, numerous other studies have shown that deer herds maintain healthy levels or even increase in the presence of substantial coyote populations, and that intensive control of coyotes may not necessarily result in significantly higher fawn survival.

Wolves. The big timber wolf (lobo) is a splendid deer hunter, but there are few wolves today in the contiguous United States. The largest single wolf population is in northeastern Minnesota. This population of northern timber wolves is a hot issue in that part of the country, with many hunters claiming that the big lobos are "wiping out the deer."

There's no doubt that the wolves prey heavily on deer all year long and are the main cause of deer mortality in areas they hunt. Nor is there much doubt that the deer population in the northeastern third of Minnesota's Superior National Forest is low and probably declining. But just how much of that decline is due to wolves and how much is caused by forest maturation (with reduction of browse) and several severe winters is tough to determine.

The timber wolf is an effective predator on all age classes and types of North American deer, but free-ranging, hunting populations of timber wolves now exist in only two regions of the "Lower 48"—in extreme northeastern Minnesota where they prey largely on whitetails, and on Isle Royale in Lake Superior where they hunt moose. (Leonard Lee Rue III photo)

A relatively high ratio of wolves to deer could limit the deer population. The fact is, however, that wolf density is rarely high enough to control a deer population. Wolf experts point out that the maximum density of the big lobos rarely exceeds one wolf for every 10 square miles. A realistic deer-kill rate per wolf is probably something like 15 adult deer per year, which means that the wolf's range must provide about three deer per square mile. If these maximum numbers applied, the wolves would probably limit the deer population. In reality, though, timber wolf density is rarely that high and deer density is rarely that low. The result is that wolf predation is unlikely to limit the deer population in reasonably good deer range.

Still, in the few remaining areas in the United States where wolves and people compete for deer, the issue of who-gets-what can be a hot one. The situation isn't helped any by wolves that appear to attack deer for the sheer joy of killing. The veteran Michigan deer biologist Ilo Bartlett once told of finding three yarded deer slaughtered by three wolves on Michigan's Upper Peninsula. The deer had been moving along a trail in deep snow while the wolves ran easily on the snow beside them. The lobos tore out the throats of the deer, took single mouthfuls of flesh from each hind-quarter, and abandoned the carcasses. Farther down the trail Bartlett found a spot where the wolves had playfully torn up cattail heads and scattered the fluff. Had they killed the deer in this same playful mood?

In spite of such incidents, it appears that wolves generally make full use of the deer they kill—and that

In this remarkable photograph, the late Tom W. Hall of British Columbia caught a timber wolf in close pursuit of a mule deer doe. For the wolf, such chases often end in failure—but nothing ventured, nothing gained. Wolves are masters at testing prey animals for weakness and exploiting any advantage.

a deer's greatest enemy is not a hungry lobo but deteriorating deer habitat. And since timber wolves are virtually extinct in the Lower 48, it seems man could afford to share "his" deer with the few wolves that are left.

Bobcats and cougars. Bobcats can and will kill deer, and in some wild areas of Pennsylvania it has been reported that bobcats live almost entirely on venison. Nor are such deer necessarily "culls." Although cats will take fawns, does, or sick animals, they are apparently capable of killing large bucks. In one case, a healthy whitetail buck weighing nearly 200 pounds was killed by a bobcat that didn't weigh over 25 pounds.

A bobcat may circle a bedded deer, creep to within a few yards and then seize the deer by the head with its forepaws. A big deer can carry the clawing bobcat into stands of saplings to tear the cat from its back, but a well-attached cat of any species is a hard critter to give the brush-off. If the cat misses on its first pounce, it may follow for a jump or two, but seldom much farther. Once on a deer's back, it locks its teeth in the deer's throat just behind the jaws. Cat-killed deer are often found with their heads sharply turned, as if they had died trying to avoid the cat's attack.

The bobcat usually begins feeding on a hindquarter, eating a portion of venison about the size of its head. One large bobcat ate the entire hindquarter of a fawn, detached the bone from the hip, ate the loin, side, and belly meat up to the ribs—including hide and hair—and exposed the intestines. But most bobcats appear to feed sporadically, alternately gorging and fasting.

Without any doubt, the most effective individual deer predator of all is our biggest cat—the cougar, or mountain lion. A single cougar may average 50 deer per year; during the cool winter months from November to April in the West one of these great cats may kill an average of one deer a week, and even more during the summer.

In early spring 1941, the late Dallas Morgan, a government hunter for the old U.S Biological Survey, trailed a huge male cougar on foot for over 70 miles in western Colorado. During the two weeks he was on the cougar's trail, the big cat never wanted for fresh meat.

"We were finding dead deer, killed along cedar benches or back in timbered pockets," Morgan said. "They were fresh kills and getting fresher, and most of them with just one good meal eaten out of them. In nine days' time me and the dogs come across nine deer that the lion had killed. He might scratch a little dirt or some pinyon needles over a deer, but he never really covered it up the way a lion will if he intends to come back.

"That old cat was just living off the land as he went,

Bobcats have been known to kill even healthy, mature bucks, but are not generally considered important deer predators. (Bureau of Land Management photo)

and he kept going pretty steady. All along his line of travel I found piles of old deer bones that I was pretty sure he had accounted for. I reckon it would be real surprising, if a man had a way of knowing just how many deer that old cat had sacked up in that country. The deer were winter-poor and pretty stringy, but Tige and the pups didn't mind. They were eatin' better than I was, at that."

Like bobcats, cougars usually stalk to within charging range of a deer, although they can catch running deer within distances of 50 yards. The big cat bounds up on the deer's back, sinks its great claws, and bites into the crest of the neck. If the deer is not killed by this bite or the subsequent high-speed spill, it is finished off with bites in the jugular region. The cougar than drags the dead deer to some secluded place under a tree or ledge before feeding—sometimes over a 1,000 feet away. The cougar usually makes its first meal of the liver, heart and lungs. Replete, it then covers the carcass with dirt, sticks, snow, leaves or anything else handy.

Cougars are well adapted to their predatory role. They are immensely strong and agile; a small, 76-pound cougar has killed a healthy elk that weighed nearly nine times as much. The cougar's clavicle is well developed, supporting powerful forelegs and shoulders for striking and holding prey. Its long, retractile claws have great ripping power and are

With the passing of the timber wolf, the mountain lion remains the most important and effective of the wild deer predators. This big cat can easily kill a large adult deer. A single cougar may take 50 deer in a year's time. (Leonard Lee Rue III photo)

designed to dig deeper as a victim struggles. The cougar's heavy jaw is formed so that it has no backward or forward play, and its skull can withstand heavy shocks suffered during attacks on grown deer. But most of all there is the ability to be more shadow than substance until it is ready to attack.

A master deer hunter, the cougar thins deer herds and in combination with other big predators helps hold deer in harmony with range conditions. In California wilderness areas where deer can't be hunted efficiently enough to control their numbers, biologists have urged that cougar populations be allowed to build up. In Sequoia National Park the thriving deer range has coincided exactly with the best-populated cougar range. And excessive populations of deer do occur when there is greatly reduced wolf, cougar, and human predation. In fact, winter starvation and huge deer die-offs have been almost unknown when big predators helped balance the deer population.

For many years there has been a persistent myth that predators deliberately cull the weak, ill, or unfit individuals from deer herds. Some of this surely occurs, since such individuals are likely to be easily taken—but a number of studies indicate that these kills are usually in proportion to the number of weaklings in the population. Most professional hunters and trappers reject the idea that cougars are selective in preying on sick, weak, or crippled deer. Some even

believe the cougar is such a skilled and able deer predator that it tends to select the healthiest prey.

Everything considered, it's risky to draw any hard-and-fast conclusions about the effects of cougar predation on western deer. There are situations in which deer show increases in spite of such predation and others in which herds are definitely suppressed or even reduced by cougars. A working cougar population, however, does tend to dampen dramatic fluctuations in a deer herd. So they help prevent the sudden upswings in numbers that, as often as not, are followed by equally sharp declines.

The cougar, then, is equipped by ages of special development to overcome the immense environmental resistance presented by the deer—but only to a degree. The deer, in turn, is equipped to survive the environmental threat offered by the cougar—but again, only to a degree. Through millions of years of selection and adjustment they have honed each other in a timeless contest of survival. Both have won, and each has contributed to the superb fitness and wild beauty of the other.

Deer defenses. Except under abnormal circumstances a healthy wild deer is superbly equipped to resist predation. It usually depends first on scent, then hearing, and probably least on vision, and all these are employed to actively detect danger. A deer's sense of smell is phenomenal, and when humidity and terrain are favorable, it can detect scents in the wind at incredible distances. In a gentle breeze a mule deer can smell a hunter for at least half a mile.

A whitetail's great ears can catch the smallest sounds, and the muley's ears may do just that much better. One doe was disturbed by a man standing downwind 75 yards away in a dense fir thicket, softly clicking his fingernails behind his back! A wary deer shows many of the listening traits of a rabbit, warping its ears in any direction. Deer are also said to have the uncanny ability to tell the difference between a human footfall and the sound of a bear-snapped twig.

In semidarkness when a man can barely see at all, a deer can see very well. And although a deer may often ignore a stationary object, it can detect the wink of an eye. It's amazingly perceptive of movement, especially any slight rapid movement, for quick moves are most often associated with predation. Although there is evidence that deer have color vision, it is not yet known to what degree deer interpret those colors.

Along with all this the deer has an overwhelming sense of curiosity. Some hunters regard this as a basic weakness that works to their benefit, confusing it with stupidity, especially in the case of the mule deer. But no creature is more curious than man himself. Curiosity is a trait of an adaptive and highly intelligent animal; the buck that studies you so naively today may be the same animal that, having slaked his curiosity, will avoid you like the plague on opening day. And, on top of all that, the deer uses curiosity to cultivate one of the most important pieces of his survival equipment—an intimate knowledge of his home range.

A deer's defenses are excellent. So good, in fact that sometimes the tables are turned. A woodsman in northern Minnesota once reported finding the carcass of a large buck deer surrounded by three dead wolves; the buck's hoofs and antlers had levied a deadly toll on a wolf pack. A New York farmer once watched his Dalmation dog, barking furiously, charge up to a deer on a snowy road. But the buck turned the tables by facing down the dog and trying to trample him. The dog took off for home with the deer close behind, still trying to strike the dog with its hoofs. This chase ended at the farmer's back porch, where the man finally drove the deer away.

The small, sharp front hoofs of deer can be effective weapons which bucks and does use by flailing or striking. A mule deer doe was seen treeing a bobcat that had threatened her fawn, and a whitetail in a similar situation chased a fox away from her fawn.

Deer hate and fear snakes. An otherwise fearless captive buck was kept from charging by the sight of a short length of rope, which a man was moving to imitate a writhing snake. But despite this instinctive dread, a deer may attack a snake. Whitetails have been

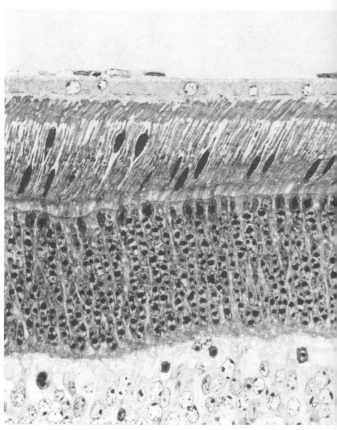

Deer may not be as color blind as deer lore has long contended. Some scientists now feel that deer have the visual equipment to discriminate among a wide range of colors. In their eyes, deer have millions of color receptors known as cones. These are the same type of nerve endings found in human eyes, which allow distinguishing among many hues.

This microphotograph, magnified thousands of times, shows a cross section of the retina of a deer's eye. The cones appear as dark, elongated shapes just beneath the surface of the retina. Below the cones, the tiny black dots are the rods, other nerve endings that enable deer to detect motion and see well in poor light.

Outdoor writer John Weiss attributes this discovery to Drs. Springer, Witzel, and Mollinhauer at the U.S. Department of Agriculture's Veterinary Toxicology and Entomology Research Laboratory in College Station, Texas. After determining the presence of cones, the biologists conducted experiments with deer and flashing colored lights to learn if the cones were really functional. They concluded that the cones in deer eyes do function in a manner almost identical to that in humans and that these cones respond to the entire color spectrum. Earlier work by biologists in Asia and Europe has confirmed color perception of other hoofed ungulates such as red deer, fallow deer, axis deer, and even sheep, goats, cows, pigs, horses, giraffes and camels.

But although the eyes of North American deer are equipped to distinguish colors, it is not known how those color signals are interpreted by the deer in terms of responses to various colors under various conditions.

known to leap up and down on rattlers with bunched hoofs until the snakes have been cut to ribbons.

The sharp front hoofs are used by both sexes and all age classes. Unlike many of the Old World deer, mule deer do not kick with their hind legs. Rather, in serious fighting, both muleys and whitetails rear on their hind legs and either jab hard or slash downward with their front legs.

MISHAPS

Just because a deer escapes wild dogs, cougars, coyotes, serious disease, malnutrition, and the hunting season doesn't mean it's assured of a long life. There is always the chance of being smashed, stabbed, or otherwise injured in some accident.

Deer can entangle themselves in fences, or catch their legs or heads in tree crotches while rearing up to feed on high browse. In such cases they often die of shock, exhaustion, or broken necks. Deer can slip and fall down snowy banks or cliffs, forever lose their footing on smooth, slippery river or lake ice, or impale themselves on sharp "stubs" as they dash through heavy timber. A whitetail doe in Montana had a foot-long, half-inch thick fir branch driven between her ribs. The stick pierced the doe's diaphragm and the point of her liver, coming to rest beneath her spine. In spite of this, the deer was healthy, fat, and had no infection. A New York buck was also lucky; he ran a poplar stub 5½ inches long and nearly 1½ inches in diameter into his chest. The stick was walled off by scar tissue and caused no ill effects.

If a deer's jaw is injured or afflicted with some condition that prevents rotary chewing, the deer may be unable to shift food from between its cheek and teeth. Food then impacts in the cheek, forming a large mass.

Another fatal encounter with fence wire: Here a mule deer buck apparently chose the wrong thing for his practice sparring. (Leonard Lee Rue III photo)

The nation's highways are toll roads for wildlife on which thousands of deer—young and old—pay with their lives. (John Goerg, New York Department of Environmental Conservation photo)

One such mass of chewed food weighing over a pound was taken from the right cheek of a Minnesota whitetail. The pressure of this food mass had caused the deer's gums to shrink and the sockets of its teeth to become highly inflamed.

Feeding on bearded wheat hay may also kill deer, if the tiny beards, or "awns," penetrate walls of the gastrointestinal tract.

Vehicle mortalities. Fatal accidents in the wild are freakish, however, and exact no serious toll on deer. They aren't nearly as common as collisions with speeding vehicles on roads and highways. In fact, such road kills involve tremendous numbers of deer. The

Weakened by winter stress, this mule deer was unable to clear a 4-strand wire fence. Such mishaps are fairly common on western deer ranges in winter. (Paul F. Gilbert, Colorado Division of Wildlife photo)

DEER AS ROAD HAZARDS

The late Tom W. Hall stopped to photograph these mule deer crossing a highway in Banff National Park, Alberta. Although vehicles take a terrible toll on deer each year, deer also exact a toll on vehicles and motorists. For an illustration of this problem, please study sequel photos on the next page.

total just keeps on growing, in part because there are more roads and there is much more traffic on them.

The 55-mph speed limit became effective on the nation's public highways in January 1974. While it may have made the roads safer for motorists, it doesn't seem to have done much for deer. In 1957, a total of 9,262 deer were killed in Pennsylvania by motor vehicles. At the time, many wildlifers thought the toll couldn't get much worse than that. So much for innocence. By 1976 (two years after the new double-nickel speed limit) the Pennsylvania road kill was 24,183. This was more than the total harvested by sport-hunting in 35 of the states!

In 1953 there were 790 deer killed on Wisconsin highways. In 1975 the figure was 14,109, a 1,786 percent increase.

Not to be outdone by the eastern and midwestern traffic toll, western drivers were racking up a good score on mule deer and blacktails. There were 8,387 deer killed by California motorists in 1967. By 1974 the figure had more than doubled to an estimated 20,000 deer, and it was still climbing. Efforts are being made to cut this terrible toll, but an effective and economic way to keep deer and motor vehicles apart hasn't been found.

LIFE SPAN

Even if a wild deer lives well away from highways, has fine winter range, and has no disease or predator problems, it can't count on a particularly long life. A northern whitetail has a potential life span of 20 years, and that potential can probably be realized only in a carefully managed captivity. One captive doe was fatally injured by a buck at 18½ years, and another was 19 years old when she broke her neck trying to escape. Such old deer often age gracefully. Grayness in the coat is no reliable sign of a deer's age, for even young deer may carry a great deal of gray. With advancing years there may be a sunken quality about the jaws as teeth wear almost to the gumlines. The oldest bucks usually have snaggy, abnormal antlers. But very old

This continues the photo sequence begun on the previous page, in which photographer Tom W. Hall catches a deer-caused vehicle accident as it happens. On the previous page, a herd of mule deer begins to cross a snowy highway in Banff National Park, Alberta. Next, in the photo at right, a passenger car with skiers stops to let the deer cross. At this moment, a truck tractor hauling two other tractors has rounded the curve ahead. The driver hits the brakes, and the tractors begin to jackknife.

The tractors cross the highway and wipe out the guardrails.

Through a ditch exploding with snow, the tractors thunder to a stop. Man and deer escape without injury.

deer are often in good flesh, and even aging does may be accompanied by fawns.

Still, deer seldom survive 15 years in the wild. In spite of their remarkable gifts, they are beset on every side by violence, disease, severe seasons, and the clever tools and stratagems of human hunters—to say nothing of certain other predators. A 15-year-old wild buck is as rare as he is lucky.

Within their biological frame of longevity, though, whitetails, mule deer, and blacktails are remarkable survival specialists. All they need from man is understanding and the kind of sound management that such understanding will foster. This and their survival skills will assure deer a long future in a world where the outlook for other large wild animals is considered by experts to be shaky at best.

DENTAL AGE CHARACTERISTICS OF WHITETAILS (2½ TO 19 MONTHS OLD) Cheekside of lower molar tooth row

Drawings courtesy of State Historical Society of Missouri, reprinted with permission from The Wild Mammals of Missouri *by Charles W. and Elizabeth R. Schwartz, published by University of Missouri Press and Missouri Dept. of Conservation, 1981.*

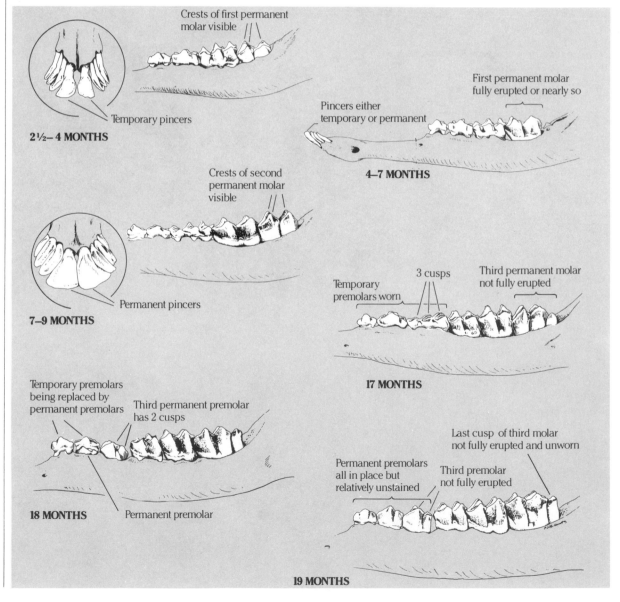

DENTAL AGE CHARACTERISTICS OF WHITETAILS (2½ TO 9½ YEARS OLD) **Cheek side of lower molar tooth row**

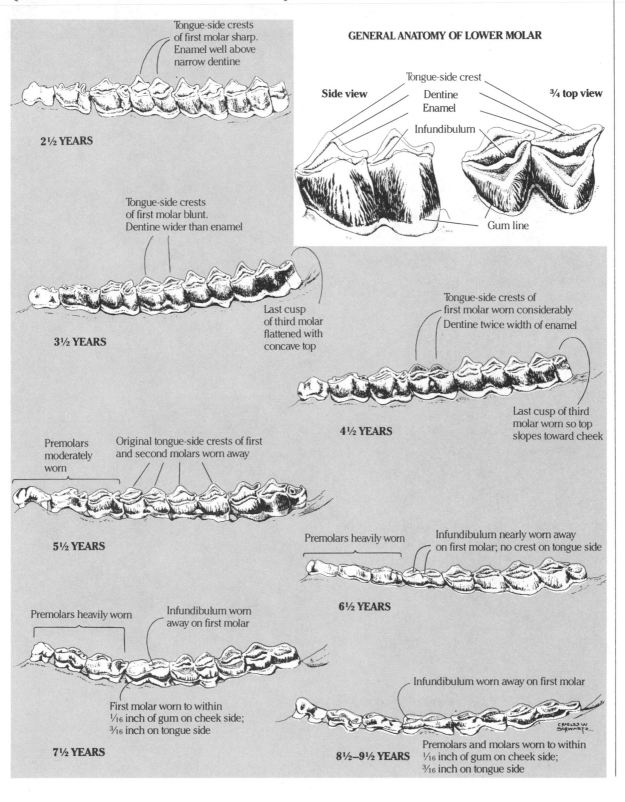

2½ YEARS

Tongue-side crests of first molar sharp. Enamel well above narrow dentine

GENERAL ANATOMY OF LOWER MOLAR

Side view

Tongue-side crest
Dentine
Enamel
Infundibulum

¾ top view

Gum line

3½ YEARS

Tongue-side crests of first molar blunt. Dentine wider than enamel

Last cusp of third molar flattened with concave top

4½ YEARS

Tongue-side crests of first molar worn considerably

Dentine twice width of enamel

Last cusp of third molar worn so top slopes toward cheek

5½ YEARS

Premolars moderately worn

Original tongue-side crests of first and second molars worn away

6½ YEARS

Premolars heavily worn

Infundibulum nearly worn away on first molar; no crest on tongue side

7½ YEARS

Premolars heavily worn

Infundibulum worn away on first molar

First molar worn to within ¹⁄₁₆ inch of gum on cheek side; ³⁄₁₆ inch on tongue side

8½–9½ YEARS

Infundibulum worn away on first molar

Premolars and molars worn to within ¹⁄₁₆ inch of gum on cheek side; ³⁄₁₆ inch on tongue side

PART 2
DEER
MANAGEMENT

When Captain Miles Standish stepped ashore on the rocky coast of New England, flintlock musket in hand and ready for action, he came into a New World where there were perhaps 2 million Indians and over ten times as many deer.

No one will ever know how many deer there were in that North American wilderness, but some recent estimates begin at about 23 million whitetails alone. The great naturalist, Ernest Thompson Seton, put the number much higher than that, figuring that some 2 million square miles of pristine whitetail range contained up to 40 million whitetails. For mule deer he calculated an original range of a quarter-million square miles and a primitive population of 10 million. For blacktails, along the Pacific, which he called "coast deer," Seton estimated a pristine range of 300,000 square miles and 3 million deer. His grand total for whitetails, mule deer, and blacktails was 53 million deer.

Seton's paper deer herds are safe enough. His numbers are probably about as good as any. His estimate was, as such estimates usually are, a carefully calculated guess that included a lot of assumptions, to say the least. His estimate of the whitetail population, for example, assumed the primary whitetail range maintained an average of 20 deer per square mile—which may be a bit high. A great deal of that range was mature, almost unbroken deciduous forest that was probably poor deer habitat at best. (Nevertheless some authorities suspect it supported more deer than now believed.) Some coastal blacktail ranges with dense conifer forests may also have been less than ideal deer habitats. And on parts of the Great Plains, mule deer may have had to compete with the bison that used brushy draws for forage and bedding.

Many of the 19th-century accounts of trappers and explorers in the Wyoming country are curiously lacking in references to deer. Most of these men were hunting almost every day for food, and while they refer often to bighorns, antelope, bison, and elk, not much mention is made of deer in their writings. Lewis and Clark saw few deer after their Corps of Discovery expedition had crossed the Bitterroots in 1805 and started down the Lolo Trail to the Clearwater River. No deer were killed as the expedition traveled down the Clearwater, Snake, and Columbia to Celilo Falls.

Michigan Dept. of Natural Resources photo

It appears that deer were unevenly distributed then, as now, because there are also some reports of abundances of deer. In 1805 the expedition found deer plentiful on the east slopes of the Beaverhead and Bitterroot mountains. Captain Lewis noted that about a hundred deer were killed between the Three Forks and Lolo Pass, west of present-day Missoula.

A similar phenomenon of deer scarcity and abundance was true of the eastern whitetail. The earliest known reference to whitetails makes a point of that. Thomas Hariot was an English mathematician in the service of Sir Walter Raleigh. He visited Virginia in 1584 and later wrote:

> OF BEASTES. *Deare,* in some places there are great store: neere unto the sea-coast, they are of the ordinarie bignes as ours in England, and some lesse: but further vp into the countrye where there is better feed, they are greater: they differ from ours onely in this, their tailes are longer, and the snags of their hornes looke backward.

Anyway, there's not much doubt that the pristine continent averaged out as pretty good deer range, by and large, with both muleys and whitetails in "great store."

Deer and the Indian culture. From the first, deer were coveted by the Indian, who hunted deer assiduously and well. Deer bones, teeth, and antler fragments are commonly found in middens (refuse heaps) and campsites thousands of years old. In fact, most of the bones found in all village sites of prehistoric Indians have been those of deer.

No other North American mammal was used as extensively by Indians over such a wide range of landscape. Elk, bison, antelope, and bighorns served many of the same purposes but none of these was as universally available as deer. Virtually every nation, tribe, and band of American Indian hunted some sort of deer. The meat was excellent. The leg bones could be shaped into needles and awls for piercing leather, the sinews of the backs and legs made excellent thread, the shoulder blades could be fashioned into hoes, the antlers were used for various tools, and the hides provided material for clothing.

Buckskin was by far the best leather the Indian had for clothing. Buffalo hide was wonderfully useful, as

Deer were coveted and eagerly hunted game to the American Indian. A source of fine leather, meat and sinew, deer were trapped, snared, "jacklighted" at night with canoe and torch, taken in communal hunts and drives with fire, hunted on snowshoes in the wintering yards, ambushed at water holes, and carefully stalked by lone hunters at all seasons. (Courtesy of Glenbow Museum, Calgary, Alberta)

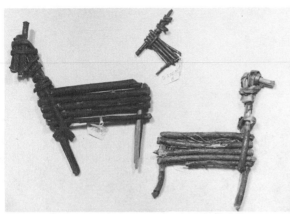

Over 3,000 years old, these split-twig effigies, possibly of deer, were found in caves in the Grand Canyon. Prehistoric Indians may have created them to ensure good hunting. (John P. Russo photo)

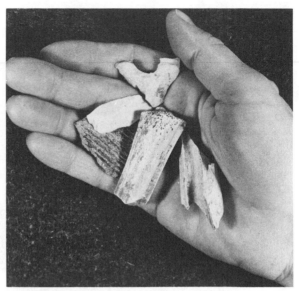

Three of the most common artifacts found in old Indian campsites: pottery sherds, flakes of worked flint, and fragments of deer bones broken for their marrow. (Dycie Madson photo)

was moose hide and elk hide. All of these had many applications, including tent-building, the making of *parfleches* that were the universal luggage of the buffalo country, and the fashioning of warm robes, footgear, and heavier clothing. But for light, soft, durable leather none could match well-tanned buckskin. It was also beautiful stuff—there were ways of working it so that it was snow white and then, with the addition of fine fringing, it might also be embroidered with dyed grasses or porcupine quills.

The frequency with which deer bones appear in primitive kitchen middens not only indicates the importance of deer, but also the skill of those Neolithic hunters. They were obviously very good with spears launched from their atlatls, or throwing sticks. They became even better with the bow and arrow, adding this great technological advance to their highly developed skills as woodsmen, trackers, and stalkers. The Indians were master deerslayers.

Dr. Saxton Pope, the California physician and bowhunter, worked closely with Ishi, discovered in 1911 as the last survivor of the isolated tribe of Yana Indians. Dr. Pope carefully studied Ishi's hunting methods and shooting skills, which were those of a wholly primitive American Indian. Ishi was not a good shot on targets, possibly because he was not particularly interested. But he regularly hit objects the size of a quail at distances up to 20 yards and Dr. Pope saw him kill ground squirrels at 40 yards. Ishi's short, flat bow (he disdained the kind of longbow that Dr. Pope used) was made of juniper. It was backed with sinews from a deer's leg, fixed in place with a glue made by boiling salmon skin. The bowstring was of sinew made from the finer tendons of a deer's shank. This bow pulled at about 45 pounds, a bit light by modern hunting bow standards, perhaps. But it was capable of driving an obsidian-tipped arrow half its length into a deer's chest, or of fracturing a deer's spine.

Indians stalked bedded deer, as in the marshes of Roanoke Island off Virginia, trying to catch the deer asleep. They sometimes baited deer with salt, or ambushed them at mineral licks. Or they stalked them with canoes by night—a two-man job with a paddler in the stern and a bowman sitting just behind a fire in the bow. They also dug pitfalls, set snares, used fire to drive deer into rivers (where hunters waited in canoes), or used lines of beaters to drive deer into large, elaborate enclosures for slaughter.

Some Indians in the Southwest supposedly dispensed with all these gadgets and simply ran the deer down. In the early 1500s the Spanish explorer Cabeza de Vaca noted that certain Indians living in what is now Texas were "so accustomed to running that, without resting or getting tired, they run from morning till night in pursuit of a deer, and kill a great many, because they follow until the game is worn out, sometimes catching it alive."

The quality of hunting equipment, and the skill with which it was used, surely varied widely among individual hunters and even between bands of primitives. There were also seasonal and regional variations in deer populations, although there's not much doubt that the average prehistoric hunter was tapping good-to-excellent deer populations. Nor is there much doubt that he got pretty good at it.

Deer and early American settlers. Deer, then, were a traditional part of the culture of the North American Indian—a tradition that was wholly beyond the understanding of the first European colonists on

When William Penn arrived in the New World in 1682, he soon won the respect of deer-hunting Indians with his fair and open dealings. The beautiful forested region that would be named "Pennsylvania" was prime deer country then, and still is. (Museum of Fine Arts, Boston)

the Atlantic coast. Few of the early English colonists had ever seen a living deer, and they probably knew deer only as royal game that no commoner ever dared hunt. Then, suddenly, they were plunged into a bewildering new land in which deer were not only plentiful and huntable, but an important part of daily life. The supply of venison was infinitely greater than the supply of beef, pork, and mutton, and the early colonists quickly learned to exploit this resource.

Jamestown, Virginia, was the first permanent English settlement in America. The colony was founded in 1607, and in its first years there was a terrible struggle for survival in which the colonists nearly starved to death. But by 1619 things were beginning to look up, and it began to look as if the new settlement might make it after all. For one thing, the colonists were evidently learning to hunt deer efficiently. Venison was becoming the principal source of meat, and Jamestown records of 1694 noted that "a good woodsman, as they call him, will keep a house in venison for there are an abundance of brave red deer."

And there were good woodsmen aplenty in the making. Within a hundred years of the founding of Jamestown a new breed of people had developed. No longer confused strangers in a strange land, they were making themselves at home on the edges of a vast continental wilderness. They were learning new ways of farming, fighting, traveling, building, and living off the land.

And through it all were the deer. America literally grew up eating venison and wearing buckskin. Buckskin was scraped, oiled, and stretched over cabin windows when there was no glass; venison was boiled and given to babies when there was no bread. Deer hides were a medium of exchange where money was scarce, as it usually was along the frontier; they were

even part of the salary of some public officials. The State of Franklin—an unsuccessful effort in 1784 to set up a new state in western Tennessee—was to have a governor whose annual salary was 1,000 deerskins.

Deer had considerable export value, too. Between 1755 and 1773, the hides of about 600,000 deer were shipped from Savannah, Georgia, to England. In 1753 alone, 30,000 skins were shipped from North Carolina. The Great American Deer Hunt had begun.

The Great American Deer Hunt. The American Revolution left an already restless people more unsettled than ever. There was a great stirring in the land; interest shifted from the settled coastal areas to the vast and unknown land beyond the Blue Ridge. Daniel Boone was over there in the Dark and Bloody Ground of Kentucky, and he helped lead the way for the flood-tide of new settlers not far behind him. More and more people pushed westward, clearing patches of the primeval forest, crowding the Indian, and killing the deer.

They were tough people willing to pit themselves against the unknown and its dangers. Many of them were now third- and fourth-generation frontiersmen, good hunters and woodsmen with the finest rifles in the world and an abiding itch to see what lay beyond the next ridge. Deer clothed them, shod them, fed them, and even helped them buy trade goods. And still there were plenty of deer.

They went west, farming and hunting; if the soil became unproductive and game grew wary, they moved on to new ground. There was, after all, no end to the land and the game that lived on it; whenever they were dollar-poor and between crops, deer could provide both dollars and meat. And just as this westering tide of Americans was nearing the Mississippi (the far boundary of the original states), the Louisiana

This idyllic scene was far more likely to be found on 19th century calendars than in actual frontier existence. One detail, however, was accurate: Early settlers made use of deer whenever they could, hunting them not only for their own use but for sale and barter as well. (Courtesy of Harry T. Peters Collection, Museum of the City of New York)

Purchase more than doubled the size of the new nation and opened up prime hunting grounds all the way to the Pacific Ocean.

The flintlock rifle gave way to the percussion caplock, the single-shot breechloaders, and finally the efficient, accurate repeating rifles. Each generation of new rifles was employed in deer hunting, and while 19th-century Americans were not wearing as much buckskin and did not depend on venison for sheer survival, both buckskin and venison were still cash crops. In December 1872, 6 tons of venison were loaded at Litchfield, Minnesota, for the Boston market. In November and December of 1877, a total of 7,490 deer saddles and carcasses and 2 tons of venison hams were shipped from Minnesota. In 1878 over 70,000 deer went to market from the Lower Peninsula of Michigan, followed two years later by 100,000 more deer—an estimated 5,000 tons of venison.

An early Texas trader built his fortune on the 75,000 deerskins he shipped from near modern Waco. In 1880 a California firm shipped 34,000 deerskins that were bought from hunters for 50 cents apiece. One team of hunters in the California mountains sold 3,000 deerskins in only one year. In 1881 the Webb boys of southern Missouri sold 4,000 pounds of venison hams and 1,500 pounds of buckskin in the fall and winter—the hams going at 8 cents a pound and the hides selling for 47 cents per pound. Still, there were plenty of deer.

Hunting by full-time professionals was bad enough, but it probably wasn't a patch on the toll of deer exacted by countless backwoods families that still depended heavily on wild game for meat, hides, and trade goods. Hunted with increasing intensity and skill, deer were given no quarter. During the Massacre Winter of 1856–57, Iowa settlers butchered the last of their

deer and elk as the animals broke through deep, crusted snow. The helpless animals were slaughtered with knives and axes.

Georgia backwoodsmen, with packs of fine hounds, wiped out their deer in the mountain coves, and mountaineers in the Great Smokies set iron deer traps in game trails. Southern slaves devised ingenious knife traps for deer, and northwoodsmen cruised lakes and rivers at night in canoes, jacklighting the deer Indian-style with torches and panfuls of glowing coals. One old New York trapper had a lifetime record kill of 2,550 deer.

Then, it ended. The close of the 19th century also saw the close of the Great American Deer Hunt, for the deer were almost gone. With them passed a considerable part of the early American culture and tradition. Suddenly, we found we had squandered one of our greatest legacies—the spectacular big game resource of North America.

Vanishing herds. The low ebb of nearly all big game east of the Mississippi came in about 1890. In the late 1890s a rumor of a bobcat or deer anywhere in southern New Hampshire was scoffed at, and a Vermont deer was a great rarity. By 1900 deer had been wiped out of the Georgia mountains and were at a low in Pennsylvania—in 1907 only 200 Pennsylvania deer were shot. The first decade of the 20th century saw the near disappearance of Michigan deer, and in the early 1920s the Wisconsin Game Commission announced: "Deer are destined . . . to cease to be a game animal in Wisconsin."

It isn't certain just how far gone North American deer really were, but they were close to being shot into oblivion. Whitetails dwindled to less than 500,000 from the pristine population that Seton estimated at

During the last half of the 19th century commercial hunting flourished, and wild game was a common item on American menus. A typical outlet was the Central Meat Market in Lincoln, Nebraska, sometime in the early 1870s. The market featured whitetails and mule deer, as well as pronghorn antelope, elk, and many kinds of waterfowl, shorebirds, and upland gamebirds—most of which were probably shot or trapped in eastern Nebraska. Within a few years such displays of big game would be part of the past, not just because commercial hunting was becoming unlawful, but because America's big game was nearly gone. (E. G. Clements/Nebraska State Historical Society photo)

40 million. Mule deer sank to a similar low, fading from an estimated 10 million to no more than 500,000. This didn't happen at once; it extended from 1890 in New England into the 1920s in many western areas. But sooner or later, East or West, the remaining fragments of the great deer populations shrank back into the swamps, deep forests, and wild canyons, or just vanished altogether. In their darkest hour, deer in the United States may have been reduced to only one percent of their original numbers.

There were efforts, almost from the beginning, to exert some sort of control on the deer kill. Closed seasons for deer hunting, bounties for deer predators, and prohibition of the sale of hides and venison had been enacted in several of the colonies well before the American Revolution. Massachusetts established a closed season for deer hunting in 1694, and New York did the same in 1705. All during the Great American Deer Hunt of the 18th and 19th centuries, there was a sprinkling of laws intended to relieve some of the relentless pressure on deer. But few of these laws

had any real teeth, and most were probably of far greater benefit to politicians than to deer.

But there was a different wind blowing in 1900. In something less than three generations, Americans had nearly wiped out the great primeval herds of bison, elk, and deer. Strict new laws were passed, and for the first time such laws were met with almost universal public sympathy and support. In the states where whitetail hunting was still lawful, rigid "buck laws" permitted only the taking of antlered deer. Does and fawns became virtually sacred, raised up on the same altar with home, mother, and the flag.

Small nucleus herds of deer were trapped and stocked on new refuges. Vermont stocked deer as early as 1898. Northern deer were released in empty Missouri ranges. Pennsylvania set up two game refuges in 1907 and stocked one with 25 whitetails. About 1,200 were imported by Pennsylvania in subsequent years, giving rise to one of the mightiest herds in North America today.

On the western mule deer and elk ranges, early efforts to save the deer generally followed the patterns being set by the eastern states: some transplanting, but mainly closed seasons, greatly restricted hunting take, establishment of refuges and preserves, and the beginnings of real game law enforcement. It was all part of a new concept called "conservation," which in those desperate early days meant severe restriction and downright preservation. It was strong medicine, but nothing else could save the dying deer population.

A NEW WAY

The simplest definition for "conservation" is "wise use," although there's really nothing simple about the concept. Wise use is obviously one thing to a lumber baron and another to a wilderness advocate. A more complete definition was given by Gifford Pinchot (Theodore Roosevelt's chief forester): "Conservation is the use of natural resources for the greatest good for the greatest number for the longest time." Clearer, perhaps, but still ambiguous; it can mean whatever a particular group wants, and the general public still doesn't know what to believe. To the hunter, using the deer resource for "the greatest good, etc." means an open season. To the protectionist it means just the opposite.

Actually, both can be right—depending on the state of a particular resource at a given place and time. Preservation can be an important part of conserving renewable natural resources. So is controlled harvest. To the public as a whole, however, conservation has a highly restrictive, hands-off connotation. Many people still can't understand how we can conserve wildlife and hunt it, too.

Some professional fisheries and wildlife workers

don't care much at all for the term conservation. They feel it is much too broad to have a precise meaning. Among themselves, at least, they're inclined to use the term "management" when referring to the system of practices they use to work with renewable resources. For example, the technical bibles in the wildlife field are *The Journal of Wildlife Management* and *The North American Journal of Fisheries Management,* and one of the nation's most prestigious resource organizations is the Wildlife Management Institute.

Game management has been defined as "the art of growing game crops for recreational use," and this is a red flag to strident antihunting groups. They claim the only goal of such a policy is producing something to kill. They don't deny its effectiveness, but presumably prefer less intensive programs that would produce fewer game animals and none at all for the purpose of hunting.

These groups decry the role of hunting as a game management method, accusing game and fish agencies of artificially inflating wildlife populations to make hunting necessary. It would be far better, they believe, to allow a "natural balance" to reassert itself and replace hunting altogether. But they overlook the fact that man has so disrupted natural environments that it would be impossible to return to anything close to the original equilibrium.

While "conservation" persists in the names of some public and private organizations, it is rarely applied to individual workers. They are more likely to be known as "wildlife biologists" and "game managers." This doesn't mean that the term "conservation" is obsolete. It's a good word, but denotes a philosophy better than an exact practice. As former Secretary of Interior Stewart L. Udall put it: "Beyond all plans and programs, true conservation is ultimately something of the mind—an ideal of men who cherish their past and believe in their future."

More recent terms are "ecology" and "environmentalism," perfectly good terms that have been thoroughly muddled by the communications media. "Ecology" means literally "a study of the home" and is a formal academic pursuit. "Wildlife ecology" is the science concerned with interrelationships between wildlife species and their environments. The genuine wildlife ecologist is not just a casual enthusiast but a trained scientist. Wildlife ecology is an essential ingredient of scientific game management.

"Environmentalism" is the broadest term of all. It implies concern with the world in which we live and the quality of life in it. Such concern can include everything from suburban sprawl to acid rain, water pollution to littering. Consciously or not, everyone is an environmentalist to some degree. Dedicated hunters, antihunters, ecologists, game managers, birdwatchers, backpackers, trout fishermen, wildflower

photographers, Sunday drivers—all are environmentalists, simply because they may be "concerned" about the environment.

What we have then, is a series of terms that progress from the very general to the very specific. *Environmentalism* is concern for our basic life support system. *Conservation* seeks to determine the wisest uses of renewable and nonrenewable resources within that life support system. *Ecology* is the study of the interrelationships of living things to that system and to each other. *Wildlife biology,* or wildlife ecology, deals with the wild animals and other living things within the system. *Game management* is the practice of producing a game species for recreational use, usually hunting. Nongame management is the practice of producing wildlife that is not hunted, such as songbirds.

Anyway, back in the early 20th century the word "conservation" was the new and only term for what was badly needed: a change of thinking about wildlife, and a change of ways. Most important of all, the public as a whole was ready for the change. Conservation was an idea whose time had finally come—and in the nick of time, at that.

The first need was to police the surviving game supply. This meant closed seasons and total protection, or highly restrictive hunting laws with new teeth in them. All of this was backed up as never before by public sentiment that railed against game hogs and market hunters.

The next step was to restock deer in game ranges that had been shot empty, and it was quickly determined that this was best done on certain public lands that could be controlled and managed for deer.

All these steps were fairly obvious. They were, after all, used for centuries by kings and barons in managing big-game populations on royal game preserves. In North America, however, it was only a beginning. These steps were followed by a growing educational effort, and as it became clear we just didn't *know* enough about deer to effectively manage them, a major fact-finding effort.

Even during the worst period of deer killing in the 19th century, the real pioneers of conservation were at work. Much of the credit for pioneering conservation is given to such men as Theodore Roosevelt and Gifford Pinchot, but others before them had laid the groundwork. In the early 1870s such national papers as *American Sportsman* and *Forest and Stream* were established as voices of the new generation of sportsmen-conservationists. These little sporting papers raised a shrill outcry against unsportsmanlike hunting and market hunting.

One editor in particular, George Bird Grinnell of *Forest and Stream,* became a driving force in early American conservation. Grinnell was a remarkable crusader, a conservationist for all seasons. He founded

George Bird Grinnell traveled widely through the Wild West when it was truly wild. In 1870 he was a member of the Othniel Marsh expedition to collect fossils in the West, and in the 1880s he explored and mapped the Montana wilderness that would later—largely through his efforts—become Glacier National Park. (Glacier National Park photo)

the original Audubon Society in 1886, and although it was Theodore Roosevelt who called the organizational meeting of the Boone and Crockett Club in 1887—a club that would be one of the most seminal wildlife conservation groups—it was Grinnell who inspired Roosevelt to do so.

The odds against such men ever really getting anything done in an age of unbridled commercialism and blind waste were incalculable. They were branded as visionaries, elitists, obstructionists to the American Way, and all-around spoilsports. But little by little, they gained ground. Such writers as John Burroughs, Emerson Hough, William Hornaday, and Ernest Thompson Seton were spreading the word with growing effectiveness, and the most telling move of all was the rise of hunter-conservationist Teddy Roosevelt to the presidency.

At the same time, certain legislators were doing their part. In 1900 Iowa congressman John F. Lacey drafted the landmark "Lacey Act" that outlawed both market hunting and the interstate shipment of any wildlife or wildlife products taken in violation of state law. This was an act that would become a vital part of future game management. It was drastic action for that time, but oddly enough there was little real opposition to its passage. At long last, the efforts of the early conservationists began to have an effect.

One of the notions beginning to emerge from all

this was the possibility of having our cake and eating it, too. Through "conservation" as defined by Gifford Pinchot, it just might be possible to save the capital of our wildlife resource while spending the annual interest. There was a distinct parallel between good finances and this new philosophy of conservation. Such well-born, affluent men as Grinnell, Roosevelt, and Pinchot certainly understood the good management of estates. It was soon apparent, however, that effective management was a lot more complicated than just clamping down on hunting and restocking game. Down on the north rim of the Grand Canyon a terrible lesson would be learned.

Under the new conservation leadership that saw the real beginnings of our national forests and wildlife refuges, the Kaibab Plateau in northern Arizona was set aside in 1906 as the Grand Canyon National Game Preserve. It was a unique area, 753,000 acres of forest and rugged canyons that held a herd of about 3,000 Rocky Mountain mule deer. It was virtually a biological island with the deep canyons to the south and west and open sagebrush plains to the north and northeast.

If there was a place in the country where a big deer herd could be safely preserved, this was it. The area was closed to all deer hunting, and since human entry could be easily controlled, poaching was insignificant. Competition from livestock was reduced, and war was declared on predators. In the 17 years between 1906 and 1923, government hunters on the Kaibab killed 674 cougars, 11 wolves, 3,000 coyotes, and 120 bobcats.

On the Kaibab, government hunters are shown with a load of deer taken during the killing episode in December 1928. Government killing was discontinued the following year. (U.S. Forest Service photo)

KAIBAB RANGE CYCLE

The Kaibab Plateau of northern Arizona is a grim example of the damage excessive populations of deer can inflict on the land—and on themselves. Over a quarter-century, photos were taken at the same location on Sowats Point on the Kaibab. The 1930 photo shows the effects of the tragic deer overpopulation that stripped the range and caused the great die-offs of the 1920s. By 1948, after years of careful deer herd control, the range had made a strong recovery. During the next six years, however, mule deer had increased greatly and by 1954 the range was again severely overbrowsed. (1930 and 1948 photos by the U. S. Forest Service; 1954 photo by John P. Russo.)

1930

1948

1954

The rationale of all this was to remove as much environmental resistance as possible, so that the deer herd could increase. And increase it did! By 1922 the original herd of 3,000 mule deer had grown to at least 20,000, and in 1924 the official estimate was 30,000 deer. Unofficial estimates put the herd as high as 100,000 animals.

As the herd increased, the quality of the range began to collapse. Many choice forage species were being defoliated, stripped of leaves and twigs, browsed into broomy little nubs or simply killed. In 1924 a special study commission visited the Kaibab, and shocked by the condition of the herd and deterioration of the range, recommended that the herd be immediately reduced by half. This, they felt, might be done by live-trapping or by regulated hunting, either by public or government hunters.

The hunting alternative was immediately opposed by protectionists, who argued that "Nature should take her course." They overlooked, as they usually do today, the fact that there was so little of the original natural conditions remaining on the Kaibab that Nature had but one option left—and in the winter of 1924–25 that option was exercised. For the next five years, each winter saw massive die-offs of the Kaibab mule deer herd; Nature mercilessly reduced it to the carrying capacity of the terribly damaged range. By 1930 the herd had shrunk to a fraction of its original size. Hunting seasons were finally opened on the Kaibab that year, but only after the tragic waste of deer and their range.

Clear-cuts of timber don't offer much in the way of fine scenery, and appear to some people to be wastelands from which deer and other wildlife have vanished. But looks can be deceiving. With the forest canopy removed and floods of sunlight let in, this clear-cut in a western forest has become a rich stand of deer food. (Leonard Lee Rue III photo)

While this was going on in the Southwest, trouble of exactly the same sort was brewing far away in Pennsylvania, Michigan, and Wisconsin. One of the problems here—or at least, a situation that helped fuel the problem—was that the protectionist era happened to coincide almost exactly with a great improvement in eastern and northern deer ranges. By the turn of the century even the most remote forests of the East and northern Midwest had had some lumbering, and many had been cut entirely. From a deer's standpoint this was wonderful.

In the wake of the lumberjacks and riverhogs who had stripped away the closed canopy of the mature forest, second-growth thrived in the open sun. Daylight, as was said, had been let into the swamp. The new shrubs, sprouts, forbs, and brush created an immensely rich new deer range. Huge areas that had been poor deer country were transformed. Small backwoods farms failed and were abandoned, leaving overgrown fields, orchards, and meadows. The great northern forests that may have never supported many deer became the finest of all possible whitetail habitats—what one expert called "brush in the sun."

With hunting greatly restricted or closed altogether, the whitetails prospered. Their range was not only improved, but vastly enlarged as well—and the whitetail deer is an animal that can take advantage of the breaks. The national whitetail herd made a surging comeback, at least doubling by 1920 when Seton announced his estimate of a million whitetails.

Pennsylvania was a prime example of this, and a prime candidate for trouble of the Kaibab sort. In about 1900, in the "morning after" the Great American Deer Hunt, the Pennsylvania Game Commission began to buy deer that had been livetrapped elsewhere, and started to restock empty game ranges. Deer were first released in state forests, and within five years they were being livetrapped from those forests and restocked in new units of a deer refuge system. The Keystone State whitetail population began to mushroom. By 1920 some of the best northern cedar swamps were already in poor shape, and deer were wintering with difficulty. By 1925 there were already too many deer in parts of Pennsylvania. Some hunting was allowed, and many deer were killed.

But whitetail deer are polygamous. One buck is capable of serving as many as 20 does in one season, and many does will have twin fawns. So a buck season rarely controls a herd. Also, Pennsylvania hunters were seeing plenty of deer, all right, but because of poor nutrition few had the forked antlers that qualified them as legal game.

The range was overstocked, the deer were stunted, and winter habitat badly overbrowsed. The die-offs of Pennsylvania herds began in the same winter that starvation struck the Kaibab. Pennsylvania deer died by the countless thousands during the winter of 1926–

Severely overbrowsed and skeined with heavily used trails dark with droppings, this northern deer yard was a barren death trap by early spring. (Leonard Lee Rue III photo)

27; a game warden found more than a thousand dead whitetails in only four townships of one county.

Tragic as it was, it nevertheless brought home an important lesson about deer conservation: protection alone is not enough. Deer need management as well. Protectionism had been carried to extremes in Arizona and Pennsylvania, and tens of thousands of deer were literally "protected to death." New ways and new leaders were badly needed.

THE NEW BREED OF WILDLIFE EXPERTS

Aldo Leopold. Born and bred a midwesterner, beginning in Iowa and ending in Wisconsin, Aldo Leopold bequeathed a matchless legacy of wildlife resource thought and work to all North America.

Trained in forestry at Yale, he took his first job after graduation in 1909 with the new U.S. Forest Service in Arizona and New Mexico territories, where a Southwestern District of the Forest Service was being organized. Green as grass, he was assigned to head a six-man crew mapping and cruising timber in the Blue Range of Arizona's Apache National Forest. By 1912 he had become supervisor of the Carson National Forest in northern New Mexico, and it looked as if the young forester was on his way to the bureaucratic heights.

Then in April 1913, he nearly died of an attack of acute nephritis brought on by exposure during a field trip. It was 18 months before he could do even office work again, but he spent the time in reading and reflection and probably began turning seriously toward wildlife work.

That was also the time when Arizona and New Mexico were becoming states, and game laws and enforcement were weak and confused. It was a situation in which a young forester might make his mark, and Leopold became absorbed in "game protection" and began writing and speaking on the subject whenever he could.

In 1915 he founded *The Pine Cone,* the little quarterly newspaper of the New Mexico Game Protective Association. Leopold edited the quarterly in his capacity as secretary of that group and approved of the new system of game protection being tried out on the Kaibab Plateau. That is, in the January 1919 issue of *The Pine Cone,* he editorialized about "Varmints," saying: "Game protection in New Mexico is going to make or break on predatory animals. Good game laws well enforced will raise enough game either for sportsmen or for varmints, but not for both. Either the lions, or the game, must go." And so he mistakenly echoed the popular, easily grasped ways of preserving remnants of the once great deer herd: restriction or complete closure of hunting, stringent predator control, and establishment of inviolate refuges within the national forest system. It was an advocacy that fit in with the ideas of the day, and won the praise of such great men as Theodore Roosevelt and naturalist William T. Hornaday.

But while the thinking of many wildlife authorities remained fixed, Leopold was a born agnostic who loved to challenge dogma with his own careful observations and conclusions. There was something wrong with the concept of protectionism as an infallible cure-all for deer problems, and Leopold soon saw all its failings. The crash of the Kaibab deer herd was just beginning in 1925 when he expressed his ideas about game management in the American Game Protective Association *Bulletin*:

"The most important single development which the past ten years have brought forth is implied in the word 'management.' We have learned that game, to be successfully conserved, must be positively produced, rather than negatively protected. The growing use of the terms 'game management' and 'game administration' reflects this change of viewpoint. In short, we have learned that game is a crop, which Nature will grow and grow abundantly, provided only we furnish the seed and a suitable environment."

Aldo Leopold, the father of American game management, is shown examining tamarack seedlings near his "shack" in southern Wisconsin in 1947, the year before his death. It was here that he wrote much of his classic book A Sand County Almanac. *(R. A. McCabe photo)*

In 1924 Leopold had accepted a transfer to the U.S. Forest Products Laboratory in Madison, Wisconsin. He stayed in that job until 1928, leaving to become a consulting forester and to develop his *Game Survey of the North Central States* for the Sporting Arms and Ammunition Manufacturers' Institute (SAAMI). Published in 1931, this survey was unique and did much to establish him as a national authority on wild game. But a growing national reputation as a wildlife expert made thin soup in a nation plunged deep in economic depression. His funding from SAAMI had run out by 1931, and few new offers were coming his way. But he somehow eked out a living and at the same time found the confidence to complete a monumental new book, his classic *Game Management*, published in 1933. "The central thesis of game management," he noted in the preface, "is this: game can be restored by the *creative use* of the same tools which have heretofore destroyed it—axe, plow, cow, fire, and gun."

Also in 1933, Leopold joined the University of Wisconsin as a teacher of game management—a position he would hold until his death in 1948. It was there that he put together his superb collection of essays, *A Sand County Almanac,* the finest evocation of wildlife ecology and the land ethic that has ever been written. The book took its title from the "sand county" region of southern Wisconsin where Leopold had built a weekend cabin on a tract of worn-out farmland that had reverted to scrub.

In this book Leopold distilled his lifelong philosophy of man's ethical obligation to land and the wildlife it supports, "a state of harmony between men and land." In taut, vivid prose he condemned the exploitation of nature for short-term profit and the despoliation of land and its wildlife, which he saw as man's alienation from the sources of strength and happiness.

One of the essays in *Sand County* completely reversed Leopold's earlier stand on predation of deer. It recalled a time in the Southwest when he had been predator hunting and shot a she-wolf. As he watched her die, he sensed that perhaps something far bigger than just a wolf was dying.

We reached the old wolf in time to watch a fierce green fire dying in her eyes. I realized then, and have known ever since, that there was something new to me in those eyes—something known only to her and to the mountain. I was young then, and full of trigger-itch; I thought that because fewer wolves meant more deer, that no wolves would mean hunters' paradise. But after seeing the green fire die, I sensed that neither the wolf nor the mountain agreed with such a view.

A Sand County Almanac was published in 1949, the year after Leopold's death. The manuscript had been turned down by several publishers, none of whom saw any potential in this odd little collection of random essays. Leopold was elated when it was finally accepted by Oxford University Press, New York. Its publication was warmly received by a little circle of naturalists and professional wildlifers but ignored by the general public. After many years, the public began discovering it. Today it is a conservation classic.

Toward wildlife professionals. Much of what Leopold wanted to see accomplished in wildlife conservation (or game management, or whatever we choose to call it) depended on solid facts gathered by trained researchers. The trouble was training of such wildlife scientists was almost nonexistent.

Leopold was not the only one concerned about this, and over in Iowa a peppery newspaper cartoonist named Jay N. "Ding" Darling was preparing to send wildlife management to college. In years to come, Ding Darling would be known as the chief of the U.S. Biological Survey who originated the federal "duck stamp," and who was the prime organizer of the National Wildlife Federation. But while he is probably best known for his role in waterfowl conservation, his efforts go to the heart of modern deer management as well.

Darling was an avid hunter from the marsh-strewn prairies of northwestern Iowa, and he never really got over ducks and duck hunting. Early in his life he had also known Theodore Roosevelt and had been deeply impressed by him. Through his long career, he drew perceptive, brilliant cartoons of resource waste and pollution, earning two Pulitzer Prizes along the way.

During the late 1920s, at the time Leopold was conducting his game survey of the North Central states, Darling was already a powerful voice in midwestern conservation. In 1931 he led Iowa sportsmen in backing a new law that took the Iowa game and fish department out of politics and set it up under a bipartisan conservation commission. It was the first such law in the nation.

The key to Iowa's game management hopes was the state's new "biological balance" law. This was defined as that condition in which all losses to a population are compensated by natural reproduction, and the law required that game and fish be managed to maintain such a balance. The Conservation Commission was designated as the sole agency to determine whether or not a biological balance existed—but it couldn't be done with a crystal ball. It meant putting trained professionals in the field, finding newer and better ways to inventory game and fish, and developing methods to increase harvestable surpluses.

Darling was a member of the new commission, and one of that board's first acts was to sponsor a state survey that would be the basis of a 25-year conser-

J. N. "Ding" Darling was a newspaper cartoonist, citizen conservationist, and dynamic leader in the new wave of resource politics. (University of Iowa Libraries photo)

Known best as "the best friend the ducks ever had," Ding Darling was the defender of any wildlife in dire straits— and that included the little Key deer of Florida. In this masterful cartoon, Darling pulled out all the dramatic stops. Driven by all the evil forces that Darling could summon up—fire, a pack of ravening hounds, and hulking brutal poachers—a buck and a tiny doe and her fawn take to the water. There the helpless deer ("The Last of the Toy Deer of the Florida Keys") will be slaughtered. The cartoon ignited public outrage and had a vital part in whipping up support for a federal Key deer refuge. (University of Iowa Libraries photo)

vation plan for Iowa. The game advisor of the survey, by the way, was the ubiquitous Aldo Leopold.

It was soon apparent to Darling, Leopold, and other members of the commission and survey team that the goals of the 25-Year Iowa Conservation Plan, and the whole concept of biological game and fish management, could never be achieved without trained people. But where to find them? Most college research on mammals and birds at the time dealt with pest species, or was in the ethereal realm of pure science. The situation wasn't much better by 1931. Something had to be done, and Iowa seemed a good place to begin doing it.

Leopold had already pointed out that the essential ingredients of game research were a skilful investigator, money to pay him, land on which to work, and a means of contacting scientists in related fields. Since most of those components already existed at state agricultural colleges, it was just a question of taking the initiative, finding the money, and getting such research training into gear.

So a fish and game management training program was set up at Iowa State College at Ames. The program's cost for the first year was split three ways: the Iowa Conservation Commission paid one third from hunting and fishing fees; the college provided an equal amount in services and materials; and Ding Darling volunteered to pay the rest from his own pocket!

The program began to pay off almost at once with badly needed information on game animals and their habitats. It was vital to the new Iowa conservation program, for running a game agency without such information is like running a store without an inventory. That was a short-run gain; the long-term value of the program was the training of men at the graduate levels. These field scientists would become leaders in the new era of wildlife research, management, and administration.

The program at Iowa State College was nearly three years old, and already a resounding success, when Ding Darling, a Republican, received a surprising request from the Democratic president, Franklin D. Roosevelt. Darling was asked to take over as head of the U.S. Biological Survey. (Some think it was an effort by F.D.R. to dilute some of the acid in Darling's editorial cartoons.) Anyway, Darling accepted and began his new job in Washington in March 1934.

He brought with him a plan to expand the Iowa training program to nine other land-grant colleges at a cost of $243,000 for three years. As in Iowa, two-thirds of the tab would be picked up by the respective state conservation agencies and the colleges themselves. But how about the remaining $81,000? Darling tried unsuccessfully to pry the money out of the Administration. Though a half-dozen New Deal bureaus were spending millions on various wildlife projects, not a dime was available for research.

Undaunted, he turned to industry. He appealed to the Sporting Arms and Ammunition Manufacturers' Institute (SAAMI), the same group that had bankrolled Leopold in his landmark game survey. And again, SAAMI rose to the occasion, pledging the needed money in 1935. Later that year, Cooperative Wildlife Research Units were established in Virginia, Oregon, Connecticut, Alabama, Texas, Maine, Utah, Ohio and, of course, Iowa. In 1936 the program received its official blessing from the federal government, and the unit program has been a state-federal function ever since. Ironically, and to Leopold's great disappointment, the University of Wisconsin was not among the first nine colleges in the unit program.

So what does all this have to do with deer management? Today there are 18 of the units. They have provided a massive amount of information about deer and their management. Probably no other wild mammals in the world have been as intensively studied, and a great deal of that work originated with the Cooperative Wildlife Research Units and the men and women trained there.

LOOKING FOR A BALANCED APPROACH

None of the efforts of Leopold, Darling, and others of the new breed solved deer problems overnight. Some of the old problems are still with us, and for the same old reasons. One is the tradition of hunting only bucks; the doe segment of the deer population is left unscathed in the name of motherhood and sportsmanship, and because that's the way grandpa always did it. The early examples of the ineffectiveness of buck hunting in controlling a deer population were generally ignored in the face of tradition. Besides, the general public asked, How can there possibly be too much of a good thing like deer?

The new breed of game manager knew all too well that there could be too much of a good thing. While herds were building up and crashing in massive die-offs, some of those wildlifers were trying their best to trim deer populations and save the range. The best way to do this, obviously, was to shoot does and other antlerless deer, along with antlered bucks. Problem herds had developed under the bucks-only laws. It was logical that a reversal of that law would reduce the herds.

There were some antlerless deer seasons early on, even in the traditional "buck states." But these were usually token seasons, because public sentiment and tradition blocked adequate deer harvests. And so the number of deer taken was always much too conservative—a limp compromise between what should have been harvested and ultracautious quotas dictated by

TRAILBLAZERS OF
MODERN DEER MANAGEMENT

East. *C. W. "Bill" Severinghaus (right) has been involved in whitetail deer research since 1939. It was recently said that "he is to the whitetail and deer hunting what Babe Ruth has been to baseball." Retired from the New York Department of Environmental Conservation, he still acts as a private consultant. (Charles J. Alsheimer photo)*

Midwest. *The late Ilo Bartlett (below) was Michigan's top deer authority from 1926 until his retirement in 1968. A quiet, unassuming biologist, "Bart" was a tireless field man and meticulous researcher—a classic example of the new breed that ushered in modern game management. (Michigan Dept. of Natural Resources photo)*

West. *"Mr. Mule Deer"—the late Gilbert N. Hunter of Colorado—served the Colorado Game, Fish and Parks Department, where he became head of the Game Division. Like Bill Severinghaus, Ilo Bartlett and others, he successfully defended the new concept of scientific deer management against great odds. (Colorado Dept. of Natural Resources photo)*

alarmed hunter-voters. And nowhere was the confusion more apparent than in Wisconsin, where not even Aldo Leopold was able to cut through the fog of deer myth and mismanagement.

For example, many Wisconsin summer resort owners resisted *any* reduction of the herds, because they wanted their guests to see deer everywhere. They even succeeded in pushing through legislation that forced the Conservation Department to winter-feed deer during the heavy snow months—a law that was in effect for 15 years and wasted thousands of conservation dollars with no real results. Making matters even worse, some hunters and naturalists reasoned that if deer were dying in winter, steps should be taken to *replace* those deer. For if deer were being lost, how could herds possibly be helped by increasing kills as those blankety-blank game managers suggested?

In 1936 a "Save the Deer" club was gathering strength in Wisconsin. That same year a forester dropped a bomb by suggesting that 14,000 deer of both sexes be killed in the Chequamegon National Forest for the good of both forest and herd. In the resultant shock wave of protest, deer management plans were thrown into chaos.

By 1943 the Wisconsin Conservation Department had managed to restore some order to their deer program. The department set a split deer season for that year—four days of buck hunting, a four-day rest period, and then four days of antlerless hunting. Over 128,000 deer were killed, and there was another storm of public alarm over what was being called "The Crime of '43." It was five years before another antlerless deer season was held in Wisconsin.

In 1943 Leopold began serving as a member of the Wisconsin Conservation Commission, a position he would hold for the last five years of his life. There he became a target of bitter personal recrimination from the thousands of deer hunters and protectionists who opposed deer herd reduction and held Leopold personally responsible for "The Crime of '43," as well as the coddling of deer predators. Many of these attacks were highly emotional and went to extraordinary lengths. As an example, here is a wartime (1945) press release by the Trego Rod and Gun Club:

> The wolf is the Nazi of the forest. He takes the deer and some small fry. The fox is the sly Jap who takes the choice morsels of game and the song birds. Can Professor Leopold justify their existence because deer meant for human consumption should be fed to the Nazi, because we must have that protection for the trees? Can he justify the Jap or Nazi because he eats a rabbit or a grouse which are meant for human food, or the song bird on its nest, which was meant by the Lord for our pleasure, because this hungry Jap must live to eat the rabbit to save the tree?

By early spring, the white cedars in an overpopulated deer yard have been evenly, neatly pruned by the starving herd. This is the hardest time of year, for although the weather is moderating, the last reserves of the herd's strength are nearly gone. (Leonard Lee Rue III photo)

Some of the most bitter attacks came from Save Wisconsin's Deer, official newsletter of the Save Wisconsin's Deer Committee. In a typical outburst, the newsletter blared:

> The infamous and bloody 1943 slaughter was sponsored by one of the Commission members, Mr. Aldo Leopold. . . . Imagine our fine deer herd shot to pieces by a man who rates himself as a Professor and uses a GUESS instead of facts?

Leopold was suprisingly patient and tolerant of such stuff, as well as the many editorials and letters that were downright insulting. He chose, generally, not to respond at all, but when a response was required he was unfailingly courteous.

In spite of the tide of sentiment against "any-deer" hunting in Wisconsin, the fact remained that forestry was big business there. It was becoming increasingly apparent that the burgeoning deer herd was interfering with forest growth and threatening the industry's future. Leopold and others didn't hesitate to offer proof of such damage, with the result that some extremists even advocated any-deer seasons *every* year.

The Wisconsin Conservation Department was not strongly in favor of this, knowing that some districts would be badly overshot, while remote problem areas would continue to be underhunted just as they'd been for years.

But, public memory of "The Crime of '43" had apparently faded and three successive any-deer seasons were held in 1949, 1950, and 1951. About 460,000 deer were shot, with results that the game department had

predicted. All hell broke loose. The state capitol was rocked by fierce protest and Wisconsin slid back to a rigid bucks-only law.

In the years to come this would be relaxed and some antlerless hunting allowed. Still, after a highly successful hunting season, the same old cry is likely to rise: "The deer have all been killed!" The D.N.R. (Department of Natural Resources, successor to the old Wisconsin Conservation Department) is forthwith exacerbated in the press, reviled at sportsmen's club meetings, and generally flayed by its critics. One of those critics recently stated this: "D.N.R.! You know what that stands for? 'Damn Near Russia'!"

To anyone not living in a northern deer state, all this may sound farfetched. But the whitetail is a way of life in the North Woods and has been the making of more than one local politician. Deer are always a front-page issue in the North, and millions of voters in Pennsylvania, New York, Michigan, Wisconsin, Maine, and other traditional deer states have a deep emotional stake in deer, not to mention a cash investment. In these states deer color the journalism, politics, education, business, recreation, and even family life.

Deer management is still heavily freighted with politics and probably always will be. Indeed, some politics are necessary—politics can work toward good ends, as well as bad. And generally, an increasingly enlightened public is supporting the sort of scientific game management that's being run by the spiritual and professional heirs of Aldo Leopold. More often than not, reason prevails.

In South Dakota's Black Hills during the mid-1950s, as one game biologist put it, "there was a deer behind every tree." Nonetheless there was local pressure for a bucks-only season. Moreover, it was pressure that had some political clout, and the new governor, Joe Foss, came out for a look-see with big-game biologists Les Berner, Wendell Bever, and Fred Priewert.

After a long day spent touring badly overgrazed, ov-

erbrowsed deer ranges, the governor said: "Well, boys, this is a democracy and the democratic way of doing things is by vote."

To this the irrepressible Priewert replied: "This isn't a matter of democracy, governor. It's a matter of right and wrong. Let's do it the biological way."

And to Governor Foss's everlasting credit, they did.

BUCKS-ONLY AND ANY-DEER SEASONS

It can't be denied that there are uncertainties aplenty in game management. But if professional wildlifers have learned anything about deer in a half-century of steady research, it is this:

1. Excessive deer result in deterioration of both deer and range.
2. If there is an effective way of controlling deer numbers by some means other than hunting, it has not been found.
3. It is impossible to curtail an overpopulation of deer by buck hunting alone.

Almost any hunter would rather shoot a whopping big buck than a doe, but his chances of doing this may be much lower if the doe isn't shot first. For one thing, starvation losses on crowded range take mostly fawns and older deer. The great majority of those starved fawns are likely to be males—a point that may be associated with the higher metabolic rates of young bucks.

In the second place, trophy bucks can't develop on badly overbrowsed deer ranges. On good range in Pennsylvania, for example, 1½-year-old bucks have sported 8-point antlers. On extremely poor range, bucks of the same age failed to grow antlers above the hair line! The trophy quality of a buck depends on his health and well-being, neither of which is possible on starvation ranges. In fact, fawns on poor range may weigh almost a third less than those born where food is plentiful.

Advocates of the bucks-only law argue that it saves does needed to bear fawns and that buck hunting is safer for hunters because more careful identification of targets is necessary. But in states where any-deer hunting is allowed, there are no more hunting accidents than in the bucks-only states. It's also been found that a bucks-only law can actually be wasteful, for antlerless deer shot either by accident or deliberately are left in the woods.

In Michigan it was estimated that about half as many deer were wasted as were taken legally from the woods. Such a kill may exceed starvation losses on overbrowsed ranges and thereby becomes a limiting factor on the size of a herd. During a Wisconsin bucks-only season, in one heavily hunted county there were two illegally killed deer left in the woods for every legal buck taken out. But when Wisconsin's party permit system began and a four-man party of hunters was allowed to take a doe in addition to four bucks, that ratio was reversed. An average of nine legal deer were taken from the woods for every four illegal kills left to the ravens.

There's little doubt that antlerless deer hunting is the most effective way to prevent herd waste. Healthier animals exist on the range and hunters get deer that would otherwise be lost naturally. Shooting a controlled number of does and fawns reduces much overwinter deer losses by maintaining the herd at a level where deer will get enough to eat.

In Michigan's Lower Peninsula, it was found that 30 percent of the does were lost during the year to legal and illegal kill, starvation, accidents, disease, and predation. Of all this, only 5 percent was legal kill. The rest was simply waste and unavoidable loss. When hunters harvested 13 percent of the doe herd, the total loss picture wasn't changed a bit; total loss was still about 30 percent, but the waste was far less. Special deer seasons can convert such waste to harvest with no net loss to the herd.

The era of protectionism began to run out of steam as the amazing resilience of deer became apparent. There are some classic examples of the capacity of both mule deer and whitetails to not only recover from drastic losses due to unlimited hunting, but also to sustain large herds with limited hunting.

Whidbey Island is a sliver of land 40 miles long and 3 miles wide off the Washington coast. Blacktail deer had nearly wiped out the island's strawberry crop, and in 1937 it was decided to wipe out the herd completely. An any-deer hunting season was held, and over 400 deer were killed. This supposedly broke the herd's back, and the following season a similar hunt was held to finish the job. But lo! Over 400 deer were taken *again*! Today, even though the strawberry patches have been largely replaced by housing developments, the deer are still there and are still being hunted.

Another classic case of basic deer production and durability was seen on a tract in southern Michigan. The Edwin S. George Reserve is a fenced 1,200-acre game range owned by the University of Michigan. In 1928 it was stocked with four does and two bucks. By fall 1933, there were 160 deer in the area and it was apparent that the herd had increased to the point where the area was being overbrowsed. Limited hunts were held beginning in January 1934, and during the next 13 years 546 whitetails were shot on the George Reserve—a fraction of the descendants of the original six.

The average harvest was a third of the winter population, but the average fawn crop had added to the carryover and increased the herd 44 percent! It is believed that a deer herd under comparable range con-

ditions can yield a harvest of one third of the winter population, year after year, if both sexes are removed in approximately equal numbers.

Repeating the original experiment, the confined George Reserve herd was reduced to ten deer by the winter of 1974–75, and none was harvested for the next five years. The results were virtually identical to before, with the herd increasing to 212 deer by 1979.

Generally, a doe harvest can actually increase the number of good bucks by reducing excessive populations and allowing more fawns to reach shootable age. Peak deer populations cannot be maintained on any range indefinitely. And the longer they are kept at peak, the more likely there will be fewer deer later, for the crash may be more severe. When overpopulation reaches the stage where fawns are starving, the herd needs to be reduced by at least half to bring the deer and range back into balance.

There are, however, two important defenses of a bucks-only season in a state with too many deer. Any-deer seasons are usually short, for the total kill mounts swiftly. Many hunters like to take annual vacations in their favorite deer camps, getting together with old sidekicks and hunting leisurely for a week or more. The deer season is the peak of their year, and they argue effectively that real fun is impossible in a slam-bank, four-day, any-deer season. Then, too, the hunting tradition itself may suffer. More often than not, the case-hardened buck hunter who spends days or even weeks outwitting a trophy buck is a deer hunter *par excellence.* Everything considered, he does more to preserve the color and traditions of the sport than the novice hunter who bags his doe the first morning.

WINTER: THE BOTTLENECK

Spring, summer, and fall are seasons of growth for deer. New fawns arrive and food is abundant, leading to expansion of the deer herd. Autumn is the annual high, and the herd is at its largest and strongest at this time. Then, in most North American deer ranges, the herd is pushed into the bottleneck of winter. If the winter is mild and doesn't tax the herd's energy reserves too severely, winter will serve as a large, easy-flowing bottleneck that most deer will pass through. Whitetails and mule deer are amazingly durable, adaptive animals that can take normal weather extremes in their stride. After all, they evolved in response to North American weather. But if there is deep snow and the deer are forced to waste precious energy in a constant, highly competitive search for nutritious food, the bottleneck closes down appreciably.

Since the earliest days of modern deer management, ways have been sought to help the deer through win-

To learn more about the food preferences of deer, Michigan game managers gave this doe her choice of several typical browse species. (Michigan Dept. of Natural Resources photo)

ter. The most obvious problem, of course, is lack of deer food—and the plainest solution to many people has been to provide it. For decades during severe winters baled hay, alfalfa, grain, molasses cake, potatoes, stale bread, horse feed, and sundry other items have been strewn over much of the northland and mountain foothills. The cost of all this artificial feeding can be staggering. But more importantly, this feeding too often has little real effect, except on the morale of the people doing it.

Deer will take food offered by man, but they greatly prefer browse plants and native grasses. Even as they accept man's handouts, they may go on damaging their already injured browse plants. If this happens, the does may come out of winter just strong enough to bear fawns and increase the herd. Next winter there are more deer around to be artificially fed and to further strip the natural range. In such cases, artificial feeding is not a guarantee that deer will not starve; it is more likely a guarantee that in upcoming winters they will starve.

Most game managers consider winter feeding of deer to be a last resort and far from a sure cure for what ails the herd. For one thing, it usually comes much too late. By the time a public outcry demands winter feeding, the deer are probably already in deep

trouble. In fact, they may be physically past the point of no return by the time a winter-feeding effort of any real magnitude can be organized. Also, the logistics of some emergency feeding programs can be horrendous. Then, too, even though the emergency food is high quality (and it is not always so by any means), it may be stuff so alien to the deer's normal diet that microflora in the deer rumen can't process it. It's not unusual to find dead mule deer with full stomachs at haystacks, where they died because they were unable to digest that food rapidly enough to receive lifesaving strength.

It is quite possible to artificially feed deer and other big-game animals enough nourishing food to bring them through a bad winter handily. It must, of course, be food that's easily gotten, readily digestible, and nutritionally similar to the deer's natural diet. It must not be withheld until the situation is critical, but fed throughout as much of the winter as possible. Colorado biologists have found that third-cutting alfalfa is a good emergency food, but only if it includes lots of leaves that the deer can eat selectively while avoiding the tough, indigestible stems. They've also had good luck with a supplemental deer ration consisting of wheat middlings, brewer's dry grain, cottonseed hulls, sun-cured alfalfa pellets, dehydrated alfalfa, corn starch, molasses, a Vitamin A, D, and E premix, and trace minerals.

Meeting all the requirements for successful winter feeding in a large northern or mountain state can pose economic and manpower problems that sorely tax the

At feeding stations like this, Patrick Karns, Minnesota Department of Natural Resources biologist, has demonstrated that starved deer on the brink of death make dramatic recovery when fed a pelletized ration loaded with nutritional grains, vitamins, and minerals. Unfortunately, many well-meaning people mistakenly attempt to save deer with hay and third-cutting crops that lack sufficient nutrients and thereby kill the deer.

This Michigan whitetail died of starvation within easy reach of a hay-filled feed bunker. Winter-killed deer are often found with stomachs full of food that the deer could not easily digest. (Michigan Department of Natural Resources photo)

resources of a game and fish department. And, as often as not, emergency winter feeding has more value as public relations than as an effective deer management technique.

A man-fed deer herd is a cardboard herd, and if food is withheld for some reason the losses may be staggering. It isn't enough to just scatter a few bales of hay here and there; food may have to be strewn out over long feeding lines twice a week. And once this concentrates the deer, it must be continued until the emergency is past.

Unlike almost every other species of game, deer will not disperse when the population outgrows food supplies. Whitetails in particular are reluctant to leave their home range and once they settle in an area, they are there for life, or death, as the case may be. Not only are they unlikely to disperse naturally, but they may be almost impossible to disperse by any other means. So when they outstrip their food supply there

are only two real alternatives: decrease the herd size or improve the herd's range.

Probably the best single way to improve whitetail range is to simply provide more "brush in the sun"—one of the factors that brought American whitetails back from the brink years ago. State and federal agencies have done this by clearing noncommercial timber, killing trees with chemicals, and by controlled burning. But nothing can match commercial lumbering for opening up forest and creating more deer browse.

A clear-cut area changes from poor to good, then back to poor deer habitat in about ten years as tree browse grows out of reach. In the meantime, deer thrive. Tops of felled trees can be left for immediate browse and the regrowth of aspen, birch, ash, maple, and many shrubs provides food for years to come. Immediately after lumbering, an acre of clear-cut hardwood timber may provide enough leafy top browse to sustain one deer for ninety days. A 40-acre deer yard cutting provides browse for 33 extra deer that the area could not support without that cutting.

In Michigan, for example, commercial operators lumbering under state permits felled enough treetop browse one year to carry 88,650 deer that otherwise wouldn't have had enough food for the winter. Michigan game managers also bulldoze blocks of forest in some deer yards, creating still more openings. They plan to selectively clear 200,000 acres of forest in a ten-year program designed to maintain an autumn population of one million whitetails.

In the northern lake states, the use of aspen for paper pulp has been important to deer. Grown aspen is worthless as deer food, but once it is cut the roots send up sprouts—up to 30,000 sprouts per acre—that can completely revitalize the deer range.

Left to itself, a heavily populated deer range quickly develops a parklike appearance with the trees neatly pruned to the "browse line" 6 or 8 feet above the ground. Such browse lines can be easily seen around lakeshores, where it often appears that high-water levels have killed all lower branches. Vast areas have few flowers, little grass, and no shrubs. Hundreds of thousands of acres may have almost no new forest growth under existing trees, and the few surviving tree seedlings may be "broomy" and distorted from ov-

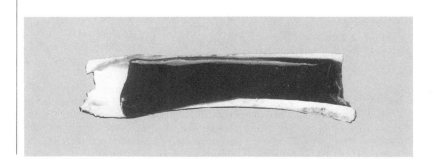

The marrow in the long bones of a healthy, well-fed deer is whitish and waxy, due to plenty of fat reserves. This marrow, dark-red and gelatinous, is a sure sign of a starved deer. (Leonard Lee Rue III photo)

erbrowsing. It is often a desert under the tree canopy—undergrowth, rabbits, hares, grouse, and wild turkey have almost vanished and lack of browse dictates a six-month deer season. Such maturation of second-growth northern forests, with a corresponding decline in carrying capacity, is the greatest problem for game managers in northeastern and lake states.

Overgrazing by cattle is primarily a western and southwestern problem that affects both muleys and whitetails, though muleys are undoubtedly harder hit. Livestock and deer can use the same range to mutual advantage, but deer and cattle alike will suffer if the range is grossly overstocked with cattle. Good range management for cattle usually favors deer, since it means the stocking rate of cattle is light. Under these conditions, cattle can graze on their preferred foods and generally leave the forage preferred by deer.

There's some overlap, of course. Cattle and deer do share certain foods, although on a moderately stocked range there is no important competition between the two. In fact, it's possible for two or more herbivores to use a particular habitat far more efficiently than just one. This always assumes, of course, that one species of herbivore, such as cattle or sheep, doesn't overwhelm the range to the detriment of everything else.

Intense competition with livestock doesn't generally

Browse provided by winter timber cutting can be meat-and-potatoes to hungry deer. It's not unusual for the sound of chainsaws to draw in deer from long distances. (Michigan Dept. of Natural Resources photo)

The greatest value of clear-cuts from winter logging is setting back plant succession to the beginning—creating the sort of "brush in the sun" habitat that whitetails favor most. (Mich. Dept. of Natural Resources photo)

But in the meantime, long before spring and the coming of succulent new second-growth, deer are quick to take advantage of the browse-rich slash of a new cutting. (Mich. Dept. of Natural Resources photo)

become a problem with whitetails, though it can with muleys, since most of the whitetail's North American range isn't subject to extensive livestock grazing. A notable exception is Texas, where whitetail deer range and livestock ranching coincide to a much greater degree. There are vast areas in Texas where whitetails suffer from brush removal and competition with cattle,

sheep, and goats. But this is also a region where many landowners appreciate the value of their deer herds. Virtually all Texas deer hunting is done on private lands, and it is not unusual for even large ranches to realize a higher annual net profit from paid hunting than from livestock sales. The commercial hunting income in Texas is well over $100 million per year. As a result, many landowners manage their deer herds with tender loving care and work closely with state wildlife managers, or even hire their own. Trophy antlers and venison—not beef—pay the bills on many Texas spreads.

To a lesser extent this is true in other western deer states as well. Private landowners may not only charge a trespass fee for the privilege of hunting, but may even charge a trophy fee based on the quality of antlers or the size of the animal. Some ranchers plow most of this revenue into game management of some kind. Too often, however, profits from big game is "found money" that is plowed back into the basic beef operation. So, even though a rancher may have a greater net income from deer, elk, and antelope hunting than from cattle, it's the cattle that have his real interest. He doesn't *want* to be a game manager. He wants to be a cattle rancher and a cattle rancher he'll be, even if he starves in the process.

Timber management offers a great range of deer

For many northern resort owners and their paying guests, deer browsing at the edges of clearings were a valuable part of the North Woods experience. . . . (see below)

(continued from caption above) . . . But unnoticed by most vacationers was the neatly pruned browse line of overpopulated deer range. Also unseen by the summer visitors were thousands of deer dead from starvation. (Leonard Lee Rue III photos)

Although cattle and deer have somewhat different tastes in foods, they can share the same pasturage without any serious competition if the range is not overstocked. These western blacktails are at ease feeding near a herd of beef cattle. (Leonard Lee Rue III photo)

The great Tillamook Burn in western Oregon resulted from a hugh forest fire and is a classic example of deer habitat resurgence when dense forest cover is removed. Although several thousand blacktails died in the fire itself, the huge burn brought a net gain in deer numbers. With an unlimited supply of new food available, resettling blacktails prospered—both in total numbers and average weight. (Leonard Lee Rue III photo)

management possibilities, but the bottom line is always diversity. That is, there should be a large variety of shrubs and herbaceous plants that offer a good selection of nourishing forage to deer. Such diversity becomes increasingly hard to find as a forest matures and the canopy overhead thickens, shutting off sunlight to the forest floor and reducing or even killing out the understory of smaller plants. Anything that opens up that forest crown to provide light for shrubs, herbs, and grasses, and releases moisture and nutrients formerly taken up by the trees is almost surely going to benefit the deer herd.

Such a release occurs to the greatest degree in lumbering clear-cuts where all the trees (except, possibly, a few seed trees) in a block of timber are removed. Selective cutting, in which only the most mature trees are removed, is not nearly as effective even though it's good for the scenery.

But then, a number of aspects of good deer management bruise tender sensibilities. Hunting tops the list, of course, but such practices as controlled burning and clear-cutting are also offensive to those who like to see Bambi cavorting over a carpet of flowers in a storybook forest.

In deer management it's possible to have your cake and eat it too, for good game management can be a corollary of sound land management, with a little extra planning. Lumbering, grazing, and burning are not only possible on deer range but may actually benefit either muleys or whitetails, *if* such land practices are slightly modified to include deer.

For years an interesting situation has existed: whitetail deer have flourished on intensively farmed croplands. The midwestern corn states all have strapping deer populations in spite of record grain production. Part of this amazing success is due to the

character of the whitetail itself—a sly, infinitely adaptable animal that may do better on the ragged edges and backyards of civilization than in pure wilderness. Some of the success, though, is also due to the tremendous diversity of habitats in most of our central farm country. For one thing, basic soil fertility there is usually high. There are such palatable foods as alfalfa, clover, and other crops. And farmland woodlands, creek bottoms, field edges, fence corners, and weed patches contain hundreds of highly palatable plant species. The plus in all this is the whitetail's amazing ability to adapt; the minus is the rapidly dwindling proportion of woodlands, forest, sloughs, and shelterbelts in its midwestern range.

For a long time, much of the nation's land development was more or less limited to the whitetail's primary range, the East. Change came to the West far more slowly. Years ago there was overgrazing in the Old West, and this led to hayfields and fenced ranges, but this left much of the mule deer range relatively unchanged. Today, many parts of the West are being developed with sprawling suburbs, summer homes, interstate highways, ski resorts, and coal and oil developments. Wildfire in western forests has been greatly reduced; in the five years from 1936 to 1940, 31.2 million acres of timber burned in the United States, most in the West. In a comparable span from 1965 to 1969, only 3.8 million acres burned. This looks wonderful on paper and may have made Smokey the Bear happy. But it also means that millions of acres of woodlands are maturing toward climax communities and have steadily decreasing value to deer.

Mule deer have been cut off from some of their traditional wintering grounds in foothill regions by interstate highways, and some of those wintering grounds are now occupied by housing developments.

An underpass beneath a heavily traveled highway can be vitally important to deer and motorists alike—especially in mule deer country where highways like this cross deer migration routes. (Don Domenick, Colorado Division of Wildlife photo)

Typical fences aren't usually serious barriers to deer. Unlike antelope, whitetails and muleys can easily jump woven wire stock fences and crawl under most barbed wire fences. But high, deerproof fences erected along highways to protect motorists can also block muleys migrating down to their winter ranges—a sure death sentence to many deer in a tough winter.

Whitetail ranges have also seen big changes since the end of World War II. Land development even spread to desert areas that were once thought to be inviolate, with housing developments and agriculture crowding into mountains and valleys of the southwestern Sun Belt. What used to be rugged backroads are now surfaced two-lane highways and country that used to be accessible only to cowboys and lonely prospectors is now hammered by trail bikes and 4 × 4s. In the snow country of the northern lake states, where deep winter used to be the silent domain of owl, lynx, and snowshoe hare, there is now a roar of snowmobiles. Not that whitetail deer mind noise. Many whitetails exist happily under the flight paths near airports. But if and when some throttle-happy snowmobiler decides to haze yarded deer, forcing deer to waste precious energy reserves in a pointless chase, the result is as deadly as a rifle bullet and a lot less merciful. Ethical snowmobilers condemn such "sport" and often work with authorities in enforcing the laws against it.

The biggest cross borne by whitetails, though, is intensified agriculture. A whitetail doesn't need a whole lot in the way of forest and fen. But even the little he did have in heavily farmed areas is now being denied him. Shaggy fencelines are being ripped out as fields are consolidated. Woodlots and windbreaks, once so important to prairie farmsteads for shelter and fuel, have matured, died, and been bulldozed away. Marshes, with their dense belts of willows and cattails, have been drained and plowed.

Some of the worst habitat destruction has occurred, and is occurring, in southern states where extensive floodplain forests have been cut and replaced with soybeans and cotton. This is often made possible by channelizing the rivers and streams of those bottomlands. In such public-works projects, the Soil Conservation Service or the U.S. Army Corps of Engineers straightens the streams and builds levees of spoil on their banks, ending the annual overflow that was a normal part of the floodplain ecology. But making those bottomlands safe for soybeans, housing, and industrial development exiles deer and other wildlife.

Of the Mississippi River's alluvial plain from the bootheel of southeastern Missouri to the Gulf of Mexico, more than 20 million acres of hardwood forests have vanished in the past 50 years. A lot less spectacular, but deadly serious from the whitetail's position, is the loss of brushy little farmland creeks that are channelized or even replaced entirely with covered, tile drains. Such unimpressive little pockets, patches, and lines of weedy and brushy cover may be anathema to the farmer who loves "clean land" and straight lines, but they're the staff of life to farm-country whitetails. The destruction of those vital coverts is the doing of modern farming: Large-scale corporate operations demand that every patch of ground produce its share of cash grain, while the family farmer is forced to put every scrap of his land into production just to make ends meet—no matter what it may cost in terms of soil, water, and wildlife losses.

This same desperation is reflected in many parts of the mule deer range, as well. Running a livestock operation costs a lot of money, and costs always seem to outrun the beef prices. Many ranchers, with the same problems as their corn-growing brethren farther east, figure the only way out is volume production. And so mule deer range may be overstocked with cattle just as whitetail range is overstocked with corn and soybeans.

Good land management and good big-game management don't always fit hand-in-glove, but they do so often it's puzzling that more ranchers and farmers don't see the long-term benefits. Some do, and successfully combine deer management with their timber, beef, or grain production.

Ideal land management is directed toward optimum crop production that does not sap the soil base. Overproduction of any crop—meaning a production level that the land is incapable of sustaining for long—is an economic mirage. Sooner or later the soil base is taxed beyond its capacity to replace its losses. Sound livestock management and deer management have much in common. In each, the productive capacity of the range and the productive capacity of the animals must be in harmony.

One or both of these factors was out of kilter for western mule deer through the 1960s and well into the 1970s. Muley populations declined in at least a dozen western states, but no one is really sure how *much* they declined or why. In the affected herds there appeared to be poor fawn survival. One California study, for example, pointed out that in the Devil's Garden area the proportion of yearling mule deer in the spring herd dropped from 38 percent during 1955–59 to only 20 percent during 1970–76. Between those periods the herd declined about 70 percent. In eastern Montana as well, declining mule deer populations showed low fawn-doe ratios.

Roughly speaking, a prosperous mule deer herd will go into winter with as many as 55 to 60 fawns per 100 does. If there are fewer than 40 fawns per 100 does at the beginning of winter, the herd is declining because the proportion of yearlings surviving their first winter is not enough to replace overall mortality (including adult deer killed by hunters) in the deer herd. Poor fawn production and/or survival wasn't proven to be the cause of this widespread mule deer decline. But it is a logical conclusion because fawns are generally more sensitive to malnutrition and predation.

At the time, many people believed that overhunting was the cause of the abrupt decrease. This may have been a factor in some locations—some overhunting theorists are knowledgeable people who aren't usually very far off base. There was no denying that during the previous decade at least 6 million mule deer had been taken by legal hunting. Still, there was something haywire in this rationale. The decline was estimated to be only about half as much in states with any-deer hunting as in those states with bucks-only seasons. So this wouldn't have been the case if overhunting was the basic cause.

It's also doubtful that the decline was caused by some mysterious new factor suddenly working against the deer. Rather, it was due to the same old insidious combination of deteriorating habitats coupled with bad winters—a combination calculated to knock the peak off any deer population.

The West was changing, and as Dr. Guy Connolly of the U.S. Fish and Wildlife Service put it: "The only generalization needed to account for the mule deer decline throughout the West is that practically every identified trend in land use and plant succession on the deer ranges is detrimental to deer. Hunting pressure and predators might be controlled, and favorable weather could permit temporary recovery, but deer numbers ultimately are limited by habitat quantity and quality."

PROFESSIONALS AND POPULATIONS

Occupations defined. Deer biology and deer management are somewhat different practices, even though there's considerable overlap and even though they generally work toward the same ends. Deer biology is simply the study of the life of the deer. The deer biologist is more than a zoologist and infinitely more than the philosophical naturalist of a century ago. He (or she) is a scientist seeking facts about deer. Like other scientists, they leave the job of putting those facts to work to the technologist and to the administrator: Within the field of wildlife conservation, the technologist is the deer manager, and the administrator is the director of the game and fish agency. The administrator translates deer facts and findings into regulations governing the hunting of deer and deer management.

Progress in the whole field of wildlife conservation basically depends on the quality of research being conducted by the wildlife biologist. Deer management programs can be no better than the facts upon which they are based, as well as the freedom with which the public allows the administrator to apply those facts to management.

Before we can manage deer with any real effectiveness and wisdom, we must know what the influences on those deer are. Deer habitats are constantly changing because of man's growing demand for more forest and farm products, living space, highway systems, fossil fuels, and minerals. And we must learn all we can of the life history, needs, and interrelationships of deer and their environments.

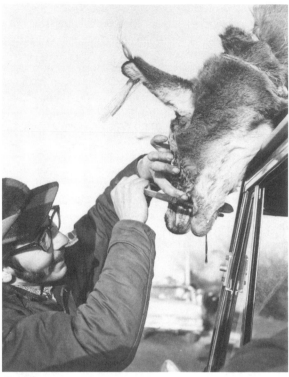

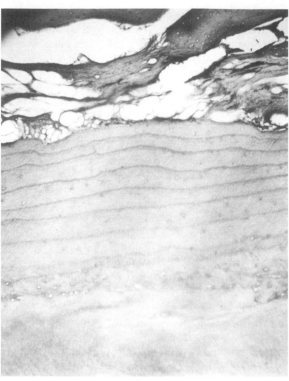

Some of the modern deer biologist's most useful information comes from aging deer by their teeth at official check stations. The proportions of age classes that make up the deer herd can reveal a healthy, balanced herd or one that is badly out of harmony with its range. (John Goerg. NY Dept. of Environmental Conservation photo)

A deer's age is reliably revealed in the lab with analysis of tooth samples. Like rings in trees, layers of cementum are laid down annually in a deer's teeth. This tooth was from a deer 8½ years old. (Leonard Lee Rue III photo)

In the wildlife field, as in any other, scientific findings don't mean much if they aren't applied. This is the job of the deer manager: putting knowledge to work, and applying special field techniques to the land and its wildlife. The only basic difference in the training of the deer biologist and the deer manager is that the biologist has usually gone further in his studies and is better trained for basic research. Sometimes their backgrounds are almost exactly the same, and in many cases titled "biologists" are largely "managers" in practice. (A common complaint of some state and federal wildlife biologists is that they do far less basic research than they feel is needed.) But by precise definition, the biologist is a finder of facts; the manager uses those facts as day-to-day working tools.

In actual practice, of course, the biologist may assume some of the field management duties as well as the basic headwork. More often than not, this is the case. But whatever his title, and however deep his academic training and abstract knowledge, it doesn't usually mean much if it is not leavened with broad field mileage. It's important that the practical deer biologist or manager know the tools of his trade: guns,

axes, tents, tractors, snowshoes, traps, canoes, boats, and perhaps even horses and airplanes. He should feel at home in the same environments as the creatures he works with.

Estimating populations. The two most important modern advances in deer management are more detailed knowledge of deer biology and enhancement of that knowledge with statistical analysis. Using information from the first and applying the second, the old ways of estimating ups and down of deer have been refined. The old European art of gamekeeping has been honed into the modern science of game management. The deer herd still harbors many secrets, but not nearly as many as it did.

The basic elements of modern deer management are: a reasonably good estimate of the local deer population; hunting regulations based on carefully gathered information, instead of partisan politics; and efficient equitable enforcement of those regulations.

At best, estimates of wild deer populations are imprecise. No one claims otherwise. The most direct method of estimating deer numbers involves a specific sampling area that is divided into units. Samples of those units are selected and exact counts of deer in them are made, often from the ground. These counts can be plugged into statistical formulas that yield a population estimate for the area.

Another method of estimating by direct observation is by the line transect—which is based simply on a predetermined baseline drawn through the deer range. Observers travel along such lines by plane and observe all the deer within sight, using these samples to calculate the deer population of the whole range. Originally developed to count ruffed grouse in their heavy coverts, the reliability of this method in making big-game estimates is yet to be verified to everyone's satisfaction. But as experience refines it, confidence in this method should grow.

Deer numbers can also be estimated indirectly by comparing the number of marked deer in a population to the unmarked animals. First, a rough calculation is obtained by trapping and marking a certain number of deer and releasing them back into the wild. Subsequent surveys (by sample area, line transect, or whatever) record the number of marked and unmarked deer. From this, the total number of deer can be estimated.

Here's how: Suppose that 50 deer were marked and set free, and that a later survey revealed 116 deer of which 14 were marked. A simple proportion can be set up to calculate the total: $\dfrac{14}{50} = \dfrac{116}{x}$

Cross multiplying obtains $14x = 5,800$, or a total of about 414 deer. The same thing can be done by comparing the number of tagged deer coming through a checking station to the number of untagged deer being examined. Obviously, the greater the sample of deer,

both marked and unmarked, the more accurate the estimate will be.

The above method is the old Lincoln Index method, as simple and straight forward as anything but a direct head count. But it has some sharp limitations, because it assumes that none of the originally marked deer have left the district, or have died, or have lost their markings in some way.

In addition to these methods that involve actual deer counts, there are ways of estimating local populations of deer by counts of their pellets and of their tracks. These techniques aren't as iffy as they might seem; the track counts of migrating mule deer under the right conditions can give a surprisingly good handle on the number of animals moving within a certain time frame along a predetermined route. The number of pellet groups left in a study area in a certain time interval, combined with the known defecation rates of deer, also gives a general estimate of the number of deer.

By another method in the numbers game, there are ways to calculate the number of deer left for each buck known to be killed by hunters. But in many states today, biologists and their administrators aren't likely to put a great deal of credence in actual counts of deer when determining the herd's condition. The public, of course, likes to have numbers—and if it's numbers the public wants, numbers they'll get. However, deer numbers in themselves may not be all that important in management.

Of greater importance are deer *trends*. Are the deer up or down in relationship to the quality and "carrying capacity" of their range? Should the hunting regulations be tightened, liberalized, or left the same? Decisions may be based on certain "indices of abun-

Deer may be live-trapped for several reasons: to remove problem deer from an area, to transplant deer from areas of high numbers to ranges needing more deer, and to examine and mark deer for study purposes. This highly portable California trap, made of fish netting and pipe, weighs only 35 pounds and can be packed into remote areas. (Leonard Lee Rue III photo)

HANDLING LIVE DEER

Drop nets may be suspended tentlike over baited areas and then dropped on deer, or cannon nets can be fired into the air over baited areas. Sometimes the net even ties up a wildlife biologist. (Colorado Div. of Wildlife photo)

Ear-tagging can provide information on a deer's age, weight changes, dispersal and travel—although such data are usually gotten only when the deer has been retrapped or taken by a hunter. If the deer dies of natural causes, the information is usually lost. (Colorado Div. of Wildlife photo)

Marking a deer with a highly visible neck collar equipped with a radio transmitter enables biologists to locate specific deer from great distances, providing valuable data on the deer's habits and movements without the need for recapturing it. (Bill Watt, Arizona Game and Fish Department photo)

HOW BIOLOGISTS TRACK DEER

Forest Service biologist Dr. Lynn Rogers shows how he employs a yagi antenna and receiver to locate deer tagged with radio transmitters. Each deer's transmitter broadcasts its own frequency, so Rogers can dial up any radio-collared deer within broadcast range and also know, in advance of sighting, which deer his receiver is picking up. Once the receiver picks up a deer, Rogers takes a bearing on it and then travels some distance perpendicular to the bearing in order to triangulate on the signal, estimate the deer's distance, and determine the place from which to begin stalking on foot. Perhaps best known for his monumental research on northern Minnesota black bears, Rogers is here conducting deer-habitat research. In one nutritional study, Rogers and his assistants traveled closely with a herd of wild and semi-tame deer around-the-clock in 26-hour stints on a weekly basis for an entire year, recording behaviors and favored foods. (Steve Durst photo)

U.S. Fish and Wildlife Service Dr. David Mech shows how yagi antennas are mounted on both sides of airplane wing struts to help him pick up transmitter signals from radio-collared deer and wolves. Widely known for his pioneering studies on wolves, Mech is here in the midst of research on deer-wolf relationships. (Lynn Rogers photo)

From a plane cockpit, Dr. David Mech picks up signals from radio-collared deer. Tracking from the air has the advantage of allowing quick spotting on animals without first needing to triangulate on bearings as is necessary when tracking from the ground. It also allows tracking in remote roadless areas. But air tracking can be done only by day in good weather. (Lynn Rogers photo)

dance" such as pellet counts, track counts, road kills, and the condition of certain browse plants. All this is sometimes leavened with the gut intuition of experienced field men.

Never sell such intuition short. At one meeting of midwestern state biologists and wildlife chiefs, there was discussion on relative deer abundance before setting hunting regulations. All were highly trained men with advanced degrees, except for one regional game manager whose schooling was limited to a high school diploma. But his education included over 30 years of solid field experience.

The biologists discussed their data, drew certain conclusions, made tentative recommendations, and then turned to the game manager. "Most of this looks good to me," he said, "but I'd like to add a comment about Area 3. All in all, the deer in there look better to me than they have for the past five years. No data. Strictly empirical, as you guys would say. But I see things happening to the browse that haven't happened for several years now. I think we could let the boys take a few more deer out of there." This opinion was plugged into the final decision, and as it turned out the game manager was right.

Of course, there's experience, and then there's experience. We once heard a particularly loud and positive sportsman-politician tell a biologist: "Listen, son. I've got 20 years of experience in those deer woods and . . ."

"No, you haven't," the out-of-patience deer man replied. "You've had one year of experience twenty times, and there's a helluva difference!"

Anyway, most deer specialists feel more comfortable working with deer trends than with deer numbers simply because they have more confidence in the trend system. It's ironic that although deer census methods have been greatly refined by advances in survey techniques and data analysis during the past 30 years, those advances have been accompanied by greater awareness of the weaknesses of census methods.

The savvy deer biologist today has few illusions. He knows that even the best of his survey methods leave a lot to be desired in determining the number of deer on a small area or the trend of deer statewide. The more he learns, the more limitations he recognizes, and that in itself is a considerable refinement of method.

PREDATORS: MAN AND BEAST

Beneath it all, the main goal of modern deer management is maintaining a healthy herd at or just below the carrying capacity of the deer range. That's really all there is to it—in principle, at least. Putting it into practice is something else.

The problem is that carrying capacities of many deer ranges are declining. And if anything is known about the population dynamics of American deer, it's that grim things happen when deer outgrow the carrying capacity of their range. We have the choice of per-

Bowhunting has added a broad new dimension to North American deer hunting. It gives the bowman a month or more of quality, unhurried, uncrowded hunting—something that may be hard to find during the relatively short, hectic gun season. (Irene Vandermolen photo)

Although good farmland is heavily cultivated and densely populated, whitetail deer can readily adapt to it. The rich soils produce trophy venison as well as trophy antlers—crops that scarcely existed in farm country fifty years ago before the advent of modern deer management. (Michigan Dept. of Natural Resources photo)

mitting adjustment by starvation and mass die-offs, or we can use hunting to make adjustments for the deer. So comes the very considerable question of how to hold deer hunts that are of mutual benefit to hunters and deer alike, palatable to the public as a whole, politially sound, and acceptable to landowners. In principle, the best interests of the deer must always come first. In practice it is sometimes necessary for the deer to share their best interests with certain practical politics.

The management of a state's annual deer harvest is almost a science unto itself. To the dismay of many hunters, the regulations in some states seem to grow more complex every year: bow-and-arrow seasons; short, long, late, and even split gun seasons; any-deer zones; bucks-only zones; trophy-deer zones; special hunt areas; and zones that are closed entirely. It may or may not be desirable to open the hunting season on a weekend. That is desirable for hunters, perhaps, but not for most landowners.

There are good reasons for such variations in hunting rules, for there are some wide variations in deer habitats, densities of deer populations, and hunting pressure. Those variations are usually less numerous and less extreme in a typical midwestern farm state than in, say, mountain states. So farmland deer seasons tend to be simpler than in the high West.

Ideally, legal deer hunting involves only the surplus animals of the herd as determined by the game biologists. Depending on the management objectives of the hunt, these may be bucks, antlerless deer, or both. Many biologists believe that managed, legal hunting is "compensatory mortality." That is, deer killed in a controlled hunt are not a net loss to the herd, since losses due to hunting will be offset by reduced losses through other causes. There is some question as to whether this applies as neatly to deer as to most small game, but the idea hasn't been discredited.

It's possible, though, to hunt deer so intensively that it becomes "additive mortality." In other words, past a certain point, hunting is simply added to all the other mortality factors instead of compensating for them. This is what happened in the virtually unlimited hunting of the 19th century, and some additive mortality is still occurring as a result of wounded deer and illegal kills both in and out of the hunting season. These losses can be substantial. Some surveys indicate that they are almost equal to the legal deer harvest in certain areas.

It's tough to tell the difference between illegal in-season kills (and wounding losses) and the estimates vary widely. But there seems little doubt that higher illegal in-season kills occur during bucks-only hunting. Five western studies showed an average illegal kill of 79 percent of the reported kill during buck seasons. In one Utah study of any-deer hunts, 35 dead deer were found left in the field for every 100 deer checked legally.

With such figures in mind, a deer manager wishing to restrict the kill on a certain deer range might be wiser to allow a modest amount of any-deer hunting rather than an all-out buck hunt. In other words, it is possible to consider wounding losses and illegal in-season kills when planning the hunting season—though such losses are tough to measure. But even tougher is getting a good handle on out-of-season kills by poachers.

Poaching. Part of the reason for poaching loss is a strange public reluctance to report poaching. In New Mexico in 1975, a research "poacher" committed 144 violations that included 19 actual kills of deer and 125 simulated kills. In the course of these 144 "violations," he was actually observed at least 43 times—but only once was he reported to authorities! This study produced an estimate that New Mexico poachers may be taking abut 34,000 deer during the closed season. This is about the same as the annual legal harvest.

In California during the winter of 1975–76, two "research" two-man poaching teams of two veteran game wardens each actually killed 21 deer and simulated a total of 134 kills. And although each of the teams was seen by the public in the course of these "violations," no reports were filed with authorities. From the information developed in this study, the California Fish and Game Department estimated that their annual out-of-season poaching kill might be as much as *twice* the annual legal kill.

Why the strange public reluctance to report actual poaching attempts? Could be that some of those wit-

There's little doubt that poaching takes a heavy toll of deer each year. Difficult to control without public cooperation, and hard for game managers to accurately gauge and adjust for, it represents a net loss to all law-abiding citizens—deer hunters or not. (Don Wooldridge, Missouri Dept. of Conservation photo)

nesses weren't all that pure themselves. Or if they were landowners, maybe they feared having fences cut or a barn burned in reprisal. Perhaps witnesses saw poachers as latter-day Robin Hoods taking King John's deer, and applauded this bold affront to the Establishment. Most likely, though, witnesses just didn't want to go to the trouble of getting involved—that peculiar modern failing that even lets thugs get away with murder.

The modern poacher is no Robin Hood. He's simply a common thief with contempt for the law and the rights of honest hunters and nonhunters alike. Undoubtedly, some poachers genuinely need the venison to feed their families, and they are subsistence hunters in the real sense. However, they are surely a tiny fraction of the total poaching community that consists largely of people too lazy, too unskilled, or too contemptuous of others' rights to take their chances during the open season.

Predator control. In the minds of many hunters, big predators are also poachers since they kill deer at any time of the year—deer that "belong" to licensed hunters and not to coyotes, wolves, or cougars. The fact that those predators are living in the only way God designed them to live is beside the point. They are taking "our" deer, and something oughta be done about it!

Predator control is one of the oldest and best-known devices in game management. It operates on the simple assumption that if competition for deer is reduced or even eliminated, there will be more deer for man. But there are many contradictions and confusions in the relationships between deer and deer predators,

and some things authorities used to be dead sure of have become less certain.

There's little doubt that reduction of predators will increase deer populations in some situations. That is, if we're to believe what happened on the Kaibab and similar ranges where the original predator populations were nearly wiped out. Cougars, wolves, coyotes and some other predators can be a major cause of deer mortality. Predators may even kill proportionately more old, sick, and very young deer than healthy adult deer, but predation is certainly not limited to a culling effect. The cougar and gray wolf are effective predators of perfectly healthy deer and cougars may actually select bucks. Even the much smaller coyote can kill healthy adult mule deer and whitetails.

Most of the recent research indicates that wild predators are rarely responsible for any widespread decline of deer, although they may trim a deer population down to the carrying capacity of the habitat. Yes, predator control can increase deer populations, especially by enhancing fawn survival or helping a herd reduced by severe winters or deteriorating habitat. But studies show that predators do not control or limit the sizes of particular deer populations. Obviously, much depends on the relative numbers of predators and deer. For example, wolves may not be capable of exerting any real control over deer if deer outnumber wolves by more than 100 to 1.

Before any real predator control effort gets off the

Weakened by winter and mired in a spring seep, this deer is easy prey for feral dogs. The importance of dogs as deer predators is uncertain, but they may be serious predators in local situations. (Michigan Dept. of Natural Resources photo)

ground, a number of questions must be answered. The usual goal is to bring deer numbers up to the carrying capacity of the range. This assumes that the range will support more deer than it does at present and that the predators are really suppressing the deer population. Then come the questions of whether or not predator control will really increase the deer, and whether such control is economical and acceptable to the public as a whole.

Each of these points must be carefully considered before a control effort gets under way, because a "no" to any one of them casts doubt on the whole plan. There are also complications that didn't exist until rather recently. For one thing, a highly vocal segment of the nonhunting public (and a growing number of hunters, too) is bitterly opposed to any predator control at all—especially the control of wild hunters such as cougars and wolves. Those species are invested with a unique glamor and appeal, and in many regions, to many people, they are at least as important and, possibly more so, than the deer they hunt.

Some of this even reflects on the coyote, but control of the little songdog is most likely to be controversial because of the means used. The deadly poison 1080 is one of the most effective coyote control agents ever developed. But it has earned an evil reputation because it persists in the food chain and winds up killing birds and other mammals. Poisoning the coyote is one thing, but when this also threatens eagles, kit foxes, and such endangered animals as the black-footed ferret, it's time to back off. The threat of 1080 is so grim that it and certain other poisons have either been withdrawn from general use or outlawed altogether.

Tight control of such low-density predators as cougars, wolves, and grizzlies is often pathetically easy to achieve. Given the incentive and funding, those wilderness species can be effectively wiped out of a game range. It's another matter with the ubiquitous coyote. Intensively hunted, trapped, and poisoned, this infinitely adaptable little wolf is expanding its range and prospering in regions where it was formerly unknown. Mounting an all-out coyote control campaign on the nation's deer range would cost far more than it would ever be worth, or that the public would be willing to pay.

Everything considered, pouring money and manhours into predator control is justified only when a specific, necessary advantage can be gained for a particular species. And that advantage must be weighed against the loss of the big predators themselves. A forest completely free of the big predators may or may not have a great many more deer than a forest with predators. But one thing is sure: if the forests ever lose their wolves, cougars, bears, coyotes, and lynxes, they will have lost something that no number of deer can ever provide. Part of their fine, *wild spirit of place* will be gone.

HUNTERS AND ANTIHUNTERS

A considerable part of deer management is people management—not only of hunters and landowners, but of the growing segment of the public that enjoy seeing deer without shooting them or rejoice in just knowing that deer are there.

There are, and probably always will be, people who object violently to the killing of deer for "sport." A big part of this may be purely emotional. They simply can't handle the thought of a "deer with dreamy eyes" being

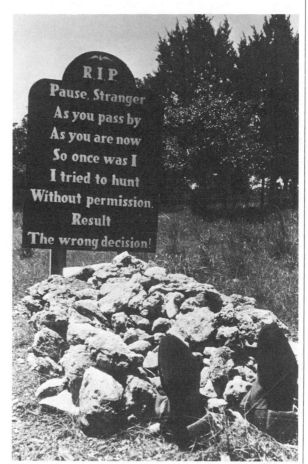

Landowners who may be otherwise sympathetic to hunting tend to develop strong dislike for those who presume to hunt posted land without permission. The result is warnings like that above. The ethical hunter must ask questions such as these: "Have I hunted with respect? Respect for the land on which I am hunting, respect for other hunters—and most of all, respect for the deer and for myself." (Leroy Williamson/Texas Parks and Wildlife photo)

wantonly shot for the fun of it. However unrealistic this antihunting attitude may be and however ignorant such people are of the real regard of most hunters for deer and deer hunting, there's no denying antihunters' rights to object to something they think is eminently wrong. Nor is there any denying that it is impossible for many antihunters to temper their deep emotional revulsion toward hunting. They probably don't understand the reasons for that revulsion any better than they understand the dynamics of deer biology or the motives of the deer hunter.

There are others who object bitterly to deer hunting for less personal reasons, and these are reasons that can't be ignored. They are people, often landowners or tenants, who may have once been tolerant of deer hunting but have been outraged by the irresponsible acts of a few hunters. They include landowners who have had livestock and farm equipment wantonly shot, who have been threatened with violence on their own property, and whose families have been endangered by the reckless behavior of deer hunters who hold property rights and public safety in contempt. The fact that such "slob" hunters are a small minority is beside the point. Those hunters are infinitely more visible and spectacular than the genuine, ethical deer hunters who keep low profiles simply because that's the best way to hunt.

Surveys show that most antihunters have been alienated by hunter behavior, rather than by the fact of hunting itself. In other words, they do not object to hunting *per se,* but to the way in which an offensive, highly visible segment of the hunting public behaves. So one of the greatest challenges in deer management and deer hunting today is not lack of deer, or even lack of places to hunt, but the negative image of the deer hunter himself. This bad image is the fault not just of slob hunters but of all hunters who tend to tolerate the slobs. It's hard to escape the conclusion that whatever the future holds for deer hunters, good or bad, hunters will be responsible.

Since public acceptance of deer hunting is the whole essence of hunter-supported deer management, any souring of public attitude toward the sport is a threat to management programs. Therefore, the committed, here-to-stay, genuine deer hunter must always weigh his act of hunting by whether he should hunt and how he should hunt.

Under the first consideration, any hunting is intolerable if it jeopardizes the deer herds. Under modern management, however, no North American deer population is jeopardized by ethical legal hunting. If anything, such hunting sustains the major wildlife resources, and there is no game species in North America today that is endangered as a result.

How hunters hunt is a reflection of the knowledge and respect hunters hold for the game. To hunt deer without knowledge and respect is not only superficial

and inefficient, it can be cruel and immoral as well. The hunter who does this is the one most likely to be a slob hunter, and it is that hunter—rather than the militant antihunter—who is the greatest enemy of sport hunting today. It is the poacher, the defiler of landscapes, enemy of landowners, the wanton killer, the arrogant slob who makes his own rules. And it is the slob hunter who alarms the average citizen and offends public decency. If the uncommitted nonhunter is persuaded to stand against hunting, it probably won't be because of any propaganda issued by the militant antihunter. More likely it will be the well-publicized offenses of the slob hunter.

Not long ago, an Illinois state trooper was at home in the evening when he heard a shot from a nearby country road. Curious, he drove down the road and found a parked car. The driver was firing a high-powered rifle out of the car window, and there was a dead doe just across the fence in a pasture. There were two more loaded rifles on the back seat. The trooper identified himself and placed the man under arrest. But as the man came out of the car, he drew a revolver and pointed it at the trooper. The officer pulled his service pistol and fired a warning shot into the ground at the man's feet. The poacher dropped his revolver and went off to jail with no further trouble. Next day the headline in the local newspaper blared:

HUNTER THREATENS TO KILL STATE TROOPER

To certain parts of the nonhunting public, that said it all. It helped confirm their suspicions about hunters in general.

More than ever, the problem usually revolves around the ways in which hunters are applying high technology to the natural world. When a hunter drives his 4×4 across a farmer's winter wheat, or gutshoots a running mule deer at 500 yards, he is abusing that technology and endangering his own interests and those of the game range as well. This seems most likely to occur when equipment becomes an end in itself, and not just a useful means to an end. It is apparent among those backcountry hunters who are more interested in jockeying off-road vehicles than in the country where they're doing it, or who care more about the rifles they shoot than the deer they're shooting at. That old American devil, the gadget syndrome!

There is grave danger when one's imagination is so entirely captured by the technology of hunting that the ethics of the hunt are ignored. Of course it's absorbing to apply a fine rifle with superb optics and a high-intensity cartridge to the problem presented by a whang-doodle mule deer buck far up the mountainside. But it is even better when this is done with some knowledge of, and sympathy for, that big buck and the mountain on which he lives. Hunting is really doomed if it is approached with high technology but

A superb trophy such as the rack of this New York white-tail can mean many things to a hunter. In the first place, it is an awesome thing—a natural masterpiece of symmetry and grace. It is a classic symbol of vigor and strength. Its rarity lends value and special interest. Heads like this are few and far between. But more than all that, such a trophy kindles memories of a hunt worth remembering, for a whitetail buck doesn't grow such antlers by being careless, foolish, or unlucky. (NY State Dept. of Environmental Conservation photo)

no ethics. In fact, the only hope for the entire environment, and not just the cherished deer ranges, lies in the ethical use of technology.

Trophy hunting. The subject of ethics can't be dismissed without some comment on trophy hunting. This is a particular burr under the saddles of many critics. They condemn the practice of killing a fine big-game animal for apparently nothing more than its antlers or horns—trophies meant to adorn the hunter's wall as an everlasting certificate of his prowess. In addition to objecting to killing for what they regard as proof of *machismo*, those critics like to point out that trophy hunting does not cull the weak and lesser males of the herd. Instead, they say, it removes the largest and most powerful bucks from the herd's gene pool.

There's little truth, if any, in that. The genetic strain that went into making a magnificent buck has already been passed on to the local deer population. It isn't as if the big buck were a virgin forkhorn on the eve of his first breeding season; he has been transmitting his genes to the herd for at least four or five breeding seasons and possibly as many as six or seven. If he is the dominant buck that his general size and great antlers purport him to be, you can lay odds that he

has already done more than a buck's fair share to improve the breed.

If a buck deer lives long enough, it is inevitable that he will peak out at his personal zenith of vigor and antler development. That zenith, of course, will be more spectacular in some bucks than in others. But just as every dog has his day, so does every buck. If he lives past his swaggering, lusty, heavy antlered prime, he will begin to deteriorate. His trophy value wanes, and as he goes over the hill there's less reason for a hunter to be after him. The genetic resources of the herd would not have suffered if that buck had been shot at the top of the hill, instead. Not that the buck has been wasted, except from the hunter's point of view. Coyotes and ravens see that old bucks don't go to waste.

Still, the critics who object so strenuously to "trophy hunting" are right in some cases. These are the offensive instances in which a big buck is killed solely for its antlers and the remainder of the carcass is discarded. Making matters even worse, it may not have even been killed "in fair chase," but taken with the direct aid of an off-trail vehicle or airplane. All of this is quite unlawful, of course. There are strict "wanton waste" laws in every state, as well as prohibition against the use of vehicles or planes in the direct taking of game. Alsaka is a prime example of this, and it can cost a guide his license to hunt game during the same day he saw it from the air, or to abandon meat in the field and pack out only trophies.

In short, there is trophy hunting and slob-style trophy hunting. Antihunting critics usually fail to understand the difference.

Trophy value isn't always a simple matter of tine count, spread of beam, and antler symmetry. A young hunter's first deer may carry a meager little rack that has trophy value beyond reckoning. Or a veteran hunter may take a particular buck whose antlers are ordinary enough, but the hunting of which was extraordinary—a grueling contest of give-and-take in which both deer and hunter surpassed themselves in an honorable pursuit that lent great credit to both species. A splendid rack of antlers is a majestic and graceful memento of a fine animal. But real trophy credit can accrue to the hunter only if those antlers were taken in fair chase, in an ethical way.

There is a common distinction made between "trophy hunting" and "meat hunting" by many deer hunters and game managers. This is unfortunate, since it often shows a lack of perception. The fact is, venison itself has high trophy value to some deer hunters. Many skilled, experienced hunters commonly pass over trophy bucks in favor of young bucks or plump does. While these hunters are not always right in their judgment of the best venison, they're right more often than not. It's a pleasure to see the tender, loving care with which such men field-dress and transport their deer, age the carcasses, and carefully do their own butchering. The pride they invest in the care of fine venison reflects trophy value as surely as any massive rack of antlers, and these hunters owe apologies to no one.

The trophy value of any big rack of antlers, of course, is purely emotional. The antlers have no intrinsic value; they are simply compounds of certain salts and minerals. To a real hunter, though, they are a repository of rich memory, of pride in himself and the splendid buck that bore them, and of the circumstances that drew them together in final contest. One thing is sure: a buck doesn't survive to grow trophy antlers by being stupid and easy to kill. He is the wariest of his tribe. And if his antlers were taken as they should have been, which is to say in a way that degrades neither deer nor hunter, they reflect certain values that are old and honorable—exalting fine bucks, the quality environments needed to produce such animals, and the respect with which genuine hunters address such bucks.

Trophy antlers taken in a trophy way exalt both hunter and hunted. They have the capacity of stopping time, of preserving some golden yesterday that will never be lost as long as the hunter can remember. Under those mounted antlers the hunter spins the oft-told and treasured yarns, stirring the memories of old friends, bringing old times and places into the room, and kindling dreams in the listening youngsters whose trophy days are still ahead. That is the essence of trophy value. It is a particular depth of experience that only a genuine hunter can understand, and his critics are poorer for not perceiving it.

"Trophy hunting is the prerogative of youth, both racial or individual, and nothing to apologize for," Aldo Leopold reflected. He went on, though, to suggest that the trophy hunter who never grows up, who never achieves any real perception of the rich, wild places in which he stalks his magnificent quarry, has a great deal for which to apologize. The genuine deer hunter, the sort characterized by James Fenimore Cooper as "the ideal man in the state of nature," instinctively recognizes quality game ranges and is keenly aware of their elements. He has a bond with the animals he hunts, knowing that they are biological indicators of environmental quality, of fine country, where a hunter too can roam free. The trophy the hunter hangs on his wall is always less than the ones he carries in his mind.

SUMMING UP

This part of this encyclopedia leans pretty heavily on the subject of ethics and the trophy behavior of hunters. That's because two of the main problems in deer management today are (1) the reluctance of some hunters to accept biological deer management programs, and (2) the reluctance of some nonhunters to accept deer hunting as valid management. Why, so often, are both the active hunter and the active naturalist opposed to conservation practices that can benefit deer, hunter, and naturalist?

One reason may be that both factions, hunter and nonhunter, are so often left out of management planning and action. Hunters in particular may feel they aren't being allowed an active role in deer management. They are expected to buy licenses and support programs, but must leave the real headwork and hands-on fieldwork to the paid professionals. They're seldom encouraged in such pet projects as winter feeding and local habitat improvement, and even their sacred institution of bucks-only hunting has been generally run down. Too often they are denied a really active role in deer management, even though many of them long to contribute. They may also feel that their enthusiasm and experience are minimized by college-trained biologists. Hunters and nonhunters alike, denied any positive voice or action, may take the negative route and become actively antimanagement or even antihunting.

However, hunters can be of immense direct value to game management, if they're willing to take up the sword against slob hunters and game law violators. It's hard to overrate the importance of this. The slob hunter who scorns field ethics and the rights of all others—fellow hunters, landowners, and the nonhunting public included—is the greatest single threat to the sport of hunting today. No one can exert more effective social pressure on such persons than the hunter whose rights antihunting sentiments endanger. The same principle applies to the problem of curbing illegal deer hunting, either in or out of season.

Deer management is based on the best game population figures and trends that the technical people can muster. That in itself is tough enough. But the factor of illegal hunting adds a variable that can throw an entire program out of balance. To compensate for this (or at least, doing what they think can help compensate for it), deer managers may have to restrict the legal harvest to a lower level than the herd might otherwise accommodate. And so a young deer hunter on his or her first hunt faces stiffer odds that are imposed by the jacklighter and out-of-season hunter.

Aside from landowners themselves, no one is more likely to detect poaching or illegal in-season kills than other hunters. They may find evidence in the woods, or along remote roads, or just hear things on the "mocassin telegraph"—casual remarks about venison for sale, or how someone has opened his own personal deer season. All of which is grist for the conservation officer. A game warden once said, "If there's an eyewitness to a deer violation, or hard evidence of illegal possession, fine. But beyond that, it's mighty helpful to just know what the boys have been hearing. Hearsay can have a way of developing into solid evidence."

So there's no reason for any hunter to ever feel he's left out of the deer management process. It is in his power to exert enormous influence on the slob hunters and game law violators who are among the greatest threats to modern sport hunting, and it's high time that he did so. Many state game and fish agencies now have special numbers to call if you suspect a hunting or fishing violation, and some states have such excellent programs as S.P.O.R.T. In Missouri this is "Sportsmen Protecting Our Resources Together" and in Pennsylvania it is "Sportsmen Policing Our Ranks Together." In both states S.P.O.R.T. wraps it all up in one educational package for schools and other groups, stressing field behavior and ethics, as well as how and when to report law violations. New Mexico and Colorado have "Operation Game Thief," Maryland has its "Turn-In-A-Poacher" and Michigan sponsors R.A.P.—"Report All Poachers." Such programs provide toll-free, 24-hour numbers for reporting violations, and some states even have special funds for rewards.

In the past 20 years immense strides have been made in hunter safety training programs, which new hunters are now required to complete in almost every state. The title is a bit misleading; at least, it doesn't tell it all. These intensive courses stress hunter and shooting safety, but much of the emphasis is on ethical field behavior, hunting regulations, and the principles of wildlife conservation. Such efforts are game management programs in every sense, and they need teachers to pass their hunting skills on to beginners.

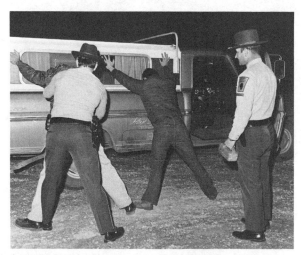

A tip from a landowner or other concerned citizen can often lead to the arrest of the thieves-by-night known as "deer shiners." In some states, conviction for such deer poaching can result in confiscation of all the equipment used in the violation—including car, truck, or even an airplane. (Illinois Dept. of Conservation photo)

Effective deer management can be an elusive goal, with each breakthrough seeming to reveal a whole new set of problems. One of the most enduring headaches is the need for a dependable way of keeping inventories. What is the most accurate way to determine the status of each segment of the state's deer herd from season to season? What are the best census methods—either by direct counts or by assessing the conditions of the range? And as the status of the deer is determined, what hunting regulations are most equitable to both deer and hunters? And above all, what are the effects on the deer herd of those inexorable land-use changes induced by growing populations, intensifying land use, and "progress" in general? No wonder some old game managers look back with nostalgia at the times when problems seemed so much clearer and more susceptible to solution.

So what does the future hold for North American deer and their hunters? Well, there's little doubt that there are generally more than enough deer. The problem in many areas is too many deer rather than not enough, and the North American deer herd could surely sustain a higher annual hunting harvest than it now does. There are places where deer are having a tough time of it, but the herds are generally in excellent shape.

Considering all data, one could conservatively estimate the North American whitetail deer population to be at least 16 million and that of mule deer and blacktails combined to be about 6 million. All of this adds up to one of the modern world's most spectacular big-game resources. There is little doubt that the strength of these herds is largely the result of an equally remarkable system of big-game management that was caused and supported by a hunting populace. That's something to crow about, but at the same time there is need to remember that big-game abundances and declines alike can occur independently of management, and sometimes unexpectedly.

So today's good deer hunting should not be taken for granted. Hunters need to do a little less bragging about the wildlife populations and what has brought them—and a little more sober thought on what is needed to maintain them—especially in view of the rising human population and shrinking land base.

Still, there's no denying that the system of scientific game management in North America is the most remarkable example of resource conservation in the world. Nowhere else have so many people hunted so much and so freely for so many kinds of game. Our game management system, like the systems of republican government in the United States and Canada, has some bad flaws. But it's far ahead of whatever is in second place, and North America big game and big-game hunting may endure and even prosper long after the fabled game ranges of the Old World have become barren.

PART 3
FIREARMS
AND SHOOTING

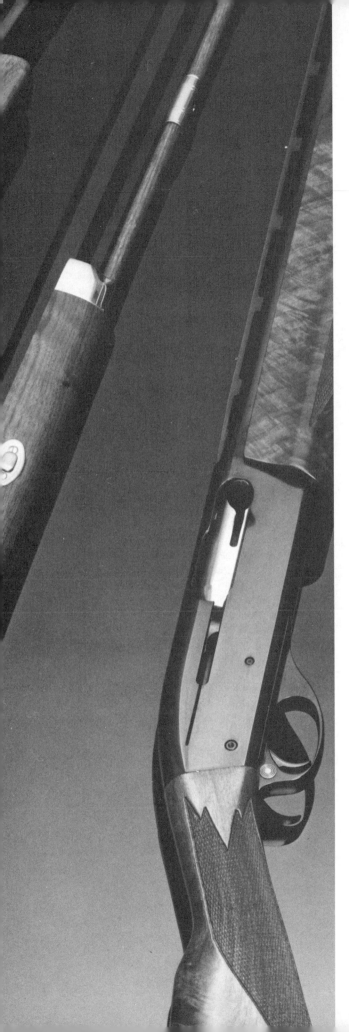

BY GEORGE H. HAAS

Drawings by Ray Pioch
unless otherwise credited

I n times past, deer hunters had little need for sophisticated knowledge of firearms. Deer hunting was a traditional sport, and hunting methods were learned from fathers and grandfathers. Hunting methods had been worked out generations before, and the kind of gun and ammunition needed to bring home the family venison was well known. Hunters often inherited a deer gun and, keeping with the tradition, used it in precisely the same way as past generations of hunters had.

That situation still exists in some areas, but today deer hunting is an evolving sport, and requirements for the appropriate and most effective firearm are changing. One reason is that today the countryside itself can change in ways that were unimagined a few generations ago, and these changes are often very rapid. Consider the many southern deer hunters who once depended on small patches of woods to produce their kills.

Because the woodlots were small, these Southerners could hunt them thoroughly and needed a firearm that could be aimed quickly and would fire a fast second shot in case the first only wounded the deer. Most often they hunted with a .30/30 lever-action carbine that had nonmagnifying sights. Or they used some other very handy short-range gun. Today many of these same hunters use a .300 Winchester Magnum bolt-action rifle or some other flat-shooting, long-range gun. The rifle usually sports a 9× scope or an even more powerful magnifying sight. Instead of walking-up deer, as a stillhunter, or participating in deer drives, these hunters sit on carefully prepared stands and wait for deer to come within range.

The reason for these new hunting practices is changed terrain. Much southern agriculture now tends toward mechanized, big-field cultivation of soybeans and grain. To make big, efficient fields, small farms have been combined, and farmhouses, kitchen gardens, and woodlots have been bulldozed. So, much of the countryside now consists of open crop fields, and there is little deer cover except in swamps that cannot be cultivated. These swamps, thick with growth, are used as bedding areas by the deer, and they are almost impossible to hunt.

Ample food and strict game laws have produced an abundance of deer in the South. But because of the generally open country in many areas, they are hard to hunt. Whitetail deer in these areas have ad-

Stanley W. Trzoniac photo

justed well to living most of their lives in open country, so the hunter who tries to approach them is playing a loser's game. And there is almost no chance of walking-up a deer in cover because there is little remaining cover and because the cover that does remain is too thick.

The best way to score is to do considerable scouting, find out where the deer are "using," and then wait for them on a stand with a long-range rifle. The stand is often elevated. Since deer in these areas feed mostly in early morning and late afternoon when the light is dim, a good riflescope is very useful. It enables the hunter to see what he is shooting at and to hit at long range. A bolt-action rifle is preferred, since it is usually (not always) more accurate than rifles with other actions. It does make a quick second shot almost impossible, but at rather long range, the deer is gone before the hunter can recover from recoil and aim again.

These southern hunters are now hunting the way hunters in the West used to go after mule deer. Scouting to locate deer was important, and a very accurate long-range rifle was used; otherwise there was little chance of making a killing shot.

Some mule-deer hunters have also found that hunting has changed since the 1950s. It used to be that mule deer were thought of as being rather stupid. Most of the animals lived out in the open in the foothills of high mountains. It was rather easy to locate the quarry, and even getting within killing range wasn't the most difficult task. But because mule deer did not inhabit heavy cover, they could spot a hunter at fairly long range. So a flat-shooting, bolt-action rifle with scope was favored.

Today mule deer in parts of the West have become much more wary. Increased disturbance of their range and more hunting pressure have taught these deer that open country is not healthy during the fall hunting season. This is especially true of old trophy bucks, and the same thing can be said of elk. Now elk and mule deer in much of the West have retreated even from the open foothills and inhabit heavily timbered land.

For hunting in this situation, western hunters are turning to short, handy, big-bore rifles with lots of punch. They need a more powerful rifle than most eastern hunters because the mule deer is bigger and more powerful on the average than the whitetail. The usual result is that the savvy mule-deer hunter who is forced to hunt in heavy cover carries a fairly powerful rifle equipped with a low-power or variable-power scope. His rifle and sighting equipment differ greatly from the flat-shooting, long-range rifle that his father used.

Examples of this need to adopt hunting methods and rifles to changing terrain and the changing habits of the deer can be cited from all over the United States and Canada. New Jersey, for instance, has an abundant deer herd, and hunting methods there have changed radically. There is an archery season and a muzzleloader season, but most New Jersey hunters go afield during the regular gun season.

Hunting deer with modern rifles is forbidden by law because the state is so heavily populated that using a long-range firearm would be dangerous. Shotguns are used instead, and hunters were formerly only allowed to use buckshot. The typical load was a 12-gauge cartridge that contained nine .33 caliber balls. The maximum effective range of this load was only about 40 yards, and many users of buckshot would not fire at a deer that was over 30 yards away. The favored shotgun was a pump gun or a semi-automatic with the original bird-hunting sight or sights. Most hunters sat in tree stands and waited for a buck to come along a heavily used deer trail. Stand-hunting was the best way to beat the odds.

Under pressure from many hunters, New Jersey officials changed the law to allow the use of rifled slugs in shotguns. These big, slow-moving chunks of lead give the hunter an effective range of 100 yards or a bit more. Many hunters bought specially made "slug barrels" equipped with adjustable rifle sights instead of bird-hunting sights. Deer began to be taken at longer ranges than was possible with buckshot loads, and some hunters tried to get more out of their slug guns by installing low-power riflescopes.

Today, in some heavily hunted New Jersey areas, deer have adjusted to the 100-yards plus-a-little effective range of slug guns. They now favor big, open fields as the right place to feed and linger during hunting season. If a field is fairly flat and several hundred yards across, a hunter simply cannot hit a deer that is out in the middle without first walking out into the field and alerting the animal.

Deer in that situation are safe from slug guns. They are also out of reach for bowhunting gear and most muzzleloading rifles, which have an effective range of only 75 yards or so when shot by the average hunter. It's a bizarre experience for an out-of-stater to jump one of these educated New Jersey deer in a patch of cover. They watch in amazement as the animal runs out into a wide open field where it would be as good as dead, if it were in a state where rifles were legal.

The best way to counter this is for a group of hunters to work together. Some walk out into the open to drive the deer from the field. Standers are posted in cover on the other side of the field, usually downwind so the deer will not get their scent. Since the deer are moving when they enter the cover, some hunters now prefer—you guessed it—buckshot-loaded shotguns. In a very short time, many hunters dropped the buckshot gun only to take it up again when the deer's habits changed.

So changes in the law can actually alter the deer's

behavior and force not only a change in the favored firearm, but the entire hunting method. With urban sprawl crowding into rural areas, more "shotgun-only" and "archery-only" counties are appearing on zone maps issued to hunters. You may find yourself changing your hunting method and equipment quite unexpectedly.

Many hunters travel a great deal, and nonresident big-game hunting is now very popular. Formerly, few hunters hunted outside their home states. Today many want to go on at least a few out-of-state hunts and can afford to do so. Most common for an easterner, of course, is the nonresident mule-deer hunt. Quite frequently, the hunting method and the preferred firearm differ from those employed at home.

And these days a hunter may suddenly find himself transferred to another area by his employer. Consider a midwestern stillhunter who is transferred to southern Mississippi or Louisiana. Because of the thick cover and swampy ground, the only effective way to hunt deer is to use a pack of hounds and post standers armed with buckshot-loaded shotguns. Where he once hunted alone with a rifle, the transferee must now adjust to sitting still on a ground stand, using a shotgun, and hunting with a tightly organized group and their dogs.

Today, it's worthwhile to have a good knowledge of the different kinds of hunting firearms and different hunting methods used in North America. But perhaps the best reason for acquiring this kind of knowledge is just that it is personally rewarding. You may not need it if you are a stay-at-home hunter and your job assignment, the terrain, and the hunting regulations do not change. But the information is fascinating in and of itself.

THE HAND CANNON

Firearms used for big-game hunting today are products of a long evolution. It all probably started in China many centuries ago with the invention of black powder, an explosive mixture of sulphur, charcoal, and saltpeter. There is no historical proof that Orientals used black powder in guns. They did use it in fireworks, set off to frighten the enemy or their horses, but later it was used in bombs and mines that probably killed people.

Black powder became known in Arabia and Europe in medieval times. At some point someone invented a primitive cannon: a tube that had one closed end and that was loaded from the muzzle. Black powder was loaded into the tube, followed by some kind of

This 15th century gunner inserted a red-hot bent wire in the flash hole to fire his hand cannon.

This cast-bronze hand cannon is the earliest hand-held firearm that can be dated with any certainty. It was found when the ruins of a castle in Germany were excavated. The castle was destroyed in 1399, so the gun predates that. The socket at the rear, in which a wooden tiller (actually a simple pole) was inserted, proves that it is a hand cannon, not a piece of small artillery mounted on a gun carriage. The opening of the touch hole is enlarged for insertion of a red-hot wire or slow match to ignite a priming charge. The rear of the bore is extra thick to provide strong walls where strength was needed most. Even so cast guns such as this frequently burst.

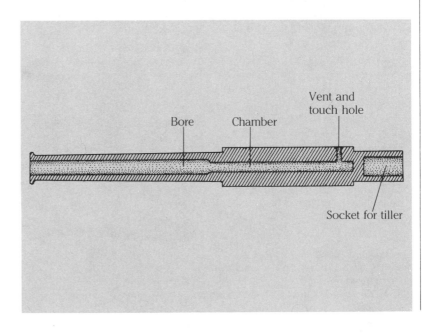

soft wad to seal in the gas pressure and a charge of shot or a single projectile. This primitive weapon was set off by inserting a burning "slow match" or a red-hot wire in a small touch hole at the closed end of the gun. Some early guns were made of metal, but others were built-up affairs made of leather strips wrapped spirally around wooden staves. Sometimes these guns fired large arrows rather than any form of bullet or shot.

At first these primitive guns were quite heavy and could not be carried by one man. Most were used in fortifications or gun emplacements. The first portable guns were crude hand cannons that had a pole protruding from the breech end. This pole or tiller could be held in the gunner's hands when the piece was fired. If the gun was a heavy one or if a very powerful charge was used, the butt end of the tiller was held against the ground and braced by the gunner's foot.

No one knows exactly when these crude hand cannons first came into use. Accuracy was miserable, and hand cannons were really useful only when fired at a formation of massed enemy soldiers or a large stationary target such as a house or fortification. Most of the specimens that have survived did not have sights of any kind, which tells us something about their accuracy. At the time when these guns were in use, many crossbows were equipped with adjustable peep sights.

Hand cannons were completely useless for hunting. The gunner could not hit a target as small as a deer, a stag, or a European bison. And walking through the woods in search of game with a burning match or a red-hot wire would have been very difficult, to say the least. Rain or even fog would, of course, put the match out or cool the red-hot wire.

For many years, these crude portable firearms were useful only to feudal soldiers, and hunters continued to rely on the longbow or the crossbow. Bows loaded faster, could be aimed with greater accuracy, and did

not require a burning match or hot wire to fire them. Thus hand cannon and longbows and crossbows existed side by side in European armies for many years. Crossbows and longbows were often used to fire at individual enemy soldiers, while the crude firearms were used only against massed troops and other large targets. It took many years of development before portable firearms became accurate and reliable enough for use against individual enemy soldiers—not to mention game animals.

The rifles we use for hunting today evolved from these crude guns, and a knowledge of this history helps the beginner to understand how modern arms function. Also, a knowledge of the early guns is useful today because of the revival of muzzleloading guns as practical arms in the United States. Formerly, muzzleloaders were discussed only briefly in books on hunting firearms. But now any book on American big-game hunting must include a very practical discussion of how to shoot two "primitive weapons"—flintlocks and percussion-cap muzzleloaders. This more detailed material appears later in this part of this encyclopedia.

THE MATCHLOCK

Efforts to improve the hand cannon were directed mostly at improving the means of ignition. By the early 1400s, the matchlock was in use in many parts of Europe, and it was soon introduced to Japan, China, and other parts of Asia. The matchlock incorporated a Z-shaped or S-shaped mechanism that was mounted on a pivot on the gun. This "serpentine" held a burning slow match in one end by means of a clip or jaws closed with a screw. The lower end of the device was the trigger.

The gunner loaded powder, wad, and a bullet or a charge of shot—or even some small stones—through

In the matchlock, powder, a wad or wads, and a bullet or a charge of shot were loaded through the muzzle. The pan was primed with fine-grain powder. When ready to shoot, the gunner swung the pivoted pan cover open and then pulled the trigger. The cock moved downward and the burning match held in its jaws touched off the pan powder which, in turn, fired the main charge in the barrel through a touch hole in the barrel wall.

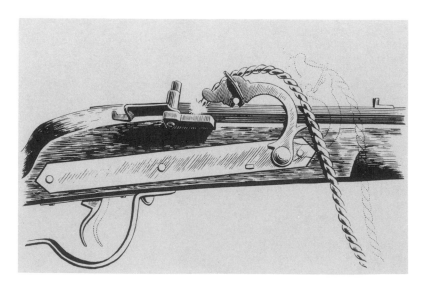

the muzzle. Then a small quantity of powder was trickled into the touchhole. When the gunner was ready to fire, he pulled the lower end of the serpentine. This lowered the burning match into the priming powder, which ignited the main charge. The exploding powder created rapidly expanding gases. These gases, contained by the closed rear end of the tube, slammed against the wadding, forcing it and the projectile down the barrel.

Later in its development, the matchlock was refined a great deal. The trigger became a separate mechanism that released a spring-loaded "cock" that held the burning match. The opening of the touchhole was expanded into a shallow pan so that more priming powder could be used for surer ignition. Finally, the pan was enclosed with a sliding or pivoted cover that kept the priming powder dry and in place in the pan. Just before the gunner fired, he manually opened the pan cover, raised the piece to his shoulder, aimed, and pulled the trigger to lower the match to the pan.

Matchlocks were a great improvement over the earlier hand cannon, and some of them were carefully made and had wooden stocks that were much more convenient than the previously used poles or tillers. There were also guns with nicely made V-notch rear sights and small blades or beads for front sights, an indication that their users could expect some degree of accuracy, at least at close range. Matchlocks were sometimes used for hunting, as evidenced by engravings of game animals on some of them. These guns were at times profusely decorated, often with complex inlay work. But the vast majority of them were crude implements used by feudal serfs serving as soldiers.

Kings and noblemen on the continent in Europe preferred to arm their serfs with crude matchlocks or crossbows because these were comparatively easy to learn how to shoot. Training a skilled longbowman was a much more difficult process. Nevertheless, the English preferred the longbow to the other two weapons because thousands of Englishmen grew up hunting (or poaching) with bows and because the Welsh longbow, adopted by the English, was a much more accurate and effective weapon. It was deadly against individual targets—game or men—and could be used with bowmen massed to fire effective flights of arrows at enemy formations. Also, with a longbow, there was no problem of the glowing, slow match that could go out just before the weapon was to be fired or that could help game or the enemy spot the shooter.

SPARK IGNITION— THE WHEEL LOCK

A quantum leap forward in firearms development came with the invention of the wheel-lock gun, which relied on spark ignition rather than direct ignition by a burning match or hot wire.

Wheel-lock ignition employed a steel wheel with a roughened or serrated edge. After loading and priming in the same way as with a matchlock, the gunner used a separate spanner or wrench to wind the wheel mechanism up against a spring. Forward of the wheel was a metal arm with a viselike arrangement at its end. In the jaws of the vise was a wedge-shaped piece of iron pyrites, which had the same function as the flint used later in flintlocks. When the gunner aimed and fired, three things happened almost simultaneously. The spring-loaded wheel began to rotate very rapidly; the pan cover slid away to uncover the priming powder; and the arm swung down toward the rear, bringing the iron pyrites wedge into contact with the serrated edge of the wheel. Contact between the moving wheel and the pyrites created sparks that fired the priming charge, which in turn fired the main charge.

Some wheel-lock guns were very accurate, and most were expensive. In some cases they were exquisitely engraved, and a few were inlaid with ivory, silver, gold, and jewels. The mechanism itself was quite complex

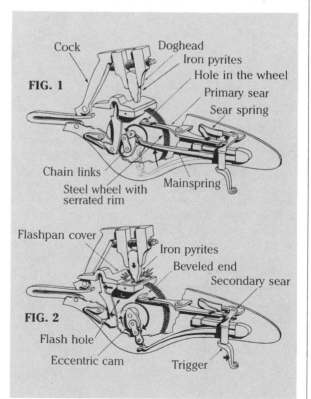

The wheel lock's complex lock relied on spark ignition created by rotating a serrated steel wheel against a wedge of iron pyrites. When the trigger was pulled, the pan opened, and the cock moved downward and sparks ignited the pan powder. The lock had to be wound up or "spanned" with a separate tool.

and therefore very expensive. Only noblemen or rulers could afford to own and use these guns. Because of the cost, it was manifestly impossible to arm a body of soldiers with these guns, though feudal lords did use them during military campaigns.

Overwhelmingly, these guns were used to hunt deer and other big game. The mechanism was seldom affected by dampness, and the ignition device was quite reliable. Since wheel locks were well made, accuracy was much better than that of most matchlocks. Finally, with a wheel lock, it had become possible for a hunter to stalk game without the revealing glow of a burning match. Hunting boar, deer, stag, European moose, and other big game with these rifles became a popular sport among the nobility of northern Europe, and wheel-lock guns made in Austria, Germany, and Bohemia were prized throughout Europe.

The wheel lock had its disadvantages, however. The complex ignition mechanism—with all its springs, levers, and linking chains—soon got out of kilter unless it was maintained by a good gunsmith. Even so, such a complex mechanism could also fail unexpectedly just when the duke had an Imperial stag or a European bison in his sights. Inevitably, gunsmiths began searching for a more dependable gun.

THE SNAPHAUNCE

The answer was a gun that also employed spark ignition—the snaphaunce. The term is almost certainly derived from two Dutch-German words: *schnap* and *Hahn.* To *schnap* is to snap and a *Hahn* is a rooster or cock. If you look at the cock (many would erroneously call it a hammer) of a spark-ignition gun or even the exposed hammers of some modern firearms and revolvers, you will see that from the side they do resemble roosters or cocks. The nose that carries the flint, or impacts on a percussion cap or firing pin, is the cock's head and beak. The rear projection, curved to suit the shooter's thumb, is the cock's tail, and its legs are represented by the downward-pointing part that pivots on the gun. Roosters or cocks constantly peck at food lying on the ground, just as the cock of a gun pecks downward when the trigger is pulled; so the name *Schnaphahn* (snapping cock)—"snaphaunce" in English—is descriptive and very appropriate. The idea that this type of gun was first used by chicken thieves is apparently quite erroneous; yet it has appeared in print many times. Chicken thieves then and now have little use for a firearm. A sack and stealth are all that are required.

There were many variations on the snaphaunce lock—German, Dutch, Swedish, Spanish, French, and English—but all of them employed a cock armed with a wedge of flint between its jaws. This was mounted to the rear of the flash hole instead of forward of it as in the wheel lock. At first the priming pan was covered with a sliding lid that was manually opened before a shot. Later it was linked to the rest of the mechanism. A third component was the frizzen, or steel. This hardened-steel part was mounted forward of the touchhole. When he was ready to fire, the gunner pulled the trigger. The flint-armed cock flew forward under the power of a spring. The flint hit the face of the frizzen or steel and scraped along it, creating sparks. The frizzen was knocked forward and out of the way on its pivot so that the sparks fell downward toward the pan. At the same time, the linked pan cover moved to uncover the priming charge, and sparks fell into the priming pan.

The snaphaunce in its many different forms soon replaced the wheel lock, except among some northern European noblemen who did not care about the high cost of the wheel lock and preferred its very reliable ignition. Snaphaunces were, however, rather complex arms because of the separate pan cover. Some snaphaunce guns were used for war, and some were used for hunting. Many were used for both.

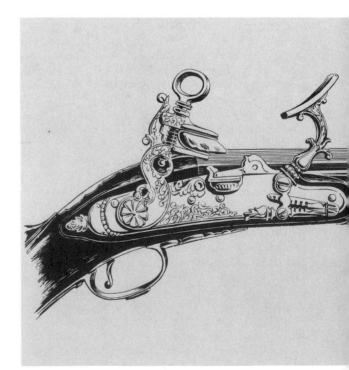

The snaphaunce had a spark-ignition lock that employed a flint wedge held in the jaws of the cock. The lidded pan was loaded with priming powder. The steel, or frizzen, was struck by the flint to create sparks. The steel was knocked out of the way at the same time the pan opened to expose the priming powder. The lock is shown in the fired position.

THE FLINTLOCK

Further simplification came when gunsmiths began combining the pan cover with the frizzen, or steel, in a one-piece part. The lower, horizontal, section of the

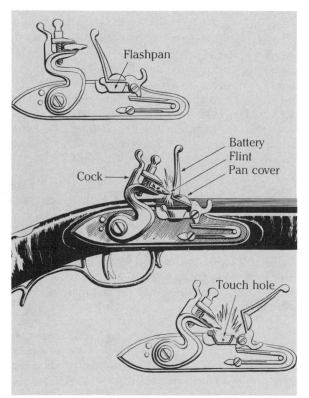

The flintlock simplified the mechanism by combining the pan cover and the steel in one pivoted L-shaped unit. When the hammer fell, it struck sparks from the steel and also knocked the whole unit forward to expose the priming charge in the pan.

frizzen was the pan cover, and the upper part was the steel on which sparks were struck. The frizzen was designed and mounted so that when the flint struck sparks, the force of the blow pivoted the frizzen upward and forward to uncover the pan and priming charge. This made for simplicity in the mechanism, and this simplicity resulted in a more reliable firearm.

Because flintlocks were simpler and comparatively cheap, they could therefore be used to arm large bodies of troops. These guns were also soon in widespread use among hunters. Flintlocks were perfected in the early 1800s but the earliest guns of this type appeared about 1620. At one time in Europe, the high nobility of the north preferred the wheel lock for hunting, while in other places snaphaunces and flintlocks were used. In some areas, all three were in use.

PERCUSSION IGNITION

With a flintlock there was a considerable time lag between the visible flash of the priming powder and the arrival of the projectile on target. This flash in the pan could be seen at a long distance, well before the report of the gun was heard because light travels quicker than sound. This was particularly annoying to a Scottish clergyman named James Alexander Forsyth, who loved to shoot birds with his flintlock smoothbore fowling piece.

In those days, gunners fired at sitting ducks and birds perched in trees. There was very little hope of "shooting flying," though some adventuresome gunners tried it. Sitting birds soon learned that the very conspicuous flash of spark ignition signified danger and took wing before the shot arrived. Archers had a somewhat similar problem. The twang of a bowstring startled many a deer into convulsive movement before the arrow arrived.

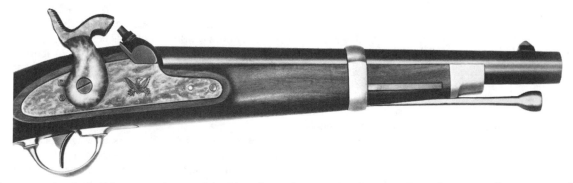

The percussion lock did not require spark ignition. Instead percussion firearms depend on a small copper cap that contains a chemical that detonates on impact. The cap is placed on the nipple under the hammer. Then the hammer is thumbed back to full cock. When the trigger is pulled, the hammer falls and crushes the cap. The priming compound in the cap detonates and the resulting flame runs through the nipple and a touch hole in the barrel to the main charge. (George Nonte photo)

Reverend Forsyth wrestled with the problem. In 1807, he patented a gunlock that was almost instantaneous in its action and produced no external flash. It relied on fulminate of mercury, a new chemical that detonated when struck violently by a mechanical force. In Forsyth's "scent bottle" lock, the fulminate was held in a reservoir that was shaped like a lady's scent bottle. This reservoir was pivoted in the middle on the lock plate of the gun. One end of the elongated reservoir was pierced with a hole that matched a hole in the side of the barrel. The other end of the reservoir was armed with a spring-loaded firing pin. After loading a charge of shot or a single ball through the muzzle, the shooter rotated the reservoir on its pivot pin, and the scent bottle deposited an automatically measured charge of the detonating powder in the vent or touchhole. The reservoir was then rotated a half turn, which brought the firing pin at the other end over the vent. When the trigger was pulled and the hammer (cock) of the gun fell on the firing pin, the pin ignited the priming powder by percussion. The resulting flame ran down the vent and ignited the main charge. There was no external flash. Its absence astonished the birds and, eventually, enemy soldiers. In fact, the lock was so quick in its action that shooting flying birds became a practical proposition.

With its obvious benefits for hunters, the Forsyth scent-bottle lock was soon in widespread use, but it had disadvantages. The scent bottle did not always measure the detonating charge accurately, and unreliable ignition could occur. Also, loose detonating powder was difficult to load into a reservoir without risking discharge of the entire amount, and dampness could affect the detonating powder in the unsealed scent-bottle reservoir. Variations on Forsyth's original lock were soon in use. Most of them were intended to provide accurately measured charges of fulminate detonating powder and to prevent deterioration of the powder. Nevertheless, Forsyth remains the inventor of percussion ignition.

THE PERCUSSION CAP

To provide safer and surer ignition, paper caps containing carefully measured charges of fulminate were introduced. These in turn were soon replaced with copper caps shaped rather like old-fashioned top hats. Copper top-hat caps are still used with some modern muzzleloaders.

The cap is placed over a nipple at the rear of the gun. A hole in the nipple leads, by means of a touchhole in the barrel itself, to the main charge. When the blunt-nosed hammer falls, the cap is crushed against the face of the nipple; the fulminate or other detonating compound is fired by the impact; and the resulting flame runs through the touchhole to the propellant charge.

It's a very simple system and much more dependable than any form of spark ignition. Millions of soldiers used percussion-cap smoothbore muskets and rifled arms in European wars and the American Civil War. The percussion cap soon replaced all forms of spark ignition for hunting, except in remote areas where percussion caps were difficult to obtain.

Some double-barreled fowling pieces were made with two different locks. One barrel was equipped with percussion ignition; the other was fired with a flintlock. When caps were available, the fowler used them; the flintlock barrel served as a backup. If caps could not be obtained, he used the flintlock. Some guns were made with two different sets of matching locks. The percussion lock could be easily removed and replaced with the flintlock if caps became difficult to obtain.

SELF-CONTAINED AMMUNITION

We use the word "cartridge" today to mean a whole unit, including a charge of powder, the primer (percussion cap), the bullet, and the cartridge case that holds them together. (A shotgun cartridge also has a wad between the propellant and the charge of shot.) It's a well-understood term among gunners, though many publications and TV commentators consistently betray their lack of firearms knowledge by using the word "bullet" when they really mean cartridge. For example, they say "The gunman finally ran out of bullets and was arrested." If that gunman had had only bullets, he could not have fired a single shot. When an antigun politician or writer makes this mistake while holding forth on firearms legislation, you can be sure that he knows nothing about guns.

The primer is seated in a pocket in the center of the head of the cartridge case. This pocket keeps the primer cap in place, and a small hole leads from the pocket to the propellant charge. Thus, the touchhole, or vent, common to all previous forms of ignition, is now located in the cartridge rather than in the barrel wall. These cartridges are said to employ "centerfire" ignition, and firearms that employ this system are called centerfire arms.

Rimfire cartridges. There is another system of ignition for self-contained cartridges—rimfire ignition. With rimfire cartridges, the priming compound is placed in a folded rim at the head of the cartridge case. The compound forms a continuous ring so that it ignites no matter where the firing pin or hammer happens to strike the cartridge head. The soft metal of the rim is designed to strike and crush the rim.

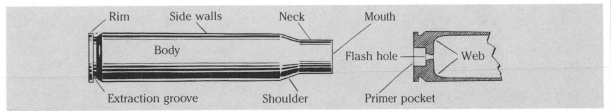

In modern centerfire cartridges, the cap (now called the primer) is seated in the primer pocket at the rear of the cartridge. When the firing pin hits the cap, the priming compound detonates and the flames reach the main charge through a flash hole.

The only modern cartridges that employ rimfire ignition are the familiar .22 Rimfire cartridges. Rimfire .22s are smallbore arms that are used for small-game shooting, target shooting, and plinking. Rimfire .22s do not develop enough energy for any form of big-game hunting.

Formerly, there were many big-bore rimfire cartridges, even including .50 caliber (half-inch bullet diameter) blockbusters. But these were loaded with black powder, which does not develop the high gas pressures generated by modern smokeless powders. It was soon found that rimfire cartridge cases could not be made strong enough to contain gas pressures needed to drive bullets at high velocities. That was because the metal in the rim had to be soft. The folded rim containing the detonating compound is much weaker than the solid head of modern centerfire cartridges.

Early cartridges. Before the invention of breechloading arms, the term cartridge did not involve a metal cartridge case. Cartridges for muzzleloaders usually consisted of a paper envelope that contained a measured charge of propellant powder and a bullet or shot. The shooter tore the envelope open, often with his teeth, poured the powder into the muzzle, and used the paper envelope as wadding. Then he rammed down the bullet with the ramrod carried in the thimbles underneath the gun barrel. He primed the gun with fine priming powder from a powder horn or other container. There are many different ways to load a muzzleloader, but this was the way in which most smoothbore guns were loaded and primed. There was no primer cap in the cartridge because ignition was achieved externally by means of sparks or a percussion cap.

Breechloaders. Many inventions and refinements bridged the gap from external to internal ignition. One fairly widespread example was the pinfire system. The cartridge case contained the propellant charge and a percussion cap, but the cap was placed on the interior wall of the case. Contacting it was a long metal pin that protruded through the opposite side of the metal case. These pinfire cartridges were fired when the

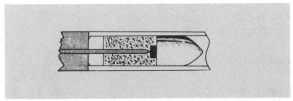

In a needle-gun cartridge, the detonating cap was placed at the base of the bullet. The cartridge walls were made of nitrated cloth or paper that burned away on firing. The gun's very long firing pin (the needle) pierced the rear wall of the case (head) and the entire powder charge before it detonated the cap. The bullet was the "anvil" against which the cap was struck. In centerfire cartridges, the anvil is contained in the primer cap, or it is an integral part of the metal cartridge case.

blunt-nosed hammer of the gun hit the pin to explode the cap. This system was ultimately discarded because the hole for the pin made the cartridge case very weak, and high-intensity ammunition could not be made with pins piercing the case wall.

Ammunition and gun designers followed many blind alleys before the advent of modern metal cartridges, developed largely by a Swiss gunsmith named Johannes Pauly. The first bolt-action rifle is a good example. It was called the needle gun and was first used by the Prussian army against the Austrians in the Austro-Prussian war of 1866. Johann Niklaus von Dreyse (1787–1867), deserves great credit for inventing the bolt-action, designed much like the familiar door bolt. The bolt contained the firing pin. The breech was closed when the shooter pushed the bolt handle forward and then turned it down into a slot in the rifle receiver. The breech-closing bolt was then in the same position as a locked door bolt. The cartridge for this firearm consisted of a fabric envelope that was nitrated to make it burn almost completely on firing. Inside the envelope was a measured charge of black powder and a bullet at its forward end. The percussion cap was attached to the rear of the bullet.

The single-shot rifle was opened by drawing the sliding bolt to the rear, and a cartridge was inserted in the open breech. The bolt contained a very long firing pin—the needle—in a hole that ran its entire length. On firing, the pin was driven forward and pierced the rear of the fabric envelope. The pin continued on through the propellant charge until it impacted the percussion cap and detonated it. The cap went off on impact only because it was backed up by the weight of the bullet which served as an anvil.

This breechloading rifle had a terrorizing effect on the Austrians, who were still using muzzleloaders. The Prussian rate of fire was many times faster. Also, the Prussian soldier did not have to stand erect to load his rifle, because he did not have to use the long ramrod. Many an Austrian soldier was killed or wounded because he stood up to load or raised his head or elbow while struggling awkwardly to do so while lying on the ground.

The Dreyse needle gun was a great improvement over muzzleloading arms, but it had a major defect that it shared with many other early breechloaders. The Dreyse bolt closed the breech of the rifle much as a cork closes a bottle. It simply slid forward and its front end entered the breech. But machine work in the 1860s and 1870s was not precise enough to make contact between the bolt and breech complete or even very close. The bottle stopper was a poor fit in the bottle neck. As a result, when the gun was fired, flame often emerged from the breech. This was extremely hazardous to the eyes, and Prussian soldiers soon learned to hold the Dreyse rifle well away from their faces. They often held it with both arms completely outstretched and the butt of the stock 10 or more inches from their shoulders. With that strange posture, accuracy was poor.

Many other breechloading systems that employed cartridges of cloth or paper (or those fired with loose charges of powder) had much the same defect. They were often more dangerous to the shooter than they were to the enemy or the game. Flame or hot powder gas could, and often did, escape from the breech. This was one very good reason why many shooters continued to use muzzleloading guns well into the breechloading era. They simply did not trust the breechloaders.

OBTURATION

Gas-leak problems were not really solved until metal cartridge cases were introduced. Of course, a metal case is much more durable than a paper or cloth case, and it is much more resistant to the intrusion of moisture, provided the seal between the case and bullet is tight. But the main reason for using metal cases is obturation (sealing against pressure). When a modern cartridge case is fired, the springy metal case expands against the wall of the firing chamber during the period of highest gas pressure. This effectively prevents leakage of flame or gas to the rear where it could injure the shooter or wreck the gun.

Obturation also prevents the loss of energy through gas leakage, which also affected shot-to-shot consistency. The amount of gas leakage varied; so the amount of energy driving the bullet also varied, often changing point of impact. The obturation of the modern metal case or plastic shotgun case not only enhances safety, it also improves accuracy. In muzzleloaders, leakage was not a problem because it only occurred through the touchhole. This is minor and consistent because the vent diameter does not change if it is kept free of black-powder fouling.

Metal cartridge cases were first introduced in the 1850s, and no really successful firearm has appeared that does not use them. Recently, there have been experiments with caseless ammunition. This type of cartridge has a propellant charge formed into a solid mass, which is fixed to the base of the bullet. It is fired either by electrical energy or by means of a jet of compressed air. Theoretically, the system should work well, but it does not because it is still difficult to mass produce gun breeches that seal well enough to prevent gas leaks. Also, without the metal cartridge case, the solid powder mass is easily damaged in handling or loading.

RIFLING

The discovery of rifling and its enormously beneficial effect on accuracy may have been an accident. Rifling was developed somewhere in Europe, probably southern Germany or Austria. Examination of many early rifles shows that the rifling was often straight; that is, shallow grooves were cut in the interior barrel wall from the firing chamber to the muzzle. These straight grooves did not improve accuracy. Their purpose was to provide room for black-powder residue. Black powder leaves behind considerable detritus after a shot, and after several shots it becomes difficult to ram another ball into the bore of a muzzleloader. This residue builds up in lumps and smears, and accuracy deteriorates since the projectile is slowed erratically by the spotty accumulation.

With a smoothbore gun firing a round ball, most shooters found it necessary to clean the barrel thoroughly after only five or six shots. One remedy for this trouble was to make the ball so much smaller than the bore diameter that it could be forced down the tube even though a great deal of residue accumulated. But the smaller size of the ball caused inaccuracy. The ball literally bounced down the barrel, and there was no shot-to-shot consistency, even when shots were fired from a barrel that had been thoroughly cleaned after each discharge. This was of no importance to a military commander whose men fired at fortifications or an enemy formation, but it made

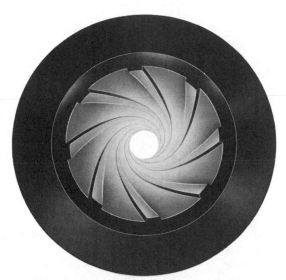

In modern rifling, spiral grooves in the barrel wall cause the rotational flight of bullets, which serves to stabilize the bullet projectile. The bullet diameter is the same as bore diameter (distance between the bottom of two opposite grooves). When a cartridge is fired, the lands between the grooves "engrave" the bullet and force it to rotate during its passage down the barrel. Rotation continues after bullet leaves the barrel. There are and were many forms of rifling, including one with no grooves at all. Instead the bore was oval in shape, and the oval spiralled throughout barrel length, rotating the bullet. Those bores were easy to clean.

round-ball, smoothbore arms almost useless to hunters except at very short range. Because smoothbore muskets could be loaded much faster, the military continued to favor them over rifled arms even after the superior accuracy of rifles had been proven. For the hunter or sniper, on the other hand, a rifled weapon had great advantages. Since these men fired at *individual* targets, human or animal, quickness in loading was not very important.

Imagine a gunsmith's shop somewhere in central Europe. The smith intends to cut straight grooves in a barrel with a metal "tooth" mounted on the end of a wooden rod. He places the tool in the barrel and pulls it through the smooth-walled tube in a spiral motion with the aid of his rifling bench. In this case the steel cutting tool was poorly made and its cutting face was slightly angled. The cutting tooth did not maintain the desired straight course but instead turned in a slow spiral. Since the first, very shallow cut spiraled, the only course was, seemingly, to start all over again. But that would have been a great deal of work and would have meant reaming out the barrel to a larger interior diameter and then starting the rifling process all over again with a new cutting tooth.

After due consideration, the smith decided to finish the first spiral cut by shaving more very thin ribbons of steel out of it. He may have thought: "What is the

difference? Even though the grooves spiral, they will still contain fouling, and that is what we want." So he completed his work by cutting several spiraling grooves with the defective cutting tool. As is usual with straight grooves, the spirals were spaced at equal intervals around the barrel wall.

When the smith completed the gun, he stepped outside his shop to test it. Loading a powder charge, wad, and ball, he fired at a mark. The bullet impacted within 5 or 6 inches of the point-of-aim, which was quite satisfactory. But the smith fired several more shots to make sure that all was well with his new gun. Much to his astonishment, five or six shots all hit within 3 or 4 inches of one another at a distance of 50 paces. After cleaning the new gun and firing again,

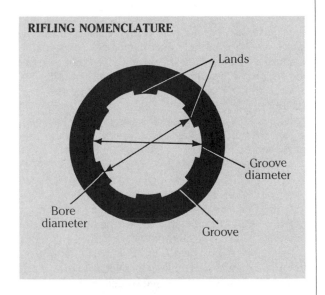

RIFLING NOMENCLATURE

This plain lead bullet recovered from soft material after firing, shows lands and grooves of the barrel in reverse. Angle or pitch of the rifling determines how fast the bullet rotates and must be carefully determined to produce best results with a given bullet within a narrow range of velocities. (George Nonte photo)

he was quite sure that the rifle was more accurate than any other he had ever made or fired.

Time passed and the gunsmith acquired a great reputation for making accurate guns. He had the common sense to recognize that spiraling grooves enhanced accuracy, but had no clue as to why. Empirically, he realized that he was onto something important, and other gunsmiths were quick to examine his work and follow his lead.

This is the widely accepted theory of the accidental origin of rifling. It may be entirely mistaken. Archers in many different places throughout the world were aware of the enhanced accuracy of a spiraling projectile, and they angled the fletching on their arrows to force the arrows to rotate in flight. Javelin throwers in ancient Greece wrapped a leather thong around their weapons in a spiral. When the javelin was thrown, the thong unwrapped because of air drag and dropped away, but not before it started the javelin rotating. On a beautifully decorated Greek bowl made centuries before rifling was invented, a competitor in the original Olympic games is shown wrapping his javelin in just this way. It may therefore be true that cutting the first spiraling grooves in a gun bore was a deliberate move to improve accuracy made by a very clever central European gunsmith whose name was never recorded.

A modern rifle bullet is said to "take" the rifling. That is, the raised "lands" between the rifling grooves bite into the bullet and force it to rotate as it moves forward. Because of inertia, the spiraling motion does not stop after the projectile leaves the bore and continues throughout its entire flight. Rotation enhances the accuracy of a projectile because the motion (around a central longitudinal axis) equally distributes all variations in weight (caused by defects in the shape of the bullet and variations in metal density). The rotation also has a gyroscopic effect that improves accuracy even if the bullet is perfectly formed (many are not).

CONOID BULLETS

Rifling also makes it possible to use elongated, conoid (conical) bullets that are more effective than round balls. The front surface of a spherical bullet has a poor aerodynamic shape. It is blunt and creates much more air drag than a long, pointed bullet. A pointed bullet, weight for weight, therefore flies farther than a spherical bullet.

Without rifling, elongated, pointed bullets couldn't be used. If a pointed bullet is fired in a smoothbore gun, it tumbles in flight and eventually flies through the air base first. Because of the tumbling, the range is very short. The base-first final flight occurs because the blunt end of the bullet is much heavier than the tapering pointed end, and laws of physics dictate that the heaviest end will lead the way through the atmosphere.

In addition, rifling also makes it possible to use heavy bullets in rifles with comparatively small bores. The weight of a round ball depends on its diameter, and that is limited by the diameter of the gun bore into which it must fit. A conoid bullet, on the other hand, can be of greater weight simply because it can be longer. Within certain limits, the cartridge designer can make a pointed bullet as long as he desires and vary its weight accordingly. To take a familiar example, the popular .30/06 rifle cartridge is factory loaded in the following weights (avoirdupois): 110 grains, 125 grains, 130 grains, 150 grains, 165 grains, 180 grains, 200 grains, and 220 grains.

The weight of a .30 caliber round ball is considerably less than the weight of the lightest of the .30/06 bullets. The only way in which heavy round balls can be used is to increase the bore diameter, and this explains why smoothbore guns firing round balls that were intended for big-game hunting had enormous bores by modern standards. With many modern big-game rifles, the hunter can use lightweight bullets for small and medium-size game and heavy bullets for larger animals. This provides great versatility in one rifle that was impossible with spherical bullets.

Rifling not only enhances accuracy, it also makes possible the use of modern elongated and pointed bullets with all their advantages. Shooters owe a great deal to that unknown gunsmith.

SMOKELESS POWDER

German, Bohemian, and Austrian gunsmiths are generally admired for their many inventions and refinements. They get the lion's share of credit for the development of firearms. But it is interesting to note that one of the most important firearms developments originated with a French chemist and engineer, Paul Marie Eugène Vielle (1854–1934). His invention of smokeless powder revolutionized military and hunting firearms.

With black powder the problem of fouling remained no matter how well the gun and ammunition were made. After comparatively few shots, the weapon had to be thoroughly cleaned if it was to be fired with acceptable accuracy. Also, many modern repeating actions—semi-automatic and fully automatic arms in particular—could not function with black powder because the fouling would stop the repeating function in a short time. Smokeless powder does leave some fouling, but it is minimal and does not interfere with accuracy or the functioning of repeaters until after a fairly large number of shots have been fired.

These benefits were originally overlooked. The

quest was for a propellant that would not generate a large gray cloud of black-powder smoke and thereby reveal the shooter's location to the enemy. This was highly important to the military. From a hunting viewpoint, smokeless powder was also a great improvement. With black powder a hunter often had to look around the cloud of smoke to see the effect of his shot. In the time that took, a wounded animal could escape.

The French Army sponsored experiments aimed at developing smokeless powder as early as 1832, but it was not until the 1880s that the new powder was available in large enough quantities for the manufacture of military ammunition. To use the new ammunition, the French developed the Model 1886 Lebel rifle, which fired an 8mm (.32-inch diameter) bullet from a self-contained metal cartridge. This rifle was also a repeater.

The Lebel of 1886 was such a great success that it started an international arms-development race: the Germans developed the famed Model 1898 Mauser rifle; the British brought forth the Lee-Enfield bolt-action rifle; the Austrians, their Mannlicher straight-pull infantry rifle; and the Americans, their famed Springfield. All these rifles were more or less basically modeled on the French Lebel, though all of them incorporated improvements. They all had comparatively small bores; they all employed repeating bolt actions; and they all fired metallic ammunition loaded with smokeless powder. And all of them could be used, and were used, to good effect in big-game hunting.

For generations, these bolt-action military rifles have served as hunting rifles. In fact, the Lebel in modified form was manufactured in this country by Remington under contract for the French Army, and thousands of them were sold as surplus to American hunters in the 1920s and 1930s.

American hunters preferred lever-action repeating rifles for most hunting before World War I, and many still do. Affluent English and German sportsmen continue to use double-barreled rifles. But it is nevertheless true that the Model 1886 Lebel can be cited as the single, most important rifle design in the development of modern hunting firearms. Most American, English, and German gun writers will dispute that statement, but their disagreement probably arises from a certain prejudice against French firearms, which have often proved to be unreliable or inefficient. That, however, does not apply to the Lebel, which was used by some French formations during World War II.

OTHER DEVELOPMENTS

Many other inventions and improvements went into the development of modern big-game rifles, and sev-

eral of the more important ones are discussed in this section. Some of these improvements were not the work of any one individual. For instance, the modern rifle stock with its sophisticated, multi-point support of metal parts of the gun originated in the crude pole or tiller of the hand cannon. Over the centuries, the stock developed very slowly indeed through the minor improvements and trial-and-error experiments of many men.

Other firearms developments came as industry learned to make new materials and to use new manufacturing methods. For instance, modern barrel steels made it possible to use high-intensity rifle ammunition that would have burst earlier barrels, and metallurgy also provided us with the springy brass that is used in obturating cartridges.

In fact, firearms inventions often had to wait for many years before they were of practical use. It was one thing for a gunsmith to spend hundreds of hours making a single firearm and suitable ammunition for a nobleman and something else to make the same gun in large quantities at a reasonable price. Samuel Colt is often erroneously thought of as the inventor of the revolver. In fact, revolving, repeating firearms of various types were "invented" by gunsmiths and arms designers all over Europe and in the United States before Colt's design, but many early repeaters were complete failures because black-powder fouling made them impractical or because obturating cartridges were not yet available in large quantities. When these roadblocks were overcome, many old ideas for repeating guns were revived or reinvented.

Very often firearms development is a disorderly process, and a particular device or invention appears out of its apparent logical time. Perhaps the best example is a fine matchlock rifle that belonged to the Austrian emperor Maximilian (1459–1519). That matchlock, a profusely decorated hunting gun, reposes today in a museum. It has all the many faults of matchlocks for hunting that were discussed earlier. Nevertheless, the gun has nicely cut spiraled rifling, which probably made it quite accurate. It is the earliest surviving rifled arm.

FIREARMS AS GAS GUNS

Most youngsters start their hunting with an air gun for tin-can plinking and sparrow shooting. At least this was true before the Daisy company reduced the power of their standard products for safety reasons; most American-made air guns now will not kill a sparrow at 20 feet. Every young air-gun plinker yearns for the time when the law or parents, or both, will allow him to have his first real gun, usually a cheap .22 Rimfire rifle. In his mind there is a world of difference between a true firearm and any air gun. That difference is mostly a matter of power.

Air or CO_2 guns actually operate on the same principle as firearms. In both types the projectile is driven by sudden gas pressure. Air is compressed mechanically in an air gun and is released suddenly to drive a round BB or an elongated projectile out of the gun barrel. In CO_2 guns the gas is compressed into a cartridge at the factory and released in bursts in the gun. In firearms the sudden increase in gas pressure results from the rapid burning of powder in a cartridge. The expanding gas at first has nowhere to go because the bullet is held rather firmly in the cartridge case. After an instant, however, gas pressure increases to the point where the grip of the cartridge case is overpowered. The bullet then moves down the bore. In all these types of guns, expanding gas drives the projectile.

Very powerful air rifles have been made in the past, and some are still made to be powerful enough for small-game hunting. Big-bore air guns were used by the Austrian Emperor Joseph II (1741–90) in a war against the Turks, and these weapons wreaked havoc on the enemy. The Turks were awed by weapons that were almost noiseless and yet killed men at a distance. Since about the same level of bullet energy is required to kill a deer and a man, it is easy to see that these Austrian air rifles (designed by an Italian engineer) could have been used for hunting. They were also quite accurate, as proved by the fact that they were used by a corps of Austrian sharpshooters that specialized in killing Turkish officers.

It would be no problem to manufacture a repeating air rifle that would be powerful enough to kill deer and other big game. But because modern firearms are simple and efficient, there is no great advantage in doing so. The only real advantage to an air gun is that it is a comparatively silent weapon. True, the escaping compressed gas does make a noise, but it is not nearly as loud as the report of a powerful firearm.

Most American states forbid air guns for hunting game animals and birds by not listing them as legal hunting weapons. Because air guns are forbidden for hunting, there is no great market for them in the United States. The reason for the prohibition is that an almost completely silent weapon would be an ideal poacher's gun (and an efficient murder weapon). If it were fired to shoot game illegally, the landowner and game warden could not hear it being used. For the same reason, hunting with firearms equipped with silencers would be of great advantage to a poacher, but federal law forbids their possession by civilians in the United States. And yet silenced weapons would be advantageous in some forms of legal hunting. A miss would not alarm the game and the hunter could settle down to fire as many shots as needed.

HUNTING ARMS OF THE FUTURE

The prohibition against powerful air guns and silenced firearms is an example of a modern tendency to eliminate some arms from the hunting scene. Formerly, every important improvement in military small arms was quickly taken up by sporting arms makers. For many years standard military rifles were regarded as excellent hunting arms. In the United States, the .30/40 Krag rifle and its successor the .30/06 Springfield were among the best arms for deer hunting. Some hunters still use them.

This relationship between military small arms and civilian sporting guns is now largely a thing of the past. The military has moved to smallbore assault rifles. These are centerfire arms, but the bullets are .22 inch in diameter. The objective of using such a small, lightweight bullet is to make it easier to supply troops and to increase the number of casualties inflicted by the average soldier. These modern assault rifles can be fired one shot at a time, but when a selector switch is turned to full automatic, they will fire the entire contents of the magazine if the trigger is held back. Infantrymen who have full-automatic capability use a lot of ammunition in action and this method of shooting would not be possible with heavy, full-power rifle cartridges such as the .30/06 military round. But the new .22 caliber cartridges can be supplied in large volume to troops in the field. Few soldiers ever fire at long-range targets, so the old full-power cartridge types are used only by snipers.

But hunters cannot use centerfire .22 cartridges for big-game hunting. The .22 cartridges are not powerful enough to kill big game reliably. Indeed, state laws forbid their use for big-game hunting, though they are legal for varmint shooting. The military has discovered, however, that wounding an enemy soldier is more advantageous than killing him outright. To care for the wounded, four men must usually man the stretcher to carry him to the rear, and whole corps of medical personnel must be maintained as well. The .22 centerfire cartridge is therefore actually more useful from a military standpoint than big-bore, full-power loads. The big-game hunter's objective is different. If possible, he intends to kill an animal with the first shot so that the quarry cannot run off.

Military and police arms will almost inevitably continue to diverge from civilian sporting arms, because they can employ arms and ammunition that would take the sporting challenge out of hunting. How about a rocket instead of a bullet? There would be no recoil to cause flinching, it would not drop in flight until the rocket fuel was used up, and it would maintain its velocity and energy at 1,000 yards or 10,000 yards. If a jet-propelled projectile or rocket for hunting seems fantastic, you have never heard of the Gyrojet pistol, which was actually marketed in the 1960s. The repeating handgun launched 13mm rockets, and it was advertised as much more convenient and deadly than a hunting rifle. Unfortunately, the weapon was poorly designed and proved to be useless for hunting or any other purpose because the propellant burned out very quickly, range was very limited, and accuracy was ludicrous. However, some bright engineer may even now be working on a small rocket launcher suitable for hunting.

Beams of energy for killing at long range may become possible in the near future. To make these long-heralded "death rays" portable, some way to miniaturize the power source must still be found. But with a death ray in hand, the hunter would not have to worry about bullet drop, range, or even the effect of wind. Shooting skill would not be required and killing game with such a weapon would be child's play.

If anyone ever attempted to use such weapons for hunting, the outcry would be very loud, and it would probably only be a short time before the futuristic weapons would be prohibited by law. Hunters themselves would be the first to call for laws prohibiting them.

In fact, many arms developments have been banned for hunting game—machine guns, poison bullets, repeating shotguns that fire more than three shots for waterfowl hunting, sophisticated crossbows because they are very accurate and silent at the same time, sniperscopes for night hunting, and many others. De-

cent hunters do not tolerate the use of arms that are too efficient. They ruin the sport.

Hunting arms cannot, therefore, be greatly improved beyond the level that exists today. Convenience, durability, dependability, and physical or esthetic form may be improved in the future, but it seems unlikely that great improvements in *killing* efficiency of hunting arms will be needed or wanted.

Some hunters are dissatisfied with the high efficiency of modern firearms already in use. They have revived archery gear for hunting, as well as the use of muzzleloading arms and black powder. They enjoy overcoming all the disadvantages. Bowhunting or use of muzzleloading "primitive weapons" is now required in many densely populated areas, but throughout much of the United States, these forms of hunting for big game are entirely voluntary. These hunters are attempting to restore the element of sport they believe is lost when efficient modern firearms are used.

The vast majority of American hunters, however, are quite content to use hunting firearms as we now know them. But it seems inevitable that today's firearms will almost certainly be regarded in the future as quaint survivals from the past, just as most hunters regard muzzleloading arms as charming replica antiques. This changed outlook of the future may even lessen the ill-advised political drive for tighter restrictions on civilian possession of firearms. If cheap plastic death-ray guns were available to criminals, as they inevitably would be, who would continue to worry about the sportsman's gun?

GASTIGHT CASES AND OTHER MIRACLES

The cartridge cases used today are miracles of mass-production metalworking. In the factory, they start out as small cylinders of brass, and through many separate "draws," they are formed into tubes that have a mouth and closed end. The most important fact is that they are durable one-piece units.

In the transition from muzzleloading arms to those using modern ammunition, a great stumbling block was the inability of manufacturers to turn out large quantities of these one-piece units. One inadequate solution to the problem was to make cartridges with metal heads and fiber or cloth bodies. Another was to use a long, coiled strip of brass as the basis for the cartridge body. Several strange European cartridges consisted of a metal tube (the cartridge body) and a metal disk that screwed into it. Other, even stranger, solutions were tried.

SHOT CHARGES AND RIFLED BARRELS

Before rifled barrels became readily available, most guns could handle a charge of shot or a single projectile, usually a round ball. The typical military musket, for instance, could be loaded with a single round ball, a charge of shot, or one large ball and several smaller balls (buckshot).

When rifling became common in military arms and civilian sporting guns, it became almost impossible to use a charge of birdshot or buckshot in these guns. Using small round lead balls of any kind frequently forced metal fouling into the grooves, and accuracy deteriorated. The caliber of guns also tended to become smaller. From the .75 caliber of the British Brown Bess Musket used in the American Revolution, caliber declined in modern cartridge arms to .50, .45, .30, and even smaller. Bores as small as this cannot contain a really useful charge of shot, even for bird-shooting at close range.

At one time, however, European and American cartridge makers provided shot cartridges for rifles. These consisted of the standard rifle case with primer and powder charge. A wooden shot container, filled with birdshot, was loaded in the case mouth. When the cartridge was fired, the wooden projectile flew down the barrel and burst on emergence or soon thereafter, leaving the shot charge to continue its flight. At best, these shot cartridges for rifles were rather inefficient. The pattern was often irregular in shape with many holes, and the shot charge was so small that it was really only useful for shooting sitting birds at close range.

In recent times, cartridges loaded with shot for rifled arms have been revived, but the shot is contained in a plastic envelope rather than a wooden bullet. Most of these cartridges are used in handguns, and they are useful for killing snakes and pests at short distances. Also, handloaders sometimes cook up this type of load for special purposes.

PUNKIN BALLS AND RIFLED SLUGS

On the other side of the coin, firing a single projectile in a shotgun has become a popular practice. In some states and in some areas close to large cities, the "shotgun-only" rule obtains for deer hunters, but they are often allowed to use a single projectile.

As late as the 1950s, solid round balls called "punkin balls" were loaded into shotgun cases and used mostly for deer hunting. In fact, these shotgun cartridges closely resembled round-ball black-powder cartridges that were often used in smoothbore military arms. But in a military musket, the bore is of a uniform diameter from breech to muzzle, so the ball could be made to fit the bore quite closely. Most shotguns, on the other hand, have some degree of choke at the muzzle. That is, the bore constricts at some point just before the muzzle is reached, and this concentrates the shot pattern for surer kills.

Because of this, the round-ball projectile for shotguns had to be made considerably smaller than the bore diameter, so that it would pass through the choke without damaging it or even splitting the barrel. These round balls literally bounced down the barrel and departed at random angles from the muzzle. Accuracy was terrible, and deer-size animals often escaped completely untouched when hunters fired punkin balls at a range of only 30 yards or so. Even if a hunter sawed off the constricted portion of his barrel, he still wound up using a ball that was too small for the bore.

This situation was remedied to a great degree by the invention of the modern rifled slug. These slugs are conoid projectiles with very blunt points. They are hollow, and the heaviest portion of the slug is at its rounded point, so that it flies through the air point first. These hollow slugs fit the standard bore diameter of each shotgun gauge much better than punkin balls did. On firing, the hollow, soft-lead "skirt" of the slug expands to fit the bore very closely, and there is no blowby of gas beyond the projectile. If there is a choke in the barrel, the soft-lead projectile is compressed slightly by the constriction and departure from the muzzle is quite consistent.

These slugs are almost always made with angled vanes on their exterior surfaces. This "rifling" is said to impart a slow rotation to the projectile in flight and to enhance accuracy moderately. In fact, these rifled-slug loads in the large shotgun gauges are fairly accurate out to 100 yards or a little more. They are very popular with deer hunters and extend the effective range of the deer-hunting shotgun far beyond what is possible with buckshot loads. The use of slugs and buckshot for deer hunting are discussed in more detail later in this section.

Even though shot charges are sometimes fired in rifled arms and single projectiles are often fired in shotguns, cartridge cases for the two types of guns are still sharply differentiated. The rifle cartridge cases are almost always made of brass, while shotgun cartridge cases almost always consist of a plastic or paper (cardboard) case body and a metallic head that includes an integral rim. Because the pressure of shotgun cartridges is lower than it is with modern high-intensity rifle cartridges, plastic, or paper bodies can be used instead of expensive brass.

THE RIFLE CARTRIDGE CASE

Rifle cartridge cases come in several different forms, but in the United States the most common type is the bottlenecked, rimless or rimmed case. A typical cartridge case of this type is shown in the accompanying drawing. This type of case is the result of the gradual evolution toward smaller and smaller diameter bullets. Formerly, most rifle cases were straight-sided. The case had the same outside diameter as the bullet or was only marginally larger. If a larger charge of powder was needed to drive a bullet of a given diameter, the only way to increase case capacity was to increase its length.

As the desirability of smaller bullets became more apparent, it became important to find some way of loading a fairly large powder charge behind a small-diameter bullet. To meet this need, the case was necked down to a small diameter at the mouth, while the case body was often expanded to take larger and larger powder charges. Some cartridge cases are now made with very short, very fat cases even though the bullet diameter is small. This permits rifle makers to produce arms that have shorter actions, and this type of cartridge case is favored for use in many military arms with full-automatic capability. For instance, the

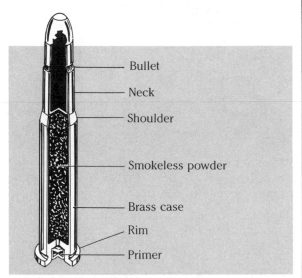

This cutaway drawing shows extreme simplicity of modern ammunition, in this case a rimmed centerfire cartridge. There are only four components: the case, the primer, the powder charge, and the bullet, though it can be said that the primer is really an assembly consisting of several components.

.308 Winchester (actually the civilian version of the former NATO standard military cartridge) is shorter than the standard .30/06, though both cartridges develop almost the same velocity and muzzle energy.

Rimless and rimmed cases. Cartridges are said to be rimless, and yet they do have rims. This is because most modern cartridges have an extractor groove just ahead of their closed heads. This groove receives the hooked extractor "claw" of most modern rifles. When the action is opened, the extractor claw pulls the cartridge case out of the rifle chamber. The extractor groove necessarily forms a rim, but this rim is the same diameter as the rear of the cartridge body, or only a bit larger. Rimless cartridges are favored for use in most modern magazine arms because they can lie side by side in a magazine without overlapping rims.

A large class of earlier cartridges were rimmed, and this type of cartridge is still used in some rifles and in revolvers. For instance, the good-old .30/30 Winchester is loaded in a rimmed bottleneck case. But most rifles that fire rimmed cases have tubular magazines in which one cartridge lies ahead of another in a series. In such magazines the rim presents no difficulty. But in general, rimmed cases are fading out, and almost every new rifle cartridge in recent years has been rimless, except those specifically designed for single-shot rifles, break-action double rifles, and combination guns.

Case configurations. The drawing on the next page shows the external configuration of typical cases, including rimmed, rimless, and other types. After the

CARTRIDGE CASES

Rimmed case   Semi-rimmed case   Rimless case   Rebated case   Belted case

Centerfire cartridge case heads: The most-common type in use today is the rimless case. Older rifle cartridges were usually designed with rims. Other forms were conceived for special purposes, as described in accompanying text.

rimmed case, the second type shown in the drawing is the semi-rimmed case. It has a rim a bit larger than the maximum diameter of the case body. About the only current example is the .220 Swift, a varmint-hunting cartridge. Presumably, the cartridge designers wanted to provide a bit more surface for the rifle extractor than would have been available with a standard rimless case. The Swift developed higher pressures, and extraction was sometimes difficult because of expanded cases. Semi-rimless cases are sometimes used for handgun cartridges so that they can be fired in both semi-automatic pistols and in revolvers. Otherwise, revolver cartridges are almost always made with rimmed cases so that they are securely seated against the rear of the multichambered cylinder. A rimless, straight-sided case would fall right through the bored-through cylinder.

A list of the *common* cartridge types now in use in the United States includes the following types:
- Rimmed bottleneck
- Rimmed straight
- Rimless bottleneck
- Rimless straight
- Belted bottleneck
- Belted straight
- Semi-rimmed bottleneck
- Semi-rimmed straight
- Rebated bottleneck

The belted case—which may be bottleneck or straight—is shown in the drawing. It is a rimless cases but has an integral belt just ahead of the extractor groove. This adds additional strength at a point where it is said to be greatly needed—the rear of the case where the rifle bolt and barrel meet. These belted cartridges are usually magnums (more powerful than standard for the bore-diameter class). And Roy Weatherby, the prominent rifle designer and manufacturer, uses this type of case in all his magnum cartridges. Another example is the 8mm Remington Magnum.

In a rebated cartridge case, the rim diameter (actually the case is of the rimless type) is *smaller* than the base diameter of the cartridge case. This type of case was originated by designers who wanted a large case for the sake of increased powder capacity while at the same time using them in arms that employed

bolts of a small diameter. The only American-made cartridge of this type is the .284 Winchester Magnum, which was used in the Model 88 Winchester lever-action rifle and the Model 100 semi-automatic. Both have been discontinued. The rim diameter is the same as that of a .30/06, but the body diameter is much larger, almost as large as that of the belted magnums. This provides a short case with a large powder capacity.

Foreign case designs. There are other centerfire cartridge case types in use, but they are not used much in American hunting. For instance, the Germans and Austrians manufacture several rimmed cartridges that are neither bottlenecked nor straight. They are extremely long and appear to taper forward toward the mouth. Actually, these cartridges do have straight-sided necks, but the case taper is so gradual that the neck is hard to see.

At first, these German and Austrian cartridges seem to be the result of some strange idea on the designer's part. What possible use could there be for these overly long and strangely shaped cartridges? In actuality, they are very useful in Continental combination guns, typically three-barreled drillings. For this type of gun, a long cartridge case is a convenient way to provide increased powder capacity. The overall cartridge design must provide a small-diameter case so that it will conform to the slender shape of the rifle barrel of a drilling, which is tucked away under the two shotgun barrels. The gradually tapering case also extracts easily in break-action rifles. It is hard to know the basic purpose behind a cartridge designer's efforts simply by examining the end product. You have to know what kind of firearm is or was used to fire it.

Taper. Almost all rifle cartridge cases have one characteristic in common—they do taper, even if the taper is so gradual that it is almost imperceptible. Calipers confirm the taper though. Some taper is necessary in high-intensity cartridge cases because straight-sided cases tend to stick in the chamber after firing. Many black-powder cases had no taper at all, or a very slight one, and when they were used later with smokeless powder, extraction was often difficult, to say the least. Overall body taper is required most of all in arms that do not have a strong extraction mechanism. For very modern short cartridges, however, extraction is not as much of a problem as it was in earlier designs with longer cases.

HEADSPACE

A cartridge must be held firmly in place in a rifle chamber in order to provide solid support for the primer in the cartridge head. If the cartridge could slide forward even a short distance, the firing pin would not strike the primer hard enough to detonate it. Also, a loosely fitting cartridge (longitudinally) may separate into two parts on firing. The determining factor for this fit is called headspace.

Headspace is the distance from the breechblock face or bolt face to the other part of the firing chamber that supports the cartridge longitudinally. A modern rimless rifle cartridge, for instance, headspaces on the

sloped shoulder; belted cartridges headspace on the forward edge of the belt; rimmed cartridges headspace on the forward surface of the rim. Rimless handgun rounds for semi-automatic pistols headspace on the case mouth. Too much headspace beyond tolerances specified for the arm may lead to separated or burst cartridges; too little headspace prevents the cartridge from seating itself properly in the chamber.

With modern American and European arms and ammunition, headspace is carefully controlled to fall within allowable limits and is of little practical concern to the shooter. With older arms and cheap, war-manufactured military surplus arms and ammunition, incorrect headspace can cause a lot of trouble. This is a very good reason for steering clear of cheap ammunition, guns made by unknown manufacturers, and guns put together hastily under the pressure of high production quotas during major wars. Many seemingly satisfactory European military rifles were actually put together from large stocks of parts left over from World War II. Bolts frequently did not match receivers, and

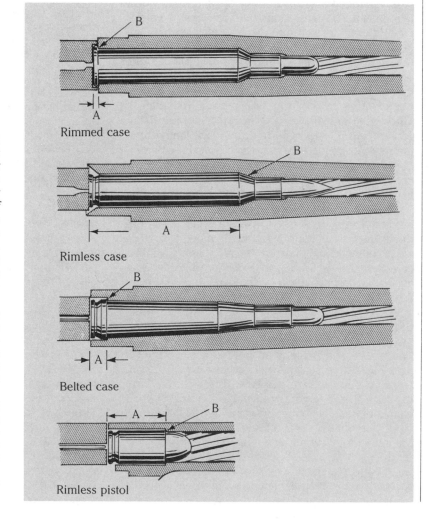

Headspace is the distance between the breechblock or breechbolt face and that part of the cartridge that stops the entry of the cartridge into the firing chamber and holds it firmly in place against the blow of the firing pin. Headspace must be carefully controlled within very narrow minimum-maximum tolerances. If headspace is too small, the firearm's action will not close on the cartridge. If it is too great, the cartridge case may separate or burst, which is very dangerous. In these drawings, A indicates headspace dimension and B indicates the forward point at which the cartridge bears on the firing chamber. With a rimmed case, top, headspace is nominally the thickness of the rim. With the rimless case, the bearing point is the shoulder of the cartridge (measured at its center). With the belted case, the forward bearing point is the front of the belt. With rimless pistol ammunition, bottom, the forward bearing point is the mouth of the case.

Rimmed case

Rimless case

Belted case

Rimless pistol

excessive headspace was common. With this type of firearm, it is always a good idea to have a gunsmith check to make sure that the gun is generally in serviceable order. Headspace should be a primary concern.

THE PRIMER

In addition to providing a container for the powder charge and support for the bullet, the metal cartridge case also holds the primer. The primer is a metal cup-like component that is inserted in the primer pocket in the case head. When the primer is struck and dented by a firing pin, the compound within the primer detonates. This sends flame through the flash hole in the case head and ignites the main powder charge. This is the same process that occurs with muzzle-loading arms employing percussion caps, but the cap and flash hole are now in the cartridge.

Rifle and pistol primers of American manufacture consist of four components: the metal cup, the explosive priming compound, the anvil, and a paper disk to protect the priming compound. The anvil is a metal piece that is pressed into place in the cup over the previously loaded priming compound. The anvil, supported by the cup and, in turn, by the cartridge case, provides a hard surface. When the firing pin strikes the soft metal cup it dents the metal inward, and some of the primer compound is crushed against the anvil. The compound detonates and the resulting flame passes through holes in the anvil. The flame then travels through the flash hole and ignites the propellant charge. This type of primer was invented by Colonel Boxer of the British Army, and it is the one used in American ammunition.

The Berdan primer, invented in the 1860s by Colonel Berdan of the U.S. Army, is used in British and Continental European cartridges. The Berdan primer does not include an anvil. Instead, the primer pocket in the cartridge case is formed to provide a hump or teat against which the primer compound is crushed by the firing pin. The primer flame is led inside the case through two small angled holes in the cartridge case head.

Americans and Europeans traded primer types. There are good reasons on both sides. Europeans prefer the Berdan primer because the anvil is an integral part of the cartridge case. The dies that form the case in the factory also shape the anvil, which cannot be separated from the case. The anvil is always there, and one possible cause of failure to fire is eliminated. This is very important in military arms, particularly machine guns. Here a failure to fire stops the firing cycle, making it necessary to remove the unfired round from the chamber and to start the cycle all over again.

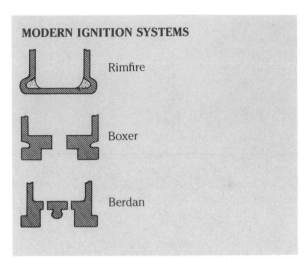

MODERN IGNITION SYSTEMS

The rimfire ignition system, top, is now used only for .22 Rimfire ammunition, not used for big game. The priming compound is placed in the folded rim all around the case. No matter how the case is placed in the firing chamber, the firing pin will crush the soft metal of the cartridge case and detonate the compound. In the Boxer system, center, of American centerfire cartridges, the primer cap is seated in a central primer pocket. The compound in the cap is detonated against an anvil contained in the primer. In the Berdan system (European), bottom, there is no anvil in the primer. Instead it is a centrally located knob integral to the cartridge case. When the primer compound detonates, the resulting flame reaches the powder charge through two small holes in the cartridge head.

In the days when ammunition manufacture was less sophisticated, and much work was done by hand, it was fairly common for Boxer primers to come off the line without anvils. The cartridge failed to fire, of course, and that was often dangerous. Americans, however, were willing to take that risk primarily because cartridges loaded with Boxer primers are easier for handloaders to reload than Berdan-primed cases.

In a Berdan primed case, unless hydraulic pressure is used (this is a mess), the primer must be removed by forcing a prick into the fired primer and prying it out. Though some European reloading tools remove Berdan primers, this is much more difficult than using a simple punch to force out a fired Boxer primer.

Primers were formerly loaded with a compound that coated rifle chambers and bores with salts. The residue attracted moisture and caused rust that ruined the accuracy of the firearm very quickly, unless it was thoroughly cleaned shortly after firing. Early primers also contained mercury, which weakened the brass cartridge case.

Modern primers are loaded with "nonmercuric, noncorrosive" primer compounds that cause little trouble. Together with clean-burning smokeless powders, the new primers make it unnecessary to clean rifle bores immediately after only a shot or two have been fired. This is a great blessing for any hunter who arrives back at camp after a really tough day.

POWDER

Provided the bore wasn't obstructed or the action defective, it was extremely difficult if not impossible to blow up a firearm using metallic cartridges loaded with black powder. The proper load was almost always enough powder to fill the cartridge case with the bullet seated at the proper depth. Since the cartridge case was made in a factory and was correctly dimensioned, there was little chance for a dangerous overload when handloaders reloaded fired cases. Black-powder cases were made so that they contained the right charge of powder to drive the bullet at the proper velocity. In general, it was also true that cases could tolerate minor variations in volume of black powder better than smokeless.

When smokeless powder became available, this margin of error vanished. The correct charge of smokeless depends on the chemical nature of the powder being loaded, the physical form of the powder granules, the type and capacity of the cartridge case, the degree of retardant coating on each powder granule, if any, and the bullet weight. If the wrong powder is used, an overload may occur and may blow up the gun.

Smokeless powders are of two basic types—single base and double base. Single-base powders are based on nitrocellulose; double-based powders include nitrocellulose with the addition of nitroglycerin. These powders are formed into many different shapes—flakes, perforated cylinders, tubes, balls—to control the burning rate. To a great extent, the existence of modern magnum cartridges depends on the availability of slow-burning powders. If all the powder in a charge burns in a very short time, the pressure peak is reached very quickly, and velocity cannot be increased after that initial burst of energy. With slower powders, energy and velocity build as the bullet moves down the barrel and much more energy is available because acceleration occurs during much of the bullet's travel toward the gun muzzle.

In factory-loaded ammunition, the manufacturer may use many different smokeless powders to charge cases of a given caliber. It really doesn't matter what powder is used as long as the resulting amount of energy is the same. The manufacturer's ballisticians simply determine what range of powders to use and the amounts needed for each type of cartridge. Then the powder charging machines are set accordingly. But handloaders have no way of determining for themselves the appropriate powder according to

burning rate and resultant energy. Therefore, they must follow recommendations of a reliable loading manual provided by the powder manufacturer or a manufacturer of reloading equipment.

It was once often said that double-base powders were more destructive of barrel steel than single-base powders, and that double-base powders containing nitroglycerin were also a bit more violent. Yet, much of this trouble with barrel corrosion was eventually traced to corrosive primers. After noncorrosive primers became universal and barrel steels were improved, this particular difficulty was largely overcome. Today the powder used is determined by the volume of gas produced, regardless of the nature of the powder.

THE BULLET

Primer and powder are of little concern to the shooter, provided he does not reload or handload his own ammunition. He usually buys loaded cartridges that suit his needs, and components of these modern cartridges have been perfected to such a degree that he seldom has any need to be concerned with them. Even if he wanted to know, he wouldn't be able to find out what kind of powder the factory used.

The bullet is another matter. A hunter who wants good performance must purchase ammunition loaded with bullets that exactly suit his particular need or, at least, offer the best possible compromise for use in several different kinds of hunting. Some modern cartridges are loaded with only one or two different bullets. Other very popular cartridges are loaded with

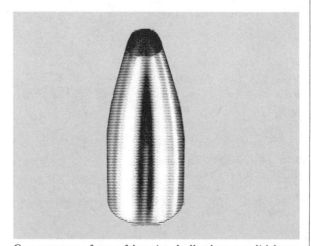

One common form of hunting bullet has a solid base. The gilding metal jacket leaves a portion of soft lead core exposed at the point. More complex forms, shown on the next pages, are usually intended for some form of long-range shooting at game in which expansion must be enhanced because of low remaining velocity.

A TYPICAL HUNTING BULLET

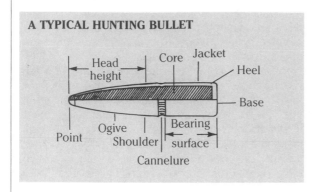

bullets of many types and weights. The accompanying illustrations show various bullet types and the captions point out the merits of each.

When the old round ball of muzzleloaders first gave way to conoid bullets, pure lead was used. Today, lead bullets are still employed in .22 rimfire ammunition and in some handgun and old rifle loads. But this lead is alloyed to harden it, because modern smokeless-powder gas tends to eat away plain lead bullets. At very high velocities, even alloyed lead is not satisfactory.

A more common type of bullet has a lead core that

MODERN BULLET DESIGNS

Fully-jacketed or non-expanding solid bullet. Only opening in jacket is at base of bullet.

Expanding bullet with round nose and soft point. Large area of lead exposed at tip with one-piece jacket covering sides and base of bullet. Cannelure aids in crimping cartridge case neck into the bullet.

Expanding bullet with round nose and soft point. One-piece jacket has slits in forward portion to weaken nose and bring on quick-controlled expansion.

Hollow-point expanding bullet. Jacket encloses sides and base but is weakened by knurling near tip to promote quick expansion.

Nosler Partition bullet has metal jacket open at both ends to expose lead. Partition strengthens base of bullet and jacket decreases in thickness toward tip. One of the best expanding bullet designs.

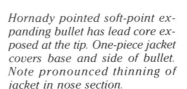

Boattail bullet is tapered at base to reduce air drag. A top bullet design for long-range shooting.

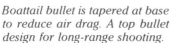

Winchester Silvertip has copper jacket that covers side and base of bullet. Tip is covered with soft aluminum case that extends back and under copper jacket. The Silvertip has good "expanding" qualities.

Remington Bronze-Point has a bronze wedge in tip that produces good expansion when it is driven to the rear of the bullet on impact.

Remington Core-Lokt is a soft-point, round-nose bullet. Forward edge of jacket has scalloped edge to insure uniform mushrooming. Bullet is strengthened by increased jacket thickness near base.

Hornady pointed soft-point expanding bullet has lead core exposed at the tip. One-piece jacket covers base and side of bullet. Note pronounced thinning of jacket in nose section.

RWS H-Mantle bullet is a semi-fragmenting bullet design. Outer jacket is steel, covered with cupro-nickle alloy. Tip cap enclosing internal cavity is copper. Jacket is indented at halfway point to separate frangible forward section from base.

Remington hollow-point Core-Lokt has shallow tip cavity for quick expansion. Jacket is purposely thin at nose to weaken it.

is completely encased in a harder metal jacket, commonly made of a copper alloy. Sometimes the copper alloy jacket is coated with a thin wash of tin to prevent tarnishing. Mild steel (low carbon content) is also sometimes used as bullet-jacket metal, and is usually used in military rounds.

Full-metal jackets are required for military use by international law (the Geneva Convention), which outlaws expanding or "dum dum" bullets on the grounds that their use is not humane. Full-metal jackets are also employed in rounds intended for semi-automatic pistols, full-automatic shoulder arms, and machine guns. In these firearms, the full jacket aids in feeding from the magazine to the chamber. A plain lead bullet or a bullet with a partial jacket often hangs up on the lip of the chamber, as the designers of early full-automatic weapons soon discovered. Many target rounds have full jackets because expansion is of no importance to paper punchers and because the jacket allows the manufacturer to tightly control bullet dimension.

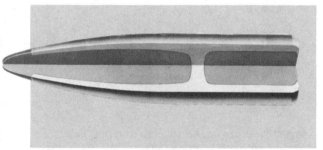

This Nosler Partition bullet has an open point to ensure rapid mushrooming of the copper-alloy jacket and lead core. The partition, integral with the jacket, protects the bullet's rear. After expansion of the nose and some loss of mass, the rear portion continues to penetrate.

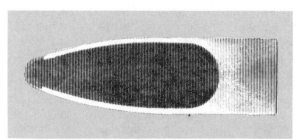

Expanding bullet with heavy base: Very heavy hard-metal jacket base and fairly large exposed lead tip indicates that the bullet designer wanted ready expansion but also needed enough retained mass to ensure deep penetration. In mushrooming, some metal frequently breaks off from the bullet, and a heavy jacket base is one way to insure adequate retained weight.

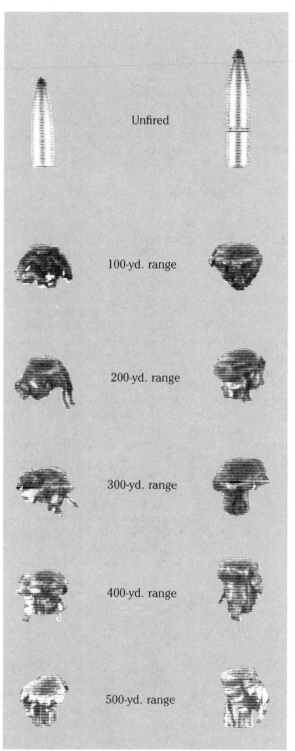

Unfired

100-yd. range

200-yd. range

300-yd. range

400-yd. range

500-yd. range

Photos at left show results of test with 100-grain bullets and 140-grain bullets in .264 Winchester Magnum cartridges. Frontal area of bullet remains fairly stable at various ranges, though it does decrease somewhat at 400 and 500 yards because of declining remaining energy. At longer ranges, the remaining energy eventually declines so much that mushrooming is not possible.

The only important use of full-metal jackets for hunting is in cartridges intended for very heavy game, such as elephants. The fully jacketed bullets provide better penetration. Without the hard point, for example, a bullet would seldom pierce an elephant's skull to reach the brain for a sure kill. With dangerous game, it does not pay to wound, and there are many authenticated stories of soft-point bullets flattening out on the skulls of Cape buffalo and other heavy game. Though an expanding bullet might be useful in some cases, penetration is clearly more important with dangerous game.

Many British cartridges and some Continental rounds intended for use in Africa are loaded with fully jacketed bullets, and a few American-made cartridges are loaded with them. For instance, the .458 Winchester Magnum is available with a full-metal jacket or an open-point expanding bullet.

The use of bullets with full jackets for hunting is prohibited by state law in the United States. Most North American big-game animals do not attain the size and ferocity of some African animals, so a full jacket is a definite disadvantage. These bullets tend to make neat bullet-diameter holes on entrance, and the exit hole is usually the same size. Unless the hunter hits the animal's brain, spine, or heart, quick kills are impossible, and the wounded animal may escape to die later in agony. The only North American animals big enough and dangerous enough to appear to merit ammunition with a full jacket are the big bears—grizzly, brown, and polar. But heavy expanding loads have been found to be sufficient.

For deer-size animals, using fully jacketed bullets is not only illegal, it is foolish. A high velocity bullet of this type commonly sails right through the animal, leaving very small wounds that often close up so that tracking by a blood trail is impossible. Expanding hunting bullets are discussed in detail later.

CARTRIDGE NOMENCLATURE

Two systems of cartridge measurement and nomenclature are in widespread use in the United States. One employs ordinary "English" inches and fractions thereof; the other involves the European metric system.

The primary identification characteristic of a cartridge is the nominal bore diameter, or bullet diameter. "Nominal" is the correct term because bullet diameter and nominal bore diameter may differ. For instance, there are many .30 caliber bullets, but the groove diameter of the rifles in which they are fired *and* the actual bullet diameter are .308 of an inch. Sometimes the maker identifies the bullet as being .30 caliber, and sometimes as .308.

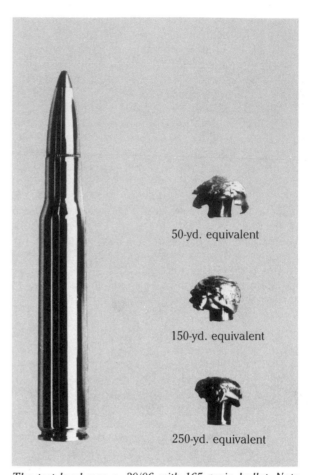

The test load was a .30/06 with 165-grain bullet. Note that the approximate frontal area of the mushroomed bullet at various ranges is about the same. This is excellent performance. In this test, the cartridge was fired straight down at water at unchanging short range, but the powder charge was proportionately reduced to provide the exact equivalent of energy attained at stated ranges. Water approximates resistance of animal tissue.

With black-powder metallic cartridge arms, the bullet diameter was given first in a multipart cartridge designation. The second number indicated the number of grains of black powder in the cartridge. Often, a third number was added to indicate bullet weight. In addition, ammunition catalogs might also state the name of the manufacturer and the length of the cartridge. The .45/70 rifle cartridge, which was adopted by the U.S. Army in 1873, is still in use. The full designation of this cartridge under the old-style nomenclature was: .45/70/405 U.S. Government. It was a cartridge loaded with a .45 caliber bullet (actually .457 in diameter), 70 grains of black powder, and a 405-grain bullet. "U.S. Government" on advertising told the consumer that the .45/70/405 was the same cartridge that the U.S. Army used in the old single-shot, "trapdoor" Springfield rifle.

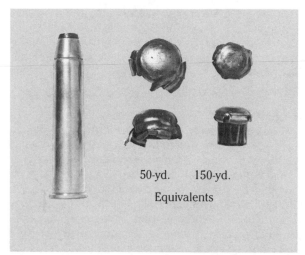

With many older, low-velocity rounds, degree of mushrooming declines very rapidly as range increases. This is the .45/70 with 300-grain jacketed hollow-point.

50-yd.   150-yd.
Equivalents

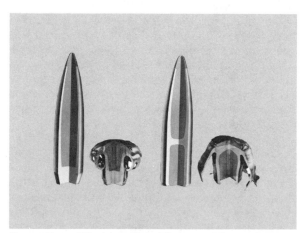

Expansion of Nosler bullets: The two different forms of Nosler bullets form differently shaped mushrooms. With the solid-base type, left, the thick jacket-metal base supports a mushroom that curls under. The partition type bullet, shown at right, provides support earlier, and the mushroom tends to splay outward. Nosler bullets are available to handloaders in a wide variety of calibers, shapes, and weights.

Caliber and bullet diameter. The difference between .45 caliber and the .457 bullet diameter provides 7 one-thousandths of an inch of bullet metal to be engraved by the rifling in the barrel, just as the difference between .30 caliber and .308 bullet diameter provides 8 one-thousandths of an inch of bullet metal for engraving. Of course, only 4 one-thousandths of an inch of this "extra" metal is present at any point around the circumference of the .308 bullet, and 4 one-thousandths of an inch is the common depth of rifling grooves in most modern American big-bore ri-

fles. This difference between actual bullet diameter and the caliber designation is present in most American cartridge designations. A few manufacturers or cartridge designers have, however, chosen to give the actual bullet diameter in their cartridge nomenclature. For instance, there are the .308 Winchester, .257 Roberts, and .351 Winchester Self-Loading.

As time went by, however, the old multi-number designation was shortened to include only two numbers. Some of the old cartridges are still in use today, but of course they are loaded with modern smokeless powders. For instance, shooters still use the .25/20 Winchester, .32/20 Winchester, and .44/40 Winchester. Even this shortened form has been further reduced. If you say you have a rifle chambered for the .44/40, fairly experienced shooters know that you are talking about the .44/40 Winchester cartridge. There is no other .44/40.

One odd exception to this system is provided by the .30/30 Winchester cartridge. This was the first American sporting cartridge originally loaded with smokeless powder, and the load at first contained 30 grains. This followed the black-powder nomenclature system. Today, the second number indicating the number of grains of powder is really useless in describing the cartridge because the actual number of grains of smokeless powder can vary a great deal. All the manufacturer worries about is using the amount of powder needed to provide the desired velocity.

Velocity. Actually, bullet velocity is a surer indicator of the type of cartridge than the number of grains of powder loaded. Velocity has been used in a few American cartridge designations, such as the .250/3000 Savage, which was originally loaded with an 87-grain bullet that reached 3,000 fps (feet per second) muzzle velocity. The attainment of this velocity, very high at the time, was a great selling point, and that fact was included in the official cartridge designation. Later, bullets of other grain weights with different velocities were loaded in this case, and the original name became meaningless. Today, we simply say ".250 Savage." In fact, almost all American cartridge designations now include only two elements—the nominal or actual bullet diameter and the name of the original cartridge designer or manufacturer.

European systems. Metric designations for cartridges usually include only two elements—the bullet diameter and the length of the cartridge case. Sometimes, the name of the designer or original maker is included. A familiar example is the 7 × 57 Mauser. This was originally a military cartridge and was first used in Mauser rifles. The bullet is 7mm in diameter (nominal), and the bottlenecked case is 57mm long. The actual bullet diameter in inch measurement is .284, and there are several American cartridges with bullets of this diameter, for instance the .284 Winchester and .280 Remington (actual bullet diameter is .284).

Many Continental European cartridges are made in two styles—rimless, for use mostly in magazine arms, and rimmed, for use mostly in break-action single-shot rifles and combination guns. If the cartridge has a rim, the letter "R" is added to the designation. For instance, 7×57R Mauser is the rimmed version of this well-known cartridge. The absence of the "R" indicates that the cartridge is the rimless version. Many European ammunition makers manufacture .30/06 Springfield rifle cartridges. The metric designation of this very popular American round is 7.62×63mm. Since all knowledgeable European shooters know that this is the popular American load, there is no reason to add any designer's name, though European catalogs sometimes help out by rather hesitantly adding "Springfield" or "U.S." in parentheses.

All in all, the European metric system with two numbers is more informative than most American designations. But the Europeans have shortened designations for some rounds so much that they too do not give much information. Typically, these shortened designations only provide the bullet diameter and the name of the designer or maker. For instance, the German military round used during both world wars is commonly called the 8mm Mauser in Europe and in the United States. The full designation is 7.93×57JS. The S indicates a cartridge loaded with a .323-inch bullet instead of the older .318 bullet. The older military cartridge, introduced in 1888, is known as the 8×57J Mauser. The *J* stands for the German word *Jaeger*, which means either infantryman or hunter depending on the context. The *S* stands for *Spitzer*, meaning pointed.

Deciphering the nomenclature. Almost everybody approaching the whole matter of cartridge nomenclature for the first time finds it confusing. The only way to fully understand the cartridge nomenclature of rounds that interest you is to read about each round in some detail. Some cartridges have long histories. At the very least, make sure that the cartridge designation stamped in the cartridge head or listed in some form on the manufacturer's cartridge box matches the cartridge designation stamped on your rifle. If not, or if you have doubts, consult someone with experience to make sure that you are using the correct round. An incorrect round may lead to serious injury. For instance, there are many 7mm cartridges on the market today. They are not interchangeable, and using the wrong one could be disastrous.

Americans have hesitantly adopted metric designations for some cartridges, but this has been mostly to differentiate a new cartridge from older ones of the same caliber. For instance, Americans have the 6mm Remington, 6.5 Remington Magnum, and 8mm Remington. Also, European cartridges manufactured in the United States usually retain part of their metric names, as in the case of the 7mm Mauser and 8mm Mauser. But the cartridge length is dropped, and this adds to the confusion.

British system. The only other system that you're likely to encounter is British nomenclature. The British also use bullet or bore diameter (nominal or actual) as the most important element in cartridge designations. Following that there is usually information on whether the cartridge has a rim, or "flange" as the British say. Sometimes British designations also give information on who designed or originally manufactured the cartridge, whether it is belted, and whether the cartridge is a magnum. For instance, there is the very popular .300 Belted Rimless Magnum H&H (for Holland & Holland).

To this rather loose "system" of cartridge designation, the British have added another element. Some British cartridge designations include two different numbers that involve bullet diameter. For instance, there is the .450/.400 Nitro Express. The cartridge is based on an older black-powder round that was loaded with .450 bullets. This was later necked down to .400 caliber. In addition, the case was shortened. Seemingly, an entirely new cartridge designation could have been used, but it was not. There are many similar cartridge designations that appeared when older black-powder rounds were altered so that they could be loaded with smokeless powder in order to attain increased velocities. With these two-number British designations, the first number indicates nominal bullet diameter of the older cartridge and the last number indicates nominal bullet diameter of the more modern round. Most of these two-number British designations are falling by the wayside since the cartridges themselves are largely obsolete.

A few British cartridges, on the other hand, have become so popular that they are regularly manufactured outside the British Isles. Their names have usually been shortened. For instance, American ammunition makers produce the .375 H&H. The full British designation for this cartridge is the .375 Belted Rimless Magnum Nitro-Express Holland & Holland. American brevity is sometimes a blessing.

So much for the general discussion of cartridge nomenclature. It provides a useful background and should help you understand how important it is to make sure that the cartridge actually fits the rifle you are going to fire. If you cannot be certain, consult a gunsmith or an *experienced* gun-shop owner. This becomes extremely important if you are considering the purchase of a secondhand rifle. Sometimes cartridges for older guns are no longer made, and the only remedy for that is handloading. Check carefully.

WHERE'S THE ACTION?

Big-city merchants often entice customers into their stores with signs that read: "Selling out! Lock, stock, and barrel must go." After the sale the business goes right on under another name, and the merchant does not really sell the door lock, the entire stock, and the barrel of junk merchandise on the sidewalk, but many people accept "lock, stock, and barrel" as a commercial phrase meaning all or everything. This expression is really a hoary piece of gun lingo.

When firearms employed spark or percussion ignition, the gunlock was a self-contained unit that was pinned or screwed to the side of the wooden stock. In those days most shoulder arms could be easily disassembled into their three main components—the lock, stock, and barrel. When repeating firearms feeding from a magazine came along, the term "gunlock" was generally replaced by the word "action." "Action" is a rather loose term. Actually, one can substitute the word "mechanism" for it. This mechanism is the means by which the firing chamber is loaded or unloaded and the cartridge is fired.

Most of the moving parts in the action of a modern shoulder firearm are contained in the "receiver" of the gun, and this term is often misunderstood. What does the receiver receive? In the usual definition, the receiver is the part of the gun that receives cartridges from the magazine. It houses the moving parts of the breech-loading action and the firing mechanism. The receiver is often tubular or boxlike in form, and the barrel usually screws into it.

A firearm type is often described by specifying the action, and the four major types of repeating actions used in sporting firearms are: lever action, pump or slide action, semi-automatic, and bolt action. It is true that a double-barreled gun or a three-barreled gun (drilling) is really a repeater, but the "actions" of these guns generally resemble break-action single-shots and are therefore discussed with that type at the end of this chapter.

THE LEVER ACTION

Lever-action, repeating firearms were developed in the United States, where they are still very popular. They are seldom used in Europe. Lever-action repeaters go back to the year 1848 when Walter Hunt of New York State patented the first lever-action gun. It fired metal self-contained ammunition that he called "rocketballs." These were odd cartridges (if they can be thought of as cartridges at all) that consisted of a long conoid bullet hollowed out to contain a propellant powder charge. The percussion cap was secured to a cardboard disk that closed the rear end of the hollow. Some of the guns were single-shots, but others

Detached Flint Lock: With either spark or percussion ignition (except the wheel lock), the entire lock is easy to remove from the stock for service or repair. This flint lock has been separated from the stock simply by removing three screws and lifting it out of the recess in the wood. This is the "lock" in the expression, "lock, stock, and barrel." (George Nonte photo)

were repeaters with a tubular magazine under the barrel.

These guns were ingenious, but they were not powerful enough to attract the interest of the military or sufficient civilian buyers. As hunting guns, they were almost completely useless. Because the bullet contained the propellant charge, it had to be hollow. Therefore, the bullet was too light in weight to be effective. And because the powder charge was housed inside the projectile, the charge could not be made large enough to drive even a lightweight bullet with sufficient velocity. This design was typical of the many failures that occurred during the transition from muzzleloading guns to breechloading repeaters. But this early failure ultimately led to very successful firearms.

With some modification this odd system was embodied in revolvers and shoulder arms made by the Volcanic Repeating Arms Company. At one time Horace Smith and Daniel B. Wesson (they later formed Smith & Wesson Co.) were stockholders, but Oliver F. Winchester, owner of a shirtmaking company, became the principal stockholder. He hired B. Tyler Henry to develop a cartridge that would work well in lever-action firearms. By 1860 Henry had developed a metallic rimfire cartridge known as the .44 Henry Flat, and he redesigned the Volcanic rifle to fire it. The new rifle became known as the Henry, and this rifle was used by some Union soldiers during the Civil War and by many hunters. This was a milestone in American arms development and set the pattern for many later breechloaders.

But the Henry had its defects, too. Its long, exposed magazine tube was easily crushed by an accidental blow, and this stopped feeding from the magazine. The magazine was loaded from the front at the muzzle, which was inconvenient, especially for a mounted man. The magazine tube was slotted to take an operating handle that compressed the long magazine spring during loading. This slot admitted dirt, and the magazine feed often hung up as a result. With dirty cartridges, the action itself often jammed.

Winchester. After the Civil War, the Volcanic Repeating Arms Company's name was changed to Winchester Repeating Arms Company, and a redesigned rifle was introduced in 1866. This was the first "modern" Winchester lever-action rifle. It loaded through a port in the side of the receiver. The port was covered by a spring-activated cover that kept out dirt. The rifleman simply pushed cartridges into the port against the pressure of the magazine spring, a system that eliminated the need for the long slot in the magazine tube. The gun had an external hammer that was cocked automatically by the lever action. With one downward and one upward stroke of his right hand, the rifleman loaded a round from the magazine into the chamber and also cocked the hammer. For its time, it was a fast and very durable action.

After many different incarnations and improvements, the Winchester company introduced a rifle that eventually became the single most popular shoulder arm ever made in the United States. This was (and is) the Winchester Model 94. The new rifle was chambered for several big-bore black-powder centerfire cartridges and for an entirely new round, a rimmed .30 caliber cartridge that contained 30 grains of smokeless powder. This .30/30 cartridge was the first American smokeless-powder round for sporting rifles. With many minor improvements, it is still used today and is very popular for short-range deer hunting. Marlin, Savage, and Colt also introduced lever-action shoulder arms, and some of them are still being made.

Today's Model 94 Winchester is a short, handy carbine that is chambered for the old .30/30 and for several new rounds—the .307 Winchester, .356 Winchester, and .375 Winchester, and the 7mm Waters. The new cartridges are intended to provide Model 94 enthusiasts with more powerful big-game rounds. The

The Model 94 Angle Eject XTR is a modern version of the pioneering Model 94 Winchester lever rifle. It ejects fired cases angled to the right instead of straight up so that a scope can be centered low over the bore. Also, the receiver has been beefed up so that a new line of more-powerful cartridges can be used. The magazine is the tube under the barrel. See inner workings on the next page.

HOW A MODERN LEVER-ACTION RIFLE WORKS (*MARLIN*)

1. *Beginning with the rifle loaded and cocked, pulling the trigger releases the upper end of the trigger from notch in the hammer, which springs forward and strikes the firing pin, detonating the cartridge.*

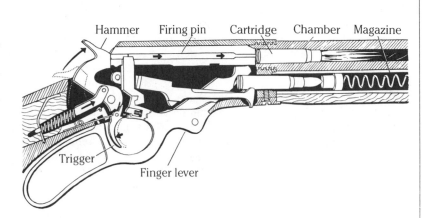

2. *Moving the finger lever forward moves the locking bolt downward, disengaging it from the bolt, and the finger lever tip engages slot in the bolt and moves it rearward. As the bolt slides back, an extractor hook pulls the fired case from the chamber and a spring-loaded ejector on the opposite side of the bolt ejects the case. The magazine spring pushes the cartridge onto the carrier and a cam on the finger lever moves carrier upward toward the barrel chamber.*

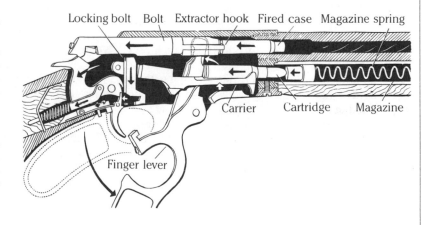

3. *As the finger lever is moved to its forward-most position and returned slightly, it engages a protruding pin on the carrier rocker and cams the carrier fully upward to the barrel chamber. As the finger lever is returned, its tip, which is engaged in the bolt slot, moves the bolt forward, pushing the cartridge into the chamber. Returning finger lever to the stock raises the locking bolt to matching notch in the bolt and aligns the safety firing pin (see Fig. 1). The gun is now ready for firing.*

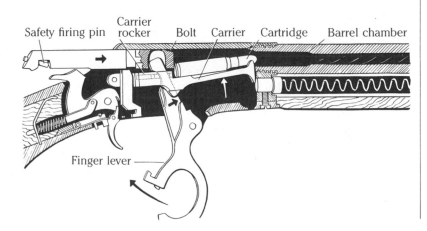

receiver and action had to be beefed up to accommodate them.

The lever action has several advantages. The most important is that the action is quite fast and can be operated to fire successive shots without removing the gun from the shoulder. This can be very important to hunters who require quick follow-up shots. In the advertising for the Model 1866 lever gun, Winchester stated that it could be fired from the shoulder without "coming off aim." This may be possible for some shooters, but most lose the sight picture during recoil and must regain it before firing again. Nevertheless, the muzzle does not move far enough off aim to cause much delay.

With the Model 94 Winchester, there is an odd disadvantage. The gun ejects fired cases through a large ejection port in the top of the receiver. This is no problem as long as open sights are being used. But if a riflescope is mounted over the bore, an ejected case can jam between the scope and the receiver or breechblock. This locks up the action and prevents feeding another cartridge.

One way to overcome this problem is to use a side-mounted scope, and side mounts for the Model 94 are available. Yet many shooters want the scope centered over the bore. In fact, this has proved to be the easiest position for the shooter, since it makes for good hand-eye coordination.

In 1984, the U.S. Repeating Arms Co., which now makes Winchester lever-action rifles, introduced the Model 94 and several improved versions of it with an ejection system that angles fired cases out of the port upward and outward. This is called "Angle Eject" and makes it possible to mount a scope centered over the bore without fear of a jam. This should greatly widen the usefulness of the venerable Model 94 and its immediate descendants.

Another defect of the Model 94 and all other arms that employ tubular magazines is that they cannot be safely chambered for cartridges loaded with pointed bullets. In a tubular magazine, cartridges lie behind one another is a straight line. If bullets were pointed, the point of one would rest on the primer of the cartridge ahead of it. Then, if the rifle were dropped on a hard surface, a bullet point might fire the primer ahead of it, and the entire magazine would probably go off firecracker fashion. To prevent this, cartridges intended for tubular magazines are loaded with flat-point bullets. The flat area is so large that it cannot dent a primer. But these flat-pointed bullets have a very poor aerodynamic shape, and this severely limits performance, especially at long range. To avoid this difficulty, other companies produce lever-action rifles that have different magazines.

The Model 94 action employs a sliding breechblock that moves forward and back within the flat receiver of the rifle. When the lever is moved downward and forward, the back of the breech-bolt cocks the rifle's external hammer. It substitutes for the shooter's thumb, which was used to cock the hammers of many earlier rifles. When the lever is pulled upward again, the bolt moves forward, strips a cartridge from the spring-loaded lifter and inserts it in the firing chamber. The breech-bolt does not actually enter the barrel; it merely covers the open end of the tube and supports the cartridge in place. The breech-bolt is locked in place by supporting struts that rise into place as the operating lever is closed. This lockup is quite strong, but the original Winchester 94 was not built heavily enough to handle cartridges much more powerful than the .30/30.

Marlin. The Marlin action employs a somewhat similar method of locking the breech-bolt. It also has a tubular magazine under the barrel and cartridges are loaded through a lidded port, but ejection is through another port in the right side of the receiver. Thus, there never was a problem about mounting a top-center scope.

The Marlin, like the original Winchester Model 94, has a good fast action, but it is not strong enough to handle very powerful cartridges. But Marlin model variations have been designed for the newly introduced .307, .356, and .375 Winchester cartridges. Most Marlins, however, are chambered for the .30/30 Winchester and .35 Remington. A few are chambered for the .444 Marlin, a close-range round intended for heavy game such as brown bears. Other Marlins are chambered for the .44 Remington, .357 Magnum, and .45/70.

Savage Arms. Walter Savage patented a different kind of lever rifle in 1893. The improved version, the Model 99, is still very much with us. The Savage rifle has no external hammer and does not have a magazine tube. The original magazine (still in use in one version) is a rotary spool type mounted in the receiver. The shooter opens the action by moving the lever down and forward, which exposes the spring-loaded spool. Cartridges are inserted in cutouts in the rims of the spool. It's a very simple mechanism that presents each cartridge for loading in line with the chamber. There is no angular movement, which sometimes batters bullets in other types of action. Other versions of this rifle are loaded with a detachable box magazine.

The Savage lockup is unusual. It is closed by a large steel block containing the firing pin. In its closed position, the breechblock is wedged against the rear end of the firing chamber and is supported in the back by vertical mortises cut in the rear end of the receiver. It is a very simple mechanism that has stood the test of time and can be used with fairly powerful cartridges. At present, the Savage Model 99 is chambered for

The Browning lever rifle is a modern design that does include an external hammer. It is loaded with a detachable box magazine, seen protruding below the receiver.

rounds that include the .308 Winchester and the 7mm/08, two very modern high-performance cartridges suitable for deer hunting. The Savage action, however, is too short to accommodate longer cartridges such as the .30/06 and other full-length loads and magnums.

Because there is no external hammer and the rifle ejects cartridge cases to one side out of the top of the receiver, there is no difficulty in mounting a scope in the top-center position.

Other lever rifles. The only remaining lever-action repeater used fairly widely in the United States and Canada is imported by Browning Arms of Ogden, Utah. It is something of a hybrid. It has the exposed hammer and lever of a typical "western" lever-action rifle, but loading is done with a detachable box magazine—a very modern feature that makes it possible to use pointed bullets.

Lockup is accomplished with a breech-bolt that moves forward and locks by means of multiple lugs. When the bolt moves forward, it also rotates in the manner of a bolt-action rifle, and the locking lugs enter recesses in the rifle's receiver ring. This is a strong arrangement and makes it possible to chamber the rifle for such powerful modern cartridges as the .308 and .358 Winchester.

But here too the action is too short to accommodate long rounds. The Browning is the only lever rifle now available that employs a rotary bolt with multiple locking lugs. Formerly, the Winchester Model 88 and Sako Finnwolf employed this kind of lockup, but both have been discontinued. These rifles are sometimes available secondhand.

PUMP (SLIDE) ACTION

Sometimes this action is called the "trombone" action because it slides like a trombone. The pump shotgun has proven itself in the very rugged sport of waterfowling. That it is very fast is demonstrated by the fact that millions of shotgunners prefer it over any other action for wing shooting. You do not have to remove

a pump gun from your shoulder to chamber a fresh round, and some shooters claim that they can cycle their pump guns just as fast as a semi-automatic. Though some shooters would not agree, many feel that the pump is slightly faster than the lever action simply because pulling the pump back tucks the butt even more firmly into the shoulder.

Formerly, several companies, notably Colt, produced big-bore pumps, and the action is used in several .22 rimfire rifles. But today only one pump-action big-bore rifle is still being offered to the American shooter. This is the Remington Model 6. The Remington Model 7600 has exactly the same action but is not as finely finished. The Remington pump rifle employs a rotating bolt with a multi-lug lockup that is very similar to the lockup of a bolt-action rifle. It has considerable camming power for extraction, and dirty or malformed cartridges work through the action better than they did in earlier pumps.

There is another good reason for considering a Remington pump when buying a deer rifle. If a shooter has grown up using a pump-action shotgun for bird hunting and small-game hunting, a pump rifle requires the same reactions. If he were to switch to, say, a bolt-action gun during the deer season he might find himself trying to pump the solid, front end of the rifle stock. This happens most often when the shooter wants to fire a desperately needed follow-up shot at a vanishing buck.

It's also worthwhile noting that the State of Pennsylvania, which has more hunters than any other, bans semi-automatic rifles for deer hunting. The idea is that many hunters would spray the woods with bullets, if pumps were legal. With the ever-growing restrictions on firearms that can be used for various kinds of hunting, other states may follow Pennsylvania's lead.

The Remington pump rifle is available chambered for good deer-hunting cartridges, including the .308 and .30/06. Though few would regard this rifle as suitable for long-range shooting, it's accurate enough for deer hunting out to 200 yards or a bit more, and sometimes individual rifles are capable of much better accuracy.

HOW A PUMP-ACTION RIFLE WORKS *(REMINGTON)*

1. *Moving the forend rearward pushes back the action bar and the bolt assembly, which in turn moves the hammer downward and ejects the empty case. Ejection is accomplished by a circular spring in the end of the bolt (see detail, showing top view) with a claw which hooks under rim of the cartridge and pulls it out of the chamber. When the case clears the chamber, the ejector spring in the bolt flips the case out. Then the magazine spring moves a new cartridge upward.*

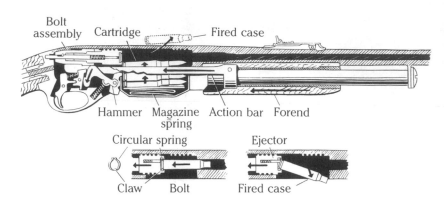

2. *Moving the forend forward locks the cartridge in the barrel chamber. The notch in the sear holds the hammer so that the rifle is cocked. As the bolt carrier is moved forward, the threads on the bolt contact the locking lugs (see detail). Continued movement of the bolt carrier causes the cam pin on the carrier to engage a curved slot in the bolt, turning the bolt and threading it into locking lugs.*

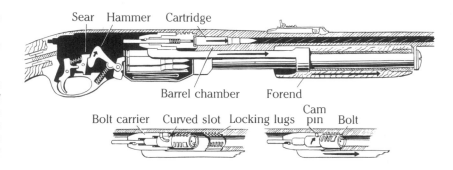

3. *Pulling the trigger disengages the sear from notch on the hammer. The main spring forces the hammer against the firing pin, detonating the cartridge. The safety lock and a disconnecting device, which prevents the rifle from going off until the action is closed, is not shown to allow maximum clarity.*

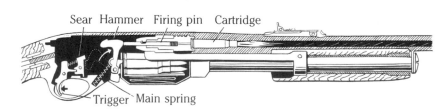

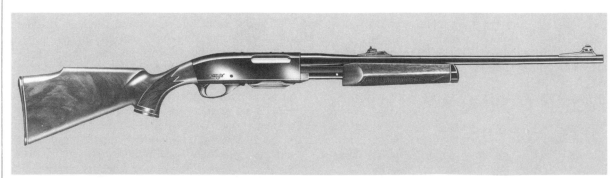

This Remington Model 6 pump rifle is among several other pump models and model variations. Loading is with a detachable box magazine (sometimes erroneously called a clip). Remington is the only manufacturer that still makes pump-action rifles, though many manufacturers make pump-action shotguns.

THE SEMI-AUTOMATIC

A semi-automatic rifle fires one shot with each pull of the trigger. The trigger must be allowed to go forward and it must be pulled again in order to fire another shot.

Before World War II almost all semi-automatic rifles operated on the recoil principle; that is, the force of recoil was used in one way or another to activate the mechanism. These rifles had their uses, but they were quite inaccurate in contrast to modern semi-automatics. Inaccuracy was inherent in these arms because of the very loose lockup of the mechanisms and the lack of rigidity caused by their two-piece stocks.

The Garand. John Garand, the Canadian-American gun designer, changed all that with his .30 caliber American infantry rifle. It fired eight shots very quickly indeed, and it was quite accurate. In fact, carefully tuned Garands and Model 14 U.S. infantry rifles (a full-auto version of the Garand) are still used in various big-bore rifle matches, and the scores are high.

Garand's design differs remarkably from that of recoil-operated semi-automatic and full-automatic arms. A small amount of powder gas is bled off through a port in the barrel. This gas enters a tube and pushes against a piston, which forces an operating arm backward to cycle the action. The rifle is clip loaded. In some other gas-operated semi-autos, the gas is fed directly into the action. The Garand has dual locking lugs that fit into recesses in the receiver.

There are so many variations on the semi-automatic rifle that it is not practical to discuss them in detail. Suffice it to say that these rifles are fast, convenient, and quite dependable. It used to be said that gas-operated autos were not desirable because bleeding gas from the barrel reduced the energy available to drive the bullet, but tests have shown that energy loss is negligible.

It has also been said often that gas-operated semi-autos jam frequently. Anyone who still holds this belief is not familiar with the excellent war record of the Garand. Shotguns of this type that are used in waterfowling do jam occasionally, and this has given rise to the mistaken belief about all gas-operated semi-autos. But waterfowling is usually a damp and muddy sport. For deer hunting, if the action and particularly the gas port, cylinder, and piston are kept clean, jams are unlikely.

The obvious advantage of semi-autos is speed, but that advantage can also cause trouble. In the hands of an inexperienced, nervous shooter, it can be dangerous. Typically, the novice fires a shot and the recoil is almost too much for him. To recover his grip on the gun, he grasps it convulsively and this desperate grip includes the trigger finger. Another shot is fired and the death grip is again applied. This continues until the magazine is empty. This is another reason why Pennsylvania bans semi-autos for deer hunting.

If you maintain a proper grip, on the other hand, the semi-auto offers a distinct advantage. After firing one shot, you don't have to make easily detected movements to load another round into the chamber. As many experienced hunters know, firing one shot often does not alarm a deer. The deer raises its head to look around, but soon goes back to browsing or some other unalarmed activity. Because no movement is required to fire again, a hunter with a semi-auto can fire accurately even when a deer is still looking for the source of all that noise. German snipers during World War I preferred semi-autos for this reason. The enemy could not spot the sniper when he chambered another round.

Today the following companies offer American hunters semi-automatic rifles that are suitable for big game: Browning Arms, Remington, Ruger, Heckler and Koch, and Springfield Armory.

Browning. The Browning Automatic Rifle (BAR) is a remarkable sporting arm. It has no relationship to

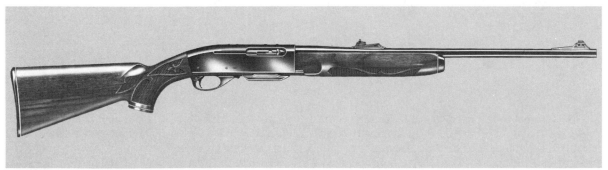

The Remington 7400 semi-automatic rifle resembles the Remington's pump, and almost all the parts are exactly the same. In fact this semi-auto rifle functions in the same manner as the pump rifle, but power to operate the action is supplied by gas pressure on a piston instead of the shooter's left arm.

HOW A SEMI-AUTOMATIC RIFLE WORKS (*REMINGTON*)

1. *Beginning with rifle loaded and cocked, pulling the trigger disengages the sear from notch on the hammer. The hammer spring forces the hammer against the firing pin, exploding the cartridge. After the bullet passes the port, residual gases are metered downward through the barrel opening into the impulse chamber in the forend.*

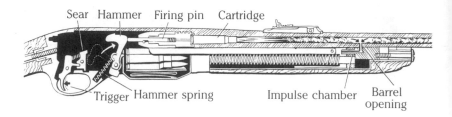

Sear Hammer Firing pin Cartridge
Trigger Hammer spring Impulse chamber Barrel opening

2. *Gases force the action bar and bolt assembly rearward, compressing the action spring, pushing down the hammer and ejecting the empty case. Further rearward travel of the bolt permits the next cartridge to raise into the path of the returning bolt. The ejection mechanism (see detail, showing top view) is the same as in the pump action.*

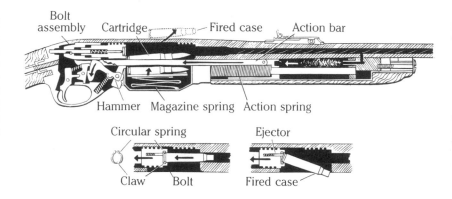

Bolt assembly Cartridge Fired case Action bar
Hammer Magazine spring Action spring

Circular spring Ejector
Claw Bolt Fired case

3. *Compressed action spring moves the action bar and bolt assembly forward, causing multiple lugs to lock the bolt into place (see detail also), sealing the cartridge tightly in the barrel chamber. The notch in the sear holds the hammer in cocked position. Pulling the trigger sets the weapon in motion as in the first diagram. The safety lock and a disconnecting device, which prevents the rifle from going off until the action is closed, is not shown to allow maximum clarity.*

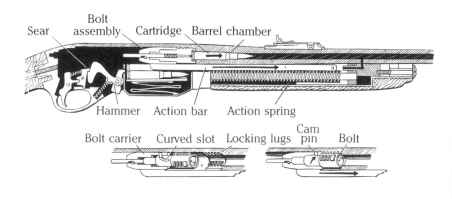

Bolt assembly
Sear Cartridge Barrel chamber
Hammer Action bar Action spring

Bolt carrier Curved slot Locking lugs Cam pin Bolt

the full-automatic BAR used by the United States during recent wars. The hunting BAR has a very strong lockup that depends on a rotating bolt and lugs at the forward end of the bolt that lock in recesses in the receiver. The BAR is a semi-automatic that operates much like a strong bolt-action rifle. Because of this, the rifle is chambered for modern high-intensity cartridges that include the .270, .30/06, 7mm Remington Magnum, and even the .300 Winchester Magnum. This last cartridge is powerful enough for the heaviest game in North America and is a flat-shooting round for long-range hunting to boot. The BAR is quite accurate—accurate enough for long-range shooting of mountain and plains game.

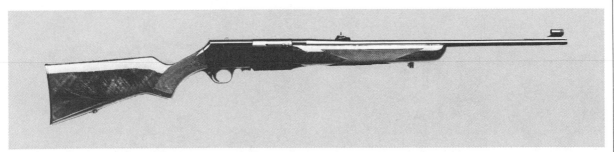

The Browning automatic rifle is a sporting rifle, not related to the military BAR used by the U.S. during World War II. The very strong action is capable of handling extremely powerful cartridges, including the .300 Winchester Magnum, and the rifle has a reputation for good long-range accuracy.

The Ruger Model 44 autoloading carbine is chambered for the .44 Remington Magnum handgun cartridge. It is a very short rifle (carbine), intended for close-range shooting at deer-size animals and works well in its intended role. It, too, is gas operated.

The German H&K (Heckler & Koch) semi-auto is the only one currently available in the United States that does not employ a gas-operated mechanism. Instead, the action is a delayed blow-back type in which the recoil of the bolt is delayed by rollers. The delay is imperceptible but it is long enough to allow pressure in the chamber and barrel to drop to safe levels before the action opens to eject the fired case. This rifle is available in .30/06. A typically German stock is used. At first, it looks very odd to Americans, but it is surprisingly comfortable. The deep hollow on top of the stock wrist gives the right hand a firm grip.

Ruger. The Ruger Standard Carbine is available in .44 Remington Magnum, which is actually a handgun round originally developed for use in Smith and Wesson revolvers. The overall length of this carbine is only 36¾ inches. That fact and the cartridge used demonstrate that the manufacturer intended this carbine for close-range woods shooting. The Ruger does just fine at its intended job.

Heckler and Koch. The Heckler and Koch semi-automatic rifle is not gas-operated. It is a delayed blow-back arm, which is locked by two rollers in the bolt that enter recesses in the barrel extension. When a cartridge is fired, the rollers remain locked until after the peak of pressure and then revolve to release the bolt head. This delay lasts long enough to allow gas pressure to drop to safe levels before the bolt actually opens. The bolt then moves forward again to chamber another round. That the action is robust is plainly demonstrated by the fact that one version of this rifle, the HK770, is chambered for the .308 Winchester and another, HK940, is chambered for the .30/06.

Accuracy is certainly good enough for short-range and medium-range deer hunting. The Heckler and Koch rifles should not be cursed with the sins of earlier "self-loading" rifles, in which the entire barrel recoiled to cycle the action. These early semi-autos had a poor reputation for accuracy because the barrel simply could not be firmly mounted in the receiver and the stock.

The H&K, however, has a strange looking stock that

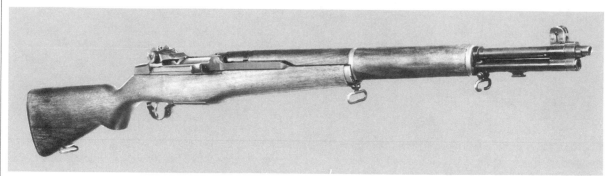

Replica Garand semi-auto rifle: This sturdy replica of the World War II and Korean War U.S. infantry rifle is made by Springfield Armory (a private company). It is widely used for competition in military-style target matches, but it is an excellent big-game rifle, too. A scope can be mounted. The cylinder for the gas piston is exposed at forward end of the stock.

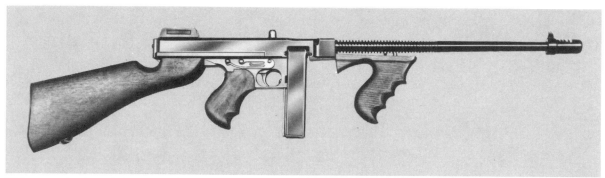

This reproduction of the famed Thompson sub-machine gun ("Tommy gun") is made by Auto Ordnance of West Hurley, New York. It is chambered for the .45 Colt Automatic pistol round. It is semi-automatic, and possession is therefore legal. Theoretically, it could be used for deer hunting in some states. Many other paramilitary arms are offered to the American buyer, but it is foolish to use them for big-game hunting even where legal because they are chambered for inadequate rounds such as the .45 Colt Auto, the 9mm Luger, and the .30 Caliber U.S. Carbine. Also, you would look rather like John Dillinger if you appeared in deer camp with a Tommy gun.

does not at first appeal to most Americans. The sharp-cornered cheekpiece is typically Bavarian. Before testing, most Americans would be tempted to go to work on the cheekpiece with rasps and chisels.

Springfield Armory. For use in the National Match, Springfield Armory, a private company in Illinois, makes reproductions of the famed M1 Garand and the Model 14 (semi-automatic only, of course). These are chambered for the .308 Winchester, certainly an adequate round for most deer hunting. If you like the military versions of these rifles because you used one in the service, you might consider buying one for deer hunting. They are heavy though.

Paramilitary Arms. The remaining semi-automatics on the American market are mostly imitations of military arms that have full-automatic capability in their original versions. They are chambered almost universally for pistol cartridges such as the 9mm Luger and the Colt .45. They are called "paramilitary" arms

in the catalogs, and that is what they look like. The magazine capacity may be as high as 30 rounds. The cartridges used are not suitable for deer hunting, and laws of many states forbid them for big-game hunting. These guns sell in large numbers to people who are called "survivalists" for want of a better name. They prepare themselves to repel a Communist invasion or put down a native rebellion. For close-range combat purposes, these guns would be fine. But don't show up at a deer camp with one unless you want to be expelled.

SINGLE-SHOTS AND MULTI-BARRELED GUNS

Among single-shot cartridge rifles, there are two basic types. One is a simple break-action or rolling-block arm sold for a low price; the other is a well-made, very accurate firearm.

Representative of the first type is the Topper Model 058 Combo Gun made by Harrington and Richardson. It is a single-shot break-action firearm that functions like a simple break-action shotgun. The barrel hinges down to expose the breech and a single round is loaded. The external hammer is thumb cocked. The Model 058 Combo Gun can be had with three different interchangeable barrels as original equipment; the barrels are chambered for the .30/30 Winchester rifle cartridge, the .22 Hornet (a varmint round not suitable for deer hunting), and the 20-gauge shotgun shell. For a moderate price, the beginner can try his hand at three different kinds of shooting, but he can only fire one round at a time before a lengthy reloading process. A scope can be mounted on the rifle barrels, but no one can pretend that the .30/30 is a good long-range deer cartridge, or even a dependable mid-range round. Other single-shot guns are supplied at even lower prices but come with only one barrel.

More expensive but still moderately priced single-shots are best represented by the Ruger No. 1 falling-block rifle. This rifle is available in many different calibers from the .22/250 all the way up to the No. 1

Tropical rifle, which is chambered for the .375 Holland and Holland Magnum or the .458 Winchester for hunting dangerous game. The selection includes fine deer cartridges such as the .270 Winchester, the .30/06, and the 7mm Remington Magnum. Good single-shot rifles in big-game calibers are also made by several European manufacturers, and Browning imports an excellent reproduction of the Sharps falling-block rifle.

Hunting with the single-shot rifle. Just why a sportsman would want to use a single-shot centerfire rifle for hunting is a matter of psychology. Of course, these rifles are reminiscent of the single-shot cartridge arms that were used by hunters on the Plains and in the Rockies, and they therefore have sentimental appeal. Another reason for using one is to boast, perhaps without saying a word. The hunter is saying to all others that he only needs one shot to make a sure kill. If he is quick at reloading his single-shot, this may not be entirely true, but using the rifle is a boast anyway.

Unless you are a very skilled shot, you probably

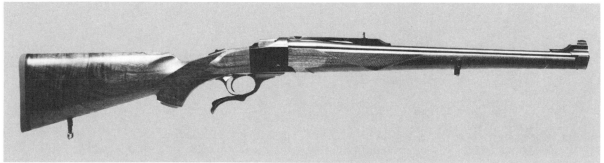

The Ruger International Model No. 1 single shot has a lever extending from the trigger guard. The lever is pressed down and forward to lower the falling breechblock. This exposes the chamber for manual loading of a single round. Falling-block actions are sturdy and almost never malfunction. This version is stocked to the muzzle in the "continental" or Mannlicher style. Half-stock models are also made.

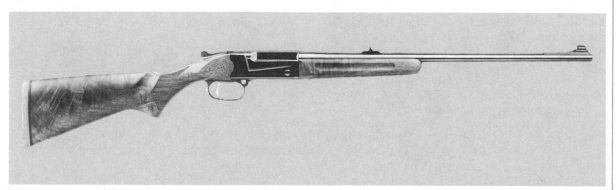

The TCR '83 single-shot rifle (from Thompson/Center) employs the break action. When the top lever is moved to the side, the barrel hinges down on pivot to expose the breech for loading a round. The action here resembles that of a single-shot break-action shotgun. But this action is more heavily built to handle higher pressures of powerful centerfire rifle cartridges.

MULTI-BARREL GUNS

German, Austrian, and Bohemian multi-barrel (combination) guns are made in many configurations. They are break-action firearms, with a selector switch that determines which barrel will fire.

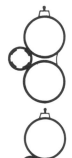

Shotgun over rifle

Double over/under shotgun with rifle barrel at side

Shotgun over big-bore rifle with smallbore rifle barrel at side

Double side-by-side shotgun with smallbore rifle in barrel rib

Side-by-side rifle and shotgun

Side-by-side shotgun with rifle barrel underneath (drilling, the most common)

Double shotgun with big-bore rifle underneath and another rifle barrel (usually .22 Rimfire) in center

Double rifle with a shotgun barrel underneath

should steer clear of these rifles, except for varmint shooting and target shooting. As a matter of fact, you should also steer clear of the moderately priced single-shots. It's often said that these guns are good for youngsters and beginners. That is a mistake. It is precisely the youngster or adult beginner who is liable to fire a wounding shot and then need a quick follow-up. It is a hunter's moral duty to make the kill quick and clean; wounding game and letting it get away inflicts needless suffering. If that is kept in mind, using a single-shot rifle for deer hunting doesn't seem attractive. And for dangerous game, it could be suicidal.

Multi-barreled guns. The best-known example of a multi-barreled (combination) gun in the United States is the Savage Model 24-V. It is a break-action firearm similar to the H&R Topper. The barrels hinge downward when unlatched exposing the breech of a rifled barrel on top and a shotgun barrel underneath. It is available in various combinations and model variations, but the shotgun barrel is .410 bore or 20 gauge, and the only rifle option suitable for deer hunting is .30/30. This is a moderately priced, dependable arm.

From that point onward and upward, you can buy

over/under, side-by-side combination guns, and double rifles imported from Europe with price tags that border on the hysterical. Winchester has introduced an over/under combination gun in 12 gauge and .30/06 with a price tag of over $2,000. Many European combination guns are priced considerably higher, and many of them are made only on individual order by custom gunshops and individual gunsmiths. Quite often, the waiting period for delivery is two years or more.

In the United States, using a two-barreled combination gun for deer hunting is usually regarded as some kind of deviant behavior, but these guns do have their uses. In Europe the hunter frequently loads the shotgun barrel with buckshot and uses a potent big-game round in the rifle barrel. Thus, he is equipped with a good rifle round for a long-distance standing shot and a buckshot load for a close-range shot at moving game.

With European three-barreled guns, the loading can be even more varied. Central Europeans often use drillings. These are break-action combination guns and usually have two shotgun barrels mounted side-by-side with a rifle·barrel underneath. In Central Eu-

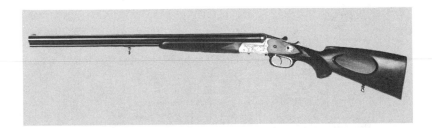

Drilling (Heym) with two shotgun tubes and rifle barrel underneath. This is the "normal" arrangement. A selector switch for barrels is located in the panel on left side. This type of firearm is preferred in parts of Europe where the law makes it difficult for a hunter to secure a permit for more than one gun.

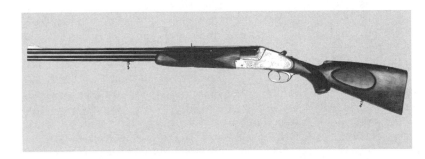

Over-and-under double rifle (Heym): If you are used to an over/under shotgun, a double rifle of this type handles beautifully. Scopes can be mounted on any of these European combination guns and doubles. The European claw mount is preferred.

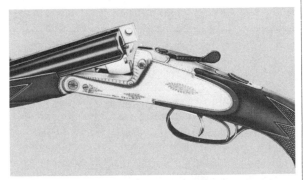

Heym double rifle with shotgun barrel underneath (photo above): At one time, this type of combination gun was popular among "one-gun" hunters in areas where dangerous game might be encountered. The double rifle in a heavy caliber was excellent for dangerous game. The shotgun barrel was used to shoot small game and birds for the pot, but it could also be loaded with a heavy slug cartridge or buckshot as a last resort against charging or wounded game at close range. Drillings with two rifle barrels are now comparatively rare, but the drilling

with two shotgun tubes is still quite popular in Europe where birds and heavy four-footed game are often shot during the same hunt. Heym (German) combination guns of many types are imported by Paul Jaeger of Jenkintown, Pennsylvania. Note the typically small German cheekpiece. Side-by-side double rifle (Heym) open for loading (photo above). Side-by-side double rifles are also made in Britain, Belgium, Czechoslovakia, Austria, and Italy. They resemble double-barreled shotguns, but actions and barrels must be much stronger.

rope big-game seasons are often open at the same time as small-game and bird seasons. The hunter can therefore load these guns with a birdshot cartridge in one shotgun barrel, a buckshot cartridge in the other, and a big-game round in the rifle barrel. So equipped, he is entirely confident that he can handle anything—unless he needs a quick follow-up shot from the rifle barrel.

The Germans, Austrians, and Bohemians also produce four-barreled guns called *vierlings*. These commonly have two shotgun barrels side by side, a powerful rifle barrel underneath and a smallbore rifle barrel in the center of the triangle formed by the other

three barrels. There are many other combinations in drillings and vierlings.

Hunting with combination guns. Prices for European combination guns and double rifles are astronomical, and using one in the United States has a certain snob appeal. In most states, however, small-game and bird seasons are not open when deer and other big-game seasons are, and vice versa. Since the European combination guns are rather heavy, it is not worthwhile for American hunters to carry around the extra weight of the off-season barrel or barrels. In some states at certain times it would be illegal. During a "shotguns-only" deer season, for instance, don't use a combination gun with a rifled barrel, even if you do not have rifle ammunition in your possession. The game warden might not believe in your innocence.

About the only region in the United States where combination guns would be practical for deer hunting is in the South. There hounds are used to move the game to hunters on stands. These hunters could use the shotgun barrel loaded with buckshot for moving deer and the rifle barrel for a standing animal. Yet most hound-hunting clubs forbid their members to use rifles for obvious safety reasons, as well as to prevent shooting a hound at long range with a misdirected or ricocheting rifle bullet.

Double rifles have been preferred for hunting dangerous game in Africa for many years. Most of the side-by-sides are made in England, and the over/unders on the Continent. These guns are available in many big-game calibers. You can order any caliber you like on a custom basis, if you have the money. Some side-by-side double rifles sell for over $10,000.

If you really want to hunt with a double rifle, it will cost you, and even so the only important advantage of these guns for American deer hunters is that they provide a very quick second shot. In the hands of an experienced shooter, a pump-action or even a lever gun can do almost as well, and a semi-automatic rifle is just as fast. Even in Africa, many hunters prefer a powerful bolt-action repeating rifle for dangerous game on the theory that two shots may not be enough to stop an elephant or a lion.

THE BOLT ACTION

A technological arms race raged after the French adopted the Model 1886 bolt-action infantry rifle with its eight-shot tubular magazine, metallic ammunition loaded with smokeless powder, and its comparatively small bore diameter. The other powers made mighty efforts to match or exceed the efficiency of the French rifle. In a few years almost every military nation dropped their old-fashioned single-shot black-powder rifles or primitive repeaters. Big-bore cartridges of .45 or even .50 caliber were replaced by "smallbore" cartridges. The French were soon outpaced, and the tubular magazine was replaced by clip loading or rotary magazines to allow use of pointed instead of blunt bullets. All the improvements in military arms that took place between 1886 and the outbreak of World War I were of great benefit to hunters.

Except for "substitute standard" arms used by the militia and in emergencies, all infantry rifles of the period were bolt-action arms. Among these weapons, the one that proved to be most serviceable for war and for hunting was the German Mauser 98, designed by Peter Paul Mauser. The Springfield Model 1903 bolt-action rifle, adopted by the United States shortly before World War I, was in fact so similar to the Mauser 98 that the American Government was obliged to pay the Mauser company royalties for a while.

After the appearance of the Mauser, many governments adopted modified Mausers, and makers of sporting arms brought out civilian versions of this rifle. Most of these modified Mausers were not really improvements on the original. The famed U.S. Springfield, for instance, has a three-piece firing-pin assembly that frequently jams or breaks. The Mauser has a massive one-piece firing pin that almost never gives trouble.

Mechanics of the bolt action. In recent years, however, several sporting rifles have appeared with real improvements over the original Mauser. Yet most of the designers have not altered the basic way in which the rifle operates. The most common type of modern bolt-action rifle has a rotating bolt with three locking lugs. Two of these lugs are located near the front of the bolt and turn down into recesses in the

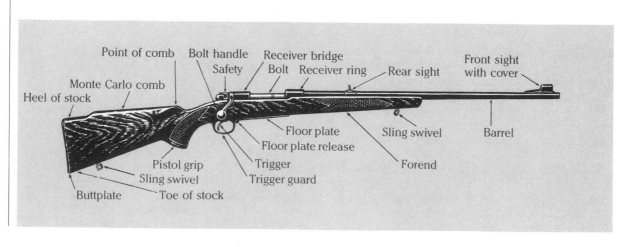

HOW A BOLT-ACTION RIFLE WORKS *(REMINGTON)*

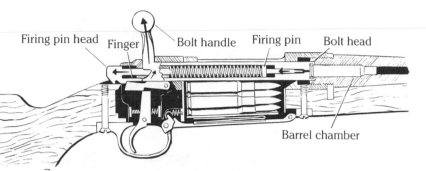

1. *Raising the bolt handle unlocks the bolt head from the barrel chamber. At the same time, the notch at the bottom of the bolt handle catches and pushes up the protruding finger of the firing pin head, pushing the firing pin to rear.*

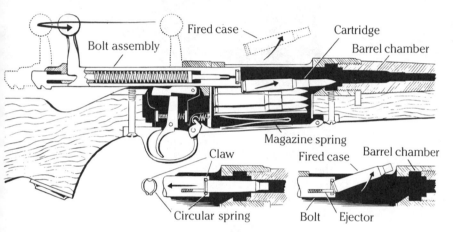

2. *Moving bolt assembly back ejects the empty case. A circular spring in the end of the bolt (see detail) exerts pressure on the claw, holding the case tightly. When the mouth of the fired case clears the chamber, the spring-loaded ejector flips the case clear. The pressure of the magazine spring now raises a new cartridge to loading position.*

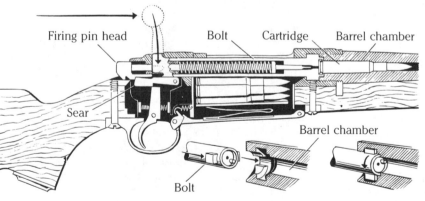

3. *Moving bolt handle forward and turning it downward locks the bolt in the chamber and seals in the cartridge. The sear engages notch on firing pin head, cocking the rifle. (Detail shows how bolt locks into barrel chamber.)*

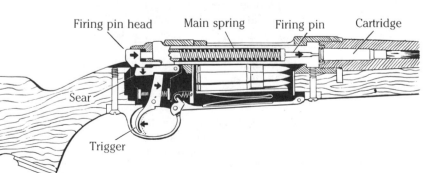

4. *Pulling the trigger disengages sear from the notch on the firing pin head. The main spring forces the firing pin forward, detonating the cartridge.*

MAUSER-TYPE BOLT RIFLE

These three bolt rifle actions are made in varied lengths by Sako, the Finnish company, for long, medium, and short cartridges, enabling the maker to shorten the overall length of the rifle and reduce its weight if it is chambered for medium or short cartridges. Removing a barrel from most modern actions is a job for a gunsmith and is seldom done except when the barrel is to be replaced. With semi-automatics, pumps, and lever rifles, removing the buttstock from the action is often a difficult job too.

receiver ring. The third lug seats itself in the receiver when the bolt handle is turned down. It acts as a "safety lug" in the unlikely event that the two front lugs fail. This is an extremely strong arrangement, as proven by the complete dependability of good bolt-action rifles in the mud and filth of World War I trenches.

Camming action of the bolt is important because it provides the power to extract bent or dirty fired cases from the breech. The camming action of this type of rifle is provided by a slanted surface (on the principle of an inclined plane) machined into the right rear of the rifle receiver bridge. On lifting the bolt handle, the root of the handle moves upward on this inclined plane, and the slanted surface forces it to the rear. This applies great rearward force to open the bolt. While the extractor hook in the cartridge extraction groove actually pulls the case out of the breech, the camming action provides the power. A good bolt-action rifle of the Mauser type has about six times as much power during extraction as the usual lever action, pump, or semi-automatic. This is the primary characteristic that makes these rifles so dependable.

The locking lug arrangement also enhances accuracy. The front locking lugs secure the bolt so firmly to the breech that there is little play. Rifles with locking lugs at the rear of the bolt are not as rigid and accuracy suffers.

These are the basic characteristics that distinguish the Mauser-type rifles in use today. Magazine feeds differ, safeties vary enormously, and other details are subject to varying degrees of ingenuity, but the lockup of the Mauser bolt is almost universally retained.

Bolt-action advantages. The Mauser-type action is also very simple and easy to service. With most of them, simply moving the bolt to the rear while holding the bolt latch open allows easy removal of the entire bolt assembly. The trigger mechanism, the magazine, and the sear remain in the receiver, but they are also usually simple in design and easy to clean and service. The bolt is the heart of this kind of rifle. With the usual Mauser type, the bolt itself is easily disassembled into its main components—the firing pin, the cocking piece, the bolt sleeve, the bolt body, and the mainspring.

The German infantryman had no difficulty in disassembling the bolt of his rifle in the trenches to get the muck out, and the modern sportsman who uses a Mauser-type rifle has little difficulty either. Once the parts have been disassembled, they are easy to wipe clean, lubricate, and reassemble. Also, because the bolt parts disassemble so readily, it is easy to find a defect and replace the part or parts. The same thing cannot be said of most lever actions, pumps, and semi-automatics. Most combination guns and double rifles should not be disassembled by anyone but a trained gunsmith who specializes in these guns. In the United States such smiths are hard to find.

The Mauser bolt offers another advantage that is important to gun owners. Remove the bolt and the rest of the rifle is useless. It can be shipped safely from place to place with little fear that it will be stolen. Gun thieves don't like to be burdened with useless guns. And there is little chance that a stolen gun will be used in a crime because it is expensive to fit a rifle with a replacement bolt. As a result, hunters

Ruger Model 77 bolt-action rifle: This is the Ruger "Tropical," chambered for heavy cartridges. Other Ruger Model 77s are made. The rifle is a Mauser type with locking lugs on the forward end of the bolt that enter recesses when the bolt is turned. The magazine release catch is inside the front of the trigger guard where it cannot be accidently opened by twigs and branches. The safety is on the tang near the shooter's right thumb.

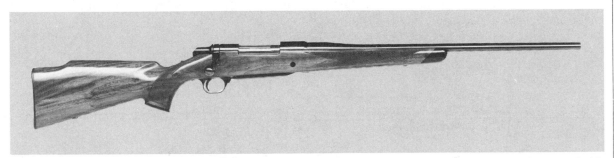

The Browning Lightning bolt rifle is another typical modified-Mauser bolt. It is, however, loaded with a detachable box magazine. The loaded magazine is inserted in a magazine well. Original military and sporting German Mausers load from the top with an open bolt. The cartridges are held in a true clip by the rims and are stripped out of it after insertion by the user's thumb. Detachable box magazines are more convenient.

The Colt-Sauer sporting rifle looks like a Mauser-type, and it is in some respects, but it does not have locking lugs integral with the bolt. Instead, this German-made rifle employs articulated locking lugs that are separate moving parts. When the bolt moves to the rear, the lugs retract out of the recesses and disappear into the hollow bolt body. When the bolt moves forward, they rise into the recesses. The bolt body does not rotate. Therefore, the entire opening and closing cycle is extremely smooth and quick. The disadvantage is complexity and more moving parts, but with careful maintenance, the rifle is easily serviceable. There have been and still are several alternatives to the Mauser bolt system, notably the well-known older Mannlicher Austrian bolt rifles.

commonly ship their boltless rifles and carry the bolt with them. The bolt by itself is not a firearm, and the rifle without the bolt is not a firearm either. This provides a ready response to overzealous policemen and customs officers who all too often use any excuse to confiscate firearms.

There are other advantages to the Mauser-type bolt-action rifle. One important feature is the overall rigidity provided by the one-piece stock. Most lever, pump, and semi-automatic rifles have two-piece stocks that do not support the barrel and receiver as firmly. It is also easy to remove the barrel and receiver of a Mauser-type rifle from the stock for servicing. Two "guard screws" are usually employed to hold the barreled action in the wooden stock, and removing them with a screwdriver is easy. After removal from the stock, it is easy to get at the trigger mechanism, the sear, and the magazine. Removing the wooden buttstock from other types of rifles is much more difficult.

For all these reasons, most sportsmen who hunt in wilderness areas far from gunsmiths prefer the Mauser-type action. Also, this type of action is preferred when a high degree of long-range accuracy is required.

Other types of bolt-action rifles have been used by military services, hunters, and competition shooters. These include the Austrian Mannlicher-Schoenauer with its rotary magazine and split receiver bridge through which the root of the bolt handle moves; the Lee-Enfield (British), also with a split receiver bridge; and various straight-pull rifles adopted by Austria, Canada, and at one time the United States Navy (6mm Lee rifle). With these straight-pull rifles, the bolt is merely pulled straight back and shoved straight forward. These is no up-and-down movement of the bolt handle. Camming action takes care of bolt rotation. And there are still other kinds of bolt-action rifles,

mostly designed by individualistic gunsmiths. At present, though, every single rifle of the bolt type offered to the American sportsman is basically a Mauser, certain proof of the desirability of this type of action.

Disadvantages. Bolt-action rifles do have disadvantages though. The most important is that a quick follow-up shot is really not possible. It is sometimes said that a really skilled rifleman can cycle a bolt-action rifle without removing it from his shoulder, but this is difficult at best and requires considerable practice. Also, thick-shouldered, short-armed men find it impossible. With a person of this body type, the stock must be short and the bolt comes back so far that it pokes the gunner in the eye if the rifle is kept on the shoulder. With pumps, levers, and semi-autos, this is not a problem.

The Mauser-type bolt-action rifle requires the shooter to move the bolt handle up, back, forward, and down—four separate motions. All this motion is

REMOVAL OF MAUSER-TYPE BOLT

The original Mauser rifle was designed for simplicity of operation and easy disassembly and cleaning by soldiers under unfavorable conditions. Sporting Mausers that closely resemble the original Mauser Model 98 retain this simplicity. This is a Fabrique Nationale (Belgian) Mauser. (Neil Soderstrom photos)

  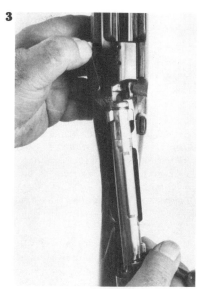

1. *Bolt is closed with bolt handle all the way down.* **2.** *Bolt handle is raised. The bolt root is about to encounter reward-slanted surface in the rear of receiver bridge that cams the bolt forcefully to the rear, readily overcoming a stuck cartridge, or dirt in the action or on the fired case. This camming action is characteristic of the Mauser design.* **3.** *Holding the bolt stop open (left thumb) permits the bolt to be withdrawn from the receiver. With the bolt absent, it's easy to inspect and clean the bore.*

DISASSEMBLY OF MAUSER-TYPE BOLT

Removal of the bolt is accomplished as shown in the previous three photos. Prior to removal, however, check the magazine and firing chamber to make absolutely sure there isn't a cartridge in the rifle. This is always the first step when servicing any firearm. Then cock the rifle as usual by manipulating the bolt handle. Next, insert a small nail or piece of wire in the hole in the bottom of the cocking piece. Pull the trigger. Remove the bolt from the receiver by disengaging the bolt stop as shown previously. (Neil Soderstrom photos)

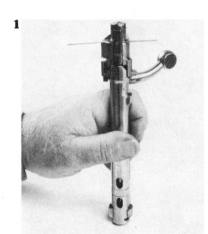
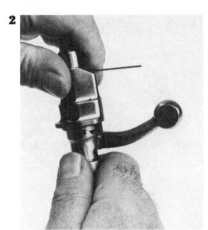

1. *Position the bolt as shown with the wire in place in the cocking piece.* **2.** *Unscrew bolt-sleeve assembly from bolt body. During the first two turns, a spring-loaded plunger in the bolt sleeve must be held in a depressed position with right thumb. In this photograph, the plunger is just contacting the bolt root during a turn. Simply push the plunger in to clear bolt root.* **3.** *Five complete turns, and the bolt sleeve (with cocking piece, firing pin, and mainspring) are free and easily removed as a unit from the hollow bolt body.*

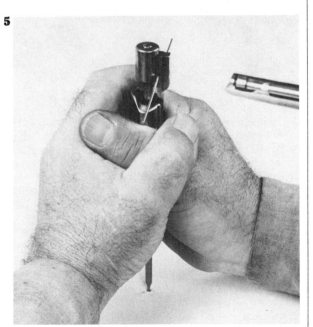
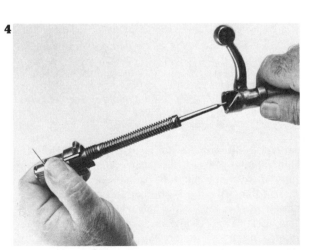

4. *As shown, the firing pin in the original Mauser design is massive and is formed in one piece.* **5.** *Place the firing-pin point on wooden surface (a clean stump will do) and press the bolt sleeve down with both hands. The mainspring will offer strong resistance, but you need only compress it about an inch.*

(Continued on next page)

(Mauser bolt disassembly continued)

6. *Hold the bolt sleeve down with one hand and rotate the cocking piece one-quarter turn to disengage slots and grooves that lock firing pin and cocking piece together.* **7.** *Lift the cocking piece off the firing pin. Meanwhile, hold the bolt sleeve down firmly against mainspring's resistance or it will get away from you.* **8.** *Slowly raise the bolt sleeve in your right hand to release the compression of the mainspring, and lift the bolt sleeve off the firing pin. The mainspring is now relaxed and simply slides off the firing pin.*

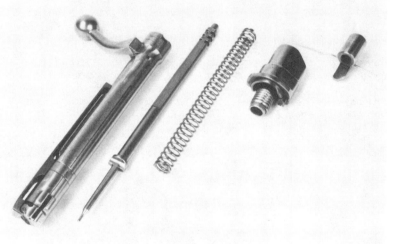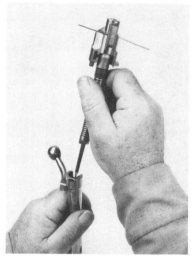

9. *All five pieces (hollow bolt body, firing pin, mainspring, bolt sleeve, and cocking piece with retaining wire still in place) are simple and easy to clean, lubricate, grease, or service in any other way. To reassemble, reverse the order of steps and insert assembly into the receiver. Later, the reassembled bolt is merely pushed into the rear of the receiver without manipulating bolt stop. To do similar work on most lever, pump, semi-auto, and break actions and many non-Mauser-type bolts takes time, tools, and trouble—and should never be attempted in the field. This is only one of the good reasons why this type of bolt rifle remains so popular among hunters.*

easily perceived by game, and each motion also makes its own characteristic noise, easily heard by deer. Even if a game animal does not run off after the first shot, as often happens, it is usually long gone by the time a bolt gun is ready to fire again. Using a bolt-action rifle therefore encourages a hunter to make his first shot count, but he does have additional rounds in the magazine.

If you weigh all the advantages and disadvantages of the various types of rifles, it's easy to see why Mau-

ser-type bolt guns are the most popular rifles in the United States. There are so many different bolt-action rifles in so many different calibers on the American market that almost any shooter will find one that exactly suits his needs and the contents of his wallet. The latest trend is to produce lightweight bolt-action rifles that have short barrels. These shortened bolt rifles, or carbines, are handy. But shooters who are sensitive to recoil will find that they kick harder than heavier full-length rifles. In powerful calibers, the muzzle blast can also be disconcerting.

SIGHTS AND SCOPES

The shortest distance between two points is a straight line, and that is the basis for open sights used on firearms. The rear sight is one point and the front sight is the other. If the sights are correctly aligned with each other, the shooter is sighting along a straight line that extends directly to the target. While this line of sight is straight, the path of a bullet is curved. That divergence leads to all the inescapable complications of making the best compromise between the two when sighting in the rifle.

In general, nonmagnifying sights are called iron sights, and within that large group there are open sights and aperture sights (also called receiver or peep sights). Aperture sights have a ring or aperture in the rear sight, and the shooter centers the front sight bead

Shallow-V   Buckhorn   Aperture, or peep

Basic types of iron sights. The buckhorn is the worst of the lot since it covers too much of the animal. The shallow-V is an improvement as it allows a hunter to see more of the game he's shooting at. The aperture, or peep, sight is the best choice for hunting because it's fast, lets in plenty of light and landscape, and the hunter simply puts the bead where he wants to hit and squeezes off.

or blade in it. Open sights have an open-topped notch of some kind in the rear sight. The shooter centers the front sight in the opening.

OPEN SIGHTS

The simplest kind of open sight consists of a V-notch (rear sight) and an upright fin (front sight) that looks like a simple post when viewed by the shooter. To aim, the shooter simply centers the front post in the bottom of the notch and adjusts the sight picture so the top of the post is level with the top of the two arms. Usually, the rear sight has a rather flat top, and this helps the shooter hold the rifle in a vertical position and avoid canting. This type of sight is almost universally employed on the cheap air guns, and since most Americans start their shooting careers with a BB-gun, many favor this type of sight. In many ways this is a pity, because this sight has distinct shortcomings.

The notch in the rear sight may be shaped in several different ways. Most common, perhaps, is a simple V-notch, but there are others: a wide, rather shallow V; a perfectly square opening; a U-shape; and the buckhorn or semi-buckhorn rear sight with its up-sweeping horns. Common front sights are simple blades, which look like posts to the shooter, or blades with a bead mounted on top. For fast shooting many

This simple open rear sight installed on rifle has a horizontal adjustment screw for windage and another screw for elevation. It is usually paired with a blade front sight, perhaps with a round bead on its top. With this type of sight, it is easy to sight-in a rifle.

shooters prefer the wide shallow V and bead. Some feel it is easier to align these "express" sights quickly. With express sights and some other open sights, the rear sight is commonly marked with a bright-colored diamond or a triangle below the rear V-notch to indicate the precise center of the shallow notch. For precise aiming with open sights, many shooters favor the U-notch, into which the shooter settles a round bead mounted on or machined into the front fin.

But the trouble with all open sights is that they obscure a great deal of the target. If you intend to hold a little high on a distant deer, the rear sight covers most of the animal. This disturbs your confidence a great deal and, even if you are quite calm, being unable to see four-fifths of your target does make it more difficult to aim. In extreme cases, holding high for a distant target makes it impossible to see the animal at all. To do this, you have to take a careful sight on the vital area you wish to hit and then raise the rifle high enough to put the bullet on it. If the animal moves while you are raising your rifle, you are completely unaware of that fact when you pull the trigger. Hunters hardly ever have time to change sight settings according to varying ranges.

To keep the game in view while holding high, some

This graduated-leaf rear sight (Griffin and Howe) is mounted on a short barrel rib. Three leaves, graduated in height, are provided for short, medium, and long range. The rearmost leaf is short and is permanently fixed in an upright position; the other two can be pivoted upward for longer ranges.

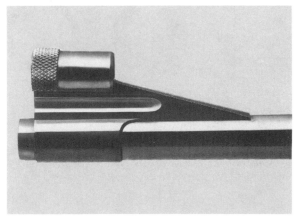

This Griffin and Howe hooded front sight is intended for rifles of heavy recoil. The barrel band circles the barrel near muzzle and supplies extra strength. A serrated ramp eliminates reflected glare. If desired, the circular hood, intended to protect blade-and-bead from being bent by accident can be removed by pulling it forward on the knurling. Hoods are not used when shooting at short range, especially with moving game.

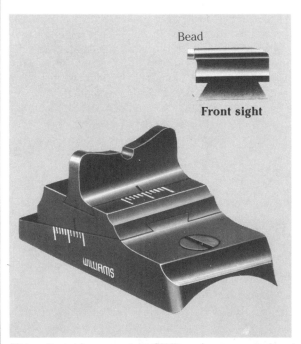

Bead

Front sight

This adjustable open sight (Williams) uses an inclined plane to achieve changes in elevation. Side-to-side adjustments (windage) are made by moving the upper part of sight in lateral dovetail. Note machining on bottom of sight to fit a curved rifle receiver. Many models are available to fit various rifles from this manufacturer and others. The bead mounted on a blade front sight with light-colored rear is excellent when teamed with an adjustable open sight.

old-time shooters are adept at taking a "coarse bead." To do so, the shooter adjusts the sight picture so that he can see more of the front sight while holding the top of the front sight on his target. In other words the muzzle is elevated so that the front sight projects above the top of the open sight. For a really long shot, the shooter may hold up the entire front sight so that its base is level with the top of the rear sight. If the shooter practices with one rifle long enough and is a good judge of range, it's possible for him to hold up the correct amount of front sight for all ranges and regularly hit the target.

A fine sight, as opposed to a coarse bead, puts the bead low in the rear notch and is often used for shooting at close range. With some open sights, the front blade or bead can be sunk so low in the rear notch that the shooter is holding low, intentionally or otherwise.

Primitive open sights, such as those found on many handguns, are not adjustable because the sights are integral parts of the metal and cannot be moved. Ingenious shooters, however, sometimes file down the rear sight to lower the point of impact or bend the front sight left or right. Most open sights on hunting rifles are fully adjustable. Commonly, the rear sight can be shifted left or right or up and down to change the point of impact by means of adjustment screws. Some sighting arrangements include a front sight that can be moved left or right, even if it is only by tapping the sight base laterally to move it in the dovetail slot near the muzzle. Some open sights include sophisticated click ajustments so that the shooter can move the point of impact a predetermined amount on target.

Open sights are difficult to use for long-range shots where precision aiming is required. But many hunters prefer them for close-range shooting in the woods and simply will not use any other kind.

APERTURE SIGHTS

With open sights, the shooter's eye must continually shift from the rear sight to the front sight to the target and back again in order to maintain the sight picture. The eye docs this so rapidly that many shooter's feel they see all three clearly at the same time. This is true, however, only of young eyes. As the shooter grows older, his eyes lose the power of accommodation, and he finds it more and more difficult to use open sights until it becomes impossible, usually in late middle age. At this point, the shooter often finds it difficult to switch to aperture sights or a riflescope because he has so many habits to break. It would be much better to start out with aperture sights, also called receiver or peep sights, because there is usually no difficulty in switching from them to a telescopic sight.

Aperture sights are seldom used on hunting rifles today, though they used to be much more common. At present most rifles come from the factory with simple open sights installed, and they are also "drilled and tapped" for scope mounts. If the shooter doesn't install a scope, he uses the open sights or goes out and buys aperture sights.

And yet aperture sights can be very precise and quick to use. With aperture sights a shooter adjusts the sight picture to center the front bead in the circle of the rear aperture. To users of V-notch sights, this seems imprecise and slow. In actuality it is not. The

The Lyman 57 Universal Receiver Sight is fairly typical of high-quality aperture sights for hunting rifles. Its mount hugs the receiver. (Another version, the 66, is made for autos, pumps, and lever actions with flat receivers.) Elevation and windage are adjustable, with audible ¼-minute clicks. A release button permits quick removal of the slide assembly so the rifle can be used with scope or open sights.

This Williams aperture sight on a break-action combination gun was mounted directly on barrels of Savage Model 24 .22 Rimfire/20-gauge combination gun. Since there is no room for the mount on the receiver of this break-action gun, barrel mounting was needed. Receiver sights should be mounted as far to the rear as possible.

human eye very easily centers a round shape within a round hole and does it with precision and speed. But you have to believe it to do it.

With aperture sights the shooter focuses his eye on the game and then interposes the sight picture between his eye and the target. The bead almost automatically centers itself in the circular opening, and the rear sight is seen only as a circular blur. As soon as the bead is on target, the rifle can be fired. With practice this becomes automatic, and even an old man can do it quite well since little eye accommodation is needed. Another advantage of aperture sights is that a fairly large aperture sight intended for hunting does not obscure the target. The deer remains almost completely in view even at long range, and the bead can be accurately moved to a vital area with ease.

If you want to use aperture sights, you'll have to buy Lyman or Williams sights and install them yourself, or have a gunsmith do so. Since most iron sights are regarded as emergency backups to be used only in the event of scope failure, most big-game hunters simply leave the factory-installed open sights in place for emergencies. Because of this, fewer and fewer hunters ever try aperture sights, and it may be that their manufacture will be dropped almost altogether in the future. However, fully adjustable aperture sights for hunting rifles are still readily available.

THE RIFLESCOPE

In the American Civil War, snipers used magnifying riflescopes effectively at long range. But riflescopes of that era were heavy and very long, and mounts used to attach them to the rifles were delicate. That type of scope was really quite useless for hunting. Today's scopes are much more rugged, are comparatively light in weight, and can be securely mounted on rifles, even those with very heavy recoil.

Sighting through a correctly mounted riflescope presents no problem to a person with normal eyesight. In fact, the process is largely automatic and unconscious. The reason why scopes are so easy to use is that the human eye has the ability to center round things in other round things. With a scope the bright circular field of view is centered in the black ring of the scope wall that surrounds it.

It's almost impossible for a shooter to center the field of view incorrectly. If, for some reason, he is in an awkward position, he will contort himself to achieve a centered field of view. Indeed, there is a built-in correction. Unless his eye is correctly centered behind the scope, the entire field of view blacks out. Try sighting through a riflescope with the field of view correctly centered "in the black" and then move your head ever so slightly left or right or up or down. You'll see this aim-correcting blackout.

The correct way to use a scope is similar to the method used with peep sights. After seeing the game, interpose the scope between it and your eye without moving your head. If your rifle fits you, the scope comes naturally to alignment with your eye, and you immediately see the game through it. Then the crosshairs can be put precisely where you wish the bullet to go.

Some hunters become so adept at this that they can trigger a shot almost immediately after the butt of the stock touches their shoulder. They are almost as quick as a good shotgunner firing at a flushed grouse or pheasant. Too many hunters have the feeling that a scope is an ultraprecise aiming device and can only be used with ponderous care and deliberation. In fact, a low-power hunting scope at fairly close range can be used just as quickly as aperture sights and more quickly than open sights.

Under some conditions, the scope is much quicker. Quite often the hunter only sees a small part of a deer, perhaps a flash of white from the ear or tail. If he's using a good sharp scope, the partial or vague view of the animal changes to a clear image as soon as he views it through the scope. Then it is easy to get a good sight picture and fire. Long-range shooting, of course, calls for more care and deliberation, but at long range the shooter usually has time enough.

Virtues of the Riflescope. It's fairly obvious that a magnifying riflescope gives the shooter an enlarged, accurate picture of his target, but scopes have other virtues. One of the most important is that images of both the game and reticle in the scope appear in the same plane. It is as though the reticle—crosshairs, or post, or what have you—were painted right on the deer. This is a valuable asset, especially to older people whose eyes have lost at least some accommodation. Younger shooters like it, too.

Good scopes also provide a much clearer, brighter image because they gather a great deal more light than the human eye. The same is true of binoculars and sporting scopes. In many cases, especially at first light and around sundown, precise aiming with iron sights becomes impossible, while the view through a scope is sharp and clear. In fact, some European makers and one American company produce scopes that are built especially for shooting in poor light. Since the

A TYPICAL RIFLE SCOPE

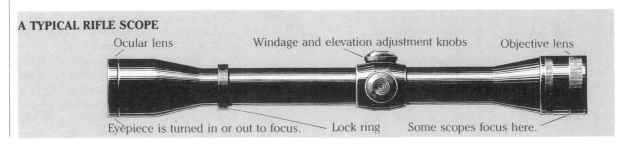

Ocular lens — Windage and elevation adjustment knobs — Objective lens

Eyepiece is turned in or out to focus. — Lock ring — Some scopes focus here.

most productive times for hunting deer are usually early and late in the day, this is something to consider.

FIXED VERSUS VARIABLE POWER

Riflescopes are available in fixed power and variable power. Fixed-power scopes may range in degree of magnification from 2× all the way up to 36×. With variable-power models the magnification can be increased or decreased merely by turning an adjustment ring.

The degree of magnification needed for deer hunting usually ranges from 2× to 6×, and the popularity of the 4× scope indicates that it is a good compromise for most deer-hunting situations. A really good shooter who hunts in open country, usually for mule deer and antelope, can make use of an 8× scope. Scopes of higher magnifications are used by varmint hunters and target shooters.

But higher magnification is bought at the price of reduced field of view. Higher magnification also lessens the light-gathering capability of the scope. Field of view is measured in terms of feet at 100 yards. One manufacturer currently lists the field of view of three

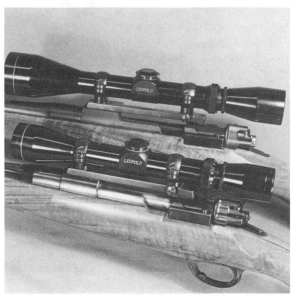

These two Leupold variable scopes of the same power are shown side by side to illustrate "miniaturization" of the latest scopes, an accelerating trend. The rearmost scope was produced about 1980. The modern counterpart is far from a miniature of the original model, but it is reduced in length, diameter, and weight. This makes for ease of handling and also helps to prevent damage, since a smaller instrument is less likely to be knocked against trees, rocks, and saddle horns. (Photo courtesy of Jim Carmichel)

of its fixed-power scopes as follows: 2× –22 feet, 8× – 14.5 feet, 36× –3.2 feet. To a target shooter using a 36× scope, the 3.2-foot diameter field of view is not an important disadvantage. He knows where his target is, and it does not move. To a deer hunter trying for a quick shot, a small field of view is a great disadvantage, particularly when he is trying to get moving game "in his scope." Limited light-gathering ability is not vitally important to a target shooter either, because the shape of the target does not change. He has it imprinted in his mind. What a hunter sees when he looks at a deer can vary enormously in shape and definition.

With a fixed-power scope of suitable power for deer hunting, however, the hunter may run into an unexpected situation. For instance, in typical brushy whitetail country he may get a long shot from time to time when deer venture out into open fields. If he is using a 2× fixed-power scope for the sake of its wide field and light-gathering capability, and spots a nice buck 300 yards away across a field, his chances of making a killing shot are limited. At the opposite extreme, a long-range mule-deer hunter with an 8× scope who suddenly jumps a bedded buck right at his feet may not be able to catch the fleeing animal in his severely limited field of view. And if he does, the animal will be out of focus because it is too close.

To overcome this difficulty, scope manufacturers introduced the variable scope. These are available from low-power 1× –4× models all the way up to 6.5× –20×. For most deer hunters a 2× –7× variable is satisfactory. The lower magnification is excellent for dim-light, close-range situations, and 7× is excellent for shots at game as large as deer all the way out to the extreme effective range of most rifles.

The only reason for buying a variable with a higher magnification is that it will be used for different purposes. For instance, a 3× –9× is a good compromise if you will be using it for varmint shooting as well as deer hunting. If you go higher than 9×, however, the low end of the magnification is greater than 3×, and you run the risk, even at the low end, that field of view and light-gathering ability will not be adequate for close-range shots at deer, particularly in dim light.

Experienced deer hunters commonly set their variables at the lowest magnification for woods hunting and only use higher power for the occasional long shot. If it is a long shot, the hunter usually has time to twirl the adjustment ring. In dim woods or under generally low-light conditions, a hunter is frequently in doubt about his target. He may see only part of the deer or only some creature that may or may not be legal game. If this situation arises, it's frequently possible to turn the scope up to the higher magnification and positively identify the animal. It's usually best to get the rifle on one's shoulder and sight the possible target through the lower magnification first.

In many states, the only legal deer is a buck with an antler (not both) showing at least 1 inch above the hairline. Few hunters can judge such minute headgear with the naked eye, or even with a low-power scope. In such situations a variable scope is a big help. Also many states have "doe seasons" or "antlerless deer" seasons that occur after the "bucks-only" season is over. The higher magnifications of a variable scope are very useful when you must assure yourself that a deer is really antlerless.

But variable scopes are bulkier and larger than fixed-power scopes, and this is another reason for avoiding variables with high upper limits. It's difficult enough to maneuver a rifle with a low-power scope in thick woods, without taking on the inconvenience of still bulkier optics. This problem is being dealt with by leading scope manufacturers through miniaturization. Variables are much less bulky than they used to be, as dimensions given in the gun catalogs show.

CALIBER AND SCOPE POWER

It makes a lot of sense to consider your rifle's caliber when you are selecting a scope. Close-range woods calibers are best teamed up with low-power scopes. It you're using a rifle chambered for the .30/30 Winchester or .30 Remington, for instance, a 2× or 3× may be adequate. It's very difficult to hit surely with this type of woods rifle beyond 150 yards or so, and higher magnifications are not usually needed. It's usually not worth the money to pay for the more expensive fixed high-power scopes. But as pointed out earlier, a variable with a fairly high upper limit may prove useful for obscured targets. A scope with 7× or 8× as the upper limit is about right, if you're using a long-range caliber in open country.

If you wear corrective eyeglasses, you may have a problem when focusing your scope. The typical hunting scope has a focusing ring that must be accurately set to suit the shooter's eyesight. Even people who have 20/20 vision should carefully move this focusing ring until the image seen through the scope is perfectly clear. The usual distance at which this is done is 100 yards. For those who wear glasses the question is: Should the scope be focused for use with glasses or without them?

In the early days of scope manufacture, it was difficult to get a good sight picture through a scope while wearing glasses, because eye relief was critical. The eye had to be a certain distance from the ocular lens or the image through the scope was blurred. This distance was often quite short. With some scopes the eye had to be so close to the scope that recoil would drive it back into the shooter's eyeglasses. So these shooters often chose to focus the scope without their eyeglasses. Then they had to remove their glasses before shooting, which took time and was very awkward. Removing eyeglasses and putting them in a pocket often takes so long that the game is gone by the time the shooter is ready to fire, and it's all too easy to drop and lose the glasses among the leaves.

Today, the eye relief of most modern medium-power and low-power scopes is not so critical, and it's possible to focus and use the scope with eyeglasses without any difficulty. Of course you should have shooting glasses with shatterproof prescription lenses for safety's sake. And you would be throwing your safety margin away if you removed them before you fired.

DEPENDABILITY

Scope manufacture is such a fiercely competitive business that hunting-rifle scopes have become very dependable and do not vary much in quality (in the same price range) from manufacturer to manufacturer. Such things as coated lenses and nitrogen-filled scope tubes to prevent fogging are universal. Optical quality is also usually very good in all American (sometimes made in Japan) riflescopes, but be prepared to pay a premium for extremely good optical quality and durability.

A scope is still a rather delicate instrument and hard usage can cause a lot of trouble. There are companies that specialize in especially durable high-quality scopes, and some of them also put a great deal of effort into providing a very sharp image. Reviewing the scopes listed in detail in a good universal catalog such as *Shooter's Bible* or *Gun Digest* will give you a good idea of the degrees of quality available. Price varies accordingly.

RETICLES

The illustrations on the next page show reticles that are available from most manufacturers. Most shooters find that some form of simple crosshair is the best choice. The cross helps them avoid canting the gun off the horizontal, which can throw shots wildly to the left or right and high. With crosshairs, the shooter instinctively holds them upright. The vertical and horizontal lines provide an almost unconscious check on the rifle's position, and this is another reason why scopes enhance accuracy.

But a simple crosshair has its disadvantages. If the crosshairs are thin enough to provide a good view of the target, they will disappear in dim light or glare, making it almost impossible to sight accurately. If the crosshairs are thick enough to remain visible under these conditions, they obscure much of the target. About 25 years ago Leupold & Stevens, an American scope manufacturer, brought out their Duplex reticle. The crosshairs are quite thick but suddenly step down to very thin lines at the center of the scope. For precise aiming at long range in good light, the shooter uses the thin lines in the center. For quick shooting in dim or glaring light, he aims with the thick lines of the cross. At close range, this is precise enough since the

eye naturally tends to center the target even if you cannot see the fine crosshairs. The apparent gap in the center of the scope can actually be used to aim at close range, even if the fine wires are entirely invisible.

This type of reticle is offered under other trade names by many manufacturers. A variation employs crosshairs that taper gradually down to very fine wires. This type of reticle makes it a bit more difficult to center the target in dim or glaring light because there is no central, sharply defined gap between ends of the thick crosshairs.

Other variations provide a central dot at the intersection of the crosshairs or even a dot without crosshairs. The central dot with crosshairs does obscure much of the target, but it is useful for quick close-range shooting, and it is a good choice for those who do not have good eyesight. A dot without crosshairs may lead to canting the rifle. Another variation is a rather thick, sometimes tapered, post with a single horizontal crosshair. Again, the thick post is useful in dim light at close range, and the single horizontal crosshair helps to prevent canting.

Sometimes Austrian or German scopes with "fence-post" reticles turn up in this country. Commonly, these reticles employ one central vertical post that is very thick and other vertical posts left and right that are thinner. The central post is usually tallest, and its pointed top is the actual aiming point. Other posts merely help the shooter locate the center post quickly and hold his rifle without canting it. These fence-post scopes are usually well made, but the many posts obscure so much of the target that an accurate shot really becomes impossible at long ranges. (This "posts" type of reticle seems like a Rube Goldberg aberration to most Americans, but it has a purpose. It is intended for use in shooting wild boar and some other game at night from a high stand, usually when snow is on the ground. The posts stand out quite clearly against the snow and make it possible to shoot accurately by moonlight or even starlight. The range is always quite short. Since shooting big game at night is universally outlawed in the United States, steer clear of this kind of reticle.)

RANGEFINDING RETICLES

Formerly, rangefinding reticles were quite popular, but few companies provide them today because hunters find them difficult to use and target shooters have no need of them because they fire at ranges known in advance. The most common type of range-finding reticle employs a double horizontal crosshair. The distance between these crosshairs on target at 100 yards

Crosshair

Dual X

Post and crosshair

Range-Finder

Dot

These Weaver reticles represent the most popular types available from most scope manufacturers today. Each type is shown both in the standard circular model and in the wide-view model.

is 18 inches, which is often said to be the distance between the top line of a deer's shoulders and the bottom line of its chest. If the deer (standing broadside, of course) exactly fills the distance between the crosshairs, the hunter knows that it is 100 yards away and holds accordingly. If the animal fails to fill the distance between crosshairs, it is proportionately farther away and the hunter must adjust his aim. If the deer fills up more space, the deer is closer than 100 yards, and the hunter has less to worry about because at that range it is difficult to miss with a flat-shooting rifle.

There is even a reticle with a range scale. Another has paired horizontal crosshairs that can be moved to enclose a deer's chest. That done, read off the range.

The trouble with all such rangefinding reticles is that it takes time to use them, and the game may be gone by the time the shooter is ready to fire. Also, deer come in various sizes. True, most mature bucks have chests that are close to 18 inches deep. But many spike deer and does are considerably smaller, and trophy deer often have very deep chests. The very use of a rangefinding scope reticle may actually throw an inexperienced rifleman off and cause a miss. This is particularly true if the rifle is used for several different kinds of game. Use this ranging method on antelope with their small bodies, or on elk and moose that are much larger than deer, and you will miss or wound for sure. Even if you only hunt deer, it takes considerable practice to learn to use a rangefinding reticle. That time is better spent practicing simple range estimation (covered in the "Marksmanship and Maintenance" section later). You should actually be conscious of the range *before* you look through any scope.

Bushnell, an American scope maker, offers the Lite-Site scope, which employs an illuminated dot powered by tiny batteries mounted in the scope. The illumination can be turned on in dim light and turned off in normal shooting conditions. This type of illuminated sight has been used by the military for many years, particularly in aircraft machine-gun sights. Such a sight could prove useful, especially for hunters with imperfect eyesight.

The future may bring illuminated scopes that also find the range automatically and move the point-of-aim automatically so that the hunter can hold dead on at any range instead of holding over or low. There's also a possibility that electrical means could be used in hunting scopes to "enhance" images. That way shooting accurately in almost complete darkness would be easy. Such scopes are available to the military. But if such scopes ever became readily available to American civilians, they would be outlawed, because they take the sport out of hunting. Accuracy is one thing, automatic accuracy is another. A sportsman is not a military sniper or a poacher.

SCOPE MOUNTS

American mounts for riflescopes are the best in the world, and European manufacturers are beginning to imitate them. Many European mounts, though, are still bulky and result in excessively high mounting of the scope.

A good mounting system, in the American view, centers the scope low over the bore. Formerly, doing this was quite difficult because the military rifles used by sportsmen had straight bolt handles that pointed up when the action was open. Scope mounts had to be so high that the rifles were almost impossible to shoot. The shooter had to have a neck like a giraffe's to see through the scope. This difficulty was overcome to some extent by simply bending the bolt handles of military-pattern rifles to clear low-mounted riflescopes. Today bolt-action rifles have bolt handles suitably shaped for low-scope mounting.

Mount bases. In a typical American mount, the base or bases for the scope are attached to the rifle with screws. Holes for the mounting screws are drilled and tapped into the rifle receiver ring and bridge. The standard 1-inch scope body is held in split rings that tighten around it. The rings fit into the bases by means of latch arrangements or dovetails. The scope and rings can be easily removed with a screwdriver or the edge of a coin that fits the screw slots. The bases remain in place. It's a simple arrangement, and the scope can be quite easily removed in the event of failure. That way the iron sights can be used for back-up.

This type of mounting can have two bases, one on the receiver ring and the other on the receiver bridge. Or there are one-base units that attach in the same places and bridge the magazine opening of a bolt rifle with a solid, integral bar of steel. This type of "bridge mount" (also called the Redfield type, after the company that first developed it) is often said to be stronger and more rigid than the two-piece type.

With both types, the bottoms of the scope bases must be machined to fit both the bridge and receiver ring. Scope makers list rifles that their mounting systems fit, and larger companies have lengthy lists. It's difficult to find a modern rifle, American or foreign, for which some scope manufacturer has not made suitable scope mounts.

Quick-detachable mounts. Several scope mounts of either type are "quick-detachable." By means of a lever or latch system, the scope can be easily removed in the field without tools of any kind. This is useful for sudden scope failures when the hunter is afield, if the iron sights have been left in place. But some of these mounts are quite expensive because they require very careful machining to insure strength and rigidity.

SCOPE MOUNTS

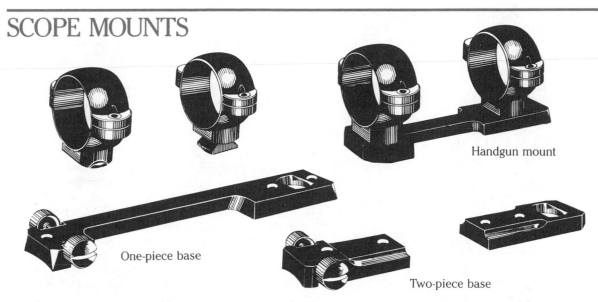

Handgun mount

One-piece base

Two-piece base

Leupold STD scope mounts: The Leupold company makes scopes and scope mounts to fit virtually all rifles except, perhaps, European combination guns and some custom rifles. For the odd rifle, a competent gunsmith can modify the shape of standard bases to fit.

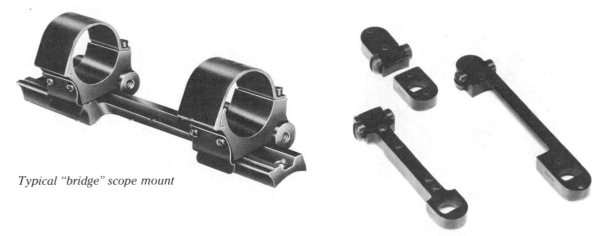

Typical "bridge" scope mount

Two-base and single-base Burris bridge mounts are made to fit practically any rifle.

1½×

2½×

This Redfield handgun scope assembly with double rings works well on most handguns. Handgun scopes must be short in length and must have a long eye relief because the sight is almost always farther from the shooter's eye than a rifle scope would be.

Rails. One American scope mounting system completely eliminates the need to drill and tap the rifle for mounting screws. Several variations of the Ruger Model 77 bolt-action rifle are made with a lengthwise rails machined into the receiver ring and bridge. These two short rails take the form of dovetails. The Ruger scope rings, supplied with the rifle, fit onto the rails by means of a matching female dovetail. Rings are clamped in place by screws. Sako, a Finnish company, makes rifles and rings that are similar. With this mounting system, the need for a permanent base or

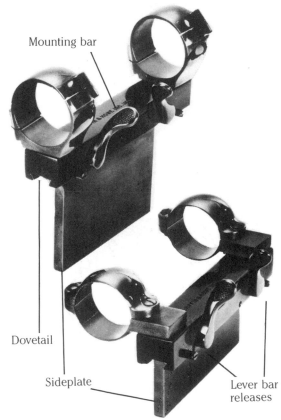

The side plate of the Griffin and Howe side mount is screwed to the side of the rifle's receiver and remains permanently in place. The mounting bar (with rings and the scope itself) is easily slid out from the dovetailed side plate. Double levers are opened to release the mounting bar and rings and are squeezed together to anchor the mounting bar in place when the mounting bar and scope are again mounted. Thus, it is easy to use one scope on several rifles if all of them are equipped with the side plate. The scope almost always returns to zero. If not, something is loose. At top is a mount intended for top-ejecting rifles such as the old (unmodified) Winchester Model 94. With that mount, the scope is offset to the left. The bottom mount is used on side-ejecting or bottom-ejecting firearms and places the scope low, and centered over bore.

bases secured by very small screws is completely eliminated, and yet the scope is easily removed. It's simple, and the average person can install his own scope in a few seconds without resorting to a gunsmith.

Special situations call for special scope mounts, and American ingenuity has developed countless variations. For instance, some hunting-handgun scopes clamp on the barrel rib.

Side mounts. Side mounts are used with the older Mannlicher rifles, a popular model that was formerly made in Austria. These rifles have an open cut in the receiver bridge and the root of the bolt handle travels through it when the bolt action is opened or closed. Consequently there is no way in which a scope base can be mounted on the receiver bridge. Griffin and Howe, the New York specialty gun company, makes a very handy side mount for these rifles that has stood the test of time. But with these side mounts the scope is centered low over the bore, not off to the side. By the way, the modern Mannlicher rifle, made in Austria by Steyr-Daimler-Puch, is really a Mauser type and does not have a split receiver bridge.

For any rifle you may have there is sure to be a workable mounting system, even if the rifle has to be slightly modified by bending the bolt handle or reshaping the receiver. A good gunsmith can advise you on the mounts that will work with your rifle if you can't find what you need in catalogs.

EMERGENCY MOUNTS

Formerly scopes were subject to frequent and disastrous failures. Condensation of moisture inside the scope was a severe problem. Scopes often fogged up inside when the air temperature changed, and rapidly changing extreme temperatures often resulted in a scope that was useless until it could be serviced at the factory.

Today, scopes are filled with nitrogen gas under slight pressure and then are tightly sealed. Internal fogging is now a thing of the past, unless the scope has been abused so much that it has a sprung a leak. Never try to disassemble a modern scope for repair. You will lose the gas. Scope repairs should be done only by the manufacturer.

Older scopes were also quite delicate. A rap on a stump or rock was often enough to dismount a lens or disable the instrument in some other way. Severe recoil could and did cause scope damage. Modern hunting scopes of good quality are so strong that this type of failure is very rare indeed.

Nevertheless, many shooters, particularly older ones who have experienced or heard about scope failures,

Williams Guide open sight, Lo-Sight-Thru Mount, and 2×–6× Guide Line Scope mounted on Remington Model 700 bolt action: With this type of installation, you can use the scope to see through the mount base to use open sights.

want to have iron sights on their rifles for use if the scope becomes inoperative. The usual way of taking care of this is to use tunneled mounts, which are manufactured in the form of figure eights. The scope is mounted in the upper rings, but the shooter can use the iron sights by looking through the lower openings. This type of scope mount always places the scope so high that the hunter has to stretch his neck upward to use the scope. (See the section "Stock Up on Accuracy" to appreciate how this type of mount affects stock design.)

Of course the "quick-detachable" feature of many scope mounts is another way of dealing with this problem, but some hunters feel that it is too slow. What they want is instantaneous access to the iron sights for the time when they throw the rifle to their shoulder and suddenly discover the scope is inoperative. Tunneled mounts meet this need, but they have other disadvantages. One is that a scope mounted very high above the bore gets many more hard knocks than a low-mounted scope, which is to some extent protected by the rifle. You'll also have a hard job putting a rifle with tunneled mounts in the average saddle scabbard. The scope is mounted so high that it usually won't fit.

Last but not least is a new scope mount made by the Williams Company, which also supplies tunneled mounts. Apparently customer dissatisfaction with the neck-stretching caused by tunnels inspired the company to come up with another solution, and they did right well. The S-O-S sight mounts an aperture rear and a bead front sight on top of the scope rings. The sight radius is rather short, of course, but this arrangement is perfectly satisfactory for close-range shooting for which iron sights are normally used.

Williams Sight-Over-Scope mounts: With figure-eight tunneled mounts, the scope must be mounted so high that the shooter must stretch his neck to see through it. With the new Williams S-O-S mounts, the scope is mounted low and a receiver sight and front bead are mounted on the scope rings. Since the scope is normally used for long-range precision shooting in which precise low head position is required, this seems to be a practical arrangement.

Mounting the sights above the scope rather than below it is logical because hunters almost always use the scope by preference and reserve the iron sights for emergencies.

Thanks to the quality of scopes and their mounts, these emergency systems will probably become rare in the not-too-distant future. Today their use is chiefly to allay the fears of some shooters. Of course, it is always possible these mounts may save the day if you go on a guided hunt in a wilderness area. But there is a better way to handle the problem—take two rifles on long hunts. Something other than the scope may fail (a broken firing pin, for instance), and then it's nice to have a complete backup gun.

THE FLIGHT OF THE BULLET

In one of the original Buck Rogers comic strips, Dr. Huer, the scientific brain behind Buck Rogers, finally found a way to penetrate the enemy's defenses against "disintegrators." Both sides in those early space wars had discovered methods of nullifying the destructive rays. After wrestling with the problem, Dr. Huer simply mounted old-fashioned artillery on the good-guy spaceships. The antique shells were not subject to dissipation or diversion and penetrated the enemy's protective energy belts to such good effect that justice and virtue triumphed. The old had also triumphed over the new, which is very nice to see once in a while.

It was a clever idea for an exciting episode, but it did not mention one great advantage of firing old-fashioned artillery pieces and small arms in outer space. Out where the stars shine with great brilliance, there is no gravity, no atmospheric drag, and no wind to disturb the course of a shell or bullet. The projectile, once launched, would continue on its course in an absolutely straight line, and it would do so for eternity, provided it did not encounter the gravitational pull of some heavenly body. A gunner could aim right at any stationary target, fire, and be relatively sure of a hit before the shell or bullet arrived on target.

On earth we have problems. Our bullets do not travel in straight lines. The bullet's course is curved, and several forces impart that curvature.

GRAVITY AND DRAG

The most important of these forces is gravity—the pull of the earth's mass. This basic force is hard to characterize because it is present every day and is so much a part of everyday life that people are hardly aware of it. But gravity is the most important reason why bullets and other projectiles, such as golf balls, footballs, and arrows, follow a curved path (trajectory).

When a shooter holds a firearm solidly just before triggering a shot, he is resisting gravity, which tends to pull him and his gun downward. After the bullet leaves the muzzle, nothing supports it, and gravity begins to have its way. This is hard to imagine because most people know that the bullet's path is comparatively straight during the first few yards of travel. But the force soon makes itself apparent, and the bullet is eventually pulled down to its point of impact with the ground.

All bullets fall at the same rate of speed—an average of about 32 feet per second during a 3- or 4-foot drop, which is typically the distance between the rifle's muzzle and the ground. This cannot be changed. But if all bullets fall at the same rate of speed, why is it that some have a comparatively "flat" (straight) trajectory and others are quite curved? The primary reason for this is that typical modern cartridges drive bullets at higher rates of speed than others. This means the bullet travels farther during the time it takes to drop in response to gravity and hit the ground. Older loads drive bullets at slower speeds, and the projectile cannot travel as far during the time interval before impact. Time, specifically time of flight, is therefore a controlling factor in determining how far a bullet can travel horizontally.

Another major factor in determining the curve of a bullet's flight is atmospheric drag. At high speeds this is a very powerful inhibiting force, and the actual mechanism is friction. The energy of the bullet is diminished rapidly by friction with the atmosphere, and this force is at work slowing the bullet from the instant the cartridge is fired. A good illustration of the power of this force is a "shooting star," which is merely a chunk of rock flying through space. When it encounters the earth's atmosphere at tremendous speed, the friction is so great that the rock heats up and burns (oxygen now being present).

Put gravity and atmospheric drag together and it's easy to understand why a bullet's flight is not a perfect arc (segment of a circle). With the barrel horizontal, the bullet leaves the muzzle at, say, 3,000 feet per second, but it must resist both gravity and atmospheric drag from the outset. Gravity is constant over time and affects the bullet equally close to the muzzle or far from it. But drag slows the bullet. At first drag has little effect, but over the bullet's course, it slows the projectile more and more. Because the bullet travels slower, gravity has more *time* to pull it down during a given segment of flight. This downward pull therefore *seems* to increase the farther the bullet gets from the muzzle. Eventually the bullet reaches a point where it is moving comparatively slowly. Gravity now has a sharply increased effect, and the bullet's path curves steeply downward. At this point in the trajectory, it becomes very hard for a shooter to hit his target because he must compensate for that sudden downward curve.

The desire to overcome this gravity/friction effect has motivated improvements in cartridges since the late 1800s. Black-powder cartridges could not provide sufficient velocity to flatten the bullet's curved path very much. But modern smokeless powders have made it possible to drive bullets at such high speeds that, over the first few hundred yards, the downward curve is negligible, particularly when one is firing at a target as large as a deer's heart-lung area. Increased velocity is the principal means by which modern designers produce flat-shooting cartridges, but they cannot go too far along this path because recoil increases as well. Quite soon, a point is reached at which the recoil becomes intolerable.

Improved bullets. Because of this recoil penalty, every other imaginable way to achieve a flat trajectory has been thoroughly explored. The result has been a continuing trend toward increasingly streamlined bullets of a smaller and smaller diameter. The smaller the frontal area of the bullet, the less the effect of atmospheric drag, and if the bullet is also sharply pointed, the effect of drag is greatly reduced.

Old-fashioned, blunt-nosed bullets of large diameter cannot be driven at modern high velocities within the acceptable recoil barrier. Modern bullets are said to have a "good sectional density" or a desirable "coefficient of form" when they are comparatively long, are of small diameter, and have a pointed aerodynamic shape. The mathematics involved in these descriptions of bullet form are too complex to be of interest to most hunters. An upcoming ballistics table provides information on bullets and the trajectories of almost all hunting cartridges. That table can be used to determine which cartridges are useful for any particular form of hunting. (See table on page 200.)

CORRECTED TRAJECTORY

A new rifle complete with iron sights or scope must be sighted-in to take the best possible advantage of the bullet's trajectory. Sights and scopes are usually not adjusted at the factory or shop, though some gunsmiths will bore sight a rifle or use an optical instrument (collimator) to adjust the sights so that they are parallel with the bore. Even if this has been done, the shooter must sight-in the rifle himself to suit his particular needs.

Whether he realizes it or not, the shooter "corrects"

the trajectory of his rifle to take the best possible advantage of the bullet's curved flight. If a rifle is held in a perfectly horizontal position and fired, the bullet immediately starts to drop in flight. In fact the bullet drops below line of bore after such a short flight that the rifle is only useful for shooting at very close range. To make consistent hits at longer ranges, the shooter must adjust his sights to tilt the bore slightly upward. In doing so, he corrects for the trajectory resulting from gravitational pull.

The accompanying drawing shows how this is done. The line of sight, with iron sights or through a riflescope, is simply adjusted so that the curved trajectory of the bullet intersects it at the desired range. The line of bore, of course, just points off into the distance in a straight line. The bullet's flight intersects the line of sight at two different points: at the target and at a short distance from the muzzle—about 25 yards—where the flight of the bullet is angled slightly upward.

The upward angle of the bore provides corrected trajectory. This is why, in shooter's language, a bullet is said to rise on exit from the muzzle. In reality, a bullet actually starts to drop below the line of the bore as soon as it exits the gun. It cannot fail to do so because there is no defying the laws of gravity.

SIGHTING-IN PRELIMINARIES

The first step is to make sure that the sights are firmly in place and that the rifle is solid in the stock. Unscrew the guard screws and take the barreled action of a bolt gun right out of the stock and check the barrel channel and other inletting. If it has not been done at the factory, coat the barrel channel with two or three coats of waterproof synthetic varnish or rub in a fairly thick coating of good furniture wax. This keeps moisture out of the wood and prevents warping. You don't want to go to all the trouble of sighting-in and then have your zero "wander" because the stock has warped and exerted varying pressure on the barrel.

After the stock is ready, put the barreled action back in the stock and tighten the guard screws. You'll need

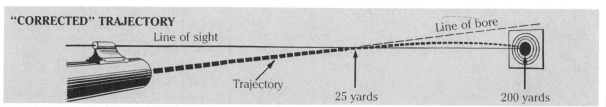

"CORRECTED" TRAJECTORY
Line of sight
Line of bore
Trajectory
25 yards
200 yards

The trajectory or path of the bullet never rises above the line of bore but crosses the line of sight. To compensate for bullet drop, the bore must be pointed upward and this is done by adjusting the rear sight so that it is higher than the front sight.

a screwdriver that fits the screws perfectly. Don't attempt to do this unless you have that all-important screwdriver. To get a perfect fit, it is sometimes necessary to grind down an oversize screwdriver so that it fits the slots perfectly. Rifles with two-piece stocks can usually be left as is because the buttstock is secured to the receiver with a massive throughbolt that pushes the wood against the receiver so firmly that very little moisture can enter. Check the forend attachment to make sure that it is solid, and if screws are used to secure it to the rifle, tighten them.

Check all sight- or scope-mounting screws for looseness. If you find one that remains loose even after pressure with the screwdriver has been applied, remove it and put a drop of Loc-Tite on the threads. Then tighten it down. Loc-Tite holds the screw in place, but not so solidly that it cannot be removed later, if need arises. If this commercial product is not available, use a drop of synthetic varnish.

The rifle bore should be clean and dry when you start out. If it is a new rifle, use your cleaning gear and solvent to remove the protective coating that is usually applied to the bore at the factory.

FIGURING DEAD-ON RANGE

The purpose of sighting-in is to make best possible use of the rifle for the kind of shooting the hunter intends to do. To accomplish this, the hunter usually sights-in to be dead on target (zeroed) at fairly long range. With most modern deer loads, that is about 200 yards or a little beyond. The dead-on range should not be too great because that could cause mid-range misses. Obviously, if the rifle is dead on at 200 yards, the bullet will be high at half that. If that half-range height is too great, and the hunter does not allow for it by holding a little low, the bullet could miss by passing above a deer's back.

To this, of course, must be added errors made by the hunter—flinching, poor sight alignment when aiming, jerky trigger control, and so forth. For most deer hunters, therefore, the mid-range trajectory height of a deer rifle should be no more than 3 inches. Expert shooters can increase that mid-range height a bit because they know how to hold low for mid-range shots, but for most hunters 3 inches is the maximum.

The following description of the sighting-in process is for a bolt-action centerfire rifle with a scope. Variations on this method that apply to other kinds of rifles are discussed afterward.

To begin, suppose you select the 150-grain .30/06 bronze-point, a good long-range deer round. By referring to the ballistics table (page 203) you see that if this load is zeroed at 200 yards, the bullet is 2 inches high at 100 yards, 1.7 inches low at 250 yards, 8 inches low at 300 yards, 23.3 inches low at 400, and a fantastic 47.5 inches low at 500 yards. On a target as large as a deer's heart-lung area, we can therefore conclude that a rifle sighted-in to be dead on at 200 yards will make a good hit (*not* taking human error into account) out to 275 yards. In fact, the shooter can hold dead on out to that range, and for mid-range shots there is no need to make a special allowance either. Beyond 275 yards, the hunter has to allow for bullet drop by holding a little high (or a great deal at extreme range). The maximum range at which no allowance is needed for drop is known as the "point-blank" range.

Looking at the figures in the table makes clear the advantages of modern flat-shooting cartridges. With many older rounds, the point-blank range is only 100 yards. If one of these older rounds is sighted-in to be dead on at 200 yards or a bit farther, the mid-range trajectory height is often 8 inches or even more—surely enough to cause a miss or wounding shot.

SETTING UP

Sight-in your rifle on a clear day with good light but little glare and when the wind is completely absent or blowing at no more than 4 or 5 mph. Your purpose is to find out what the rifle can do without variations caused by the wind or human error. You want to know where the rifle and cartridge will hit at various ranges before adding other variables.

Don't forget to bring along protective earplugs or muffs, or both. In any fairly long shooting session, you need good ear protection, and many shooters wear both plugs and muffs. Shatterproof shooting glasses are also a source of mental calm. Your ammunition should be the same loads you intend to use for hunting, here Remington 150-grain bronze-points. Never sight-in with one load and then hunt with another. Even if the bullet weight is the same, point-of-impact variations can result from differences in the bullet shape, differences among manufacturers in loading a given cartridge, and other factors. This should also tell you that you must sight-in again if you do change loads—for example, to go varmint hunting in the spring with a 125-grain or 130-grain bullet instead of a deer-hunting .30/06 load.

To eliminate human error as much as possible, the rifle should be supported very solidly. If you have access to a rifle range and solidly anchored shooting benches where you can sit while firing, by all means take advantage of that fortunate situation. If a shooter's bench-rest pedestal and sandbag are available, do use them. But you can set up on the hood of your car or even shoot prone from a rest and do fairly well.

You must have a firm, but not hard, rest for your rifle and a flat, unobstructed piece of ground over

HOW TO SIGHT-IN A RIFLE

1. *If the bolt can be removed from rifle, center the target in the bore as shown and then adjust the iron sight or scope to center on the same impact point. This is a coarse adjustment, best done at 25 yards or a bit more.*

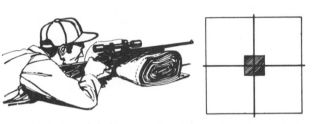

2. *With three rounds loaded and a steady rest, carefully aim at the target (a 1-inch black square is best with a scope, larger with iron sights) and fire three shots.*

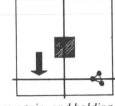

3. *Aim precisely at the black square again, and holding rifle steady, move the sight vertically until the crosshairs move into line vertically with the group of bullet holes.*

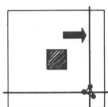

4. *Then move the crosshairs horizontally so they center in the shot group. In effect, you move the sight to the point where the rifle is shooting.*

5. *You are now sighted-in to be dead on at 25 yards. Since the bullet, as shown in an earlier drawing, crosses the line of sight twice, at 25 yards or a bit more and again at a bit over 200 yards, you are also sighted-in to be dead on at about 225 yards. Your bullet will be 2 or 3 inches high at 100 yards. Fire at 100, 200, and longer ranges to check. Make fine adjustments, if needed.*

which to shoot. You must also have a good backstop, such as the side of hill, to halt your bullets. Some shooters use a heavy cardboard box and make cutouts at its ends in which to rest the rifle's forend and the stock just in front of the trigger guard. A tightly rolled coat or blanket is just as good, if less convenient. Never take a rest against a hard object unless you put your hand between the rest and stock. On firing, a rifle bounces away from a hard object and causes wild shooting.

BORE SIGHTING

Set up an aiming point 25 yards from the firing point. For a rifle with a fairly powerful scope, the best aiming point is a 1-inch square of black tape stuck on a white sheet of paper. Use a big sheet of paper or mount a smaller sheet on a large piece of cardboard. A big cardboard box of the kind used to ship refrigerators or washing machines is excellent. It stands up by itself without stakes and provides a big surface so that you

can see where all shots go, even if some of them are way off at only 25 yards. Of course, if you are shooting at a formal rifle range, you will have to use the target frames provided by the club.

Remove the screw-on covers from the windage (horizontal) and elevation adjustment dials of your scope and take the bolt out of the rifle as shown. Sight through the bore and maneuver the rifle on your rest until the black square is dead center in the bore. Now hold the rifle steady and use the windage adjustment to move the scope's crosshairs so that the vertical wire cuts the square into two halves. Then move the horizontal crosshair up or down so that the black aiming point is exactly quartered by the scope's crosshairs. In doing this, you are moving the sight so that it points exactly where the rifle's bore is pointing. If it is done with care, bore sighting should put your first few shots right on the aiming point, or close to it.

It is difficult to adjust the elevation and windage dials (or knobs) while you're holding the rifle, but if you're careful and have a good rest, you can hold the stock at the pistol grip with one hand and use a screwdriver or coin to turn the dials with the other.

An easier way is to hold the rifle solidly with both hands and have someone else adjust the scope in response to your directions.

Firing at 25 yards. After bore sighting, replace the bolt in the rifle and wait a bit so that you will be steady. Practice a bit by dry firing at the aiming point, again quartering the black square with your crosshairs. This is particularly important if the rifle is new and you are not used to the trigger pull.

Take your time and fire three shots with the crosshairs perfectly on target, using the steadiest hold and best trigger control you can muster. The goal is shot-to-shot consistency.

Sighting-in at 100 yards. If the group is dead on, congratulate yourself heartily and go on to shooting at 100 yards. But for one reason or another, you may find that the three-shot group of bullet holes is a few inches away from the aiming point.

In this case, put another 1-inch square of tape over the group of bullet holes so that you will be able to see it clearly through your scope. By the way, the bullet holes in a three-shot group at 25 yards should all be within a 1-inch-square area. If a rifle won't hold a 1-inch group at 25 yards, something is terribly wrong with it, the scope, the ammunition, or the shooter's technique.

Now steady your rifle again and put the crosshairs on the *first* aiming point. Then walk the crosshairs across the paper onto the *new* black square, holding the rifle very steadily while doing so. This time you have moved the sight so that it points at the exact place where the rifle is shooting.

As we have already seen, a bullet intersects the line of sight at two points—close to the muzzle and out at long range. The first point of intersection with scopes mounted 1½ inches above the bore line (the most common mounting height for powerful scopes) is 25 yards from the muzzle, or close to it, and that is why bore sighting and preliminary shooting is done at that range. Because you are dead on at 25 yards, you should also be close to the plotted trajectory of your chosen load out at longer ranges.

But this is the real world, and rifles do vary from the ideal for many reasons. Therefore, set up a new aiming point at 100 yards and fire a three-shot group from a steady rest as before.

Walk down to the target and place a new black square over the center of the three-shot group. If two holes are close together and one is quite distant, ignore the "flier." Out-of-group shots like that are usually the result of shooter's error, not the rifle's. You may have jerked the trigger, for instance. Again, walk the crosshairs across the paper from the first aiming point to the new one so that they quarter the new aiming point, vertical adjustment first, then the horizontal. You

are now sighted-in to be dead on at 100 yards. With a new aiming point, fire another three-shot group to make sure.

But to take the best possible advantage of our 150-grain .30/06 load, you should be 2 inches high at 200 yards, not dead on. It's simple to make this adjustment. Put up a new 1-inch aiming point exactly 2 inches below your dead-on 100-yard group center. Measure center to center on the squares. Hold the rifle solidly, aim at the original square, and then move the crosshairs down to the new one. The point of impact is now 2 inches higher than the crosshairs indicate.

Finally, you should be able to aim confidently at new aiming points and have all your shots hit 2 inches high, or very close to it, in a tight group. Fire a few groups to make sure. Be as precise as you can at this short range. Remember that groups open up as the range increases and that a small error at 100 yards becomes much greater at longer ranges.

This method of sighting-in is convenient and easy. You don't have to worry about the adjustment markings on your scope's dials or knobs, and that's very comforting, because it's easy to make mistakes when reading them. For most hunters, this method is much better than the usual system of making on-target measurements with a ruler and then adjusting the scope up or down by the necessary number of "clicks."

In any long shooting session, sighting-in or practice, remember that you are working with a hunting rifle. Don't fire too rapidly, because that could heat the barrel a great deal and cause it to expand, changing the point of impact. When you see a buck in the woods, you'll fire maybe two shots, at most three, and that doesn't heat the barrel of most rifles enough to cause trouble. Target shooters fire rapidly in some matches and need to know where their shots will go when fired from a hot barrel.

Long-range. If you think your sighting-in is all done, you are mistaken. You must fire at longer ranges to make sure of what your rifle will do way out there. In this case with the 150-grain loads, the objective is to have a 200-yard zero. Set up a target at that range and fire a group. You should be dead on. If not, and it's entirely possible, put up a second aiming point on your group and walk the sights across the paper just as you did at 100 yards. Normally, you will only have to work with the elevation adjustment because windage remains the same, no matter what the range. Of course, you should be doing all this long-range shooting on a windless day.

You should also fire at 250 yards and 300 yards to check the exact curvature of the bullet's path. For many different reasons, a bullet may drop more quickly than the ideal curve in the ballistics table, and if that is true, you should know about it. Write the exact impacts (how many inches low) at 250 and 300 yards (closer intervals if you so desire) on a piece of tape and stick it on the rifle's stock for ready reference during practice. After a while you should have these figures memorized.

The reference mark. Most scopes have a reference mark that can be moved to register the zero of your rifle. After making sure that you are dead on at long range (200 yards in this case), move this reference mark to the 0 marked on the vertical adjustment dial and leave it there. Then do the same with the windage dial or knob. This is your 200-yard zero. If you do make minor adjustments in elevation or windage at some future time, always "return to zero" after you are through.

Most scope adjustments are graduated in minutes of angle and parts thereof. Directions furnished with your scope will tell you what markings on your scope adjustments actually mean. A minute of angle, for all practical purposes, is 1 inch at 100 yards, 2 inches at 200, 3 inches at 300, 4 inches at 400, and so forth. If the scope is graduated in quarter-minute "clicks" (the most common graduation), it is necessary to change the scope adjustment by four clicks to move point of impact on target 1 inch at 100 yards, eight clicks for 2 inches, and so forth. This information may come in handy if you have to make temporary minor adjustments, but it's really not important if you sight-in as described previously by moving the crosshairs to point of impact.

To sight-in any other cartridge, first look up its trajectory in the table (page 200) to determine how high you should be at 100 yards and what the long-range zero should be. Then sight-in accordingly. For instance, it's usually thought best to sight-in the 150-grain .300 Winchester Magnum so that it is dead on at 250 yards. To do that, you need to be 2.6 inches high at 100 yards. With less-powerful rounds, the zero range is shorter, and the 100-yard impact point varies too.

OTHER RIFLES AND SIGHTS

With iron sights, it's usually best to use a square 4-inch, or even larger, aiming point so that you can see it clearly. But the sighting-in process is much the same, except that it's best to start out with the preliminary bore sighting and shooting at only 12½ yards. This applies also to low-power, low-mounted scopes that are less than 1 inch above line of bore (center to center). The bullet's path intersects the line of sight closer to the muzzle with low-mounted sights of any kind.

Iron sights are almost always used at fairly close range when hunting. With most short-range rifles and loads, it's usually enough to be able to keep your shots within a 4-inch area at 100 yards when using iron sights. A bullet's trajectory and the nature of its downward curve at long range are of very little interest to a deer hunter if he hunts in heavy cover. In typical whitetail habitat, most deer are shot at only 50 or 60 yards. Some are taken at only 50 *feet* or less, particularly when shooting from a tree stand over or near an established deer runway or scrape. For this kind of hunting, it's almost always best to sight-in to be dead on at 100 yards to allow for moderately long shots that may come along and let it go at that. Many lever-action rifles and other short-range guns really

If the bolt of the rifle cannot be conveniently removed, a bore-sighting device such as this Bushnell Bore Sighter is useful. The stud enters the barrel to keep the optical tube parallel to the bore. The shooter looks through scope and lines up on a grid to adjust the sight and barrel to the same point of impact. Several different types are sold. These bore-sighting devices are also useful to check sight setting without firing after the rifle has been zeroed. A check can be made without firing shots that might alarm game. This shooter's setup for sighting-in includes a cardboard box with cutouts to hold the rifle steady. It works, but it is not as good as a solid shooting bench anchored in the ground and a shooter's bench-rest pedestal or sandbags. (Vin Sparano photo)

don't shoot within 4 inches at 100 yards anyway; so there's little use in trying for precision.

It's easy to remove the bolt from a bolt-action rifle so that it can be bore sighted as a preliminary step, but bolts or breechblocks of other kinds of rifles are difficult or impossible to remove. If this is the case with your rifle, a gunsmith can use his collimator to adjust sights or scope so that the line of sight is parallel to the bore. This usually puts you nicely on paper at only 12½ yards.

Inexpensive bore periscopes are available. You simply open the rifle's action, slip the periscope into the breech end of the barrel, and do your bore sighting by peering through the instrument. After bore sighting,

you proceed as with a bolt-action rifle, using the periscope when you walk your crosshairs across the paper. Yes, you *need* adjustable sights.

UPHILL AND DOWN

Obviously, any bullet's flight is curved to the greatest degree when the barrel is horizontal or close to it. If the barrel is elevated more and more toward the vertical, the effect of gravity is lessened because the horizontal flight is shorter and shorter. If the barrel were exactly vertical (very unsafe), gravity would only act

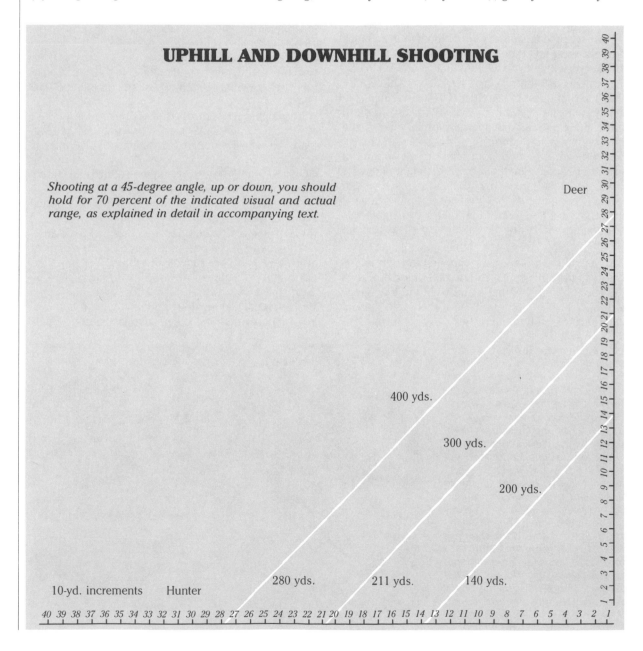

UPHILL AND DOWNHILL SHOOTING

Shooting at a 45-degree angle, up or down, you should hold for 70 percent of the indicated visual and actual range, as explained in detail in accompanying text.

Deer

400 yds.

300 yds.

200 yds.

280 yds.   211 yds.   140 yds.

10-yd. increments   Hunter

on the bullet to slow it down, and atmospheric drag would do the same. The bullet's flight would be perfectly straight. Surprisingly, the same thing is true if a hunter is firing downhill at a fairly steep angle. If the rifle's bore were exactly vertical, and the bullet came straight down out of the sky toward the earth, it's flight would again be perfectly straight. Gravity and drag could only speed up the bullet.

This concept is difficult for many hunters, but it is true that a steep downhill *and* a steep uphill shot elevates the point of impact a bit higher than the normal point of impact when firing horizontal shots. In other words, for a steep downhill or a steep uphill shot, hold a bit lower than normal in order to compensate. The question is, how much? In hilly country, this becomes a matter of some importance.

People judge range mostly by the apparent sizes of objects. The farther away something is from you, the smaller it looks, and that is what allows you to estimate the range fairly accurately. This process is largely unconscious, but most hunters do quite well at range estimation. If you cannot, you need practice or eyeglasses.

Assume that you are in the bottom of a valley and spot a mule deer buck on the crest of the sloping valley wall. The upward angle is 45 degrees and the buck appears to be 300 yards away.

You are, of course, using the same ammunition that you used when you sighted your rifle in—the 150-grain Remington bronze-point load. You know that you are dead on at 200 yards, and carefully memorized numbers tell you that the bullet will impact 8 inches low at 300 yards. You therefore hold 8 inches high to compensate and then fire. If you do that, the bullet will almost surely fly over the animal or merely crease his back because you failed to take the steep upward angle into account.

The 70 percent rule. It's possible to calculate the effect of shooting uphill or downhill (Kentucky elevation) with pencil and paper, provided you have time to do it or you can use a computer. Doing either is impossible when you are hunting, but there is a simple way to compensate.

Imagine how far away the target would be if it were on the same horizontal plane as yourself. If you drop the mule deer buck (seen at a 45 degree upward angle) straight down to your own level, you will find that he is only 210 yards away.

It may help to refer to the diagram on the accompanying page. It shows a right triangle with one short side horizontal and the shooter at its base angle. The deer is at the top of the triangle above the hunter. If the distance to the deer is 300 yards, the distance along the horizontal leg is 210 yards—70 percent. The buck looks 300 yards away because of his diminished apparent size and that is the actual distance the bullet

must travel, but you hold for the 210-yard (70 percent) range with your 150-grain load. Remember that you are sighted-in to be dead on at 200 yards! Ten yards is too small a distance to worry about, so you hold dead on the center of the buck's chest, just behind the shoulder, and drop him in his tracks.

This 70 percent rule would apply uphill or downhill for shots of 45-degree angle, and holds for all ranges. For instance, if the upward-angled range is 400 yards, the hold is for 280 yards—again 70 percent. Anything flatter or steeper technically requires a different percentage, and you could work out a whole set of numbers to cover all the angles. In actuality, just keep 70 percent in mind for quite steep shots and hold pretty much as usual for anything less steep. If you ever get a shot steeper than 45 degrees, you will have to hold even lower. It seems unlikely that you will ever fire straight up at a deer since they cannot fly. Besides, all shots should be backstopped for safety's sake. It is also unlikely that you would ever shoot straight down.

THE WIND

In woods hunting at a maximum range of 100 yards or so, allowance for the wind is not important. The close range and damping effect of vegetation diminish the importance of wind. But for long-range shots a hunter must allow for wind, which can move a bullet off a straight course to an astonishing degree. Take an extreme example: the old-fashioned .32 Winchester Special with its 170-grain round-nose bullet. If the wind is blowing 10 mph at right angles to the bullet's path, the bullet will curve off course by about 9 inches at 200 yards. That's often enough to cause a complete miss. Double the wind velocity and the deflection more than doubles, causing a sure miss if you hold dead on. To give an example at the opposite extreme, the fast-stepping .300 Weatherby Magnum with a 180-grain bullet is only deflected 2½ inches at 200 yards by a 10 mph crosswind.

Kentucky Windage. It's obvious that a modern fast-moving cartridge lessens the allowance that must be made for wind. Hunters do not have the time to "click off" their sights to allow for wind deflection like target shooters. Instead, they hold into the wind to compensate. This is known as "Kentucky windage."

The chief stumbling block in allowing for wind by holding off is estimating the wind velocity. But experienced hunters are seldom really aware of the wind in terms of miles per hour. They adjust their shooting by the feel of the wind on their face and hands and by how much it moves bushes and grass. Using one rifle and one load over a long period both in practice and when hunting provides a largely unconscious scale of allowances for wind.

The angle at which the wind impinges on the bullet varies a great deal, and most experienced hunters constantly register wind direction without really thinking about it. Wind blowing from straight ahead or directly behind has little or no effect on a bullet. At a slight angle, the wind is not really important either, though you might hold off a few inches to compensate for a strong breeze. In practical terms, most hunters stillhunt game by approaching into the wind because downwind approach would allow game to pick up human scent at long distances. In most circumstances, therefore, the wind is blowing toward the hunter, and its effect on the bullet's path is mild. It only lowers the point of impact slightly.

Tables of wind deflection for sporting cartridges are not readily available, though they do appear in some reloading manuals. Glancing through these tables is useful because it gives the shooter a general idea of how much wind affects bullet flight, but these tables are calculated in terms of wind blowing at right angles to the bullet's path. The shooter must determine what the effect would be at other angles. Another problem is that wind can fishtail across a considerable arc in a very short time. It's also true that the perfect right-angle wind is seldom encountered.

You must also estimate the wind velocity, no matter what it's angle. For a hunter, anxious to get off a shot at a distant deer, conscious estimation and calculation is impossible. One is forced to the conclusion that only patient practice provides the skill needed to make accurate allowances for wind.

If you refuse to take shots at extreme range, you cut down on the need for wind allowance, especially if you use a load with high velocity. Do both and you have few problems. But high velocity in deer-killing calibers means a hard kicker, and anticipation of heavy recoil could throw your shot off more than any wind that ever blew, short of a hurricane. Every factor in shooting accurately is subject to some sort of compromise.

STOCK UP ON ACCURACY

If you examine a collection of old-time muzzleloading rifles, you'll find that these guns have a great deal of drop at heel. That is, the stock falls away at a quite steep angle from the centerline of the bore (and the line of sight). The development of modern rifle stocks has tended to reduce the steepness of that angle. The two reasons for this change are to provide better access to the sights—iron or glass—and to reduce the effects of recoil.

When a flintlock rifle is fired, there's considerable flash in the open pan and burning particles erupt. A caplock rifle usually has no visible flash at the vent, but if a cap bursts, there is a quite violent flash and metallic fragments fly through the air. With early breechloaders, such as the British Ferguson screw-breech military rifle, the U.S. Hall infantry rifle (with its hinged breechblock), and the Prussian Dreyse rifle, a great deal of hot powder gas and sometimes flame leaked at the breech.

MUZZLELOADER HAZARDS

The shooter tried to keep his face away from all the potential destruction. Even so, many shooters were injured or even blinded, at least in the right eye. During a black-powder shooting match, you'll see that many of the competitors try to keep their faces as far from

the gunlock as possible. They have reverted to the firing stance of the early black-powder shooter, which was developed at least partly to preserve the shooter's eyesight. Of course, some black-powder shooters wear shatterproof glasses. Others do not because they feel it would interfere with their "image" as shooters of primitive firearms. That's foolish.

A SLOW EVOLUTION

With the introduction of metallic cartridges, smokeless powder, and improved actions, danger to the face and eyes was almost completely eliminated. Even if a cartridge bursts, gas ports in the rifle action and flanges direct powder gas away from the shooter's face. As riflemen and shotgunners gained confidence in the new gear, they began to bring their faces forward and to lower their cheeks onto the stock.

This provided remarkable benefits. It brought the eye closer to the rear sight, which permitted quicker and more accurate alignment. Mutual support between the stock, and therefore the whole rifle, and the shooter's head was improved. Most shooters think that their heads are firmly anchored on their shoulders and that if they hold still, their heads remain steady. This is rarely true. There is always considerable tension in many directions in the neck. It causes inescapable

Flintlock stock: When spark ignition or percussion caps were widely used, the shooter tried to keep his face as far from the lock as possible in order to protect his eyes. This flintlock rifle's stock shows the extreme drop that resulted. Since shooter's neck and head had to be held erect in order to keep face as far back as possible, the stock had to drop considerably below line of bore to properly butt against his shoulder. Believe it or not, rifle stocks are still being made with extreme drop because the tradition has been handed down all the way from flintlock days!

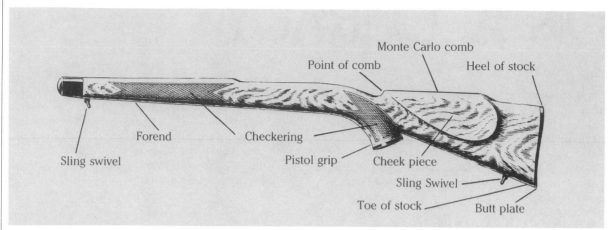

Monte Carlo stock: This racy number has all the preferred features of the "California style." Theoretically, the heightened comb aligns eye with sights while drop is adequate to allow fairly erect head. In actuality, the stock is quite crooked because of the large amount of drop. This tends to cause the rifle to pivot upward in recoil and bang the cheekbone quite hard. In heavy calibers, this is like a punch in the face and causes flinching in many cases. Yet, some shooters are more accurate with this type of stock than any other and experience little discomfort.

trembling, moves the eye, and can affect eye alignment with the sights.

Most rifle coaches tell beginners to "spot weld" their cheek to the stock. This gives support to the head and lessens trembling. Also, with the cheek against the stock and the cheekbone hooked over the top of the comb, there is fairly solid support for the stock.

This type of spot-welded head position is very difficult to achieve if the stock angles downward sharply. For this reason, rifle manufacturers have considerably lessened the drop in their stocks over the past two decades. Some of them have gone so far as to produce rifles with so little drop that the shooter simply cannot lower his head below the line of iron sights. This is a problem for shooters who have very large cheekbones, and they often combat this problem by shaving down the comb.

As the heel of the stock rose, the comb inevitably came closer and closer to the horizontal. Today many shooters want a comb that is either horizontal (parallel to the rifle's bore) or actually slopes *downward* from rear to front, as it does in some stocks with Monte Carlo combs. The traditional comb that slopes downward at a steep angle to the rear is disappearing from rifle design, particularly in bolt-action guns. Unfortunately, the old-fashioned, sharply angled comb is still all too common on lever-action rifles.

STOCKS AND SCOPES

The problem of crooked stocks is still very much with us, even though stocks are straighter than they used to be. The reason is that most manufacturers adjust comb height and overall straightness to provide easy access to iron sights. These are usually mounted just a bit less than an inch above the line of bore. Low-power scopes with their small lens diameters are also mounted at this height above bore or only a bit higher. So most modern, comparatively straight stocks bring the shooter's eye into fairly close alignment when he places the butt against his shoulder.

If a more powerful scope is used, the rear and front bells of the scope are much larger, and the scope must be mounted higher—usually 1½ inches above the bore, centerline to centerline. With many factory stocks, the shooter must stretch his neck to align his eye with a high-power riflescope. This lessens the "spot weld" quality of his hold and makes putting the crosshairs on target more difficult. Ideally, stocks intended for use with high-power scopes have higher combs so that it is easier and quicker to line up on a target. But almost all manufacturers make stocks that are really intended for use with irons sights.

To a certain extent, the shooter can correct this defect by building up his rifle's comb with a carved, wooden add-on piece. It's best to start by adding so much wood that the eye is above ideal alignment with the scope. Then shave the appliqué comb down until the best eye-scope alignment is achieved. Flexible plastic add-on pieces are also sold complete with adhesive for this purpose. Both work, but they are usually ugly. The only real solution is a new stock that actually fits.

There is an even greater problem with comb height if the shooter uses tunneled scope mounts. These mounts allow the shooter to see under the scope so that he can use the iron sights if the scope fails for some reason. Because the forward and rear mounts are tunneled, they place the scope still higher above the bore and this calls for an even higher comb. Some of these tunneled mounts place the scope 2 inches or more above the bore (centerline to centerline). If the shooter raises the comb enough for scope alignment, it is too high to use the irons sights!

Most big-game shooting today is inevitably done with fairly powerful scopes, but stocks are still really built for use with iron sights or low-powered, low-mounted scopes. This is a sad situation because well-made scopes are now so dependable that they seldom fail, and they certainly provide greater accuracy at medium and long range than any form of iron sights. In fact, many experienced shooters either buy rifles that are not equipped with iron sights or remove them so that the scope can be mounted as low as possible. Yet many shooters still like to have iron sights on their rifles in case the scope fails.

MONTE CARLO PROBLEMS

The Monte Carlo stock configuration was introduced in the United States in a big way by Roy Weatherby, a California gunmaker, and it is still very popular. This type of stock includes a high comb that drops down sharply at the rear. This sudden jog permits a big drop at heel for shooters who like that sort of thing (perhaps they have long necks), and yet permits a comb height that works well with riflescopes. This type of stock, however, has a distinct disadvantage. The stock is actually just as crooked, if not more so, than old-fashioned stocks intended for use with iron sights. When the rifle goes off, this steep angle pivots the whole rifle upward and bangs the comb into the shooter's cheekbone. In extreme cases it's like being hit with a stick across the side of the face, and the blow is angled sharply upward under the cheekbone. With powerful modern loads, this often results in severe flinching.

The only sensible solution to this problem is a level comb adjusted to scope height without the sudden Monte Carlo dropoff. This is the configuration that many modern shooters and riflemakers favor, particularly in expensive big-bore hunting rifles and varmint rifles.

All this is of little concern to hunters who use short, handy carbines for woods shooting at close range and who rely on low-power scopes and iron sights. These firearms are commonly chambered for low-power cartridges and recoil is not a problem. The shooter's primary concern is to have a short rifle (carbine) that is easy to carry in woods and brush and comes to the shoulder without tangling in brush because of excessive length. With a very short gun and its necessarily short stock, the whole unit *must* be rather crooked,

and a spot-welded cheek hold is almost impossible unless you have cheekbones as prominent as an elephant's. But for this type of shooting, precision aiming is not nearly as important. The following discussion relates mostly to bolt-action rifles and long-range shooting.

Comb comfort. Another important rifle-stock dimension is the thickness of the comb. When shooters kept their heads back, the comb could be any shape, and many stock designers adopted the very thin sharp comb. This has a racy, aristocratic appearance reminiscent of European shotguns, but in a powerful rifle it almost tears off your cheekbone. Most modern stocks, particularly American ones, have a fairly plump, rounded comb that fits the curve under the cheekbone quite comfortably. If this is not true of your rifle, you can solve the problem with add-on wood or plastic or a new stock.

THE CHEEKPIECE

Most Monte Carlo combs are accompanied by cheekpieces—raised wooden panels on the left side of the stock against which the shooter's cheek rests. Other rifles also have them. These cheekpieces were originally intended to solve a problem that no longer exists in most American factory-made rifles. European rifles and shotguns made by custom riflesmiths and quality manufacturers usually had some degree of cast-off in the stock; that is, the stock was angled slightly to the right (for a right-handed shooter). Cast-off permitted the shooter to face the game and the rear of his gun more squarely. With cast-off, he could get behind his gun better than with an in-line stock. Cast-off is still built into many quality shotguns, but it is rare in hunting rifles.

With a fair amount of cast-off, say, half an inch or so measured from centerline of the bore, the shooter's face contact with the stock is less without a cheekpiece because he must align his eye with the sight. To compensate for this, the stock designer or custom stocker provides the shooter with a filler in the form of a cheekpiece.

If there is no cast-off, there is little need for a cheekpiece unless you have a very hollow cheek; yet it is used in many rifles that have no cast-off at all. Omitting the cheekpiece but retaining the Monte Carlo comb is one modern stock design.

Elevating the entire top line of the stock and making it perfectly level, or with only a slight slope, is a growing trend. One great advantage of the level comb is that no matter where along its length the shooter happens to apply his cheek, his eye has exactly the same relationship to the line of sight. Some shooters hold their heads fairly far back in calm moments when shooting targets, but when game is in view, nervous tension leads them to "crawl the stock" toward the receiver. If the comb is sharply sloped, the eye's height changes accordingly, and this makes accurate shooting more difficult. Topflight trap shooters are very aware of this, and many of them prefer guns with perfectly level combs.

ACHIEVING GOOD FIT

Of course, you can have a custom stocker make you a custom stock with a perfect fit. You will certainly spend a great deal of money in the process. Another solution is to replace the factory stock with one you carve yourself to a satisfactory fit, but that is time consuming and difficult if you aren't handy with wood tools. A third method is to alter the factory stock with add-ons or by cutting away some wood. For instance, if you have very short arms, you may find it advisable to shorten the stock a bit. This is usually quite easy to do. But if you go at a stock with wood tools, proceed cautiously. Take off only small amounts of wood until you approach, and finally reach, the correct dimension.

Actually, if you buy a well-designed straight-stocked rifle, you'll probably do quite well. Rifle-stock dimensions are not so critical as those for shotguns because the rifleman most often uses front and rear sights or a scope to aim precisely at a small distant target. A small amount of squirming, stretching, or squinching to get a good sight picture is really not much of a problem. Also, a hunting rifleman shoots in many different positions—offhand (standing), kneeling, sitting, squatting, prone, and others, depending on the circumstances.

Shotgunners almost always shoot while standing or while sitting down on a bench in a waterfowl blind, and positions do not differ much. The precision shotgunner, particularly the skeet and trap competitor, therefore finds it worthwhile to determine the perfect stock dimensions for his physique and shooting style.

A rifleman's case differs because of the many shooting positions he will inevitably assume. For instance, a short stock is good for prone shooting, but it would be too short for offhand shooting. "Perfect" fit in a rifle stock is really a compromise.

HOW TO SHOP AROUND

If you're just getting your feet wet, one way to determine the type of stock that will work best for you is to visit a gun shop that has a large number of used rifles in open racks. Go down the line, picking out rifles that are basically suited to your type of shooting. Shoulder each one in turn, sight on a mark, and swing left and right. Note the quickness with which the sights come to bear when you shoulder each piece. You'll be amazed at how good some guns feel and how impossible others feel.

If you belong to a gun club or some other shooting group, seize every opportunity to handle or shoot the rifles of other members. Don't make a pest of yourself, but try to investigage other stock conformations as much as you can. In a short while, you'll have a very good idea of what suits you best. Eventually, you may decide to have a custom stock made in order to achieve perfection, but remember that the dimensions of every rifle stock really embody a great deal of compromise.

Of course, there are many other stock dimensions

Factory stocks: The top stock is a plain factory item for hunters. The middle stock is a dolled-up Monte Carlo number with cheekpiece on either side and raised comb. Bottom is a target stock with enlarged forend for the sake of improved grip, though some hunters find this feature useful, too. Note the level comb of the target stock. No matter at what point one's cheek touches a level comb, one's eye is always at the same height. If comb height is properly adjusted, the eye will always be properly aligned with the scope or iron sights the moment that the rifle is mounted.

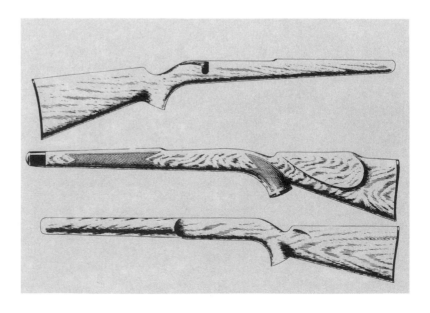

and configurations other than drop, comb height, and degree of cast-off (if any). The shooter will also be concerned with the curve of the pistol grip, the cross section of the forend, the curve of the buttplate, if any, the length of pull from the pistol grip to the trigger, and several other factors. In general, however, you'll find that most bolt-action, long-range hunting rifles that have a straight stock and a level comb usually have other dimensions that are quite satisfactory. For instance, no rifle designer in his right mind would give this type of hunting rifle a forend with a square cross section. That type of forend is hard to hold solidly and adds unnecessary weight to the rifle. The forend cross section should be rounded.

There is a general type that best suits the long-range rifle. It is often called the classic style, though it is very modern and not antique in any sense. Merely flipping through gun catalogs is enough to isolate the makes and models that embody this style.

ACCURACY AND THE STOCK

The previous sections have dealt with how well the stock fits you. How well the stock fits the rifle barrel and receiver is also important because wood-to-metal fit has an effect on shot-to-shot consistency, which is only another term for accuracy.

The traditional material for gunstocks is wood, and European and American walnut are preferred today, though early American gunsmiths often used hard maple (sugar maple) and wild black cherry, which are still employed by some custom stockers. Plainer woods, such as birch, beech, and sycamore, have been pressed into use for mass-produced guns as the price of decent walnut has risen. Some tropical hardwoods are used, and sometimes an American custom stocker has a go at myrtle or madrone. Believe it or not, a quite satisfactory gunstock can be made out of dense longleaf pine, but that wood does not lend itself to decorative staining or cut checkering. The primary need is for a wood that is light in weight, that can be carved or machined easily, and that responds well to staining to bring out the grain. No better stock wood has been found than walnut.

Checkering is the crosshatch pattern of grooves that forms raised diamonds on the forend and pistol grip. Its primary purpose is to provide a sure grip, particularly when the hands are sweaty, but well-done checkering is very attractive too. Good wood checkers easily, and that is another reason why walnut is preferred.

A lot of money is spent on fine wood for gunstocks for custom rifles. Thousands have been spent on a

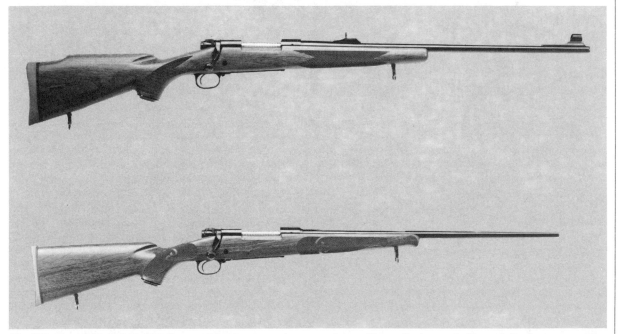

The Winchester Model 70 XTR Sporter Magnum, top, has a moderate Monte Carlo comb. Essentially the same action is used in the Winchester Model 70 XTR Featherweight, bottom. The top rifle weighs 7¾ pounds; the bottom rifle weighs 6¾ pounds, some of the weight saving made possible by the Featherweight's stock style, which is of the classic type with nearly level comb. The "Schnabel" (German for "beak") forend finial is a mark of current lightweight rifles, but it has little practical use, though some long-armed shooters do hold the rifle just behind the schnabel and claim that it makes for a steadier hold. Winchester offers many stock variations in its various models.

ONE MAKER'S BOLT-ACTION STOCKS

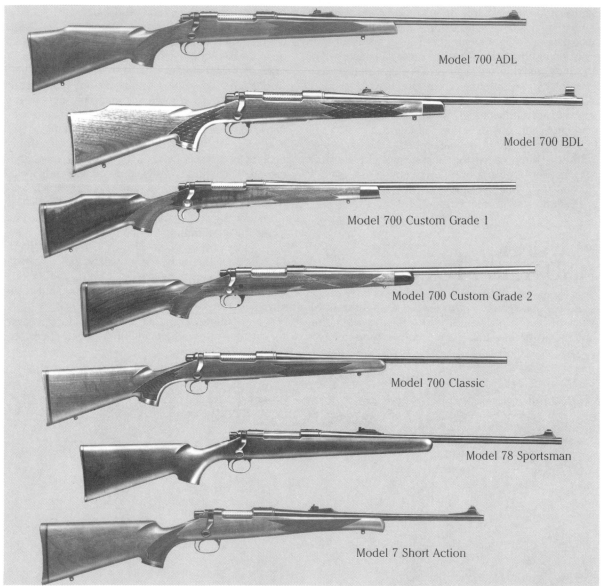

Model 700 ADL

Model 700 BDL

Model 700 Custom Grade 1

Model 700 Custom Grade 2

Model 700 Classic

Model 78 Sportsman

Model 7 Short Action

These Remington stocks are used on rifles that employ essentially the same action, usually designated the Model 700. From top to bottom, the M 700 ADL has moderate Monte Carlo without cheekpiece on the left side; M 700 BDL has plastic forend tip, much the same comb, and a cheekpiece. The next two rifles are Grade 1 and 2 M 700s turned out by Remington's Custom Shop. Remington Grade 3 and Grade 4 (not shown) custom rifles have even finer finishing and engraving. Practically any stock configuration known to man can be ordered from the Remington Custom Shop. The top custom rifle is the moderate Monte Carlo style; the Grade 2 is in the classic style, but with the addition of a plastic forend tip, without white line spacer, however. The M 700 Classic, next in
the lineup, is just that—classic—finely finished with excellent checkering but without Monte Carlo comb, cheekpiece, forend tip, and other showy features. This type of stock is gaining in popularity. The M 79 Sportsman (actually an M 700 action) has a very plain stock without checkering, intended to keep the price down. But note that the lines of the stock are actually much the same as the lines of the Classic. The Model 7 Short Action has a shortened Model 700 action intended for cartridges of moderate length such as the .308 Winchester. Moderate cartridge length helps to reduce the overall length and weight of the rifle. Stock is really of the classic type but the schnabel forend finial indicates it is a lightweight, in this case only 6¼ pounds.

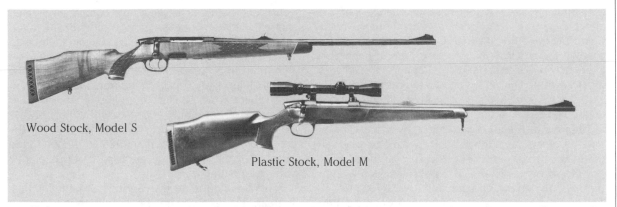

Wood Stock, Model S

Plastic Stock, Model M

Both of these rifles are made by Steyr-Daimler-Puch, an Austrian company known for quality arms. Both employ essentially the same action, though the Model S (top) is shown with double set triggers and the bottom rifle, a Model M, has a single trigger. The top stock is wood, however, and the bottom stock is made of special, very strong plastic. It has been colored and grained to look as much like wood as possible. The plastic stock reduces weight of the rifle by about 1¼ pounds. Note the extreme curvature of the pistol grip, needed to keep the rifle from rising excessively during recoil when very powerful magnum cartridges are used. Plastic stocks are impervious to moisture. Thus swelling, shrinking, and warping do not occur, which greatly enhances a rifle's ability to retain its zero.

single superb European walnut blank that showed exceptional figured grain and color, but a perfectly satisfactory stock can be made out of almost any fairly hard, lightweight wood. The "worst" effect of using an "inferior" wood is that the checkering cannot be cut so fine. But that's a small defect. The overall stock configuration and the wood-to-metal fit are much more important.

To inlet a stock, a craftsman carefully cuts away wood to let the rifle receiver and barrel into the stock blank. He also drills holes for the guard screws that attach the stock to the rifle and provides slots through which the magazine and trigger project downward. In a bolt-action rifle, the stock is a one-piece affair, and to achieve a close fit, the stocker must work with different dimensions at the same time. It's a very difficult task, and few handcraftsmen attain real proficiency.

Factory stocks are inletted by machines, and the millwright who sets up the machines for this task usually works from a master hand-carved stock. Some factory stocks are so accurately inletted that they are superior in this respect to many stocks turned out by custom stockers who have not quite mastered the difficult inletting chore.

Here again, the concern is mostly with bolt-action rifles and their one-piece stocks. The two-piece stocks used on most lever-action, semi-automatic, pump, and single-shot rifles are much easier to fit. The buttstock is commonly held in place by a massive throughbolt, and the forend attaches easily with screws or a latch. Because there are two separate units, dimensioning of the wood by hand or machine is much easier than it is with a one-piece stock. If the inletting is close, however, a one-piece stock is more rigid and this enhances accuracy.

Warping and vibration. The use of wood for gunstocks poses several problems. First, since wood is a natural material its characteristics vary greatly from piece to piece. Even if two stock blanks are taken from one tree, density may vary and this results in varying degrees of moisture absorption. No matter how much waterproof finish is applied to a wooden gunstock, it does absorb at least a little moisture. Dimensions change as it swells and warps, and again as it dries.

Varying temperature can also warp a gunstock enough to set up stresses that actually force the barrel to move, thus changing the point of impact. A rifle sighted-in at sea level in a damp climate may be quite far off if it is suddenly taken to a high, cool place where there is little moisture in the air. When returned to the place where the rifle was sighted-in, the stock almost always returns to its original dimensions and configuration. Dimensional alterations in the stock are the principal reasons why a rifle should be checked for zero by firing after a long trip to a different location. You're asking for a miss if you don't do it.

A rifle barrel vibrates a great deal when a shot is fired, and much of this vibration takes place before the bullet exits the barrel. The barrel may be pointing slightly upward, downward, or to one side when the bullet exits the muzzle. As long as this vibration does not vary much from shot to shot, the shooter is usually quite unconscious of it and does not need to worry about it. Sighting-in the rifle automatically assures that the rifle will shoot to much the same point as long as the same cartridge is used and some other condition does not change the angle of departure.

But other conditions *do* change, and the most important one is usually pressure from the wooden stock on the rifle barrel. If, for instance, the stock absorbs moisture and warps, barrel vibration changes and angle of departure changes too. As a rifle barrel heats up during rapid fire, it expands and exerts more pressure on the stock. This increased pressure can also alter angle of departure and point of impact in relation to the sights. This is a very good reason for firing slowly when you are sighting-in. Many other variations occur as a result of the use of wood in gunstocks.

The primary means of preventing stock-barrel problems is close metal-to-wood fit in the first place. If the fit is good, there is less tendency for the point of impact to move. Tight guard screws, and a tight throughbolt and forend latch are also very important. The less the barrel and receiver can move, the better.

Adjusting the fit. Some rifles throw extremely large groups, and checking the tightness of the screws or latch is usually the first step in curing the trouble. If this does not work, remove the barrel and receiver from the stock and check for dark areas where they have worked unevenly against the wood. These areas become easier to recognize as continued wear creates more distinct marks on the wood surface. Sometimes removal of very thin layer of wood with sandpaper fixes the problem. In other situations, a plastic shim is needed. For instance, if a rub is evident on one side of the barrel channel, a plastic shim inserted between the barrel and wood on the other side may equalize the pressure and tighten your groups.

This sort of adjustment can also be done if the receiver is not contacting the wood equally on all surfaces. It's a delicate operation, and its best to try shims first. Resort to wood removal only if the shim does not work.

A shim in the bottom of the barrel channel near the tip of the forend pushes the barrel upward slightly and also evens other pressures. Sometimes, this simple alteration markedly improves accuracy. Plastic credit cards provide hard but flexible material for shims. Take the barrel and receiver out of the stock, insert the shim, and then tighten up on the guard screws or other holdfasts. But don't be surprised if the shim makes the trouble worse. Considerable fiddling around is often needed to effect a cure.

A complete seal against moisture is impossible, but good "waterproof" finishes help a great deal. Refinish promptly if the finish wears away or is damaged. Surprisingly, many factories apply waterproof finish to the outside surfaces of the stock, but do little to waterproof the barrel channel and receiver inletting. If this is the case with your rifle, apply several coats of waterproof finish to interior surfaces. Allow each coat to dry and sandpaper lightly before applying the next coat so that each adheres firmly to the one beneath it.

Free-floating and glass bedding. If shot-to-shot consistency is not achieved by the comparatively mild methods, some shooters resort to more drastic alterations. One is to cut out the barrel channel a bit with inletting tools (gouges and rasps) and sandpaper so that there is no contact between the barrel and the wood whatsoever. This is called free-floating the barrel. If there is no contact, a migrating stock cannot affect barrel vibrations, and they will almost always be the same from shot to shot. This solution to the problem is employed by many target shooters, and target rifles and varmint rigs are often factory-equipped with free-floating barrels.

A hunter should be very cautious about trying this. If a barrel is correctly free-floated, there is a gap, no matter how tiny, between the barrel and the wood. Water can enter this gap, and the results can be disastrous. If the temperature goes below freezing, the water freezes and expands, thus applying considerable pressure on the barrel with resultant alterations in point of impact. If the gap is wide enough (as it often is), all sorts of dust and debris can get in and exert pressure on the barrel.

The best way to prevent this sort of thing is to work a good-quality furniture wax into the gap. Even with a rifle that has not been free-floated, working a quality wood wax into the crevice between barrel and stock is a good idea. Once in a while, remove the barrel and action from the stock and clean the inletting to prevent a build-up of trouble-causing debris.

The fit of the stock should be square and accurate in order to prevent movement and shot-to-shot variation. Again, looking for non-symmetrical rubs is one way to get a clue to movement and its direction. After you have located trouble, delicate wood removal or a shim may provide a cure. If not, many rifle owners resort to glass bedding.

First, the inletting of the receiver and barrel is uniformly enlarged by a small amount with inletting tools, and then the cavity is coated with liquid epoxy. The receiver and barrel are coated with a release agent that prevents a bond between the metal and the epoxy. Then the barreled action is replaced in the stock, and the guard screws are tightened. After the plastic hardens, the barreled action can still be easily removed from the stock in the normal fashion. If the trouble is caused only by barrel contact, bed the barrel in glass and leave the receiver alone. "Glass-bedding" kits with directions are readily available. Theoretically at least, glass bedding provides a new surface that is molded precisely to the shape of the metal. Sometimes it cures wandering zeros, but not always. Target shooters and varmint hunters often employ this method, but few big-game hunters ever find it necessary.

If all else fails and the trouble is definitely caused by an ill-fitting stock, you might try ordering a new stock from the factory or a semifinished inletted stock from one of the many suppliers.

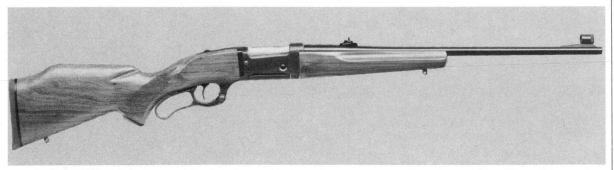

Savage Model 99-C has the two-piece stock used in most lever, pump, and semi-auto rifles. The rifle's receiver separates the forend and buttstock. The buttstock is usually held in place with a massive through bolt that screws into the rear of the receiver. Two-part stocks are often said to be inherently less accurate than the more-rigid one-piece stocks of bolt-action rifles, but some of these guns will surprise you with the tightness of their groups. This Savage lever gun is somewhat unusual in that it has a Monte Carlo stock. Most two-part stocks have traditionally styled straight combs, sloped down to the rear (some excessively) and no cheekpiece.

Resort to alterations last. All these methods of enhancing accuracy should be approached with caution. Don't try them unless you have searched for other, more easily cured defects, such as loose guard screws, loose scope mounts or iron sights, a jerky trigger pull on your part, a case of unconscious flinching, or other troubles. Many a riflestock has been butchered when the accuracy problem was really a defect in the shooter. If you're in doubt about this, try to get an experienced marksman to shoot several five-shot groups from a bench rest with your rifle. If he can get markedly smaller groups than you do, work on your shooting rather than your rifle.

If you are not skilled with tools, don't attempt to alter the inletting of your rifle in any way. Go to a good gunsmith and explain the trouble. He may be able to make tiny alterations that cure your accuracy problems.

Acceptable accuracy. It's also good not to be too demanding about the accuracy of a big-game rifle. If a bolt-action big-game rifle fired from a bench rest produces five-shot groups that measure 2½ inches or a bit less at 100 yards, you're getting about as much as you paid for in that rifle. A 3½-inch group at the same range is just fine for most semi-automatics and pumps. With most lever actions, 4 inches is really quite good.

Big-game rifles are not intended for match shooting or long-distance varmint hunting. It's best to go out and buy specialized rifles for those sports if you want to pursue them seriously. Some out-of-the-box hunting rifles do considerably better than the figures given here, but they are rare. If you are lucky enough to have one, think a long, long time before you make any alterations. The best course is usually to make every effort to preserve that accuracy through good maintenance.

PLASTIC STOCKS

Plastic stocks have been in use among those super-accuracy enthusiasts, the bench-rest shooters, for many years. In fact, in some bench-rest matches, wooden stocks are entirely absent from the firing line. A plastic stock is impervious to moisture and does not change enough dimensionally to influence accuracy, no matter how conditions vary. But many shooters appreciate the beauty of wood so much that they reject the idea of plastic automatically.

Besides dimensional stability, plastic stocks can provide a marked reduction in weight, if that is what you need. Hunters of mountain game find that they can take a pound or more off the total weight of their rifles, and that is very important if you must climb a great deal or go long distances on foot. Older people and those who are not so robust also find that these lightweight plastic stocks are a blessing.

Several companies, including Weatherby and Steyr-Daimler-Puch (Austrian makers of modern Mannlicher rifles), now each offer one model apiece that is factory-equipped with plastic stocks. Several custom stockers will make a plastic stock for your rifle, but the cost is high. Accuracy Products, of Wonder Lake, Illinois, offers "drop-in" plastic stocks for a variety of popular rifle models. These stocks are completely inletted. They are simply attached to the barrel action by tightening the guard screws. The company provides a list of rifles for which these stocks are available.

If you can live with the plain, dull finish of one of these plastic stocks (some are painted in camouflage colors), you can solve weight and some accuracy problems. But plastic poses one possible hazard—the rifle may be too light. If you get down to 6 or 6 ½ pounds with a big-bore hunting rifle, you may experience unacceptably heavy recoil, and this is one of

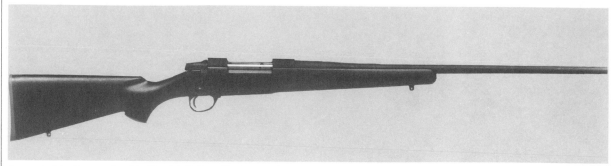

Imported by Stoeger's, this Finnish Sako rifle has a plastic stock, but its shape is of a traditional type. The rifle weighs a hair over 7 pounds, on average, about a pound lighter than its wood-stocked counterpart. This rifle is made in calibers up to and including the .338 Winchester Magnum and the .375 H&H Magnum. But you'll need to hang onto your rifle if you fire these powerful cartridges in this lightweight Sako.

the greatest enemies of accuracy. The pounding soon makes the shooter afraid to fire. He may not even be aware of it; nevertheless, he flinches just before the rifle fires, and that can cause wild misses.

With some plastic stocks, it is possible to add a bit of weight. Simply drill a hole in the butt of the stock and add lead shot, or even a lead bar cushioned with cloth. Add the weight a little at a time until you find the optimum amount, and then seal the hole with two-part epoxy or a buttplate. This, of course, shifts the balance point of the rifle to the rear and could itself cause problems. You pay your money and you make your choice. But if you add so much weight that the rifle weighs just as much as it did with the wooden stock, you have wasted your money.

Plastic stocks are quite durable; the military now uses them and the plastic stock of the U.S. M-16 is almost indestructible. Very early plastic stocks tended to crack or shatter, particularly in cold weather, but the problem has been solved through improved plastics.

Laminated wood stocks are more dimensionally stable than the standard wooden stocks, and are used in many target rifles and some varmint rifles. Just as good plywood resists warping better than a plank, each ply of wood in a laminated stock works against adjacent plies during expansion and contraction. Two different woods are usually used in alternate plies in this type of stock. Thus the tendency to warp is at least partially dampened by the tension set up between the different layers. These rifle stocks are even heavier than ordinary wood stocks, however, because of the large amount of adhesive between layers. One sometimes encounters a big-game rifle with a laminated stock, but they are usually custom jobs. A plastic stock would be a better solution.

CORRECT CARTRIDGE AND RIFLE

Which came first, the chicken or the egg? This old quandary has some bearing on firearms. Which comes first when buying a rifle, the cartridge or the rifle?

If you're wedded to a certain type of rifle, say a lever action, you have only a few cartridges to choose from. The choice for a pump action rifle is even more limited, since only the Remington pump is still in production. With semi-autos the list is longer, and with bolt-action rifles the choice is very wide.

If you have no strong feelings about the type of rifle you want to buy, it's a good idea to first consider all the available cartridges and then choose a rifle to fire the one you select. In the process a great deal of useful knowledge comes to light.

ENERGY

Many authorities agree that a minimum of 1,200 foot-pounds of energy on target is needed to kill deer effectively with one shot. A foot-pound is loosely defined as the amount of work done to lift a 1 pound weight 1 foot in the air or, conversely, the amount of energy developed by a 1 pound weight dropping 1 foot. Of course, deer are often killed by those who use firearms with much less energy than 1,200 foot-pounds, but these kills are most often made by lucky accident or at very short range where perfect bullet placement is possible. For effective kills, you need 1,200 foot-pounds of energy, and some cartridges don't develop that much power at the *muzzle,* much less on target. It's important not to opt for one of these weakling cartridges, but many hunters do so, particularly when buying a secondhand rifle. At the other end of the scale, some cartridges develop more energy than is needed for deer hunting, and if you hit a deer with one of these loads, you may destroy as much as one-fourth of the edible meat, sometimes more. A fast-moving, heavy bullet often shatters bones and the splinters turn the meat into bloody fragments.

On upcoming pages, you'll find the table "Ballistics of Popular Cartridges," reproduced from the Remington Arms catalog. It lists almost all the rifle cartridges manufactured in the United States. It includes many cartridges that were originated by other companies, such as Winchester and Savage Arms, and several that

were designed by U.S. Army ordnance engineers. The Remington table was chosen because it provides a great deal of useful information. For instance, the table includes information on bullet flight out to 500 yards and also lists remaining energy out to that range.

The following discussion is intended to give the reader a basis for evaluating cartridges for deer hunting. Every manufacturer's cartridge catalog changes from year to year as new loads appear and others are dropped. The important thing is to develop a standard of judgment that will work even if the load in question is not listed in the ballistics tables.

THE VARMINT LOADS

Several rifle cartridges were developed with varmint hunting in mind and should never be used for deer hunting. Among these are the .17 Remington, .22 Hornet, .222 Remington, .222 Remington Magnum, .223 Remington, .22/250 Remington. The .17 Remington is the only current factory cartridge with a bullet diameter of less than .223. All of these cartridges are loaded with bullets that weigh 55 grains or less. Because of their lack of mass and their small diameter, they do not develop sufficient energy for deer hunting, even though velocity may be very great. They are just too small to be effective on deer.

Most of the bullets for these cartridges have very thin jackets and are designed to expand readily in small animals such as woodchucks, marmots, and even crows. They often expand or blow up immediately on impacting anything more solid. These bullets are also preferred by varmint hunters because they fragment readily when they hit twigs, hard earth, or rock. This reduces the possibility of a dangerous ricochet.

One load for the .223 Remington, however, has a "metal case" bullet, which is used for target shooting, not for deer hunting. It does not expand at all. One varmint load listed here—the .22/250 Remington—does have an expanding bullet and does develop over 1,200 foot-pounds of energy at 100 yards. This load would undoubtedly be adequate for deer out to 100 yards in the hands of a skilled shooter, but it should not be used for deer hunting. At best, it is barely ad-

BALLISTICS OF POPULAR CARTRIDGES
(REMINGTON)
(Approximately actual size)

.17 Remington

.22 Hornet

.222 Remington

.222 Remington Magnum

.223 Remington (5.56mm)

.22–250 Remington

Remington Ballistics

CALIBERS	REMINGTON Order No.	BULLET Wt.-Grs.	BULLET Style	Primer No.	VELOCITY FEET PER SECOND Muzzle	100 Yds.	200 Yds.	300 Yds.	400 Yds.	50 Yd
17 REM.	R17REM	25*	Hollow Point Power-Lokt®	7½	4040	3284	2644	2086	1606	12
22 HORNET	R22HN1	45*	Pointed Soft Point	6½	2690	2042	1502	1128	948	8
	R22HN2	45	Hollow Point	6½	2690	2042	1502	1128	948	8
222 REM.	R222R1	50	Pointed Soft Point	7½	3140	2602	2123	1700	1350	11
	R222R3	50*	Hollow Point Power-Lokt	7½	3140	2635	2182	1777	1432	11
	R222R4	55	Metal Case	7½	3020	2562	2147	1773	1451	12
222 REM. MAG.	R222M1	55*	Pointed Soft Point	7½	3240	2748	2305	1906	1556	12
	R222M2	55	Hollow Point Power-Lokt	7½	3240	2773	2352	1969	1627	13
223 REM.	R223R1	55	Pointed Soft Point	7½	3240	2747	2304	1905	1554	12
	R223R2	55*	Hollow Point Power-Lokt	7½	3240	2773	2352	1969	1627	13
	R223R3	55	Metal Case	7½	3240	2759	2326	1933	1587	13
22-250 REM.	R22501	55*	Pointed Soft Point	9½	3680	3137	2656	2222	1832	14
	R22502	55	Hollow Point Power-Lokt	9½	3680	3209	2785	2400	2046	17
243 WIN.	R243W1	80	Pointed Soft Point	9½	3350	2955	2593	2259	1951	16
	R243W2	80*	Hollow Point Power-Lokt	9½	3350	2955	2593	2259	1951	16
	R243W3	100	Pointed Soft Point Core-Lokt®	9½	2960	2697	2449	2215	1993	17
6mm REM.	R6MM1	80**	Pointed Soft Point	9½	3470	3064	2694	2352	2036	17
	R6MM2	80**	Hollow Point Power-Lokt	9½	3470	3064	2694	2352	2036	17
	R6MM4	100**	Pointed Soft Point Core-Lokt	9½	3100	2829	2573	2332	2104	18
25-20 WIN.	R25202	86*	Soft Point	6½	1460	1194	1030	931	858	7
250 SAV.	R250SV	100*	Pointed Soft Point	9½	2820	2504	2210	1936	1684	14
257 ROBERTS	R257	117*	Soft Point Core-Lokt	9½	2650	2291	1961	1663	1404	11
25-06 REM.	R25061	87	Hollow Point Power-Lokt	9½	3440	2995	2591	2222	1884	15
	R25062	100*	Pointed Soft Point Core-Lokt	9½	3230	2893	2580	2287	2014	17
	K25063	120	Pointed Soft Point Core-Lokt	9½	2990	2730	2484	2252	2032	18
6.5mm REM. MAG.	R65MM2	120*	Pointed Soft Point Core-Lokt	9½M	3210	2905	2621	2353	2102	18
264 WIN. MAG	R264W2	140*	Pointed Soft Point Core-Lokt	9½M	3030	2782	2548	2326	2114	19

*Illustrated (not shown actual size).
**Interchangeable in 244 Rem.

.243 Winchester

6mm Remington

.25-20 Winchester

.250 Savage

.257 Roberts

.25-06 Remington

6.5mm Remington Magnum

.264 Winchester Magnum

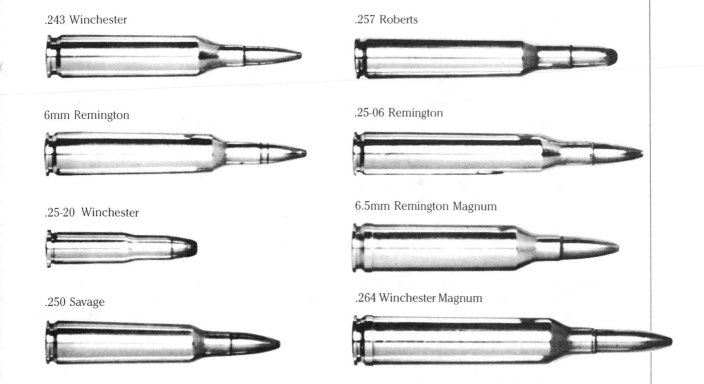

									TRAJECTORY†		0.0 Indicates yardage at which rifle was sighted in.									
							SHORT RANGE Bullet does not rise more than one inch above line of sight from muzzle to sighting-in range.						**LONG RANGE** Bullet does not rise more than three inches above line of sight from muzzle to sighting-in range.							
		ENERGY FOOT-POUNDS																		
Muzzle	100 Yds.	200 Yds.	300 Yds.	400 Yds.	500 Yds.	50 Yds.	100 Yds.	150 Yds.	200 Yds.	250 Yds.	300 Yds.	100 Yds.	150 Yds.	200 Yds.	250 Yds.	300 Yds.	400 Yds.	500 Yds.		
906	599	388	242	143	85	0.1	0.5	0.0	−1.5	−4.2	−8.5	2.1	2.5	1.9	0.0	−3.4	−17.0	−44.3	24″	
723	417	225	127	90	70	0.3	0.0	−2.4	−7.7	−16.9	−31.3	1.6	0.0	−4.5	−12.8	−26.4	−75.6	−163.4	24″	
723	417	225	127	90	70	0.3	0.0	−2.4	−7.7	−16.9	−31.3	1.6	0.0	−4.5	−12.8	−26.4	−75.6	−163.4		
1094	752	500	321	202	136	0.5	0.9	0.0	−2.5	−6.9	−13.7	2.2	1.9	0.0	−3.8	−10.0	−32.3	−73.8		
1094	771	529	351	228	152	0.5	0.9	0.0	−2.4	−6.6	−13.1	2.1	1.8	0.0	−3.6	−9.5	−30.2	−68.1	24″	
1114	801	563	384	257	176	0.6	1.0	0.0	−2.5	−7.0	−13.7	2.2	1.9	0.0	−3.8	−9.9	−31.0	−68.7		
1282	922	649	444	296	198	0.4	0.8	0.0	−2.2	−6.0	−11.8	1.9	1.6	0.0	−3.3	−8.5	−26.7	−59.5		
1282	939	675	473	323	220	0.4	0.8	0.0	−2.1	−5.8	−11.4	1.8	1.6	0.0	−3.2	−8.2	−25.5	−56.0	24″	
1282	921	648	443	295	197	0.4	0.8	0.0	−2.2	−6.0	−11.8	1.9	1.6	0.0	−3.3	−8.5	−26.7	−59.6		
1282	939	675	473	323	220	0.4	0.8	0.0	−2.1	−5.8	−11.4	1.8	1.6	0.0	−3.2	−8.2	−25.5	−56.0	24″	
1282	929	660	456	307	207	0.4	0.8	0.0	−2.1	−5.9	−11.6	1.9	1.6	0.0	−3.2	−8.4	−26.2	−57.9		
1654	1201	861	603	410	272	0.2	0.5	0.0	−1.6	−4.4	−8.7	2.3	2.6	1.9	0.0	−3.4	−15.9	−38.9		
1654	1257	947	703	511	363	0.2	0.5	0.0	−1.5	−4.1	−8.0	2.1	2.5	1.8	0.0	−3.1	−14.1	−33.4	24″	
1993	1551	1194	906	676	495	0.3	0.7	0.0	−1.8	−4.9	−9.4	2.6	2.9	2.1	0.0	−3.6	−16.2	−37.9		
1993	1551	1194	906	676	495	0.3	0.7	0.0	−1.8	−4.9	−9.4	2.6	2.9	2.1	0.0	−3.6	−16.2	−37.9	24″	
1945	1615	1332	1089	882	708	0.5	0.9	0.0	−2.2	−5.8	−11.0	1.9	1.6	0.0	−3.1	−7.8	−22.6	−46.3		
2139	1667	1289	982	736	542	0.3	0.6	0.0	−1.6	−4.5	−8.7	2.4	2.7	1.9	0.0	−3.3	−14.9	−35.0		
2139	1667	1289	982	736	542	0.3	0.6	0.0	−1.6	−4.5	−8.7	2.4	2.7	1.9	0.0	−3.3	−14.9	−35.0	24″	
2133	1777	1470	1207	983	792	0.4	0.8	0.0	−1.9	−5.2	−9.9	1.7	1.5	0.0	−2.8	−7.0	−20.4	−41.7		
407	272	203	165	141	121	0.0	−4.1	−14.4	−31.8	−57.3	−92.0	0.0	−8.2	−23.5	−47.0	−79.6	−175.9	−319.4	24″	
1765	1392	1084	832	630	474	0.2	0.0	−1.6	−4.7	−9.6	−16.5	2.3	2.0	0.0	−3.7	−9.5	−28.3	−59.5	24″	
1824	1363	999	718	512	373	0.3	0.0	−1.9	−5.8	−11.9	−20.7	2.9	2.4	0.0	−4.7	−12.0	−36.7	−79.2	24″	
2286	1733	1297	954	686	484	0.3	0.6	0.0	−1.7	−4.8	−9.3	2.5	2.9	2.1	0.0	−3.6	−16.4	−39.1		
2316	1858	1478	1161	901	689	0.4	0.7	0.0	−1.9	−5.0	−9.7	1.6	1.4	0.0	−2.7	−6.9	−20.5	−42.7	24″	
2382	1985	1644	1351	1100	887	0.5	0.8	0.0	−2.1	−5.6	−10.7	1.9	1.6	0.0	−3.0	−7.5	−22.0	−44.8		
2745	2248	1830	1475	1177	929	0.4	0.7	0.0	−1.8	−4.9	−9.5	2.7	3.0	2.1	0.0	−3.5	−15.5	−35.3	24″	
2854	2406	2018	1682	1389	1139	0.5	0.8	0.0	−2.0	−5.4	−10.2	1.8	1.5	0.0	−2.9	−7.2	−20.8	−42.2	24″	

†Inches above or below line of sight. Hold low for positive
numbers, high for negative numbers.

(Continued on next page)

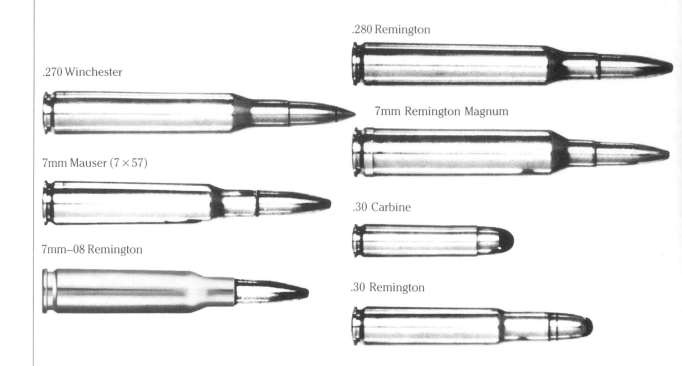

.280 Remington

.270 Winchester

7mm Remington Magnum

7mm Mauser (7×57)

.30 Carbine

7mm–08 Remington

.30 Remington

Remington Ballistics (continued)

CALIBERS	REMINGTON Order No.	Wt.-Grs.	Style	Primer No.	Muzzle	100 Yds.	200 Yds.	300 Yds.	400 Yds.	500 Yds
270 WIN.	R270W1	100	Pointed Soft Point	9½	3430	3021	2649	2305	1988	169
	R270W2	130*	Pointed Soft Point Core-Lokt	9½	3060	2776	2510	2259	2022	180
	R270W3	130	Bronze Point	9½	3060	2802	2559	2329	2110	190
	R270W4	150	Soft Point Core-Lokt	9½	2850	2504	2183	1886	1618	138
7mm MAUSER	R7MSR1	140*	Pointed Soft Point	9½	2660	2435	2221	2018	1827	164
7mm-08 REM.	R7M081	140*	Pointed Soft Point	9½	2860	2625	2402	2189	1988	179
280 REM.††	R280R1	150*	Pointed Soft Point Core-Lokt	9½	2970	2699	2444	2203	1975	176
	R280R2	165*	Soft Point Core-Lokt	9½	2820	2510	2220	1950	1701	147
7mm REM. MAG.	R7MM2	150*	Pointed Soft Point Core-Lokt	9½M	3110	2830	2568	2320	2085	186
	R7MM3	175	Pointed Soft Point Core-Lokt	9½M	2860	2645	2440	2244	2057	187
30 CARBINE	R30CAR	110*	Soft Point	6½	1990	1567	1236	1035	923	84
30 REM.	R30REM	170*	Soft Point Core-Lokt	9½	2120	1822	1555	1328	1153	103
30-30 WIN. "ACCELERATOR"	R3030A	55*	Soft Point	9½	3400	2693	2085	1570	1187	98
30-30 WIN.	R30301	150*	Soft Point Core-Lokt	9½	2390	1973	1605	1303	1095	97
	R30302	170	Soft Point Core-Lokt	9½	2200	1895	1619	1381	1191	106
	R30303	170	Hollow Point Core-Lokt	9½	2200	1895	1619	1381	1191	106
300 SAVAGE	R30SV3	180	Soft Point Core-Lokt	9½	2350	2025	1728	1467	1252	109
	R30SV4	180*	Pointed Soft Point Core-Lokt	9½	2350	2137	1935	1745	1570	141
30-40 KRAG	R30402	180*	Pointed Soft Point Core-Lokt	9½	2430	2213	2007	1813	1632	146
308 WIN. "ACCELERATOR"	R308W5	55*	Pointed Soft Point	9½	3770	3215	2726	2286	1888	154
308 WIN.	R308W1	150*	Pointed Soft Point Core-Lokt	9½	2820	2533	2263	2009	1774	156
	R308W2	180	Soft Point Core-Lokt	9½	2620	2274	1955	1666	1414	121
	R308W3	180	Pointed Soft Point Core-Lokt	9½	2620	2393	2178	1974	1782	160
30-06 "ACCELERATOR"	R30069	55*	Pointed Soft Point	9½	4080	3485	2965	2502	2083	170
30-06 SPRINGFIELD	R30061	125	Pointed Soft Point	9½	3140	2780	2447	2138	1853	159
	R30062	150	Pointed Soft Point Core-Lokt	9½	2910	2617	2342	2083	1843	162
	R30063	150	Bronze Point	9½	2910	2656	2416	2189	1974	177
	R3006B	165*	Pointed Soft Point Core-Lokt	9½	2800	2534	2283	2047	1825	162
	R30064	180	Soft Point Core-Lokt	9½	2700	2348	2023	1727	1466	125
	R30065	180	Pointed Soft Point Core-Lokt	9½	2700	2469	2250	2042	1846	166
	R30066	180	Bronze Point	9½	2700	2485	2280	2084	1899	172
	R30067	220	Soft Point Core-Lokt	9½	2410	2130	1870	1632	1422	124

††280 Rem. and 7mm Express Rem. are interchangeable.
*Illustrated (not shown actual size).

.30-30 Winchester "Accelerator"   .308 Winchester "Accelerator"

.30-30 Winchester   .308 Winchester

.30-40 Krag   .30-06 "Accelerator"

.300 Savage   .30-06 Springfield

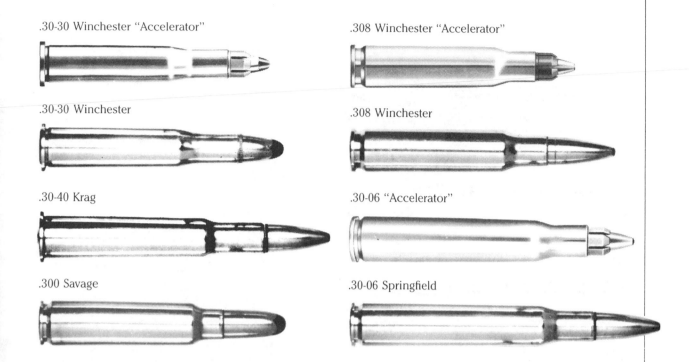

| ENERGY FOOT-POUNDS | | | | | | TRAJECTORY† 0.0 Indicates yardage at which rifle was sighted in. | | | | | | | | | | | | | |
| | | | | | | SHORT RANGE Bullet does not rise more than one inch above line of sight from muzzle to sighting-in range. | | | | | | LONG RANGE Bullet does not rise more than three inches above line of sight from muzzle to sighting-in range. | | | | | | | |
Muzzle	100 Yds.	200 Yds.	300 Yds.	400 Yds.	500 Yds.	50 Yds.	100 Yds.	150 Yds.	200 Yds.	250 Yds.	300 Yds.	100 Yds.	150 Yds.	200 Yds.	250 Yds.	300 Yds.	400 Yds.	500 Yds.	
2612	2027	1557	1179	877	641	0.3	0.6	0.0	-1.7	-4.6	-9.0	2.5	2.8	2.0	0.0	-3.4	-15.5	-36.4	
2702	2225	1818	1472	1180	936	0.5	0.8	0.0	-2.0	-5.5	-10.4	1.8	1.5	0.0	-2.9	-7.4	-21.6	-44.3	24″
2702	2267	1890	1565	1285	1046	0.4	0.8	0.0	-2.0	-5.3	-10.1	1.8	1.5	0.0	-2.8	-7.1	-20.6	-42.0	
2705	2087	1587	1185	872	639	0.7	1.0	0.0	-2.6	-7.1	-13.6	2.3	2.0	0.0	-3.8	-9.7	-29.2	-62.2	
2199	1843	1533	1266	1037	844	0.2	0.0	-1.7	-5.0	-10.0	-17.0	2.5	2.0	0.0	-3.8	-9.6	-27.7	-56.3	24″
2542	2142	1793	1490	1228	1005	0.6	0.9	0.0	-2.3	-6.1	-11.5	2.1	1.7	0.0	-3.2	-8 1	-23.5	-47.7	24″
2937	2426	1989	1616	1299	1035	0.5	0.9	0.0	-2.2	-5.8	-11.0	1.9	1.6	0.0	-3.1	-7.8	-22.8	-46.7	
2913	2308	1805	1393	1060	801	0.2	0.0	-1.5	-4.6	-9.5	-16.4	2.3	1.9	0.0	-3.7	-9.4	-28.1	-58.8	24″
3221	2667	2196	1792	1448	1160	0.4	0.8	0.0	-1.9	-5.2	-9.9	1.7	1.5	0.0	-2.8	-7.0	-20.5	-42.1	
3178	2718	2313	1956	1644	1372	0.6	0.9	0.0	-2.3	-6.0	-11.3	2.0	1.7	0.0	-3.2	-7.9	-22.7	-45.8	24″
967	600	373	262	208	173	0.9	0.0	-4.5	-13.5	-28.3	-49.9	0.0	-4.5	-13.5	-28.3	-49.9	-118.6	-228.2	20″
1696	1253	913	666	502	405	0.7	0.0	-3.3	-9.7	-19.6	-33.8	2.2	0.0	-5.3	-14.1	-27.2	-69.0	-136.9	24″
1412	886	521	301	172	119	0.4	0.0	-2.4	-6.7	-13.8		2.0	1.8	0.0	-3.8	-10.2	-35.0	-84.4	24″
1902	1296	858	565	399	316	0.5	0.0	-2.7	-8.2	-17.0	-30.0	1.8	0.0	-4.6	-12.5	-24.6	-65.3	-134.9	
1827	1355	989	720	535	425	0.6	0.0	-3.0	-8.9	-18.0	-31.1	2.0	0.0	-4.8	-13.0	-25.1	-63.6	-126.7	24″
1827	1355	989	720	535	425	0.6	0.0	-3.0	-8.9	-18.0	-31.1	2.0	0.0	-4.8	-13.0	-25.1	-63.6	-126.7	
2207	1639	1193	860	626	482	0.5	0.0	-2.6	-7.7	-15.6	-27.1	1.7	0.0	-4.2	-11.3	-21.9	-55.8	-112.0	
2207	1825	1496	1217	985	798	0.4	0.0	-2.3	-6.7	-13.5	-22.8	1.5	0.0	-3.6	-9.6	-18.2	-44.1	-84.2	24″
2360	1957	1610	1314	1064	861	0.4	0.0	-2.1	-6.2	-12.5	-21.1	1.4	0.0	-3.4	-8.9	-16.8	-40.9	-78.1	24″
1735	1262	907	638	435	290	0.2	0.5	0.0	-1.5	-4.2	-8.2	2.2	2.5	1.8	0.0	-3.2	-15.0	-36.7	24″
2648	2137	1705	1344	1048	810	0.2	0.0	-1.5	-4.5	-9.3	-15.9	2.3	1.9	0.0	-3.6	-9.1	-26.6	-55.7	
2743	2066	1527	1109	799	587	0.3	0.0	-2.0	-5.9	-12.1	-20.9	2.9	2.4	0.0	-4.7	-12.1	-36.9	-79.1	24″
2743	2288	1896	1557	1269	1028	0.2	0.0	-1.8	-5.2	-10.4	-17.7	2.6	2.1	0.0	-4.0	-9.9	-28.9	-58.8	
2033	1483	1074	764	530	356	0.4	1.0	0.9	0.0	-1.9	-5.0	1.8	2.1	1.5	0.0	-2.7	-12.5	-30.5	24″
2736	2145	1662	1269	953	706	0.4	0.8	0.0	-2.1	-5.6	-10.7	1.8	1.5	0.0	-3.0	-7.7	-23.0	-48.5	
2820	2281	1827	1445	1131	876	0.6	0.9	0.0	-2.3	-6.3	-12.0	2.1	1.8	0.0	-3.3	-8.5	-25.1	-51.8	
2820	2349	1944	1596	1298	1047	0.6	0.9	0.0	-2.2	-6.0	-11.4	2.0	1.7	0.0	-3.2	-8.0	-23.3	-47.5	
2872	2352	1909	1534	1220	963	0.7	1.0	0.0	-2.5	-6.7	-12.7	2.3	1.9	0.0	-3.6	-9.0	-26.3	-54.1	
2913	2203	1635	1192	859	625	0.2	0.0	-1.8	-5.5	-11.2	-19.5	2.7	2.3	0.0	-4.4	-11.3	-34.4	-73.7	24″
2913	2436	2023	1666	1362	1105	0.2	0.0	-1.6	-4.8	-9.7	-16.5	2.4	2.0	0.0	-3.7	-9.3	-27.0	-54.9	
2913	2468	2077	1736	1441	1189	0.2	0.0	-1.6	-4.7	-9.6	-16.2	2.4	2.0	0.0	-3.6	-9.1	-26.2	-53.0	
2837	2216	1708	1301	988	758	0.4	0.0	-2.3	-6.8	-13.8	-23.6	1.5	0.0	-3.7	-9.9	-19.0	-47.4	-93.1	

†Inches above or below line of sight. Hold low for positive numbers, high for negative numbers.

(Continued on next page)

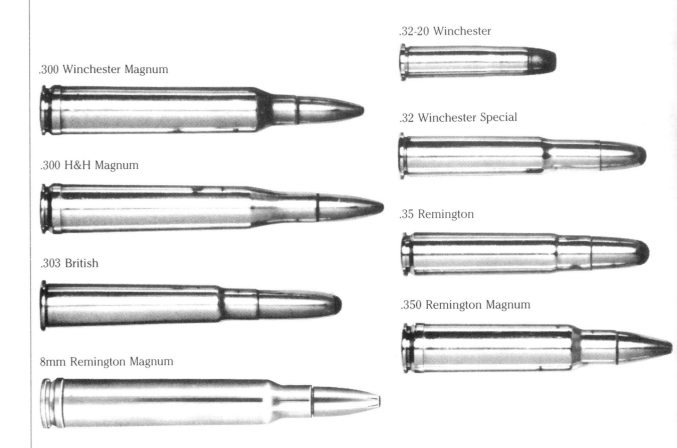

.300 Winchester Magnum

.300 H&H Magnum

.303 British

8mm Remington Magnum

.32-20 Winchester

.32 Winchester Special

.35 Remington

.350 Remington Magnum

Remington Ballistics (continued)

CALIBERS	REMINGTON Order No.	BULLET Wt.-Grs.	BULLET Style	Primer No.	Muzzle	100 Yds.	200 Yds.	300 Yds.	400 Yds.	5(Y
300 H. & H. MAG.	R300HH	180*	Pointed Soft Point Core-Lokt	9½M	2880	2640	2412	2196	1990	17
300 WIN. MAG.	R300W1	150	Pointed Soft Point Core-Lokt	9½M	3290	2951	2636	2342	2068	18
	R300W2	180*	Pointed Soft Point Core-Lokt	9½M	2960	2745	2540	2344	2157	19
303 BRITISH	R303B1	180*	Soft Point Core-Lokt	9½	2460	2124	1817	1542	1311	1
32-20 WIN.	R32201	100	Lead	6½	1210	1021	913	834	769	7
	R32202	100*	Soft Point	6½	1210	1021	913	834	769	7
32 WIN. SPECIAL	R32WS2	170*	Soft Point Core-Lokt	9½	2250	1921	1626	1372	1175	10
8mm MAUSER	R8MSR	170*	Soft Point Core-Lokt	9½	2360	1969	1622	1333	1123	9
8mm REM. MAG.	R8MM1	185*	Pointed Soft Point Core-Lokt	9½M	3080	2761	2464	2186	1927	16
	R8MM2	220	Pointed Soft Point Core-Lokt	9½M	2830	2581	2346	2123	1913	17
35 REM.	R35R1	150	Pointed Soft Point Core-Lokt	9½	2300	1874	1506	1218	1039	9
	R35R2	200*	Soft Point Core-Lokt	9½	2080	1698	1376	1140	1001	5
350 REM. MAG.	R350M1	200*	Pointed Soft Point Core-Lokt	9½M	2710	2410	2130	1870	1631	14
375 H. &. H. MAG.	R375M1	270*	Soft Point	9½M	2690	2420	2166	1928	1707	1!
	R375M2	300	Metal Case	9½M	2530	2171	1843	1551	1307	1
44-40 WIN.	R4440W	200*	Soft Point	2½	1190	1006	900	822	756	
44 REM. MAG.	R44MG2	240	Soft Point	2½	1760	1380	1114	970	878	8
	R44MG3	240	Semi-Jacketed Hollow Point	2½	1760	1380	1114	970	878	8
444 MAR.	R444M	240	Soft Point	9½	2350	1815	1377	1087	941	8
	R444M2	265*	Soft Point	9½	2120	1733	1405	1160	1012	8
45-70 GOVERNMENT	R4570G	405*	Soft Point	9½	1330	1168	1055	977	918	8
458 WIN. MAG	R458W1	500	Metal Case	9½M	2040	1823	1623	1442	1237	1
	R458W2	510*	Soft Point	9½M	2040	1770	1527	1319	1157	1(

*Illustrated (not shown actual size).

.375 H&H Magnum

.44-40 Winchester

.444 Marlin

.44 Remington Magnum

.45-70 Government

.458 Winchester Magnum

ENERGY FOOT-POUNDS						TRAJECTORY† 0.0 Indicates yardage at which rifle was sighted in.														
						SHORT RANGE Bullet does not rise more than one inch above line of sight from muzzle to sighting-in range.						LONG RANGE Bullet does not rise more than three inches above line of sight from muzzle to sighting-in range.							
Muzzle	100 Yds.	200 Yds.	300 Yds.	400 Yds.	500 Yds.	50 Yds.	100 Yds.	150 Yds.	200 Yds.	250 Yds.	300 Yds.	100 Yds.	150 Yds.	200 Yds.	250 Yds.	300 Yds.	400 Yds.	500 Yds.	
3315	2785	2325	1927	1583	1292	0.6	0.9	0.0	−2.3	−6.0	−11.5	2.1	1.7	0.0	−3.2	−8.0	−23.3	−47.4	24″
3605	2900	2314	1827	1424	1095	0.3	0.7	0.0	−1.8	−4.8	−9.3	2.6	2.9	2.1	0.0	−3.5	−15.4	−35.5	24″
3501	3011	2578	2196	1859	1565	0.5	0.8	0.0	−2.1	−5.5	−10.4	1.9	1.6	0.0	−2.9	−7.3	−20.9	−41.9	
2418	1803	1319	950	687	517	0.4	0.0	−2.3	−6.9	−14.1	−24.4	1.5	0.0	−3.8	−10.2	−19.8	−50.5	−101.5	24″
325	231	185	154	131	113	0.0	−6.3	−20.9	−44.9	−79.3	−125.1	0.0	−11.5	−32.3	−63.8	−106.3	−230.3	−413.3	24″
325	231	185	154	131	113	0.0	−6.3	−20.9	−44.9	−79.3	−125.1	0.0	−11.5	−32.3	−63.6	−106.3	−230.3	−413.3	
1911	1393	998	710	521	411	0.6	0.0	−2.9	−8.6	−17.6	−30.5	1.9	0.0	−4.7	−12.7	−24.7	−63.2	−126.9	24″
2102	1463	993	671	476	375	0.5	0.0	−2.7	−8.2	−17.0	−29.8	1.8	0.0	−4.5	−12.4	−24.3	−63.8	−130.7	24″
3896	3131	2494	1963	1525	1170	0.5	0.8	0.0	−2.1	−5.6	−10.7	1.8	1.6	0.0	−3.0	−7.6	−22.5	−46.8	24″
3912	3254	2688	2201	1787	1438	0.6	1.0	0.0	−2.4	−6.4	−12.1	2.2	1.8	0.0	−3.4	−8.5	−24.7	−50.5	
1762	1169	755	494	359	291	0.6	0.0	−3.0	−9.2	−19.1	−33.9	2.0	0.0	−5.1	−14.1	−27.8	−74.0	−152.3	24″
1921	1280	841	577	445	369	0.8	0.0	−3.8	−11.3	−23.5	−41.2	2.5	0.0	−6.3	−17.1	−33.6	−87.7	−176.4	
3261	2579	2014	1553	1181	897	0.2	0.0	−1.7	−5.1	−10.4	−17.9	2.6	2.1	0.0	−4.0	−10.3	−30.5	−64.0	20″
4337	3510	2812	2228	1747	1361	0.2	0.0	−1.7	−5.1	−10.3	−17.6	2.5	2.1	0.0	−3.9	−10.0	−29.4	−60.7	24″
4263	3139	2262	1602	1138	844	0.3	0.0	−2.2	−6.5	−13.5	−23.4	1.5	0.0	−3.6	−9.8	−19.1	−49.1	−99.5	
629	449	360	300	254	217	0.0	−6.5	−21.6	−46.3	−81.8	−129.1	0.0	−11.8	−33.3	−65.5	−109.5	−237.4	−426.2	24″
1650	1015	661	501	411	346	0.0	−2.7	−10.0	−23.0	−43.0	−71.2	0.0	−5.9	−17.6	−36.3	−63.1	−145.5	−273.0	24″
1650	1015	661	501	411	346	0.0	−2.7	−10.0	−23.0	−43.0	−71.2	0.0	−5.9	−17.6	−36.3	−63.1	−145.5	−273.0	20″
2942	1755	1010	630	472	381	0.6	0.0	−3.2	−9.9	−21.3	−38.5	2.1	0.0	−5.6	−15.9	−32.1	−87.8	−182.7	24″
2644	1768	1162	791	603	498	0.7	0.0	−3.6	−10.8	−22.5	−39.5	2.4	0.0	−6.0	−16.4	−32.2	−84.3	−170.2	
1590	1227	1001	858	758	679	0.0	−4.7	−15.8	−34.0	−60.0	−94.5	0.0	−8.7	−24.6	−48.2	−80.3	−172.4	−305.9	24″
4620	3689	2924	2308	1839	1469	0.7	0.0	−3.3	−9.6	−19.2	−32.5	2.2	0.0	−5.2	−13.6	−25.8	−63.2	−121.7	24″
4712	3547	2640	1970	1516	1239	0.8	0.0	−3.5	−10.3	−20.8	−35.6	2.4	0.0	−5.6	−14.9	−28.5	−71.5	−140.4	

†Inches above or below line of sight. Hold low for positive numbers, high for negative numbers.

equate at 100 yards, and the small bullet does not have enough weight to penetrate consistently. The load is in fact intended for long-range varmint shooting and for the larger varmints such as foxes and coyotes.

THE OLD-TIMERS

The ballistics table also lists other cartridges that are inadequate for deer hunting. Among these are old-time loads, most of which were designed for use with black powder. They are loaded with smokeless powder today, but they are still inadequate for deer hunting. This class of cartridges includes the .25/20 Winchester, .32/20 Winchester, .32 Winchester Special, and the .44/40 Winchester. None of them develop sufficient energy.These cartridges are still manufactured because numerous rifles that fire them are still in existence. The .44/40, the most powerful among them, only develops 629 foot-pounds of energy *at the muzzle.* The least effective load, the .25/20, turns up a measly 272 foot-pounds at 100 yards. To use this cartridge on deer is like trying to make the kill with a low-powered handgun.

Also inadequate is the .30 Carbine, which was originally used in the semi-automatic M1 Carbine developed during World War II. This arm was intended to provide American soldiers with a close-range weapon to replace the .45-caliber Colt pistol, and the cartridge is a wounding round rather than a killing one when it comes to deer-size targets.

The .44 Remington Magnum is a marginal load for deer hunting. Several rifles have been chambered for this round, which is still the most powerful widely used handgun cartridge available as a factory load. Many deer and larger game, even grizzly bears, have been killed with this cartridge fired from a revolver. Yet the round develops only 1,015 foot-pounds of energy at 100 yards in a rifle with a 24-inch barrel. Handgun hunters are (or should be) careful about the range at which they shoot and the placement of their shots. In the hands of a real handgun expert, this cartridge is effective for deer-size targets at close range. But if you're going to hunt with a rifle, it would be foolish to employ a rifle chambered for this round except for close woods shooting. That is doubly true for the popular .357 Magnum handgun round (not listed in the table), which is used in some rifles.

SHORT-RANGE DEER LOADS

With the criterion of a minimum of 1,200 foot-pounds of on-target energy, it's easy to pick out cartridges that

are effective on deer out to 100 yards or a bit more. These include the .250 Savage, .257 Roberts, .30 Remington, 150-grain and 170-grain .30/30 Winchester loads, .300 Savage, 8mm Mauser, .35 Remington, and .45/70 Government.

Most of these cartridges, as loaded by Remington, are effective on deer to 150 yards. But some are loaded to higher velocities (and energy levels) by other companies. For instance, there's the 8mm Mauser (7 × 57JS). This was the original full-power load for the famed Mauser 98 German infantry rifle. Remington only makes a 170-grain load, which has 1,463 foot-pounds of energy at 100 yards and drops off to 993 at 200. The Remington version is really a 150-yard deer load in the hands of the average rifleman.

But loads from other companies, available in the United States, develop more energy. For instance, the Swedish company Norma has a 196-grain 8mm load that turns up 2,097 foot-pounds at 100 yards, 1,562 at 200, and 1,152 at 300 yards. In the Norma loading, the old 8mm Mauser turns out to be a good deer cartridge for use at ranges out to about 275 yards and surely qualifies as a medium-range load.

If you have an 8mm Mauser rifle, and there are thousands of them in the United States as a result of widespread availability after World War II, it pays to shop around for European loadings that are more effective than American ones. This also applies to other cartridges that were originally military. For some of these military surplus rifles, you can buy only European ammunition—for instance, the 7.7mm Japanese and the 6.5 Italian Carcano. But to go out and buy a rifle chambered for these former foreign military rounds would be ill-advised because more effective cartridges are readily available.

One cartridge in this class has characteristics that should warn you off of a certain type of loading. This is the .45/70 Government, which was originally adopted by the U.S. Army in 1873 for the single-shot "Trapdoor" Springfield rifle. It is representative of a whole class of old-fashioned black-powder cartridges that employed big bullets and large charges of black powder. In the modern smokeless load by Remington, the .45/70 with its 405-grain bullet has 1,227 foot-pounds of energy at 100 yards and should be used for deer hunting at no more than that range. A deer hit in a vital area with this very big, very heavy bullet at close range usually goes down in its tracks. Beyond 100 yards, there is insufficient energy, and the looped trajectory of the heavy bullet also renders it ineffective at medium and long ranges. Referring to the trajectory figures in the previous table, you'll see that, when sighted in to be dead on at 150 yards, the .45/70 is 22.5 inches low at 250 yards and 39.5 inches low at 300. Holding more than 3 feet over the target and making a hit is impossible for most hunters. To cite a very extreme example, the .45/70, when sighted-in to be dead on at 150 yards, is 140.4 inches low at 500 yards. To hit where you aim at 500 yards, you would have to hold over 11 feet high! That figure is revealing when you remember all the ancient tales about killing an Indian on a galloping horse at "half a mile" or even more with this cartridge.

If you hunt where shots at deer are never available at any more than 100 yards, this cartridge and similar ones are just fine. Otherwise, they are really useless. Trajectory figures as well as the energy figures should always be consulted before settling on any hunting cartridge.

MEDIUM-RANGE DEER LOADS

Two hundred yards is only medium range as modern cartridges go, but it is a long distance nevertheless. It's the combined length of two football fields.

At that range, with the criterion of 1,200 foot-pounds of energy, the worthwhile cartridges have more varied uses than the short-range loads discussed previously. These cartridges are commonly available with bullets of differing weights and expansion capabilities.

A good, but simple, example is the .308 Winchester, a load that was originally designed for military use in the Model 14 U.S. Army rifle and in machine guns. The cartridge was intended to replace the old standby .30/06 and had to be a bit shorter than that round for use in automatic weapons. The .308 is known in military parlance as the 7.62 (mm) NATO, and it has turned out to be a very useful hunting cartridge.

Three Remington loads are available. One has a 180-grain "Soft Point Core Lokt" bullet. This cartridge has 1,572 foot-pounds of remaining energy at 200 yards and therefore qualifies as a medium-range deer round. The designation "Soft Point Core Lokt" is Remington's way of telling you that the bullet is not a sharp-nosed spitzer type and that the bullet jacket has been solidly secured to the lead core so that it will seldom separate during penetration. It is a very satisfactory hunting load at medium range and at short range, and the recoil is not excessive for the average rifleman.

The 180-grain *Pointed* Soft Point Core Lokt round in .308, if you refer to the energy figures, is obviously a long-range load. It has 1,269 foot-pounds of energy at 400 yards, and the trajectory figures show that the bullet path does not curve down very abruptly. With the rifle sighted-in to be dead on at 200 yards, the bullet is only 9.9 inches low at 300 yards. To drop a deer at that range when the animal is broadside, it's enough to hold on the top of the back. Some target shooters may find the recoil of this round fairly pun-

ishing, but hunters don't fire enough to take a bruising from it.

The third Remington load for this cartridge employs a 150-grain bullet, which is a "Pointed Soft Point Core Lokt." The remaining energy at 300 yards is 1,344 pounds, and the trajectory is quite flat. The recoil is mild because of the light bullet. This cartridge is obviously a good compromise between the other two rounds.

The .308 Winchester is so versatile that it is both a medium-range and a long-range cartridge depending on the bullet weight, the velocity, and remaining energy. Of course, all three .308 loads would be effective at short range, though the 180-grain round-nose bullet is perhaps the best for this use. A rifle chambered for this round is therefore very versatile.

The all-time champion in terms of versatility is the .30/06 Springfield. The Remington catalog lists eight different bullet weights for this cartridge. The 125-grain load is intended for varmint shooting and has a light jacket not suitable for deer. The 220-grain load has an exceptionally heavy jacket and is intended to achieve deep penetration on heavy game, such as moose and elk, before it expands fully. It should never be used for deer hunting because it usually passes right through a deer with little or no expansion and therefore is not a sure killer. The remaining six loads are excellent for deer hunting, and a little study of the varying bullet characteristics and trajectories should reveal their intended uses. The 165-grain bullet is usually regarded as the best possible compromise between a heavy load with a rather curved trajectory and a light load with a very flat trajectory.

It should be noted that both the .308 and the .30/06 are available as "Accelerator" cartridges. These rounds fire a 55-grain .22 bullet encased in a plastic sabot, which drops away a short distance from the muzzle. These Accelerator cartridges are intended for varmint hunting and should never be used for deer. Accelerator cartridges are also available for the .30/30 Winchester.

In addition to the cartridges already described, the following are also useful for medium-range deer hunting out to 200 yards, sometimes a bit more: .243 Winchester, 100-grain bullet (80-grain loads are really varmint cartridges); 6mm Remington, 100 grains; .25/06, 100 grains; .300 Savage, 180-grain pointed bullet; and the .303 British (another military survivor), 180 grain.

By this time, it should be apparent that unless the ballistics table indicates that the bullet is pointed, it is in fact a rather round-nosed projectile intended for use at medium ranges or less. "Power Lokt" and "Core Lokt" indicate that the jacket and the lead bullet core are firmly held together to prevent separation during penetration. Other ammunition manufacturers have their own ways of designating the type of bullet.

LONG-RANGE DEER LOADS

This class of cartridges delivers at least 1,200 foot-pounds of energy at 300 yards, and some of them do so at considerably longer ranges. For instance, the .300 H&H (Holland & Holland) Magnum with its 180-grain pointed bullet has 1,292 foot-pounds of remaining energy at 500 yards! Many of these cartridges are "magnums"—more powerful than usual for the given bore diameter.

Also in this broad class are several cartridges that deliver the required energy at 300 yards and drop below that level shortly thereafter. For instance, there is the old .30/40 Krag, a former U.S. Army round which has a retained energy of 1,314 foot-pounds at 300 yards. In other words, this class includes very powerful cartridges, as well as some of only moderate power. There are many different cartridges in this category; the problem is to select the right one for your kind of hunting.

One way to go at it is to choose a cartridge that delivers the needed energy out at 400 or even 500 yards and use if for all deer hunting, even close-range shooting at whitetails in heavy cover. But this is the wrong solution. For shooting in heavy cover, you need a short, handy rifle or carbine that can be put on target with a minimum of deliberation. To fire the long-range magnum cartridges, you'll probably be obliged to buy a bolt-action rifle that weighs quite a bit and is slow to shoot. The recoil of these big cartridges is also quite punishing. This is no problem when you're hunting, but it makes for a sore shoulder and jaw and flinching when you sight-in or fire target rounds. With these powerful firearms you can build up a severe case of flinching that makes it almost impossible to shoot them accurately when you do go out hunting.

Another type of hunter goes for a magnum rifle because he intends to eventually hunt moose, elk, mountain goats, or even the big bears—grizzlies or brown bears. In the meantime, he uses the powerful rifle for deer hunting. This is not a good practice. These very powerful rifles are a definite safety hazard in heavily populated areas. They carry a long way and can severely wound or kill way out there at 2,000 yards or more, should the bullet strike another hunter or a farmer working on his crops. During deer drives with 10 or 12 hunters participating, it's a frightening experience to hear a big magnum rifle go off. That bullet may reach you through the brush if the shooter lets go in the wrong direction. Or it may go right through a deer, angle off in an odd way and hit another hunter, even though he is in a supposedly safe position.

The best advice is to choose a deer cartridge that is lethal out to the normal, fairly long range at which shots are taken where you hunt. Defer buying a magnum until you really need one.

All this applies to whitetail hunting under conditions found in the East and to mule deer in heavy cover. If you intend to hunt mule deer or even Columbia blacktails in open country where long-range shooting is the norm, you'll need a flat-shooting magnum, and you'll just have to get used to recoil as best you can. However, there is no earthly reason to use a .300 H&H or a .300 Winchester Magnum in the eastern and midwestern deer woods. Using the kind of rifle that takes this load puts you at an extreme disadvantage, and at close range you will ruin a lot of venison if you do make a hit.

The list of effective deer cartridges at 300 yards or greater range, as loaded by Remington, includes: .25/06, 120-grain bullet; 6.5mm Remington Magnum; .264 Winchester Magnum, 140 grain; .270 Winchester, 130 grain; .270 Winchester, 130-grain Bronze Point; .270 Winchester, 150 grain; 7mm Magnum, 140 grain; 7mm–08, 150 grain; .280 Remington, 150 grain; 7mm Remington Magnum, 150 grain and 175 grain; .30/40 Krag, 180 grain; the suitable .308 Winchester and .30/06 loads already discussed; the .300 H&H Magnum, 180 grain; and the 150-grain and 180-grain .300 Winchester Magnum loads.

If there is any choice, always select pointed bullets, including the Bronze Points, over round-nosed or flat-nosed bullets. If possible, before you buy any of the big magnums, it might be a good idea to test fire the cartridge you select to make sure that you can really stand up to the recoil. If you are very sensitive to recoil, the .243 Winchester is about the least you can get away with as an effective deer-hunting cartridge, but the .257 Roberts or the 6mm Remington are worth consideration.

THE HEAVY RIFLES

The last class to be listed here really requires little consideration because the loads are too heavy for deer hunting. For instance, there is the 220-grain .30/06 load, already mentioned. Also in this class are the 8mm Remington Magnum, .350 Remington Magnum, .375 H&H, .444 Marlin, and .458 Winchester Magnum. You'll note from the previous ballistics table that the .458 Winchester and the .375 H&H are available with "Metal Case" bullets. These bullets have full metal jackets with no exposed lead and are intended for deep penetration on such heavy game as African Cape buffalo and elephant. They do not expand at all.

OTHER SOURCES

The Remington ballistics table was used here because it provides so much information. But you should also study the Winchester, Federal, Norma, Weatherby, and Patton and Morgan tables. They list several cartridges that are not loaded by Remington.

For complete ballistics information, it's best to consult *Shooter's Bible* or *Gun Digest.* Both are issued annually, and are usually available at a good gun shop or in some public libraries. The ballistics tables they contain have practically every factory cartridge used in North America. These books also list and illustrate an enormous variety of rifles and other firearms.

In interpreting the ballistics tables, however, it's important to use the criteria for load choices given above, even if the table does not include full information on such considerations as trajectory. Many ballistics tables only give the mid-range trajectory height at 100, 200, and 300 yards. But with the listed energy figures, bullet weights, and bullet descriptions, you can get a good picture of the intended use of the cartridge.

The physical appearance of a given load also provides information. A pointed bullet with only a little bare lead exposed at the tip is obviously intended for high-velocity shooting at fairly long range. A round-nosed or flat-nosed bullet with a large amount of lead left uncovered for the sake of easy expansion is obviously intended for close-range woods hunting.

If you become interested in one or more rifle cartridges and require more detailed information than the usual ballistics tables provide, consult the latest edition of *Cartridges of the World* by Frank C. Barnes, published by DBI Books, Inc. This softcover book is usually available in better gun shops, and you may find a copy in a good public library. It includes a history of each cartridge plus ballistics and handloading data.

A little caution. Ballistics tables should be used with a little caution, however, because the figures in them are usually produced by a computer, not by firing test rounds from rifles. Your particular rifle may produce results that differ considerably from published figures.

It's also a very good idea to consult the regulations booklet issued to hunters for your home state or the state where you will be hunting. Some states specifically bar low-powered cartridges such as the .44/40 or the .30 Carbine, and there are other strictures that you should know about before you select a cartridge and buy a rifle to fire it. In most hunting areas of North America, however, rifles that fire cartridges of .243 caliber or greater are legal for deer hunting, provided you do not use full-metal-jacket ammunition (military or target).

THE RIFLE

After your deer load has been selected, you're all set to choose your rifle. A little research before you hie yourself off to the gun shop is advisable. I'd run through *Shooter's Bible* and *Gun Digest* to check out all the rifles that fire the cartridge. If you can't find something you really like that sells for the right price, select another cartridge and try again. Some rifle-cartridge choices are very, very simple. For instance, if you want to fire a magnum, long-range load in a lever-action rifle, you will have to buy the Browning BLR in .300 Winchester Magnum. There is no other choice. If you want to hunt deer with a pump-action rifle, you'll be obliged to purchase a Remington pump rifle, which is chambered for only six different calibers. Again, there is no other choice. With semi-automatics and bolt-action rifles, the choice is wider, but you now have the standards that you need to make a wise selection.

SECONDHAND GUNS

Typically, someone the beginning hunter knows is offering a real bargain in a used deer rifle. How about a nice scope-equipped rifle that will knock down a big buck out at 300 yards without fail? Be cautious! There may be a good reason why the seller wants to get rid of that gun. It may be chambered for a round that is no longer factory loaded, and many old rifles are chambered for low-powered rounds that are illegal or useless, or both, for deer hunting.

Then there's the physical condition of the rifle. Many things can be out of kilter, and some of them are not apparent to the untrained eye. You can see a cracked stock right away, but a wildly roaming zero is not detectable unless you actually fire the rifle, and the cause may be mysterious. If you can do so, borrow the rifle and shoot a box of ammunition with it before you lay out any cash.

In cases of serious doubt about the safety of a rifle, it's best to test fire the arm by placing it on its side in a tire. Slip the butt into the hollow on one side and tie the rifle down on the other side of the tire with a rope. Snuggle yourself down behind a thick tree and pull the trigger with a lanyard. Do this several times with the heaviest loads available in the given caliber. Then check the rifle again, but don't make a superficial examination. Take the barreled action out of the stock and examine all parts carefully.

Remember that you don't get a manufacturer's warranty when you buy a secondhand firearm. If you pay for it, you're stuck with it. The only recourse, if the rifle is defective, is to try to sell it to someone else. If you do, you have a moral obligation to tell the prospective buyer about the defects, or you're just as much a cheat as the man you bought it from. If the rifle is actually dangerous, you should destroy it or bury it somewhere to make sure that no one can be injured or killed by using it.

Many gun shops have racks of used firearms, and sometimes it's possible to pick up a real bargain. A reputable gun shop owner, particularly a capable gunsmith, tries to avoid losing his reputation for fair dealing, and he is unlikely to try to stick you with a lemon. But there are many fly-by-night operators. In some cases, gun shop owners, though honest, do not have time to examine in detail every firearm they take on for resale.

You can buy new, dependable firearms for moderate prices, though they may lack such conveniences as a hinged magazine floorplate for easy unloading or such refinements as extra-fine checkering. But you can rely on the manufacturer's warranty. Why take on a pig in a poke by purchasing a secondhand gun that may turn out to be inaccurate or a danger to life and limb?

There have been several horrendous cases, but only one is needed to emphasize this point. An inexperi-enced Pennsylvania hunter was offered a Savage lever-action rifle chambered for the .300 Savage cartridge. That's a good rifle and a good load for eastern deer hunting, and the rifle appeared to be in very good condition. He bought it and paid the full price in cash, even though he did not know the seller well. At the range, the rifle blew up. The chamber burst, but for-tunately the fragments flew straight up and did not injure the shooter. It could easily have been otherwise.

Later it was discovered that the rifle had been in a fire and that the heat had taken the temper out of the barrel, though there was no obvious damage to the metal. The original owner, perhaps innocently, equipped the rifle with a replacement stock before selling it. After it blew up, he denied that he knew there had been any real damage to the gun, though he admitted that the original stock has been burned away. No one will ever know whether the seller really intended to cheat the buyer. It's possible that he simply did not know that intense heat can ruin a barrel. In fact, instead of cheating him, he almost killed him. That's something to remember when you buy or sell a secondhand gun.

"Proofing" a rifle: Proof loads as used by manufacturers and Euro-pean proof houses to test rifles are not available to the public, but you can use the heaviest available fac-tory load to test a secondhand gun. For instance, with a .30/06, use the 200-grain factory load. Tying the ri-fle into a tire as shown and pulling the trigger with a long lanyard from a safe position is wise. Use a thick dead tree, a solid stump, or some other safe, non-ricocheting, bullet-devouring backstop. (Neil Soder-strom photo)

MARKSMANSHIP AND MAINTENANCE

Ernest Thompson Seton, the well-known naturalist, praised deer in his monumental book *Lives of Game Animals* by saying that whitetail deer trained the armies of the American Revolution. In part, this was true. Frontier farmers often killed a deer a week as food for their families, and they did so throughout the year. Stalking the animal to get close enough for a killing shot with a short-range flintlock rifle provided essential training for men who later stalked British soldiers in irregular warfare.

Today the situation is quite different. In most American states, the hunter is permitted to kill only one buck deer per year. A youngster in colonial times often learned to shoot by actually firing at game. Most hunters now must learn to shoot before they go hunting. Of course, small-game hunting provides a lot of training that will be useful when a youngster goes out after deer for the first time, but small-game seasons are only open for a few weeks in the fall. Most big-game hunters therefore learn to shoot through practice, and all practice shooting is artificial to one degree or another. To become a competent shooter, it's best to make the practice resemble the hunting as closely as possible.

THE TARGET

The whitetail deer is not a large animal, and to make a killing shot at medium to long range, a hunter must have a fair degree of skill. At close range, usually when the deer is moving—sometimes at an astonishing speed—the emphasis is on quick gun handling rather than pinpoint accuracy. On the average, the mule deer is slightly larger than the whitetail, but in terms of size of target, the difference is not great enough to matter.

Most hunters aim for the heart-lung area. A hit there is usually fatal. A bullet driven through one or both lungs causes death by suffocation since internal bleeding fills the lungs with blood. If the bullet hits the heart, death is very quick. When viewed broadside, the entire chest area of the deer is usually said to be 18 inches in height and *about* 22 inches in length. But the target is actually smaller. In fact, the heart-lung vital area is about the size of an $8\frac{1}{2} \times 11$ sheet of typewriter paper. Turned with its long dimension horizontal, a sheet of typewriter paper makes a good target for the beginning deer hunter. If you can consistently hit that target, the "boiler room," your marksmanship is good enough for most deer hunting.

Aiming for the "boiler room" is wise because it is the largest target you have when deer hunting. And even if you miss by a small margin, the bullet may still kill. If you shoot a little high, the bullet may hit and smash the spine, and then death is almost instantaneous. If you are just a bit too far back, the bullet may hit the liver or the diaphragm, and death is usually quick. In fact, these hits may kill the deer quicker than a bullet through both lungs, but it's better not to actually aim to hit them.

Always try for the biggest target. It's possible for a bullet to pass below the spine and above the lungs. The deer will almost surely die eventually, but you may not find the animal if it runs a long distance. Aiming for the liver or diaphragm isn't wise because a bullet that hits slightly to the rear will strike the paunch, and a deer often runs for miles after that kind of hit. Aim for the heart-lung area and regard any other killing hit as a lucky bonus. If you do hit the spine by accidentally shooting a bit high, and the deer drops dead instantaneously in its tracks, smile quietly and assume a superior attitude. The old-timers will know, however, that you actually missed your intended target.

The hydrostatic shock of a high-speed bullet makes these "near miss" kills more common than they used to be. The tremendous energy released inside a deer's body by an expanding bullet can easily disrupt bodily functions and either kill at once or drop a deer because the shock momentarily interrupts the functioning of its nervous system. When the hit is nonlethal, however, the nervous collapse may end quite suddenly. This is the reason for the sudden recovery of many deer that dropped at the shot. Even if you are sure that your shot went where you aimed it, get there quickly if the deer falls. It may get up again, and sooner than you think.

Very few hunters ever aim for the brain, because it is a very small target and a deer's head is in almost constant motion. A shot to the head may also destroy the antlers. Some older hunters prefer to aim for the neck in an effort to break the spine. This target is also difficult to hit because the deer's neck angles upward, allowing only a little windage and elevation error. Hunters who try this type of shot are primarily intent on saving meat. Neck meat is only good for stew and second-grade chop meat anyway; so destroying it is no great loss. Actually, a bullet through the lungs destroys even less edible meat. Aiming for a neck hit is really not a good idea unless the range is very short or the rest of the deer's body is behind a tree or brush.

But standing broadside shots are not very common. Quite often, the animal is facing the hunter or facing directly away from him. And then there are angled shots anywhere between these two extremes. If the animal is facing you, try to place the bullet at the base of the throat, a bit low. It may hit the heart, or it may pass above the heart and drive into the diaphragm or liver. If the deer is facing directly away from you, aim right at the rectum. The bullet will almost always pass through the abdomen and impact the liver, diaphragm, heart, or a lung. With either longitudinal shot, if you are a little off left or right, the bullet will probably hit a lung.

Angled shots are best visualized as shooting at a rectangular block with 8½ × 11 sides and a thickness of about 7 inches. If you measure a 1-gallon metal syrup or oil can, you'll find that all of its dimensions are an inch or two smaller than these measurements. These cans make excellent targets for the aspiring deer hunter. Place them on their sides and fire away. Your target has the shape of a deer's central vital area, and by varying the long axis, you can get a good idea of how hard it is to hit an end-on or angling deer. The fact that the can is a bit smaller than reality is good, because it tends to make you a better marksman than with a larger target. Besides, you may find yourself shooting at a small, young buck or doe. In fact, these cans are better for practice than any flat piece of paper or even life-size pictures of deer, complete with scoring rings. The only better practice target is a full-size foam-plastic deer of the type sometimes used by bowhunters. These targets cost a great deal more than used gallon cans.

MINUTE OF ANGLE

When you sighted-in your rifle, your intent was to put it on target at hunting ranges. To do so, you used a firm rest to eliminate as much human error as possible. After sighting-in and firing your rifle from a rest at long range, your intent should again be to reduce human error as much as possible. If you have a rifle that shoots rather large groups and then you add a substantial degree of human error caused by trembling, lack of accurate range estimation, failure to allow for the wind, and similar problems, your shooting can be so wild that you will miss a big buck at 50 yards. It's been done many, many times, and sometimes by highly experienced hunters.

Accuracy is really shot-to-shot consistency. The man/rifle team should be able to place all shots within a reasonably small area. Shooters commonly speak of accuracy in terms of minutes of angle. For all practical purposes, a minute of angle is 1 inch at 100 yards, 2 inches at 200, 3 inches at 300, and 4 inches at 400.

It should be apparent that if you have a minute-of-angle rifle, it can hit a deer-size target quite handily out to all practical hunting ranges. A rifle that makes a 4-inch or 6-inch group at 100 yards (common with lever-action guns) is deadly at that range. But as the range increases, rifles with groups that large quickly become incapable of making consistent hits on deer. If the shooter adds several minutes of angle to the equation through human error, even an accurate, flat-shooting rifle is really quite useless for deer hunting or hunting almost anything else.

REALISTIC PRACTICE

A rifle range is a good place to sight-in and do a little preliminary practice, but if you want to become a good game shot, it's best not to visit them too often. They're really very artificial places. The ground is always flat, and this eliminates realistic practice for downslope or upslope shooting. The distance to the target is always known in advance. If you're in a 100-yard stage, you know that for sure, and you can adjust your sights accordingly. The same is true of 200-yard or 800-yard shooting.

Target shooters always adjust their sights according to this known distance and shoot right at the target. Many of them also adjust their sights to allow for the wind. After adjusting the sights, the target shooter can hold dead on the center of the target, and this is a great help in making a high score. Hunters seldom do this because the game may vanish if they take time to adjust the sights. Instead, they hold high or low, or left or right, to allow for range and the wind. For all these reasons, conventional target shooting is not good practice for hunting.

Target shooting may also give the hunter an inferiority complex. To practice for hunting, he should use his hunting rifle. But even in an informal pick-up "match", he will shoot with riflemen equipped with finely tuned, specialized target rifles with very light trigger pulls and all kinds of sophisticated refinements. Inevitably, his scores don't measure up, and he may give up in disgust. If you do shoot at a formal target range, shoot when only a few shooters are banging away informally, and don't pay any attention to their scores.

Lately, "silhouette shooting" has come on strong as practice for hunting. In this game the shooter fires at metallic silhouettes of animals and birds from various ranges. All shots must be fired from the offhand position (standing), and slings and other supports are not allowed. The heavy steel-plate targets must be hit almost dead center or they will not topple over, which is the way you score a point. Therefore, fairly heavy calibers must be used, and this is said to make this

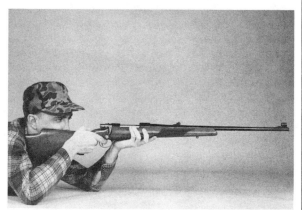

The prone position is the steadiest of them all because the shooter's body is almost completely supported by the ground. The farther you get from ground support, the shakier you are. The forearms form a solid bipod. Feet are spread fairly wide and as flat as possible to tense the legs just a bit. This posed picture represents the ideal position on flat, smooth ground. Rocks, brittle stubble, twigs, and so forth almost always make it necessary to modify the ideal position when hunting. You cannot assume the prone position if the ground slopes downward toward the target. (Neil Soderstrom photos)

The sitting position is quite steady, too, and it is preferred if grass and brush or the nature of the ground make it impossible to shoot from prone. The elbows go slightly beyond the curve of the knees so that muscle tension holds the legs together to form a solid base. Mistakenly placing elbows inside the knees forces legs apart and weakens the bipods formed by the legs and forearms.

kind of shooting very realistic for hunters.

It's almost heresy to disagree, but someone should point out that the range is known in advance and that almost all shooters do adjust their scopes and hold dead on. Also, shooting all shots at silhouettes from the offhand position is excellent practice for offhand shooting, but few hunters would fire offhand if a steady rest were available or if they could assume a steadier sitting, kneeling, or prone position. Silhouette shooting is a lot of fun, and it *is* more realistic than other forms of target shooting, but it's not the best practice for hunting.

Actually, silhouette shooting developed in Mexico as a live-target competition. A local honcho, such as a cantina owner, brought several domestic animals, and staked them out on a flat piece of ground. Local hotshots paid an entrance fee, and everyone got a chance to shoot at the tethered live targets. He who killed got to eat the turkey, goat, chicken, or what have you. Money prizes were paid out of the fees, the honcho took a big percentage, and everyone had a lovely time. In it's original form, Mexican silhouette shooting was a bit more realistic than shooting at metallic silhouettes. Animals could and did move around

In the kneeling position, the rifle wobbles and weaves much more than it does when you are sitting because the right elbow is no longer supported and the bipod effect is lost. Nevertheless, it is steadier than shooting offhand (standing erect). In high grass or low brush, always kneel and shoot over the top of the vegetation if that is possible rather than shoot from the offhand position. (Neil Soderstrom photos)

Offhand is wobbly because the entire body weaves in many directions to maintain the erect position, even if you are just standing there without a rifle. In this position, the shooter is forced to resort to the "squeeze and stop" method, even if he doesn't use it when closer to the ground. When sights are on target, squeeze; when sights wobble off, stop. Finally, the rifle goes off. All this of course applies to stationary targets. With moving game (always at close range), the rifle must move with the game and then ahead of it to attain the needed lead. A steady, smooth swing, pivoting from hips is best. The rifle has four support points: shoulder, right hand, cheek, left hand. To a considerable extent, a steady hold results from opposing these support points against one another firmly but not so firmly as to cause avoidable trembling.

on their tethers. But the game was never intended to provide good practice for hunting, and its more humane American variant isn't really good practice either.

DOWN IN THE DUMPS

One of the best places to practice hunting marksmanship is a town dump located well away from the nearest house so that the firing won't alarm nervous residents. Some dumps are off limits to shooters, but many of them can still be used, even if you have to get permission from the sanitation department or some other local official. It's axiomatic in hunting and all forms of target shooting that you should have a good backstop to stop your bullets. A mound of trash and garbage is usually quite satisfactory, but avoid firing at solid metal objects because ricochets can angle off in unexpected directions. Sunday afternoon is usually a fine time to shoot because sanitation people are not interested in visiting the dump on a holiday.

Repair there with your rifle, some ammunition, a spotting scope, and a friend. Find a place where you can shoot safely from the standing position, sitting, kneeling, and prone. Start at reasonable range and in the prone position. Let your friend pick out a target such as the plastic jug at the bottom of the slope or the oil can halfway down. Your goal is to hit it solidly in as short a time as possible. If satisfactory targets are not available in the dump, bring some square gallon cans and place them at odd intervals where firing at them will be safe. It's not considered fair to pace off the distance when you walk back to your firing point, particularly if there is a little money riding on the afternoon's shooting.

Fire a few shots and then change off with your friend so that your rifle cools down and the zero does not wander. Try to surprise each other with unexpected targets at fairly close range. After you are both hitting

fairly well at 100 yards or so, try the same thing in the sitting position, then try kneeling, and finally, offhand. After you get good hits, move farther from the target area and run through the positions again. After a few sessions like this, you'll both come up against the fact that there is an ultimate distance at which you cannot hit a deer-size target. That's the point where serious practice is required. By firing fairly often, you can push this limit farther and farther away, but then you'll reach the point where you and your rifle cannot hit. Engrave that range in your mental imagery and never try to hit a game animal at that distance. For many hunters this ultimate range is only 150 yards or so.

After you and your compadre can hit at most practical hunting ranges, try to surprise your partner by selecting several long-range targets and then one that is very close. Vary the ranges suddenly. In many dumps, you can also call for a downhill shot or an uphill shot. The aspiring hunter who practices this way is forced to spot his target quickly and estimate the range accurately, and he must be conscious of the wind and hold accordingly. There is no better practice.

A spotting scope with very high magnification is useful in this type of shooting. The backup shooter focuses the scope on the target he intends to announce and then calls for the shot. He can almost always spot where the bullet hits and can inform the shooter so that corrections can be made. The same thing can often be done in long-range shooting afield.

Another excellent place for this kind of practice is a recently plowed and harrowed field that is fairly dry. You can almost always spot the misses by the puffs of dust. A sloping field is essential, however, because it backstops the bullets. Never shoot this way on a flat field or one that only slopes a bit because the bullets can ricochet.

If you intend to hunt long-range game, such as mule deer, in open country, practice should be a bit more

An excellent way to develop your aim for shooting running game is to place a target inside an automobile tire and have a partner roll it down a hill.

formal. Take some time to fire regularly at long range in the various positions. Use a full military sling to steady your aim; you'll find that it is a great help. But don't become dependent on it. You may not have time to lock into a shot with a sling when you're hunting. That applies even to a "hasty sling" in which the left arm is merely twisted through the sling or carrying strap.

With rolling ground and a safe backstop, you can even practice on moving objects. A round metal can rolled down a slope has a great ability to avoid bullets. A rubber tire with a cardboard cutout tucked into the hole is an excellent target because it bounces a lot when it rolls, just like a bounding "pogo stick" mule deer. This sort of thing is fairly realistic, and it's a lot of fun, too, particularly if you compete with a partner and make small bets.

Even if you can't find someone who wants to shoot with you, you can go it alone. Select the targets for yourself. Try for the long-range can and then suddenly try for a quick offhand shot at a close-range target. You'll be competing only with yourself, but if you are a severe critic, your shooting skills will improve enormously. The practice is much more realistic than anything you can do at a formal target range.

And don't practice only on nice calm days when the sun is shining. Also go when the wind is blowing and visibility is limited. You can't cancel your match with a trophy buck merely because the wind may blow your bullet off target or misty rain dims the light.

VARMINT SHOOTING

Shooting at "pest" animals and birds, such as woodchucks, sitting crows, magpies, prairie dogs, and jackrabbits (where they are on the unprotected list) is excellent practice for big-game hunting, and it can be done at almost any time of year. Even in the northern states where burrowing animals and most pest birds vanish with the onset of winter, you can still go out for coyotes and foxes, which is a very demanding sport in itself.

Varmint hunters have contributed a great deal to the development of accurate rifles, but if your objective is to develop your skills as a big-game hunter, don't rush down to the gun shop and invest a thousand dollars or more in a 20× scope and a super-hotshot varmint rifle. Use your hunting rifle for varmints and fire the hunting load you shoot during the big-game season. If the noise is too much for the neighbors, use the lightest available load. In a .30/06, for instance, fire the 125-grain varmint load during most of your varmint shooting, but switch to the heavy hunting load for a few sessions as the deer season approaches.

There is another alternative if your hunting rifle is a .30/30 Winchester, .308, or 30/06. Remington makes

Accelerator cartridges for these rifles so that it is possible to fire a .22 caliber bullet in hunting rifles with accuracy at least as good as with your pet full-power hunting load. Of course the trajectory of the .22 Accelerator bullets will vary a great deal from your hunting load, and for that reason you have to sight-in differently. Just before the hunting season, sight-in again for the hunting load.

Because a varmint is a living creature, you do not know what it will do next, just as you do not know what a deer will do. Trying to score on a woodchuck sitting up near its burrow and showing signs of nervousness is excellent practice. He may go down his burrow before your are precisely on target and ready to squeeze off, so you hurry a bit and miss him completely. The sitting crow suddenly decides to walk on to the next bunch of spilled grain just as you squeeze off a shot. Can you stop the shot in time and catch him a few seconds later when he settles down? It's just like shooting at a skittish mule deer.

As with practice in a dump, varmint shooting is better with a partner. He can spot your shots for you with a spotting scope or even a good binocular. This will tell you whether you missed high or low, left or right, and leads to constructive correction. It's very difficult to see the strike of a bullet when you are firing a high-powered rifle. Commonly the recoil lifts the scope so that you can no longer see the target. Even if you score a hit, you may not see it through your scope.

Why do big-game hunting guides smile and buy a beer for everyone when they learn that the client is a gung-ho varmint shooter? It's because the guide knows that the hunter will almost always center the game after that long climb up the mountain or riding a horse all day. Formal target shooters are not half so adept, especially when the slope is steep and the range is puzzling.

TAKE A REST

In all big-game hunting, you'll do better if you take a rest—both kinds of rest. If you're breathing hard and your heart is pounding after a steep climb or hard run, it is almost impossible to make a hit. Rest a while, even if the deer looks like he might bolt. Steady down before you fire. Dont risk wounding a fine game animal because you were too anxious to get off a shot.

Resting a bit may also give you time to spot a rest in the second sense—a rest for your rifle. A tree crotch, a fallen log, a rolled up coat, a binocular case, anything to steady your aim, particularly if you are still trembling a bit after hard exercise. This advice is often given to shooters without saying that it is not intelligent to rest a rifle stock, much less the barrel, on a hard object. It is unwise because the rifle will bounce away

The kneeling position is steadier than shooting offhand (standing upright) but not as steady as sitting. Yet it raises the rifle fairly high in case the shot must pass over high grass or weeds. The hinged lens covers on the riflescope protect the lenses when not in use. (Grabeklis/ Soderstrom photo)

from the hard object when it is fired and cause a very wild shot. Place your hand on the rest and then put the rifle on your hand. If the rest (a coat or whatever) is soft, but fairly firm, put the rifle forend on it and then reach around or across the rest to grasp the stock. Taking a rest in both senses is something that you should practice regularly, particularly if you will be shooting at long ranges.

TRIGGER CONTROL

Almost all military triggers were of the "two-stage" type, and many of these triggers are still used for hunting in military-surplus and war-souvenir rifles. With this type of trigger, the shooter takes up considerable slack and then encounters firmer resistance. This tells him that the rifle is about to go off, and he settles the sights on target before applying the last ounces of pressure to fire. Two-stage triggers have a bad reputation among hunters, but it's hard to see why. This kind of trigger was developed to give a soldier more control over his rifle, particularly in cold weather when the fingers are numb and when the shooter is often wearing gloves. If you get used to it, there's nothing wrong with a good two-stage trigger. Actually, the two-stage arrangement got a bad reputation because the final let-off was usually very stiff, and this required a great deal of pressure, which sometimes threw off the shot. A gunsmith can rework the mechanism to lighten the final trigger pull.

Quality sporting rifles have single-stage triggers that "break" as clearly as a glass rod. However, even a single-stage trigger has something of a two-stage action. The shooter applies preliminary pressure, but this does not move the trigger; it only compresses the soft tissues of the trigger finger. Finally, the needed additional pressure is applied, and the rifle fires.

Set triggers are designed to give the shooter a very light let-off, a matter of mere ounces. The most common type is the single-set trigger. It can be used as

an ordinary one-stage trigger, but if it is pushed forward just before firing, the let-off is very, very light. Continental Europeans, particularly Germans and Austrians, make many sporting rifles with double-set triggers. Arrangements vary, but usually the forward trigger is pulled to set the mechanism, and the rear trigger is pulled to fire the rifle. To fire with normal trigger tension, use the rear trigger without setting. Some Americans like double-set triggers, but many others feel that the mechanism is very complicated and subject to malfunctions. Also, there's no denying that the combined movements of the additional parts in single-set and double-set triggers can throw off the aim just prior to cartridge ignition.

With any kind of set trigger, remember to unset the mechanism if you do not fire. It comes as a shock when the rifle goes off unexpectedly at the touch of a blade of grass because the trigger mechanism is still set. In many bolt-action rifles, the mechanism is unset by simply opening the bolt, but there are other arrangements.

Trigger pull is a subject of great debate among riflemen. Commonly, target shooters like a very light trigger pull, while hunters need a fairly stiff pull. When wearing gloves or trembling after physical exertion, it's almost impossible to fire accurately with a very light trigger pull or a set trigger. Some pulls are so light that merely touching the trigger with the finger fires the rifle, and this can be very dangerous for someone who is not used to it. Also, if the rifle goes off prematurely, you are almost sure to miss the animal entirely or to merely wound it.

American single-stage triggers are usually set at about 6 pounds for safety's sake, but some triggers are considerably heavier than that. Most hunters cannot use a trigger effectively if it has a pull lighter than 3 pounds, but there is no clear rule. Determining the ideal trigger pull for your rifle depends a great deal on your dexterity and nervous control, and the quality of the rifle let-off.

Formerly, many quality American rifles had adjustable triggers. The weight of the let-off could be changed by turning a screw. Another screw adjusted the backlash—that is, the distance the trigger traveled after let-off occurred. Backlash adjustment was important because sudden travel after let-off could move the rifle and cause a wild shot.

Today many rifles are made without adjustable triggers, and some companies fill the adjustment mechanism with epoxy so the trigger pull cannot be lightened. Accidental injuries—and expensive lawsuits—resulting from rifles that went off prematurely brought this about. American riflemakers are so afraid of the lawsuits that adjustable triggers on sporting rifles are no longer widely available. It is possible to pick the epoxy out of the adjustment mechanism or dissolve it (usually with vinegar), but if you do so, don't set the trigger too light. If you reactivate the adjustment mechanism, you assume full responsibility for the disaster that may ensue.

If the trigger is not adjustable, you can get used to it or have a gunsmith lighten the trigger. This is no job for a home-workshop tinkerer. Again, if you have the trigger pull lightened, the manufacturer has no legal responsibility. Target shooters often have access to a trigger scale that reliably measures trigger pull in parts of an ounce, but hunters can measure trigger pull accurately enough merely by cocking the rifle, bracing it in a vertical position and then placing a weighted cord across the trigger. Add weight until the rifle fires.

Actually, for deer hunting, it's best to leave the trigger strictly alone, unless the pull is really excessive. The only exception is the long-range shooter who really has to have a delicate let-off. Many of these sportsmen buy a separate adjustable trigger mechanism and install in on their long-range rifles. The devices are available from several suppliers.

THE SHOT

For a shot at a standing deer, the hunter usually puts his sights on the part of the animal he wishes to hit, adjusts the sight picture, and then starts his trigger squeeze. It used to be said (too often) that a good shooter does not have to know when the rifle will fire. Instead, he supposedly holds his sights on target and applies slow pressure until the rifle finally fires. He attempts to maintain a perfect sight picture throughout the trigger squeeze. In actuality, this method of shooting is more appropriate to target shooting than hunting. A hunter usually cannot maintain a perfect sight picture (including hold-over for range or hold-off for windage) throughout the trigger squeeze because most hunting rifles have a heavier trigger pull.

Whether they know it or not, most hunters watch the sight picture very carefully while applying trigger pressure. If the sights move off the vital area, the application of pressure on the trigger is stopped. When the crosshairs or the bead move back on target, pressure is again applied, and finally the rifle fires. But because the hunter is familiar with his rifle, he really does know when the rifle is about to fire. He has to know because if he goes too far and the animal moves unexpectedly, he cannot stop the shot and he will wound or miss it.

DRY FIRING

Familiarizing yourself with the sight picture and the trigger isn't easy, but fortunately, it can be practiced at home by dry firing. Make sure the gun is unloaded and then take a sight on a small object in the room. A speck on a light-colored wall will do, or you can make a small mark with a pencil. Take aim, maintain the sight picture, and squeeze. Practice until you develop good trigger control.

Dry firing can teach you a great deal about accuracy. With no cartridge in the rifle, there is no recoil, and you can easily see where the rifle was pointing when let-off occurred. It's astonishing how far off the mark this can be. There is no use in buying a very accurate, expensive rifle if you can't exercise precise trigger control. And it really is a good idea to develop this ability somewhat before firing live ammunition.

Don't worry about dry firing centerfire rifles of modern design. The mechanism can stand more dry firing than you'll ever do. Rifles of older design may break if they are let off too often with an empty chamber, but a short, once-a-week session shouldn't cause trouble.

RANGE ESTIMATION

Estimating the range accurately is perhaps the most important element of making a hit. It is not as important as it once was, however, because the trajectories of modern high-velocity cartridges are so flat the "point-blank" range is quite far out. For instance, consider the .30/06 with a pointed 150-grain bullet. As the Remington ballistics table provided earlier in this section shows, if this cartridge is sighted-in to be dead on at 200 yards, it is only 3.2 inches low at 250 yards. For all practical purposes, you can therefore aim directly at a deer's 8½ × 11 vital area and expect to hit without hold-over at fairly long range. Other long-range cartridges are even flatter than the 150-grain .30/06, but many older cartridges have very curved trajectories. If you hold dead on with these old cartridges even at moderate ranges, you'll miss the deer entirely.

It's obvious that every cartridge, no matter how "flat," reaches a point where it drops rather suddenly. You should know that point and hold high accordingly.

With many older cartridges, the drop is so sudden and so steep that beyond a rather short range it actually becomes almost impossible to hit anything, even a rhinoceros. With these cartridges, range estimation is still extremely important.

Most people have little need to estimate range unless they are using a firearm. They spend much of their lives indoors, and if they do go out of the house, it's usually to ride around in a vehicle. So practice at estimating range is usually needed. The best way, of course, has already been described—impromptu targets at unknown ranges that must be estimated. But you can also practice merely by taking a walk—perhaps on your way to the railroad station or bus stop.

First, determine the length of your average stride or pace. Ideally, this is 3 feet, but only very tall men actually cover 36 inches in one stride. The best way to determine the length of your stride is to walk 100 yards at a normal speed several times and average the number of paces you take. If, for instance, your standard pace is 33 inches, it will take 109 paces. Call it 110 for the sake of an even number. This gives something to use as a guide. Two hundred yards is 220 paces, 300 is 330, and so forth.

As you practice pacing near home, look to one side for a few steps and then suddenly look ahead. Estimate the range to the first object that catches your eye, and then pace it off to see how correct you are. You may be amazed at how wrong you can be. In bright clear light with an unobstructed view, 400 yards may look like 200. In rather dim light with many objects such as trees, dogs, moving people to distract you, 100 yards may look like 200, or even 300. Consistent practice, however, will give you the skill to estimate ranges

Quick-detachable sling swivels: The screw enters the rifle stock and is permanently installed. When the stud is pressed, the spring-loaded bar moves aside so that the bar can be inserted in the hole in the screw. This makes it easy to take the sling off the rifle or put in on as need arises. In thick brush, a sling catches on every obstruction and makes a lot of noise. Also available are detachable sling swivels with rings that go around the barrel.

quite accurately. Each time you estimate range, call up a mental image of how you would hold on a deer-size target in various positions—broadside, end-on, angled, and so forth—until the imaginary sight picture comes to mind automatically. This works much better than any hand-held rangefinder or rangefinding reticle in a scope.

For a long-range shot, a beginning shooter should go through a simple mental checklist. First estimate the range, and determine the needed hold-over, if any; then consciously determine wind direction, its strength, and degree of hold-off needed. Ask yourself about your elevation above the target or how much you are below it; and think about holding a bit low (See the previous section on cartridges and ballistics.) Then settle yourself into the best possible shooting position, preferably with a rest, and steady your rifle

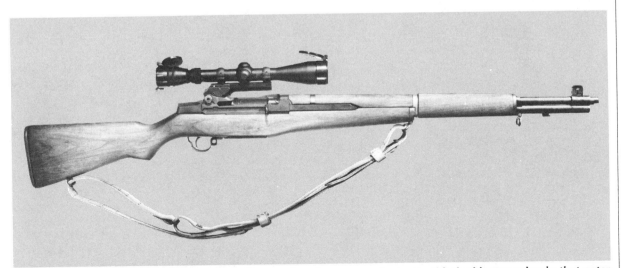

Two-part sling on replica Garand rifle: The sling consists of two separate straps with double prong hooks that enter a series of twin holes in the forward strap so that length can be adjusted. Both straps can be adjusted for length, and the entire sling can be adjusted for overall length. Make the adjustments for the offhand position and then practice getting into the sling-supported position. If you must shorten or lengthen the sling, it's easy to do.

USING A SLING

In the following photos, the rifleman is using a two-part, military-style American sling, not a simple carrying strap. These two-part slings are most useful in the offhand, kneeling, and sitting positions. In prone, the two-part sling must be readjusted for proper length, and few hunters would bother to take the time since prone is a very steady position without use of a sling. Target shooters frequently use slings when shooting prone. But getting into a sling loop is usually not worth the trouble when hunting if a steady external rest is available.

Offhand with minimal sling support

This can be done with a simple one-piece carrying strap as well as with a two-part military sling. Insert the left arm between the sling and the rifle stock. Grasp the forend as usual and push to the left with your elbow. If enough steady tension is achieved, this steadies the rifle a great deal and many shooter's find that it is all the additional support they need. Also, this can be done very fast. (Neil Soderstrom photos)

Offhand with hasty sling

After inserting your left arm between sling and rifle, move your left forearm to the left so that sling crosses wrist. Push your left elbow to the left and push your left hand forward. The twisting effect of the tense sling gives some additional support. With practice, it's very quick, too. Practice this use of a sling and the previous one in all positions except prone.

Offhand with full sling support

1. *Insert your left arm through the sling loop.* **2.** *Loop should go quite high on the arm.*

3. *With right hand, shove the leather "keeper" down on left arm to lock the loop in place.* **4.** *Insert your left hand under the forend as usual with sling tight across the back of the hand. Push your left hand firmly forward toward the sling swivel. Using a sling this way steadies the rifle enormously, and it also takes a lot of tension off the right hand. This makes a careful trigger squeeze easier to achieve.*

on target. Firm up the sight picture and move the safety to the off position. Put your finger on the trigger. Now take a few fairly deep breaths, hold the last one, let out just a little air, and start your trigger squeeze. If the sights wander too far off target, or if you begin to tremble, release the trigger, take a few additional breaths and start all over. Of course, experienced shooters go through this checklist almost unconsciously, but a beginner has to think about it, step by step. Never, never be afraid to cancel a shot and rest if you realize that you cannot shoot accurately. You're shooting at long range, and presumably, the game is not alarmed. You can take your time. And even if the animal does move off, you may be able to make another stalk and try again. If you fire and miss, on the other hand, you may wound or thoroughly spook the animal and never get another chance.

Even with a one-minute-of-angle rifle, most accomplished hunters will not fire at a deer at over 300 yards. True, a few really superb shooters who use magnum bolt-action rifles of fine quality can hit deer consistently at 400 yards. Beyond that, even if you can hit, remaining energy has dropped so much that a good hit may only result in a wounded animal. For most hunters, 250 yards is the outside limit, even with a one-minute-of-angle rifle.

MOVING TARGETS

So far, the discussion has only been concerned with marksmanship when firing at stationary game. With moving targets, there's little time for a fine sight picture and a slow, deliberate trigger squeeze. Many hunters simply will not fire at a moving animal because they know that they lack the ability to make a killing shot, but most will try a shot if an animal is walking slowly at close range, or is moving straight away, straight toward, or at a slight angle to the hunter.

The most difficult shot of all is a target that moves at a right angle, or close to it, at high speed. Hitting a buck running at a right angle out at 100 yards or more is nearly impossible for most weekend hunters. You have to discover your capabilities through practice shooting, and since this is the most difficult form of rifle practice, few hunters develop much ability.

Actually, firing at a close-range moving target is largely instinctive, and the hunter shoots much like an upland bird hunter. The game appears and the shot is fired without conscious sighting or thinking about the trigger pull.

Shooting this way may involve leading the target. Even if the angle is slight, you don't shoot directly at the animal's vital area, but at the point where that vital area will be when the bullet arrives. This is achieved either by "snap shooting"—simply aiming at the future point of impact and firing the shot—or by some other form of conscious lead.

If you have a practice area where it is safe to fire at moving targets, you may be able to develop some ability, or at least find out if you should swear off this kind of shooting. But it's sometimes difficult to find a place to practice. If that is the case, you can try skeet shooting, which will inevitably teach you a great deal about how to lead a target at various angles. It's true that skeet shooters use open-choke shotguns that have a wide pattern and fire at close range, but the principles involved in hitting a moving target are the same as in deer hunting. At the very least, you will find out about your own innate ability to lead and hit a moving target.

If you cannot hit a crossing clay pigeon with a charge of shot from the middle stations on a skeet

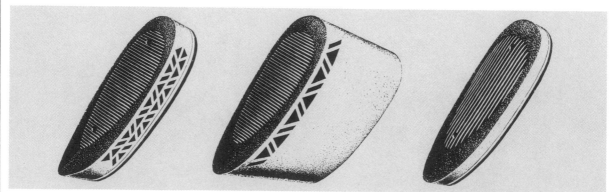

Three recoil pad designs: The vented pad, left, is preferred when stock is to be lengthened. The slip-on pad, middle, has detachable as well as recoil absorbing feature. The solid pad, right, is preferred for rifles with magnum recoil. The slip-on pad lengthens the rifle for use when only a shirt is being worn. Take the pad off when you're wearing heavy clothes. In this way, the rifle's length is altered to suit the circumstances. When it is cold afield, heavy outer clothing absorbs the recoil instead of the pad. One cause of inaccurate shooting is fear of recoil (flinching), and using some form of padding, especially in long practice sessions, helps a great deal.

field, you should not consider a right-angle shot at a galloping buck at 200 yards. Deer hunters can learn a great deal on the skeet field, and perhaps the most important lesson is to refrain from attempting difficult shots at moving targets.

CLEANING AND MAINTENANCE

Only a few years ago, shooters cleaned their firearms immediately after any use. Today, with noncorrosive primers, smokeless powders, and jacketed bullets, many shooters clean their guns thoroughly only once or twice a year. The residue in the barrel actually forms a protective coating that prevents, rather than causes, damage. Under most circumstances, your own (acidic) sweat is much more damaging to metal than the aftereffects of firing the rifle.

It's usually enough to wipe down the exterior parts of the rifle with an oily cloth and to store it in a dry place. The temperature should remain fairly even so that condensation does not deposit moisture on metal faces. *Much* more careful cleaning is required if you use old ammunition or if you live in a very damp climate, particularly on the coast near salt water. Under such circumstances, clean your rifle thoroughly every time it is used.

Many accomplished target shooters do not clean the bore of their rifles until the point is reached where accuracy is about to deteriorate, and they know when because they have fired long strings of shots through the bore many times. Accuracy is affected by powder residue and gilding metal from bullet jackets left in the bore. Rifles vary in the number of shots that can be fired before these deposits begin to affect accuracy. Some rifles have rougher bores than others, for instance, and the abrasion can strip a lot of metal off the bullet jackets in only a few shots. If you practice shooting fairly often, you'll learn when a thorough cleaning should be done in order to forestall too great a buildup.

Cleaning Procedure. Hoppe's No. 9 "Powder Solvent" is a favorite bore-cleaning liquid, but there are several others. The name "Powder Solvent" is actually something of a misnomer. The liquid contains chemicals that dissolve powder residue, but another component acts on copper alloy and turns it into a soft, gray-green substance that is easily wiped out of the bore.

When cleaning is needed, dip a bronze or brass brush into the solvent and run it through the rifle bore several times with your rod. If possible, remove the bolt and insert the cleaning rod from the rear. This

prevents damage to the lands and grooves at the muzzle, which can ruin the accuracy of any barrel. If it is not possible to remove the bolt or breechblock, you must work from the muzzle, but make an effort not to touch the barrel with the cleaning rod. You can purchase funnel-like soft-metal guide tubes that guard the muzzle from damage. Or make your own from a suitable small-bore cartridge case by drilling a hole through its head. If you use these devices, make sure that you remove the guide and clean the muzzle itself after the main cleaning job has been done.

After scrubbing the bore with the solvent, put a clean cloth patch on your cleaning rod and wipe the bore out as thoroughly as possible. Use several patches until one comes out entirely free of powder residue and greenish matter. If a bore has been neglected for a considerable period, you may have to clean it once and then do the job all over again the next day or even on a third day.

If so, clean as thoroughly as possible, and then dampen the bore with solvent again. Place the rifle on its side in a safe place and leave it for a few hours. Then turn the rifle over so that the solvent will seep onto the other half of the bore, and let some additional time pass. The idea is to allow time for the solvent to work on the copper-alloy residue. Then go to work with your brush and patches again and repeat until the last patch comes out perfectly clean.

Cleaning schedule. At least once a year, the firearm should be disassembled as completely as possible and thoroughly cleaned. Some guns disassemble quite easily—at least down to the major components, such as the trigger group. Others, such as double-barreled rifles with box locks, should never be disassembled except by an experienced gunsmith. Whatever the case, take the gun down as far as you can and go to work with powder solvent, a small brush, swabs, and perhaps a toothpick or two. You'll find plenty of gunk if the rifle has been used fairly often.

Clean all parts as thoroughly as possible, and then coat them with a light coat of gun oil. Do not use too much. Dirt combines with oil to form a thick gunk that can actually stop the function of moving parts. If the mechanism is especially difficult to clean because of parts that cannot be dismantled, soak it in solvent, let it dry and then take the mechanism to an automobile service station and use the air hose to blow out the wet gunk.

If you hunt in an area where the temperature goes far below freezing, lubricate moving parts with gun oil that is guaranteed to remain liquid at extremely low temperatures. Clean and wipe the mechanism dry and then apply the low-temperature lubricant sparingly. In extreme cases, it is best to use some form of dry lube or graphite compound, instead of a liquid. The most common failure caused by very low tem-

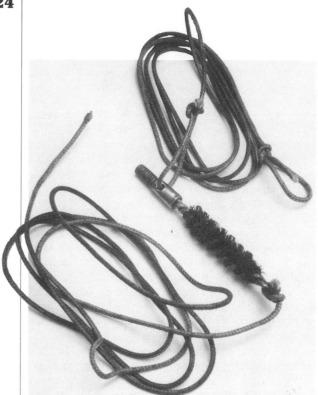

This home-modified pull-through for rifle cleaning is made of 125-pound-test Dacron fishing line, which is not affected by gun-cleaning solvents. It is also so stiff that it can be pushed through bore. The brush is an ordinary screw-on type, intended for use on a bore-cleaning rod. A small hole is drilled in the shank of the brush assembly to take the line. The brush is pulled back and forth in bore. To avoid scratching the bore, line and brush must be clean, so carry pull-through in a film canister. (Neil Soderstrom photo)

peratures is the failure of a firing pin to impact the primer with enough force to detonate it. It's very frustrating to hear the firing pin fall when your sights are on on a deer. You never hear it if the rifle goes off.

Condensation. Condensed moisture on a hunting arm can result in a lot of damage, and is usually caused by bringing the rifle into a warm room after a hunt in cold weather. If the temperature change is very great, moisture will form on all metal surfaces. One way to avoid this is to leave the rifle in an unheated room or outside shed. Keep the rifle out in the cold, and moisture will not condense on it or the scope. If this is not possible, use a soft gun case or some other tight-fitting bag to prevent a sudden temperature change. Leave the case outside in the cold when you go hunting. When you come back, put the rifle in the case, close it partway, and squeeze out as much air as possible. Then close the case completely and bring it indoors. The case or bag warms up very slowly and transmits this warmth even more slowly to the rifle. Because warm air does not suddenly come in contact with the metal, very little moisture, if any,

condenses out of the air. Next morning, however, make a quick inspection, and if any moisture is present, wipe metal surfaces down with an oily rag. Check the bore too.

The pull-through. A good one-piece cleaning rod is best for thorough bore cleaning at home. You should also have the right size brush, a good supply of solvent, gun oil, and precut patches. Jointed rods that screw together for easy transport are really too weak to be useful. The threads between sections soon strip or break, and these rods bend easily.

For use on a hunting trip, a pull-through is usually enough to clean the bore thoroughly, and everything you need can be carried in a small bag. You can make pull-throughs out of 125-test Dacron fishing line with a patch tied into a noose in the middle and a small lead weight on one end. Drop the weight through the barrel and pull the patch back and forth through the bore. You can even modify a metal bore brush so that there is a metal loop on each end. Tie the brush in the middle of the pull-through cord and pull it back and forth in the bore. In general, cleaning a hunting rifle during a hunt should not really be necessary, unless the rifle is soaked or you suspect that there is salt in the bore. If you start out with a clean, dry bore, it should remain clean enough to fire accurately several times.

Cleaning the bore of a bolt rifle is quite easy because the bolt can be removed. With a lever gun, pump, semi-auto, and many single-shots, the bolt or breechblock is very hard to remove. If this is the case with your rifle, place a piece of white paper or a wad of cotton wool at the rear of the open breech. Hold the breech end of the rifle to a bright light and look through the muzzle to inspect the bore. Enough light will be reflected into the tube to make close inspection for any remaining dirt and metal fouling possible. This is a good way to check for bore obstructions such as sand or even a twig that could cause a burst barrel.

Loose screws. On an extended hunting trip, screwdrivers are much more important than a cleaning kit. You should have a screwdriver that fits the screws that hold your sight or scope bases on the rifle, one to fit the screws of the split rings, plus a third larger screwdriver that fits the guard screws holding the barreled action in the stock. Rifles and scopes sometimes get hard knocks in transport, and sudden changes in temperature and moisture can cause dimensional changes in the stock.

All of this can loosen screws holding an action and barrel, or sights or scope, in place, and movement of these parts results in shot-to-shot inconsistency. Nothing infuriates a hunter more than to spend thousands of dollars for a guided wilderness hunt, only to arrive in camp with a loose scope and find that no one has the right size screwdriver. In this situation, all your rifle practice doesn't matter a tinker's damn. Inspect your rig for loose screws as soon as you arrive in camp, and tighten anything that moves. Check the zero afterward by firing the rifle.

It's also a good idea to have a packet of photographer's lens tissue in your pocket at all times if you use a scope, and to have another one tucked away in a dry place in case the one in your pocket gets wet. Wipe exterior lens surfaces only with this tissue. *Clean* lens tissue will not scratch the lenses. Transparent plastic lens caps are useful, too. They protect scope lenses during transport. Some shooters keep them in place during hunts and actually sight through them, except when there is time to remove them for a long, more deliberate shot. Spring-loaded lens caps are available. Pressing a button or a lever swings the lens caps aside just before the hunter fires.

Storage. To store a rifle for a long period, it's usually enough to clean all metal surfaces and then coat them with rust-inhibiting grease intended for use on firearms. Store the rifle in a dry place. Don't forget to coat the bore thoroughly, and don't forget to remove the thick grease when you reactivate the rifle. Thick grease can cause a split or burst bore if the rifle is fired.

Years ago, many hunters fired a "fouling shot" before they started hunting. This was intended to foul the bore before a shot was fired at game. It was done because hunters believed that the first shot fired from a clean, dry bore would have a different point of impact than subsequent shots fired from a fouled bore. Today, powder residue and jacket metal build up so slowly that second, third, and so on shots do not wander at all, or only a small amount. The best advice is to refrain from fouling shots. There should be very little difference between the impact point of a shot fired from a clean, dry bore and one fired from a dirty bore. You can check this during practice shooting.

Blocked bores. Water in a bore can cause bulged or burst barrels, particularly if it freezes and forms hard ice. If it's raining, it's best to carry your rifle with the barrel slanted downward. You can even sling a rifle over your shoulder with the muzzle slanted downward, but don't make the angle too steep or it will point at one of your feet. G. I. Joe, during World War II and the Korean War, commonly placed a small tin can over the muzzle so that he could carry the gun slung with the muzzle up and still keep the rain and moisture out. The trouble with this is that the can rattles around and falls off or is pulled off by twigs. It's much better to place a short length of thin waterproof tape over the muzzle. Don't worry—the tape does not affect accuracy when you fire. Air pressure builds up ahead of the moving bullet and either bursts the tape or blasts it off before the bullet arrives at the muzzle.

Rifles are still heir to all sorts of troubles, but thank your lucky stars for modern arms and ammunition. They are so well made, strong, and dependable that they seldom cause serious trouble during a hunt. A little care is enough to guarantee sure functioning. This, of course, does not apply to a luxurious firearm embellished with superb checkering, inlay work, a finely finished stock, and goodness knows what else in the way of decoration. If you own that kind of rifle, you may spend most of your time worrying about it during a hunt, instead of actively trying to kill a decent buck. My advice is to leave such rifles at home in a securely locked or hidden gun cabinet. Take a plain practical rifle on your hunting trips. The ultimate snob, of course, buys a finely finished, custom piece and treats it like an unaltered military rifle. That kind of one-upmanship is unwelcome in most hunting camps.

GUN SAFETY

Older books on shooting usually included a long chapter on gun safety or, at least, the once popular "Ten Commandments of Gun Safety." Times have changed. With the revival of muzzleloader shooting and the growing popularity of handgun hunting, plus the increasing use of shotgun slugs, safety has become a more complex problem. A short discussion can't possibly cover all the hazards. Yet, many hazards are discussed in detail where appropriate in this text.

Fortunately, however, most states now make it mandatory for first-time hunters to take a hunter-safety course. In these courses, the shooter learns a great deal about arms and ammunition and archery tackle, but the emphasis is on avoiding accidents. These courses are given by sportsmen's associations with the guidance of state game departments, and they logically concentrate on the kinds of hunting done in the hunter's home state. The emphasis is very much on safe gun handling. The course can teach you more than any printed material since demonstrations are given. Even if your home state does not require that you take a hunter-safety course in order to obtain a license, it's best to take the course on a voluntary basis anyway. You'll probably learn more than any publication could tell you.

Actually, however, one safety rule does deserve emphasis: Keep your firearm pointed in a safe direction at all times, even if you believe it is unloaded. If you maintain your firearm in good condition and follow that single rule, you will *never* shoot anyone else by accident and you will *never* shoot yourself. Could anything be simpler? In reality, you are much safer at the target range or out hunting than you are when driving a car, many times safer, but that's no reason for being careless.

SMOOTHBORE HUNTING: BUCKSHOT AND SLUGS

A repeating shotgun loaded with buckshot shells is a fearsome firearm. There are nine .33 caliber lead balls in the 12-gauge 2¾-inch 00 Buckshot load, a very popular cartridge. With four shells in the magazine and one in the chamber of a repeating shotgun, the gunner can trigger off 45 projectiles in five shots. Each ball is a third of an inch in diameter, and the muzzle velocity is about 1,300 feet per second. Because each pull of the trigger launches nine projectiles, they leave the muzzle at least as fast as rounds from a submachine gun, and most submachine guns have only a 20-round magazine capacity.

Big-bore shotguns loaded with buckshot have been used to kill polar and grizzly bears, African horned game, and lions. Buckshot-loaded shotguns are often used by game wardens and professional hunters when following up a wounded leopard in heavy cover. A heavy buckshot load is more than enough to kill a leopard or even a lion if the shot is taken at close range, and a good shotgun is quicker to put on target than any rifle.

The awesome reputation of buckshot makes it puzzling for a first-time user when he finds that, for deer hunting, it is quite ineffective at ranges that exceed, at most, 60 yards (with the most powerful loads). And a deer is a rather small animal that is actually quite easy to kill.

A SHORT-RANGE FIREARM

The accompanying drawing shows the actual size of buckshot used in the United States. A single .36 caliber lead ball (000 Buck, called *triple-Oh)*, the largest available, weighs about 71 grains. At a muzzle velocity of, say, 1,300 feet per second, energy at 100 yards has dropped to 84 foot-pounds. The reason for this sharp drop is that a round ball has a very poor aerodynamic shape. A pointed rifle bullet would retain its energy much better if fired at the same velocity. The 84 foot-pounds of energy is about the same energy retained by a .22 Rimfire Long Rifle bullet at 100 yards, and shooting deer with a .22 Rimfire is universally forbidden by state laws.

In the 3-inch 12-gauge 000 Buck load, there are 10

shot of .36 caliber. Multiplying 84 foot-pounds of energy by 10, we come to the conclusion that, roughly, the 100-yard energy of this heavy deer load is only 840 foot-pounds. This is quite a bit less that the 1,200 foot-pounds of energy that is generally considered satisfactory on-target energy for a deer-hunting rifle. This very powerful shotgun deer load is obviously not effective at 100 yards, and yet, many inexperienced

| No. 4 | No. 3 | No. 2 | No. 1 | No. 0 | No. 00 | No. 000 |
| .24 | .25 | .27 | .30 | .32 | .33 | .36 |

Buckshot diameters in inches: No. 000 buckshot was introduced only a few years ago. It adds several yards to the maximum effective range of buckshot. For deer, however, 00 buck in a 12-gauge gun is the more popular.

hunters will fire it at a deer at that range and expect an instantaneous kill. These great expectations, usually harbored by hunters who have previously used only centerfire rifles, are the reason why buckshot loads have a bad reputation for wounding deer.

Even if you could hit a deer with 840 foot-pounds of energy in a heavy buckshot load at 100 yards, you probably would not kill the animal. You would have to hit the deer with all 10 shot, and that's difficult. For best results, you would have to hit the vital heart-lung area with all the shot, and that is impossible. Remember that the heart-lung area of a deer is approximately the size of an 8½×11-inch sheet of typewriting paper, if you have a broadside shot. You'd be very lucky indeed if you managed to put three of the 10 pellets in that area at 100 yards, and three of these pellets would yield only 252 foot-pounds of energy. Penetration would be shallow because of low energy and because of the blunt, rounded shape of the projectiles. Of course, the other seven shot might connect with the deer, and it's faintly possible that one or two would hit the spine, cut an artery, or penetrate the brain, but you simply cannot depend on it.

On the average, what is the extreme effective range of buckshot loads when used in deer hunting? Exact ranges are impossible to determine because so many factors enter into the "equation." But approximations can be developed by considering each factor in turn. This will also give a lot of useful information about these deer loads.

SHOT SIZE AND NUMBER OF PELLETS

The diameter of buckshot ranges from .36 inch in 000 down to .24 inch in No. 4. The larger and heavier the projectile, the longer velocity and energy are retained during flight since muzzle velocity in buckshot loads does not vary a great deal from load to load. For this reason alone, most hunters opt for 000 or 00 Buck and ignore the smaller sizes, but that may be a mistake.

A few years ago, 00 Buckshot, then the largest size, had a poor reputation for accuracy. The most popular load was the 2¾-inch 12-gauge shell with nine shot. In tightly choked guns, patterns were so wide and spotty that the hunter was lucky to hit any part of a deer with three or four pellets, much less put enough lead in a vital area to make a sure one-shot kill. For that reason, many experienced shotgunners opted for the smaller sizes, particularly No. 4, the smallest in 12-gauge guns. In the standard factory-loaded 2¾-inch shell, this load contains 27 pellets. At reasonable ranges, the hunter could, therefore, expect to hit a deer with 10 or 12 pellets, and in most cases four or five of them would hit the vital heart-lung area when shooting broadside. For a then unknown reason, the small No. 4 Buckshot produced denser, more even patterns than the 00.

But the smaller pellets had less retained energy out at 45 or 50 yards; so penetration was less, and many gunners would not shoot at a deer with No. 4 in a 12 gauge at any more than 30 yards or so. Some hunters compromised by using No. 1 Buck in the standard 12-gauge shell (16 pellets) or No. 0 (12 pellets). This is one dilemma of using buckshot. Heavier pellets have greater individual energy, but there are fewer of them than there are of the smaller sizes when loaded in the same capacity shell. The problem is often to find an acceptable compromise between retained energy and the number of shot that hit the target.

The problem was partially solved when buffered buckshot loads were introduced. In these shells spaces between the projectiles are filled with granulated plastic. This prevents most shot deformation caused by firing, by bouncing of shot against bore, and by "jostling" of shot during passage down the barrel. The buffering also greatly improves pattern density and uniformity of buckshot fired from tightly choked guns. All major manufacturers of buckshot cartridges now offer buffered loads. Not using them limits the effective range of your shotgun quite a bit.

It used to be said that large buckshot formed tighter, more even patterns when fired from open-choke shotguns. But with buffered loads, tight patterns are produced by 000, 00, and 0 Buckshot when fired from tightly choked shotguns. Use of the smaller sizes in 12-gauge guns is no longer so common.

GAUGE

Buckshot loads are made in 10 gauge, 12 gauge, 16 gauge, and 20 gauge. Twenty-eight gauge and .410 shells, smallest of them all, are not available with buckshot charges. The small number of buckshot of any size that these two shotguns could fire make them completely ineffective for deer hunting.

The nominal bore diameters (some manufacturers vary slightly) of the six shotgun gauges are shown on the next page.

In other words, the largest bore available today is larger than ¾ of an inch, and the smallest one that is useful with buckshot to any degree is bigger than the bore of a .50 caliber American machine gun.

The larger the gauge, the greater the number of shot in the shell, all other things being equal. With the mighty 3½-inch 10-gauge Magnum, the only two buckshot loadings at present are charged with 18 00 Buckshot or 54 No. 4. Both are manufactured by Federal Cartridge. With the small size of No. 4 buckshot, the loading is obviously intended more for fairly close-range shooting at moving deer. The very heavy 00 Buckshot load is best at longer ranges.

Before you go out and buy a 10-gauge gun, however, you should note that they are expensive, very heavy (11 pounds or so), bulky, and that the recoil is punishing for most shooters. Shorter, less powerful 10-gauge loads are available.

Twelve-gauge loads are available in many different sizes of buckshot from 000 down to No. 4. Twelve-gauge shotguns are chambered for the 2¾-inch shell or the 3-inch magnum. These lengths, as with all shotgun shells, refer to the unfolded length of the case after firing. The 3-inch 12 gauge has a greater capacity than the shorter case. If you have a gun chambered for the 3-inch shell, you can also fire the shorter shells in it. The short shell is loaded as a magnum (more shot and more energy) or with "standard" 2¾-inch charges. This gives the shooter three broad classes of 12-gauge buckshot (and birdshot) loads to choose from and makes for a great deal of flexibility. If you have a gun with 3-inch chambers, you have the option of firing progressively lighter loads if the heavy ones prove too much for you or if the gun does not handle them well.

BORE DIAMETERS OF SHOTGUN GAUGES

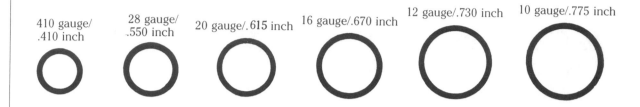

The 28-gauge and .410 bore are too small to be effective with buckshot or slug loads in big-game hunting. The 12-gauge is by far the most popular, but very heavy buckshot and slug loads are now available in 10-gauge. Some manufacturers vary from the bore dimensions given here by a thousandth of inch or several. By coincidence, the 12-gauge bore is almost exactly the diameter of a U.S. dime, but a dime will not actually enter the muzzle of most 12-gauge guns because of choke constriction.

The heaviest 12-gauge 3-inch magnum is loaded with 10 pellets of 000 Buckshot, and a dozen other 12-gauge loadings are currently available. These include 000 Buck, 00, 0, No. 1., and No. 4. Obviously, you can easily change your load quite a bit to suit changing hunting needs. Even if you do not have a 12 that will take 3-inch shells, there are eight different 2¾-inch loads.

A great variety of 12-gauge shotguns is available. Pump, semi-automatic, double-barreled, single-shot, and even bolt-action 12-gauge guns are on the market in countless model variations. Prices range from moderate to a king's ransom. With the other gauges, particularly the 10 and the 16, the variety is extremely limited. In 20 gauge there is a good variety of guns, but the 20 has severe limitations when used with buckshot.

Sixteen-gauge guns are being phased out, and very few of them are being made, even in Europe. If you're buying a new shotgun for any purpose, it's best to avoid the 16 because the variety of loads available in this gauge constantly declines. Currently, the only 16-gauge buckshot load is 12 pellets of No. 1 Buck, a compromise between a long-range and a short-range shell.

The choice in 20-gauge buckshot loads is limited, too. You can use a 20-gauge 3-inch magnum of No. 2 Buck (18 pellets) or a 2¾-inch load of No. 3 Buck (20 pellets). The larger buckshot sizes are not available in 20-gauge shells. It's obviously best to avoid using a 20-gauge gun with buckshot because of this lack of versatility and because the small number of pellets in the available sizes severely limit effective range.

In leafing through ammunition tables for useful buckshot loads, you'll find odd gaps. For instance, using 00 Buckshot in a 20-gauge gun might seem like a good way to increase effective range, but doing so

is not possible. Too few 00 projectiles could be loaded in the small case. Also, 00 Buck is .33 inch in diameter, and the 20 gauge has a .615 bore diameter. Two of these shot equal .66 inch in diameter, which is only .045 larger than the bore. In other words, two balls could easily jam in the bore on firing, causing a bulged barrel or even a burst one. For similar reasons, many "logical" or "improved" buckshot loads are lacking.

CHOKE AND PATTERN

One of the most important considerations is the choke of the shotgun. Without going into great detail, most modern shotguns are choked Extra Full, Full, Improved Modified, Modified, Improved Cylinder, and Cylinder. Extra Full is the tightest choke available, and a shotgun bored Cylinder has no constriction at the muzzle. Choke is intended to concentrate the shot into an even, dense pattern at long ranges. With buckshot, the objective is to place as many shot as possible in the small vital area of a deer and, for this, the obvious choice is the tightest possible choke.

The usual method of determining the degree of choke is to fire at a large paper target at a range of 40 yards. If a 30-inch circle drawn on this target encloses over 75 percent of the pellet holes, the choke is Extra Full. Full is 65–75 percent; Improved Modified, 55–65 percent; Modified, 45 to 55; and Improved Cylinder, 35 to 45. A Cylinder bore usually throws a 25 to 35 percent pattern. Many authorities differ on the precise percentages for each degree of choke, and most American guns are labeled Full, Modified, Improved Cylinder, and Cylinder.

But a 30-inch circle is much larger than a deer's

vital area, and percentages taken with buckshot will probably not match the choke marking on your gun barrel.

The only way to check out your shotgun is to put up a full-size paper target of a deer of the type used by bowhunters and fire at it with various buckshot loads. If full-size deer targets seem expensive to you, buy only one and cut out the deer's image. Then trace the outline on large sheets of paper.

Start out at a reasonable range, say 30 yards and fire a few shells. Then increase the range in 5-yard increments until the pattern disperses to such a great degree that putting three pellets in the heart-lung area becomes merely a matter of chance. Most hunters agree that if you hit the heart-lung area with at least three pellets, you'll make a quick kill. If you hit the heart death is almost instantaneous, and if three pellets pierce the lungs, you won't have to track the deer very far. The point at which you simply cannot put at least three pellets into the vital area should be considered your maximum effective range with that particular load. Doing all this will also give you a good idea of where your pattern is actually going in relationship to your shotgun sights. With buckshot, it's best to use the single-bead or double-bead sighting equipment that is installed on bird-hunting guns.

Don't be surprised if the results are terrible. In some guns marked Full, 00-Buckshot pattern is so thin at only 30 yards that it is completely useless at that short range. Because of all the variables that go into buckshot performance, a beat-up, barbed-wire scratched pump gun that cost only $90 secondhand may fire a better buckshot pattern than a fine new shotgun. Choke markings on barrels are often meaningless. You may find that a Cylinder-bored skeet gun fires a tighter, more even pattern than an Extra Full, long-range duck gun.

If one load does not work, try another. Dropping down one size in the diameter of the buckshot may improve the density of the pattern, and doing just the opposite may have the same result. Sometimes, a very heavy magnum load does not perform well in a given shotgun. You may even find that you have an old-fashioned doughnut pattern in which most of the shot tends to impact at the edge of the pattern, leaving the center empty. Holes in the pattern are to be avoided because the hole may coincide with the small heart-lung area.

In patterning buckshot, it's also wise to remember that you may fire at a deer that is facing you, and in that case, the maximum heart-lung area is only 6 or 8 inches wide. If you're wise, you won't fire at a deer that is facing straight away from you because the penetration of buckshot is very limited. Even the largest shot entering from the rear will often fail to penetrate all the way to the vital area. In patterning on a full-size picture of a deer, pay very little attention to hits in the head and neck area. They're a matter of good luck, at best, unless you are firing at close range.

Some shotguns simply will not handle any buckshot load well. If such is the case with your gun, it's best to beg, borrow, or buy another that patterns well. Wounding a deer with buckshot so that it gets away to die in agony is wrong, whether you do it with a shotgun or a rifle.

MAXIMUM RANGE

Because good buckshot performance depends on so many different factors, some of them not clearly understood, it's obviously impossible to determine precise maximum effective ranges for these loads. Experience and testing on paper targets counts more than mere calculation. But some generalizations can be made. Listed below are maximum effective ranges for buckshot-loaded shotguns, using the heaviest buckshot loads—those with the largest projectiles. It is assumed that buffered loads are used and that the gun fires a dense, even pattern.

With smaller buckshot, you must shoot at shorter ranges under most circumstances, but sometimes you'll come across a shotgun that throws very dense, very tight patterns with it. At medium ranges these patterns enable you to put more shot on target than you can with the larger sizes of buckshot. In other words, you increase the total energy by increasing the number of pellets rather than the size (and weight) of each projectile. If you have such a gun, hang onto it. They're hard to find.

Many hunters will disagree with the maximum ranges listed below. Some old-timers have never fired the new buffered loads or are unfamiliar with magnum shells. They will say that these ranges are too long. Other hunters have killed deer at longer ranges, and

MAXIMUM RANGES FOR BUCKSHOT LOADS

Gauge/Shot	Yards
10-gauge 3½-inch Magnum, 00 Buck	60
12-gauge 3-inch Magnum, 000 Buck	55
12-gauge 2¾-inch Magnum, 000 Buck	50
12-gauge 2¾ inch standard loading, 00 buck	40
16-gauge No. 1 Buck	35
20-gauge 3-inch Magnum, No. 2 Buck	30
20-gauge, 2¾-inch shell, No. 3 Buck	25

they will say the ranges are much too conservative. But these maximums are intended only as a general guide. Test your gun until you yourself find out what the best load is and its maximum range. Never exceed it.

Range estimation is obviously important when using buckshot. If you're shaky in this area, practice regularly, using the methods described earlier, in the section on marksmanship. Those who regularly hunt with centerfire rifles are often very accurate when estimating ranges in excess of 100 yards, but when it comes to telling the difference between 50 and 65 yards, or 25 from 30, they simply can't do it.

RECOIL AND ACCURACY

The recoil of heavy buckshot loads is so great that some shooters simply cannot handle it. This is particularly true when these loads are fired in lightweight bird-hunting guns. The heavier the gun, other things being equal, the less the felt recoil. If recoil does bother you, using a gas-operated semi-automatic shotgun helps a bit because the gas mechanism helps to dampen the impact. A thick recoil pad on the butt of the shotgun helps, too. The worst gun for heavy loads is probably a side-by-side double shotgun with a European-style splinter forend and a high, sharp comb.

Recoil can have a subtle effect on accuracy. Many heavy, powerful men say that the recoil does not bother them at all. Yet, I've seen such people make astonishing misses at quite close ranges when using these loads, even though they are very accurate with light bird-hunting cartridges and when shooting trap and skeet. The only possible conclusion is that, unknown to themselves, they do fear the recoil of heavy shells and do flinch when they pull the trigger. If you're a good shot with light loads and yet miss a great deal with heavy ones, this is probably the case with you. If so, you have no choice except to use lighter loads and limit the range at which you fire.

THE HUNTING SITUATION

In many parts of the South, deer are hunted with shotguns and dogs. The gunners are posted in place on stands, and the huntsman and his helpers take the hounds around to the other side of the cover and drive deer to the standers. This form of hunting often takes place in very heavy cover where nothing can be seen beyond 20 or 25 yards. For this type of hunting, the emphasis is on more pellets in the load instead of long-range killing capability with heavy buckshot.

You must be able to see the deer or you cannot fire with reasonable accuracy. If you can see the deer, it is obviously only a short distance away, and there are holes in the cover for the buckshot to travel through. You're better off with, say, 27 pellets of No. 4 Buck in a 12-gauge gun that you are with only eight 000 Buckshot. Besides, most southern dog packs include at least one good tracking hound that can be used on leash to go after a wounded deer. Of course, every decent hunter wants to put the deer down with one shot, but if you don't succeed, following the deer by means of a hound makes it possible to get in another shot or track it to the place where it has died.

Outside the South, almost every state and Canadian province forbids hunting with hounds, and if you actively hunt deer with a shotgun, you'll eventually find that big buckshot works better, on the average, than smaller sizes. With hounds, the deer are almost always moving when the shot is taken. In stillhunting, if you're skilled, you'll get standing shots, often at rather long range. For this, large sizes are more effective.

But many deer are shot from tree stands and ground stands, and some of these shots may be only a matter of 20 yards, if that. In this situation, many hunters rely on the smaller sizes, feeling that the advantage of more shot outweighs greater penetration. Actually, if the deer is very close, large-diameter buckshot does very well. If, on the other hand, you do get a shot at long range from a stand because the deer simply refuses to come closer, you're equipped for it. It's also true that a few large buckshot ruin less meat than half a handful of smaller shot.

One way to be ready for what comes along is to use a double-barreled shotgun and load one barrel with heavy buckshot and the other with lighter (smaller) shot. For a moving shot at close range, trigger the smaller pellets; for a long-range standing shot, use big buckshot. The disadvantage is that you only have two shots to fire, and if the deer is at long range, you only have one effective load. Most hunters, therefore, prefer to use a pump gun or a semi-automatic and load it with only one kind of shell best suited to the type of shot that they usually get.

One dodge is to load a repeater with short-range loads but put a heavy long-range load in the chamber. If a long-range standing shot offers, fire the heavy load. If the gunner doesn't score at long-range, the thinking goes, he wouldn't get another shot anyway because the deer often gets beyond maximum range very, very quickly once a shot is fired. If, on the other hand, a moving animal appears at close range, the heavy load is fired, followed as quickly as possible by the short-range load or loads. If the heavy shell puts the deer down, well and good; but if the deer keeps going, you'll get on target quickly with the other shells. Sometimes, it works just fine. Sometimes it doesn't.

PRACTICE

Simply patterning your shotgun and determining maximum range is sufficient training for firing at stationary deer. For moving deer, you have to acquire many of the skills of a wingshooter, and this is particularly important for those who participate in deer drives with dogs or human drivers. Fortunately, practicing for moving targets is a lot of fun, and the name of the game is skeet.

It's true that the ranges in this clay-target game are very short, but the principles of lead are the same, and the velocities of the shot do not differ from heavy buckshot loads. Skeet is better than trap shooting because the angles vary more greatly. Shoot starting from a low-gun position. You can't walk around in the woods with a shotgun already mounted on your shoulder, and by all means, use your regular hunting shotgun rather than a specialized skeet gun. But load your gun with No. 8 or No. 9 skeet shells. You won't shoot high scores, but you'll become a better deer hunter.

RIFLED SLUGS

The factory-loaded rifled-slug cartridges available in the United States are of two basic types. The American or "Foster" slug is a hollow-based projectile made of soft lead. The hollow in the base is very large and forms a skirt that is easily compressed by a shotgun's choke so that it will pass through the constriction without causing any damage to the gun.

The soft skirt first expands on firing because of the upsetting of the soft lead. The expanded skirt fills the bore and provides a bearing surface that guides the slug down the barrel without tilting, but if choke of any degree is present, the skirt contracts on reaching it. The expanding and contracting skirt provides some gas sealing (obturation), and these slugs are backed by soft wads that also seal the barrel against gas leakage.

American rifled slugs fly point first (if the blunt forward end can be called a point) only because the point contains a much greater weight of metal than the thin skirt. The angled "rifling" vanes on the exterior surface of the skirt are said to impart a spin to the projectile because of the action of atmospheric drag on the angled surfaces. Some investigators report that there is a very slow rotation; others report none.

German Brenneke slug loads, widely available in North America, were first used in Europe during the 1890s and have certainly proven themselves as reasonably accurate ever since. Europeans once had a wide variety of slug designs, and the French are still

turning out new ones, but the Brenneke survives all competition. The Brenneke slug is solid soft lead, though a deep circular groove in the base of the slug does allow some compression. Because the Brenneke slug is solid, it is shorter in length than the hollow American slug. If it were not rather short, it would have to be so heavy that the force needed to propel it would cause intolerable recoil.

Short, solid projectiles fired from smooth bores tumble shortly after leaving the muzzle, and slow rotation provided by the angled exterior rifling, if any, would not overcome this tendency. Brenneke solved this problem by attaching wads solidly to the slug by the simplest possible means—a wood screw. A Brenneke slug travels with its blunt point forward simply because the attached lightweight wads are the rear part of the projectile. As with the American Foster slug, this puts the weight forward. This screw also centers the solid slug on the wads and prevents side-to-side movement or tilting during travel down a slightly oversize bore.

Rifled slugs of both kinds are vast improvements over the single, round "punkin balls" that were formerly used in shotguns for deer hunting. Primarily, slugs are better because they fill the bore completely by means of expansion or attached wads. The punkin ball had to be made smaller than the tightest choke in any gauge so that it would pass through it. As a result, the ball bounced down the bore and the angle of departure varied greatly from shot to shot.

The old round-ball loads in 12-gauge shotguns would kill a deer or a black bear very dead if they hit a vital area, but making that kind of shot at anything more than 20 yards was only a matter of luck. By contrast, 6-inch three-shot groups at 100 yards are common with good scope-equipped 12-gauge shotguns firing slugs from a rest. Some guns handle one type much better than the other for reasons that would take a full-fledged ballistic investigation to determine. Just why one gun is very accurate with Foster-type slugs and wildly inaccurate with the Brenneke, and vice versa, is a mystery. Common sense indicates that the Brenneke with its longer bearing surface in the barrel should be more accurate, but in a given gun, it may not be.

ENERGY

Rifled slugs are available in all common shotgun gauges from 10 to .410, except that there is no 28-gauge slug load. The .410 slug weighs only ⅕ of an ounce, and the muzzle energy is only 650 foot-pounds, so don't be tempted to fire at deer with them. They are intended for such game as fox and, at most, coyotes, provided you can get within very close range.

RIFLED SLUGS

Slugs shown are all 12-gauge (from left): Remington one ounce, Federal one ounce, Brenneke (German) one ounce with attached wad, Federal 1¼ ounce.

The Brenneke slug cartridge: The compression groove in the base of the slug permits firing through tight chokes. Wads are attached to a soft lead slug with a simple wood screw.

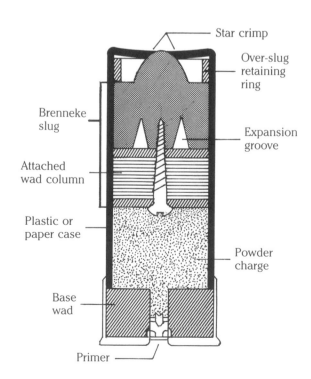

- Star crimp
- Over-slug retaining ring
- Brenneke slug
- Expansion groove
- Attached wad column
- Plastic or paper case
- Powder charge
- Base wad
- Primer

The Vitt slug is made in the United States and is sold mostly to hand-loaders. It has attached wads, but there is no raised ring at the base of the hollow lead slug, and the angled vanes are deeper than the vanes of other slugs. This, Vitt claims, assures rotation in flight and improved accuracy.

The 12-gauge slug is most popular, and a 1-ounce slug in this gauge has about 1,300 foot-pounds of energy at 50 yards and about 900 foot-pounds at 100 yards. This depends on many factors, including the precise fit of the projectile and wads in the bore. But it's a sure killer at 50 yards because it exceeds the commonly accepted minimum of 1,200 foot-pounds of on-target energy. At 100 yards, the energy falls below the theoretical minimum, but another factor enhances the destructive power of these large projectiles, and that is enormous size and weight.

Many deer rifles fire .308 diameter bullets. A 12-gauge slug is almost ¾ of an inch in diameter, and this big bullet makes a very large and destructive wound channel. Also, rifled slugs are made of soft lead and expand readily in animal tissue. Quite often, a 12-gauge slug expands to 1¾ inches. The great weight of the slug also helps. The heaviest .30/06 rifle load includes a bullet that weighs 220 grains, but a 1-ounce 12-gauge slug weighs in the neighborhood of 400 grains, depending on which manufacturer turned it out. If it hits solidly in a vital area at 100 yards, the deer usually goes down in its tracks.

The only real weakness of big-bore slugs is limited penetration. The noses of these slugs are very blunt, the lead is soft, and expansion takes place soon after entrance, especially with the new hollow-point slugs. Because of this, a shot fired into a deer from the rear may not penetrate far enough forward for a sure kill. Therefore, it's best to avoid these shots. A deer quartering away, however, is a satisfactory target. If you're a good shot, aim just forward of the point of the hip and the slug will enter the chest cavity diagonally. You can aim for the neck, but it takes a fine shot to hit it.

RANGE LIMITATIONS

With the 1-ounce 12-gauge slug, you may have enough energy to kill a deer at ranges longer than 100 yards—say, out to 120—but other limitations make it unlikely. One reason for this is the steep drop of the heavy, blunt projectile, which is highly subject to aerodynamic drag. Out to 100 yards, the trajectory is only bit more curved than the one followed by a fast-stepping modern rifle load, but beyond that the drop is so steep that compensating hold-over is difficult to determine. In this, slug-loaded shotguns resemble the older slow-moving, big-bore rifle loads that are unsatisfactory for long-range shooting. It's also true that the best slug-loaded big-bore shotguns are not as accurate as good rifles. Even with a scope-sighted slug gun, you cannot hold a tight group at long range, and for this reason alone, it's unwise to take long shots.

Federal recently introduced a 10-gauge slug load with a 1¾-ounce projectile and a 1¼-ounce 12-gauge slug load. These two new shells have slightly higher energy at all ranges but, so far, the 1-ounce 12-gauge slug remains the most popular loading. The 16-gauge ⅘-ounce slug has about 700 foot-pounds of energy left at 100 yards, and it is only a bit smaller in diameter than the 12-gauge slug. Experience has proven that deer can sometimes be killed with these 16-gauge loads at 100 yards, but it is really best to limit their use to no more than 75 yards. If you're interested in buying a new slug gun, however, don't opt for a 16-gauge because they are being phased out of production. Buy a 10 or a 12, though the 12 is the better choice for reasons discussed earlier in the section on gauges. The ¾-ounce 20-gauge slug and the ⅘-ounce 20 are effective at shorter ranges, and the only real reason for using them is that the hunter has a 20-gauge shotgun and is unwilling to buy another for slug use.

MAXIMUM RANGE

The table below lists maximum effective ranges for slug-loaded shotguns. Again, it is based partly on available energy but mostly on experience in the field. In every case it is presumed that the gun is accurate, that it is being fired from a rest or from a very solid shooting position, and that it is equipped with a scope sight in the larger gauges (adjustable sights for the short-ranged 20 gauge).

Tests and computations carried out by Briarbank Ballistics Laboratory (the ballistics laboratory of *Outdoor Life* magazine) show that the Federal 1¼-ounce 12-gauge slug retains 1,200 foot-pounds of energy at 130 yards. And the Federal 1¾-ounce 10-gauge slug retains 1,200 foot-pounds of energy at the astonishing range of 180 yards! But the 10-gauge slug's trajectory is very curved because of its great weight. To hit with it at ranges that amount to good rifle ranges for most lever rifles, it would be necessary to sight-in carefully, use a carefully mounted scope, and practice a great deal. Probably, the real advantage of the heavy 10-gauge Federal slug is that it makes kills at moderate

EFFECTIVE RANGES FOR SLUG-LOADED SHOTGUNS

Gauge	Nominal Weight of the Slug (oz.)	Range (Yards)
10	1¾	125
12	1¼	120
12	1	100
16	⅘	75
20	¾	50
20	⅝	45

ranges much more certain. Nevertheless, enterprising shotgunners can experiment with the heavyweight until they can use it to its full potential. The ranges given in the table, on the other hand, are for the average gunner with the average shotgun, and they are only reasonable after considerable practice shooting.

Again, some hunters will dispute these ranges, but as with buckshot loads, you won't wound many deer if you adhere to the maximums. And many hunters will find that the maximum effective range with their own gun is much shorter.

THE GUN

Pump and semi-automatic shotguns are the best slug guns because they can be used to fire quick follow-up shots. Double-barreled side-by-side shotguns are really unsatisfactory because the barrels almost always shoot to very different points of impact. Over/unders do better in this respect, but they're less satisfactory than a single-barreled repeating shotgun.

Nevertheless, a double of any kind can be useful in some circumstances. Install a receiver or a scope sight and sight-in your most accurate barrel for use with slugs. Load a heavy buckshot load (where legal) in the other barrel, and you're prepared for a distant standing shot with the slug or a running shot with buckshot, whichever comes first. Of course, you'll find that the adjustable iron sight or scope, when sighted for slug use, is way off when you fire the buckshot load, but most shotgunners can make allowances for that. With good adjustable iron sights or a scope adjusted for the slug, the buckshot load will almost always hit low, but test to make sure.

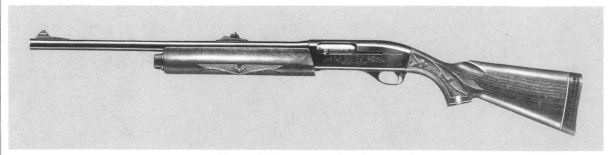
The short barrel of the Remington Model 870 pump slug gun makes it handy in the brush. This is the 12-gauge.

Pump with slug barrel: The Ithaca Model 37 is a lightweight shotgun, known for quick handling. Here it is shown with the slug barrel mounted.

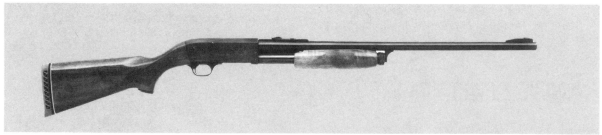
A semi-auto slug gun: This Remington Model 1100 is the left-handed model. If you are left-handed, using a left-handed pump or semi-auto is essential. Otherwise, fired hot shells, gas, and powder fouling are ejected much too close to your eyes and face.

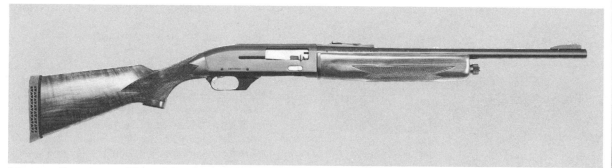

10-gauge Deerslayer—The mighty Ithaca MAG-10 is the only repeating shotgun capable of firing the Federal 10-gauge 1¾-ounce slug loads. The barrel easily interchanges with bird-hunting barrels.

The Colt-Sauer drilling (three-barreled, break-action gun) is available with two side-by-side shotgun barrels in 12 gauge and a .30/06 rifle barrel underneath. One way to load this type of gun is with a buckshot load for close-range moving deer, a heavy slug for standing deer at medium range, and a rifle cartridge for long-range shooting. Selecting the right barrel is very important. In the excitement of seeing a good buck, it would be a mistake to touch off the buckshot load at a deer that is 200 yards away.

A bolt-action shotgun has its uses. Marlin and Mossberg both make bolt guns intended for use with heavy waterfowl cartridges. The barrels are extremely long, but a gunsmith can cut them to 20 inches or even 18 for use with slugs, and improved sights are easy to install. As mentioned earlier, the rigidity of a bolt-action firearm enhances accuracy, and a bolt gun for use with slugs has a built-in accuracy advantage over less-rigid shotguns. A few hunters have discovered that a Marlin or Mossberg bolt gun especially adapted for slug shooting works very well at long slug ranges. Have the bore lapped if it is too rough for slugs.

Few hunters install slings on their slug guns, but having one available is a great help, not only when you're carrying a gun a long distance but also for the sake of accuracy. A simple carrying strap can be used to steady the gun by employing the "hasty sling" illustrated earlier. When you're using a scope or good iron sights, steadiness of aim is just as important at long slug ranges as it is with a rifle.

THE SIGHTS

The usual single-bead or double-bead shotgun sights are really rather useless for slug-gun shooting. For the needed accuracy out to 50 or 75 yards, most shooters must have adjustable V-notch sights or aperture sights. At longer ranges, a 2× or 3× scope is essential. If you intend to have a scope installed on your shotgun, don't attempt it with any gun that has a lightweight aluminum-alloy receiver. The heavy recoil of these loads soon causes the threads to become distorted, and the scope is soon shooting so loose that it is useless. The same goes for the mounting screws of iron sights.

"Add-on" temporary iron sights are available for those who have only one shotgun and must use it for bird hunting as well as deer hunting. One variety is simply a flat strip of sheet metal bent upward at the rear end and at the front. The rear end is cut to form a V-notch rear sight and the front end is an inverted

The Holden Ironsighter see-through scope mount is shown on a pump shotgun. Rifle sights on the slug barrel can be seen through the lower portion of the figure-8 mounts. A wide variety of scope mounts is available.

V front sight. This Slug-Site attaches to the receiver with a special adhesive. After the deer season, it is easy to remove. But, as with rifles, open sights are not as inherently precise as aperture sights or a low-powered scope. For long-range shooting with slugs, you need something better.

REPLACEMENT BARRELS

Major American manufacturers of shotguns offer a specialized pump or semi-automatic shotgun intended especially for deer hunting, and many foreign companies export these guns to the United States. Slug guns are almost always altered versions of the company's usual production pump or semi-automatic. The barrel is only 20 inches long or 18 inches-and-a-fraction (shorter than 18 is illegal). These short barrels are handy in the woods, and longer ones are not needed to fully utilize the energy developed by slug loads. There is no choke; the barrel has parallel walls all the way to the muzzle. Most often, some effort is made to polish the bore to a fine finish. Roughness could distort and possibly tilt the slug, the wad, or both, and accuracy would deteriorate. The barrel is

fitted with a blade front sight and an adjustable V-notch rear sight.

Buying a specialized shotgun for deer hunting is not necessary if you already have a modern pump or semi-automatic that you use for bird shooting. Simply buy an extra slug barrel. It's easy to remove the barrel from the receiver and replace it with another if you have a gun of recent manufacture. No tools are needed, and it only takes a few seconds. If you want a scope or aperture sights, however, the receiver will have to be drilled and tapped to take mounting screws in most cases, though some scopes with long eye relief can be mounted on the barrel. In use, however, this is a bit awkward. An aperture rear sight should always be mounted as far to the rear as possible, and that means mounting it on the receiver.

SIGHTING-IN

Sighting-in a shotgun for use with slugs is much the same as sighting-in a rifle (see page 183), but since the shooter doesn't have to worry about point of impact at long rifle ranges, it's simpler to do with a slug gun. Fire at short ranges first to get on the paper, just as you would do with a rifle, and then settle down to make sure of your zero at longer range. Sight-in from a padded rest.

With adjustable iron sights of the V-notch variety, 50 or 60 yards is about maximum for accurate shooting with heavy slugs. With bird-hunting sights, it's much shorter; with aperture sights, a 75-yard zero is about right. With a good scope, you can usually hit accurately out to the maximum ranges stated in the table "Effective Ranges for Slug-loaded Shotguns" on page 234, provided you have a good rest or a solid shooting position, and everything else is up to snuff, including yourself.

The Brenneke people have published a theoretical trajectory table. As a sample, here is what you can expect in inches above or below point of aim from a 12-gauge gun using their ammunition:

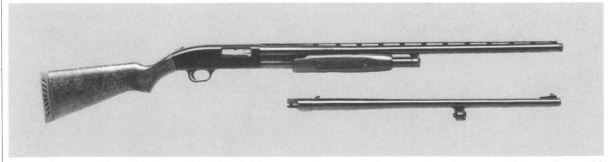

Pump shotgun with replacement slug barrel: Most manufacturers make repeating shotguns with interchangeable barrels. This is the Mossberg pump with bird-hunting barrel in place and slug barrel with rifle sights. Changing barrels takes only a minute or two.

BRENNEKE SLUG TRAJECTORIES

IRON SIGHTS: LINE OF SIGHT 0.79 INCH ABOVE CENTERLINE OF BORE

25 yards	50 yards	75 yards	100 yards
+0.24	0	−1.62	−4.96
+0.75	+1.06	0	−2.79
+1.46	+2.48	+1.69	0

SCOPE SIGHT: LINE OF SIGHT 2.0 INCH ABOVE CENTERLINE OF BARREL

25 yards	50 yards	75 yards	100 yards
−0.35	0	−1.02	−3.85
−0.08	+0.71	0	−2.52
+0.51	+1.93	+1.89	0

The trajectories of American 12-gauge slugs won't vary a lot from these Brenneke figures, at least in theory, but you must shoot in order to find out for sure. Note that the midrange trajectory heights in this tabulation are not enough to cause midrange misses on a deer-size heart-lung area. Results with other gauges will vary a great deal from these 12-gauge trajectories.

You can sight-in for short or long range, just as you can with a rifle. It's up to you to select the optimum zero for the type of hunting you do and for the quality of your shooting and equipment. The figures for iron sights should be used with caution. Even if the trajectory figures are accurate for your gun, few gunners can hit much with iron sights at 100 yards, so it's best to ignore the bottom line of the table and select the 50-yard zero for open sights and the 75-yard zero for aperture sights at least to start.

When sighting-in, however, you may be in for some surprises. Slug guns and slug cartridges are not as precisely made as rifles and centerfire rifle ammunition and there are other factors that limit shot-to-shot consistency. For practical deer shooting, many experienced hunters simply determine the maximum range at which they can consistently group almost all shots within a 6-inch circle when firing from a good rest. They regard that as the maximum range. After it is determined, the sights are adjusted to be dead on at that distance. After that is done, these conservative shooters practice a bit in the prone, sitting, kneeling, and offhand positions to get a very clear idea of the maximum ranges at which they can make three-shot, 6-inch groups. They never take longer shots when hunting. It's a good system.

Remember that the maximum ranges given previously are for good equipment in the hands of an excellent gunner with a good rest or solid position. It's one thing to knock over a deer at 100 yards with a 12-gauge slug from a steady prone position with a rest. It's quite another to attempt the same shot from the very unsteady offhand position, or even when kneeling or sitting. It's just like rifle shooting, except that the wind does not affect heavy slugs a lot because of the short ranges involved.

Of course, this discussion has been about firing at standing deer. Shooting at a moving animal is much more difficult, and it takes a lot of practice to develop the skill. In fact, it takes a fair amount of practice to hit consistently even if the animal isn't moving.

But few hunters really practice with slugs. Many rifle nuts think nothing of burning up two boxes of ammunition during an afternoon of practice shooting, but few slug shooters make even the minimum effort needed to sight-in with any degree of precision. In the first place, slug cartridges are expensive; in the second place, the recoil with heavy slug loads can be punishing. Yet, it pays to persevere.

Practice in the manner previously described for riflemen. And if that becomes too expensive, consider reloading slugs with cheap hand tools (see the reloading section at the end of this part of the book) and eliminate some of the expense. There is no really valid excuse for wounding a deer and letting it get away, even if you are shooting a slug gun instead of a rifle. With slugs, the first consideration is to fire only at reasonable ranges.

EFFECTIVE RANGES FOR SLUG-LOADED SHOTGUNS

Gauge	Slug weight (ozs.)	Muzzle velocity	Yards						Range at which bullet is 3 inches low (yds.)
			25	50	75	100	125	150	
10	1¾	1,280	1.8	3.0	2.3	−0.5	−5.6		114
12	1¼	1,490	1.5	2.8	2.8	1.0	−2.6	−8.3	127
12	1	1,560	1.5	2.9	2.6	0.5	−4.0		120
16	⅘	1,600	1.5	2.9	2.6	0.4	−4.1		120
20	¾	1,600	1.4	2.8	2.8	1.2	−2.4	−8.2	128
.410	½	1,830	1.3	2.7	2.9	1.4	−2.0	−7.8	130

These are probable average trajectories for slugs of various gauges. It is easy to sight-in a slug gun with adjustable iron sights or a scope. A given gun may fire these loads with a more curved or a slightly flatter trajectory, but the figures give you a good idea of what to expect. This table was developed by Jim Carmichel, Outdoor Life's *shooting editor. Note the flat trajectory of the .410 slug, but remember that it is useless for hunting deer because of the extreme lack of energy.*

HANDGUN HUNTING

In the early 1970s, Jack O'Connor, then undoubtedly the foremost gun writer in the United States, was asked an important question by William E. Rae, the editor of *Outdoor Life.* "Why," Rae asked, "don't you write about handguns once in a while?" Interest in hunting with handguns had been increasing, and Rae felt that the subject should be dealt with occasionally in O'Connor's shooting column.

O'Connor's reply was forthright: "I hate the damn things, Bill. If you want to go out and hunt, you should use a gun that you can depend on, not a handgun."

O'Connor never did turn in a column on handgun hunting, but his remark embodied an attitude that is fairly common among some hunters and the public at large. Many people, particularly Easterners, are prejudiced against handguns, and many hunters feel that a handgun is inadequate for deer hunting, much less heavier game.

AVAILABLE ENERGY

Experience has led most rifle hunters to use fairly powerful firearms for deer. As discussed in detail earlier, deer rifles should deliver 1,200 foot-pounds of energy on target if one-shot kills are to be made. Even if the average hunter isn't conscious of the exact numbers, he knows from personal experience and the advice of others that a less-powerful rifle cannot be trusted to put a deer down for keeps. Even the good old .30/30 with a 170-grain bullet delivers only 1,355 foot-pounds at 100 yards, and most hunters realize that this cartridge is not really reliable for deer hunting beyond 150 yards.

Energy confusion. In discussing revolver energy, it's best to be aware that the subject is still somewhat confused by an industry practice that is no longer followed. The .357 Magnum revolver cartridge was the first of the modern handgun magnums. Later, the .44 Magnum and the .41 Magnum were added to the lineup. These three cartridges are the most popular factory loads for handgun hunting. But when these rounds first appeared, they were listed in ammunition company catalogs with very impressive velocities and energy levels at various ranges. The cartridges were fired in test barrels to determine velocity and energy, and the barrel length was not specified. In addition, test barrels had fully enclosed breeches. That is, test barrels were closed with breechblocks so that all the expanding powder gas was used to propel the bullets. They were in effect rifle barrels.

In revolvers, there is a gap between the mouths of

One limit on handgun accuracy is comparative lack of steadiness. This shooter takes a rest on tree but does not let the gun touch it. If the gun does touch a solid object, it bounces away on firing and this can cause a miss. (Chuck Adams photo)

the chambers in the cylinder and the rear of the barrel. Some powder gas always exits through this gap so that the energy level attained by a revolver using a given cartridge never equals the level reached when the same cartridge is fired from a barrel with an enclosed breech. Because of all this, ammunition catalogs published only a few years ago attributed unrealistic energy levels to the three popular handgun cartridges.

But handloaders and other shooting enthusiasts who had chronographs soon discovered the discrepancies, and the outcry was quite loud. Finally, ammunition companies altered the test procedure, and now these three revolver rounds are tested in "vented" barrels that duplicate the gas loss through the cylinder gap in a revolver. The test barrel used is almost always 4 inches in length. In other words ammunition makers are now bending over backward to be realistic. The current energy figures developed with these 4-inch barrels are useful, even though most hunting revolvers have longer barrels, generally 6 or 8 inches (give or take a few eighths of an inch). But the energy developed is only slightly greater than from 4-inch barrels.

The reader should also bear in mind that velocity and energy figures may differ among various individual revolvers. For instance, a bullet can be slowed down by an overly obtuse angle of the wall in the barrel's throat, a minimum barrel diameter (though within accepted tolerances), or by a rough-finished barrel. When you are looking at ammunition tables, the figures seem so exact that they suggest a degree of precision that really isn't there, especially with revolvers. Actually, there may be some variation in energy developed with precisely the same cartridge when different revolvers are used, even if those revolvers were

ENERGY LEVELS
4-INCH VENTED BARRELS—REMINGTON BALLISTICS

Bullet	Muzzle velocity (fps)	Muzzle energy (foot-pounds)	50-yard energy	100-yard energy
.357 Magnum 158-grain	1,235	535	428	361
.41 Magnum 210-grain	1,300	788	630	526
.44 Magnum 240-grain	1,350	971	749	608

ENCLOSED-BREECH—10-INCH BARRELS

Bullet	Muzzle velocity (fps)	Muzzle energy (foot-pounds)	50-yard energy	100-yard energy*
.357 Magnum 158-grain	1,450	735	592	484
.41 Magnum 210-grain	1,500	1,050	823	658
.44 Magnum 240-grain	1,470	1,151	905	728

*100-yard energy levels developed by Briarbank Ballistic Laboratory

made by the same manufacturer. Remember that you're dealing with approximations when you consider the reported exterior ballistics of revolver cartridges. Sophisticated handloaders almost always have chronographs and know how to figure foot-pounds of energy at the muzzle and downrange for various firearms and loads. If you know one, maybe he will be willing to work up figures for your revolver. They can be very revealing.

If you do not have access to a chronograph, it might be a good idea to conduct a penetration test on water-soaked newspapers or old telephone books. This test was described in the section on muzzleloaders. If the bullet penetrates 3 inches of this material, which is roughly equivalent to blood-filled animal tissue, you can be sure of penetrating the chest wall of a deer, even at a fairly sharp angle. Determine that range, and refrain from trying to kill beyond it.

The accompanying table, "Energy Levels," gives velocity and energy figures for the three most popular revolver cartridges for hunting (factory loads) fired from 4-inch vented barrels. Also listed are energy figures for the same factory ammunition fired from fully enclosed barrels with no energy loss because of a cylinder gap. These figures apply to 10-inch barrels, a common length in single-shot break-action and bolt-action hunting handguns. The 100-yard energy figures for enclosed-breech guns were developed by Briarbank Ballistic Laboratory, *Outdoor Life's* research facility, operated by the magazine's shooting editor Jim Carmichel.

The figures show clearly the drop in energy out to 100 yards. Even when fired from a single-shot handgun with a fully enclosed breech and a 10-inch barrel, the heavy, factory-loaded .44 Magnum cartridge only de-

velops 1,151 foot-pounds of energy at the muzzle, 905 foot-pounds at 50 yards, and 728 foot-pounds at 100 yards. The energy figures for the other cartridges are even lower.

Yet the generally accepted minimum for one-shot deer kills in modern shoulder arms is 1,200 foot-pounds of on-target energy. Even in a *rifle* with a 20-inch barrel, the 240-grain .44 Magnum develops only 1,015 foot-pounds of energy at 100 yards. Quite rightly, most experienced hunters regard .44 Magnum rifles as short-range arms for brush-country hunting that cannot be depended on to make sure one-shot kills at much more than 100 yards. But many gun writers have said that the big .44 factory load in a *handgun*, including long-barreled revolvers, is good for deer kills out to as much as 150 yards. Some have even gone so far as to say that the .357 factory load will do the same. That cartridge when fired from a revolver has only 361 foot-pounds of energy left at 100 yards, about what you would need to kill a raccoon.

To make a comparison, the .30 caliber U.S. carbine cartridge with a 110-grain soft-point bullet develops 600 foot-pounds of energy at 100 yards from a 20-inch barrel, and that cartridge is almost universally banned for deer hunting on the grounds that it is much too puny. It's easy to see that numerous statements about long-range shooting with these three handgun cartridges are, to say the least, ill-advised. But the tide is turning. Recently, several gun writers have hinted that perhaps the .357 should not be used for deer hunting, except at very close range.

Of course, these are factory cartridges and a handloader can up the energy figures quite a bit, say about 20 percent. That doesn't increase effective range a great deal.

There is another side of the coin, however. These rounds fire heavy, large-diameter bullets. On-target momentum is rather high. If jacketed open-point hunting bullets are used (as they always should be), the wound channel is quite large and a lot of tissue is destroyed. Still, their effectiveness should not be exaggerated on this score.

The following are recommended maximum effective revolver hunting ranges for one-shot kills on deer with a well-placed bullet in the heart-lung area of a deer. These figures are more conservative than the generally accepted ranges, but they reflect a realistic appraisal of killing power. Minimum barrel length is 4 inches:

Bullet	Yards
.357 Magnum, 158-grain	35
.41 Magnum, 210-grain	55
.44 Magnum, 240-grain	75

Suggested maximum ranges for single-shot handguns with fully enclosed breeches and barrels 10 inches in length or a bit longer are:

Bullet	Yards
.357 Magnum, 158-grain	60
.41 Magnum, 210-grain	80
.44 Magnum, 240-grain	100

The reason for the difference in ranges between the revolvers and single-shots is not based solely on available energy. These long-barreled handguns are somewhat more powerful, it is true, but they also have a longer sight radius, are often equipped with aperture sights or scopes, and allow the hunter to take a very firm grip because of the forend. Good hits are therefore easier to make.

Adequate caliber. Some handgunners point out that very heavy game has been taken with the .44 Magnum, and this includes elk, moose, grizzlies, and Alaskan brown bears. The reasoning is that if the big .44 is capable of taking such large animals, it is surely adequate for deer. But this is false reasoning if we are talking about the average deer hunter. The often cited elk, moose, and bear kills were made by very capable handgun marksmen who were skilled enough to get within very short range and restrained enough to turn down all long-range shots. It takes a particular kind of steely nerved marksman to come within 50 yards or less of a big brown bear and fire accurately, even if he is accompanied by a guide with a backup rifle. Few people are capable of it. The usual weekend hunter finds it very difficult or impossible to get within handgun killing range of a deer by stalking. More often than not he either spooks the animal and fails to get a shot, or is tempted into firing at long range and misses or wounds the animal.

In fact, many deer are killed with handguns not by stalking them but by taking a stand, often an elevated tree stand, and waiting for the deer to appear. This is also true of hunting with other short-range arms—muzzleloaders, slug-loaded shotguns, and archery tackle. In a good stand, the hunter usually has time to take a steady rest, aim carefully, and squeeze off the shot. The range is often as short as 20 or 30 yards. Locating the stand in the right place is the principal skill, not marksmanship. It works best with whitetail deer. Also, rattling old antlers sometimes brings bucks to the hunter.

Part of the misunderstanding about available energy in handguns arises from the use of .38 Special revolvers by the police and the .45 Colt semi-automatic pistol by the U.S. Army. The .38 Special delivers only 200 foot-pounds of energy *at the muzzle* in the usual police load, and the big .45 Colt auto churns up only 335 foot-pounds at the muzzle with the factory-loaded 230-grain bullet. In terms of killing energy for deer, these are pip-squeak arms, yet they are used to kill armed men. Since a deer and a man have about the same bulk and weight on the average, the reasoning goes, these handguns should be adequate for deer hunting and, therefore, the .357, .41 and .44 magnums should be more than adequate.

The reasoning is completely false, however, because police combat shooting is commonly done at very short range. FBI studies indicate that shots fired at armed criminals with handguns are triggered at an average range of only 7½ yards. Try to get that close to a deer! Also, a criminal commonly gives up to save his life if wounded. Deer, on the other hand, don't give up to save their lives. They simply run off and present the hunter with a tracking problem. The .45 Colt auto is also inadequate for deer hunting for much the same reason. It's a reliable one-shot man-killer at close range, but it's really quite useless for deer hunting.

With lesser handgun calibers, the energy level is laughable. For instance, the .32 Smith & Wesson Long develops only 115 foot-pounds at the muzzle. At 50 yards, it's only 98 foot-pounds. Anyone who would use this type of cartridge for deer hunting has to be ignorant of ballistics or callous about wounding game.

THE HANDGUNNER'S REPLY

Experienced handgunners who know their ballistics admit to the facts above, but they reply by saying that a skilled marksman and hunter can overcome the disadvantage by stalking to very close ranges and putting heavy handgun bullets through both lungs, through the heart or through the spine in the neck. It's done

Here are four factory-loaded handgun cartridges suitable for deer hunting. The .357, .41, and .44 magnums are popular revolver cartridges, and a few semi-automatic pistols have been chambered for the .357 Magnum. The .357 Remington Maximum is a newer handgun cartridge that develops 1,168 foot-pounds of energy at the muzzle in a revolver with a 10½-inch barrel (889 foot-pounds at 100 yards). This exceeds performance of any factory .357 Magnum load and rivals the .44 Magnum—and without very heavy recoil. Two makers of revolvers have tried to develop revolvers for the new cartridge. So far, however, trouble with excessive powder fouling has made them impractical. Currently, the cartridge is used in single-shot pistols. Note the large capacity of the extremely long case, which is same diameter as the .357 Magnum. This is only one reason why the use of powerful factory loads and wildcats is limited almost exclusively to single-shot handguns.

.357 Magnum

.357 Remington Maximum

.41 Magnum

.44 Remington Magnum

HANDGUN BALLISTICS
TABLE (REMINGTON)

CALIBER	Primer No.	Wt.- Grs.	BULLET Style	VELOCITY (FPS) Muzzle	50 Yds.	100 Yds.	ENERGY (FT LB) Muzzle	50 Yds.	100 Yds.	MID-RANGE TRAJECTORY 50 Yds.	100 Yds.	BARREL LENGTH
357 MAG. Vented Barrel	5½	158*	Semi-Jacketed H.P.	1235	1104	1015	535	428	361	0.8″	3.5″	4″
	5½	158	Soft Point	1235	1104	1015	535	428	361	0.8″	3.5″	4″
	5½	158	Metal Point	1235	1104	1015	535	428	361	0.8″	3.5″	4″
	5½	158	Lead	1235	1104	1015	535	428	361	0.8″	3.5″	4″
	5½	158	Lead (Brass Case)	1235	1104	1015	535	428	361	0.8″	3.5″	4″
357 REM. "MAXIMUM"**	7½	158*	Semi-Jacketed H.P.	1825	1588	1381	1168	885	669	0.4″	1.7″	10½″
	7½	180	Semi-Jacketed H.P.	1555	1328	1154	966	705	532	0.5″	2.5″	10½″
9mm LUGER AUTO. PISTOL	1½	115*	Jacketed H.P.	1155	1047	971	341	280	241	0.9″	3.9″	4″
	1½	124	Metal Case	1110	1030	971	339	292	259	1.0″	4.1″	4″
380 AUTO. PISTOL	1½	95	Metal Case	955	865	785	190	160	130	1.4″	5.9″	4″
	1½	88*	Jacketed H.P.	990	920	868	191	165	146	1.2″	5.1″	4″
38 AUTO. COLT PISTOL	1½	130*	Metal Case	1040	980	925	310	275	245	1.0″	4.7″	4½″
38 SUPER AUTO. COLT PISTOL	1½	115*	Jacketed H.P. (+P)†	1300	1147	1041	431	336	277	0.7″	3.3″	5″
	1½	130	Metal Case (+P)†	1215	1099	1017	426	348	298	0.8″	3.6″	5″
38 S. & W.	1½	146*	Lead	685	650	620	150	135	125	2.4″	10.0″	4″
38 SPECIAL Vented Barrel	1½	95	Semi-Jacketed H.P. (+P)†	1175	1044	959	291	230	194	0.9″	3.9″	4″
	1½	110	Semi-Jacketed H.P. (+P)†	995	926	871	242	210	185	1.2″	5.1″	4″
	1½	125	Semi-Jacketed H.P. (+P)†	945	898	858	248	224	204	1.3″	5.4″	4″
	½	125	Semi-Jacketed S.P.	945	908	875	248	229	212	1.3″	5.3″	4″
	1½	148	"Targetmaster" Lead W.C.	710	634	566	166	132	105	2.4″	10.8	4″
	1½	158	"Targetmaster" Lead	755	723	692	200	183	168	2.0″	8.3″	4″
	1½	158*	Lead (Round Nose)	755	723	692	200	183	168	2.0″	8.3″	4″
	1½	158	Semi-Wadcutter	755	723	692	200	183	168	2.0″	8.3″	4″
	1½	158	Metal Point	755	723	692	200	183	168	2.0″	8.3″	4″
	1½	158	Lead (+P)†	890	855	823	278	257	238	1.4″	6.0″	4″
	1½	158	Lead H.P. (+P)†	890	855	823	278	257	238	1.4″	6.0″	4″
	1½	200	Lead	635	614	594	179	168	157	2.8″	11.5″	4″
38 SHORT COLT	1½	125*	Lead	730	685	645	150	130	115	2.2″	9.4″	6″
41 REM. MAG. Vented Barrel	2½	210*	Soft Point	1300	1162	1062	788	630	526	0.7″	3.2″	4″
	2½	210	Lead	965	898	842	434	376	331	1.3″	5.4″	4″
44 REM. MAG. Vented Barrel	2½	180*	Semi-Jacketed H.P.	1610	1365	1175	1036	745	551	0.5″	2.3″	4″
	2½	240	Lead Gas Check	1350	1186	1069	971	749	608	0.7″	3.1″	4″
	2½	240	Soft Point	1180	1081	1010	741	623	543	0.9″	3.7″	4″
	2½	240	Semi-Jacketed H.P.	1180	1081	1010	741	623	543	0.9″	3.7″	4″
	2½	240	Lead (Med. Vel.)	1000	947	902	533	477	433	1.1″	4.8″	6½″
44 S. & W. SPECIAL	2½	246*	Lead	755	725	695	310	285	265	2.0″	8.3″	6½″
45 COLT	2½	250*	Lead	860	820	780	410	375	340	1.6″	6.6″	5½″
45 AUTO.	2½	185	Metal Case Wadcutter	770	707	650	244	205	174	2.0″	8.7″	5″
	2½	185*	Jacketed H.P.	940	890	846	363	325	294	1.3″	5.5″	5″
	2½	230	Metal Case	810	776	745	335	308	284	1.7″	7.2″	5″
45 AUTO. RIM	2½	230*	Lead	810	770	730	335	305	270	1.8″	7.4″	5½″
38 S. & W.	1½	–*	Blank	–	–	–	–	–	–	–	–	–
32 S. & W.	5½	–	Blank	–	–	–	–	–	–	–	–	–
38 SPECIAL	1½	–	Blank	–	–	–	–	–	–	–	–	–

†Ammunition with (+P) on the case headstamp is loaded to higher pressure. Use only in firearms designated for this cartridge and so recommended by the gun manufacturer.
**Will not chamber in 357 Mag. or 38 Special handguns.

every hunting season by capable handgun hunters.

In fact, this form of hunting is so difficult that making killing shots on deer-size and larger game by still-hunting and stalking is actually something of a "stunt." That word is a red flag to most experienced handgunners because riflemen often believe that pulling off a stunt should not be the primary reason for going hunting. Sometimes, of course, this attitude is caused by jealousy of the handgunner's skills.

Most handgun hunters come to the sport from intensive target shooting with handguns. Shooting at metallic silhouettes is very popular with them. In hotly contested target matches of one kind or another, the handgunner develops superb marksmanship skills. One day, the thought occurs to him that deer are fairly large animals and that hitting them solidly with a handgun would not be difficult. This kind of handgun enthusiast is a good shot when he first goes hunting, but his woodsmanship and hunting ability are often inadequate. If a handgunner wounds a deer, for instance, he has to track, and tracking is a fine art. Merely stalking a deer within the effective range of a handgun is difficult too. It sometimes takes years before a skilled handgun target shooter develops the hunting and tracking abilities that he really should have on tap when he first goes afield. Fortunately, hunting with a handgun is so fascinating to the dedicated handgunner that he often keeps at it until he becomes a superb hunter as well as a fine marksman. He often starts with a stand, but with experience, he may become an expert stillhunter and stalker.

Handguns have other roles to play in hunting that are seldom mentioned. One is on a hunt in remote country where the hunter has to pack in all his own gear on foot. A good hunting handgun fits easily into a backpack or can be hung very conveniently over the shoulder on a carrying strap. Because of reduced bulk and weight, these guns are much easier to carry than any rifle or even a carbine. In remote country where few hunters venture, hunting handguns are quite effective, too, because the game is not so wary, and the handgunner can often stalk the quarry to very short range. It's also true that handguns are very useful in thick brush where shooting is commonly done at close range. As any experienced hunter will tell you, some cover is so thick that it is almost impossible to get through it while carrying a shoulder gun. In that kind of cover, a handgun is very convenient, and if you do get a shot, it will be at short range indeed. It is easier to get a handgun on target when you must fire fairly quickly, too, because of its short length. It doesn't hang up quite so often on branches, vines, and twigs. In hard-hunted areas, deer often spend the entire hunting season in thick lowland swamps, and a powerful handgun in that situation is a blessing. There's nothing better than a good handgun when you are following up a deer that has run into very thick cover

after being wounded in open country with a rifle. This is particularly true if you are trying to control an eager hound on a leash with one hand.

HANDGUNS ONLY?

At one time there was a push in some states to set up a "handguns-only" deer-hunting season that would closely resemble the bowhunting-only and muzzleloader-only seasons. This movement failed, probably because most riflemen simply did not want an additional hunting season in which they could not participate. The bowhunting season and the muzzleloader season were more than enough from their point of view.

Perhaps this was fortunate, though some handgunners protest vigorously that they too should have an exclusive season. Bowhunters, for example, used to be a small band of brothers, and every one of them was an enthusiast. When bowhunting was only permitted during the rifle season, no one would go afield with a bow unless he really loved archery. With the coming of bows-only seasons in many states, a whole new group of bowhunters jumped on the bandwagon. These people were not archers first and hunters second; they were hunters willing to use any legal weapon to kill a deer, provided using it gave them a chance to take an additional deer or two.

Many riflemen take up bowhunting today only because doing so gives them a second deer season and more venison in the freezer. Unfortunately, many of these bowhunters do not put in the many hours of practice needed to develop adequate hunting marksmanship with a bow, and they tend to wound more animals than they should.

Many very enthusiastic bowhunters now regret that their sport has been diluted by the influx of these "two-season" hunters. Much the same can be said for muzzleloader seasons and those who participate. Dedicated handgunners should really be grateful that they have not been granted exclusive seasons. Because handgunners must hunt during the regular gun season, only those who really prefer to hunt with handguns do so. If that situation changed, there would be many unskilled handgunners charging around the woods with nickel-plated .32 revolvers and other inadequate firearms. It wouldn't be long before handgunning for big game would be forbidden by law. Some states have never permitted it.

In a few states "either-or" laws are in effect. If you opt to hunt during the bow season in these states, you can't hunt during the gun season and vice versa. Under this kind of law, unskilled bowhunters opt for the rifle season. The same type of thing has been applied to muzzleloaders in a few instances, and it could be used to "purify" handgun hunting too.

HOW TO GET STARTED

These strictures are not intended to deter anyone from taking up handgun hunting; they're meant to provide a realistic picture of the sport and the opposition to it.

If you have never used a handgun before, you have a long road to travel before you should hunt deer. Commonly, beginners are advised to purchase a good .22 rimfire revolver with adjustable sights and practice with it until they develop the needed marksmanship skills. The mild recoil of the .22 is said to be conducive to good marksmanship, and the .22 can be used to hunt squirrels, cottontails, and even jackrabbits as training for big-game hunting. Actually, buying a .22 handgun may be an unnecessary expense, and practicing with it can actually be disadvantageous. A quality .22 revolver is an easy gun to shoot, and it is superbly accurate. But if a shooter gets used to it, graduating to a heavier firearm becomes difficult. The recoil and muzzle blast of a full-power .357 Magnum may seem intolerable if you are used to a .22.

A more intelligent choice is a .357 Magnum revolver with a 6-inch or longer barrel. These revolvers shoot a variety of ammunition. They chamber all .38 Special loads, including the .38 Special Wadcutter, a low-power target round that is adequate for small-game hunting. You can start out with that cartridge for paper targets, tin cans, and small game. Then you can graduate to a .38 Special full-power load in your .357 and finally to a .357 Magnum hunting round.

After you develop good marksmanship, you can use the same revolver with heavy loads for deer hunting, provided you can get within 35 yards of the animal and track successfully if you wound. Finally, you can graduate to a big .44 Magnum. Even with that gun, however, a less-powerful practice load is available. Revolvers chambered for the .44 Remington Magnum also fire the .44 Special, which has fairly mild recoil. This cartridge is also superbly accurate for target shooting and small game, though the factory load develops only 310 foot-pounds of energy at the muzzle and is therefore inadeqate for deer hunting.

The big jump is from the .357 or .44 Special to the full-power .44 Magnum load, and though some shooters simply cannot make it, you should make every effort to do so in order to use the powerful factory-loaded cartridge. If you cannot take the heavy recoil and muzzle blast, you can sell your .44 and try a .41 Magnum revolver. It's midway between .357 and the big .44 and is just the ticket for some people. One disadvantage is that there is no comparatively mild factory round for practice with a .41 Magnum revolver. You can use the comparatively mild plain-lead-bullet police load for practice, but the recoil is still quite impressive. If you have a friend who handloads and offer to buy the dies for his press, he may be willing to brew up practice loads in .41 Magnum cartridge cases.

PRACTICE AND EXECUTION

Realistic practice is important, and the beginning hunter should develop an ongoing marksmanship-improvement program for himself similar to the one for riflemen outlined earlier in this section. If anything, you'll have to spend more time practicing with a handgun than you would with a rifle. Taking a rest whenever possible is very important, even if you use the preferred two-handed hold on your handgun, and you should use it.

You should also practice in all worthwhile shooting positions. A two-handed hold in the prone position with a good rest is obviously the steadiest, but it's not possible when you are shooting in brush or high grass or weeds. The sitting and kneeling positions, again with a two-handed hold, are quite steady, and these do get you up above the top of the grass and low brush. If possible, shoot from the sitting position with your back against a tree. This steadies your aim a great deal.

In the standing (offhand) position, you'll find that your sights will wobble even if your hands are rigid on the gun, but sometimes it is impossible to shoot from the steadier positions. For this type of thing, some experienced handgunners use a strong lanyard or narrow leather strap. It can be attached with a snap to the bottom of the gun butt on a lanyard loop that usually must be installed by a gunsmith. The loop is placed around the shooter's neck or over one shoulder and under the other armpit. Holding the revolver firmly with two hands, the shooter pushes the revolver away from is body until the lanyard comes taut. It will steady your hands a great deal. The difficulty is adjusting the loop to precisely the right length for shooting in the offhand, sitting, and kneeling positions. Lanyards are seldom used in the prone position. Another way to use the strap is shown in photos on page 249.

Another dodge is to use a short length of stick to steady the aim. Place one end of the stick on top of your right shoulder and grasp the other end with your left hand as though it were a rifle's forend. Place your left elbow on your left hip in the familiar rifleman's offhand target-shooting position to steady the shooting stick. Now put the revolver butt on top of the stick but do not allow the hard butt to touch the stick since recoil might cause the whole gun to jump away from the hard surface and throw a wild shot. Instead, hold the stick with the fingers of your left hand and rest the revolver butt on the heel of the same hand. Many shooters find that a shooting stick used in this way makes it possible to hit consistently in the offhand position. A stick can also be stuck into the ground and used as a rest in the kneeling or sitting position.

In some ways practice with a revolver is less difficult than it is with a rifle. You should never try to shoot beyond your effective killing range, and even with a .44 Magnum revolver that is never more than about 75 yards. So practice at extended range is not needed. Sight-in to put the bullet on target at maximum effective range. If you do this, the midrange height of the trajectory should not be great enough to cause a miss. If it is in actual practice, holding a little low is easy.

Tight groups. Just as a good rifleman does (see the earlier discussion on rifle marksmanship), fire at various ranges in various positions, always moving away from the target, until you establish the maximum ranges at which you can fire satisfactory groups. As stated earlier, this is usually considered to be six inches, at most eight inches, when shooting under good conditions at paper targets. Even though the vital heart-lung area of a deer is larger than that, allow a few inches for excitement when shooting at game and the fact that you may not be able to assume a really solid shooting position and may be trembling after a climb or other exertion. When you find out the maximum ranges at which you can fire good groups, never exceed them when shooting at deer. In the great majority of cases, these ranges will be *shorter* than the maximum effective ranges of the cartridges as determined by retained energy. If you continue regular shooting practice, you'll gradually extend your effective ranges until they reach the maximum ranges determined by the energy level of your cartridge. To give one example, it is difficult indeed to fire a 6-inch group from a .44 Magnum revolver at 100 yards!

SIGHTS

Adjustable sights are important because the revolver must be zeroed for mild practice rounds and then for full-power loads. A bright-colored plastic insert on the front sight is a big help, and many shooters like a rear sight with a square notch outlined in white. Old-fashioned nonadjustable V-notch sights should be avoided. Aperture sights are seldom used on handguns. The square-notch rear and square-post front sights are preferred.

Low-power handgun scopes and mounts are available and some capable marksmen use them. Buying anything stronger than a 3× scope is inadvisable, however, because the maximum effective range even with the most powerful .44 Magnum loads is so short.

TYPE OF ACTION

Many handgun hunters prefer single-action revolvers. With these guns, the shooter must thumb-cock the hammer for each shot. With a double-action revolver, the hammer can be cocked, just like the single-action, for deliberate shots, and the revolver can also be fired rapidly in the double-action mode. With the hammer down, the shooter takes aim and pulls the trigger. The hammer rises and then falls again to fire the cartridge. But accurate double-action shooting is difficult. Double-action revolvers can fire several fast shots, and all police revolvers must obviously have this capability.

Handgun hunters often say that there is no excuse for double-action firing at deer or other big game. The idea is to cock the hammer, take sure aim and slowly squeeze off the shot. Many of these handgunners therefore prefer the single-action revolver because, in general, these revolvers have fewer working parts to get out of kilter.

However, there is a common situation in which the double-action capability is desirable. Say that you have

The Ruger New Model Super Blackhawk .44 Magnum is a good example of the single-action, heavy framed revolver, which must be cocked with the thumb for each shot. This type of revolver loads through a gate in the right side of the frame at the rear of the cylinder.

The Ruger New Super Blackhawk, Stainless Steel, is the same as the previous model but in stainless steel with an untapered bull barrel of greater length. Ruger makes many different revolvers in .357, .41, and .44 Magnum, single action and double action.

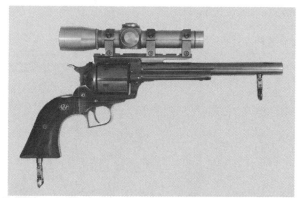

The Virginian Dragoon: Heavy .44 Magnum single-action revolver made in the United States by Interarms Industries Inc. Basically, all single-action heavy revolvers intended for hunting are externally modeled on the old Colt single-action "Peacemaker" revolver, which originally appeared in 1873. Though many have tried, no one has improved much on the shape of the old Colt for single-action shooting. The gracefully curved grip is intended to slide smoothly through the hand on recoil, thus lessening its effect. Note absence of checkering because of this design element. The large, shapely hammer is designed for quick, easy cocking with thumb.

Mag-na-Port Adaptation of a Ruger Revolver: The barrel has twin slits just behind muzzle. This vents powder gas upward so that vertical muzzle jump is reduced. Carrying-sling swivels have been added at bottom of the butt and barrel. The sling can also be used to steady the revolver when firing. The scope mount has a long mounting bar and three sets of rings for increased strength. For long-range revolver shooting, this adaptation is excellent. Similar porting and other adaptations can be done on any revolver by Mag-na-Port and others.

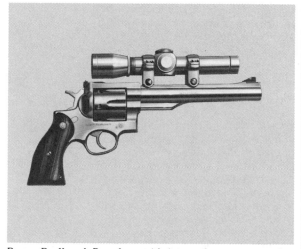

Heavy Smith & Wesson Double-Action Revolver: This is the Model 29 with a 8⅜-inch barrel in .357 Magnum. Other models are available for the .357, and the .41 and .44 magnums. The "saw handle" grip with checkering is not intended to slide through the hand when gun recoils. Because double-action revolvers can be fired rapidly by pulling the trigger without thumb-cocking, they must be designed to be held without movement in the hand during recoil. Successive shots can be fired by pulling the trigger without the need to re-establish the grip. These revolvers load by "side-wheeling." When the latch behind the cylinder is pressed forward, the entire cylinder can be swung out to the left, exposing the rear of six chambers for loading. Loading can be accomplished much more quickly than is possible with a single-action revolver.

Ruger Redhawk Revolver with integral scope-mounting system: The two-point scope mount fits into two cutouts in barrel rib. The simple but strong system permits quick removal of the scope. Handgun scopes must have long eye relief so that they can be used with eye at much greater distance from the rear lens than is the case with long guns.

Llama Super Comanche IV in .44 Magnum: This is a moderately priced but serviceable heavy revolver made in Spain by Gabilondo and imported by Stoeger Industries. It is available in .357 and .44 Magnum calibers.

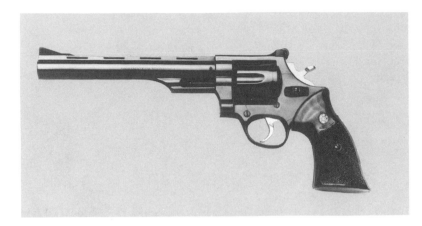

Williams top mount and scope on Thompson/Center Contender pistol: The contender is, perhaps, the best-known of the single-shot hunting handguns. There are many model variations, but with all of them, barrels are interchangeable within certain limits, so that one gun can be used for many purposes from varmint shooting to big game. The Contenders are break-action guns. The barrel hinges down to expose breech. Many calibers, factory and wildcats, are available, including some rifle calibers.

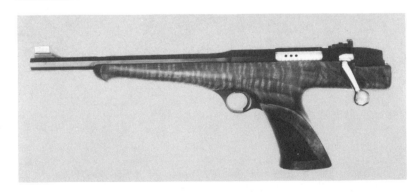

Wichita Classic single-shot bolt-action handgun: The bolt handle is on the left so the hunter will hold the gun in his right hand and load with his left. Other models are available. These pistols are made in any caliber up to and including .308 Winchester. This includes many popular wildcats. Guns with magazines are available on special order.

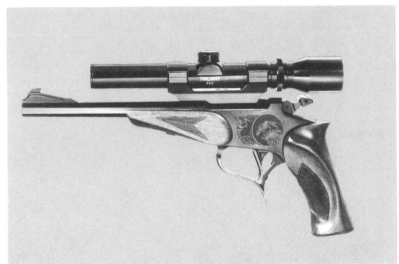

The Wichita MK-40 Silhouette Pistol with plastic stock resembles previous model, but the highly durable, waterproof stock precludes warping.

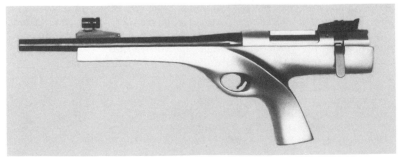

The Wichita Hunter International Pistol resembles a semi-automatic repeating handgun. But it is a break-action single-shot made in many calibers, including .30/30 Winchester. For shooters who are accustomed to semi-auto handguns, this look-alike would be easy to shoot.

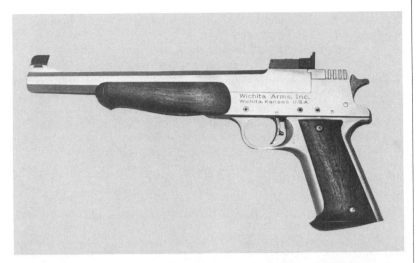

Dan Wesson .44 Magnum Pistol Pac: Interchangeable short and long barrels are quickly installed, and butts can be changed quickly, too. This system allows different configurations for different shooting.

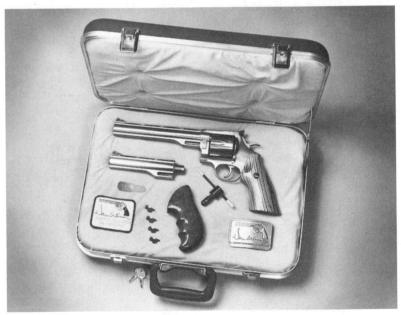

dropped a deer with a deliberately aimed shot and walk toward it. Quite suddenly, the wounded animal jumps up and begins to run. When approaching a downed deer, you should of course have any revolver cocked for just this kind of thing. But if you fail to put the deer down with this second shot, you will find a single-action firearm is slow to cock and fire again. You may need to fire several shots very quickly, and at such times, it's convenient to have a double-action revolver. The shooting commonly takes place at very close range, but double-action practice is essential for accurate shooting in this situation.

Finishing off a wounded deer, by the way, is about the only time a handgunner should fire at a moving animal. Shooting a handgun accurately is difficult enough without trying to hit moving game.

UPPING THE ENERGY

Handloading can substantially increase the power of the hunting handgun. For instance, the .44 Magnum can be upped to about 1,300 foot-pounds of muzzle energy with a 240-grain bullet by loading the cartridge to maximum safe pressure levels. This results in more on-target energy down range, but it also increases muzzle blast and recoil. The .357 and .41 magnums can be similarly improved. In fact, most accomplished handgun hunters are proficient handloaders, and they experiment to develop heavy loads that they can fire with an acceptable degree of accuracy. Handloading can also be used to load very mild cartridges for practice so that you can work up gradually to heavy hunting loads. Handloading metallic cartridges is not difficult and is covered in the next section.

Other handgun hunters opt for firearms that are even more powerful than the .44 Magnum revolver. Some of these handguns were developed for metallic silhouette shooting, but they can be used for hunting, and you can obtain them chambered for rifle cartridges. For instance, the Thompson/Center break-action single-shot Contender is available in .30/30 Winchester and .35 Remington—both rifle cartridges—as well as in an assortment of handgun cartridges, including wildcats. Many Contender barrels are interchangeable on the same frame, which is very convenient and saves a lot of money if you are content with a single-shot handgun. Wichita Engineering offers single-shot, bolt-action handguns in .308 Winchester plus other heavy rifle calibers on special order.

If you really want to find out if you're capable of flinching, try something like a .45/70 in one of these handguns. It's an unforgettable experience. Yet, many accomplished shooters use these guns effectively. These powerful handguns have very long barrels. The Thompson/Center barrels are 10, 13½, or 14 inches in length. With this type of firearm, you're into something that is midway between a true handgun and a carbine or short rifle.

These guns have fully enclosed breeches, and it is therefore possible to have a forearm under the barrel. With revolvers, gripping the gun anywhere forward of

Two-handed revolver grip: Grasp the butt as usual with right hand. Then place left hand over the right and tighten up. Most hunters cock the hammer with the left thumb. Usually, a lot of practice is needed to develop the uniform two-handed grip that works best for an individual shooter. (Chuck Adams photo)

the cylinder is unwise because metal is sometimes shaved from bullets at the cylinder gap and may wind up in your hand or wrist. The escaping gas from the gap hurts too. With forearm-equipped single-shots, the shooter can safely grasp the forend to steady his hold while the trigger hand firmly holds the grip. This is a lot like rifle shooting, particularly if you can take a rest, and you may find that a 3× or even a 4× scope is very useful with this type of handgun in a rifle caliber.

Using these very long handguns is a bit awkward at first, but practice helps a great deal. The lack of the ability to fire a quick second shot is also a disadvantage. Some hunters, however, prefer this type of firearm. Using one undoubtedly increases your effective range, but you must have a remarkably strong physique, and steady nerves to handle one.

This type of firearm in a rifle caliber should only be used by a very experienced shooter. It's the worst possible choice for a beginner. Firing one shot from a .308 Winchester handgun may be the last handgun shooting the beginner ever tries. As with all other shooting, you should wear earmuffs or plugs when practicing. Wearing both at the same time is best when you shoot these hand cannons.

THE AUTO PISTOL FOR HANDGUNNING

At one time the .44 Auto Mag handgun was available for handgun hunting, but at present it is no longer manufactured. It fired a very heavy .44 semi-auto wildcat cartridge, but these cartridges are available from several custom loaders. The Wildey semi-automatic (gas operated) handgun fires the extremely powerful .45 Winchester Magnum handgun cartridge with a muzzle velocity of 1,001 foot-pounds. But the Wildey pistol is an on-again off-again proposition. Samples were delivered to gun writers in 1979 for testing, but the gun was not available to the public until years later. The price is well over $1,000.

Perhaps this situation with semi-auto hunting pistols says something. Surely, if demand for these guns were great enough, some manufacturer would be producing them in quantity at affordable prices. A very powerful semi-automatic for hunting is an intriguing idea, but there are definite disadvantages.

Chief among them is the undeniable fact that this type of gun functions best with full-metal jacketed bullets that do not hang up from time to time on the top of the chamber or loading ramp. Plain lead or bullets with open points commonly do so. It's true that soft-point jacketed loads have been developed for use in semi-autos, such as the Colt .45 Government, but most experienced shooters know very well that

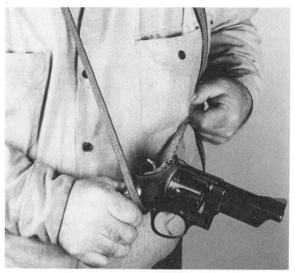

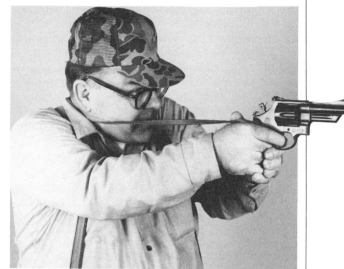

Handgun support with a strap: Here a leather dog leash with a snap on one end and a metal ring on the other is used. Cut the strap to proper length to form a circle that goes over your right shoulder and under your left armpit. The strap goes around the revolver grip behind the cylinder and under your hand. With two-handed grip, push the revolver away from you. Tension on the strap steadies the revolver a great deal. The strap can also circle to a specially installed lanyard loop under the handle butt. (Neil Soderstrom photos)

they risk unreliable feeding. In any case, full-metal jacketed bullets are forbidden for hunting big game.

A semi-auto is subject to more mishaps than a revolver, principally jamming because of a small amount of dirt in the works. At present most hunters find that a heavy revolver is the better choice, and this is reflected by the absence of a true hunting semi-auto .41 or .44 in today's gun market. However, two semi-automatics chambered for the .357 Magnum cartridge are now available.

PRACTICE OF ANOTHER KIND

Most beginners will find that it's not too difficult to develop the marksmanship required for handgun hunting. All that is needed is steady target practice. But another kind of practice is also needed. To use a handgun effectively, you have to get within very close range of the deer, and that's very difficult indeed, unless you hunt from a stand. You also need tracking skills in case you wound a deer. Here is an unusual suggestion that may be amusing to experienced hunters. A beginner needs to get out into the woods as much as possible to practice tracking and moving quietly. Small-game hunting with a shotgun or a .22 rifle or handgun provides good practice in moving quietly of course, but you don't find out how to track.

For practice at tracking, work with a partner and take turns moving around in the woods and finding

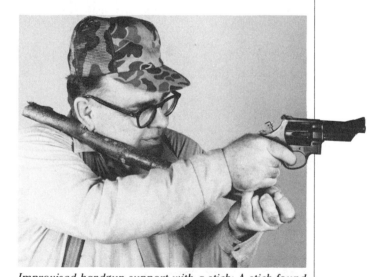

Improvised handgun support with a stick: A stick found or cut in the woods can be used to steady a handgun a great deal. The stick goes over the right shoulder and is held by left hand with left elbow resting on the point of the hip or against the body (if you have short arms). With firm one-handed grip with the right hand, the revolver butt is rested on top of the fingers of left hand. Particularly when sitting down with rear end of stick against a tree and left forearm on your knees, the handgun feels a lot like a carbine. A stick can also be used as a steadying post by placing one end on the ground and resting the hands in two-handed grip on the top end. A long staff is needed for the offhand (erect) position. Many variations are possible. A steady rest is even more important with a handgun than it is with a shoulder arm. (Neil Soderstrom photo)

one another. When a hunter walks through the woods, he leaves telltale signs, such as bent grass, broken twigs, drag marks of his heels in soft ground, and so forth. Deer leave much the same telltale traces. If you can follow these signs and get within handgun range of your partner without letting him know you are there, you're developing an ability that is just as important as good marksmanship.

Experienced outdoorsmen who grow up hunting acquire these skills without thinking about it, but a city hunter who elects to use a handgun for hunting should do a lot more than practice marksmanship. It will stand you in good stead when the hunting season opens. If you doubt that this is true, talk to bowhunters. They have much the same problem, and many of them manage to solve it only by hunting from a stand and waiting for the deer to come to them. A really skilled hunter should also be able to go to the game.

CLEANING

Cleaning a revolver differs from cleaning a rifle in that the six chambers in the cylinder must be cleaned as well as the barrel. Also, fouling or bullet jacket metal accumulates in the throat of the barrel, on the face of the cylinder, and the breech of the barrel at the cylinder gap. Careful cleaning in these areas is very important, and if the gun has been neglected you may have to soak the fouling with solvent. Then remove it with improvised aluminum or brass chipping tools, soft steel or brass wool. If you don't, the cylinder may freeze and hang up the whole gun. Moving parts inside a revolver are also rather small and require fairly frequent cleaning too. If metal fouling accumulates in the barrel throat and part of the rifling, it may ruin the accuracy of the handgun. To remove it, special kits are available that employ a cleaning patch made of bronze screening. It is hard enough to scrub out the residue but too soft to harm the barrel steel.

NEW DEVELOPMENTS

Experiments by handloaders and wildcatters constantly lead to new developments in the continuing effort to increase the effectiveness of handguns, and these efforts sometimes lead to new handguns.

For instance, Remington brought out the .357 Remington Maximum, which is simply a lengthened .357 Magnum with a greatly increased powder capacity. Fired from a 10½-inch barrel, this cartridge develops 1,168 foot-pounds of energy at the muzzle and 668 foot-pounds at 100 yards, putting it in the .44 Magnum class, but with much less recoil. This cartridge is currently used in some single-shot handguns. Two revolver makers built revolvers for this round, and one was marketed for a while. But rapid erosion of the barrel throat caused by the very large powder charge caused it to be withdrawn, and the other revolver was never put on the market, presumably for the same reason. The quest for more powerful rounds in revolvers continues.

The Texas-based Freedom Arms Company introduced a truly massive revolver for the .454 Casul cartridge, which is available from the company as factory-loaded rounds. The cartridge is so powerful that the cylinder is made with only five chambers instead of six in order to provide the extra metal needed to strengthen the cylinder sufficiently. This round is about 20 percent more powerful than the .44 Magnum revolver load. It is so powerful, in fact, that only experienced handgunners can tolerate the recoil and muzzle blast. Revolvers are, of course, harder to control than single-shot handguns because of the lack of a forearm that can be held by the left hand.

Wildcatters constantly come up with new cartridges (often based on modified rifle cases) that develop high energy levels, and some of these may eventually develop into factory-loaded rounds. At that point, a handgun manufacturer may begin to make revolvers or single-shots to fire the round. Normally, these cartridges are fired in standard handguns that have been modified by reaming out their chambers (or cylinders).

A few specialist gunsmiths modify existing handguns to make extraordinarily powerful cartridges. One man, who has killed several elephants with his own wildcat cartridges in modified single-shot handguns was asked if he would build a single-shot bolt-action handgun for the .458 Winchester Magnum round—a rifle cartridge intended for the very heaviest African game. His reply was: "No, that's a bit too much. But I will build one for my own shortened .458 Magnum wildcat." That cartridge is *only* 2 inches long. It's more than enough for almost anyone.

With all this development work, new cartridges and new guns are undoubtedly in the offing, and most experienced handgunners follow these developments avidly. It may eventually be possible to develop handguns with extremely effective recoil-absorbing capability so that very heavy cartridges could be fired without damaging recoil or felt recoil of any kind. If that ever happens, many hunters would undoubtedly prefer handguns over rifles. The very effective recoil-absorbing devices used in modern artillery may be a fertile area for handgun experimenters to investigate.

Who knows what the future will bring?

MUZZLELOADERS

That muzzleloading rifles are capable of superb accuracy was forcefully demonstrated in 1876 during the International Match at Creedmoor, New York, when a member of the Irish rifle team put all 15 shots from his muzzleloading percussion rifle into a 3-foot circular bull's-eye at 1,000 yards. It was arguably the single greatest rifle-shooting feat of the decade, and his praises were sung on both sides of the Atlantic. It was no doubt a fine achievement, but other riflemen often came close to his perfect score at the 1,000-yard stage.

But this was target shooting from the prone or "back position." The shooter lay on his back with his feet toward the target, held the butt of the rifle firmly in the bottom of his armpit, and supported the barrel with his legs and even his feet. At the time those who used muzzleloaders often shot as well or better than those who used breechloading target rifles (usually Remington or Sharps) in this type of match.

The stories of these early international matches and the mythical feats of long-range shooting described in American fiction and semi-fiction of the period often inspire modern users of muzzleloading hunting rifles to expect much too much from their rifles and themselves. The long-range target-shooting of the 1880s grew out of military riflery, and many of the shooters were military officers. It was recognized that the matches were intended not as practice for hunting but rather for war. The shooter was trying to hit a target as large as a horse and rider or a military ammunition wagon with the hope of blowing it up.

At this international target match in the 1880s, the rifleman on left employs the prone position favored by Americans. The rifleman on the right is in one form of the "back position" just before firing. His feet are toward the target and the very long rifle is supported by his right leg. The rear sight is mounted far to the rear on the stock. The back position was favored by shooters from the British Isles and was often used by British snipers in the Napoleonic Wars.

In fact, the long-range target in these matches was 12 feet long and 6 feet high. Even a hit on the 2-foot-wide end zones counted two points. In war the target was often a group of the enemy, and the shooter didn't care much which man he killed or wounded. Military men knew very well that at ranges over 200 yards or so, a bullet from a big-bore, heavily charged rifle almost always wounded rather than killed. However, wounding a soldier creates more trouble for a civilized enemy than killing him outright.

For deer hunting even a maximum load in a big-bore muzzleloader is a sure killer only out to 125 yards. Most fairly powerful hunting loads are effective at much shorter ranges, precisely because a hunter wants to kill his deer outright and not wound it. If the legends of long-range shooting attract you, it's probably best to forget about hunting with the muzzleloading rifle. In fact, muzzleloading rifles have been revived precisely because they are short-range arms. To kill his deer, a muzzleloading rifleman must therefore be a better hunter, on the average, than those who use modern long-range centerfire rifles.

A large number of people are attracted by the sheer nostalgic satisfaction of using the firearms of the pioneers and mountain men, though most of them are aware of the limitations of these firearms. These are the people who participate in reenactments of Revolutionary War and Civil War battles or dress up in coonskin caps and fringed buckskins for matches and frontier celebrations. It's startling to meet an authentically dressed mountain man in the deer woods. But some of these romantics do become accomplished hunters.

Firing accurate shots with a muzzleloader involves a complicated loading procedure, painstaking cleaning and maintenance of the firearm, lots of practice, and willingness to put up with inevitable and fairly frequent failures to fire. If you have the patience, it's great sport; if you don't, stay with modern arms.

WHAT THE LAW ALLOWS

A few hunters voluntarily use flintlocks rather than percussion guns because they feel they are more authentic, but the very unreliable ignition of flintlock arms, especially in damp weather, makes them much less reliable than caplock arms. If you have ever tried to prime the open pan of a flintlock with loose powder when the wind is blowing, you have experienced true frustration.

In a few states, notably Pennsylvania, using a caplock rifle during the special muzzleloader deer season is forbidden by law; so hunters in these states must rely on the flintlock. Pennsylvania also recently banned use of anything except round balls during the muzzleloader deer season. This is symptomatic of a trend in hunting regulations as they relate to muzzleloaders.

Formerly, regulations allowed the hunter to use almost any kind of firearm, ammunition (including conoid bullets), accessories, and other gear as long as loading took place through the muzzle, not the breech. This is changing. At first muzzleloader deer kills during the special seasons were quite small, and the regulations were liberal. But as more and more hunters took up the sport and the efficiency of the shooters and their equipment improved, annual kills rose beyond expectations.

To cut down on the kill and keep it within limits that game biologists feel are needed to maintain the herd, additional restrictions are being imposed. For instance, some hunters use low-power scopes on their muzzleloaders, but several states now forbid it. If you're about to purchase a muzzleloader for deer hunting, carefully study the regulations of the state or states in which you wish to hunt before you consult the catalogs or go to the gun store.

In general, eastern and midwestern states have more restrictive regulations than western and southern states, though there are exceptions. In about 20 states (the number changes from time to time), there are no regulations simply because there are no separate muzzleloader seasons. In these states you're free to use a muzzleloading gun, but of course, you'll be competing with those who use modern cartridge arms.

The status of the muzzleloading handgun in such states is often in doubt. In at least a few of these states (those that allow handguns for big-game hunting and make no stipulation on minimum muzzle energy), you

could legally use a handgun for deer hunting, but it's a foolish thing to attempt. The most powerful replica muzzleloading revolver develops only about 300 foot-pounds of energy *at the muzzle,* and these arms are therefore really quite useless for deer hunting, except as backup guns with which to kill a wounded deer at 1 or 2 feet with a shot through the neck.

If you want to use a muzzleloading revolver (they actually load through the front of the cylinder) or even a single-shot front-loader handgun, check the regulations carefully. In some states any repeating gun is illegal during the muzzleloader season. In others it is illegal to carry any handgun, concealed or not, without a special license. This is part of the criminal law, not the hunting regulations.

Even if you have a "carry permit" for a modern repeating handgun, it's not a good idea to holster it during the muzzleloader-only deer season as a backup gun. The game warden may decide your intent is to use the cartridge handgun to shoot the deer in the first place and that your muzzleloading long gun is only a prop. In many states the law is very vague about such things, and if you ask two game wardens, you often get contradictory answers.

ORIGINALS AND REPLICAS

Many people formerly used original antique arms for target shooting and hunting, but today the trend is very much toward replica muzzleloaders. Original antique muzzleloaders, including issue arms of the Civil War are now quite valuable, and few people use them because firing these guns inevitably leads to deterioration and lessens their value. Also, in spite of being

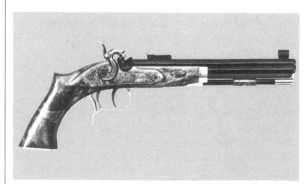

Thompson/Center Patriot Pistol: Available in .36 or .45 caliber, this single-shot percussion handgun is useful only for target shooting or as a backup gun for dispatching wounded deer. Muzzleloading handguns, including revolvers, do not develop enough energy for hunting because of their very short barrels. Use of handguns for any type of hunting is forbidden in many states.

This .50 or .54 caliber Lyman Plains Pistol is traditional in form and lacks bright metal. The simple curved grip slides in the hand readily on discharge rather than being stopped immediately by a more conventional saw-handle grip. This type of grip is the distant ancestor of all single-action American revolver grips.

genuine antiques or because of it, many of these guns are not in good enough condition to be accurate or safe. The metal used in modern replicas is vastly superior to the metal used in originals, and a well-made quality replica will last a lifetime if properly maintained. For all these reasons, it's best to use original muzzleloaders as wall-hangers.

Good replicas are mass-produced in modern factories in the United States and Europe, particularly in Italy. In some cases, the Italian arms factories that produced original Civil War arms for export are again producing the same arms with some of the original tools.

Another class of muzzleloaders is produced in Europe. These are cheap muzzleloading smoothbores intended for use by African natives where the law forbids them to possess modern cartridge arms. Many of these guns are poorly made and many of them are unsafe. In one case, the barrels were actually made from water pipe. Every once in a while, some American fly-by-night importer tries to make a killing by buying such guns at a low price and selling at much higher prices to unsophisticated shooters in the United States. Yet, the prices are attractive. The guns are easily detected, however. Finish is poor and the whole weapon is badly fitted, so badly that parts rattle in the lock and the barrel is loose in the stock. Don't be tempted by low prices unless you can tell the difference between a decent gun and a piece of junk. Muzzleloaders regularly listed in *Gun Digest* and *Shooter's Bible* are dependable. Beware of very cheap guns with unknown maker's marks or no marks at all. They are sometimes encountered in discount houses and cheap sporting-good's stores.

There is still another class of muzzleloaders. These are handmade firearms produced by individual gunsmiths. In some parts of North America, people have continued shooting muzzleloaders since pioneer times, and local gunsmiths have gone right on producing excellent guns. Also, many modern gunsmiths have learned the art of building custom muzzleloaders. If you tell one of these gunsmiths that the rifle he makes is a "replica," you might get a violent reaction. These smiths follow traditional practices but they design each firearm individually, often to satisfy a customer's specifications. Though built in modern times, these guns are in no sense replicas. They are modern originals. But they are often so beautiful and so interesting that they should not be used for hunting or even for target shooting. Many of them are also very expensive. In one interesting case, the historic restoration at Williamsburg, Virginia, maintains a complete Colonial gunsmith's shop and the smith will make a muzzleloader for you. But the price is steep because of all the hand labor, and a premium is charged to cover pride of ownership in possessing a "Williamsburg original."

POWDER, BALL, AND CALIBER

Black powder, a granulated mixture of charcoal, saltpeter, and sulfur is available in varius granulations intended for different purposes. They are Fg (for fine grain), FFg, FFFg, and FFFFg. Fg is very coarse and is used to load big-bore shotguns and cannon and signal guns in war reenactments. The finest granulation, FFFFg, is used to prime the pans of flintlock arms. Because of the fineness of the granules, it burns very rapidly and is excellent for priming, but it burns too rapidly to be used for the main propellant charge. FFg is usually used for rifles of .54 caliber or greater, and three-F is for rifles of smaller caliber.

Smokeless powder merely burns when it is not confined, but that is not true of black powder, which often detonates even when in an unconfined state. This detonation can be caused by sparks. Therefore, powder cans, flasks, and other containers for black powder used by shooters are not made of steel, and steel or iron ramrods are not used. Black powder also creates a great deal of thick, blue-gray smoke when fired, and black-powder fouling is thick and quite hard to remove.

Pyrodex RS (rifle and shotgun), a substitute for black powder was developed to lessen some of these disadvantages. It produces much less smoke, fouling is not so bad, and it does not ignite (or detonate) so easily. Nevertheless, use Pyrodex RS with the same degree of caution you would employ with black powder. Unfortunately, the fact that Pyrodex is harder to ignite creates ignition problems when it is used in a gun. It is therefore seldom used in flintlock arms. Even in percussion rifles, special hot caps are often needed to ignite it.

Loading a gun properly with Pyrodex and a hot cap is a good way to avoid the necessity of falling to one's knees to look under a cloud of smoke to see the results of a shot. Yet many traditional shooters will not use Pyrodex because it sullies the mystique of hunting with a muzzleloader. In many black-powder shooting matches, the use of Pyrodex is barred for the same reason and to put all competitors on an even footing.

Pyrodex loads match black-powder loads on a volume-to-volume basis. You can, therefore, use the same powder measure that you use with black. But weighed charges do not match because the weight of the two powders differs. The usual procedure is to determine the volume of the black-powder charge and then use the same charging cup or other measure to meter the volume of Pyrodex.

Never use anything except Pyrodex RS or black powder to load a muzzleloader. If you do you may find yourself attending the next frontier rendezvous in the sky. Also, it's very hazardous indeed to try to make your own black powder. True, the formula is very simple, but the procedures are not, and many fully equipped, well-run black-powder mills have blown up. Home tinkerers beware!

Storing black powder in your home is legal in many states and cities, but some specify the quantity that can be stored and others require a special permit. Inquire at your local fire department. It's best to store black powder in small lots. Five separate containers, one pound each, stowed in different locations is better than one 5-pound container. A 5-pound black-powder explosion is a real blast!

THE BULLET

Two basic types of bullet are currently used in muzzleloading arms—round balls and conoid (conical) bullets. Both are made of pure lead, not lead alloys such as type metal. Round balls, rather surprisingly, are more accurate in many rifled arms than conoid bullets. But because of their light weight in comparison to conoids of the same caliber, they do not develop as much on-target energy and are usually used for small game and target shooting. In large-bore muzzleloaders though, round balls can kill deer-size animals effectively at moderate ranges.

The Minié "ball" was developed by a Frenchman and named after him. This type of bullet was used in many wars, including our own Civil War. At first the hollow bases of these projectiles contained a soft iron cup, which expanded on firing and drove the lead skirt into the rifling of the bore. The minie ball of today (both initial capital letter and the French accent mark are no longer used) is made entirely of lead without cups or expanding plugs since the lead skirt expands quite well without them. The minie ball is not a ball, of course, and American soldiers always called them Minny balls, as though they had been cooked up by Aunt Minerva. Some modern writers refer to these projectiles as mini-balls or just plain minis, and this causes confusion because they are in no sense smaller than round balls.

If the bore size is the same, a minie ball is heavier than a round ball, and this provides greater energy. But there are other advantages. For best accuracy a round ball in a rifle must be "patched"—enclosed in a greased piece of cloth that "takes" the rifling. The ball never touches the rifling, and this helps keep the ball as round as possible during loading. The tightly compressed cloth between the ball and the rifling is gripped by the lands and grooves and imparts stabilizing spin to the bullet as it travels down the bore.

The need for a patch makes the round-ball loading procedure time consuming and complicated. But a wad or a patch is not needed with minie balls because the skirt of the soft-lead bullet expands into the rifling

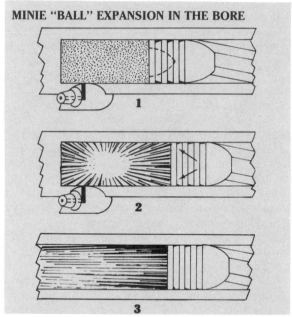

MINIE "BALL" EXPANSION IN THE BORE

Cutaway view shows how minie balls seal the bore: 1. As first loaded, bullet rests on the powder but is not in firm contact with walls of the barrel or the rifling's spiraling lands and grooves. 2. When the main charge goes off, gas pressure expands base of the bullet so that the soft lead engages rifling and spins the bullet. 3. Expanding gas moves the spinning bullet down the tube. The bullet is now a bit shorter than before firing because of the expansion of the base.

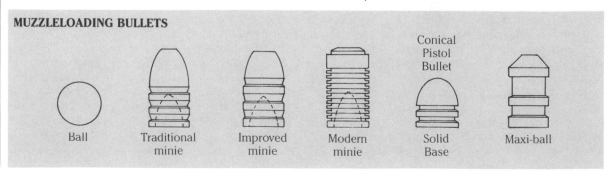

MUZZLELOADING BULLETS

Ball   Traditional minie   Improved minie   Modern minie   Conical Pistol Bullet / Solid Base   Maxi-ball

and seals the bore when the gun is fired. The bullet is engraved by the lands and grooves, which also impart a spin to the projectile. Minie balls are easily inserted in the muzzle and are easy to push down on the powder with the ramrod, provided the bore is fairly clean. This makes for faster, more convenient loading. In some military loads, the minie ball was so small that it actually dropped down the bore for the first few shots. A ramrod was used only after the bore became heavily fouled.

Round balls are comparatively light in weight because of their shape; minie balls are a bit heavier, but their weight is limited because of the hollow base. To provide a heavier projectile, Thompson/Center Arms developed the Maxi-Ball. Predictably, the word "ball" is used in spite of the fact that the bullet is conoid. Superficially, Maxi-Balls look like minie balls, but they are solid rather than hollow based. Bore size for bore size, Maxi-Balls provide more weight and therefore more on-target energy.

Round balls in rifles are loaded with greased cloth patches for hunting (the old-timers used greased leather) to lubricate the bore, soften black-powder fouling, and prevent rusting. Minies and Maxi-Balls have grease grooves, which are filled with thick grease (store-bought or homemade). With minie balls, bore sealing is accomplished through expansion of the skirt.

With Maxi-Balls, there is little expansion of the projectile on firing. So the Maxi-Ball has three "bearing bands" and two grease grooves. The first and second bearing bands are approximately bore sized and enter the muzzle quite easily during loading. The top band is oversized and must be forced into the muzzle. When this is done, the rifling engraves the bullet and seals the bore quite effectively. On firing, the bottom bearing band expands and "takes" the rifling. A somewhat similar bullet, the REAL (rifling engraved at loading), enters the bore in much the same way.

These solid bullets are therefore harder to load into the bore than round balls or minies. For this reason, many hunters load a Maxi-Ball at home or in camp where it is possible to take one's time and do the job carefully. After firing in the field, they reload their rifles with a minie ball. This makes for quicker loading, an advantage if one must follow up a wounded animal.

CALIBER

The caliber designation of many modern rifles is the groove diameter of the bore, which is the same as the diameter of the bullet, give or take a bit. For instance, the familiar .308 Winchester has a .308-inch groove diameter, and the bullet is .308 of an inch in diameter. Muzzleloading rifles are most often described by the land diameter; that is, the distance between opposite

lands. Most hunting rifles, flintlocks, and caplock rifles today are of the following mass-produced calibers: .32; .36; .45; .50; .54; and .58. Some smoothbores are larger. Original handmade arms, mostly flintlocks, were often made in "odd" calibers because the gunsmith supplied a mold to go with every rifle he made, and everyone cast their own round balls—the only bullets used. Also, once the soft steel of the bore wore so badly that accuracy was lost, the smith "freshed the barrel out" by cutting new rifling. Of course, this enlarged the bore and often resulted in an odd bore size. Since mass-produced rifles and bullet molds prevail today, calibers have been more or less standardized. Many smoothbores are designated as to caliber by the gauge system, and most are actually 12 gauge or close to it.

Because you know the caliber designation of the rifle, you should not assume that you know the diameter of the bullet. For instance, a .54 caliber rifle is most often loaded with a .535 ball, the "extra" room being taken up by the cloth patch. The same .540 bore will take a .533 minie ball, which expands to seal the bore. The table on the next page shows bore and bullet sizes.

Smoothbore guns are often used in battle reenactments and for hunting in states where rifled muzzleloaders are not allowed for big-game hunting. These guns are mostly of military pattern. For instance, there are replicas of the British Brown Bess .75 caliber (nominal) musket used by the British in the American Revolution and many other wars. These smoothbores should always be used with round balls for deer hunting. A conoid projectile tumbles in flight soon after exit from the muzzle of a smoothbore.

For deer hunting, smoothbores are best when loaded with a slightly undersize ball and a lubricated patch. The patch softens the fouling and lubricates the bore. Because it fits tightly in the bore, the patched ball also prevents moisture from reaching the powder charge and keeps the bullet firmly seated on the powder charge.

If a bare round ball is used, it may become dislodged and move forward in the bore, leaving an air space (very dangerous). Or it may even roll right out of the barrel. Bare round balls with paper wadding on top of the powder were used by infantrymen for the sake of quick loading, but embers from the burned paper wadding left behind in the bore often ignited the next charge of powder loaded. The patched ball is much safer if it is properly loaded.

If there are no specifications on ball size and loading instructions for a gun, write to the company or importer before buying it and find out if reliable information is available. If not, buy some other model. Too often cheap smoothbore guns are sold without such information precisely because the guns themselves are unreliable and poorly made.

BLACK-POWDER LOADS FOR RIFLES AND REVOLVERS (LYMAN)

The data in the following tables were developed by Lyman Products for Shooters. The information is printed here in abbreviated form with only a minimum and maximum load for each barrel length. In the *Lyman Black Powder Handbook*, many loads are given between the powder-charge minimum and the maximum. Lyman and this publisher accept no responsibility for use of the data. Only the shooter is responsible for the manner in which he loads a black-powder arm. Maximum loads are intended only for arms that are in very good condition.

Barrel Length	Bullet Type & Diam.	Bullet Weight (grains)	Powder (grains)	Muzzle Velocity (fps)	Muzzle Energy (ft. lbs.)	100 yard Energy (ft. lbs.)
RIFLE .36 CAL. (.365 BORE DIAMETER)						
Min. 28"	.360 ball	71	25	1329	278	84
Max. 28"	.360 ball	71	60	2090	688	135
Min. 32"	.360 ball	71	25	1335	281	84
Max. 32"	.360 ball	71	60	2108	700	137
Min. 37"	.360 ball	71	25	1384	301	87
Max. 37"	.360 ball	71	60	2192	756	144
Min. 43"	.360 ball	71	25	1521	364	95
Max. 43"	.360 ball	71	60	2292	827	154
.45 CAL. (.453 BORE DIAMETER)						
Min. 28"	.445 ball	133	30	1089	349	N/A
Max. 28"	.445 ball	133	75	2025	1209	341
Min. 32"	.445 ball	133	30	1240	453	N/A
Max. 32"	.445 ball	133	75	2057	1248	352
Min. 36"	.445 ball	133	30	1294	493	N/A
Max. 36"	.445 ball	133	75	2055	1245	351
Min. 40"	.445 ball	133	30	1327	519	N/A
Max. 40"	.445 ball	133	75	2009	1190	338
Min. 28"	.454 minie	265	30	782	359	295
Max. 28"	.454 minie	265	65	1472	1273	789
Min. 32"	.454 minie	265	30	715	300	245
Max. 32"	.454 minie	265	65	1489	1303	805
Min. 36"	.454 minie	265	30	1041	636	477
Max. 36"	.454 minie	265	65	1506	1333	820
Min. 40"	.454 minie	265	30	825	399	327
Max. 40"	.454 minie	265	65	1547	1406	856
Min. 28"	.455 Maxi-B	230	30	939	449	292
Max. 28"	.455 Maxi-B	230	65	1588	1286	527
Min. 32"	.455 Maxi-B	230	30	1017	528	326
Max. 32"	.455 Maxi-B	230	80	1746	1554	598
Min. 36"	.455 Maxi-B	230	30	927	438	286
Max. 36"	.455 Maxi-B	230	80	1735	1535	592
Min. 40"	.455 Maxi-B	230	30	1065	578	344
Max. 40"	.455 Maxi-B	230	80	1803	1657	628
.50 CAL. (.503 BORE DIAMETER)						
Min. 26"	.498 ball	180	50	1348	725	304
Max. 26"	.498 ball	180	120	2041	1663	432
Min. 28"	.498 ball	180	50	1333	709	300
Max. 28"	.498 ball	180	120	2009	1611	515
Min. 32"	.498 ball	180	50	1445	833	327
Max. 32"	.498 ball	180	120	2101	1762	565
Min. 43"	.498 ball	180	50	1506	905	343
Max. 43"	.498 ball	180	120	2243	2008	657
Min. 26"	.503 Maxi-B	370	45	1033	875	559
Max. 26"	.503 Maxi-B	370	70	1286	1357	718
Min. 28"	.503 Maxi-B	370	50	1067	934	581
Max. 28"	.503 Maxi-B	370	85	1442	1706	819
Min. 32"	.503 Maxi-B	370	50	1116	1022	612

Barrel Length	Bullet Type & Diam.	Bullet Weight (grains)	Powder (grains)	Muzzle Velocity (fps)	Muzzle Energy (ft. lbs.)	100 yard Energy (ft. lbs.)
Max. 32"	.503 Maxi-B	370	85	1435	1689	814
Min. 43"	.503 Maxi-B	370	55	1212	1205	672
Max. 43"	.503 Maxi-B	370	90	1542	1951	895
.54 CAL. (.540 BORE DIAMETER)						
Min. 28"	.535 ball	220	80	1453	1030	436
Max. 28"	.535 ball	220	150	2008	1967	699
Min. 30"	.535 ball	220	80	1466	1048	440
Max. 30"	.535 ball	220	150	2024	1998	712
Min. 34"	.535 ball	220	70	1439	1010	431
Max. 34"	.535 ball	220	140	1973	1899	676
Min. 43"	.535 ball	220	70	1527	1137	462
Max. 43"	.535 ball	220	140	2113	2178	784
Min. 28"	.533 minie	410	50	739	497	N/A
Max. 28"	.533 minie	410	120	1505	2059	1192
Min. 30"	.533 minie	410	60	897	732	580
Max. 30"	.533 minie	410	130	1620	2386	1346
Min. 34"	.533 minie	410	50	941	805	627
Max. 34"	.533 minie	410	120	1614	2368	1337
Min. 43"	.533 minie	410	60	1089	1087	772
Max. 43"	.533 minie	410	130	1718	2683	1498
.58 CAL (.575 BORE DIAMETER)						
Min. 22"	.560 ball	260	100	1249	899	440
Max. 22"	.560 ball	260	170	1648	1566	613
Min. 24"	.560 ball	260	110	1329	1018	469
Max. 24"	.560 ball	260	180	1783	1833	685
Min. 26"	.560 ball	260	120	1306	983	459
Max. 26"	.560 ball	260	190	1669	1606	623
Min. 32"	.560 ball	260	110	1352	1056	478
Max. 32"	.560 ball	260	180	1737	1739	659
Min. 22"	.575 minie	505	50	607	413	349
Max. 22"	.575 minie	505	120	1195	1599	1124
Min. 24"	.575 minie	505	60	791	701	587
Max. 24"	.575 minie	505	130	1253	1758	1198
Min. 26"	.575 minie	505	90	979	1073	852
Max. 26"	.575 minie	505	160	1340	2011	1317
Min. 32"	.575 minie	505	80	971	1056	841
Max. 32"	.575 minie	505	150	1393	2173	1393

Barrel Length	Bullet Type & Diam.	Bullet Weight (grains)	Powder (grains)	Muzzle Velocity (fps)	Muzzle Energy (ft. lbs.)
REVOLVER .44 CAL. (.440 BORE DIAMETER)					
Min. 8"	.451 ball	138	19	706	153
Min. 8"	.451 ball	138	22	752	173
Min. 8"	.451 ball	138	25	805	198
Min. 8"	.451 ball	138	28	885	240
Min. 8"	.451 ball	138	31	933	266
Min. 8"	.451 ball	138	33	979	293
Max. 8"	.451 ball	138	37	1032	326
Min. 8"	.450 conical	155	19	705	171
Min. 8"	.450 conical	155	22	768	203
Min. 8"	.450 conical	155	25	882	267
Max. 8"	.450 conical	155	28	861	255
REVOLVER .45 CAL. (RUGER OLD ARMY, .442 BORE DIAMETER)					
Min. 7"	.457 ball	185	30	858	301
Max. 7½"	.457 ball	185	40	917	344
Min. 7½"	.454 conical	185	26	860	303
Max. 7½"	.454 conical	185	35	905	335

RIFLE CALIBERS AND CHARGES

The table "Black-Powder Loads for Rifles and Revolvers" was developed from the *Lyman Black Powder Handbook,* a very useful publication for anyone who shoots a muzzleloader. The table lists only minimum and maximum charges for various rifle calibers and varying barrel lengths. Many intermediate charges are given in the Lyman handbook, but you can work with these abbreviated tables to select a moderate charge for your muzzleloading deer rifle.

The Lyman handbook states that the company does not take any responsibility for accidents that occur when using these loads because the shooter is the only one who can take responsibility for safe loading procedures. The recommended charges will work in a firearm that is in good condition, provided the shooter loads properly and, above all, measures the powder charge accurately. If you don't, you're the sole cause of any mishap.

The satisfying boom of a big-bore muzzleloader is a joy in itself, but the effective range is limited. To avoid wild shots and wounded game, the hunter must carefully determine maximum effective range in practice sessions. (Rick Hacker photo)

LOADING INSTRUCTIONS

The following discussion of loading procedures is not intended to tell you how to load any particular gun. Instructions on proper loading, including the correct charge and the correct projectile, should be obtained from the manufacturer of your gun. Most makers are happy to supply this information. For instance, Thompson/Center supplies an instructional booklet with every muzzleloader it sells, and this manual states: "Thompson/Center Arms is not responsible for loading information printed in sources other than this booklet."

The upcoming instructions are intended solely for those who have never used muzzleloaders before, so they will know what to expect in general if they take up this demanding sport.

Looking over the table "Black-Powder Loads for Rifles and Revolvers" tells a great deal about muzzleloading rifles. First of all you can rule out the .36 caliber rifle and the even smaller .32 as not powerful enough for deer hunting. The maximum 100-yard energy level is only 154 foot-pounds, and that is only enough for small game. At the opposite end of the scale is 1,498 foot-pounds at 100 yards, achieved with a minie ball in a .54-caliber rifled musket with a 43-inch barrel. Most hunting muzzleloaders have much shorter barrels and develop less energy. That's certainly enough to kill a deer, but maximum range is only about 125 yards, and actually much less if accuracy is poor as it often is in big-bore rifles loaded with maximum charges.

Many of the .58 caliber loads listed in the table are not as powerful as the .54 caliber maximum in terms of foot-pounds of energy, but the heavier, larger projectiles make up for this to some degree. Nevertheless, 125 yards is about maximum for sure kills with the heavy minie-ball loads. Deer are killed at about 100 yards every season with .45 and .50 caliber rifles loaded with minie balls or Maxi-Balls. Though the energy is less at 100 yards than the 1,200 foot-pounds often used as the minimum for modern rifles, the bullets weigh so much and bullet diameter is so large that the damage done is enough to kill effectively. But killing deer with lesser loads, particularly round-ball loadings, is a chancy thing at any more than 75 yards. Fifty yards is the effective maximum with many of the lighter loads. Actually, everything said earlier about shotgun slugs and effective range applies about equally to heavy muzzleloading charges.

It's also quite obvious from the energy figures that if the law allows you to use a conoid bullet, you're much better off than you are with the traditional round ball, nostalgia or not.

RIFLING TWIST

Modern muzzleloaders are made with rifling that has a slow twist (one complete turn in 66 or 68 inches is common) or a fast twist—almost always one complete turn in only 48 inches. Slow-twist rifles are intended mostly for use with round balls. The fast twists almost always work best with minie balls or Maxi-Balls. In buying a rifle for hunting, it's best to choose a rifle with a fast twist so that you can use the more effective conoid projectiles. Most manufacturers supply a booklet or at least an information sheet about their guns, and some catalogs also specify rifling twist. If you're interested in a particular rifle and information on twist is not readily available, write the manufacturer.

Many rifles will, however, handle both round balls and conoids with fair accuracy regardless of rifling twist. In fact, it's quite common to find that a slow-twist rifle handles conoids better than round balls and vice versa. These arms are much more individualistic than modern cartridge arms, and you'll only find out what your rifle will do by shooting it, and shooting it quite a bit at that.

HUNTING LOADS

The Lyman manual and information from the rifle manufacturer will provide details on loads for your rifle. The same sources will specify the correct percussion-cap size.

After you have familiarized yourself with the rifle and loading procedures, the next step is to work up your deer-hunting load. You want maximum energy and maximum accuracy, but you can't have both, and a compromise is in order. The usual procedure is to start with a low-power or medium-power load, and fire a group or two. Then increase the powder charge by a small amount, fire again, and so on. When groups open up to such a large size that the load would be useless for deer hunting, drop back down to a satisfactory load. If the rifle will fire the maximum safe load fairly accurately, count your blessings. Never exceed the maximum listed charge.

Many shooters strive for a 6-inch group and stop right there when they get it. A 6-inch, three-shot group (five shots are better) is a bit smaller than the heart-lung area of a mature deer, but remember that the group is achieved at a target range with a paper target.

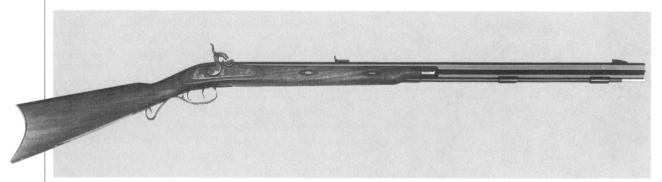

Lyman Great Plains Rifle: Plainly finished with hunting in mind, the Lyman Great Plains rifle is something of a compromise with its 32-inch barrel in .50 or .54 caliber.

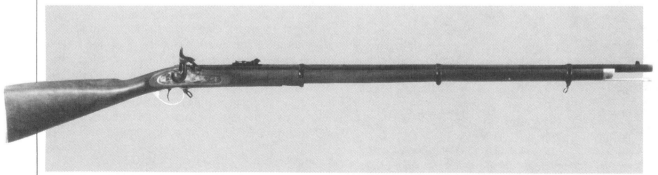

A rifled musket: A few long rifles of military pattern are also available. This one is the 2260 London Armory Company three-band Enfield Rifled Musket, imported by Euroarms of America. Barrel length is 39 inches and overall length is 54. Military-pattern rifles have the disadvantage that the barrel is difficult (almost impossible) to remove for servicing and cleaning. But, for the same reason, they are very sturdy.

Allow a few inches for nervousness when firing at a live animal, an inconvenient or unsteady shooting position, a jerky trigger pull, and all the other things that cut accuracy in the field. If the rifle will hold a 6-inch group only at ranges shorter than 125 yards, you'll have to limit the maximum range at which you take a shot.

Since muzzleloaders are perforce short-range arms, it's usually enough to determine the range at which the rifle produces 6-inch groups and then determine the midrange trajectory height. This is seldom great enough to produce midrange misses, but if it is, simply hold a bit low for midrange shots. If you hold on the bottom of the body for a heart shot at moderate range and the bullet flies a bit high, you will pierce the lungs if the deer is standing broadside or close to it. Sighting-in procedures are much the same as they are with modern rifles and practice is much the same too, or it *should* be. Bore sighting is, of course, impossible.

Though the size of the group may be satisfactory, the energy may not be. If you do not have access to a chronograph to determine the bullet velocity, you cannot determine the foot-pounds of energy developed at any range. Though the Lyman manual lists foot-pounds of energy for many different loads, your rifle and your loading procedure may produce considerably less energy, and it may be insufficient for deer hunting. Muzzleloaders differ from modern cartridge arms in that they may not produce anything like the expected energy listed in the tables. The only way to be sure is to chronograph your favorite load and work out the energy level at various ranges. Sometimes this leads to great surprises.

Another way to test energy levels is to soak newspapers or old telephone books overnight in water, and then set up a thick block of them as a test target. The wet paper roughly approximates the resistance offered by animal tissue. If the bullet penetrates three inches of wet paper, it will get through the chest wall of a deer to penetrate lungs or heart, even on an angling shot. If it won't, shorten the range at which you will take a shot. Because of limited penetration with these guns and loads, it is best to pass up shots on deer directly from the rear. Also, a brisket shot from the front is chancy because of the small size of the target. Yes, elephants and Cape buffalo have been killed with muzzleloaders in modern times, but six-gauge and four-gauge rifles were used. The rifles discussed here are of reasonable caliber and charges, and intended for deer hunting.

THE POWDER MEASURE

Say that you are working up a hunting load for a .50 caliber Maxi-Ball in a Thompson/Center Hawken or Renegade rifle. The company's instruction manual, furnished with their rifles, lists three powder charges— 80, 90, and 100 grains of FFg. Start with the 80-grain load. If it produces a satisfactory group, try the medium load and finally the maximum. Then choose the one that gives best accuracy. For an individual rifle, it may be somewhere between listed loads.

In the old days a rifleman never thought of the actual weight of his charges. Most of the time, the riflesmith supplied a charging cup that held the exact amount of powder to be used in the rifle. The smith was experienced enough to judge how much powder to use, and he fired the piece to make sure, increasing or decreasing the load if necessary. But a frontiersman without a powder measure could roughly estimate the charge. He simply held the right-size ball in the palm of one hand and poured powder over it until the ball was completely covered. The smaller the ball, the less powder was needed to cover it and vice versa. Then a charging cup was made to contain that amount. The frontiersman then shot the rifle for a while, and if an adjustment was needed, he shortened the measure or made a larger one. It was a rough-and-ready method, and it was often unsafe. There's no reason to employ it today. Besides, it does not work with conoid bullets.

Today very few shooters weigh black-powder charges in grains avoirdupois with a reloader's powder scale. Instead a measuring powder flask or a graduated powder measure is used. These metering devices simply measure the charge in terms of volume equivalents of weight. Say that firing the rifle shows that the best compromise between accuracy and sufficient energy is the 90-grain load. Use a volumetric measuring device to measure out that charge and then make a charging cup that contains just that amount. If you know someone who reloads, however, he may be willing to check your metering device and your charging cup to determine the weight of powder that is actually being used. This is certainly a wise precaution when you're using the maximum charge or close to it.

If you carry a powder horn or flask, never pour directly from it into the bore. Instead pour from the big container into your charging cup and then into the barrel. If the small measured charge does go off prematurely, there will only be a small blast.

One of the chief joys of using a muzzleloader is that you can vary the load considerably for different purposes. For instance, a .50 caliber rifle can be loaded with a Maxi-Ball, a minie ball, or a round ball. Powder charges will vary considerably. If you use, say, a ball for plinking, a Maxi-Ball for your first shot when hunting, and a minie ball for quick follow-up shots, you'll need three different powder measures. Mark them very clearly to show the charge and be careful not to use one for the other because the results of making that mistake can be startling.

Charges for flintlocks are worked up in the same way, but charging the pan of a flintlock does not involve weighing or metering charges by bulk. The best procedure is to open the pan, hold the rifle (or smoothbore) in a horizontal position, and fill the pan until the priming charge comes level with the flash hole but does not cover it. Particularly on a damp day, it often helps to poke a few powder granules into the flash hole with your vent pick to make ignition of the main charge surer. The FFFFg priming powder is carried in a small powder horn or, better still, a special pan-charging flask with a long spout and a spring-loaded stopper.

SIGHTS

In states where they are legal, a low-powered scope is obviously a good investment, not only because it permits more accurate shooting, but because using one gives a better sight picture in dim light. Aperture sights are useful, but few muzzleloaders come equipped with them. If you feel you need them, they usually must be installed. Some states prohibit their use.

Most muzzleloading rifles come equipped with simple V-notch or U-notch open sights, some adjustable and some not. But even with so-called non-adjustable sights, you can usually use a file to open up the rear notch slightly or even move it left or right to change point of impact. Fill up the old notch by soldering and painting the metal black. Front sights are almost always fitted into a dovetail near the muzzle and they can be drifted left or right with a brass hammer, leather mallet, or with a brass drift and a machinist's tap hammer. Front sights can be filed down to raise the point of impact, and almost any home craftsman can easily add a little height to a blade front sight if lowering point of impact is in order. Bring your tools to the range, and shoot and shoot again until you have the sights right. Then lock them into place as securely as possible. With open sights this usually means soldering or brazing them in place or peening to slightly distort them in the mountings so they cannot move.

Some rifles are supplied with old-fashioned buckhorn sights that look like two long cow horns curving up and around the target. Users of cartridge arms abandoned them years ago because they obscure too much of the target. If they are installed on your rifle, they should be replaced with more modern sights. If open sights are installed, a rather large U-shaped notch is preferable to any form of buckhorn or semi-buckhorn.

TRIGGERS

Many black-powder guns have simple one-stage, non-adjustable triggers that work a great deal like the triggers on modern rifles and shotguns. Others have adjustable single-stage triggers, and some are supplied with set triggers—single or double—and these are, of course, adjustable. They are so adjustable in fact that the final let-off can be a mere feather's touch.

Set triggers of any kind on a hunting muzzleloader are unnecessary and can be dangerous. They may be useful on the target range, but they are delicate in the field, and by using them, you risk accidental discharge. Muzzleloaders with heavy loads are inherently so inaccurate that delicate set triggers make no real contribution to hunting accuracy. A simple adjustable trigger is probably the best one, but a gunsmith can smooth out and lighten most nonadjustable triggers. For information on safe trigger pulls and set triggers, see the "Marksmanship and Maintenance" section earlier. Even if a rifle has a set trigger, that doesn't mean you must use it. Simply fire without setting the trigger first.

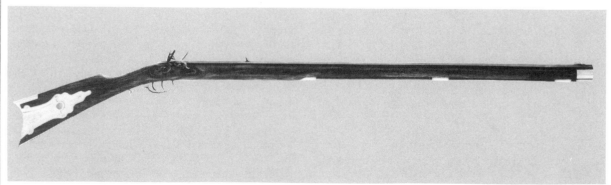

CVA Pennsylvania Long Rifle: This rifle is more traditional in styling. Caliber is .50, and the barrel length is 40 inches, which permits full combustion of heavy powder charges. That advantage, however, must be considered in the light of the long barrel, which can be awkward in the woods.

THE RIFLE

Early rifles made by colonial gunsmiths were mostly of the "Jaeger" type that was used in southern Germany, Switzerland, and Austria. These guns had slow-twist rifling and were of large bore—.60, .70, .75, .80, and sizes in between. They were loaded with a round, unpatched ball that was pounded down the bore with a sturdy ramrod and a mallet. The ball was engraved by the rifling when it was loaded, but all that violence distorted the sphere and lessened accuracy.

Rifles of this type were needed in central Europe, then a very wild place, because hunters often encountered wild boar and Eurasian brown bear. Both animals attacked humans now and then, and the hunter needed a powerful rifle to put them down with certainty. Even though a hunter might be trying for something as inoffensive as the small European roe deer, he could run into dangerous game at any time. Also, a heavy rifle was very useful if you wanted to penetrate the light body armor worn by tax collectors, the baron's bailiff, and other representatives of the tyrannical aristocracy. The German-speaking Catholics of central Europe fought their own peasant revolts, and they had the arms to do so with some effect. They brought these rifles and smoothbores to Colonial America.

Colonial frontiersmen soon learned that the very heavy Jaeger rifles were not needed. The American black bear seldom attacked human beings, and there were no other animals that had to be feared. The only really dangerous creature in the dark eastern forests was the American Indian, and a man is about as easy to kill as a deer.

In addition, lead and powder were expensive and hard to obtain in many parts of Colonial America. Soon it was recognized that a "smallbore" rifle was effective and much more economical than a big-bore Jaeger. So gunsmiths developed a new style by reducing bore diameter to reasonable calibers that fit the circumstances better. With a reduced bore and load, heavy, thick, and clumsy Jaeger stocks were also not needed. Patched-ball loading came into widespread use because it helped to protect the small balls from damage during loading and improved accuracy.

In a generation or two, the heavy rifles of Central Europe had been transformed into the slim and beautiful "long rifles," of colonial America. These arms are often called "Kentucky rifles," in spite of the fact that most of them were made farther east, notably in Pennsylvania. They acquired their popular name because many of them were used in Kentucky by Pennsylvanians who settled in that area.

Then American frontiersmen moved westward over the mountains onto the Great Plains and started the long trek that eventually led to the Pacific. They now encountered dangerous heavy game, indeed— the grizzly bear. They also encountered the buffalo, which weighed as much as 3,000 pounds. To kill a grizzly or a buffalo, the frontiersman needed a heavier rifle, and bore sizes were again increased. Because of the heavier loads, stocks had to be made heavier and stronger too, and a new rifle style was born. It is often

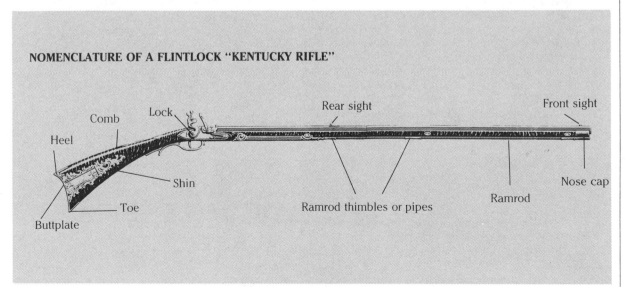

NOMENCLATURE OF A FLINTLOCK "KENTUCKY RIFLE"

The flintlock depends on sparks struck from steel to ignite powder charge. A sharp piece of flint is clamped between the jaws of the cock in a patch of rawhide or a piece of sheet lead. With hammer at full cock, the shooter pulls trigger, the hammer falls and, when the flint hits the frizzen or steel, it strikes sparks. The frizzen flies upward to uncover the flash pan. The sparks ignite the fine powder in the pan. In turn, the main powder charge is ignited through the flash hole.

called the "plains rifle," though it was also used by mountain men in the Rockies. Instead of being stocked to the muzzle or close to it, the new rifle usually had a half stock. It was also shorter than the Kentucky rifle, partly because mounted men often used these rifles, particularly during buffalo hunts.

The plains rifle was really a reversion to something that resembled the German Jaeger rifle. The long rifle and the plains rifle are still with us in replica form, though many rifles of the plains type are called "Hawken rifles" in memory of two brothers who made many fine rifles in St. Louis for frontiersmen.

If you're interested in several kinds of muzzleloader shooting—say small-game hunting, deer hunting, and target shooting, you might buy a replica Kentucky rifle with a slow twist and load with patched balls. If the rifle is .45 caliber or greater, you'll do pretty well with deer if you confine yourself to close-range shooting, and some of these guns will handle conoid bullets fairly well.

If your interest is primarily deer hunting with hopes of hunting heavier game in the future, the best choice is a Hawken type rifle. It should be at least .45 caliber and have a fast rifling twist intended primarily for shooting conoid bullets. For hunting you might also consider a big-bore replica of a military rifled musket,

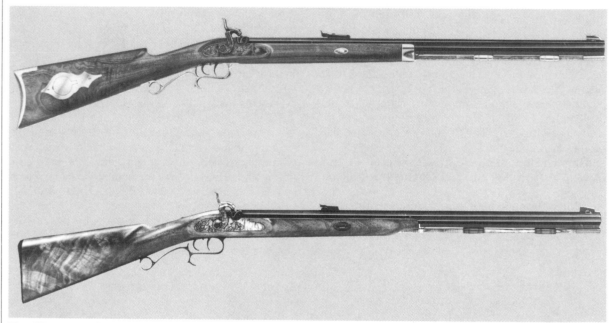

Two Thompson/Center Percussion Rifles: The Hawken, top, is available in .45, .50, or .54 percussion and .50 or .54 flintlock. It is a well-thought-out design with a barrel of moderate length for easy use in the woods. Comparatively short barrel, however, limits energy developed by black-powder charge. The Renegade rifle, bottom, available as a percussion rifle in .50 or .54 caliber has an even handier 26-inch barrel and metal work is dull in finish and therefore more suitable for hunting. Thompson/Center produces several other models in various calibers, flintlock and percussion, but the Hawken and the Renegade are preferred by many hunters for big game.

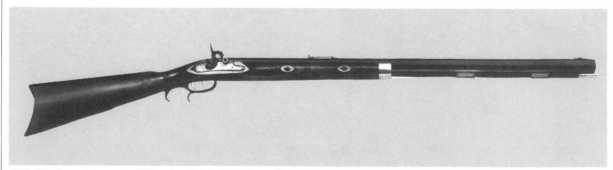

CVA Big Bore Mountain Rifle: Available in .54 or .58, this rifle is equipped with double set triggers, which will fire either set or unset, allowing the hunter to use the "hair trigger" for target shooting and the unset trigger for hunting. Barrel length is 48 inches. The .58 caliber version is one of the few .58s available.

though these guns are long, heavy, and somewhat awkward in the woods.

You can use round balls in Hawkens and rifled muskets, and if you wish to do so, you can reduce the powder charge for target shooting and small-game hunting. But there is no valid reason for using a round-ball long rifle in the East for deer hunting unless the law requires it. A big-bore Hawken or a rifled musket is more effective, even though you may use it on Daniel Boone's home turf. You can be sure that he would have used it too, had it been available.

Try to avoid rifles for hunting that are decked out with a lot of brass or pewter furnishings. The flash of bright metal in the woods alarms game at long distances. If a rifle has the characteristics you want except that there is a lot of bright metal, paint it with matte black or dull-green paint. All that bright metal is intended to bag gunstore customers, not game.

Modern Muzzleloaders. There is a fourth basic type of rifle. These are sometimes called "modern muzzleloaders" because the designs have no relationship to the Kentucky, Hawken, or plains rifles.

Typical of these rifles is the MAC Wolverine. It employs straight-line ignition and there is no external hammer. It is a percussion gun, but instead of a percussion cap on a nipple, ignition is accomplished with a shotgun primer inserted in the firing chamber. The primer cannot fall off the nipple and the big, very hot shotgun primer provides sure ignition. The stock resembles that of a modern rifle.

Learning to use this type of gun is easy for those who are accustomed to cartridge rifles. Yet it is a muzzleloader because the bullet and powder are loaded from the front end of the gun. This rifle is available in .45, .50, and .54 caliber.

Several other modern muzzleloading guns have been taken out of production, though they still can be bought secondhand. One of these was a break-action gun. The barrel was hinged down to open the breech, and a primer was loaded in a chamber, fully enclosed by the breech when the gun was closed. It was a very sure ignition system. The rifle was fired by an external hammer. Powder and bullet were loaded from the front. The fact that the MAC is the only modern hunting muzzleloader still in production is due to outright bans on various types of modern muzzleloaders in several states and the nostalgia craze.

One severe problem with most muzzleloaders is that hunters can fire only one shot before going into a rather time-consuming loading procedure. In the meantime a wounded animal can get away. Using a double-barreled rifle is one solution, though they are outlawed for deer hunting in many states because they are really repeating arms. The Kodiak double rifle is made in .50 and .58 caliber and interchangeable barrel sets are available. One set is made up of a rifle barrel and a 12-gauge smoothbore barrel; another set mates two 12-gauge shotgun barrels. But the best for deer hunting is the set with two rifle barrels. This rifle gives the hunter a quick follow-up shot.

If you do buy a double-barreled muzzleloader of any kind, be very careful when loading. Do not fire one barrel and then load another powder charge and bullet on top of the unfired load by mistake. The gun will almost surely blow up. Also, if you fire one barrel and want to reload it, keep your hand and the rest of yourself well away from the barrel that is already loaded. An accidental discharge is always possible. The hammer of the loaded barrel should always be lowered to safety half cock before reloading the fired barrel. Don't make the mistake of believing this accident can't happen. It was common when muzzleloading shotguns were widely used.

States vary in their regulations on the use of muzzleloaders for deer hunting, and this makes the Hopkins and Allen "Pennsylvania Hawken" (an appropriate name) an attractive choice if you may hunt in

Design of the MAC (Michigan Arms Company) rifle dispenses with tradition. Bullet and powder are loaded through the muzzle. A percussion cap is not used. Instead, a modern shotgun primer is loaded in a chamber at the rear end of the barrel through what amounts to a bolt action. The rifle is a "slam-loader." When bolt handle is turned down, much like operating a safety catch, and the trigger pulled, the bolt slams forward and a projection on its face discharges the primer. It's a safe, simple, very dependable ignition system. This is the stainless-steel version, which can be painted with camouflage paint for hunting. A stainless-steel barrel helps enormously when you are cleaning the gun or refrain from doing so. A blued steel version is also available.

A double-barreled rifle such as this Kodiak gives the hunter a second shot, but most states forbid use of repeating guns during muzzleloader seasons, and a double is a repeater. Check regulations before you buy one. (Rick Hacker photo)

several states. A conversion kit makes it possible to change this firearm from percussion to flintlock and vice versa.

Gun Digest and *Shooter's Bible* make something of a specialty of muzzleloading arms and the illustrations and specifications are an excellent guide to what is available currently. It's a fluid field. New rifles are announced with fanfare but they often vanish after a year or two. Therefore, looking at the current *Gun Digest* to find out what you can buy is wise. Never limit yourself to the small number of models that are usually available in the average gun shop.

Many muzzleloaders are offered in kit form as well as fully assembled. By buying a kit and assembling the rifle in a home workshop, you can reduce the price by about one-third. It's a pleasant project if you're handy and have a few tools.

READYING THE PIECE

Kentucky rifles are usually received from the manufacturer in one piece and the barrels are never removed from the stock except for serious repairs or modifications. Half-stock Hawkens are usually packed in the box broken down into the stock (with lock attached) and the barrel. With these rifles the breech is equipped with a large hook that fits into the recess in the tang, which is held to the stock by screws. The barrel is secured by inserting the hook into place and then driving a wedge through the stock and a pierced hanger attached to the barrel. Easy removal of the

barrel from the stock makes the Hawkens easy to clean and service. Replicas of military rifled muskets are one-piece affairs and are seldom disassembled.

New rifles are shipped from the factory with their metal parts covered with heavy grease to prevent rust. You must remove all of it with a solvent, such as Hoppe's Number 9 or lighter fluid. Buy (or adapt by grinding) the screwdrivers you need to remove the lock from the stock. Put the screwdrivers aside and use them only for working on your rifle. The blades of the screwdrivers should fit the screw slots exactly because screws must be tightened down very firmly when you reassemble the gun. After removing screws that hold the lock in the stock, tap the lock gently with a soft mallet to loosen and remove it from the stock. Do not pry the lock out or you will damage the wooden walls of the lock recess.

With the lock out of the stock, go over it carefully and remove all heavy protective grease. With a copper wire, pipe cleaners, and solvent, clean the vent, the nipple, and the bolster, or drum, to which the nipple may be attached. Most manufacturers supply a nipple wrench as part of the package, but if not make sure you buy one that fits the nipple perfectly. And while you're at it, buy two spare nipples for use when the first one wears out or becomes so battered that it is useless. Remove the nipple from the lock and clean it thoroughly. Take out the screw that closes the bolster clean-out hole (if your rifle has one), and clean the hole and the screw too.

With everything cleaned up, examine the lock closely so that you thoroughly understand how it works and how it is attached to the stock. Grease fric-

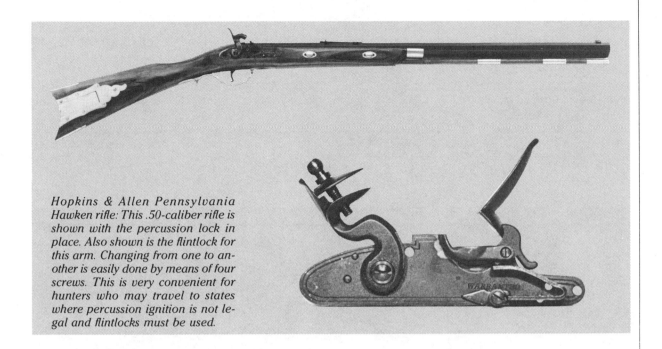

Hopkins & Allen Pennsylvania Hawken rifle: This .50-caliber rifle is shown with the percussion lock in place. Also shown is the flintlock for this arm. Changing from one to another is easily done by means of four screws. This is very convenient for hunters who may travel to states where percussion ignition is not legal and flintlocks must be used.

tion points of the lock to assure easy operation. If you plan on long hunts far from home, consider buying a complete spare rifle lock to take along with you. It is infuriating to go on a long hunt and find that the lock is out of kilter.

Thoroughly clean the protective grease from the bore, and then coat the bore with light machine oil to prevent rust. If the barrel has been removed from the stock, rub down the inside of the stock with boiled linseed oil to protect it. Do the outside for the same purpose and to enhance the appearance of the wood.

If the manufacturer has supplied printed information on how to load and service the rifle, read it thoroughly with the disassembled rifle in front of you so that you understand the directions completely. Finally, reassemble the rifle, making sure that the screws are tightened properly. Care at this stage will save a lot of trouble at the range and afield.

LOADING

The accompanying photographs and captions show one way to load a rifle. It's the classic frontiersman's method with round ball and patching material that must be cut off with a patch knife. Loading a minie ball or a Maxi-Ball differs considerably, and the patched-ball procedure can be simplified for easier loading.

There are three different situations in which loading takes place. In a camp or at home, a hunter can take his time in a nice dry place and load his piece so that he's almost certain it will go off for the first shot, *hopefully* the only shot of the day. At the range, when firing many shots to work up a load or when practicing, it's possible to load with some care too. But if you decide to enter a match, you'll have to fire fairly rapidly, and you will have to worry about bystanders and other shooters. Match shooters work hard at developing their own reliable, fast methods of reloading and wiping out the bore with solvent between shots or strings of shots. In the field, after firing the first shot, you'll often find that reloading is quite difficult, particularly if the wind is blowing, your fingers are cold, or the day is damp or rainy.

For the first shot of the day, the bore should be cleaned of all protective oil or grease. Use a patch wet with solvent on the end of your cleaning rod to dissolve oil or grease, and then wipe the bore dry with fresh dry patches. Clean the touch hole or nipple with a vent prick or nipple prick and a pipe cleaner dunked in solvent; then run dry pipe cleaners through the hole. In this procedure, you also remove any moisture that may have accumulated, and this makes for surer ignition.

Why, some beginners ask, is it necessary to be so particular about removing all oil or grease when you are about to load a ball encased in a greased patch or a minie or Maxi-Ball covered with lube? If the bore is oily or greasy, you can't pour a new powder charge into it without running into trouble. A lot of the powder will stick to the bore and remain there, particularly in the grooves. Then, when the ball or bullet is loaded, the granules are crushed against the rifling. This reduces the effective charge, and the amount lost varies from shot to shot, which makes for very inaccurate shooting. After firing your first shot in a properly cleaned firearm, the bore is lightly fouled. But you can shoot four or five new loads without cleaning before accuracy is lost. Some target shooters, however, wipe their bores clean after every shot. Rifles vary considerably in their ability to fire long strings without losing accuracy, and this is something you can determine by practice firing at the range.

Loading safety. Almost every writer on muzzleloaders states that it is important to keep all parts of your

A LOADING PROCEDURE WITH PATCHED ROUND BALL IN A RIFLE

1. *The hunter measures out a powder charge by filling a brass measuring cup from his powder flask.* **2.** *The powder charge is poured down the barrel, which has been previously cleaned of all oil or protective grease. (Clean the nipple, too!)* **3.** *The patching cloth is coated with grease. Many hunters prefer to carry pre-cut, pre-greased patches.*

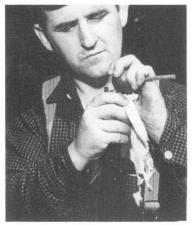

4. *The greased cloth is draped over the muzzle, and the ball is then centered in bore. Round ball of bullet starter's handle is then used to push bullet down flush with the muzzle. Some bullet starters have two arms, one very short, which is used for this purpose.* **5.** *With the bullet just below muzzle, a patch knife is used to cut cloth off flush with the muzzle.* **6.** *A short one-armed bullet starter is used to push patched ball about 8 inches down the bore. Bullet starters are used in order to preclude damage to the long ramrod.*

(Photo series by Leonard Lee Rue III)

7. *With the rifle butt resting on ground, ramrod presses the bullet down onto the powder charge. This should be a one-hand operation unless the barrel is becoming fouled. Use care to keep hands and fingers relatively safe from accidental discharge, rather than using the unsafe methods shown. The bullet must be firmly seated on the powder with no air space between them.*

8. *With the rifle at full cock, the rifleman is at last ready to fire. There are many ways to shorten this lengthy procedure. See text.*

body away from the muzzle so that if an accidental discharge takes place, you will not be injured. Yet in the drawings and photographs that accompany these strictures, you'll often see hands, arms, and even faces right over the muzzle. This is mostly because the illustrations are done with the *first* loading in mind. The rifleman knows that the piece is unloaded (always check) and that it has not been fired for quite some time. That means he can be certain there are no lingering sparks from the previous shot.

Nevertheless, do your best to keep out of the way. When loading powder and ball, even for the first shot, place the butt on the ground and angle the piece away from you. It is possible to load without risk, and if you *always* load that way, you form the right habits. Don't grasp the ramrod like a broomstick. It should be held tightly between forefinger and thumb, and the projectile should be seated on the powder with one smooth stroke. That way if there is an accidental discharge, you'll probably only lose a little skin, not a finger. After the bullet is firmly seated, don't bang the ramrod down on it several times to make sure. This distorts the soft lead and makes accurate shooting an impossibility. Never fire so many shots that black-powder fouling builds up so much that loading becomes difficult. That leads to using muscle on the ramrod and gripping it with the entire hand or both hands. You'll sometimes see a shooter with his ramrod in the bore thrusting it at a tree or fence post like a bayonet to drive the bullet down the bore. That's asking for big trouble. Fouling can build up to the point where even if the bullet can be seated on the powder, the next shot will blow up a rifle or smoothbore because the bore is obstructed. It happened many times to infantrymen who had to go on loading and firing to save their own lives during a battle.

If you load at home and carry the rifle to your hunting area, you violate the law in many states against carrying a loaded firearm in a vehicle. But a flintlock or caplock rifle cannot be fired if it isn't primed, and transporting a muzzleloader without a cap on the nipple or charge in the pan of a flintlock is legal in many states. At the end of a day's hunting, you can remove the cap or discard the pan charge and take the piece home loaded to be used the next day.

Don't always depend on this, however. If a game warden is checking you, he'll probably be aware of all the laws, but a state highway patrolman or a policeman may not be. For this reason and for safety's sake, many hunters load afield and discharge their pieces into a stump or soft ground at the end of the day. If you do this, you must reload the next day, but that assures you that you have a fresh charge in your piece. You have to decide on the best procedure according to the circumstances of the hunt.

Patched-ball loading. The patched-ball loading procedure shown here is the most complicated one but there are shortcuts. Instead of using patching material, you can buy perfectly round precut patches of the size needed for your rifle. Lubricate them thoroughly and carry them in a plastic container with a secure lid. It's best to lube the patches a day or two before you shoot so that the cloth absorbs the lubricant.

Another shortcut for loading in the field is to use a loading block. This is a piece of hardwood with

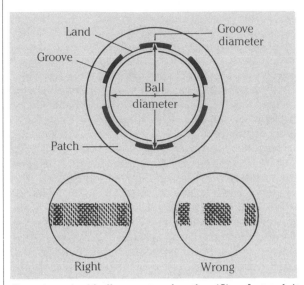

Round patched ball never touches the rifling. Instead, it is loaded encased in a cloth patch. Cloth engages rifling and spins the ball. Patch drops away a few yards from the muzzle. Patch should be thick enough to mark soft lead ball over the grooves of rifling as well as the lands. If impression of cloth shows only over lands when you pull a loaded ball, the patch is too thin or the ball you are using is too small. This permits gas to pass the ball and lowers power.

several holes drilled in it. The balls are patched and driven into the loading block just as though each hole were the muzzle of the rifle. Then the excess patching cloth is cut away if precut patches are not being used. The holes are slightly countersunk to fit over the muzzle of the rifle. When loading, the block is slipped over the muzzle and the ball is driven from the block into the bore with a one-armed bullet starter. Then the ramrod is used to seat the ball.

The best material for bullet patches is usually bedticking or unbleached muslin sheeting. These are tough enough to survive the necessary degree of violence in loading and coarse enough to absorb your favorite patching lube. The gun's manufacturer usually recommends the type and thickness of cloth to be used for patches, and some sell the cloth or precut patches suitable for their rifles. After firing during practice sessions, try to recover patches—they can be informative. If there are cuts in the patches made by the rifling, the ball is too large for the bore or the patch material is too thick. If the patches are burned through in the center, the patch material is much too thin.

In centering a ball on a patch, either on the muzzle or over a loading-block hole, make sure the sprue (cut-off pouring neck formed during casting) is straight up (facing toward the muzzle). The round side of the ball should face the powder charge. In this way, a con-

sistent surface is presented to the powder gas during firing, and this helps accuracy. Some shooters who cast their own rifle balls spend a little extra time with a knife or file to remove all traces of the sprue. If this detail worries you, buy a good supply of factory-made swaged balls. They have no sprue.

Loading minie balls and Maxi-Balls. With minie balls and Maxi-Balls, there is no patch to worry about, and this speeds up the loading process. These bullets should be greased on all surfaces that bear upon the rifling, and the grease grooves should be full. Though there are faster ways to do this, the best procedure is to smear the grease on with your fingers so that you are forced to inspect the results while you're doing it. The hollow bases of minie balls are filled with grease, too, and don't omit this step. The thick grease helps to hold the minie ball in place on the powder. Minie balls should fit the bore tightly enough so that they do not move in the bore when the rifle is carried in the field, but the grease helps.

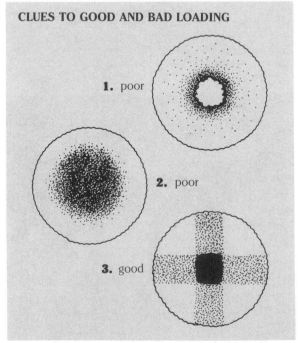

CLUES TO GOOD AND BAD LOADING

1. poor

2. poor

3. good

After a shot, the patch can often be recovered a few yards from muzzle. Examining these tells a lot about your loading **1.** *If center has been burned away, the patch is much too thin to seal the bore.* **2.** *If most of the patch has been charred and is covered with fouling, the patch is still too thin, though rifle may function fairly well.* **3.** *Patch of the right thickness shows folded portions that weren't in contact with bore. They are clean, and patch will show a cross. If patching material seems to be thick enough, but gas still passes the ball, the ball itself may be too small for bore. Most shooters lubricate their patches with patch lubricants*

Nevertheless, check on bullet seating now and then by passing a marked ramrod down the bore. If the projectile has moved forward, leaving an air space, the barrel may burst. Properly cast Maxi-Balls actually enter the rifling at the muzzle and usually stay firmly in place, but some shooters check occasionally anyway. After a loaded gun bounces around in a vehicle a while, check to see that the bullet is safely down on the charge.

Seating bullets. Consistency is the name of the game in all shooting, but it applies especially to loading these black-powder arms. Once you have developed a pet hunting load, don't vary the powder charge, bullet, lubricating grease, patch, cap, or anything else. In particular don't change the way in which you seat the bullet.

Never seat a round ball by using only the ramrod. Inevitably, you will damage the rod or the bullet. Start round balls with the short arm of a two-pronged ball starter, then use the long arm, and finally the ramrod. When using a loading block, a one-pronged bullet starter with a 6- or 7-inch rod works well. In some rifles a one-pronged bullet starter must be used to load a minie ball, but in others merely seating the bullet in the muzzle with the fingers works well, provided you're careful with the ramrod. Maxi-Balls, because the top band is larger than bore diameter, require a little force to get them into the bore. Some shooters use a two-pronged bullet starter, but others find that a one-prong tool is adequate. When firing many shots at the range, some riflemen use a wooden or leather mallet to drive the bullet into the rifling at the muzzle. One moderate tap does the job; greater force distorts the bullet.

Marking your ramrod with a notch or paint helps to assure safe loading. After you have worked up your favorite load, insert the rod so that it rests on top of the bullet and mark the rod. Next time, if the rod goes down to the marked depth, you can be sure that the bullet is seated securely on the powder and that there is no air space between them. If you vary your loads—for instance, a round ball for plinking, a Maxi-Ball for the first shot when hunting, and a minie ball for follow-up shots, you will have three marks on the rod.

Make sure that you remove the ramrod from the barrel after loading powder and bullet. No, it's not funny. Many a soldier was killed by a ramrod left in the bore by an enemy soldier. A rod in the bore also increases gas pressure and can cause a lot of trouble, especially in a lightly built long rifle.

Field reloading kit. Afield, it's convenient to carry powder and bullet in specially made plastic containers. These are readily available at most good gun stores. With one type, a measured charge is poured into the container, and the open end is stoppered with the ball or lubricated Maxi-Ball. It's not a good idea to use minie balls with the bases full of grease as stoppers because the grease remains in contact with the powder for a long period. Instead, carry lubricated minie balls in a plastic tube of the right size with a stopper for the open end. Another type of container has both ends open and a partition in between. The small chamber is for the priming charge of a flintlock, and the larger chamber for the main charge.

Actually, you can improvise containers from plastic pill bottles and film containers. Whatever form is used, the chief advantage is that the powder charge can be carefully metered at home where the wind does not blow. One good method for a patched-ball rifle is to carry metered charges in containers and round, patched balls in a loading block. With a little experience, you'll soon develop the best method for your rifle and circumstances.

It is a rule that powder and bullet should be loaded before the piece is primed with a cap on the nipple or a priming charge is placed in the pan of a flintlock. Never, never prime first and then load the bore. Doing so is asking for an accidental discharge.

THE HAMMER

After loading the main charge and the bullet, you must manipulate the hammer of the gun to put the primer cap on the nipple, and this is where things can go astray. Most shooters are so used to hammerless cartridge arms and the various forms of safety catches that they find it hard to use the hammers of muzzleloaders.

The hammers of most muzzleloading guns have three positions—all the way down (the position just after a shot); half cock, sometimes called safety half cock; and full cock. With this type of hammer, pull it back to half cock so that you can get at the nipple or open the flash pan by moving the frizzen forward. In doing so keep your finger well away from the trigger. Touching it, even slightly, can interfere with the slight movement of the trigger as it assumes the half-cock position and may result in insecure engagement. Theoretically, at least, a hammer that falls from the half-cock position will not strike with sufficient force to detonate a cap or make enough sparks to set off a flintlock priming charge. But don't depend on it. Dropping the gun could knock the hammer out of the half-cock position with sufficient force to fire the gun. Of course, the gun must always be kept pointed in a safe direction.

With the hammer at half cock, place a percussion cap on the nipple. Push the cap all the way down. It should fit quite tightly without splitting if you are using the right size. If it is a little loose, pinch the mouth of the cap between your forefinger and thumb to close it slightly and put it back on the nipple. Many hunters use a capping device that holds a dozen or so caps in a magazine and presents each one in turn to an opening by means of a follower spring. Cappers are a great convenience when your fingers are cold and stiff. If you use one, though, check the cap afterward to see that it is solidly on the nipple. A cap that is not all the way down can cushion the impact of the hammer and cause a misfire. With a flintlock put the hammer at half cock, open the pan, and prime as previously described.

With the bore loaded and the piece primed, you're ready to fire. You can ear the hammer back to full cock and then apply your trigger squeeze immediately, but most hunters load their guns and then spend quite some time before they are ready to fire. If that is the case, leave the gun on safety half cock until you get a shot. Then ear it back to full cock, aim, and fire. You can't walk around in the woods with the hammer at full cock. That's much too dangerous. The half-cock safety notch is the only safety device on most replica muzzleloaders.

Some shooters carry their rifles with the hammer all the way down and touching the primer on the nipple. They feel safer this way than they would if they relied on the half-cock safety, which can fail, but rarely does in a well-made gun. But with the hammer all the way down, a sharp blow to the hammer or dropping the gun upside down on a hard surface will fire the piece. Most shooters strongly agree that the half-cock notch is safer.

When you do decide to fire and ear the hammer

Capping the nipple: Almost all muzzleloaders available today take No. 11 size caps. The open mouth of the cap can be pinched slightly to ensure a snug fit. Nevertheless, check frequently to see that the cap is still on the nipple when hunting. They fall off all too often.

back to full cock, you will probably find that there is a very loud click. This is audible to deer at surprisingly long distances, and the unnatural sound often alarms them. To avoid making this noise, grip the hammer firmly with the thumb while it is in the half-cock position. Pull it back slightly and then pull the trigger. Then move the hammer all the way back to full cock and let the trigger go forward. Let go of the hammer. If the lock is working properly, your piece is ready to fire and there has not been a sound.

But suppose that the deer vanishes, and you wish to move on. How do you make the gun "safe" again? You cannot simply hold the hammer with the thumb, pull the trigger, and ease the hammer forward to the half-cock position. The lock is so constructed that the hammer will pass the half-cock notch. The lock had to be made this way, or the hammer would catch the half-cock notch every time you tried to fire. The proper procedure is to let the hammer go down, controlled by your thumb with the trigger pulled back, until it touches the primer for an instant. Then remove your finger from the trigger and pull the hammer back normally to the half-cock position.

Many hunters will not hunt with any hammer gun that cannot be cocked safely in complete silence because they hunt mostly where close-range shots are the rule. If your rifle won't do it, take it to an experienced gunsmith who is used to working with muzzleloaders. He'll probably be able to cure the problem in a short while. If not, you need a replacement lock.

In order to do all this, the lock must be in good condition, and it's best if you understand precisely how it functions. That is why it's so important to study the working of the lock thoroughly when you have it out of the gun just after you buy it.

The reason for putting the hammer on safety half cock when priming with a cap is to provide room for your fingers or a capping device. But some muzzleloaders are not made this way. Notably, the Thompson/Center guns, very fine hunting arms, have a half-cock notch that is so far down that there's no way to put the cap on the nipple if the lock is not at full cock. With this kind of lock, you have to prime in the full-cock position. It's not really dangerous if you are careful to keep your finger away from the trigger, and the gun is pointed in a safe direction. The theory behind this type of hammer is that when it is at half cock, it is already so far down that failure of the half-cock mechanism will not cause a discharge because there isn't enough energy to snap a cap. But, as usual, it's best to handle the gun safely at all times. Don't rely solely on mechanical devices.

Some cheap caplock muzzleloaders, mostly poorly made imports, have only two hammer positions—all the way down and full cock. You have to walk around in the woods with the hammer down on the cap or at full cock, and this increases the risk of an accidental discharge. Don't buy one. Remember, the money you save by buying a cheap, unreliable gun could cost you your foot or your life.

After you fire a caplock gun, make sure that the hammer nose is clear of cap fragments before you put another cap on the nipple. Sometimes bits of soft copper adhere to the hammer nose and prevent it from hitting with a sufficient force to detonate the next cap.

"POSSIBLES"

At some point in most discussions of muzzleloaders, it is customary to give the reader a list of gear that he must carry with him when shooting. The list, of course, varies according to the type of gun and the circumstances of the hunt. If you are on a long trip, you must carry a lot of gear in order to maintain your piece in firing condition. When hunting close to home and gun

One kind of container for main charge and bullet consists of a blind-ended plastic tube. The pre-measured powder charge is poured into the tube, and the open end is plugged with the bullet, in this case, a Maxi-Ball. Containers of this type and many others are available in gun shops. Their use speeds up the loading process.

shops, the list is quite short. If you use a caplock firearm, the list is shorter than it is for a flintlock. Some hunters do carry everything they might possibly need, and therefore the bag in which they carry it is called a "possibles" bag. It is quite large.

For practical hunting—rather than an authentic appearance at a shoot or rendezvous—it's best to carry as little as possible. Take what you really need and leave the rest at home or in camp. You don't need a powder horn or a flask on a strap that can catch on bushes or a bulky possibles bag that flaps at your side when you're trying to run up a slope. Load premeasured charges in separate containers, and you can eliminate a lot of encumbrances. In fact, all you really need when afield with a caplock gun can be boiled down to: the ramrod in the gun thimbles; measured charges and minie balls or Maxi-Balls in plastic containers; caps in charger; a nipple wrench and a nipple prick (plus a spare in case you drop the first one); and a one-armed or two-armed bullet starter. All this gear fits easily into one large pocket or one small pouch.

The list is longer if you use patched round balls in a caplock gun or use a flintlock, but not by much. Leave everything else at home or in camp where it won't weigh you down. All the gear needed for maintenance and servicing the piece has been mentioned in the text or will be. Develop a checklist for use when you go on a long trip.

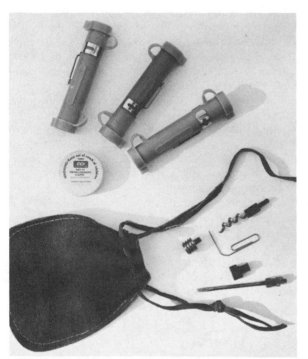

The "possibles" bag contains, theoretically, everything that a hunter will need afield (aside from rifle and ramrod). The list varies according to the firearm used and the loading procedure. In this case, the assortment includes: bullets and powder charges in plastic speed loaders; percussion caps in watertight can; a worm (corkscrew device) that screws into ramrod tip for removing lost patches and to pull balls if the rifle fails to fire; a paper clip used as a nipple prick; a nipple cap to keep the rifle's nipple dry; a cleaning jag for the ramrod; and a small screwdriver, which has many uses, including tightening lock screws and removal of the cleanout screw, if any, in the rifle's cleanout port.

FAILURE TO FIRE

No matter how carefully you load and maintain your piece, a failure to fire now and then is well-nigh inevitable. This happens more frequently with flintlocks than with caplocks because moisture can enter the pan and because of dull or poorly mounted flints. A new gunflint, squarely mounted, is only good for 15 or 20 sure ignitions and should then be replaced. On damp days it helps to discard the pan charge now and then and replace it. Moisture is the primary culprit. With a caplock, fire two or three caps without a main charge before loading powder and bullet. Some shooters do this every time they load for the first shot of the day; others do it only when the air is damp. With a flintlock, wipe the frizzen and the pan with an absorbent dry cloth before loading the bore.

What happens if a loaded piece fails to fire? The main charge and the bullet are in the bore and are not easily removed so that you can reload. In the field one thing to try is removing the cap (which may have been defective) and replacing it with another that may fire. If that doesn't work, remove the nipple with your wrench and pick out some of the main charge. Always use a copper or brass prick or some other nonferrous wire, never steel, which could spark. Push some fresh powder into the hole, and fire a fresh cap. The same can be done through the vent of a flintlock. By this time, of course, the deer will be long gone, but at least you can reload in the field and resume hunting.

If all of this does not work, you'll have to resort to a ball screw to remove the bullet and then pour out the powder, perhaps after stirring it a bit with a vent pick. A ball screw is nothing more than a sharp, self-tapping, tapered screw, the threaded base of which screws into a ferrule mounted on your ramrod or a heavy duty cleaning rod. It is used with conoid bullets. Removing a bullet in this way is best done at home, or at least in camp where someone else can hold the rifle, or the barrel removed from the stock, while you work on the stubborn bullet.

If you do it at home, the gun or the barrel should be mounted in a padded vise to hold it steady. But before you do that, remove the nipple or open the pan and soak the whole breech end of the gun in hot water for a full hour. You're going to be working with a heavy rod and a metal tool in the bore, and an accidental discharge would be disastrous. Then put the piece in an upright position and pour hot water into the barrel to soften fouling if any is present. Pour out the water and then push the rod into the bore until the ball screw rests on the bullet. Press it down firmly and rotate it with one hand while you tap the end of the rod with a mallet. It may take several tries, but eventually you will drive the screw into the bullet and may be able to pull it out. A special sturdy rod that almost fills the

bore probably should be used for this task. Your ramrod may be much too delicate. Round balls are much easier to remove than Maxi-balls or other, similar conoid bullets.

As a last resort, if the ball screw does not work, you may want to try disassembling the rifle and removing the breech plug to get at a conoid bullet. The wrench must fit the plug perfectly, and some muzzle-loader companies sell special wrenches for this purpose. With some guns, however, it is next to impossible to take the barrel out of the stock yourself so that you can get at the breech plug. With others the plug is next to impossible to turn out. Considerable force must often be used, and unless you know what you're doing and have the correct equipment, you may actually bend or twist the barrel. If you run into this situation, the best thing to do is to take the whole gun to a competent gunsmith and let him go to work.

If you get the breech plug out yourself, it's usually a simple matter to tap out the bullet with a sturdy rod and a mallet. Never use steel or iron rods for this purpose. They can damage the rifling, and if the powder charge is not removed first or rendered inert, it's just possible to strike a spark and cause a blast. Thompson/Center's manual states that breech plugs should *always* be removed by a gunsmith because the barrel is so easily damaged.

If you manage to move a bullet partway down the bore by introducing fresh powder through a rear opening, don't put still more powder in and try again. In this situation, there is an empty air space between the powder and the bullet that can cause the barrel to burst. Instead, it's best to resort to the ball screw or breech-plug removal.

In loading or cleaning, it sometimes happens that a round-ball bullet patch or a cleaning patch becomes lost in the bore. Never ignore this and load the barrel on top of it. Use a worm—a two-pronged head for your rod with both prongs in the form of a corkscrew—to catch the piece of cloth and remove it. If you don't, you are risking a burst or bulged barrel.

CLEANING

Black-powder fouling is extremely hygroscopic. This is, it readily absorbs moisture from the air and retains it, which causes very rapid rusting of steel. Fortunately, the fouling dissolves readily in hot water, and pouring or pumping hot soapy water through the bore is a good cleaning method. You'll need a brush that fits the bore and clean, dry patches used with a jag or slotted head on the rod.

If the barrel can be easily removed from the stock, do so by all means. Fill a bucket with hot soapy water (not detergent), remove the nipple or open the frizzen and remove the vent bushing (if any), and submerge the breech end of the barrel in the bucket. Put a tight-fitting patch on your rod and push it all the way to the breech plug. Then move the rod up and down and pump the water into and out of the bore until your arm begins to hurt. Then use clean dry patches and a brush to work into the grooves and repeat the hot-water treatment again. Put the piece aside, muzzle down so that water will drain, and then wait a bit for the hot barrel to cause evaporation. While the metal is still hot, oil or grease all metal surfaces. Cleaning this way must be done before rust can start, and that means cleaning your rifle the same evening whenever it has been fired. When men's lives depended on their rifles, they cleaned their pieces before eating their evening meal.

If the barrel cannot be removed from the stock, you can slip a tight-fitting plastic tube over the nipple and put the other end in a bucket of hot soapy water. Pumping the patch on the rod up and down sucks water from the bucket into the bore. Flintlocks are a problem if the barrel cannot be removed. About all you can do is mount the gun in an upright position and pour two gallons or so of hot soapy water through the muzzle. A little ingenuity, however, may enable you to make a pierced plug that fits in the vent and allows you to attach a plastic tube to it for discharge into a drain. This saves the stock from a harmful soaking.

Today there is a wide variety of liquids that chemically duplicate the effects of hot water and speed the process. And yet many experienced shooters stick to the hot-water method and regard it as safer. It certainly is less costly. Solvents are usually sold as part of a complete cleaning kit on the first go-round and in separate containers thereafter. If you use solvents be cautious and inspect the rifle for rust at short intervals until you are sure the solution works. Solvents are useful at the range for quick wiping between strings. Detailed instructions are furnished with the bottle or are printed on the label.

Now and then remove the entire lock and clean it thoroughly, too.

HOW LONG?

If a muzzleloader is loaded with care, how long can it be relied on to fire dependably? There is no real answer. Inevitably, moisture will work into the powder or the priming and the load will "go dead." How long this takes depends mostly on the degree of moisture in the air. In the desert, a muzzleloader can be left loaded much longer than is advisable if you live near water. If you do leave the main charge in place, however, always remove the cap or the pan charge as a safety measure.

Military chronicles are full of stories about military arms that failed to fire in dangerous situations, and soldiers constantly worried about it when they went into action. The common practice was to "draw charges" (round balls) or fire the pieces at fairly short intervals and reload.

THE FUTURE

Current regulations governing use of muzzleloaders in the Commonwealth of Pennsylvania during the special seasons read, in part, as follows: "Only single barrel flintlock ignition long guns of a type manufactured prior to 1800, or any reproduction thereof, .44 caliber or larger with open iron sights propelling a single spherical lead ball are permitted. Telescopic, peep, or aperture sights, minie balls, and Maxi-Balls are prohibited."

What can Pennsylvania do to further cut down on the kill and keep enough deer available for those who hunt with cartridge arms—the really big pressure group? About the only thing left as regards firearms would be to prohibit the use of rifled frontloaders and force hunters to use smoothbores. Some states have already done this. It seems a shame that these regulations force hunters to use firearms that are less effective than they could be. It can only result in more wounded deer. Perhaps a better solution would be to shorten the special muzzleloader season or limit the number of hunters by employing some form of lottery to draw permits.

This sort of thing is no problem in states that now have deer herds that equal or exceed carrying capacity. In those states, limits are liberal and there are enough deer for every hunting group. But in one-deer-per-year states with limited herds, officials are going to have to face up to this problem. The future of deer hunting with muzzleloaders depends on it.

SHOULD YOU LOAD YOUR OWN?

Writers on reloading invariably state that the cost of rifle, handgun, or shotgun ammunition can be cut by one-third or one-half by reloading fired cartridges. Then these writers go on to say that reloading is, in itself, a fascinating and satisfying hobby. They point out that there are two forms of this pursuit—(1) reloading of fired cartridge cases to duplicate factory loads and (2) handloading fired cases or empty virgin brass to develop loads not available in factory cartridges.

Of course, the enthusiastic handloader puts the emphasis on handloading rather than mere reloading. He declares that the handloader is a creative hobbyist who may even develop a new cartridge. Who knows? The cartridge may eventually prove so useful that it will be named after him and be taken up as a factory load by one or more of the major manufacturing companies. This has happened many times. Consider, for instance, the .257 Roberts, a very fine deer and varmint cartridge named after Ned Roberts, the well-known gun writer.

Writers on reloading and handloading are enthusiastic target shooters and hunters. Most of them use handguns and shotguns, as well as rifles. That type of enthusiast uses a vast amount of ammunition every year. Reloading and handloading make it possible for him to afford the ammunition he needs. Having set up an expensive press for reloading metallic ammunition and another for shotgun ammunition, he goes on to experiment with entirely new loads in an effort to enhance the performance of the wide variety of firearms he owns. For him handloading is not only an interesting hobby—it's a necessity.

THE DISADVANTAGES

For many hunters, reloading, not to mention handloading, is not really worthwhile in dollar savings. Deer hunters often fire only a few shots every year. They may fire once or twice before the season opens to make sure that their rifles are still properly sighted-in. After that, the season in one-deer states is over when the hunter takes his buck, preferably with one shot. One 20-round box of ammunition may last for years.

The enthusiasts also usually neglect to mention that reloading saves money only because the hobbyist replaces factory labor. The "profit" or saving results only because the hobbyist replaces a factory worker. If you had to pay someone to use your reloading equipment

to produce ammunition, factory ammunition would be much cheaper than home-brewed loads. The savings represented by reloads, if you do a little arithmetic, "pay" the loader only two or three dollars per hour of work, but if you're willing to work for such low wages, it can be "profitable" to reload. Still, many find it a satisfying hobby, aside from dollar savings.

It's also true that reloading is a demanding task because it requires careful, consistent, and very repetitious work. After the reloader has determined the components he will use, reloading amounts to low-level factory work, but it demands very close attention because a mistake could result in a wrecked gun or serious personal injury. You are entirely responsible for damage done by defective reloads. There's no one to sue.

It's better not to take up this activity unless you have a liking for the work and can devote undivided attention to it when you're loading. It's not advisable to turn the radio on when you're loading or to let anything else distract you. A fascinating item in a news broadcast could result in disaster. Reloading is not dangerous, however, if you pay attention and follow recommended safe procedures.

VARYING THE LOAD

Besides economy and enjoyment of a hobby, there are two other reasons for taking up reloading or handloading. One is to vary the loads when factory ammunition is only available in one bullet weight and type. For instance, the very fine 6.5 Remington Magnum cartridge is now factory loaded with only one bullet, a 120-grain Core-Lokt Pointed Soft Point intended for long-range big-game shooting. One reloading manual lists seven other loads ranging from an 87-grain bullet for varmint shooting up to a 160-grain bullet for heavy game. Obviously, if you own a rifle chambered for the 6.5 Remington Magnum, it's a good idea to take up handloading. You'll provide greater versatility for your rifle, and this may make it possible to avoid the purchase of another firearm, such as a varmint rig. Several modern rifle cartridges are factory loaded with only one or two different bullets. With all these cartridges, handloading may be worthwhile because it increases the usefulness of the rifle.

No one is chambering rifles for the 6.5 Remington any longer, and the day may come when factory loading of the cartridges will cease. In fact, this is almost inevitable as rifles in this chambering wear out. Sooner or later, demand for the cartridge will sink so low that profits for the factory will vanish completely. Some companies are good about keeping an unprofitable cartridge in the line. This is because a firm that manufactured a particular rifle does not wish to leave purchasers high and dry, but this practice cannot continue indefinitely.

When the cartridge is finally discontinued, the handloader who has several hundred cases on hand can go on cooking up his own loads for years. Dies for practically every cartridge—modern, old, and ancient—are available from RCBS and other companies. On special order, you can buy dies for cartridges that were discontinued many years earlier, as well as dies for many popular wildcat cartridges.

THE RELOADING MANUAL

All reloaders rely heavily on a reloading manual, usually supplied by makers of reloading equipment and components. These manuals often include detailed directions for safe operation of the press, but these may be supplied separately. Presses vary slightly in their construction and operation, so the manufacturer's instructions should be followed carefully. No overall discussion of the reloading process can possibly detail all steps involved in operating the great variety of presses currently available.

Reloading manuals, such as the exceptionally complete one supplied by Lyman for metallic-cartridge loading, list loads for various cartridge cases. They specify proper primer, powder type, powder charge weight, cartridge case length, overall cartridge length after loading, and other information. For a given bullet weight, the cartridge can be loaded to low velocities, very high velocities, and to a whole range of velocities in between. Naturally, as velocity increases, gas pressure also increases. Therefore, the manuals list a maximum powder charge, and it's very unsafe to exceed it. Even the maximum charge listed as safe may be too much for some old rifles, and the manuals advise hobbyists to approach the maximum with caution. In other words, start out with a light or medium load, and increase the powder charge very carefully—small batch by small batch—looking for signs of too much gas pressure, such as protruding primers, when the rounds are fired.

CASE TRIMMING

After a cartridge case has been reloaded and fired several times, the brass stretches, and the case increases in length. If this is not controlled by trimming back the case mouth, it can create a dangerous condition. The case mouth may eventually lengthen so much that the beginning of the rifling squeezes the case mouth tightly around the bullet, making it progressively difficult for the bullet to "break free" of the case on firing. In turn, this means that the gas in the cartridge case is confined longer than normal, which could result in a burst case. Therefore, the reloader must check case length carefully after a few reloads and trim them back to the correct length as needed. Reloading manuals list minimum and maximum safe

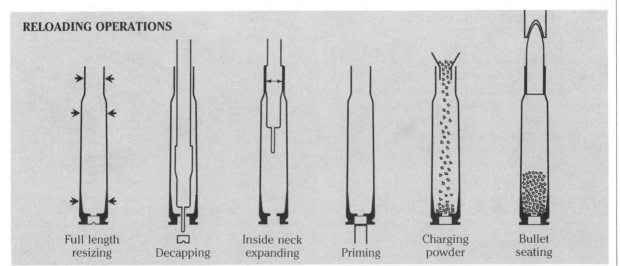

RELOADING OPERATIONS

Full length resizing   Decapping   Inside neck expanding   Priming   Charging powder   Bullet seating

A modern bench-mounted press performs the six operations shown here, but on some makes certain operations may be combined so that they are accomplished with one pull on the handle. Almost all presses, for instance, combine full-length resizing of the case and decapping.

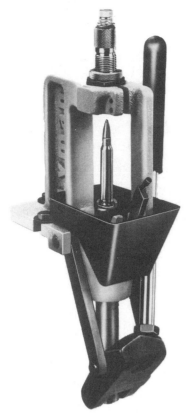

The Lyman "Orange Crusher" press for metallic cartridges is an example of the "O" type press, so named because the frame forms a complete "O" or a square. The older "C" type presses with only one support leg are being phased out. This photo shows a complete cartridge in place, held by the shell holder on the ram just after the bullet was seated.

case lengths for each cartridge case and several case-trimming devices are available. A chamfering tool is used to remove burrs in the case mouth.

A rather simple bench-type reloading press for rifle and pistol cartridges can be purchased for a bit over $100, and a two-die set for rifle reloading costs about $30. All the odds and ends also needed—calipers, brushes, powder scale, powder measure, lubricating pads, loading blocks, and so forth—should cost no more than an additional $100. So you can start out as a reloader with a fairly sophisticated set of tools for about $250. Components—primers, powder, and bullets—also cost money, of course, but at savings of up to half on factory ammunition, the investment is soon recovered if you shoot a lot. Many manufacturers sell complete sets of basic reloading equipment for prices that are less than the combined prices of all units. Take advantage of a package deal if you can find one that suits your needs.

HAND TOOLS

There is another method of loading rifle, pistol, and shotgun ammunition that does not involve as large an outlay of money for equipment. This is to use hand tools instead of a bench press. The Lyman 310 tong tool, for instance, can be purchased for about $50,

complete with dies for one caliber. The tool functions like a nutcracker. Dies are screwed into one handle, and the cartridge case is seated in a shell holder in the other. When the handles are squeezed, the case is driven into the die. You'll need a few other items, such as a powder-metering device, but you can set up for handloading for about $100 and turn out high-quality metallic ammunition.

With the Lee Loader set of hand tools, the empty cartridge case is driven into the die with a soft mallet and powder is measured by volume with a hand-held dipper. The tools in the set vary according to use—shotgun or metallic ammunition. It's possible to turn out very fine ammunition with this set too, and the cost is only about $30, including a few needed items that do not come with the kit.

All hand tools, however, have one principal disadvantage. They are much slower than reloading with a bench press. And yet, an accomplished user of these tools can turn out a box of 25 slug-loaded shotgun shells in less than an hour, for instance. Most hand tools do not full-length resize rifle and handgun shells; so the reloads should be fired in the same gun that discharged them.

Using these hand tools is a good way for you to get started in handloading, and if you do not require large amounts of ammunition, speed is not really essential. If you buy a good set of hand tools, you can load enough cartridges for practice shooting and the hunting season during the closed season when you have a lot of free recreational time. Later, if you become interested in target shooting, you can invest in faster, more expensive equipment. But you'll never throw

The Lyman 310 Tong Tool consists of the tongs and four screw-in dies: neck sizer and decapper, primer seater, neck expander, bullet seater and case-head adapter. The tong tool is the descendant of similar tools used by frontier hunters and soldiers to load brass black-powder cartridge cases. This tool and other hand tools turn out excellent ammunition if used with care. The disadvantage is slowness; the advantage is that you need only about $50 to get started in handloading.

Lyman tong tool partially resizes case by forcing it into a die screwed into handle. (Jim Carmichel photos)

Extraction of lubed case from die is accomplished by pulling the handles apart.

your hand tools away. When your bench press is all set up and finely tuned to turn out large quantities of skeet or trap loads or metallic cartridges for target shooting, the hand tools can be used for specialty loads. That way, you don't have to reset the press.

RELOADING FIRED RIFLE CASES

The usual reloading process with a bench press is quite simple. A fired rifle case is lubricated so that it will not stick and is then forced into a hollow resizing die that returns it to its original dimensions. During this operation, the fired primer is also forced out of the primer pocket by the depriming punch. A new primer is inserted in the primer pocket. Then the cartridge case is charged with a metered or weighed charge of powder. The bullet is seated in the case mouth at the proper depth with the bullet-seating die. With almost all rifle cases, only two dies are needed.

The photo series at the end of this section shows the process in some detail as done by a very careful reloader, who is intent on achieving an extremely high degree of accuracy. If you want to do the same, follow his methods quite closely, allowing, of course, for the fact that you will probably be using a press made by a different manufacturer and so must follow the manufacturer's operating instructions. But the average hunter who is reloading fired cases for a short-range deer rifle does not need to be so much of a perfectionist. For instance, the pictures show priming as a separate step. For best accuracy, priming should be done separately as shown in the photo series, but it can also be done as part of the resizing step, and

most hunters follow that practice. The pictures also show the use of virgin brass (cases that have never been fired before), specially purchased so that the cases will always be loaded in the same manner with the same dies in the same press (not the factory dies first and then the reloader's). Most hunters find fired cases perfectly satisfactory.

But there is one part of the process that cannot be simplified and that is careful inspection of the cases and the completed cartridges. Cases should be examined closely for dirt in the primer pocket, incipient separation of the case body, and other defects. If a case is too long, it must be trimmed back with a case trimmer or else the excess length could cause a lot of trouble. All defective cases should be discarded for safety reasons. Don't try to get "just one more reload" out of any case that is defective. Throw it away. After a batch of cases has been reloaded, the rounds should be carefully inspected again for defects such as dents in the brass cases, split mouths caused by the reloading process, exceeding maximum length, and so forth. Carefully dispose of all defective rounds in a manner that keeps them out of someone else's rifles and prevents playful experiments by children. Don't thow them in the garbage; bury them instead. If you neglect these precautions, you're risking a lot of serious trouble.

Beginners often ask how many times a rifle case can be reloaded. There is no simple answer to that question. With mild loads, the reloader *may* safely get 25 or 30 reloads. With high-velocity, hot loads, only five or six reloadings may be possible. Most hand tools do not full-length resize, so the cartridge cases eventually enlarge to such a degree that they will not enter the rifle's chamber. With hand tools, the number of reloadings therefore seldom exceeds five or six.

HANDGUN AND SHOTGUN AMMO

Reloading ammunition for a revolver, single-shot pistol, or semi-automatic pistol is much the same as reloading for a rifle, except that the mouths of most handgun cartridges must be crimped into a groove in the bullet to hold them in place. To accomplish this, the reloader needs four dies instead of only two. Reloading manuals explain clearly how to do it.

Shotgun reloading is a bit more complicated than loading metallic ammunition because another component must be employed—the wad between the powder charge and the shot or a rifled slug—and because the case mouth must be closed over a shot charge. Almost all modern shotgun cartridges are closed by means of a folded crimp (also called a "star" crimp), and this involves two dies that are not needed in metallic-cartridge reloading.

On the other hand, shotgun ammunition does not require very precise sizing of cases or trimming. The equipment is therefore less massive and not as closely machined. You can buy a simple non-progressive press (one operation at a time) for as little as $100. Fewer additional tools are needed and they are less expensive than those for metallic-cartridge reloading. But if you are a skeet and trap enthusiast and you fire a large number of shells, you may need a high-volume progressive press. A press of that type can cost in the $500 range.

BUCKSHOT AND SLUGS

Those who use their shotguns for deer hunting, however, are usually not interested in volume production. They make up a few buckshot or slug loads, and only need very simple equipment.

Buckshot is loaded much like birdshot, but there is one important difference. Birdshot is usually measured either by volume with a hand-held dipper or automatically by the reloading press. Buckshot is loaded by counting the number of these large pellets prescribed for each different load. For instance, if you are loading 00 Buckshot, the usual count prescribed in the manual is nine pellets for a 2¾-inch shell. Factory-loaded buckshot loads for deer hunting cost about 80¢ apiece, and this cost can be cut substantially by reloading. But most deer hunters who use shotguns need only a few loads per season; so it may be best to buy factory ammunition.

Shotgun-slug loads for deer hunting are easy to assemble. A new primer and the powder are loaded as usual. Then a wad or wad column is loaded over the powder and a slug is seated on top of the wads. With most slug loads, the case mouth is not folded into a star crimp, however. Instead, the plastic or cardboard case body is folded over onto itself in a "roll crimp," and this crimp holds the slug in place. A special tool is needed to make the roll crimp.

Rifled-slug loads cost nearly $1 apiece, and again, you have to fire a lot of shots to justify the cost of buying the equipment needed to load them. Usually, it's advisable to undertake this effort only if you use the press to make other loads in large volume, such as trap and skeet target ammunition. If this is so, reloading slugs with a press is worthwhile, particularly because it gives you a comparatively cheap source of ammunition that you can fire in target sessions before deer season. Ordinarily, slug loads are so expensive that many deer hunters do not sight-in carefully or practice enough to shoot well. But if you reload them yourself, you won't mind shooting 20 or 30 of them.

German Brenneke slugs with attached wad (discussed earlier) are usually available in gun shops that cater to reloaders, but no one sells the American Foster-type as reloading components. Several small companies sell slugs for reloading, but these products dif-

Typical American rifled-slug load (left) has wads that fall away a short distance from the muzzle. Slugs shown are all 12-gauge (from left): Remington 1 ounce, Federal 1 ounce, Brenneke (German) 1 ounce with attached wad, Federal 1¼ ounce. The .30/06 bullet (right) illustrates relative masses.

fer in design from the two standard types. Some of the better-known, non-standard slugs are the Vitt and Boos Aerodynamic slug, Ballistics Research Laboratories SABO Slug, and the Balle Blondeau (an imported French slug). These slugs are priced rather high, and the result is that little or no money is saved by loading them. Shooters usually buy them because they are more accurate than the standard types in some guns. They are often sold direct to the consumer through the mail. Slugs for reloaders are available in 12-gauge and (sometimes) 20-gauge but at present slugs of any other gauge are not sold as components.

But you can cast your own slugs and really cut the cost. Lyman sells molds for 12-gauge and 20-gauge Foster-type slugs, but you'll need several other items such as a ladle and perhaps an electric furnace. These slugs must be cast from soft lead; so you can use salvaged metal such as old cable sheathing or lead pipes. Avoid alloyed lead since it is harder than pure lead and may damage the choke in your gun. Follow the loading manual carefully when loading slugs. The Lyman shotgun reloading manual and the Lyman cast-bullet manual (see bibliography at back of book) are good on this subject.

Home-cast slugs *a la* Lyman don't have the angled vanes that are said to impart rotation to the projectile in flight. Lyman formerly sold a special die that swaged vanes into these slugs, but there was so little demand for the die that it was discontinued. Customers are apparently satisfied with the accuracy of vaneless slugs. In many shotguns groups fired with slugs are so large because of other factors that stabilization through rotation would not really make much of an improvement.

CAST BULLETS

You can also cast your own lead rifle and handgun bullets, either with specially alloyed lead sold in bars or by alloying the metal yourself to increase its hard-

ness, though this is a messy task. For deer hunting, however, cast-lead bullets have a disadvantage in that they cannot be driven at very high velocities. The hot powder gas damages the base of the bullet, and this can cause inaccuracy. To avoid this, some reloaders use gas checks—zinc or copper-alloy cups crimped onto the base of the bullet with a die. The savings to be had by going to all this trouble are not great, and a gas-check lead bullet does not expand as well as a carefully designed, manufactured bullet with an alloy jacket. Jacketed bullets for reloading are readily available.

CREATIVE HANDLOADING

Creative handloading is the darling of many experts. They like to develop loadings that have never been manufactured or even listed in any manual. Sometimes this is a legitimate practice when a specialized load is needed, but it's usually not worthwhile for someone who hunts deer almost exclusively. Because deer hunting is such a popular sport, the ammunition companies have developed a great number of loads that are primarily intended for this kind of hunting, and handloading manuals are replete with many others engineered by ballisticians employed by the manufacturers of reloading gear and components.

It's best to stick to factory loads or loads that are listed in authoritative manuals because they have all been carefully designed and tested. Later on perhaps, particularly if you take up target shooting or varmint hunting, you may become a creative handloader too. It's a fascinating hobby, but it can be very dangerous if you don't know exactly what you're doing. Who knows? Maybe you'll even design a new cartridge case. These are known as "wildcats," and developing your own pet cat is the very zenith of the game.

RELOADING OF A RIFLE CARTRIDGE CASE

1. *New brass: Serious handloaders always purchase new, unfired cases instead of reloading fired cases. There are many reasons for this. Most important is the uniformity of interior dimensions within one brand name and one manufacturing lot. This alone gives you an advantage in achieving constant velocities and good tight groups. Stay away from bargain brands, foreign Berdan-primed cases (American cases are Boxer primed), and military surplus. Buy boxes of new brass with the same lot numbers and purchase enough cases to last through a long loading program.*

Photo series by Stanley W. Trzoniac

2. Lubing cases: *Rifle cases must be lubricated so they won't stick to the walls of the sizing die. The lubricant is applied with a lube pad. You can roll seven or eight cases at a time on the impregnated pad. All die-making companies also market a case lubricant that works best with their dies. Do not lubricate the shoulders of the case, which only invites shoulder collapse when the lube is forced down on this part of the case by the sizing die. While minor dents in the shoulder are blown out on firing, large dents often lead to early case failure or even case separation, which can damage your rifle or you.*

3. Case neck lubrication: *Give the inside of the neck a tingle of lube to help it slip over the neck-expander button incorporated in the sizing die. This plug expands the case mouth so it has a uniform inside diameter and achieves a tight fit on the bullet.*

4. Inserting the sizing die: *After snapping the correct shellholder onto the press ram, the sizing die is threaded into the top of the press. The first step is to size all new factory cases in order to match the sizes machined into your particular die set. All die sets for a given caliber are made to the same standard dimensions, but most dies tend to have a personality of their own. By sizing all new cases as your first step, one variable is eliminated. To set up the sizing die, first move the ram to the top of the strike by pulling the operating handle. Screw the sizing die in until it touches the shellholder and then lock it in place by tightening the set screw in the locking ring. This is your setting for full-length sizing. With a two-die rifle set, in this single operation, the case is sized, it is decapped (if it has been fired), and the neck is expanded to take the bullet.*

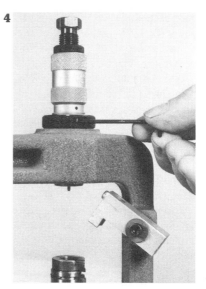

5. Full-length sizing: *With the handle pulled down, the cartridge case is now up into the sizing die. A mild sensation of resistance will accompany this operation, especially if the case has been fired before. On the way down, during the return stroke, additional resistance will be felt, which simply means the expander plug is doing a good job.*

6. Measuring and trimming cases: *After cleaning all cases of lubricant with a soft cloth impregnated with mild solvent, measure all the empty cartridge cases. The .30/06 case shown should be no longer than 2.494 inches to chamber smoothly. But it can be trimmed back to 2.484 inches to allow the case to grow in length as you fire. The overall lengths for all cartridges are listed in all good handloading books. Most cases need minor trimming after five or six loadings. There are two ways to trim a case back to the correct length. One is to use a trim die; the other is to use a horizontal tool called a case trimmer, which resembles a small lathe. With the former, you file the case down until it no longer protrudes through the top of the die. The latter lathe-type tool has pilots and collets.*

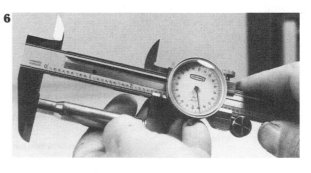

7 & 8. Deburring: *To remove burrs, use a deburring tool, which costs only a couple of dollars. This little tool chamfers the inside of the case mouth (**7**) or cleans up the outside of the neck (**8**) with one deft twist.*

9. Priming preparation: *Fill the primer magazine with primers and screw it into the press.*

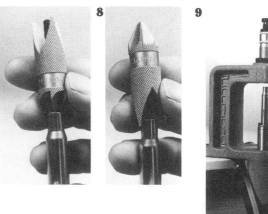

10. *Readying the press:* With the case in the shell-holder, raise the ram to clear the priming punch. Then, upward pressure on the handle will seat the primer in the base of the case.

11. *Seating the primer and selecting loads:* Do not touch the primer with your fingers. The photo shows how the primer punch is moved into the slot in the ram. Primers are seated flush with, or a little below, the flat head of the case. Use the primer specified for your caliber. For beginners, start at a point 5 to 6 percent below the maximum powder charge listed in your manual. Bullet weight is tailored to the game.

12. *Setting the powder measure:* With bullet weight and powder charge selected, set your powder measure to deliver a charge just short of the predetermined charge, which will be achieved on a balance scale (not shown).

13. *Charging the cases:* When you are satisfied that the powder weight is exact, pour the powder into the case. Do one case at a time, and move each charged case to the back of the loading block away from the empties. This avoids "double charging," which is possible when you are assembling some reduced loads. Finish up by looking into each case to make sure the powder level is the same in all of them.

14. *Bullet seating:* This die seats the bullet at the proper depth in the case. It also crimps the case mouth tight against the bullet to hold it in place if that is required. After you have started a few turns into the threads, stop and remove the top part or bullet stem.

15. *Adjusting the seating die:* With the ram in its highest position, screw the die in until you feel a slight resistance. This is the crimping part of the die coming in contact with the case neck. At this point, back off about half a turn to allow some working freedom between the two. Lock the die in place with the black locking ring. This is the no-crimp position used for most rifle cartridges.

16. *Starting the bullet:* With the die set and locked, place a bullet in the case mouth. It should be straight and true. Only a small portion of the bullet will enter the case.

17. *Adjusting the bullet stem:* Elevate the ram until the bullet enters the die. Carefully screw in the bullet stem until it comes in contact with the bullet. Then, tighten it down one or two more full turns. This will force the bullet into the case far enough to allow you to back off with the ram without the bullet falling out of the case. The next step is to raise and lower the ram while screwing the seating stem downward until the proper overall cartridge length, including the bullet, is reached. With the die and die stem properly adjusted, you can load bullets into all your cases with a single power stroke for each case. (Caution: Loads should be boxed and carefully labeled as to load. A record book should show more detailed data.)

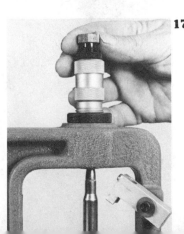

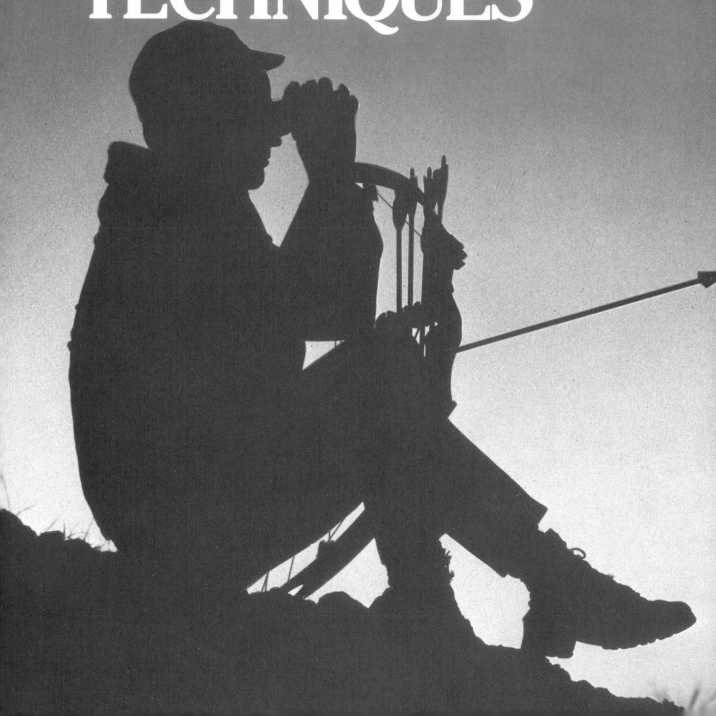

PART 4
BOWHUNTING TACKLE AND TECHNIQUES

BY CHUCK ADAMS

Photos by the author unless otherwise credited. Drawings by Lloyd Birmingham.

Use of bow and arrow to hunt deer is more widely enjoyed today than ever before. There are many factors that have contributed to this current popularity, but chief among them are the excellence of modern hunting bows and arrows, widespread incidence of special archery-only deer-hunting seasons before and after general gun seasons, the uniquely quiet and peaceful nature of pursuing game with a bow, and increased limitations on hunting deer with guns in many parts of North America. This is not to mention the innate challenge and thrill of matching wits on a personal, close-range basis with the sharpest game animals in North America. As more and more woodsmen discover the special advantages of hunting deer with "string guns," this primitive sport gone modern will continue to increase in popularity.

Not long ago, becoming proficient with archery equipment was tedious and time-consuming. In addition, basic bow-shooting gear was less dependable and required more maintenance. Bows and arrows were prone to warp, crack, or break when used in excessively damp or warm conditions. The equipment was also hard to shoot longbows were inefficient and muscle-rending, while wooden arrows proved fragile and inconsistent.

By contrast today, the average compound bow with its fiberglass limbs, fine synthetic finishes, and computer-tested metal parts is practically indestructible. Arrows composed of aluminum or fiberglass are similarly dependable. This equipment is so easy to shoot that an average hunter can quickly perfect his target-hitting skills.

Virtually every part of the United States and Canada currently has generous bowhunting seasons for deer—seasons that can give the average hunter more time in the field. In some areas bowhunters can also shoot extra deer on special archery-only permits. This is a distinct advantage today, considering that shrinking habitats and increased hunter pressure have led to shorter gun seasons in most areas. As a result, as much as 40 percent of all deer hunters now participate in archery-only seasons for deer, and these hunters include a fair number of hard-core firearms enthusiasts. This chance to increase dramatically the amount of time spent scouting and hunting deer each year makes bowhunting especially attractive today.

Bowhunting deer is a quiet, unobtrusive sport. It allows quality hunting of relatively calm, unspooked animals—even in areas where plenty of archers are stand-hunting or silently slipping through the trees. Such tranquility afield is appealing to many hunters because it represents a dramatic change of pace from the hustle and bustle of life today. It also allows views of truly trophy-size bucks that seldom poke their noses out of the brush once opening-day guns go off.

Many game-management experts believe that bow-hunting is destined to become increasingly important in the United States, because in the years to come, available deer habitat will probably continue to shrink in the face of urban sprawl, accelerated mining and timber-cutting activity, intensified agricultural production, and other factors that have eaten away at woodlots, brushfields, and forests. Even though mod-

ern archery tackle is incredibly dependable and enjoyable to use, bowhunting remains a relatively low-yield sport. That means a large number of hunters can practice their skills without significantly reducing deer populations. Bowhunting provides a maximum number of recreational hours per animal taken and makes it ideal wherever deer harvests must carefully be monitored.

The challenge of bagging bucks with a bow and arrow is downright addictive for many serious hunters. Once an archer encounters a deer or two at eyelash-batting distance, he is usually hooked on the sport—even if he fails to bag his venison. Though the vast majority of American bowhunters actively hunt with firearms as well, most harbor a special fondness for bowhunting, the comparatively primitive phase of their yearly deer-hunting activity.

Much of the challenge of bowhunting for deer lies in the need to approach or bring deer into shooting ranges that are closer than required for most firearms. This makes you match wits with some of the wariest game in North America, such as this big whitetail. (Leonard Lee Rue III photo)

EVOLUTION OF TACKLE

Bows and arrows were used by European hunters at least 100,000 years ago. Ancient cave drawings prove this. Egyptians used simple longbows in war nearly 6,000 years ago, and Assyrians dominated the Middle East around 1800 B.C. with short, laminated recurve bows made of leather, horn, and wood. In 1200 B.C., Middle Eastern Hittites carried bows in chariots to outmaneuver and outshoot their opponents in battle. From the birth of Christ until the Middle Ages, bows were primary inplements of war in both Europe and Asia.

In North America, archaeological digs show that Indians used bows in hunting and war as much as 5,000 years ago. Beyond this, the history of American archery is very murky at best.

It is generally acknowledged among primitive-weapons experts that the bow and arrow has not been *widely* used as long as the layman might expect. Most hunters of American, European, and Asian prehistorical times probably used hand-thrown or atlatl-thrown spears for taking animals. Such hunters grew up with these simple hunting tools and were unquestionably deadly with them at 50 or 60 yards. This viewpoint is not supposition, because modern-day primitives such as Australian aborigines use spear-throwers and short, light spears with incredible accuracy.

Careful studies of obsidian, flint, and other stone-age projectile points support the theory that bows and arrows are relatively recent hunting implements. A lightweight, feathered shaft shot from a crude bow such as those used by native Americans in colonial times was armed with a relatively small point to promote decent down-range trajectory. Even so, the average bow of the Plains Indian could launch an arrow less than 75 yards when shot at a 45-degree angle! By

The atlatl, in effect, extended the arm and helped hurl projectiles with heightened velocity.

contrast, an atlatl-thrown spear with a larger, heavier head will fly as far or farther with more energy and greater down-range killing capacity.

In most parts of the world, smallish arrowhead-size stone projectile points begin showing up in archaeological digs about the time when prehistoric tribes switched from nomadic to sedentary and agrarian cultures. Nomadic peoples tend to be less warlike than those who occupy property that can be raided and must be defended. The bow and arrow was undoubtedly a far superior implement of war when compared to the hand-thrown or atlatl-launched spear. The spear was fine for hunting, but the bow could be shot in rapid-fire fashion to drive off attackers.

It was a standard rule of early-American mountain men never to approach closer than 100 yards to bow-toting groups of Indians until the intentions of these "savages" were clearly known. The best Apache and Commanche bowmen reportedly could launch five arrows before the first one hit the ground, their hands a blur as they plucked arrows from their shoulder quivers, drew, and released in a rhythmic, completely fluid motion. A volley by several quick-shooting braves would invariably wound or kill several attackers inside 60 or 70 yards—even if those attackers were armed with muskets or rifles.

Exactly when the first especially brainy warrior attached a thong to a springy piece of wood will never be known. However, bows were important for several thousand years of hunting and fighting in prehistoric times, and continued to be important in war until the advent of the first crude firearms several centuries ago. The famous English longbow was a major factor in medieval battles, and the short, wicked recurve bows of the Mongols made these people a fearsome fighting

Primitive cave art proves that hunters have been using bows and arrows for many thousands of years. These drawings were rendered in a remote grotto near Spain's Valltorta Gorge approximately 100,000 B.C.

Small Stone-Age projectile points contrast sharply with a modern hunting broadhead. The oldest primitive arrowheads found in North American excavations date back to 3,000 B.C.

force throughout the Middle Ages. Bows probably were first used for warlike purposes, but naturally became hunting implements as well.

The notion of sport hunting with a bow is a relatively new concept. Bowhunting for sport as we know it today officially began in August of 1911 when America's last recorded "wild Indian" was cornered by dogs in a slaughterhouse near Oroville, California. This Indian was subsequently adopted and studied by professors of anthropology at the University of California in San Francisco.

Ishi, as he was called, was the last of the California Yana nation, and soon attracted the curiosity of Dr. Saxton Pope—an instructor at the university's school of medicine—and Pope's good friend Art Young. During the five years before his death of tuberculosis in 1916, Ishi taught Pope and Young the basics of hunting with bow and arrow equipment—basics these avid outdoorsmen took to heart. In subsequent years, Pope and Young hunted many big-game species with their crude longbows, including Alaskan grizzly bears, moose, and African lions.

This pair of enthusiastic California adventurers can be considered the first recreational archery hunters of the 20th century, and paved the way for this unique and challenging sport. The famous Pope and Young Record Club, instituted in 1961 for the recording of outstanding big-game trophies taken by bow and arrow, was named after these pioneers.

Since the early 1900s, bowhunting has enjoyed slow but steady gains in popularity. Through the exploits and promotional activities of well-known hunting archers and archery-equipment manufacturers such as Howard Hill and Fred Bear, state game agencies eventually recognized bowhunting as a legitimate

sport and instituted special archery-hunting seasons. Bowhunting began gaining ground during the late 1940s and early 1950s, and by the mid-1960s it was widely recognized as a popular, effective method of hunting deer. Today there are over 2 million registered bowhunters in the United States alone, and the number creeps upward each year.

As the sport has evolved during the past few decades, so have bows and arrows. The crude longbows used by Ishi, Pope, and Young around 1915 resembled broomsticks bent by stout pieces of twine. The arrows were hewn of wood and were terribly rough by modern manufacturing standards. By the early 1950s, longbows had given way to better balanced, more efficient recurve bows with laminated, S-shaped limbs. That decade also marked the introduction of tubular aluminum hunting arrows, and from that time, there began a rapid decline in the manufacture of shafts made of pine, cedar, and other fragile woods. In the late 1960s, the cable-and-pulley compound bow quickly proliferated in the marketplace, and by 1980 over 95 percent of modern bowhunters were using this "newfangled, Rube Goldberg contraption." Today bows and arrows only vaguely resemble the whittled-out longbows of 1915, and perform with efficiency that would have amazed Ishi, Pope, and Young. As far as accurate and dependable archery equipment is concerned, bowhunters have never had it so good.

By the mid-1930s, there were enough bowhunters in the United States to form small, active archery clubs. These bowhunters used simple, relatively crude longbows and wooden arrows.

Hunting with the durable, laminated-limb recurve bow carried here by renowned archer Fred Bear, left, became popular in the 1950s. During this decade other equipment refinements, such as bow quivers, also became commercially available. (Bear Archery photo)

CHOOSING TACKLE

At best, selecting a modern bow/arrow combination is a complicated task for archers with some experience. So it is especially important that a beginning archer shop at a reputable equipment outlet. Well-qualified sales personnel can help make intelligent equipment selections. There are literally dozens of hunting-bow models, hundreds of draw-length/draw-weight combinations, and thousands of specific bow/arrow/accessory setups possible to accommodate a myriad of physical statures, individual shooting styles, and personal druthers. The archer who buys his bow-and-arrow setup at a department store or through the mail has little chance of being properly outfitted for a hunt—the result: strained muscles, poor shooting, and severe frustration.

There are over 8,000 authorized archery pro shops in the 48 contiguous states—shops that usually have experienced sales experts and bow-shooting facilities for their customers. All beginners should purchase their gear at one of them. One compound-bow model alone may be available with a dozen different wheel sizes, half a dozen draw-weight ranges, three or four bow-grip shapes, and two or more arrow-rest configurations. Only one combination of such variables is best for an individual bowhunter. Add to this the fact that some 35 hunting-arrow sizes are currently sold—only one of which is likely to shoot well from a particular hunting bow—and the beginning or interme-

Correctly chosen archery products yield accuracy of this kind on targets and game. By contrast, haphazardly purchased gear results in mediocre performance and plenty of frustration to match.

A well-stocked pro shop is the only sensible place to purchase archery equipment. These outlets carry top-quality products, and their salesmen can help ensure gear selected will meet your personal needs.

Selecting a hunting bow is no easy matter. With several hundred models to choose from, a would-be archer should understand basic bow design and strengths and weaknesses of a specific model.

diate deer hunter has little chance of coming up with the correct combo without some help.

The single most critical thing every bowhunter must keep in mind is how vitally important the proper shooting setup is. Far too many hunters merely buy what seems to be a good-looking bow, add a dozen arrows of any old size, and ignorantly expect shooting accuracy to follow. This makes as much sense as pur-

chasing a .30/06 rifle and some .270 ammunition, and heading afield without any sights. It is impossible for a hunter to shoot a mismatched bow/arrow combination with any degree of accuracy. It is equally impossible for him to end up with a *matched* combo unless he seeks out professional advice. Buying equipment through a reputable archery dealer is the only sensible way to go.

MODERN HUNTING BOWS

Modern hunting bows can be divided into three classes—longbows, recurve bows, and compound bows. Although compound bows of one sort or another have dominated the market for several years, both longbows and recurve bows still have small, faithful followings of nostalgic, back-to-basics bowhunters. But today's longbows and recurve bows bear little resemblance to the originals; instead they are made of contemporary laminated materials and have fine modern finishes.

HOW A BOW OPERATES

Hand-held bows consist of a central riser section with springy limbs projecting from either end. The limbs support the bowstring and give it the necessary tension. The archer grasps the bow by the contoured handle grip near the middle of the riser and "nocks" an arrow—that is, he nocks the arrow over the bowstring. Then, by drawing the bowstring back, he bends the limbs. This bending creates and stores energy for the shot. Longbow limbs bend in a simple arc; recurve limbs unfold from a deep S-shape into a less pronounced S-curve; and compound limbs bend only slightly under the tremendous mechanical leverage of tip-mounted wheels or oval-shaped cams. When the bowstring is released, the bow limbs snap back to their original shape and, in doing so, impart a high percentage of their stored energy to the arrow, hurtling it toward the target. If the bow and arrow are properly matched, if the bow/arrow setup is correctly tuned, and if the archer's shooting form is up to snuff, the arrow will follow the correct trajectory and hit on target.

Crossbows are gunlike, shoulder-mounted bows now legal for deer hunting in a few areas of North America. Both recurve and compound crossbow designs are currently available to hunters. These bows work in the same fashion as hand-drawn bows, except that there is a trigger mechanism to release the bowstring and release the arrow.

ARROW SPEED AND TRAJECTORY

The selection of a particular deer-hunting bow should be based primarily on a bow's reputation for accuracy and dependability. Bow manufacturers are extremely

Limbs of hunting bows bend under drawing pressure and impart stored energy to the arrow when the bowstring is released. With a proper bow/arrow setup, the arrow sizzles to the target with amazing accuracy.

fond of promoting their wares on the basis of raw arrow speed produced. The novice is often duped by such sales propaganda and selects the "hottest" new bow instead of the one with a sound track record for consistently satisfactory performance. Experienced bowhunters know that the slight edge in speed of one model may be more than offset by increased shooting noise and decreased bow-limb and bowstring longevity. Fast bows are often problem-plagued rattletraps with little practical value in the field.

When a bow manufacturer offers a "fast" new model, he's usually emphasizing a relatively minor increase in basic arrow velocity. The average modern longbow generally casts arrows between 160 and 180 feet per second (fps); the average recurve, between 180 and 200 fps; and the average compound, between 190 and 220 fps. These speeds are peanuts compared to the projectile velocity produced by handguns, rifles, and shotguns. What is more important, the practical difference between 175 fps and 210 fps in the woods as a deer strolls past a stand 20 yards away is *almost nil.*

Any bow/arrow combination can be tested for speed by means of this type archery chronograph. Although many bowhunters mistakenly stress velocity produced above all other hunting-bow characteristics, this should be a relatively minor consideration for selecting a bow.

AVERAGE TRAJECTORIES FOR STANDARD 29-INCH ALUMINUM HUNTING ARROWS

This table shows that no matter what sort of hunting bow is used, arrow trajectory is still quite arching compared to the path of a big-bore rifle bullet. Even the flattest-shooting compound bows still require pinpoint distance estimation. (Courtesy of Ranging Inc.)

Bow	Arrow Shaft Size	Total Arrow Weight (grs)	Arrow Velocity At Various Distances (fps)								Trajectory For Various Sight-In Zeroes (in inches)							
			10 Yds.	15 Yds.	20 Yds.	25 Yds.	30 Yds.	35 Yds.	40 Yds.	45 Yds.	10 Yds.	15 Yds.	20 Yds.	25 Yds.	30 Yds.	35 Yds.	40 Yds.	45 Yds.
45-lb. Recurve	1918	522	162.8	162.0	161.3	160.6	159.5	159.0	158.8	158.3	+ 3.4	0	- 6.3	-16.2	-29.6	-46.4	-66.8	-91.0
											+10.2	+10.4	+ 7.2	0	-9.2	-22.7	-39.7	-60.2
											+20.1	+25.3	+27.2	+25.7	+20.8	+12.4	0	-15.1
45-lb. Recurve	2016	493	166.5	165.6	164.7	163.8	163.1	162.4	161.7	161.2	+ 3.1	0	- 6.3	-15.9	-28.8	-45.1	-64.8	-88.0
											+ 9.7	+ 9.9	+ 6.9	0	- 8.9	-21.7	-38.0	-57.8
											+19.5	+24.6	+26.4	+25.1	+20.5	+12.6	0	-13.5
50-lb. Recurve	2016	493	172.3	171.3	170.4	169.5	168.7	167.9	167.2	166.6	+ 3.2	0	- 5.3	-14.0	-25.9	-41.1	-59.4	-80.8
											+ 8.9	+ 9.0	+ 6.1	0	- 8.7	-20.9	-36.2	-54.7
											+18.0	+22.6	+24.3	+23.0	+18.6	+11.0	0	-13.5
50-lb. Recurve	2018	542	165.7	164.9	164.0	163.3	162.7	162.0	161.5	161.0	+ 3.4	0	- 5.8	-15.2	-28.2	-44.3	-64.1	-87.0
											+ 9.8	+ 9.9	+ 6.8	0	- 9.2	-22.2	-38.6	-58.6
											+19.6	+24.6	+26.5	+25.0	+20.3	+12.3	0	-14.0
55-lb Recurve	2018	542	176.5	175.6	174.7	173.9	173.2	172.4	171.8	171.2	+ 2.9	0	- 5.3	-13.8	-25.1	-39.4	-56.8	-77.3
											+ 8.6	+ 8.7	+ 5.9	0	- 8.2	-19.8	-34.2	-51.8
											+17.0	+21.4	+23.0	+21.7	+17.5	+10.4	0	-13.0

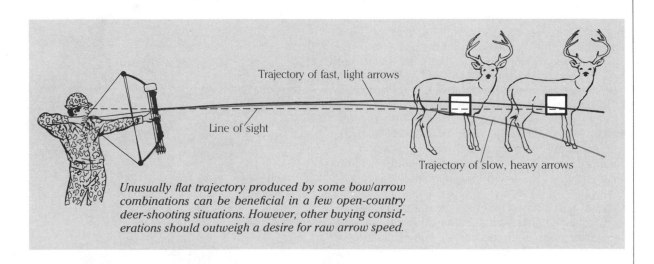

Trajectory of fast, light arrows

Line of sight

Trajectory of slow, heavy arrows

Unusually flat trajectory produced by some bow/arrow combinations can be beneficial in a few open-country deer-shooting situations. However, other buying considerations should outweigh a desire for raw arrow speed.

Bow	Arrow Shaft Size	Total Arrow Weight (grs)	Arrow Velocity At Various Distances (fps)								Trajectory For Various Sight-In Zeroes (in inches)							
			10 Yds.	15 Yds.	20 Yds.	25 Yds.	30 Yds.	35 Yds.	40 Yds.	45 Yds.	10 Yds.	15 Yds.	20 Yds.	25 Yds.	30 Yds.	35 Yds.	40 Yds.	45 Yds.
55-lb. Recurve	2117	535	177.3	176.3	175.4	174.5	173.7	172.9	172.2	171.5	+ 2.9	0	- 5.2	-13.5	-24.8	-39.0-	-56.2	-76.5
											+ 8.5	+ 8.6	+ 6.0	0	- 8.0	-19.4	-33.9	-51.4
											+17.0	+21.4	+23.0	+21.7	+17.6	+10.5	0	-12.5
55-lb. Compound	1918	522	182.0	181.0	180.0	179.2	178.4	177.7	176.9	176.3	+ 2.7	0	- 5.0	-13.1	-23.8	-37.3	-53.7	-73.1
											+ 8.1	+ 8.3	+ 5.7	0	- 7.5	-18.3	-32.0	-48.4
											+16.1	+20.2	+21.7	+20.5	+16.5	+ 9.8	0	-12.2
55-lb. Compound	2016	493	185.9	184.8	183.8	182.8	181.9	181.0	180.1	179.4	+ 2.8	0	- 4.5	-12.1	-22.4	-35.2	-51.0	-69.5
											+ 7.7	+ 7.9	+ 5.4	0	- 7.3	-17.7	-30.7	-46.7
											+15.5	+19.5	+21.0	+19.9	+16.2	+ 9.8	0	-11.3
60-lb. Compound	2016	493	192.4	191.3	190.2	189.2	188.2	187.3	186.4	185.5	+ 2.5	0	- 4.3	-11.4	-21.0	-33.0	-47.8	-65.0
											+ 7.4	+ 7.5	+ 5.3	0	- 6.5	-16.0	-78.3	-43.0
											+14.6	+18.4	+19.8	+18.8	+15.3	+ 9.4	0	-10.2
60-lb. Compound	2117	535	186.3	185.3	184.3	183.4	182.5	181.6	180.8	180.0	+ 2.8	0	- 4.5	-12.0	-22.1	-35.0	-50.6	-69.0
											+ 7.8	+ 7.9	+ 5.4	0	- 7.2	-17.5	-30.4	-46.3
											+15.5	+19.5	+21.0	+20.0	+16.3	+ 9.9	0	-10.9
65-lb. Compound	2117	535	192.2	191.1	190.0	189.1	188.1	187.2	186.4	185.6	+ 2.5	0	- 4.4	-11.5	-21.1	-33.3	-47.8	-65.1
											+ 7.4	+ 7.5	+ 5.3	0	- 6.6	-16.2	-28.3	-43.1
											+14.6	+18.4	+19.8	+18.8	+15.3	+ 9.4	0	-10.2
65-lb. Compound	2018	542	191.4	190.4	189.4	188.5	187.6	186.8	185.9	185.2	+ 2.5	0	- 4.5	-11.6	-21.3	-33.6	-48.2	-65.8
											+ 7.4	+ 7.5	+ 5.2	0	- 6.7	-16.5	-28.8	-43.7
											+14.7	+18.9	+19.8	+18.7	+15.2	+ 9.2	0	-10.5

In long-range bow-shooting situations, such as hunting mule deer on sagebrush flats, an arrow-speed spread of 35 fps *can* make the difference between a solid hit and a complete miss. But other factors are usually far more important—factors like the archer's basic range-estimating skills and ability to restrain his tendency toward buck fever. No matter what hunting bow an archer uses, he must estimate shooting distances within a few short yards or he'll miss the mark entirely. Even the fastest "barnburner" bow on the market cannot flatten arrow trajectory enough to eliminate the need for determining shooting range accurately.

A 500-grain deer-hunting arrow shot from an average compound hunting bow has only 50 foot-pounds of energy as it leaves a bow—barely half as much as a lowly .22 rimfire Short cartridge. The fastest-shooting compound sold produces only 10 to 20 foot-pounds more—again, a mere drop in the bucket in terms of raw deer-killing power. But exact arrow energy has little to do with how an arrow kills a deer—the key is the design of the broadhead being used.

Projectile energy bears directly on deer-killing efficiency in firearms. The little .22 Short with its muzzle energy of about 100 foot-pounds is ill-suited for taking deer while the .270 Winchester with its energy of 2800 foot-pounds is a fine deer-hunting cartridge. But a beginning bowhunter should pay less attention to bow manufacturers' boasts about arrow speed and energy because these factors are not of major importance in hunting deer. Instead he should concentrate on other important factors, such as dependability of basic design, purchase price, shooting smoothness, bowstring-drawing stress on shooting muscles and bowstring fingers, and level of bow-shooting noise.

HUNTING LONGBOWS

A modern hunting longbow is precisely what its name implies—a long, slim, simple shooting tool. It has a short handle riser, slender grip section, and straight, relatively narrow limbs. The average longbow measures about 70 inches from tip to tip after being strung, and describes a smooth, continuous arc from tip to handle to tip.

Longbows are the *least* efficient of all contemporary bow designs. They store less energy in their limbs during the draw and impart a lower percentage of this energy to the arrow when the bowstring is released. More importantly, longbows do not draw as smoothly as other kinds of bows. Bow poundage rises abruptly near the full extent of the draw instead of being distributed evenly throughout the drawing stroke. Longbows also tend to "kick" or recoil in a shooter's hand at the instant of arrow release, a phenomenon which intimidates many archers.

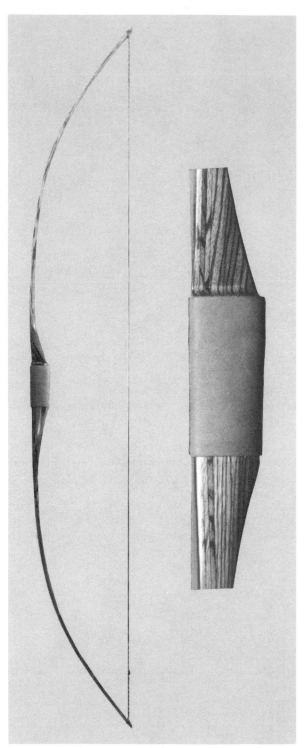

The modern longbow is a sleek design with limbs composed of maple and fiberglass laminations. Although not the sluggish shooting tool of yesteryear, this bow is still relatively unsophisticated compared to recurve and compound bows. The handle section is short and trim with a grip wrapped in slip-resistant leather. The grip seldom contours to fit the hand and recoils noticeably whenever you take a shot.

Modern longbows are quite dependable and reasonably resistant to normal amounts of dampness and heat encountered afield. This is due in large part to laminated limbs made of good-quality maple, yew, or other hardwood bonded with epoxy to outer layers of top-grade unidirectional fiberglass. These limbs are usually coated with polyurethane or epoxy-base finish—ample protection from the elements. By contrast, old-style longbows of the 1920s and 1930s were made of solid wood, assembled with animal glues, and finished poorly to boot. The result was unexpected breakage and inconsistent arrow cast (speed) depending upon the temperature and humidity of the day. Today, longbows are certainly dependable by former bow-construction standards.

The chief drawbacks of contemporary longbows include their long, awkward overall length, and the previously mentioned uneven draw and tendency to recoil. In addition, such bows require an archer to hold the full force of the bowstring with his muscles and fingers as he aims—a problem compound bows eliminate. Despite these disadvantages, the price tag for a longbow is still considerably more than the average price of a top-grade hunting recurve bow. This is largely due to the fact that most modern longbows are made in custom shops and aren't mass-produced like other kinds of bows.

An estimated 1 in every 200 American bowhunters currently hunts with a longbow. Usually, this archer belongs to a longbow club that emphasizes traditional bowhunting values and the simple beauty of our most basic bowhunting tool.

RECURVE BOWS

Recurve bows were the predominant deer-hunting bows during the 1950s and 1960s, and still enjoy a limited following today. The hunting recurve bow usually has a medium-length handle riser and broad, thinly constructed S-shaped limbs on either end. The recurving limb design stores and releases more energy per pound of draw weight expended upon the bowstring than the straight limbs of a longbow, and also yields a smoother, easier draw. On the average, hunting recurve bows measure about 60 inches from tip to tip when strung.

Recurve bows have limbs constructed of the same laminated hardwood and fiberglass as longbows, but they are more fragile than longbows because they are broader and thinner. The bow limbs need not be babied, but cannot be slammed in car doors or left strung for many days without possibly warping or twisting.

Recurve bows are characterized by quiet shooting performance, compact handling length, and light physical weight. Some models quickly disassemble into three separate sections for transport in an airline

Recurve bows like this one have been used by deer hunters for several decades. They are characterized by relatively compact size; light carrying weight; smooth, quiet shooting; and rugged dependability in the field.

case or bowhunting backpack.

The one disadvantage of a recurve hunting bow is that the full force of the bow limbs is held by the archer's bowstring fingers and shoulder muscles as he aims prior to taking a shot. In other words, a 50-pound recurve bow places a full 50 pounds of stress upon the archer every time he shoots. Careful muscle conditioning is therefore needed for reasonably good accuracy.

Only about four percent of all archers currently use recurve bows for hunting deer. Most bowhunters prefer recurves because these bows are relatively inexpensive, or because they enjoy using what they consider to be traditional and esthetically superior bow-shooting equipment.

THE RECURVE HUNTING BOW

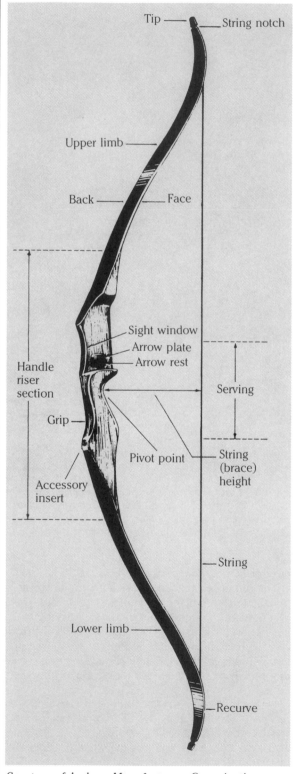

Tip — String notch

Upper limb

Back — Face

Sight window
Arrow plate
Arrow rest

Handle riser section

Serving

Grip

Pivot point

String (brace) height

Accessory insert

String

Lower limb

Recurve

Courtesy of Archery Manufacturers Organization

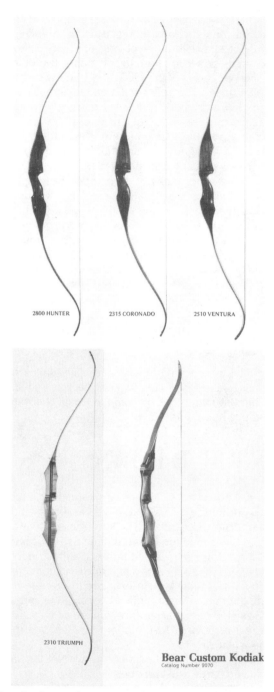

2800 HUNTER   2315 CORONADO   2510 VENTURA

2310 TRIUMPH

Bear Custom Kodiak
Catalog Number 2070

Standard one-piece recurve bows are available in a variety of pleasing shapes and wood colorations to match any hunter's tastes. Most measure about 60 inches from tip to tip when strung and ready to use. The bow at bottom right is a three-piece take-down recurve bow. It is easy to transport—especially on backpack bowhunting trips. When disassembled, the handle section and limbs tuck neatly in any tote sack or padded carrying case.

COMPOUND BOWS

A wide variety of so-called "compound bows" have been introduced since the first four-wheel version was offered commercially in 1968. Although initially regarded with suspicion by traditional archers, the compound design quickly captured most of the hunting market because of its many advantages.

No one can seriously say that a mechanical wheel-and-cable bow is handsome, but such a bow is certainly compact, fast-shooting, accurate, and thoroughly dependable. The deer-hunting compound bow usually measures a scant 45 to 50 inches from tip to tip, which makes it easy to tote through brush or stow in the back seat of a car. The mechanical advantage of eccentric wheels or oval cams near the ends of the limb tips stores more energy in a compound's stiff, stubby limbs than can be mustered by simply bent longbow or recurve limbs. Slight increases in speed and shooting power are relatively minor advantages in bowhunting, but do raise the average deer-hunting archer's chances slightly in open country where longer shots are the rule instead of the exception.

The primary advantage of the compound bow is that it "lets off," or relaxes, in draw weight at full draw. The average 60-pound hunting compound exerts a full 60 pounds of bowstring pressure on an archer's fingers and drawing muscles at half draw. Then it eases off to approximately half as much bowstring tension as the compound wheels roll on over to a full, aiming position. This lets the archer line up on target while holding only 30 pounds with his fingers and back

The modern two-wheel hunting bows are quiet, accurate, dependable, and relatively inexpensive to buy. They are sold in a variety of configurations to suit any personal tastes and needs.

A compound bow's major advantage over other designs is its draw-weight let-off feature. The peak drawing weight is reached at half draw, then decreases about 50 percent as you pull back farther to aim and shoot.

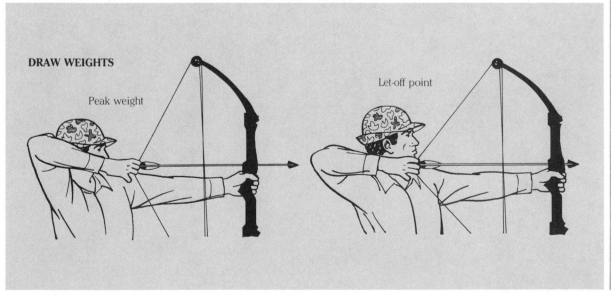

DRAW WEIGHTS

Peak weight

Let-off point

THE COMPOUND HUNTING BOW

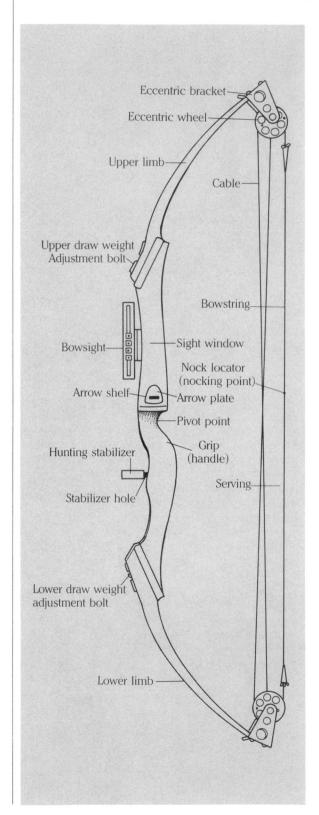

Eccentric bracket

Eccentric wheel

Upper limb

Cable

Upper draw weight
Adjustment bolt

Bowstring

Bowsight

Sight window

Nock locator
(nocking point)

Arrow shelf

Arrow plate

Pivot point

Grip
(handle)

Hunting stabilizer

Serving

Stabilizer hole

Lower draw weight
adjustment bolt

Lower limb

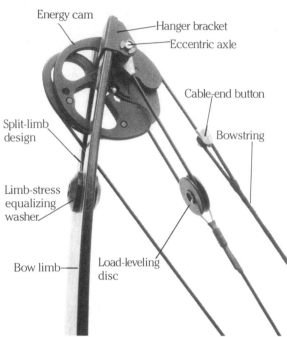

Energy cam

Hanger bracket

Eccentric axle

Split-limb
design

Cable-end button

Bowstring

Limb-stress
equalizing
washer

Bow limb

Load-leveling
disc

An oval compound cam stores more bow-limb energy than a conventional eccentric wheel and thus produces higher arrow speed. However, this speed is often accompanied by noisy, unstable bow performance.

The first compound bows had four or more wheels and fairly complex cable assemblies. All those moving parts certainly produced speed and power, but sometimes led to malfunctions.

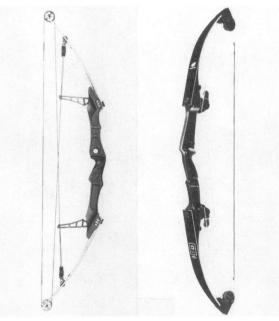

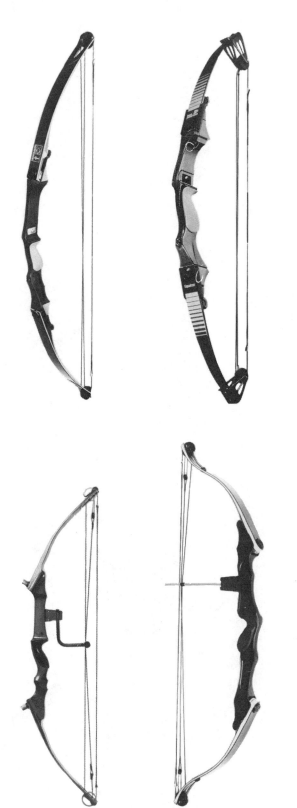

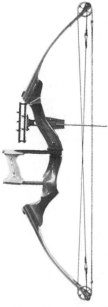

Unusual compound configurations like this forward-grip bow appear on a regular basis as manufacturers experiment with new designs. Most serious deer hunters rely on conventional models instead.

muscles—a major aid in steady, accurate shooting. A bowhunter using a compound bow must still master shooting form, but he can do so with less time spent building muscles. He also runs far less risk of developing bad shooting habits that stem from tired, strained muscles and a poor attitude.

Compound hunting bows fall into two basic categories—round-wheel bows, and cam-operated bows. The round-wheel bows tend to be smoother shooting, quieter, and easier to draw than those with egg-shaped cams, but the cam-bows produce some 10 to 15 percent higher arrow velocity. Cam-bows have proved to be less dependable than conventional round-wheel bows because the cams store more energy in limbs. This puts more stress on all parts of the bow when a shot is taken. Consequently cam-bows are prone to limb breakage, cable separation, extreme shooting noise, and touchy, only marginally accurate arrow flight.

Cam-bows are favored by some open-country deer hunters who place a premium on flat arrow trajectory. But the average deer hunter is best advised to purchase a regular round-wheel compound bow that shoots with quiet, dependable accuracy. The best-designed round-wheel compounds currently available are two-wheel bows, which feature the rugged simplicity of only two wheels and two connecting cables.

Compound hunting bows have one notable disadvantage. The average two-wheel compound weighs about 5 pounds—easily twice as much as the average

These four two-wheel hunting bows are quiet, accurate, dependable, and relatively inexpensive to buy. They are sold in a variety of configurations to suit any personal tastes and needs.

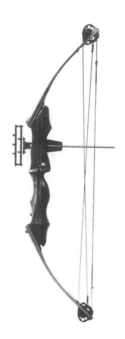

Compound bows are sold to meet virtually every bowhunting need. The child's model shown here is scaled down in size, draw weight, and price tag to accommodate a young but growing archer.

The typical two-cam configuration on this bow is favored by those who want a simple, fairly trouble-free "string gun" for long-distance shooting. For flat arrow trajectory, nothing can match a well-designed hunting cam-bow.

This bizarre compound bow has a recurving upper limb, a large lower cam, and only one driving cable. Surprisingly, the design enjoys a reputation for accuracy and dependability.

hunting longbow or recurve bow. All those wheels, cables, and related metal parts add to carrying weight—something a deer hunter must consider. However, the draw-weight let-off feature alone makes compound bows the overwhelming favorite of bowhunters.

CROSSBOWS

As mentioned earlier, a few North American states and provinces allow hunting with crossbows. A crossbow is theoretically superior to hand-drawn bows because, when aiming, the hunter does not have to hold back the bowstring and employs top-notch telescopic or open sights for pinpoint aiming. In reality, though, crossbows are not usually accurate past 30 or 40 yards. This is primarily because the short, ultralight arrows (called bolts) are somewhat unstable in flight when tipped with hunting-sized broadhead arrowheads.

Several dependable deer-hunting crossbow models are sold at archery stores, including bows with conventional recurving limbs and more advanced com-

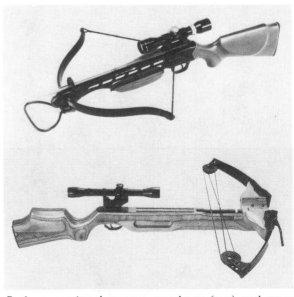

Both conventional recurve crossbows (top) and more advanced compound crossbows (bottom) are available. When coupled with telescopic sights, the bows are fairly accurate in steady hands.

pound-wheel setups. Some experimentation with arrow sizes and sight settings can yield fairly good accuracy from these trigger-operated shooting machines—accuracy good enough for taking deer at short to medium range.

Because relatively few places allow crossbow hunting for deer, and because this sort of "bowhunting" falls outside the traditional notion of bowhunting as a Robin Hood-style sport, a mere handful of nimrods use crossbows to take their venison.

OTHER BOW DESIGNS

Manufacturers are constantly experimenting with hand-drawn arrow launchers of one sort or another. No one can divine what designs will emerge in coming years. Several odd-looking four-limbed hunting bows have already been offered commercially, though they have not been well received. Predictions are difficult, but it seems likely that one form or another of the two-wheel compound bow will probably be the mainstay of deer-hunting archers for many years.

The deer hunter who enjoys workshop construction has one interesting bow option that is worth considering. Several top-notch bow companies offer compound and recurve kits at reduced prices—kits that allow hobbyists to assemble and finish hunting bows themselves. Serious hunters can custom-shape the grips and otherwise produce unique, personalized bows. Bow kits are not recommended for beginning archers. It takes an old hand to know exactly what modifications are required to create a "perfect" deer-hunting bow.

LAMINATED VS. FIBERGLASS LIMBS

Until the early 1980s, bow limbs composed of wood-and-fiberglass laminations were generally considered superior to limbs made of solid fiberglass material. Laminated limbs were lighter in weight and springier and yielded faster, more consistent arrow flight. However, the aerospace industry developed an improved fiberglass and this has completely changed the role of solid fiberglass in quality bow-limb production.

The conventional laminated bow limb is a top-performing, but extremely fragile, part of any hunting bow. Wood cores in limbs tend to soften or crack if moisture seeps in, and laminated bow limbs invariably lose poundage over the years as they take a permanent, irreversible set under bowstring and cable tension. In addition, laminated limbs will explode if they become too hot to touch, as when left near a roaring campfire

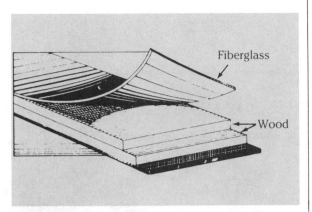

A conventional laminated bow limb consists of two or more strips of straight-grained maple sandwiched between layers of unidirectional fiberglass. The combination is springy and light in weight, but fairly fragile.

or in a closed vehicle on a hot day. By contrast, modern solid-glass limbs are almost indestructible. They do not take a permanent set and produce arrow-flight speed and consistency on a par with the best laminated limbs. As a result, some manufacturers are phasing out laminated limbs in their compound bows.

Hunters who harbor old prejudices about the inferiority of solid fiberglass bow limbs should discard these antiquated notions. Solid-glass limbs in compound bows are now superior to laminated limbs, and will serve a hunter far better over the long haul.

Unfortunately, the long power stroke of recurve and longbow limbs still requires lighter-weight laminated construction for decent shooting results. Solid-glass limbs are simply too heavy to be used on these non-mechanical bows.

FEATURES IN BOWS

No matter what sort of bow a deer hunter decides to buy, he should insist on having certain important features. The majority of modern bows have them, and those that do not should be avoided.

First and foremost, the handle riser of every hunting bow should be drilled and tapped to accept bowsights and a hunting-bow stabilizer. Sights are generally mounted with two screws to the right side of a right-hand bow. A stabilizer is affixed to the front of the bow handle just below the area where the archer grips the bow. If a bow does not have threaded holes or bushings to accept these accessories, look for another model.

Most good-quality hunting bows are drilled and tapped or bushed to accept bow quivers and screw-adjustable arrow rests as well. Some bow quivers attach at the same holes where a bowsight is anchored—others require a separate mounting arrange-

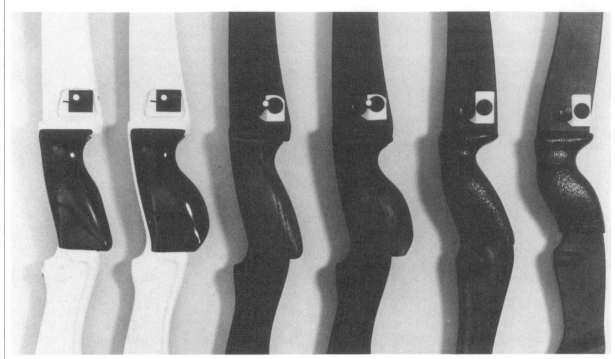

Most experienced compound-bow shooters insist on bow models with interchangeable grips to fit any hand size and shape. A comfortable grip is one key to very accurate shooting.

ment. A bow without provisions for quiver and adjustable-rest mounting can sometimes be altered to suit the customer at an archery pro shop.

In addition to standard threaded holes for sights, stabilizer, quiver, and arrow rest, top-quality hunting bows often have other features worth shopping for. These include adjustable draw weight in compound bows, factory camouflage finishes, a quick-takedown feature for convenient backpack bowhunting, and interchangeable bow grips to custom-fit the hand. Such options are not essential for bowhunting deer but certainly are good to have. When selecting any hunting bow, be sure to discuss these and similar features wih an archery dealer. He can help determine which will benefit you most.

DRAW WEIGHT

The heavier the draw weight of a bow, the faster that bow tends to shoot arrows and the more penetrating power the arrow has. In longbows and recurve bows, the draw weight rating of a bow is determined by how many pounds of pressure it takes to pull the bowstring back exactly 28 inches from the front side of the handle riser. In compound bows, draw weight is the same as peak weight—the maximum poundage it takes to pull a bow past half draw before the wheels roll over and drawing weight subsides. Although draw weight

and the arrow energy produced by a bow only roughly correlate, a deer hunter should follow some general guidelines to ensure that his bow produces the energy needed to cleanly kill an animal.

In recurve bows and longbows, where an archer must hold the full draw weight of his bow as he aims

RECOMMENDED DEER HUNTING DRAW WEIGHTS

RECURVE BOW

	Young Teenagers	Adult Women	Adult Men
To begin with	25–35	30–40	35–50
After lots of regular practice	30–40	35–45	45–60

COMPOUND BOW

	Young Teenagers	Adult Women	Adult Men
To begin with	30–40	35–45	45–60
After lots of regular practice	35–45	45–60	50–75

to shoot, the average adult male can comfortably and accurately use a bow with a draw weight of 50 to 55 pounds. Adult women usually perform best with bows of 40 to 50 pounds draw weight. When used with the proper arrow, a longbow or recurve bow of 40 to 55 pounds will drive arrows deep into deer for quick, humane kills.

Because compound bows let off in draw weight at full draw, hunters generally select bows with draw weights 10 to 15 pounds heavier than those they would otherwise use. Bows of 60 to 70 pounds are commonplace among adult men using compounds, and many women comfortably shoot compound bows of 50 or 55 pounds. Such heavier-draw bows yield deeper arrow penetration and the flatter arrow trajectory preferred by many archers.

The key to selecting a proper bowhunting draw weight is choosing a weight that is comfortable to

Most hunting bows are checked on this type machine at the factory for exact draw weight. This allows you to purchase gear with confidence and also figures in correct selection of hunting-arrow size.

Most compound bows allow draw-weight adjustment like this—with the turn of a sturdy Allen wrench. The adjustment feature lets a hunter choose draw-weight levels matching his own physical strength. Beginning bowhunters should leave draw-weight adjustment to a competent archery dealer.

An archery-store employee will use an ultra-accurate scale when changing and double-checking draw weights of bows. Draw-weight monitoring is important in compound bows with weight-adjustment capability.

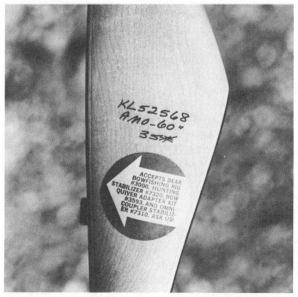

Look on the handle riser or lower limb to find the draw weight of a bow. This maple-handled recurve bow requires 35 pounds (note "35#") to draw the string a standard 28 inches from the front side of the bow.

shoot. A fellow who shakes like a bowl of jelly whenever he draws his 65-pound bow is not nearly as likely to hit a deer as the more practical hunter who chooses a 50-pound bow and aims with steady muscles and rock-solid precision. Fortunately for compound-bow users, most better bows allow draw weight adjustment over a 10- or 15-pound range. This lets archers experiment with draw weights to determine which suit them best, and also lets them raise bow poundage as their muscles strengthen with regular shooting practice.

The draw weight or weight-adjustment range of a hunting bow is normally marked on the handle riser or lower limb of the bow. Recurve or longbow users who habitually draw longer or shorter than 28 inches must add or subtract 3 pounds of draw weight for every inch longer or shorter than the standard 28-inch draw weight marked on a bow. For example, a long-armed archer who draws a 30-inch arrow in a recurve marked 50 pounds is actually holding 56 pounds on his bowstring fingers as he aims.

Every bowhunter must know the exact draw weight of his bow because this is vital when selecting the proper arrow to match that bow.

The "yardstick" method of determining draw length is easy to figure. The distance from the base of the throat to the tips of the outstretched fingers is the hunter's correct draw length.

DRAW LENGTH

Before any bowhunter buys a bow, he must determine precisely what his proper draw length is. There are two methods for accurately gauging draw length. One is called the "yardstick-against-the-throat" method; the other is the "knuckles-against-the-wall" method.

To use the "yardstick" method, an archer places one end of the yardstick against the base of his throat immediately above the collar bone. He holds the stick in this position between his fingertips with both arms fully outstretched directly in front of him as shown in the accompanying photo. The distance from the throat to the middle fingers of the outstretched hands will be the shooter's proper draw length.

Using the "knuckles" method requires the help of a friend. An archer stands facing at right angles to a wall with feet spread about 18 inches apart. Without leaning into the wall, he places his clenched bow hand (left hand for right-handed shooters) against the wall and turns his head to face the wall (see photo, right). A helper measures the exact distance from the wall to the right corner of the archer's mouth (left corner for left-handed shooters). This distance will be the proper bowhunting draw length.

Determining draw length is important for two reasons. First, a compound bow must be purchased with wheels or cams of the correct size to match the draw length of an individual shooter. Second, bowhunters cannot select hunting-arrow size or length without knowing their draw lengths ahead of time. In addition,

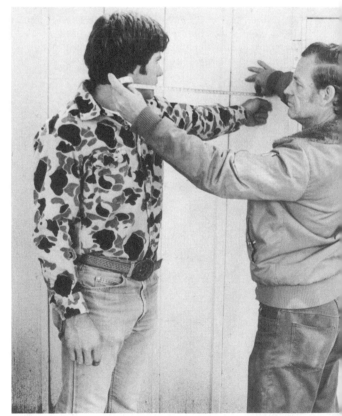

The "knuckles" method of pinpointing draw length is very accurate but requires a helper with a tape measure. The distance from the wall to the corner of the mouth is the proper draw length.

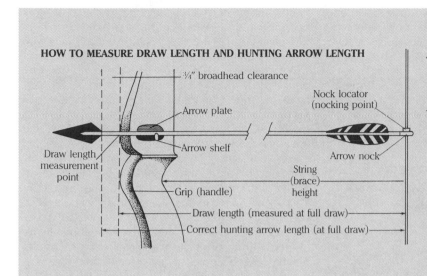

HOW TO MEASURE DRAW LENGTH AND HUNTING ARROW LENGTH

¾" broadhead clearance

Arrow plate

Nock locator
(nocking point)

Arrow shelf

Draw length
measurement
point

Arrow nock

String
(brace)
height

Grip (handle)

Draw length (measured at full draw)

Correct hunting arrow length (at full draw)

A bowhunter's draw length is the distance from the throat or bottom of the arrow nock to the front of the bow when he aims to take a shot. Arrows are generally cut ¾ inch longer than this to allow broadhead clearance during the draw.

bowhunters who prefer to use longbows or recurves cannot accurately determine the actual draw weights of these bows prior to buying them unless they know their draw length. Remember, a shooter with a 30-inch draw holds a full 56 pounds when using a recurve or longbow marked at an even 50 pounds.

Far too many hunters purchase their bows without considering draw length. The result is almost always a compound bow that draws too short or too long for proper shooting form, reasonable shooting comfort, or tolerable shooting accuracy. If the bow selected is a recurve bow or longbow, draw weight is seldom what the archer expects. It is either too light for adequate power on deer, or too heavy for painless and productive shooting. A hunter should know his draw length prior to purchasing any bow!

DETERMINING MASTER EYE

Most would-be bowhunters automatically assume that a right-handed person should shoot a right-handed bow and a left-handed person should shoot a left-handed bow. In the vast majority of cases this assumption in absolutely correct. However, the critical factor is choosing between a left-hand and right-hand bow should not be a shooter's favored hand at all—it should be his dominant, or master, eye.

In most instances, a right-handed person has a right dominant eye and a left-handed person has a left dominant eye. However, a fair number of shooters with right- or left-dominant hands have dominant eyes on the opposite sides. Since a hunter using a bow, gun, or any other shooting tool tends to aim automatically

Determining master eye is easy. First, you should point your finger at a distant object with both eyes open. Without moving, close one eye, and then open it and close the other. The eye that aligns with both target and finger is your master, or dominant, eye. A bowhunter with a right master eye must use a right-hand bow.

with his master eye, the shooter who crosses over between dominant hand and dominant eye tends to *crossfire,* or attempt to use his dominant eye to aim at an angle across a gun barrel or past a bowstring. Crossfiring is the kiss of death for archers and won't allow even mediocre accuracy. Avoid crossfiring at all costs when learning to shoot a bow.

The first step in eliminating a crossfiring inclination is to determine the master eye. To do this, a shooter

Proper bow accessories can make the difference between hunting success and failure. This archer used a bow quiver, stabilizer, and sights to drop his whitetail.

points his finger at a distant object with both eyes open. Next, he closes one eye at a time while continuing to point at the object. The eye that aligns with the finger and the target is the master eye.

With any luck at all, a hunter's master eye will be on the same side as his dominant hand. If it is not, he should buy a bow matching his master eye—not his dominant hand. A right-handed shooter with a left master eye should purchase a left-handed bow, and a left-handed shooter with a right master eye should purchase a right-handed bow. It's as simple as that.

In order to hit a target exactly, a bowhunter must align his dominant, aiming eye with the bowstring. This is impossible to do if the dominant eye is several inches to one side of the string because a wrong-handed hunting bow is being used. Fortunately, an archer with an opposite master eye and dominant hand quickly becomes accustomed to holding a bow in the nondominant hand in order to achieve dead-center bow-shooting accuracy.

OTHER TIPS FOR SELECTING BOWS

The final choice of a hunting bow almost always involves a few subjective factors only the shooter himself can evaluate. After trying several test bows at the archery store, a hunter usually decides that one *feels* better than the rest because the grip is more comfortable in his hand; or the bow seems to shoot more smoothly with less arrow-release recoil; or the bow seems to balance better in the hand before, during, and after a shot is taken. Perhaps one model is simply light enough to ease muscle strain or heavy enough to allow an especially steady aim. The careful archer selects his bow objectively according to factors previously discussed. But he also pays attention to small intangibles that make one hunting bow more comfortable to shoot than the rest.

HUNTING-BOW ACCESSORIES

A well-chosen deer bow without the proper accessories is no more effective than a new automobile is without decent tires and the correct kind of fuel. A few intelligently selected accessories for a pet hunting bow cost no more than an equal number of ill-chosen accessories, and they invariably make the critical difference between pleasant, accurate shooting and hair-tearing frustration.

When an archer purchases a deer-hunting bow, he should also buy several important add-on items. There are literally dozens of bow accessories sold at archery stores. Some of them are helpful and some are not. But to begin with, the shooter needs only eight or ten items to help ensure shooting and hunting success.

BOWSIGHT SELECTION

Prior to 1960, the use of sights on hunting bows was generally viewed with scorn. This was the heyday of the recurve bow and longbow—implements tradition-ally aimed and shot by "feel" instead of by mechanical precision. Today, the hunter *without* sights on his bow is very rare indeed. A bowsight allows equally precise aiming at a bull's-eye or a deer and is especially easy to use with compound hunting bows. These bows do not strain drawing muscles during a long, deliberate aim.

There are dozens of excellent hunting bowsights on the market, but the best have sturdy aluminum attachment brackets with four or five separate metal sight pins for different shooting ranges. Such pins are generally made of brass and have independent adjustment knobs for elevation and windage. Top-quality hunting sights invariably attach to a bow with two mounting screws. A few incorporate horizontal-bar rangefinding devices, which help determine the distance to nearby deer. But since most bowhunters today prefer optical rangefinders that they can carry on their belts, sight-attached rangefinders are really not an important bowsight accessory.

When selecting a hunting bowsight, avoid any

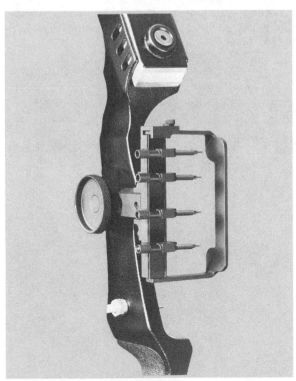

A hunting-bow sight should be made of metal to resist bending upon impact. Here a wrap-around guard protects the brass pins from accidental bumps on the target range and in the field.

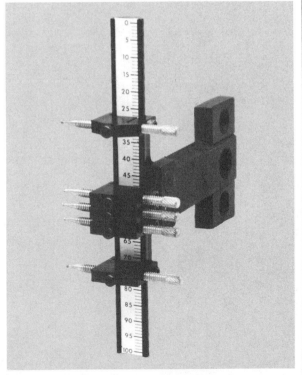

This five-pin bowsight is finely calibrated to ease the sighting-in process. It also features a rugged aluminum attachment bracket and independent adjustment for elevation and windage.

models with brackets or pins made of flimsy plastic or other fragile materials. A bowhunting sight should be stoutly constructed to survive plenty of rough-and-tumble use and abuse—otherwise, the device is apt to be out of kilter when that one all-important shot presents itself. *Simple* and *sturdy* are the two words to remember when choosing any multiple-pin bow-sight for hunting.

BOW STABILIZERS

A bow stabilizer is a short, stubby bar that screws to the front of a bow just below the grip section. A stabilizer performs two important functions. First, it helps eliminate accuracy-impairing bow torque during a shot—even when a hunter displays poor shooting form and visibly grabs the bow with his hand. Second, a stabilizer absorbs vibrations that naturally course through a bow as the limbs and bowstring snap taut—a function that lessens shooting noise and reduces bow recoil.

A myriad of hunting stabilizers are available at archery stores. Designs include simple bars of brass or steel, screw-cap models designed to hold survival gear, and spring-loaded styles that theoretically soak up more than the normal amount of shooting shock waves. A beginner can quickly become confused as he views this wide array of gimmicks dreamed up by clever marketing experts.

As in bowsights, simple and sturdy is best. A stabilizer should measure about 8 inches in overall length—a good compromise between effectiveness and carrying compactness—and should weigh between 6 and 16 ounces. The heavier the better, provided the physical weight does not seem to tire your arm or radically unbalance your bow. The best way to select a hunting-bow stabilizer is to try a few on the practice range of the archery dealership.

BOW STABILIZERS

Bow stabilizers vary considerably in length, weight, shape, and construction. Three common configurations are: a slender bar tipped by a heavy knob; a hollow design with internal add-on weights held in place by a silencing spring; and a simple, mildly tapering bar. All are effective on deer.

A bow stabilizer is screw-attached here below the hand grip to minimize hand torque during a shot. It also dampens shooting noise by absorbing vibrations that course through a bow. Shiny stabilizers, such as this one, must be camouflaged prior to hunting.

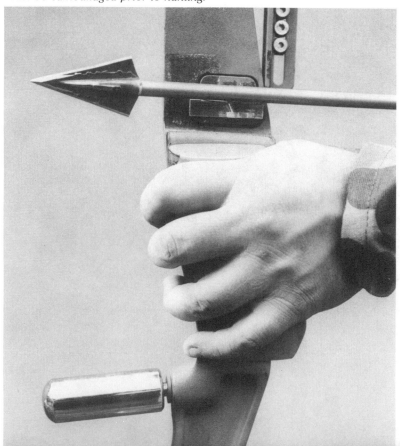

BOW QUIVERS

Over 95 percent of bowhunters carry their arrows in some sort of quiver attached directly to a bow. A bow-mounted quiver offers several important advantages, including carrying ease in the woods, quick access to arrows, and safe, silent storage of several backup shafts. Every beginning bowhunter should purchase one of these quivers when he buys his bow.

When selecting a bow quiver for deer hunting, look for these features. The quiver should fully enclose sharp hunting broadheads beneath a sturdy plastic or metal hood. This protects the archer from dangerous cuts, and protects the broadheads from rust-causing moisture or abrasion against trees, bushes, and similar outdoor obstacles. A bow quiver should also hold shafts individually in snug, rubber arrow grippers that absolutely prevent arrows from accidentally dislodging as an archer walks along. Such grippers also prevent arrow-against-arrow rattle when a bow is carried and shot—a sound guaranteed to alert deer.

BOW QUIVERS

A bow-mounted quiver like this one is the choice of most hunters. It keeps six or eight shafts within easy reach for backup shots, and allows convenient arrow transport no matter what the terrain or ground cover.

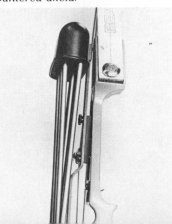

A good-quality bow quiver holds sharp hunting broadheads beneath a stout, roomy hood like this one. The hood protects the archer from accidental cuts, and shields broadheads from the edge-dulling moisture and abrasion that are often encountered afield.

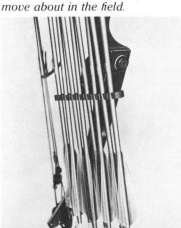

The best bow quivers hold shafts snugly and apart from each other in rubber grippers. This allows easy arrow access, prevents fletching from rattling noisily together, and guards against the danger of razor-sharp arrows dislodging as you move about in the field.

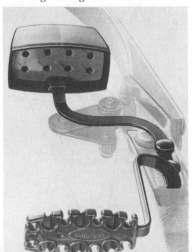

A decent bow quiver attaches solidly to a hunting bow to prevent noisy, game-spooking vibration during a shot. This model attaches directly to bowsight-mounting holes with two hand-tightening lock-down bolts.

A third feature all good bow quivers should have is a quiet sturdy mounting system. Most top-quality bow quivers bolt to a bow at two separate points to ensure solid, silent hookup. Quivers that attach at only one point must lock down with no rattle or play. Because a bow quiver rides to one side of a hunting bow and torques forward during a shot, it tends to vibrate loose during regular shooting unless mounted very securely.

The best bow quivers hold six or eight hunting arrows compactly and close at hand. They flare arrows just enough at the rear to prevent noisy fletching-to-fletching rattle, and cluster broadheads closely beneath the protective hood in a deep layer of good-quality foam rubber. Deer hunters seldom shoot away half a dozen arrows during the course of a single hunting day, but having extra shafts is good insurance in the event of unusual shooting flurries.

BOWSTRINGS AND ACCESSORIES

The average hunting bow comes complete from the factory with a fat bowstring consisting of 14 or 16 strong Dacron strands. Every hunting-bow design requires a string of a unique overall length, from 72 or 74 inches to accommodate longbows to somewhere between 30 and 43 inches to accommodate various compound bows.

A bowhunter should purchase one or two spare bowstrings of the proper size at the time he buys his bow. Bowstrings wear out over time, and sometimes break unexpectedly or become nicked or cut in the course of a hunting trip. Thus, a hunter should always have a replacement bowstring close at hand.

There's nothing complex about bowstring design, but serious archers choose their strings with care. The best and most durable strings have monofilament wrapping in the middle to protect the strands from finger wear, and have looped ends similarly wrapped

with nylon or Dacron thread. Such wrapping is called *serving,* and should be inspected before you buy the bowstring to make certain it is not frayed and is tightly wrapped about the bowstring. One or two well-made backup bowstrings cost very little but sometimes make the difference between a successful bowhunt and a disappointing disaster. One careless swipe with a razor-sharp broadhead can reduce a hunter's bow to a heap of tangled parts.

Replacing a bowstring is easy if a hunter owns the proper bowstringing tool. Since every bow make and

Restringing any hunting bow requires an appropriate bow-stringing device. For example, most recurve bows are strung and unstrung with a rope-type stringer that slips over the tips of the limbs.

BOWSTRING SELECTION TABLE

Draw weight of bow (lbs.)	Number of Dacron strands
25–35	10
35–45	12
45–55	14
55–70	16
70–85	18

Rubber bowstring silencers are a must for quiet bow performance. Three popular styles are (bottom to top): a cluster of "catwhisker" filaments similar to those used in bass-plug skirts; a flexible one-piece silencer with vibration-absorbing fingers; and a flat, V-shaped wrap-around silencer.

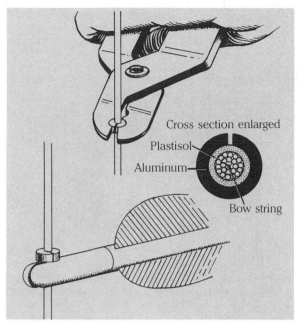

A clamp-on nock locator is practical in bowhunting. It will not slip accidentally but allows easy adjustment so that you can fine-tune your bow/arrow combination.

model is at least slightly different in design, there are several dozen varieties of bowstringing tools available. When buying a bow, a hunter should also buy a bowstringing tool that matches his bow. This tool will ensure quick, easy string changing without the possibility of damage to the bow or danger to the archer.

Rubber bowstring silencers should also be purchased and installed before a hunting bow is shot. Several styles of silencers are currently being sold, but the most popular by far are so-called "catwhisker" silencers. They are composed of tiny rubber filaments similar to those in the skirts of bass plugs. Silencers absorb most of the guitarlike twang made by a string during a shot, calming a shooter's nerves and reducing the chance that deer will hear a bowstring strum and so wheel to run away. Since bowstring silencers alter the way a bowstring vibrates and oscillates once it leaves a shooter's fingers, silencers must be installed prior to shooting to prevent changes in the way a hunting bow casts its arrows. Silencers should also be attached to spare bowstrings to eliminate frustrating equipment inconsistencies later on.

One other gizmo should be installed on a hunting bowstring at the time the bow is selected. This is the nock locator, sometimes called the nocking point. Such a locator ensures consistent arrow nocking on the bowstring from shot to shot, which in turn leads to accurate shooting on targets and game.

There are several varieties of nock locators sold at archery stores, but the most practical and popular is a clamp-on model. This consists of an aluminum-alloy ring cushioned underneath by a thin layer of plastisol (pliable rubber). When securely clamped to the bowstring with special nocking-point pliers, this nock locator stays firmly put and lets a shooter nock arrows beneath it with machinelike consistency. Unlike other nock locator designs, the clamp-on variety can be moved about later as a hunter carefully tunes his bow. To begin with, most archery dealers will set a nock locator on the string about ⅜-inch above right angles to the arrow rest—an average location that promotes decent arrow flight as a hunter learns his bow-shooting basics.

ARROW RESTS

An arrow rest holds and guides an arrow as it is drawn and shot at the target. Every arrow rest consists of two basic parts—the shelf, on which the bottom of an arrow shaft rests; and the plate, against which the side of an arrow shaft rests.

ARROW RESTS

Simple, nonadjustable arrow rests seldom provide decent arrow-flight characteristics. They also tend to wear out quickly with regular shooting. Although most top-quality hunting bows come from the factory with one-piece rests attached, for best shooting results the factory-installed rests should be replaced at once.

A springy rest has different springs designed to match exact bow poundage. The rest itself is virtually indestructible and yields excellent arrow flight when properly adjusted. Some springy rests come complete with Teflon sleeves that slip over the rest/plate section to ensure quiet arrow passage across contact points.

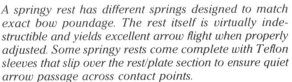

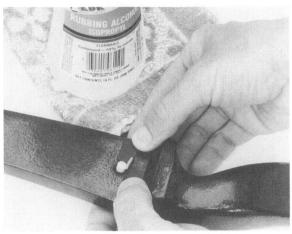

The flipper portion of a flipper/plunger combination rest (left) is adhesive-backed for easy installation. Once the rest area on a bow has been cleaned with rubbing alcohol, a flipper will securely attach in place. The plunger portion (below) of an arrow rest consists of a Teflon plate button and a spring-loaded plunger arm that move in and out of a threaded housing under spring tension. When screw-attached to a bow, the plunger helps cushion arrow vibration during shots, and this leads to improved accuracy.

Selection of an adequate arrow rest is one of the most critical factors in first-rate bow-shooting accuracy. Unfortunately, most bow manufacturers ship their products with second-rate, one-piece rests attached. Cutting arrow-rest quality is a sin even the best bowyers are guilty of, and the biggest favor any bowhunter can do himself is to replace a cheap factory rest with a sturdy, accurate, and fully adjustable model instead.

Arrow rests to be avoided on hunting bows include most one-piece wonders made of molded rubber or plastic. Such rests do not allow fine plate adjustment for accurate bow tuning, and tend to quickly break or chew away with repeated shooting. Far too many deer hunters struggle along until these factory-supplied rests fall off or fall apart. It's better to discard them at once and start from scratch.

There are several top-notch arrow rests to choose from. The very best and most fully adjustable of the lot are the springy rest and the flipper/cushion-plunger combination.

The springy rest consists of a threaded brass or aluminum adjustment arm attached to a simple coil of spring steel. This coil acts as the plate portion of the rest. The end of the spring coil extends outward from the plate section to form a shelf for the arrow to rest upon. The springy arrow rest is horizontally adjustable with a turn of its threaded arm, and the coil-spring construction of this simple plate/shelf configuration helps cushion an arrow as it is launched to enhance shooting accuracy.

Springy rests are available in different spring gauges from 10 through 25 ounces. Most deer hunters find that 15-ounce or 20-ounce springy rests are most accurate for bows in the 50- to 70-pound draw-weight category. Because a springy rest is an all-metal design with bearing surfaces made of hardened steel, this rest is almost indestructible.

The flipper/cushion-plunger combination rest is less durable but slightly more accurate than the springy rest. This is a two-piece rest consisting of a spring-loaded, straight-wire shelf that flattens out as an arrow passes by, and a fully screw-adjustable, spring-loaded metal-and-Teflon plate portion that can be moved in and out of the bow's handle-riser section. The flipper shelf on this particular rest attaches to the bow with good-quality adhesive backing.

As will be explained in the upcoming section on tuning a hunting bow, both springy rests and flipper/plunger rests promote the easiest and most accurate hunting-bow tuning.

In addition to these two primary full-adjustment rests used by many bowhunters, a few one-piece arrow rests are also acceptable when attached to recurve bows and longbows. Among these are the adhesive-backed Pro Rest and Super-Pro Rest by Hoyt, which have been dependable standbys for many, many years. Although not adjustable like the springy rest and flipper/cushion-plunger combination, these alternate rests do incorporate durable Teflon and yield good service on bows that are not drilled to accept more versatile, screw-adjustable rest designs.

CABLE GUARDS AND CABLE SAVERS

A cable guard is a simple, slim-line bar that extends backward from a compound-bow handle riser. Such a guard performs two important fucntions on compound bows. First, it holds compound cables well away from the path of a fully drawn arrow, which contributes to decent accuracy. Second, it quiets noisy cable strum typical of some compound models. If the bow you decide to buy does not have a cable guard, ask your archery dealer if one should be installed. Some compound models are designed to function without a cable guard, but others perform better with one.

The only other major hunting-bow accessory an archer should consider is a so-called "cable saver" device. This small nylon or plastic gizmo is meant to be used in conjunction with a compound-bow cable guard and reduces wear caused by contact with the metal guard. A cable saver costs next to nothing but can easily triple the life of cables in a regularly used compound bow.

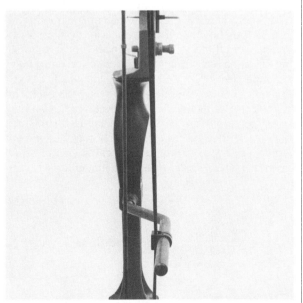

A cable guard is a simple metal bar extending backward from the handle riser of a compound bow. This bar holds compound cables well away from an arrow's path to ensure accurate, nonwobbly flight.

ARROWS FOR HUNTING

The hunting arrow is undoubtedly the single most important part of any archer's gear. The correct arrow will fly with superb accuracy from a wide range of hunting bows, but improperly chosen arrow just will not fly well no matter how expensive or skilfully designed the bow happens to be. A bowhunter can get along just fine with a sound but moderately priced bow, but he should never, never skimp on the quality of arrows he shoots at deer.

A hunting arrow is composed of four separate parts—a central shaft section, a nock and fletching glued to the rear of the shaft, and some sort of arrowhead affixed to the front. Like the links of a chain, all of these components must be first-rate for the arrow as a whole to do its job correctly.

ARROW NOCKS

Beginning at the very rear of the arrow is a plastic nock that slips or snaps securely over the bowstring. A nock is a small, seemingly insignificant part of a hunting arrow and weighs less than 2 percent of the overall arrow's weight. However, this little rear-end attachment can make or break accurate shooting.

A serious bowhunter must look for two important features in all the nocks. First, nocks must snap securely over a bowstring to ensure safe and convenient shooting. Second, nocks should be top-quality designs that glue precisely in line with arrow shafts each and every time. Extensive tests by several major archery manufacturers have determined that an arrow nock only a few thousandths of an inch out of alignment with a shaft can promote noticeably erratic arrow flight. For trouble-free shooting, a hunter must be cer-

Millions of factory-assembled arrows are sold each year to hunters. Some are well-made products and others are marginal offerings that hamper an archer's ability to hit what he shoots at. Getting the best of the lot requires a careful, systematic procedure.

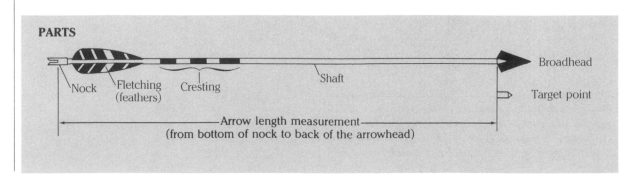

PARTS

Nock | Fletching (feathers) | Cresting | Shaft | Broadhead | Target point

Arrow length measurement
(from bottom of nock to back of the arrowhead)

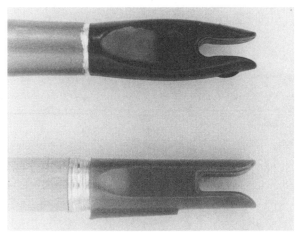

Arrow nocks vary considerably in appearance, from streamlined models with pleasantly curving surfaces to slab-sided designs with rough-hewn features. However, any nock is acceptable if it is glued on true and snaps snugly to a string.

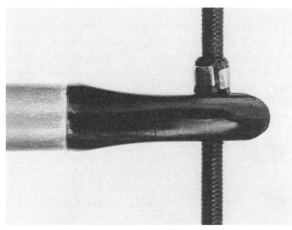

A nock that grips a bowstring (under nock locator shown) securely is not apt to fall off accidentally. This helps prevent broadhead cuts—which can be harmful or fatal—and also ensures smooth, unimpeded shooting at deer.

tain his arrow nocks snap to a string and align correctly.

Unfortunately, quite a few el cheapo arrow nock styles are attached to factory hunting arrows or are sold separately over the counter. Some of these show noticeable warping when inspected carefully. Others slide over a bowstring in loose, sloppy fashion, virtually guaranteeing that hunting arrows will fall off the bowstring—usually at the worst possible times.

A few nocks incorporate small indexes, or wings, so that hunters can nock arrows properly by feel instead of looking down to rotate each arrow fletching correctly before nocking the arrow. Such indexes are a definite aid that many bowhunters prefer.

ARROW FLETCHING

The feathers or plastic vanes on the rear of a hunting arrow create the air resistance or drag necessary to spiral the arrow in flight for consistent shooting accuracy. Such fletching must be of the proper shape, size, and material for true arrow flight, and must also be attached correctly to a shaft or erratic performance results.

Nearly all modern hunting arrows are fletched with plastic vanes of a streamlined, parabolic shape. A few archers still use feather fletching instead, especially those hunting with longbows and recurve bows. Plastic fletching is many times more durable than feather fletching, does not flatten out or mat down in damp weather, and effectively steers an arrow on a true, unveering path. Feather fletching is advisable with longbows and recurve bows because it flattens to closely pass the bow handle section and therefore doesn't throw an arrow off course. But feather fletching tends to fray and tatter with regular shooting, and must be waterproofed with silicone or hair spray whenever inclement weather is expected. Stiffer, less yielding plastic vanes work best with compound bows because such bows usually have more of a "center-shot" handle riser. This style allows vanes to pass by the handle

Modern plastic arrow vanes are impervious to snow, rainwater, and other forms of moisture that wilt older-style feather fletching. As a result, most archers insist on plastic fletching for deer hunting.

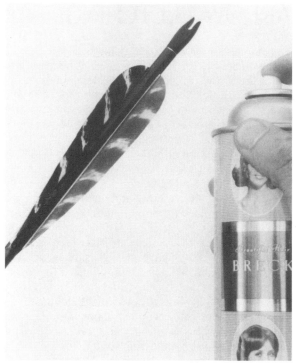

Feather fletching must be coated with hair spray or silicone to help prevent matting in excessively damp hunting conditions.

Fletching on deer-hunting arrows must be 5 inches long and strongly spiraled to create stabilizing rear-end drag in flight. Big deer-hunting broadheads are especially prone to fly erratically unless matched with large, spiraling fletching.

without colliding severely enough to throw the arrow off course.

Although a few bowhunters prefer to shoot arrows with four fletches, the standard three-fletched arrows commonly used for deer hunting cannot be beat for accuracy. The only drawback of a three-fletched arrow is the fact that the cock vane, which is usually a different color than the other two, must be pointed away from the bow each time the arrow is nocked. Otherwise, this vane will collide with the bow and ruin ac-

curacy. By contrast, four-fletched arrows will neatly clear a bow no matter how they are nocked.

Arrow fletching must be a full 5 inches long to ensure arrow stability, and should noticeably spiral around a shaft instead of being glued in a straight line. Fletching less than 5 inches long and/or fletching that does not spiral an arrow in flight will usually fail to promote top shooting accuracy—especially when deer-hunting broadheads are used.

ARROW SHAFTS

The arrow shaft is the single most important part of any hunting arrow. The weight, stiffness, and straightness of a shaft all contribute to or detract from accurate shooting. A bowhunter should carefully choose arrows with proper shafts to avoid major bow-shooting headaches.

There are currently three major types of shaft material used by arrow manufacturers. Hunting archers should be aware of the pluses and minuses of each.

Wooden shafts. Shafts of wood hark back to prehistoric times when the bow itself came into use. Modern wooden arrow shafts are usually made from cedar logged along the northern coast of Oregon. This cedar is inexpensive, is fairly light in weight, and has very straight grain. But the reason cedar shafts can still be purchased at some archery stores is that they are cheap.

For any serious hunter, cedar shafts represent false economy. The shafts tend to break or splinter whenever they hit solid objects like logs, trees, and rocks. Also, cedar shafts tend to warp or twist in damp weather. On top of these drawbacks, cedar shafts are never identical in straightness, physical weight, and innate stiffness—factors that must be consistent for consistent accuracy.

A few nostalgic bowhunters use cedar shafts with longbows and recurve bows, and others purchase such shafts in a futile attempt to save money. However, in the long run an archer will spend less money and achieve better accuracy with shafts made of modern materials.

Fiberglass shafts. Arrow shafts made of tubular fiberglass are touted by manufacturers as the strongest and most durable available. This may be true, but a relatively small percentage of bowhunters go after deer with them because fiberglass is a heavy material that produces a looping arrow trajectory. There is also a pronounced lack of quality control on factors important to accuracy—rigid straightness, consistency of weight, and consistency of stiffness. But fiberglass arrow shafts are impervious to moisture and are not bent by hitting solid objects.

Fans of these shafts are quick to point out that fiberglass is either straight or broken—never bent after a missed shot or when an animal rolls onto it after being hit. Unfortunately, the average top-grade fiberglass shaft is already 10 to 20 thousandths of an inch out of straightness at the time of purchase, and this creates accuracy problems for the very best bowhunters.

Aluminum shafts. The most expensive arrow shafts on the market are made of aircraft-grade aluminum tubing. However, despite their relatively high cost, aluminum shafts are currently used by over 90 percent of all bowhunters. The reason is abundantly clear to any serious shooter—aluminum shafts are the most accurate available today.

Top-grade aluminum arrow shafts are drawn to size in successive stages from 1-inch tubular stock. This procedure work-hardens the metal and prepares it for a special heat-treating process. The end result is a lightweight, tubular shaft that is rigidly uniform in weight, strength, stiffness, and straightness. The average XX75 aluminum hunting shaft—the favorite of most archers—is straight within .003-inch over its entire 33-inch length and weighs exactly the same as any other shaft of the same designated size. Such a shaft is also identical to others in stiffness—a fact that can be tested with a simple arrow-spining machine. The result of such rigid manufacturing perfection is extremely accurate shooting on both targets and deer. It's no wonder that all state, national, and international archery tournaments in recent history have been won with top-quality aluminum arrow shafts.

Aluminum shafts do bend slightly under heavy im-

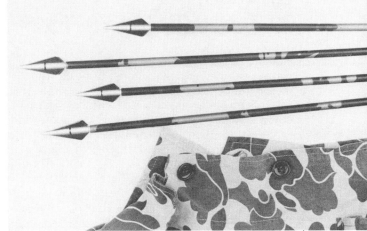

Modern aluminum arrow shafts are dull-anodized in several woodsy colors. One popular pattern is a patchwork of medium green and black, which camouflage.

The XX75-alloy shaft is considered standard bowhunting equipment. The aluminum shaft is drawn from the best quality aircraft tubing and is usually marked with its size as well as alloy designation somewhere near the fletching area.

pact, but can be quickly straightened at any archery pro shop for a small fee. Shafts are anodized in a wide variety of dull, woodsy colors to help bowhunters hide from deer. Another plus is the fact that aluminum shafts are manufactured in over 30 different hunting sizes to match any hunter's specific arrow-size or arrow-weight preference.

The only disadvantage of aluminum shafting is its cost, but aluminum arrows are affordable initially and are cheaper to use over the long haul because they don't splinter like wood and seldom break into pieces like fiberglass. Bowhunters in-the-know insist on arrows with good-quality aluminum shafts.

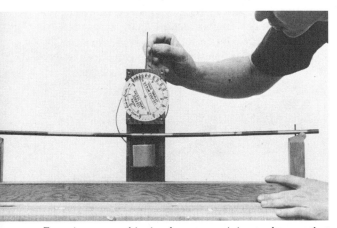

Experiments on this simple arrow-spining tool prove that aluminum shafts are rigidly consistent in stiffness. Such consistency yields superb shooting accuracy on both targets and game—accuracy that cannot be equaled by other shaft materials.

ARROWHEAD ATTACHMENT SYSTEMS

Hunting arrowheads are attached to arrows in one of two ways—they are either glued in place with hot-melt ferrule cement, or screwed into the ends of arrows. Screw-attachment of arrowheads is far more convenient than glue-on attachment, but some of the very best deer-hunting broadheads sold today must be glued to arrows or glued to screw-in adapters.

With wooden hunting shafts, an archer has little choice but to buy glue-on arrowheads and attach these to the 5-degree tapers on the shaft ends. With fiberglass and aluminum, a hunter can choose between arrow-end inserts that allow screw-attachment or the older-style glue-on attachment. Unless a hunter prefers a specific type of arrowhead that must be glued on, he is best advised to have his archery dealer set up shafts for easy screw-attachment.

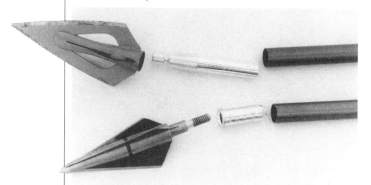

There are two basic ways to attach arrowheads to arrow shafts—old-style gluing (top) and the more modern screw-attachment. Once glue-on or screw-in adapters are cemented to the ends of arrow shafts, arrowheads can be installed.

SHAFT STIFFNESS

Matching arrow-shaft stiffness to a particular hunting bow is vitally important to accuracy. Arrow manufacturers have devised complex shaft-selection charts to aid the archer in choosing shafts of the proper stiffness—an impossibility without such expert guidance.

When a hunting arrow is released, the shaft flexes slightly as the bowstring propels the arrow from the rear end and sends it sizzling out of the bow. The degree of this arrow flex (called archer's paradox) must be exactly right or the arrow will wobble side-to-side after it leaves the bow. For this reason, selecting the wrong size generally results in badly missed shots and/or poor penetration of game.

SHAFT SIZE

In order to select the correct shaft size to match his hunting bow, an archer must know his exact draw length and the exact draw weight of his bow. Once these two statistics are plugged into the appropriate columns on a shaft-selection chart, determining the correct arrow size with the proper stiffness is easy and automatic.

In the case of aluminum hunting arrows, more than one shaft size of near-identical stiffness might fly well from a given hunting bow. This allows the archer to select a lightweight shaft for flatter trajectory or a heavier shaft for deeper penetration on large-bodied deer. Generally speaking, bowhunters are best off choosing medium to heavy arrow shafts unless they plan to bowhunt deer in open country where shots over 30 or 40 yards are the exception instead of the rule. A light, fast shaft tends to be less stable and slightly less accurate than a heavier shaft, and most definitely penetrates less deeply than a heavier shaft which retains more of its initial in-flight energy.

Once a deer hunter determines which arrow-shaft size is best, he should have his archery dealer cut off shafts ¾-inch longer than his draw length and install screw-in or glue-on inserts in the shaft ends. A dozen arrows is plenty to begin shooting with, although most hunters start deer season with two or three dozen shafts.

PARTING NOTE

To recap, a serious deer-hunting archer should buy arrows with top-quality snap-on nocks, noticeably spiraling fletching 5 inches long, and good-grade aluminum shafts. Shaft size should be carefully chosen by consulting a shaft-selection chart to ensure top-notch accuracy. Once shafts have been cut to length at the archery store and fitted with glue-on or screw-in arrowhead inserts, they are ready to shoot.

A bowhunter should ask his archery dealer to cut arrow shafts to proper length on a high-speed cut-off tool of this type. The tool ensures consistent arrow length and a square arrow-end cut. This makes for precise, accurate arrowhead alignment.

EASTON ALUMINUM HUNTING SHAFT SELECTION TABLE

This Easton table tells you which shaft size or sizes will fly well from your hunting bow at your personal draw length. Without such a table, you have next to no chance of choosing arrows that will fly accurately. The shaft size in boldface type of each box is the most widely used, but you may decide to shoot a lighter shaft for flatter trajectory, or a heavier shaft or greater durability. Also, large variations in bow efficiency, bow design, shooting style, and release may require special bow tuning or a shaft size change to accommodate these variations.

ACTUAL BOW WEIGHT (At your draw length)	CORRECT HUNTING ARROW LENGTH (Your draw length plus ½- to ¾-inch clearance)																COMPOUND BOW PEAK WEIGHT	
	26½–27½ 27"		27½–28½ 28"		28½–29½ 29"		29½–30½ 30"		30½–31½ 31"		31½–32½ 32"		32½–33½ 33"		33½–34½ 34"			
	Shaft† size	Arrow‡ weight	Shaft† size	Arrow‡ weight	Shaft† size	Arrow‡ weight	Shaft† size	Arrow‡ weight	Shaft† size	Arrow‡ weight	Shaft† size	Arrow‡ weight	Shaft† size	Arrow‡ weight	Shaft† size	Arrow‡ weight	30% let-off	50% let-off
35–39	1913* 1815□ **1816**	415 424 440	1913* 1915□ **1916** 1818	426 447 471 490	2013* **1916** 1917□	451 481 501	2114 **2016** 8.4^M 1917□ 1918	486 507 508 511 537	**2114** 2016 2115□ 1918 8.5^M	496 517 524 549 565	2213* 2115□ **2018** 8.6^M	505 535 583 619	**2213*** 2117	514 587			41–46	47–52
40–44	1913* 1915□ **1916** 1818	415 438 461 478	2013* **1916** 1917□ 1820**	442 471 490 530	2114 **2016** 8.4^M 1917□ 1918	476 496 497 501 526	**2114** 2016 2115□ 1918 8.5^M	486 507 513 537 553	2213* 2016 **2018** 8.6^M	495 524 571 612	2213* **2117** 2018 8.7^M	505 575 583 675	**2117** 2216	587 587			47–52	53–59
45–49	2013* **1916** 1917□ 1820**	433 461 479 517	2114 **2016** 8.4^M 1917□ 1918	466 486 487 490 514	2114 **2016** 2115□ 8.5^M 1920**	476 496 502 541 559	2213* 2115□ **2018** 8.6^M	485 513 558 598	2213* **2117** 2018 2020 8.7^M	495 563 571 609 660	2117 **2216** 2020 8.7^M	575 575 622 675	**2216** 2217□	587 609	2219	658	53–58	60–66
50–54	2114 **2016** 1917□ 1918	456 475 479 503	2114 **2016** 8.4^M 2115□ 1920**	466 486 487 492 546	2213* 2115□ 8.5^M **2018** 1920**	475 502 541 546 559	2213* **2117** 2018 2020 8.6^M	485 551 558 595 598	2117 **2216** 2020 8.7^M	563 563 609 660	2216 2217□ 8.7^M	575 596 675	2216 2217□ **2219**	587 609 644	2219	658	59–64	67–72
55–59	2114 **2016** 8.4^M 2115□ 1920**	456 475 477 481 534	2213* 2115□ 8.5^M **2018** 1920**	465 492 529 534 546	2213* **2117** 2018 2020 8.6^M	475 539 546 582 585	2117 **2116** 2020 8.7^M	551 551 595 645	**2216** 2217□ 8.7^M	563 584 660	2216 2217□ **2219**	575 596 631	2217□ **2219**	609 644	2317 2219	648 658	65–70	73–79
60–64	2213* 8.4^M 2115□ **2018** 1920**	455 477 481 522 534	2213* **2117** 8.5^M 2018 2020	465 527 529 534 568	2117 **2216** 2020 8.6^M	539 539 582 585	**2216** 2217□ 8.7^M	551 571 645	2216 2217□ **2219** 8.7^M	563 584 617 660	2217□ **2219**	596 631	**2317** 2219	634 644	2317	648	71–76	80–86
65–69	2213* **2117** 2018 2020	455 515 522 555	2117 **2216** 2020 8.6^M	527 527 568 571	**2216** 2217□ 8.7^M	539 558 629	2216 2217□ **2219** 8.7^M	551 571 603 645	2217□ **2219**	584 617	**2317** 2219	621 631	**2317**	634	2317	648	77–82	87–93
70–74	2117 **2216** 2020	515 515 555	**2216** 2217□	527 546	2216 2217□ **2219**	539 558 589	2217□ **2219**	571 603	**2317** 2219	607 617	**2317**	621	**2317**	634	2419	685	83–88	94–100
75–79	**2216** 2217□	515 533	**2216** 2217□ 2219	527 546 575	2217□ **2219**	558 589	2317 **2219**	594 603	**2317**	607	**2317**	621	2419	670	2419	685	89–94	101–107
80–84	**2216** 2217□ 2219	515 533 562	2217□ **2219**	546 575	2317 **2219**	580 589	**2317**	594	**2317**	607	2419	656	2419	670	2419	685	95–100	108–114
85–89	2217□ **2219**	533 562	2317 **2219**	567 575	**2317**	580	**2317**	594	2419	641	2419	656	2419	670			101–106	115–121
90–94	2317 **2219**	553 562	2317	567	2317	580	2419	627	2419	641	2419	656					107–112	122–128
95–99	**2317**	553	2317	567	2419	612	2419	627	2419	641							113–118	129–135
100–109	2317	553	2419	597	2419	612	2419	627									119–129	136–149
110–119	2419	583	2419	597	2419	612											139–142	150–163

*Available in XX75 only. **Available in GAME GETTER only. □Indicates Jim Dougherty "Naturals" †NOTE: The shaft sizes 1815 through 2419 are contractions of actual physical dimensions of the tubes. (Example: **2016** has a **20**/64″ outside diameter and a .**016**″ wall thickness.) ‡NOTE: The arrrow weight in grains (437.5 grains per ounce) includes a 125-grain broadhead, 30-grain insert and 35 grains (average between plastic vanes and feathers) for nock and fletching. 8.4^M, 8.5^M, 8.6^M and 8.7^M are Bear Metric Magnum & Metric Hunter shaft sizes. The indicated spines are recommended by Bear Archery.

This table tells you which shaft size or sizes will fly well from your hunting bow at your personal draw length. Without such a table, you have next to no chance of choosing arrows that will be accurate.

DEER HUNTING ARROWHEADS

Experienced bowhunters use several types of arrowheads to fulfill a variety of target-shooting and in-the-field requirements. Arrowheads include broadheads, field points, steel and rubber blunts, and Judo points. A bowhunter should learn when and where to use each type of head.

THE HUNTING BROADHEAD

A broadhead is a streamlined, multibladed arrowhead designed to penetrate and drop deer with quick, humane efficiency. Although bowhunters use several other sorts of arrowheads for target practice and secondary pursuits, choosing the proper deer-hunting broadhead is most important. A hunting broadhead can be every bit as accurate as a target point and every bit as effective on game as a big-bore rifle bullet—provided this head is properly designed. When selecting deer-hunting broadheads, a bowhunter should insist on the following positive features:

Accurate design. Because broadheads are relatively large, multibladed arrowheads, they tend to catch air in flight. This can steer speeding arrows off course in the same way a rudder steers a ship. Erratic arrow flight caused by excessive, uneven action of air on broadhead blades is called planing, and it can frustrate a bowhunter to tears as broadhead-tipped arrows dip, dart, and swerve through the air instead of flying true to the mark.

Of primary importance in choosing an accurate hunting broadhead is matching the weight of the head to the weight of other arrowheads regularly used. A hunter cannot tune his bow to shoot 125-grain field points and expect 145-grain broadheads to fly even moderately well. If a favorite hunting broadhead weighs 145 grains, field points, blunts, and other heads must weigh the same so that a bow shoots all with equally clean, accurate arrow flight.

Some broadhead models are inherently more accurate than others because they are aerodynamically designed to minimize the effects of air on the blades. When choosing any hunting broadhead, look for the following: First, the overall design should be clean and streamlined like a rocket, with no obvious friction-causing elements such as flat frontal surfaces and ultrawide blade extensions. Second, overall diameter of a broadhead should never exceed 1½ inches, with 1⅛ to 1¼ inches being optimum for the best accuracy. Third, broadhead blades with vents or cutouts tend to promote the most accurate, nonplaning flight be-

This big mule deer buck was shot at 50 yards with a streamlined broadhead design. The arrowhead did an excellent job of penetrating both lungs for a near-instant kill.

THE HUNTING BROADHEAD

A knowledgeable hunter insists upon certain broadhead characteristics. This popular deer-hunting head has 11 positive features well worth considering—features yielding accurate flight, dependable performance, and trouble-free attachment and maintenance.

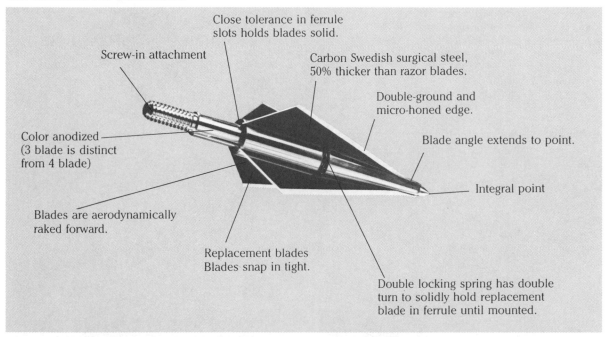

Screw-in attachment

Close tolerance in ferrule slots holds blades solid.

Carbon Swedish surgical steel, 50% thicker than razor blades.

Double-ground and micro-honed edge.

Color anodized (3 blade is distinct from 4 blade)

Blade angle extends to point.

Integral point

Blades are aerodynamically raked forward.

Replacement blades
Blades snap in tight.

Double locking spring has double turn to solidly hold replacement blade in ferrule until mounted.

The proper broadhead will fly like a missile and bring down deer with machinelike dependability. The wrong head will cause a world of problems.

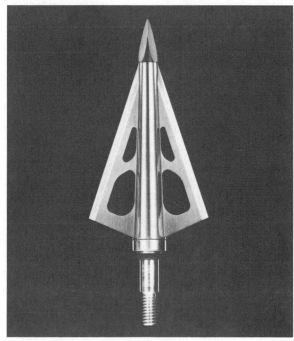

Some large hunting broadheads incorporate blade vents or cutouts like these to allow horizontal air flow as heads rotate during flight. This helps ensure accurate shooting.

HOW TO SHARPEN ARROWHEADS

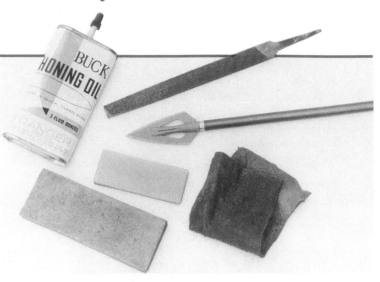

To properly sharpen a broadhead to hair-shaving keenness, you need a coarse mill file, good-quality honing oil, medium and fine sharpening stones, and a rectangle of leather.

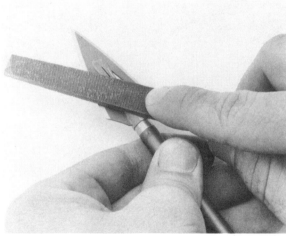

1. *Broadhead edges should be filed to an approximate 22-degree angle. Use the back of the broadhead center section (ferrule) as a file guide during the operation to get the correct angle.*

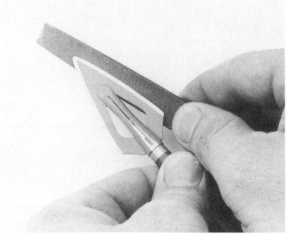

2. *File the tip to a spade to make it strong and to guard against tip curling on collision with a deer's heavier bones. Finally, the file should be drawn backwards along all edge tapers to remove the majority of filing burrs.*

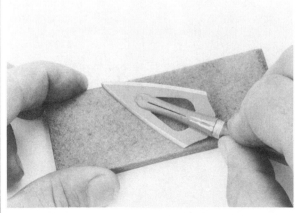

3. *The first honing phase is accomplished on a medium-grit stone, such as this good quality Arkansas stone. Again, the broadhead ferrule should be pressed against the stone to ensure a consistent honing angle.*

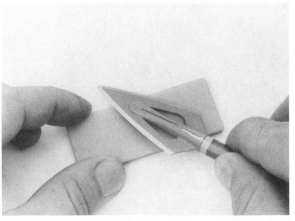

4. *Final honing should take place on a hard, fine-grained finishing stone. At the end of this process, all file marks should be gone from the edge tapers, and the cutting edges should reflect no light at all.*

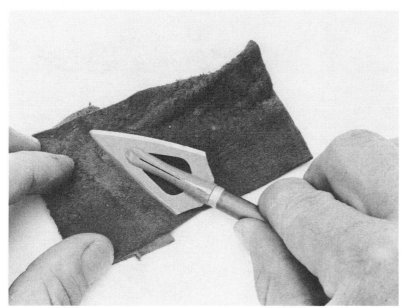

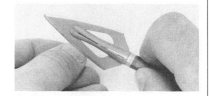

5. *To finish off the edges, each blade taper should be stroked* backward *along a piece of leather. This step, called stropping, removes microscopic honing burrs and produces a super-keen cutting edge.*

6. *To test sharpness of a broadhead: If all edges grab a thumbnail (top) instead of sliding smoothly over it, the head is adequately sharp. Or if edges easily slice medium-weight paper, or neatly sever a stretched rubber band with very little downward pressure, they're ready to take afield. Some bowhunters prefer to test broadhead edges by shaving a little hair from an arm or leg, but this procedure can be dangerous.*

cause such vents allow through-the-blade air flow.

If a broadhead conforms to the foregoing, if all arrowheads weigh the same, and if a bow is tuned to shoot such arrowheads without wobble, broadheads should fly extremely well.

Broadhead durability. A hunting broadhead must be accurate, and it must also be strongly constructed to penetrate a deer's muscle, gristle, and bone without bending or breaking apart on impact.

A surprisingly high percentage of the broadhead designs currently sold are far too flimsy for practical bowhunting use. The weak point in these broadheads is blade design. Many heads have paper-thin blades that crack or disintegrate as they enter a deer, destroying or limiting their ability to cut a decent killing hole. When selecting a broadhead, an archer must be certain the blades are at least .015-inch thick for adequate strength, though .020 to .025 inches thick is preferable.

The most rugged hunting broadheads also have stout, beefy center sections with hardened steel noses that resist bending or curling to the side upon impact. A careful, commonsense inspection of various designs will reveal a lot. And some serious shooting into target bales, dirt banks, and rotten stumps with a few experimental broadheads will quickly show which withstand the most bowhunting abuse. Any head that breaks or bends easily upon impact won't drop deer worth a hoot, and should be avoided.

Broadhead durability is especially important in

hunting areas with hard or rocky ground, lots of trees, or other obstacles that can be hit with misdirected shots. It is convenient and less expensive in such situations to shoot stout broadheads instead of "one-shot heads" that self-destruct upon impact with almost anything in sight.

Keen cutting edges. In order to do its job correctly, a big-game broadhead must have blades that are honed to a scalpel-sharp, hair-shaving edge. Such an edge promotes massive blood loss and tissue damage in deer for efficient, humane kills.

About half of all hunting broadhead models currently available come fully sharpened from the factory. The other half must be carefully sharpened by hand. Since most bowhunters are not capable of honing an edge to hair-splitting perfection, or simply do not wish to take the time to try, they are best off purchasing factory sharpened broadheads. A hunter who is a whiz at honing steel and doesn't mind spending 10 or 15 minutes on every broadhead he shoots can consistently drop deer with a good hand-sharpened arrowhead. It is practically criminal to bowhunt with dull-edged broadheads because they cripple and wound rather than kill.

Adequate cutting size. The best bowhunting broadheads have three or four blades that cut a hole between 1 inch and 1½ inch in diameter. Broadheads that are smaller than this or carry fewer blades tend to cause inadequate tissue damage in deer.

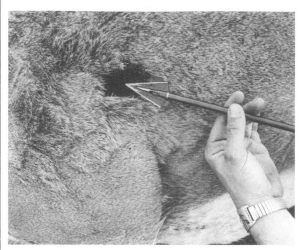

A big, razor-sharp broadhead slices a large, fatal wound in a deer. The wound bleeds profusely, produces an excellent blood trail and promotes the quick, humane kill every conscientious hunter demands.

Some bowhunters elect to shoot ultrasmall broadheads that provide fairly accurate flight even when a bow is not properly tuned; others use broadheads with only two cutting blades because such heads are easier to hand-sharpen and/or fly well without planing from a poorly tuned bow. However, a hunting broadhead with a diameter under 1 inch or a head with only two blades will reduce somewhat the chances of making a kill.

Penetrating ability. A hunting broadhead cannot drop game efficiently unless it penetrates deeply. Penetration must be virtually friction-free to fully use the meager in-flight energy of an arrow. A deer-hunting bullet requires substantial power to violently expand it and cause major tissue damage; by contrast, the proper broadhead cuts a sizable hole in flesh by slicing through it easily. Slight differences in projectile speed and energy are not important in dropping deer with a bow. A well-designed hunting broadhead cuts with very little energy behind it, while a poorly designed head wastes most projectile energy no matter how great that energy happens to be. A puny 40-pound recurve hunting bow shooting arrows with top-notch broadheads will invariably outpenetrate a 60-pound compound bow shooting arrows with high-friction heads.

A broadhead with excessively wide blades, jagged "ripping hooks," or other nonstreamlined features will usually produce inadequate pentration. By contrast, any streamlined, razor-sharp hunting broadhead penetrates at least fairly well in deer.

All else being equal, the key to penetration by a broadhead is the design of its frontal nose section. The majority of modern broadheads have cone-shaped

Broadheads with jagged blades are difficult to sharpen and penetrate poorly on deer. The heads may look deadly to beginning archers, but should be avoided in favor of simpler, more streamlined arrowhead designs.

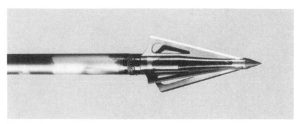

Broadheads with cone-shaped noses of hardened steel penetrate reasonably well on deer, provided noses are fairly small in size to minimize entry friction in flesh. Avoid heads with large-diameter nose cones.

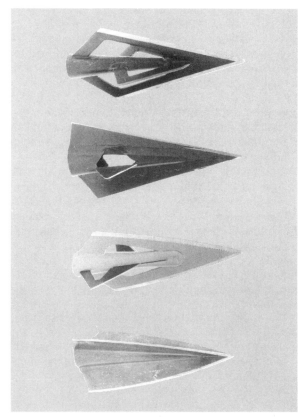

Many deer-hunting broadheads have sharpened, chisellike noses that penetrate with very little friction. Unfortunately, most do not allow quick replacement of blades after an edge-dulling shot.

or pyramid-shaped noses made of steel. They penetrate reasonably well on game, provided nose size is fairly small to minimize plowing friction as a broadhead enters flesh.

The best penetrating broadheads on the market do not plow through flesh at all. These feature chisellike noses that slice deep from the point on back. Sharp-around-the-nose broadheads of this sort outpenetrate nose-cone or pyramid-point heads by some 20 to 30 percent, but do not allow quick replacement of dull blades with sharp ones. Unless an archer is using a bow with a draw weight under 50 pounds, the difference in penetrating ability between top nose-cone, pyramid-point, and chisel-point broadheads is probably less important than other factors related to broadhead design.

Convenience. Some broadheads are simply more convenient to use than others. For example, one of the best heads instantly screw-attaches to an arrow and allows quick replacement of blades with the turn of a knurled blade-locking nut. By contrast, some other basically desirable heads must be carefully glued to arrows or aluminum screw-in adapters and must be sharpened by hand each time an edge is dulled. Similarly, some broadheads feature stainless-steel blades that resist edge-dulling rust in damp bowhunting conditions, whereas others have carbon-steel blades that rust unless oiled regularly on a hunt. If two or more bowhunting broadhead designs have suitable primary characteristics, the final choice should hinge on which is most convenient to attach and maintain.

There are dozens of decent bowhunting broadheads available. However, they are not all created equal. Every bowhunter has unique needs and personal druthers, but the best deer-hunting broadheads are invariably accurate, durable, razor sharp, moderately large in size, designed for deep penetration, and convenient to attach and maintain. Hunting broadheads should always be selected with these factors in mind.

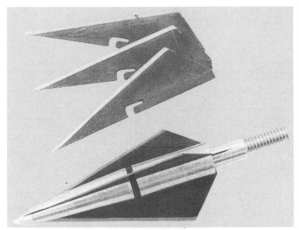

Replaceable-blade broadheads are most convenient to use in the woods. Dull or rusty blades can be instantly discarded and replaced with new, shaving-sharp extras from the factory. Most such heads also screw in and out of arrows in seconds.

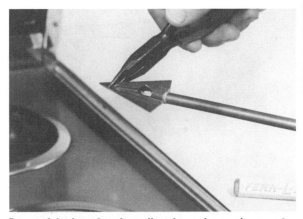

Some of the best deer broadheads on the market require time-consuming glue-on arrow attachment. This is not as convenient as the screw attachment, but provides a strong arrow-to-broadhead bond when hot-melt arrowhead cement is used.

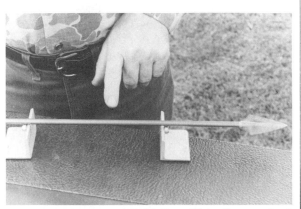

One of the best ways to ensure arrowhead alignment is to spin arrows on commercial rollers. This allows a check for wobble at each broadhead tip. Most quality broadheads screw or glue in place with excellent alignment.

OTHER ARROWHEADS

A smart archer complements his deer-hunting broadheads with several other arrowhead types of identical weight. Here are three common secondary arrowheads used by virtually all active bowhunters.

Field points. A field point is a simple, rugged steel arrowhead designed for target shooting and casual plinking in the field. Most hunting archers spend the majority of their off-season time using field points instead of broadheads because these heads will not tear up targets and target backstops. In addition, field points pull easily from a target, do not disintegrate upon impact with solid objects they accidentally hit, and cost considerably less.

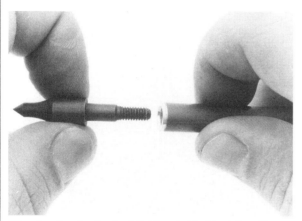

The simple, sturdy steel field point is ideal for all sorts of backyard target practice. This head does not tear up target butts and easily pulls free after shots. It is also quite accurate because of its streamlined design.

A field point is generally the arrowhead used by beginners as they perfect their shooting skill and tune up their bow/arrow combinations. As long as a bow *is* properly tuned, field points that weigh the same as broadheads always fly to the same point of impact.

Blunt arrowheads. A bowhunter should purchase a few blunt arrowheads of steel and rubber for serious in-the-field shooting at natural targets. Blunts do not wedge tightly into half-rotten stumps, trees, and solid soil the way field points often do, making extensive field practice prior to deer season more enjoyable and trouble-free. Solid steel blunts are best in areas with relatively few rocks and iron-hard stumps and logs; rubber blunts absorb the shock of hitting hard objects the best and tend to prevent valuable arrows from bending in rocky and heavily treed hardwood forests.

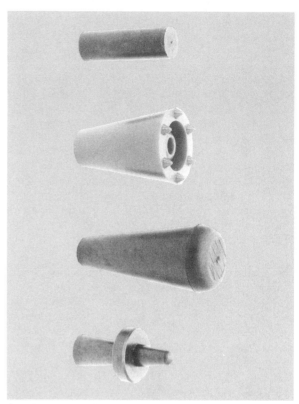

A wide variety of blunt arrowheads can be used for in-the-field shooting practice. Some common designs are (top to bottom): simple steel blunt; plastic bludgeon blunt; HTM rubber blunt; and steel shocker blunt.

Judo points. The Judo point is a unique arrowhead with a field-point nose and four spring-wire arms extending outward from the nose. This one-of-a-kind design will not skip away through the grass or slide out of sight beneath deep layers of matted leaves as other heads often do. The Judo point is regarded by many as an unlosable arrowhead, and should replace field points or blunts whenever a hunter decides to practice in areas where ground-hugging undergrowth

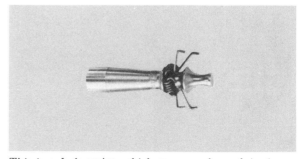

This is a Judo point, which many archers claim is unlosable in the field. Its front spring-wire arms dig in and tumble an arrow upon impact instead of allowing the shaft to slip beneath matted grass or leaves.

or debris threatens to literally gobble up arrows tipped by other practice arrowheads.

MATCHING ARROWHEAD WEIGHT

It is worth reiterating here that all arrowheads used by a bowhunter should be of the same weight. The best way to be sure is to check the grain-weight of various arrowheads on an ordinary gunpowder measuring scale. Far too many archers attach and detach heads of various weights willy-nilly without the slightest inkling how this alters the arrow's flight. Field points, blunts, Judo points, and broadheads not only fly erratically when they differ significantly in weight; they also group into different general areas in relation to a hunter's bowsight pins. Matching weight is easy upon purchase.

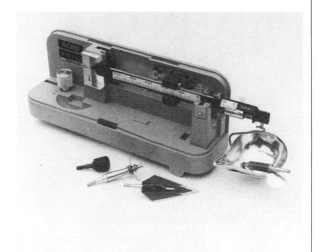

Weight-matching ensures accuracy and consistent points of impact. A handloader's gunpowder scale can be used to double-check the grain weights of all arrowheads.

SHOOTING NECESSITIES

Aside from a bow, arrows, and related equipment, a bowhunter needs several other items before he can perfect his target- and field-shooting abilities. This gear is far less expensive than a bow and set of arrows, and it's important to shooting enjoyment and success.

ARMGUARD FUNCTIONS

Every archer needs some sort of armguard to hold down the baggy sleeve of his shirt or jacket and to protect his forearm from painful bowstring slap

A baggy shirtsleeve can send arrows wild if the bowstring even slightly rakes it during a shot. A sleeve can also cause excessive bowstring slap, which often frightens deer. An armguard flattens a sleeve and prevents these shooting problems.

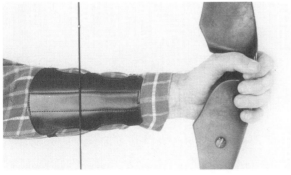

An armguard protects a shooter's forearm from painful bowstring slap during a shot. The guard should be positioned so that the bowstring bisects it visually when the bow is held in the normal predraw position.

whenever a shot is taken. A few naive bowhunters insist on target practicing and pursuing deer without armguards in place, but this invariably degrades accuracy—not to mention the possibility of raising wicked purple welts where a bowstring has whacked the forearm.

Even if a bowhunter's basic shooting form somehow keeps his forearm out of the way, the slightest contact between bowstring and sleeve can ruin accuracy. Such contact alters vibrations coursing through the bowstring and arrow after a shooter releases and generally sends the arrow careening on an entirely unexpected course. A noisy "slap" generally results too—a sound guaranteed to scare any nearby animal.

A standard bowhunting armguard measures about 6 inches long and 4 inches wide. It clips or buckles to the forearm halfway between the elbow and wrist with three elastic bands. A few archers with unorthodox shooting styles require a longer armguard that protects the bow arm from mid-biceps all the way to the wrist. But a beginner should start using a standard armguard and replace this with a longer one only if shooting troubles develop.

FINGER GLOVES AND TABS

The drawing fingers must be adequately protected from direct bowstring abrasion with some sort of leather guard. Most bowhunters use gloves or tabs to cushion their fingers and provide a somewhat smoother arrow release than can be accomplished with bare fingers alone.

Beginning and intermediate archers usually find that a conventional bow-shooting glove feels most natural when drawing and releasing the bowstring. This glove covers the first three fingers of the hand to the second joint and is held securely about the wrist with a thin leather strap.

A bow-shooting glove should fit the fingers snugly but not so tightly that it hampers circulation or pinches nerves in the fingertips. Although a few companies sell plastic bow gloves, leather gloves are more durable and usually produce smoother, more accurate shooting.

A shooting tab consists of a flat, oval piece of leather or several layers of leather and rubber designed to protect the bowstring fingers and produce a slick, accurate release. Tabs feel a bit awkward to beginners,

A finger glove protects the bowstring fingers during the draw and the shot. Most beginners prefer the natural feel of a soft leather glove despite its tendency to produce a high-friction, and less-accurate release.

A shooting tab takes some getting used to, but allows the slickest possible finger release. Quality tabs generally protect shooting fingers from abrasion with two or three layers of leather and/or rubber.

but for experienced shooters these finger protectors actually promote better accuracy than gloves. A glove invariably becomes deeply grooved over a few weeks or months of shooting, and these grooves tend to hang up the bowstring, leading to sloppy, high-friction arrow releases. By contrast, a shooting tab never becomes grooved and thus provides a smoother, more consistent release. The best shooting tabs feature calf-hair bowstring surfaces that further promote slippery, accurate releases. It's certainly okay for beginning archers to start with a glove, but most deer hunters will enjoy better shooting results if they eventually change over to using a tab.

MECHANICAL BOWSTRING RELEASES

Although still fairly rare in deer hunting, more and more mechanical bowstring releases are being used. Most such releases grip the bowstring just below the nocked arrow with one or two small steel fingers. To shoot with a mechanical bowstring release, an archer simply snaps this release over the bowstring, draws the bow, and squeezes a gunlike trigger to send the arrow on its way. In practiced hands the mechanical

release provides more accurate shooting than is possible with three separate, quivering fingers.

Although a few expert archers use mechanical releases on deer, these devices have several drawbacks

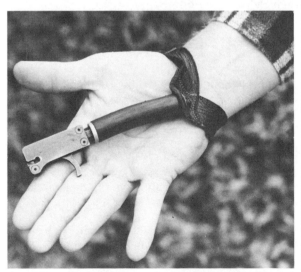

A mechanical release grips the bowstring securely and allows gunlike shooting with the squeeze of a trigger. These devices yield superb accuracy, but tend to be noisy and slow in the field. (See photo, next page.)

The trigger release shown on the previous page is here demonstrated in use.

that make them questionable deer-hunting aids. For one thing, a release is extremely slow and awkward to use, especially when nocking a second arrow for a follow-up shot. For another, the release produces louder-than-normal shooting noise that can scare a target animal out of the path of the arrow. A third problem is that a release sometimes malfunctions like all mechanical devices. Because releases often cause more field-shooting problems than they solve, deer hunters should not consider using them unless the hunters have great difficulty releasing a bowstring accurately with their fingers.

RANGEFINDERS

Next to the compound bow, the bowhunting rangefinder is probably the single most important innovation in deer-hunting archery to appear since the late 1960s. Some staunch, conservative bowhunters were slow to accept this newfangled gadget, but today the rangefinder is an esssential part of most bowhunter's basic gear. There is absolutely no doubt that a top-quality rangefinder can greatly improve a hunting archer's ability to score.

Hitting targets with bow-and-arrow gear is not particularly easy, but steady practice and proper instruction will turn most neophytes into decent shots at known distances in a relatively short period of time. With normal coordination, decent eyesight, and acceptable shooting form, the average practiced bowhunter can consistently hit a 4-inch circle at 20 yards and a 9-inch pie plate at 40 yards. This degree of ac-

curacy is good enough to nail deer-size animals every time because the average whitetail buck measures 14 or 15 inches from backline to brisket and offers a broadside heart-lung zone easily ten inches in diameter. Hitting a zone of this size would not be all that difficult out to 40 yards, provided a bowhunter always knew the exact distance of his shots.

Rangefinders are regarded as standard equipment by savvy bowhunters. The best bowhunting optical rangefinders are compact and very light in weight. Most come complete with padded belt pouches that silently unzip for easy access.

The trouble is, a bowhunter *never* knows the distance to target animals without using some sort of rangefinding aid. He may be relatively good at guesstimating shooting distance, but a fair share of the time he'll misjudge range because of broken terrain, poor light, dense foliage, or any number of other factors. Without the ability to pace off the range to his target or look at a handy distance marker like those found on archery ranges, a bowhunter's odds of hitting an animal are not especially good.

In order to understand just how critical distance estimation is, consider the following: When coupled with a 500-grain arrow flying at close to 200 feet per second, a 55-pound compound bow will neatly drop deer every time when arrows hit a vital zone. The problem is, arrows from this and any other hunting bow fly with incredibly arching trajectory. If the bow/arrow combo just described is zeroed at 15 yards with a modern bowsight, the arrow will drop 13.1 inches below line of sight at 25 yards, 37.3 inches low at 35 yards, and a whopping 73.1 inches low at 45 yards! Obviously, a misestimation of only 5 yards at 25 yards or 2 yards at 35 or 40 yards will result in a crippling hit or clean miss on a deer as the arrow sails high or low. When compared to a high-powered rifle bullet, which is seldom more than one inch above or below line of sight out to 100 yards, a flying arrow requires

This shooting table shows how in-ability to guess the correct distance causes missed shots when using the 20-yard aiming pin and shooting at various distances. Figures given as-sume a perfect shot. From this table it's easy to see that given the 10-inch vital chest zone on a deer, even the flattest-shooting compound bow or cam-bow still requires accurate range estimation for effective, quickly fatal hits. (Courtesy of Ranger Inc.)

IMPACT POINT OF AN ARROW

Bow & arrow combination	10 yds.	15 yds.	20 yds.	25 yds.	30 yds.	35 yds.	40 yds.
55 Lb. Compound/2016 arrow 28" draw	5.0" High	3.8" High	◎	6.3" Low	15.4" Low	27.0" Low	41.4" Low
60 Lb. Cam/2117 arrow 30" draw	3.8" High	2.8" High	◎	4.8" Low	11.5" Low	20.0" Low	30.6" Low
65 Lb. Compound/2117 arrow 30" draw	4.1" High	3.1" High	◎	5.2" Low	12.4" Low	22.0" Low	33.5" Low
70 Lb. Cam/2219 arrow 30" draw	3.2" High	2.4" High	◎	4.0" Low	9.7" Low	17.0" Low	26.1" Low

HOW A RANGEFINDER WORKS

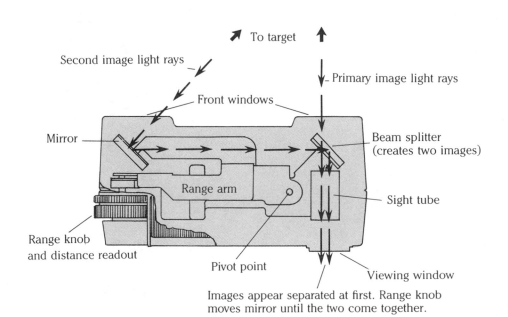

An optical bowhunting rangefinder mechanically triangulates on target with the simple turn of a dial. This unit is valuable in both stalking and stand-hunting situations where shots over 15 or 20 yards are expected.

astoundingly accurate range estimation to ensure decent hits.

The fact that arrows generally drop over 6 feet between 15 and 45 yards complicates bowhunting immensely. However, the optical rangefinder has made long shots far less difficult. The first rangefinders were fairly crude and inaccurate, but today the devices are very precise and totally dependable. Top designs can be carried on a belt in a padded pouch, allowing easy access immediately before taking a shot.

Rangefinders optically zero on a distant object with the simple turn of a dial—when two separate images of the target object merge perfectly into one, the distance to that object can be read off a handy distance scale. Archery rangefinders are usually accurate to within half a yard out to 50 yards, and some models are this precise at even longer ranges.

A bowhunting rangefinder is normally used in one or two ways. Archers in tree stands or ground blinds generally predetermine the distance to several nearby landmarks such as rocks, trees, or logs beside trails where game is likely to appear. This eliminates the need to pace off shooting distances in the stand area—a time-consuming practice that also tends to saturate the immediate vicinity with game-spooking human scent. Hunters who prefer to stalk or stillhunt on foot use a rangefinder to check the distance to the deer itself, once the animal has been sighted. Walking bowhunters do not always have the time to use a rangefinder prior to taking a shot, but when this is possible the result is generally pinpoint accuracy.

ARROW-QUIVER DESIGN ALTERNATIVES

A bow-mounted quiver is used by most deer hunters because of its obvious advantages. However, several alternate arrow-quiver designs are available to accommodate special preferences or needs. Every archer should at least consider these when studying available bowhunting accessories.

Hip quivers. Hip quivers are quite similar to bow quivers in basic arrow-holding design. The best models have roomy protective hoods that fully enclose sharp broadheads, and sturdy rubber arrow grippers that hold six or eight shafts firmly and keep them from rattling. However, a hip quiver is attached to a hunter's belt instead of directly to his bow, and this has both advantages and disadvantages.

The chief plus of a good-quality hip quiver is that it leaves a hunting bow lighter and slightly more maneuverable. Some archers prefer to shoot with an unencumbered hunting bow. Arrows are still very close to an archer's hand, making possible fairly quick

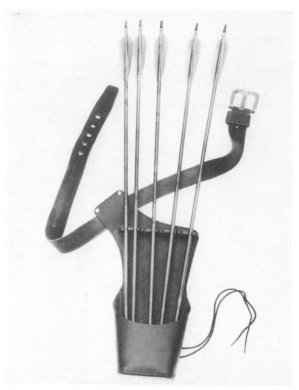

A good hip quiver fully covers keen-edged arrowheads and holds shafts firmly in rubber arrow grippers. The setup ideally flares arrows to prevent fletching from rattling noisily together.

Bowhunters who prefer light, maneuverable bows often opt to use hip quivers. In fairly open deer country where brush does not hinder easy walking, hip quivers work exceedingly well.

second and third shots. Hip quivers are substantially less expensive than bow quivers too, which makes them attractive to bowhunters with a tight budget.

The primary drawback of a hip quiver is that it tends to be awkward to use in the field. This quiver can hang up in heavy brush and sometimes slaps an archer's leg annoyingly as he walks or sneaks along. Also anytime a hunter scales a fence or climbs in and out of a vehicle, the quiver must usually be removed first, and then slipped on again once an archer is in the clear. Many woodsmen simply will not put up with such inconvenience.

Shoulder quivers. Old-style shoulder quivers have been used for centuries by hunters and Indian warriors. Their primary advantage is extremely quick over-the-shoulder arrow access—access that allowed American Indians to launch arrows with steady, blinding speed. However, shoulder quivers are seldom used by modern hunters because they hang up on high bushes and low-hanging limbs, allow arrows to rattle noisily together, and dull broadhead edges by permitting contact in the quiver. A few staunch traditionalists annually grab their longbows and go after deer with shoulder-mounted quivers. But, for hunting, these quivers are a mistake.

Back quivers. So-called back quivers are special-purpose, larger-capacity arrow holders designed to be carried like a small hiking backpack. Commercial back quivers can hold up to 24 arrows—arrows that can be plucked free for use by a careful reach to the rear. Back quivers are somewhat awkward and noisy to carry through heavy cover, although they do not ride above the shoulder as shoulder quivers normally do.

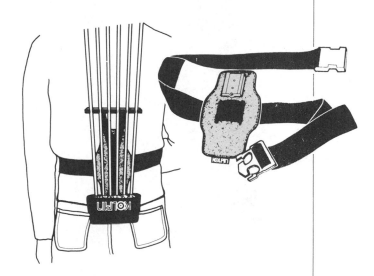

A back quiver positions arrows in the middle of a hunter's back. Some designs hold 18 to 24 arrows to allow plenty of serious shooting. Arrows are plucked free with a backward grasp of the hand. The model shown here is simply a bow quiver attached to a back-quiver belt.

The best back quivers fully cover sharp broadheads and snugly grip individual arrow shafts. These quivers are not practical unless an archer expects to be hunting all day in areas where lots of long-range shots are likely and more than the normal six or eight shots will be needed.

Target quivers. In addition to a hunting quiver, every archer needs a simple, tube-type hip quiver to hold field-tipped arrows for regular backyard shooting. A belt-attached target quiver is inexpensive and convenient. Various models are usually available at well-stocked archery stores.

The old-style shoulder quiver is not an acceptable deer-hunting design. It allows arrows to rattle together, dulls sharp broadheads, and causes arrows to collide with every bush and limb in their path.

Serious bowhunters will get good use from an inexpensive tube-type target quiver. It holds arrows close at hand for backyard shooting sessions and other target activities.

SHOOTING-RANGE EQUIPMENT

Before perfecting his bow-shooting skills, every would-be deer hunter must set up a simple shooting range. The range should allow a minimum of 30 yards for practice at various distances, but 40 to 60 yards is preferable. Naturally, this setup must be safe, with a large vacant area beyond the target location or a high, sturdy wooden fence or similar backstop capable of stopping a misdirected arrow. If you use a backstop, be sure the area beyond it is not frequented by children or other passersby who may be struck by an arrow going over the backstop.

Target butts. To begin shooting, an archer needs an arrow-stopping target butt to attach targets to. There are several commercial target butts, and one home-made butt that many prefer. First, the commercial target butts:

One of the most portable, durable, and generally available bowhunting target butts is the Indian rope-grass mat. This is a round, brown-colored butt made of tightly woven natural rope-grass fibers. Rope-grass mats are approximately 6 inches thick and can be purchased in diameters of 24 inches up to 48 inches. When periodically dampened with water to swell the rope-grass fibers, these mats will stop and hold arrows shot from the heaviest hunting bows.

The only disadvantage of the rope-grass mat is that arrows with hunting broadheads quickly tear it apart. However, for regular field-point shooting practice this mat is hard to beat. It can be stored in a garage or basement when not in use and then rolled to the range. Rope-grass mats can be propped against trees, fences, or other existing supports, or they can be set up on commercial metal easels.

Another popular bowhunting target butt is the ethafoam butt. Ethafoam is an ultralight, ultratough space-age material that stops both field points and broadheads extremely well. A target butt made of Ethafoam is fairly expensive, but represents the ultimate in target-butt portability. This butt normally measures about 2 feet across and about 1 foot thick, and features a round, replaceable center section.

A bean-bag butt is another fine backyard target butt. It consists of a large burlap-type bag loosely stuffed with cotton or other impact-absorbing material. The stuffing stops arrows cold, allowing only slight penetration.

Although commercial archery butts all do a fairly good job of stopping arrows from hard-shooting hunting bows, ordinary straw or hay bales cost a fraction as much and usually last several times as long. The most durable bales are made of wheat straw, which is an especially tough and fibrous material. Three bales cost next to nothing at a feed store and make

TARGET BUTTS

A rope-grass mat is one of the most durable target butts for serious backyard shooting. It can be used with a commercial target stand (right) or simply leaned against a tree, as below.

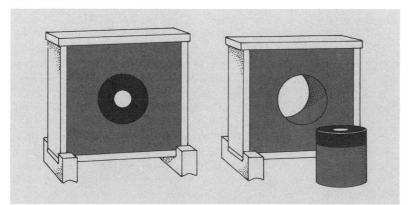

An ethafoam target butt is lightweight but durable. Better-quality versions allow quick replacement of round, center sections that take a beating in regular shooting. Ethafoam butts stand up well to practice with field points and broadheads, too.

A beanbag butt stops arrows in fairly loose, impact-absorbent stuffing. This butt normally attaches to a metal stand. One reversible design features aiming spots on one side and a deer on the other.

Straw bales make dandy arrow stoppers when several bales are stacked together. To keep the bales high and dry regardless of weather, two worn-out auto tires, as shown, should be used as a target-butt foundation.

a dandy bow-shooting butt when stacked on top of one another like building blocks. For best results with this do-it-yourself target butt, stack bales on top of two old automobile tires. This keeps them high and dry no matter how damp the ground happens to be. When the middle bale begins to wear out from lots of shooting, rotate the bales to position a fresh one in the center where most of the arrows hit. A target butt made of bales will generally last for an entire year of regular shooting—a bargain in anybody's book!

Targets. Active bowhunters use a wide variety of backyard targets to fine-tune their shooting skills. The targets every archer should begin on are ordinary paper bull's-eye targets. Archery stores are full of suitable commercial targets and these include black-and-white field archery targets in several different sizes; colorful American round targets with brilliant gold centers fringed by red, blue, and black; and distinctive blue-and-white PAA targets designed for shooting at 20 yards. In addition, you can easily convert ordinary 9-inch white paper plates into excellent targets. Use a black felt-tipped pen to draw aiming spots in the centers of the plates. Any bull's-eye target of this type is excellent for ordinary backyard bow-shooting practice.

A serious bowhunter accumulates other kinds of targets as he becomes more proficient. Various commercial animal targets are especially enjoyable to shoot at and help teach a hunter to aim for the animal's vital area. Most bowhunters devote at least a little time each year to shooting at deer targets to help sharpen their aim.

Two other types of targets can be beneficial. These are commercial three-dimensional deer targets made of Ethafoam, and homemade cardboard silhouettes of deer. The 3-D Ethafoam targets most closely approximate live deer but are too expensive for most bowhunters. Silhouettes of deer cut from cardboard

make fairly realistic targets when there are no markings on them to help an archer aim. One important skill in bowhunting is learning to shoot precisely at a small vital spot on the side of a deer—a skill sharpened by regular shooting at brown cardboard silhouettes.

Other shooting-range equipment. The dedicated, year-round archer might wish to purchase or make a few other items for his backyard shooting range. These might include commercial racks for hanging up bows between shooting sessions, or distance markers placed at regular intervals away from the target butt. However, a backyard range is simple and inexpensive to set up, and will provide convenient, regular shooting practice.

PREPARING TACKLE FOR SHOOTING

Once a bowhunter assembles the basic bow-shooting equipment, he's almost ready to begin honing his target-shooting skills. Almost, but not quite. Prior to shooting that first arrow at the target, a hunter must prepare his tackle so that it performs smoothly and gives him every chance of hitting what he's aiming at.

Lubrication of bow parts. One of the very first things that should be done to any new hunting bow is a careful lubrication of all moving parts. The manufacturer does some of this, but you should double-check all friction points on a bow, and oil or grease any that seem to be dry and prone to wear, squeaking, or rust.

On any compound hunting bow, axles that pass through wheels or cams should be lubricated regularly. Thoroughly drench axle ends with a top-grade penetrating lubricant such as WD-40. Allow the oil to seep into working parts for at least an hour, and then wipe away any excess on limbs and wheels. Repeat this process once or twice a year to keep wheel action smooth and quiet, and to prevent excessive wear.

Another bow part needing occasional oiling is the draw-weight adjustment bolt, which holds each compound limb to the handle riser of the bow. Bolts that become dry and rusty can freeze in a bow and create major draw-weight adjustment problems, and at the very worst, the bolts are weakened over time by thread-destroying rust. Any name-brand penetrating oil will do an excellent job here too.

A Dacron hunting-bow string is invariably dry as a bone when a new bow is purchased. Lubricate it with bowstring wax before shooting to retard wear between the strands of the string. Wax should be rubbed in

TARGETS

A variety of commerical bull's-eye targets are sold at archery stores. Two common types are American Round targets with multicolored rings and simpler black-and-white field archery targets.

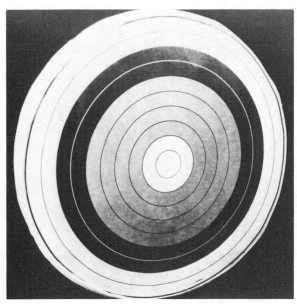

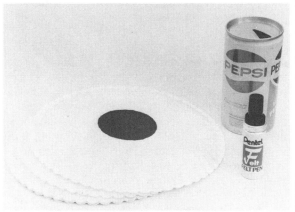

You can make inexpensive bull's-eye targets from 9-inch paper plates by outlining the bottom of a soft drink can with a black felt-tipped pen. Once the bull's-eye is colored in, the target provides a highly visible aiming spot.

A wide variety of paper animal targets are sold at archery stores. No matter what animal or bird the targets portray, they teach a shooter to pick an aiming spot.

Wheel axles on a brand-new compound bow should be oiled to ensure quiet, friction-free performance. Any good penetrating oil, such as WD-40, will do just fine.

until it forms a heavy coat over the entire string and makes it difficult to see individual Dacron strands.

Bowhunters who use a flipper/plunger arrow rest should also carefully disassemble the plunger part of the rest and lubricate the adjustable plunger spring with light oil or powdered graphite. Such lubrication prevents the plunger from grabbing or sticking, which can cause wild shots.

Attaching major accessories. You should reserve a few hours for attaching all accessories to your bow prior to shooting. This includes bolting or screwing a bow quiver in place, solidly anchoring a bowsight to the handle riser section, twisting a bow stabilizer into the handle, and fitting bowstring silencers to the string according to manufacturer's instructions. All the accessories must be installed tightly so they do not rattle loose during regular shooting. The hunter who *does not* mount bow accessories before he begins shooting will discover later on that there is a difference in the feel and shooting characteristics of a naked bow from that of one with accessories attached.

Setting the bowsight. Before beginning backyard target practice, set the top bowsight pin about 3 inches above the arrow rest. The aiming bead should be clearly visible about ½ inch from the sight window in the handle riser of the bow. This sight position should yield arrow hits somewhere near the target on the first few shots from 10 to 15 yards. And it will

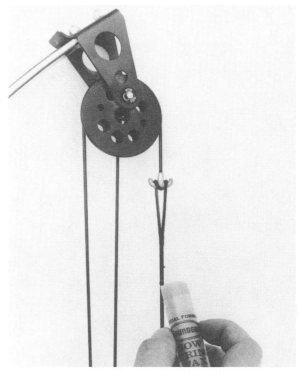

A new bowstring should be heavily waxed before shooting. This prolongs string life by cutting friction between the strands and reducing the chance of surface fraying during normal contact with rocks, trees, and other natural obstacles.

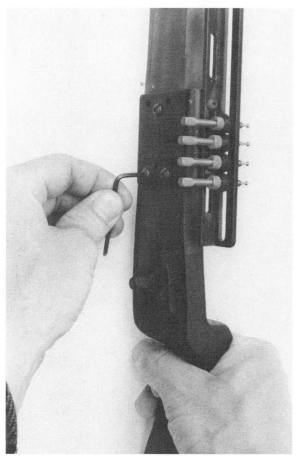

The bowsight should be snugly bolted in place. A loosely mounted sight can buzz noisily during shots—an unpleasant distraction that may also spook game.

Bow quivers will vibrate loudly and occasionally separate from bows unless solidly mounted in place. Tighten thumbscrews or lock-down nuts on quivers to avoid noise problems later.

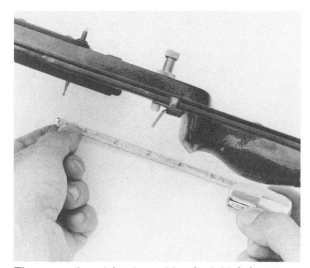

The proper bowsight-pin position for initial shooting practice is approximately 3 inches above the arrow rest (left-hand photo) and ½ inch away from the bow (right-hand photo). With this setting arrows should hit reasonably close to the bull's-eye when shots are taken from 10 or 15 yards.

Most hunting bows shoot best when arrows are nocked slightly above right angles to the arrow rest. To begin with, position the nock locator so nocking height is about ⅜ inch above 90 degrees.

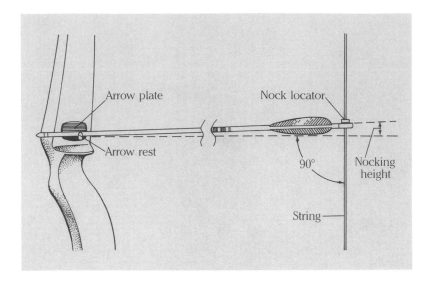

eliminate wild shots and lost or dangerously careening arrows. As you shoot and perfect your basic bow-shooting form, you can adjust the sight-pins for hits in the exact center of the target.

Setting the nocking point. As mentioned earlier, the nocking point on a bowstring should be set initially at about ⅜ inch above the line running at a right angle to the bowstring from the arrow shelf portion of the arrow rest. To do this correctly requires nocking-point pliers and a bow square. So most beginning archers ask their archery dealer to set the nocking point for them and then purchase the necessary do-it-yourself tools later.

Adjusting bow poundage and tiller. On compound bows there are two adjustments that are absolutely critical for comfortable and accurate shooting. The first is setting draw weight at a point that feels comfortable to your finger, arm, and back muscles. The second is setting bow tiller—a complicated procedure that ensures upper and lower wheels on a compound bow will roll over in harmony during the draw and the shot. Since both of these adjustments require an intimate knowledge of compound-bow mechanics, a beginning or intermediate bowhunter should leave the adjusting to a qualified archery dealer. But you should be aware that draw weight and tiller adjustments are necessary, and make certain they have been made before heading to the archery range.

Arrow-rest adjustments. Solid, one-piece arrow rests are pressed on the handle riser with the hope that they will automatically produce decent shooting accuracy. Adjustable arrow plates on adjustable springy rests and flipper/plunger combinations should be preset at the time-tested location that usually yields

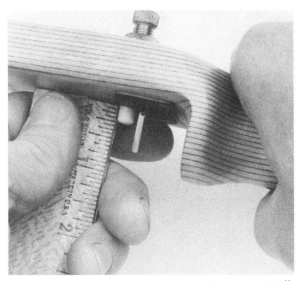

The plate portion of the arrow rest should be set initially about ¼ inch away from the bow. This position generally yields at least passable arrow flight if the proper arrow size is used.

the very best in accuracy. This plate location is exactly ¼ inch away from the surface of the handle riser section (see accompanying photo). Setting the arrow plate there usually allows arrow fletching to adequately clear the bow and also places the energy thrust of the bowstring in near-exact alignment with the centerline of the arrow shaft. This leads to relatively wobble-free, accurate arrow flight from the outset.

Tightening arrowheads in place. One of the major vexations of beginning archers is loose, rattling field points on target arrows. Heads sometimes unscrew in target butts and are lost forever. More often, they vibrate wildly during shots and throw arrows off course. The solution is to tighten field-point arrowheads on the ends of the shafts with a stout pair of pliers. Once tightened in this way, arrowheads stay put and cause no shooting problems. Few bowhunters possess the physical strength to hand-tighten arrowheads on shafts.

SHOOTING BASICS: STEP BY STEP

Beginners and experienced bowhunters alike can benefit by analyzing their basic bow-shooting form. Most bowhunters learn how to shoot "by the seats of their pants" without ever paying much attention to specifics or realizing how important a systematic approach is. The result is almost always a whole rash of bad shooting habits that undermine accuracy.

Shooting a hunting bow should be a careful, step-by-step procedure. For the beginner, each step should be consciously considered and systematically executed. Although experienced archers display a wide variety of bow-shooting styles, all true crack shots follow the same basic series of steps when shooting. There is nothing haphazard about shooting a hunting bow with acceptable accuracy—each shot consists of deliberate, carefully practiced moves.

It is far easier to learn bow-shooting correctly than to attempt to break shoddy shooting habits later. A beginning archer who consciously shoots step by step for several months prior to deer season will eventually be able to shoot automatically and subconsciously in fine style whenever a deer ambles into range. The experienced hunter who has developed poor shooting habits will have a tougher time perfecting his skills because old mistakes will be deeply ingrained and very tough to overcome. However, *anyone* who practices shooting a bow in step-by-step fashion will eventually smoothen up his act on both targets and deer.

Here are the eight basic steps in correct bow-shooting form. They are followed with minor modifications by all top bowhunters and tournament archers and virtually guarantee pinpoint accuracy when rigidly followed. Shooting a bow in this way may seem awkward at first, but with practice it quickly becomes second nature.

Step 1: How to stand. To begin with, stand facing at a 90 degree angle to the target with your feet planted comfortably 12 to 18 inches apart. Both toes should be pointed at right angles to the target, and your weight should be evenly distributed on both feet. If you are

The stance

Most archers enjoy tight arrow groups if they practice standard bow-shooting steps. Consistently proper shooting form leads to excellent accuracy on targets and deer—something a haphazard approach will never allow you to accomplish.

Addressing the target

a beginner, take your first practice shots at relatively short distance—10 yards is a practical initial range.

If you are right-handed, grip the bow loosely in your left hand as you assume a proper shooting stance. Once your feet are planted solidly at the correct angle to the target, turn your head to face the target.

Step 2: Nocking the arrow. Once you have the proper stance in front of the target, nock an arrow directly below the nocking point on the bowstring. The arrow should be snapped positively over the string so that the cock vane (off-color fletch) on the arrow is facing away from the bow. Once the arrow is firmly snapped to the bowstring, position the shaft on the arrow rest of the bow and hold it there lightly with the index finger of your bow hand.

Step 3: Gripping string and bow. After nocking an arrow, assume a proper grip on both bowstring and bow. To grip the string, curl the first three fingers of your bowstring hand (right hand for right-handed shooters; that is, with right master eyes) around the bowstring. Nestle the string deeply in the first joints of all three fingers. Your index finger should be above

Holding the arrow on the rest

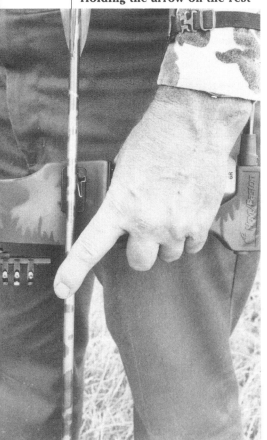

Conventional bowstring grip

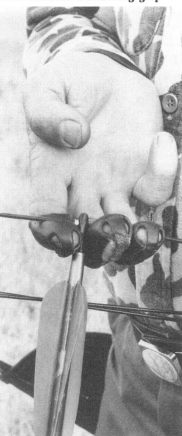

Gripping the bow prior to the draw

the arrow and your next two fingers below it. When the bowstring is correctly gripped, your hand forms a modified Boy Scout salute.

The correct way to grip a bow is by lightly curling all your fingers around it in firm but relatively relaxed fashion. In the beginning you may need to hold the arrow on the arrow rest with your index finger as you draw to shoot, but an experienced archer drops his index finger to grip the bow prior to beginning the draw. Once a bow is drawn, your grip should remain firm but not white-knuckle tight. The bulk of drawing pressure should focus on the web of your bow hand between the forefinger and thumb.

Step 4: Drawing the bow. To draw the bow, extend your bow arm directly at the target, then smoothly pull the bowstring back to the right side of your face (left side for left-handed shooters). During the draw, keep your bow arm straight and keep your hold on the bow relaxed with all fingers lightly wrapped about the grip. Your bowstring fingers should be deeply curled to safely and positively hold the string.

During the draw, you may have trouble keeping the arrow on the arrow rest. This trouble disappears once you learn to roll the bowstring slightly in your fingers

to torque the arrows against the plate of the arrow rest. Initially, you can continue to hold the arrow on the rest with your index finger during the draw, but this should not become a habit. That is because use of the index finger to hold the arrow tends to tighten muscles in the bow hand, which in turn leads to erratic shooting performance.

Step 5: Anchoring the string hand. Once the bow is drawn, you must anchor your string hand solidly against the side of your face. The most common bowhunting anchor, and the one every beginner should use, is placing the index finger of the bowstring hand firmly in the corner of the mouth. When this anchor is properly positioned, the point of your jaw nestles neatly in the pocket between your index finger and thumb of your bowstring hand with the thumb dropped below the jawline. Depending upon the exact shape of your face, the bowstring will be slightly to the right or to the left of your aiming eye once your bowstring hand is anchored.

A solid anchor to the face accomplishes two important things. First, it transfers some of the bow's draw weight from your shoulder muscles to muscles in your neck and middle back. This leads to steady

Beginning the draw

Proper drawing grip

aiming. Second, a consistent anchor is similar to the back sight on a hunting rifle—it ensures consistent aiming from shot to shot because your aiming eye is in the same place in relationship to the arrow and the bowsight each and every time. Archers who faithfully practice their anchors become quite consistent about aiming at bull's-eyes and venison on the hoof.

When you draw and anchor solidly to your face, the forearm of your bowstring arm should align quite closely with the arrow. This alignment is least stressful on shooting muscles and greatly enhances accuracy.

Step 6: Aiming at the target. The next step is aiming at the target. To do this, you slowly and smoothly swing the bowsight toward the bull's-eye. Hold the sight pin dead center for a split second before releasing the string. Both eyes should be open during the aim and should be focused on the target—not on the bowsight pin. The bowstring should appear as a dark, out-of-focus bar to the right or left of your aiming eye (master eye) during the entire aiming process. Always hold a hunting bow with bowsights in a vertical position as you aim and shoot—canting a bow as old-

style longbowmen once did leads to inconsistent aiming and varying points of impact with modern hunting bows.

Consistency is the key to accuracy with a bow. Consequently, you should learn to be consistent about how you swing your sights on target. If you like to raise your sights from below, do this each and every time. Most hunters do come *up* on the target because this allows the clearest view above the cluster of bowsight pins. However, some excellent archers drop on target from above or swing in from the right or left. It really doesn't matter how you move your sight into position, as long as you do it the same way from shot to shot.

A few bowhunters prefer to aim without the aid of sights. This is never as accurate as using a carefully adjusted bowsight pin, but so-called "instinctive aiming" can be effective after lots of serious practice. Virtually all nonsight bow-shooters consciously or subconsciously use the tips of their arrows as crude bowsights when they aim, "gapping" between the target and the arrowhead, and releasing when the gap looks exactly right. Because gap-shooting take years of practice to perfect, and because it never yields accuracy on a par with skillful use of a bowsight, be-

Anchoring the bowstring hand

Proper elbow alignment with the arrow

ginning archers should use some sort of commercial sight to refine aiming skills.

Step 7: Releasing the string. Once the aim looks right, smoothly release the bowstring to send the arrow on its way. Releasing smoothly is more easily said than done because your bowstring fingers are under pressure and tend to jerk when you attempt to loose the arrow. The proper way to release a bowstring is by simply relaxing your three string fingers and letting the string slip away under its own power. Attempts to forcibly throw open your bowstring fingers or pluck the string with your fingers (like the string of a guitar) invariably send arrows sailing wild.

With a proper bowstring release, your bowstring hand remains solidly pressed against the side of your face. It will always slide backwards along your jaw an inch or two as the drawing muscles are relieved of bowstring pressure, but it never leaves your face. Rough, high-friction bowstring releases generally cause your bowstring hand to fly away from your face. You should practice relaxing your bowstring fingers and holding your hand firmly in the proper anchor position as the string slides free and the arrow speeds

away. A smooth, unobtrusive release with very little hand motion is by far the most accurate way to go.

Step 8: Following through. A proper follow-through is one of the most important elements of step-by-step bow-shooting and is one of the most commonly ignored. The average bowhunter drops his bow and raises his head the instant he releases the bowstring in an attempt to see where the arrow has hit. Unfortunately, breaking good shooting form in this way is a major cause of misdirected shots.

An arrow requires a split second to sizzle past the handle riser after the string is released. To allow an arrow to clear the bow—and more importantly, to ensure that you don't drop your bow *before* you release the string—you should continue to aim solidly until the arrow actually hits the target. A hunting bow will naturally recoil to one side as the bowstring comes taut. But when you *try to hold your sight on the target until the arrow hits,* you will generally achieve a smooth release without plucking the bowstring or prematurely dropping your bow.

Many archers mistakenly believe that they should watch an arrow fly to the target. In reality you should

Aiming at the target

Correct follow-through

never see the arrow until it hits the mark. Your eyes should remain fixed on the target, your bow arm rigidly outstretched and your bowstring hand snugly pressed against your face.

SIGHTING-IN

As you shoot arrow after arrow with your attention focused on the individual steps of proper form, your confidence will grow steadily. Bow shooting is really not too difficult when approached in systematic fashion. However, complete confidence is never achieved unless you're actually hitting the bull's-eye. As a result, you should start adjusting your bowsight at once to sight-in the bow and put your arrows directly on the money.

To sight-in a bow, you simply move the bowsight pin to where arrows are hitting. For example, if initial shots are grouping high and left, move the sight pin up and to the left. If arrows are hitting low and right, move the aiming pin down and to the right. A little experimentation will lead to sights that are properly set.

Once you become confident in your skill at 10 or 15 yards, you will want to begin shooting at longer ranges, such as 20, 30, and 40 yards. Sight pins for longer yardage are always positioned lower than pins for shorter yardage—the lower the pin, the higher the bow is held during the aim to compensate for greater

shooting distance. By shooting regularly over several weeks, you can eventually adjust four or five separate pins on your bow to achieve dead center accuracy at ranges of 20, 30, 40, 50, and 60 yards.

STYLE VARIATIONS

Every archer should learn to shoot using the basics just described. However, later on a seasoned bow-hunter may want to experiment with shooting-style variations that may improve his ability to hit targets and deer. The shape of every archer's arm and upper body is somewhat unique, and these variations in physical build will sometimes require slight deviations from textbook-perfect shooting form.

Variations in stance. Although most archers seem to shoot best when standing with toes pointed at right angles to the target, a fair number also shoot while using a more "open stance" with toes pointed slightly *toward* the target. An open stance is especially desirable if you have trouble with the bowstring hitting your armguard or the bow-arm side of your chest. Facing the target slightly with your feet tends to move the bowstring farther away from your chest and arm during the draw and shot, which can in turn enhance bow-shooting accuracy.

In virtually every instance, archers who try to shoot with toes pointing *away* from the target more than 90

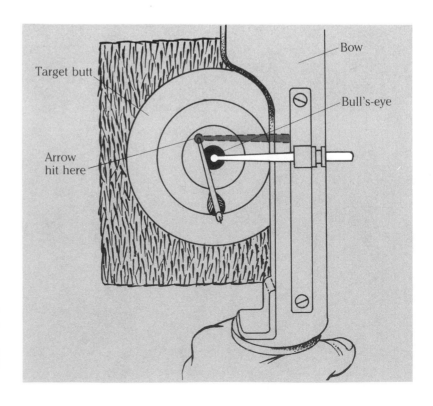

To sight-in a bow, a shooter simply moves the bowsight pin to where the arrows are grouping. For example, if arrows are consistently impacting high and to the left, the pin should be moved up and to the left.

Normal stance

Open stance

Conventional bowstring grip

Apache draw

degrees will experience problems with bowstring collision against the chest and bow arm. Many bowhunters unconsciously shoot with their feet rotated too far away from the target, naively handicapping their hitting ability in the process.

Variations in bowstring grip. Although most bowhunters find that they shoot best by drawing with one finger above the arrow and two below, a few prefer the so-called "Apache draw" with all three fingers beneath the arrow. Those who do draw in such fashion are invariably shooters who prefer not to use bow-

sights. The Apache draw brings arrows closer to the aiming eye than a conventional bowstring hold. This allows you to aim down the arrow like sighting over a gun barrel. "Gun barreling" is especially popular with hunters who usually take deer from tree stands at very close range where precise aiming is not especially critical.

As you perfect your bow-shooting ability, you will also naturally experiment with different methods of placing pressure on the drawn bowstring with your fingers. The average shooter distributes bowstring weight fairly evenly on all three drawing fingers, but

A high anchor

Anchoring along side of chin

Anchoring under chin

many archers find that they achieve smoother string releases by placing the bulk of the pressure on the upper two fingers, the lower two fingers, the middle finger, or the outside two fingers. Everyone's hand is shaped uniquely, so you should experiment to determine what sort of finger-pressure distribution makes for maximum shooting comfort and tightest arrow groups.

Variations in anchor. Placing the index finger in the corner of the mouth is the most common method of anchoring the bowstring hand. However, variations in facial shape or other factors sometimes cause archers to use a different anchor. For example, bowhunters who prefer to gun-barrel shoot with an Apache draw often anchor higher than normal on their face to bring the arrow into even closer alignment with their aiming eye.

Bowhunters who shoot fairly light-draw bows with relatively arching trajectory often anchor on or beneath the chin so arrow trajectory is raised and more bowsight pins can be used for longer shooting ranges. As long as an anchor is solid and consistent, and as long as it produces a special desired effect, never be bashful about using it to hunt deer.

Variations in bow grip. The majority of shooters use a so-called "straight grip" on their bows. This grip places the top of the bow hand more or less in line with the top of the forearm. However, a unique bow-handle configuration, the peculiar shape of a bowhunter's hand, or another factor sometimes requires a grip of a slightly different sort for maximum comfort and efficiency. A common alternative to the straight grip is the high-wrist grip, which angles the bow hand downward at a fairly steep angle.

A less common grip is the low-wrist, or heeling, grip, which transfers pressure against the bow hand from the web of the hand downward along the palm and heel of the hand. The low-wrist grip is not especially accurate compared to higher wrist grips. But it does help distribute drawing weight over a larger area of the hand if an archer has a weak or injured wrist.

TIPS ON SHOOTING PRACTICE

A bowhunter should begin diligently practicing with his bow at least three months before hunting season. Practice should be a slow, deliberate process emphasizing the steps of accurate shooting. To begin with, a shooter should release only 20 or 30 arrows per practice session, and should practice no more than three times per week. As shooting muscles strengthen, he should increase the number of shots per session until he can shoot 60 to 100 arrows over a two-hour period without becoming wobbly and badly fatigued. A hunter who has been shooting several months can keep his muscles and aiming instincts sharp with weekly practice sessions of 60 to 75 arrows.

BETTER ACCURACY

Most bowhunters do not shoot nearly as well as they could. Part of the problem is a lack of well-tuned shooting gear—something that will be discussed later. But often bowhunters simply do not realize how deadly accurate they could become with regular practice and a positive mental attitude. Most people never exceed their personal expectations, and most bowhunters do not expect more than mediocre shooting from themselves and their equipment.

Here are some shooting goals any normally coordinated person with decent eyesight should be able to meet within six or eight months of regular bow-shooting. At 20 yards, an archer should be able to group 90 percent of his arrows within a 4-inch bull's-eye. At 40 yards, 90 percent of his shots should hit a standard 9-inch paper plate. Many experienced bowhunters shoot even better than this, achieving arrow groups of 2 or 3 inches at 20 yards and 5 or 6 inches at 40.

A bowhunter who cannot meet these standards def-initely has room for improvement, and should consciously, and patiently strive to do better. The result will be more shooting enjoyment on targets and more venison in the freezer.

COMMON SHOOTING PROBLEMS

As an archer perfects his basic bow-shooting ability on the target range, he's bound to experience problems that cause temporary setbacks in his progress toward greater accuracy. Here are a few of the more common troubles.

Target panic. Target panic, or freezing, is a common psychological problem. Panic is usually caused by excessively tired muscles, but can develop into a severe mental hangup if an archer does not readily identify and work to counter it before it becomes deeply ingrained.

Basically, target panic occurs when a bowhunter begins freezing off target with his sight pins. Muscles seem to lock up, and no amount of effort will bring the sights to the center of the target. Characteristically, a shooter who freezes off target releases the bowstring after wobbling about a bit, and the result is usually a poor, inaccurate shot.

Half the battle in beating target panic is to avoid becoming worried about it. It usually rears its ugly head because a shooter is fatigued and is physically

Straight grip

High-wrist grip

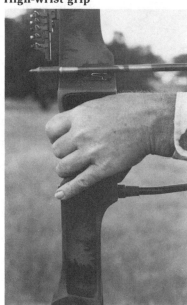

Low-wrist grip

not up to swinging the bow to the bull's-eye for a solid aim and smooth bowstring release. The best cure is immediately ending a practice session whenever such physical symptoms arise. Do not try to fight the situation—this will only make it worse.

Bowhunters who become psychological freezers can cure the ailment in systematic fashion. The easiest way is merely aiming at the target repeatedly without actually releasing the bowstring. A hunter with target panic can usually swing right on target if he knows he isn't going to shoot, and enough such "dry practice" will eventually allow solid aims and actual shots.

Target panic may sound like a bizarre bow-shooting problem, but virtually every archer locks horns with it at some point in practice sessions.

Plucking the bowstring. Overly tired shooting muscles can also cause bowstring plucking. In this case a hunter begins strumming the bowstring with his fingers during the release instead of simply relaxing his fingers and letting the string slide smoothly away. The bowstring hand invariably flies out from the shooter's face during a pluck, and the arrow usually hits to the right of center (for right-handed shooters). Resting the fingers and consciously releasing the bowstring smoothly is the best cure for a string-plucking habit.

Caving in. A bowhunter who caves in drops his bow as he releases instead of holding it up and following through correctly. Caving in usually results in a low-and-right point of impact and can only be solved with conscious follow-through effort. As with most bow-shooting problems, caving in is caused by overly tired shooting muscles during a practice session that is too long.

Grabbing the bow. A hunting bow should be gripped firmly but not tightly during the entire draw, aim, and bowstring release. Some archers tend to grab at the bow (tighten up their bow hands) as an arrow is released—a mistake which generally sends an arrow from a right-hand bow sailing off to the left. An archer should consciously make his bow hand *feel like a stump* as he aims to take a shot—relaxing the tightly closed hand will eliminate bow-grabbing and enhance accuracy considerably.

Diligent shooting practice gets the game. Joanne Adams regularly takes deer with bow-and-arrow gear out to 30 or 40 yards—solid testimony to her well-practiced bow-shooting form.

TUNING THE BOW/ARROW COMBO

The average bowhunter purchases a bow, arrows, and accessories, shoots a few arrows at a bale of hay during the week prior to deer season, and naively believes his gear is ready for the hunt. Even meticulous archers often fail to realize how important proper bow/arrow tune-up is to accuracy and limp along for years with setups that launch wobbly, only marginally accurate shafts. Most of them never even know their arrows are flying poorly because the wobble is too fast and too subtle to detect with the naked eye. Nonetheless, wobbly arrow flight produced by 99 percent of hunting bows in the field degrades accuracy considerably and results in many missed shots.

ARROW WOBBLE

The most accurate bow/arrow combinations shoot shafts that do not wobble at all. Anytime an arrow does wobble in flight, it tends to veer at least slightly

A hunter can shoot extremely well with a properly tuned bow. Good shooters prove this on occasion by actually splitting one arrow with another. Such a feat is called a "Robin Hood" by target buffs, and requires perfect arrow flight.

off course and also loses important deer-penetrating energy. Hunting broadheads with their wide, air-catching blades magnify arrow-wobble inaccuracy tenfold, often causing shafts to dart and veer wildly. This phenomenon, called "broadhead planing," is one that every longtime bowhunter has witnessed and marveled at. Unfortunately, all too often a hunter discovers planing as his arrow sails harmlessly past the largest buck he has seen all season long.

There are two kinds of wobble a bowhunter must tune out of his arrows—up-and-down wobble, called porpoising; and side-to-side wobble, called fishtailing. As often as not, both forms of arrow wobble occur at once, causing the tail end of an arrow to describe a slight circular motion in flight.

Bowhunters who practice for months with field points often become confident in their shooting prowess—even with untuned bows—because field-point arrows can wobble considerably and still hit more or less where they are aimed. However, a proper bow tune-up to eliminate arrow wobble will instantly improve a shooter's target and field shooting performance no matter what kind of arrowhead he is using. The effects of such tuning are more dramatic when broadheads are being used.

INITIAL TUNING STEPS

As mentioned earlier, to produce tolerable arrow flight, it is necessary to select the proper arrow size to match a bow, and to set the arrow rest and nocking point correctly. If the arrow plate portion of the rest is set about ¼ inch away from the bow, and if the nock locator on the bowstring is about ⅜ inch above right angles to the arrow rest, arrow wobble should be less than horrendous for most bow/arrow combinations. However, in 999 cases out of 1000, both arrow rest and nock locator will need to be fine adjusted before arrow wobble is completely eliminated.

TUNING WITH A BARE SHAFT

The only foolproof method of fine-tuning a bow also happens to be very easy. This method is called bare-shaft tuning, and it requires two items besides a hunting bow—a field-point-tipped arrow *without* fletching attached, and a large, pure-white piece of paper or

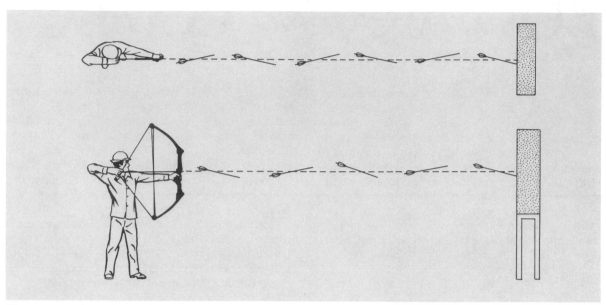

There are two basic kinds of arrow wobble—side-to-side wobble (top drawing), called fishtailing; and up-and-down wobble, called porpoising. Both varieties severely reduce accuracy, especially when deer-hunting broadheads are attached to shafts.

The stark-white background provided by a tuning target lets a shooter clearly see how bare tuning shafts fly. This allows deliberate nocking-point and arrow-plate adjustments to eliminate the slightest arrow wobble.

cardboard with a small black aiming dot in the center. The bare, fletchless shaft must be exactly the same in every other detail as the arrows an archer normally shoots. It can be made by cutting away the vanes or feathers from an ordinary arrow. *Warning: a bare, bow-tuning shaft should never be shot with a broadhead attached because dangerously erratic flight can result!*

To tune a bow using the bare-shaft method, the archer should affix the large white tuning target to a butt and begin shooting the bare shaft at a distance of about 10 feet. As he shoots, he should watch the shaft against the stark white background to see which way its tail end veers in flight. A bare shaft does not wobble as it flies because it has no fletching to keep the tail end in tow—instead, the nock end of the shaft swings farther and farther in whichever direction it is misaligned as it leaves the bow. Tail leaning is clearly visible when a shaft is silhouetted against a close, white target and tells the archer instantly how he must adjust his bow to correct for wobble.

Adjusting a bow to cure arrow wobble is easy when using a bare shaft. If the shaft flies tail high, the nock locator on the string must be moved down. If the shaft flies tail low, the nock locator must be moved up. If the shaft flies tail left, the arrow-plate portion of the arrow rest must be moved to the left. If the shaft flies tail right, the arrow-plate portion of the arrow rest must be moved to the right.

With a cushion plunger arrow plate, very slight tail-right or tail-left tendencies in a bare arrow shaft can be eliminated by loosening the plunger spring when shafts fly tail-right and tightening the spring when

ADJUSTING THE NOCKING POINT

A test session will help you determine whether your nocking point is too high or too low.

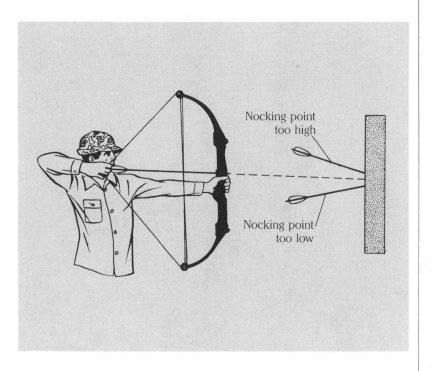

A bowstring square allows precise placement of a nocking point in relation to the arrow rest. The square is inexpensive and makes elimination of arrow porpoising a whole lot easier than randomly moving the nock locator about.

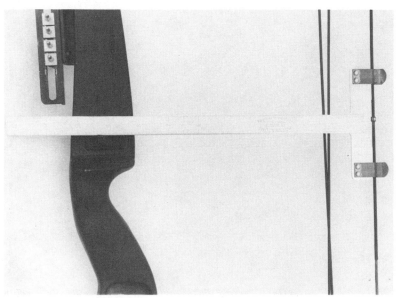

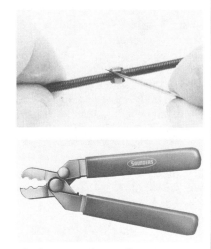

A shooter can easily pry open a clamp-on nocking point (top photo) with the thin blade of a knife. Once this nock locator is loosened, it can be adjusted on the string and clamped tightly again with inexpensive nocking-point pliers.

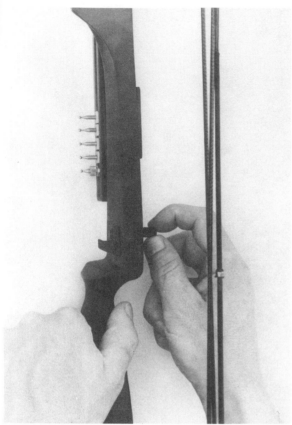

Any screw-adjustable arrow plate greatly diminishes side-to-side arrow wobble. A solid plate like this model will not yield quite the accuracy of a cushion-plunger or springy rest setup, but it is capable of doing a fairly decent tuning job.

FINE POINTS ON BOW TUNING

Any change a bowhunter makes in his bow-and-arrow combination or in his basic shooting style will generally require another tune-up session. For example, if arrowhead weight is changed, arrows that were previously tuned immediately begin to fishtail (wobble side to side). Similarly, removing a bow quiver from a bow that was tuned with the quiver in place will cause noticeable arrow wobble. A hunter who switches from a straight-wrist grip to a high-wrist grip, begins anchoring in a different place on his face, or changes the way he grips the bowstring will throw the fine tuning completely out of kilter. This is crucial to remember because almost every archer makes occasional changes in shooting equipment and basic shooting style.

Certain natural changes in a hunting bow over time also require an occasional check of the fine tuning by the bare-shaft method. For example, most laminated hunting-bow limbs tend to relax or let down in draw weight as the years go by, a subtle change that can yield not-so-subtle results on targets and game. Similarly, a Dacron bowstring will stretch minutely throughout its shooting life, which in turn changes a bow's thrusting power slightly. These and similar changes in bow components are overlooked by many unknowing bowhunters. But the careful shooter checks the tune of his bow at least twice a year and makes necessary adjustments that let him continue to hit exactly where he aims.

Proper bow-tuning produces excellent bare-shaft flight and perfect projectile entry into a target butt. Once the bow-tuning is completed, regular fletched arrows should fly superbly to the target.

shafts fly tail-left (reverse these directions for left-hand bows). A cushion plunger plate can be adjusted until arrow flight is positively perfect because it allows very fine plunger-spring adjustments.

Most often, bare shafts shot from untuned bows will require both arrow-rest and nock locator movement. For example, a hunting bow might initially cast a bare shaft tail high and right. To eliminate such tendencies, the nock locator must be moved down ¹⁄₁₆ inch at a time and the arrow plate moved to the right ¹⁄₁₆ inch at a time until the bare shaft flies like a dart with no tail lean at all.

Once a hunting bow shoots bare arrow shafts perfectly, it will shoot fletched shafts with superb accuracy. If extensive arrow-rest and nock-locator adjustment fails to straighten out bare-shaft flight, an archer is using the wrong arrow size for the bow and must experiment with other sizes until arrows *do* straighten out. An experienced archery dealer can help any archer select an arrow size that *will* fly well from a hunting bow set at a particular draw weight and draw length.

OPTIONAL SHOOTING EQUIPMENT

As a bowhunter perfects his basic shooting skills and experiments with variations in style, he is likely to try out quite a few optional items that may or may not improve shooting performance. Archery-store shelves are lined with so-called aids to pinpoint shooting—some of which are time-tested winners while others are the misbegotten creations of marketing experts who are more interested in getting your buck than helping you hit the buck you are after. Here are a few of the most beneficial optional shooting items preferred by serious bowhunters.

Wrist slings and finger straps. A wrist sling or finger strap literally ties an archer's hand to the bow handle. Slings and straps are used by hunters who have chronic problems with grabbing their bows at the instant of bowstring release. To prevent the inaccuracy which results from bow grabbing, they shoot with their bow hand open fully and rely upon slings

or straps to prevent their bow from falling to the ground as shots are taken.

Wrist slings and finger straps are somewhat inconvenient to use because they must be slipped off to rest the bow hand or put down the bow. However, if an archer is prone to grab his bow, these aids can improve his shooting performance tremendously.

Bowstring peeps and kissers. A bowstring peep is a round or oval gizmo that attaches directly to a bowstring in line with a shooter's eye. This peep is similar to the rear peep sight on a rifle because it ensures perfectly consistent eye alignment with the front sight on each and every shot. A bowstring peep with a large aperture hole is favored by many bowhunters because it forces them to anchor in exactly the same place from shot to shot. This eliminates changing points of impact caused by a less than perfect, "floating" anchor.

A kisser is a small plastic bowstring attachment that also promotes a consistent anchor. This disc-shaped item is positioned on the bowstring so that the archer can press it against his lips and/or teeth on every shot. A kisser is no cure-all for inconsistent anchoring but

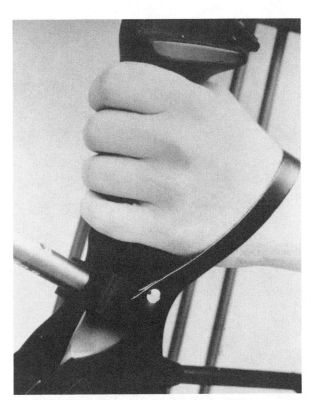

A wrist sling literally ties a shooter's hand to the handle of a bow. This ensures an accurate, fully relaxed grip during a shot—something a few archers cannot seem to master without this important bow-shooting aid.

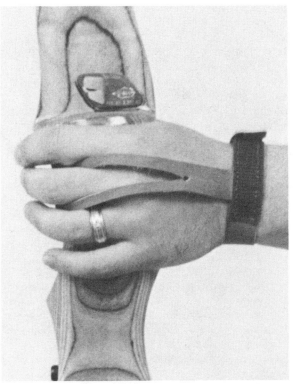

One form of finger strap features snug Velcro attachment for a shooter's wrist. An accessory of this sort can be a nuisance in the woods, but for some hunters the only alternative is regularly missing shots at deer.

A target-shooting bowstring peep (above left) has a very small viewing hole to ensure exact eye alignment from shot to shot. By contrast, a bowhunting peep has a large aperture that ensures good visibility.

A peep, at right, must be attached to the bowstring in exact alignment with your natural eye position. This sight is similar to the back sight on a rifle and can greatly increase shooting accuracy.

does provide an extra reference point to help a shooter aim from shot to shot.

Arrow holders. An arrow holder is a simple, spring-loaded device that attaches to a bow near the arrow rest and holds the arrow on the rest as an archer watches for deer. Holding an arrow on the rest with the index finger can become tiring over several hours of hunting, and can also be insufferably cold in chilly weather when mittens are advisable. An arrow holder allows a hunter to stop worrying about physically holding the arrow in a ready position. It automatically and silently flips out of the way the instant the draw begins.

Game trackers. A game-tracker device consists of a large spool of fine but very strong thread that mounts on the bow. The leading end of this thread is attached to a hunting arrow so that it pays out after the arrow has been shot. Game trackers are used primarily by deer hunters in very heavy forests where finding mortally wounded animals can be difficult. Trackers are especially useful in rainy weather that can wash out all signs of a blood trail.

Once a deer is hit with a game-tracker arrow, the fleeing animal pulls hundreds of yards of thread behind it to aid in the recovery operation. Because a game-tracker thread tends to drag down an arrow at medium-to-long range, shooting with this accessory should be limited to a maximum of 20 to 25 yards.

An arrow holder snugly grips a shaft and keeps it on the rest until an archer begins to draw. Then, the holder flips out of the way to allow unimpeded arrow flight.

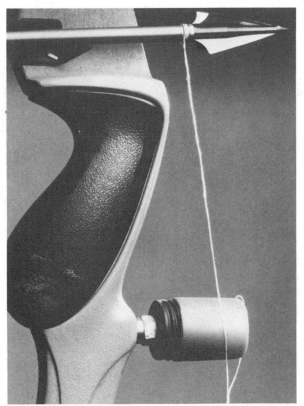

A game-tracker spool is screw mounted in the stabilizer hole in a bow. The thread pays out smoothly behind the arrow. If the shaft hits the mark, the archer can follow the thread to the mortally wounded animal.

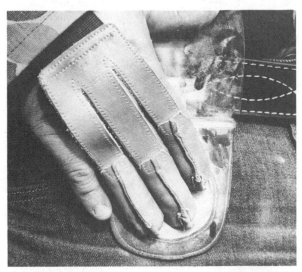

A belt-carried powder pouch has two uses in the field. First, it lubricates a glove or tab for slick, accurate bowstring releases. Second, it discharges talcum powder to indicate the direction of even slight breezes.

Powder pouches. Special belt-attached talcum-powder pouches are designed to enhance hunting and shooting performance. These pouches can be filled with any scented or unscented talc and release talc through a special opening when gently tapped with the hand. Their purpose in the woods is twofold—talc released on a shooting glove or tab allows a smooth, slippery bowstring release for better accuracy; and a tap on the pouch releases powder that floats in the direction of the slightest breeze. Since slick string releases and keeping track of wind direction are both important in bowhunting deer, many archers regard powder pouches as standard field equipment.

Illuminated bowsight pins. Several companies sell illuminated bowsight pins that are powered by small batteries similar to those in hearing aids. Light-up pins are favorites of deer hunters who frequently shoot at first or last light of day. Illuminated sight pins are especially well suited for stand-hunting of whitetail deer because whitetails often leave heavy bedding cover late in the evening. Shooting under these circumstances is generally possible with conventional brass

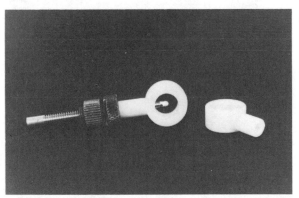

One bowsight-pin design consists of a phosphorescent ring around a fine aiming bead. In low-light deer-shooting situations, the ring shows up clearly to allow accurate arrow placement. (Bohning Inc. photo)

bowsight pins, but illuminated pins clarify aiming and increase the odds of a solid, vital hit. These special bowsight pins are not for everyone, but they certainly are worth checking out at the local archery store.

Spare arms. A spare arm is composed of one or two fabric-covered metal hooks that cradle a hunting bow when an archer needs both hands free for tasks such as using a binocular or riding a horse. A single-hook spare arm attaches to a hunter's belt and makes

A spare-arm hook is handy. A hunter can hang his bow from this belt-attached hook by the handle or by the string, leaving both hands free for other tasks.

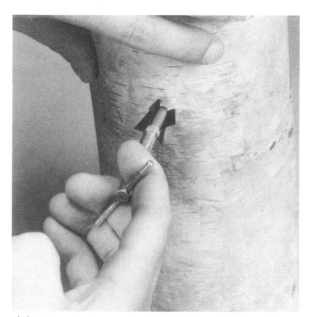

A hunter using screw-in arrowheads can generally salvage a shaft that accidentally hits a tree. However, a better solution is retrieving the arrowhead as well with the help of a T-handle arrowhead puller.

A two-hook spare arm is ideal for carrying a bow on horseback, walking steadily along, or otherwise moving about with both hands free. However, this accessory does not allow lightning-fast access to a bow.

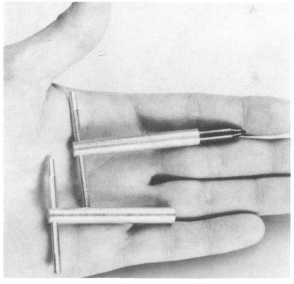

One popular arrowhead puller features a threaded female end for removing arrowheads and a threaded male end, too. When not being used to salvage misdirected shots, this handy accessory doubles as a tree-stand bow-hanging hook.

a handy hook for hanging a bow by its string or grip; a double-hook spare arm suspends beneath an archer's armpit from a shoulder-harness setup. The double hook is best for more active pursuits such as walking or horseback riding because a bow is more solidly cradled in place. Spare arms of the belt-attached, single-hook variety are especially popular with on-the-go archers who periodically pause to glass surrounding terrain.

Arrowhead pullers. Every archer occasionally misses the mark and buries an arrow in a tree, log, or stump. The arrow can usually be retrieved by unscrewing it from the arrowhead, even if the head itself is deeply lodged in place. However, an arrowhead puller allows a hunter to extract all but the most tightly wedged broadheads and field points. The puller normally screw-attaches to the threads of an arrowhead, allowing the shooter to grasp the T-handle of the puller and slowly lever the arrowhead free. Many bowhunters in heavily wooded areas carry a small, stout arrowhead puller at all times.

Other shooting aids. There are literally dozens of other shooting gadgets for a bowhunter. Most of the practical ones look it, while the worthless gimmicks generally stand out for exactly what they are. However, only experimentation with these items will tell a hunter exactly which ones are best for him and the conditions in which he hunts.

FINAL PREPARATION BEFORE A HUNT

An archer who selects proper shooting equipment and learns the basics of using this equipment is well on his way to becoming a top-notch bowhunter. However, prior to actually heading afield it is wise to make some final alterations of the bow/arrow combination and also to fine-tune field-shooting as well as target-shooting abilities. Conventional backyard practice on bull's-eyes is important to success at deer hunting, but so are the following preparations for an actual hunt.

READYING BOW AND ARROWS

The careful bowhunter oils and otherwise maintains the bow/arrow setup from the moment he pulls his gear from the factory boxes. However, another sort of shooting-gear preparation is every bit as important. This is silencing the creaks and rattles in a bow that often accompany carrying and shooting.

The most common noisemakers are a bow quiver that rattles against the bow during a shot, arrows inside a quiver that rattle together or vibrate against the quiver or bow itself, loose bowsight pins that hum like bees at the instant the bowstring is released, and loose screw-mounted bow components, such as a stabilizer, bowsight bracket, or adjustable arrow plate. All such parts must be somehow silenced to prevent alarming a deer before the arrow hits.

The best way to detect rattles and hums in the bow and quiver is not by actually shooting. Instead, a hunter should rap the handle riser of the bow firmly

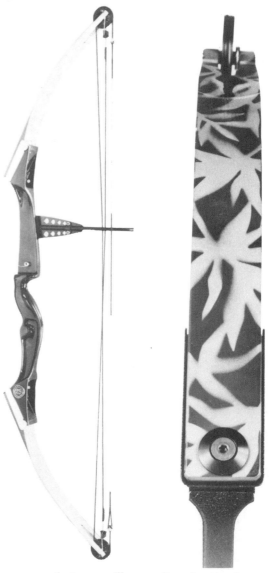

Some manufacturers will camouflage hunting bows on a special-order basis.

Discussing the fine points of gear preparation with good friends is one of many pleasures enjoyed by bowhunters. Comparing notes often leads to better setups.

with his fist and listen for telltale noises. A properly silenced bow will thud dully when smacked in such a fashion. Any extraneous noise should be located by repeated raps on the bow. Loose bolts and accessories should be tightened up; vibrating parts between bow, quiver, and arrows must be hushed with adhesive-backed rubber weather stripping or plastic tape. It's also a good idea to glue down all locking bolts on the bow quiver, sight, and other bow attachments with vinyl arrow-fletching cement. Available at archery stores, the cement prevents bolts and screws from working loose during the hunt and can be removed at any time with thinner.

BOW CAMOUFLAGE

The average hunting bow comes from the factory with shiny and light-colored surfaces meant to attract a buyer's eye across a store counter. A few bows are camouflaged on a special-order basis by the manufacturer, but most must be carefully camouflaged by the owner prior to hunting.

There are three basic ways to eliminate the mirrorlike shine of bow limbs and mute light-colored factory finishes. Some bowhunters use so-called bow-limb sleeves, which are simple tubes of camouflage cloth slipped over the limbs and ends of a bow's handle riser section. Other archers carefully adorn the flat or semi-flat surfaces of their bows with commercial camouflage tape in pleasant leaf-print patterns. However, the vast majority of veteran deer hunters spray-paint their bows in two or three nonglare, contrasting colors that blend very well with the woods.

Cloth bow-limb sleeves are inexpensive and quick to install, but they never completely cover all shiny surfaces and tend to soak up water during foggy or rainy weather. Wet sleeves can retard the action of bow limbs and also tend to give hunters an unwelcome shower as limbs suddenly come taut during the release of an arrow. Camouflage tape is a better bet, but takes a long time to apply and never fully covers all parts of a bow. Tape also sometimes leaves gummy residue when removed.

Spray-painting a hunting bow is best of all because a thin coat of nonglare paint covers completely and takes very little time to apply. Colors can be changed or freshened once a year with ease, and the camo paint can be scrubbed off with special remover supplied by manufacturers. Whether sprayed in alternating bands of contrasting colors such as black and light brown or more carefully camouflaged with a leaf-print design as shown in the photos on the next page, a camo-painted hunting bow will blend neatly into the surroundings and won't catch the wary eye of a nearby deer. A variety of special nonglare bow paints are available at well-stocked archery stores.

Cloth sleeves (below) adequately hide the mirrorlike surfaces on bow limbs, but do not camouflage the bow handle itself. Sleeves are seldom used by deer hunters with much field experience. Adhesive-backed leaf-print tape (photo right) is available in a variety of woodsy colorations. But tape is time-consuming to install and never fully covers a bow for complete deer-fooling camouflage.

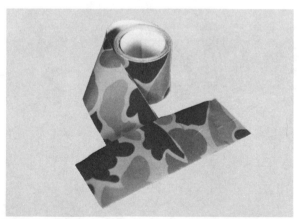

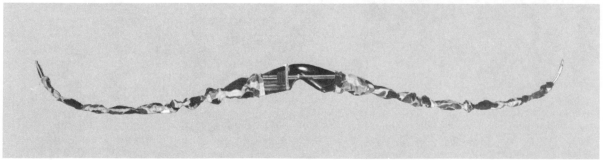

HOW TO CAMOUFLAGE-PAINT A BOW

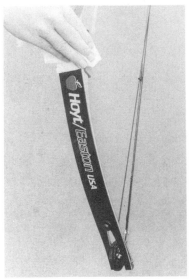

1. *Before camouflaging a bow with spray paint, degrease all surfaces with a paper towel soaked in rubbing alcohol. This mild cleaner in no way harms a bow and evaporates very quickly.*

2. *Once a bow is clean and dry, lightly coat all surfaces with good bow-camo paint in a medium-tone color, such as tan or light brown. Let the paint dry for several hours.*

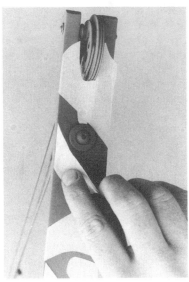

3. *Next, cut leaf-shaped decals from wide masking tape and lightly press these on bow limbs and handle to form a pleasing pattern. Exact decal shape and distribution are strictly personal preference.*

4. *Once decals are in place, spray the entire bow with dark paint, such as jet black or forest green. This second coat should be allowed to dry at room temperature.*

5. *The final step is removing the masking-tape decals. Take care to avoid scuffing the paint during this phase of the bow-camouflaging operation.*

6. *The finished product blends with a wide variety of deer-hunting backgrounds. All mirrorlike surfaces have disappeared, and so have light-colored, eye-catching areas.*

BACKYARD PRACTICE

As a bowhunter perfects standard target-shooting form on a backyard range, he'll gradually build his muscles and develop excellent hand/eye coordination with a bow. Development of muscles and skills is essential to shooting at deer and leads to smooth, accurate bow-shooting as the weeks of practice roll by.

Once an archer has bow-shooting basics mastered, he should begin moving back to more distant shooting ranges, such as 40, 50, 60, and even 70 yards. Trying to hit a target at these ranges can be demoralizing at first, but regular practice will allow fairly accurate shooting out to 70 yards. Virtually all top-notch shooters can hit a 12-inch bull's-eye almost every time at 70 yards, provided they know the exact distance of the shot.

Shooting at longer ranges accomplishes two important things. First, it prepares a hunter for those occasional instances when closer shots aren't possible. Second, it makes shots of 15, 20, or even 30 yards seem like a piece of cake, thus bolstering confidence and increasing potential to make good hits on nearby animals.

As time goes along and deer season approaches, bowhunters should supplement their regular textbook shooting sessions with some practice shooting from awkward body positions. Bowhunters are usually able to shoot at deer from a classic upright stance, but sometimes they're required to kneel, sit, or twist about at awkward angles to make shots in heavy foliage. Practicing from unusual positions prepares a hunter for the worst and improves the odds of making those nasty little twisting or bending shots that sometimes decide the outcome of the entire deer-hunting season.

Shooting uphill and downhill. One of the most common errors deer-hunting archers make is failing to practice uphill and downhill shooting prior to season. Arrow trajectory is significantly altered by upward and downward angles—altered enough to cause complete misses on stationary, broadside deer. Only practice can teach hunters how to compensate for various ups and downs encountered afield—shooters must develop a feel for this sort of thing.

The most common downward shooting situation in the woods is experienced by tree-stand hunters. Anyone perched 15 or 20 feet above the ground must shoot sharply downward at deer, and this requires a dramatic change in aiming. Arrows always hit higher than normal when shot downward, and hundreds of nice bucks escape every year because bowhunters either do not know to hold low when shooting out of trees or forget to do so in the heat of the action. Generally, a hold at the bottom of the brisket hits a deer dead-center through the chest as the animal strolls beneath a tree

stand. A tree-stand bowhunter should carefully practice downward shooting from an elevated platform such as a flat rooftop or tree stand itself to learn how to compensate with his own bow/arrow combination.

Uphill shooting is a bit trickier than downhill shooting because arrows initially fly higher than normal, then drop off as gravity slows them down. Most archers hold slightly low on uphill shots out to 30 yards and hold a bit above normal as distance increases to 50, 60, or 70 yards.

There is absolutely no substitute for *knowing* how arrows will fly in various shooting situations. The bowhunter who practices diligently at unorthodox shooting will hit most deer *on purpose* instead of flinging arrows haphazardly and merely hoping for the best.

Finding your mark. One of the most important skills to perfect prior to heading afield is learning to hit silhouette targets that approximate an actual deer. It is far easier to aim at a bull's-eye than at the uniformly gray brown side of a deer, and most archers who are accustomed to bull's-eyes alone tend to blow shot after shot at both silhouette targets and live deer.

Commercial deer targets force a hunter to shoot precisely, even when there are no bull's-eyes to help in zeroing in. Most beginning archers mistakenly tend to shoot at an entire deer instead of concentrating on a small, vital part of the anatomy.

Every archer has a tendency to shoot in the general direction of the whole deer instead of aiming at a small, imaginary spot in the deer's vital area. Careful bowhunters can overcome this urge to spray arrows at a deer by practicing on commercial animal targets, deer-silhouette targets of cardboard, and 3-D deer targets made of tough, durable Ethafoam. Even practice at an ordinary brown paper bag can help a shooter learn to *pick a spot* on the bag instead of shooting at the entire, uniformly colored target. Spot-choosing skill is necessary to consistently shoot deer squarely through the lungs instead of hitting them any old place.

ORGANIZED SHOOTING PRACTICE

Many successful bowhunters learn their shooting craft on a backyard range. But supplementing this informal practice with organized shooting can be fun and beneficial.

Virtually every mid-sized metropolitan area has some sort of archery club that offers structured shooting opportunities and the chance to socialize with bowhunters. Many clubs maintain indoor and outdoor bow-shooting ranges, and quite a few sponsor periodic archery competitions for trophies or cash prizes. Some tournaments are relatively informal events enjoyed by club members alone; others are larger-scale invitational shoots with the sponsorship of such national organizations as the National Field Archers Association (NFAA) or the National Archers Association (NAA). Organized archery shooting is not everybody's cup of tea, but it certainly is an opportunity worth considering.

Three basic types of organized bow-shooting can benefit a serious bowhunter. The first is outdoor field-range shooting, which usually involves walking around a course of 14 or 28 targets set up at ranges between 15 feet and 80 yards. Most field ranges are laid out in country similar to that inhabited by deer, and the targets used on these ranges can vary from ordinary bull's-eye faces to 3-D or paper deer targets. The experience of shooting field courses is not unlike that of playing golf.

A second bowhunter-oriented shooting activity is indoor winter shooting at fairly close range. Most larger archery clubs have access to 20-yard indoor bow-shooting facilities that allow target practice during the colder, stormier times of year. Some shooting takes the form of competitive leagues similar to those in bowling; other indoor practice is strictly relaxed and

Indoor bow-shooting during the winter months sharpens your eye and keeps bow-drawing muscles fit. It also provides enjoyable companionship with other hunters.

Organized silhouette shooting is steadily gaining popularity with American bowhunters. This form of target competition requires rapid, accurate shooting at ranges between 20 and 80 yards—good practice for deer season.

noncompetitive in nature. Many serious hunters rely on off-season indoor shooting to keep their muscles and aiming eyes in shape for summer and fall hunting seasons.

Silhouette target shooting is a relatively new but extremely enjoyable organized bowhunter event. Such formal competition is patterned after the silhouette shooting enjoyed by riflemen and pistoleros, and pits the archer against 12 lifelike bird and animal silhouettes at ranges between 20 and 80 yards. The sheer fun of trying to knock over three chickens, three pigs, three turkeys, and three rams within a two-minute time limit makes bowhunter silhouette competition worthwhile. Also the chance for trophies and the satisfaction of serious competition makes this sport exceedingly popular.

One of the most gratifying dimensions of organized bow-shooting practice is being able to socialize with other archers who have an equally strong interest in hunting deer and other kinds of game. Swapping hunting stories and comparing equipment notes with other shooters is highly enjoyable and can also expand one's knowledge of deer hotspots, bow-shooting variations, and in-the-field hunting skills. For many hunting enthusiasts, archery is both a social sport and a solitary hunting pastime.

LEARNING TO SHOOT IN THE FIELD

Conventional target practice alone cannot entirely prepare a bowhunter for that all-important moment when a deer steps into shooting range. However, enough field-shooting practice at natural targets can bring the average archer quite close to game-shooting expertise.

Actually launching arrows at natural objects in the woods teaches several skills that are vital for bagging deer, including the ability to accurately estimate range; the knack for shooting over, under, and around natural foliage; and a feel for hitting targets while dressed in bowhunting clothes. Nothing exactly duplicates the heart-throbbing excitement and tension of drawing down on a live buck, but practice shooting in natural settings injects all shooting elements of the hunt except for the intense excitement.

There are many places an archer can safely shoot in the field. Any patch of woods without human habitation will do, provided access is legal and terrain is broken enough to present plenty of soft, natural target backstops, such as dirt banks, sand hills, and rotten logs. Excessively rocky areas should be avoided because these tend to destroy practice arrows, and very flat terrain allows arrows to skip and slither out of sight forever.

A bowhunter should learn to shoot over, under, and around intervening foliage during preseason field-shooting sessions. That preparation can pay off big when a live deer suddenly appears beyond major obstacles such as limbs and clumps of leaves.

Shooting afield requires no special preparation except dressing in regular deer-hunting clothes and tipping arrows with blunts or no-skip Judo points. At the stage of field practice, the bow/arrow combo should be fully ready for hunting. This includes having sight pins zeroed for distances out to 50 or 60 yards and string silencers, bow quiver, and other accessories solidly and silently installed.

Field shooting, or roving, is a simple, enjoyable endeavor that can be practiced alone or with companions. Archers simply stroll about the woods, shooting repeatedly at targets such as leaves, grass clumps, sticks, and soft dirt clods. To be most effective, shooting practice should concentrate on objects that test a hunter's skills. Shooting sharply uphill and downhill, choosing targets at a wide variety of distances, and

Uninhabited areas with plenty of soft dirt banks, sand hills, and other natural backstops are ideal places to perfect field-shooting ability. An archer who wanders about the woods and shoots repeatedly at leaves, dirt clods, and other targets improves his skill at estimating distance by eye and accurately shooting over broken terrain.

picking situations that require kneeling or twisted shots past intervening bushes and limbs all help sharpen one's ability to hit under pressure.

In-the-field practice also tests out the hunting clothing and other gear. An afternoon or two of ambling over hill and dale with a bow in your mitts will clearly reveal any flaws in selected gear—rattles in the bow/arrow combo, a hat that bumps the bowstring, a baggy sleeve that puffs out around an armguard and collides with the bowstring. Such seemingly minor defects can ruin a shot at a deer, and should be corrected before the hunt.

At its very best, in-the-field practice with companions is highly gratifying. Most roving archers make a game out of practice shooting by playing follow-the-leader and awarding points for arrows that come closest to the selected targets. For example, if three bowhunters head for the hills together, Archer A selects the first target to aim at and gives it his best shot. Archers B and C follow suit, with the arrow closest to the mark receiving one competitive point. Next, Archer

B selects a target while Archers C and A wait their turn to shoot. The first shooter to reach a predetermined point total—say 25 points—is the winner of the game. Actually, all three archers will be winners regardless of score because they'll all be sharpening their abilities to estimate distances and hit targets.

One other form of preseason field practice deserves special mention here. This is small-game hunting with a bow and arrow. Virtually every part of the country harbors jackrabbits, ground squirrels, woodchucks, or similar vermin that can be hunted prior to deer season. Small animals inject an extra dimension into field shooting because they must be pursued and taken under the same challenging circumstances a deer hunter often faces. Granted, bagging a one-pound rodent is not nearly as exciting as bagging a 150-pound buck, but the little animal is far more difficult to hit and possesses the same alert senses and survival instincts. The bowhunter who can regularly bag pint-sized varmints will often find it surprisingly easy to shoot at deer with high accuracy.

THE ULTIMATE TEST: SHOOTING AT DEER

With diligent preparation, a bowhunter puts the odds of bagging a deer in his favor. However, there are certain things that only shooting at deer can teach effectively. These include learning to control excitement in the presence of big game, learning when and when not to take a shot, and learning to perform smoothly when a second shot is required or when some other unexpected difficulty arises. Aside from hunting deer for several years and learning by making mistakes, the best an archer can do is to try to anticipate shooting problems and decide in advance on the best solutions.

BUCK FEVER

The primary obstacle most deer hunters need to overcome is becoming uncontrollably excited when they get within close range of game—a phenomenon known as buck fever. The strain of finding yourself in close range of a deer is apt to cause a bona fide case of the jitters that so weakens muscles and jangles normally clear senses that accurate shooting is next to impossible. There are authentic cases of fever-stricken bowhunters throwing their bows at deer, running away through the woods, or becoming physically unable to draw back when deer suddenly popped into view. Extreme buck fever is not very common, but virtually every bowhunter suffers at least a touch of "the old buck" when he first begins seeing and shooting at animals. Controlling adrenaline levels and making critical shots count is tough but entirely possible if an archer anticipates the problem of excitement prior to ever drawing down on a deer.

The best way to control excitement in the presence of game is to merely regard the situation as no big deal. Too many bowhunters take themselves and their sport far too seriously, and this attitude can heighten tension enormously when a deer presents itself. The archer who recognizes these tendencies in himself should convince himself to regard a shooting opportunity as fun instead of a sacred test of ability. Mental attitude is the sole means of controlling excitement, and an archer can usually psych himself up to perform calmly when the shooting time rolls around. Mental preparation plus lots of hunting experience combine to let seasoned archers nail animals time after time.

The act of shooting at a deer takes just a few seconds to accomplish but often determines the outcome of an entire hunting season. An archer must learn to control his excitement at this moment to make a killing hit.

SETTING UP THE SHOT

Once a deer does present a shot inside reasonable bow range, an archer must do three things in the following order. First, he must accurately determine the distance of the shot to prevent misses high or low. Second, he must time his shot so that the animal's body angle is right and so the deer cannot see him draw. Third, he must choose a specific vital place on the deer to aim, concentrating on this aiming spot instead of shooting at the entire animal.

Range. In most instances, a deer hunter can use a belt-carried rangefinder to take accurate distance readings around a deer stand on notable landmarks such as rocks, trees, and stumps. If a deer appears near such landmarks, the archer can generally estimate the shooting range within a yard or two for an excellent hit. In addition, bowhunters who stillhunt deer often use rangefinders as well to pinpoint shooting distances on the animals themselves. This is best done when deer are feeding or otherwise can't see the hunter.

To be in best control of the rangefinding, a bowhunter should be well practiced at estimating distance by eye as well. That way he can handle situations when it is not possible to use an optical rangefinding device. For example, a walking hunter who pokes his noggin above a ridgeline and finds himself staring at a dandy buck can do little but guesstimate the range and then draw back and hope the animal stands until the arrow hits. Fumbling with a rangefinder at a time like this is a mistake because no deer will stand still for such nonsense—not for one second. Bowhunters who field shoot a lot before deer season generally develop an ability to estimate distance by eye, although this skill is never as surefire as using an optical rangefinder.

Timing. Once an archer has decided upon the shooting range to a deer, the next step is to properly

In unexpected eyeball-to-eyeball encounters with wary deer at close range, your only hope is visually estimating distance and drawing your bow to shoot. This is no time to monkey with hand-held rangefinding devices.

time the shot. There is usually one best time to shoot at an animal, and that time is invariably when the creature is least likely to see the archer draw and aim. In wide-open areas, the only feasible time to draw is when the animal is facing almost directly away. A deer's peripheral vision is extremely good, so any deer will instantly catch the movement of the draw if its head is anywhere near broadside to the bowhunter. Whenever possible, an archer should wait until a deer's head is obscured by a bush, tree, log, rock, or another deer before raising the bow. This allows an unnoticed draw and an unrushed, deliberate aim.

Hundreds of "gimme" shots are muffed each year by bowhunters who impatiently try to draw at once instead of waiting for an angling-away shot at a deer or waiting until the animal's eyes are blocked by natural cover. The only relatively safe time other than those mentioned is when a bowhunter is perched high above a deer in a stand. Deer cannot see at sharp overhead angles unless they actually crane their necks to scan the sky. This makes a downward shot a relatively safe one no matter what a deer's body angle happens to be.

Whenever possible, precisely determine the distance to a deer with a rangefinder.

Aiming. As in all forms of shooting at deer, a bowhunter must direct his arrow to an area with vital or-

Deer have superb peripheral vision. As a result, bowhunters should take their shots when the eyes of a target animal are completely hidden by grass, brush, or similar natural cover. Otherwise, drawing and aiming a bow will alert the deer.

A deer cannot see directly overhead unless it twists its neck to gawk at rakish upward angles. For this reason, a tree-stand hunter can generally draw and shoot without being detected. Note the safety belt here.

gans or major blood vessels. This means a deliberate aim for the center of the chest cavity or the large part of the ham. The particulars of where to aim at deer with gun and bow will be illustrated and discussed later in this book. But what needs to be stressed here is the importance of *consciously aiming at a small, vital part of a deer's body.* Practice on animal targets helps perfect this ability, and so does remaining cool and collected.

JUMPING STRING

One problem every bowhunter occasionally encounters is a situation in which the target deer jumps string (ducks or sidesteps the arrow). Some bowhunters believe that deer actually see the projectile coming, but in reality it's probably the noise of the bow being shot or the shooting motion of the hunter that triggers a deer's arrow-evading reaction. Regardless of cause, it's a fact that deer have the reflexes to avoid a well-aimed shaft that takes less than one-third second to travel 25 yards. It is one of bowhunting's greatest disappointments to set up a close-range shot at a deer, successfully draw and aim the bow, and watch your arrow slice empty space as the animal does everything but turn wrongside-out in a frantic attempt to get away. Obviously, the longer the shot at a deer, the greater the chance the animal has of making a clean getaway.

Bowhunters cannot control every shooting situation, but they can minimize the risk of deer jumping string in several important ways. First, they should hush their bows as much as possible with bowstring silencers and tight lockdown screws. Second, they should avoid shooting at deer that are likely to see a draw or the

This muley buck was stalked in wide-open country well above timberline. In terrain such as this, the well-practiced ability to hit long-range targets is a big advantage.

slight motion of hands as a shot is actually released. And third, they should always try to set up close-range shots that reduce a deer's odds of moving completely out of the path of an arrow. Jumping string is a phenomenon that must be seen to be believed, and every dedicated bowhunter is sure to witness this frustrating event eventually.

SECOND SHOTS

Once a shot is taken at a deer, it is the archer's responsibility to pay close attention to exactly where that arrow hits. If it hits the animal, knowing *where* it has hit will definitely influence what an archer does next. If an arrow misses entirely, the hunter who sees where it hits in relation to the deer can oftentimes

adjust his aim and make a killing hit with a second shaft if the deer becomes confused and lingers in the area. Exact follow-up procedures for deer hit in various places with arrows will be discussed in detail later in this book. The archer who neglects to note where his arrow has hit seldom makes intelligent follow-up steps.

There is a definite knack to making a second shot pay off on a deer when the first one hits high or low. Shooting over or under a deer is the most common mistake an experienced bowhunter makes because the most difficult part of field shooting is accurately estimating target distance. A bowhunter who incorrectly estimates distance sometimes enjoys a reprieve as the deer stands to gawk about uncertainly. At this point, the canny archer notes where his arrow has hit in relation to the deer, raises or lowers his sights to compensate for the error, and drives the second arrow deep into vital tissue. Second-arrow shooting during field-practice sessions prior to season is the very best way to develop the skill of making that second shot pay off.

HOW FAR IS TOO FAR?

One of the most common questions raised by beginning bowhunters is how long is too long a shot. Unfortunately, there is no pat answer. Each bowhunter must set his own shooting limit based on an honest assessment of his skills. Some excellent bowhunters are relatively poor shots and as a result never shoot at deer beyond 20 or 25 yards. Others have the ability to consistently bag bucks at 40 or 50 yards, provided these animals are not alarmed and present perfect broadside body angles. Each deer hunter should limit his shooting to ranges at which he can consistently hit the 10-inch vital chest area on a deer—such self-imposed restraint leads to quick, humane kills.

PARTING NOTE

Consistent shooting success is never accidental. An ill-prepared bowhunter might get lucky once in awhile, but a dedicated bowhunter makes his own luck by selecting proper shooting equipment to begin with, refining the performance of this gear and his own shooting ability, and constantly striving to improve control over the variables involved getting within range of deer and then staying cool.

CARE OF EQUIPMENT

Bowhunting equipment is durable and fairly trouble free—far more so than ever in the past. As long as equipment is kept in protective cases, it will hold up quite well during routine transport and storage. However, there are certain extra measures that should be taken to protect shooting gear.

BOWS AND COMPONENTS

The two primary enemies of a hunting bow are heat and moisture. Most laminated bow limbs are apt to literally explode if they become too hot to touch. Similarly, steady rain, melting snow, or condensation on a bow is likely to creep into the core wood of limbs—which can cause weakening or breakage—and may also rust vital moving bow parts such as wheel axles, draw-weight adjustment bolts, and the spring in a cushion-plunger arrow rest. Rust can cause noisy performance and can also ruin the straight-shooting capability of a bow.

It is easy to protect a hunting bow from heat and moisture, once an archer is aware that they destroy a bow. Keeping equipment in a case when not in use is one excellent protection. But there is more. A hunter should *never* leave his bow in a closed-up car or truck, especially beneath the curving windshield or rear window. He should likewise protect his bow from the direct heat of campfires, stoves, and other sources of heat. In addition, he should wipe his bow dry after every hunt in the rain or snow. Ordinary hunting exposure to moisture will not hurt bow limbs as long as they do not remain soaked for 24 hours or longer. A final bow-care precaution is to avoid carrying a bow from cold weather into a warm tent or room. This can cause instant condensation on all parts of a bow, which sometimes leads to rust.

Naturally, it makes good sense to prevent a bow's becoming coated with dirt or grime. Gritty material can work into wheel axles and rapidly wear these moving parts. Similarly excessively rough treatment can bend bowsight pins, break arrow rests, fray bowstrings, crack compound wheels, or cause fractures of bow limbs.

Modern archery gear is designed to withstand heavy doses of inclement weather and rough-and-tumble use. A coating of snow every once in awhile in no way damages a quality bow or arrows. The photo model here is no escaped convict. It's renowned archery hunter, writer, and equipment manufacturer Fred Bear in striped pajamas.

Long-term exposure to moisture can soften or crack the wooden cores in laminated bow limbs. Hunting in wet weather causes no problem, provided you towel-dry your bow at the end of every soggy day.

Dacron bowstrings are fairly fragile, fraying or breaking with alarming regularity unless carefully coated with wax. For best results, wax the string about once a month.

For longtime performance of compound-bow parts, a hunter should occasionally lubricate wheel axles, draw-weight adjustment bolts, and the cushion plunger spring with penetrating lubricant. This prevents rusts and ensures smooth, quiet performance.

No matter how careful a hunter is, he must inspect his bow periodically for damage and routinely maintain, repair, or replace worn parts.

Bowstring care. The bowstring is probably the most fragile part of any bow and eventually wears out no matter how careful a hunter is. A Dacron string should be heavily waxed with beeswax or a good synthetic bowstring wax about once a month to protect it from surface fraying. The wax also lubricates individual strands so friction among them during shots will not cause premature breakage. Even so, a bowstring of the best quality will eventually wear out—generally at the point where the arrow is nocked on the string. To prevent a broken string and hazards of flying cables and other bow parts, a string should be replaced after about a year of weekly shooting.

Arrow rest care. Another part of the hunting bow that needs occasional replacement is the arrow rest. Even the best quality flipper rests and springy rests either break off after a year or two of regular shooting, or need new noise-dampening plastic or nylon sleeves.

Bowsight maintenance. Every bowhunter should inspect his bowsight regularly to make sure pins have not been knocked or bent out of alignment. It's surprisingly easy to drop a bow or smack the sight and this can throw the sight out of kilter.

CARE OF ARROWS

Hunting arrows are relatively maintenance free—especially the aluminum arrows most serious archers prefer. They are impervious to the elements, do not bend easily, and can be restraightened if they *do* become bent when shot into targets, game, or natural obstacles, such as trees and rocks.

Shaft and fletching care. Bowhunters who use feather fletching on their shafts instead of plastic fletching must realize that feathers sometimes become matted even though they have been thoroughly coated with silicone spray (or ordinary hair spray). Matting most commonly occurs during a real downpour or after an arrow passes completely through an animal. Matted feather fletching can be restored to its original shape by letting it dry, then steaming it briefly over the spout of a teapot. If feathers are covered with blood, they should be washed out with soapy water before letting them dry and steaming them until they regain their original shape.

Aluminum shafts with plastic fletching can be cleaned of blood and grime after a hunt by scrubbing them in warm, soapy water. Bent shafts can be straightened on an inexpensive arrow straightener or

SHAFT AND FLETCHING MAINTENANCE

Matted feather fletching pops back to original shape like magic when steamed over a teapot spout. However, plastic arrow vanes never flatten down, making them the choice of most bowhunters.

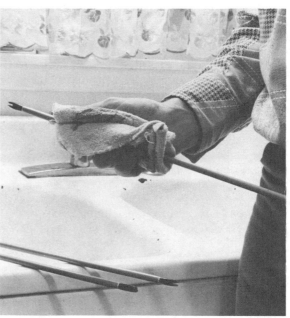

Unlike old-style wooden shafts, modern aluminum arrows are easily cleaned with warm, soapy water. Shafts have hard-anodized surfaces that never deteriorate on contact with moisture, blood, or grime.

A moderately priced arrow-straightening tool quickly restores bent aluminum shafts to brand-new straightness tolerances. Most serious bowhunters own arrow straighteners of one sort or another to keep their "ammunition" in tip-top shooting condition.

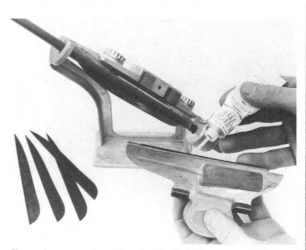

Even the most durable plastic fletching eventually cuts or tears. Although any archery pro shop can replace damaged fletching for a moderate fee, many archers handle this job themselves with inexpensive arrow-fletching tools and fletching cement.

taken to an archery store to have this done for a small fee. Cut or tattered fletching can also be replaced at the archery store. Some hunters replace fletching themselves with an arrow-fletching tool. In fact, most serious bowhunters own arrow straighteners and fletching tools to cut costs and make arrow repair more convenient.

Arrow-nock replacement. The nocks on arrows occasionally break or pop off shafts that hit hard objects such as rocks. Damaged nocks or pieces of them that adhere to shafts should be carefully pried loose with a knife. Apply a thin coating of arrow-fletching cement on the nock tapers of the arrow shaft and twist on the replacement nock. Let the cement dry for 30 minutes, and the repaired arrow will be every bit as good as new.

Broadhead care. Every time a broadhead is shot, it becomes dulled, and blades must be resharpened or replaced. If a broadhead hits a rock or hard object, it may be bent or broken beyond repair.

Many broadheads can be straightened with a sturdy pair of pliers after becoming bent. If broadhead blades and center section can be manually straightened, the broadhead will be ready to shoot again once the edges have been resharpened to shaving keenness. To ensure razor-sharp edges during both a hunt and off-season months, broadheads should be periodically oiled and inspected.

EQUIPMENT CASES

Every archer should buy protective cases for transporting and storing his gear. Cases for bow, arrows, and accessories come at extremely reasonable cost—

a small extra price to pay to ensure undamaged, top-performing equipment.

Semisoft bow cases. For average bowhunting, some kind of semisoft case will adequately protect a bow. The most popular of these are so-called square-end cases, which fully enclose a compound bow complete with bow quiver full of arrows. They are zippered for ease of use, and protect bows well from all but the worst impact, dampness, or dust and grime. They also tend to shield a bow from excessive heat—the most dreaded enemy of laminated bow limbs.

One of the best semisoft bow cases is made of two tough cordura nylon layers with thick protective foam rubber sandwiched in between. Not only will this case fully enclose a bow complete with quiver in place, it also has two roomy zippered side pouches for extra arrows, armguard, tab, bow stabilizer, and a myriad of other shooting accessories. This particular semisoft

Semisoft bow cases provide ample protection in most transport situations. Cases of this sort are available in a wide variety of color patterns and configurations, including a few with extra pouches for arrows and other shooting accessories.

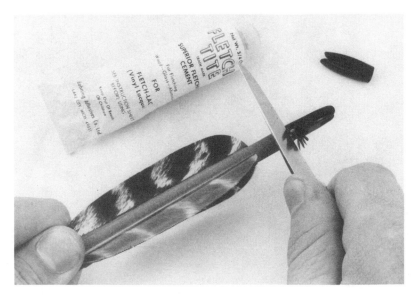

Damaged arrow nocks can be removed and replaced in a matter of seconds with a sharp knife and fletching cement.

case, has nearly indestructible nylon construction and superb internal padding. Many others nearly as well designed are also sold at archery stores.

Rigid bow cases. Although a top-flight semisoft case like the model just described is fine for most bow-hunting transport and storage needs, a rigid plastic or aluminum bow case is needed if you travel by air. The rigid case will support baggage piled on top of it, dampen impact from rough handling, and seal out water, heat, and grime. Rigid bow cases can be ordered through any archery store.

Arrow cases. In most circumstances, an archer can adequately protect his main hunting arrows by leaving them in a bow quiver inside his semisoft bow case.

However, the majority of archers own far more than the six or eight arrows generally held in such a quiver. As a result, manufacturers offer several excellent rigid cases designed specifically for protecting larger quantities of quality hunting shafts. Some of these are standard clamshell plastic cases similar to larger bow cases—others are round plastic tubes with internal brackets for holding a dozen or more hunting arrows.

Another first-rate container for hunting shafts without broadheads attached is an ordinary fishing-rod tube made of durable plastic. A tube about 4 inches in diameter will easily hold three dozen shafts without badly mashing fletching, and will completely protect them from bending or becoming moist or dirty.

Other containers for archery gear. In addition to standard cases for bows and arrows, a serious archer can use commercial or homemade containers to protect hunting broadheads and other small but important shooting items. For example, several companies sell plastic broadhead boxes that fully enclose razor-sharp heads and thus keep them dry, clean, and sharp. One excellent home-grown solution to storing and transporting broadheads is pressing them into an oil-soaked Styrofoam block packed inside a large, airtight freezer tub.

For the myriad of other items a bowhunter accumulates and uses, there's no better container than a medium-sized, good-quality fishing-tackle box. The box will hold items such as extra armguards, shooting tabs, and arrow rests.

Rigid plastic and aluminum cases are best for worry-free airline transport of hunting bows and arrows. They cushion expensive archery products in thick foam rubber and shield them from the roughest baggage treatment.

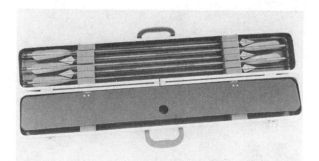

A rigid clam-shell case holds broadhead-tipped hunting arrows snugly in foam-rubber grippers. The case allows safe, convenient transport of extra deer-hunting shafts.

Pressing razor-keen broadheads in oil-soaked styrofoam is one excellent way to store such heads during off-season months. A large, airtight freezer tub serves well.

PART 5
HUNTING GEAR

BY CHUCK ADAMS

Photos by the author unless otherwise credited. Drawings by Lloyd Birmingham.

An individual hunter needs no more than a small fraction of the treasure trove offered by hopeful and smiling retailers, and he should choose those items to match his special outdoor requirements. An early-autumn whitetail hunter in the hot and humid swamps of Florida needs heavy wool mittens about as much as a late-season muley hunter in frigid Wyoming needs a thin camouflage tee shirt.

Beginning deer hunters seldom know exactly what equipment will suit their needs, and even seasoned veterans are constantly on the lookout for new and better equipment. As a result most hunters experiment with a variety of gear. Tinkering can be fun and also leads to sensible gear combinations that help in the serious task of bagging a deer.

A few hunters take their love for gadgetry to an extreme, toying incessantly with every new doodad that appears on store shelves. In sharp contrast, a few others are nothing short of miserly about spending hard-earned cash on equipment, making do with next to no gear besides a rattletrap rifle, a pocketful of bargain-basement cartridges, and a rusty old pocket knife.

The most practical and productive attitude toward deer-hunting equipment falls somewhere in between. A deer hunter with a moderate, no-nonsense assortment of equipment will usually enjoy himself immensely and end up bagging deer on a regular basis. In comparison, the gung ho accessory addict will clank and rattle like a worn-out washing machine as he struggles along through the woods, scaring every deer within earshot. For different reasons the chronic skinflint will also miss chances at game, fighting instead of enjoying what little hand-me-down gear he does happen to have. And even when he does break down and buy a binocular or other important deer-hunting aid, he's likely to skimp on quality and end up regretting his second-rate choice.

There's really no substitute for a careful, sensible approach to selecting outdoor equipment. First, you should survey the wide variety of items available. Second, you should assess your personal needs and decide what general *types* of equipment are apt to increase your comfort and effectiveness in camp and in the field. Third, you should purchase good-quality, name-brand products with features that satisfy your requirements. The most expensive item isn't always best when it comes to meeting a hunter's unique outdoor needs, but where deer-hunting equipment is concerned, that old saw certainly tends to be true— you *do* get what you pay for.

BINOCULARS AND TELESCOPES

Selection of a proper binocular or field glass is one of the most important decisions every deer hunter must make. Although a few hunters head afield each year without any such optical aid, it is safe to say that every outdoorsman will benefit by carrying a binocular no matter what his preferred hunting style, chosen terrain, or favorite kind of deer.

The ability to see the surrounding habitat through some sort of magnifying device serves three important purposes—it allows a hunter to discover animals he otherwise might not see; it lets him make a telescopic determination of a deer's sex, antler size, body angle, and other details that might determine how and when a shot is taken; and it adds tremendous enjoyment to any hunt by providing close-range looks at deer and all sorts of other interesting wildlife. Almost every experienced, successful deer hunter feels naked in the field whenever he accidentally leaves his favorite hunting binocular at home.

Telescopes for deer hunting are available in a wide range of physical sizes and magnification levels. The smallest type is called a monocular, and is basically just half of a binocular. Larger telescopes providing more powerful magnification are usually called spotting scopes, and must be affixed to tripods for solid, steady viewing. Although optical aids of this type do have definite applications in hunting deer, they are really special-purpose tools required by a small minority of hunters.

It is important to note here that the scope sight on a deer-hunting rifle is in no way a suitable substitute for a binocular or hunting telescope. A riflescope is designed for one purpose—to direct shots at stationary and moving deer. To ogle other hunters, haphazardly scan the countryside, or merely watch wildlife through the aiming mechanism on a deadly shooting tool is irresponsible and dangerous. Besides, the best-quality riflescopes available allow poor, extremely narrow views compared to those through well-made binoculars and telescopes. A riflescope is not designed for anything other than shooting, and should *never* be regarded as a substitute for other hunting optics.

BUYING BINOCULARS

Selecting a proper hunting binocular should not be done in a haphazard way. Hunters often unknowingly rush out and buy the first binocular they see at a bargain price, or use hunting optics received as a birthday or Christmas gift, or choose a binocular based on superficial qualities like color, shape, or case design. But a deer hunter should shop carefully for that one field glass that best fits his needs. A well-chosen, good-quality binocular will be a solid joy to use throughout a lifetime of hunting. The wrong glass will produce dim and fuzzy images, cause headaches with

Versatile deer hunters own quality binoculars and spotting scopes to accommodate a variety of glassing needs. In open country with a long-distance view, these optical aids are essential for locating game.

Contrary to general belief, a binocular can help bag deer in an area with heavy brush or trees. A magnified view of a nearby animal obscured by foliage can reveal its sex, body angle, and small holes in cover that might afford a shot.

extended viewing, fog unexpectedly in less-than-perfect weather, and subtly torture a hunter in many other ways. The only good thing about most poorly designed binoculars is that they eventually malfunction, causing the hunter to throw them into the trash, where they belonged from the beginning.

Because most successful deer hunters spend hundreds of hours each year with their eyes glued to binoculars, it makes no sense to rush binocular choice or to skimp on the purchase price. With a little looking, anyone can find a top-notch binocular that is perfectly suited to his own deer-hunting needs.

Magnification. The viewing magnification provided by a hunting binocular is clearly marked somewhere on the unit. One common binocular magnification is 7× (7-power), which means this binocular makes viewing images seven times as large as the same images seen with the naked eye.

Every deer hunter must decide how much magnification will suit him best in the field. On the surface it might seem that the more binocular magnification, the greater the advantage a hunter has. But as binocular power increases, hand tremor becomes more noticeable and makes steady viewing more difficult. Tremor can cause eyestrain and headaches with extensive viewing and is the primary factor that limits how much binocular magnification is practical in the woods.

Binoculars with 6×, 7×, 8×, 9×, and 10× magnification levels are all used by expert deer hunters. All five levels can be hand-held effectively, but 7× is generally considered ideal for an average viewer with moderately steady hands. A 6× glass is the steadiest to use in unusually jiggly hunting circumstances, such as glassing from horseback or using a binocular in windy weather. Glasses of 8× to 10× provide the additional magnification often needed by hunters who must scan big canyon country or who must attempt to size up the trophy quality of distant bucks.

A hunter who has especially steady hands or intends to do most of his glassing from a sitting position with elbows locked against his knees will usually do fine with an 8× or 10× binocular. Similarly, a commercial or homemade elastic binocular keeper can provide hand-steadying pressure similar to that of a shoulder sling used in offhand rifle shooting—pressure that allows the trouble-free use of high-magnification binoculars. However, for average, midrange viewing in deer-hunting situations, a 7× binocular can't be beat.

Also important is the physical size of field glasses. Generally speaking, the higher the magnification a binocular provides, the larger it is in size and weight.

Field of view. Field of view in a binocular is defined as the diameter of the viewing area that is contained within the magnified image at a distance of exactly 1,000 yards. Field of view varies tremendously from one binocular to another, and must be considered carefully.

As a rough rule of thumb, a suitable deer-hunting binocular should have a field of view no smaller than 300 feet at 1,000 yards. Looking through a binocular with a narrower field of view is similar to looking through a water pipe—the view is severely restricted. This makes locating distant objects difficult at best, and also limits the amount of terrain a hunter can effectively scan. By contrast, a top-notch binocular with a field of view in the 350- to 500-foot range allows a pleasant, panoramic look at the countryside and lets a hunter raise his glass and instantly find whatever he wishes to see somewhere within the wide viewing frame.

All else being equal, the higher the magnification, the narrower the field of view. For example, a 6× glass in a particular model will have a wider field of view

HOW TO MAKE A BINOCULAR KEEPER

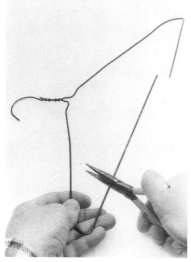

1. *To make a binocular keeper, first cut a straight, 8-inch piece of wire from a coat hanger. Sturdy multi-purpose pliers with wire cutters serve best.*

2. *Next, double-over the heavy gauge wire, and bend in a fishhook shape as shown. Grip the wire with pliers to prevent cuts to your hands.*

3. *Once the double-wire hook is fashioned, wrap it tightly with plastic electrician's tape from one end to the other. This prevents rust and safely covers the ragged wire ends.*

4. *A 2-foot length of surgical tubing makes the best binocular-keeper band. Force one end of this tubing over the back half of the hook.*

5. *Then tie the free end of the surgical tubing to the binocular as shown. Attach the hook end to a belt loop during this process. Tie the tubing to take up all slack.*

6. *The keeper holds the binocular snugly against your chest when not in use, and the elastic tension steadies your view whenever you raise the glasses to your eyes.*

As a general rule, binoculars of higher magnification are larger and heavier than those of lower power. This is graphically illustrated by the 10× glass on the left and the midget 6× model beside it.

For scanning in open country, you need a binocular with a fairly wide field of view. This lets you cover plenty of country with a single slow sweep of the terrain.

than a 10× glass of the same design. As a result, hunters who place a premium on wide field of view usually opt to buy glasses of lower magnification. A few optical companies offer special wide-angle binoculars with fields of view between 500 and 600 feet at 1,000 yards—however, these are usually heavier, bulkier glasses than the norm. An ideal field of view for average deer hunting is somewhere near 400 feet.

Light-gathering ability. Basic light-gathering capability is one factor that clearly separates top-quality hunting binoculars from their not-so-nifty counterparts.

It's common for hunters to compare binoculars by looking through them during primary daylight hours. More often than not, the inexperienced hunters with low-cost, poor-quality binoculars snort contemptuously after such comparisons and declare their glasses on a par with the best in the group. But these comparisons almost always fail to test light-gathering ability. Any realistic comparison of binoculars should be made during the dim light of dawn or dusk, not when light is full and strong. Morning and evening are the times when deer hunters see the bulk of their game. These are also the times when a mediocre glass fails miserably, while the honest-to-gosh winner transmits bright, perfectly clear images.

The ability of any binocular to gather light until the last gasp of day is dependent upon three basic factors—objective lens diameter, level of magnification, and special hard coating on all exterior glass surfaces.

A binocular's objective-lens diameter determines in part how well that glass transmits light to your eyes in low-light situations. Other factors contributing to light-gathering ability include magnification level and quality of hard coatings on lens surfaces.

The front lenses on a binocular are called the objective lenses. The larger these are, the more light they transmit to the eye—the same as larger windows in a house allow more light to enter than smaller windows. The diameter of an objective lens is generally marked in millimeters on the binocular immediately after the magnification-level designation. For example, one popular deer-hunting binocular is a 7 × 35—a seven-power glass with objective lenses 35 millimeters in diameter. All else being equal, a similar 7 × 50 binocular will exhibit better light-gathering characteristics in low-light situations because its objective lenses are larger in diameter.

Magnification of a binocular significantly affects its ability to gather light. As a rule, the stronger the magnification, the less light-gathering ability a particular model has. For example, a 7 × 35 binocular allows brighter viewing early and late in the day than a 9 × 35 glass of the same basic design.

Exit pupil: A binocular buyer should pay close attention to both the magnification level and objective-lens diameter. An excellent rule of thumb when assessing the relative light-gathering abilities of various binoculars is to divide the diameter of the objective lens in millimeters by the magnification power. This simple process yields the size of a binocular's "exit pupils"—the two bright circles seen in the eyepieces of a binocular when it is held approximately 1 foot away from the eyes. For example, a typical 7 × 35 binocular has an exit pupil of 5mm (35 ÷ 7). By contrast, a 7 × 50 binocular has an exit-pupil diameter of 7.1mm (50 ÷ 7). The greater the exit-pupil rating of a binocular, the better its inherent light-gathering ability will be.

To understand why the exit-pupil size in a binocular determines its ability to transmit low-light images, consider how the human eye itself functions. In bright light, the pupil contracts to a mere pinpoint, and in low light it widens to a fairly large disk. The larger the exit pupil a binocular has, the more efficiently it transmits light to the large, low-light pupil in a hunter's eye. As a rule, if the exit pupil of a binocular is as large or larger than the pupil of a hunter's eye, the hunter will see images almost as bright as *without* the aid of binoculars.

Binocular manufacturers have researched the varying pupil diameters of the human eye, and have designed binoculars to meet a wide variety of light-gathering needs. The very brightest and most efficient low-light binoculars are those of fairly low power and large objective-lens size—glasses such as 7 × 50 marine binoculars often used for nighttime viewing. Unfortunately, the brightest binoculars are also the biggest and bulkiest because they do have very large frontal lenses.

When choosing any hunting binocular, insist upon an exit pupil size of 4mm or larger. A 6 × 24 glass has such an exit pupil (24 ÷ 6 = 4) and so does a 7 × 28 (28 ÷ 7 = 4). Another popular trophy-hunting binocular size, the 10 × 40, also has an exit pipil of 4mm (40 ÷ 10 = 4). A hunter after ultra spooky whitetail deer or other deer that are prone to show themselves only in the gray dimness of dawn and dusk might be best advised to use a binocular with an exit pupil of 4.5 or 5.0 for a little brighter view.

Lens coating: A third factor that contributes to light-gathering ability is the hard nonglare coating on all air-to-glass surfaces. The coating prevents a significant percentage of light from bouncing off the curving objective lenses and eyepieces. The best hunting binoculars feature either bluish magnesium fluoride lens coating or amber coating. These coatings can increase through-the-lens light transmission to a hunter's eye by up to 50 percent. Binoculars with uncoated lenses seldom allow clear low-light viewing.

A hunting binocular with a fairly large exit pupil and hard-coated lenses will allow clear views of deer until the last light of day—views nearly as bright as those seen with the naked eye alone. In comparison a mediocre binocular poops out long before the eye itself, yielding dark-gray to jet-black views when the unaided eye can still pick up good detail at fairly close ranges.

Since most deer are seen in fairly dim light, a hunting binocular's light-gathering ability must be first-rate. Anyone who has suffered through using a dull, lifeless low-light binocular will certainly agree!

Viewing clarity. Excellent viewing clarity, or resolution, is an important feature all top-notch binoculars share. There are very few objective guidelines to help a binocular buyer sort the clearest glasses from those that transmit marginal images. Usually, the better name-brand binoculars with higher price tags ensure top viewing clarity because their makers are sticklers for detail. To a certain degree, you can merely compare several likely brands by checking them out in the sporting goods store parking lot. Provided your eyes are normal, clear is usually clear, and fuzzy is fuzzy when looking through various glasses.

Several factors contribute to the ability of a binocular to transmit sharp, crystal-clear images. One is the precision with which the internal magnifying optics have been ground and polished at the factory. Shoddy optical shaping leads to soft or fuzzy images—images that are obviously inferior to those seen through a high-quality binocular.

Another factor determining clarity is collimation (alignment) of the individual viewing barrels during binocular assembly. Basically, a binocular consists of two separate mini-telescopes fastened rigidly together, and these telescopes must be precisely parallel to one another so that both eyes can naturally look in the same direction. An alarming number of low-cost, slapdash binoculars are not precisely collimated at the factory, requiring a viewer's eyeballs to perform Olympic-style gymnastics as they look down two slightly different paths at the same time. Lack of collimating precision produces fuzzy viewing, and prolonged binocular use results in eyestrain often accompanied by headaches, dizziness, and temporary loss of clear vision with the naked eye. Poorly collimated bargain-brand binoculars are never the bargains they seem to be initially.

Many of the best deer-hunting binoculars incorporate internal ultraviolet filters that cut haze to allow clearer viewing through fog, smoke, and other particulate pollution in the air. The quality of optical grind and collimation are not noted in manufacturers' literature, but most binocular makers do note the presence of UV filters in various field-glass models.

Size and weight. The size and weight of a hunting binocular are extremely important factors in selection. A glass that is too large and too bulky can be a pain to carry all day, especially if this larger size also means excessive weight. A tiny binocular is equally undesirable; it seldom yields suitable optical performance and prevents steady viewing because it telegraphs every pulsebeat and body quiver directly to the eyes.

Most quality modern binoculars have lightweight aluminum-alloy bodies instead of older-style frames made of brass or heavy base metal. Nonetheless, the largest binoculars are still backbreakers when carried all day on a neck strap. And despite their superior

Author Chuck Adams used a large 10×50 binocular to spot and size up this record-class muley buck in big, open country. A glass this large borders on being too heavy for comfortable carrying but certainly allows excellent long-range, low-light views.

light-gathering and steady viewing properties, many hunters shun them. Lightweight, so-called mini-binoculars that literally disappear in a closed fist can be carried in a shirt pocket but seldom yield even a marginally acceptable magnification level, field of view, or light-gathering ability—not to mention their serious lack of viewing stability. A sensible hunter strikes a balance between the two extremes, realizing that there is no perfect product and that compromises must always be made.

As a general rule, deer hunters are best served by a binocular weighing somewhere between 15 and 30 ounces. There are dozens of excellent models to choose from within this range—models with suitable magnification, excellent field of view, top-notch light-gathering ability, and superb viewing clarity. Hunters who especially loathe the chore of carrying glasses on a neck strap should purchase a binocular weighing no more than 1 pound; hunters who favor the higher magnification, better light-gathering qualities, and steadier viewing weight of a larger glass might decide instead to invest in a binocular weighing nearly 2 pounds.

There are superb binoculars weighing 50 ounces or more, and handy little glasses on the market that run a mere 10 or 12 ounces. However, such extreme models are not practical for the majority of deer-hunting needs.

One other size dilemma deer hunters face is whether to buy a standard porro-prism binocular or a sleeker, more compact roof-prism model. A porro-prism glass has eyepieces significantly closer together than the objective lenses, with both halves of the binocular displaying an obvious dogleg appearance. By contrast, the trimmer roof-prism design, sometimes called a "coke-bottle binocular," consists of two relatively straight viewing barrels. These transmit light directly from objective lens to eyepiece instead of routing this light along a zigzagging path.

A roof-prism binocular weighs approximately 25 percent less than a porro-prism glass of identical optical power. It is significantly less bulky as well because of its straight, coke-bottle-shaped viewing barrels. However, roof-prism binoculars are more difficult to manufacture and thus cost considerably more than porro-prism glasses of comparable quality. Both designs serve hunters well—the big decision must be

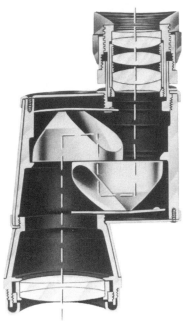

A standard porro-prism binocular transmits its viewing image along a zigzagging path, with light entering by way of the objective lenses and finally being directed through narrower eyepieces. This optical setup is most commonly seen in deer-hunting glasses.

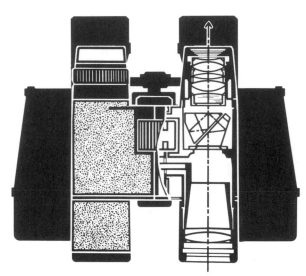

This cutaway of the roof-prism design shows why a roof-prism binocular is less bulky than the silhouetted porro-prism version. The roof prism configuration transmits images in a straight line from objective to rear lenses.

Both binoculars shown here are excellent choices for hunting deer. The smaller roof-prism model is a 10 × 40; the larger porro-prism model is a 7 × 50 glass designed for late-evening viewing.

whether the compact, lightweight construction of the roof-prism design is worth the extra money.

Other important characteristics. Magnification level, field of view, light-gathering ability, viewing clarity, and physical size are the primary characteristics a deer hunter should consider in any binocular. However, the following features must also be taken into account.

Focusing mechanism: There are several common focusing mechanisms. The vast majority of modern field glasses feature handy, one-dial center focusing. A few excellent glasses require individual eye focus instead. Each basic design has certain advantages and disadvantages well worth considering.

Center-focus binoculars are ordinarily made in three basic configurations. The most common of all has a central dial that moves focusing elements *inside* the body of the binocular. Almost as frequently seen is the so-called German center-focus design. On this type, a central dial moves an entire, *external* eyepiece assembly back and forth to facilitate crystal-clear focusing. German-style glasses become longer or shorter depending upon exact focusing-dial position. In addition a few of the best binoculars have a central "insta-focus" pedal that rocks up and down at the ends to allow rapid focusing with either hand.

For quick, handy focusing, nothing beats the insta-focus pedal system. However, a conventional center dial allows more precise focusing when time permits, making it popular with many hunters. The German-style focusing system is least desirable of all because the moving focus mechanism is susceptible to becoming gritty in the field. In addition this system is more fragile because critical moving parts are exposed. Nonetheless, with proper care, all three center-focus systems are worthy.

Center-focus binoculars are easily set to match the shooter's eyes. First, you focus the left eyepiece on a distant object by using the center focusing dial and keeping your right eye closed. Next, the right eyepiece is focused to match the left focus by turning a separate focusing dial on that eyepiece. The left eye should be closed during this second focusing phase. Once this two-step procedure is accomplished, the binocular will focus both eyepieces at any distance with the center dial or pedal alone.

A top-of-the-line binocular that requires separate eyepiece focusing offers two important advantages over center-focus models. First, this type of glass has sturdier hinges holding the two barrels together than a center-focus design, making it harder to knock them out of collimation (alignment) by rough-and-tumble use. Such extra strength is possible because there is no fragile center-focusing mechanism located between the halves of the binocular.

A second major advantage of a glass with separate eyepiece focusing is the fact that it is the only type that can be made completely waterproof and fogproof. Because there is no center-focus setup to break the internal seal of viewing barrels, the binocular barrels can be nitrogen purged inside to remove all moisture and then hermetically sealed. Not all individual-eye-focus binoculars are top designs, but most quality products can be submerged in water indefinitely without causing internal damage. Likewise, dramatic temperature changes that sometimes fog a conventional binocular will have no effect on hermetically sealed designs.

The primary disadvantage of a binocular with two separate eye-focus rings is that it is inconvenient to focus both eyepieces for every viewing distance. However, several such binoculars are designed to be in perfect focus all the way from 100 or 150 feet on

A center-focusing dial is the favorite of most binocular users. The dial allows quick, precise adjustment of internal optics for crystal-clear viewing at various ranges.

This center-focus glass features an insta-focus pedal for fast use in action situations. The German-style eyepieces on this binocular move in and out to facilitate focusing.

Some binoculars require individual eyepiece adjustment instead of allowing quick center-dial focusing. Glasses of this type are somewhat slow to use, but most are completely waterproof and significantly more rugged than center-focus models.

out to infinity once individual eyepieces are correctly set. So these glasses are completely functional in most deer-hunting situations without any additional focusing adjustment.

Most hunters prefer some sort of center-focus binocular for general use, but a glass featuring individual eye focus is clearly best in situations where binoculars must endure rough treatment, exposure to very moist weather, or sudden changes in temperature.

Rubber coating: A few excellent deer-hunting binoculars are sold with rubber coating on exterior parts instead of the more common baked enamel and leather-grain vinyl. Such "armored binoculars" are designed to resist moisture and shock a bit better than standard-issue models, and also prevent noisy clanks and clatters when a glass unexpectedly collides with a gun, tree, rock, or another hard object. In addition, armored glasses have nonglare camouflage surfaces in black, green, or two-tone colorations—a solid plus when sharp-eyed deer are likely to be nearby.

Both gun hunters and bowhunters use rubber-armored binoculars, but these are especially popular in bowhunting because they reflect no light and make less incidental noise than glasses with regular hard finishes. The rubber coating on good-grade binoculars requires no special maintenance, and only deteriorates when regularly exposed to gun oil or other petroleum products.

Retractable eyecups: Virtually all well-made binoculars have retractable eyecups on the eyepieces to allow clear viewing through prescription eyeglasses and ordinary sunglasses. Any form of spectacle holds binoculars farther from the eyes than normal, requiring eyecups to be retracted for clear scanning and normal field of view. Most binocular eyecups are the fold-

over rubber variety or plastic screw-in design. Either style is suitable for all sorts of deer hunting.

Interpupillary adjustment: The two individual telescopic barrels of a binocular are always joined to-

Rubber-coated binoculars are soft and quiet—a good match for other close-range deer stalking gear, such as wool clothing and boots with pliable soles. Optics armored with rubber also absorb shocks of handling extremely well.

gether with one or two sturdy, wig-wagging hinges. These hinges allow eyepieces to be swung farther apart or closer together to perfectly match the set of the viewer's eyes.

Unfortunately, a few binoculars commonly sold at stores will not swing wide enough to align properly for hunters with unusually wide-set eyes. So check the hinge-swing width on likely glasses to make sure they will fit your eyes and those of hunting companions. Inadequate interpupillary swing is especially common among miniature binoculars weighing less than 10 or 12 ounces.

Carrying straps: The majority of binoculars are sold with second-rate, cord-type carrying straps that dig into the neck during a long walk or while waiting on stand. Avoid purchasing binoculars based on carrying-strap quality because many excellent glasses are coupled with thin, flimsy straps.

Unfortunately, the wrong binocular strap is literally a giant pain in the neck. As a result, all but a few binoculars should have their straps removed and replaced with fairly wide straps made of nylon webbing or pliable leather. Many 35mm camera neckstraps work well for this purpose.

To prevent excessive binocular swing while hunting, adjust your binocular strap so that you can barely slip it over your head. This positions glasses high on the chest with just enough strap slack to allow unencumbered viewing. Binoculars that regularly swing like a pendulum near the navel are a real nuisance and also tend to prevent quiet movement and smooth shooting of gun or bow.

In addition to shortening the binocular strap to minimal length, many hunters rig up some sort of

An armored binocular can be fully protected with plastic cups that cover delicate exposed glass surfaces. If the cups are attached directly to a carrying strap, they can be pulled out of the way when you use your optics.

elastic or surgical-tubing chest keeper to hold a glass snugly against the body when it's not being used. A chest keeper also aids steady viewing by cushioning hand jiggle and the effects of strong winds.

Binocular cases: Every quality hunting binocular should be stored in a protective case. Most good binoculars come with cases. Also a wide variety of binocular cases are sold at sporting goods stores. Cases of rigid construction with snapping closure flaps are most common, but semisoft zippered cases are also fairly standard.

One company makes a "quick-draw" case meant to be carried on the shoulder. This design dumps a binocular into the waiting hand with the flick of a wrist. Another company offers an armored binocular with two wide, plastic cups that attach directly to the carrying strap and slip on and off the objective lenses and eyepieces. Aside from these novel yet well-designed cases, binocular cases should be left in a vehicle or the hunting camp whenever the glasses themselves are being used. Unfurling a cased-up binocular in the heat of the action is usually a noisy, time-consuming process guaranteed to frighten deer.

Every unarmored binocular deserves a well-designed padded carrying case to match. A semisoft zippered case is an excellent choice for keeping internal components of a glass in perfect shape and for protecting its baked-enamel and leather-grain outer surfaces.

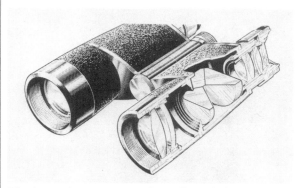

The internal components of a well-made binocular are glued solidly in place to withstand reasonable jars and bumps. By contrast, optical parts in second-rate glasses often shift or rattle free after a few months of use.

Zoom binoculars: Although so-called zoom binoculars with variable magnification are sold by a few outdoor companies, these binoculars have a reputation for fuzzy image transmission, poor light-gathering ability, and fairly fragile construction. A binocular designed to zoom from 6× to 15× or 7× to 20× is also heavier and bulkier than a fixed-power model. Furthermore, most zoom glasses begin at 6× or 7× and zoom upward to 15×, 18×, 24×, or another high level of magnification that cannot be steadily hand-held anyway. As a general rule, zoom binoculars are impractical contraptions with little application in the deer woods.

Binocular cost: Placing a strong emphasis on low purchase price and selecting a "bargain glass" seldom turns out to be a bargain at all. A binocular with a significantly reduced price tag may appear to be a sound investment, and may even seem to meet all the basic criteria of a decent deer-hunting glass. However, cheap binoculars are often poorly constructed. This shoddy workmanship cannot be readily seen, but it eventually comes back to haunt the buyer.

A few things commonly go haywire with bargain-basement binoculars. First, internal lenses are often fixed in place with glue and pop loose after warranty coverage expires. The resulting effect is not the least bit desirable—the combo of aluminum and loose internal glass does not even make a decent baby rattle. Similarly, inexpensive binoculars usually have sloppy metal-to-metal and gear-to-gear fit in the focusing mechanism. This may be temporarily disguised by heavy grease on all moving parts to fill in the gaps. But grease rapidly collects debris during use, and the dirt eventually jams up the works or at least makes focus adjustment sound like a gravel truck slowly dumping its load. This is not to mention the poor collimation, wretched or nonexistent lens coating, and terribly fuzzy views of cheap binoculars.

By contrast, a fairly expensive binocular has internal optics that are mounted to stay put, extremely close tolerances on all moving mechanical parts, and many other positive features discussed earlier in this section. In the long run, a hunter will *save* money by investing in one good binocular to begin with instead of purchasing three or four second-rate glasses over a period of years.

TELESCOPES

There are two basic types of telescopes used by deer hunters—hand-held monoculars and much larger tripod-mounted or gunstock-mounted spotting scopes. Both designs have relatively limited application in deer hunting, but do help in a few situations.

Monoculars. Monoculars, or hand-held telescopes, are not very popular with hunters. This is because there's really nothing a monocular can do that a binocular cannot do better.

The chief advantage of monoculars is extremely light weight. Most of these little telescopes weigh only 5 to 8 ounces and easily slip in any shirt pocket. However, monoculars typically display poor light-gathering qualities (because of a small exit pupil) and have a relatively narrow field of view. The only hunters who strongly favor such glasses are those who have clear vision in only one eye and thus gain nothing by carrying a binocular.

Spotting scopes. High-power spotting scopes are extremely valuable for some kinds of deer hunting. For example, they are particularly beneficial in sizing up trophy bucks at fairly long range. Their primary drawbacks are that they are bulky and must generally be carried into the hills with a tripod to allow rock-solid viewing. Less than five percent of America's deer hunters ever have reason to use spotting scopes afield, but those who do should choose practical, dependable models.

Features to look for in any spotting scope include magnification level, light-gathering ability, field of view, size, weight, and viewing clarity. The two most important factors—aside from quality, name-brand

A monocular's primary selling point is extremely light weight and unequaled carrying compactness. These tiny telescopes are offered to hunters by several companies, but they never perform as well as binoculars.

SPOTTING SCOPES

A compact, lightweight spotting scope with a 20× magnification is ideal for trophy-spotting needs. It allows close-range views of bucks at long-distance.

A good spotting scope features a sliding frontal sun visor, a handy, top-mounted focusing dial, and a threaded tripod collar underneath. Hunters should look for these features before buying any telescope.

Spotting scopes are available in configurations to suit a variety of personal needs. Two styles commonly used by deer hunters are a rugged rubber-armored version and a scope (below) with 45-degree eyepieces, which allows you to use it while standing up.

SCOPE ACCESSORIES

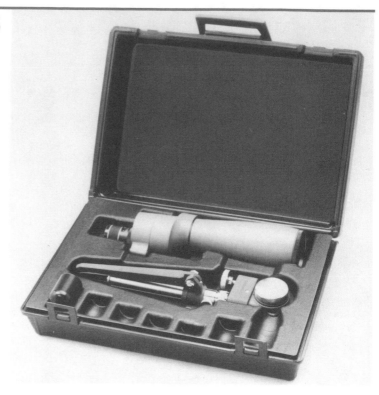

An expensive spotting scope should always be stored and carried in a padded protective case. The best containers close and carry like briefcases and have ample room for compact tripods and accessories.

Tripods of many different types for spotting scopes are sold at sporting goods stores and camera shops. Some of these are tiny models with truncated, telescoping legs and small carrying pouches; others are larger, somewhat sturdier designs.

design—are magnification level and light-gathering ability. Unfortunately, these two positive characteristics work against one another in any telescope. Invariably, the higher the magnification level, the lower the light-gathering ability tends to be.

The most popular deer-hunting magnification in spotting scopes is 20×. This allows a fairly close-range view of all but the most distant animals and still preserves an exit pupil of 3mm or more in most models for decent low-light viewing. Telescopes are available with magnifications up to 60×, but high-power scopes tend to be large and heavy, to accentuate hand tremor considerably even when tripod-attached, to have very narrow fields of view, and to have exit pupils of 1mm or less. A telescope in the 30× to 60× range also accentuates heat waves in the air between the hunter and animals being viewed. On all but the coolest days in extremely dry climates, heat shimmer almost completely obliterates a long-distance view through any telescope over 30×.

Good-quality 20× spotting scopes measure about 12 inches long and weigh in the neighborhood of 36 to 40 ounces. Most have a field of view of 100 to 150 feet at 1,000 yards and provide excellent viewing clarity when attached to a tripod or similar support.

Special features to consider: Spotting scopes can be purchased with a number of special features that may or may not help a hunter. A few excellent models are sold that zoom between such practical powers as 15× and 30×. Unlike zoom binoculars, zoom spotting scopes have an excellent reputation for dependability. Other features available in hunting telescopes include rubber armored finishes on a few models, a 45-degree viewing eyepiece that allows standing hunters to look *down* into their scopes, and a sliding front sun visor to help shield optics from glare.

Most hunting telescopes come standard with easy-to-use focusing dials, a hard coating on all external glass surfaces to enhance light gathering, and tripod-mounting collars.

Telescope accessories. The majority of good hunting telescopes come complete with padded protective cases that shield the scopes from grime and damaging impact. Get one if not provided with your binocular.

A myriad of ordinary tripods for telescopes and cameras are sold. The best are made of light, strong magnesium, but less expensive aluminum tripods work nearly as well if a shooter doesn't mind carrying the extra weight. The most practical tripods feature telescoping legs to level them out in any kind of deer-hunting terrain.

Although most deer hunters end up backpacking spotting scopes and regular tripods into the hills, a few make use of car-window mounts for telescopes and shoulder-mounted spotting-scope stocks (similar to gunstocks). Alternative spotting-scope supports can be ordered through many larger sporting goods dealerships.

CARE AND CLEANING OF OPTICS

Optics must be handled carefully to minimize impact and abrasion to external surfaces. A few minor dents and scratches appear on any binocular or telescope as the hunting years go by, and such blemishes do not impair in-the-field use. However, hard bumps and jars *can* loosen internal components and can also throw even the best binocular out of factory collimation. Similarly, exposure to sandstorms, dust-laden air along dirt roads, and other grimy situations can damage viewing lenses and gum up external moving parts with fine grit.

All but completely sealed and gas-purged optics are susceptible to internal fogging when temperatures change or weather is damp for long periods. Some models are better sealed against moisture than others, but all should be kept reasonably dry whenever possible. Hunters frequently make the mistake of bringing binoculars and spotting scopes from icy weather into very warm tents, cabins, or hotel rooms. This often causes condensation inside a binocular or telescope—condensation that can totally fog glasses for many days on end. It's far better to leave hunting optics out in the cold inside a locked automobile or beneath a weatherproof tarp. This generally prevents optical fogging altogether.

For clearest viewing, the objective and eyepiece lenses on binoculars and telescopes should be cleaned periodically to remove dust, water spots, dribble marks left by spilled soft drinks, and other common smudges. There is a right way and a wrong way to clean fine optical lenses. Unfortunately, most hunters do it the wrong way.

The only proper method of cleaning optical glass is to first dust if off with a photographic blower brush and then to gently cleanse and dry the delicate coated surfaces with special lens tissue. A blower brush, lens tissue, and liquid cleaner (used with the tissue) are all available at any camera store for a very small price. These simple products ensure unscratched binocular lenses and first-rate light transmission to the eye. (See photos and captions on the next page.)

By contrast, any hunter who scrubs lenses with saliva-moistened toilet paper, the tail of his hunting shirt, or any other handy wipe will slowly but surely grind away the coating on lenses. This also leaves tiny but severely light-reflecting and image-degrading scratches in the glass. The result is often a fuzzier, dimmer view through a clean lens than through a soiled but unscratched lens.

HOW TO CLEAN BINOCULAR LENSES

To keep binocular lenses clear and bright, you need three basic items—a bottle of liquid cleaner for camera lenses, a packet of lens-cleaning tissue, and a photographer's blower brush.

  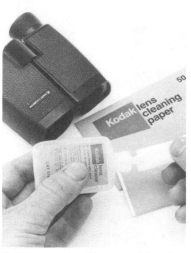

1. *Cleaning lenses the correct way is easy. The first step is to vigorously blow away loose particles on all lenses with the squeeze-bulb blower (brush removed). This takes just a few seconds.*

2. *Next, gently dust lenses with a soft camel-hair brush attached to the blower bulb. Squeeze the bulb repeatedly during this phase to blow away loosened abrasive particles.*

3. *Once you've blown and brushed all lenses, roll a few sheets of cleaning tissue into a cylinder. Dampen one end of this tissue roll with lens-cleaning fluid.*

4. *Using only moderate pressure, wipe lens surfaces with the dampened end of the tissue. This removes smudges, stains, and water spots that reduce the chance of clean binocular viewing.*

5. *Once you've thoroughly scrubbed the lenses, dry them with the other end of the rolled lens tissue. This prevents cleaning fluid from seeping around the edges of lenses and fogging internal optics.*

KNIVES AND OTHER CUTTING TOOLS

Every deer hunter should carry some kind of knife into the field. Without a knife, a hunter cannot field-dress a deer after a kill, or perform other related chores, such as skinning, quartering, and removing a deer's legs to facilitate transport. This is not to mention the myriad of other tasks a handy field knife can be used for—peeling an apple for lunch, whittling a wooden plug to repair a stripped-out rifle-carrying sling, or shaving fine tinder for a fire.

Most experienced woodsmen own *several* knives to perform a variety of camping, in-field, and at-home duties associated with hunting. In addition to one or more blades suited for carrying into the wilds, savvy hunters usually have separate cutting implements for skinning a deer carcass back at camp, caping a trophy head, cutting up meat for the freezer, fleshing a deer hide to be tanned at a later date, and doing other hunting-related chores. A single knife can be pressed into service to accomplish all such outdoor tasks—provided it was chosen carefully to begin with. Yet it is best to have knives that fit specific chores, be they slitting, slicing, or carving.

Here are some guidelines to follow when selecting one or more knives for deer hunting.

BLADE LENGTH

The important decision on blade length can be mind-boggling because there are dozens of lengths to choose from.

It's fairly common in heavily congested hunting areas to see novice hunters carrying ponderous belt knives with handles rising to their midriff and blades dangling almost to their knees. These "toad-stickers" are often of the Bowie knife design, which history tells us won the West by warding off "redskins" and slaying grizzly bears. Be that as it may, these big knives are impractical for deer hunting and give veteran woodsmen a hearty laugh whenever a greenhorn packing one pops from the shrubbery. A deer hunter needs a much smaller, less cumbersome cutting tool.

Any deer knife with a blade over 3 inches long is bigger than it has to be, except for cutting up meat to be packaged. Three well-shaped inches of proper steel will perform any camp and field chore a hunter will encounter, from gutting a buck, boning it out, and skinning it to dicing up groceries for supper. In most instances a knife with a blade only 2 or 2½

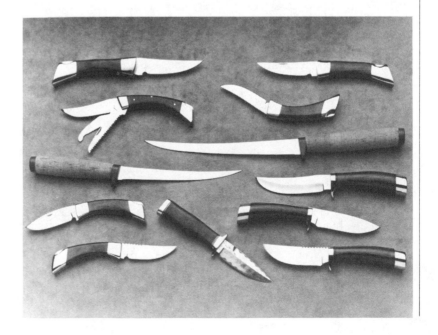

A mind-boggling array of knives is available to hunters. These cutting tools come in every imaginable shape and size, combining practicality with sturdy assembly and good looks.

Every hunter needs at least one well-designed knife to perform essential deer-care chores. The carefully selected blade will gut, skin, and quarter an animal with ease and efficiency.

inches long will stand a hunter in very good stead. And for some special-purpose assignments, a tiny blade only 1 inch long can perform like an absolute champ.

Purchasing a knife with a blade much longer than needed increases carrying bulk and weight, and in many instances also hampers a hunter's ability to do a proper, easy cutting job. Here are some recommended knife-blade lengths for specific deer-hunting tasks.

One-inch blades. When carefully caping deer heads, hunters seldom use more than the first inch of steel on any blade. Skinning out the ears, delicately cutting around eyes and nose, and carefully splitting the lips on a trophy buck is ticklish business best done with a small blade. Similarly, removing flesh from a deer hide to be salted requires a short cutting edge of no more than 1 or 1½ inches. Blades up to 3 inches long will perform such tasks, but a hunter generally ends up holding the rear part of such a blade instead of the handle in order to get closer to the working tip.

Two-inch blades. All field-dressing, skinning, and other related chores can be accomplished with a knife blade only 2 inches long. This blade, found on most common pocket knives, can even be used to quarter a deer and remove the legs at knees and hocks. The only chore a 2-inch blade is *not* ideally suited for is reaming out a deer's anus during field-dressing. Two inches of steel simply doesn't have the reach to slickly perform this operation—although a little extra whittling will eventually do the trick in slightly ragged fashion. Of course, a 2-inch knife blade is *not* suited for many *noncarcass* operations around camp, such as slicing spuds, cutting cheese, etc.

Three-inch blades. Knife blades with three-inch overall length are the most versatile of all in deer-hunting situations. They will do a good caping job on a deer head if the hunter is careful and grips the blade itself instead of the handle. Three-inch blades perform all other deer carcass jobs in fine style and have the edge length to be used for most camping jobs as well. A knife with a 3-inch blade is too large to carry com-

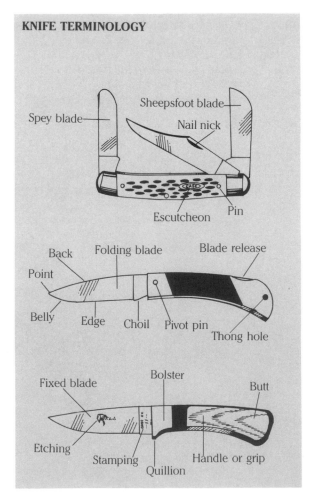

KNIFE TERMINOLOGY

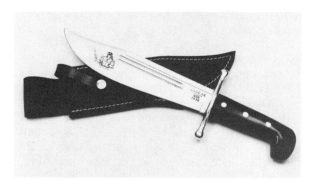

Long, heavy knives like the legendary Bowie appeal to many deer-hunting novices. But they have little value unless you expect hand-to-paw combat with a bear.

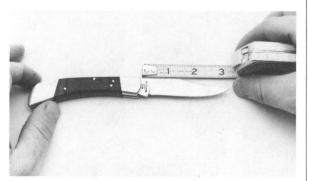

The most practical blade for deer-care chores is about 3 inches long. This blade is also fairly useful for performing secondary tasks around a hunting camp.

fortably in a pants pocket and has more bulk than a model with a shorter blade. But it represents the best working compromise when only one knife is carried afield.

Blades over 3 inches. Butchering a deer carcass requires a blade between 4 and 8 inches long to slice up steaks, roasts, and other cuts in quick, easy fashion. Such a blade is also best for long kitchen cuts needed in slicing bread and halving sandwiches. A knife with a blade over 3 inches long is best left in camp or the kitchen because it has no place in the woods at all—unless a hunter has plans to ward off bears.

BLADE SHAPE

Knife manufacturers offer literally thousands of subtle blade-shape variations with both practicality and esthetic appeal in mind. Knife aficionados are fond of naming exact blade shapes, and consequently there are enough blade types listed in journals and catalogs to baffle even the experts. Among the more traditional blade shapes are the clip, spear, spey, sheepsfoot, pen, hawkbill, razor, coping, pruning, and square-end configurations. The fact that knife makers and knife collectors do not agree on the names of all blade shapes adds a substantial dash of confusion to any heartfelt, scholastic study of blade design.

Fortunately, a deer hunter can lump the majority of blade shapes into four primary categories. Subtle variations in these shapes are not important in practical outdoor tasks. The four basic blade shapes are shown in the accompanying drawings. Each has practical field applications.

Clip point. A clip-point blade is the most commonly seen shape in knives of all varieties. This configuration

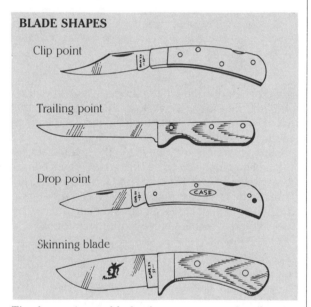

BLADE SHAPES

Clip point

Trailing point

Drop point

Skinning blade

The four primary blade shapes seen on deer-hunting knives are (top to bottom): the clip point with its unique peaked back; the trailing point, which has a relatively straight back; the drop point, displaying a strong arched back; and the skinning blade, characterized by a sharply curving edge near the tip.

is easily recognized from the notable peak on the top or back of the blade and the strongly upswept point at the front. A clip-point blade is an excellent all-around deer-hunting shape. The front edge curves enough to facilitate easy cutting and skinning, the point is sufficiently slender to easily penetrate hide, and the wider rear portion of the blade is strong enough to allow a certain amount of heavy use, such as chopping through the pelvic area on a deer.

The only notable drawback of the clip-point shape is the fact that the tip of the blade sweeps up enough to make gutting a deer mildly difficult. When held up-

The clip-point blade shape is the most common in hunting knives of all varieties. Although slightly awkward to use in field-dressing, the blade is strong and has a slender tip for easy penetration.

side down during the gutting process, a clip-point tip tends to slide along very close to the paunch; this may result in an accidentally sliced stomach and the smelly mess that results.

A hunter can carefully slit the belly sheath of a deer with a clip-point blade while holding the paunch away from the blade with his other hand, but doing so requires some extra effort and care. So this disadvantage to the clip-point blade is minor, and many successful deer hunters use this blade without any trouble.

Trailing point. The back of a trailing-point blade is nearly flat instead of peaked like that of the clip-point design. This makes for a fairly slender blade that is light and easy to wield. Because the trailing point is narrower from top to bottom, it lacks the rough-and-tumble strength of the beefier clip-point configuration. However, it has the clip point's curving front edge radius and slender penetrating point. It's really a toss-up between this design and the clip point, unless blade strength is a prime requirement. In 99 cases out

of 100, a trailing point will do everything a clip point will in hunting.

Drop point. The drop-point blade is the most practical deer-hunting shape available. This unique configuration is exactly what its name implies, having an arched back and a point positioned lower on the blade than seen in the clip-point and trailing-point designs. A drop-point blade is the strongest available for hunting and allows the easiest deer-gutting because the back of the blade tends to hold the innards away from the point.

The only drawback of the drop point is that it requires more pressure to penetrate a deer's hide with the point of the blade than slimmer, more friction-free blade points. This is a small objection overruled by the majority of avid woodsmen.

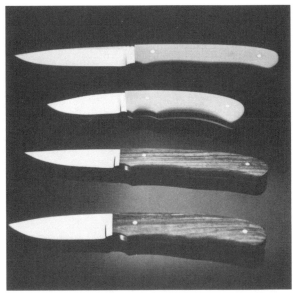

Drop-point blades of various lengths and sizes are the most versatile of all configurations. These blades are strong and represent the best compromise of such characteristics as edge curve and tip-penetrating ability.

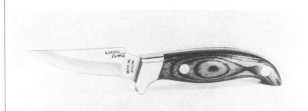

A trailing-point blade has a flat or slightly concave back. This makes the tip a bit weaker than in other blade designs, but cuts down knife weight and enhances penetrating ability by slenderizing the tip.

Skinning blade. A skinning blade is characterized by a uniquely shaped belly (cutting edge). This edge is more sharply curved near the tip than other blades to provide a fairly long cutting edge in a fairly short blade length. When properly used, this tight-radius edge is rocked in an easy, efficient slicing motion. Since the front working edge on this blade is longer than normal, it doesn't dull as fast as the other three basic blade types. Because a skinning blade is seldom used to *puncture* skin, it usually has a fairly blunt, strong tip.

A typical, special-purpose skinning knife has a markedly curving blade that provides more cutting edge up front where it counts. The knife is usually wielded with a smooth, rocking motion that quickly parts the hide from a deer carcass.

Other blade shapes. Some knives—notably folding pocketknives—have blade shapes that markedly deviate from the four hunting shapes just described. Some of these will do a passable job on game, and others will not. For example, the so-called spey blade in many three-blade pocket knives is merely a modified drop-point shape and is thus okay for gutting and skinning if it's 1½ to 2 inches in length. By contrast, another common pocketknife blade, called the sheepsfoot, has a perfectly flat edge with little application in the field.

Which blade shape is best? The clip-point, trailing-point, and drop-point blade shapes are all fine for general deer-hunting use, provided blade *length* is acceptable. The drop point is most practical of all, but only by a slight margin. A hunter who plans to process several deer per year might wish to own a second knife with a special-purpose skinning blade, but such a knife should be considered luxury and not necessity.

BASIC KNIFE DESIGN

There are three basic kinds of knives commonly carried by hunters. These are the folding pocketknife, the folding belt knife, and the fixed-blade knife. Each has pluses and minuses well worth considering.

Folding pocketknives. A well-designed pocketknife can be a handy little tool. At its best it is no more than 4 inches long when folded up—preferably 3 or 3½. To fit snugly and unobtrusively in a trouser pocket, the handle must be fairly slim from top to bottom and extremely thin from side to side. A pocketknife is not the most versatile deer-hunting knife available but certainly is easy to carry and use. In a pinch, it can be used to gut, skin, and quarter an elk, let alone a

conventional-size deer, and performs dozens of other routine field chores. Most pocketknives have two or more blades, although a few modern styles have only one blade.

There are four traditional pocketknife configurations worth mentioning here. A penknife has a large clip blade at one end and a smaller drop-point blade at the other. A jackknife is also a two-blade folder with clip and drop-point blades, but both blades fold out from the same end of this particular design. A stock knife is a three-blade pocketknife with clip and

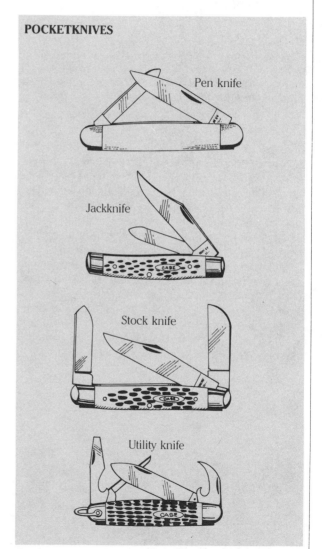

POCKETKNIVES

Pen knife

Jackknife

Stock knife

Utility knife

Folding pocketknives are extremely handy hunting tools. Regardless of exact blade configuration or knife size, these little cutting implements can be used to field-dress a deer in a pinch and perform a variety of other incidental tasks. Four traditional pocketknife shapes are (top to bottom): two-blade penknife, two-blade jackknife, three-blade stock knife, and utility knife of the Boy Scout configuration.

A Swiss army knife is the ultimate utility folder, incorporating over a dozen blades and other accessories in the most elaborate models. This pocketknife tends to be somewhat bulky but still slips into any pants pocket.

sheepsfoot blades at one end and a spey blade at the other. A utility knife, sometimes called a camper's knife, is a pocket folder with four or more blades and other folding tools attached. One common utility knife is the traditional Boy Scout knife with drop-point blade, leather punch, cap-lift/screwdriver, and can opener. Another is the Swiss army knife, which sometimes has over a dozen blades and other accessories.

Most deer hunters own several pocketknives and carry one regularly for use in camp and in the field.

Folding belt knives. The folding belt knife, sometimes called the lock-blade folder, is a working knife used by more deer hunters than any other design. A pocketknife is a handy and convenient tool for light

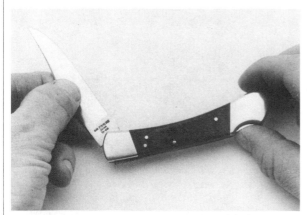

The best folding belt knives have locking blades to prevent accidental closure during use. Most models lock and unlock with the action of a thumb-press spring located on the back of the handle.

field work—by contrast, a folding belt knife takes the toughest job in stride and does it very well. This is usually all a one-knife hunter really needs if the blade has a clip-point, trailing-point, or drop-point shape about 3 inches in overall length.

Folding belt knives vary somewhat in size and shape, but the average model with a 3-inch blade measures about 4 inches long when folded up; features a relatively stout, easy-to-grip, flat-sided handle section averaging ½ inch wide and 1 inch deep; has one heavy-duty working blade; and incorporates some sort of positive blade-locking system that prevents the blade from closing accidentally on a hunter's hand during use. The most common blade-locking device on a no-nonsense folder is a stout thumb-press spring somewhere on the back of the handle.

Blade-locking devices on folding belt knives vary in placement and action. One manufacturer offers a sturdy drop-point design with a sliding "bolt-action" locking button that allows completely safe slicing and carving.

A folding belt knife is not quite as stoutly constructed as a rigid, fixed-blade knife because it has moving parts and an internal spring assembly to snap the blade securely open during use. Folding belt knives have a blade slot in the handle to protect both the blade and the user when the blade is closed, and this slot is prone to collect blood, meat, hair, and other debris that can be a minor nuisance to remove. Nonetheless, a knife that is only 4 inches long when closed and a rigid 7 inches long when open is unquestionably handy to use and carry.

Fixed-blade knives. Fixed-blade knives are the strongest hunting knives. These are sold in various shapes and sizes, but all consist of a blade that is pinned, glued, or welded to some sort of grip.

Fixed-blade knives are easiest to clean after use because the handles do not have blade slots. For hunters who tend to abuse knives by using them to chop through the pelvic area on deer and forcibly pry through deer spines during the quartering chore, this

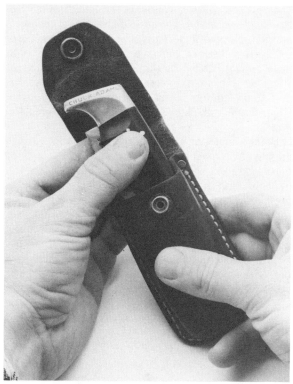

Because folding belt knives are typically too bulky to carry in a pocket, they are usually carried in sturdy leather sheaths with snap-down closure flaps. Belt-attached sheaths hold knives securely and unobtrusively, but allow instant access whenever you need a blade.

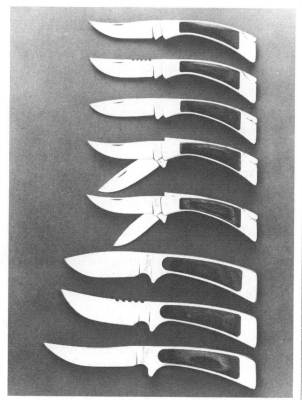

Folding belt knives (top five) are often nearly identical to fixed-blade knives when open. However, the fixed-blade models are at least twice as long when sheathed and not in use. Fixed-blade knives are sold in a wide variety of sizes. They represent the ultimate in functional simplicity, require little care, and cost less than knives with folding blades. Like the knives themselves, sheaths for these knives are longer than those of folding knives.

kind of knife will hold up long after a lock-blade folder gives up the ghost.

At its best, a fixed-blade hunting knife is a handsome, serviceable tool with a full, easily gripped handle made of antler, micarta, hardwood, plastic, ivory, or metal. The simple, functional lines of such a knife makes it the favorite of custom knife makers everywhere, and in factory knives this plain-Jane design is less expensive than folding models because there are fewer parts to manufacture and assemble.

The primary drawback of any fixed-blade knife is its unchanging overall length. Even the fixed-blade caping knives with their short blades are significantly longer than general-purpose folders, creating a minor carrying problem in the outdoors. A lock-blade folder in its compact belt sheath is forgotten until it's needed; a fixed-blade hunting knife measuring 7 or 8 inches long tends to remind a hunter of its presence as the butt nudges his ribs and the sheath slaps gently against his leg. This knife is also easier to lose afield than a folding model because snagging brush can pluck it from the best-designed sheath.

Most knives with blades over 4 inches long are fixed-blade models simply because a folding knife loses

A size comparison of a folding-knife sheath (far left) and several fixed-blade sheaths shows why many hunters prefer folding knives.

compactness—its major selling point—once blade length reaches 4½ or 5 inches. As a result, most excellent butcher knives with blades between 5 and 10 inches long are simple, fixed-blade cutting tools.

Many hunters prefer fixed-blade knives because they are sturdy, fill the hand exceedingly well, clean up easily, and carry a moderate price tag when mass-produced. For these hunters, a slight carrying disadvantage is no big deal, and it's tough to argue with their logic.

Other knife designs. A few other knife designs show up around hunting camps: so-called belt-buckle knives that fold up inside integral belt buckles to provide a cutting edge in survival situations; specialized pointless rope knives for cutting lines used in tent setup; patch knives used in muzzleloader shooting; and other one-of-a-kind configurations. But the woodsmen who use such blades carry them because of special interests or druthers—not because they need the knives to work on deer.

Fine points on knife construction. Most brand-name knives sold today are adequately designed for use in deer-hunting situations. However, a discerning knife buyer picks and chooses from one or more models that fit his needs and tickle his personal fancy. Here are some major design factors worth considering.

Knife weight and balance: Ideally, a hunting knife balances nicely in the hand with no unnecessary weight to tire muscles during use. Most working knives have blades somewhere in the neighborhood of 0.1-inch thick for good strength and relatively light physical weight. Knives with thicker blades are unnecessarily stout for working on deer and too heavy to satisfy the average user. Knife balance is a subjective thing, but most experienced users prefer a knife with a balance point somewhere near the center of the grip.

This lets the knife lie solidly in the hand during use.

Grip shape and material: The shape of a knife grip and the material it is made of are largely a matter of personal preference. However, any deer knife should have a grip that is not slippery—even when wet or smeared with animal secretions or fat. To meet this end, many hunters prefer a grip with finger grooves. Other hunters like a knife with a rough or corregated grip.

Handle material has as much to do with positive gripping as physical shape and texture. Dense-grained hardwood like ebony or rosewood is basically nonslip in nature, and so is staghorn and micarta. Plastic knife grips are fine as well, provided surfaces are slightly rough instead of polished smooth. One favorite fixed-blade handle material is rough-textured aluminum with surfaces similar to heavily sand-blasted steel.

Grip shape and material are also important to anyone who enjoys the artistic aspect of knives. A slim, neatly contoured knife handle made of rosewood or top-grade staghorn is far more pleasing to the eye than a slab-sided chunk of plastic—something that may

A rough-surfaced staghorn knife handle provides a no-slip grip for serious deer-care tasks. It is also pleasing to the eye.

Grip shape and grip material are largely a matter of personal preference. These folding belt knives all incorporate practical deer-hunting grips (left to right): rough-surfaced plastic, flat-sided rosewood, contoured rosewood, and flat-sided rosewood/brass combination.

not affect durability but certainly can influence the user's enjoyment of his primary cutting tool.

Window dressing: A few deer hunters insist upon using a knife that is ornately decked out with skrimshaw on the grip or etching on the blade. Window dressing on a knife does nothing to improve its usefulness afield, but hurts nothing either, all else being equal. To each his own.

KNIFE STEEL

The principal factor in determining the quality of a hunting knife is the quality of steel in the blade. Excellent steel makes an excellent knife, and poor steel makes a poor knife. Other factors such as blade shape and overall knife design are certainly important, but every knife is a cutting tool and the steel in the blade determines how well that blade performs.

What is good knife steel? There is no such thing as perfect knife steel. If there were, this material would display three primary characteristics. First, it would never rust. Second, it would never break. And third, it would never need to be resharpened. Unfortunately, the three positive knife-steel characteristics are somewhat incompatible in any single billet of steel. Metallurgists have tried for centuries to concoct a steel that excels in all three areas. But the best modern knife steels are still working compromises with one superb quality and two others that leave at least a little to be desired.

The type of steel in a hunting knife is often stamped near the back of the blade along with other particulars like the model name and place of manufacture. Steel quality makes or breaks a knife and should be a major factor in shopping.

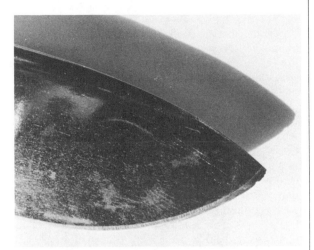

There is no perfect knife steel. For example, 440-C stainless is almost completely rust-resistant and holds an edge extremely well, but tends to chip with very heavy use (see tip of blade).

All knife steels are composed largely of iron with other elements added to produce specific working characteristics. For example, one of the most popular knife steels today is 440-C, which has unusually high chromium content. This makes it virtually stainless even when used near saltwater. Another knife steel, F-8, is unusually high in tungsten and vanadium, which makes it superb in the edge-holding department. A third steel, D-2, is high in molybdenum and displays unusual resistance to breakage.

Unfortunately, like all knife steels, each of these sacrifices certain traits to excel in one category. 440-C holds an edge fairly well but is brittle and suffers edge chipping or actual blade breakage with very heavy use or abuse. F-8 readily rusts and is so brittle it sometimes shatters when accidentally dropped from waist level on a rock or similar unyielding object. D-2 holds an edge fairly well but rusts with incredible rapidity if given half a chance.

The very elements in steel that ensure one ideal trait tend to degrade the level of another. However, the best factory-produced hunting knives have blades that embody excellent working levels of corrosion resistance, durability, *and* edge-holding ability. These blades are tempered in various ways to enhance their serviceability. The best factory knives have blades measuring 55 to 60 on the Rockwell scale (a method of determining hardness using a diamond point to indent the steel). A high Rockwell blade rating helps ensure edge-holding ability.

The majority of factory blades are made with some variety of 440-series stainless steel to inhibit rust and diminish blade care. Quality blades that are not made of stainless steel are generally composed of high-carbon tool steel, which will rust but not readily. Most high-carbon tool steels hold an edge extremely well. No matter what the blade material, most decent factory blades will not readily chip or break unless severely abused.

Before buying a hunting knife, consult manufacturer literature to determine the quality of steel in various models. Steel quality is generally reflected in the price tag, so a little comparison shopping generally tells the tale. Excellent knife steel is simply more expensive to buy, temper, and test than run-of-the-mill steel, and manufacturers pass on this cost to consumers. A smart customer double-checks the Rockwell rating of any blade he wants to buy, spends a little time talking to well-informed sporting goods dealers to learn which knives have the best reputations in the blade-steel department, and strictly avoids knives with alluringly low price tags.

A knife with excellent steel is a joy to use, and a knife with poor steel is worse than worthless to own. Unfortunately, there are dozens of cheap folding and fixed-blade models on the market—models with low-Rockwell steel that will not take or hold an edge. Other knives display fairly good sharpening characteristics but rust into fine red dust whenever a damp cloud passes overhead. A hunter need not be a metallurgist to avoid such dime-store wonders—all he needs to do is shop intelligently and remember that he'll probably get what he's willing to pay for.

CUSTOM, OR BENCH-MADE, KNIVES

Well-made factory knives are completely satisfactory for most deer hunters. But a handful of knife connoisseurs prefer custom-made hunting knives. Bench-made knives are uniquely designed, finely crafted products of superb steel and grip materials. These one-of-a-kind creations carry big price tags to match, costing up to 20 times more than similar looking factory-made deer knives.

For hunters who appreciate superbly polished steel, near-perfect blade-to-grip fit, and other signs of bona fide craftsmanship, bench-made knives are well worth their relatively high cost. However, given the excellent quality of factory knives, the only *practical* justification for using a custom-made blade is something special about the steel it is fashioned from.

Many custom knives are made of the same steel found in assembly-line blades. For example, 440-C stainless is a very popular custom knife steel. A bench-made, drop-point knife with a 440-C blade will perform no better on deer than a 440-C factory knife costing much less—only the status appeal and careful hand-crafting of the custom knife make it more desirable. In contrast, some handmade knives incorporate steel

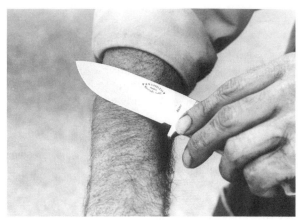

The best custom knives are made of steel that takes and holds a hair-shaving edge incredibly well. However, the need for these expensive superknives for deer hunting is an oft-debated question.

that is too expensive or too difficult to work with to allow assembly-line production. For example, F-8 is a common custom steel that holds an edge far better than any factory-knife steel. This blade material is extremely brittle, requiring meticulous grinding, tempering, and finishing with the tender loving care of a craftsman. Once sharpened, an F-8 blade will gut, skin, and butcher several deer without becoming dull—a fact that appeals to some deer hunters. Other custom-knife steels like 0-1 and 154-CM also embody higher levels of edge-holding ability than standard-issue factory blades, making them popular with some.

At best the practical value of a custom deer knife over a factory knife is debatable matter. A hard, superior edge made of F-8 or comparable custom steel usually presents problems every bit as substantial as those the steel is supposed to solve. For example, once such a blade *does* dull down from regular use, it is difficult for the average owner to quickly hand-sharpen himself. In some instances custom knives with ultrahard steel blades must be sent back to their makers for costly machine resharpening—a time-consuming nuisance at best. Similarly, many extra-hard custom blades rust quite easily, requiring unusual maintenance to keep them functional and attractive.

There is no doubt that a custom hunting knife displays superior workmanship and embodies the unique collectability of any work of art, but the best factory hunting knives sold today perform deer dressing and related functions every bit as well. A few knife experts will even argue that the quality, factory blade embodies a better balance of important properties—edge-holding ability, strength, and rust-resistance—than more specialized steels used in many custom knives.

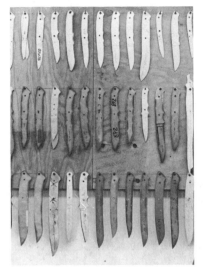

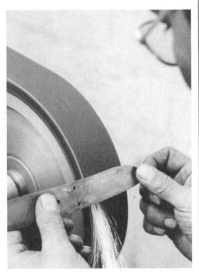

Most custom knife makers offer dozens of different shapes and sizes to choose from. Once a customer selects a personal favorite, the craftsman outlines the knife on a billet of steel, then cuts and grinds it to basic shape.

SHARPENING STONES

With the exception of a few custom knives made of ultrahard, exotic types of steel, every deer-hunting knife must be sharpened by its owner from time to time. There are several sharpening implements that work quite well.

The majority of deer hunters sharpen their knives on quality honing stones. When used with special honing oil, which prevents stone pores from becoming clogged, honing stones can quickly restore blade edges to hair-shaving keenness. Stones are especially desirable for hard steel with a Rockwell rating of 58 or more. This steel cannot be sharpened easily on a ceramic sharpener or other alternate honing device.

Although knife-honing stones composed of man-made materials like Carborundum are sold at sporting goods stores, the best honing stones are made of natural, fine-grained novaculite rock quarried in Arkansas. Arkansas stones offer several advantages over man-made honing stones. First, they have a fairly fine grain structure that removes knife-edge steel at a slow, even rate. Second, they are porous enough to soak up honing oil—oil that suspends steel particles and ensures consistent edge-sharpening throughout the life of a stone. Because of their oil-retaining properties, Arkansas stones are often called oilstones. By contrast, most man-made sharpening stones are relatively coarse-grained yet too dense to accept adequate levels of honing oil. The result is a rough, deeply scratched knife edge and a stone soon clogged with fine steel particles.

The harder and more abrasion-resistant a knife steel

Arkansas oilstones are made of fine-grained novaculite rock that hones an edge to hair-splitting perfection. Stones are available in several sizes to match any hunter's personal needs.

happens to be, the more difficult it is to sharpen. The very abrasion-resistant properties in the best edge-holding blades resist resharpening efforts every bit as well as they resist initial dulling from grit, grime, and friction against various parts of a deer. As a result, sharpening a quality deer knife takes some old-fashioned elbow grease plus proper sharpening technique.

Edge taper. The key to honing any edge with a stone is retaining the sharpening angle of the blade throughout the honing process. Steel must be removed along both edge tapers of a blade until these tapers meet at a clean, sharp edge completely free of nicks, burrs, and flat places. The best edge taper is approximately 22 degrees (about the same as for arrow broadheads)—a working compromise between a thin, fragile edge that is razor sharp, and a fat, chopping edge that is strong but not especially keen. Most factory knives have such edge angles already; so a hunter is best advised to closely scrutinize the tapers on a blade and maintain these as best he can during the resharpening process. For people who have trouble retaining edge angle by eye, several companies make honing-angle guides that clamp to the back of a knife blade. These guides produce sharp, consistent knife-blade edges when held firmly against a stone during the honing process.

Sharpening technique. To sharpen a blade on a honing stone, a hunter should first make sure the stone can be held in place without getting his hand too close to the blade during the sharpening process. Although most honing stones are sold without wooden cradles or bases, it is wise to purchase a cradle, or to epoxy the stone to a large plywood base. This lets you keep your hand away from the stone itself as you work a blade over it.

During sharpening, hold edge tapers firmly at the proper angle and slice across the stone with firm, fluid strokes (see accompanying photos). The more pressure you exert against the stone, the quicker the edge will reach hair-shaving perfection. The common technique of sharpening by moving the blade in a circular motion does not work nearly as well because this makes retaining a precise edge angle far more difficult. Squirt honing oil liberally on the stone throughout the sharpening process—too much is better than too little.

Hunters test the keenness of their knife edges in several ways. Most common is shaving hair from an arm or leg, but this can be dangerous unless carefully done. A knife edge that grabs a fingernail instead of sliding over it smoothly is plenty sharp enough, and so is a blade that slices medium-weight typing paper with ease.

Most knife owners use only one honing stone during sharpening, but a few begin with a medium-grain stone and finish off with a hard, fine-grain stone to achieve slightly better keenness. As long as both edge tapers meet at a clean, burr-free edge, a blade honed by either method is sharp enough for work on deer.

SHARPENING STEELS

A sharpening steel is a cylindrical, rattail-shaped tool that is held in one hand while the knife edge is passed across it with the other. Some small sharpening steels have a surface impregnated with ceramic particles, diamond chips, or similar abrasive material that removes knife steel and brings an edge back to functional sharpness. These are commonly called sportsman's steels. Larger sharpening steels used by professional butchers are made of ultrahard tool steel with a slightly rough surface and seldom have any abrasive added.

Most knife-sharpening steels are best used on blades made of fairly soft material. Butchers in particular prefer long sharpening steels and knives with relatively soft, durable blades. This combination allows quick, repeated sharpening throughout a full day of cutting meat. A few sportsmen's steels—especially

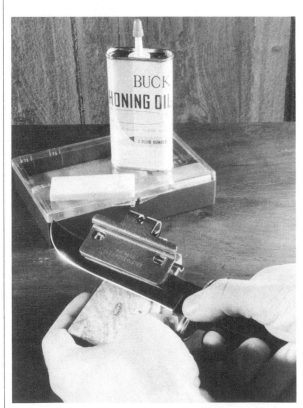

A knife-honing guide clamps to the back of a blade to ensure proper edge-sharpening angle. This is a practical accessory for anyone who has trouble maintaining consistent edge angle by eye.

HOW TO SHARPEN A HUNTING KNIFE

Before starting to hone a knife edge, coat the oilstone with liberal amounts of commercial honing oil. The oil suspends steel particles during the sharpening process to prevent stone pores from becoming clogged.

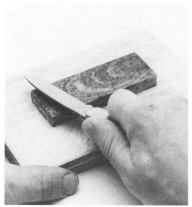

Holding the blade at an approximate 22-degree angle, bear down hard and slice the blade, cutting edge first, across the stone in one fluid motion. This removes steel evenly along the entire cutting edge.

Repeat the honing stroke on the opposite side of the edge in the opposite direction. By alternating strokes back and forth with steady downward pressure, you can quickly produce a keen cutting edge. (Continued on next page)

(Continued from previous page)

Once you believe your blade to be sharp, burnish the edge tapers by dragging them backwards *along a piece of wood or leather. This is called stropping, and enhances blade keenness by removing microscopic burrs.*

A small, diamond-impregnated sportsman's steel is handy for minor edge touch-up in the field. This Eze-Lap model can be carried in a shirt pocket like a ballpoint pen and easily unscrewed to expose the rattail-shaped sharpening surface.

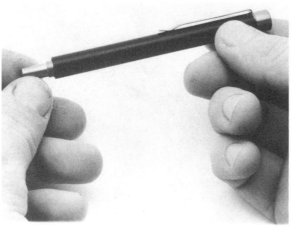

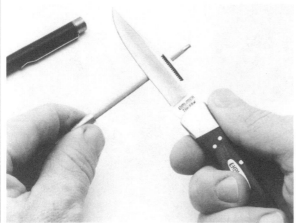

those impregnated with diamond chips—are abrasive enough to sharpen a knife blade made of hard steel. Most deer hunters own compact steels of one sort or another for touching up edges in the field during field dressing, skinning, and caping—edge honing is a time-consuming process reserved for spare time at home. Some of these steels can actually be clipped in a shirt pocket like a ballpoint pen, making them handy to carry and use when knife edges begin to dull.

To use any sharpening steel, hold it by the handle and draw knife edges *toward* you across the top and bottom of the steel in alternating strokes. A little practice at this ensures fairly consistent edge angles and quickly removes edge nicks and burrs that hamper knife performance in the field. Before using any sharpening steel, ask for a demonstration at the sporting goods store to ensure that you know how to wield a steel safely and properly. Because knife edges are drawn toward you when you use a sharpening steel, improper technique can lead to dangerous and painful cuts.

A sharpening steel characteristically puts a fairly rough, serrated edge on a knife. This cuts meat well but dulls faster than a smoothly honed edge. The serrated edge is also prone to collect moisture and rust more easily than the edge produced by a honing stone.

OTHER SHARPENING AIDS

Several other sharpening aids are sold at sporting goods stores. All can be used to bring a knife edge to hair-shaving keenness, provided you learn to handle them properly.

Crock sticks. So-called crock sticks made of ceramic are rapidly gaining popularity. Two round sticks are mounted on a wooden base to form a sharpening V (see photos on next page). Edge tapers are alternately passed across the sticks to produce a keen, nick-free edge. A little practice at using a crock-stick setup allows you to sharpen knives quickly and with consistency. Because the knife blade is stroked downward instead of horizontally during sharpening, this sharpening device is one of the safest available.

Disk-type sharpeners. An ordinary kitchen-knife sharpener consisting of intermeshing disks of hardened steel will adequately sharpen hunting knives that have only moderately hard blades. A disk setup produces a relatively ragged, serrated edge that needs frequent resharpening, but there's no easier way to sharpen a blade.

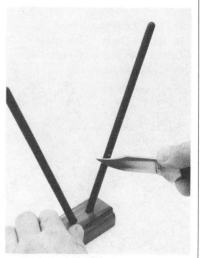

A V-type crock-stick sharpener consists of a compact wooden base and two ceramic rods that store inside. The components assemble quickly for sharpening.

To use a V-type crock-stick, grasp the knife firmly and stroke the blade downward and backward alternately against each crock-stick arm in smooth slicing motions.

To ensure proper edge angle, hold the knife blade straight up and down throughout entire strokes on both sides of the crock-stick.

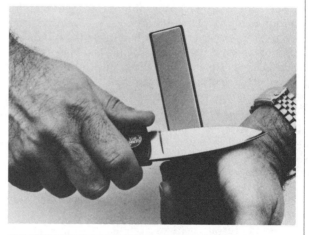

A disk-type sharpener (above) consists of intermeshing, hardened-steel disks that remove softer knife-blade steel in short order. The resulting edge is somewhat ragged and serrated, but it cuts meat like a charm.

Flat sharpeners. Several companies offer flat, pocket-sized sharpening devices for knife touchup in the field. Some of these are made of solid ceramic; others are composed of ultrahard, rough-surfaced steel or steel impregnated with diamond chips. Although no substitute for a full-blown honing job, flat sharpeners are handy in the field if a knife edge begins to dull.

Glass. This is one of the hardest, finest-grained substances known. Although seldom used as a honing surface, any thick piece of glass can be employed like an Arkansas stone to put an ultrafine edge on steel. Using glass to hone a knife takes time because very little steel is removed with each pass of a blade. But for the keenest edge achievable on any knife, a careful honing on glass cannot be matched. In survival sit-

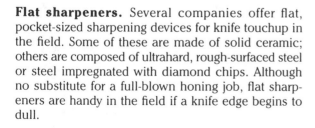

Small, flat tools for touching up edges (middle photo) are impregnated with diamond chips or composed of solid ceramic; others are made of ultrahard, rough-surfaced tool steel. Thongs and cases add protection.

uations or when you simply forget your oilstone, you can use the bottom of a glass jar, an old mirror, or any other relatively flat glass surface to refine a knife edge to hair-splitting perfection.

KNIFE TRANSPORT AND CARE

Good hunting knives need very little care aside from occasional resharpening. But you should always protect your blade from moisture, abrasion, and impact during use to ensure that it lasts many hunting seasons.

The best way to carry most hunting knives is in a quality leather sheath designed specifically for that purpose. Aside from pocket knives, almost all decent hunting knives come complete with a sheath from the factory. The sheath protects both the knife and the hunter who carries it.

Hunting knives should be washed periodically with mild, soapy water to remove blood, fat, dirt, and other debris prone to accumulate on the blade and handle. Once a knife is clean, rinse it in clean water and dry it thoroughly to inhibit rust. Lubricate all moving parts on a folding deer knife with light machine oil to prevent rust and ensure smooth folding and blade-locking action. Likewise, lightly oil the blade itself to keep the edge keen and free of corrosion. Knives made of 440-C stainless steel seldom stain or rust no matter how badly they are treated.

A knife is not a hatchet or a pry bar, and should not be used as such. Too many hunters use knives to pound through pelvic bones and other bony parts of deer, sometimes using a rock or limb to hammer against the back of a blade to expedite matters. Another common stunt is twisting and prying with a blade to sever the backbone or cut off the legs of a deer. These chores are better accomplished with a hatchet or meat saw, and using a knife to do them can ruin the parts of a folding knife or actually snap a hunting blade in two. A knife is designed to cut and slice only—any other tasks should be considered abuse.

SAWS AND HATCHETS

Saws and hatchets are handy deer-hunting tools, both for working on animal carcasses and performing necessary chores about camp.

The primary function of a saw in deer hunting is cutting through larger bones during field dressing, quartering, butchering, and trophy care—bones such as the pelvis, spine, legs, and skull. Secondary uses of a saw include cutting firewood, pruning limbs around a tree stand, and making tent stakes.

A hatchet, sometimes called a hand axe, can also be used for hacking through the bigger bones on a deer. If properly designed, this chopping tool will also perform menial camp duties, such as splitting kindling for fires, pounding in tent pegs, and fashioning simple wooden camp furniture.

When choosing hunting saws and hatchets, shop with care and buy well-made, time-proven designs.

Field saws. Deer-hunting saws fall into three categories—folding pull saws, rigid push saws, and bow saws. Each has advantages and disadvantages worth considering.

Folding pull saws: A folding pull saw vaguely resembles an oversized folding belt knife. The best designs measure 8 to 12 inches long when closed and incorporate some sort of blade-locking device to prevent accidental blade closure during use. The blade on a folding pull saw is lightly curved to enhance cutting ability, and has teeth that *point toward the user.* This means that the saw cuts only when pulled, not pushed—a major advantage in the field.

A saw that must be pushed tends to bind up in bone and cause the blade to buckle unless it is stoutly constructed. By contrast, a pull-saw blade can be relatively light in weight because pull-cutting does not bend or buckle a blade. A folding pull saw will perform any field dressing or butchering chore to perfection, and is the smallest, lightest saw available to the hunter. Many deer hunters carry one of these saws for cutting small-gauge firewood, pruning limbs around a tree stand or blind, and performing necessary cutting jobs on the carcass once a deer is down.

Rigid push saws: Although not as compact or light in weight as folding pull saws, several excellent push saws for deer hunting are sold at sporting goods

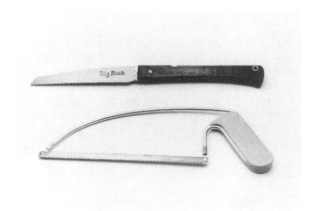

Folding pull saws (top) and bow saws are both used by hunters to cut through the bony areas of deer carcasses. Pull saws are especially desirable because they fold to compact size and cut when pulled—*this eliminates blade binding or bending.*

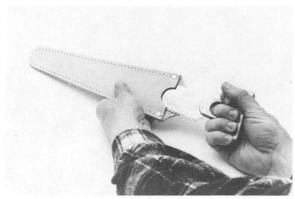

A rigid push saw is favored by many hunters because it has a long blade and two rows of teeth to accomplish both bone-sawing and wood-cutting duties. It is normally carried in a leather belt sheath.

stores. The most popular of these has a compact, T-shaped handle with a finger hole in the center to provide a solid, no-slip grip. The 12-inch saw blade has teeth on both edges—fine teeth on one side for sawing through bone, and coarser teeth on the other for cutting firewood and pruning limbs. This saw has a stout steel blade, and coupled with its leather belt sheath, it weighs several times as much as a folding pull saw. However, its long working blade and double-purpose rows of teeth make it a popular choice with hunters.

Bow saws: Bow saws for field use are available in a wide variety of configurations to serve a number of different purposes. All these saws consist of a springy bow of tubular steel with a blade fixed to the ends under tension. Some have separate handles; others are used by gripping the bow itself. The smallest bow saws are similar in size to regular metal hacksaws—under 10 inches long—and are used exclusively for cutting the bony parts of an animal.

Larger versions of these saws measure 12 to 24 inches long and are used for no-nonsense animal butchering. These so-called butcher's saws will quickly cut a deer carcass in two from neck to tail, precisely spitting the spine lengthwise as no other variety of saw can do. A saw of this sort is favored by hunters who like to cut and wrap deer meat with the sliced-up bones attached to the venison.

The largest bow saws measure several feet in length and are used primarily for cutting wood around a hunting camp. Most of the better brands are manufactured in Scandinavia, which is why these saws are often called "Swedish saws" by woodsmen.

Deer-hunting hatchets. Hatchets for hunting can be separated into two different categories—light duty and heavy duty. Each is perfectly suited for certain specific jobs.

A light-duty hatchet generally weighs less than 10

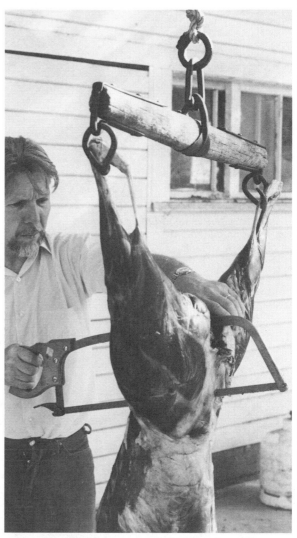

A bow-type butcher's saw is ideal for halving a deer carcass lengthwise and accomplishing other major bone-cutting needs.

ounces, measures less than 12 inches long, and has a cutting head only slightly wider than the blade on a sturdy fixed-blade knife. This hatchet generally displays a balance point about halfway between the head and the handle. As often as not, a light-duty hatchet comes complete with a belt sheath that snaps securely about the head.

A light-duty hatchet is meant to do what its name suggests. When kept sharp with a file, it will neatly split a deer's pelvis during field dressing, chop open the brisket to aid carcass cooling, and hack through the spine of a deer being cut into quarters. It will *not* safely perform heavier chores, such as cutting firewood, because it has neither the mass weight nor the overall length to power through big chunks of wood. Many hunters prefer one of these hatchets to a folding

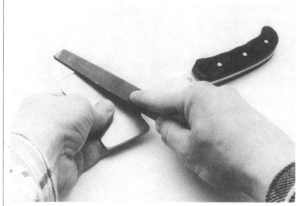
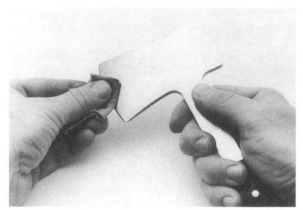

A hatchet like this light-duty, belt-carried model should be kept sharp with a mill file and oiled from time to time to prevent edge-dulling rust. To protect the edge, and yourself too, cover the head of any hatchet not in use with a leather sheath.

The best heavy-duty hatchets balance just behind the head, measure over 12 inches long for easy chopping, and incorporate heavy, flat-backed heads suited for pounding stakes and serving like a wedge head to split stubborn logs.

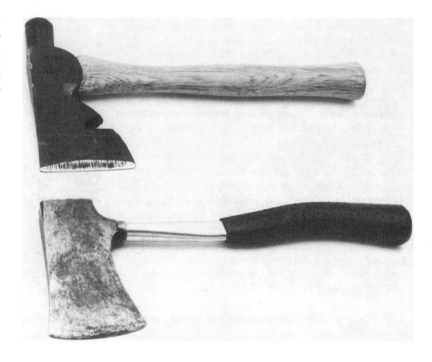

saw because it is easily carried on a belt and can be used in an emergency to chop small-gauge firewood.

A heavy-duty hatchet usually weighs a pound or more, making it too heavy to be carried afield. Its head normally tapers from a wide back to a thinner cutting edge, and its balance point is generally directly behind this head. Most heavy-duty hatchets measure between 13 and 14 inches from front of head to back of handle, allowing a longer, more energy-efficient power stroke for bone-chopping, wood-splitting, and stake-driving jobs. The extra weight makes them safer for big jobs because, with a lightweight hatchet, you must flail wildly to achieve adequate splitting power.

Most deer hunters use a heavy-duty hatchet in every

camping situation, supplementing it with a small meat saw or light-duty hatchet for field dressing and carcass jobs.

Using saws and hatchets. A sharp tool is usually the safest tool, and saws and hatchets are no exception. They should be inspected frequently for tooth or edge wear, and must be oiled periodically to prevent edge-dulling rust. Dull saws should be replaced or professionally resharpened; dull hatchets can be quickly returned to original keenness with a few strokes from a mill file. Sharp saws and hatchets cut easily and surely, saving a lot of elbow grease and preventing accidents as well.

DEER-HUNTING STANDS AND BLINDS

A deer stand can be defined as any elevated platform or enclosure used by a hunter to wait for and ambush deer. A deer blind, on the other hand, is an ambush enclosure positioned at ground level. Both stands and blinds are used extensively by deer hunters with excellent success—especially in areas where deer are wary and foliage is especially dense.

Deer seldom look up for danger, so an elevated stand allows you to wait without an animal seeing you before you take a shot. Minor body movements in a lofty tree stand, tower stand, or similar contrivance seldom catch a deer's attention, so camouflage precautions need not be as meticulous when stand-hunting. Another advantage of a deer stand is that above-ground air currents generally sweep away human odor and are too high for deer to smell. Waiting for animals at ground level is always a gamble as breezes swirl about, but an elevated position largely cancels out this problem.

As a rule, ground blinds should only be used for deer when taking an elevated stand is impossible or when local laws prohibit the use of aboveground stands. Blind enclosures *do* help you take animals by allowing you to hide behind camouflage netting or a similar shield. You can then make casual shifts in position to remain comfortable during long waits for deer, and can also prepare to shoot without alerting a deer.

An elevated stand allows a clear view of surrounding terrain and keeps you well above the eyes and noses of deer. As a result, most hunters who prefer to ambush their venison use stands.

A stand allows close-range shots at wary deer. As a result, most successful bowhunters use stands exclusively to make the most of their short-range shooting tools.

A wide variety of commercial and homemade stands and blinds are used. Learning about them and deciding which will work best in particular hunting situations is enjoyable, and so is building custom stands and blinds at home. The only factor to consider when selecting stands and blinds, aside from hunting practicality, is local legislation regulating their use. Tree stands in particular are subject to laws in some parts of the United States and Canada—laws governing how high stands may be, how they can be fixed to trees, and what safety features they must have. A few deer-hunting areas do not allow use of tree stands at all. Before shopping for stands or blinds, check out local laws.

CLIMBING TREE STANDS

The most popular commercial deer stands sold today are the so-called climbing stands. These vary somewhat in design configuration, but all allow you to inch up a straight-trunked, relatively limbless tree by using the stand itself as a climbing device. Climbing tree stands are especially popular in deer areas with straight, tall hardwoods and pines.

Climbing tree stands offer several advantages worth considering. First, most of them are small enough to

be backpacked into prime hunting areas far from vehicle access points. Second, they allow quick, silent ascent once a suitable stand location has been found and thereby provide spur-of-the-moment hunting versatility. Third, climbing stands can be removed at the end of every hunting day, preventing other hunters from using or even stealing them when you are not around. And fourth, stands of this type let hunters take elevated positions on limbless trunks.

A typical climbing tree stand consists of a platform section and a separate hand-climber section that grips a tree above the platform. To use the stand, the hunter first bolts both sections around the tree, then slips his toes under elastic foot straps located on the stand platform. Next, he grips the hand-climber tool and slides it as far up the trunk as possible. Then, by hanging from the hand climber and pulling his knees upward, he lifts the platform section a foot or so up the trunk. Both hand-climber and platform sections are designed to slip up a trunk easily and lock around it whenever there is downward pressure from the hunter's weight. With a little practice you can inchworm up a trunk in fluid, rhythmic fashion. Once you reach the desired height, you can use the hand-climbing section as a comfortable tree-stand seat.

Although climbing stands with hand-climbing sections are the most common design, there are other types. The seat climber, for example, lets a hunter sit down as he climbs up a tree. This type is by far the easiest to use. Another type of stand requires a hunter to hug the tree trunk as he climbs aloft—a muscle-straining chore that can cause abrasions of the chest,

Climbing tree stands are best used in areas with clusters of straight-trunked, relatively limbless conifers and hardwoods. Deer often inhabit such thickets.

THE PARTS OF A TYPICAL CLIMBING TREE STAND

1. *Upper blade (for gripping tree) made of ⅛- to ¼-inch aluminum or steel. May be angled or flat. Inside edge beveled for gripping tree trunk.* **2.** *Arms made of ⅛- or 1/16-inch aluminum (1-inch square channel).* **3.** *Lower blades (for gripping tree) made of ¼- or ⅛-inch flat aluminum bolted or riveted to platform.* **4.** *Toe strap made of ½- to 1-inch nylon web or bungee cord.* **5.** *Heel strap is ½-inch bungee cord attached to underside of platform and runs through holes drilled in platform.* **6.** *Locking bolt is ¼ × 2-inch steel bolt.* **7.** *Wing nut removes to attach stand to tree.* **8.** *Braces are ⅛-inch aluminum or steel.* **9.** *Metal angles are ⅛-inch aluminum or steel to which platform is secured.* **10.** *Platform is ½- to ¾-inch plywood, marine grade.*

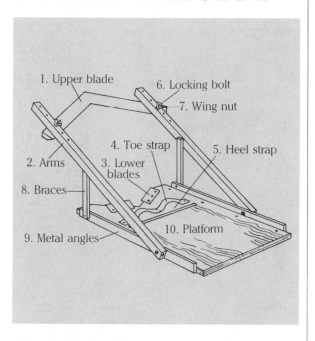

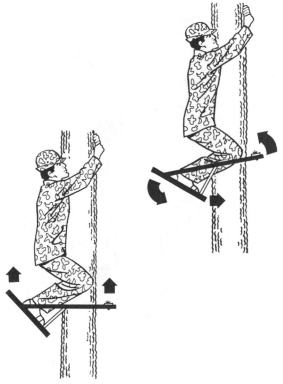

Basic stand-climbing technique is relatively simple. You grip a tree with your arms or a climbing tool, then bend your knees to lift the stand platform and secure it higher up the trunk. When repeated, such a move allows you to inch up any straight limbless trunk.

A hand-climbing tool allows you to use a climbing tree stand without needing to hug the trunk of a tree directly. This minimizes muscle strain and prevents abrasion of your face, arms, and chest.

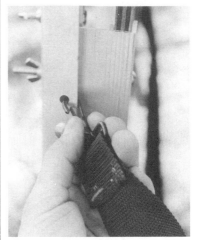  

Most commercial climbing stands allow quick attachment of backpack straps for easy transport. Once straps have been clipped in place and stand components have been bolted flat, the entire climbing unit can be carried, leaving both hands free to shoot.

arms, and face. Climbing stands with separate seat-climbers or hand-climbers are by far the best way to go.

When selecting any climbing tree stand, look for certain positive features. The frame should be made of sturdy aluminum or steel, and assembly bolts should be large enough to hold the unit to a tree safely and solidly. Also, tree-gripping blades should be designed so they will not slip, and the stand platform itself should be made of heavy-duty all-weather plywood. The platform should be roomy enough to make waiting on the stand comfortable and shooting in several directions easy—20″ × 20″ is a good average size, and many models have even larger platforms for extra comfort. Lastly, the stand setup should have backpack straps and some sort of integral tree-stand seat.

A stand with all these features will weigh 15 pounds or less, making it fairly easy to transport. It should serve well wherever straight, smooth-trunked trees grow in abundance.

TREE-SLING ASSEMBLIES

A tree sling is a compact, lightweight seat-harness assembly that makes it possible to sit comfortably 20 or 30 feet above the ground and "walk" your way around a tree trunk to shoot in various directions. This "hammock for the derrier" suspends the hunter in a sitting position from one or more sturdy ropes or cords. Slings don't allow you to stand up and move about, but they are popular.

Primary selling points of the tree sling are compact transport and ultraquiet installation in a tree. The average sling weighs only 4 to 6 pounds, making it easy to carry about the woods. If you decide to take an

A seat-climbing stand allows you to sit down as you work your way aloft. This provides the ultimate in leisurely tree-stand climbing, just about eliminating muscle strain.

Bolts on any climbing tree stand should be stout to prevent any possibility of breakage. To ease assembly, most quality stands have finger-tightening wing nuts instead of hex nuts requiring a wrench.

A stationary sling is the most compact and portable tree-stand setup. It is ideal in remote deer areas with plenty of easily climbed trees, allowing elevated stands where ordinary climbing platforms will not function effectively.

elevated stand, the sling unit goes up even more quietly than a rigid platform-type climbing stand. A tree sling also allows selection of almost any tree.

There are two basic kinds of tree slings—stationary slings and self-hoisting slings. Each has important pluses and minuses.

Stationary slings. A stationary sling is usually small enough to be carried in a pants pocket or frameless backpack. First the hunter climbs to a desired tree-stand height by utilizing available limbs or portable tree-stand steps. Once aloft, he simply ties the suspension lines on the sling to a sturdy limb and sits down in the sling to wait for deer.

From the standpoint of portability, nothing can match a stationary tree sling. Some models weigh barely 3 pounds yet safely hold a hunter high above the ground. The major drawback of this type of sling is that it must be used in a tree that is easy to climb hand over hand.

Self-hoisting slings. A self-hoisting tree sling consists of a bench-type seat connected to a safety harness that wraps about the legs and waist. This seat assembly is attached to a strong nylon rope and a ratchet-type climbing hoist. The hunter straps himself into the seat assembly, tosses the rope over a sturdy limb at a suitable stand height, and pulls himself upward with the mechanical hoist. Descent from a tree is equally easy because the action of the hoist can be reversed with the flip of a lever.

A self-hoisting tree sling is usually carried across the shoulder on some sort of strap assembly. This sling weighs more than a stationary sling, but seldom more than 6 or 7 pounds. Its primary advantage over a stationary sling is the self-climbing feature—its major

A typical climbing tree sling is carried over the shoulder in compact, out-of-the-way fashion. Most often, all sling components are stored inside the seat assembly itself.

HOW TO USE A CLIMBING SLING

To use a climbing tree sling properly, first toss the climbing rope across a stout overhead limb and thread the end back through a ratchet-type climbing hoist. Next, tie bow, gun, and other equipment to the free end of the rope. Then, by carefully pulling the rope through the ratchet block, you can slowly but surely ascend.

Once at the desired height, pull up the hunting gear attached to the free end of the rope. A climbing tree sling allows complete shooting flexibility with gun or bow because you can twist in any direction and actually "walk" around a tree. To descend smoothly, flip a reversal lever on the climbing ratchet box.

drawback is carrying weight and a fairly high price tag. But all in all, the self-hoisting tree sling is one of the most versatile tree-stand setups.

OTHER COMMERCIAL TREE STANDS

A wide variety of nonclimbing tree-stand platforms are sold at sporting goods stores. Most of these are mounted with chains, ropes, or wires. No matter what the design happens to be, the platform stand is usually pulled up on a rope—after a hunter first climbs up the tree to the desired spot. Some small, highly portable commercial platform stands are easily installed in trees by a lone hunter—others are too large or too tricky to fasten in place unless two or three people team up on them.

Nonclimbing tree stands can be extremely useful in areas where trees are easy to climb and deer display predictable behavior patterns. Because these stands are difficult to install, they are generally left in place for several weeks at a time. In areas where tree-stand theft occurs, a nonclimbing platform should be designed so that it can be securely padlocked to a tree.

PLATFORM LADDERS

Many excellent deer-hunting areas are devoid of trees large enough to accommodate a regular commercial tree stand. In places with clumps of willows or other varieties of small-diameter trees or bushes, a platform ladder might be the ideal elevated stand.

Basically, a platform ladder consists of a sturdy aluminum ladder with a roomy plywood platform at the top. This setup can be leaned against any tree or high-growing bush with a trunk over 3 inches in diameter, and secured in place with a wraparound chain. The ladder itself holds most of a hunter's weight when he is on top of the platform—the bush or tree merely steadies the stand and keeps it in a rigid upright position.

Most platform ladders are 10 or 12 feet high—enough elevation to place a hunter above a deer's eyes and nose and to give him a decent view of surrounding terrain. Platform ladders tend to be heavy and cumbersome to carry for long distances in the woods, but they allow elevated stand-hunting in areas devoid of full-size trees.

Nonclimbing commercial tree stands usually require two or more people for initial setup. However, once chained or roped in place, the stands often provide the ultimate in comfortable, roomy waiting for deer.

A tripod tower stand is ideal for ambushing deer in brushy terrain devoid of trees suitable for a stand. This stand allows decent views into undergrowth and provides shots at animals often hidden from ground-level hunters.

TRIPOD TOWER STANDS

Deer sometimes reside in very brushy areas where stand hunting is a must but where trees and high-growing shrubs are impossible to find. There the only feasible elevated stand is an artificial tower. The majority of commercial tower stands are tripod stands that sit high above the ground on three sturdy metal legs. Such stands are fairly expensive and relatively difficult to pack and set up properly. But they allow a hunter to peer down into brush fields that completely blot out ground-level views of deer.

The tallest commercial tripod towers put a hunter 12 to 15 feet above the ground—high enough to provide the movement and air-current camouflage of an ordinary tree stand or platform ladder. Tripod tower stands are popular in flat, brush-choked country typical of Texas and the American Southwest, and in creek-bottoms crammed with short, thin-stalked willows or other plants too flimsy to support a platform ladder.

HOMEMADE TREE PLATFORMS

A wide variety of permanent, homemade tree-stand platforms are used. Some of these platforms are truly "tree houses," roomy enough for several hunters and

Homemade platform stands are inexpensive and easy to make. The model shown here chains to the tree. It has a V-shaped cutout on one end and neatly jams against other tree trunks or outward-projecting limbs to provide superb platform stability.

enough equipment to stall a one-ton truck. Others are barely large enough for one hunter. A pile of lumber, a bag of nails, a hammer, and a little imagination will enable any hunter to build safe, serviceable tree stands.

The accompanying illustrations show just a few sensible homemade tree-stand designs. Exact tree-stand shape, size, and construction will depend on the shape, size, and orientation of trees and limbs.

Remember two important things when building any permanent tree stand. First, use sturdy lumber and construct the stand to ensure absolute safety aloft. Second, erect a permanent homemade stand only where it is legal to do so and—on private land—with the landowner's permission.

Not as versatile as portable tree stands, permanent homemade tree stands are relatively inexpensive to erect and work exceedingly well in areas where deer display consistent year-in, year-out movement patterns. Obviously, erecting a stand with saw and hammer is a very noisy procedure, and should be done during off-season months. That way the deer have time to calm down and resume natural movement patterns after the stand has been completed.

HOMEMADE TOWERS; PLATFORM LADDERS

A hunter who is handy with wood can make both tower stands and platform ladders to match specific hunting needs. Many hunters with access to private property scatter homemade towers or platform ladders throughout favorite deer locales, leaving them in place all season long and sometimes for several years.

The Texas homemade vehicle tower deserves special mention. It is mounted on a pickup or jeep so that a hunter can scan brush country along roads from an elevated position while the vehicle is driven. Vehicle towers are used in Texas both to scout heavy brush areas for concentrations of deer and to hunt deer from roads. It is legal to shoot from a vehicle in Texas—a law unique to the Lone Star State—and vehicle towers provide the only feasible way of spotting scattered mule deer and whitetails in some arid, brushy parts of this deer-hunting mecca.

TREE-STAND ACCESSORIES

In addition to the stand itself, a hunter needs an assortment of accessories designed to make his sport safe and enjoyable. Most deer hunters regard the following as standard equipment whenever they take an elevated stand.

TREE STANDS YOU CAN BUILD

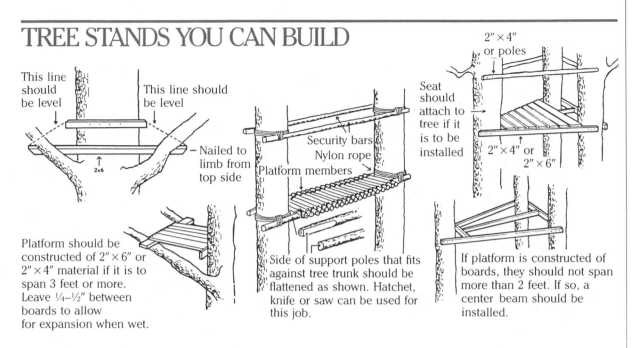

This line should be level

This line should be level

2×6

Nailed to limb from top side

Platform should be constructed of 2″×6″ or 2″×4″ material if it is to span 3 feet or more. Leave ¼–½″ between boards to allow for expansion when wet.

Security bars

Nylon rope

Platform members

Side of support poles that fits against tree trunk should be flattened as shown. Hatchet, knife or saw can be used for this job.

2″×4″ or poles

Seat should attach to tree if it is to be installed

2″×4″ or 2″×6″

If platform is constructed of boards, they should not span more than 2 feet. If so, a center beam should be installed.

Homemade tree-stand platforms can be built in a myriad of sizes and shapes. More often than not, the exact configuration depends upon the location and orientation of supporting trees and limbs. (Drawings reprinted with permission from The Original Tree Stand Handbook *by Richard C. McGee Jr.)*

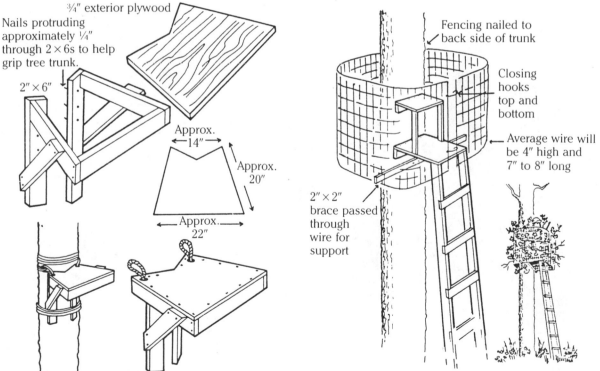

¾″ exterior plywood

Nails protruding approximately ¼″ through 2×6s to help grip tree trunk.

2″×6″

Approx. 14″

Approx. 20″

Approx. 22″

Fencing nailed to back side of trunk

Closing hooks top and bottom

Average wire will be 4″ high and 7″ to 8″ long

2″×2″ brace passed through wire for support

A semiportable, homemade stand held in place by ropes is easy to construct from 2×6 lumber and a small piece of ¾-inch plywood. This stand can be installed without making a lot of noise and is ideal for setting up on the spur of the moment in deer-rich areas.

A homemade platform ladder surrounded by a roomy fence-wire cage completely hides a hunter from the prying eyes of deer. The stand can be nailed permanently to a tree or chained in place to facilitate easy removal.

A Texas vehicle tower allows hunters to scan brush-country deer as they drive along a road. The homemade setup shown here has steering column, gearshift, clutch, and brakes in the tower itself.

Tree-stand steps. Tree-stand steps make it easy to climb and descend in safe, easy fashion in many situations. There are several dozen commercial designs available at stores, and most are sturdy, dependable creations. The most common screw into a tree and provide a foothold just wide enough for safe, secure climbing. A few cinch to a tree with chain or rope—a must in areas where laws prohibit steps that penetrate living trees. In addition, several home-grown varieties are used by hunters, including wooden steps nailed to trees and sturdy eyebolts screwed solidly in place.

Regardless of design, tree-stand steps perform several important functions in the field. In some cases they provide the only way to climb a limbless tree trunk to reach a suitable stand elevation. In other situations tree-stand steps merely simplify your life, allowing you to ascend and descend without having to inch your entire climbing tree stand up and down each and every hunting day. In areas where tree-stand theft can be a problem, you can remove steps as you climb down, rendering your stand inaccessible to others.

The handiest tree-stand steps are compact, fairly light in weight, and sturdy enough to easily hold your weight. They attach solidly to a tree in short order, ideally with one-hand installation so that you can safely climb as you affix them. In most deer-hunting situations, screw-in steps satisfy these requirements.

Sturdy tree-stand steps allow safe, easy ascent and descent on any limbless trunk. The handiest of these screw in place, letting you climb a tree as you install steps one by one.

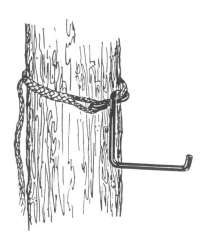

Rope-on tree-stand steps are excellent alternatives to screw-in steps in areas where laws forbid steps that penetrate living trees. Rope-attached models are more difficult to install than screw-in steps but provide secure footing.

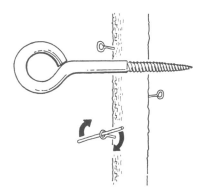

Large, heavy-duty eye-bolts make excellent tree-stand steps. The eyes perform two important functions—they help with mounting (passing a steel bar or stout stick through the eye gives extra leverage), and they also prevent your feet from slipping off the steps as you climb.

Rope ladders. For sheer climbing convenience and safety, nothing can beat a rope ladder. It provides easy access to any tree stand already in place, and can be pulled up after a hunter reaches his stand. This prevents it from swinging in the breeze and spooking deer that stroll by.

Rope ladders are especially favored by hunters using climbing tree stands or stands in trees with lots of low-growing limbs. Using ladders is much easier than inching a climbing stand up and down each day or climbing up from limb to limb. Several excellent commercial tree-stand rope ladders are manufactured.

Safety belts. Every stand hunter should have a top-quality safety belt and securely strap himself to the tree the instant he gets up to hunting height. Most stand-related accidents occur when hunters fall out of the stand, usually from many feet above the ground. A safety belt completely eliminates the chance of a dangerous fall as a hunter moves about his platform, shoots at deer, and prepares to descend from the stand.

A proper tree-stand safety belt is made of strong nylon webbing. It usually has a strap that secures about the trunk of a tree, and another strap that buckles about a hunter's waist. These two straps are connected by a short nylon coupler to allow some freedom of movement about a stand platform. If the

A rope ladder is compact to carry and easy to climb. Several outdoor companies sell ladders made of strong nylon rope with reliable hardwood rungs.

Once you reach a suitable hunting height, fasten your safety belt high about the tree. There should be enough slack for comfortable sitting and for easy shooting from a standing position.

A safety belt is a must for worry-free hunting high above the ground. The belt allows shooting at deer from positions that would be hazardous without harness support.

hunter does slip and fall, a belt of this sort will not cinch up like a hangman's noose, causing injury. The best tree-stand safety belts have quick-release buckles similar to those on automobile seat belts and are strong enough to hold several thousand pounds without breaking.

A safety belt offers one major advantage aside from safe, worry-free hunting high above the ground. A hunter who is solidly strapped to a tree can lean into his belt and bend at the waist to take shots at deer directly below his platform. He can also pivot in various shooting directions that might be dangerous without this solid support.

Backpack straps. As mentioned before, many commercial tree-stand packages include backpack straps for easy transport in the woods. Straps are also sold separately by several tree-stand makers; this allows the do-it-yourselfer to pack homemade stand platforms the same way. The alternative is hand-carrying a stand to a hunting location—a royal pain.

Stools and cushions. Most decent commercial stands incorporate comfortable stools or seats. However, for homemade stands and commercial models without integral seats, you can buy some sort of folding stool. Standing up for hours can tire muscles to the point that you feel unsteady on your feet. At the

very best, standing up all the time is plain hard work, and it can be unsafe. A person who sits comfortably on stand will be fresh, alert, and steady of hand when that trophy deer finally appears out of the brush.

For vigils in excessively cold weather, an insulating seat cushion is advisable. One company even offers a heat-up cushion to prevent fanny frostbite in bitterly cold conditions.

Urinals. A hunter who answers nature's call over the edge of his tree stand will saturate the entire area with game-spooking human odor every bit as effectively as a dog marks his home territory. As a result, smart stand hunters carry a urinal aloft whenever they plan to spend several hours on a stand. Any waterproof con-

An ordinary bleach bottle makes an excellent tree-stand urinal when painted a dull, medium color to blend with the treetops. The handle allows easy hoisting aloft on a rope, and the screw-on cap prevents the spread of odor and accidental spills.

tainer will serve the purpose well enough, as long as it blends reasonably well with surrounding foliage. A white bleach bottle painted green or brown is an excellent choice, and so is a small plastic bucket. The best urinals have watertight caps or lids to contain odor and prevent accidental spills.

Final notes on tree-stand accessories. Most veteran tree-standers prefer to have an equipment pouch or ditty bag close at hand to hold a lunch, flashlight, spare ammunition, camera, and specialized gear such as a small thumb-ring limb saw. Some tree-stand seats have gear pouches underneath, and several companies sell separate ditty bags that can be hung on handy limbs or regular gun/bow racks. In addition, an ordinary canvas stuff sack makes an excellent place to store and carry tree-stand hunting accessories.

A compact, thumb-ring saw is one of several gadgets used by stand hunters. The saw quickly removes small limbs that impede tree climbing or clear shooting at hunting height.

A tree-stand seat with a zippered gear pouch underneath is handy for storing such miscellaneous items as a lunch, camera, and limb saw. Or a ditty bag can be hung on a handy tree limb or screw-in hook.

COMMERCIAL BLINDS

As a rule, hunting deer from a ground blind should be resorted to only when climbing to some sort of elevated stand is impossible. Although a ground blind does help cover your movements as you wait for deer, animals often see you anyway and are able to smell you anytime breezes blow the wrong direction.

The best commercial ground blinds consist of nylon, leaf-print netting held up by lightweight aluminum stakes. Blind wall height is usually about 4 feet, and

Ambushing deer in very open areas will probably require a ground blind. A hunter needs this artificial barrier to mask his human form and hide shooting movements.

wall lengths are 8 and 16 feet. The best blinds have four or five stakes and the netting walls can be rolled tightly around them to form a compact package for over-the-shoulder carrying. Although a few commercial deer blinds are sold with walls of cardboard or other relatively stiff materials, these are difficult to transport in and out of the woods.

HOMEMADE BLINDS

Many hunters build their own blinds from common materials. One popular type consists of a ring made of chicken wire interwoven with natural branches and grasses. Another has wooden wall stakes draped with GI camouflage netting. In brown, late-fall settings, a simple ring of haybales or strawbales stacked three high makes a dandy, inexpensive blind. A hunter who has need of a blind in very open areas can use his imagination to create a homegrown solution to deer-hunting problems. Any enclosure that hides the ambusher, blends well with the landscape, and allows quick, easy shooting usually works just fine.

CLOTHING FOR DEER HUNTING

Most avid deer hunters own clothing to match outdoor situations they are likely to encounter. Choosing correct apparel is the single most important task for any would-be deer hunter. Wearing the correct outdoor garb can make a particular hunting situation highly enjoyable, while the wrong duds can absolutely ruin it with hours of physical discomfort.

A sensible deer hunter always selects his clothing with care. He tries to consider every aspect of every situation he's likely to encounter, and matches these

Hunters wear a variety of clothes with good success. A gathering of any motley deer-camp crew will show that every hunter has his own ideas about what's most comfortable and practical for existing weather conditions.

considerations with clothes that are likely to yield the utmost in comfort and deer-dropping efficiency. Here are some points to consider when selecting apparel.

LAWS ON CLOTHING

In the majority of states and provinces, deer hunters are legally required to wear red or blaze-orange clothing to ensure their safety in areas swarming with other hunters. Most laws require that hunters wear a specified number of square inches of red or blaze orange in plain sight. For example, several states set 400 square inches of blaze orange as the minimum

amount. Every hunter must make it his business to find out about clothing laws. Compliance is for his own safety as well as to meet legal requirements.

A wide variety of clothes are made in red and blaze orange to ensure hunter visibility. The most common fabrics seen in blaze orange are plastic, nylon, cotton, and knit synthetics like Orlon, but a few 100-percent virgin wool garments have also been introduced. Wool is the most difficult to dye in this highly visible color, so blaze-orange garments made of wool are relatively expensive.

The majority of deer hunters wearing blaze orange or red opt to don garments of solid color—bill caps, stocking caps, vests, shirts, jackets. It is not certain how well deer see colors or interpret colors, if they see them. However, large patches of blaze orange are bona fide game-spookers in close-range shooting situations. As a result, several garment companies offer leaf-print clothing with blaze-orange shapes intermixed with darker, more subdued colors such as red, brown, or green. Such mottled clothes probably look natural to deer, but they stand out like the proverbial sore thumb to any hunter.

Even in areas where red or blaze-orange duds are not legally required for hunting deer, it's always a good idea to wear such gear whenever lots of other hunters are lurking around. Blaze orange in particular glows

In many areas, clothes incorporating blaze-orange coloring are required for legal big-game hunting. Hunters who value camouflage but wish to comply with safety laws often wear brilliant but mottled duds that deer don't distinguish from natural settings.

like a beacon in any sort of deer habitat, protecting hunters from the misdirected bullets of overly excited, irresponsible gunners.

CLOTHING COMFORT

A deer hunter must consider three factors when choosing clothes to ensure personal comfort in the field. First, a garment must provide adequate protection from the elements—rain and snow, wind, and average outdoor temperatures. Second, clothing must accommodate a hunter's own temperature and moisture output as he tries for deer. Physical exercise can create body heat and perspiration that must be dissipated at the proper rate for maximum comfort. Third, clothing must fit properly to allow comfortable, easy movement in the field.

RETAINING BODY HEAT

The primary function of any garment is protection from the elements. In order to choose clothing that does this properly, you must know something about the weather you'll be hunting in—either from personal experience or by asking others who know. But more often than not, staying warm enough, without becoming too warm, is the key because deer habitat is often at least moderately chilly during fall hunting seasons.

Any garment, from hats and jackets to trousers and socks, keeps a hunter warm by retaining his own body heat in air pockets between the skin and outer surface of that garment. The more efficiently a piece of clothing traps body heat, the warmer that article is likely to be. Several standard types of materials are used in top-grade cold-weather clothing because they have proven quite effective over the years. These include goose down, polyester fiberfill, polyester Hollofil, polyester Quallofil, Thinsulate, wool, and cotton. All in some way trap radiated body heat to keep a hunter warm.

Goose down. This is one of man's oldest and most effective clothing insulators. It is characterized by extremely light weight and more than average bulk when dry and properly fluffed to do a decent insulating job. Down is generally contained in spaces between an inner and outer fabric shell of nylon, cotton, or cotton/synthetic blend. This provides an excellent barrier against the cold. Goose down has two primary drawbacks—it is worthless if it becomes thoroughly soaked by water, and the very fluffiness (called loft) that makes it an excellent insulator results in relatively bulky clothing. Despite its bulk and vulnerability to becoming wet, goose down still provides the best

clothing insulation known to man. Pound for pound, it retains heat better than any synthetic clothing material.

Synthetics. Various modern polyester clothing insulators such as Hollofil and Quallofil trap body heat in a maze of tiny synthetic filaments. Ordinary polyester filaments (called fiberfill) retain heat quite well, but more advanced hollow filaments like Hollofil (with one internal chamber per filament) and Quallofil (with four separate internal chambers) retain even more body heat. Like goose down, polyester clothing insulation is normally sandwiched between an inner and outer layer of nylon or other durable fabric. All polyester insulating material remains fairly warm even when wet, is extremely resilient to pressure (will not permanently compress or lose its loft), is less bulky than conventional goose-down insulation, and is quite supple for comfortable body movement. From the standpoint of clothing thickness and bulk, polyester fibers of one sort or another insulate better inch for inch than any other natural or manmade material.

Thinsulate is a relatively new clothing material made of thinly layered polyester microfibers to provide a dense, warm insulating layer. Although not as warm as down or polyester fill, inch for inch, this space-age material is extremely thin and keeps the body warm even when wet. Garments incorporating Thinsulate are lightweight, and they hug closely to a hunter's body—a feel many prefer.

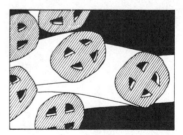

Polyester fibers of various sorts provide good insulation for clothing. Although a mass of ordinary solid fibers traps heat fairly well, more advanced hollow fibers (with one or four separate chambers) retain body warmth even more efficiently.

Wool. In various weaves wool is a longtime standby of serious cold-weather hunters. This natural material traps body heat reasonably well and keeps the body quite warm when wet. One of wool's major selling points is that among natural fibers it is unmatched for durability. It wears like iron in any situation. By contrast, insulation-filled garments with shells of nylon or other common fabrics occasionally tear, and eventually become threadbare. When hit by sparks from a campfire or stove, the shell fabric often melts, leaving small holes in the material. Meanwhile, wool breezes along largely unchanged by heavy use and abuse. The two primary drawbacks of wool are its fairly heavy weight and its tendency to itch on contact with sensitive skin.

Cotton. If woven in a porous manner that creates air pockets between the threads, cotton clothing can be quite warm. Cotton garments are relatively inexpensive, last a long time, and provide fairly good protection from the elements. Once soaked with water, though, cotton offers next to no protection from cold weather.

RAIN AND SNOW

Precipitation can make a hunter miserable unless he's properly dressed. As mentioned before, certain garment materials like goose-down fill and cotton provide little protection from moisture and lose their insulating ability once they do become wet. Other materials like the polyesters and wool do soak up water but continue to keep a hunter warm. Ideally, however, anyone who expects to encounter severe wet weather should wear some sort of garment that completely sheds moisture to keep inner clothing dry. A few parkas and jackets combine moisture protection with inside insulation, and these have their fans. Other hunters prefer to throw a thin waterproof garment over other clothes when needed.

Several clothing materials are used for rainwear. The most common is ordinary rubber, which is usually bonded to canvaslike fabric to give a garment strength. Several companies offer rubberized coats, parkas, and pants of this basic design—duds guaranteed to shed water like the roof on a house.

Another favorite moisture-proof substance is a space-age material called Gore-Tex. This is a micro-thin coating used on many sorts of clothing—most often laminated with nylon—that effectively blocks rainwater and other external moisture. Gore-Tex offers a major advantage over conventional rubberized garments because it is microporous—that is, it allows

In hot early-season hunting situations, a thin, short-sleeved shirt and cool cotton pants help dissipate body heat and perspiration.

For the ultimate in protection from cold, damp, and windy weather, hunters often wear a head-to-toe combination of polyester Thinsulate coated with Gore-Tex film. Such outerwear provides total warmth and dryness without insulating bulk.

body perspiration to pass outward but blocks external moisture from passing inward. More about this important feature later.

WIND

As a rule, garments suited for shedding rainwater and snow are best for windy conditions. Wind robs the body of stored-up heat by penetrating other types of clothing. But wind also reduces the effective temperature of surfaces it buffets; so a hunter in cold, windy conditions must wear insulating garments beneath a windbreaker of rubberized fabric or Gore-Tex.

The windchill factor caused by steady breezes will drop the effective temperature on the surface of a hunter's clothing approximately one degree Fahrenheit for each mile per hour of wind velocity. For example, a wind of 30 mph will turn a 30-degree thermometer reading into a zero-degree comfort situation—something a hunter should never forget. Harsh winds blowing against windproof garments can still make a hunter miserable unless he bundles up underneath to completely offset the windchill factor.

In a nutshell, wind can destroy hunter comfort in two primary ways—by penetrating clothing and robbing stored body heat, and by lowering effective temperature through the windchill factor. To combat these wind-related problems, woodsmen must bundle up more than normal in heavy winds and wear windbreakers that completely block the flow of air.

BODY HEAT AND PERSPIRATION

Many hunters purchase clothing solely with protection from the elements in mind. This can be a mistake, because excessive body heat and perspiration can cause every bit as much discomfort as outside influences. Clothing should ideally carry perspiration away from the skin to prevent you from swimming in your own body juices and should not be too warm in situations when you are exerting yourself or when outside temperatures rise to balmy levels.

In downright hot weather, a hunter should wear thin, airy garments that allow body heat and perspiration to readily escape. Thin cotton clothing is tough to beat when temperatures soar into the 70s and above.

In mid-fall stand-hunting situations, where the hunter is moving very little if at all, perspiration and excessive body heat are seldom a problem. However, an on-the-go walking hunter can work up a healthy sweat and turn normally excellent cold-weather duds into a portable sauna unless he chooses gear with care.

Precipitation and wind can make a hunter absolutely miserable unless he's dressed to fully combat conditions. With a rubberized parka, a hunter can smile even when weather takes a nasty turn.

There is no perfect cold-weather set of clothing, but some garments work decidedly better than others at keeping a hunter sufficiently warm without making skin clammy and overly hot. The best garments breathe away moisture and excess heat instead of trapping it and making the user miserable. Goose down and polyester both do a fairly good job of passing excess heat and moisture, provided the shells around these insulating fills are somewhat permeable.

Rubberized clothing tends to trap moisture most when a hunter overheats and sweats profusely. More modern Gore-Tex waterproofing is much, much better because it passes moisture in an outward direction when air inside a garment expands from excess body heat and humidity. The expansion creates slightly greater air pressure inside the garment than out, actually *forcing* moisture-laden air to exit through microscopic holes. The fact that Gore-Tex breathes away body vapors while completely keeping out rain and wind makes it one of the most popular parka and coat materials.

Aside from using clothes made of top-grade fabrics that insulate yet breathe, you can control your body

Experienced hunters usually dress in layers to accommodate changing daytime temperatures and levels of body heat. For moderate mid-fall weather, a cotton tee shirt, long-sleeved flannel shirt, and lightweight goose-down vest provide excellent layering versatility.

warmth and perspiration level in two other important ways. First, you should simply unzip clothing from the top if you become overly warm to allow heat and moisture to rise away from your body. Second, you should always dress in layers to allow adding or shedding of clothes to match changing internal and external temperature levels. Although bulky garments may be perfectly warm in ultracold conditions when you are stationary, they are far less versatile than several thinner garments layered over one another. One heavy coat can only be unzipped or removed to change a hunter's body temperature; by contrast, when several garments are used together, they can be shed or added to maintain maximum body comfort.

Typically, good upper-body wear for deer-hunting in fairly chilly October weather might consist of a cotton tee shirt, a thin wool shirt over the top, a goose-down vest over that, a polyester-fill coat over the vest, and a Gore-Tex windbreaker over the coat. A hunter who leaves camp in this attire at the crack of dawn for some careful sneaking about the woods will be toasty warm until the sun comes up and begins to warm surrounding air. As he feels himself warming up and beginning to perspire, he can shed the windbreaker, coat, and vest to maintain maximum comfort.

Many deer hunters carry frameless packs on all-day hikes to hold layers of clothing they wish to shed or add to accommodate changing weather and changing body temperature.

ENSURING PROPER FIT

One key to clothing comfort is proper fit. On the surface of things, fit might seem too obvious even to mention. However, many beginners purchase pants, shirts, jackets, and other gear with weather protection in mind and completely forget the importance of wearing comfort. Pants that bind in the crotch or jackets with too-short sleeves can chafe and otherwise torture you. Some hunters dislike the feel of bulky goose-down upper-body wear, and others *prefer* soft, lightweight down over stiffer, thinner insulating fabrics like Thinsulate or wool.

Every hunter should try on clothing for fit and make sure the garments he buys are completely comfortable and practical for moving about and shooting at deer.

CLOTHING FOR CLOSE-RANGE HUNTING

A hunter who expects to find himself within 50 or 75 yards of deer must consider other factors aside from comfort. A gunner sneaking through heavy brush will generally encounter deer at extremely close range, and so will any person hunting deer from a tree stand in close-knit clusters of timber. Similarly, a bowhunter must ideally close the shooting gap to 50 yards or less. In these and other point-blank deer-hunting situations, clothing must be well camouflaged and extremely quiet as a hunter moves about.

Clothing camouflage. A deer has sharp eyes capable of instantly spotting a human shape or off-colored object inside 100 yards. Deer hunters who characteristically shoot at long-range or running deer have no great need for camouflage clothing, but setting up a close shot at an unalerted deer requires carefully chosen garments that hide a hunter's human outline and blend well with surrounding terrain.

Any mottled, contrasting pattern of clothing colors will effectively break up a hunter's human shape and fool the wary eyes of deer. Standard World War II leaf-print patterns with smallish blotches of green and brown work quite well in many hunting areas, and so does Vietnam camouflage with its larger patches of color. Equally effective is plaid clothing because it also breaks up the telltale human shape.

Every bit as important in camouflage as a broken pattern is the overall coloration of garments. This coloration must match the terrain in order to fool deer. A standard leaf-print outfit blends well with any deep-woods deer habitat, but stands out dramatically against light-colored desert terrain and snow-covered backdrops. In light-gray sagebrush country, a deer hunter who wishes to blend with the topography must wear camouflage that is lighter in color than normal—gear like that used by late-fall duck hunters in dead-brown environs. Similarly, special light-colored snow camo is best in wintry settings because it all but disappears against snow-covered hillsides.

Because deer are relatively color-blind, hunters should think black-and-white when selecting any camouflage clothing. If in doubt about the effectiveness of a particular camo garment, you can test-photograph it in black and white in a typical deer-hunting setting. As mentioned before, the inability of deer to distinguish color well makes red and blaze-orange camouflage extremely effective on deer at very close range. Colorful plaids like a black-and-red wool coat perform equally well where hunters wish to be recognized by other hunters but ignored by sharp-eyed deer.

In many hunting situations, upper-body camouflage is far more important than camouflage below the belt. Low-growing shrubbery generally obscures a walking hunter's trousers anyway. A camouflage shirt or jacket alone provides a major advantage in close-range encounters with deer.

Choosing quiet clothing. A hunter-wise deer can sometimes hear and recognize the scrape of hard-weave fabric against bushes and trees at ranges over 100 yards. The truly sneaky deer hunter takes pains to wear soft-surfaced clothing that never whines or shrieks audibly as he moves about or waits on stand.

The majority of hard-weave fabrics are too noisy for close-range hunting of deer. Prime offenders are rip-stop nylon, 60/40 cotton/synthetic blend, tightly woven cotton, and Gore-Tex shells. By contrast, wool and soft cotton are extremely quiet to move about in—even in heavy brush. To test any fabric for quietness, simply drag your fingernails across the surface and listen for sound. If this test produces a rough, scratchy noise, the garment is ill-suited for close-range hunting.

Any noisy garment can be used in close-range deer hunting as long as a quiet-surfaced garment is worn over the top to prevent deer-spooking sound. For example, a nylon-surfaced, goose-down vest can be worn beneath a soft wool jacket with excellent results. In this way, a person can remain comfortable in chilly weather without spooking every deer within earshot.

WHAT CLOTHING WORKS BEST

There are countless different hats, shirts, jackets, pants, gloves, boots, and other kinds of clothing sold at well-stocked sporting goods stores. Styles seem to change by the year, and materials constantly improve as manufacturers research and develop. However, certain basic types of clothing are longtime favorites

It's hard to beat standard World War II leaf-print camouflage in many hunting areas. Outline-breaking garb is essential for pistol hunters and bowhunters who must set up close-range shots at deer.

Vietnam camouflage with its fairly large patches of color blends well with any medium to dark forest background. This deep-woods clothing usually works best where evergreen trees are prevalent.

Special hunting situations require special kinds of camouflage. For example, snowy backdrops are best matched with mottled duds incorporating large blotches of white. These pants neatly fill the bill.

A deer's wide, flaring ears can detect the slightest un-natural sound. As a result, close-range hunters must wear quiet-surfaced clothing that does not make noise when it scrapes against overhanging limbs and underbrush.

The Jones-style hat is a traditional hunting favorite. Hats of this kind are available in a variety of colors from fluorescent orange to leaf-print green, and most models are treated to shed moisture effectively.

of well-informed deer hunters. Here are guidelines to follow when choosing hunting apparel.

Headgear. A comprehensive collection of hats and caps used by deer hunters over the years would fill a very large warehouse. But certain basic styles reign supreme.

One is the ordinary bill cap—a simple design available in airy summer models, insulated winter styles, and many other designs. Another is the Jones-style hat, with a short frontal brim which rolls up at the sides and back. A third is the western felt hat, available in a variety of brim sizes and shapes. All three designs protect the face from sun and dripping rain, shield the top of the head from wind and cold, and keep your hair more or less in tow. A few have pull-down ear muffs to combat extra-cold wind and weather. The choice is largely a matter of personal preference.

For bitterly cold hunting, nothing beats a wool or synthetic stocking cap. The best of the lot have internal face masks which can be pulled down to shield the face entirely against the elements. In milder weather, a stocking cap can be rolled up above the ears or dropped over them depending upon exact wind and temperature conditions.

In addition to fairly standard hat styles for hunters, sporting goods stores also sell special-purpose head-

A well-designed stocking cap has a mask that can be pulled down to protect the entire face in bitterly cold conditions. In milder weather, this versatile chapeau can be worn atop the head like any other hat.

Heavily insulated head protectors are nice to have when weather turns especially cold. The warmest are stuffed with goose down or polyester fibers to hold in virtually all body heat.

To ensure successful close-range stalks on deer, hunters need to fully cover their light, shiny complexions. A leaf-print camouflage headnet offers one excellent way to accomplish this.

gear for unusual outdoor situations. Specialized hats include rubberized rain hats and pull-over head protectors stuffed with polyester or goose-down insulation. Bowhunters and others needing to sneak really close to deer can also purchase camouflage headnets to hide their shiny, light-colored faces.

Underwear. For the majority of deer-hunting situations, ordinary cotton or cotton/synthetic underwear will work just fine. The general tendency of beginning hunters is to slap on thermal undergarments the instant temperatures drop near freezing— a move that is usually a monumental mistake. Using long johns should be considered a last resort for any hunter who plans to hike around the hills. Long johns become insufferably hot as the body heats up and perspiration begins to flow. Stand hunters in bitter weather do need some kind of thermal underwear to combat the cold. But regular cotton underwear with standard cold-weather outer-garments will usually keep them warm until the thermometer drops below 20° or 25° F.

Hunters who do need thermal underwear have a variety of styles to choose from. Conventional medium-weave cotton "long handles" are relatively warm, provided they fit a hunter's body snugly but not tightly. Better, more modern weave patterns incorporate two or more separate layers of fabric with plenty of warmth-

trapping air space in between. One unique underwear construction is fishnet fabric, which appears to be precisely what its name suggests. The gaping holes in this netting-type thermal underwear would seem to defeat its intended purpose, but in reality the netting creates air pockets between the skin and outer garments. These pockets fill with warm air, and also allow migration of perspiration away from the skin.

Most name-brand thermal underwear works exceedingly well. A hunter who expects subzero weather should certainly invest in one or more pairs of long johns—especially the hunter who plans to sit motionless on stand for several hours at a time.

Shirts, jackets, and vests. The majority of deer hunters wear shirts made of cotton, wool, or cotton/synthetic blend. All these shirts can be purchased in a wide variety of colorations, from blaze orange to subdued plaids to leaf-print camouflage.

Shirt selection should be tempered by the sort of weather expected. A hunter trying for deer during hot August hunting seasons like those in California and Alaska might opt for a thin, short-sleeved cotton tee shirt or thin, long-sleeved work shirt made of cotton or synthetic. Medium-weight flannel shirts are popular for mid-fall hunting when daytime temperatures hover in the 40 to 60-degree range. For colder weather, wool

More than one kind of upper-body garment will often meet the same outdoor needs. This pair of buck hunters took trophies the same day, but one hunter wore a medium-weight wool sweater while the other preferred a heavy flannel shirt, which provides adequate warmth in average mid-fall weather and makes no noise.

For upper-body raingear, two common choices are a ¾-length parka with protective hood (left) and a lighter-weight waist-length jacket with water-shedding collar.

shirts made of medium to heavy fabric are excellent, providing good warmth with little bulk, remaining warm even when wet, and lasting for many years.

In moderately cold weather, an ordinary button-up shirt provides ample warmth and protection from the elements. In the chilliest conditions, a turtleneck sweater of wool, heavy cotton, or acrylic holds in body heat much better. Heat under the clothing naturally rises and escapes around the neck, and any garment that bottles up this heat is especially warm to wear.

There are so many kinds of jackets sold at sporting goods stores that a detailed description of every one would fill a book all by itself. Most of the better ones are made of wool/synthetic blend or a sandwich of down or polyester fiber between layers of durable nylon or cotton/synthetic blend. How warm such garments are depends largely on the heaviness of the fabric used and the thickness of internal insulation. No single jacket performs well in all situations; so most hunters own two or three to satisfy a variety of requirements. Thin jackets of wool or Thinsulate are ideal for only moderately cold conditions—bulkier jackets of heavy wool or thick insulating material work best in subzero hunting situations.

Thin parkas and rain slickers made of rubberized fabric or Gore-Tex can be real lifesavers in areas where rain and snow are the rule. Such garments vary in configuration, from ordinary waist-length parkas with rain-protective hoods to ankle-length slickers providing full protection. Some of the best deer-hunting rain gear is specialized duck-hunting garb in brown fall colors. Duck hunters endure more inclement weather

than any other outdoors group, and top-grade clothing designed with waterfowl shooting in mind is invariably comfortable and practical to wear.

Vests of one sort or another are extremely popular with deer hunters. A vest insulates the torso but allows freedom of movement for the arms. Most deer-hunting vests consist of ripstop nylon shells heavily stuffed with goose down or polyester fiber. A few are made of wool with heavy, extremely warm fleece lining. A vest that buttons, snaps, or zips in place keeps a hunter toasty warm while allowing him to shoulder and shoot any hunting gun easily.

One sort of vest commonly used by deer hunters is a thin plastic or nylon over-vest in highly visible blaze orange. The vest is worn outside other clothing to ensure safety and comply with blaze-orange hunting laws.

When selecting shirts, jackets, and vests for hunting deer, a person should concentrate on buying several thin to moderately heavy garments that can be layered over one another for warmth and dryness. Except in ultracold conditions, extremely bulky, heavily insulated garments are more often a handicap than a blessing.

Trousers. In shirts, jackets, and vests, a few basic sizes fit most people well. As a result, manufacturers seem to concentrate on lining store shelves with upper-body wear. By contrast, every kind of trouser must be stocked in a dozen or more sizes to accommodate the various leg lengths and waist measurements of customers. For this reason, deer hunters have fewer special-purpose pants to choose from than garments worn above the waist.

Many deer hunters wear ordinary blue jeans or other cotton pants exclusively. Such department-store trousers fit most people well and stand up to plenty of

An insulated vest keeps the torso warm while allowing free movement of the arms.

All-wool clothing, including trousers, is favored by many cold-weather hunters. Wool is warm even when wet— a plus when stalking a deer for a long distance in damp, snowy conditions.

abuse through low-growing brush and the climbing of trees. Only when weather turns decidedly foul must a hunter turn to special cold-weather pants.

Heavy wool trousers are standard garb in cold hunting areas like the East, Midwest, Rocky Mountain West, and far North. Such pants are loose-fitting to allow the use of thermal long johns underneath; they also shed snow and rain well, and retain body heat as well as any other material. Although quilted pants with goose-down or polyester insulation are available at stores, these are very bulky and not nearly as durable as wool or cotton trousers. Quilted pants are excellent for a stationary hunter on stand but have little other use in the field.

Brush pants are another kind of deer-hunting trouser. These have tough nylon shields sewn to the fronts of the legs to protect against briars, stinging nettles, and heavy brush. A variation of such pants are nylon chaps that pull over regular trousers. The drawback of nylon is that it is noisy compared to other fabrics.

An innovative deer hunter can camouflage cotton pants to match specific kinds of terrain. Bowhunters in particular often have trouble finding durable, well-fitting pants that blend with the woods. Light-colored cotton trousers are easily tie-dyed in mottled patterns, and blue jeans can be tie-bleached to produce tough, two-tone camouflage pants.

Tough, tight-weave nylon chaps provide superb leg protection whenever a hunter "beats the brush" for animals in thickets. Special-purpose brush pants with sewn-in front shields also are popular for heavy cover.

TIE-BLEACHING BLUE JEANS

Tie knots in each leg moderately tight but not so tight that they will be hard to undo later. Then as shown, bunch the area above the crotch of the pants. Secure it with a rubber band or a cord.

Mix 2 cups of laundry bleach with 2 gallons of water to create a fast-acting bleaching solution. A plastic or metal bucket makes an ideal container for soaking trousers.

Press the pants to the bottom of the bleaching container. As soon as all visible fabric fades to light tan— usually within 2 hours—take the pants out, untie them, and machine wash in cold water.

Coveralls. Although a few hunters prefer to wear ordinary or camouflage coveralls afield, these are perhaps the least versatile of all deer-hunting garments. Even if coveralls fit well—a not-so-common occurrence—they cannot be quickly donned or shed to accommodate changing weather conditions. A hunter should only consider coveralls if weather conditions promise to be especially stable. Several companies sell insulated coveralls for cold-weather hunting.

Mittens, gloves, and hand warmers. In icy weather, a hunter's hands tend to become uncomfortably cold sooner than any other part of his body. As a result, most deer enthusiasts wear some sort of hand protection in very cold or windy conditions.

A good-quality mitten is the warmest hand protection available because it pools heat from all the fingers and also allows free finger movement to generate additional warmth. Unfortunately, a mitten does not allow as much manual dexterity as a glove—dexterity needed to shoot, climb tree-stand trees, and skin deer. Still, many hunters prefer to wear cold-weather mittens and pull them off when they need to use their fingers.

The best mittens for deer hunting are made of wool or a sandwich of insulating materials. All-wool mittens, such as the liners used inside military goose-down mittens, will keep a hunter's hands reasonably warm without excessive bulk. In the coldest conditions, regular ski mittens insulated with down, acrylic fiber, or Thinsulate provide better comfort. Because a person's hands tend to sweat inside insulated mittens, the best designs have shells that allow free passage of body vapor. Mittens covered with nylon and Gore-

The result of tie-bleaching is a pair of two-tone jeans that blend well with many woods settings, though not this one. As long as bleach is quickly washed away, fabric remains strong and durable.

Insulated mittens provide the ultimate in cold-weather comfort for the hands. Mittens pool warmth from all the fingers and allow complete freedom of hand movement to further generate heat.

A belt-attached hand warmer can be an extremely worthwhile cold-weather accessory. A hunter can jam one hand at a time into this giant mitten when walking along or sitting on stand, keeping fingers warm until he needs both hands to shoot.

Although not as warm as mittens, gloves allow greater manual dexterity, which is needed to fire a weapon. Gloves are made with several kinds of insulation, including fleece, goose down, acrylic fibers, and Thinsulate microfibers.

Tex work best of all, with leather-shell mittens being a close second.

A few special hunting mittens incorporate finger slits to let hunters poke out their trigger fingers to take shots in very cold weather. These mittens are never as warm as regular wool or ski-type models, and most hunters prefer to simply shuck a better-quality mitten when the time to shoot finally rolls around.

Some excellent hunting gloves are sold at sporting goods outlets. The thinly constructed gloves commonly called "shooting gloves" are probably the worst of the lot because they provide only marginal protection from the cold. Better gloves are fleece-lined leather models and bulkier gloves insulated with down or acrylic. Fairly new, compact gloves lined with Thinsulate are developing a good reputation. Gloves never keep hands as warm as mittens do, but again, they do allow manual dexterity.

One item designed to keep a hunter's mitts warm in sub-zero conditions is a belt-attached hand warmer. This is merely an oversized mitten that you can jam your hand into as you walk or wait. When coupled with a small commercial pocket heater, a belt-attached hand warmer can keep fingers downright hot in decidedly wintry situations.

Although not commonly used in the deer woods, thin camo-net gloves are favored by a few bowhunters for close-range sneaking and stand-hunting situations. Such gloves in no way warm the hands, but do hide light, shiny skin.

Footgear. Like clothing, hunting shoes and boots must fit well and protect feet from moisture and cold. They must also give good ankle support for steady walking in rough terrain, cushion the soles of feet to absorb walking shock, provide a nonslip grip in a variety of terrain, and allow reasonable walking comfort. That's a lot for one boot or shoe to accomplish, but literally dozens of contemporary models do the trick.

There are three basic types of footwear worn by savvy hunters—standard calf-high leather boots, rubber boots of varying height, and combination leather-and-rubber pacs. Each has specific applications in the field.

Hunting boots must be well-designed to keep feet warm and dry, provide traction in a variety of terrain, and provide firm but flexible wearing comfort. They must also be durable.

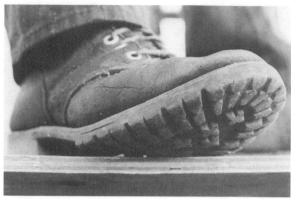

Vibram-type lug soles provide the most stable footing on tree-stand platforms, steep hillsides, and other surfaces where hunters cannot afford to slip. These soles also wear like iron, usually outlasting the leather uppers to which they're attached.

Leather boots: A typically good all-around leather hunting boot stands 6 to 10 inches high, with an 8-inch boot being by far the most common. This boot generally has a Vibram-type lug sole that wears like iron and grips rocks, dirt, and other surfaces incredibly well. It laces tightly about the ankle and lower leg for good lateral support, and provides at least fairly good protection from outside moisture.

There is no such thing as a completely waterproof leather boot, despite manufacturers' claims. Some silicone-treated models come fairly close, especially those with soles glued instead of sewn (welted) to leather uppers. Nonetheless, every leather boot will leak at least a little water if subjected to unusually wet conditions. The best a hunter can do is realize this fact and treat his leather footwear regularly with heavy doses of silicone or wax-type sealant especially made for boots.

It is important to note that calf-high boots can be separated into two basic leather types—silicone-impregnated and oil-tanned. Silicone-treated boots are the ones advertised as being waterproof, and most have glued-on soles. These boots should *never* be waterproofed with oils like Mink Oil or waxes like Sno-Seal—to do so can deteriorate the leather and ruin the leather-to-sole bonding agent. By contrast, oil-tanned boots can be waterproofed with any commercial product designed to do the job. Sno-Seal, with its waxy consistency, is a favorite of many hunters using untreated boots in heavy rain, sleet, snow, or swampy walking conditions.

Leather boots are available in insulated and uninsulated models. The insulated models are heavier in weight but more comfortable from the outset. Boot insulation is usually some sort of closed-cell foam between the outer shell of the boot and the inner lining. This foam traps body heat for cold-weather com-

A calf-high, insulated, oil-tanned boot with a welted (sewn-in) Vibram sole is the choice of many deer hunters. When treated with waterproofing wax or oil, the boot serves admirably.

fort, and also gives with a foot to minimize the amount of wearing time needed to break in a boot for hunting. Interestingly enough, insulated leather boots are seldom hot to wear even in warm early-fall hunting weather. As a matter of fact, many professional firefighters wear such boots to *insulate against* the intense heat from forest fires.

Uninsulated boots—especially those made of strong, thin kangaroo leather—are the lightest on the market but require initial break-in prior to heavy use to prevent blisters on the heel, toes, and other tender parts of the foot.

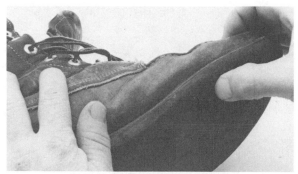

The quietest neoprene hiking soles are soft enough to give with the press of a thumb. These soles do not resist wear as well as Vibram, but allow quiet close-range deerstalking.

A silicone-impregnated boot with a glued-on sole is the most completely waterproof of all leather footwear. This particular boot is made of lightweight kangaroo leather and features a pliable neoprene sole—both of which enhance walking ease and comfort.

Although Vibram soles are the very best gripping soles available for hunters, bowhunters and close-range stalkers with guns are better off wearing boots with soft neoprene soles. These soles do not wear quite as well as Vibram, but provide sure footing and make far less walking noise than harder Vibram soles.

A myriad of leather-boot styles are sold at sporting goods stores. A hunter can buy just about any color, toe design, lace-up system, and sole-tread pattern imaginable. Shopping for leather boots can be a real eye-opener, and careful shopping will result in a purchase that pleases both eye and foot.

Rubber boots: Insulated and uninsulated rubber boots are best where footing is sloppy wet. No leather boot can stand up to hours of trudging through water, mud, or wet snow. And once leather becomes water-soaked a hunter will quickly become miserable. In deep, wet snow, some hunters tape their rubberized rain pants to the tops of calf-high rubber boots to form a waterproof seal. Others simply don hip-high rubber boots or even chest waders to stay dry in fairly deep water or snow.

All-rubber boots are never as comfortable to walk in as top-quality leather boots, but foam-insulated rubbers can be every bit as warm. Rubber footwear does not breathe away body vapors at all, which can cause a foot-sweating problem if a hunter is actively moving about in fairly warm weather. However, in

Calf-high insulated rubber boots are ideal whenever the ground is sloppy wet. This footwear completely blocks all outside moisture but also holds in perspiration.

some circumstances, all-rubber boots are definitely the way to go.

Leather-and-rubber pacs: In light snow or moderately wet footing, many deer hunters prefer to wear pacs with leather uppers and rubber lowers. Combo

A quality leather-and-rubber pac is completely moisture repellant below the instep while also allowing calf and ankle comfort that only flexible leather can provide. The best pacs are insulated for warmth and have soles that give good traction.

boots combine some of the best features of both all-leather and all-rubber boots—complete rubber waterproofing for about 3 inches above ground level plus the breathability and walking flexibility of leather in the ankle and calf areas. A few pac-type boots have rubber lowers and heavy, moisture-resistant Cordura nylon uppers to further enhance breathability and walking ease. Leather-and-rubber pacs are not quite as comfortable to hike in as leather boots, nor are quite as waterproof as all-rubber boots, nor do they wear as well as boots with Vibram soles. However, they are an excellent choice for sneaking about snow-covered hillsides or swamps.

Tips on boot size: To prevent blisters on the feet, smart deer hunters wear two pairs of socks whenever they slip on hunting boots of any sort. This lets the socks rub against one another instead of one sock rubbing against skin. To accommodate two socks—most often a heavy sock over a thin sock—a hunter must buy boots one to two sizes larger than the shoes he normally wears. The extra room provided by a larger boot also traps heat and dissipates perspiration through the double layers of sock material.

Other outer footwear: Most longtime deer hunters wear other footwear besides standard types of boots. This includes slippers or conventional shoes around hunting camp, goose-down "booties" in camp and in bed, and old tennis shoes. Constantly wearing heavy, serviceable boots around camp as well as in the field

can be bothersome and uncomfortable—something to consider before heading for the hills.

Socks for deer hunting: The most popular socks are made of cotton, wool, or wool/synthetic blend.

Cotton socks are quite comfortable for most deer-hunting needs. They absorb and carry away foot perspiration fairly well and provide soft comfort against the skin. Wool and wool-blend socks are warmer, especially when wet, but should be worn over inner socks to prevent chafing and rashes on the skin.

As mentioned before, you should always wear two pairs of socks to help prevent blisters. Inner socks should be fairly thin. Any sock made of nylon, Orlon, acrylic, cotton, or a combination of these common materials will work quite well as an inner sock. So-called insulated or thermal socks with integral air pockets for trapping body warmth make excellent inner socks, provided these are relatively thin. A few hunters with sensitive feet wear silk inner socks because these are slippery and help eliminate blisters. Outer socks can be of cotton or wool, and should be fairly heavy to insulate and cushion the foot. These sock recommendations hold true no matter what the weather conditions.

In bitterly cold stand-hunting, some hunters prefer to wear electric, battery-operated socks to ensure toasty warm feet. Electric socks are not the most comfortable for walking, but they keep the feet warm no matter what the weather.

This hunter is enjoying the cushioned warmth of goose-down booties as he waxes his regular Vibram boots.

SELECTING CAMPING GEAR

An old, grizzled deer-hunting veteran put it best when he said, "No matter how much campin' stuff a fella has, there's always room for more!" Any experienced hunter will verify this claim with a loud "amen!" Store shelves are jam-packed with nifty gizmos that promise to make camping easier and more comfortable—a tantalizing assortment of gear guaranteed to part shoppers from their money whenever they wander into the sporting goods department. As a result, a hunter's mountain of camping equipment invariably continues to grow throughout his active hunting years.

For many people, life around hunting camp is every bit as important as stalking the woods for deer. Even diehards who tramp the hills from dawn till dusk can greatly enrich their outings with a few well-chosen camping items. Given the mind-boggling array of tents, sleeping bags, stoves, utensils, lanterns, ice chests, and other standard camping gear available today, no hunter needs to rough it in semimiserable fashion as he wiles away the hours between tries for game.

CAMP TYPE

Many deer hunters accumulate their camping gear in piecemeal, willy-nilly fashion. However, it's more sensible to make some initial decisions about need requirements prior to purchasing a basic camping setup. A systematic approach saves both shopping time and money and results in a superior deer camp with more than average comfort.

There are as many specific camping-gear assortments as there are individual hunters. However, deer camps can be generally divided into three classes. They are, from the simplest to the most elaborate: backpack camps; camps for horseback, boat-in, and fly-in situations; and roadside camps. Each sort of camp requires particular types of gear to satisfy unique needs and limitations.

Many deer hunters pursue more than one type of hunting and thus require more than one set of camping equipment. The key to choosing proper gear is deciding in advance whether that gear must be carted in a backpack, stuffed in pack boxes attached to a horse or mule, piled in the bow of a motorboat, lashed to the transport brackets on a trail bike, or heaped in the back of a truck or jeep. Once this decision is made, a hunter can begin his never-ending career as a collector of useful camping paraphernalia.

BACKPACKING GEAR

Aside from the backpack itself, which will be discussed later, a walk-in hunter needs a compact, lightweight assortment of camping items that ideally

Hunting camp can be a comfortable home away from home if gear is selected with care. The setup need not be elaborate to be efficient—too much camping equipment can be as troublesome as not enough.

A backpacking deer hunter must trim camping food and gear to 20 or 25 pounds to save his back muscles and keep the hunt enjoyable. Beginning backpackers tend to overload their packs to ensure camping comfort—which usually leads to fatigue and, sometimes, to strains and sprains.

weighs no more than 20 or 25 pounds. The best place to look for special carry-in camping gear is any well-stocked backpacking or mountain-climbing shop. Most of this equipment is highly specialized and seldom seen in a department store or even a local Army-Navy outlet.

It's safe to say that the average deer hunter tries to carry everything but the kitchen sink on his first attempt at backpack hunting. Into the pack go all sorts of poorly chosen items—a heavy cast-iron skillet, a cotton-duck tent, plenty of nourishing canned goods . . . in other words, all the things he just cannot do without. After lugging this stuff for several miles over rough terrain, the novice learns that he *can* do without many traditional roadside camping essentials. This lesson is driven home by aching back muscles and accompanied by a decidedly sour mental attitude.

Man is not a pack mule. The newly educated hunter begins his second wilderness trek by replacing the heavy skillet with a lightweight aluminum model,

buying a small, ultralight tent, packing freeze-dried food instead of hefty canned food, and otherwise lightening the load. With experience, he discovers that lightweight camping embodies some comfort sacrifices but is all in all a fairly comfortable way to go.

A backpacker needs the same basics every camper requires—some sort of cooking setup, shelter from the elements, a source of nighttime light, sleeping accommodations, a water container, and so on. But these things should be chosen with ultralight weight in mind. Backpacking gear is generally more expensive than heavier camping equipment, but is well worth the money.

It's important to note that motorbiking into remote deer areas requires the same basic equipment setup as backpack hunting does. Keeping weight down might not be quite as critical, depending upon the payload of the bike being used, but it's tough to load much more bulk on a motorbike than a hunter can carry on his back.

Specific necessary items for backpack and motorbike hunting will be discussed a little later.

HORSEBACK, BOAT-IN, FLY-IN SETUPS

In some areas, a hunter needs a horse, boat, or light airplane to reach productive deer country. Camping equipment to accommodate these modes of transportation need not be as compact or lightweight as in backpacking, but the entire food/equipment setup must be carefully selected for safe, easy transport. As

The amount of camping equipment used on horseback hunts is largely dependent on how many pack animals are available. On the average, gear plus food should not exceed 75 pounds per person for a 10-day hunt.

A small pile of well-selected duffel will usually allow trouble-free camping in boat-in or fly-in situations. Deer hunters in wilderness must always sacrifice a little comfort, but intelligently assembled camps can be surprisingly comfortable.

The best deer camps are permanent cabins, as shown, or big RVs with most of the niceties of home. However, a tent-camper can be almost as comfortable if he uses quality equipment.

a rule, complete camping gear plus food for a 10-day horseback, boat-in, or fly-in hunt should weigh no more than 100 pounds per man, and preferably only 40 or 50 pounds. How elaborate a horseback camp can be is only limited by the number of pack animals available, but boats and light aircraft have payload safety limitations that must be observed.

Many hunters carry regular backpack camping gear when using horses, boats, or planes—supplementing this setup with heavier food and a few heavy convenience items such as a gasoline lantern and a roomier tent. Gigantic water jugs, big ice chests, and other roadside camping conveniences are far too bulky for transport by pack animal, boat, or airplane. Both bulk and weight should be carefully considered.

ROADSIDE CAMP SETUPS

Most deer hunters who camp use some sort of roadside accommodation. The lucky ones have access to permanent cabins or live out of elaborate motor homes, camper trailers, or oversized pickup campers. The rest must laboriously set up a conventional tent camp in a handy campground or spot beside the road.

Roadside tent-camping is really not difficult, provided you have a trim assemblage of quality gear. The amount of gear needed depends upon the capacity of the transport vehicle and the number of hunters involved. Equipment weight is usually not a problem in roadside camping—most hunters bulk out long before they overload their vehicles.

The key to selecting practical roadside camping aids is gauging how quickly and how easily these items

Roadside deer camps may not look like the Hilton but they can provide ample comfort between tries for deer. Camping can be fun, even in foul weather, provided you are properly equipped.

can be unpacked, set up, and packed away again after the hunt. Aside from those few camping fans who don't mind puttering for days to set up a comfortable home away from home, hunters usually prefer to set up the camp as quickly as possible.

Quality tents, stoves, and other camping items are designed with rapid setup as well as efficient function in mind. A roadsider who chooses first-rate gear and refrains from cluttering camp with dozens of useless or marginally useful items can set up a truly wonderful camp in less than two hours and take it down just as fast.

So much for generalities about camping needs. Here are some specifics about such major camping items as tents, sleeping bags, and portable stoves. By paying close attention to these guidelines, anyone can choose sensible camping equipment no matter what his preferred method of hunting.

TENTS

Regardless of size, shape, weight, or material, a top-quality tent should have two important characteristics. First, it should set up with a minimum of time and effort. Second, it should completely protect the user from wind and precipitation. Any tent that meets this pair of camping requirements is well on its way to being a solid winner in the field.

Tent designs are too diverse and ever-changing to thoroughly cover here. Literally hundreds of shapes and sizes are displayed in manufacturers' catalogs—tents made of nylon, polyester, cotton duck, cotton drill, and other durable fabrics. Common shapes include the classic peak-roofed wall tent, geodesic dome, round tepee, and flat-sided umbrella tent. These and less conventional tents are available in a wide array of heights, lengths, and widths, weighing as little as 2 or 3 pounds in backpacker models and as much as 75 pounds in large roadside designs. There's a good-quality hunting tent to fit every need and every pocketbook.

A close comparison of several manufacturers' brochures is one of the best ways to select tents that will satisfy particular needs. A hunter must know how many people are apt to be using the tent. He must decide whether cooking needs to be done inside or outside the tent—a factor largely determined by weather. He must consider other tent features, such as bug-proof netting shields over windows and doors, an awning over the door to create a shady patio area, a durable floor to keep out ground moisture, and so on.

Tent manufacturers offer many design options worth considering. For example, some full-sized models come complete with awnings to create shady patio areas and protect against wet weather.

Certain camping tents are solid standbys in some situations. A large, floorless cotton-duck wall tent about 10 × 12 in size is a favorite of hunters setting up long-term roadside camps. This tent characteristically pitches over ropes or a permanent pole frame and has a stove-pipe hole so that a wood-burning stove can be used inside. A more portable, more easily pitched roadside tent is a similar-sized wall tent with aluminum framing, nylon or polyester walls, and a roof of treated, water-shedding cotton drill. Such wall tents generally weigh 35 to 50 pounds and house five or six people with ease.

By contrast, a highly popular tent for horseback, boat-in, or fly-in hunting is a small four-man wall tent or geodesic dome weighing 15 or 20 pounds, meas-

Floorless wall tents made of durable cotton duck are roadside favorites. They normally pitch over permanent pole frames or taut networks of rope. Larger models allow the use of wood stoves and provide superb shelter.

Tents ideal for horseback, boat-in, and fly-in situations usually weigh about 20 pounds and provide 60 to 80 square feet of usable floor space. These tents are most commonly sold in peaked versions (with walls) and energy-efficient dome configurations.

uring 8′ × 8′ or 8′ × 10′ across the floor, and having a "hunch-over" height of 4 or 5 feet at the peak. A tent of this type is normally pitched with aluminum poles and features nylon construction throughout, a waterproof floor, and waterproof fly stretched over the roof. In smaller tents of this variety, walls must breathe to prevent condensation on internal surfaces.

Backpackers' tents are the most specialized of all because they must allow a modicum of sleeping and lounging comfort in a very small space. Both wall tents and dome tents are popular, although the domes are more wind-resistant, provide the most internal room per square foot of tent fabric used, and are easiest of all to pitch. The average two-man backpackers' tent complete with aluminum poles weighs about 6 pounds, and three-man versions weigh 10 or 11 pounds. Some tiny one-man tents weigh under 3 pounds.

Tents of this persuasion are invariably made of thin, tough nylon supported by slender aluminum poles. The best have fairly porous walls and waterproof floors and flies. Because the average person snoozes away two pints of moisture during one night of sleep, any small tent without breathable construction will literally rain on the occupants in a few short hours of use.

The best backpackers' tents provide relatively cramped quarters for hunters, but allow easy carrying, set up quickly, and afford excellent protection from the elements.

No matter what the hunting need, there are tents available to fill the bill. Finding that just-right model can be a highly enjoyable exercise, provided the shopper knows approximately what he wants and studies manufacturers' literature with care.

Backpackers' tents are designed with light weight and easy setup in mind. Dome shapes provide the most interior space per square yard of fabric used, and also withstand higher winds than backpacking wall tents.

SLEEPING BAGS

After a hard day of hunting, there is nothing better than a night's sleep in a toasty warm sleeping bag, and nothing worse than being too cold and shivery to get any sleep at all. Every hunter should keep this in mind and regard the selection of his sleeping bag as one of the most important outdoor decisions he's likely to make.

There are several things to look for when shopping for a sleeping bag. If you consider each of them care-

The lightest and most energy effi-cient sleeping bags are mummy bags (top two). Spacious rectangular bags allow more sleeping move-ment—which many nonbackpack-ing outdoorsmen prefer.

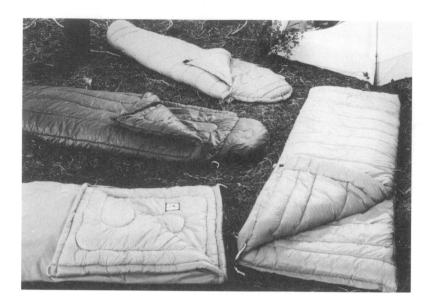

fully prior to reaching for your checkbook, you'll end up with a comfortable, long-lasting investment.

Warmth. Generally speaking, most hunters tend to buy sleeping bags that do not have enough insulating material to keep them warm in many nighttime camp-ing situations. All quality sleeping bags are assigned "temperature ratings" by manufacturers—ratings that give a general idea how low the thermometer can dip before the user becomes uncomfortably cool.

The temperature ratings of sleeping bags are only rough selection guidelines because there is no ac-curate, absolute way of measuring bag warmth. Me-tabolism varies from individual to individual. Heavy people need less bag insulation than thin people and well-fed people need less than hungry people. Simi-larly, dry weather is usually more conducive to sleep-ing-bag warmth than damp weather, all else being equal, and calm conditions are always more com-fortable than windy conditions at exactly the same thermometer reading. Still, a hunter can definitely use the temperature ratings of bags to good advantage.

As a rule, when shopping for an adequately warm bag, select a bag with a temperature rating 15 to 20 degrees *below* the lowest temperature likely to be en-countered. For example, a hunter who will be camping during late fall in an area where unusually low night-time temperatures hover around 20° F is best advised to purchase a bag with a 0-degree or 5-degree tem-perature rating. The rationale for this is simple enough—a hunter can always cool down by unzipping an overly hot bag to allow outside air flow, but a cold bag is a cold bag no matter what. A hunter should always hedge in the direction of extra warmth when selecting a sleeping bag to ensure sleeping comfort.

Weight. There are two basic categories of sleeping bags available: (1) those designed to be as light and compact as possible for backpacking and (2) all the rest.

Backpacking bags are carefully manufactured to al-low maximum warmth-to-weight efficiency—accom-plished by using top-grade, high-loft goose-down insulation and lightweight nylon shell construction. These bags compress into relatively small stuff sacks yet bounce back to full fluff when unpacked at day's end. Depending upon the comfort rating and corre-sponding volume of goose-down insulation used in a given backpacking bag, the bag may weigh as little as 2 pounds and as much as 6 pounds.

Sleeping bags other than special backpackers' models are usually insulated with a polyester fiber. Such fiber is heavier than goose down, but provides adequate warmth when ample amounts are used. Covers or shells on these bags are usually cotton sheeting or nylon fabric; liners are most often soft flannel. The average sleeping bag of the nonback-packing variety weighs between 6 and 12 pounds.

Shape and size. Sleeping bags are available in three basic shapes—rectangular, tapered, and mummy. The rectangular shape is most common in mild-weather bags with fairly high temperature ratings. Bags that taper toward the foot are more energy efficient because there is less volume to keep warm. As a result, this design is often used in bags with medium temperature ratings ranging from 15 to 30 degrees. Mummy bags surround the user like a loose-fitting mitten, leaving no extra internal space to heat and thus utilizing body warmth most efficiently. All backpacking bags are mummy bags because this shape is both heat-efficient

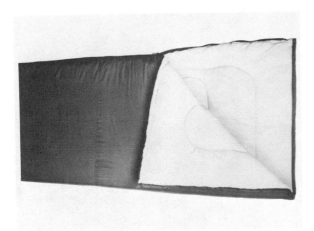

*A tapered sleeping bag represents a compromise be-
tween the efficiency of a mummy bag and the roominess
of a rectangular model. A tapered bag is generally used
in moderately cold weather.*

and much lighter than rectangular and tapered bags.

There is no perfect sleeping-bag shape. Rectangular
bags are the roomiest and allow the most movement
inside the bag but are the heaviest and least heat-
efficient of the lot. On the other end of the spectrum,
mummy bags are lightest and most heat-efficient but
constrict movement of arms and legs. If weight is not
a concern, a spacious, heavily insulated rectangular
bag is probably the best choice for most people.

Most good-grade sleeping bags are available in several lengths to accommodate people of different
height. It's better to own a bag that is a bit on the
long side than to have one that jams the feet and constantly creeps away from neck and shoulders.

Durability. The best sleeping bags are constructed
to last despite heavy use. Seams are tightly stitched
with stout thread and double or triple-stitched at stress
points, such as at fabric corners. Outer fabric is tightly
woven and virtually snag-proof under normal conditions. Ideally, zippers are made of self-healing nylon
to prevent corrosion and permanent zipper damage.
Liners are made of soft but tough material like flannel
or fine-mesh nylon. Such careful construction provides
many years of trouble-free service.

Other desirable features. A would-be camper
should carefully compare the secondary selling points
of basically high-quality sleeping bags. Some are easily
machine washable; others must be dry-cleaned for
best results. Some unzip and "mate" with similar bags
to provide comfortable sleeping for two. A few have
an extra heat-retaining edge by incorporating full-
length zipper flaps to insulate this vulnerable part of
any bag. These and other positive, secondary design
features are highly touted by manufacturers, and often

prove to be the deciding factor on that just-right bed
away from home.

MATTRESSES, COTS, AND SLEEPING PADS

Throwing a sleeping bag down on hard, bare earth
ensures sleeping discomfort. A few rugged individu-
alists with a broad streak of masochism may prefer
to bed down on the ground, perhaps digging a shallow
hip hole to fit the body's contour or piling up pine
boughs to form a makeshift mattress. But these attempts at comfort are only *necessary* in bare-bones
survival situations.

Several conventional types of sleeping cushions are
used by sensible hunters—cushions which give with
the body and help insulate against the cold ground.
These include air mattresses, foam sleeping pads,
cots, and foam-filled or inflatable backpacker pads.

Air mattresses. Inflatable air mattresses at their best
provide two important advantages. First, they are extremely compact and light in weight when deflated
and folded up. Second, they conform to a sleeper's
body to provide excellent resting comfort.

The primary bugaboo of the air mattress is its tendency to spring leaks at the worst possible times. A
leaky mattress is worse than worthless, torturing you
throughout the night as you blow yourself blue in the
face, only to find yourself back on hard ground shortly
after you doze off to sleep again. The best air mattresses made of rubberized, laminated fabric are fairly
reliable and come complete with patching kits similar
to those used on auto tires. Finding the precise location of an air leak in the middle of the night can
make a magician's best trick look like child's play,
but quality air mattresses can be fixed. Avoid "cheapo"
models made of thin plastic.

Air mattresses are available in a variety of sizes,
and some can be hitched together with snaps to accommodate more than one sleeper. Most require a
hearty set of lungs to inflate, but a few incorporate
foot-pump inflating devices to save time and dizziness.
Some hunters love air mattresses—especially in
backpacking situations—and others wouldn't touch
one because of past experiences with leaks. Every
hunter must make his own decision about air mattresses, but quality models are usually reliable if handled carefully.

Foam pads. Foam sleeping pads are among the best
sleeping cushions available to campers. Ordinary
sheets of open-cell mattress foam sold at furniture
stores and military surplus stores work the best for
hunting use. The most practical and comfortable

Mattress open-cell foam (left) compresses to about the same insulating thickness as closed-cell foam (right). But open-cell foam is far more comfortable to lie on, although it is much bulkier and heavier to transport. (Neil Soderstrom photo)

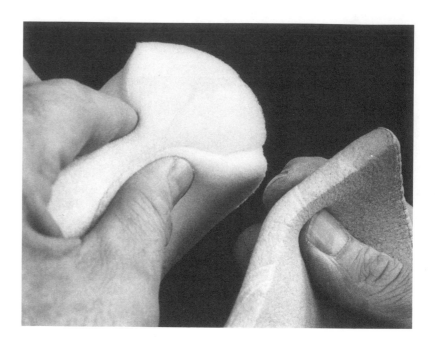

thicknesses are 3 and 4 inches. These pads work best when encased in GI mattress covers or similar home-made covers, which keep out grit and grime.

Foam sleeping pads are somewhat bulky and heavy to carry around, but this is no real problem unless a hunter needs to backpack into remote areas. The insulating and cushioning properties of a foam sleeping pad provide an excellent night's sleep in any circumstance.

Cots. Folding cots have been a traditional favorite of campers for many decades. Most are made with hardwood frames and canvas sleeping surfaces. They are heavy and bulky to transport, but keep a sleeping hunter 18 to 24 inches above the cold, clammy earth. In rattlesnake country, cots also provide insurance against the odd snake looking for a warm place to spend the night. Needless to say, snakes have crawled in with more than one hunter sleeping on the ground.

A folding cot is by no means as comfortable to sleep on as a foam pad, but it provides one important advantage inside a stove-heated tent. The extra foot or two of elevation on a cot positions the sleeper in a fairly warm band of air—often 15 to 20 degrees warmer than ground level. That is because heat rises and cold air sinks in a tent.

In big wall tents with wood stoves, hunters sometimes engage in good-natured squabbles about the temperature level. Fellows sleeping on cots may be sweltering hot in their bags and want to open the tent flap to cool things down; hunters at ground level may be shivering at the same time and want to throw more wood on the fire. An elevated cot definitely provides warmer sleeping inside a heated tent.

Backpacker's pads. Backpack hunters often carry thin, body-length or ¾-length closed-cell foam sleeping pads that roll up tightly and weigh less than one pound. Such pads insulate well but are not particularly comfortable. More-comfortable pads are thick and spongy, open-cell foam covered with durable nylon; others have airtight, rubberized covers with an open-cell foam structure that requires mouth-inflation for full sleeping comfort. Simple spongy foam pads are heavier and bulkier than inflatable models but cost considerably less. Inflatable pads are more dependable than regular air mattresses because their internal foam structure reduces necessary inside air pressure.

Unless a hunter has problems with cold feet and calves, ¾-length backpacking pads are every bit as comfortable as full-length models because they completely cushion the shoulders, buttocks, and area in between. These pads are obviously lighter in weight for easier carrying.

CAMP STOVES

Hunters who camp cook their meals over a wide variety of heat sources. Unless it's raining or snowing, charcoal-burning grills and smokers work well *outside* tents and campers. These items should never be used in closed-in places because they release deadly carbon monoxide. Similarly, a hunter in fair weather can cook over some sort of campfire/grill arrangement. However, stoves using white gasoline or propane are easier to use, making them the all-around favorites of hunters.

You can make a simple rock stove by drawing a rough frying-pan shape in an area cleared of dry grass and other flammable material. Make the round portion of the "pan" about 2 feet in diameter before scooping out the interior of the drawing in the dirt to form a depression roughly 4 inches deep.

Ring the round portion of the rock stove with dry, relatively round stones. Pack the gaps between stones with dirt to hold in heat and contain the fire. Fringe the pan-handle section of the grill with large, flat rocks of nearly equal height. Rocks must be dry and unporous to prevent heat-splitting and minor explosions once a fire is started.

After building a sizable fire inside the ring of rocks, rake coals from the edges and work them under a small backpacker's grill across the panhandle section. This setup allows you to cook comfortably away from searing heat of the main fire.

Liquid fuel versus propane. For conventional camp stoves—no matter what the size and shape—a hunter's major decision will be whether to go the liquid fuel or the bottled-gas route.

Liquid fuel, sometimes called stove and lantern fuel, is all basically the same white-gasoline formula no matter who the manufacturer happens to be. This fuel is most economical to use, costing less over the counter than a like amount of bottled gas and yielding about the same heat output and length of burn. Liquid fuel lights easily in all weather conditions, will not clog or gum up stove parts, and is available in virtually every grocery store and sporting goods store in North America. Its major disadvantages are that it must be poured into a stove with the aid of a filtering funnel, and the stoves must be manually pumped up to pressure once the fuel is in the tank.

Portable two-burner stoves are extremely popular in roadside camping situations. Both gasoline models (top) and handier propane-bottle configurations work well, provided they have a heat-production capability of approximately 25,000 BTUs. The better stoves incorporate wind baffles at the sides and fold to suitcase size.

Propane fuel, a liquified gas, is sold in pressurized cannisters that instantly screw-attach to any gas-operated stove. The containers are bulkier than cans of liquid fuel, and cost significantly more per hour of burning time provided. However, bottled propane is more convenient and less messy to use than liquid fuel.

Stove configurations. Camp stoves vary from large three-burner units measuring nearly 3 feet long to palm-sized, one-burner backpacking stoves. Each has specific features worth considering.

For most roadside camping needs, a two-burner camp stove delivering about 25,000 BTUs of heat from both burners combined will work just fine. The best models have stainless-steel cooking heads, wind baffles around the cooking area, sturdy, tight-knit grills to allow the use of any pot or pan, and heat-adjustment controls for precise cooking needs. The most popular stoves of this sort fold up to suitcase size for easy transport and storage.

Handy accessories such as Teflon-coated griddles, camp ovens, and waist-high metal stands are often available for standard-size roadside camping stoves. These items allow cooking technique nearly on a par with that possible at home.

Smaller two-burner and one-burner stoves providing BTU output of 10,000 to 20,000 are favorites of hunters on horseback, boat-in, and fly-in deer-hunting excursions. Scaled-down one-burner stoves with miniature fuel containers provide bare-bones cooking and beverage-heating convenience for hunters who backpack into remote areas. Most tiny stoves produce over 5,000 BTUs of heat and are engineered for reliability on the most grueling wilderness expeditions.

Wood stoves for tents. A variety of rectangular and barrel-type wood stoves provide heat inside large,

Some wood-burning stoves are designed to work inside cotton-duck tents. The best of these are compact, have flat top surfaces for easy cooking, and incorporate internal baffles to increase heating efficiency.

floorless cotton wall tents. The best have baffled interior construction for more efficient heating and incorporate a flat surface on top for simple cooking and the heating of water.

CAMPING UTENSILS

For roadside camps, the same basic assortment of utensils used at home will work well enough. But, because dishwashing is difficult in the wilds, many hunters lean toward disposable paper plates and plastic knives, forks, and spoons.

Some utensils are specially designed for backpacking and are made of lightweight aluminum; other products are merely tougher and more durable than the glassware and stoneware used around the house. Plates, glasses, and cups for camping are best made of plastic or similar non-breakable material—coated steel containers for eating and drinking are commonly sold as well, but conduct heat so well they tend to burn the hands and mouth while letting food and drink cool off rapidly.

For compact or lightweight transport in backpack or horseback situations, nothing can beat an aluminum mess kit that nests several pots, pans, plates, and other utensils in one compact package. These kits plus lightweight frying pans and other incidentals line the shelves of any backpack shop or well-stocked sporting goods store.

LIGHT SOURCES

It can be miserably dark in hunting camp if you fail to pack along a lantern or other source of light. A campfire alone yields poor nighttime working light and dazzles the eyes instead of providing light where it's needed. Automobile headlights work in a pinch around a roadside camp, but cannot be considered a sensible alternative to a lantern.

Some sort of lantern is the standard light for roadside and horseback camps. Both liquid-fuel (white gasoline) and propane lanterns are commonly used in the woods, and the same basic pluses and minuses of each kind of fuel apply here as they do with camp stoves. The liquid-fuel lanterns are cheaper to run but require pouring, pumping, and refilling; propane models are more expensive to operate but far more convenient.

Lanterns for hunting camp are not too difficult to choose once you decide on liquid fuel or propane. The primary buying points to consider are compactness, length of burning time, and single- or double-mantle construction.

Most lanterns measure about 14 inches high, with

Traditional gasoline lanterns are available in two-mantle versions (left) and more compact one-mantle models (right). Although two-mantle lanterns are more popular with outdoorsmen, one-mantle lanterns are more fuel-efficient and throw ample light.

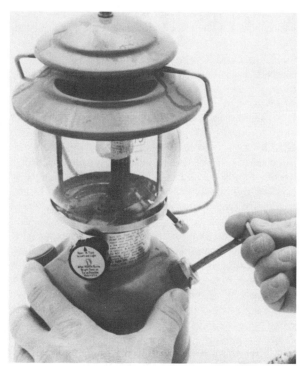

Liquid-fuel lantern tanks must be pressurized by hand pumping. On the average, 30 to 40 strokes are necessary for a bright, smoothly burning mantle.

propane models being a little taller than gasoline versions. A few models are under 12 inches high.

Burning time is important from a convenience point of view. Most double-mantle gasoline lanterns burn about 10 hours per pint of fuel on a medium light-output setting. Propane models burn longer per one-pint fuel cylinder—up to 20 hours depending upon the model and the light-output setting. Convenience-conscious hunters usually select the longest-burning models available, provided these lanterns generate adequate light.

Necessary light-output in a lantern is highly debatable. Most consumers assume that more light is better, making double-mantle, high-output models the most popular and widely sold today. However, the human eye dilates or contracts to adjust to different levels of illumination, effectively cancelling out slight differences in lantern light levels. A single-mantle lantern, with its moderate light output, is about 30 percent more fuel efficient than a comparable double-mantle model and throws entirely adequate light for tents and outdoor situations. This type of lantern commonly burns over 15 hours per tank of liquid fuel and over 30 hours on one canister of propane fuel. Most hunters use double-mantle lanterns, but single-mantle models are really more practical.

Backpacking hunters seldom carry lanterns because they weigh so much. A few tiny backpacking lanterns are available, but serious hikers generally use special long-burning candles around camp to supplement firelight and flashlights. A backpacker must cut corners to minimize weight on all equipment, and this includes camp lighting at night.

A propane lantern requires no fuel-pouring or pumping and usually burns longer than a gasoline lantern of comparable size. However, this light is significantly more expensive to use.

ICE CHESTS

Ice chests and smaller one-hand coolers are strictly roadside camping items. They are available in a variety of configurations and capacities to suit any outdoor situation.

No matter what the size or shape, the best coolers and ice chests have cases made of lightweight polyethylene or a combination of polyethylene and steel. Internal insulation in the bottom, walls, and lid is usually tightly packed urethane foam. All-polyethylene coolers and chests are more durable than steel-belted models, surviving impact tests that badly dent or crack metal. However, coolers with metal-belted sides and tops have been available for several decades, making them the traditional favorites of many.

Most one-hand coolers have storage capacities somewhere between 8 and 16 quarts. This makes them ideal for one-day hunts that require a lunch or two plus a six-pack of drinks. Full-sized ice chests vary in capacity from 25 to 80 quarts, satisfying any roadside camper's needs.

For deer enthusiasts who hunt out-of-state on a regular basis, having meat packaged and quick-frozen at packing plants near hunting sites makes good sense, provided a huge ice chest is on hand when transporting meat back home by automobile. A few camping companies sell colossal ice chests that hold a whopping 160 to 180 quarts of payload, but very few hunters are aware of them. One of these magnum models is ideal for transporting the frozen quarters or packaged meat from deer. On the average, an ice chest with a capacity of 175 quarts will hold the boned, packaged meat of four mature deer with ease and will keep the meat frozen hard for two or three days without the need for dry ice.

Some ice chests and coolers are designed to double as camp stools, and a few even feature vinyl cushions on top. Most incorporate removable deep-dish trays, water drains, and sturdy two-way handles.

WATER CONTAINERS

Hunters often dry-camp a long distance from clear, drinkable water. These situations require the use of one or more airtight, easy-to-handle water containers. Several types of commercial water jugs are available for camping, from standard plastic five-gallon pour-containers to more sophisticated large-capacity jugs with faucets. For the horseback, boat-in, or fly-in hunter, thin-walled, collapsible water jugs are ideal.

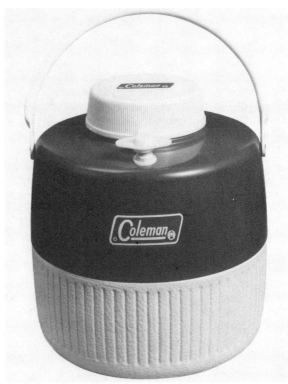

Any water container is fine for roadside camping, provided it has ample storage capacity, keeps water clean, and allows easy access to water. Simple airtight models with pour spouts are favored by many hunters.

In addition, a myriad of homegrown solutions to water-carrying problems range from simple plastic buckets to stainless-steel dairy-farm milk cans. Any container that holds ample water, keeps water clean, and allows easy carrying and access will work just fine for the average hunter.

A quality ice chest often has an all-polyethylene case insulated with urethane foam. It is durable and extremely well insulated for camping use.

FOOD

Food is a highly personal thing. One man's delicacy is another man's tripe; one man's delight is another man's disappointment. However, the *weight and bulk* of food used by hunters must be considered whenever this food will be carried in a backpack, on a beast of burden, across a motorbike, or in a motorboat or airplane.

The most expensive and lightest-weight of all is freeze-dried food sold specifically for backpacking. Water is the heaviest single ingredient in conventional food, so removing water greatly lightens the load. Some surprisingly good-tasting freeze-dried meals are available these days—perhaps not restaurant fare, but close enough for a hungry hiker.

The hunter on a budget can do quite well without buying freeze-dried foods if he shops carefully at the local grocery store. A wide variety of nourishing dry foods like cereal, soup mix, dried fruit, and the like are available at any market—foods that taste great when mixed or boiled.

Hunters who need to pare down bulk and weight of food for horseback hunting or similar pursuits can usually get by with a mix of dry grocery items and a carefully selected assortment of canned goods. Perishables like bacon and sandwich meats are obviously out for long trips away from roads, but most of these items can closely be duplicated in dried or canned commodities. Food selection, when weight is a potential problem, is largely a matter of common sense and personal taste.

OTHER CAMPING ITEMS

Other handy camping items include a variety of ropes made of nylon and other materials, and nylon and treated-cotton tarps. Rope has many uses around any hunting camp, from making a clothesline inside a tent and hanging deer to lashing down tent flies during a storm. Tarps of various sizes can be used for covering equipment during inclement weather, wrapping a deer carcass to keep off dust and grime, providing a waterproof ground cloth for a small backpack tent, and many other things.

As time passes, a serious deer hunter adds item after item to his basic camping setup as new needs arise or new products appear. Carefully browsing a well-stocked camping equipment section of any large store takes several hours and turns up all sorts of nifty little goodies that are hard to resist.

MISCELLANEOUS EQUIPMENT

The basic equipment needs of an all-around deer hunter go on and on. A good many of these items are really necessities but do not fall into any of the broader categories already discussed. For example, a hunter without a flashlight is greatly hampered at night.

The following items, then, are essential on many deer hunts, but are categorized here as miscellaneous gear. But do not be fooled into thinking they are un-important. It's safe to say in most cases they would be sorely missed on a hunt.

BACKPACKS, BELT PACKS, DUFFEL BAGS

Every deer hunter should own at least four types of packs or bags—(1) a frameless shoulder-carried day-pack, (2) a full-sized expedition backpack with ex-ternal frame, (3) a compact belt pack or fannypack, and (4) a large, well-made duffel bag. All these gear-toting bags have features in common, but each has specific applications in the field.

Backpacks. For many all-day hunting situations, a woodsman is best off carrying a frameless backpack. This pack will hold a lunch, bone saw, flashlight, spare ammo, spotting scope, coat, and/or other items a hik-ing hunter might need. Some hunters find carrying daypacks a nuisance, and prefer to pare down gear to belt-pack size whenever possible. However, for long treks afield the carrying capacity of a light, shoulder-wide pack is essential.

A full-sized, external-frame backpack, on the other hand, is not a debatable item when a hunter intends to walk far away from roads for an extended hunting trip. Similarly, this pack is essential for carrying the meat, hide, and head of a deer over several miles of rugged terrain.

Backpacks of the frameless and larger external-frame types should have certain important features. For one, they should be made of durable, heavy-duty nylon. All closure zippers should be made of self-healing nylon rather than metal because metal will eventually corrode and bind up with heavy use. Shoulder straps should be heavily padded and fully adjustable for comfort. And hip belts—available on some frameless as well as all external-frame packs—should be wide, strong, padded in the hip-bone areas, fully adjustable, and easy to buckle and unbuckle with the squeeze of a button, lift of a tab, or twist of a hook.

The frames on full-sized expedition packs should be made of aircraft aluminum or even lighter-weight magnesium. Solid frames with welded joints are the strongest and quietest during use, and are thus the odds-on favorites with hunters. Frame size should be chosen at a regular backpack shop to match a par-ticular hunter's physical stature. A few extra-strong frames called "freighters" are sold for carrying fire-wood and other heavy loads, and these are ideal choices if you expect to be backpacking meat and other loads weighing over 60 pounds on a regular ba-sis.

Packsack design for external-frame packs varies tremendously from model to model. To choose a suit-

A roomy frameless backpack is standard equipment for many deer-hunting hikers. The pack will carry a lunch, flashlight, bone saw, coat, and similar day-use items.

HOW TO ADD A SACK TO A FRAME PACK

A standard external-frame pack can be made even more useful by attaching a smaller commercial pack below the primary sack. Components for a two-sack pack are available at any backpack store.

1. *Line up grommet holes on the lower sack along the pack frame in suitable position and mark hole placement on the frame with a lead pencil.* **2.** *Carefully drill holes in the metal pack frame to accommodate the secondary sack. Determine drill-bit diameter by the diameter of mounting pins purchased with the lower pack.*

3. *The lower pack can be quickly mounted with grommet pins and a pack-assembly pin bar. Note that only two pins are used to fasten this three-hole pack—unnecessary holes drilled in a pack frame can slightly weaken construction.* **4.** *For optimum deer-hunting results, a backpack frame should be stripped of its packs and sprayed with nonglare camouflage paint. This helps hide it from the wary eyes of deer.* **5.** *A two-sack arrangement allows optimum gear transport to a remote campsite. Once actual hunting begins, you can shed the larger sack and cruise the hills with the smaller day sack in place.*

able type, a hunter should spend some time thinking about his needs as he browses in a backpack store and pores over manufacturers' literature.

One packsack setup worth considering for hunting is two separate sacks attached to one frame—something any hunter can create by wielding a tape measure and drilling a few extra holes in a frame. This pack can be used with both sacks in place for packing to and from a major wilderness campsite. During the actual hunt, a hiker can remove the top sack and hike with the frame and lower sack on his back to carry day-use items. If a deer is bagged, the entire animal or individual quarters can be lashed to the frame above the lower sack with stout nylon rope.

Belt packs. Belt packs, sometimes called fanny-packs, are usually constructed of heavy Cordura nylon and feature nylon, self-healing zippers. These are available in two basic types—a compact model with belt loops for attachment to a regular leather belt, and

A small belt pack is ideal for transporting a few well-selected day-use items like food, extra ammo, and a compass. If a hunter can stuff all necessary equipment in one of these packs, he has no need to haul around a larger, heavier shoulder model.

a more spacious version with its own integral belt. Both configurations work quite well in deer-hunting situations, holding such vital equipment as a small lunch, flashlight, and fire-starting material. If a hunter can stuff all essential day-use gear in a belt pack and his pockets, he'll enjoy unencumbered movement as he hikes over hill and dale.

Duffel bags. A duffel bag is a flexible, sausage-shaped container with handle straps on top and some sort of positive closure system.

Duffel bags vary somewhat in size, material, and

Large fanny packs and well-designed duffel bags are both favored by hunters in the know. Items like these are ideally constructed of tough, heavy-duty Cordura nylon.

specific construction, but all are practical for carrying clothes, food, and other resilient hunting items. Unlike hard-shell suitcases and pack boxes, duffle bags can be tossed about and stuffed in nooks and crannies without incurring any damage. For airline travel, transporting gear by boat or horse, or merely tossing equipment in the bed of a pickup truck, nothing beats a duffle bag.

The duffel bags many old-timers are familiar with are GI models made of tough green canvas. These are still available at surplus stores, and close at one end with a series of large grommet holes and a steel padlock loop. Although these simple duffel bags are inexpensive and relatively useful, modern duffel bags are many times better.

A typical contemporary duffel bag is made of the same tough Cordura nylon used in backpack sacks and belt packs. A few top-notch models are made of canvas or heavy cotton-synthetic cloth. Regardless of basic material, a good duffel bag has a full-length zipper on top made of self-healing nylon, and features nylon carrying straps that wrap entirely around the girth of the bag to prevent strap seams from tearing loose. A top-opening zipper allows easy access to all gear stored inside. Some elaborate duffel bags have several external zippered pockets for extraneous gear or items a hunter wants especially quick access to.

Duffel bags of the sort just described vary in length from 18 inches to over 3 feet. Average circumference is about 4 feet. There's nothing elaborate about a good duffel bag, but it will serve you well, provided you choose a practical size for your needs.

ORIENTEERING GEAR

When one says Orienteering* gear, he means maps and compasses. This equipment can be extremely important in the field, both for moving precisely about the woods during a hunt and for responding sensibly to life-and-death survival situations. Here are guidelines on choosing maps and compasses for deer-hunting application.

Compasses. Basically, a compass is a straightforward device with a needle or dial that points toward the magnetic north pole of the Earth. When used in conjunction with maps of hunting areas, or merely used with some personal directional knowledge of a section of woods, a compass will allow you to move about in confidence when visibility is obscured by fog, a blinding snowstorm, or heavy foliage.

Compasses are seldom used in deer areas with sparse cover and plenty of relief to topography—in this terrain, a hunter can keep track of his location from landmarks alone. However, a smart hunter always carries a compass anyway just in case visibility drops to near-zero and landmarks disappear. In positive, nonstress hunting situations, compasses are more routinely used in fairly flat, monotonous country with uniformly clustered trees or brush. A hunter traversing this terrain can keep track of his movements

by using a compass—even on heavily overcast days when the sun is not visible to help give direction. Many experienced woodsmen seldom use a compass, even though they keep one on hand as a confidence builder, allowing free movement with the knowledge that a compass is available to double-check directional intuition.

For average hunting needs, any good, name-brand compass will serve the purpose. The simplest, least expensive models consist of a magnetic directional needle surrounded by a ring of bearing marks numbered in a clockwise direction from 0 to 360 degrees. More elaborate designs include Orienteering compasses with sighting mirrors, notch-type directional sights, and rotating graduated dials; and lensatic compasses with their unique magnifying dial viewers and thin-wire sighting lines.

Unless a deer hunter needs to guide himself to and from a precise point on the map, such as the end of a road or a small cabin in deep, uniform forest, the more elaborate compasses have little use in the field. A hunter who learns to use a compass properly can make fairly accurate declination adjustments and follow a reasonably straight line of travel without slowly, precisely moving from one landmark to another with the aid of mirror-type or lensatic sighting compasses. These compasses cost just a few dollars more than simpler models, and some hunters like to cover their options with the most precise direction-finding gear

A wide variety of compasses are sold at sporting goods stores. Common types are (left to right): a simple, liquid-filled sportsman's compass with bearing marks; a air-filled, balance-type compass with protective cover; and an elaborate Orienteering compass with sighting mirror, sight notch, rotating bearing dial, and luminous needle.

*Orienteering is a registered trademark.

A lensatic compass opens up from a compact metal case to allow precise directional movement about the woods. This unique sort of compass has a magnifying dial viewer and thin-wire sighting line.

available. It's really a matter of personal choice.

Certain design features *are* important to consider when buying any compass. The best have liquid-dampened dials or needles for smooth, accurate pointer rotation. Less expensive models merely balance a directional needle on a pivot; this causes the needle to dance and dart continually for jerky, wiggly direction indication. The magnetic needles and other important parts of compasses are generally luminous to allow easy use even in the dark. The most desirable compasses also incorporate some means of attachment to the user. Most pin to a shirt or have sturdy rings for attachment to a zipper or key chain. A few have wrist bands like watches or come complete with lanyards for carrying about the neck.

Top-quality compasses cost only a few dollars and ensure confident movement about the field. Every hunter should own a compass, know how to use it, and carry it as standard procedure.

Maps and map sources. Unless you know an area intimately, it's wise to use maps to familiarize yourself with the terrain you plan to hunt. Such preparation will fix major landmarks and landscape directions in mind prior to an outing, and carrying a map in the field during the actual hunt will further aid familiarization. In places with flat, featureless terrain, a map and compass can be used together to plot a course despite the lack of prominent orienting landmarks.

Maps are valuable for things other than safe movement about a particular region. Properly chosen maps can give a hunter important information about where deer are likely to be and which hunting strategy might be best—all before an area is seen firsthand. For example, good topographic maps show the exact relief of landscape, clearly delineating flowing creeks in canyons, steep hillsides, shallow valleys, and other details about the land. Contour lines showing elevation on such maps tell the well-informed hunter a great deal about vegetation types and temperatures he's likely to encounter, which areas are roughest and most inaccessible, where deer can water and seek midday shade, and so on.

No matter what the purpose—be it strictly orienting or a combination of orienting and deer-scouting—the best maps are by U.S. and Canadian federal agencies. They are available at many backpacking shops, survey equipment stores, and well-stocked bookstores. They show year-round and intermediate streams, roads of

Topographic maps allow you to familiarize yourself with a particular area before you see the countryside first-hand. Such maps also ensure exact orientation when used in conjunction with a well-made compass.

Maps of one sort or another are used extensively by avid hunters to aid in deer-scouting efforts. Careful studies of maps help pinpoint areas (as noted) that are likely to produce excellent hunting sport.

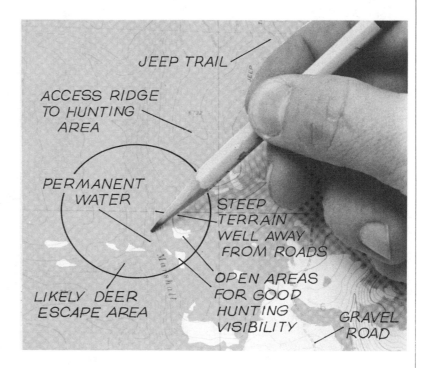

various types, contour lines giving elevations and an indication of the shape of the terrain, and an accurate grid indicating scale in miles. As with most maps, these also have meridian lines delineating the direction of true, static north plus a notation of declination to allow compass correction away from magnetic north. Hunters who study and carry such maps will probably never become "turned around" if they carry good-quality compasses, and will also know a great deal about the region before venturing out.

To obtain U.S. topographical maps by mail, write to the U.S. Geological Survey for an index in map form showing positions of topo maps within the state you are interested in. For areas east of the Mississippi River, including Minnesota, write to Branch of Distribution, U.S. Geological Survey, 1200 South Eads Street, Arlington, VA 22202. For areas west of the Mississippi River, write to Branch of Distribution, U.S. Geological Survey, Box 25276, Federal Center, Denver, CO 80225.

For Canadian maps, write Canada Map Office, 615 Booth Street, Ottawa, Ont., CANADA K1A 0E9. These maps are now based on the metric system.

When you receive the state or province index map, locate the area you plan to go to. It will have one or more rectangles over it showing map borders with the name of each map printed inside. Then, write to the appropriate U.S. Geological Survey (or Canadian) office requesting the maps you want, identifying them by name, series, and state (or province).

Maps other than those by U.S. and Canadian agencies can also help you keep your bearings. Road maps, maps issued by state and provincial game depart-

ments, and others all indicate true north in relation to the landscape, and all good ones also indicate magnetic declination to allow compass adjustment. Also, for home use and wall display, you can obtain plastic raised-relief maps (scale models of hunting regions) from Hubbard Scientific, Northbrook, IL 60062. For guidance on adjusting for declination and using map and compass together, refer to Part 10 of this book.

CANTEENS AND BOTA BAGS

A hunter's throat can become as dry as sterilized cotton in short order. As a result, deer hunters in all but the most water-laced country should carry canteens or water bags wherever they go.

Two conventional deer-hunting canteens are regular GI-issue bottle-type models and round, shoulder-carried canteens.

GI canteens are usually made of aluminum or tough plastic, although a few lucky hunters own genuine stainless-steel canteens of World War II vintage. The stainless models are most durable but are almost impossible to find anymore. Those of aluminum and plastic are excellent values too. The canteens are meant to be carried in canvas pouches on a woven military multipurpose belt.

Round, shoulder-carried canteens usually have semiflat sides to aid in toting. These canteens are not

A hot, thirsty hunter never enjoys himself as much as a well-watered one, and seldom probes difficult terrain a hunter with backpacker plastic water bottles is willing to investigate. (Neil Soderstrom photo)

A leather-covered bota bag holds ample liquid for a full day of hunting, makes no carrying noise, and slings out of the way across a hunter's shoulder or compresses to fit into a pack.

practical for carrying afield because they are bulky, heavy, and batter a hunter's ribs as he walks along. A round shoulder container is used primarily for fetching camp water from nearby creeks and streams.

One often-overlooked canteen style is perhaps the best of all for hunting deer. This is the bota bag—a flexible leather-covered water bag with a neoprene liner and handy screw-off cap. The bag is carried over the shoulder on a short, sturdy cord. Unlike other canteen styles, a flexible bota bag does not slosh water noisily or bang loudly on contact with rocks, tree limbs, a hunter's rifle, or other solid objects. This quietness alone makes such a water bag ideal for close-range bowhunting and rifle-hunting.

In addition to the foregoing canteens, a hunter can buy a variety of lightweight plastic water bottles and flasks designed with backpackers in mind. These containers are often carried in belt pouches; some must be carted in frameless backpacks with other gear.

FLASHLIGHTS

The only field flashlight worth a hoot is a sturdy, fairly expensive name-brand model. Although many hunters limp along with tiny disposable flashlights or cheap C-cell and D-cell models, these are apt to malfunction at the worst possible time. Actually, *anytime* a flashlight malfunctions is the worst time because without it a hunter cannot see what he's doing. In some sit-

Police lights made of black-anodized aircraft aluminum are the best of all hand-held flashlights. They are easily carried in leather belt loops for instant access in the field.

uations, flashlight malfunction is only mildly frustrating and worth a good laugh later. In others, the results can be tragic.

Several things can and do go wrong with poorly designed flashlights. Commonly, the off/on switches break, corrode, or simply wear out. On second-rate lights, electrical contact points between batteries and bulb also fail with regularity. These flimsy products are extremely easy to break because they incorporate thin, weak battery compartments made of plastic or base metal.

The best flashlights for the field are tough name-brand models with durable bodies made of heavy plastic, aluminum, or steel. Most hunters prefer a field light of the 2-D or 2-C cell configuration because such a model is compact and relatively lightweight. Coupled with the right bulb and long-lasting alkaline batteries, a 2-D or 2-C light will shine brightly for several hours as a hunter trails a crippled deer after dark or hoofs it back to camp.

A relatively large six-cell flashlight cannot be beat for use around a roadside hunting camp. This light throws a strong, long-lasting beam and usually takes heavy abuse without giving up the ghost.

The best of all sportsmen's flashlights is the so-called police type—a rugged design with black-anodized, aircraft-aluminum walls, and a sturdy switch guaranteed not to malfunction. This light is relatively heavy because its walls are thick enough to withstand being run over with an automobile. A flashlight this strong is not likely to fail a hunter in emergency situations. Police-type lights are sold in both D-cell and smaller C-cell configurations, generally hold an extra bulb in the rear end, and can be carried with tough leather belt loops made specially for this purpose.

For camp use only, a regular flashlight is fine. However, a larger, heavier six-cell flashlight throws a stronger beam and lasts longer on a battery too. Doz-ens of different six-cell light designs are sold at stores, and most are dependable.

FIRST AID AND SNAKEBITE KITS

Every deer hunter should own one or more first aid kits to handle minor and major outdoor emergencies. Most woodsmen carry two separate first aid kits afield—a fairly large, well-stocked kit for use around a roadside camp, and a shirt-pocket version for carrying in the field.

There are dozens upon dozens of excellent first aid kits sold in a myriad of places. The full-sized models need no great elaboration here—they are standard equipment and are not just designed for hunting. They usually include mild painkillers like aspirin or Tylenol, Emperin or other stronger painkiller, tablets for diarrhea, burn ointment, a tourniquet, antiseptic cream, assorted bandages, eyepads, gauze pads, adhesive tape, scissors for cutting bandages, tweezers for removing thorns and splinters, and so on. A hunter should always inspect the contents of a camp-size first aid kit, make sure it meets his basic needs, and add any special-purpose items needed for hunting, such as insect repellent and bite cream.

Smaller first aid kits for backpacking and day use in the field come in a variety of configurations, ranging from curving, molded-plastic containers that slip into any pocket to kits housed in small nylon stuff sacks. The contents of such kits are necessarily limited by space, but aspirin, bandages, antiseptic cream, gauze pads, and adhesive tape are all fairly standard.

A hunter adds to existing first aid kit contents for long stays in the field. He increases the supply of gauze, tape, and bandages, perhaps adds a thermometer for checking on a fever, and doubles aspirin or Tylenol supplies. There's nothing complex about the contents of first aid kits. If you are in doubt about unique field problems you may encounter, consult your physician and a druggist.

Some camp-size first aid kits come complete with snakebite kits. Deer sometimes inhabit the same country as poisonous snakes, such as rattlesnakes and water mocassins, making the possibility of snakebite very real. Only a tiny percentage of people actually die from snakebite in America, but a poisonous bite almost always results in hospitalization. Having a snakebite kit with scalpel, suction cups, possibly some antivenin, and instructions on how to use these items can minimize pain, reduce damage to tissue in the bite area, and lower the possibility of fatality. A hunter in snake country should always carry a snakebite kit on his person and add another to his camp first aid kit if it does not already have one.

First aid kits are available in many configurations. One of the handiest is a Scout-type shirt-pocket model with a tough plastic case. (Neil Soderstrom photo)

Nothing can warm body and soul like a campfire. A sensible deer hunter always carries fire-starting equipment on his person to provide comfort and ensure emergency field survival.

TRAIL MARKERS

In heavy forest a deer hunter should always carry ample trail-marking material to help him flag important landmark locations and mark trails to downed deer. It is amazingly easy to permanently lose a deer carcass if you have to leave it in the field for a time—a heartbreaking occurrence easily avoided if you drape marker material along the way between your kill and the nearest easily found landmark. Similarly, important but hard-to-find places like trailheads in heavy brush, waterhole locations, and food caches are best marked in a highly visible manner to prevent wasted time.

The best trail-marking material available is fluorescent-orange surveyor's tape. This thin plastic material is available in large rolls at survey supply stores and stands out in the woods. Other tape colors, such as red, blue, and yellow, work all right too but sometimes blend with fall leaves and branches. An alternate marker material is toilet paper in any bright color. This sometimes blows away in winds or washes away in downpours but is certainly better than nothing if a hunter heads for camp to get help to drag out his deer or wishes to mark a newly found spring of cold, clear water. The only alternative to carrying trail-marking material is blazing a trail on trees with a pocket knife or belt hatchet—that wounds trees and takes up precious time.

FIRE-STARTING GEAR

For sake of safety as well as convenience, you should always carry fire-starting gear in the woods. In dry

One simple but effective fire-starting kit consists of ordinary, strike-anywhere matches inside a waterproof 35mm film canister. This combo slips in any pocket and provides fire when you need it.

HOW TO MAKE TOILET-PAPER FIRE STARTERS

1. *To make a toilet-paper fire starter, first melt a quantity of paraffin inside a glass jar. To do this without danger of fire, boil the jar in a pan of water.*

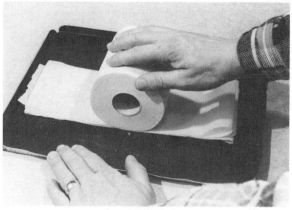

2. *Roll six or eight layers of ordinary toilet paper onto a metal cookie sheet. Paper color is a matter of personal preference, but yellow shows up best if accidentally dropped on snow or onto a dry forest floor.*

3. *Once the paraffin is completely melted, pour it liberally over toilet-paper layers. The toilet paper will soak up the wax and thereby form one contiguous sheet of paper and paraffin.*

4. *Allow the paraffin to solidify for a minute or two. While the wax is firm but still warm to the touch, use the edge of a spatula to scribe around the toilet paper and separate it from the overflow.*

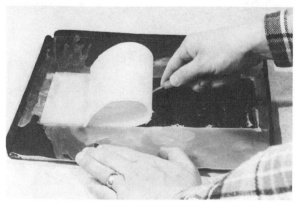

5. *Carefully remove the sheet of wax-saturated toilet paper from the metal sheet while the paraffin is still warm and moderately pliable. If wax sets up cold and hard, it will stick to a cookie sheet like glue.*

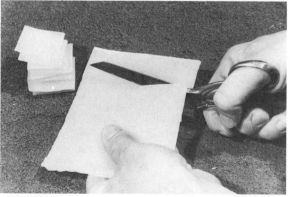

6. *Cut the sheet of TP firestarter into 2-inch squares with an ordinary pair of scissors. Again, this step should be accomplished before the wax cools and becomes semi-brittle in consistency.* (Continued on next page)

(Continued from previous page)

6. *Toilet-paper fire starter is best stored in small plastic sandwich bags that prevent waxy residue from rubbing off on clothing. A dozen firestarter squares can be carried in any shirt or pants pocket.*

7. *A toilet-paper fire starter square lights instantly at the corner and burns for several minutes even in wet outdoor situations. Three or four squares will usually dry out and ignite damp, small-gauge twigs and limbs.*

weather, when natural tinder is abundant, any source of flame is enough for making midday campfires, emergency signal fires, or fires for heat at night. If weather is apt to be damp, some sort of long-burning substance should also be carried to dry small twigs and get a fire going.

Most expert woodsmen carry matches and butane cigarette lighters for starting fires. Both work well, but butane lighters are more dependable in wet weather. Matches carried in a waterproof container such as plastic 35mm film cannisters are fairly dependable bets, and matches with the heads dipped in paraffin are even better.

If newspaper, toilet paper, or another easily ignited starter is available, a so-called Metal Match that sparks and ignites its own metal shavings is also a fine source of flame—especially in survival situations.

Most savvy deer hunters carry some sort of long-burning substance to help start fires in wet weather. Commercial fire-starting tablets work fairly well, but tend to burn hot and go out quickly. Wax paper or dry slivers of pitch pine also work well. A stub of wax candle is even better and burns steadily under damp tinder for several minutes. Perhaps the best wet-weather fire-helper is toilet-paper fire starter, which can be made at home by pouring hot paraffin over several layers of toilet paper (see photo series beginning on previous page). When cut into squares, "TP fire starter" can be carried in a pocket for starting fires in any situation.

In a real pinch, any sort of lubricating oil or penetrating oil can be used to coat damp tinder and get a fire going. A little WD-40 or heavy gun oil has saved more than one hunter on a cold, shivering night in the field.

GAME-CARE PRODUCTS

Deer hunters normally use several special-purpose items in caring for a deer carcass once it is ready for transport back to camp. Such game-care aids include hanging gambrels, deer bags, deer hoists, and deer drags.

Gambrels. A gambrel is a simple double-hook device for hanging a deer by its hind legs. Gambrels vary in design from simple one-piece models of steel or aluminum to more elaborate versions incorporating scales for weighing a trophy once it is hung. As long as a gambrel has a ring at the top for attachment to

A deer-hanging gambrel is usually a simple, one-piece device with a hanging loop at the top and two leg hooks spread about 2 feet apart. This game-care aid is sometimes used with a spring scale to accurately determine trophy weight.

a rope and two hooks below spread about 2 feet apart, it will work well for hoisting deer above the ground.

Deer bags. Deer bags are sold at sporting goods stores and perform two important functions in the field. First, they fully enclose a carcass or carcass quarters to keep out meat-damaging blowflies and carnivorous insects. Second, they surround a deer with a sun-reflecting white surface to keep meat cooler and help minimize chances of spoilage.

There are good deer bags and not-so-good deer bags. The best are made of sturdy, rough-weave cotton cloth that resists ripping. They also have drawstrings at the top to allow tight, bug-discouraging closure. The poorest deer bags are unfortunately the most commonly sold. These are made of thin, see-through gauze that tears easily, does not shield out heat, and clings to a carcass, keeping it moist and allowing in-

Deer-quarter bags adequately protect the parts of an animal if made from white, close-knit cloth. At best, such bags incorporate drawstrings to fully shield meat from flies and other insects.

sects to eat and deposit eggs right through the mesh.

Most deer bags are large enough to cover an entire deer, but smaller deer-quarter bags are also sold at some stores. These work equally well, provided a hunter doesn't mind cutting his deer into four pieces. In a pinch, old pillow cases can double as quarter bags, and so can burlap sacks.

Deer hoists. Small block-and-tackle setups and ratchet-arm hoists are commonly sold to allow hunters to hang deer all by themselves. Two hunters can easily hoist a deer by hand with a rope and gambrel alone, but mechanical leverage is almost a must if a hunter must hang a full-size deer all alone.

Deer drags. In fairly flat country where dragging a deer is the most feasible transport method, nothing beats a special commercial deer-drag harness. One end of this harness attaches to the head or antlers of a deer, and the other end wraps about the hunter's waist or shoulders. With such a rig, the hunter can trudge along with both hands free as the deer slides along behind. Anyone who has dragged deer a long distance by hand knows how tough this exercise can be on hands and arms, not to mention other muscles strained during the awkward, body-twisting process. Deer drags of various types are commonly available. They cost relatively little and do a splendid job if terrain is not too rugged.

VEHICLE GEAR

Hunters should check out vehicle accessory equipment designed to aid off-road driving and give access to firearms in vehicles. Winches, tire chains, and sim-

A good winch can be a bona fide godsend in slippery off-road situations. This accessory can make the difference between deer-hunting fun and outdoor misery when tires suddenly spin and refuse to move any farther on their own. Tire chains can also prove invaluable.

ilar rough-road or foul-weather equipment can improve a hunter's chances of getting in and out of productive deer areas. Special automobile gun racks can prevent firearm damage on bouncing roads and also provide easy gun access. These and similar vehicle-related items are sold at auto parts stores and well-stocked gun shops.

PART 6
HUNTING METHODS

BY CHUCK ADAMS

Photos by the author unless otherwise credited. Drawings by Lloyd Birmingham and Charles W. Schwartz.

Man is a natural hunter with all the physical attributes needed to efficiently pursue and kill big-game animals. Zealous anti-hunters who deny this statement blatantly ignore some basic human facts. Like all meat-eating predators, men have eyes in the front of their heads to gauge distance to their prey and make accurate pounces or projectile aims. Their legs are designed to walk long distances in search of game, and their arms and fingers are free to wield weapons and reduce animals to eating-size portions. Mankind is blessed with a dental structure and gastric system equally suited to eating meat and vegetables.

Man's very temperament is also that of the hunter, with adrenaline flooding and preparing his body for action whenever the quarry appears. Polite, sedentary society may dull natural hunting instincts, but the basic biological mechanisms remain largely unchanged. When given half a chance, man becomes a highly effective hunting machine.

Successful, reflective deer hunters unabashedly enjoy their innate predatory instincts and make no apology for them. Instead of burying inbred outdoor abilities, they seek to refine and channel them for maximum game-getting potential. They learn to become fully aware of their surroundings and spot deer with wolflike keenness. They heighten their ability to silently pad through the woods or sit unobtrusively on stand, stalking deer with catlike stealth or lying in ambush like hawks after meadow mice. They become attuned to the subtle sounds of the forest, learn to read sign like a large-print children's book, and consciously develop hunting and shooting habits that help them get the game. In so doing, avid hunters fit into the ecosystem as neatly as any coyote, mountain lion, or similar predator.

It has often been said that 10 percent of the hunters take 90 percent of the deer, and this statement is largely fact. Deer hunters as a group have the desire and driving instinct to pursue animals, but the successful minority *work* at their sport by combining instinct with conscious effort and a strong determination to improve. These individuals keep tabs on current deer regulations, actively scout before season to locate pockets of animals, and make certain their shooting skills are up to snuff. They also consider the basic habits and habitats of deer they plan to hunt and match these variables with strategies. Successful hunters also make it a point of learning where to aim on deer and what to do once bullet or arrow hits are made. Such attention to detail usually makes the difference between success and failure.

Leonard Lee Rue III photo

PRESEASON GROUNDWORK

The importance of preseason preparation for deer hunting is best illustrated with examples. Here is how two different gunners proceeded with their North Woods hunting trips.

The first hunter was a robust, physically fit young fellow with enthusiasm in his eye. He had dreamed of huge bucks throughout the year and shot his rifle often to be fully prepared for action. He had never actually taken a deer, but had seen a few afield and felt especially ready this year. On opening day, he tramped into a hardwood forest near home—a place his father had hunted successfully for many, many years. The leaves were damp and quiet, and no other hunters were in the vicinity. But he sneaked about this area all day long without seeing even one scraggly doe or fawn. During the week that followed, he canvassed his dad's old stomping ground from one end to the other, still confident a trophy buck would suddenly materialize. At season's end, he was still dreaming about giant racks and cursing his bad luck.

The second hunter was also young, lean, and enthusiastic. He lived in the same town as the first hunter

Nice bucks like this high-racked blacktail fall consistently to well-practiced hunting skills. It's no accident that a majority of deer are bagged by a minority consisting of the highly skilled hunters.

Man is well equipped for hunting deer. His eyes spot game and estimate distance. His hands wield weapons, and his legs pursue game.

and shot on the very same rifle range. This was his first deer hunt, but he had read quite a bit on the subject. He impatiently awaited opening day. The month before season, he called his state game department and talked with the head deer biologist for nearly an hour. The weekend after that, he gathered up some dog-eared maps and spent all day Saturday driving around and walking through the hardwood forests near his home. On Monday, he called the game department again, talked briefly, and then called the local game warden for another short but lively chat. On opening morning of deer season, he drove a short distance from home, parked his vehicle, and eagerly entered the woods.

Late the same afternoon, this second hunter was gutting a fat-laden buck with antlers spreading well beyond its ears. He had seen seven other deer throughout the course of the day, including another smaller buck.

The first hunter is typical of many well-meaning but unprepared outdoorsmen. He hunts his heart out and curses his luck if deer do not appear. By contrast, the second hunter knows he must *make* his own luck.

A key to deer-hunting success is locating areas with ample populations of deer. Equally important for many hunters is pinpointing places with particular *kinds* of deer—a high percentage of trophy-antlered bucks, plenty of fat, healthy meat animals. Once a productive habitat that suits the hunter's requirements is found, the next step is to pattern the habits of deer in this area. That makes it possible to develop a hunting strategy. All successful hunters lay such deer-getting groundwork well before the season actually begins.

DECIDING WHEN AND WHERE TO HUNT

The best way to begin planning a deer hunt is to consult current hunting regulations to determine facts about upcoming deer seasons. In most U.S. states and Canadian provinces, biologists modify yearly season dates and bag limits to accommodate changing deer populations. Factors such as hunting pressure, availability of deer food, and weather all directly affect deer-population dynamics and in turn determine hunting season length, season dates, and deer-tag availability. There is no such thing as a deer-hunting area that is always good. Population levels and trophy-producing potential constantly fluctuate. Since hunting regulations in different hunting districts reflect the condition of deer populations, check first on regulations.

Hunting regulations also answer certain other practical questions—questions like how expensive a deer tag will be, whether or not a hunting guide is required, which firearms are legal and which are not, what hunting methods, if any, are illegal, and so on. A hunter who pores over deer regulations governing his own state or other areas where he might wish to hunt can *plan* a hunt that fits his time schedule, bank account, and preferred deer-hunting technique. For example, a hunter who has vacation time coming in October and wants to fill his freezer with venison can shop for a season that allows multiple deer tags in October. By contrast, another hunter who wants to bag one trophy buck during the November rut will search regulations for an area and season accommodating these requirements. Even the undecided or neophyte hunter can benefit by studying current regulations because they will define his hunting options.

Consulting deer biologists and game wardens. A conscientious hunter follows up his perusal of state or provincial regulations with more substantive study of upcoming deer hunts. Research into hunting areas and seasons is smart for anyone planning to try a new state or area for the first time, but it's also advisable for hunters planning to return to favorite hunting spots. The worst mistake any hunter can make is *assuming* that an area is good for deer just because it was last year or in years past. One harsh winter, one summertime logging operation, or one outbreak of animal disease can ruin a high-yield deer area in a matter of months. Likewise, a variety of factors can turn formerly poor deer habitat into superb hunting terrain. The best deer hunters remain flexible in hunting-area selection and double-check deer conditions each year.

The easiest and most dependable way to research deer areas is to contact local game wardens and state or county deer biologists. These experts monitor game

Careful deer-scouting gets the game. Do your preseason homework and you will know where animals are when opening day rolls around. That way you can concentrate on actually hunting deer.

populations on a month-in, month-out basis and often have an active influence on annual hunting regulations. As a result, they are abundantly qualified to say where deer herds are healthy and where hunting is apt to be marginal. They can also recommend *when* hunting is apt to be the best—a determination based on such factors as likely changes in weather, predictable deer-migration trends, and so on. A polite hunter can often obtain valuable deer-hunting information by calling game biologists and game wardens at their regular places of business. Any state or provincial game department office will readily supply the names and telephone numbers of qualified experts on deer.

Researching trophy hotspots. Some hunters are avid trophy buffs. But the disorganized enthusiasts usually only dream about big antlers and don't get the chance to take a trophy. By contrast, savvy hunters concentrate their efforts in established antler-producing hotspots with the necessary remoteness, weather, food, minerals, and genetic potential to grow wall-hanging racks. An amazingly high percentage of trophy hunters neglect this vital research and waste years of effort in places devoid of bragging-size bucks.

The trick to bagging a trophy is to hunt hard in areas with a recent history of record trophies. These areas are not difficult to locate if you know how to proceed. To a minor degree, state game biologists can steer trophy hunters in the right direction. However, as a group such professionals tend to pay more attention to deer *numbers* than average antler size. Even biologists who *are* trophy oriented seldom give away their favorite big-buck haunts to strangers who telephone them.

Far more dependable gauges of trophy production

are the American hunting record books, such as the Boone and Crockett Club *Records of North American Big Game* and the Pope and Young Club *Bowhunting Big Game Records*. These two books are the trophy hunter's official bibles. They are available through most public libraries and bookstores, and are also sold at many sporting goods stores. The books are important because they list when and where the top bucks have been taken in North America. When properly used, they indicate where trophy hunters should concentrate their efforts.

Take Columbian blacktail deer as an example. These small, Pacific Coast deer are abundant within a 200-mile-wide habitat that stretches from central California northward through Oregon, Washington, and southern British Columbia. However, certain parts of this range produce bigger racks than others. The record books bear this out. For example, the Boone and Crockett book lists over 300 exceptional blacktails taken by modern sport hunters—nearly 150 from California, about 100 from Oregon, approximately 75 from Washington, and only a dozen or so from British Columbia. On the surface, this seems to indicate that California is the best place to hunt record-size deer. However, many of the record-book deer were taken decades ago when habitat and hunting conditions were different. So, a researcher should look only at *recent* entries to formulate an accurate trophy-hunting strategy.

Blacktail bucks shot during the past decade indicate that the long-term trend still holds true today; California is the trophy-producing king. A close look at California listings shows that three counties reign supreme as trophy producers—Trinity, Siskiyou, and Mendocino. These counties are adjacent to one another in the northwestern part of the state, and together

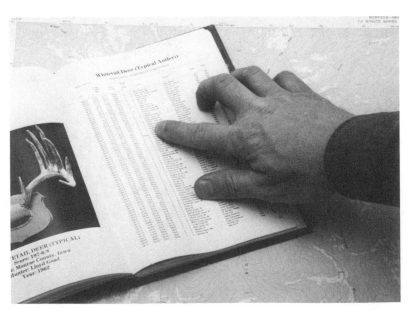

A careful look at record lists tells you when and where the biggest bucks of various species have been taken. This helps narrow the field of potential trophy-producing hotspots.

form a trophy blacktail hotspot. Most other parts of coastal California, although loaded with blacktail deer, fail to make the record lists.

A similar analysis of record books will show where trophy mule deer, whitetail deer, and other varieties are apt to be found. Record books are excellent trophy-trend indicators because for every "book" animal entered from a particular region, many others have not been entered or were tremendous racks but did not quite measure up to record class.

Once a trophy hunter isolates a specific hotspot he'd like to explore, he can refine his hunting plans by contacting the deer biologist familiar with this area. The result will be a wealth of information about topography, deer numbers, suggested hunting techniques, and related factors.

Finding meat deer. As mentioned before, the majority of state and provincial deer biologists are concerned primarily with deer numbers—not with trophy size. As a result, these experts are *the* people to ask about first-rate meat-hunting areas. The hunter who wants to fill a freezer instead of a trophy room needs access to lots of animals to have the best chance for success. In some cases, lots of animals and trophy animals go together. However, more often the two do not. So a meat hunter should deliberately find an area with plenty of deer per square mile and not concern himself with trophies.

Other factors. Careful deer hunters try to anticipate problems connected with a hunting trip long before they leave. For example, they find out how remote and how rugged various potential deer hotspots are, and also learn what weather conditions are apt to be. Hunters who always hunt deer close to home already

know such things, but those planning out-of-state deer excursions should do some digging to find out. A hunter who wants to set up a cozy roadside deer camp will be out of luck if the animals are ten miles away from pavement. Or an enthusiastic but overweight hunter will be heartsick to discover that pitons, ropes, and climbing spikes are required to get to a chosen hotspot.

PRESEASON SCOUTING TIPS

If at all possible, scout chosen deer areas prior to season or during the first few days of a hunt to *precisely* locate concentrations of animals. Deer invariably gravitate to the especially comfortable living situations where there is ample water, excellent food, shady bedding cover, and good terrain protection from hunters. A hunter's first in-the-field task should be to discover where the best deer pockets are within a generally productive area. Such pockets may shift around from week to week, month to month, or year to year as external situations change. A consistently successful hunter cannot sit on his laurels and *assume* he knows where animals are.

Making educated guesses. Most longtime deer hunters can make some fairly accurate guesses about the whereabouts of deer within general deer-rich areas. For example, after season opens in accessible places, deer tend to migrate to little out-of-the-way hideaways where they are not often disturbed by hoards of hunters. These are sometimes rugged can-

Once opening-day guns go off, deer will move away from hunting pressure, sometimes seeking out torturous hellholes with steep and/or brushy topography like this.

Deer seldom stray far from ponds (shown in background) and other reliable sources of water. In average weather, most deer drink once a day—in extremely hot conditions, they may drink two or more times in one 24-hour period.

Knowledgeable hunters seek out hunting areas with excellent feed for deer, so your preseason scouting should include analysis of plant growth. Places with ample browse like oak brush and nutritious grass like wild oats (above) generally hold deer in very good numbers.

yons or draws, and sometimes just dense thickets of brush and trees.

Similarly, experienced hunters know what kinds of food deer prefer in their favorite hunting districts—corn or alfalfa in a typical farmland whitetail area, sagebrush or snowberry in a foothill mule-deer haunt, or manzanita and oak brush in high-country blacktail terrain. Hunters educated in basic deer needs can make guesses on the whereabouts of deer that usually hit the nail on the head.

Seasoned hunters new to a particular deer habitat seldom have difficulty locating deer. They know that animals of a particular variety have certain standard habits no matter what the location. A scouting hunter who pores over topographic maps of an area and then eyeballs it firsthand can often guess exactly where deer will be before he ever tramps the woods. He does this by knowing that heavy bedding cover grows in certain places, that year-round streams and lakes are most likely watering places for animals, that certain canyons are roadless and thus not visited by lots of hunters, and so on. Such educated guessing, based on past experience, provides a skeletal framework. Firsthand scouting fleshes it in with facts.

SCOUTING FOR SIGN

After a hunter decides on the general area and makes some educated guesses about where animals are likely to be, the next step is to go out into the woods and scout for sign. The sign will substantiate hunches about exact locations of game. Even if deer are tucked away in thickets dense enough to strangle a wood mouse, the sign they've left behind is solid evidence of their day-in, day-out movements.

Sign takes several forms and reads like a book to savvy woodsmen. The following sections describe the various types of sign and how to "read" them.

Tracks. The most common form of deer sign and one of the easiest to locate and analyze is the hoofprint. No matter how cagey a deer happens to be, the animal leaves telltale tracks in mud, soft dirt, and snow. Areas littered with deer tracks usually have plenty of deer.

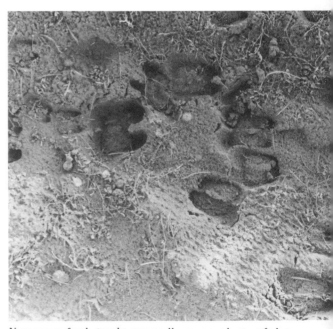

Numerous fresh tracks generally mean plenty of deer nearby, especially when tracks seem to be meandering in more than one direction. Savvy hunters look for tracks prior to season as they attempt to pinpoint hotspots.

When scouting for tracks, pay attention to the number of tracks, direction, and freshness. Each of these considerations is important.

Deer-rich areas usually have tracks almost everywhere—so many that casting about is unnecessary. But in some areas deer do not roam widely during hunting season. Then you must walk extensively until you locate one or more little draws or pockets where there are plenty of tracks.

In most decent deer areas, tracks meander in all directions instead of being lined out on one basic course. An area with all tracks pointed in a single direction is invariably a migration area—a place that might provide red-hot hunting if you intercept the migration. For instance, certain intermediate elevations are excellent for hunting migratory mule deer when the first heavy snows hit high-up summer range.

But there are hazards in trying to ambush migrating deer. More than one naive gunner waiting in ambush along a migration trail has twiddled his thumbs for days on end because herds of mountain mule deer are already dozens of miles below him. When deer move from summer to winter habitat, they often do so quickly, leaving tantalizing but worthless sign behind. Such sign is obviously old to experienced woodsmen, but openly inviting to novices.

Generally, a small area with plenty of fresh tracks pointing in various directions will have huntable numbers of deer. Fresh tracks are easiest to identify in mud and snow, and most difficult to identify in dry dust. No matter what the footing, the freshest tracks (under two days old) have sharp edges with little or no debris like leaves and twigs inside. Older tracks in mud tend to be light-colored and dry around the rim, and older tracks in snow have poorly defined edges, often partially melted away. Fresh tracks in powdery snow are sometimes fuzzy in shape, but are obviously fresh because breezes have not yet sifted new snow over them.

A deer track left in the dust can appear fresh for days if there is no breeze or precipitation. However, old tracks in dust tend to lack clean, sharp edges and generally contain leaf segments and similar natural litter. In addition, a close scrutiny of such deer tracks usually shows tiny insect trails across the hoof impressions—evidence the prints were made some time back.

Trails and fence crossings. A few deer areas—especially whitetail areas—are too heavily overgrown with grass to show clear tracks in soil. In such areas, a scouting hunter can still determine if huntable numbers of deer are present by paying close attention to trails and fence crossings. Deer moving about a patch of woods tramp down a network of body-wide trails, mashing foliage underfoot and shouldering brush out of the way. Similarly, deer generally belly fences where

The best deer areas are laced with regularly traveled trails. Even when grass, leaves, and other debris make hoofprints impossible to see, well-defined trails ensure that you'll see deer.

they cross and sometimes leave a little hair behind on barbed-wire strands. Well-beaten deer paths plus telltale fence crossings indicate the presence of deer, even where tracks are nearly impossible to see.

Droppings. Deer droppings are even easier to age than tracks. Deer litter feeding areas with small piles of pellets—pellets that quickly harden and age. Deer dung that is fairly fresh is black in color and soft when squeezed. Dung less than 24 hours old is usually quite soft and somewhat slippery on the surface. By contrast, old dung pellets are brown or off-white and hard or crumbly. An area with abundant, fresh deer pellets usually holds animals in huntable numbers.

Deer beds. Deer are simple creatures that eat, drink, and rest periodically throughout the day and night. They generally bed in the same basic areas day after day, creating oval, washtub-sized beds in the grass or dirt. Some beds are easier to identify than others, but all are relatively obvious to an experienced hunter.

A fresh deer bed in the grass is tough to find. Grass

Recent deer droppings are nearly black in color and extremely soft to the touch. The freshest dung also has decidedly slick surfaces. Deer droppings are abundant near regular feeding areas.

is merely flattened in all directions from hours of lounging around. Deer usually rise and swap ends periodically as they rest, thoroughly leveling all plant growth underneath. Signs of a bed in grass do not last, however, because foliage springs upright again not long after the deer leaves.

In soft dirt, pine needles, or leaves, deer generally paw out shallow depressions for added resting comfort. These little dishes are easy to spot as you cruise the woods. The fresh ones are obvious because dirt is disturbed and recently scuffed by hoofs and moving

bodies. Like old tracks, old deer beds are littered with debris and lack the sharp, clean lines of freshly disturbed soil.

Deer beds are found in different sorts of terrain, depending upon the species, weather situation, and time of year. Generally speaking, whitetails bed in heavy brush and trees, and mule deer bed in wide-open country or semi-open areas with scattered trees and brush.

Beds in snow can be analyzed much like tracks in snow, discussed earlier.

Antler rubs. All buck deer shed their antler velvet sometime between late July and mid-September. Exact timing depends on the latitude and elevation of the place where the deer live. During the process of shedding velvet, bucks vigorously scrape their racks against trees and bushes, scarring and sometimes denuding them of branches.

Later on, during the rut, bucks again attack foliage with their racks. These mating rubs are more vigorous and more damaging to bushes and trees, leaving unique sign that are easy to spot.

The value of antler rubs in scouting is fairly obvious. During summer deer seasons, freshly thrashed limbs betray the presence of bucks. During the fall mating season, fresh, unhealed rubs on willows and other foliage mean a mature buck is frequenting the area. So the hunter knows he is not wasting his efforts in an area without bucks.

Buck scrapes. Scrapes are a specialized form of sign created by rutting whitetail bucks. These are bare,

Deer bed on and off throughout the day and night. If you keep a sharp eye out, you will spot washtub-size depressions or flat areas the deer leave behind. This sign promises decent hunting in the immediate vicinity.

First-rate deer areas have plenty of buck rubs. Deer make minor rubs in late summer as they strip velvet from their antlers. Major rubbing occurs when bucks enter the rut and thrash foliage in mating frenzy.

Lovelorn whitetail bucks roam their territories during rutting season, chasing receptive does and fighting other bucks. The territories are marked by scrapes pawed in the ground to attract area females that are in heat. (Russell Thornberry photo.)

sexually frustrated bucks. Bigger, better established scrapes are visited frequently by both bucks and does. Bucks regularly urinate in these sexual meeting places to attract does, making major scrapes ideal places for hunters to wait in ambush. Any whitetail area with lots of minor and major scrapes in late fall is a top bet for hunting.

GLASSING FROM A DISTANCE

Deer are quite secretive by nature, making them fairly difficult to find during the midday hours when most hunters do their preseason scouting. However, the hunter who gets out before dawn or stays afield until dark can sometimes spot deer with the aid of powerful field glasses. Deer are most active early and late in the day, and often betray movement patterns at these prime feeding times.

There is no substitute for searching out tracks, droppings, beds, rubs, and other deer sign, but actually spotting deer with a binocular gives sign extra meaning and helps a hunter put venison in the bag.

There are two basic types of binocular scouting. In fairly flat farm country, typical of many productive whitetail areas, hunters working from roads glass likely feeding fields near dawn and dusk. In more mountainous terrain inhabited by mule deer and blacktail deer, the accepted procedure is walking ridgetops and scanning terrain from elevated knobs, bluffs, and other vantage points. If terrain is a mixture of hills and flat-

pawed-out places on the ground used by a dominant buck to mark his territory and attract a doe. Scrapes take two forms—minor scrapes, generally less than 2 feet in diameter; and major scrapes, which are sometimes bigger than bathtubs.

Both minor and major scrapes are always formed beneath fairly low overhead limbs projecting from trees or bushes. There is some speculation about why this is the case, but rutting bucks experience some sort of positive sensation by grasping overhead foliage in their mouths as they paw out scrapes with their hoofs. Some say these animals are leaving scent on foliage with glands located near their eyes. Others claim the branches merely tickle the supersensitive noses of bucks to provide a rut-related pleasure. Whatever the case, scrapes are always found beneath limbs a buck can reach with his mouth and nose.

Minor scrapes are usually the one-time creations of

Glassing from a distance is one of the best ways to scout for farmland whitetail. Deer usually come out to feed in crop fields just after sundown.

land, the best bet is sitting high in one spot at dawn and dusk or moving about just enough to enjoy two or three different expansive views.

A hunter who scouts with a binocular can learn three things about deer behavior before season actually begins. First, he can locate feeding areas and the general bedding areas the animals use. Second, he can often pinpoint particular areas deer pass through with regularity between beds and feeding places. At best, scouting will actually show which trails are most frequently used by deer, letting him erect productive stands later. The third advantage of pre-season scouting is evaluating the trophy quality of animals. A scouter with a binocular can often spot trophy bucks and devise strategies for taking these *specific*

animals. By contrast, the trophy hunter who enters an area cold or merely checks for sign can only surmise the antler size and number of mature bucks in the immediate vicinity.

Glassing deer from a distance can provide one other important bit of information. In some hard-hunted areas, deer tend to be nocturnal and move long distances under cover of darkness. In such situations, tracks and other sign may be worthless because they indicate where deer are during illegal hours. The only way to be sure of where deer actually are is by watching them poke their noses out of brush at last light and slip into cover again at the first blush of day. Otherwise you may set up a stand or hike about a track-tattooed area that is devoid of animals during the daytime.

Take the gung-ho, but inexperienced, whitetail hunter who located a well-used trail meandering through wide-open fields of alfalfa and erected a stand in the only tree for half a mile around. On the opening afternoon of deer season, this fellow climbed hand over hand to his 25-foot-high perch and settled in to wait patiently. If tracks were any indication, he thought, action will not be long in coming.

Seven days later the hunter climbed his stand for what seems like the umpteenth time, still convinced his strategy was right. However, his sour face reflected the fact that not one deer had appeared despite clear views in all directions. For the first time, the hunter had a binocular around his neck, and as twilight fell he began to canvas the surrounding terrain. .

Holy Toledo! At least 75 deer appeared magically in his field glass—all hugging a densely wooded river bottom 1,000 yards away. Suddenly a light went on within the hunter's head. All those deer were drifting

An inexperienced hunter who sits on stand in an open field full of tracks may wait for weeks in vain. That is because the wary deer only venture out into the field during the night.

in his direction, sure enough, but none were yet visible to the naked eye. He realized his stand was probably surrounded by deer at midnight or 2 A.M., but never during legal hours. All those smoking-hot tracks along the trail directly below were nighttime tracks—tracks of hay-hungry but hunter-wary deer!

Not all geographical regions are conducive to scouting for deer with binoculars. For example, the dense swamplands of the Deep South, the flat, featureless brush-country of south Texas, and the rainforests of the Pacific Northwest seldom allow long-distance viewing. In those places scouting for deer sign is the best a hunter can do before opening day.

SCOUTING AT NIGHT

In places where deer are heavily pressured by hunters and have become somewhat nocturnal, scouting at night with spotlights or automobile headlights can be highly productive. Night scouting is not legal in all areas, but some states and provinces allow the spotlighting of deer provided scouters do not have firearms in their possession at the time.

Whitetail deer in agricultural habitat are especially susceptible to diligent nighttime scouting. Even animals that hug heavy cover throughout the day often venture into ankle-deep hayfields or knee-deep stretches of stubble after dark. Scouting at night reveals exactly how many deer are using particular feeding areas, and also betrays the presence of trophy bucks that are seldom seen during casual daytime scouting sessions.

FLYING LIKELY TERRAIN

An increasing number of truly dedicated deer hunters also use an airplane in their deer scouting. Thirty minutes or an hour of flying time in a Super Cub or similar aircraft can tell a hunter more about deer areas and the animals that live there than weeks of on-the-ground scouting. Flying deer habitat is especially productive in semiopen terrain because animals are fairly easy to spot during peak feeding hours. In addition, a hunter gets a good idea of the lay of the land from an airplane tour of a foothill area or mountain range. For example, he can see exactly where access roads are located, where remote and inaccessible places lie, how dense foliage is, and so on. Such information can be gleaned from a topographic map too, but nothing can match a bird's-eye view of the terrain itself.

A few hunters own their own airplanes. However,

Shed deer antlers like this one show the trophy potential of given areas. Thus you should scout for cast-off racks in areas you plan to hunt.

the overwhelming majority must hire a pilot to chauffeur them around. Charter flights are fairly expensive, but can easily be arranged at most major airports. Generally speaking, airplane scouting is most beneficial for mule deer and least beneficial for bottomland whitetail deer. Areas with ample roads are easily scouted without the use of a plane. But mountainous muley haunts, the least accessible to vehicular traffic, are ideal for airplane scouting.

EVALUATING SHED ANTLERS

One form of deer scouting is largely overlooked by all but a few serious trophy hunters. This is searching for shed antlers and evaluating an area's trophy potential based on cast-off racks. Because whitetail deer most often frequent the same territory throughout the year, shed antlers reveal the presence of big bucks even if the animals themselves remain hidden. Hunters looking for shed antlers usually canvass chosen hunting areas during off-season months with their eyes riveted to the ground. Patience generally yields plenty of picked-up antlers and a fairly decent notion how big the bucks are.

Hunters familiar with the movement patterns of

mule deer and blacktails can also use shed antlers to gauge available trophy size. However, these highly mobile types of deer sometimes drop their racks dozens of miles from where they are during open hunting season, making dropped-antler speculations far more chancy. It is a common mistake of beginning hunters to waste their time hunting in a wintering area where they found lots of shed mule-deer antlers. Meanwhile, the deer are far away in cool, high-country summer habitat.

ADVANCED SCOUTING TECHNIQUES

Searching for sign and looking for deer at a distance are the two primary scouting techniques used in preseason preparation. However, a few dedicated hunters with the free time go even further to ensure success. Elaborate scouting measures are important in deer areas with short hunting seasons because locating deer and discovering movement patterns can waste valuable hunting time. But the techniques are most commonly used in areas where cover is very thick and observation of deer is almost impossible.

Dusting trails is one of the most useful scouting methods. To do this, you simply slip into likely deer habitat at midday and dust away all tracks on several well-established deer trails with a branch or hat. You then return the next day and observe how many new tracks have been laid down. Several dusting sessions can tell you precisely how many deer pass a particular point per day, and which directions the animals are moving. This shows the best places to locate a tree stand or ground blind.

The most elaborate form of preseason deer scouting is to actually set up a trial hunt, minus gun or bow. To do this the hunter plans his strategy, erects a tree stand or blind, and waits during prime hunting hours to see what passes by. Although a few walking hunters attempt trial hunts, tramping about the hills tends to spook deer and ruin the real hunt. A stand hunter seldom alerts deer and thus benefits by a trial run; a walker is better off waiting for the season to open.

SCOUTING HEAVILY HUNTED AREAS

In deer areas likely to receive heavy hunting pressure, even careful scouting efforts may be rendered useless once opening-day guns go off. Deer tend to change their movement patterns dramatically in the face of severe hunting pressure—a fact every hunter should consider prior to spending large amounts of time learning what deer are doing *before* the season begins.

Virtually every longtime hunter has suffered the heartbreak of scouting plans gone sour. This can happen quite rapidly when other hunters interfere. Take the hunter who watched several trophy-size muley bucks and numerous does eat, drink, and sleep in one high mountain basin for several weeks before season. Well before dawn on opening day, he made his way noiselessly toward the lower, downwind edge of his secret hotspot. He crouched behind a table-size granite rock, waiting for daylight and shivering with the cold and excitement. His rifle was tuned to drive tacks at 100 yards, his clothing carefully chosen to blend with surrounding terrain, and his backpack stuffed with bone saw, drag rope, and other deer-care necessities. He knew the bucks were well inside shooting range, knew his own shooting capabilities, and knew he would have a solid rifle rest.

Sunrise was still a faint, off-color blush when the hunter's well-laid plans began to disintegrate. A car door slammed far below, followed by someone's raucous laugh. The hunter cringed and bit his lip. Seconds later, a horn honked along the distant road, then honked again. Daylight oozed slowly across the horizon, a hemorrhage of reds and pinks and blues.

Suddenly, the angry buzz of a chainsaw ripped through the mountain air. The hunter cocked his head in disbelief. No, he decided, it was not a chainsaw at all—it was a damnable motorbike. His hopes sinking and his stomach queasy, he realized the machine was droning closer and closer. A cloven foot scuffed nervously in the darkness and air whistled through animal nostrils close by—sounds rapidly followed by clattering rocks and thundering hoofs. With daylight less than 15 minutes away, an iron-clad scouting plan was quickly coming unhinged.

The end arrived five minutes prior to legal shooting light. With sickening steadiness, the distant snarl became a deafening roar. A motorbike suddenly popped through the predawn haze barely 20 yards away, its double upholstered seat bristling with arms, legs, and gun barrels. The heartsick rifleman spun on his heel and trudged away through the gloom.

Many rich but easily accessible hunting areas become worthless on opening day when hoards of inept and noisy hunters descend on them. However, a savvy hunter can generally anticipate disruptive hunting activity near roads and actually use it to good advantage. For example, if you believe the deer will exit an area on opening morning, you can take up your vigil before daylight near likely animal escape routes. In places where people are apt to congregate once hunting season begins, you can try to anticipate and turn the human activity to your advantage.

DEVELOPING HUNTING SKILLS

No matter what sort of shooting tool a hunter uses, the same basic skills are needed to set up the shot. Bowhunters must refine their skills to an especially high degree to get within 50 yards or less, but successful riflemen, shotgunners, or muzzleloading enthusiasts practice the same techniques when bagging their deer. The common notion that bowhunters must use some mysterious tactic that gun hunters don't is just plain bunk.

In a nutshell, every deer hunter pits his senses and hunting skills against those of wary, hunter-shy animals. This sounds simple enough, but it takes time for a hunter to perfect his abilities. A deer has finely honed survival instincts, an ultrasensitive nose, razor-keen eyes, extremely alert ears, and the ability to move quickly over rugged terrain to get away from danger. By contrast, a man has a relatively poor nose, fairly good ears, and exceptionally keen eyesight. Were it not for his superior brain, man would be no match for the deer. As it is, the contest is often extremely close, with deer winning the majority of encounters.

A skilful hunter keeps two basic things in mind in the woods. First, he attempts to use his own senses—eyes, ears, and nose—to locate the deer before it locates him. Second, he never forgets that to get a shot he must penetrate a deer's defense system. Deer hunting at its best requires many diverse and subtle skills, but at bottom it's a simple game. The hunter is trying to outwit a deer's senses and prevent its detecting danger and taking flight.

USING YOUR SENSES TO BEST ADVANTAGE

You should polish your ability to see, hear, and smell deer. A hunter who regularly detects game before it becomes aware of him will usually get the shot, while less alert hunters stumble ineffectively about. Here are some tips on perfecting hunting senses.

Developing a first-rate game eye. "There he goes!" the hunting guide suddenly hissed to his client, anxiously tugging the rifleman's vest. "Shoot 'im before he gets away!"

"Where . . . where?" the hunter gasped in astonishment and gawked about.

"Over there, darn it!" the guide hissed again, kneeling to stare through his binocular. "Right there in front of you. A giant buck. Shoot!"

It's safe to say that thousands of deer escape from hunters every year simply because the hunters never see them. Having good "game eyes" has relatively little to do with how well these eyes measure up in an optometrist's office. Many hunters with 20/20 vision have extreme difficulty seeing deer in the field, while others with less than perfect sight can pick out distant deer with incredible efficiency. The keys to seeing deer are knowing what to look for and knowing where to look.

There is no good substitute for experience when learning what to look for in the deer woods. Deer seldom stand out in wide-open places like bucks on calendars and picture postcards. They just are not normally relaxed or naive enough to expose themselves to such easy scrutiny. Invariably, only bits and pieces of deer are visible through existing foliage and the hunter must learn to look for these bits and pieces. That is all there is to see as the deer hugs the forest edge and remains surrounded by brush, trees, rocks, and other outline-breaking cover. It is a matter of consciously looking for puzzle pieces instead of the entire puzzle—the amber curve of an antler, the soft glow of an eye or nose, the subtle movement of an ear flicking flies, or the telltale shape of a leg below the brush. Longtime deer hunters habitually look for such things as they sneak along or wait patiently on stand, knowing full well that they won't often see the complete deer on the hoof.

One of the keys to seeing deer is knowing what *color* these animals are. The color of deer varies by area and time of year. Typically, summertime deer have reddish brown coats. Later on, as the weather cools down, this coat is replaced by a heavier winter coat of gray or dark brown. A bowhunter or muzzleloader buff who goes after deer in August will have trouble seeing them if he's looking for gray animals, and a hunter in late fall with an eye peeled for red will completely overlook most nearby game. It is essential to find out the basic coloration of animals in the area to be hunted.

Knowing where to look is a skill that can only be perfected over time. Deer gravitate toward certain terrain and foliage. For example, whitetail deer in farm country are generally seen along forest edges around dawn and dusk—not smack dab in the middle of open fields. Similarly, mountain mule deer usually stay near substantial patches of sagebrush or stunted junipers and pines—not stands of mature, large-trunked trees.

Finding the right places to look is usually far more complex than this, however, because a number of factors determine where deer are likely to be at a par-

Sharpening your game eye is the only way to locate deer through intervening foliage or in tricky lighting conditions. Always look for parts of an animal—not the whole deer. Can you find all of the deer in these four typical field situations?

ticular time. For example, in hilly country deer are usually on the downwind side of a ridge when a stiff breeze is blowing, but may be on the opposite, sunny slope if weather is calm and very cold.

A deer hunter eventually learns such things about deer behavior and automatically looks to those places where deer will logically be. A beginner must learn by trial and error, but the knowledge does come with time.

Learning to hear deer. The thin, mournful wail of a black-and-tan hound dog split the early-evening air. The stump-sitting hunter cocked his head in admiration, fondly remembering similar southern deer drives in the past. The canine music was so intoxicating a tiny nearby noise almost went unheard. However, the clearly audible crunch snapped the hunter back to reality. He swivelled, spied the buck, and threw up his shotgun in one well-oiled motion. An instant later, a fat little eight-point buck lay floundering on the ground, laced by half a dozen buckshot. The animal never knew what hit it as it sneaked before the hounds.

A hunter's ears are vital for detecting deer before they hear him. Deer make a variety of telltale noises, from bleats and snorts to thuds, crunches, and crackles. The experienced hunter can sort out these sounds from the thump of an acorn dropped by a squirrel, the rustle of birds among the treetops, and other natural forest noises. Getting in tune with natural sounds requires concentration and time, but an alert hunter gradually develops this all-important skill.

There are three basic deer-related sounds a hunter should listen for in the field. First are the normal crunches and clatters deer make as they walk about, shift positions in their beds, feed on bushes and limbs, or run away from a hunter. Second are less common sounds, such as the rattling antlers of fighting, rut-crazed bucks; the bleats of a fawn; the snorts and asthmatic wheezes of a frightened buck or doe; and the grunts of a dominant buck during the mating season. Third are sounds, not made by deer, that nevertheless signal their presence—sounds such as the screaming of a blue jay or the scolding chatter of a squirrel. This kind of racket is often started by a deer moving near these small, noisy critters. If you keep alert for these sounds, you will be alerted whenever deer are near, giving you a decided edge in the contest between predator and prey.

Here are some typical instances when a hunter's ears can help put him on alert. Deer often betray their presence when they stroll between bedding and feeding areas at about dusk. An alert stand hunter can generally hear animals approaching before they actually pop into view, allowing him to get ready to take a shot. Another case is when animals jump and run or sneak away from a hunter, or unknowingly move

Jays often scold nearby deer with shrill, piercing screams. This is an important clue to keep in mind.

toward him to get away from other hunters. If you hear thudding hoofs you can track the sound and prepare to shoot when the deer breaks into the clear. Natural deer sounds such as antlers batting together, vigorous thrashing in the brush to remove antler velvet, sneezing, and so forth can also help you zero in on a deer and set up a shot at a reasonable distance.

Using sense of smell. Man has a notoriously poor sense of smell—by animal standards. Smell is the hunter's least important sense, but it occasionally helps locate nearby animals. For instance, rutting whitetail bucks throw off a pungent glandular scent a keen-nosed person can detect at close range. Similarly, deer that leap up and sneak away in dry weather sometimes stir up dust that sometimes can be smelled.

LEARNING TO MOVE SILENTLY

All too many hunters walk through the woods like the proverbial bull in a china shop. In addition to the kettledrum "clump, clump, clump" of heavy boot-clad feet, the tyro's clothing usually whines and shrieks against foliage like a muted rock guitar. This rhythmic tune is often complemented by music of jangling cartridges, spare change, and other hard objects in the pockets. These noises may not bother a man in the least, but they terrorize all deer within earshot.

Deer are finely tuned survival machines. When those big ears cup forward and those piercing eyes stare suspiciously ahead, the deer is usually only seconds from hightailing it away.

Learing to walk silently in steep, brushy terrain takes plenty of practice plus proper clothing and footwear. But you have to master quiet walking skills if you want to get the deer.

In sharp contrast, a good hunter slips along like a cat with little or no noise. He realizes that the big, cupped ears on a deer have more than decorative value, and knows that when these ears fan forward alertly, the animal is as sensitive as a finely designed electrical sound detector. It is not always possible to move silently enough to approach deer. This is especially true when the weather is warm and the forest floor is covered with what might as well be a thick bed of potato chips. But a careful, experienced hunter can do a good job under most circumstances.

Walking *technique* is a principle factor in quiet movement about the woods. A hunter accustomed to tramping sidewalks and pavement seldom thinks about how he walks, and it shows when he first enters the woods. However, a hunter with a few deer seasons experience has generally learned how to pad softly. The quietest walkers lift their feet fairly high to avoid shuffling debris underfoot, plant their boots delicately with every step, and watch where they put their feet to avoid especially noisy footing. Only practice can perfect silent walking technique.

Being smart about selecting the route ahead is half the battle in walking quietly. A savvy hunter skirts noisy rockslides, clumps of brittle pine needles and leaves, stands of dry grass, and tangles of thin, noisy match-stick limbs. Instead, he seeks out a path over soft dirt, solid rock, and other relatively quiet routes. Whenever possible, he follows deer trails that have been pounded into fine, quiet powder. A hunter who barrels cross-country without weaving to avoid the noisiest footing seldom gets a shot at a deer.

Naturally, speed of movement has plenty to do with quiet walking. Generally, a slow, careful walking technique is least obtrusive. But fast walking is sometimes better in deer hunting than the take-a-step-and-wait-two technique often recommended in deer-hunting manuals. There will be more about advisable walking speeds in the upcoming section The Fine Art of Hunting on Foot. The point to be made here is simple enough—if quiet walking is difficult in a particular area because of rough terrain, close-growing foliage, or excessively dry weather, slow down to help mute an otherwise noisy stretch.

Selection of footwear and clothing is a key to silent movement. On a calm day, a normal deer can hear the crunch of leaves and twigs beneath hard-sole boots several hundred yards away. Similarly, the whine of limbs and brush against hard-weave clothing sends deer packing immediatcly. A quiet hunter dresses in relatively soft-soled boots and fairly soft-surfaced clothing.

Proper footwear and clothing for hunting deer are discussed in detail earlier in Part 5 of this book. But to recap, neoprene boot soles are best for close-range sneaking because they give with underfoot debris. By contrast, Vibram boots are fine for long-distance deer shooting but tend to make more noise. In the clothing department, wool and soft-woven cotton are the quietest hunting materials—a must in areas with dense brush and trees. Ripstop nylon, hardweave cotton/synthetic blends, and other canvaslike fabrics make significant noise against brush and tree limbs.

A hunter must make certain nothing he carries makes a deer-spooking sound. Loose cartridges in a pocket can rattle noisily, a binocular on a long strap can swing about like a pendulum, and two belt canteens in close proximity can bang loudly together. These and similar noisemakers never go unnoticed by deer.

One other noise, the human voice, is the absolute kiss of death when hunting. On calm days, normal conversational chatter can sometimes be heard *several miles away* by another hunter, let alone a deer with even sharper hearing. Even voices dropped in quiet conversation travel amazingly well across draws and canyons, tipping deer off to danger. The only short-range talking sound a hunter can safely make is a whisper. This does not utilize the vocal cords, and seldom carries more than a few yards in the woods.

A final note on being quiet when hunting deer: Too many tree-stand sitters and ground-blind users underestimate their prey and fail to worry about being silent as they wait. In reality, the slight scuff of a foot or scrape of a garment on stand often spoils the best laid ambush.

READING AND USING THE WIND

If humans smelled as bad to one another as they do to deer, words like "companionship" and "togetherness" would not be in the dictionary. Deer will occasionally hear an unnatural sound or see a suspicious movement and still linger in the area. However, one whiff of human odor sends deer tearing toward the next county. Despite this fact, many hunters pay little attention to wind direction.

Before wind-doping tactics can be discussed, a common myth about human odor must be dispelled. Many hunter believe that freshly laundered clothes and regular baths cleanse them of smells a deer can easily detect. Such misguided individuals are quick to snort their disapproval if another hunter smokes tobacco, wears clothes more than one day afield, or otherwise defiles his person with a strong-smelling substance.

In reality, a deer's schnozzle is so sensitive that the animal can smell hunters no matter how fastidious their personal hygiene or how fresh their clothes. When breezes blow from a hunter downwind to a deer, the animal *always* catches the scent and departs immediately. There are no ifs, ands, or buts about it.

Human odor moves on air in precisely the same way that ink moves in water. Ink released from an eyedropper will slowly expand in all directions in perfectly calm water, weakening in color as it expands and dilutes in all directions. In moving water ink spreads freely in the direction of the flow, fanning out and diffusing but remaining quite dense and potent near its point of origin. Similarly, a hunter standing in dead-calm conditions emanates a scent that spreads around him very slowly. In a breeze, a steady stream of scent flows with the wind in fairly concentrated form. By visualizing human scent as ink in water, a hunter can easily understand which situations alert the supersensitive nose of a deer.

If a noticeable breeze is blowing, a hunter's scent is traveling the same direction as the wind and at the same speed. In slight breezes, a hunter may be able to walk as fast as his scent and thus effectively hunt with the wind to his back. However, such situations are relatively rare. As a rule, you must walk directly into the wind or in a cross-wind direction to keep your scent from drifting toward a deer you will approach.

A stand hunter should pay every bit as much attention to currents of air. If there is no appreciable breeze, his scent will slowly slip away in all directions—a decided disadvantage unless he is sitting high above the ground. As he approaches a stand site, the hunter should always move with the wind in his face to avoid scaring a nearby deer that might move into range a little later. If possible, a stand should be elevated at least 20 feet. This helps carry human odor away on upper-air currents, instead of wafting this odor to

Elevated stands give you a definite edge on deer. As long as your stand is a minimum of 20 feet above the ground, your scent is usually carried safely above deer on upper-air currents. (Hunting laws may limit stand height.)

nearby animals. *Anytime* a hunter's scent blows to a deer within 200 or 300 yards, the animal will instantly recognize the smell and move away.

Deer are capable of sniffing out human trails through the grass and leaves like fine hunting dogs. The more moist foliage is, the longer human odor lingers. As a result, an archer or gunner who walks to an early-morning tree stand leaves telltale scent on the dew-moistened ground and all grass that brushes against his pants. The odor lingers for several hours and scares away deer that encounter it. Walking to stand in drier afternoon hours also leaves human scent, but scent trails tend to dissipate within an hour or two if weather is relatively warm.

Leaving scent trails to deer stands is not a major problem, provided hunters approach their stands in the direction opposite that which approaching deer are likely to take. To further blot out foot trails, many experienced hunters squirt commercial odor-masking scents on their boot soles and pant legs. A good alternative to this in cattle country is wiping boot soles across a soft, cow pie before walking the last 300 or 400 yards to stand.

Camouflage your approach trail to a deer stand by squirting commercial scent on your bootsoles and pant-legs. Otherwise deer can sniff out your scent trail.

Failing to mask scent trails can ruin any chance of stand-hunting success. Take the case of a bowhunter after Pacific Coast blacktail deer. The fellow scouted long and hard, discovered an oak-brush flat teeming with bucks and does, and erected a climbing stand in a tall pine. He sneaked to his tree two hours prior to sundown, climbed aloft, and nocked an arrow on the bowstring. With any luck at all, he thought, something would wander into range.

Just before sundown, a dandy, record-size 4 × 4 buck popped out. The archer fidgeted nervously, his heart pounding as the buck picked nearer and nearer. At 75 yards, the animal suddenly snorted in surprise, swapped ends like a barrel-racing horse, and charged away in a cloud of dust. In seconds a dozen other deer were blowing noisily across the flat. Only then did the bowhunter realize the buck had picked up his scent on the approach trail to the tree. A little acorn scent smeared across his boot soles might have prevented that.

When it comes to wind-borne scents, the key is determining wind direction. In strong, steady winds, there is no problem. Lighter winds are more common though, and hunters use a variety of methods to monitor the direction. Some toss a little dust in the air and watch it drift away. Others attach a fine thread to the tip of their gun barrel or bow limb and keep an eye on this makeshift wind sock. A few carry leather pouches full of unscented talcum powder and drop a pinch once in awhile to check the wind. One of the simplest and most effective wind-direction gauges is an ordinary butane cigarette lighter. The flame leans before the slightest breeze.

Deer hunters planning major walks need to know in advance what prevailing winds will be to maintain an upwind direction. Those who have hunted particular areas a lot can predict wind patterns from past experience.

Wind direction in most mountainous terrain follows some basic patterns. For example, early-morning and late-evening "thermal breezes" usually flow downward along major slopes because air is cool and heavy. On warm, sunny days, winds switch to an uphill direction as air heats up and begins to rise. But weather fronts and other disturbances can unbalance normal thermal patterns, making planning for wind direction as hard as predicting the weather itself.

Fickle breezes are the undoing of many hunters despite well-laid plans. In unstable weather, breezes often become maddeningly unpredictable. Similarly, many deer areas with broken terrain tumble and swirl the wind in complex and irregular patterns. To a certain extent, hunters can alter their movement to remain more or less downwind of terrain they want to hunt. But a sudden and unexpected about-face in wind direction is never out of the question.

There's no pat solution to coping with unpredictable

Keeping tabs on wind in a number of directions is easy with simple techniques: You can toss a little dust in the air as shown. Or you can attach a fine, breeze-responsive thread to a gun or bow or flick a butane lighter to check flame direction.

breezes. Some straight-shooting hunters manage to pot their deer on the run even after wind changes have ruined a surefire setup. Bowhunters, by contrast, are out of luck if wind movement betrays their presence. It helps to attempt to predict wind direction based on past experience and to always try to move in an up-wind or cross-wind direction. A hunter's only other precaution is using some sort of commercial odor-masking scent to at least partially cover his human smell.

FACTS ABOUT ODOR-MASKING SCENTS

Many experienced hunters use an odor-masking scent to cover their human odor. A variety of potent masking scents are commercially available and they fully or partially cover a hunter's odor. How well scents work is highly controversial, but there is little doubt among experts that good-quality scent at least confuses deer by mixing with human odor and camouflaging it. That confusion gives the hunter a few extra seconds to take a shot. At best, there seem to be times when scents

completely cover a hunter's body odor—especially when breezes shift just enough to leak slight sniffs to nearby animals. In any case, odor-masking scent is good insurance.

Which odor-masking scent is best? The choice can be confusing to a beginner because there are dozens of different scents available to match different situations and druthers. But they can be divided into three categories—food scents, natural scents, and sex scents.

Common food scents for deer include wild grape, acorn, apple, sweet corn, and sunflower. Natural scents include pine, cedar, skunk, red fox urine, and earth scent. Most sex scent is natural doe-in-heat odor, although some manufacturers sell rutting-buck urine as well.

Both food scents and natural scents are concocted to mask a hunter's human odor. Although a starving deer might occasionally be attracted to the smell, food scent is not considered a deer lure at all. Sex scent is occasionally used for masking human odor at the height of the rut, but it is most commonly used to lure rut-crazy deer into range.

When selecting scent to cover human odor, buy a brand name product with a reputation for potency and accurate duplication of natural in-the-field odors.

Food scents, such as acorn, are ideal for masking human odor. You can squirt odor-masking scents on a handy, removable scent pad as shown. This technique keeps clothing itself free of odor.

Natural scents can markedly improve your chances of success because breezes can shift suddenly. Strong, but pleasant, odors like earth, cedar, and pine are far more desirable than potent, awful-smelling skunk scent. Sex scents work superbly when the deer rut reaches its peak. Properly used, these commercial odors lure in amorous bucks and does like flies to strawberry jam.

Salesmen at any sporting goods store can recommend quality brands of scent. The second thing to remember is to match the scent to particular hunting environments. This should be a matter of common sense, but all too many hunters ignore it. When hunting in the piney mule-deer woods, pine scent is the logical thing to use. Near fields of yellow corn or sunflowers, scents duplicating the odors of these plants will work like a charm. But wild grape scent used in high alpine areas without wild grapes can scare animals as badly as human odor can. The same is true of red fox urine or apple scent used in places where these scents do not exist naturally.

Doe-in-heat and buck-urine scents deserve separate elaboration here. These scents are used during the rutting period. They actually lure bucks and does to stand sites when sprinkled on nearby bushes and trees or squirted directly in active scrapes made by rutting bucks. The doe-in-heat odor draws bucks from long distances, and buck urine attracts does that are ready to be bred. Sex scents work only during the deer rut, which generally occurs sometime late in the fall.

Some hunting scents are more pleasant to use than others. Skunk scent is the most potent available and works well in most places because skunks abound throughout whitetail and mule deer habitat. But this scent is too strong for many hunters to tolerate. A little *eau de polecat* might be okay on bushes and trees around a stand, but acorn, apple, cedar, or other less offensive smells make more sense in the majority of deer-hunting situations. Similarly, red fox urine is not nearly as pleasing to sniff as sunflower or wild grape. Stronger, less pleasant odor-masking scents are fa-

vored by some archers and gunners who expect close-range shots, but the scents are always squirted on commercial scent pads instead of directly on clothing or boots.

Some deer hunters prefer to use natural odor-masking scents instead of commercial products. One common technique is to cut the smelly tarsal glands from the hind legs of deer and tying or pinning the glands to pants or shirt. The glands can be frozen and stored from year to year inside plastic sandwich bags. A few deer hunters simply crush the needles of pines, leaves of pepperwood trees, or parts of similar strong-smelling plants and rub the juice on their clothing or shoes. Natural odor-masking precautions might well make a

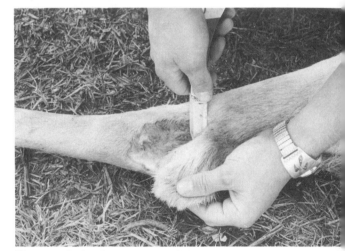

The tarsal glands near a deer's hocks are laden with potent natural odor. You can cut these glands from deer and pin them to your clothes to hide your scent.

positive difference if breezes switch unexpectedly, but are no substitute for paying strict attention to wind direction.

THE FINE ART OF CAMOUFLAGE

A rifle hunter trotted up a long, shallow wash between banks of crumbling rock. At the head of the draw, he cut sharply to the right, slowed his pace considerably, and peeked across a prominent mound of dirt. There, less than 500 yards away, stood the muley buck of his dreams. The massive 5 × 5 rack rolled bewitchingly as the animal gobbled brush. The hunter surveyed intervening terrain, noted another shallow dip curving directly toward the buck, and confidently eased ahead. Another 150-yard stalk and the trophy was his for sure.

Suddenly, a flicker of movement caught the stalker's

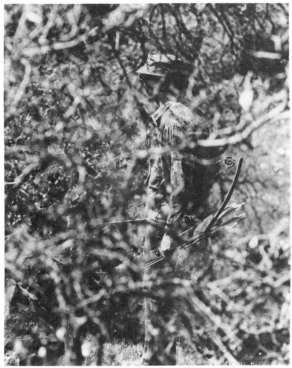

Hunter-wise deer instantly recognize the telltale human shape. You should wear camouflage clothing and use foliage to help break up what a deer sees as the clear, unmistakable outline of danger.

eye. An old scrawny, propeller-headed doe walked into view barely 100 yards ahead, nibbling half-heartedly at scattered clumps of grass. The hunter grinned and froze like a tree in his tracks. He had heard that deer cannot recognize stationary objects, and decided to simply let the emaciated doe pass. A heavy clump of brush provided excellent hiding cover less than 3 feet away, but the confident rifleman was tired of crouching and stood his ground.

The doe walked steadily toward the hunter: 75 yards, 60, 45. At 30 yards, she turned dead broadside, pausing to uproot tender shoots. The wind was fanning the hunter's face directly, and he could still see the distant trophy buck. The doe plucked free a solid mouthful of grass, switched her tail at flies, and lazily looked around.

The old biddy suddenly froze. Her eyeballs rolled in her head as she stared at the stationary hunter and her muscles bunched as she made ready to run. The rifleman's smug expression vanished as the doe craned her neck to look, stiffly raised her foreleg, and solidly stamped the ground. A split-second later, the deer blew like a fireplace bellows and tore off the ridgeline—directly toward the giant buck. The hunter stood in horror as the doe galloped closer to the big-racked muley and finally spooked him into the brush.

Through one tragic error in judgment, the hunter had lost his buck.

Contrary to old tales accepted as gospel by armchair experts, *deer can see and identify stationary hunters.* Any experienced woodsman—particularly a bow-hunter—can testify that deer do not merely walk past motionless people as if they were tall stumps or bushes. If those keen animal eyes recognize a suspiciously human shape, the animal charges away like a turpentined tomcat.

A deer sees both stationary and moving objects with unbelievable ease. Its eyes are set to the sides of its head like those of all prey species, giving it superb peripheral vision as well as vision to the front. A deer cannot see directly rearward and has a blind spot directly overhead. However, anything to the front and sides is seen with superb clarity—even objects several hundred yards away.

All deer are relatively color-blind. As a result, a hunter need not worry about the colors of his clothing so much as the pattern they present when seen in black and white. As was discussed in the section on hunting clothes, any garment will help camouflage a hunter if it matches basic shades of existing terrain and has a mottled, two-tone coloration to break up a hunter's human outline. Standard World War II issue leaf-print duds and Vietnam camouflage both serve the purpose, and so do plaid and tie-dyed garments. In areas congested with other hunters, many hunters wear blaze-orange or red camouflage. This is highly visible to humans but blends well to the color-blind eyes of deer.

Covering the shiny, light-colored skin of your face with a head net is important in close-range sneaking or stand-hunting situations. This extra precaution is practically a necessity when you are bowhunting.

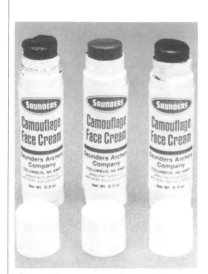

Camouflage cream is available in both applicator sticks and plastic squeeze-tube containers. This makeup is messy and time-consuming to apply and remove, but provides unexcelled camouflage.

In close-range deer-hunting situations, a hunter should camouflage his light, shiny complexion with a head net or with commercial camouflage makeup. If deer are most often spotted and shot at ranges beyond 100 yards, elaborate camouflage precautions are really not necessary. Long-range deer hunting typical of that in big, open canyon country seldom requires *any* sophisticated camouflage. Solid-colored clothes and hats make acceptable garb. However, all-white shirts, yellow straw hats, and other highly visible garments alert deer at several hundred yards, especially when hunters are moving instead of standing like statues. For most medium-range hunting situations, mottled upper-body wear is sufficient to destroy a hunter's telltale human shape and trick the deer.

The most meticulous hunters take special pains to completely camouflage their equipment as well as their bodies. Many spray their canteens, binoculars, and other potentially shiny gear with nonglare primer paint. A few go so far as camouflaging their rifles or shotguns with two contrasting shades of dull paint to prevent light reflection from gun barrels and other metal surfaces. In addition, commercial gun-carrying slings, handgun holsters, and other shooting accessories are available in leaf-print patterns to satisfy the most zealous camouflage fanatic.

A great deal of fuss is made over camouflage clothing and equipment in various hunting books and magazines. However, the gear *alone* does not provide effective hunting concealment. It must be complemented by proper camouflage *technique*—something not discussed nearly so often.

Very light clothing can alert even distant animals. This buck-rattler would have blended well enough if he'd left the cowboy hat at home.

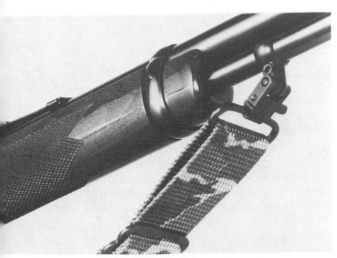

Gun slings and other shooting accessories are available in camouflage leaf-print patterns. In close-range shooting situations, camouflaged equipment is bound to help.

A smart hunter wears and carries multicolored, nonglare gear. An even smarter hunter uses camouflage skill, as well as gear. He uses available terrain and existing cover to help him hide from deer because the most carefully selected leaf-print garb still sticks out like sore thumb if silhouetted against the sky, if seen moving rapidly across sunny openings, or if spotted in areas that do not blend with the black-and-white shade of the camo.

Successful deer hunters always use foliage and terrain to hide their bodies or at least break up their human profiles. A sneaking hunter never walks the top of a ridgeline when he can stalk along below the crest and occasionally peek over with only his forehead and eyeballs exposed. A smart stand hunter never plants himself in wide open areas when he can back into outline-breaking brush and virtually disappear.

The best deer hunters are extremely sensitive to the effects of sunlight and shadow on camouflage. They know that direct light can make them stand out, especially when poised in front of shadowy backdrops. If possible, they always hug the deepest shadows and forsake the sun, realizing that deer cannot see as well in shadows and also knowing that medium-colored clothing blends best in darkest areas. If circumstances permit, savvy hunters also move along with the morning or evening sun low behind their backs. This forces deer to squint directly into blinding rays and thus reduces their ability to see and recognize danger.

Deer invariably pick up fast movement with their eyes more readily than they see slow, deliberate progress. Hunters who know this always creep along

Use foliage and sunlight as well as proper clothing to avoid being seen by deer. Wear something white (below left) and you stand out in any deep-woods situation. By contrast, head-to-toe camouflage (middle photo) helps you blend fairly well against bushes in broken sunlight and shade. You just about disappear when you really hug the shadows.

whenever deer might see them, and often sneak right past animals that would be spooked by maneuvers at normal speed. At times, when you must cross a sunny opening without adequate cover, you can slow to a snail's pace and slip along undetected. Similarly, stand hunters who elect to wait on the ground are far better off sitting *in front of* cover than hiding behind it. A gunner or archer who crouches behind brush or limbs must constantly bob his head like a tom turkey to see and shoot, creating deer-spooking movement. By contrast, a hunter who backs against cover can survey terrain without the twitch of a muscle.

LEARNING BASIC DEER HABITS

One rifleman had never hunted whitetails in his life. But he'd taken dozens of nice mule-deer bucks on his father's ranch in Colorado, and he believed a deer was a deer no matter what. So when the tight-racked Arizona whitetail barreled up a hillside 200 yards away, he waited patiently for the animal to stop near the crest and gaze back downhill. That was the way Colorado mule deer had always behaved. Imagine the hunter's surprise when the buck kept on going as if it had been scorched by a cattle prod.

A successful deer hunter must know the habits of animals he's after. All the other hunting skills together are useless if you cannot find deer in the first place or predict where they will go and what they will do next. A deer hunter must perfect basic hunting skills, but he must also master the animals themselves to set up shots to best advantage.

The first step in mastering deer behavior is learning their basic habits. Mule deer, whitetails, and blacktails each display characteristic habits and temperaments. Here are some facts about the three major types of deer.

Whitetails. These deer are noted for being particularly nervous by nature. As a group, they display a preference for heavy bottomland cover. Whitetails are not often migratory, usually inhabiting the same stretch of country on a year-round basis. They are most often seen early and late in the day as they forsake thickets to canvass open areas for food. Whitetails are quite adaptable and thrive in close proximity to man despite heavy hunting pressure. When pressed very hard, they tend to become nocturnal and remain in cover during daylight. Yet as a group whitetails have fairly predictable habit patterns that make them vulnerable to a well-planned ambush.

Mule deer. These deer can be cagey but display a calmer temperament than their whitetail cousins. These animals usually live in mountainous or foothill areas with scattered openings and cover, and often display a preference for open bedding ground with a view. Mule deer are generally migratory, spending the summers in high alpine areas and moving up to 100 miles to lower terrain where winters are less severe.

Mule deer do coexist well near man, and so are most often found in fairly remote locations. But today mule deer sometimes live in densely timbered areas, surviving by borrowing the whitetail's secretive, thicket-loving ways. Mule deer tend to wander randomly over a large home territory, and this unpredictability makes them extremely difficult to ambush from stands.

Blacktails. These deer combine the fairly nervous nature of whitetails with the unpredictable movement patterns of mule deer. Blacktails inhabit a wide variety

In some areas, deer will pause like this one on the crest of a hill to gawk at you. By contrast, deer in more heavily pressured country seldom make such a potentially fatal mistake. To become a successful hunter, you must know the habits of animals in specific regions.

of terrain on the Pacific Coast, from coastal rainforests to semiopen oak-and-grass savanna country. Most commonly, blacktails are heavy-cover animals. Some blacktail herds migrate in mule-deer fashion; others live out their lives in small home territories. Blacktails can live in close proximity to man and become nocturnal when hunted hard. They are known for their ability to remain in hiding while letting an unsuspecting hunter walk by at close range.

DEER HABITS IN SPECIFIC AREAS

Any basic deer-hunting textbook outlines the typical traits of various kinds of deer. What many of them fail to point out is the extreme variation of habit patterns within a single species of animal.

There are literally thousands of mini ecosystems in North America—ecosystems containing deer with unique habit patterns adapted to existing food, water, terrain, and hunting-pressure conditions. Quite often, whitetails on one stretch of river bottom display different habits and respond differently to hunting pressure than whitetails living only five or ten miles away. For whitetails generally, deer in one herd may stay put within a small home territory when hunted hard by gunners. But other whitetails may pack their bags and move to less stressful surroundings.

Similarly, there are many documented studies of blacktail and mule deer showing that animals in one drainage prefer open, tabletop country with a view. But deer of identical genetic makeup only 20 miles away hole up in brush like cottontail rabbits when resting or resisting hunter pressure. Some mule deer migrate 75 miles between summer and winter ranges, while others of identical breeding live along the same migration path but prefer to stay in lowland winter range all year long. The list of subtle and not-so-subtle differences in deer habits goes on and on.

An observant person who regularly hunts one particular deer area learns the habits of local deer and develops a hunting strategy based on this knowledge.
• If the deer prefer open ground and keep hunters at long-range, the hunter slips on sophisticated camouflage clothing and carries an accurate, long-range rifle.
• If deer hole up in brush and stay there throughout the hunting season, the hunter climbs into a tree with a good downward view or routs out animals and shoots them on the run.
• If bucks in a particular swamp respond well to rattling antlers because there's a high buck/doe ratio and resulting competition for females, a hunter carries rattling antlers and uses them frequently.
• If every buck has a dozen does to himself and turns

Match your shooting tool to the precise habits of deer you are after. For example, a tight-shooting, scope-sighted rifle (left) is best in open areas where deer look for danger from a distance. By contrast, a faster-handling, but less accurate, carbine with open sights might be best where deer hug cover and leap out unexpectedly.

up his nose at fighting sounds, a gunner still-hunts through the undergrowth and surprises trophies preoccupied with harems of does.
• If mule deer or blacktails in one area like to bed in low-growing bushes, a hunter may sit on vantage points all day to glass for bedded animals across major mountain canyons. But if the same varieties of deer in another area hug big pine thickets, a hunter must sneak up on the animals, drive them out with the help of other nimrods, or attempt to ambush them along forest edges at first and last light.

Anyone who hunts deer in a new area is obviously handicapped at first by his ignorance of local animal behavior. However, experienced hunters have learned to observe carefully, ponder deer behavior they see during the first few days of an outing, and attempt to construct an accurate picture of existing deer-habit patterns. The result is generally a sensible hunting strategy.

THINGS ALL DEER HAVE IN COMMON

All big-game animals are extremely comfort oriented. No matter what the species of deer or specific locale, a hunter can bank on the fact that deer are moving and bedding with optimum luxury foremost in mind.

Deer are usually found near dependable souces of food. This buck was ambushed in a field of ripe commercial grain and was easily dragged to a vehicle.

For example, deer are seldom more than a stroll away from first-rate food and easily accessible water. Similarly, they invariably bed on sunny slopes in frigid weather and tuck away in shady areas when daytime temperatures soar. If stiff winds are blowing, deer nestle on the lee sides of ridges, swales, or wind-breaking foliage. A sharp hunter realizes these things and goes where the deer are most likely to be on a particular day or in a particular kind of terrain.

In the face of heavy hunting pressure, deer do whatever it takes to avoid direct confrontation with hunters. In dense foliage, they often hole up and refuse to move unless literally stepped on by hunters or routed out by dogs. As a result, animals are often abundant in forests where noisily tramping hunters complain bitterly about the obvious lack of deer. In country with less "escape cover," deer generally migrate into little roadless pockets or places too dense or steep and rugged for the average person to go.

Hunters as a group are just as comfort oriented as deer and prefer to linger near the car and the beer cooler instead of hoofing it into steep draws or nasty tangles of brush. In mule-deer terrain, some of the biggest and smartest trophy bucks are found *below* roads. This is because hunters prefer to hunt *above* roads where meat packing is a fairly easy, downhill operation. Hunters in places with heavy gunning pressure can always find game if they stop to figure out where deer have drifted to avoid the hunters' beaten path.

PRACTICE MAKES PERFECT

No one turns legal hunting age and instantly becomes an expert deer hunter. Like athletes of all sorts, hunters slowly develop the necessary skills and know-how to excel. Some progress faster and further than others as a result of greater desire, more innate hunting talent, and lots of time in the field. Those who truly wish to be expert at deer hunting usually do, becoming a part of that elite 10 percent of hunters that bags 90 percent of the deer.

The greatest single ingredient in becoming a good deer hunter is spending lots and lots of time in the field—time studying animals, learning terrain, and developing basic hunting skills. The best basketball players, bowlers, and golfers all got where they are through day-in, day-out practice, and deer hunters are no different. The more a hunter practices his sport, the more skilful and experienced he becomes.

PHYSICAL AND MENTAL CONDITIONING

A person with superior skills and knowledge is not necessarily the most effective hunter. To be top-notch at his sport, a deer hunter must also be in good physical and mental condition. Such conditioning does not magically happen—it takes hard work and concentrated effort.

Physical conditioning. The most arduous deer hunts require hunters to be tough and fit. In big mountain country, the more terrain a hunter covers, the more likely he is to score on deer. Similarly, a hunter capable of dropping into torturously steep canyons or bucking thick, body-restraining brush can penetrate areas where deer are plentiful and other hunters are few.

A soft, out-of-shape hunter can never stalk deer as well as a physically fit one. Unfit hunters often spot animals they cannot get to at all or cannot reach quickly enough to make a killing shot. Even stand hunters need to be in shape because they must be able to pull themselves up into trees.

When a deer is finally knocked down, good physical condition is certainly worth a lot. Grunting out a deer with a deer drag or across the shoulders is pure, unadulterated torture for a hunter who is out of shape.

Hunters can keep in shape in a number of different ways. Some jog, others cross-country ski or swim, and many more use exercycles or regular bicycles to keep muscle tone and the cardiovascular system in good condition. Man is by nature a walker, and most doctors recommend hiking as the best exercise of all. Hunters who live in metropolitan areas devoid of hills and mountains often walk or trot up and down flights of stairs or the bleachers in football stadiums to keep their legs in shape and their wind completely up to snuff. A hunter who is seriously out of shape should consult his physician to devise an exercise program that is both safe and effective.

Mental conditioning. One of the most important ingredients in consistently successful deer hunting is undying perseverance. Persistence and mental confidence pay off big in hunting, turning potentially sour outings into sweet success.

A hunter who probes one extra canyon, walks one extra mile, or sits one extra hour on stand increases his chances of success considerably. Often he will drop a wary buck while less ambitious hunters are taking it easy in camp. The woods is no place for easily discouraged tyros because most deer are earned by conscientious effort—not short-lived hopes and prayers.

Developing a die-hard hunting attitude is not as difficult as some might think. A hunter who merely realizes the difficulty of matching wits with alert, hunter-wise deer is more than halfway home. Once the task has been realistically assessed, a few successful, difficult hunts tend to cement a hunter's resolve to never give up trying. In even the poorest deer-hunting situations, the best hunters generally scrounge up deer through unswerving, hard-headed tenacity.

STAND HUNTING FOR DEER

It was the last evening of a two-week hunting trip, and altogether the bowhunter had spent many hours up on the tree stand, waiting with determined patience for his trophy buck to appear. But time was running out for this trip—shooting light was fading fast. Suddenly, there was a faint crunching sound as something nearby moved across the frozen forest floor. Up on his tree stand, the bowhunter perked up at the sound and slowly swiveled around, his heart already racing. There was no mistaking the steady footfalls of a walking whitetail deer—he had heard them many times before. The bowhunter squeezed his half-numb fingers around the bow grip, pulled the mitten off his bowstring hand with his teeth, and shifted his feet farther apart against the tree for safe, steady shooting.

Seconds later the approaching deer popped out of a willow thicket less than 50 yards away. In the dim twilight it was impossible to see antlers at that distance, but the animal appeared to be a big one, and a real butterball. As the animal approached, the hunter strained his eye to detect bone above the ears, but still nothing showed. Only when the deer passed directly underneath the stand did its tight basket rack become visible, contrasting faintly against its broad steel-gray shoulders.

The archer drew back, leaned out slightly in his climbing tree sling to track the deer with his 20-yard sight, and let the bowstring slip from his already chilly fingers. The aluminum shaft struck home with the sound of a fist slamming against a side of beef, and the buck leaped forward into a cluster of cottonwoods. The hunter shivered—not just from the cold—and settled down to wait a bit before following up the shot. Thirty minutes later, he was gutting out his prize—a handsome, eleventh-hour trophy with heavy eight-point antlers.

Stand hunting is one of the easiest yet most effective techniques for bagging deer. It requires a minimum of physical effort, a minimum of hunting skill, and a minimum of shooting expertise. Stand hunting places a deer at a decided disadvantage once the animal moves into range because the hunter is theoretically motionless. More often than not, shots are moderately close and the animals have not been alerted. The shooter can take his time, wait for that perfect moment, and then lower the boom.

The key to stand-hunting success is ironclad patience. Many hunters are too high strung and fidgety to make decent stand hunters. Even when they know they've set up a stand in a productive area, these fellows often move around and make too much noise

Ambushing deer from a well-placed stand is one of the easiest and most surefire hunting methods. Animals are seldom spooked as they move by, allowing excellent, high-percentage shooting opportunities.

to fool deer. A few flatly cannot tolerate waiting for more than short periods of time. By contrast, a good stand hunter is stoic and solid, suffering through rain, wind, cold, and heat with the resolve of a postal service letter carrier. His reward is a chance to shoot at wary but completely unalerted deer—often the honest-to-gosh trophies rarely seen by more active hunters on foot.

WHICH DEER FROM STANDS?

Stand hunting only works well on certain types of deer. The most popular stand-hunting target is the bottom-land-dwelling whitetail, primarily because this deer displays fairly habitual movement patterns between water, bedding cover, and agricultural feeding fields. Whitetails in nonagricultural hardwood and softwood forests can also be taken from stands. Here stands are placed to provide shots at deer as they move about normally or slip around the hoards of walking hunters or trained deer dogs.

Blacktails and mule deer are also vulnerable to stand hunting in certain situations despite their less predictable natures. The most practical stand-hunting areas for these animals are dense thickets of juniper, manzanita, oak brush, and other close-growing plants. This kind of cover makes other hunting methods virtually impossible.

A deer hunter who tries taking a stand for any kind of deer in open country invites bitter disappointment. In high alpine country where muleys and blacktails often reside, the animals are spread so thin and display such haphazard movement patterns that consistently fruitful stand hunting is not possible. A hunter may wind up sitting several weeks without so much as one shot. Even open-ground whitetails—and there are quite a few in parts of the Midwest, Rocky Mountain states, and Canada—are poor bets for stand hunting. These deer generally avoid ground blinds and seldom stray within shooting range of tree stands. A hunter should only take a stand when the deer in a particular area seem vulnerable to this sedentary hunting technique.

WHERE STANDS WORK BEST

Tree stand and ground blind hunting techniques do not work worth a hoot in some deer-rich areas. Obviously, tree stands require suitable trees for decent hunting height and safe waiting aloft. But in areas of brush or small-trunked trees, commercial or home-made tripod stands or platform ladders can be used. Blinds, on the other hand never work well unless there is at least a little ground cover to help them blend with terrain.

The very best stand provides a bowman or gun hunter with a view out to the maximum range of his

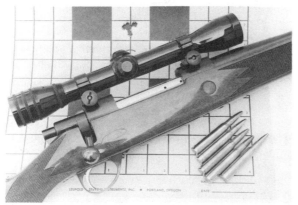

An accurate, long-range rifle like this .30/06 provides the ultimate in stand-hunting reach on deer in fairly open areas. If a stand setup is ideal, a rifleman can command nearly ¼ mile of terrain in any direction.

weapon. For example, a rifleman shooting a scoped .270 Winchester can effectively cover an area nearly ¼ mile in any direction, especially if his stand allows a solid aiming rest. By contrast, a shotgunner with slugs can command a view of only 100 yards in any direction, and a bowhunter 50 yards or less. Stands allowing clear views to maximum shooting range provide optimum chances for success.

STAND HUNTING IN SPECIFIC REGIONS

Hunting techniques vary from one part of the country to the next. This section tells where stand hunting is most useful for bagging deer.

The Northeast and Great Lakes Region. This region extends from Maine, Michigan, and Wisconsin southward into Ohio, Pennsylvania, Maryland, and Delaware. The area has hardwood forests and wood-lots mixed with some farms and many major population centers. This part of the United States teems with whitetail deer despite dense human populations, and hunting is a popular pastime during the fall.

Stand hunting here is the primary hunting method because deer are wary and because leaves, brush, and debris on forest floors make a quiet approach on foot impossible. Many hunters tramp the woods during gun season, but *successful* hunters generally sit in tree stands and let the walkers push animals their way. In some farmland areas, it is also possible to ambush deer near the edge of a field just before dark.

Rut hunting for bucks in November is also popular with both bowhunters and gun hunters throughout the Northeast. At this magic time of year, patient tree-stand sitters wait near fresh buck scrapes that they have sprinkled with commercial sex scent. This coupled with judicious grunting and snorting calls by hunters often lures the biggest trophy bucks into range.

The Southeast. The Southeast—including all states east of the Mississippi River and south of the Mason–Dixon line—is another geographical region tailor-made for hunting deer from stands. Like the Northeast, the predominant deer here are heavy-cover whitetails. Foliage varies dramatically throughout this region, from dense hardwood stands, farmland bottoms, and scattered woodlots to pine-covered ridges and thick, overgrown swamps.

Tree stands along agricultural fields and stands in heavy timber (with other hunters serving as drivers) are both popular throughout the Southeast. However, deliberate drive hunting of deer past strategically located tree stands and ground blinds is a time-honored tradition in this part of the country, and groups of 10 or 15 well-organized hunters are common. In areas where it is legal, dogs are often used to hound deer past hunters in tree stands or well-selected blinds.

The Great Plains Region. This region extends from eastern Montana south into eastern Colorado, eastward to the Mississippi River. This is primarily farmland habitat with both whitetail and mule deer herds. Stand hunting here usually takes two basic forms: simple tree-stand or ground-blind ambushes laid along agricultural fields of corn, wheat, and alfalfa; and stands taken along vegetation-clogged watercourses or woodlots where walkers can drive deer past waiting hunters.

In this transition zone between pure whitetail habitat and that used by mule deer as well, muleys are taken from stands nearly as often as whitetails. Some truly huge whitetails are also killed from stands during Midwestern seasons, which correspond with the late fall rut.

In the parts of the Great Plains that are wide-open prairie, stand hunting is not an effective hunting technique.

The Southwest and South-Central United States. The expansive region from California to Texas, Missouri, and Arkansas includes a wide variety of landforms and types of vegetation. The eastern fringe of this zone is strictly whitetail country, with dense hardwood forests, agricultural riverbottoms, and Gulf Coast swamps. Here, stand hunting is popular along forest edges, where other hunters keep deer moving and organized deer drives are feasible.

Farther west the land becomes increasingly arid, trees become sparse, and brush fields provide the main cover. Texas hunters take most of their whitetail deer from homemade tower blinds and vehicle towers attached to pickups and jeeps. Many of these animals are ambushed at water holes. Others are called in with rattling antlers or are lured by sex scent sprinkled in rutting scrapes. The whitetails and mule deer of western Texas, and points west, are seldom stand-hunted at all because the country tends to be open and more conducive to stalking and stillhunting efforts. A few deer hunters try coastal California blacktails from stands, but the hot, brushy country yields more deer to serious walking hunters.

The Rocky Mountain West. The Rocky Mountain West is famous for its abundance of mule deer, but there are plenty of whitetail deer here as well. Mule deer are generally not hunted with stands. But deer drives appear to be increasingly popular throughout this mountainous zone because muleys have permanently forsaken open country in many hard-hunted areas. Mule deer are also hunted from stands positioned near major migration trails at the time of year when these animals move en masse from high-country ranges to lower wintering grounds.

Rocky Mountain whitetails are most frequently seen along watercourses choked with cottonwoods, willows, and other excellent cover. However, populations are spreading into many higher ranges covered by pine, fir, and other softwood timber.

The best stand hunting for Rocky Mountain whitetails is enjoyed along fields of alfalfa and grain near dawn and dusk. Rifle-toting hunters often hide in haystacks instead of more conventional commercial stands. For Rocky Mountain whitetails, stand hunting near scrapes and drive hunting along narrow creekbeds are also popular techniques.

The Pacific Northwest. Stand hunting is almost required in dense coastal forests in Oregon, Washington, and points north into Alaska. Blacktail deer inhabit this region and they are slippery little critters that are tough to take by methods other than sitting patiently in wait.

Stand hunters in the Pacific Northwest often plant themselves in deer-rich areas and simply wait until animals wander by. Drive hunting patches of timber surrounded by clearcuts is also popular in this region, and so is luring blacktails toward elevated stands with commerical bleating-fawn calls.

In the central Pacific Northwest, blacktails and mule deer migrate miles from summer habitat to lower wintering areas. These deer are often ambushed along major migration trails by hunters using ground blinds and elevated stands.

SELECTING STAND LOCATIONS

There is nothing more frustrating than sitting on stand in an area devoid of deer. It is a futile exercise that can drive any hunter batty within a few short days of waiting. What is more important is that it can be avoided by scouting generally productive locations.

Good stand locations have three important characteristics. First, they allow clear views of trails, feeding areas, water holes, or other places that deer are known to frequent on a regular basis. Second, they are on the downwind side of areas where deer are likely to appear and also allow the hunter to approach the stand from the downwind side. Third, they facilitate concealed placement of a tree stand or ground blind while also allowing a clear field of fire at deer that do move into view.

Scouting for deer sign and deer themselves will satisfy the first requirement. Deer tracks along trails, droppings, and other sign ensure sightings of animals from a stand. Time spent glassing the area at dawn

Author Chuck Adams waylaid this record-size blacktail from a stand in an area laced with fresh tracks and heavily used water holes. This type of sign indicated a well-placed stand might be effective. It was.

The most productive tree stands are usually erected within shooting range of well-established deer trails. Stands near heavy bedding cover provide the best shots at deer in the late evening.

and dusk also helps. Checking a potential stand area firsthand also provides information on prevailing winds and reveals certain general locations with especially commanding views conducive to shooting at game.

Particulars on stand locations. Aside from the three basics of choosing stand locations, there are other factors to keep in mind when selecting stand sites. For one thing, the stand itself should be well above a deer's line of smell and sight. All too often, well-meaning neophytes erect tree stands in trees that are rooted in the bottoms of ravines. This puts a hunter at the same level as deer that come by on the flanks of nearby ridges. Similarly, a hunter who erects his stand 30 feet up in a tree atop the crest of a hill may actually be 75 or 100 feet above lower ground where deer are likely to mosey by. This extreme elevation serves no practical purpose.

One interesting technique used by savvy stand hunters in extremely brushy areas is to hack out trails through foliage at the ideal shooting distance from the stand. Deer quickly take to these artificial runways, preferring them to the thornier going along natural paths. This way hunters funnel deer toward their stands instead of erecting stands to accommodate the deer.

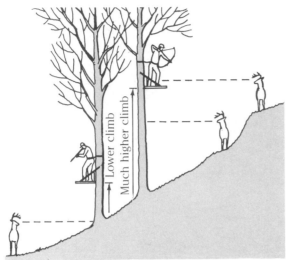

Select a tree and stand height that makes the most of existing terrain. If deer are likely to appear sharply downslope, stand placement need not be particularly high to avoid alerting the deer. By contrast, extra-high stands are needed to ambush animals on the upslope.

THE PROPER STAND OR BLIND

Nothing can match a commercial or homemade platform stand in accessible deer areas with plenty of sizable trees. For very remote stand locations, a more portable tree sling works best. Deer habitat with flimsy trees like willows or high-growing bushes is often tailor-made for some sort of platform ladder. In brushy areas devoid of trees, a tripod stand or tower blind provides the best elevated stand. When all else fails, any area with sparse clumps of grass or brush can be hunted with fairly good results from a commercial or homemade ground blind. Stands and blinds are discussed in detail in Part 5 of this book.

In some situations, a well-camouflaged deer hunter can take a stand by simply backing up against bush, tree trunk, stump, or similar outline-breaking object. These impromptu stands usually work as well as ground blinds. The only drawbacks here are that body odor remains at ground level and that a hunter is not above a deer's direct line of sight.

WHEN TO ERECT A STAND OR BLIND

Any major, noise-making activity involved in setting up a stand should be accomplished several weeks before deer season actually begins. Most portable trees

Natural stands or ground blinds sometimes provide adequate ambush cover. For example, a convenient haystack (above) provides excellent concealment, and so does a tree trunk (below) that breaks up your outline.

stands, tree slings, and ground blinds go up quickly and quietly, but stands that creak and groan during setup or that must be hammered in place tend to ruin deer hunting in the immediate vicinity for several days.

Take the case of a well-meaning bowhunter who watched a lush alfalfa field for several weeks prior to an early-September bowhunting season. He noted that the best bucks in the field trooped out each night from directly under a tall cottonwood tree with a wide, three-pronged crotch some 20 feet above the ground. So he slipped into the field with hammer, saw, lumber, and nails the afternoon before opening day and built a dandy three-sided platform in the crotch of the tree. The next afternoon, he tiptoed to the stand well before sundown with the wind squarely in his face, climbed upward on solidly nailed wooden steps, and settled down to wait for dusk. To his amazement, dozens of deer popped into the field near sundown, but every one was 400 yards away at the opposite end of the field. The nice bucks in the bunch gawked suspiciously toward him until dark, remaining half a dozen long bow shots away. After dark, the bowhunter headed back to his pickup, thoroughly frustrated and confused.

The cause of this hunter's consternation is patently obvious to any veteran bowhunter. All that hammering and sawing the day before season scared the daylights out of deer bedded 200 yards away in heavy willow thickets. The lure of the hayfield was too strong for these animals to stay away, but they changed their normal entry point and gave the tree-stand site very wide berth.

Many stand hunters grossly underestimate the animals they are trying to bag. Any deer will avoid places with sudden and unexpected human activity—and that includes careless, noisy stand building.

HOW AND WHEN TO TAKE A STAND

Always approach your stand from the downwind side to eliminate the chance of alerting nearby deer. Move in cautiously and quietly, actually stalking the stand as if it were a deer. To help mask your foot trail, cover your soles with commercial odor-masking scent or another scent-squelching substance.

Try to reach your stand at least two full hours before you expect deer to pop into view. The two common times to sit on stand in agricultural areas and other places where deer feed in leisurely fashion are early in the morning and late in the evening. Reaching a stand in mid-afternoon for an evening hunt is usually easy enough to do, but climbing into a morning stand well before the rooster crows means leaving the sack early and fumbling through pitch-black woods. Despite the inconvenience of reaching stand two hours prior to daylight, this is the only way a hunter can expect to see deer once dawn breaks. A hunter who reaches his stand *at first light* seldom has a chance because nearby animals have been spooked and his scent trail is still fresh. Deer feeding at night in fields near a stand will drift back out to eat if danger passes nearby well before daylight. But a late morning approach drives deer into heavy cover for good.

In situations when deer are likely to be moving about all day—such as during the whitetail rut; when

Stand hunting deer over water holes at midday can be a deadly technique. Ideal hunting locations near water's edge are easily found by looking for concentrations of tracks in mud.

the woods are full of eager, walking hunters; or when mule deer are migrating heavily during a storm—a deer hunter is best advised to stay on stand all day long. Similarly, in many heavily hunted areas, deer have learned to alter their normal habits and feed only during midday hours when the majority of hunters are back at camp. A savvy and patient hunter can cash in on such adaptive deer behavior by staying on stand throughout the daylight hours.

One other specialized stand-hunting situation deserves mention here. This is sitting over water holes and other areas where deer regularly get their water. The mud around such places is always tattooed with fresh tracks, and hunters can glass watering areas during the off-season to confirm deer activity. Animals usually water at least once per day in moderate weather—often twice or more when temperatures are really warm. Most often, deer visit watering spots during full daylight hours. This makes stand hunting near these spots ideal midday bets. Gung-ho hunters often sit on morning and evening stands near deer-feeding hotspots, and spend the balance of the day on separate stands overlooking heavily used watering holes. Many deer—particularly whitetails—are waylaid on the banks of water holes.

TREE-STAND SAFETY

Every tree-stand hunter should follow a safe, established procedure from the moment he lifts his stand from the pickup truck until he stores it away again at season's end. A very high percentage of hunting accidents occur in and around tree stands—accidents that run from scrapes and bruises to fatalities.

The first step in tree-stand safety involves carrying a stand to the site. All too many hunters attempt to carry gear as well as stands in their hands—an awkward procedure inviting dangerous falls. The correct way to transport any stand is to backpack it to the site. This leaves both hands free to hold a rifle, shotgun, or bow and also to steady a hunter in rough terrain.

The second safety step is to select a proper tree for climbing. Any slippery-barked tree or tree covered with ice is a poor choice because it invites slips and falls. This type of tree is especially deadly when a climbing platform stand is attached because the tree-gripping blades will not solidly engage.

A dead tree or tree that is too small in diameter can be spooky and downright dangerous for tree-stand use. In either case the tree may fall or break off in a heavy

Some trees are safe for tree-stand use and others are not. One of the poorest bets is a dead tree with loose, rotting bark. Biting or stinging pests such as scorpions and ants often live under the bark, and decaying trees sometimes fall or break in heavy winds.

The only safe way to carry a tree-stand platform is by means of backpack straps. This leaves both hands free to carry a gun or bow and allow good handholds and balance over rough terrain.

wind. This has happened more than once to unsuspecting hunters and has resulted in broken legs or arms, internal injuries, and worse. A dead tree can be dangerous for another reason, too. Biting and stinging critters such scorpions, wasps, ants, and bees often live under the loose bark of long-dead trees. These pests can unexpectedly swarm a climbing hunter and cause him to fall. So select a stout, living tree to climb.

Once you select a suitable tree, tie your bow, gun, knapsack, and other essential gear to a long piece of rope and place these items safely to one side of the tree. After tying the other end of the rope to your belt, begin climbing cautiously upward. Attempting to tote equipment aloft during the initial climb is always awkward and risky. At worst it can lead to an accidentally discharged gun or a fatal fall on razor-keen hunting arrows.

When climbing, always proceed with extreme caution. If you're using a climbing stand, make sure the stand is solidly assembled and securely attached to the tree. If you are climbing hand over hand with available limbs or tree-stand steps, maintain a two-point grip on the tree for optimum safety (two hands or one hand and one foot). Otherwise, a limb or tree-stand step that gives way unexpectedly can result in a serious fall.

An approved safety belt is an absolute must for safe tree-stand hunting. The belt will not cinch dangerously around your waist if you trip and fall, and it features a quick-detach buckle similar to that of car seat belts.

Once you have reached the desired height, immediately attach a certified safety belt around your waist and the trunk of the tree. This belt should be positioned on the tree to allow for both standing up and sitting down. An ordinary rope should never be used as a safety belt because it can cinch about your middle during a fall. Sometimes this causes serious injury and leaves the hunter helplessly dangling like a crawfish on a line.

After carefully buckling yourself to the tree, you can relax and hoist up your gear by the rope attached to your belt. Once this equipment is untied and hung on handy limbs or tree-stand hooks, you are almost ready to wait for deer. Almost.

Prior to settling down, take a minute to walk about the platform and familiarize yourself with its limits. It is easy to accidentally step over the edge of an unfamiliar stand, especially in the excitement as game approaches. At little orientation shows you how to restrict your movements and reduce chances of a mishap later.

Always sit on a stool or integral tree-stand seat during long waits to prevent excessive fatigue or lightheadedness. Standing up for hours can become uncomfortable as muscles tire and blood settles from the head toward the lower body. At worst, too much standing can cause stumbles and falls or even fainting. Sitting down prevents these problems and makes the wait for deer more comfortable.

One other note on tree-stand safety: According to a recent study by one of America's largest tree-stand manufacturers, the vast majority of tree-stand accidents occur when hunters become excited by the presence of game. With surprising regularity, tree standers simply forget they are high above the ground after seeing or shooting at deer, stepping into space or attempting to or even attempting to run after their

Climb the tree first, **then** *haul your equipment up on a hoist rope. This is the safest, easiest way to mount a tree stand. Your gun should be unloaded before the hoist.*

prey. The result is often disastrous if a hunter is not using a safety belt. At the least, it leads to a bruised body and a badly bruised ego to match.

When climbing down from a stand at day's end, reverse the safe-climbing procedure outlined above.

PROCEDURES FOR WAITING ON STAND

Waiting in ambush for deer is a relatively easy technique once a productive location has been scouted. But you must still exercise certain precautions and practice certain skills to ambush a wary deer.

First and foremost, make as little noise as possible from the time you reach your elevated stand or ground blind until you are ready to walk back to your vehicle. Move about the stand or blind to detect and eliminate any underfoot debris or nearby limbs that might make noise during the wait and the taking of a shot. Some tree-stand platforms creak and groan insufferably when a hunter first moves about, so you should shift your weight repeatedly to work the creaks out of noisy tree-stand joints. Similarly, you should experimentally draw your bow or shoulder your gun toward places

Think safety when you climb to any elevated stand. This bowhunter tried a one-hand climb up the steep side of a haystack and was rewarded by a fall with something extra—a solid wallop from the top bale. Fortunately, this hunter learned his lesson without serious injury.

deer are likely to appear. This shows what shooting lanes are open and completely clear of foliage. Lap off any branches impeding noise-free movement and shooting, by using a small saw or knife.

When actually waiting for deer, remain relatively motionless and quiet. Too much thumping of boots against a tree-stand platform will alert nearby animals, and so will the fairly subtle rustling of clothing created when you move about and crane your neck to look. Avoid coughs, sneezes, and similar noises. Deer have sensitive ears capable of picking up relatively slight human sounds.

A tree stand high above the ground helps keep your movements away from a deer's direct line of sight. However, deer are wise to danger in trees in many parts of the country, and some keep a wary eye toward the sky. As a result, stand hunters after pressured whitetail deer and other species must move slowly even when they are aloft. There's nothing more frustrating than waiting for hours on stand, only to spook a nearby deer by excessive movement.

In fairly dry conditions that allow stand sitters to hear a deer approaching, many hunters relax and read a good book to wile away the hours. This curbs impatience and minimizes movement on stand. If you are constantly raising your binoculars to look about, strolling the perimeter of your platform, or otherwise fidgeting, you will hamper your chances.

DEER SCENTS

As mentioned earlier, conscientious stand hunters usually squirt an odor-masking scent on their boot-soles and pantlegs before approaching a stand. In addition, most also sprinkle scent liberally on bushes and tree trunks near their stands just in case down-drafts waft human odor to an approaching deer. The scent should match the terrain and time of year. Some sort of food scent or natural scent is favored early and late in the fall. Sex scents are preferred at the height of rutting activity.

PATIENCE

Stand hunting is largely a game of patience. First you must be patient as you scout for sign and glass for deer. You must also be patient as you seek out ideal ambush locations and build or erect adequate tree-stand structures. And you must be patient as you wait for hours and hours on the random movements of animals.

For those who like hunting game on stand, the pre-hunt legwork, educated scheming, and waiting all become worthwhile in that one moment when hoofs scuff the forest floor and a deer pops into shooting range.

THE FINE ART OF HUNTING ON FOOT

An outdoorsman skilled in hunting deer on foot can take deer with machinelike consistency. Hunting from a well-placed stand is best in some noisy environments, and is sometimes most effective on ultraskittish trophy bucks. But the hunter who can move like a cat through the woods is far more versatile than a hunter who relies on stands exclusively and lacks the ability to actively pursue game.

Hunting on foot is by far the most difficult hunting technique because you become an active aggressor, risking detection with every step. In contrast to a passive tree sitter or blind user, a walking hunter attempts to slip past a deer's network of survival senses and make a vital shot. No matter where an animal is or what the terrain peculiarities happen to be, a really good hunter can weasel into range with patience and a little good luck. This near-total control of hunting situations gives a satisfaction unequalled by any other type of deer hunting.

Because there is nothing easy about hunting deer on foot, many hunters balk at the very idea of trying. Others plod about the forest with no concept of what being sneaky is really all about. But those conscientious, do-or-die individuals who hang tough and perfect their skills are versatile, deadly deer hunters who seldom draw a blank. If stand hunting seems the best approach, these hunters do not hesitate to try it out. However, they do not helplessly wring their hands if deer are hanging tight in cover or feeding and

watering well beyond shooting range of practical stand locations. Instead, they go after the deer.

There are five separate methods for pursuing deer on foot and a versatile hunter should learn them all. The methods are stillhunting, stalking, jumpshooting, drive hunting, and tracking. Each has specific applications in the field.

STILLHUNTING BASICS

Stillhunting can be defined as moving steadily and carefully in search of unseen deer. This is the most difficult of all the methods because it requires constant vigilance and stealth. A stillhunter never knows when he'll round a bush or poke his head above a rise and find himself face to face with game. As a result, he can never drop his guard—an intense, demanding requirement.

Stillhunting is best accomplished in areas with relatively dense foliage and few, if any, long-distance views. Such areas ideally harbor dense enough populations of deer to make encounters likely. Footing should be relatively quiet and undergrowth broken enough to allow careful, silent walking. Stillhunting is particularly popular in northeastern hardwood forests, rolling brush country typical of the American

Hunting on foot is difficult but very rewarding. Hunters who can sneak within shooting range of game can create more opportunities than those who rely only on stands.

Southwest, and rain forests of the Pacific Northwest. However, any overgrown, deer-rich area that can be quietly traversed is ideal for stillhunting.

Whitetails and blacktails are most commonly still-hunted with good results. Mule deer in their typically mountainous, semiopen habitat are best pursued with other methods of hunting on foot. However, *any* place with restricted views and ground cover that can be walked on quietly is well suited for stillhunting.

A stillhunter goes to work at times when deer are likely to be up and feeding or moving about. Generally, this means early morning and late evening. But cool or stromy weather can make midday a productive stillhunting time.

Stillhunters can be likened to tomcats hunting mice in a field overgrown with weeds. The hunter moves along slowly, inspecting terrain before him for telltale sights and sounds of deer. Since views in stillhunting areas are invariably restricted to less than maximum shooting range, the hunter's primary goal is spotting animals before they detect him and run or sneak away. Once a deer is located, a stillhunter can generally shoot at once unless foliage blocks his shot.

Here is how one eastern stillhunter made his skill pay off. The countryside he was hunting in was eastern hardwood forest, a hodgepodge of hogbacks, shallow ravines, and hollows. Tree-stand hunting would have been a moderately effective technique on the white-

Shooting at deer in stillhunting situations is often fast and furious. In densely wooded areas, shotguns with slugs or buckshot are as effective as rifles.

tails living there, but local regulations outlawed the use of elevated stands. As a result, the hunter entered the woods on foot in predawn darkness, skulking along after daylight had penetrated the leafy overhead canopy. The forest floor was littered with leaves, but recent rains had softened and muted debris to allow almost noiseless walking. The hunter eased along with eyes and ears straining for nearby animals. He kept the wind in his face and his slug-loaded shotgun poised for a shot at the moving "flag" of any departing whitetail deer. Visibility in the tight-knit woods was seldom more than 60 yards.

The hunter knew the woods held ample deer, and he paused after each step to survey every bit of terrain before him. Animals would be up and feeding, preoccupied with their bellies and making moderate noise. By hugging occasional willow clumps and blending close to trees, the hunter knew he was nearly invisible and likely to get his chance.

Without warning, something flickered almost imperceptibly along the edge of a swale to the left, then dropped out of sight. The hunter froze, canvassed the area and strained his ears. Seconds later, a hoof thudded audibly against the forest floor in direct line with the movement he had seen earlier. The hunter waited, noting the breeze in his face with satisfaction. Something flickered above the swale again—an unmistakable golden glint of polished antler.

The hunter raised his shotgun with infinite care, cradled it against a handy maple sapling, and leveled the sights in line with the antler. Thirty seconds passed like slow, heavy heartbeats. Then, without warning, the deer strolled into plain view, head down and broadside. The hunter crushed the trigger and the small, mud-fat six-point buck dropped as if beaned with a 12-pound sledge. Stealth and patience had made the morning successful.

This stillhunting adventure is repeated thousands of times each year across North America. The foliage may vary from sun-heated sagebrush to ice-coated hardwood, and the deer may be a 200-pound whitetail or 100-pound blacktail. But the slow, deliberate, ever-watchful hunting approach gets results.

Because ideal stillhunting country is usually thick with foliage and footing is littered with debris, successful hunters using this method invariably wear soft-surfaced clothing and footwear with pliable soles. Garb is carefully chosen to blend with surrounding terrain. These clothing precautions are necessary because deer are usually encountered well within the range of their probing eyes and big, sensitive ears.

Bowhunters and gun hunters alike get results by walking quietly, hugging the shadows, and exercising other basic sneaking skills. Exact walking speed and other precautions for maintaining silence are governed by footing conditions, how far ahead a hunter can clearly hear and see, and how dense deer populations

Stillhunters wear camouflage clothing that makes little or no noise in the densest foliage. Encounters with deer are usually unexpected and sometimes point-blank, owing to the hunter's stealth.

are in the particular area. Soft, rain-soaked footing allows faster movement than brittle warm-weather footing, and 100-yard views allow less perfect stealth than views that invariably place wary deer smack in a hunter's lap.

The old, hackneyed deer-sneaking rule of "take a step, then wait two" is good advice in most stillhunting situations. But in very noisy conditions a hunter might be advised to take a step and then wait five or ten. In areas with relatively silent walking and very few deer per square mile, a hunter should move faster to cover more ground and increase the odds of bumping into game. Walking speed and caution level are always judgment calls in stillhunting—calls a hunter must base on past experience with deer.

The majority of dedicated stillhunters use some sort of odor-masking scent to hide their own body odor just in case fickle breezes suddenly shift. In close-range stillhunting situations, the scent will sometimes confuse deer just long enough to allow a shot.

Stillhunting is a highly demanding deer-hunting technique that separates the veterans from the novices. Stealing within close range of a deer in fairly heavy cover taxes every stillhunting skill to the utmost and requires continuous vigilance and mental concentration. Since a stillhunter seldom knows when he'll suddenly encounter an animal, he can never drop his

guard. But that also makes stillhunting the most rewarding of all methods of hunting on foot.

STALKING BASICS

Stalking is the skill of spotting game from a distance and then deliberately sneaking into shooting range. Although similar to stillhunting, stalking does not involve a blind search for deer. A stalking hunter always knows where his quarry is *prior* to moving in for the kill.

Any deer habitat with long-range views is suitable for stalking. Big canyon country and relatively open flatlands both nicely fill the bill. Although some whitetail range is tailor-made for stalking—most particularly the sparsely wooded habitat of Coues deer (desert whitetails)—this technique is predominantly used on mule deer and on blacktails residing in mountains and foothills. These environs let a hunter cruise ridgelines or sit atop knobs and points, patiently probing hillsides, swales, and valleys with binocular and naked eye until deer are spotted and approach strategies devised.

A stalking deer hunter must be in especially good physical condition to move about broken country, hoof it up and down hills of varying elevation, and walk long distances to unalerted deer. Compared to stalking, stillhunting is generally a physical piece of cake. As often as not, a stalking hunter must move quickly and surely over rugged terrain to intercept moving deer or reach stationary animals before they bed in heavy thickets.

A stalker's primary allies are well-made hiking boots

Small southwestern Coues deer (desert whitetail) inhabit semiopen terrain that is well suited to spot-and-stalk hunting techniques. But most whitetail deer are taken by stand hunting or stillhunting in fairly heavy cover. (Craig Boddington photo)

A stalking hunter must spot deer from a distance, devise a sensible approach route, and then execute the sneak as skillfully as possible. Stealing within shooting range of wary deer is seldom easy.

Wide-open foothill country like this is typical mule-deer habitat and is tailor-made for stalking. In this country, a hunter must use existing hills, gullies, and canyons with uncanny skill.

and a first-rate hunting binocular. The binocular is used to scan large tracts of countryside in search of feeding or resting deer. In trophy hunting, a field glass is also employed to size up antlers at a distance. Finally, a good-quality glass allows the stalker to analyze terrain between himself and his prey—a process vital to planning a quiet, unobtrusive approach. The need for excellent boots becomes obvious—often painfully so—to anyone who attempts a long-distance stalk for the very first time.

Stalking is not as mentally draining as stillhunting because a hunter need not be fully keyed for action each and every second of an entire morning or evening outing. First, the stalker moves or sits with eyes working overtime until he locates a deer he wants to put in the bag. In most cases, this phase of the game occurs during the first three hours of morning or the last three hours of evening—those times when deer are active and feeding.

But, in some areas and under certain weather conditions, spot-and-stalk hunting can occur throughout the day. For example, a hunter after mule deer in semiopen sagebrush country can often see bedded animals and stalk them at any daylight hour. Similarly, brush-country blacktail deer habitually rise to feed off and on all day long, allowing a patient hunter on a high perch to spot animals in thick brush between 10 A.M. and 4 P.M. In cool, drizzly midday conditions, all varieties of deer are prone to move in and out of protective cover, thus playing into a stalker's hands.

Once an animal is spotted, the next step is plotting a feasible approach route. This is occasionally easy, but usually it is fraught with complications. Sometimes other deer block an easy walk to the target animal, threatening to spook every deer in sight. Sometimes the target deer is steadily moving as it feeds or heads

for bed, creating uncertainty about how best to intercept its progress. Often, terrain and foilage make an out-of-sight approach difficult, or threaten to prevent a clear shot once a hunter steals within shooting distance.

In devising a likely approach strategy, a stalking hunter must also try to second-guess wind directions along the approach—a tough and sometimes impossible task in areas where breezes dart, swirl, and roll across uneven upslopes, downgrades, bowls, and flats. To make matters worse, some deer-stalking areas are littered with noisy obstacles, such as shale slides, brush patches, and areas with ankle-deep leaves. As any experienced mountain hunter will testify, an easy stalk is a rare and wonderful deer-hunting opportunity.

Exact stalking strategies are as numerous as moves on a chessboard. A simple stalk might require a hunter to tiptoe down the north side of a long knife ridge, ease over the top at a designated spot, then blast a buck with his rifle as it contentedly chews its cud and stares the other way. A complex stalk might entail weaving in and out of half a dozen other deer, slipping past those on the upwind side and scaring those on the downwind side in a direction well away from the target animal. It might involve four major shifts in wind direction—depending upon where the hunter has to go—and might also require some ticklish sneaking over precarious and noisy shale in plain view of an animal feeding at a long distance. If the hunter does get close to his target, the deer might feed off at a rapid pace into foliage that blocks any possible shot, might bed in cover too heavy for a ground squirrel to wiggle through, or might detect the hunter and bound away at high speed. Stalking is a complicated game. The initial spotting of animals is the easiest part.

A spot-and-stalk hunter locates his animal, wracks

his brain for a few intense minutes to decide how to make his approach, then executes the stalk to the best of his ability. During the entire stalk, he pays strict attention to basic walking skills, monitors the wind, and remains as quiet and unobtrusive as possible. He changes movement speed to suit the moment. The initial 200 yards may be covered at a lope because terrain fully covers his approach. The last 50 yards may take an hour or a minute to traverse, depending upon footing and the location of the deer being stalked.

One other note on stalking technique: All deer have superb peripheral vision, allowing them to instantly spot movement even when their heads are lowered in a broadside feeding position. Many stalking deer hunters—especially close-range bowhunters—blow otherwise perfect setups by attempting to move in plain view of alert, broadside deer. Feeding animals are the easiest to stalk because they are rustling foliage and chewing vigorously, which impairs their ability to hear. But the animals can see well unless their eyes are completely blocked by terrain or foliage—an important fact every stalker learns one way or another.

Stalking is a highly rewarding endeavor. It is perhaps the most exciting deer-hunting method of all because hunters see their targets long before shots are possible.

Open-country deer can be stalked to within close range by a patient and well-practiced hunter. This huge Sitka blacktail buck was nailed in the Alaskan high country with one shot at 25 yards.

This allows suspense to build during the approach. Stalking with bow-and-arrow is by far the most difficult version of this taxing technique, but first-rate bow-hunters pull off masterful stalks with regularity. Stalks with guns are usually easier and shorter in duration, but by no means easy.

JUMPSHOOTING BASICS

Heat ghosts danced weirdly across decaying stumps of distant mesas as the solitary hunter picked his way along. A giant, colorless sun hung soddenly above in the West, injecting the sultry and windless afternoon with nearly unbearable heat. The rifleman paused, mopped his brow, then stepped out on a weathered lava shelf. The sidehill canyon below was choked with manzanita brush—a perfect place for deer.

The hunter scanned the ravine for several minutes, then scooped up a fist-size rock, balanced the projectile in his palm, and hurled it into the thickets below. The stone clattered against limbs, then bounced and rolled loudly down the gully. A thin cloud of dust rose slowly into the hot afternoon air. The hunter watched intently for the gray-black flicker of deer slipping out of the draw and listened for the crunching and crackling of hoofs. Nothing stirred below. After a minute he picked up and heaved another rock, followed by a third, and then a fourth. The canyon echoed with noise and boiled with dull red dust, but no deer materialized through the haze.

The fifth rock did the trick. As it careened off an ancient manzanita stump and bounced out of sight into the dry bushes, a stone rattled faintly on the left. The hunter turned just in time to see a sleek, high-racked buck slip between two stunted oak trees, lunge through a crack in the rim barely 50 yards away, and barrel uphill across open ground toward a thicket *behind* the hunter.

The hunter spun and snapped up his rifle in one fluid motion, squeezing the trigger as the crosswires cleared the charging deer's massive chest. The firearm roared and the animal did a complete somersault, its sleek white belly flashing as it tumbled tail over tea-kettle onto the ground. Minutes later the hunter was happily gutting his prize—a 200-pound mule deer with massive 4 × 4 antlers (western count; 4 tines to each side). Jumpshooting had paid off once again.

With minor variations, this is how jumpshooting is practiced across the country. In hard-hunted areas dotted with patches of heavy cover, deer of all varieties often prefer to stick tight and let hunters walk by. These tactics are a favorite of whitetail deer, but mule and blacktail deer use them too. The only way to see and shoot deer under these circumstances is to rout

Throwing rocks into brushy hiding places often extricates nervous deer. At times, several stones are hurled before animals become rattled enough to leave cover.

them from their beds and then shoot well.

Hunter-wise deer are prone to hang tight in any area with protective thickets. Whitetails in swamplands of the Deep South, mule deer in broken, brush-dotted mesa country of the Southwest, and blacktails in post-oak tangles of the Pacific Northwest all react the same way provided cover is adequately heavy. These deer are especially hard to flush out of brush during midday hours, and they often huddle like bobwhite quail within just a few feet of passing hunters. The deer blend quite well and only jump up when they realize they have been seen, when hunters linger nearby for long periods, or when the immediate area is pelted by rocks or invaded by hunting dogs.

Deer hide in a variety of cover, but jumpshooting technique only works well in places where animals must cross open country once they do leap up and run. Typical jumpshooting hotspots include terrain with choppy draws dotted with a patchwork of thickets and meadows; woodlot country with small islands of timber surrounded by agricultural fields or logging clearcuts; and flat topography with scattered openings and foliage. The key to jumpshooting deer is being able to see and shoot at animals once they decide to run. Areas too thickly overgrown for one or two hunters to jump and see deer must be hunted with organized deer drives, not jumpshooting techniques.

Routing animals from their beds is half the battle in successful jumpshooting. This can often be accomplished by throwing rocks into likely bedding

HOW TO MAKE A STONE-THROWING SLING

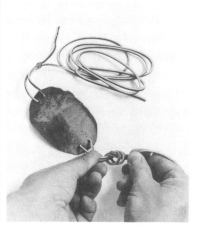
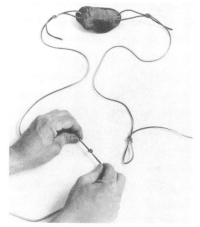

You can hurl stones great distances by means of this homemade sling, which you can fashion from new boot laces and an old boot tongue. Create pouch holes by means of a leather punch or a nail, and (left) fasten the laces to the pouch with simple loops. Then loop one free end of lace to serve as a finger thong and knot the other (middle photo) to align with the looped end when the pouch is suspended. To hurl stones, grip lace ends as shown and whirl the sling over your head, like an airplane propeller, increasing centrifugal force until you are ready to release the knotted end and thereby fire the stone in the intended direction.

thickets. The rocks can be hurled by hand or with the aid of homemade rock-throwing slings (see accompanying photos). Because holed-up deer are wise to the ways of gunners, a single thrown rock often fails to get them moving. In many instances, a dozen or more stones must be tossed before the ruckus is sufficient to unglue deer from cover.

In some hunting areas, the oldest and wisest deer are difficult to move even with thrown projectiles. Unless brush is pelted until rocks actually smack into a hidden deer, animals might refuse to move. As a result, a few jumpshooters work with partners, alternately playing dog and hunter to thoroughly thrash likely cover. No deer will stick tight if his bedding area is invaded directly by humans. This allows one person to wade the rough foliage and chase out deer to a waiting hunter.

One jumpshooting variation that works extremely well is to use a well-trained jumpdog to nose about within rifle range and to shoo out nearby deer. This technique is illegal in most parts of North America, but is very popular in some brushy states like California and Texas. Dogs used to jump deer include fox terriers, rat terriers, terrier/beagle crosses, and other hot-nosed breeds. These dogs typically move a deer, chase it with high-pitched yips for 100 yards or less, and then return to the hunter. Such dogs are also ex-

tremely useful in tracking down crippled deer, usually circling and holding a wounded animal at bay with short, choppy barks.

As mentioned before, jumping deer in the first place is half the battle. The other half is hitting animals once they break into open areas. As often as not, attempts are merely snapshots as deer flash through very small openings. In canyon country, shooting is sometimes long as deer break from cover and climb distant slopes. Occasionally, pressured deer will attempt to sneak away by holding their bodies low and their chins only inches from the ground. But most run hell-bent for leather. Hunters who jumpshoot deer with regularity become extremely good at making shots count, learning to lead moving animals and shoot the instant a sight picture looks correct.

DRIVE HUNTING BASICS

Driving deer is highly enjoyable and is a traditional method of hunting throughout much of North America. A deer drive requires several hunters for a decent chance of success, making it a major social event as well as a dandy way to hunt. It is also an exciting way of taking deer—suspense builds from the time hunters plan their strategy and then slowly, methodically bring events to an adrenaline-charged conclusion.

Organized drives work the best in substantial, uninterrupted patches of extremely heavy foliage—foli-

Fox terriers, rat terriers, and similar yapping jumpdogs are often favored for routing deer out of heavy cover— where this technique is legal. This hunting strategy is especially popular in California, Texas, and other dry and brushy states.

Drive hunting uses several walking hunters to flush deer toward gunners on stand. As long as prevailing breezes blow from drivers to standers, deer generally move out of cover along fairly predictable avenues of escape. Depending on terrain, drivers might be spaced as much as 100 yards apart, preferably within sight of one another.

age too thick for stillhunting, stalking, or jumpshooting deer. Drive hunting is especially popular on deep-woods whitetail deer, but works equally well on blacktail deer and heavy-cover mule deer. A solitary hunter rarely gets a crack at these animals. They run or sneak away from him and generally circle behind or beeline for places a long distance away.

Stand hunting often works every bit as well as drive hunting in brushy or heavily wooded areas with relatively little hunting activity. However, heavy-cover deer that are regularly pressured by man usually become nocturnal about feeding and watering habits, making deer drives the only feasible approach. Even in lightly hunted areas, drives are enjoyable, as effective as waiting on stand, and ideal when several people prefer to hunt together.

A basic deer drive consists of several drivers and several standers. First of all, the hunting party studies a particular patch of woods, decides which directions driven deer are likely to flee, and then splits into drivers and those designated to wait for animals to move by. Observant hunters who have driven particular areas in the past can usually predict with fair accuracy which escape routes animals will take. In unfamiliar places, hunters must do some educated guessing based on the lay of the land.

The most effective way to drive any deer area is placing stand hunters on the downwind side—either dropping them off by automobile or giving them ample time to sneak into position undetected. In many traditional drive-hunting hotspots, hunters have erected permanent tree stands near well-used trails that deer favor for escape. In other areas, standers must back against existing foliage to hide their human outlines. The best places also afford a fairly good view of terrain.

Once stand hunters are in position, drivers begin moving slowly toward these standers with the intention of scaring deer ahead. There are two schools of

thought among serious drive-hunters. One philosophy holds that drivers should shout, whoop, throw rocks and sticks, and otherwise make a major ruckus. The other philosophy dictates that drivers quietly stillhunt along as if there were no stand hunters at the end of the line.

Both noisy and quiet drives have their fans. However, in most cases quiet driving seems to yield better results. Since drivers are ideally moving with the wind at their backs, the animals need no fanfare to realize danger is near. A noisy drive certainly pushes deer to waiting stand hunters, but these deer are often thoroughly spooked and running hard. In addition, noisy drivers undoubtedly scare some deer into sticking tight instead of slipping away as they would under less intimidating circumstances. A quiet drive also invites deer to try circling back between the drivers. This gives walkers ample opportunity to score themselves as they move along in a ragged skirmish line. Those deer that are driven straight ahead tend to slink along instead of running all-out, and this gives waiting hunters relatively easy shots. The only major advantage afforded by noisy deer drives is that stand hunters can keep close tabs on the positions of the drivers moving their way.

Specific deer-drive setups are as diverse as individual plots of ground. A classic drive in a perfectly rectangular section of woods usually spots two or three stand hunters on the downwind end, one stander along each flank to intercept deer squirting out the sides, and three to five drivers walking parallel to one another in a relatively straight line. In areas of continuous forest, hunters usually drive random portions of cover with standers sitting wherever major deer trails leave the driven plots of land. Narrow, heavily wooded creek bottoms are easiest of all to drive, with one or two standers setting up downwind as one or two walkers work ½ mile to one mile of upwind terrain.

COMMON DEER-DRIVE SETUPS

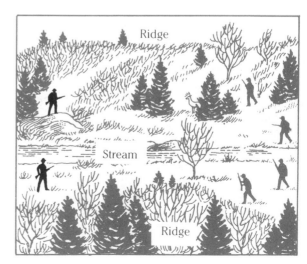

In brushy or timbered canyons, hunters often fan out with one or two in the bottom, one on each flanking ridge, and one or two waiting patiently at the end of the drive. Such a setup is especially effective where ridges are semiopen and the canyon bottom heavily treed. Most deer either run directly toward the waiting hunters or peel off to the sides and provide shots to the ridge-walking flankers. As long as a deer drive positions waiting hunters downwind and drivers with the breeze more or less at their backs, animals are apt to move the desired direction and give someone a shot at success.

One time-honored technique is called the southern deer drive. This unique method uses deer-trailing hound dogs and is employed primarily in the Deep South and other lushly overgrown areas south of the Mason–Dixon line. Southern deer drives with dogs add the spine-tingling music of hounds to an already exciting technique, and work better on deer dwelling in truly thick cover than drives using human hunters alone.

A southern deer-drive setup is basically the same as any other, with several hunters on stand along likely escape routes, such as old trails. However, drivers lead dogs to the other end of the area to be driven, then turn these hounds loose to cast about for fresh deer scent. Drivers move toward standers, but hounds invariably hit hot deer tracks and really begin stirring up the woods.

Hounds are used in southern deer drives to follow hot tracks and make plenty of noise in the process. This stirs up deer while hunters jockey about in hopes of intercepting the hard-pressed animals.

Many sorts of deer hounds are used in southern drives. They range from pure-bred Walkers, blueticks, redbones, and black-and-tans to mixed-blood hounds of questionable ancestry. Many excellent deer hounds are cast-off coon dogs or foxhounds that owners failed to break from trailing deer. The best dogs for southern deer drives are those with relatively "hot" noses. Cold-nosed dogs capable of trailing old tracks can follow deer sign for hours on end before tracks warm up and a deer is actually jumped. By contrast, a hot-nosed hound only runs a fresh, pungent track. That means the deer is moving nearby and ideally past waiting guns.

In southern deer drives, drivers as well as standers have excellent chances of bagging venison once hounds begin chasing deer around. Southern white-tails generally circle repeatedly before a persistent, bawling canine and move about within a fairly small home territory. If deer are not dropped as they streak or sneak past stand hunters initially, gunners can jockey about the woods and attempt to intercept the crying hounds and moving deer on subsequent circles through the area.

Deer hunting with hounds embodies both advantages and drawbacks. The dogs definitely keep deer moving, maximizing the chances for waiting gunners. When deer are crippled or dropped stone dead, pursuing hounds usually bay them up or stay with carcasses until lucky shooters are able to arrive. Unfortunately, most hounds will follow live deer for several hours and sometimes several *days,* making dog recovery a major problem. In a few parts of the South, following deer hounds on horseback is preferred for keeping close tabs on dogs and increasing the odds of seeing the deer being followed.

Deer drives are popular and effective no matter what weapon a hunter uses. In truly dense whitetail habitat, shotguns loaded with buckshot are best for drive hunting. In canyon country, rifles work the best. Even bowhunters can benefit by driving deer, provided animals are pushed quietly to allow stationary or slow-moving shots as deer sneak along.

BASICS FOR TRACKING DEER

Tracking is not a particularly popular technique. There are two basic reasons for this. First, deer can only be tracked in fresh, soft snow—a circumstance seldom encountered in many deer-hunting areas. Second, deer tracking takes considerable time, skill, and patience, and that tends to discourage the majority of hunters.

In areas with lots of animals, there is little need to find a deer track and follow it for hours. It is far easier to stillhunt and count on bumping into unalerted deer.

Tracking deer in soft, fresh snow can be exciting and productive. It is especially practical in areas where deer are few and far between. Once you find a fresh track, you must dog it persistently until an animal appears or darkness finally falls.

Deer tracking comes into its own in areas where animals are few and far between. There a hunter's best bet is walking or loping cross-country until a fresh track is found. Then the hunter follows that track, dogging it persistently until the deer that made it jumps into view or otherwise appears.

Here is how one hunter tracked down a big buck. One Friday night toward the end of whitetail season an inch of soft, dry snow suddenly fell. This hunt happened to be in the Northeast, although it could have occurred almost anywhere. The hunter drove to his favorite patch of woods just before daylight, grabbed his short-barreled slug gun, and began tramping rapidly along an old dirt road that bisected the rolling, hardwood forest.

Thirty minutes later, the tracker found two fresh sets of tracks crossing the road—a medium-size set and a markedly smaller set. From past experience, he realized these footprints had been made by a doe and

fawn, and elected to pass up the animals in hopes of finding a lone dry doe or buck. He continued down the road another mile without success, then veered into the forest edge. Fifteen minutes passed, and he suddenly hit the fresh, meandering trail of a big, wide-hoofed deer. The animal was heading into the most remote, roadless tract in the area, but the hunter took up the trail like an excited hound. Part of the time he followed the track directly, and part of the time he walked nearby ridges to get a little better view. The snow was soft and silent underfoot, the air biting and still.

Two hours of slow tracking produced no results, but the hunter noted that his deer had ceased to meander and feed. The animal was walking steadily now, apparently heading for bed. The hunter slowed his pace, increasingly alert for the slightest sight or sound of the animal. Fortunately, a light breeze blew against his face.

The end of the trail came suddenly and unexpectedly. One instant, the tracks were beelining straight ahead with no deer in sight. The next, a slight rustle caused the hunter to look to the right. A heavy, wide-racked buck was standing barely 30 yards away, gawking in disbelief at the unexpected intruder. As the hunter shouldered his gun to fire, the buck whirled to duck into nearby foliage. But the big, 1-ounce 12-gauge slug caught the buck and dropped it cold.

The wary old buck had buttonhooked before bedding down so that it could scrutinize its backtrail—a common precaution for hunter-wise deer. But the gunner's stealth and quick-shooting ability had caught the buck by surprise.

Deer tracking is always a dramatic way to hunt. Hoofprints promise action at the end of the line, and a patient tracker usually enjoys exactly that. To be successful at tracking, a hunter must be a skilful sneaker, must constantly think about where the target animal is heading and what its intentions might be, and must remain poised to shoot quickly and accurately. Deer are occasionally trailed and surprised in their beds but most often are shot or just shot at as they run off.

Contrary to popular belief, nobody can determine with absolute certainty the sex of a deer by its track. Especially large, boxy tracks are likely to be those of a buck, but a few does with overly large feet inhabit any tract of land. The smallish hoofprints of fawns are instantly recognized by any hunter worth his salt, and fawn tracks accompanying larger tracks usually mean a doe with offspring. But in fresh snow, a tracker can only guess whether buck or doe will end up in his sights.

One other tip on tracking deer. This technique is most feasible immediately after a fresh snow. With rare exceptions, older snow becomes crusted and silent walking is impossible.

OTHER HUNTING TECHNIQUES

The great majority of hunters rely solely on stand-hunting methods and traditional foot-hunting variations to pursue deer. But there are other, though more limited, game-getting techniques. These are calling, float hunting, hunting on horseback, baiting deer, and hunting from vehicles. Each can work like a charm in certain situations.

DEER CALLING TECHNIQUES

Deer, like most animals, are vulnerable to certain calling techniques. Many hunters know that rutting bull elk can be lured into point-blank shooting range with bogus bugles and grunts, and that a bull moose responds passionately to calls imitating the lovelorn moans of a cow moose in heat. But relatively few people realize that whitetails, mule deer, and blacktails can all be coaxed into close range with skilful and well-chosen calls.

Calling deer can be a startlingly effective technique, especially in heavy-cover areas. If animals decide to respond, they often run or sneak into point-blank range.

Bleating calls. A common sound that lures in bucks and does alike is the plaintive bleat of a hurt or frightened fawn. This call seems to work the best on Pacific Coast blacktail deer, but mule deer and whitetails also respond sporadically. Several outdoor companies sell bleating deer calls—calls that are extremely easy to master. In addition, a hunter can make his own bleating call by sandwiching a rubber band between two slightly bent Popsicle sticks.

Bleating calls are most effective in dense cover where deer feel fairly secure and must closely approach the sounds to get a look at what is happening. No one knows exactly why fawn bleats work so well

This commercial deer call imitates the bleats of a fawn in pain or terror. The sounds arouse the curiosity or, perhaps, the protective instincts of adult deer, effectively luring them to you.

on deer, but most experts feel the animals respond out of pure curiosity, genuine concern for the safety of a young animal, or a combination of the two. Luring in deer with a bleating call is popular in the dense grass-and-alder tangles along the coast of British Columbia and southern Alaska.

Rattling antlers. A traditional whitetail-hunting technique in Texas and Old Mexico is rattling antlers together to simulate the sounds of two bucks fighting over a doe. Hunters all over the continent have used this technique with varying success in recent years. Some swear *by* it; others swear *at* it.

The necessary tools for rattling up whitetail bucks are two stout, well-matched antlers attached by a long thong at the bases to make carrying them easy. When such antlers are clashed vigorously together over a period of 5 to 15 minutes, rut-crazy bucks in the immediate vicinity sometimes sneak or run toward the sound. For best results, a hunter should assume a concealed position in a tree stand or ground blind. Breezes should be blowing from areas where deer are apt to be. Some gung-ho deer rattlers claim that adding

secondary sound effects to the rattling procedure helps draw in wary bucks. These special effects include antlers smashing brush and trees and the hunter stamping the ground with his feet to duplicate the sounds of deer pushing each other around.

Although arguing about the best size and shape of rattling antlers is a popular pastime around hunting

HOW TO MAKE A BLEATING-DEER CALL

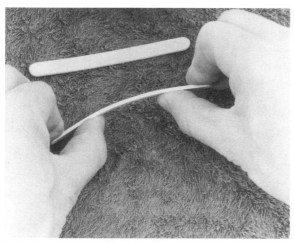

1. *Make a homemade bleating-deer call from two ordinary Popsicle sticks. First, wet the sticks with water, and then bend them by using your thumbs and forefingers as shown.*

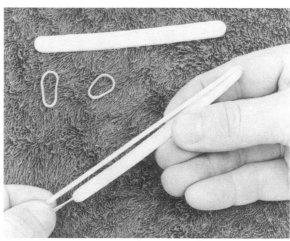

2. *Let the bent sticks dry completely. Then stretch a medium-sized rubber band over one stick lengthwise. You will need two smaller rubber bands to assemble the completed call.*

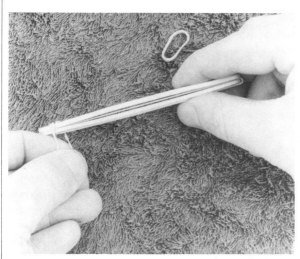

3. *Press the two halves of the deer call together with concave surfaces toward the center. Now lash the ends tightly in place with smaller rubber bands.*

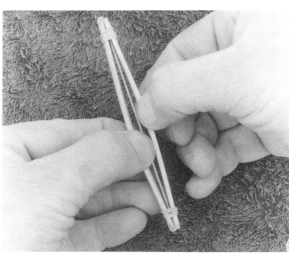

4. *Once the deer call is assembled, pull the wooden sides apart to ensure adequate bowing away from the central rubber-band reed. Repeat this procedure whenever Popsicle sticks begin to flatten during use.*

To use the call shown on the previous page, blow between the sticks while holding them firmly between your teeth and lips. The tighter you clamp the sticks and the closer they come to the rubber band, the higher-pitched the bleats become.

During the late-fall rutting period, rattling antlers sometimes lures in whitetail bucks. Do your antler-rattling from an elevated stand or well-concealed ground blind to avoid being spotted by responding bucks.

camps, the truth is that *any* antlers will do an excellent job. Many successful whitetail rattlers use antlers from mule deer, elk, or caribou to call in bucks, and a few use bamboo sticks instead of antlers. All of them produce a sound close enough to the genuine article, and effectively bring in bucks that happen to be in a responsive mood.

What motivates whitetail bucks to approach rattling antlers? Experts agree that the main reason is a shortage of receptive does in a particular area. In other words, parts of the country with a relatively high number of bucks per doe are best for rattling because competition for females is high. A rutting whitetail in northern Pennsylvania, where hunting pressure is heavy and buck/doe ratios are doe heavy, might ignore rattling antlers because he has all the does he can handle. By contrast, in lightly hunted south Texas, with its 50–50 buck/doe ratio, bucks might run to sounds of a fight in hopes of ushering away the doe being fussed over.

Similarly, time of year strongly influences the effectiveness of rattling on whitetail bucks. During the month prior to the rutting peak, relatively few does come in heat. This makes competition for females especially intense. As a result, rattling tends to work much better during the prerut preliminaries of October and early November than during the peak in late November or early December.

Other effective calls. Rutting whitetail bucks can also be called into point-blank range by a skilful tree-stand hunter perched near an active scrape. The scrape is a meeting place for receptive does and bucks—a place where does in heat patiently wait until a dominant male swaggers by. Bucks check out scrapes with regularity during the entire mating season, leaving themselves vulnerable to careful calling.

Calls that work best near a scrape are the grunt and the snort. These are the challenge calls of rutting whitetail bucks and they are meant to warn off less dominant bucks. When challenged with grunt and snort, any dominant, red-eyed whitetail in the area will strut in to whip the noisy intruder. A hunter who is able to make the bleating grunt of a buck and follow this sound with an airy snort can often set up point-blank shots at trophy deer. Because deer do come so close to mating calls, the technique works extremely well for shotgun hunters and archers.

Instructional tapes on calling rutting deer are available at sporting goods stores. They can help a hunter learn to imitate the mating noises of whitetail bucks by using just his mouth or by using a commercial grunting and snorting call. If conditions are right, calling rutting bucks near scrapes can be exceedingly productive.

FLOAT HUNTING BASICS

A few ultradense deer areas are laced by backwaters, sloughs, or running streams. Such places allow the unique opportunity to hunt from a boat for animals hiding in nearby thickets.

When float hunting, you must pay careful attention to standard boating safety procedures. Wear a certified flotation vest like this camouflage model.

Free-floating a moving stream or paddling along a standing body of water is a silent and deadly way to slip through deer-rich areas. In locations with open areas along the shore, hunters can float hunt early and late in the day and have a good chance of catching feeding animals unawares. In uniformly overgrown habitat, a midday floater can often surprise a deer taking a drink at water's edge. Using a boat is simpler and quieter than walking, and often produces fairly close shots at completely unalerted deer.

A variety of boats can be used for float hunting. The most common are canoes, flat-bottomed johnboats, and aluminum V-hull car-toppers in the 12- to 14-foot class. If the boats are camouflaged with nonglare paint, so much the better.

A float hunter should always adhere to standard boating safety procedures, such as wearing an approved flotation vest and keeping the equipment load under a boat's published payload. On fairly long boat-in trips in remote areas, a hunter should never travel alone and should carry a sizable first aid kit for unexpected mishaps.

HUNTING FROM HORSEBACK

Hunting deer from horseback has been lavishly romanticized by outdoor writers for many years. In reality, this technique is seldom all it's cracked up to be. A horse is a superb vehicle of transport to and from a remote hunting camp, and provides the best of all means for packing out heavy loads of venison. But actually cruising the countryside for deer atop a sway-backed nag can end up being far more trouble than it's worth.

In theory, a horseman pursuing mountain mule deer or blacktail deer can ride ridges and sidehills until a deer jumps up, then leap off, pull his rifle from its scabbard, and neatly blast the animal. In reality, most deer are frightened witless by horses and the crunching, plodding sounds they make. Toting a scope-sighted rifle in a scabbard is an excellent way to ruin its zero, and shooting near skittish horses almost guarantees a long, tiring walk back to camp.

In remote areas where animals have not learned to fear hunting horses, hunters can ride ridges and established trails with excellent chances of seeing fairly docile deer. Walking is always better, if a hunter can manage the chore, but hunting from horeseback is a legitimate technique for aging or out-of-shape individuals.

One long-standing fairy tale in the hunting world tells of the good ol' huntin' hoss that walks quietly about muley country all day long, then stands like a rock while the rifleman pops his deer from the saddle.

Although hunting from horseback is an oft-romanticized adventure, beasts of burden sometimes cause more trouble than a hunter expects. A minor rodeo in the hills tends to dampen romanticized notions about horseback hunting, and it certainly isn't conducive to bagging bucks.

No horse in the history of the world ever stood like a rock; invariably they sway, shudder, or at least quiver. The majority will put a rodeo bronc to shame when subjected to a point-blank rifle blast. So gunners must tie their horses up and shoot from conventional positions away from the horses.

DEER BAITING METHODS

A few states allow baiting of deer. This is not a particularly glamorous way of dropping the yearly venison, but certainly works if a proper bait is used near an elevated stand or ground blind.

Deer display a definite weakness for several common baits. They frequent blocks of cattle salt during active feeding periods, licking this delectable mineral with pleasure. They also enjoy eating alfalfa hay, yellow corn, wheat, and similar crops. When such foods are made constantly available to deer over several weeks or months, the animals visit baiting sites with regularity and provide relatively easy shots for nearby hunters.

The morality and sportsmanship of baiting deer has been seriously questioned by many hunters. Black bears, wild pigs, and some African animals have been hunted over bait for many, many years, and few hunters seem to object to this. But baiting deer seems to be far less acceptable to the hunting populace at large. This technique works with deadly efficiency in areas where it is legal, but whether or not the overall experience is rewarding and palatable is something every hunter must answer for himself.

HUNTING FROM VEHICLES

Very few states or provinces legally sanction shooting from motor vehicles. A notable exception is Texas, where special deer-tower rigs are commonplace and fully accepted by residents.

Road hunting—not road shooting—is by contrast a common practice all over the continent. This method of looking for deer is esthetically bankrupt and betrays a definite laziness on the part of the hunters who cruise for deer in this way. There is a definite knack

Four-wheel-drive vehicles can be a godsend in rough, steep, or muddy deer-hunting areas. But ethical hunters in most states regard them as modes of transportation— not mobile blinds.

to spotting deer from a moving vehicle, and the most straight-laced deer hunters keep a weather eye peeled for game as they drive to and from their favored deer-hunting hotspots. However, spotting an occasional deer from the pavement and going after it on foot is a far cry from deliberately scouting and shooting at bucks from a plushly padded vehicle seat.

Anyone taken with the notion of actively hunting from motor vehicles should check local laws first. Most states make it illegal for hunters to drive maintained roads with gun barrels bristling in every direction, and nearly all prohibit the possession and discharge of a loaded firearm in a vehicle or near a roadway. These laws are based on more than a general repugnance for hunting game from a vehicle; shooting from or across a roadway can endanger people in the vicinity.

In Texas, hunting from vehicles is a legal and time-honored convention. Many deer rigs have permanent tower stands attached—stands that allow superior views in flat and brushy terrain.

ALL ABOUT SHOOTING AT DEER

The act of shooting at deer takes just seconds to accomplish, but often determines the outcome of an entire hunting season. For this reason, it is just good sense to learn as much as possible about how to proceed once your sights settle on the gray-brown hide of a deer. Where you aim, how calmly you take your shot, how observant you are about an animal's reaction to hits and misses, and how you follow up potential hits all contribute to the final outcome.

BEING COOL UNDER PRESSURE

Shooting at deer is normally an invigorating event. Beginners get the jitters in the presence of game and miss the shot because of it. Even longtime hunters occasionally have trouble dealing with the tension when gigantic trophy bucks appear or when shots have been very long and difficult in coming. When excitement rises to fever pitch, the adrenaline flows, muscles become rubbery and weak, and cool-headed judgment may vanish. Then comes the missed shot that in a calmer moment the hunter would have put precisely on the mark.

Similarly, many hunters merely lack the patience to wait for that one perfect shot to materialize. They exercise patience until a deer appears in range, then lose all self control and begin slinging lead before a good shooting opportunity arises. More than one gunner or bowhunter has shot repeatedly at a distant deer, or one obscured by heavy cover, only to have the animal become confused and present a perfect close-range shot after all the ammo is gone. Or a poorly timed shot merely scares a deer away and bollixes a potentially perfect chance. Such heartbreaking events can be avoided by some forethought and the resolve to maintain control when deer finally do appear.

Facts about buck fever. Excitement and flow of adrenaline are not necessarily negative features of a hunt. These mechanisms have helped man take game for thousands of years. But modern hunters have not been exposed to the hunting situation often enough to learn to steel their nerves and properly channel their primordial hunting drives. Only long experience in the woods and plenty of shots at deer completely smooth a hunter's ragged emotional edges and allow him to shoot with intense but rigidly controlled excitement.

Buck fever at its worst can be both tragic and positively hilarious. Most veteran deer-hunting guides can reminisce for hours about their experiences with tenderfoot hunters: those who shot wildly in the air and then fled from the deer; those who froze and stared in dumbfound amazement at nearby bucks; and those who emptied their rifles by ejecting all rounds *unfired* only to swear they shot in normal fashion. Fortunately for most hunters, the average case of jitters is not so dramatic. Most often a hunter merely shakes

The shot itself takes relatively little time to accomplish, but determines the outcome of an entire hunting trip. Smart hunters prepare themselves for this crucial moment with a gun rest if feasible.

uncontrollably or becomes too weak to shoot his gun or bow. A hunter who spends ample time afield eventually overcomes this lack of control. Time and experience pay off.

Aside from simple exposure to hunting, the only thing a hunter can do to curb buck fever is to have a serious talk with himself before heading into the field. Many hunters become overwrought simply because they place too much importance on making the kill. Shooters who convince themselves that deer are nifty *bonuses* on otherwise enjoyable outings do not place so much importance on actual kills. So they tend to function better because their expectations are not geared solely to the kill. It's ironic indeed, but wanting something too much often ruin, or at least hampers, a person's ability to perform.

Learning to shoot at the proper time. There is usually a right time and a wrong time to shoot at every animal a hunter sees. Even if buck fever doesn't get the best of a hunter in shooting situations, he still might not make correct judgments about when to release the bowstring or carefully squeeze the trigger. The results of such miscalculation are usually missed or crippled deer.

Shooting at the proper time is a function of self-control and experience in the field. A hunter who forces himself to *think* about potential shots instead of reacting emotionally often makes correct shooting choices. Past experience helps a lot in making sensible decisions because a hunter ideally learns from his mistakes.

Here are a few examples of when and when not to shoot at deer. For one thing, a deer obscured by foliage is not a decent shooting bet, especially when the animal is unalerted and apt to step into open terrain. Hunters sometimes take calculated risks and attempt to drive projectiles through or around limbs, leaves, and other intervening obstacles. But this type of shooting only makes sense if chances of setting up a better try are nil. Similarly, hunters should attempt to shoot when animals present ideal body angles. A deer walking straight away can be decked with a rifle, but only at the expense of tasty steaks and chops. The rear-end shot is okay *when no other is likely to present itself,* especially when a hunter does not expect to see another deer. In like fashion, a chest-on shot is not as desirable as a broadside try because it also ruins more meat.

Deer hunters are often guilty of trying difficult shots when easier ones are likely to materalize. For example, a buck feeding 100 yards away with only its head and neck exposed presents a fair target for a crack rifleman with a rock-steady rest. However, hitting the large rib cage area is a much better bet if the gunner has patience to wait for a shift in body position. A deer lying down 20 yards from a bowhunter with only its head exposed also presents a potential shot at success, but the archer is best advised to wait until the animal stands up and exposes a larger vital area. Hunters too frequently fidget, become impatient, then blow their chance.

Haste often makes waste in deer-shooting situations. But another old saw can be equally true—he who hesitates is lost. As often as not, inexperienced deer hunters blow shooting opportunities by piddling around when they ought to be shooting. For instance, when a deer does present that perfect broadside target within good range, the shooter should hop on the chance and squeeze off a steady, accurate shot as

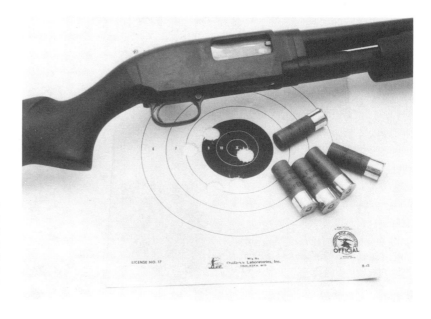

You must know the accuracy capabilities of your weapon to make critical aiming decisions during the hunt. For example, the average slug-shooting shotgun throws 5-inch groups at about 50 yards—not nearly good enough to deliberately hit a deer in the head or neck.

soon as possible. Otherwise, the animal might spook or merely walk away.

Another situation where shooters sometimes miscalculate is when a deer appears at a walk, trot, or out-and-out run. If the animal is heading toward nearby cover, it's generally a case of shoot now, or forever hold your (hunting) piece. In brushy or heavily wooded areas where deer are hunted hard and prone to allow only brief shooting opportunities, the difference between consistently successful hunters and those who never score is often the ability to shoot fast and shoot accurately before the opportunity evaporates.

The best hunters with gun or bow usually know how the animals they hunt will behave and can better judge when to take a shot. In one lightly hunted mule deer area, for example, even the oldest bucks might still display the once common trait of running up a ridge, then pausing to look back at the hunter. In another more typical muley haunt pounded by armies of eager shooters, no self-respecting mule deer would think of stopping that way. Knowledge of these patterns is vital and can only be gathered through observation.

SHOT PLACEMENT

Every hunter should know in advance where to aim on deer for quick, humane kills and minimal damage to meat. This requires at least rudimentary knowledge of animal physiology and how a hunting projectile does its job.

Basic deer physiology. Every deer has three vital systems that keep it alive—the *respiratory system,* which provides a constant supply of oxygen to the blood; the *circulatory system,* which pumps oxygen and nutrient-laden blood throughout a deer's body; and the *central nervous system,* which controls the respiratory and circulatory systems via the brain and spinal cord.

When a hunter kills a deer, he does so by destroying one or more of these body systems. No matter whether he uses a rifle bullet, shotgun slug, buckshot, or razor-sharp arrow, he'll drop his animal if he (1) destroys the respiratory system by puncturing or collapsing the lungs; (2) prevents the circulation of oxygen-rich blood

DEER ANATOMY

Well-placed projectiles drop deer with high efficiency. Every responsible hunter strives for quick, humane kills that are possible only when you know where to aim.

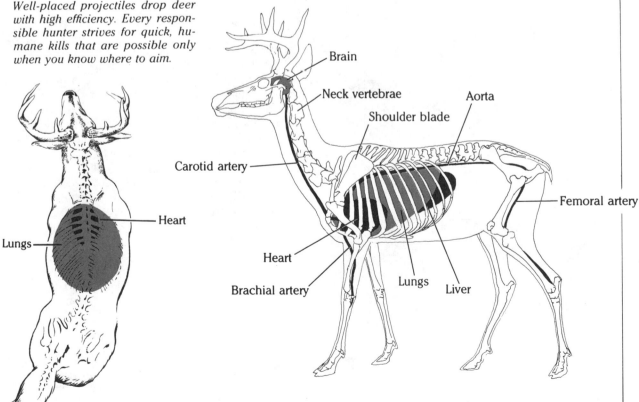

Brain

Neck vertebrae

Aorta

Shoulder blade

Carotid artery

Femoral artery

Heart

Lungs

Heart

Brachial artery

Lungs

Liver

by damaging the heart or creating a wound that drains the animal's arteries of blood; or (3) disables the central nervous system by damaging the spinal cord or brain.

Whether or not a bullet or arrow drops a deer quickly depends on two important factors—where it impacts the body and how well it disrupts vital functions once it penetrates flesh. If the projectile is directed to a vital anatomical area, and if it successfully knocks out one or more of a deer's three basic systems, the animal will expire in short order.

How projectiles drop deer. So much for basic deer physiology. Next, let's look at how various hunting projectiles perform once they enter flesh.

Before it hits a deer, a normal soft-nosed rifle bullet, shotgun slug, or buckshot pellet is a concentric, streamlined piece of metal. Upon impact, pressure forces the projectile to widen, or "mushroom." How quickly and how dramatically mushrooming takes place depends on several factors, including projectile design, projectile speed, and where the projectile strikes a deer. All well-made, copper-jacketed hunting bullets enlarge as much as 100 percent before stopping or exiting on the far side of a deer. Rifled slugs and buckshot pellets mushroom less fully, often flat-

Hunting bullets begin as concentric cones. Upon impact with flesh, they expand with violence—a process that causes massive tissue destruction.

Rifled shotgun slugs of various sizes often incorporate concave noses that ensure rapid expansion in game. This increases the deer-dropping potential of these projectiles.

tening only slightly because of their lower velocity.

All projectiles create a "flash hole" in soft tissue as they plow through. This hole is an oversized cavity around the projectile that is opened and closes up in a microsecond. The hole is somewhat wider than the expanding projectile itself because flesh is violently shouldered out of the way by the lateral force of expanding metal. This force ruins vital tissue on a fairly major scale.

The exact diameter of a wound channel is determined in large part by the speed of the bullet. As a general rule, the slower the projectile, the less dramatic mushrooming is and the smaller the wound channel. Other factors like projectile diameter and composition also influence mushrooming characteristics, but projectile speed is most important. A 180-grain .30/06 Springfield bullet moving 2700 fps (feet per second) invariably creates more damage than a 1 ounce 12-gauge shotgun slug traveling at 1500 fps, despite the much larger diameter of the shotgun slug. A smaller, slower-moving buckshot pellet does even less damage to deer, but relies on total damage from all the pellets in a pattern.

It is a common myth that firearms kill deer through massive, explosive shock. This is indeed the case when a bullet or slug impacts the shoulder blade, spine, or another large, unyielding mass of bone. The result is an explosion of metal and bone fragments that often blows a deer completely off its feet. However, when a firearm projectile penetrates soft tissue and misses major bones, it has little if any explosive knockdown power. It drops the deer through damage to one of the deer's three vital systems.

All firearm projectiles kill deer in basically the same way, but a hunting arrow is an entirely different matter. Here a sharp, multibladed broadhead is driven into flesh with next to no penetrating friction. The average deer arrow is traveling less than 200 fps and embodies less than 50 foot-pounds of energy when it hits a deer. But an arrow makes far more efficient use of energy than a firearm projectile. A bullet, rifled slug, or buckshot pellet does damage by using tremendous impact energy to widen out and create a tissue-destroying flash hole. By comparison, an arrow slides into flesh and cuts a deadly hole exactly the diameter of its broadhead blades. The hole is every bit as large as the flash holes created by many medium-power hunting guns, and thus damages ample flesh. Damage is coupled with almost no blood coagulation because an arrow slices instead of pulverizing flesh. The result is massive, uninhibited bleeding for quick, humane kills.

Contrary to popular belief, hunting arrows and bullets kill equally well with hits in nonbony parts of the anatomy. Broadheads slice deeply—often penetrating all the way through a deer—while jacketed bullets and shotgun projectiles commonly penetrate less deeply but create slightly larger wound channels. Hits in bony areas are an entirely different matter because an arrow's meager energy cannot blast through bone the way a fast-moving, energy-packed bullet can. Arrows that hit the shoulder blade, spine, skull, and other bony areas do sometimes penetrate into vital flesh, but often stop cold with little effect.

Where to aim on deer. A hunter cannot always control where he hits an animal, but he should know what types of hits cause death, how much meat damage different shots produce, and how animals normally react.

The chest-area hit: All experienced hunters prefer to aim at a deer's chest cavity because this is the largest vital target area and because hits here cause quick death with very little loss of meat. The chest contains the lungs, heart, and major arteries leading away from the heart. A broadside shot at the chest is best of all because a bullet or arrow passes behind the shoulder and damages heart, lungs, and/or arteries with little or no damage to edible meat. Shots into the chest from various frontal angles often connect with one or both shoulder blades, which bloodshots and ruins venison. An angling-away shot into the chest is an excellent choice, but sometimes ruins the off shoulder and surrounding roasts and chops. A downward shot from a tree often hits the spine before entering the chest. This also ruins meat.

A chest shot can kill deer in several different ways. If the projectile punctures one or both lungs, these quickly collapse and the animal dies from lack of oxygen within 15 or 20 seconds. If the heart is hit, blood circulation stops and the animal drops in 10 to 15 seconds from lack of oxygen to the brain. If the projectile somehow penetrates the chest but misses all major organs, the lungs will collapse as outside air rushes in—a phenomenon that drops deer within a minute or two. Any projectile that penetrates the chest will quickly kill a deer, but the more damage created, the faster the animal will drop.

One selling point of aiming at the chest is the fact that near misses still drop animals very quickly. A hit too high will sever the spine, a hit too far back can catch the blood-rich liver, a hit too low will sometimes damage arteries in the brisket, and a hit too far forward can break one or both shoulders.

A deer hit in the chest will seldom go down immediately unless spine or shoulders are smashed by the bullet. A hit directly through the lungs generally produces a "death run" of 75 to 150 yards, the animal charging frantically with body held low to the ground. A hit in the heart or major arteries produces a similar run, but the animal is less prone to crouch and gallop with abandon.

The spine hit: A direct hit in the spine with bullet or arrow generally kills a deer on the spot. Spine hits

WHERE TO AIM

(Continued on next page)

forward of the shoulders kill a deer quickly because they stop the action of the lungs and/or heart. Hits farther back paralyze a deer's hindquarters and usually require a finishing shot unless blood loss is massive. Because the aortic artery runs the full length of a deer's body directly beneath the spine, spine hits often *do* cause major bleeding in addition to disrupting the central nervous system.

A spine-hit deer sometimes bleats loudly, a giveaway for this particular shot. Deer seldom make a sound unless the spinal cord is damaged.

Any spine hit ruins plenty of excellent meat—especially hits to the rear of the shoulders. A misplaced bullet to the middle of the spine generally damages the backstraps, which many hunters regard as the best meat on any big-game animal.

The head/neck hit: A deer shot in the upper skull drops like a rock; the central nervous system is totally destroyed and no damage is done to edible meat. Hits in the jaw or fleshy part of the neck will often kill deer in the long run, but seldom slow animals immediately. This makes recovery next to impossible unless a projectile severs the carotid artery or jugular vein. Both of these blood vessels bleed profusely when damaged, leading to very rapid death. Although some riflemen who fancy themselves crack shots prefer to nail stationary deer in the neck or head, the primary objection to these aiming points is worth considering. Pinpoint hits in the spine or brain yield instant results, but near misses can result in slow death. The deer runs off as if unhurt, and may survive for several days.

The ham hit: The solid ham hit, sometimes jokingly referred to as the "Texas heart shot," is very deadly but extremely damaging to meat. A solid hit with bullet or arrow in the large part of the ham invariably severs major arteries—either the large femoral arteries or branches from it running inside the legs. The result is rapid blood loss and a very quick demise. In addition, many ham hits with bullets pulverize large leg bones, often breaking the deer down on the spot.

A deer hit in the ham generally sags in the rear end or falls and gets up again, greatly reducing speed as it finally moves away. More often than not, bleeding is so profuse that hunters can see the point of impact clearly surrounded by red.

Gunners generally prefer not to hit deer in the hams. This hit is not a bad one *with an arrow* because it gets the job done quickly with relatively little damage to meat. By contrast, a ham hit with a high-powered rifle or shotgun slug mangles lots of good meat. A few finicky hunters in areas swarming with animals pass up shots at deer that are running or standing straight away. But most hunters take a butt shot if no better opportunity presents itself. The old hunter's philosophy that "half a deer is better than none" is a sound code to live by in areas where one shot per season is all that most hunters can expect.

(Where to Aim continued)

One rear-end shot placement deserves special mention here. This is directly between the hams on a perfectly straight-away deer—in other words the old bung-hole shot. Such a shot misses both hams and ranges forward through the paunch into the vital chest region. If properly executed, this shot on running or standing animals seldom ruins a single ounce of meat and drops deer with authority.

The paunch/liver hit: The general instinct of beginning deer hunters is aiming at the exact center of broadside deer. This is a mistake, because the center of a deer is occupied by the paunch—one of the very worst places to hit with bullet or broadhead. If projectiles impact the pyloric artery that runs low through the paunch, a "breadbasket" hit, it can kill quickly due to major loss of blood. Otherwise, the animal will hump up with head lowered and hobble or trot away. The deer will be capable of giving any hunter the slip, but it is destined to suffer—sick but mobile—for several hours before finally dropping dead. The hunter who paunch-hits a deer and recognizes the reaction should do his level best to get in finishing shots before the animal moves out of sight.

The liver is a large blood-filtering organ located just forward of the paunch. Hunters who aim too far back occasionally hit this organ—a happy circumstance for them. A liver-hit deer reacts in similar fashion to a paunch-hit animal. But it bleeds profusely and seldom lives for long—rarely over ten minutes with dead-center projectile placement.

Fringe hits on deer: Unfortunately, hunters occasionally nick deer around the edges instead of scoring solid, killing hits. Most such nicks draw blood but seldom cause lasting damage or pain.

Two sorts of fringe hits on deer do produce noticeable results. One is a lower-leg hit, and the other is a hit that lightly clips the spine or smacks a buck in the antlers.

Deer hit in the lower legs can run with surprising agility. One or two broken legs will certainly handicap an animal and seal its long-term fate. In many cases, leg-hit deer can be recovered by persistent trailing hunters—especially when dogs are used to find and bay them. The hunter who does break a deer's lower leg can usually tell because the animal stumbles dramatically at the time of impact. Dangling legs are also easily seen. A hunter who leg-shoots a deer should make every conceivable effort to follow up his shot and finish off the suffering animal.

A bullet that barely clips the spine or hits the base of an antler will sometimes coldcock a deer as surely as a solid hit in the brain or spine. Such a fringe hit temporarily stuns the animal but seldom causes lasting damage. Many a hunter has squeezed the trigger, seen his target animal somersault and roll with feet pointed toward the sky . . . and then stared in amazement as the deer leaped up and charged away like a bee-stung horse. Hunters should always be prepared to shoot again when deer drop at once because a small percentage of deer are alive and may run off.

Using buckshot on deer. Buckshot is legally required for deer in many heavily populated parts of the country—most notably states east of the Mississippi River. Using buckshot on deer is different than other forms of shooting because a single, well-directed projectile is not involved. Instead, a gunner must place his pattern of pellets in the *general* part of a deer where it is apt to do the most good. Because individual buckshot pellets lack the energy and tissue-damaging ability of rifle bullets and shotgun slugs, deer taken with buckshot are usually dropped from the cumulative effect of several pellets simultaneously damaging several parts of the anatomy.

Except in point-blank shooting situations where buckshot patterns are extremely tight, experienced

When using deer-sized buckshot, always aim at the base of the neck to direct the pattern toward vital tissue in the front half of an animal. This increases the odds of killing hits.

shotgunners always aim for the base of an animal's neck. There are more vital zones in the front half of a deer than in the rear, and a neck hold with a shotgun directs most pellets toward chest, spine, and/or head. One lucky pellet through the brain, heart, lungs, or spinal cord can neatly drop a deer all by itself, and several vital hits do an even faster job. By contrast, a dead-center hold on the chest with buckshot directs much of the pattern toward the undesirable paunch area of a deer.

AFTER THE SHOT

One of the least-discussed, but most important, aspects of hunting deer is deciding exactly what to do

Mortally hit deer often run away instead of keeling over on the spot. As a result, you should always follow up shots with a careful search.

after a shot has been taken. Hunters talk for hours on end about a variety of subjects, from their pet firearms to time-tested hunting techniques. However, the subject of what to do after the hit seldom pops up in casual conversation. But every hunter should be aware of what he must do immediately after a shot. It can make the difference between easily recovering animals and losing them altogether.

Here is the procedure every hunter should follow after shooting at deer. This step-by-step method works like a charm for gun hunters and bowhunters alike.

Step 1: Watch for animal reactions. As described earlier, deer often betray whether or not they've been hit with characteristic reactions. Even those deer that run or walk away as if unscathed are sometimes mortally or at least superfically hit. An observant, cool-headed shooter always watches target deer for any clue about where shots have hit. Close observation also reveals the direction a deer is heading—facts that can aid in recovering the animal.

Step 2: Wait, look, and listen. Once the target deer is out of view, stay put for several minutes and watch and listen for further clues to the whereabouts of the animal. Some hard-hit deer stop for a while to get their second wind, then move again. This lets the hunter hear or see their progress. Other deer become confused and back-track, allowing shooters to finish them off with backup shots. A hunter who presses forward immediately after taking his shot risks pushing a crippled deer into a final bid for escape—a situation far less desirable than hanging back and giving the animal ample time to expire or calm down and bed near the place where it was hit.

Step 3: Mark the place the shot was taken from. All too many hunters shoot at deer, barrel after the animals immediately, then become confused about where the action originally took place. This mistake is especially easy to make in monotonous stands of trees or uniform patches of brush. Once a shooter does lose his bearings, he may never again locate where he shot from or where he last saw his animal.

Experienced outdoorsmen always carry some sort of highly visible marker material to aid in finding deer. Top choices are fluorescent surveyor's tape and brightly colored toilet paper. Either one tied to a tree or draped across a bush will clearly mark a shooting site and make deer recovery a less haphazard procedure.

Step 4: Go to where the deer disappeared. A hunter should always follow up his shots—even when he believes he probably missed the mark. All too many gun-toting hunters blast at distant deer, then walk away without checking the results because animals did not pile up immediately. This stunt wastes many trophies each and every year and is irresponsible.

A running deer's footprints are unmistakable in soft soil or mud. The cloven toes are noticeably splayed, and the dewclaw marks deeply indented behind. Recognizing such tracks for what they are often makes it possible to trail a wounded deer even when no blood can be found.

Once you have observed an animal's reactions, waited a short period of time, then marked the location you shot from, cautiously proceed to the last place you saw the animal. An alternate plan is having a hunting partner investigate while you watch from your original position. In canyon country with a view, it is especially advisable for one gunner to move toward a potentially hit deer while another stands guard with rifle at the ready. This tactic sometimes nets crippled animals that initially hide and then run when pressed by close-range hunters. Even when an investigating hunter is not able to shoot, his partner across the canyon can finish off the fleeing deer.

Step 5: Look for signs of a hit. Once you reach the place where the deer was last seen or heard, look for signs of a hit. If the animal is not dead on the spot, a study of nearby terrain might turn up blood or tufts of hair. In soft soil or mud, a fleeing deer's hoofprints are often highly visible—splayed, running tracks with dewclaw depressions behind. If signs of a hit are not apparent, follow tracks or cast in ever-widening circles, keeping your eyes peeled for blood and hair. If diligent searching reveals definite signs of a hit, begin the trailing chore at once. If you find no blood or hair but still believe the animal was hit, settle down for a perhaps long and difficult search.

Never leave a potential hit site unless searching proves the target animal was totally untouched.

TRAILING WOUNDED DEER

A smart hunter hangs with the trail of a potentially crippled deer like a hungry coyote after a rabbit. Begin by cruising the possible hit site for obvious clues, such as blood and hair, but do not give up if you cannot find any. Good trackers often search on hands and knees with eyes only inches from the ground, knowing that tiny, match-head-size flecks of blood or a single hair dislodged by impacting bullet or arrow can be the beginning of a productive trail. Also search for less obvious but equally important signs of a hit— signs such as a moist spot on a log where stomach fluids have dripped, a tiny chunk of bone or meat blown from a wound, or a bit of half-digested food from a central paunch hit. Also hunt for signs indicating that you might have missed the mark entirely, such as a bullet hole in a tree well above the place where a deer was standing; or an arrow in the dirt with absolutely no blood, hair, or body fluid covering it. Here as elsewhere, you should be patient and tenacious. Use your brain as well as your eyes to determine the probable outcome of shots.

When no blood is present. At times a shooter *knows* he scored a hit because of animal reaction— even when the hit site shows no positive signs at all. At others, the odds may seem at least 50–50 that an animal escaped unscathed. However, in any case a sensible hunter presses the search even farther, following running tracks with care or crisscrossing a deer's likely travel route when there are no tracks.

Observant hunters become quite good at second-guessing the movements of animals that run away, knowing that even scared or wounded deer tend to follow established game trails and the easiest or most direct routes to safety. For example, a liver-hit buck on a steep hillside will sometimes climb a short distance if a wide path runs uphill to the nearest heavy cover in sight. The same animal in a different setting might swing directly sidehill along the best trail in the area, or might descend because a convenient ravine angles into heavy brush and pines.

Hit and unhit deer display two relatively predictable traits when scared by hunters: they take the course of least resistance as they make their getaway; and they head for the safest place nearby. Since deer have four strong driving legs, the course of least resistance might be steeply uphill, provided the going is fairly smooth and safety lies in that direction. A "safe place" might be a thicket for a whitetail or blacktail deer, and it might be a distant but completely open ravine for a prairie-dwelling mule deer. There is absolutely no substitute for your knowing the animals in your favorite deer area when you are called upon to guess where wounded deer might go.

When blood is present. Quite often, a solid hit with bullet or arrow leaves at least a little blood to follow. If searching reveals blood, take up the trail carefully and systematically.

Analyzing blood: Different blood colors and consistencies provide important clues to the location of a hit. Analyze the kind of blood along a trail immediately to further understand the plight of the animal. Pink, frothy blood invariably signals a lung hit and indicates that the animal is dead on its feet. Thin, bright-red blood betrays an artery hit or a hit in the heart, especially if blood seems to have been squirted out under pressure instead of merely dripping to the ground. Large quantities of bright blood usually mean a dead deer not far away. Thick, dark-red blood, by contrast, is not a particularly good sign, especially if dripped sparsely on the ground. Such blood can be shed by a dying deer, but often comes from surface vessels and means a superficial hit. A frontal liver hit or hit in the jugular vein of the neck sheds dark red blood so that hunters should always follow this blood sign as carefully as any other.

Greenish or colorless fluid coupled with dark red blood clearly points to a hit in the stomach region.

Track to one side of a deer's trail, not directly down the middle. This eliminates the chance of accidentally wiping out a blood sign.

Leap-frogging two trail markers is the best way to follow a skimpy blood trail. One marker is left at the last sign found, the other carried ahead to mark the next clue.

Such paunch fluid is seldom plentiful and usually peters out entirely inside 50 or 75 yards.

Proper trailing procedure: Follow blood by walking to one side of a trail instead of directly in the tracks of the deer. A clumsy trailing attempt often obliterates important sign when blood is sparse and difficult to find. Your boots may blot out blood on the ground or turn over leaves and rocks bearing telltale droplets. By paralleling actual sign instead of stamping over it, you leave blood as it is for double-checking and increase your chances of success.

If a mortally wounded deer is losing lots of blood, a hunter can sometimes trot from hit site to animal along a foot-wide path of red. More often, deer bleed internally and leave less obvious trails. Unless bleeding is profuse, a hunter should move at a snail's pace so that he misses nothing and stays on track.

Really skimpy blood trails require special techniques. When droplets are five or ten feet apart and extremely difficult to see, you are best advised to leapfrog two trailing markers, placing one beside the last blood found and casting ahead with the second marker to locate additional sign. White handkerchiefs, fluorescent strips of tape, or toilet paper squares all work well. This methodical follow-up saves time and eliminates the chance of temporarily losing a trail in heavy brush or trees.

Throughout the blood-trailing, keep your eyes ahead

for a dead animal or one trying to escape. Hunters sometimes become too engrossed in blood trailing alone and miss prime chances to finish off nearby deer or to walk directly to already downed trophies.

Knowing where to look: Experienced blood trailers save time and increase their odds of success of looking for blood in likely places. Blood shows up best on uniformly colored or nonporous objects such as leaves, logs, and rocks, and blends diabolically well with dirt, grass, pine needles, and other broken surfaces. A smart hunter on a tough trail often jumps from one easy trailing place to another along a deer's path. He checks out rocky areas, piles of leaves, downed logs, and other blood-showing objects, instead of scrutinizing each and every square inch of ground.

Experienced hunters search for blood above the ground as well as directly underfoot. Deer often spray or smear blood on grass, bushes, and trees up to waist level. This facilitates fast and accurate trailing.

Special trailing clues: An observant blood trailer can sometimes recognize special clues about where an animal is hit. For example, a deer's front hoofs are always larger than its hind hoofs because extra traction is needed up front for running and climbing steep slopes. A blood trail in which one front track is always full of blood indicates that the deer is hit somewhere in the chest or shoulder region. Similarly, an animal that smears blood along the right side of a trail about 30 inches above the ground is obviously hit in the right side in a solid body area. Clues of this sort help bolster confidence and give the hunter a better idea of what to expect at the end of the line.

TYPICAL TRAILING SITUATIONS

With minor variations, hunters generally encounter one of six typical trailing situations when following up shots. You should learn to recognize each situation so that you know exactly how to proceed.

1. The first situation is the most desirable. A hunter walks ahead, looks around, and finds his deer as dead as a stump a few feet from where it was hit. Usually, the animal has been shot through the head, spine, or shoulders.

2. A second situation is almost as convenient as the first. In this case, he finds a liberal trail of blood, quickly follows it 50 to 200 yards, and finds his deer has been killed with a chest shot, ham hit, or artery hit. No muss, no fuss.

3. This situation starts out looking good and ends up in total disappointment. A liberal blood trail is found at once—a trail the hunter follows with high hopes. The blood is dark red in color, and lies upon the ground in large droplets and pools. Gradually, the trail deteriorates over 100 to 300 yards until only pin-head-sized specks are visible every 5 to 15 feet. Finally, no more blood can be found, and no amount of canvassing nearby terrain produces sign of an animal. In this instance, the deer was almost certainly hit in surface muscle and offers next to no chance of recovery. The animal will probably survive unless a leg has been broken.

4. This deer-trailing situation starts out disappointingly and ends up with success. Here, a hunter finds no sign of a hit at all, circles wider, and still finds nothing. He lines out on the deer's tracks or follows several likely escape routes. Suddenly, he stumbles across a wide trail of blood some 25 to 75 yards away from where the animal was hit. A short, fast walk brings him to his deer, which was shot squarely through the chest.

Deer often fail to leave blood initially because they bleed internally until the body cavity fills to bullet-hole level. Lung hits are generally the culprits here, especially those slightly high of center. A deer hit in the chest usually charges away, sometimes covering close to 100 yards prior to spouting blood externally. Dead-center hits between a deer's hams sometimes produce the same effect. Delayed-bleeding hits probably account for more lost deer than any other type.

That is because inexperienced hunters see the deer run away, search briefly in the immediate hit area, and then give up in disappointment.

5. This situation occurs when a skimpy but steady trail of blood is found. This trail can be caused by several types of wounds, most of which are fatal. Liver hits, very high lung hits, paunch hits, and off-center hits in the ham can all produce a skimpy trail. Blood color can be a real helper in this trailing situation. It tells the hunter if he nailed the bright-blood ham area, dark-blood liver or paunch, or pink-blood lungs. A sparse pink-blood trail is seldom longer than 150 yards, and a dead lung-hit deer is usually waiting at the end. A bright-blood or dark-blood trail is often longer, and there is the distinct possibility of a living and semimobile animal at the end of the trail. Persistence on skimpy but steady blood trails most often turns up deer, and hunters should follow these trails with patience and confidence.

6. This trailing situation is the nonexistent blood trail. Most often, the reason for lack of blood is a cleanly missed shot. Less frequently, a deer is found nearby that bled internally altogether from a very high chest-cavity hit. On rare occasions, persistently canvassing a no-blood area turns up a living, but very sick animal, hit squarely in the paunch. Because the outside chance exists that a dead or wounded animal will spill no blood at all, a hunter *must* look long and hard even when chances are great he merely missed.

Using dogs to locate deer. In some areas, it is legal to trail crippled deer with dogs. Dogs can be a bona-fide godsend. A keen-nosed, deer-wise mutt is capable of doing in two minutes what a hunter might never accomplish. If blood sign is on the ground, the dog will cruise along the hot scent trail and eventually encounter the deer. In iffy situations, a dog can often sniff out a dead or holed-up animal without any blood scent to follow.

It is important to note here that not just any old dog can skilfully track down deer. The best breeds are hounds, bird dogs, livestock dogs, and small-game terriers. Ideally, the dog should be experienced at following trails of healthy and crippled game.

SAFETY PRECAUTIONS FOR TRAILING

Any wild animal can be dangerous when hurt or cornered. Deer are normally shy, retiring creatures, but occasionally attack trailing hunters if no easy escape route exists. The danger is relatively remote, but deer *can* cause serious damage with antlers or flying forefeet if pressed. As a result, wounded deer should always be given wide berth and never taken for granted.

PART 7
AFTER THE DEER IS DOWN

BY CHUCK ADAMS
Photos by the author unless
otherwise credited. Drawings
by Lloyd Birmingham.

Every experienced deer hunter knows stories about beginners who mishandled their first trophies. These yarns are often exaggerated in the telling, but they do illustrate how far wrong a neophyte can go, even after his animal is down.

Just how bad is that? Take this example of a completely inexperienced hunter. It took him a while to settle down after making the kill. Then he dragged his deer to a road, hung it in a tree, and transported it on the hood of his pickup truck to town the following day. After four hours of cruising Main Street to show off the prize, he went to see an experienced deer hunter to brag a bit and get some much-needed advice on skinning and butchering. The experienced hunter couldn't believe his eyes when the proud hunter drove his truck into the driveway. What was obviously once a nice buck was completely coated with dust on the hot truck hood and abuzz with eager blowflies and bees. Furthermore, the deer had bloated like a giant football—the animal's stomach still inside it and swelling in the warm afternoon sun.

The experienced hunter caught a whiff of the critter on a vagrant breeze, politely stifled a gag, and moved around to a more pleasant upwind position. All the while, he wondered how to break the news to his pal that the meat had already spoiled, that the hair was slipping from the hide, and that the paunch was a stink bomb just waiting to be set off. Only the antlers were salvageable, and they were apt to smell like the city sewer for many months to come.

Tales like this one are told around backwoods campfires; yet an appalling number of seasoned hunters—not to mention the beginners—don't know how to take proper care of a deer once it has been killed. Many hunters who have well-honed hunting and shooting skills consistently bungle postmortem procedure, allowing their neatly shot deer to spoil, get grimy, and become tainted by egg-laying or carnivorous insects. This is not to mention the laughable, energy-wasting antics of some hunters when they attempt to move the carcass from a kill site to a pickup point.

Being a fine hunter and a crack shot is all well and good, but there is still a lot to do after the bullet has found its mark. As any expert hunter knows, the difference between tender, veallike cuts of meat and gamy venison given away to "friends" is often determined by the nature of initial carcass care. Similarly, a slick, lifelike deer head above the mantle might well have been a mangy-looking flop without prompt and proper trophy care in the field.

APPROACHING THE ANIMAL

Just because a deer is down does not necessarily mean it is down *and out* for good. More than one hunter has dropped a deer, hustled forward to claim his prize, and found himself grappling with an animal that is very much alive and fighting-mad. More commonly, a theoretically dead deer leaps up at the last instant and charges away for parts unknown, leaving the hunter flat-footed and flabbergasted. The very first step any hunter must take is making certain his animal is down for keeps.

Safety precautions. Instances when a wounded deer actually goes after a hunter are few and far between. More often a hunter trots up to a deer with gutting knife drawn, straddles his supposedly dead trophy, and finds out suddenly that the animal has plenty of life left to kick and cavort about. Having a tiger by the tail would certainly be worse, but hanging onto a struggling 200-pound buck's antlers is a difficult and dangerous task.

When approaching any downed deer, be sure to move in behind the animal, preferably from an uphill side. This gives the deer a clear escape path if it is only playing possum, and makes access to you slower and more difficult if the crippled deer indeed decides to take revenge.

Minimizing a deer's chance of escape. When moving in on a downed deer, think about the setup instead of just charging forward. All too many hunters let out a war whoop when a buck goes down, and take the shortest, easiest path toward the animal. This is seldom the best approach, and usually gives the deer a chance to escape if it still has the ability. So determine which approach route will allow the clearest shooting if the animal gets to its feet and tries to run or hobble away.

At best, you should *stalk* downed game much the same way you would stalk a bedded and fully alert animal. Work into the wind, make as little noise as possible, and watch the trophy carefully for any signs of life. Chart a course that leaves abundant shooting lanes open, and stick to high ground if possible to enjoy the superior views it affords. In this way the animal will be less likely to detect your approach if it is indeed alive and mobile. When it does finally sense nearby danger, you should be close enough to take a relatively easy finishing shot.

Approach a downed deer cautiously. Look for batting or closed eyes, heaving sides, and other signs that show the deer might be down but not out. Be ready to make a quick finishing shot.

As mentioned in Part 6 of this book, it is best for two hunters to work as a team when approaching crippled deer in choppy canyon country. One hunter remains in an elevated shooting position while the other drops into a draw to investigate the results of a shot.

How to tell if a deer is dead. Certain telltale signs can tell you whether your downed trophy is dead or not. The most obvious is the condition of the animal's eyes. Any deer with wide-open, blank, unblinking eyes has probably expired. By contrast, a deer with eyes closed is always alive and a potential threat. Obviously, if eyes are open and rolling or blinking, the critter is still alive.

Careful hunters watch a deer for several seconds from close range before deciding that it is dead. A down-and-out animal sometimes kicks or quivers spasmodically for several minutes, but any deer that continues to breathe rhythmically has by no means given up the ghost. Watch a deer's ribs and belly for the heaving movement of breathing, and either wait awhile or apply a finishing shot to any breathing animal.

The final intelligent thing to do before setting your weapon aside is to nudge the animal's rear end with the toe of your boot, gun muzzle, or tip of your bow to make sure no lively reaction results. If the deer's eyes are open and unmoving, if its sides are not heaving in and out, and if a sharp poke to the rear meets with no reaction, the trophy is down for good.

DEER-CARE BASICS

There are a few basic principles of proper carcass care. First, a deer must be kept as cool and dry as possible to inhibit spoilage of its meat and hide by bacteria. Second, in most cases animal parts must be transported to a cooling plant or taxidermist as soon as possible for professional handling of meat and trophy hide. Third, a deer should be protected from carnivorous and egg-laying insects that are often prevalent in deer season. Fourth, meat should be protected from grit and grime whenever possible. And fifth, a deer should be handled and hung so that predators such as coyotes and bears cannot despoil the carcass. If you follow these deer-care basics and handle your animal accordingly, you will be rewarded with first-rate steaks and a lifetime trophy mount.

BACTERIAL ACTION

Bacteria begin to break down and rot all parts of a deer the instant the animal hits the ground. An experienced hunter realizes this and works quickly to retard bacterial action.

Bacteria thrive and multiply in a warm, moist environment. As a result, every possible effort must be made to cool and dry the carcass of a downed deer. The first step is to field-dress the animal. This means removing the stomach and intestine and thus allowing cool and dry air to circulate to inner body walls. The second step is transporting the carcass back to camp or home as quickly as possible so that the animal can be skinned to further aid cooling and surface drying of the meat. Large deer in exceptionally warm weather should be quartered on the spot to accelerate meat cooling and surface drying. Meat and hides that are quickly cooled once a deer is dropped *and kept cool* (preferably below 50 degrees) will remain in good condition for at least two days—long enough to transport them to a freezer or commercial cooler.

If outdoor temperatures are below freezing, carcass care is usually easy and bacteria are seldom a problem. In shirtsleeve weather, on the other hand, time works against you as you gut, carry, skin, and quarter your hard-earned prize. A dead deer that lies untouched for four or five hours can spoil completely or at best end up tasting second-rate. Likewise, a buck left hanging in direct sunlight for one afternoon can rot on the spot from accelerated bacterial action. Allowing maximum air circulation to animal parts in the coolest available place retards bacterial activity and preserves the quality of steaks, chops, and roasts.

Bacteria also quickly damage a warm, moist hide. Within a few short hours, the hair can slip (loosen from the skin), and this creates a taxidermist's nightmare. A hide that is stretched out to air in a cool, dry place will resist spoilage considerably longer.

So bacterial action is the hunter's number one enemy once a deer is dropped. The warmer the weather, the more pressing the problem of meat and hide spoilage. *Heat, moisture,* and *time* will all be against you as you care for your trophy.

MEAT AND INSECTS

Next to out-and-out spoilage, egg-laying pests such as blowflies and carnivorous insects such as meat bees are the biggest threat to the trophy and carcass.

Experienced hunters hate flies with a passion because these filthy creatures deposit blows (eggs) en masse on all exposed and moist animal parts. At best, yellowish clusters of fly blows must be painstakingly scraped or wiped from a deer's edible areas. At worst, these blows will hatch within a day or two and infest a carcass with putrid, writhing maggots.

Blowflies appear like magic around a freshly killed deer unless the weather happens to be very cold. It is amazing indeed that these pests converge so rapidly on fresh meat—even when you haven't seen a single fly in the area for hours before the kill. The most remote, placid grove of trees comes alive with these black, buzzing egg-layers within minutes after a deer has been dropped.

Carnivorous insects like bees are seldom a serious problem in the woods, but these critters *can* make sizable and unsightly dents in meat if they swarm a carcass completely unchecked. They also bite or sting hunters with alarming regularity if allowed to crawl willy-nilly about a deer.

Hunters use several methods for discouraging blowflies and meat-eating bees. These will be discussed a little later.

MEAT AND GRIME

There's nothing more disgusting to a hunter who is a perfectionist than a carcass caked with dirt, leaves, grass, twigs, and other forest debris. Practically speaking, a little natural crud on deer meat does not hurt flavor, but a coat of grime does require careful cleanup and trimming later. The local butcher will charge extra for this and it will reduce the amount of edible meat left behind. It is disconcerting to bite down on a venison chop and feel grit or the sharp crunch of a twig between your teeth. Sloppy field-dressing, transport and butchering cause this.

Grime from transporting an uncovered deer along dusty roads or from dragging a deer across a dry forest floor can lead to major meat-cleanup problems later. Natural debris and dirt on venison does not hurt the taste but does reduce the number of edible portions.

BEARS AND OTHER SCAVENGERS

In many deer-hunting areas, bears and smaller scavengers like coyotes, wild dogs, foxes, and raccoons are relatively abundant. These keen-nosed animals will home in on the smell of a freshly killed deer from up to a mile away. A hunter who leaves his deer unattended or hangs the animal in a vulnerable spot may wind up being robbed of his trophy by these skulking, sharp-toothed scavengers. A pack of coyotes can completely devour a deer in one glorious night, and a black bear or grizzly will characteristically drag away an entire carcass, gobble up the choicest parts, and defile the rest. Hunters never underrate the possibility of scavengers nabbing their deer and take the steps necessary to foil them.

PRESERVING A TROPHY HIDE

As mentioned earlier, heat and moisture will quickly sour a hide and cause the hair to slip. Trophy-conscious hunters should also be aware that deer hair is extremely fragile stuff. It can be broken, kinked, or rubbed away with relative ease—irreversible damage that ruins a wall rug or head-and-shoulders mount. There will be more about specific hide-care procedures later, but this is one *basic:* Deer hides for a professional taxidermist or home tanning project must be handled with kid gloves from the very start if they are to turn out properly.

FALLACIES

Many misinformed hunters insist on cutting a deer's throat immediately after it has been killed. This process supposedly "bleeds" the animal to ensure first-rate meat. In reality, any bullet or arrow wound completely drains an animal of blood, effectively negating the value of slicing the critter's throat. Aside from being a total waste of effort, cutting a trophy buck's throat also ruins the cape completely.

Another fallacy is the theory that a deer's genitals and hock glands must be cut away quickly to prevent them from tainting the meat. How on earth anyone could believe that undesirable deer musk or hormones from these peripheral body parts could magically course through dead muscle tissue is a puzzle, but this old tale persists among veterans and beginners alike. The tarsal glands in a deer's hocks and its genitals in no way affect venison once the animal is down.

THE FIELD-DRESSING PROCESS

Every hunter should know how to field-dress (gut) an animal before he goes out hunting. Unfortunately, all too many beginners blast their venison and then wonder what the heck to do next. But removing the innards from a deer must be accomplished within a few minutes after the animal is dropped to ensure sweet, tasty meat.

A fair number of neophyte hunters learn basic field-dressing from a father, uncle, or hunting friend. But this simple process is just as easily mastered from a book such as this in which clear, step-by-step photographs show just how to do it.

WHY FIELD-DRESS?

Field-dressing a deer accomplishes four important purposes. First, it removes paunch, intestine, and other inedible internal tissue, and thereby accelerates the dissipation of a deer's body heat. This cooling of the meat and hide retards bacterial action. Second, field-dressing eliminates the paunch with its smelly stomach acids and quickly expanding gasses. These too can ruin potentially delicious meat. Third, this process allows blood to drain completely from the body cavity—blood that will quickly sour and taint all flesh it touches. And fourth, field-dressing lightens a deer carcass by about 20 percent to allow easier transport from the field.

A big-game animal that has not been promptly gutted will bloat up, develop a rank odor with incredible speed, and begin to rot from bacterial action. Every deer should be field-dressed immediately to prevent this kind of waste.

FIELD-DRESSING BASICS

Gutting a deer is relatively easy to describe but is more difficult to carry out. The upcoming photos illustrate proper field-dressing technique and should serve as a guide for any beginner. The deer in these pictures was shot in the upper neck; so the body cavity would be relatively free of fluids for the photo sequence shown. This "clean" body cavity is unusual, and most field-dressing chores are accompanied by plenty of abdominal or chest-cavity blood. Seasoned hunters are seldom bothered by the messiness, and they wash up afterward in a nearby stream or with water from their canteen.

To start field-dressing, turn the deer upside down so that its feet point toward the sky. If terrain permits, position the head and shoulders uphill from the paunch and hams. This allows the insides to roll out freely. Now begin slitting the belly hide and muscle layer encasing the paunch from brisket to genitals. Take care not to slice open the stomach itself. Ream the anus from the body as though it were the core of an apple. This frees the intestine so that it can be pulled out of the animal along with the paunch.

Now you have three options for proceeding. You can merely empty the body cavity by groping forward into the chest and cutting the esophagus (the tube which connects the throat of the deer with the stomach) and the windpipe. Then you just pull out the paunch, intestine, lungs, and heart. This technique satisfies basic field-care requirements if weather is cool and you are faced with a grimy drag or carry that would dirty a more fully opened carcass. For a more complete and generally more desirable field-dressing job, split the chest all the way to the shin with a knife and compact saw. Pry open the chest cavity and remove the windpipe, heart, lungs, paunch, and intestine in one neat operation. Many hunters go one step further and split the pelvic bone to completely open the carcass. This thoroughly cools a deer and allows drying of internal surfaces to better retard bacterial action. But more meat is directly exposed to dust, twigs, leaves, and similar junk as you carry or drag your trophy back to civilization.

Study the photos shown here to learn the fine points of field-dressing a deer with a knife and saw. A clean, neat job like this one allows no belly juices to squeeze

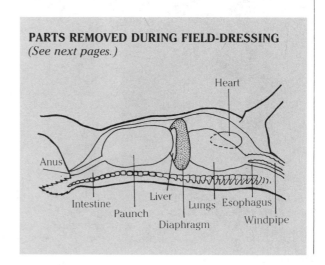

PARTS REMOVED DURING FIELD-DRESSING
(See next pages.)

Heart

Anus

Intestine

Liver

Paunch

Diaphragm

Lungs

Esophagus

Windpipe

out and taint meat, empties the body cavity of useless dead weight, cools down the carcass quickly, and keeps the meat in the best possible condition. With enough practice, a hunter can do the whole field-dressing job in five or ten minutes.

SPECIAL EQUIPMENT

Any medium-sized deer knife will perform the field-dressing chore to perfection. The best of all, however, is a drop-point blade because this tip makes it easier to steer clear of the paunch during the belly-slicing

operation. (See the knife illustrations in Part 5 of this book.) Similarly, any hatchet or compact bone saw will handle the bone-splitting necessary for a thorough stem-to-stern field-dressing job.

A few outdoor companies sell so-called "gut kits" designed to make field-dressing less messy. These kits generally include rubber gloves to protect the hands and towelettes to wipe up with afterwards. Relatively few experienced hunters bother with such niceties, but if blood irritates your skin or insults your sensibilities, by all means slip on hand and arm protection before cutting open a deer. Commercial gut kits are especially practical in areas where wash-up water is not apt to be handy once a deer is down.

HOW TO FIELD-DRESS A DEER

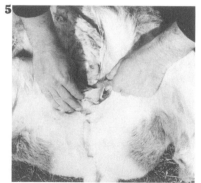

1. *To begin field-dressing, roll the deer onto its back with legs pointed toward the sky. Feel around, as shown, to find the base of the brisket—the place where bone ends and soft stomach tissue begins.* **2.** *Carefully slip your knife (blade edge* up*) beneath the hide just below the brisket. Use two fingers from your free hand to guide the blade and hold the hide away from the belly muscles as you cut.* **3.** *Slice the hide, and hide only, from brisket to anus. Cut to one side of the deer's genitals along the way. Hold the knife at a shallow angle to avoid cutting muscle.*

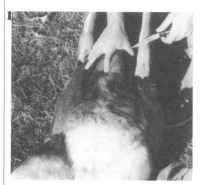
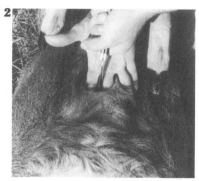
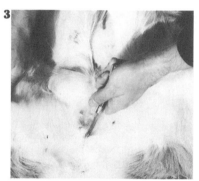

4. *After slitting the hide from brisket to anus and using two carefully spread fingers to guide your knife, insert the blade through the thin layer of belly muscle below the brisket as shown, and begin slicing toward the tail.* **5.** *Continue the belly incision to the pelvis, where the thin belly muscle lining ends. Use extreme care when making this cut— a slip will slice the belly itself, creating a smelly mess.* **6.** *Done properly, the gutting incision opens the stomach cavity to fully expose the paunch. In healthy deer, this tough, gray food sack is often seamed with white fat.*

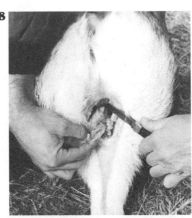
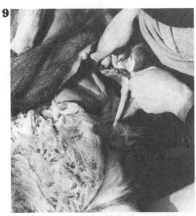

7. *Cut all around the anus, slicing just deep enough to completely penetrate the hide. The circular incision that results should be about 2 inches in diameter.* **8.** *Carefully ream around the anus by thrusting the blade deep between the hams and whittling around the tough, rubbery anal canal. Your knife should penetrate about 4 inches during this procedure.* **9.** *A thin, reddish muscle membrane, called the diaphragm, separates the paunch from the front of the chest cavity. Locate diaphragm below the back of the brisket and cut it away from the ribs on both sides.*

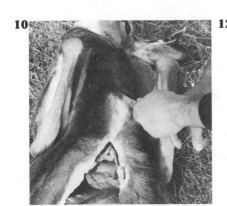

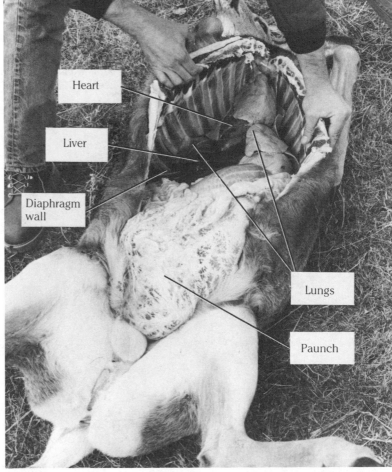

Heart

Liver

Diaphragm wall

Lungs

Paunch

10. *The carcass will cool faster if you slice the hide from the brisket all the way to the chin.* **11.** *Using a bone saw or hatchet, cut through the brisket bone toward the deer's throat. This opens the chest cavity for easiest access to heart and lungs, and also accelerates cooling of a deer's front end.*

12. *Neat incisions through hide, muscle, and bone clearly show all internal organs. Many people eat the liver and heart. Lungs, paunch, and intestine (which leads from paunch to anus) are always discarded.*

(Continued on next page)

(Field-dressing continued)

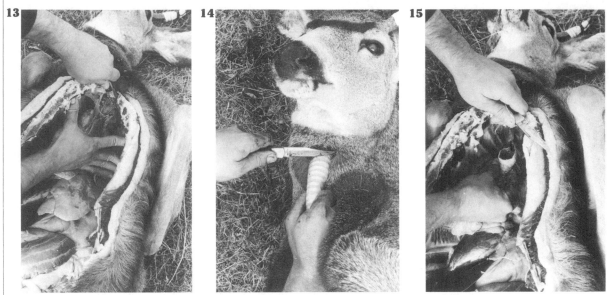

13. *Heart, lungs, and stomach are attached to the esophagus (back of throat) and windpipe at the front of the chest cavity. To do a "quicky" field-dressing job without sawing through the brisket, you must grope into the chest and cut through esophagus, windpipe, and surrounding tissue as shown.* **14.** *If you opt to open the chest and neck, cut off the windpipe and esophagus just under the chin to aid cooling of the neck. These food and air canals pull free from surrounding tissue with a moderate tug.* **15.** *Once windpipe (the larger, stiffer tube) and esophagus are severed and pulled free from the neck, the innards are ready to be pulled out. At this point, it's best if the deer's head and shoulders are positioned slightly higher than its rear end.*

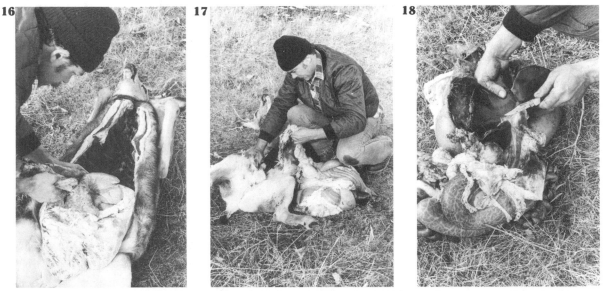

16. *Gripping the windpipe and esophagus, pull backward stiffly to roll all internal organs out of the deer in one contiguous mass. If heart, paunch, or lungs adhere stubbornly to the body cavity, carve them free.* **17.** *Roll the insides to one side of the body cavity. Grasp the intestine that extends backward from the paunch, and pull this out from between the hams. If you have reamed the anus completely, the entire anus, intestine, and bladder should slide out easily with no deer pellets or urine spilling.* **18.** *Roll the insides away from the carcass so they won't be underfoot. If you plan to save heart and liver, take care to keep these parts clean. The liver is a large, dark-red, two-lobed organ positioned directly in front of a deer's paunch and directly behind its diaphragm. Cut it free where it attaches to the paunch.*

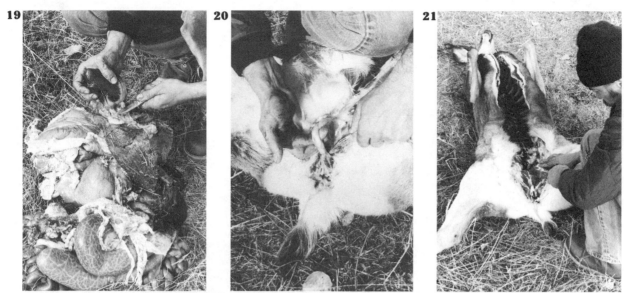

19. *The heart has a unique flavor. To remove this muscle from the pile of innards, slice through the tough artery tissue extending from its larger end.* **20.** *Most hunters prefer to split the pelvis at the same time they perform initial field-dressing. On a buck, the penis must first be carved from between the legs and severed at its root near the base of the tail. The testicles should be left attached to the hide.* **21.** *Using knife and saw or hatchet, slice down to the center of the pelvis and cut through this thin plate of bone. On small deer the pelvis can sometimes be split with a stout knife alone.*

22. *The deer is now fully field-dressed from throat to tail, and internal meat is quickly cooling and glazing over. This neck-shot buck had very little blood in the body cavity, but many animals are partially full of blood.*

23. *Roll the deer over to allow the body cavity to thoroughly drain of blood. To keep meat clean, drain the carcass in a grassy area or drape the animal across a nearby bush or rock.*

TRANSPORT OUT OF THE WOODS

In many ways hunting becomes just plain hard work once you drop a deer. Nothing can be harder than moving a field-dressed deer weighing upwards of 100 pounds across uneven terrain laced by downed trees, running streams, and other natural obstacles. Just how tough the chore happens to be depends upon many factors, including where you choose to hunt, where your deer falls, and how many friends you have on hand to share the sweating and muscle strain. But unless your deer drops smack in the middle of a passable road, you'll want to devise a sensible strategy to get the animal out of the woods with a minimum of effort and time.

Unfortunately, the best deer-hunting areas seldom make for easy hauling. During hunting season, deer don't stay in areas that can be cruised with vehicles or easily covered on foot. These places are generally swarming with people—a circumstance that drives deer into less accessible places. Some lazy hunters actually plan their hunts to make hauling the carcass easier (such as hunting only the uphill side of a road). But these individuals are usually destined to failure. By contrast, a good hunter goes where the animals are apt to be and worries about packing or dragging *after* he fills his tag. You should definitely consider the problems before heading afield, but don't let potential difficulties stand in the way of hunting in productive, hard-to-reach locales.

In areas congested with other hunters, always cover your deer with a bright-colored wrapping, preferably blaze-orange, to ensure that you are not mistaken for a deer by another hunter during the pack. Covering meat also helps keep it clean.

SAFETY

Always keep safety in mind when hauling your deer out. For example, guard against overexertion or physical injury when lugging out a deer. Accidental slips and falls are more likely to happen when a hunter is pushing too hard. Beyond that, safety is a matter of common sense. Obviously, a hunter with a heart condition should never wear himself to a frazzle in the field, and a hunter with a bad back would be ill-advised to hoist a 150-pound buck across his shoulders. Similarly, toting a top-heavy backpack full of venison across sheer cliffs and treacherous shale slides makes no sense at all. It invites injury.

Another danger when hauling out a deer is the possibility of being shot at by trigger-happy bozos who shoot first and ask questions later. In all but the most remote areas, carrying a deer across your shoulders can be a very grave mistake. The shoulder-high glint of an antler or the flash of gray-brown hair can draw gunfire, and several hunters are killed by accident each year as they muscle out whole, uncovered deer.

Smart hunters in heavily hunted areas usually drag their animals, cover them entirely to hide deerlike parts, or adorn them with blaze-orange surveyor's tape. A deer that is dragged along the ground is tough for any other hunter to see, and the guy doing the dragging is generally seen first in his red or blaze-orange garb. If you drop a deer in an area where backpacking or carrying up on your shoulders is the only sensible transport procedure, you should wrap the carcass in a blaze-orange cloth, a bright-yellow raincoat, a white deer bag, or other highly visible and totally un-deerlike covering. If a deer drape is not available, surveyor's tape festooned from antlers, legs, and neck clearly flags the critter and minimizes danger from hunters in the vicinity.

KEEPING THE CARCASS CLEAN

Keeping a deer carcass white glove clean while hauling it out is impossible in most situations. But there are some things you can do to reduce the amount of meat-tainting debris picked up on the way out of the woods. First, never skin deer in the field unless the carcass or parts can be completely wrapped up in tarps, game bags, old sheets or other coverings during the transport process. Second, always try to prevent direct meat-to-ground contact during dragging or carrying. Use the hide itself as a shield unless it is destined for the taxidermist. Third, in really dirty situations, you can actually sew the body cavity shut on a field-dressed deer. Make holes in the belly skin with a knife and stitch the gutting incisions tight with nylon rope. There's no reason to be fanatical about keeping deer meat clean, but a few precautions minimize cleanup chores later.

DEER-DRAGGING METHODS AND GEAR

On relatively-level ground and in downhill situations, dragging a deer out of the woods is often the easiest way to go. The problem with deer dragging is getting a solid pulling grip on the carcass. A mature buck's antlers make a fairly good handle to drag by, especially when two people grab opposite sides of the rack and pull along together. A doe or spike buck is more difficult to grip. Here, the front ankles offer the best non-slip handles.

Dragging any deer by antlers or feet can severely tire hand, wrist, and forearm muscles if transport distance is long—especially if you tackle this chore alone. A commercial deer drag can help with this problem. The strap assembly cinches around a deer's

Dragging a deer is often the easiest transport method when terrain is level and fairly free of obstacles. For short drags, two hunters can merely grab hold of antlers or front hoofs.

head or antlers and loops about your waist or upper body. The deer drag leaves both your hands free to tote gun or bow, and lets you plug along digging in with both feet in straight-ahead fashion. In a pinch make your deer drag from rope or a leather belt.

Some people who always hunt in level terrain covered with grass and leaves believe dragging is the only way to haul out deer. However, dragging makes no sense at all in uphill situations, over very broken terrain, or when you want to have a deer's hide tanned with the hair left in place. Even a runty 90-pound yearling buck can wear you to a frazzle on a short uphill drag, and choppy or rock-strewn country hangs a deer up so often that dragging is almost impossible. In all but the grassiest, most stone-free terrain, the friction of dragging a deer will rub away hair in a matter of minutes, leaving giant bald spots in the hide and ruining what little hair is left. In places where dragging is too much work or too darn tough on a trophy hide, carrying a deer is a much better way to go!

CARRYING DEER

Many hunters grimace at the thought of shouldering a deer and packing it out of the woods. But in many situations carrying is much faster and requires far less effort than dragging. As long as the load weight is not overtaxing, and as long as terrain is not too dangerous to negotiate, backpacking deer is an excellent way to proceed.

There are several methods of carrying a deer on your back. A small animal—under 100 pounds—can be slung across both shoulders like an elongated sack of barley. Heavier deer in the 100- to 130-pound class can be lugged out whole by a strong, persistent individual. Here, all four of the deer's legs must be doctored with knife and rope to form relatively comfortable shoulder slings (photos next page). If two hunters are available for the carry, cut the deer in half with knife and saw to form two loads of equal weight. To do this, slice the sides of the deer vertically between the fifth and sixth ribs (counting from the back) and sever the backbone at the point where these between-the-rib incisions meet. Halving a deer distresses a few hunters who like to hang their animals whole in camp. But anyone caught far enough from a road will gladly sacrifice a 120-pound tradition in exchange for a 60-pound load.

Backpacking deer hunters who drop animals several miles away from roads generally prefer to bone out carcasses on the spot. They carefully skin deer, separate edible meat from the bones, and stuff the meat in backpack sacks. It makes no sense to grunt out useless bones and hide that would only be discarded later anyway.

In remote areas where safety is not a problem, a small deer can be slung across both shoulders like a sack of grain. Carrying is often easier than dragging in steep or rocky terrain. But a fairly heavy deer can be modified to allow easier carrying out of the hills. First, cut the skin on the hind legs and slip the front legs through the incisions, as shown left. Tie the legs in this position with rope or twine to create slings for the shoulders. Not as comfortable as a commercial backpack, but much better than nothing. If there's a chance that other hunters are in the area, drape the deer with a bright covering so you don't get shot.

Boning a deer takes about an hour for an expert to accomplish and easily cuts deer-carrying weight in half. A field-dressed deer's weight consists of approximately 25 to 35 percent head and hide, 25 to 35 percent bones, and 30 to 50 percent edible meat. For details on how to separate a deer from its bones, study the upcoming section on boneless deer processing at home.

DEER-TRANSPORT AIDS

Certain types of deer terrain lend themselves to special deer-hauling techniques. For example, in relatively open foothill country covered with knee-deep sagebrush, a hunter can usually haul out his deer in a wheelbarrow or similar homemade gurney with a bicycle wheel up front. If the ground is smooth enough, a gurney makes quick work of long-distance carting.

Another item some hunters use is a deer stretcher. This homemade gizmo is exactly what its name im-

plies—it looks just like a conventional medical stretcher or litter. Once the deer carcass is strapped in, two hunters, one at each end, are needed to lift the stretcher and walk it to the nearest road. Obviously, a deer stretcher is only practical in flat or mildly sloping terrain.

USING PACK ANIMALS

A horse or mule may be a pain to feed and keep tabs on in the hills, but nothing beats a well-trained pack animal for transporting of deer. Beasts of burden are seldom used for hauling game unless kill sites are rough and remote, where the only alternative is boning-out deer and backpacking 50 to 100 pounds of meat over several miles of leg-wrenching terrain.

In many western muley areas, successful hunters hire professional meat packers to carry out deer on horses or mules. It is best to arrange for such services before hiking into hellholes where only horses and helicopters can easily salvage meat.

Pack animals can be a nuisance to feed and control on wilderness hunts, but all that grief seems well worthwhile once a sizable deer is down. A well-trained mule or horse can lug out loads guaranteed to break a hunter's back. This mule, named Herkimer, refused to be saddled with this buck until his eyes were covered with a jacket.

USING VEHICLES

There are few things more gratifying than killing a deer and then discovering that the animal can be reached with a motorbike, all-terrain vehicle, or a car or truck. This is the sort of rare occurrence every hunter dreams about at night.

If topography permits use of a vehicle, you'd be a fool to carry a carcass out on your back. Some well-heeled hunters keep an off-road trail bike or compact ATV on hand to aid in deer retrieval. Others use four-wheel-drive vehicles with excellent results. Vehicles can be used in areas laced with old logging roads—especially if you have a chainsaw to remove any deadfalls that block the way. A little forethought and intimate knowledge of abandoned roads in a hunting area can save many hours of deer-packing grunt work.

HOW NOT TO TRANSPORT DEER

A fair number of books on deer show photos of hunters carrying out their game on long, stout poles. An animal's legs are usually lashed to the pole with a pair of hunters, one in front and one behind, shouldering the burden. Whoever started the trend of illustrating this wretched deer-transport method deserves to have his publishing and hunting licenses permanently revoked.

Pole-carrying deer is a technique all experienced hunters avoid like the plague. Even if a suitable carrying pole can be found, the infernal thing digs into the shoulders like a medieval torture device. To make matters worse, the deer being carried invariably swings from side to side like a pendulum. Pole-carrying also adds the weight of the pole itself to what is already a heavy burden. Finally, the method is only suited to places where the terrain is almost perfectly flat. But even in ideal, table-top country, this is a third-rate method.

Nothing beats dropping a deer where a vehicle can easily go. Vehicle access is seldom good in the better hunting locales, but good access saves plenty of strenuous work when you do luck out.

FROM FIELD TO FREEZER

Now that the basics of field-dressing and packing a deer carcass have been covered, it is time to get to some specific techniques for preserving your trophy. The following pages give valuable tips for keeping hard-won venison in the best possible condition, as well as showing how to butcher it yourself. Ways of preserving hides and trophy heads for the taxidermist are also discussed.

HANGING THE DEER

Hanging a deer facilitates cooling, maximizes air circulation, and keeps the animal away from scavengers. You should always hang a deer as soon as you get it back to camp or home. Also, if immediate transport out of the woods is impossible, hang the field-dressed carcass at the kill site.

Deer should be hung as soon as possible to allow maximum air circulation and rapid meat cooling. Hanging a carcass by the hind legs is usually best because it lets heat rise from the chest cavity and makes removing the head easier.

A deer can be hung by the head or by the hind legs. Although hunters use both techniques, hanging a deer by the hind legs is better for three reasons. First, this position allows body heat to rise freely from the chest cavity area, and this accelerates rapid cooling to ensure decent meat. Second, a deer hung by the back legs can be fully skinned or caped—including removal of the head. By contrast, an animal hung by the head itself cannot be decapitated. This retards meat cooling in the neck area and makes salvaging a trophy head impossible. Third, a rope attached around the deer's neck will gall the cape beyond repair, and a rope lashed to the antlers may break or crack antlers or the skull. Experienced hunters who hang deer by the head usually hunt in fairly cold climates and do not care about saving a head and cape for the taxidermist.

Always hang a deer in a cool, shady place. Direct sunlight can quickly warm a carcass, resulting in soured or off-tasting meat.

PREVENTING CONTAMINATION

It is a common misconception that deer meat is either excellent or rotten. Unfortunately, venison quality is not so black or white. A deer that is quickly field-dressed, quickly hauled out of the woods, quickly hung, and quickly skinned in moderate-to-cool weather usually produces meat of excellent flavor. But it must be *kept* cool and rushed to a butcher shop within two days after the kill.

By contrast, meat that is less expertly handled declines in quality by degrees. Many people who swear they hate the taste of deer have sampled meat that was neither superb nor positively spoiled. Strong, gamy flavor usually results from the following: letting a carcass lie on the ground overnight; leaving the deer ungutted for several hours; hanging the carcass in partial sunlight for several days; or otherwise allowing the carcass to stay warm when it should be very cool to the touch. The meat actually rots if you leave the carcass draped across a hot auto hood or hung for days in the warm autumn sun.

Once you hang a deer, skin it at once and then trim away all blood-shot venison with a sharp knife. A bullet or arrow usually pulverizes at least a little meat, pervading surrounding tissues with jelled blood. Such reddish, spongy wound areas must be cut away immediately after skinning because they tend to sour or

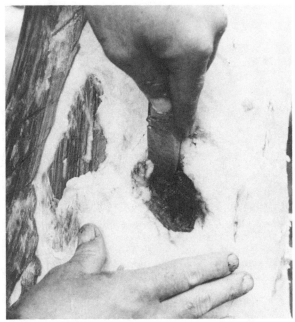

Trim away blood-shot tissue on a carcass promptly. This pulverized flesh tends to spoil quite rapidly, tainting surrounding meat and thereby generally degrading the meat's flavor.

taint surrounding meat with incredible speed, even in fairly cool weather.

Once a carcass has been hung, skinned, and trimmed, it should be covered with a white commercial deer bag. The bag allows air circulation to the meat but keeps out blowflies, meat bees, and similar pests. If you don't have a deer bag, coat all exposed surfaces of a skinned carcass with lemon juice or pepper to ward off flies and meat-eating bugs. When handled in this manner, a carcass will quickly "glaze" over—that is, surface meat will become dry to the touch. Cool, glazed deer meat will remain in good condition for two or three days if temperatures stay below 40 or 50 degrees.

In areas where bears might possibly raid your hunting camp and chow down on hanging deer, hang carcasses from sturdy ropes and high in the air. Black bears climb almost as well as monkeys; so hang deer away from tree trunks and other easy access points.

BASIC DEER SKINNING

Skinning a deer is a relatively easy task not unlike removing the peel from an orange. Skinning is important because it accelerates carcass cooling and allows surface meat to glaze or dry. Deer need not be skinned immediately in extremely cold weather, but experienced hunters usually decide to complete this operation at once.

A deer is normally skinned from hocks to throat as shown in accompanying photographs. This technique produces a complete, uniformly shaped hide suitable for tanning. It is also the quickest way to do the skinning even if you plan to throw the hide away. By contrast, trophy bucks for the taxidermist must be caped carefully for professional shoulder mounting—a procedure requiring entirely different incisions. Before hacking away with your knife, consider these two deer-skinning options.

CAPING

A trophy buck requires careful caping to ensure a handsome taxidermy job. If you drop a buck large enough to grace your living-room wall, you have two caping options: the cape-and-freeze technique or complete shoulder-to-nose skinning.

If your hunting situation allows you to remove the cape and entire head, double-wrap this part in plastic garbage bags and rush it to a freezer within a few hours. This is the best way to go. Skinning out a buck's head is painstaking business, and a professional taxidermist can handle it far better than a hunter. If you do not have direct access to a freezer—a common occurrence on wilderness hunts—you'll have to skin the cape from shoulders all the way to nose, as shown here. A slow, careful approach will usually result in a nick-free job even if you have never completely caped a deer head in your life.

FIELD CARE OF TROPHY HIDES

Both full deer hides and completely skinned capes must be properly handled to prevent hide spoilage and resulting slippage of hair. If at all possible, trophy hides should be rushed to a taxidermist. Or freeze the hide within 24 hours after the animal has been killed. A hide or cape can be frozen in double plastic garbage bags for up to one year before damaging freezer burn occurs.

In a pinch any deer hide or cape can be preserved in the field. First, trim every scrap of fat and meat from the fleshy side of the hide, taking care not to cut through the hide itself. Next, heavily coat all surfaces not covered by hair with salt. Roll up the salted hide or cape, hair out, and set it aside. The salt will draw moisture from the hide and pickle it against bacterial action. Shake out the moist salt about 24 hours later, replace it with a fresh supply, and either stretch the hide, hair down, for drying or roll it up again for shipping to taxidermist or tannery.

HOW TO SKIN A DEER

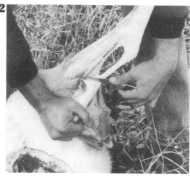

1. *Roll the deer on its back. After slicing the hide along the insides of both hind legs from below the hocks to mid-hams, completely girdle each hind leg about 5 inches below the hock, as shown. Take care not to cut leg meat. The lower legs need not be skinned out because these will be discarded.* **2.** *Skin the hide away from both hocks with smooth, careful strokes. Don't cut through the large Achilles tendons on the backs of the legs.* **3.** *Using a bone saw, cut off the hind legs about 3 inches below the hocks. If a saw isn't handy, use a sharp knife on the "knee" joint in this part of the leg.*

4. *Insert a meat-hanging gambrel in both hocks and hoist the deer until the head barely touches the ground. Without a gambrel, hang the deer by tying a rope through one of the hocks.* **5.** *Finish slicing the hide from pelvis to hock on the inside of each hind leg. Simply run your blade beneath the skin and cut upward away from the meat as shown.* **6.** *Begin skinning the deer's hams by pulling downward on the hide and wielding your knife with smooth, even strokes. This skin should cut away easily.*

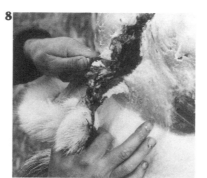

7. *Part skin from muscle over the backs of both hams, being careful not to nick the hide. Even if you do not plan to save the skin, accidentally slicing through it deposits messy hair on the meat. As you skin the rump, pull the hide away from the meat to allow easier knife work. Fat is often thickest here, making skinning especially easy.* **8.** *Carefully skin around the tail. Then grasp it and cut it off at the base with firm strokes of your knife. There's no edible meat here.* **9.** *The flanks and back of the deer are easily skinned with downward pressure on the hide and careful blade work. On younger deer, the skin here often peels away with hard tugging alone.*

10. *With special care, skin the ribs down to the front legs. Here, thin meat layers cling tenaciously to the hide, slowing progress and requiring shorter, more careful blade strokes.* **11.** *Continue removing hide across the middle back and downward to the shoulders. A combination of hand pressure on the hide and moderate slicing usually makes for fast work here.* **12.** *Once you reach the front legs, slice the hide along the back of each between the knee and "armpit." Keep the knife at a shallow angle and cut upward to avoid slicing leg meat.*

13. *Skin around each front leg and across the shoulders as shown. Cut the hide off directly below the knees to allow removal of the lower legs.* **14.** *Using a bone saw, sever both front legs at the knee. As with the hind legs, a sharp knife can be used in lieu of a saw to slice through the knee joint.* **15.** *Skin down across the shoulders and brisket to the base of the neck. At this point, blade work becomes slower because hide begins to hug muscle more tenaciously.*

16. *A deer's neck is the most difficult part to skin. Heavy downward pulling on the hide and patient knife strokes remove the hide here.* **17.** *After you skin to jawline (if legal), sever the head from the body with a bone saw. Some states require that you leave head and body intact until the deer is ready to be cut and wrapped. Inspect the carcass for blood-shot or grime-covered meat, and trim away and discard all tainted areas.* **18.** *Enclose the hanging carcass with a white, fine-mesh deer bag to ward off blowflies and carnivorous insects. This bag should be tied tightly above the gambrel to keep pests out completely.*

HOW TO CAPE A DEER FOR MOUNTING

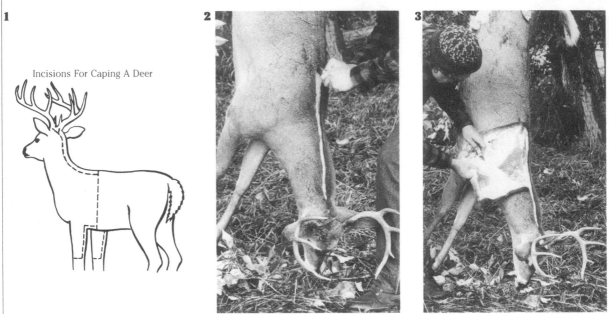

1 & 2. *To cape a trophy deer head for the taxidermist, make a straight incision in the hide along the middle of the spine between the back of head and back of shoulders.* **3.** *Make a second incision at right angles to the first well behind the shoulders. Peel the hide from the shoulders with slow knife work, being careful not to nick the cape.*

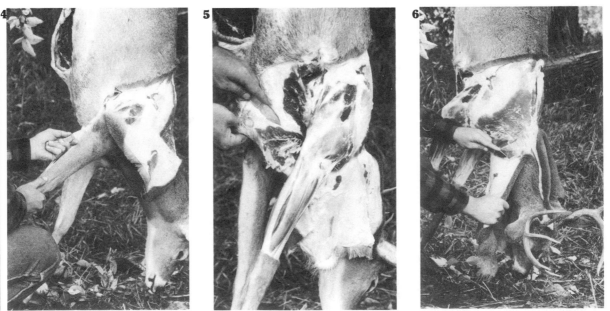

4. *Beginning at the knee on each front leg, slice the hide along the back of the foreleg. The incision should join the cut behind the shoulder in the "armpit" of the deer.* **5.** *Girdle the front legs at the knees and carefully part the skin from the upper legs and brisket. A little tugging on the hide will help separate it from the meat.* **6.** *Finish girdling the deer's body behind the shoulders by slicing the hide as has been done here. Skin down the neck with painstaking care while pulling steadily downward on the hide.*

7. *When you reach the deer's throat, carefully cut through the meat to the spine all the way around the neck. Avoid accidentally slicing the cape.* **8.** *Twist the head from the body with a firm wrench of the hands. If you've deeply girdled the neck at the back of the head, the spine should pop in two with a begrudging crunch.* **9.** *If quick access to a freezer is possible, double-wrap the head and cape in three-ply plastic garbage bags and freeze it at once. Otherwise, you'll have to skin out the head completely, as shown on upcoming pages.*

PRESERVING ANTLERS

There are two basic ways to preserve trophy antlers. The first is by skinning and fleshing the entire upper skull, and then salting it to completely eliminate odor (see upcoming photos). This preparation is necessary if you want to mount the rack on a plaque with the entire skull attached. This is called a European mount. Leaving the entire upper skull intact also adds some insurance against the antlers being broken apart during transport. A whole skull is considerably stronger than a small section removed with a saw. (See page 572.)

A second way to preserve antlers is simply sawing out the upper skull plate (see drawing). This easy technique is all that is necessary for normal plaque mounting or for sending antlers and fully skinned-out capes to taxidermists for head-and-shoulders mounts. You should heavily salt the sawed-out portion of deer skull to prevent bacterial odor. On antlers to be plaque mounted, the scalp can be removed from the skull plate or left to dry in place. For details on full-skull European mounts and traditional plaque mounts with and without the scalp, see Part 8 of this book on home taxidermy.

HOT-WEATHER CARE

Late-summer and early-fall deer seasons are sometimes accompanied by extremely warm weather. When midday temperatures soar above 70 degrees, care for a deer carcass becomes a truly nerve-racking chore. The most important factor in such situations is *speed*—quick initial carcass care, fast carrying or dragging out of the woods, and hasty transport to a meat-cooling plant. However, on occasion a hunter must tend to meat for several warm days before transporting it to a refrigerated locker.

Deer meat can often be preserved for two or three days in warm weather with special cooling techniques. Here's how to proceed. First, hang and skin the carcass immediately in the deepest constant shade available. Cover the meat with a thin cotton deer bag, and allow it to hang until dawn on the following day. Before sunrise, ease the deer to the ground and thoroughly wrap it in one or more sleeping bags, blankets, or similar insulation. Hoist up the deer once more after darkness falls, wrap it on the ground again at dawn, and so on. This process chills meat at night, and keeps it cool throughout warmer daylight hours. A deer that would totally spoil within 24 hours of constant hanging can be saved in this way.

FINAL PROCESSING

The final step in handling deer meat is cutting and wrapping for the freezer. The majority of hunters prefer to leave this to a competent butcher. However, a fair number of do-it-yourselfers butcher game themselves both to save money and to enjoy the satisfaction of self-sufficiency.

HOW TO SKIN OUT A HEAD FOR THE TAXIDERMIST

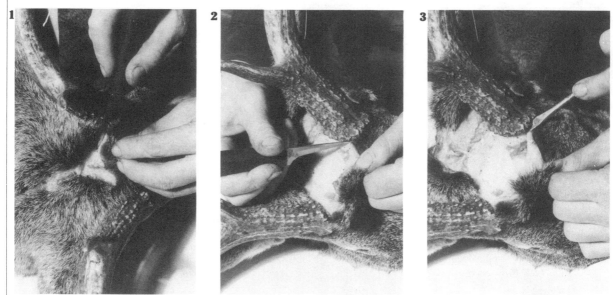

1. Make two short incisions from the back of the head forward to the antler bases. These incisions should form a "Y" on top of the head. **2.** Carefully peel the scalp from between the antlers using a short, sharp knife for good blade control. Avoid nicking the hide throughout the head-skinning chore. **3.** Using a screwdriver or similar blunt instrument, force the hide away from the bases of the antlers. The cape clings tenaciously here, but slow, careful prying will do the job neatly.

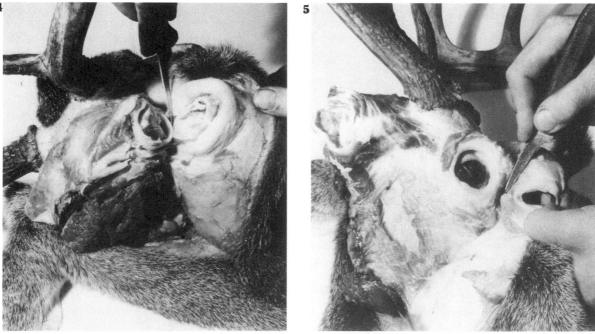

4. Skin between the antler burrs and ears. At the ears, cut through the cartilage that attaches them to the head. Avoid slicing the hide. **5.** After skinning forward toward the eyes and separating the eyelids from the eye sockets with short, careful knife strokes, work the knife deep into the tear duct depression in the skull, as shown, to skin out intact this thin, sunken segment of hide. Eye-socket and tear-duct cuts must be delicate.

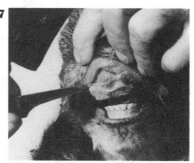
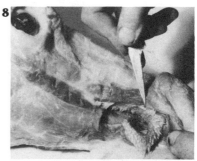

6 & 7. *Move to the mouth and make shallow incisions along the inside edges of both upper and lower lips. The lip skin folds inward about ¼ inch along the full perimeter of the mouth, and a knife incision along this inner line prevents your cutting away lip skin when you cape from the underside of the hide later.* **8.** *Once inner lip incisions are made, continue peeling away the cape along the nose and jaw. Your knife will intersect the inner lip incisions, leaving the entire inner and outer lips intact.*

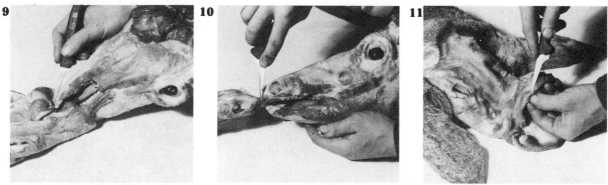

9. *Carefully skin toward the end of the jaw and free the hide from the chin with short, delicate strokes. Work slowly and carefully to avoid nicking this thin-haired part.* **10.** *Peel the hide forward to the nostrils, cautiously cut through the cartilage beneath the nostril holes, and skin over the end of the nose. After a few final blade strokes, the cape is separated from the skull.* **11.** *Next, split the fatty tissue on the underside of the deer's lips. This flattens out the lips where they normally roll into the mouth, allowing salt to penetrate deep and prevent spoilage of thin skin.*

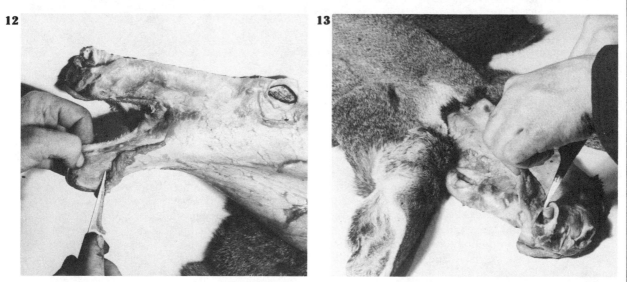

12. *Carefully strip the head skin of all clinging meat and fat that can block salt penetration and thus lead to spoilage. Excess meat must usually be whittled away from the chin.* **13.** *The nostril area generally also needs fleshing. A layer of fatty tissue adheres in this region and must be stripped away.*

(Continued on next page)

(Caping continued)

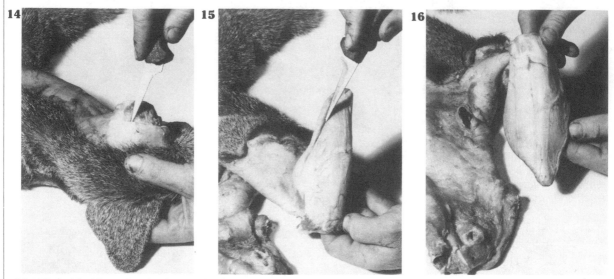

14, 15 & 16. *Meticulously skin the backs of the ears. Turn the ears inside out while leaving the ultrathin frontal ear skin attached to the cartilage that gives the ear its shape. As long as the backs of the ears are skinned completely to the rims of the cartilage, spoilage and hair slippage will not occur.*

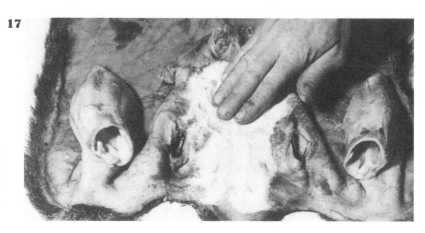

17. *A deer cape must be heavily salted immediately after skinning to stop bacterial action and potential spoilage. Rub salt over all inner surfaces, including the ears, eyes, split lips, and nostrils.*

Whether you butcher your own or entrust this task to a pro, here are important meat-processing tips well worth considering.

About aging meat. Among experienced deer hunters there's been an ongoing controversy about the aging of venison. Some insist that venison should be cut and wrapped as quickly as possible. Others contend that the deer should hang one to three weeks in a cool environment before final processing. According to one theory, extra days of hanging outdoors in chilly weather (36 to 38 degrees is considered ideal) or inside a meat locker ages and tenderizes meat through controlled bacterial action. Strong advocates of deer aging claim that subtle improvements occur in the flavor and texture of venison over time, especially in old, lean animals. At best these claims are subject to debate.

Most butchers and open-minded hunters feel that 7 to 10 hanging days neither hurt nor help meat, provided the proper temperature is maintained. Most professional meat cutters hang game for a week or more at controlled locker temperatures because they are too busy to do the job immediately. The only hazard involved in hanging meat outdoors at home is the possibility of unwanted warm weather and the resulting flavor deterioration.

The important thing to remember is that well-handled deer meat *can* be hung a week or so with no ill effect at temperatures in the mid to high 30s. This buys time if you plan to cut up a deer yourself.

HOW TO PREPARE A SKULL FOR THE EUROPEAN MOUNT

Preserving the entire upper skull of a deer is relatively quick and easy if ample salt is on hand. In remote locales, hunters often process several trophies in this way during the course of a single hunt.

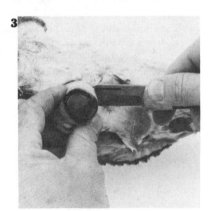

1. *To preserve a deer's entire upper skull, first slice the hide backward from the back of the mouth on both sides. Force the lower jaw downward and backward until it unhinges from the skull. Knife work in the jaw-hinges might be needed.* **2.** *Remove the hide from the front half of the upper skull with a sharp knife. No special care is needed here because the hide will be discarded. Do not cut into the bone itself. Whittle around the antler burrs, as shown, to remove the bulk of the scalp. Remove as much meat and fat along with the hide as you can. Then carefully carve away any remaining skin and cartilage about the antler bases.* **3.** *Cut around each eyeball until it pulls free from the skull. The eyes will adhere stubbornly. Avoid cutting the socket bones. Then cut away most of the meat and fat.*

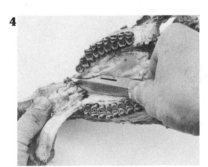

4. *Carefully remove the palate tissue. This resists peeling in much the same way as the hide around a neck. Patience and pulling prevail.* **5.** *Using a double-over length of stiff wire, scramble and scrape out the brains through the small Atlas hole in the back of the skull. This takes time because the Atlas hole is small and the brains are reluctant to budge.* **6.** *Liberally coat the skull with salt, pouring plenty into the eye sockets and nostril slits. Completely fill the brain cavity via the Atlas hole.*

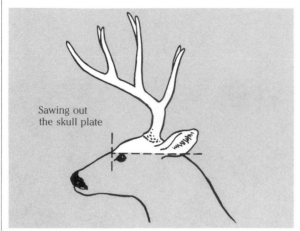

This option to the European skull mount on the previous page is to saw out the skull plate.

Tips on home butchering. There are two basic ways to butcher a deer—with and without the bones. Professional butchers with meat bandsaws almost always dice up venison with bones attached because this takes less time and energy. The same process can be accomplished at home with a hand saw, but it requires considerably more effort. As a result, most knowledgeable deer hunters remove the bones from meat as they cut and wrap—a process illustrated in accompanying photos. Boneless venison takes up less room in a freezer too—an energy-saving plus.

There are three ways of wrapping deer meat for the freezer. Some butchers merely double-bag the cuts in one-gallon zip-lock containers. Others wrap meat in heavy aluminum foil. The most popular, and most meat-protective method, is using plastic-coated freezer paper. It is available at any grocery store or butcher shop.

Generally speaking, meat wrapped in freezer paper can be frozen at least one year before it begins to dry out and lose its flavor. Venison enclosed in plastic bags or foil begins to show freezer burn somewhat sooner—normally within eight or ten months. Deer meat frozen over two years is palatable but decidedly dry, leathery, and flat in taste.

Tip: Write the name of contents on the outside of each package. Even transparent plastic bags tend to fog up in a freezer, making it impossible to get a look at the contents. A black grease pencil or children's crayon does the job.

Making venison jerky. Jerky is a tasty, lightweight, and nutritious food, ideal for carrying on hunting trips. With a proper recipe, you can easily convert your deer meat to jerky.

Most hunters prefer to use marginal, traditionally tough cuts for jerky—meat from the neck, shoulders, lower legs, and ribs. However, true jerky connoisseurs sometimes make jerky from tender meat as well. An average deer weighing 120 pounds field-dressed produces approximately one shopping bag full of jerky—a lot of enjoyable gnawing and munching.

There are dozens of excellent recipes for venison jerky in wild-game cookbooks. Most require meat to be cut in ¼-inch strips, marinated in spicy sauces, and then slowly dried in an oven or smoker for a prescribed period of time. Oven jerky is easy to prepare; smoker jerky has the distinct wood-smoke flavor but requires extra effort. Both varieties will last several years when properly prepared and stored, although jerky seldom lasts long with hungry hunters lurking about.

To prevent mildew, always store jerky in a container that allows ample circulation of air. A brown paper bag or tightly knit cotton sack is ideal, and so is a glass jar with a few small nail holes punched in the lid. For maximum longevity and freshness, jerky should always be stored in a freezer, refrigerator, or cool kitchen pantry.

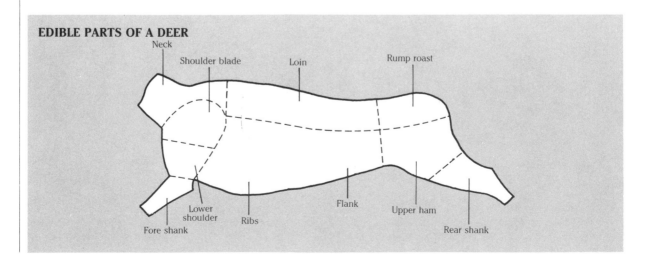

EDIBLE PARTS OF A DEER

BUTCHERING VENISON

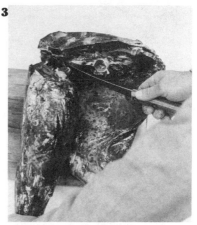

1. *To debone and cut up a deer, first remove both hams from the carcass by slicing through the backbone area with knife and saw. A meat-cutting board is a handy aid.* **2.** *Remove one ham from the pelvis by cutting deep with a knife. An incision here will intersect the joint that connects the hip with the rest of the body.* **3.** *A sharp twist of the hip will pop the ball-and-socket joint from the pelvis. A few more passes with the knife frees the ham entirely.*

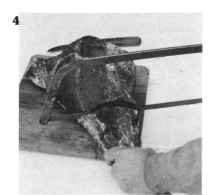

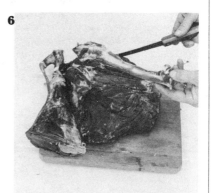

4. *Separate the lower leg or rear shank from the rest of the ham by slicing through the meat with a knife and cutting the leg bone with a sharp saw.* **5.** *The rear shank (left) is tough, sinewy meat ideal for stew, burger, mincemeat, or jerky. The upper ham (right) provides some of the best steaks.* **6.** *To remove the large bone from the upper ham, make a vertical incision along the outside of the ham and cut around bone until bone is completely free.*

7. *Cut the now boneless upper ham in two pieces along the channel left by the bone. The resulting chunks of venison are ready to be cut into round steaks.* **8.** *Keeping knife cuts parallel, slice the two halves of the upper ham into round steaks—½-inch to 1-inch thickness is fairly standard.* **9.** *Remove the bone from the rear shank with deft cuts of the knife. Dice this meat into small chunks for stew, burger, or mincemeat—or slice it into strips for jerky.*

(Continued on next page)

(Butchering continued)

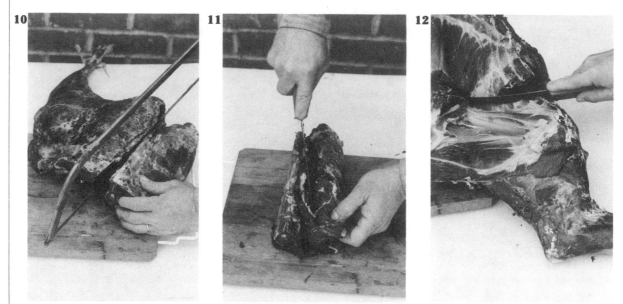

10. *Using a meat saw, cut through the backbone and pelvis from the top to separate the rump roast from the opposite ham and roast. There's plenty of bone to saw through here; so be prepared to use some elbow grease.* **11.** *Remove the meat from the backbone and pelvis bone in the rump roast cut. This leaves a tender, boneless piece of meat that is superb when properly cooked. Next, process the second ham and rump roast as already described.* **12.** *Separate the shoulders and front legs from the deer by slipping a sharp knife between shoulder blades and ribcage. There are no ball-and-socket joints here; so shoulders slice free easily.*

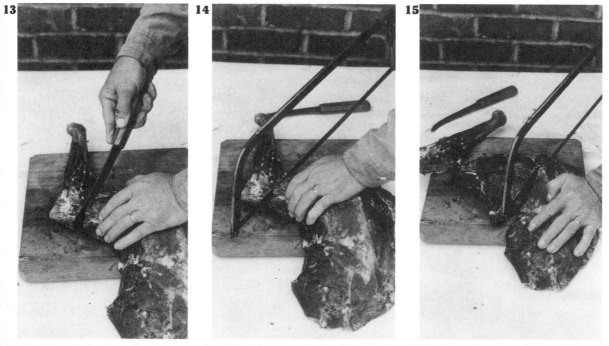

13 & 14. *Cut the fore shank (lower front leg) from each shoulder blade with knife and saw as shown. This cut should be positioned directly above the "elbow" of the front leg.* **15.** *Cut the lower shoulder (left) from the upper shoulder blade (right) with knife and saw. This separates shoulder into two equal parts that must be deboned.*

16 & 17. *Remove the bone from the lower shoulder. The resulting meat can be sliced into shoulder steaks, which are tasty and moderately tender, or left in one piece as an excellent roast.* **18.** *Carve the meat from the upper shoulder blade bone, which is flat with a central ridge, making deboning somewhat more time-consuming than with ordinary round bones.*

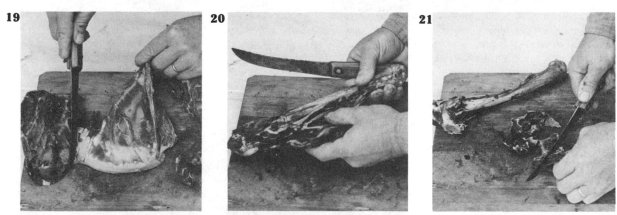

19. *The two chunks of meat from the shoulder blade are somewhat tough and stringy, making them the logical choice for burger, stew, mincemeat, or jerky. Shoulder-blade venison also makes very good roasts.* **20 & 21.** *Like the rear shank, the fore shank is sinewy and chewy in texture. As a result, the boned-out meat should be diced and tossed in the pile for stew, burger, mincemeat, or jerky. Repeat this process on the second shoulder and leg.*

22. *The loin (backstrap) is the long, thick band of meat on each side of the backbone above the ribs and between the hams and neck. Cut this out next. Work close to the ribs and spine with your knife.*

23. *Slice the loin into thick, oval chops as shown. Loin chops are the best part of any deer. They have superb flavor and unequaled tenderness even in older deer. Remove second loin from the carcass and repeat the slicing procedure.*

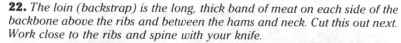

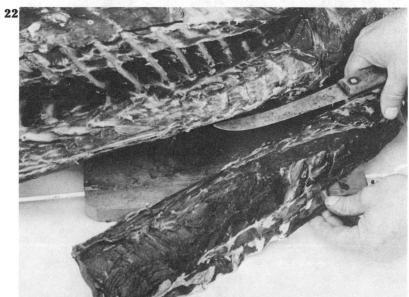

(Continued on next page)

(Butchering continued)

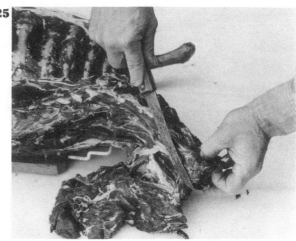

24. *Remove all peripheral venison from the ribcage, spine, brisket, and flank. Although many hunters discard these leftovers, meat of this sort is ideal for making burger, stew, mincemeat, and jerky.* **25.** *Beginning at the throat, carefully peel the neck meat from the irregular bones in this area. Because this venison is somewhat tough, most hunters convert it to burger, stew, mincemeat, or jerky. However, the entire slab of neck meat makes a fine roast as well.*

26. *If you have the time and inclination, cut the meat from between the ribs for burger, jerky, or mincemeat. These strips are thin, and all combined do not yield much meat.*

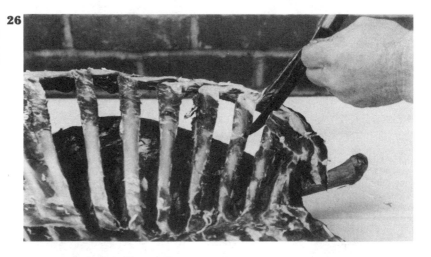

27. *With little experience, you can completely debone and cut up a deer in less than an hour. When boning animals in the field for easier packing, the same basic procedure is used except that bones are left intact and larger chunks of meat are removed from around them.*

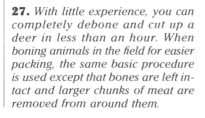

HOW TO MAKE JERKY

To make one excellent kind of oven jerky, you'll need about 3 pounds of venison, a sharp knife, and a container for marinade. Typical marinade ingredients include garlic powder, onion powder, black pepper, soy sauce, Worcestershire sauce, seasoned salt, and Accent.

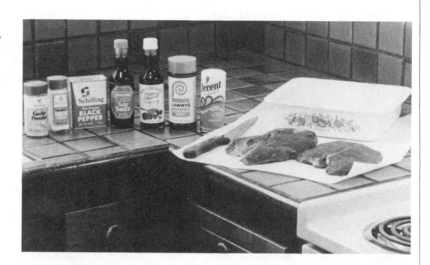

1. *Slice the meat into strips about ¼-inch thick and 5 or 6 inches long. The meat cuts most easily when still semifrozen. For easiest chewing later on, cut across, not with, the grain of the meat.* **2.** *To make a jerky marinade, combine ¾ cup soy sauce, ½ cup Worcestershire sauce, 1 tsp. Accent, ½ tsp. seasoned salt, 1 tsp. garlic powder, 2 tsps. onion powder, and 1 tsp. black pepper.* **3.** *Stir the marinade to mix ingredients thoroughly. Marinate the strips of venison 8 to 12 hours, stretching them out in the marinade to ensure thorough saturation and optimum flavor. Turn strips occasionally for best results.*

4. *Lay the marinated strips on the oven rack and heat them 7 to 8 hours at 150 degrees with the oven door left open just a crack. Delicious smells will fill the kitchen. The end result is melt-in-your-mouth jerky quaranteed to put a smile on anyone's face. To prevent mildew, store the jerky in a container that breathes, such as a cloth sack or paper bag.*

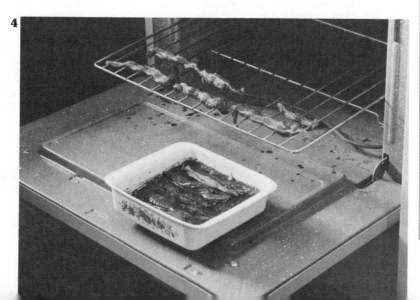

RECIPES FOR VENISON

When properly handled in the field, venison is generally fine-grained, tender, and delicious on the table. It has a distinctive, delicate flavor most people enjoy. Old bucks—particularly those taken after the late-fall rut—tend to be somewhat tough and dry in texture, and often have a strong or gamy taste. But it is a mistake to assume that all trophy bucks are less tender or tasty than younger animals. Any deer in its early-summer prime can be melt-in-your-mouth good, be it a young buck or old boss of the woods.

Like most wild meat, venison does not marble and retains a relatively dry texture—even in deer thickly laden with lard. Domestic beef is usually 25 to 30 percent fat, whereas deer meat seldom has a fat content higher than 5 or 10 percent. A sleek, fat deer tends to be juicier, tastier, and more tender than a lean, rundown deer. But visible fat should be trimmed from *all* venison prior to cooking. Deer fat is invariably strong tasting, degrading the overall flavor of steaks, roasts, and chops.

Aside from improper handling afield, the primary reason many people turn up their noses at venison is the fact that they have sampled deer cooked in ways intended for conventional domestic meat. This usually results in rubber-tough, objectionably-dry, and nearly flavorless meat that anyone would prefer to toss to the dogs. All decent wild-game cooks prepare venison in especially moisturizing ways, often larding by insertion of domestic fat, or barding (placing strips of bacon, salt pork, or pure suet over cooking meat). Similarly, venison should be cooked for a shorter period of time than beef, pork, or mutton. Inexperienced wild-game chefs tend to overcook venison, a process that removes what little moisturizing fat is originally present. Venison stews, casseroles, and other moist preparations are especially popular because the meat stays juicy and tender.

As in domestic meat, certain venison cuts are more tender than others. Meat from the neck, shoulders, and shanks (lower legs) tends to be tough and stringy, making it ideal for hamburger or stew. Choice cuts from backstraps and hams are usually the most tender of all. As in all kinds of meat, judicious marination will tenderize and disguise the flavor of tough or gamy venison.

JOANNE'S VENISON BOURGUIGNONNE

1¼ lb. venison round steak,
  all fat trimmed
2 large onions, chopped
4 tbsps. butter
6 slices bacon, diced
3 tbsps. flour
1 cup Burgundy wine
1 tsp. tomato paste
1 clove garlic, minced
1 carrot, diced
2 cups beef bouillon
½ to 1 cup small fresh mushrooms
salt and pepper

Cut meat into 1½-inch cubes. In a large skillet, brown onion in butter. Add bacon and brown. Remove onion and bacon, and set aside in separate bowl. Add meat to butter and bacon drippings, and brown on all sides. When brown, stir in flour and cook for 1 minute. Stir in Burgundy, beef stock, tomato paste, garlic, and carrot. Season with salt and pepper. Cover and simmer 1½ hours. Add onions and bacon, and simmer ½ hour longer. Add mushrooms and simmer 15 minutes. Serve over rice or noodles. Makes 4 servings.

VENISON ORIENTAL

2 lbs. venison round steak, all fat trimmed
3 tbsps. peanut oil
3 tsps. sugar
½ cup soy sauce
2 cloves garlic, minced
¼ tsp. pepper
½ tsp. ground ginger
6 green onions, cut in 2-inch lengths
2 green peppers, cut in strips
3 carrots, cut in thin slices
½ lb. fresh mushrooms, sliced
1 can water chestnuts, sliced
1 small can bamboo shoots, drained
3 tbsps. cornstarch
¼ cup water

Cut meat into thin strips, 3 inches long. Heat oil over medium heat. Add meat and brown well. When meat is browned, pour off drippings and save. To drippings add enough water to make 1½ cups. Mix with sugar, soy sauce, garlic, ginger, and pepper. Add to meat, cover, and simmer 50 minutes. Add remaining vegetables, cover, and cook 20 minutes. Mix water and cornstarch to thicken for gravy. Serve over hot rice.

DEER HUNTER'S PIE

2 lbs. venison round steak, cut in 1-inch cubes
4 tbsps. butter
1 16-oz. can of tomatoes
2 onions, chopped
1 bay leaf, crumbled
¼ tsp. thyme
1 tsp. garlic powder
½ tsp. parsley
1 tbsp. paprika
¼ tsp. red cayenne pepper
1 tbsp. Worcestershire sauce
1½ cups beer
3 carrots, thinly sliced
1 raw potato, diced
½ cup celery, sliced
1 tube of refrigerated biscuits

Melt butter in frying pan. To melted butter add meat and brown on all sides. Add all remaining ingredients except for potatoes, carrots, celery, and biscuits. Cover and simmer mixture for 1 hour. Add potatoes, carrots, and celery; cover and simmer for 20 minutes. Preheat oven to 425°. Place mixture into a deep round casserole dish or a 9″ × 13″ pan. Place biscuits on top and bake for 15 minutes or until golden brown.

BUDDY'S VENISON STROGANOFF

2 lbs. venison round steak, all fat trimmed
1 large onion, chopped
2 cups fresh mushrooms, sliced
2 tbsps. shortening
2 tbsps. butter
3 cups boiling water
3 beef bouillon cubes
1 tsp. dry mustard
1 tsp. salt
2 tbsps. catsup
¼ tsp. freshly ground pepper
3 tbsps. flour
½ cup water
1 cup sour cream
4 cups cooked noodles or rice

Cut venison into 2-inch strips. Strips should be thin. Melt butter and shortening in skillet, sauté onion and mushrooms in butter and shortening until golden brown. When onion and mushrooms are brown, remove from skillet. Add meat and brown on all sides for 15 minutes. Dissolve bouillon cubes in boiling water. When bouillon is dissolved, add mustard, catsup, salt, and pepper. Mix well and pour mixture over meat. Cover and simmer for 1½ hours. Mix water and flour together to make a smooth paste. Add paste slowly to meat mixture and bring to a boil. Stir constantly. Reduce heat and add onions, mushrooms, and sour cream. Heat, but *do not* let mixture come to a boil. Serve over hot noodles or rice.

VENISON SWISS STEAK

1½ lbs. venison round steak, cut 1½ inches thick
1 tsp. salt
½ tsp. pepper
½ cup flour
¼ cup butter
2 large onions, chopped
1 large can tomatoes
1 green pepper, thinly sliced
1 large stalk celery, diced
½ cup Burgundy wine

This contrasts the marbeling fat of beef, on the right, with the near absence of it in venison. Beef may run 25 to 30 percent fat. Venison goes about 5 to 10. (John Weiss photo)

½ cup beef bouillon
2 cloves garlic, minced
2 tbsps. Worcestershire sauce
1 tsp. sweet basil

Preheat oven to 350°. Mix together the flour, salt, and pepper. Leave the round steak whole and dredge with seasoned flour. Melt butter in an ovenproof skillet. Brown meat on both sides in melted butter. Add remaining ingredients. Cover and bake in oven 1½ hours or till meat is tender.

VENISON PEPPER STEAK

1½ lbs. venison round steak, fat trimmed
¼ cup Burgundy wine
2 cloves garlic, crushed
½ tsp. ginger
⅓ cup soy sauce
¼ cup cooking oil
1 cup green pepper, cut in squares
1 cup green onion, thinly sliced
2 stalks celery, thinly sliced
1 cup water
2 tbsps. cornstarch
2 tomatoes, cut into wedges

Cut venison into thin strips. Mix wine, soy sauce, garlic, and ginger. Add steak. Stir and set aside. Prepare vegetables. Heat oil in wok or frying pan. Add steak and stir over high heat until browned. Cover and simmer for 1 hour. Increase heat and add vegetables. Stir-fry vegetables for 10 minutes. Mix cornstarch and water together. Add cornstarch mixture to meat and vegetables, and cook until it thickens. Add tomatoes.

VENISON STEW

2 lbs. venison round steak, cut in cubes, all fat trimmed
3 tbsps. shortening
2 cloves garlic, minced
2 tsps. Worcestershire sauce
1 tbsp. salt
½ tsp. pepper
1 bay leaf
1 tsp. paprika
1 tsp. sweet basil
½ tsp. marjoram
dash ground allspice
1 large onion, chopped
4 potatoes, quartered
3 stalks celery, sliced
6 carrots, quartered

Melt shortening in a Dutch oven. When shortening is hot, add meat and brown well on all sides. After meat is browned, add next 9 ingredients and 2½ cups boiling water. Cover and simmer for 2 hours. Remove bay leaf and then add vegetables. Cover and cook for 40 minutes.

SPANISH-STYLE VENISON

2 lbs. venison round steak, all fat trimmed
⅓ cup flour
1 tsp. salt
½ tsp. pepper
⅓ cup shortening
1 onion, chopped
2 cloves garlic, minced
1 green pepper, sliced
1 pound can tomatoes
1 tsp. sugar
1 tsp. celery salt
1 tsp. chili powder
½ cup stuffed olives, sliced
½ cup beef bouillon

Cut meat into 8 single-serving-sized pieces. Mix together flour, salt, and pepper. Dredge meat in flour mixture. In a large skillet, melt 2 tbsp. shortening. Sauté onion, garlic, and green pepper about 5 minutes. Remove onion, garlic, and green pepper from skillet and add remaining shortening. Add meat to shortening and brown on both sides. Drain off all but 2 tbsp. drippings. Add remaining ingredients plus green pepper, onion and garlic; cover; and simmer 1½ hours.

VENISON SHERRY

2 lbs. venison round steak, all fat trimmed
2 cans golden mushroom soup
1 pkg. dry onion soup mix
2 tbsps. Worcestershire sauce
1⅓ cups sherry wine
2 cloves garlic, minced
1 large onion, chopped
1 large can mushrooms, drained
½ cup celery, diced

Cut steak into thin strips. Mix together mushroom soup, dry onion soup, wine, Worcestershire sauce, and garlic. Set aside. Place meat in a casserole and top with onion, mushrooms, and celery. Pour soup mixture over meat. Cover tightly and bake in a 325° oven for 3½ to 4 hours. During the baking time it may be necessary to add more wine or water. Serve over rice or noodles.

HUNTER'S STEW

2 lbs. venison stew meat, all fat trimmed
8 slices bacon, diced
1 large onion, chopped
1 cup carrots, sliced
2 cloves garlic, minced
3 cups beef bouillon
⅓ cup red wine vinegar
1 tbsp. Worcestershire sauce
½ cup Burgundy wine
1 tsp. salt

Here 8-ounce slices of venison are browned before being combined with other ingredients in a casserole. (John Weiss photo)

½ tsp. pepper
1 green pepper, sliced
¾ cup uncooked rice

Cut meat into 1½-inch cubes. In large frying pan, cook bacon until most of the fat is rendered. Remove bacon and set aside. Pour all but a thin film of the bacon fat out of pan. Sauté onions until transparent. Add garlic and carrots, and sauté 3 minutes. Return bacon to pan. Stir in vinegar, 2 cups beef broth, Worcestershire sauce, wine, meat, salt, and pepper. After mixture has reached a boil, reduce heat, cover, and simmer for 2 hours or until meat is tender. Stir in rice, pepper, and remaining broth. Bring to a boil and then reduce heat. Cover and simmer for 20 minutes. Turn off heat and let mixture stand for 5 minutes.

VENISON HUNGARIAN GOULASH

2 lbs. venison round steak cut into cubes, all fat trimmed
¼ cup oil
1 large onion, chopped
1 clove garlic, minced
1 tsp. salt
¼ tsp. pepper
2 tsps. paprika
1¾ cups beef bouillon
1 cup carrots, diced
1¼ cups potatoes, diced
½ cup tomato sauce
1 8-oz. pkg. egg noodles

Heat oil in large frying pan. Sauté onion and garlic until transparent. Add meat and brown. Add beef broth, paprika, salt, and pepper. Cover and simmer for 1 hour. Add potatoes, carrots, and tomato sauce. Cover and simmer 30 minutes. Serve over noodles.

CHUCK'S BUCK AND BEER

2 lbs. venison round steak, cut into 1½-inch cubes
2 large onions, sliced
7 tbsps. butter
flour
salt
pepper
2 cups beer
3 cloves garlic, whole

Melt 4 tbsps. butter in frying pan. Add onions and cook until lightly browned. Remove onions. Flour steak cubes lightly. Melt remaining butter in pan. Add steak and brown on all sides. Return onions to pan, and add salt and pepper to taste. Add beer and garlic and bring to a boil. Reduce heat, cover, and simmer for 1½ hours. Serve over hot noodles.

ITALIAN-STYLE VENISON

2 lbs. boneless venison loin chops, all fat trimmed
flour
salt and pepper
½ cup cooking oil
2 tbsps. butter
1 clove garlic, minced
¾ cup prosciutto, thinly sliced
⅓ cup beef bouillon
⅓ cup sherry wine
½ tsp. sweet basil
½ tsp. oregano
⅓ lb. sliced fresh mushrooms
1 small can stewed tomatoes

With a meat mallet, pound chops to ⅛-inch thickness.

Dredge chops in flour, salt, and pepper to taste. Heat oil in large frying pan. Brown meat on both sides and remove from pan. Drain all but 2 tbsps. of oil. Add butter to oil and melt. Add prosciutto to butter and oil, sauté for 3 minutes. Add mushrooms and sauté for 5 minutes. Return the chops to pan along with all remaining ingredients. Cover and simmer slowly for 20 minutes.

BARBECUED VENISON

4 venison steaks or chops, all fat trimmed
1¼ cups red wine
¾ cup olive oil
2 cloves garlic, minced
¼ tsp. oregano
¼ tsp. freshly ground pepper
1 bay leaf
juice of 1 lemon

Combine all ingredients to make a marinade. Place meat in marinade for at least 8 hours. Keep refrigerated. Meat can be barbecued or broiled. Baste while cooking. Cook to desired doneness.

TOMMY'S VENISON CHOPS

8 venison chops, all fat trimmed
2 tbsps. oil
2 tbsps. butter
3 tbsps. milk
2 eggs
2 cups cracker crumbs
1 tsp. sweet basil
2 cloves garlic, finely minced
½ tsp. rosemary
1 tbsp. parmesan cheese
salt and pepper to taste

Heat butter and oil in pan over medium heat. Beat milk and eggs together. Add garlic, basil, rosemary, and parmesan to cracker crumbs and mix. Dip chops into egg and milk and then coat in cracker mixture. Fry chops over medium heat on both sides till done.

TERIYAKI VENISON

8 venison loin chops, all fat trimmed
⅓ cup soy sauce
2 tbsps. finely chopped onion
3 cloves garlic, minced
1 tbsp. brown sugar
1 tsp. dry mustard
½ cup vegetable oil
1 tsp. ginger
2 bay leaves, crushed

Mix all ingredients except chops to make marinade. Pour marinade in a dish and add chops. Cover and refrigerate overnight, turning occasionally. Drain meat and place on broiler rack. Broil 10 minutes. Brush periodically with the marinade. Turn and broil to reach desired doneness.

CHICKEN-FRIED VENISON STEAK

1½ lbs. venison steak, all fat trimmed
¼ cup oil
1 beaten egg
1 tbsp. milk
1 cup flour
1 tsp. salt
¼ tsp. pepper
1 tsp. garlic powder
½ tsp. sweet basil
¼ tsp. onion powder

Cut steak into serving-sized pieces. With a meat mallet, pound each steak to ¼-inch thickness. Beat together egg and milk. Combine flour, salt, pepper, basil, garlic, and onion powder. Dip steaks in egg mixture and then in seasoned flour. Heat oil in large frying pan. Slowly brown meat for 15 minutes on each side, turning meat only once.

WESTERN BARBECUED VENISON

3 lbs. venison round steak, all fat trimmed
2 cans tomato sauce (8 oz. each)
1 large onion, chopped
¼ cup sugar
⅓ cup Worcestershire sauce
½ cup vinegar
½ cup water
½ tsp. celery salt
½ tsp. garlic salt

Combine ingredients in roasting pan. Cover and bake at 325° for 3 hours. Punch with potato masher until meat shreds. Serve on French rolls or buns.

VENISON STEAK DIANE

4 venison steaks, all fat trimmed
⅓ cup butter
1 tsp. dry mustard
salt
pepper
2 tsps. Worcestershire sauce
4 tbsps. fresh lemon juice
3 tsps. diced chives

Pound steak with a meat mallet to ⅓-inch thickness. On one side of each steak, sprinkle salt, pepper, and ⅛ tsp. dry mustard. Dredge meat in mixture. Repeat on other side of each steak. Melt butter in frying pan. Add steaks to melted butter and cook for 3 minutes on each side. Remove steaks and keep warm. To the drippings add the Worcestershire sauce, lemon juice, and chives. Bring mixture to a boil and serve over meat.

MARINATED AND BARBECUED VENISON CHOPS

6 venison chops, all fat trimmed
6 Italian sausages

2 cups Burgundy wine
1 cup butter
1½ tsps. celery salt
2 cloves garlic, crushed
½ tsp. seasoned salt
½ tsp. sweet basil
1 tsp. onion powder
½ tsp. rosemary
½ tsp. oregano

Melt butter in large saucepan. Add wine and spices to butter and stir till thoroughly mixed. Remove from heat and add sausages and chops. Do not cook, but let the meat marinate in wine mixture for 2½ hours. Stir occasionally. Barbecue sausage and chops till done, basting meat frequently with wine marinade. Heat remaining marinade and serve with meat if desired.

VENISON PATTIES
    1 lb. venison burger
    ¼ lb. pork sausage
    ¼ cup onion, chopped very fine
    1 shredded raw potato
    1 tsp. garlic salt
    1 tsp. salt
    ¼ tsp. freshly ground pepper
    1 egg lightly beaten
    2 tbsps. shortening
    1 tbsp. Worcestershire sauce
    1 tbsp. parsley

Combine venison and sausage with all ingredients, except shortening. Shape mixture into patties about 1-inch thick. Melt shortening in frying pan. Fry patties over medium heat until browned on both sides and done.

SWEET AND SOUR VENISON RIBS
    3 lbs. venison short ribs
    ⅓ cup shortening
    2 cloves garlic, coarsely chopped
    1 large onion, sliced
    1 bay leaf
    ⅓ cup vinegar
    ⅓ cup brown sugar
    ⅓ cup catsup
    1½ cups hot water
    ½ cup flour
    1 tsp. salt
    ¼ tsp. pepper

Cut ribs into serving sizes. Remove all fat. Mix together flour, salt, and pepper. Coat ribs with seasoned flour. Melt shortening over medium-high heat and brown meat on all sides. Remove ribs and sauté garlic and onion until golden brown. Combine remaining ingredients. Return ribs to skillet and pour mixture over the meat. Cover and simmer over low heat for 2½ hours.

ROAST VENISON
    3 lb. venison roast, all fat trimmed
    ⅓ cup shortening
    ¼ tsp. garlic powder
    ¼ tsp. celery salt
    ¼ tsp. seasoned salt
    ¼ tsp. freshly ground pepper
    1 package dry onion soup
    1½ cups water
    ½ cup Burgundy wine
    ½ cup milk
    ¼ cup flour

In a Dutch oven, brown meat in shortening. When meat is brown, sprinkle with seasonings, along with 1 tbsp. of dry onion soup. Add remainder to bottom of pan. Add water and wine to pan. Cover roast and cook at 325° for about 2 hours or till tender. When roast is done, remove from pan and add flour to drippings. Mix well. Add milk to flour mixture while stirring until thickened.

MARINATED ROAST VENISON
    6 lb. venison roast, fat trimmed
    2¾ cups Burgundy wine
    ¾ cup apple cider
    1 tbsp. Worcestershire sauce
    5 peppercorns, crushed
    2 bay leaves
    1 clove garlic, minced
    salt
    ⅓ cup butter
    1 cup marinade, strained

Combine wine, apple cider, bay leaves, garlic, peppercorns, and Worcestershire in a pan. Place roast in marinade and refrigerate overnight, turning periodically. Place roast on a roasting rack and sprinkle with salt. Insert meat thermometer. Place roast in a 325° oven. Melt butter and add 1 cup strained marinade. Baste meat with marinade and butter mixture during roasting. Roast 25 to 30 minutes per pound.

BUSTER'S ROAST VENISON
    1 4–5 lb. venison roast, all fat trimmed
    4 slices bacon
    1 pkg. dry onion soup mix
    2 cloves garlic, minced
    1 can cream of mushroom soup
    1 cup water

Preheat oven to 325°. Line bottom of roasting pan with enough foil to fold over and cover the meat completely while roasting. Spread half of the mushroom soup on foil. Place meat on foil and spoon remaining mushroom soup on roast. Add water. Place bacon slices on roast. Sprinkle dry onion soup and minced garlic on top of roast. Wrap foil tightly around roast and bake 2½ to 3 hours.

PART 8
TAXIDERMY AND TANNING

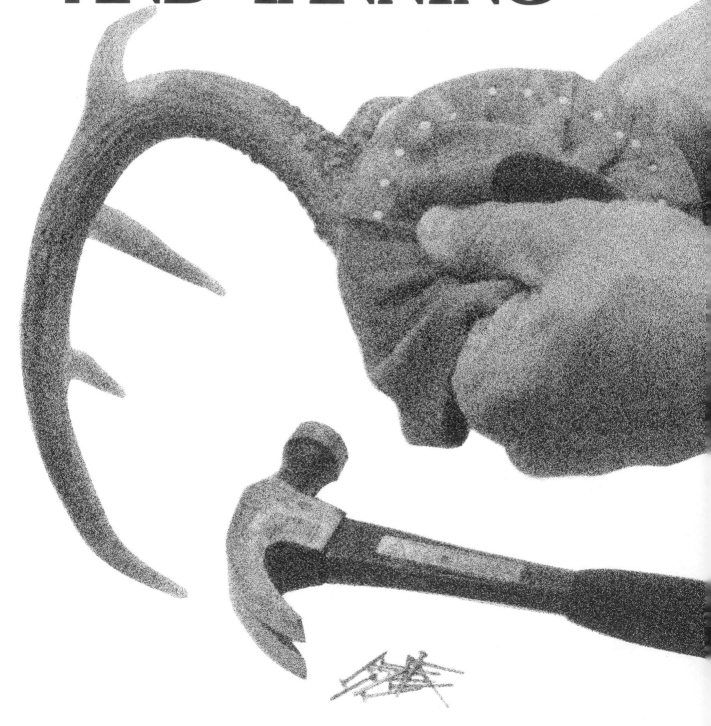

BY CHUCK ADAMS
Photos by the author unless otherwise credited

O ne of the many rewards of a successful deer hunt is the trophy—a deer head, hide, or set of antlers on the wall. Memories of the hunt fade and venison steaks soon disappear. But home-mounted or taxidermist-processed trophies provide constant reminders of hunting successes and good times gone by.

Deer trophies can be decorative or functional. Decorative items include head-and-shoulder mounts, plaque-mounted antlers, and hides tanned for the wall. Soft-tanned buckskin jackets, antler buttons, and deer-hoof coat racks are among the functional trophies. Obviously, trophies can be both decorative and functional, as are clothing racks fashioned from antlers or hoofs.

Functional trophies such as buttons or coat racks are most often made from picked-up antlers or similar deer parts found in the woods. For the average woodsman, the personal satisfaction of dropping a nice buck makes cutting up its rack for buttons or otherwise altering its original form something close to a sacrilege.

When it comes to actually making the trophy, you can either hire a professional taxidermist or do the job yourself. *Always* hire a taxidermist to handle major jobs such as mounting a deer head and soft-tanning hides. These procedures require real expertise and many special tools and materials. A good taxidermist can also handle less complex trophy-processing tasks, such as mounting antlers on plaques; converting deer hoofs to racks, bookends, or ashtrays; and restoring cracked and weathered antlers to original condition. But because professional taxidermists can be expensive, hunters often prefer to do simpler jobs themselves.

Home taxidermy has its own rewards. Plaque-mounting antlers, designing deer-foot or shed-antler racks, making buttons, and restoring weathered antlers can be accomplished with grocery-store and hardware-store materials. Your trophy of these simpler projects can be as good as a professional job if you take your time and closely follow instructions. You can save considerable money by processing hides, antlers, and hoofs yourself. Plus you eliminate the relatively long wait for a pro taxidermist to deliver the finished goods.

USING THE PROFESSIONAL TAXIDERMIST

A skilled taxidermist is nothing short of a miracle worker. He takes an odoriferous bundle of hide and antlers, works magic with chemicals, time, and artistry, and recreates the front one-third of your deer in startlingly realistic detail. If you've done your part in caring for the hide from field to freezer, the outcome should be a sleek, lifelike mount that seems ready to step straight out of the wall. Similarly, a pro can complete wall rugs, hoof racks, antler mounts on plaques, and other fairly simple projects.

Problems you might encounter. A few avid deer enthusiasts use taxidermists on a regular basis and know they will get a thoroughly professional job. However, the average hunter uses a taxidermist infrequently at best—perhaps only once or twice in his life. This generally occurs when he drops an especially big trophy buck with antlers just too nice to toss in the attic or tack over the garage door. Here, it pays to shop for a top-notch taxidermist with care.

Few things are more heartrending than shooting a nice buck, proudly carting the head to a taxidermy shop, waiting 12 to 18 long months, and then being stuck with a bad mounting job. A deer mounted by an experienced perfectionist is handsome. But a bad taxidermist might give you a bug-eyed, bulb-nosed, propeller-eared disaster. There are many fine taxi-

Mounted trophies are among the most gratifying rewards of successful hunts for deer. A good buck head on the wall serves as a lasting reminder of enjoyable times in the field. (Photo courtesy of professional taxidermist Wayne Lundberg)

dermists today, but there are also hacks who unabashedly sing their own praises, eagerly pounce on your money, and then ruin your trophy. Anyone can hang out a taxidermist's shingle, but the advertisement in no way guarantees customer satisfaction.

Shopping for the right taxidermist. Selecting a competent taxidermist is not an especially difficult task if it is done systematically. First, make a list of local taxidermists by checking the Yellow Pages of your phone book. Second, visit these professionals in person to chat a bit and take a look at the heads hanging in their shops. Third, ask for references from the taxidermists who seem responsible and seem to turn out good work. Any well-established professional will gladly give you the names and telephone numbers of several customers for whom he has recently completed deer heads. Call these customers and ask how satisfied they were with the work they received. If possible, make arrangements to see one or two of the recent mounts to satisfy yourself about their quality. Sometimes deer heads displayed in a taxidermy shop are not at all typical of a particular taxidermist's work, or may not even have been done by him.

Reinforce this initial research with some other word-of-mouth recommendations. Talk to local deer-hunters and ask to see recently mounted heads they own. Ask about especially lifelike deer heads hanging in sporting goods stores to find out who did the mounting and when. Finally, mull over all the facts and leave your precious deer head with the taxidermist you tend to trust the most.

The best taxidermists are usually very busy fellows—especially near the end of deer-hunting season when a flood of hides and antlers enters their doors. As a result, you can expect to wait a minimum of six months to one year for trophy completion—often twice that long. A taxidermist with lots of time on his hands is seldom first-rate and probably should not be trusted with the best buck you've ever bagged.

One final word on selecting a taxidermist: You generally get what you pay for in taxidermy. If you shop for a bargain-basement price, you're apt to end up with a deer head suitable only for hanging in the basement. If you shop for quality and don't balk at paying for it, your odds for complete satisfaction are greatly improved.

WHAT A TAXIDERMIST EXPECTS FROM YOU

Competent taxidermists can tell plenty of horror stories about irresponsible hunters. To get off on the right foot with any taxidermist, you should carefully handle

Since many taxidermy studios receive trophies for mounting from throughout the world, as well as local deer, you can expect to wait a year for quality work. This photo gives a good idea of volume, scope, and backlog at a good studio. (Courtesy of American Taxidermist.*)*

the cape or full hide of your deer as outlined in Part 7 of this book. A good taxidermist can do wonders with antlers and skins, but he cannot replace tattered or slipping hair. Similarly, a deer cape with the throat cut or improper incisions is a nightmare for any pro to patch and salvage, and the end result is always second-rate at best. You have every right to expect a realistic mounting job from the taxidermist, but you must deliver an unblemished, unspoiled cape in the first place.

Deer vary as much in individual body and facial structure as people. As a result, some perfectionistic hunters prefer their trophy mount duplicate as closely as possible the unique appearance of the original animal. Most hunters do not care about such nitpicking duplication. But if the swollen neck, high Roman nose, or broad, blocky brow of your deer is something you want faithfully preserved, be sure to submit several

good photos of the downed animal from various angles at the time you deliver your trophy for shoulder mounting. If you have a tape measure in the field, taking three measurements of your deer's head will also help the taxidermist to do his job—nose tip to front of eye, nose tip to back of head, and circumference of throat immediately under the chin. These help preserve the deer's original appearance.

Be sure to discuss custom neck and facial work with your taxidermist well in advance. Some pros use commercial mounting forms for deer and do not want to bother with custom sculpting the facial and neck features of individual animals. Other taxidermists charge an extra fee for such personalized service.

Because some customers never pick up finished deer heads, your taxidermist will probably require a cash deposit on the work to be done. This is a standard procedure in the business.

DO-IT-YOURSELF PROJECTS

Complex and ticklish taxidermy projects should be left to a competent professional. As mentioned earlier, special skills and equipment are needed for shoulder mounting of heads and soft tanning of deer hides. Most beginners know to leave well enough alone when it comes to full-blown mounts, but a surprising number tackle hide tanning with zeal. Readily available books on tanning have contributed to this. The books characteristically extol the virtues of home tanning while grossly downplaying the difficulties. Even most longtime taxidermists prefer to send hides to tanneries. That way they avoid laborious, tricky tanning procedures and the need for exotic (and sometimes dangerous) tanning chemicals.

These big jobs aside, there are several *practical* home-taxidermy projects any deer hunter can try. These include various methods of plaque-mounting antlers, making shed-antler coat racks, forming buttons and other useful articles from antlers, refurbishing bleached and weathered antlers, constructing deer-hoof nicknacks of various types, and tanning a deer hide in *hard* form to display on any wall.

The following projects can be accomplished by any moderately handy deer hunter with ordinary tools and readily available materials. By taking your time and carefully following the accompanying step-by-step instructions, you will get professional results at a substantial financial saving.

MAKING PLAQUES

Plaques (sometimes called shields) of one sort or another are necessary for many home-taxidermy projects, including the antler mounts and hoof and antler racks. The deer hunter can buy ready-made plaques at a taxidermy studio, have a cabinet-maker produce plaques of a specific size and shape, or make his own.

Some hunters prefer particular wood species such as oak, walnut, or mahogany—woods that can be stained and finished to match other plaques or furniture in a room. Plaque shape and size are matters of personal preference, so long as they do the intended job. Some popular plaques for deer mounts have the same stylishly curving and routed edges as the finest hardwood furniture. Others are crudely simple but highly effective in setting off the antlers or hoofs they display. To each his own.

For the average hunter with no specialized shop tools and a fairly small bank account, a plaque made of good-grade ¾-inch plywood fills the bill. Plywood can be shaped with a hand saw and wood rasp or plane in minutes, costs next to nothing to make, yet turns out to be strikingly attractive when stained and edged in black. Unless you have unlimited funds and a solid preference for finely finished hardwood, consider the accompanying plywood-plaque procedure.

HOW TO MAKE ANTLER PLAQUES

Plywood plaques are inexpensive and easy to make, yet attractive. Shapes and sizes for home-taxidermy projects are only limited by your imagination. Here are just a few possibilities.

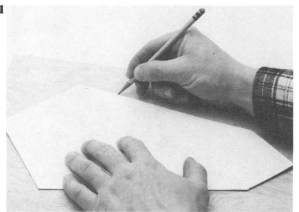 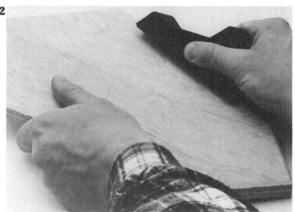

1. *To make a simple plaque, start with good-grade ¾-inch plywood. Using a cardboard pattern as a guide, mark the outline of the plaque on plywood veneer (species your choice). Any hand saw with medium to fine teeth will make a quick, splinterless cut.* **2.** *Bevel the front edges of the plaque to a 45-degree angle with a small hand plane or wood rasp. The finished beveled surface should be about ¼-inch wide. Next, sand with fine sandpaper.*

 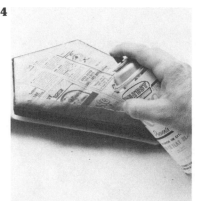 

3. *Apply wood stain appropriate for the veneer to simulate oak, walnut, mahogany, whatever. If you use a combination stain/sealant, there is no need for a finish coat of varnish. Once the finish dries, mask off the front of the plaque right out to, but not including, the bevels.* **4.** *Spray the bevels and sides with flat black enamel or automobile primer. This black border hides plywood laminations and sets off the wood grain.* **5.** *Drill a hole about ½-inch deep in the back of the plaque near the top. Then position a metal plaque hanger over the hole and secure it with screws as shown. Hang the plaque by slipping it over a stout nail or screw on the wall. Plaque hangers are available at any hardware store.*

ANTLERS WITH NATURAL SCALP INTACT

One of the fastest and easiest plaque mounts employs a deer's natural scalp as a skull-plate covering. When correctly done, this yields an odorless, sanitary antler mount with a natural look many hunters like. Scalp-mounting is especially attractive when deer are taken in their full winter coats—hair is long, thick, and silky.

All too many slapdash home taxidermists merely saw out the skull of a deer, fold any excess scalp hide beneath the bone, and nail or screw the rack to a board or plaque. The ratty-looking end result with its dry and decaying flesh quickly develops a rank odor and eventually loses its hair to moths and other bugs. By contrast, plaque-mounting deer antlers the *right* way with natural scalp intact is a neat, professional, and lasting taxidermy technique. The photos on the next pages show how.

HOW TO MAKE SCALP MOUNTS

To many people, the hair-on scalp mount is more pleasing than bare bones.

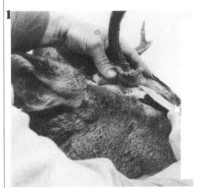

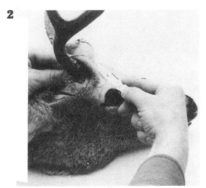

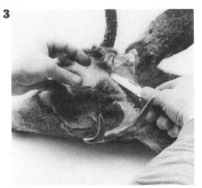

1. *Slice the skin on each side of the head. Cut along a straight line from above the ear to the middle of the tear duct in front of the eye.* **2.** *Join both side cuts with an incision across the bridge of the nose. Skin back the hide to the fronts of the antler bases, taking care not to nick the skin with your knife.* **3.** *Cut across the back of the head from ear to ear. Then skin the scalp forward to the backs of the antler bases. Leave as little meat as possible.*

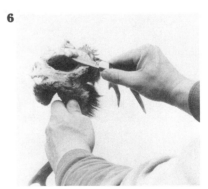

4. *Using a bone saw, cut vertically through the middle of both eye sockets, as shown. Hold the scalp away from the blade to prevent damage to the hair.* **5.** *Remove the skull cap and antlers from the head by making a second saw cut from directly above the ears forward through the centers of both eye sockets. Again, hold the scalp safely out of the way.* **6.** *Next, use the tip of a knife to scoop out brain tissue from under the skull cap.*

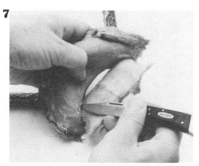

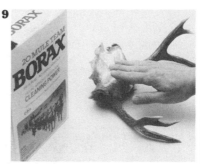

7. *With careful blade work, separate the scalp from the skull until the scalp adheres only around the base of each antler. Take care not to nick the hide during this ticklish procedure.* **8.** *Carefully scrape away all fat and flesh from the underside of the scalp and from the skull with a sharp knife.* **9.** *Rub Borax cleaning powder on the skull and fleshy side of the scalp. This deodorizes and bugproofs the mount, pickles the hide, and accelerates scalp drying once the mount is complete.*

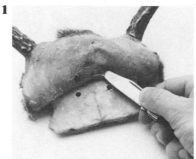

10. *Drill two holes through the front of the skull cap roughly 2 inches apart, as shown. Make holes approximately ¼-inch in diameter—big enough for stout 1¼-inch or 1½-inch wood screws to slip through easily.* **11.** *Cut ¼-inch slits in the scalp directly over screw holes in the skull. Mounting screws will be inserted through the slits after the scalp has been securely sewn in place.* **12.** *Fold the edges of the scalp under the skull cap and sew them together using strong carpet thread and a heavy-duty needle. Continue stitching from edge to edge until the scalp is tightly stretched over the upper skull from all angles.*

13. *Position the skull plate in the center of your plaque, insert wood screws through scalp and skull, and drive the screws in tight. If you use a hardwood plaque, first drill pilot holes in the plaque. Finally, smooth the scalp hair with your hand to completely conceal heads of the mounting screws. Cure the mount in a cool, dry place for about two weeks prior to display.*

MOUNTING ANTLERS WITH LEATHER OR VELVET

The most popular method of plaque-mounting covers the skull cap with pliable leather or velvet. This favorite technique of expert taxidermists requires a little time and effort, but is something any careful beginner can accomplish with professional results. The end product appears especially refined and finished—a handsome addition to any living room or den.

Two notes on this plaque-mounting method. First, the exact shape of the plaster-covered, plywood-backed skull-cap section is entirely up to the home taxidermist. Many hunters prefer a perfectly round cap as shown in the accompanying step-by-step photos, but others opt to cut plywood backing in a teardrop or triangular configuration and contour this with plaster. Second, choice of velvet or leather skull-cap covering is largely a matter of taste. Do-it-yourselfers use many colors of cloth and leather. However, any covering used must stretch to conform to the skull cap's curving plaster surfaces. Of the leathers, thin buckskin and chammy (also *chamois*) are easiest to work with and produce the most professional result. Both can be purchased at most taxidermy shops, leather-goods stores, and automobile-care centers. An alternate—and easier—version of the basic leather or velvet plaque-mounting project is to sand the plaster dome especially smooth and then just paint it. Use non-glare enamel in a woodsy color such as brown or green.

HOW TO MAKE LEATHER- OR VELVET-COVERED MOUNTS

An ornate, router-edged hardwood plaque looks especially good with leather-mounted antlers.

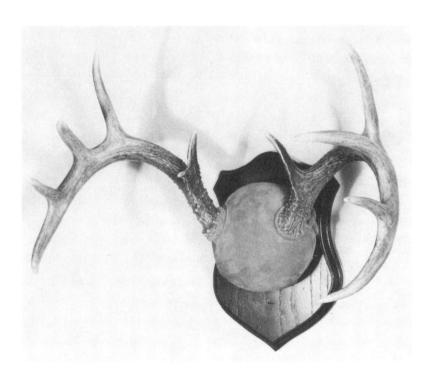

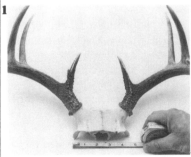

1. *Saw out the skull cap with two right-angle cuts through the eye sockets. (See previous serious of photos on scalp mounts for details.) Completely skin and flesh the skull. Then measure the skull cap at its widest dimension.* **2.** *Draw a circle on ³⁄₄-inch plywood. Make the circle slightly larger in diameter than the width of the skull cap. Saw out the circle, following the outline as closely as you can.* **3.** *After drilling two ¹⁄₄-inch holes through the top of the skull cap about 2 inches apart, attach the skull cap to the plywood disk with stout 1¹⁄₄-inch or 1¹⁄₂-inch flathead wood screws as shown.*

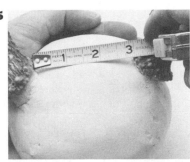

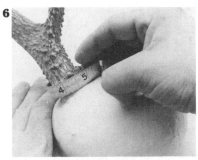

4. *Using a putty knife, fill nooks and crannies between the round plywood baseplate and the skull cap with wet plaster of paris. Then sculpt over the skull to the antler bases to form a smooth, round dome. You will need about two cups of plaster of paris.* **5 & 6.** *Once the plaster of paris hardens (about 10 or 15 minutes), smooth out any rough spots with medium-grit sandpaper. Then measure the inside spread and circumference of the antler bases with care. These measurements are necessary to ensure that the leather fits properly.*

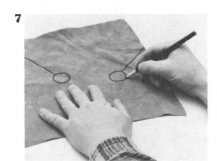

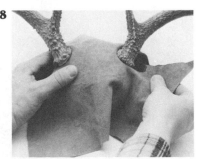

7. *Transfer the exact circumference and spread measurements of the antler bases to a large piece of leather or other covering material. Next, draw the two seam lines outward and backward from antler-base circles at a 45-degree angle. Cut your covering material along these lines.* **8.** *Drape the covering across the skull dome with antler bases in their holes and seam cuts angling toward the rear.* **9.** *Stretch the leather tightly over the dome and tack it with ½-inch nails to the back of the base plate. Overlap edges of the seam behind the antler bases for a tight, wrinkle-free covering of the plaster dome. Cut away excess leather with scissors.*

10. *Next, cut two strips of leather 1 inch wide and 10 inches long. Roll them into tight cylinders for use as trim beneath the antler bases.* **11.** *Wrap the leather strip snugly around an antler base, cross behind the base as shown, and nail both ends to the underside of the base plate. Repeat this for the other antler base. Rolled strips dress up a plaque mount and hide seams behind the antler bases.* **12.** *Drill and countersink two holes through the back of a plaque. Then drive flathead wood screws into the base plate.*

EUROPEAN PLAQUE MOUNTING

One of the most striking of all antler mounting techniques is attaching the bleached-white upper skull of a buck to a dark, contrasting plaque. This technique, called European mounting, is *the* standard method of displaying antlers and horns in Europe. It enjoys a large following in North America as well.

Like plaque-mounting with leather or velvet, European mounting requires some physical effort and artistic ability. The most time-consuming—though by no means difficult—part of this project is boiling, fleshing, and bleaching the skull. This might seem messy and tedious to some, but the outcome makes the work worthwhile.

A European mount has a stark, uniquely captivating beauty. This mount is also the most durable because the entire upper skull is left intact. Such mounted antlers will endure much more rough-and-tumble abuse without breaking apart.

The plaque used with a European mount must be especially long and narrow to provide a proper backdrop for the oblong upper skull.

HOW TO MAKE A EUROPEAN PLAQUE MOUNT

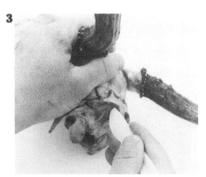

1. *Flesh the entire upper skull and then boil it in soapy water. Use a pot large enough to submerge the skull up to the antler bases. Boil the skull outdoors over a camp stove because this is a mildly smelly process. Add water every 15 minutes or so to keep the level even with the antler bases. Boil the skull for one hour—no more. Excess boiling weakens the bone.* **2.** *Boiling loosens meat and cartilage from the skull. Most of the flesh curls up at the edges and can easily be removed by hand. Reach into the nose orifice and remove the eye-socket cartilage, as shown, and paperlike sinus bones in the nose orifice, which should pull free easily.* **3.** *With a plastic knife, which will not scratch the skull, scrape all skull surfaces to remove pockets of remaining flesh. The back of the skull takes time because cartilage clings stubbornly there.*

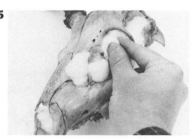

4. *Use a toothpick to dig debris from the many pockets and holes in the skull. Remove all flesh to prevent unwanted odor and invasion by bugs later.* **5.** *Fill the eye sockets, tear-duct holes, nose orifice, and other depressions with sterile cotton balls.* **6.** *Wrap a layer of sterile cotton batting around the skull in a lengthwise direction. Batting can be found in the first aid section of any well-stocked grocery or drug store. Then wrap the skull with another sheet of cotton in the opposite direction to completely cover the skull, as shown in the next photo.*

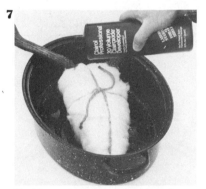

7. *After tying the batting in place with twine to prevent slippage, place the cotton-covered skull in a shallow pan and thoroughly soak it with 20-volume peroxide used for bleaching hair. This type of peroxide is sold in drug stores.* **8.** *Using more sterile cotton balls dampened with peroxide from the bottom of the pan, fill in gaps where skull bone is exposed—especially under the antler burrs. Wash your hands immediately to prevent bleaching and burning of fingers. To ensure even bleaching, periodically dip peroxide from the pan with a cup and pour it over the skull.* **9.** *Allow the cotton-covered skull to bleach for 24 to 30 hours. Then remove the cotton and thoroughly rinse the skull with cold tap water. Now the bone should be ivory white.*

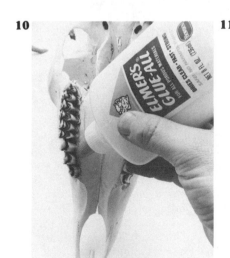

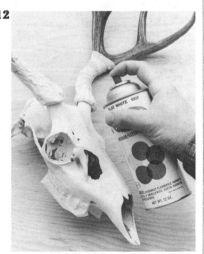

10 & 11. *After the skull has dried for several hours, use white glue to secure loosened parts. The teeth and bony plates over the nose commonly need gluing.* **12.** *Due to high fat and blood levels in some deer skulls, the bone sometimes remains a yellow-gray in color even after bleaching. This can be remedied by masking the teeth and antler beams with tape, and spraying the skull with flat white enamel.*

(Continued on next page)

(European plaque mounting continued)

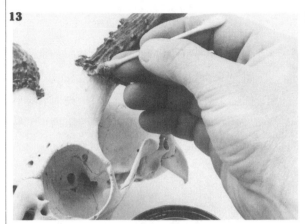

13. *Bleaching a skull sometimes whitens antler bases unnaturally. To restore normal color, touch up these areas with a cotton swab dipped in dark walnut stain. Take care not to spill stain on the skull.*

14. *To attach the trophy to a plaque, drill two small pilot holes in the skull—one in the thick bone just forward of the Atlas hole at the rear of the skull, and one in the middle of the palate (area between the teeth).*

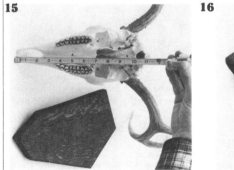

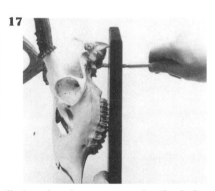

15. *Measure both skull and mounting plaque so clearance holes can be drilled in the plaque to match pilot holes in the skull. When properly mounted, the skull should be centered on the plaque.* **16.** *Countersink the clearance holes in the back of the plaque and screw the skull to the plaque. Flathead screws 2 inches long are usually just right.* **17.** *A European mount makes a striking trophy for any wall. Because the full skull is used, these mounts rarely break between the antlers.*

MAKING ANTLER COAT RACKS

Many hunters salvage shed antlers they find on woods hikes. These are nifty mementos of outings and also make excellent decorative items for any hunter's home. Some hunters display shed antlers above a fireplace or set them on furniture as other nicknacks. Other hunters go one step further and convert shed antlers to useful as well as attractive items.

One of the easiest but most practical shed-antler projects is an antler coat rack. The accompanying photos clearly show how. When mounted on a plaque so primary tines jut slightly upward, any antler from a thin spike to a massive cluster of points makes an excellent coat hook. The simple one-antler rack illustrated here works well indeed, but some hunters go whole hog and design longer coat racks with several antlers attached.

Inventive do-it-yourselfers can make a myriad of other useful shed-antler items. Candleholders, lamps, door handles, and bookends are just a few possibilities. Visits to various taxidermy studios, a few books on taxidermy nicknacks, and a little imagination will give you plenty of shed-antler ideas.

HOW TO MAKE ANTLER COAT RACKS

An antler coat rack is simple but decorative and useful. Mount it in bedroom, entranceway, or other place where clothing is normally hung.

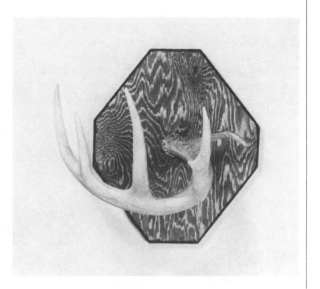

1. *Ingredients for an antler coat rack are few—one or more shed deer antlers, a wooden plaque, epoxy glue a ¼-inch bolt several inches long, a nut, and a washer.* **2.** *File the base of the antler flat so that it will mount solidly on the plaque. The fibrous bone is relatively easy to remove with a coarse file.* **3.** *Drill a ¼-inch hole in the antler base at approximate right angles to the flattened surface. Make the hole no deeper than ½ inch to avoid drilling out of the side of the antler. Caution: A bench vise would be safer than shown for stabilizing the antler.*

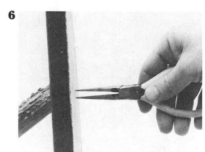

4. *Epoxy the bolt in the hole as shown. Use plenty of epoxy to ensure a solid bond. Five-minute hardening mix allows you to complete the project quickly.* **5.** *Once the epoxy has thoroughly hardened, shorten the exposed part of the bolt to ¾ inch with a metal hacksaw. File off burrs on the bolt end so that the nut attaches easily.* **6.** *Drill a hole in the center of the plaque for the mounting bolt. Countersink the back to accept a washer and nut below flush with the surface. The nut can be tightened with a pair of needle-nose pliers.*

HOW TO MAKE ANTLER BUTTONS AND MORE

Antlers without sentimental value to you can be sawed into useful items as shown. The best antlers for buttons, key-chain ornaments, watch fobs, belt buckles, and similar doodads are fairly fresh, solid antlers that have not become white or cracked through exposure to the elements. When lightly coated with varnish, such cross-sectional bits of antler retain their denseness and beauty for many years.

Antler buttons look especially appropriate on jackets, vests, and other garments made of buckskin. Buckskin clothing is sold off the rack at many leather shops, or can be tailor-made to a customer's specifications. A few hunters or their spouses actually make garments from buckskin. They either use buckskin from the deer they have taken or buy it from a taxidermist, tannery, or leather-goods outlet.

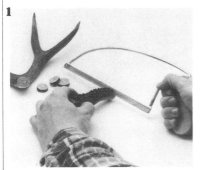

1. *To make buttons you need a solid deer antler. Start with cross-sectional saw cuts ¼-inch apart. A fine-toothed bone saw or metal hacksaw makes quick work of it.* **2.** *Next, bore four ¹⁄₁₆-inch holes in each piece of bone so that the buttons can be sewed on a garment. (To be safer, mount the buttons in a vice before drilling.) Then use fine-grit sandpaper to smooth top and bottom faces of each button. Round button edges slightly so that they will not wear through clothing. Lastly, coat each with satin polyurethane varnish.* **3.** *You can make key-chain ornaments and watch-chain fobs from antler cross sections.*

HOW TO RESTORE A WEATHERED RACK

Many hunters have the bad habit of tacking up antlers outdoors on a barn or garage door. In a few years, the racks invariably bleach and crack, ruining their appearance and eventually causing them to fall apart. Similarly, complete racks or single shed antlers that lie afield for more than a year or two rapidly deteriorate from weathering, if not consumed first by gnawing critters. Fortunately, you can refurbish any weathered but reasonably solid antler with a little effort and know-how. If you've mistakenly let a nice rack go bad over the years, inherited an outstanding but weathered trophy from a relative or friend, or found a shed antler or complete set of "bones" in the woods, the accompanying photos and instructions show you how to restore the trophy.

1. *A deer rack that has been found afield or allowed to deteriorate can be refurbished with dark walnut stain, rubbing alcohol, ordinary epoxy glue, and a relatively small amount of elbow grease.*

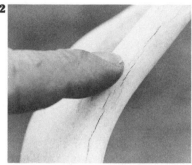

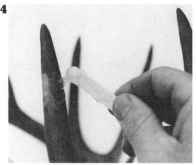

2. *Exposure to sunlight, wind, and precipitation slowly ruins any deer rack. The first signs of serious deterioration are whitening in color and hairline cracks running lengthwise with the beams.* **3.** *Restoring weathered antlers is easy. First scrub them down with a paper towel or lint-free cloth soaked in rubbing alcohol. Then apply a medium-to-dark walnut stain as evenly as possible with a cloth as shown. For best results, test one or more stains first on a backside part of the rack to ensure you will get the natural tone you want.* **4.** *After the stain dries, mix up some 2-hour (not 5-minute) epoxy glue. Apply a thin coating to all areas of the rack that have hairline cracks. On badly whitened antlers, this often means coating all surfaces with epoxy. Then rub away all the wet epoxy you can with a coarse, lint-free cloth. This fills cracks with glue and leaves a thin protective coating on antler surfaces.*

5. *Once the epoxy hardens, lightly sand all surfaces with ultra-fine, 400-grit sandpaper. This removes any unnatural epoxy shine and also creates lighter-colored ridges and bumps (normally seen on freshly taken antlers).*

DEER HOOFS

Nicknacks made with deer hoofs are very popular with hunters. Simple one-hoof racks (shown next page) multiple-hoof gun racks with larger and more ornate hardwood shields, hoof-and-wood bookends, and deer-hoof ash trays are just a few of the more common designs. Taxidermy supply houses sell special hardware for more complicated creations such as hoof ash trays, and most how-to taxidermy books illustrate various nicknacks like bookends and hoof racks.

Some professional taxidermists skin and completely debone lower legs to be used in deer-hoof projects. Once the hoofs and leg skins have been pickled in a tanning solution, they are mounted around commer-

cial or homemade leg forms. But this kind of project is too difficult for the average hunter and is only slightly less complicated than shoulder mounting a buck.

Fortunately, there is an easier and perfectly suitable hoof-preserving method for amateurs. Many expert taxidermists use this technique themselves—proof positive it works like a charm. The procedure is illustrated step-by-step here. In a nutshell, you need only to clean the marrow from the lower leg, bug-proof the leg and foot in a simple solution, bend the hoof to a desired position, and allow it to dry thoroughly in a cool place. Then saw the leg to proper length and attach it to a plaque, bookend, ash tray, or similar support. The result is as handsome, sleek, and long-lasting as more complex hoof-conversion procedures.

HOW TO MAKE A DEER-HOOF RACK

A single-hoof rack is ideal for hanging hats and coats. Multiple-hoof racks are great for guns, hunting bows, and similar items.

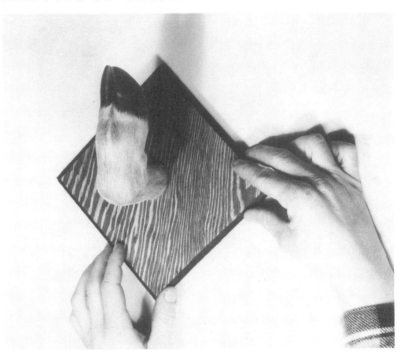

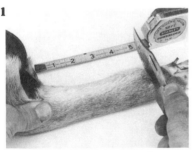

1. *Start this project by girdle-cutting the hide about 5 inches away from the ankle-bend of the hoof. Then, using a saw, sever the bone along the knife cut. This cut need not be square or neat because this section of bone will be discarded later.* **2.** *Double over a piece of coat-hanger wire 10 inches long and use the rounded end to scrape out all marrow in the leg bone.* **3.** *Mix 1 cup of Borax powder in 1 gallon of water and submerge the hoof in this solution for several days. This bugproofs, deodorizes, and pickles the bone and hide.*

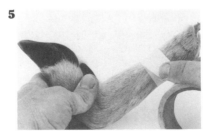
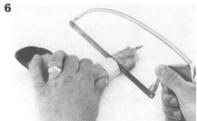

4. *Using a block of wood and twine, bend the hoof to a 90-degree angle. Let it dry completely in a cool place for 10 to 14 days.* **5.** *After drying the hoof, measure outward from the dewclaw and tightly wrap the leg with masking tape. The tape's outer edge should be 3 inches from the dewclaw.* **6.** *Using a fine-toothed bone saw or metal hacksaw, carefully make a square cut along the outer edge of the tape. Next, remove the masking tape from the hoof, being careful not to break or rumple hair underneath.*

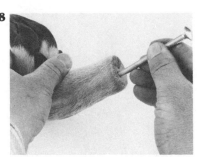
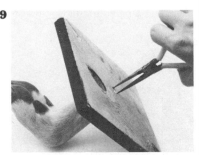

7. *Scrub inside the leg bone with a cotton swab soaked in acetone or rubbing alcohol. This degreases the bone for a solid epoxy bond.* **8.** *Cover the end of a long ¼-inch bolt with five-minute epoxy glue, then press the bolt into the bone-marrow hole. You may need a hammer to tap in the bolt on small deer legs. Once the glue hardens, saw the bolt to leave only ¾ of an inch exposed.* **9.** *Drill a hole in the center of a plaque to mount the hoof. Countersink the hole on the backside of the plaque. Use needle-nose pliers as shown to tighten the mounting nut.*

HARD-TANNING A HIDE

As mentioned before, soft-tanning deer hides with or without the hair is a tedious and tricky job requiring hard-to-find and sometimes hazardous chemicals. As a result, even full-time taxidermists normally ship deer hides to tanneries instead of tackling the processing themselves. But any neophyte can safely and easily *hard-tan* a deer hide to preserve the skin and hair for an attractive mount on the wall. The accompanying step-by-step photos show how.

For a wall rug, hard-tanning is just as good as professional soft-tanning. Since deer hair is fairly brittle stuff, placing a pliable, tannery-processed hide on the floor or draping it across furniture is never a good idea. The hair is quickly ruined. So a home-tanned wall rug, which dries flat and hard, is as desirable as a flexible wall rug that no one touches anyway. Both look alike, and the hard-tanned version can be produced at home for very little money.

If you have the time and inclination, try hard-tanning.

HOW TO HARD-TAN A HIDE

Hard-tanning leaves the hide stiff, rather than pliable. Since deer hair is brittle anyway, it should not be used as a rug or chair cover. And hard-tanning saves you considerable money compared to costs for hide soft-tanned by professionals.

(Continued on next page)

(Hard-tanning continued)

1. *Flesh out the hide completely. This means removing all fat and meat from the underside with a sharp knife—a process taking upwards of an hour.* **2.** *Mix 1 gallon water with 1 pound alum, ½ pound salt, and ¼ pound washing soda in a container with a lid. Shake thoroughly to mix the chemicals. Then pour the hard-tanning solution into a plastic bucket or trash can large enough to hold the deer hide. Add another gallon of water to completely immerse the hide.* **3.** *Submerge the hide in the solution in loose folds. If it tends to bob to the surface, weight it down with a large stone. Leave it submerged for 6 to 8 days.*

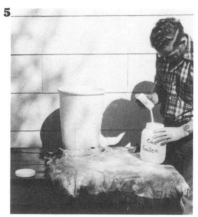

4. *Remove the hide and use a garden hose to rinse it thoroughly on both sides with cold water.* **5.** *Add ½ pound Borax to 1 gallon water in a clean container. Shake or stir to dissolve the Borax completely, then pour the solution into a clean 5-gallon bucket or can. Immerse the hide in the Borax solution for 2 to 4 days, making sure the hide is completely submerged. If 1 gallon will not cover the hide, mix and add another gallon of solution. Finally, after the Borax soak is complete, give both sides of the hide a 5-minute, high-pressure rinsing with a garden hose. This removes excess chemicals and prepares the hide for drying.* **6.** *Spread the hide, hair down, on a sheet of plywood. Spacing nails about 1 inch apart along the edges, stretch the skin as taut as possible in the shape you want to see on the wall. After 2 weeks of drying in a cool place, the deer hide should be as hard and flat as a board. Remove the nails and carefully smooth the hair with a brush.*

TROPHY CLEANING AND CARE

A first-rate mounting or tanning job is too attractive and too expensive to be allowed to go downhill through neglect or abuse. Trophies require relatively little upkeep, but some regular care is needed to keep them in good condition.

Hanging heads and rugs. Deer heads and rugs should be handled as little as possible to avoid unnecessary rumpling of the hair. Hang them carefully and then avoid touching or moving them unless absolutely necessary.

The first step in hanging heads and rugs is deciding *where* these things should go. Decorative arrangement is a matter of personal taste, but two other factors should also come into play when displaying heads and hides.

First, excess heat and moisture are natural enemies of all taxidermy creations. Heat from a fireplace, stove, gas heater, or large window in the summer will slowly but surely dry and crack the nose, eyelids, and hide of any mounted head, and will also cause subtle color changes in deer hair over time. Direct sunlight is especially destructive to heads and hides because the ultraviolet rays accelerate deterioration and fading of natural hair color. Similarly, moisture-laden air near a door or other damp area can promote mildew and bacterial action in a head or hide. This in turn ruins hair and skin. So do not hang trophies where they will be exposed to excess heat, moisture, or sunlight.

A second factor to consider when hanging heads is the possibility of accidental bumps and deliberate handling by friends or children. Hanging trophies in inaccessible places—preferably fairly high on walls—prevents unnecessary handling and other causes of abrasion to hair.

When moving or hanging any mounted deer head, always grasp it by the antlers or nose with one hand and the bottom of the brisket with the other. Never handle a head by the ears or neck, and never dig your fingers into the hair.

Routine trophy cleaning. Deer heads and hides should be dusted at least once a month with a lint-free cloth or feather duster. A vacuum cleaner with a soft-bristled furniture attachment can also be used, especially in areas with longer hair such as the neck. When dusting or vacuuming any head or hide, always brush in the direction the hair lies—never against it.

The eyes and nose of a deer should be lightly polished with a soft cloth to maintain their original shine and sparkle. Never rub these areas hard—doing so can dull or remove artist's paints on nostrils and eyelids.

The antlers on plaques and mounted heads require very little maintenance. If excessively dirty, antlers should be scrubbed with a damp cloth. Apply a little furniture polish to antlers from time to time to restore their original sheen. Never varnish the antlers on trophy mounts—this produces an unnatural shine.

Major trophy cleaning. Neglected deer heads and rugs often become too dirty to clean with a cloth or vacuum cleaner alone. Hard, smooth areas like the eyes, nose, and antlers can be washed clean with a cloth and mild soapy water. Dry these parts immediately to prevent damage. It is harder to restore hair on a grimy head or hide to original condition. The best way is to use ordinary grocery-store carpet cleaner according to directions. Let the cleaner set up and remove it several hours later with a soft-bristled brush. Be sure to use a carpet cleaner suitable for natural fibers like wool—a few synthetic-only cleaners will ruin deer hair in short order.

Trophy repair. Old or neglected deer heads often need repair, ranging from a home touch-up of nose and eyelids with fresh paint to a complete remount by a professional taxidermist. A relatively new head can also develop unexpected problems like splitting eartips or shrinkage cracks around the nose, eyes, or lips. Even with the best care, color in the nose and eyelid areas will often fade after many years on the wall.

A hunter can easily touch up fading nose and eye colors with nonglare model paints. The paint is inexpensive, lasts a long time, and can be obtained at any hobby store. A small natural-bristle brush is best for applying these paints and allows precise touch-up in the tight eyelid and nostril areas.

You can match and brighten faded colors around a trophy mount's nostrils and eyes with a little nonglare model airplane paint. Use a small, soft-bristled artist's brush.

Hairline cracks in the nose or eyelids of a mount are often easy to disguise with model paint. But large cracks, loose eyeballs, splitting eartips, moth-eaten or broken hair, and other major problems are best left to a professional. At the very worst, a taxidermist might have to acquire another deer cape and mount a dilapidated trophy head from scratch. This drastic measure costs as much as an original mount but is well worth the price if the buck being refurbished has especially large antlers or sentimental value.

PART 9
TROPHY HUNTING

Irene Vandermolen photo

BY DWIGHT SCHUH
Photos by the author unless
otherwise credited. Drawings
by Lloyd Birmingham.

The terms *trophy* and *trophy hunting* are commonly used by hunters, but these terms often mean something different to each hunter. By dictionary definition, a trophy may be "something symbolizing victory or success . . . a mounted fish, animal's head, etc." Given that definition, almost any deer can be a trophy.

If a beginning hunter strives to bag a buck, and instead legally shoots a doe, then he's still enjoyed a victory, and even a photograph of this doe might be considered a trophy. Most hunters would allow that view, but that's not what most mean when they talk about trophies. Over the years, the word *trophy* in deer hunters' parlance has come to mean a big set of antlers. A forked horn is not considered a trophy buck, but a 4-point mule deer (western count) or a 10-point whitetail (eastern count) by most hunter standards certainly would be.

Yet, even agreement on the minimum number of antler tines leaves room for disagreeing personal opinion as to the relative quality of such trophies. So some hunters have devised antler-measuring systems that quantify trophy size. Using a set formula, it's possible to measure a deer's antlers in relation to universally accepted standards for North America and achieve world recognition for those antlers that score above established minimum standards.

As you might have guessed, measuring systems have spawned official record books. Now many hunters define a trophy buck as a "record-book buck." Two major organizations maintain records of such trophy bucks as well as other big game. The Boone and Crockett Club accepts qualifying animals taken by any legal method, including bow and arrow. And the Pope and Young Club accepts only trophies taken with bow and arrow.

This part of the encyclopedia centers on the record-keeping clubs and their measuring systems. *Trophy* will here be defined as antlers that would qualify either for listing in the Boone and Crockett Club's periodically updated *Records of North American Big Game* or the Pope and Young Club's *Bowhunting Big Game Records of North America.*

THE BOONE AND CROCKETT CLUB

To many hunters, the name "Boone and Crockett" means certification of record big-game trophies, but the club didn't originate as a record-keeping organization. It began as a conservation group.

In 1883 when Theodore Roosevelt was 24 years old, he traveled to North Dakota to hunt bison and antelope. He returned there to run a ranch from 1884–86. During this time, he witnessed the destruction of game herds and observed the ravages of soil erosion that followed logging, overgrazing, and fire.

Roosevelt was appalled at the waste of wildlife he saw. On returning east in 1886, Roosevelt called a meeting of leading explorers, writers, scientists, and politicians to discuss the problem and what to do about it. This group formed the nucleus of the Boone and Crockett Club. Established in 1887 and limited to 100 regular and 50 associate members, the club was dedicated to preserving big game in North America.

One of its first projects involved Yellowstone National Park. Congress had officially established Yellowstone in 1872, but no laws specifically protected park resources. So poachers, timber cutters, vandals, and trappers continued to take their toll on Yellowstone's natural resources and scenic wonders. The Boone and Crockett Club fought for strong laws to stop this destruction. Finally, in 1894 Congress passed a bill that spelled out penalties for violations within park boundaries, and a new era began there.

That victory was only the first of many conservation projects taken on or financially supported by the Boone and Crockett Club.

The Record Book. The first American record book, called *Records of North American Big Game,* was published in 1932 by Prentiss Gray. The scoring system for that book was simple, and measurements consisted mainly of length and spread, with rankings on length alone. That system worked well enough for the African antelopes of the Rowland Ward System, but it proved inadequate for North American species such as those in the deer family.

In 1949 the Boone and Crockett Club formed a committee to improve the measuring methods further, and in 1950 the club adopted scoring methods that are basically the same as those used today. In 1952 the Boone and Crockett Club published the first record book based on the current system.

For antlered and horned game, a fairly complex system of scoring is used, as illustrated for deer later in this section. Bears and cats are scored by a simple combined total length and width of skull. To bring the system within reach of average hunters, Grancel

Record books provide valuable background for planning a trophy hunt. Records of North American Big Game *(left), published by the Boone and Crockett Club, indicates where you'll find the finest specimens for all big-game species.* Bowhunting Big Game Records of North America *(front), published by the Pope and Young Club, tells where archers have scored. (Neil Soderstrom photo)*

Fitz—a member of the revision committee—wrote a booklet called *How to Measure and Score Big-Game Trophies.* Published in 1963, this book became the standard and was the only such book available.

Awards programs. The Boone and Crockett awards programs began in 1947, but since 1970, they've been held every three years. Top animals entered in each huntable category undergo a final awards judging by the Boone and Crockett Club. Species include all hoofed big game, as well as bears and the big cats. At that time a panel of judges measures the trophies—to eliminate the possibility of bias. Trophies invited for final judging are displayed publicly. Then at a banquet concluding the three-year awards period, the Boone and Crockett Club presents medals or certificates for the winning trophies.

The top three trophies taken by fair chase receive First, Second, and Third place awards. (Fair chase is defined on the score charts, shown later in this section.) Other trophies, such as picked-up heads, are eligible only for Certificates of Merit. In addition to these honors, the Sagamore Hill Award, the highest award given by the Boone and Crockett Club, is presented occasionally for truly outstanding trophies.

Following each awards banquet, the club publishes brochures containing the scores and photos of all trophy antlers entered during the scoring period. In addition, the official record book, *Records of North American Big Game* (commonly called the Boone and Crockett book), is published about every six years or when significant changes take place in trophy rankings or in categories and requirements. An awards records book is published every three years, following the close of the entry period.

In 1973 Boone and Crockett and the National Rifle Association joined forces to cosponsor the record-keeping task under the name North American Big Game Awards Program (NABGAP). This joint effort continued through 1980, when Boone and Crockett Club again took over as the sole record-keeping body.

Membership in Boone and Crockett. Entering a trophy head in the Boone and Crockett awards program does not entitle a hunter to membership in the club. To be considered for membership, a candidate must be referred by four active members. He must also have an outstanding record in hunting and conservation and have taken three adult male animals in fair chase with a rifle. Regular membership is limited to 100. There are also associate and honorary memberships, but these are few in number, and today the club has only about 60 such members, bringing total membership to about 160.

In addition to the record books, the Boone and Crockett Club publishes books on conservation and wildlife management. For more information, contact: Boone and Crockett Club, 205 South Patrick St., Alexandria, VA 22314.

THE POPE AND YOUNG CLUB

In 1911 Ishi, the last surviving member of the Yana Indian nation, emerged from the foothills of the Sierra Nevada in California and was discovered near Oroville. As an anthropological curiosity, Ishi was taken to San Francisco where he lived at the University of California's museum. Dr. Saxton Pope was called in to give Ishi a medical examination. Pope had grown up on the western frontier, where he gained an appetite for outdoor knowledge. So Ishi's primitive lore intrigued him, and they became good friends. Although Ishi died of tuberculosis five years after he met Pope, his knowledge of hunting kindled in Pope a keen interest in bowhunting.

Pope's enthusiasm affected Art Young, an energetic and athletic man who hunted with rifle and shotgun, and Pope and Young began to bowhunt together regularly. They took deer and bear in California, and they traveled to Alaska to kill grizzly bears and to Africa to hunt lions. The two hunted with homemade straight bows and wooden, hand-fletched arrows. Pope described many of their exploits in his book *Hunting with the Bow and Arrow.* Their adventures and feats during the 1920s became widely known and helped springboard the bow and arrow onto the modern hunting scene. During the 1930s, several states for the first time established archery seasons or set aside special archery-only hunting areas.

Ishi, last surviving Yana Indian, demonstrates his unique bowhunting form. (Photo is property of Lowie Museum of Anthropology, University of California, Berkeley, courtesy of Pope and Young Club.)

Art Young (left) and Dr. Saxton Pope photo: courtesy of the Pope and Young Club.

Evolution of the Pope and Young Club. In 1940, the influence of bowhunting made itself felt in the realm of organized archery competition. The National Archery Association (NAA) had existed since 1879, but it was oriented strictly toward target archery. With the rising interest in bowhunting, many archers wanted target competition that emphasized hunting conditions, and in 1940 some NAA members broke off to form the National Field Archery Association (NFAA).

In 1956 the NFAA established a Hunting Activities Committee. Chairman Glenn St. Charles and his committee sent questionnaires to state archery groups, wildlife departments, and individuals. The response showed that bowhunting was still viewed with uncertainty by the public and many wildlife managers. Archers needed a vehicle to show that the bow and arrow was a valid method of hunting and that bowhunters were dedicated to conservation of wildlife.

St. Charles thought an organization similar to the Boone and Crockett Club would work for bowhunters. He and his committee pulled together all the trophy heads and bowhunter records they could find and drew up guidelines, and they got permission from Boone and Crockett to use that club's official score charts to measure bow-killed animals. St. Charles and his committee recommended this material to the NFAA as a means of keeping bowhunting records.

The NFAA approved, and in June 1958 the first awards program was held at Grayling, Michigan, in conjunction with the NFAA's annual tournament. A second awards program followed in 1960, and many participants agreed that an organization separate from the NFAA was needed to fulfill the record-keeping and conservation goals of bowhunters. The NFAA finally acknowledged this need and released its trophy records to Glenn St. Charles and his group.

With these records as a base, the Pope and Young Club was formally established on January 27, 1961. Glenn St. Charles, the primary force behind the club, was elected temporary chairman and later served as

president. The club, of course, was named after Saxton Pope and Art Young, who helped make bowhunting a popular sport in North America.

Bow-and-arrow records. The Pope and Young Club now holds an awards program and banquet every two years. As with the Boone and Crockett Club, top trophies entered during the biennium are measured by a panel of judges, and awards are presented for the top trophies. Top trophy antlers are displayed at the biennial Pope and Young banquet. First, Second, and Honorable Mention plaques are awarded.

In addition, the Pope and Young Club occasionally presents the Ishi Award—equivalent to Boone and Crockett's Sagamore Hill Award—for truly outstanding trophies. Following each awards banquet, the club issues a booklet listing all top entries for the scoring

The Ishi Award is the highest honor the Pope and Young Club gives for a big-game trophy.

period. The club also publishes a book called *Bowhunting Big Game Records of North America*. The first edition was published in 1975. Revised editions are published every few years.

Pope and Young membership. Anyone can join the Pope and Young Club as an associate member. Associate membership isn't limited, but prospective members must have taken at least one adult deer or other big-game animal by bow and arrow. The animal must be taken under the rules of fair chase, as defined on the official score charts shown later in this section.

Regular membership is limited to 100 persons. Regular members move up through the associate ranks. To qualify as a regular member, the candidate must have taken with bow and arrow at least three species of North American big game, and at least one of these must be listed in the record book.

Senior membership is not limited in number. To

qualify as a senior member, candidates must have five years seniority as a regular member. In addition, they must have taken at least four species of North American big game, and three of these must be listed in the Pope and Young records.

For more information, contact: Pope and Young Club, 1804 Borah, Moscow ID 83843.

NRA AND OTHERS

NRA Big Game Awards Program. The most broad-based program for trophy recognition is the National Rifle Association's (NRA) Big Game Awards Program. Certificates are presented in four categories: modern long rifle, modern handgun, muzzleloader, and bow and arrow.

To receive a certificate of recognition, the hunter measures his trophy himself and submits the measurements along with a photograph of the trophy. Awards are presented for 14 species of North American big game. For deer, the requirements are minimal: whitetails and mule deer must have four points on at least one side of the rack, and blacktail and Coues deer must have three points on at least one side.

In addition to certificates for general recognition, the National Rifle Association makes a special presentation, called the Leatherstocking Award, for outstanding animals. Trophies entered for this award must be measured by official Boone and Crockett or Pope and Young scorers. Only animals killed during

This world-record typical whitetail was taken by James Jordan in Wisconsin in 1914. Official score is 206⅛. (Boone and Crockett Club photo)

the preceding calendar year may be entered. Winners in each of the four categories—rifle, handgun, muzzleloader, and bow and arrow—receive Leatherstocking statuettes.

For more information, contact: National Rifle Association, Attn: Hunter Services Div., 1600 Rhode Island Ave., N.W., Washington, DC 20036.

Other record-keeping organizations. Those discussed above are the major groups that keep records and present awards for North American trophy deer. However, many U.S. state and Canadian provincial groups also publish records. In most cases, the Boone and Crockett scoring system is used, but generally the minimum scores are relatively low. For more information on the existence of state and provincial trophy-record groups and record books, contact appropriate government wildlife departments. Most government agencies don't keep records, but they can direct you to groups that do.

STORIES BEHIND WORLD-RECORD HEADS

Most serious deer hunters would like to get into the record books and, in fact, not all world-record bucks were taken by veteran trophy hunters. Some were taken by rank beginners, and others weren't killed by hunters at all. The Boone and Crockett Club honors all trophy heads regardless of how they were taken, and the term "Picked Up" is used for antlers that were found.

Whatever the circumstances, world-record stories provide fascinating lore for serious hunters. Here are some stories of how world-record heads were taken and how they found their way into the record books.

Boone and Crockett typical-class whitetail. On November 20, 1914, James Jordan, who was 22 years old at the time, followed tracks of several deer in the fresh snow on a crisp, sunny morning near the town of Danbury in northwest Wisconsin. Three of the tracks were average size, but one track was huge and it drew Jordan on.

Near a railroad line, he stopped to watch. When an approaching train blew its whistle, Jordan saw the deer he'd been following rise from tall grass near the tracks. One of them was a huge buck, and Jordan shot at it. The deer sprinted away, and Jordan fired several more times. He continued following the buck and then saw it wade the Yellow River. Taking careful aim he dropped it in its tracks on the far side. When Jordan finally reached his buck, he was astounded by its antlers and massive body. Jordan said the buck weighed close to 400 pounds.

That was the simple part of the story, but from there

it turned into a Sherlock Holmes mystery that remained unsolved for more than 60 years. A part-time taxidermist named George Van Castle offered to mount the impressive head for $5, so Jordan took him up on the deal. But then Van Castle moved to Minnesota, and later to Florida, and Jordan was never able to track him down to recover his prized deer. For over 50 years, Jordan had no idea where the antlers were.

Then in 1964 Robert Ludwig, an antler collector and a distant relative of Jordan's, paid $3 for a moth-eaten deer head at a rummage sale in Sandstone, Minnesota. Ludwig showed the antlers to Jordan, who also collected antlers, and Jordan claimed those antlers came from the buck he'd shot in 1914. Ludwig didn't believe Jordan and kept the rack.

Ludwig recognized the outstanding nature of the head and had it measured by a Boone and Crockett scorer. The official score came out at 206⅝ (which was later revised to 206⅛), larger than any other typical whitetail ever measured. The head was entered in the Boone and Crockett book as a new world record, but the hunter was listed as "Unknown." In 1968, Ludwig sold the antlers to a New Hampshire antler collector named Charles Arnold for $1,500.

In 1977 outdoors columnist Ron Schara wrote up Jordan's story for the Minneapolis *Tribune*. As a result of that story, the Boone and Crockett Club investigated Jordan's claims and in 1978, the club officially recognized James Jordan as the man who killed the world-record typical whitetail. Unfortunately, Jordan died just two months before he received official recognition for his accomplishment.

Boone and Crockett nontypical-class whitetail. It was the fall of 1981 when Dave Beckman of St. Louis, Missouri, drove home from a successful deer hunt. He'd killed a 10-point whitetail and checked it in with conservation officer Mike Hellend. He figured his excitement had ended for the season.

But on the way home, he noticed a buck lying off the road. He investigated and found the enormous whitetail dead just on the other side of a fence. Beckman contacted Hellend, and they returned together. Hellend could find no evidence that the deer had been shot; so he assumed the buck had died of natural causes or had killed itself trying to jump the fence.

Hellend later had the rack scored officially by a Boone and Crockett measurer and found it would qualify as a new world record. The buck was finally panel-measured at 333⅞ inches. This eclipsed the previous record, a Texas buck killed in 1892, by more than 47 inches. The head now belongs to the Missouri Department of Conservation.

Pope and Young typical-class whitetail. Mel Johnson began hunting with a bow and arrow in 1959,

The world-record nontypical whitetail was found dead along a road near St. Louis, Missouri. Its official score is 333⅞. (Photo courtesy of Missouri Department of Conservation)

Bowhunter Mel Johnson killed this typical whitetail near Peoria, Illinois, in October 1965. It scored 204⅛ points and is the only trophy head to win both the Sagamore Hill and Ishi awards. (Pope and Young Club photo)

when he was in his mid-20s. He hunted in Wisconsin, Colorado, Missouri, Pennsylvania, and his home state of Illinois. At that time he hunted with a 72-pound Damon Howatt recurve, Microflite glass shafts, and Zwickey Black Diamond broadheads.

During his first five years of bowhunting he killed six whitetails, but no large bucks. With growing experience he started passing up the smaller animals, trying for something big. Johnson hunted near home in Peoria after work each evening during the week, but he knew chances for a trophy buck so close to civilization were slim. So each weekend he drove to Wisconsin to look for big deer.

Ironically, his trophy hunting didn't go according to plan. In 1964, during an evening hunt near a major highway 20 minutes from Peoria, he glimpsed two big bucks in the timber at the edge of a soybean field. He didn't get a shot, but those animals piqued his interest. Beginning October 1, 1965, opening day of the bow season, he concentrated his efforts on that soybean field. For the first few weeks he saw plenty of deer but no large bucks, and he never loosed an arrow.

On October 29, a clear, warm day, he visited the field after work as usual. Normally, he hunted from a tree stand that overlooked the edge of the field, but because of the clear weather, Johnson thought the deer would emerge later than normal. So he chose to take a ground stand in brush on the far side. He wore camouflage clothing and a mask to hide his face.

After several hours with no action, Johnson suddenly realized he was looking at a deer walking slowly from the timber into the field. It was a buck—a big one. As the deer walked toward him, Johnson began to sweat, fearing his camouflage might not hold up at eye level.

The buck passed by so close that Johnson remained frozen, knowing the slightest movement would alert the deer. When the big whitetail was directly in front of Johnson, mere feet away, he turned and stared at the hunter. Seeing nothing out of the ordinary, the buck walked on. When he'd gone by, Johnson rose slightly, drew, and released an arrow. The range was less than 20 feet. The buck leaped into the air and ran out across the field out of sight over a small rise. Johnson found him lying dead over the rise in the middle of the field.

The buck was so huge that Johnson had to get help from a nearby farmer to load the animal into his car. Field-dressed, the buck weighed 270 pounds.

More remarkable was the massive 12-tine rack. The buck officially scored 204⅛ points. This was large enough to surpass a buck killed by John Breen in Minnesota in 1918, making it then a new Boone and Crockett world record (Johnson's buck has since been surpassed). In addition, Johnson received the Boone and Crockett Club's Sagamore Hill Award for the finest animal taken during the scoring period.

After that the buck was recognized as a new bow-hunting world record and won the Ishi Award, the highest honor bestowed by the Pope and Young Club. Johnson's trophy head is the only one to receive both of hunting's highest honors—the Sagamore Hill and Ishi awards.

Boone and Crockett typical-class mule deer. Doug Burris, a native Texan, got trophy-buck fever chasing big whitetails in South Texas, and in 1969 he decided to carry that fever to new ground in search of mule deer. Record-book study and conversations with knowledgeable hunters led him to the southwest corner of Colorado, near the town of Cortez, where many record-book bucks had been killed.

The first three years he hunted there, Burris passed up many small bucks and each year killed 30-inch bucks, outside spread. By the time he and three friends returned to Cortez in 1972, Burris knew the country well and could pinpoint five locations he considered prime big-buck spots. The country was broken by many canyons and mesas, and the vegetation consisted primarily of oak brush, aspen groves, and scattered pines. Burris considered thick oak brush the major factor for growing trophy bucks because it affords protection even when hunters are numerous.

Doug Burris killed this world-record typical mule deer near Cortez, Colorado, in 1972. It has an inside spread of 30 inches and an official score of 225⅝. (Wm. H. Nesbitt, Boone and Crockett Club photo)

To hunt this country, Burris combined stillhunting and watching with a binocular from high rims and other vantage points. The third day of the 1972 hunt dawned drizzly and dark. After dropping off his companions, Burris set out alone, hunting into a breeze drifting down from higher country. As he worked toward the head of a rough canyon, he spotted two bucks a half-mile away. Even at that distance, he could see their racks with his naked eye. They had to be worthwhile bucks. He set out after them.

For part of the stalk, he could see the bucks feeding, but then they disappeared into a patch of high brush. Burris felt confident they were still there, and when he'd approached within 200 yards, he bumped a doe that sprinted away in the direction of the bucks. Burris ran into an opening where he could see, and he got ready to shoot. The two bucks bounded into view, but before Burris could shoot, a third buck emerged. It was even larger than the other two. When Burris swung on the buck and fired, the huge deer stumbled and hit the ground, dead. Burris didn't know it at the time, but he'd killed a mule deer buck with the largest antlers ever recorded.

On March 24, 1974, at the Fifteenth Awards Program in Atlanta, Georgia, Burris's trophy received official recognition as the new world record for mule deer, and it also won the Sagamore Hill Award.

Pope and Young typical-class mule deer. Through a series of conversations, Lee Kline, an official measurer for the Pope and Young Club, located a mule deer rack wired to the rafter of a barn in Colorado. Kline's discovery unearthed the finest mule deer antlers ever recorded for bow and arrow.

It all began in 1972 when Bill Barcus, then 18 years old, took up deer hunting. Barcus had never killed a

Bill Barcus killed the Pope and Young record mule deer in Colorado in 1979. This great rack measured 203⅝ points. (Lee Kline photo)

deer, but he decided to take the tough route anyway—bowhunting. For five years he hunted diligently, staying out for as long as two weeks by himself. Not until 1977 did he finally kill his first deer, a doe.

Barcus's years of experience may not have produced an impressive kill record, but they'd sharpened his hunting skills. What is more, he found a lonely ridge where there were many fine bucks and he never saw another bowhunter. When the 1979 season arrived, the stage seemed set for big success.

His hunting territory was on the White River National Forest and consisted of oak brush tangles on lower ridges that gave way to aspens high on a seemingly inaccessible mountain. Barcus normally hunted alone, but in 1979 his parents went along to keep him company in camp.

He hunted the first four days on the lower oak brush slopes, but hot dry weather made hunting poor there. On the fifth day, he decided to tackle the aspen mountain, his secret hideaway for big bucks. He started hiking an hour before dawn to reach a small clearing near the mountain top just after sunrise. During the course of the day, he stalked four bucks feeding together but spooked them, and later he missed a 45-yard shot at a 5 × 5 buck (western count).

Late in the afternoon he stillhunted slowly down a game trail, moving a few cautious steps and then stopping to inspect a series of terraces on the steep hillside. A faint movement in tall grass 85 yards below caught his attention, and through his binocular, he made out a fuzzy antler tine. Then he saw another. It was so far from the first he assumed two bucks were bedded near each other. But then the antler tines moved simultaneously. They belonged to the same buck.

Dead aspen branches littered the hillside and there was little cover, so Barcus studied the area carefully to plan an approach. Inch by inch, he descended toward the unsuspecting buck. Slow movement and full camouflage were his major allies, and they paid off. After an hour, Barcus stood 15 yards from the bedded buck. Concentrating on a spot below the deer's spine, Barcus aimed and released an arrow. The shaft disappeared exactly where he'd aimed. The buck quivered and lay still. Barcus's legs were rubbery with excitement as he approached his first buck.

But when he got close, he noticed the deer's eyes were closed. It wasn't dead. Before he could nock another arrow, the animal leaped up and raced downhill out of sight over a terrace, leaving Barcus with a sinking feeling of loss. In desperation he ran to the point where he'd last seen the buck, and there, 30 yards below, lay his trophy.

Back in camp that night, Barcus told his parents of his success, but he scarcely mentioned the antlers. His main concern was the deer's size. The next day Barcus, along with his father and mother, spent from early morning until dark packing meat back to camp. Incredibly, Barcus and his father considered leaving the cumbersome antlers there, but Mrs. Barcus would have none of that. She sawed the antlers off and carried them out herself.

And it was because of her efforts that Lee Kline had an opportunity to measure those antlers wired to a rafter in a barn on the Barcus's farm. The 7 × 7 antlers had an enormous 38-inch outside spread and a 30-inch inside spread. Kline came up with a score of 203⅝, well over the previous world record of 197. Bill Barcus had killed a world-record buck, but Lee Kline was far more excited about it than Barcus himself.

Pope and Young blacktail. George Shurtleff isn't the kind of person you'd picture as a world-record holder. This retired security guard is just a fellow who hunts for the pleasure of it. He's never taken long vacations to pursue trophy game around the world; instead, he just hunts on weekends and holidays near his home in Portland, Oregon. But he has found a combination of location and method that produces trophy blacktails.

Shurtleff killed the Pope and Young world-record blacktail in 1969. This buck also won the Ishi Award as the outstanding trophy measured during the scoring period ending in 1979, and it was listed as the Boone and Crockett world record in the 8th edition of *Records of North American Big Game*. (It has since been surpassed.)

Shurtleff hunts primarily in the Cascade foothills bordering the east side of Oregon's Willamette Valley. He thinks the biggest bucks are taken within a mile of farmland. Hunting from stands is nothing new to eastern whitetail hunters, but in 1969, when Shurtleff took his world-record buck, most westerners didn't

know the meaning of "stand." Shurtleff had tried stalking and stillhunting, the methods used by most western hunters, but he found that in the rainy forests of western Oregon, those methods offered only a slight chance for trophy bucks. So he began hunting from stands, and in that sense he helped pioneer stand-hunting in the West.

One day while fishing near Silverton, Oregon, Shurtleff discovered a well-used deer trail that contained one very large track. On October 2, during Oregon's general rifle season—it was legal to hunt during both the bow and rifle seasons at that time—Shurtleff took a stand on a rock bluff overlooking the trail. He didn't have long to wait. About 7 A.M., he saw antlers coming

George Shurtleff holds his world-record blacktail rack, which scores 172⅞. The antlers on the far left measure 163⅞, and the middle rack would have scored over 160, but Shurtleff split the skull and thereby mistakenly disqualified the antlers from official recognition.

his way through the blackberry brambles, and a huge buck emerged from cover and walked directly below him, 20 feet away. When the buck had gone past, Shurtleff drew his bow and sent an arrow quartering forward through the buck's chest. He was elated to see the animal go down a short distance away.

Shurtleff's story is remarkable for two reasons. First, he killed that buck while competing with Oregon's hordes of rifle hunters. He thinks competition actually gave him an advantage because other hunters probably pushed the buck by his stand.

Second, that isn't Shurtleff's only trophy-class buck. In 1977 while hunting from a tree stand (again during

George Shurtleff killed this blacktail with a score of 172⅞ in Western Oregon in 1969. This world-record head also won the Pope and Young Club's Ishi Award.

the general rifle season), Shurtleff killed a blacktail that scored 163⅞ and ranks No. 2 in the Pope and Young record book. In 1978 he killed another huge buck, but because he knew nothing about scoring at that time, he unfortunately split the skull to lay the antlers neatly on his pack. That disqualified the head from official recognition, but the buck unofficially scored about 162, which would place it high in any record book. A couple of years later, Shurtleff killed yet another blacktail. That one scored over 140, perhaps an anemic encore for George Shurtleff but certainly the accomplishment of a lifetime for most hunters.

Boone and Crockett blacktail. Even as George Shurtleff's buck, or the previous world record killed in 1962 by Clark Griffith near Elk City, Oregon, topped the Boone and Crockett listings, an even larger buck hung in obscurity in Washington. The story behind that buck began in 1953 with Lester Miller of Forks, Washington.

Miller regularly hunted upper Lincoln Creek in western Lewis County, and several times he saw a group of three bucks, one of them an exceptional trophy. Miller considered himself a meat hunter and wasn't really looking for a big buck, but the sight of that deer kept drawing him back. Other hunters had seen the buck too, and were trying their best for a crack at him.

One day Miller was walking down a road when the

The world-record blacktail, taken by Lester Miller in Washington in 1953, went unrecognized for nearly 30 years. With a score of 182⅖, it exceeded the previous world record by 10 points (inches). (Boone and Crockett Club photo)

buck jumped from the brush and bounded across a rock slide. Miller dropped him with his Model 1894 Winchester .30/30. For years he tried to get people interested in his big buck, but nobody realized the significance of the head. Finally, for lack of room in his house, Miller gave it to his nephew Bruce Mulligan.

Then in February 1980, Mulligan took the head to a sports show in Portland, Oregon, where rough measurements seemed to indicate that this was a world-record-contender blacktail. In 1983 Lester Miller's blacktail was accepted as a new world record with an official score of 182⅖.

FIELD-JUDGING TROPHY QUALITY

If you're seriously hunting for a record-book animal, you must be able to gauge antler measurements within an inch or two in the field. You can learn techniques, but without actual practice, you'll never perfect the art of judging trophy racks. First, become familiar with the dimensions of deer antlers by measuring as many racks as possible. Once you've learned the fundamentals, take that knowledge to the field and apply it to deer on the hoof. Practice is the only way to develop a proficient trophy eye.

The following discussion uses Boone and Crockett minimums as a base. If you're hunting with a bow and arrow and want to kill a buck that qualifies for the Pope and Young book, the same principles apply, since Pope and Young employs the same scoring system. However, record-class dimensions are smaller, and you can learn them by studying measurements listed in *Bowhunting Big Game Records of North America.*

The principles. Primary measurements are length of main beams, inside spread, length of tines, and mass. Many hunters place greatest emphasis on spread, but if you're looking for trophy-book heads, don't be misled. Under the Boone and Crockett system, spread is only a small percentage of the score, and excessive width actually can reduce the total score. Antler height, which indicates long tines, combined with width is the combination that adds up to a high score.

Mass also inspires awe among hunters, and few would pass up any buck with massive antlers that look as heavy as oak limbs. But in terms of scoring, mass, like width, can be deceiving. Circumference measurements comprise a relatively small percentage of the overall score. Length and height add much more to the score of a rack.

John Wootters, in his excellent book *Hunting Trophy Deer,* analyzed the top 100 whitetail deer listed in one edition of the Boone and Crockett record book. He found that length of the main beams plus cumulative tine length made up 70 percent of the total score. Circumference (mass) accounted for 18 percent, and width only 12 percent. You can see that lengths of main beams and tines are the most important elements in a high whitetail score, and the same holds for other deer categories.

Also, remember that symmetry plays a big part in score, and you can gauge this fairly quickly in the field. Rather than looking at all tines and trying to add them up in your head, look only at the poorer side and double that. That works because all differences in measurements between the left and right side are subtracted from the score. In essence, total score is a bit less than the poorer side doubled. For example, if a buck has three points on one side and four on the other, he'll actually be scored like a symmetrical 3-point. The additional fourth tine on one side does not affect the total score.

Field-estimating whitetails. General dimensions of a whitetail's head help you gauge the size of his antlers. Average tip-to-tip ear spread on a mature whitetail measures about 16 inches, and on a big buck it may go 18. The ears are about 7 inches long, and distance from the tip of the nose to the antler base is 10 to 12 inches, depending on the size of the buck. These figures provide a rough yardstick for field judging.

Width: Most Boone and Crockett bucks have a spread of at least 20 inches. If you can see 2 inches or more of daylight between the main beams and the tips of the ears, you know the buck is potentially in the trophy class. Be cautious about gauging width from the rear, especially if the deer has his ears laid back, because it will appear much wider than it actually is.

Main beams: Wide spread is essential, but don't estimate the quality of a rack strictly on width. The world-record whitetail, which scores 206⅛ points, has an inside spread of only 20 inches. Where that buck really picks up score is the length of main beams (30 inches on each side). Main-beam length may be the single most important measurement on a buck; so gauge it accurately.

A buck just about has to have 25-inch beams to make the record book. John Wootters, in his analysis of Boone and Crockett whitetails, found that the average length of main beams was 27½ inches. Remember this was for the top 100, most of which scored more than 180.

How do you estimate beam length? Essentially, it's a function of width and curve. For that reason, spread may be more important as an indicator of beam length than as an actual measurement in itself. On some whitetails, the antler tips curve toward each other over the buck's nose until they come within a few inches

of each other. If a buck has a spread of at least 20 inches with tips that curve close together, you can bet the main beams exceed 25 inches.

Exceptional main beams will extend forward as far as a line drawn vertically from the tip of a buck's nose. Wootters suggests that spacing of tines indicates length of the main beams. If a buck has 5 points on each side—typical conformation—and the tines are widely spaced, the main beams are long. If little space separates the tines, the main beams probably aren't outstanding.

To gauge the quality of antlers in the field, you must know general dimensions of the deer's head. Whitetail bucks have ears about 7 inches long.

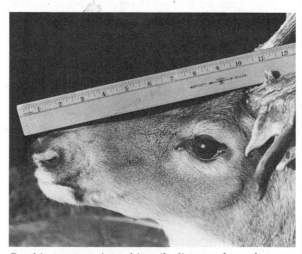

On this average-size whitetail, distance from the nose tip to antler base measures about 10 inches. On a large buck, this could be 11 inches or more.

Most Boone and Crockett whitetails have an antler spread (left) of 20 inches or greater. Average tip-to-tip ear spread is 16 inches; so you should see at least 2 inches of daylight between ear tips and inside of main beams. Main beam length (right) contributes a major percentage to a whitetail trophy score. Beams must be at least 25 inches long to put a buck in Boone and Crockett class. If main beams curve forward to a line drawn vertically from the tip of the buck's nose, they're probably in the 25-inch range.

Tines: First priority goes to the number of tines. Mature whitetail bucks typically grow four, five, or six points on each side and a rack just about has to have at least five per side to qualify for the record book. (The Boone and Crockett score chart accepts up to seven per side.) Out of 440 typical whitetails listed in a recent edition of *Records of North American Big Game*, only 10 had as few as four points on one side, and the highest scoring 4 × 4 was listed No. 211.

Tine length varies greatly. The brow tines on most Boone and Crockett bucks are 4 to 6 inches long, and most other tines are no shorter than 6 to 8 inches. Of course, the fewer in number, the longer each individual tine must be. You can use ear and nose lengths to gauge the length of tines.

Nontypical whitetails (asymmetrical antlers) are scored identically to typicals; so the same guidelines apply in each category. The only difference is that on nontypicals all abnormal points are added to, rather than subtracted from, the score.

Coues deer, or Arizona whitetails, are measured by the same method as northern whitetails, but the dimensions are smaller. Mike Cupell has scored dozens of Coues deer. He says the flared ears on a Coues deer measure 10 to 12 inches, tip to tip, across the skull; distance from the antler base to the tip of the nose is 8 to 9 inches; and the chest is 14 to 16 inches deep. These measurements provide a rough guide in the field.

Cupell says most Coues whitetails large enough to make the book have an inside spread of at least 13 inches, so you must see daylight between the tips of the ears and the inside of the main beams.

Main beams generally must be 16 inches or longer. The average Coues deer has three points per side, but it's a rare 3 × 3 that will make the book. Cupell said a buck just about has to have at least four points on each side to make it. The brow tines must be at least 3½ inches long—almost as long as an ear—and the second points must be 7½ to 8 inches for the buck to score well. Again, nontypical Coues deer are measured like typicals; so the same general dimensions apply.

Field-estimating mule deer. The ears on an average buck are 9 to 10 inches long. Most large bucks measure about 20 inches from ear tip to ear tip—provided the ears are spread out. But on younger bucks, tip-to-tip distance may be only 18 inches, and it could be 22 on a huge old buck. From the base of the antlers to the tip of the nose measures about 10 inches. Chest height is about 20 inches. Remember that antler judgment is relative to an animal's size. Average antlers may look enormous on a 3-year-old buck that weighs 150 pounds and has a small head, and big antlers may look average on a 7-year-old buck that weighs 300 pounds.

On mule deer, the average ear length is about 9 inches. This is an average-size buck, but ears on a huge deer could be longer.

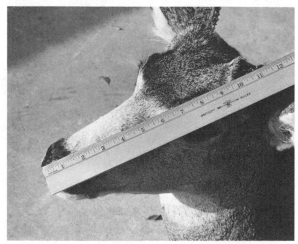

From nose tip to antler base, this mule deer measures just under 10 inches. However, the face could be a bit longer on a huge buck.

Width: Wide-racked mule deer inspire great awe. The generally accepted standard for a "big buck" is a 30-inch spread, but in most hunters' minds that means maximum outside spread. Any buck with 30-inch antlers is a sight to behold, but in the Boone and Crockett measuring system, outside spread means little. It's the inside spread of the main beams that counts.

Inside spread of record-book mule deer varies from less than 20 inches to greater than 30 inches. However, a majority of bucks listed in the book have inside spreads of 25 inches or more; so that is a good general guideline. If a large buck has main beams that extend outside his ears at least 2 to 3 inches, you know he has an inside spread of 25 inches or more.

Main beams: In his book *How to Find Giant Bucks*, Kirt Darner says he considers 27 inches to be the cutoff point for main-beam length. Most bucks with beams shorter than 27 inches fail to make the book. The book supports his contention. A large percentage of mule deer listed have main beams longer than 27 inches. Very few are shorter than 25 inches.

Darner suggests that the main beams on an outstanding buck will curve forward to a line drawn vertically from the tip of the buck's nose. Another means of judging beam length is antler conformation. Mike Cupell, who measures for Boone and Crockett and other record books, says he defines two styles of racks—box shaped and basket shaped. A basket rack generally angles up from the head and continues fairly straight or in a gentle curve. A box-shaped rack commonly extends almost straight out from the head and then curves sharply upward. Given equal inside spread and height, box-shaped antlers will have longer main beams than basket antlers because they have a much greater curve.

A high rack generally scores better than a wide rack for the same reason. Cupell says he gauges antler height in relation to a buck's chest. To receive serious consideration, a rack should be at least as high above the deer's head as the chest is deep (20 inches), and most record-class mule deer antlers, Cupell says, measure 22 to 24 inches high. In other words, antler height exceeds depth of the chest.

Tines: Given adequate spread and main-beam length, the next major consideration is number and length of tines. Typical configuration for mule deer is four even points to the side plus brow tines, or a total of five points to the side. Only seven out of 311 bucks listed in a recent *Records of North American Big Game* are even 4 × 4 bucks (4 points on each side). Many are 5 × 5, and many have more points than that, which indicates the presence of abnormal points. That shows the importance of brow tines in overall score.

Given the required number, tines must be long. The middle points must be 10 to 12 inches long, and the back tine (listed as G-2 on the score chart) generally

The average tip-to-tip ear spread (left) for mule deer is about 20 inches. If the inside curve of the main beam extends 2 to 3 inches beyond the ears on each side, you know the buck has an inside spread of 25 inches or more. If (right-hand drawing) the main beams on a mule deer's antlers sweep forward to a line drawn vertically from the tip of the buck's nose, the antlers may be of record class.

Generally, mule deer racks can be classified as box shaped (left) or basket shaped (right). For a given width and height, box-shaped racks often will score a bit higher than basket racks because the main beams and tines will be longer.

is 18 inches or longer. Here again, given equal height and spread, a box-shaped rack generally scores better than a basket rack because the tines are longer.

Blacktails. Principles used to judge mule deer apply to blacktails, although the dimensions are smaller. Tip-to-tip ear spread of a mature blacktail buck is about 17 inches, and the ears measure 6½ to 7 inches long. Length from the tip of the nose to the antler base is 8⅛ to 9 inches.

For blacktails, very few record-book bucks have an inside spread less than 16 inches; so as a rule of thumb, the antlers must be at least as wide as the ears to assure adequate width. Main-beam length generally must exceed 20 inches. Just as with mule deer, blacktails must have four typical points to the side, plus brow tines. Boyd Iverson, a veteran blacktail hunter, has found that on blacktails, either the front fork or the back fork is typically weak; so you must look carefully to be sure both forks on each side are deep and long. Individual tines on the main forks should be 7 to 8 inches long, and brow tines must be 2 to 3 inches long.

HOW TO LOCATE TROPHY BUCKS

For this discussion *trophy buck* is defined as an animal that qualifies for the Boone and Crockett or the Pope and Young record book.

Regardless of where you hunt, there is no guarantee you will have a chance to kill a record buck. According to figures compiled from states and provinces, hunters kill roughly 2.5 million whitetails in the United States and Canada each year. Some records experts estimate that only 1 in 70,000 whitetail bucks killed would qualify for the record book.

However, some areas produce a disproportionate number of large animals, so the odds may be much better in them. Your challenge as a trophy hunter is to locate those regions.

Research sources. Surprisingly, guides and outfitters may not be a good route to a record-book buck. Guides must maintain a reputation for success, and if they held out specifically for record bucks, their clients would rarely kill any deer. In addition, many areas with good trophy potential have few if any guides, and in heavily guided regions, most outfitters are stuck with one small area, which may not be producing big bucks at the moment. With a reputable guide, your chances of taking a respectable buck are good, but killing a record-book deer, for the most part, is a do-it-yourself project.

The Boone and Crockett book *Records of North American Big Game* serves as the primary reference for trophy research because it helps pinpoint areas that produce the very largest animals. Most good deer areas produce bucks large enough to meet minimum Pope and Young scores, so bowhunting records more accurately portray distribution of archers than areas capable of growing huge bucks. In the discussion below, the "record book" will mean the Boone and Crockett book.

The record books are only a starting point and must be supplemented. Hunting statistics and big-game surveys from wildlife agencies and big-game biologists, as well as hunting regulations, hunter information services, maps, and other sources can lead you to a big buck.

Finding a region. Record books reveal one important point—some regions produce many book heads, and others produce virtually none. So location may play the biggest part in trophy hunting. Given some luck, a novice in a good spot can kill a Boone and Crockett buck, but a skilled hunter will surely fail in a place with no big bucks.

Heredity: The most fundamental quality is heredity. If a deer herd doesn't contain the genes to produce big antlers, then age, good feed, minerals and other necessities don't mean much. Through record-book study, you can identify areas where bucks have the tendency to grow big antlers. Above right is a rough breakdown of the top states and the percentage of Boone and Crockett animals taken there.

Many other states and provinces have scattered list-

RECORD-BOOK HEADS

Whitetails	Percent
Saskatchewan	12
Wisconsin	9
Texas	8
Minnesota	8
Nebraska	5
Montana	5
Ohio	5
Missouri	4
Iowa	4
Kansas	3
Washington	3
Mule Deer	
Colorado	36
Idaho	12
Utah	9
New Mexico	9
Arizona	8
Wyoming	7
Montana	5
Oregon	3
Washington	2
Saskatchewan	2

ings, but the figures above reveal states that have shown the most impressive yields, from a hereditary point of view.

Of course, other factors come into play. One is the percentage of total deer harvested that will make the book. Jack and Susan Reneau, in their book *Colorado's Biggest Bucks and Bulls,* emphasize this point. For example, Utah with 51 entries ranked higher for mule deer in the 1981 record book than Arizona with 47. However, comparing these figures with total harvest for the past 30 years, the Reneaus conclude that the odds for a record-class buck are much higher in Arizona—1 in 17,048 compared to 1 in 63,657 for Utah.

In any one state, small localities normally produce the best bucks. Texas had 62 whitetails listed in a recent *Records of North American Big Game,* and more than half of those came from a cluster of counties south of San Antonio, with Webb and Dimmit counties leading the way. In Montana, Flathead County is the focal point for big whitetails, with quality radiating out from there.

In Colorado a cluster of counties—Mesa, Garfield, Eagle, Delta, and Montrose—have given up a majority of the Boone and Crockett mule deer. In Arizona the North Kaibab and the Strip—the northwest corner—have yielded every record head.

So, in record-book analysis, it's smart to try to pinpoint specific counties, national forests, and drainages that have produced the largest deer.

Current conditions: Because of changing land use, increased hunting pressure, and other influences, an area today may be falling far short of its hereditary potential.

Again, the record book serves as good background, and here the date of kill is most important. Consider these examples: Overall, Colorado has produced 36 percent of the Boone and Crockett mule deer, but since about 1970, that state has produced more than 50 percent, giving it a firmer grip on first place. Wyoming has improved its ranking from 7 percent overall to 12 percent since 1970. Utah, in contrast, has slipped from 9 percent of the total mule deer entries to less than 2 percent since 1970. In short, some states are producing a higher percentage of trophy bucks now than in the past, and others have fallen off. Thus, you would be wise to concentrate on states with improving figures.

Next to heredity, age may be the most important factor in making big bucks. In most cases bucks reach their maximum antler growth at 5½ to 6½ years. Given today's intense hunting pressure, few areas grow many bucks that old. And after 7½ years, an old buck's set of antlers tends be smaller each year.

Harvest figures can point you toward the better ones. If harvest data show that 80 percent of the bucks killed in a game management unit are yearlings, then you know that turnover is high and few animals there live more than a couple of years. On the other hand, if 60 percent are 4-point or better bucks, you know plenty of bucks reach maturity.

Not all wildlife agencies break harvest figures down that way, but most survey herds, and their buck-doe ratios can tell you a lot about the quality of bucks in a given unit. As a rule of thumb, the higher the buck-doe ratio, the better the trophy potential. In some units the buck-doe ratio may be as low as 5 bucks per 100 does, which indicates a high annual harvest. In units where permits are limited or where private land or rough terrain limit access, the ratio may be as high a 50 bucks per 100 does. Many authorities agree that a ratio of at least 30 per 100 assures the best trophy hunting. You can get such information from reports by wildlife departments or by talking to big-game biologists.

Hunting regulations: You can forecast potentially good trophy hunting by reading hunting regulations and following management trends. In particular, watch for limited hunting. In portions of some states, the firearms season may be as short as one to three days. Such limited hunting time allows sneaky bucks to live to old age, and such regions may produce trophy whitetails.

In the early 1970s, hunting in Nevada had deteriorated badly. So in 1975 the Nevada Department of Wildlife restricted the number of deer tags for the entire state. By 1980 overall hunting success exceeded 60 percent, and in many units more than half the bucks taken were 4-points or larger. Other states restrict hunting in specific units, and if these contain proven trophy genes, the chances for taking good bucks there are excellent.

Watch for units that have been closed for some time too. Much of southern Utah was closed through the early 1980s following a drastic decline in deer population. Under total protection many bucks lived to old age, and when the units were reopened, hunters reported seeing monstrous bucks. Historically, this area had produced Boone and Crockett animals so potential obviously was there.

One thing to avoid is special "trophy units." Many of these carry "4-point or better" regulations. Under that rule, you'll see lots of bucks, but because all hunting effort is directed at the biggest bucks each year, you'll see few truly exceptional deer.

Weather trends can give you clues about where, or where not, to hunt. Winter weather plays a big part in the quality of bucks. During hard winters, big bucks that have expended much of their fat reserves in the fall rutting season are among the first deer to die. So hard winters often spell bad news for trophy hunting for at least three or four years. Even if the deer don't die, bucks may grow smaller antlers than normal, because nutrients go toward restoring body condition. A wet spring and summer generally yields excellent forage and, as a result, healthy bucks with bigger-than-normal antlers.

In some ways fire can be a constructive force because it can improve ranges for deer and may help produce trophy bucks.

Severe conditions may work in reverse, too. Some South Texas hunters say the biggest bucks are taken following a dry winter, possibly because mesquite produces an unusually heavy mast crop—nutritious deer food—during dry years.

Fire generally may benefit deer range because it opens up heavy forests and destroys decadent brush to make way for more nutritious browse. Much of the California Coast Range is choked with chaparral, a poor deer food. During the 1970s, public agencies began a burning program there, and that brought about a marked increase in deer numbers and size.

Specifics of habitat quality may vary from year to year, but one principle remains constant. It is that conditions change. The same buck that would make the Boone and Crockett records on a good year might fall short when times are tough, and vice versa. Keep an eye to the weather, hunting regulations, fire, and other variables and stay flexible to hit prime regions the year you will hunt.

Fine tuning for trophies. Once you've settled on a region that is producing big bucks now, step two involves pinpointing the haunts of the biggest bucks. Well-known outdoor writer-photographer Erwin Bauer feels the exact spot—such as a small woodlot, creek bottom, swamp, or grainfield edge—that once produced a record-book buck is the place to look for another. Quoting Bauer: "I firmly believe that the same set of circumstances that yielded one big buck will produce another—maybe more. So I submit that the combination of terrain, excellent habitat, high-quality and nutritious browse, plus superior genes, has been producing bigger, healthier whitetails in that one spot than in the surrounding areas."

Although Bauer refers specifically to whitetails, the same holds for mule deer. Kirt Darner, who has killed several Boone and Crockett mule deer, has made a science of locating record-class bucks. Although he lives in the best region in North America for trophy mule deer—southwest Colorado—he still researches constantly to identify trophy localities. Anytime he hears about a big buck, whether it has been killed or just sighted, he investigates because he knows circumstances that produced one giant buck could grow another.

His method of following reports of big bucks clearly produces results. Hunting one rugged canyon near Montrose, Colorado, Darner killed a nontypical buck with a 38-inch spread that scored 273% points, placing it well up in the record book. Another year he returned to that exact spot and killed a buck with a 39-inch spread.

Remarkably, he killed those bucks on public land looking down on a paved highway. To select that spot he analyzed the country carefully. From maps he learned that land above the canyon rim was private, and landowners wouldn't let hunters in from above. To come up from the bottom—which is how Darner got there—he had to wade a river and scale some cliffs. Those impediments—along with the fact that the place seemed too obvious to be any good—ap-

A backpack hunter surveys mule deer country in the Rocky Mountains. Authorities on trophy hunting say that specific conditions in a small locality produce trophy bucks year after year. Study the region you intend to hunt to locate pockets that might grow big bucks.

Kirt Darner, shown here, has specialized in hunting trophy mule deer, and his record proves the value of diligent research. Darner here poses with some of his trophies, among which are several Boone and Crockett record-book deer.

parently discouraged other hunters, and Darner had it to himself. Lack of hunting pressure undoubtedly accounted for trophy bucks there.

Not all good spots are that rough, but they all have something in common: Hunting is restricted in some way. You can get a lead on many such places by studying maps. Acquire county, public-land (such as U.S. Forest Service), and topographic maps, and study them closely. Discover pockets of land isolated by private land, dense vegetation, steep canyons, or other natural barriers, and you've probably located good trophy-buck locations.

Never overlook the most obvious research source—other people. Follow up any reports you hear of big bucks, and try to discover exactly where they came from. In particular, talk to local authorities, such as state game biologists, foresters, loggers, hunters, sport shop owners, and anyone else who might give accurate information. This will help you get a clear picture of present conditions and the precise localities of big bucks.

Other considerations. Locality may be most important, but method and timing play a role too. Most trophy hunters emphasize one point—big bucks differ from small bucks. You may be able to kill an average buck hunting during the regular season, but for a wizened old-timer, you have to do everything possible to give yourself an advantage.

Timing: Many states offer special early-season hunts, and these can benefit mule deer hunters in particular. In August and September, many bucks live above the timberline where they're most visible. If one of these

Choose hunting methods geared to take advantage of the weaknesses of older bucks. For mule deer, use a binocular to spot bucks from a distance.

early hunts takes place in a proven trophy region, check it out.

At the opposite end, some hunts take place in late November and December when deer concentrate on relatively small winter ranges. That's when they're easiest to find and see, so never overlook the potential of a late hunt.

Finally, watch for hunts during the rut. Most hunters know that bucks, and in particular old bucks, are most active during the breeding season and lose some of their natural caution. Also, during the rut whitetail bucks will respond to antler rattling, which gives you an added edge.

Don't shun primitive weapons hunts. Many muzzleloader and archery seasons take place in early fall before general rifle seasons, in late fall on winter ranges, and during the rut. The advantages of timing often outweigh the limitations of the weapons, and some of the biggest bucks each year fall to bow and muzzleloader hunters.

Hunting Methods: Regardless of when you hunt, choose hunting methods geared to trophy hunting. Most proficient trophy hunters agree that big bucks act differently from small bucks, and that you must hunt accordingly.

For mule deer concentrate on methods that emphasize spotting from long distances. Young bucks running from hunters often bound into the open, but old mule deer bucks tend to sneak, and they'll slip away undetected from moving hunters. By observing from a distance with a good binocular or spotting scope, you can locate an old buck without alerting him and plan a sound strategy.

For whitetails and blacktails that live in dense country, tree stands have revolutionized trophy hunting. Dave Boland, a Minnesota trophy hunter and measurer for Boone and Crockett, says far fewer big bucks would be killed if hunters could not use tree stands. He believes that holds for gun as well as bow hunters.

Boyd Iverson, an Oregon hunter who has taken several record-class blacktails, echoes that view. "In blacktail habitat, stand hunting offers your only chance for a trophy," Iverson said. "You'll rarely see the biggest bucks if you're moving on the ground. Just as important if you're trophy hunting, you must have time to judge the size of a rack. Hunting on foot, you may catch only a glimpse, but from a stand you have time to judge trophy quality."

TROPHY MEASURING AND SUBMISSION

At first the scoring system for deer may seem complicated, but once you've measured a few antlers,

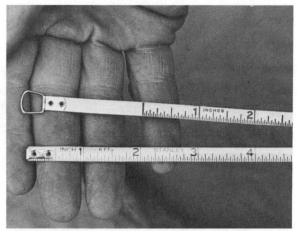

The only tool you need for measuring deer antlers is a ¼-inch-wide steel tape measure. You can do the complete job with a hook-end tape, shown on the bottom here, but the measuring of circumferences is easier if you use a ring-end tape.

you'll find it straightforward and simple. The only equipment needed is a quarter-inch-wide steel tape measure. One tape with a hook on the end is adequate, but a tape with a ring on the end helps in making circumference measurements. In addition, you need a copy of the appropriate scoring chart (you can photocopy the appropriate chart shown later in this section). It also helps if someone else holds the antlers and writes down scores as you measure. (Charts begin on the next page.)

Measuring a trophy. Steps for measuring a rack are outlined on the scoring charts. Since differences in technique can yield substantial variations in score, it's important to conform to standard methods. Official Boone and Crockett measurer Elvin Hawkins offered many of the following suggestions.

Before starting, it is worthwhile to note a couple of points about the scoring system. It's all right to "green-score" a trophy for your own satisfaction, but for official recognition, the antlers must dry for at least 60 days. Also, notice that all fractions are measured to the nearest ⅛ inch, and to simplify addition, these fractions are recorded in ⅛-inch increments. They are not reduced to the lowest common denominator. So ½ inch and ¾ inch would be recorded as ⁴⁄₈ and ⁶⁄₈ respectively.

Noncounting measurements: You first count the points. A point is defined as a projection at least 1 inch long. However, it must also be longer than the width of its base. In other words if a projection measures 1½ inches long, but it's 2 inches wide at the base, it's not counted as a point. Record the total number of measurable points on line A of the scoring chart.

Measurement B is tip-to-tip spread. Here you simply

OFFICIAL SCORE CHARTS

Records of North American
     Big Game

BOONE AND CROCKETT CLUB

205 South Patrick Street
Alexandria, Virginia 22314

Minimum Score:
    whitetail 170
    Coues'   110

TYPICAL
WHITETAIL AND COUES' DEER

Kind of Deer _____

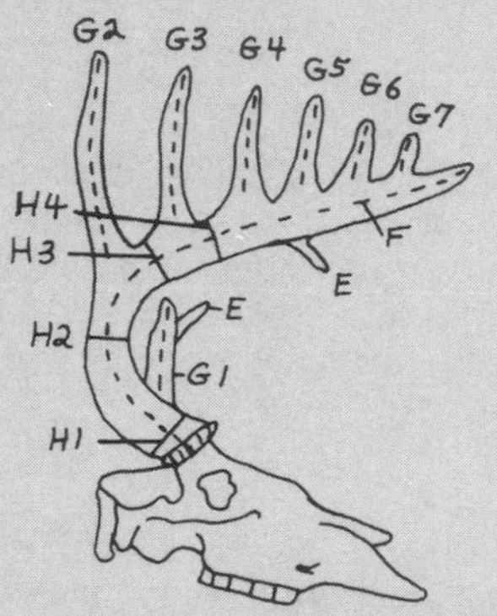

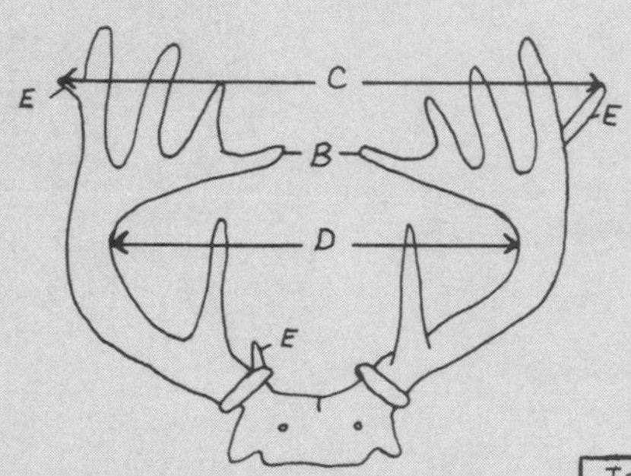

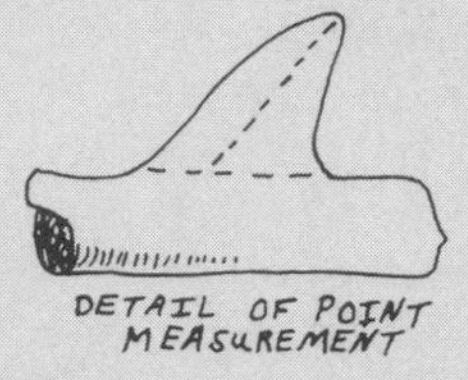

DETAIL OF POINT
MEASUREMENT

Abnormal Points	
Right	Left
Total to E	

SEE OTHER SIDE FOR INSTRUCTIONS		R.	L.	Column 1 Spread Credit	Column 2 Right Antler	Column 3 Left Antler	Column 4 Difference
A.	Number of Points on Each Antler						
B.	Tip to Tip Spread						
C.	Greatest Spread						
D.	Inside Spread of Main Beams — Credit may equal but not exceed length of longer antler						
IF Spread exceeds longer antler, enter difference.							
E.	Total of Lengths of all Abnormal Points						
F.	Length of Main Beam						
G-1.	Length of First Point, if present						
G-2.	Length of Second Point						
G-3.	Length of Third Point						
G-4.	Length of Fourth Point, if present						
G-5.	Length of Fifth Point, if present						
G-6.	Length of Sixth Point, if present						
G-7.	Length of Seventh Point, if present						
H-1.	Circumference at Smallest Place Between Burr and First Point						
H-2.	Circumference at Smallest Place Between First and Second Points						
H-3.	Circumference at Smallest Place Between Second and Third Points						
H-4.	Circumference at Smallest Place between Third and Fourth Points (see back if G-4 is missing)						
	TOTALS						

ADD	Column 1		Exact locality where killed
	Column 2		Date killed By whom killed
	Column 3		Present owner
	Total		Address
SUBTRACT Column 4			Guide's Name and Address
FINAL SCORE			Remarks: (Mention any abnormalities or unique qualities)

Use this and upcoming official scoring charts for measuring trophies for Boone and Crockett recognition. Similar charts are used by Pope and Young. Four charts are needed for measuring all deer species: typical whitetail, nontypical whitetail, typical mule deer, nontypical mule deer. The whitetail chart is used to score the Coues deer (a whitetail subspecies of the U.S. Southwest.) And the typical mule-deer chart is used for blacktails and Sitka deer.

I certify that I have measured the above trophy on _____ 19____
at (address) _____ City _____ State _____
and that these measurements and data are, to the best of my knowledge and belief, made in accordance with the instructions given.

Witness: _____ Signature: _____
OFFICIAL MEASURER

INSTRUCTIONS FOR MEASURING WHITETAIL AND COUES' DEER

All measurements must be made with a ¼-inch flexible steel tape to the nearest one-eighth of an inch. Wherever it is necessary to change direction of measurement, mark a control point and swing tape at this point. Enter fractional figures in eighths, without reduction. Official measurements cannot be taken for at least sixty days after the animal was killed.

A. Number of Points on Each Antler. To be counted a point, a projection must be at least one inch long and its length must exceed the width of its base. All points are measured from tip of point to nearest edge of beam as illustrated. Beam tip is counted as a point but not measured as a point.

B. Tip to Tip Spread is measured between tips of main beams.

C. Greatest Spread is measured between perpendiculars at a right angle to the center line of the skull at widest part whether across main beams or points.

D. Inside Spread of Main Beams is measured at a right angle to the center line of the skull at widest point between main beams. Enter this measurement again in Spread Credit column if it is less than or equal to the length of longer antler; if longer, enter longer antler length for Spread Credit.

E. Total of lengths of all Abnormal Points. Abnormal points are those nontypical in location (points originating from points or from sides or bottom of main beam) or extra points beyond the normal pattern of up to eight normal points, including beam tip, per antler. Measure in usual manner and enter in appropriate blanks.

F. Length of Main Beam is measured from lowest outside edge of burr over outer curve to the most distant point of what is, or appears to be, the main beam. The point of beginning is that point on the burr where the center line along the outer curve of the beam intersects the burr, then following generally the line of the illustration.

G-1-2-3-4-5-6-7. Length of Normal Points. Normal points project from the top of the main beam. They are measured from nearest edge of main beam over outer curve to tip. Lay the tape along the outer curve of the beam so that the top edge of the tape coincides with the top edge of the beam on both sides of the point to determine baseline for point measurements. Record point lengths in appropriate blanks.

H-1-2-3-4. Circumferences are taken as detailed for each measurement. If brow point is missing, take H-1 and H-2 at smallest place between burr and G-2. If G-4 is missing, take H-4 halfway between G-3 and tip of main beam.

* * * * * * * * * * * *
FAIR CHASE STATEMENT FOR ALL HUNTER-TAKEN TROPHIES
To make use of the following methods shall be deemed as UNFAIR CHASE and unsportsmanlike, and any trophy obtained by use of such means is disqualified from entry for Awards.
I. Spotting or herding game from the air, followed by landing in its vicinity for pursuit;
II. Herding or pursuing game with motor-powered vehicles;
III. Use of electronic communications for attracting, locating or observing game, or guiding the hunter to such game;
IV. Hunting game confined by artificial barriers, including escape-proof fencing; or hunting game transplanted solely for the purpose of commercial shooting.
****
I certify that the trophy scored on this chart was not taken in UNFAIR CHASE as defined above by the Boone and Crockett Club. I further certify that it was taken in full compliance with local game laws of the state, province, or territory.

Date_____ Signature of Hunter _____
(Have signature notarized by a Notary Public)

Records of North American
Big Game

OFFICIAL SCORING SYSTEM FOR NORTH AMERICAN BIG GAME TROPHIES

BOONE AND CROCKETT CLUB

205 South Patrick Street
Alexandria, Virginia 22314

NON-TYPICAL
WHITETAIL AND COUES' DEER   Kind of Deer

Minimum Score:
whitetail 195
Coues'   120

DETAIL OF POINT MEASUREMENT

SEE OTHER SIDE FOR INSTRUCTIONS			Column 1	Column 2	Column 3	Column 4
			Spread Credit	Right Antler	Left Antler	Difference
A. Number of Points on Each Antler	R.	L.				
B. Tip to Tip Spread						
C. Greatest Spread						
D. Inside Spread of Main Beams	Credit may equal but not exceed length of longer antler					
IF Spread exceeds longer antler, enter difference						
E. Total of Lengths of Abnormal Points						
F. Length of Main Beam						
G-1. Length of First Point, if present						
G-2. Length of Second Point						
G-3. Length of Third Point						
G-4. Length of Fourth Point, if present						
G-5. Length of Fifth Point, if present						
G-6. Length of Sixth Point, if present						
G-7. Length of Seventh Point, if present						
H-1. Between Burr and First Point						
H-2. Circumference at Smallest Place Between First and Second Points						
H-3. Circumference at Smallest Place Between Second and Third Points						
H-4. Circumference at Smallest Place Between Third and Fourth Points						
			Total to E			

Abnormal Points	
Right	Left

TOTALS			
ADD	Column 1		
	Column 2		
	Column 3		
	Total		
SUBTRACT Column 4			
	Result		
Add Line E Total			
FINAL SCORE			

Exact locality where killed	
Date killed	By whom killed
Present owner	
Address	
Guide's Name and Address	
Remarks: (Mention any abnormalities or unique qualities)	

I certify that I have measured the above trophy on _____ 19___

at _____ (address)   City   State

and that these measurements and data are, to the best of my knowledge and belief, made in accordance with the instructions given.

Witness: _____   Signature: _____

_____ OFFICIAL MEASURER

INSTRUCTIONS FOR MEASURING NON-TYPICAL WHITETAIL AND COUES' DEER

All measurements must be made with a ¼-inch flexible steel tape to the nearest one-eighth of an inch. Wherever it is necessary to change direction of measurement, mark a control point and swing tape at this point. Enter fractional figures in eighths, without reduction. Official measurements cannot be taken for at least sixty days after the animal was killed.

A. Number of Points on Each Antler. To be counted a point, a projection must be at least one inch long and its length must exceed the width of its base. All points are measured from tip of point to nearest edge of beam as illustrated. Beam tip is counted as a point but not measured as a point.

B. Tip to Tip Spread is measured between tips of main beams.

C. Greatest Spread is measured between perpendiculars at a right angle to the center line of the skull at widest part whether across main beams or points.

D. Inside Spread of Main Beams is measured at a right angle to the center line of the skull at widest point between main beams. Enter this measurement again in Spread Credit column if it is less than or equal to the length of longer antler; if longer, enter longer antler length for Spread Credit.

E. Total of Lengths of all Abnormal Points. Abnormal points are those nontypical in location (points originating from points or from sides or bottom of main beam) or extra points beyond the normal pattern of up to eight normal points, including beam tip, per antler. Measure in usual manner and enter in appropriate blanks.

F. Length of Main Beam is measured from lowest outside edge of burr over outer curve to the most distant point of what is, or appears to be, the main beam. The point of beginning is that point on the burr where the center line along the outer curve of the beam intersects the burr, then following generally the line of the illustration.

G-1-2-3-4-5-6-7. Length of Normal Points. Normal points project from the top of the main beam. They are measured from nearest edge of main beam over outer curve to tip. Lay the tape along the outer curve of the beam so that the top edge of the tape coincides with the beam on both sides of the point to determine baseline for point measurement. Record point lengths in appropriate blanks.

H-1-2-3-4. Circumferences are taken as detailed for each measurement. If brow point is missing, take H-1 and H-2 at smallest place between burr and G-2. If G-4 is missing, take H-4 halfway between G-3 and tip of main beam.

* * * * * * * * * *

FAIR CHASE STATEMENT FOR ALL HUNTER-TAKEN TROPHIES

To make use of the following methods shall be deemed as UNFAIR CHASE and unsportsmanlike, and any trophy obtained by use of such means is disqualified from entry for Awards.

I.   Spotting or herding game from the air, followed by landing in its vicinity for pursuit;
II.   Herding or pursuing game with motor-powered vehicles;
III. Use of electronic communications for attracting, locating or observing game, or guiding the hunter to such game;
IV.   Hunting game confined by artificial barriers, including escape-proof fencing; or hunting game transplanted solely for the purpose of commercial shooting.

* *

I certify that the trophy scored on this chart was not taken in UNFAIR CHASE as defined above by the Boone and Crockett Club. I further certify that it was taken in full compliance with local game laws of the state, province, or territory.

Date _____   Signature of Hunter _____

(Have signature notarized by a Notary Public)

OFFICIAL SCORING SYSTEM FOR NORTH AMERICAN BIG GAME TROPHIES

Records of North American Big Game

BOONE AND CROCKETT CLUB
205 South Patrick Street
Alexandria, Virginia 22314

TYPICAL
MULE AND BLACKTAIL DEER

Kind of Deer _____

Minimum Score:
mule 195
blacktail 130

DETAIL OF POINT MEASUREMENT

	Abnormal Points	
	Right	Left

SEE OTHER SIDE FOR INSTRUCTIONS	Column 1 Spread Credit	Column 2 Right Antler	Column 3 Left Antler	Column 4 Difference
A. Number of points on Each Antler R. L.				
B. Tip to Tip Spread				
C. Greatest Spread				
D. Inside Spread of Main Beams Credit may equal but not exceed length of longer antler				
IF Spread exceeds longer antler, enter difference				
E. Total of Lengths of Abnormal Points				
F. Length of Main Beam				
G-1. Length of First Point, if present				
G-2. Length of Second Point				
G-3. Length of Third Point, if present				
G-4. Length of Fourth Point, if present				
H-1. Circumference at Smallest Place Between Burr and First Point				
H-2. Circumference at Smallest Place Between First and Second Points				
H-3. Circumference at Smallest Place Between Main Beam and Third Point				
H-4. Circumference at Smallest Place Between Second and Fourth Points				
TOTALS				

	Column 1		Exact locality where killed	
ADD	Column 2		Date killed	By whom killed
	Column 3		Present Owner	
	TOTAL		Address	
SUBTRACT Column 4			Guide's Name and Address	
FINAL SCORE			Remarks: (Mention any abnormalities or unique qualities)	

Total to E

I certify that I have measured the above trophy on _____
at (address) _____ City _____ State _____ 19____
and that these measurements and data are, to the best of my knowledge and belief, made in accordance with the instructions given.

Witness: _____   Signature: _____
OFFICIAL MEASURER ☐☐☐

INSTRUCTIONS FOR MEASURING MULE AND BLACKTAIL DEER

All measurements must be made with a ¼-inch flexible steel tape to the nearest one-eighth of an inch. Wherever it is necessary to change direction of measurement, mark a control point and swing tape at this point. Enter fractional figures in eighths, without reduction. Official measurements cannot be taken for at least sixty days after the animal was killed.

A.   Number of Points on Each Antler. To be counted a point, a projection must be at least one inch long and its length must exceed the width of its base. All points are measured from tip of point to nearest edge of beam as illustrated. Beam tip is counted as a point but not measured as a point.

B.   Tip to Tip Spread is measured between tips of main beams.

C.   Greatest Spread is measured between perpendiculars at a right angle to the center line of the skull at widest part whether across main beams or points.

D.   Inside Spread of Main Beams is measured at a right angle to the center line of the skull at widest point between main beams. Enter this measurement again in Spread Credit column if it is less than or equal to the length of longer antler; if longer, enter longer antler length for Spread Credit.

E.   Total Lengths of all Abnormal Points. Abnormal points are those nontypical in location such as points originating from a point (exception: G-3 originates from G-2 in perfectly normal fashion) or from sides or bottom of main beam or any points beyond the normal pattern of five (including beam tip) per antler. Measure each abnormal point in usual manner and enter in appropriate blanks.

F.   Length of Main Beam is measured from lowest outside edge of burr over outer curve to the tip of the main beam. The point of beginning is that point on the burr where the center line along the outer curve of the beam intersects the burr, then following generally the line of the illustration.

G-1-2-3-4. Length of Normal Points. Normal points are the brow and the upper and lower forks as shown in the illustration. They are measured from nearest edge of beam over outer curve to tip. Lay the tape along the outer curve of the beam so that the top edge of the tape coincides with the top edge of the beam on both sides of the point to determine baseline for point measurement. Record point lengths in appropriate blanks.

H-1-2-3-4. Circumferences are taken as detailed for each measurement. If brow point is missing, take H-1 and H-2 at smallest place between burr and G-2. If G-3 is missing, take H-3 halfway between the base and tip of second point. If G-4 is missing, take H-4 halfway between the second point and tip of main beam.

FAIR CHASE STATEMENT FOR ALL HUNTER-TAKEN TROPHIES

To make use of the following methods shall be deemed as UNFAIR CHASE and unsportsmanlike, and any trophy obtained by use of such means is disqualified from entry for Awards.
I.   Spotting or herding game from the air, followed by landing in its vicinity for pursuit;
II.   Herding or pursuing game with motor-powered vehicles;
III. Use of electronic communications for attracting, locating or observing game, or guiding the hunter to such game;
IV.   Hunting game confined by artificial barriers, including escape-proof fencing; or hunting game transplanted solely for the purpose of commercial shooting.
****

I certify that the trophy scored on this chart was not taken in UNFAIR CHASE as defined above by the Boone and Crockett Club. I further certify that it was taken in full compliance with local game laws of the state, province, or territory.
Date _____   Signature of Hunter _____
(Have signature notarized by a Notary Public)

Copyright © 1981 by Boone and Crockett Club
(Reproduction strictly forbidden without express written consent)

Records of North American Big Game

OFFICIAL SCORING SYSTEM FOR NORTH AMERICAN BIG GAME TROPHIES

BOONE AND CROCKETT CLUB

205 South Patrick Street
Alexandria, Virginia 22314

NON-TYPICAL MULE DEER

Minimum Score: 240

DETAIL OF POINT MEASUREMENT

SEE OTHER SIDE FOR INSTRUCTIONS		Column 1	Column 2	Column 3	Column 4	Abnormal Points	
		Spread Credit	Right Antler	Left Antler	Difference	Right	Left
A.	Number of Points on Each Antler	R.	L.				
B.	Tip to Tip Spread						
C.	Greatest Spread						
D.	Inside Spread of Main Beams	Credit may equal but not exceed length of longer antler					
	IF Spread exceeds longer antler, enter difference						
E.	Total of Lengths of Abnormal Points						
F.	Length of Main Beams						
G-1.	Length of First Point, if present						
G-2.	Length of Second Point						
G-3.	Length of Third Point, if present						
G-4.	Length of Fourth Point, if present						
H-1.	Circumference at Smallest Place Between Burr and First Point						
H-2.	Circumference at Smallest Place Between First and Second Points						
H-3.	Circumference at Smallest Place Between Main Beam and Third Point						
H-4.	Circumference at Smallest Place Between Second and Fourth Points						
	TOTALS						

		Column 1		Exact locality where killed	
ADD	Column 2			Date killed	By whom killed
	Column 3			Present Owner	
	TOTAL			Address	
SUBTRACT Column 4				Guide's Name and Address	
Add Line E Total	Result				
FINAL SCORE				Remarks: (Mention any abnormalities or unique qualities)	

I certify that I have measured the above trophy on _____ 19___

at (address) _____ City _____ State _____

and that these measurements and data are, to the best of my knowledge and belief, made in accordance with the instructions given.

Witness: _____ Signature: _____ OFFICIAL MEASURER

INSTRUCTIONS FOR MEASURING NON-TYPICAL MULE DEER

All measurements must be made with a ¼-inch flexible steel tape to the nearest one-eighth of an inch. Wherever it is necessary to change direction of measurement, mark a control point and swing tape at this point. Enter fractional figures in eighths, without reduction. Official measurements cannot be taken for at least sixty days after the animal was killed.

A. Number of Points on Each Antler. To be counted a point, a projection must be at least one inch long and its length must exceed the width of its base. All points are measured from tip of point to nearest edge of beam as illustrated. Beam tip is counted as a point but not measured as a point.

B. Tip to Tip Spread is measured between tips of main beams.

C. Greatest Spread is measured between perpendiculars at a right angle to the center line of the skull at widest part whether across main beams or points.

D. Inside Spread of Main Beams is measured at a right angle to the center line of the skull at widest point between main beams. Enter this measurement again in Spread Credit column if it is less than or equal to the length of longer antler; if longer, enter longer antler length for Spread Credit.

E. Total of Lengths of all Abnormal Points. Abnormal points are those nontypical in location or points beyond the normal pattern of five (including beam tip) per antler. Mark the points that are normal, as defined below. All other points are considered abnormal and are entered in appropriate blanks, after measurement in usual manner.

F. Length of Main Beam is measured from lowest outside edge of burr over outer curve to the tip of the main beam. The point of beginning is that point on the burr where the center line along the outer curve of the beam intersects the burr, then following generally the line of the illustration.

G-1-2-3-4. Length of Normal Points. Normal points are the brow and the upper and lower forks, as shown in the illustration. They are measured from nearest edge of beam over outer curve to tip. Lay the tape along the outer curve of the beam so that the top edge of the tape coincides with the top edge of the beam on both sides of the point to determine baseline for point measurement. Record point lengths in appropriate blanks.

H-1-2-3-4. Circumferences are taken as detailed for each measurement. If brow point is missing, take H-1 and H-2 at smallest place between burr and G-2. If G-3 is missing, take H-3 halfway between the base and tip of second point. If G-4 is missing, take H-4 halfway between the second point and tip of main beam.

* * * * * * * * * * * *

FAIR CHASE STATEMENT FOR ALL HUNTER-TAKEN TROPHIES

To make use of the following methods shall be deemed as UNFAIR CHASE and unsportsmanlike and any trophy obtained by use of such means is disqualified from entry for Awards.

I. Spotting or herding game from the air, followed by landing in its vicinity for pursuit;
II. Herding or pursuing game with motor-powered vehicles;
III. Use of electronic communications for attracting, locating or observing game, or guiding the hunter to such game;
IV. Hunting game confined by artificial barriers, including escape-proof fencing; or hunting game transplanted solely for the purpose of commercial shooting.

* *

I certify that the trophy scored on this chart was not taken in UNFAIR CHASE as defined above by the Boone and Crockett Club. I further certify that it was taken in full compliance with local game laws of the state, province, or territory.

Date _____ Signature of Hunter _____

(Have signature notarized by a Notary Public)

measure the distance between the tips of the main beams.

Measurement C is maximum outside spread. Hold the tip of your tape on the point protruding farthest from one side and measure to the point extending farthest from the other side. This measurement must be taken at a 90-degree angle to the head, not diagonally. Measurements A, B, and C do not enter into the final score, but correct measurements are needed for accurate records.

Inside spread: Measurement D—inside spread of the main beams—is the width measurement that really counts. For this measurement, place the end of your tape on the inside of one main beam and extend it across to the other. Move the entire tape up and down along the inside curve until you've determined the widest point. Remember again, this measurement must be taken at a 90-degree angle to the skull axis. In other words don't hold the tape on an angle because you will distort the score.

Also, note the relationship of this measurement to length of the main beams. You get no credit for width greater than the length of the longer main beam. If width exceeds the longer main beam, you enter the beam length rather than the width in "Spread Credit" on line D. That may seem confusing the first time through, but it will become clear when you measure the beams (line F).

Abnormal points: Before you do that, you must record the cumulative length of all abnormal points. Again, remember a point is any projection an inch long, provided it is longer than the width of its base. (The correct method for measuring individual points, or tines, is described below.) Any point that doesn't conform to the typical pattern is considered abnormal. Score charts show the typical pattern. For mule deer, typical conformation includes four points—two branches—on each side, plus brow tines. If more than one brow tine grows on either side, you must judge which one most closely conforms to the typical pattern, and measure the others as abnormal points.

The same holds for whitetails. Normal tines must grow up directly from the main beam. Notice, however, that the score chart allows for as many as seven tines.

Main beams: Line F calls for measurement of the main beams. It's important to determine the correct starting point or the entire measurement will be wrong.

Hold the antlers so you get a direct side view. From this angle you're looking directly at the outer curve of the beam, and you should measure along this outer curve, starting at the burr (the rough base of the antler). This point should be directly in line with the deer's eye. From the score chart you can see that if you extend the dotted line on the main beam down through the skull, it will bisect the eye. Use the eye as a guide to the starting point.

To measure a main beam, catch the 0-inch mark

Elvin Hawkins, an official Boone and Crockett scorer, measures the inside spread of the main beams. To do this, place the tape end inside one beam, and then move the tape up and down until you've determined the narrowest point. Be careful to keep your tape horizontal and the imaginary centerline of the antlers vertical.

This blacktail has an even 4×4 rack (5×5 counting brow tines), but the tine Elvin Hawkins points out must be considered abnormal because it grows from an atypical position. Record the length of this and other abnormal tines on line E of the score chart.

In measuring the main beams, it's important to start at the right location. A line drawn through the eye socket and up the main beam indicates the starting place. Start your tape right where this pencil laid across the eye hits the burr (base of antler).

of your tape on the burr and extend the tape up the beam, always keeping it on the crest of the antler. Follow the natural lines on the antler as a guide. As long as the beam is straight, continue to extend your tape, but wherever the antler turns slightly, you must mark that point with a pencil and turn your tape. Let's say the first 6 inches is straight but then the antler curves. At the 6-inch mark, make a pencil line on the antler. Keeping the 6-inch mark on the tape exactly on that pencil line, turn the tape and extend it up the beam. If the antler continues to curve, then make another mark at 7 inches. Turn the tape and so forth out to the very tip of the main beam.

As long as the main beam or tine is straight, you can continue to extend your tape without turning it. But where a beam or tine curves, you must mark the spot and then turn the tape. As long as the antler curves, continue to mark 1-inch increments and move tape.

Tine measurements: Next come point measurements, listed as G-1, G-2, and so forth on the score charts. A couple of cautions are in order. First, you must determine the proper base of the tine. To do this, lay your steel tape along the beam from which the tine originates. Curve the tape around the tine you plan to measure. Make a pencil mark along the edge of the tape (see photo at right). Elvin Hawkins suggests that you visualize grinding off the tine you're going to measure; you gauge the base of the tine as if the tine didn't even exist.

Now measure from that baseline directly along the outside curve of the tine. If it curves, mark the point with a pencil and move the tape just as you did on the main beams. If an abnormal point grows out from the tine, you must run your tape around the point, taking the shorter side. In other words don't distort the tine measurement by curving your tape around the wider side of an abnormal point.

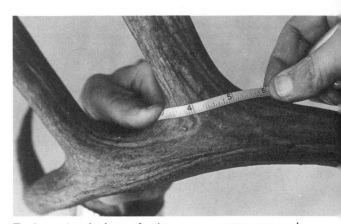

To determine the base of a tine, wrap your tape around the tine and draw a pencil mark along the bottom tape edge. Visualize the base as if the tine weren't there.

Use this same procedure to measure and record each typical point on the score chart.

Circumferences: Finally come the circumference measurements listed as H-1, H-2, and so forth on the score charts. The charts show the four locations. The major caution is to keep your tape at a 90-degree angle to the axis of the antler at that location. Here again, if you allow any diagonal angle at all, it will throw off the score. Many antlers have lots of bumps and knobs near the base, particularly between the brow tines and the burr. You simply loop your tape around them and measure over them. To get an accurate measurement, work up and down the antler until you locate the smallest circumference at each of the prescribed points.

If a tine is missing, the score chart tells how to fill out each line. For example, H-1 is taken below the brow tine and H-2 is taken above. If the brow tine is missing, which is common on mule deer, you simply measure the smallest circumference between the burr and the first major fork and record that circumference on both the H-1 and H-2 lines.

That concludes the measuring process. Now you total up each column and add these columns together. Note that Column 4 calls for the difference between

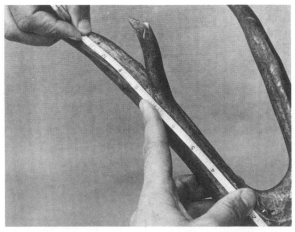

Abnormal tines sometimes grow from a main point. Taking the shorter side, measure around the abnormal tine. Keep your tape as close to the outermost curve of the main tine as possible.

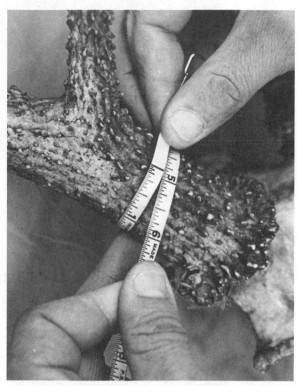

To measure the circumference, be sure to keep the tape at right angles to the antler, and work it up and down until you've found the smallest circumference. Measure right over any bumps and burrs on the antler. As shown, the ring-end tape is better for taking circumference measurements.

Columns 2 and 3. To compute these, simply subtract the smaller measurement from the greater and record the difference. For example, if one main beam measures 21 inches, and the other 19, the difference is 2 inches, so you enter a 2 in Column 4 on Line F. This amount is subtracted from the total score, which shows why symmetry is so important for a high score.

The totaling process is identical for typical and nontypical heads, except that for typicals you subtract the cumulative length of abnormal points, and for nontypicals you add it.

Obtaining an official measurement. Now that you've measured your buck's antlers and think they may qualify for the record book, you must contact an official measurer who will remeasure (record-keeping clubs won't accept your measurements). If you don't know any scorers, write to the Boone and Crockett Club or Pope and Young Club (if you're a bowhunter), and they'll send you a list of official measurers in your state.

Call the nearest one and make an appointment. Remember, most measurers are busy, and they donate their time for measuring. So don't bother them to measure green antlers that will have to be rescored later. Wait the 60 days before submitting your trophy.

If your animal qualifies for either record book, you then must sign a fair-chase affidavit and have it notarized, which verifies that you took the animal by legal means and within guidelines shown on the official entry form. You send the score chart and the affidavit to the appropriate club. Along with this package, you must submit a processing fee (the scorer can tell you how much it is) and three photos of the trophy rack—right, left, and front views.

Incidentally, any rack is eligible for entry into the Boone and Crockett book. If you come across antlers from a deer killed many years ago, or find a record-class animal dead in the field, you can still enter that rack in the book. The idea behind record books is to maintain the most complete and accurate record possible, so all entries are welcomed.

However, animals taken illegally cannot be entered. The head from an illegally killed animal may make its way into the book, but not by the person who shot it. If, for example, a state game department confiscates a record-class animal from a poacher, the game department then becomes the owner. That game department then can enter the head, and the hunter will remain anonymous and listed as "picked up" or "unknown." That way the trophy head receives recognition but the law violator does not.

The Pope and Young Club will accept heads killed years ago, but picked-up heads and illegally taken animals are not accepted. The animals must be taken by legal means with archery tackle only.

PART 10
SAFETY, SURVIVAL, AND FIRST AID

BY DWIGHT SCHUH

Photos by the author unless otherwise credited. Drawings by Lloyd Birmingham.

The many books and articles on survival attest to the popularity of the subject. But just what is survival, anyway? To some writers survival means little more than returning safely from an afternoon picnic with the family. To others it implies back-country emergencies. Still others view survival as the ability to live off the land for a year with no more basic gear for starters than a knife and no more clothing than a loin cloth.

For deer hunters survival probably falls somewhere in middle ground. Deer hunters do indeed prowl wild and threatening lands that present the potential for life-and-death predicaments, and deer hunters do die in the field each year. At the same time, modern deer hunting shows little kinship to exploring uncharted and uninhabited regions. Deer hunts should be planned occasions, and far more deer hunts take place in wood lots on the back 40 than they do in remote wilderness areas.

Survival books usually offer a great deal of information and survival lore, but much of it has little practical value for deer hunters. These books assume you'll be thrust suddenly and without prior knowledge into a remote region where your only hope lies in long-term survival skills. In that case, knowing the edible plants and knowing how to build snares may keep you alive, but few deer hunters will ever face such conditions. A person can survive for days or even weeks without food. And most lost hunters are found within a day or two of their emergency. So gathering wild edibles is not essential.

Besides, eating the wrong wild foods can be far worse than going hungry. For example, several experienced outdoorsmen were rafting Oregon's Owyhee River when they ate roots from water hemlock, apparently mistaking them for parsnips. One of them died within minutes and five others had to be airlifted to a hospital in Boise, Idaho. Lack of food is rarely, if ever, a threat to your survival. Unless you specialize in the study of edible plants, you're much better off going hungry. Starving to death should be the least of your worries.

Much writing on survival misses the mark because few hunters will ever bother to learn it. Few hunters have ever tried to start a fire with a fire bow or drill. For most deer hunters, the sole aim is to enjoy a few days or weeks in the woods each year, to hang some venison on a meat pole, and to return home safely. They won't take time to learn primitive survival skills. Such knowledge is nonessential because it will probably never be applied.

ESSENTIALS FOR HUNTING SURVIVAL

The real core of survival knowledge is prevention. Survival doesn't necessarily involve the knowledge to live through emergencies, but it does require the foresight to avoid them.

Safety knowledge—prevention—is probably the most fundamental aspect of survival. Hunting safety involves proper handling of firearms and bows, knives, and axes; accident prevention in various camping-related activities; an understanding of weather and the effects it can have on your body; and knowledge of dangerous animals. The ability to use a map and compass can be considered a safety measure too, because it can prevent your getting lost.

Safety involves gear preparation too. As a deer hunter, you're not likely to be thrust into drastic, unpredictable situations. When you go deer hunting, you have a plan in mind. You know where you'll hunt and what to expect in the way of weather, terrain, and vegetation. You can plan for the equipment you'll need ahead of time, so you have little excuse for getting caught shorthanded.

To say you'll never suffer an accident would be naive, of course. A priority in survival is to admit that you're human. You may break a leg, you may get lost, you may get stranded by heavy snows. These things

may happen. For that reason survival skills must include rescue procedures and first-aid skills.

As you mature as a hunter, you may want to go beyond the basics to master primitive survival skills. But for now, study the essentials for deer-hunting survival that are covered in the following sections. If you remember these basics, you'll return safe and sound. You'll survive.

The modern deer hunter can plan ahead and take all the gear he needs for survival. Even at that, he handles dangerous weapons and explores rugged country; so he must hunt safely and carry with him a knowledge of rescue and first aid techniques.

Statistics show that many firearms injuries occur at close range and that many of them are self-inflicted. Unload your rifle when you are in camp. Never point the muzzle at yourself or another person.

SAFETY

WEAPONS SAFETY

The North American Association of Hunter Safety Co-ordinators reports an average of more than 1,500 hunter weapons accidents each year, about 13 percent of them fatal. Compared to total hunting activity, accidents are rare, but if you're a victim, the odds don't matter. That is why hunting-arms safety plays a big part in outdoor survival.

Causes of accidents. Accident figures for a recent three-year period are in the accompanying table. An analysis of these figures reveals the major points of safety. As you can see, the first three categories, which collectively took the highest toll, involve two hunters, one the shooter and one the victim. In many cases shooters were careless, but the underlying problem is visibility. Victims were not visible to the shooters.

WEAPONS ACCIDENTS

Type of accident	Total	Percent fatal	Percent self-inflicted
Victim out of sight of shooter	684	8	—
Victim mistaken for game	674	26	—
Victim hit by shooter swinging on game	638	6	—
Shooter stumbled and fell	410	24	68
Careless gun or bow handling	323	11	69
Trigger caught on object	295	10	66
Victim moved into line of fire	207	19	—
Removing or placing firearm in vehicle	191	31	57
Unloading firearm	141	9	38
Defective firearm or bow	140	9	61
Firearm fell from rest	136	13	67
Discharged firearm in vehicle	135	22	56
Improper crossing of obstacle	125	56	69
Loading firearm	113	14	41
Ricochet	101	2	15
Horseplay with firearm	71	22	41
Fell from tree	62	32	100
Used firearm as a club	29	45	79
Other or unknown	462	11	47

You can go a long way toward preventing such accidents by making yourself more visible.

Hunter orange. Studies show that by far the most visible color under all lighting conditions is blaze (hunter) orange. Many states have mandated the use of hunter orange during big-game seasons, and results since its inception have been dramatic: In Nebraska, shooting accidents dropped by 60 percent. In Michigan the number of shooting accidents dropped from 288 in 1974 to 116 in 1980. Colorado and Arkansas reported a 50 percent reduction in accidents. Every state polled reported fewer accidents with no reduction in deer harvest.

Even in states with no clothing laws, you're wise to wear hunter orange. Mik Mikitik, a hunter-safety officer in Washington, says: "Preventing shooting accidents is the responsibility of the victim as much as the shooter. In most cases hunters shot accidentally in the woods are wearing brown or other subdued colors, and they're as much to blame for accidents as the shooters."

Careless gun handling. Judging from the three categories at the top of the table, you'd assume getting shot by a stranger at long range poses the major threat while deer hunting, but that's not true. Those cases make up only 40 percent, while other categories, which could roughly be classified as "careless weapons handling," comprise 60 percent.

True stories taken from accident reports in various states illustrate common circumstances:
- A man using his rifle as a crutch to climb a hill fell and shot himself in the head. He died instantly.
- A deer hunter blew off two fingers as he slipped his rifle into a saddle scabbard.
- When a hunter tripped over a log, his gun went off and shot his partner in the back.
- A man was unloading his rifle in camp when the gun went off and killed his hunting partner.
- As a truck bounced along a rough road, a loaded rifle lying in the bed of a truck discharged. The bullet hit the driver in the hip.
- As a man pulled his rifle from the gun rack in his truck, the trigger got caught and the gun went off. The bullet hit the man in the chest, killing him instantly.
- A hunter's pistol fell from its scabbard and shot him in the leg.
- A hunter was walking a log when bark on the log gave way and the man crashed to the ground. His rifle discharged and shot him in the leg.

Obviously, many accidents are not the result of stray bullets flying around the woods; they're the result of carelessness. Mik Mikitik said 60 percent of all injuries

This rifle is an accident waiting to happen. Surveys show that many hunters are shot because of careless gun handling like this. Support firearms so that they cannot fall.

are either self-inflicted or involve members of the same hunting party, and figures from Oregon show that nearly 75 percent take place at ranges of 10 yards or less. And the survey by the hunter safety coordinators' association shows that fully 35 percent are self-inflicted. To put that another way, most victims have no one to blame but themselves.

Rules for safe gun handling. The most obvious rule is never allow a gun to point toward any person. When loading, unloading, or cleaning your rifle, point the muzzle at the ground. When pulling the gun from a car or gun rack, remove it butt first so that it's not aimed at you (or anyone else). If you're hiking up a steep hill with rifle slung over your shoulder, watch the barrel. Otherwise, it could point directly at your hunting partner uphill from you.

Never carry a loaded gun in a vehicle. In most states it's illegal; so you should be fined for doing it. But even worse, it's dangerous. To be totally safe, unload the magazine as well as the chamber. One hunter who always kept cartridges in the magazine, "just in case," but "never" left one in the chamber, pulled the trigger on his .30/06 and blew a hole in his living room ceiling.

As you can see from the table on hunting accidents, many hunters are injured by guns that have fallen over, or that have discharged when the hunter fell. Never lean a loaded gun against an unstable rest. Unload your rifle before crossing fences, climbing cliffs, negotiating deadfalls, or moving into any situation where there is a possibility of slipping or falling. Of course, a rifle should never be used as a club or crutch.

BOWHUNTING SAFETY

A bow and arrow must be handled with great respect. The most important rule here is never hunt with an arrow nocked until you're ready to shoot. That may seem overly cautious at first. But one hunter told of stumbling and driving a broadhead deep into his thigh. Through fast action he slowed the bleeding and got to a doctor, but he could have died. Besides posing a danger to himself, a hunter swinging a nocked arrow around could easily stab a nearby partner.

Many bowhunters have been hurt by falling on their own arrows while hunting. Hunt safely, as this hunter is doing, and don't nock an arrow until you're ready to shoot.

Choose a good quiver. Probably the most frightful gadget ever invented was the unhooded bow quiver. Fortunately these have pretty well passed from the scene, but you still see some around. Avoid them like a skunk, and only use a quiver that fully encases the broadheads on your arrows.

If you use a back quiver, pad it to hold the arrows tightly. An accident in Colorado illustrates the reason for this. A bowhunter who used only a long bow and leather back quiver killed an elk deep in the backcountry; so he hired an outfitter to pack the animal. On the way out, the riders had to jump a log with their horses. When the bowhunter went over, his saddle slipped sideways. As he fell, the arrows dropped from his back quiver and hit the ground with broadheads pointing up. He landed directly on his arrows and died a few hours later.

Check your arrows. One hunter shot a couple of aluminum arrows into a target, and inadvertently creased one arrow by hitting it with another. When

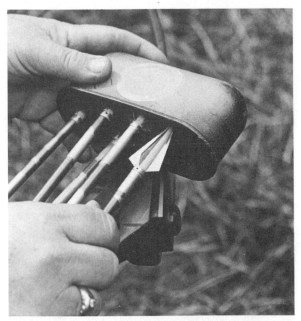

In bowhunting use a hooded quiver that completely covers the broadheads, and make sure your quiver holds the arrows securely so they can't fall out at any time while you're hunting.

he went to shoot the creased arrow, it broke and drove through his thumb to produce a gruesome wound. So for safety's sake discard badly creased arrows, and always check for and discard cracked wooden and glass arrows.

Make sure of your target. It would seem impossible for hunters to shoot each other with a close-range weapon such as a bow and arrow, but accidents aren't uncommon. Definitely one of the most dangerous practices in bowhunting is trying to "surround" an animal. It simply puts you in position to shoot your partner—or to have him shoot you.

In one case two brothers were elk hunting. When they saw a bull elk, they split up to work the animal from different directions. The elk finally came within range of one of them. That hunter hadn't seen his brother for three hours and had no idea where he was; so he took the shot. His arrow flew high over the elk and disappeared down a hill. When the hunter heard a scream, he ran 100 yards down the hill and found his brother with the arrow in his back. The wounded brother died shortly afterward.

Most states do not require bowhunters to wear blaze orange during archery seasons, but obviously the need

To keep both hands free for climbing and to avoid falling on your weapons, always pull your rifle (left) or bow into a tree stand with a rope. Never pull up a loaded rifle with a rope. Unload it first. Many hunters have died by falling from tree stands. If your stand doesn't have a railing, always use a safety belt (shown right) to prevent falls.

for visible clothing exists. Take the case of a bow-hunter who had removed his shirt to cool off on a warm day. Another archer, who mistook the man's tanned skin for the hide of a big-game animal, sent an arrow through his chest.

TREE-STAND SAFETY

One category—"fell from tree"—mentioned in the hunter safety coordinators' association survey deserves special attention. One-hundred percent of these were self-inflicted, and 32 percent were fatal.

Before using any tree stand, check screws, bolts, and other structural points. Make sure steps leading up to the tree stand are securely fastened. To keep both hands free for climbing and to prevent falling on your rifle or bow, pull the weapon up on a rope after you're securely in your stand (obviously, your rifle should not be loaded). Build permanent blinds with a rail to prevent falls, and with portable blinds, always use a safety strap to keep you from falling.

KNIFE SAFETY

One hunter had begun gutting a deer when he noticed blood pouring down his wrist. Even though he felt no pain, he could see he'd slit his wrist to the bone. Blood was spurting everywhere. He jammed his thumb into the cut and ran to a nearby farmhouse, and from there he was rushed to a hospital. He lived, but if he hadn't noticed the blood quickly and found help close by, he might not have been so lucky.

Kirt Darner, in his book *How to Find Giant Bucks,* tells of a similar experience. Hunting remote country, he was cutting the leg tendons on a buck when his knife slipped and cut completely through his hand between the thumb and index finger. Blood spewed out both sides. He wrapped it with a hanky and staggered to a sheepherder's camp, his legs wobbly and his eyes burning. As the herder took him to town, Darner passed out and didn't wake up until the following morning. He spent three days in the hospital getting blood transfusions.

Another Colorado hunter wasn't so lucky. He'd killed a cow elk and apparently was pulling the knife toward himself to split the brisket. The knife slipped and stabbed deeply into the man's thigh, cutting the femoral artery. The man was later found dead, lying on top of the elk.

Gunshot, arrow, and knife wounds should be treated in the same manner as other major injuries. See the first aid section later for details.

Serious knife wounds are not uncommon among deer hunters. Gutting and skinning may present the most dangerous moments. Use caution as you work inside an animal, and cut away from yourself as you skin and slice tendons.

SAFETY AROUND CAMP

Axes and hatchets. Axes and hatchets should be handled with as much care as a hunting knife. In using an ax or hatchet, always swing it straight down toward a chopping block, not in a circular motion toward yourself. One hunter ignored this point while splitting wood, and when he missed the wood, he split his leg instead. Fortunately he didn't hit a main artery, but many stitches were required to close the gaping wound.

Then there was a camper who was chopping wood. His ax caught an overhead branch, and he looked up just in time to catch the ax blade with his face. He lived, but he carried a disfigured eye and deeply scarred cheek for the rest of his life. Chop in the open away from obstructions, and stay away from tents and vehicles near which other people will be walking. One other point should go without saying: Never leave a double-bit ax stuck in a chopping block. Someone might fall on it; so put it in a sheath.

Fire. A group of hunters was camped in a travel trailer when apparently a gas line to the stove began leaking. During the night, the trailer filled with gas, which finally exploded. None of the hunters died, but they bear some terrible burn scars. Another hunter was burned severely when a wood stove set his canvas wall tent on fire.

If you use gas appliances, keep a close eye on all

Synthetics, such as the nylon in this backpack tent, can burn almost explosively. Never cook inside a tent. Put your stove outside on bare ground.

Gas appliances need watching. Regularly check fittings, pipes, and hoses for leaks. Hunters have been burned badly when gas stoves and lanterns exploded.

fittings and pipes. In tent camping make sure wood stoves are sound, and in particular inspect and replace fittings where the stovepipe exits the tent. Nylon and other synthetics burn like tinder; when using back-packing tents and other synthetic gear, build fires beyond spark-popping distance. And never operate a stove inside a nylon tent. Set it outside on the ground.

Picking a good campsite. Flat ground isn't the only criterion for a good campsite. Look overhead too. One night a man and his wife were sleeping in their tent when a strong wind came up. The wind broke loose the dead top of a tree and sent it crashing onto the tent, killing the man.

Dead limbs have deservedly earned the name "wid-ow maker." Look around before you set up camp, and stay away from snags or trees with dead limbs. Along the same line, avoid hunting during heavy winds, es-pecially in forests with lodgepole pine or abundant dead timber.

Flat ground may seem like the most important part of locating a campsite, but look overhead too. Never camp under snags or trees with big dead limbs. A falling limb can go through a canvas tent like a dagger.

Thinking safety. In all hunting, safety comes from common sense. Data from the National Center for Health Statistics show that in a recent year alone, 155 Americans died by falling off cliffs. In many regions, cliffs and deer hunting go together, and even in flat country, one slip off a rock or log may result in a broken leg. Carelessness, especially if you're alone, may result in tragedy. You face alternatives in all hunting—whether to climb a cliff or go around, to walk a log or step over it—and your survival rests on the wisdom of your choices.

WEATHER

Without question, weather is the most discussed topic in America, and it's probably the most overwritten survival subject. Books on outdoor survival usually list numerous cliches about predicting weather: *Red sky in morning, sailors take warning, red sky at night, sailors delight; smoke rising from a campfire means fair weather, but smoke drifting low to the ground means a coming storm; dew on the grass indicates clear skies and fair weather.* These principles have some scientific basis, but most meteorologists wouldn't stake their lives on such signs.

The same can be said for clouds and wind direction. Certain clouds generally attend given weather conditions, but the average hunter would only be guessing if he tried to make extended predictions from them. In general, the wind preceding a storm system in North America blows from the south or southwest, but that's not always true. Nor is it always true that a shifting wind or an east wind foretells storms.

Jim Campbell, a meteorologist with the severe weather branch of the National Weather Service, says: "Wind direction and the direction of shift depend on the source of a storm front, and a person in the field has no way of knowing that; so you can't make any accurate predictions based on wind direction. That's particularly true in the mountains where terrain and elevation affect the weather in unusual ways.

"Trained meteorologists with their computers and satellites can't predict weather accurately; so it's not likely the average outdoorsmen can, just by looking at signs in the field. In some cases, it's almost more dangerous to try to second guess what's going on than to just play it safe."

Observing weather signs in the field may enhance your experience, but don't bet your life on them. To be safe, understand the general nature of weather in a given locale and prepare for the worst.

SUMMER WEATHER

Perhaps the most dangerous type of summer weather is the thunderstorm. In simple terms, these storms are products of local weather conditions where rising hot air meets cool, high-altitude air. The result is huge white thunderheads. These massive cloud columns often begin to pile up about noon. A couple of hours later the sky blackens and the wind whips violently, and then comes the lightning and thunder.

Thunderstorms can occur anywhere in North America during the summer, but they're particularly violent and frequent in the high mountains. You can just about count on intimidating storms every afternoon at high elevations, such as in the Colorado Rockies. They're frequent in the Southwestern deserts, the Plains States, and the Southeast too. Anyone hunting early seasons in August and September must understand the dangers of these storms.

Lightning. Because thunderstorms build gradually before your eyes, dealing with them isn't so much a matter of predicting them as reacting wisely when they do occur. The major threat comes from lightning.

Make no mistake—lightning can kill you. The National Center for Health Statistics says that lightning kills about 125 people each year and injures another 500. A biologist surveying big game by helicopter in Colorado witnessed the devastating power of lightning when he noticed some animals lying on a grassy slope above timberline. He had the pilot set down and they found 17 dead elk scattered about. They'd all been electrocuted by lightning.

Lightning is a very powerful charge of electricity. As a thunderstorm travels over the earth, a negative electrical charge in the cloud induces a positive charge in the earth, a charge that follows the cloud like a shadow. It grows stronger as the negative cloud charge increases, and it flows up into high points, such as trees, buildings, and poles, trying to reach the cloud. Air resistance prevents the flow of electricity until the charges develop such power—as much as 100 million volts—that they're able to overcome the resistance and flow together. Then the result is a lightning bolt. The lightning bolt rapidly heats surrounding air, and the violent expansion of the heated air creates thunder.

Seek shelter before a storm hits. To gauge the distance of a storm, watch for lightning and then start counting the seconds until you hear thunder. Divide the number of seconds by five to get a rough mileage. If the storm starts 3 miles away (a 15-second count) and suddenly you find it's only a mile away (5-second count), you'd better move fast.

Because ground charges flow into high points, you should stay away from lone trees, high peaks, and ridges. Get in a depression or below a cliff. If you're above timberline, get downhill into the trees, but avoid tall, prominent trees. Instead, crouch under low, dense trees or brush. Stay away from water or metal objects such as fences, which are excellent conductors. They can carry an electrical charge to you from a long distance.

If you're caught in the open and feel your hair standing on end, you may be acting as a lightning rod. Instantly squat down and wrap your arms around your knees. Don't lie flat because this exposes more of your body to the wet, conductive ground. If at all possible, get to your car before a storm hits. An all-steel vehicle is about the safest place you can be,

1. *The negative charge in a thundercloud induces a strong positive charge in the ground underneath, and the positive earth charge follows the cloud like a shadow. This charge constantly climbs into high points on the ground. When the charges build up enough voltage to overcome air resistance, they flow together **(2)**, and the result is lightning.* **3.** *Take lightning seriously, and seek refuge before a lightning storm hits. In particular get off high, exposed ridges and stay away from tall trees or other prominent features.*

because it conducts electricity around you into the ground. The rule doesn't hold for vehicles with canvas tops.

First aid for a person struck by lightning primarily involves mouth-to-mouth respiration to restore breathing, and inspection and treatment for burns (see the First Aid section).

Summer storms also present the potential for chilling. When you're caught in a thunderstorm, chances are you'll get soaked, and wind from the storm could supercool you in minutes. Even in summer, beware of hypothermia and prepare accordingly. Exposure problems are covered on upcoming pages.

Flash floods. Flash floods also pose a serious threat, particularly in the Southwest and prairies where thunderstorms are common and runoff-slowing vegetation is scarce. Many heavy summer storms release as much as 4 inches or more of rain in a few hours. In 1970 thunderstorms dumped more than 11 inches of rain on parts of Arizona within 24 hours, and ensuing flash floods swept away trees, huge boulders, cars and buildings. Twenty-three people died. In 1972 thunderstorms over South Dakota's Black Hills produced flash floods that killed 230 in the Rapid City area.

To prevent disaster from flash floods, never set up camp in a dry streambed, arroyo, or other low spot that will channel runoff from higher ground. Remember, too, that just because rain isn't falling at your location doesn't mean you won't get hit by floods. A storm several miles upstream could send a gully washer your way. Especially during any thunderstorm activity, beware of flash floods.

During a flash flood, never try to drive or wade across stream bottoms awash with flood waters. In Arizona signs along many paved highways warn against driving through flooded dips. All too frequently motorists ignore these warnings, and in some cases they have been drowned.

Flash foods pose another summer weather danger. Notice the wall created by water that has flushed down this dry wash. Never camp in creek bottoms, and during thunderstorm activity, stay on ground above flood areas.

Heat. In general, heat isn't a problem during deer seasons, but during early seasons, there is a potential for heat-related problems. In hot weather, rest to avoid overheating and drink plenty of liquids to prevent dehydration. The effects of heat on the body are discussed fully in the upcoming section on physiological injuries.

WINTER WEATHER

In contrast to summer storms that develop locally, winter storms—beginning roughly in late September and continuing until spring—develop over the oceans and in Arctic regions, and sweep over mainland North America as huge weather fronts. These storms can move rapidly, and a bright beautiful morning can quickly give way to a drizzling, dank afternoon. That's why signs such as dew on the grass are far from foolproof. Winter storms can change the prognosis in a matter of hours—or less.

Early in the fall, winter storms generally bring rain ranging anywhere from a drizzle to a deluge, and later they'll bring snow, occasionally in the form of blizzards. And, of course, low temperatures and high winds are also part of winter weather.

In contrast to the acute, violent nature of summer storms, winter storms are chronic and determined, often lasting for hours or days. The danger here is not so sudden as being struck by a bolt of lightning. Instead it is being soaked for days by interminable rain, becoming bogged down in roads that have turned into muddy quagmires, or being stranded by deep snows.

Winter storms travel long distances from oceans and Arctic regions. In this satellite photo, you can see a large storm front sweeping in from the Pacific Ocean to the coast of Oregon and California. (NOAA photo)

Winter storms can wear you down with chronic fog, snow, and cold. The primary defense is to prepare ahead of time for the worst possible conditions.

Forecast dangerous weather. If you're traveling from home to the mountains to hunt, listen for warnings of threatening weather conditions. Postponing a hunt doesn't appeal to anyone, but it beats forging ahead with bullheaded determination and getting stranded in a blizzard.

The most reliable weather predictions come from the National Weather Service. Most large towns have weather offices where you can get immediate forecasts. Of course, you can get some form of weather news over radio or television, although most meteorologists warn that popular weather reports can be inaccurate.

A network of very high frequency (VHF) radio weather stations provides the most accurate weather information. Nearly 400 stations now operate across the U.S. to reach an estimated 90 percent of the American population. You can get a complete list of stations at your local weather service office, or by writing to: National Weather Service, Attn: W/OM 15 × 2, National Oceanic and Atmospheric Administration, Silver Spring, MD 20910. Or you can buy a battery-powered VHF weather radio from most radio and stereo shops for the price of a couple of boxes of rifle ammo.

Professional weather forecasters use standard terms to indicate specific weather conditions, and you should know them. You can get a complete list from the National Weather Service, but they include the following:

- Winter storm watch—severe winter weather may hit your area.
- Winter storm warning—severe conditions are imminent.
- Heavy snow warning—expect at least 4 inches of snow in 12 hours.
- Blizzard warning—heavy snow and 35 mph winds for several hours.
- Severe blizzard warning—heavy snow, 45 mph wind, and temperatures of 10° Fahrenheit or lower for several hours.

Preparing for winter weather. Even in hunting camp, you're wise to listen for such warnings. But you may be camped where you can't pick up a station, and it may be too late to get out once you've heard a warning. So defense against winter weather consists of preparation.

For any fall and winter hunting, expect terrible weather that could leave you stranded, and camp accordingly. Locate your camp in such a way that you can escape during bad weather. If you have to use four-wheel drive to reach camp under dry conditions, chances are you won't get out if deep snow blankets the ground.

And always prepare your gear for the worst possible conditions of rain, snow, and cold. Check tires, antifreeze, battery, spare tire, oil, and other vital components before any major trip. And carry tools and repair and safety equipment equal to the worst conditions: Bumper jack, tire chains, tow chain, jumper cables, shovel, ax, powerful flashlight, tool kit, baling wire for emergency repairs, first aid kit, spare fan belt, and emergency rations. Also carry flares for emergency signaling, available at marine-supply stores.

Your camp, whether it consists of tents, a camper, or travel trailer, must have a good stove or other heating system. Make sure you know how to set your gear up so that it's windproof. More than one hunter has had a wall tent crash down on him during a midnight windstorm. Winter preparation, of course, includes adequate clothing, discussed in Part 5 of this book.

Getting snowed in. In Wyoming and other Plains States, blizzards frequently strand motorists even on interstate highways. If you're caught in heavy snow, stay with your car and wait for help. Don't try to walk out during a blinding snowstorm and don't try to dig yourself out. Snow can pile up a lot faster than you can clear it away. The National Weather Service reports that more people die of heart attacks from overexertion during blizzards than from exposure. If you run the car engine for warmth, be careful to keep fresh air flowing through the passenger compartment. Blowing snow can seal a car air tight and suffocate you. Also, keep the exhaust system free of snow so that carbon monoxide and other exhaust gases flow freely away from the car.

If the storm is bad enough to paralyze an entire region, rescue crews will be on the prowl for your car. If that's not likely, you're still wise to wait until the storm passes to make any kind of move.

WINDCHILL FACTORS

Air Temperature (°F)	WIND SPEED (mph)								
	5	10	15	20	25	30	35	40*	
	Equivalent Chill Temperature								
40	35	30	25	20	15	10	10	10	
35	30	20	15	10	10	5	5	0	**LITTLE**
30	25	15	10	5	0	0	−5	−5	**DANGER**
25	20	10	0	0	−5	−10	−10	−15	
20	15	5	−5	−10	−15	−20	−20	−20	
15	10	0	−10	−15	−20	−25	−30	−30	**INCREASING**
10	5	−10	−20	−25	−30	−30	−35	−35	**DANGER** (flesh may
5	0	−15	−25	−30	−35	−40	−40	−45	freeze
0	−5	−20	−30	−35	−45	−50	−50	−55	within one minute)
−5	−10	−25	−40	−45	−50	−55	−60	−60	
−10	−15	−35	−45	−50	−60	−65	−65	−70	
−15	−20	−40	−50	−60	−65	−70	−75	−75	
−20	−25	−45	−60	−65	−75	−80	−80	−85	**GREAT**
−25	−30	−50	−65	−75	−80	−85	−90	−95	**DANGER** (flesh may
−30	−35	−60	−70	−80	−90	−95	−100	−100	freeze
−35	−40	−65	−80	−85	−95	−100	−105	−110	within 30 seconds)
−40	−45	−70	−85	−95	−105	−110	−115	−115	

Moving air speeds up cooling of the body through the process of conduction, and the windchill factor is designed to take this into account. You can see that a moderate 40° temperature coupled with a 30 mph wind produces the chilling equivalent of calm 10° weather.

*Winds above 40 mph have little additional effect

PHYSIOLOGICAL INJURIES

The National Center for Health Statistics reports that in a recent year, heat killed 305 people in the United States and cold killed 666. Most victims probably weren't hunters, but those statistics point out the potential for heat- and cold-related injuries.

It's easy to forget a list of symptoms and first aid measures, but if you learn the principles of body-heat regulation, you'll instinctively do the right thing when an emergency arises. The core of your body—heart, lungs, liver, and other vital organs—must remain at about 99 degrees to function properly. Your skin acts as a radiator, and blood vessels are the cooling system. In winter when freezing temperatures cool your skin, blood vessels near the skin close down to reduce circulation. This shunting process is necessary to keep the vital organs at the proper temperature. In extreme cases the body will sacrifice extremities to preserve vital organs.

In summer when too much heat becomes the problem, the process is reversed. Then blood vessels dilate to increase flow to the skin, where excess heat dissipates and prevents central-body overheating.

COOLING PROCESSES

Muscular activity generates heat much as friction does in a car engine. The greater the activity, the greater the body heat. To maintain the proper temperature, your body must preserve this generated heat in winter and get rid of it in summer. That's why it's important to understand ways in which the body cools itself.

Radiation. As blood carries heat from the core body to the skin, the heat radiates from your body much as waves radiate from a rock splash on calm water.

Evaporation. As water evaporates (that is, turns into a gas), it absorbs heat and the result is a cooling effect. Many air conditioners operate on this principle. Sweating is a natural mechanism, and cools the skin through evaporation. But whether you get wet from sweat, rain, or falling into a stream, the effects of evaporation are the same—rapid cooling.

Convection. Moving air speeds up heat loss too, and this process is called convection. Even in calm air, heat radiates from your body, but in a breeze the moving air draws off more heat from exposed skin. The stronger the wind, the faster the cooling. That's where the terms "windchill" or "chill factor" come from. As you can see from the accompanying chill-factor table, on the previous page, a 40-degree temperature combined with a 40 mile-per-hour wind yields the equivalent of a calm, 10-degree temperature.

Conduction. If you sit on snow or any other cold material, body heat passes directly from your body to the other material. Some materials, such as metal, snow, water, and hard plastics conduct heat away rapidly, whereas cloth, rubber, and wood are poor conductors (to put it another way, they're good insulators).

Respiration. This process accounts for significant loss of body heat. Each breath you inhale is warmed in your lungs, and body heat used to warm the air is expelled as you breath out. You can't do much to avoid or enhance heat exchange through respiration, except to control your rate of breathing by not overexerting yourself.

HYPOTHERMIA

Most deer hunting takes place in mid to late fall in cool weather; so without question the major temperature-related threat to deer hunters is hypothermia, or lower than normal body temperature. When the temperature of vital organs drops below the normal core 99 degrees, the result is hypothermia. It's commonly called "exposure."

Preventing hypothermia. Studies on hypothermia at the University of Victoria, British Columbia, have shown that a person in 32-degree water will die of hypothermia within about 1 ½ hours, and in 50-degree water, in about three hours,

Under milder conditions, the process may take longer, but you can suffer hypothermia even in moderate weather. Referring to the windchill chart, you can see that a 40-degree temperature combined with a 20-mile-an-hour wind produces the chill equivalent of 20 degrees. Getting wet accelerates cooling even more; so even relatively mild 40-degree air combined with the chilling forces of wind and water can cause a serious case of hypothermia.

That's why you must retard the cooling processes discussed above during any cool weather. First, stay dry. Obviously, in snow or rain, you must wear waterproof outer clothing, but it's just as important to pre-

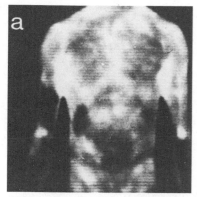 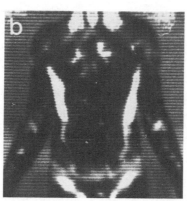 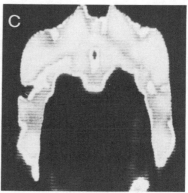

*Photo A shows a man before immersion into cold water. The gray area represents skin temperature range from 71° to 91°F., black being colder, white warmer. As you can see, skin temperature is fairly uniform throughout the upper body. **Photo B** shows the same man after immersion in cold water, where he remained still. White coloration indicates warmest skin areas, and the most critical areas to protect in cold conditions. Notice that these white surface areas with little insulating muscle and fat (neck, sides of trunk, and groin) are most critical. **Photo C** shows a man who has been swimming in cold water. Exertion has increased the critical heat-loss area. In dry conditions, exercise can generate needed body heat, and this heat can be trapped by heavy clothing. But in water, exertion brings vital body heat to the surface, and the heat is drawn off. In cold water, you can survive much longer by holding still and protecting critical heat-loss areas than by swimming.*

vent sweating. As you hike, take off heavy clothes to allow heat to escape, and wear underclothes that wick moisture from your body. Fishnet weaves, wool, and some synthetics, such as polypropylene, wick moisture from your body much more efficiently than cotton garments.

When you're less active, put on clothing before you get cold. A down or synthetic jacket traps radiated body heat and reduces heat loss through convection and conduction. Wear a windbreaker to prevent heat loss in heavy wind. Avoid sitting on wet logs, metal, snow, or other materials that will conduct heat from your body.

In particular protect critical parts of the body. Heat transfer is most rapid in thin-walled areas where blood vessels flow near the skin's surface. Dr. John S. Hayward, who conducted hypothermia studies at the University of Victoria, says:

"The arms lose heat quickly, but once they've cooled they don't lose much more heat, and areas with heavy muscles and fat, such as the lower trunk and legs, aren't critical. In severe conditions, I'd concentrate on protecting the neck, head, and chest. These are the vital areas."

In other words, wear a warm hat, scarf, and jacket or vest. If you're sitting, hold your arms in against your sides. Through regulation of clothing and activity you can maintain a comfortable and safe body temperature under most cold conditions.

Signs of hypothermia. Shivering—involuntary muscle activity to generate heat—is an initial sign of hypothermia. It doesn't, however, indicate immediate

danger. Dr. Hayward's studies show that a person soaking wet in 30-degree temperatures for several hours may outwardly seem to be freezing, but as long as they're still shivering, their core body temperature has probably not dropped more than 1 degree.

"People that cold will feel like they're dying, but it's only peripheral cooling. Severe chilling affects motor performance and probably the will to survive, but your body is still okay. After prolonged cold, we estimated a 40 percent decrease in mental performance and physical ability. That brings about strange

Since blood vessels flow close to the skin in the head and neck, these parts of the body lose heat rapidly. In cold weather wear a hat and scarf to reduce body cooling.

behavior, but it doesn't indicate a cold heart, which is life threatening.

"The average person in a hypothermic condition can hold deep body heat for several hours, but then they become exhausted and run out of the energy required to shiver and exercise. That's when deep hypothermia sets in," Dr. Hayward said. "It's hard to see shivering when a person is moving, so you must stop frequently to watch. Failure to shiver indicates exhaustion, and that's when you can quickly fall into a deep level of hypothermia."

Deep hypothermia. If you're alone and begin to shiver violently, or one of your buddies is shivering hard, don't ignore the sign. Take time to stop and warm up. Once hypothermia goes beyond a certain point, you may not be able to reverse it.

In a person exhausted by cold, core body temperature will drop steadily. As it reaches 90 degrees, shivering will cease and muscles will stiffen. The victim may become disoriented and move erratically. At 85 degrees he may become totally irrational, and when core body temperature drops to 80 degrees, he'll pass out and die.

First aid for hypothermia. The first step in treatment of hypothermia is to prevent further heat loss. Get the victim out of the wind and strip off wet clothing to, in essence, get him out of the water.

The second step depends on conditions. Once the core body has dropped below 95 degrees, the victim's body probably can't generate enough heat to rewarm itself; so an external heat source is needed. If you're within a few minutes of town, get the victim into a bathtub of 110-degree water—mildly hot to the touch. Keep his arms and legs out of the water so the central body is warmed first.

Obviously, you won't find a hot bath near most deer-hunting camps, so you'll probably have to take other steps. For a mildly hypothermic person who's shivering hard but still has his faculties, build a big fire and give him hot liquids. That may be enough.

If a person has stopped shivering, strip him and wrap him in a sleeping bag with another person inside it. The more skin-to-skin contact the better, because it will speed up rewarming. Remember that simply putting a hypothermia victim in a sleeping bag by himself will do no good because a bag doesn't generate heat; it only preserves heat, and a hypothermic person is producing very little heat.

FROSTBITE

Frostbite—the destruction of flesh through freezing—is another serious injury associated with cold weather, and the procedures outlined above for hypothermia also apply to the prevention of frostbite. Because poor circulation underlies frostbite, it's important to wear loose-fitting clothes. Wrist elastic on your windbreaker should not impair circulation to your hands. If your boots fit tightly, loosen them periodically to enhance blood flow to your feet. During rest breaks, sit on a foam pad or your pack to prevent conductive heat loss, and always wear gloves when you handle metal or other cold objects. Gasoline evaporates rapidly even in cold weather; so use it cautiously. Spilled on your hands in cold weather, gasoline can cause frostbite quickly.

Watch for early signs of frostbite. You can warm frost-nipped fingers by holding them under your armpit, and you can rewarm a frosted cheek or ear by pressing your warm hand over it.

But if you or one of your party actually has suffered frostbite, special first aid measures must be taken to prevent major tissue damage. Beware if a part of the body hurts severely and suddenly goes numb. It may be frozen. Frozen tissue normally has a white, yellow-white, or blotchy blue color and will be firm and insensitive.

First aid for frostbite. A person with frostbite should be hospitalized for two reasons. Warming frostbitten parts in the field presents the danger of refreezing, which can cause drastic tissue damage. Also, a person probably can walk out on frostbitten feet, but once those feet are rewarmed, the victim will have to be carried out. For these reasons, treatment should begin only when the patient won't have to move under his own power and where refreezing is not a possibility.

When these conditions are met, the frozen parts should be thawed quickly by immersion in water between 100 and 112 degrees F. When sensation and color return, the extremity should be removed from the water. The affected area may turn deep purple and large, clear blisters will develop. That's a good sign. Following this treatment the affected area should be held stationary in a clean environment. The primary object of aftercare is to prevent infection. New skin will replace the old within several weeks.

Some myths surround treatment of frostbite, and these can cause irreparable damage. Never treat frostbite by rubbing with ice, snow, or cold water. Thawing frostbite rapidly near intense heat or in very hot water can literally cook the flesh, and any rubbing or rough treatment can also destroy tissue cells.

HEATSTROKE

Heatstroke, or sunstroke as it is commonly called, is the flip side of the body temperature problem. In hypothermia the body fails because of low internal temperature; in heatstroke it fails because of high temperature.

Extreme air temperature, say higher than 110 degrees F., can cause heat stroke even among inactive people. That's because blood flowing near the skin is heated to air temperature (which is higher than the normal 98.6-degree body temperature), and this "hot" blood returning to the heart overheats the core body.

That situation would be rare for deer hunters, because hunting-season weather generally isn't that hot. Nevertheless, heatstroke can occur when the body produces heat faster than it can get rid of it. That's possible even in milder weather if you're exerting hard without rest.

Preventing heat stroke. If you're hiking hard or struggling to drag a deer off a mountain during warm, early seasons, it's important to rest often enough to cool off.

At the same time, do all you can to enhance the cooling processes. Wear lightweight clothing that allows heat to radiate from your body, and wear a light, protective hat that prevents the sun from overheating blood flowing to your neck and head. Allow any breeze to blow freely through your clothing to evaporate sweat. In very hot weather, sprinkle water on your skin and clothes to increase cooling through evaporation.

Above all, drink plenty of fluids. Dehydration underlies heatstroke, so drink as much water as you can to keep your cooling system—that is, your bloodstream—running smoothly.

Symptoms of heatstroke. Heatstroke can strike rapidly, particularly in a person who is out of shape. At first a victim will sweat heavily and become irritable and tired, and he may get a severe headache and feel dizzy and nauseated.

As his body temperature rises to 105 degrees, the person probably will collapse, and his skin will become hot, dry, and red. Dry skin is a sure sign of heatstroke. Once the sweating mechanism ceases, body temperature rises even more rapidly, and when it hits 108 to 110 degrees, the victim will die. This can happen in a matter of minutes; so you have no time to seek help. First aid must be given immediately.

First aid for heatstroke. You must lower body temperature quickly. If you can, immerse the victim in ice water. When that's not possible, move him into the shade, strip off his clothes, and pour water over his entire body. Fan him to increase cooling through evaporation. Keep pouring on water and fanning until his body temperature returns to normal. Then take him to a doctor.

HEAT EXHAUSTION

A hunter who sweats long hours, day after day, and who fails to replace lost liquids, may gradually suffer dehydration and resultant heat exhaustion. Prevention consists of adequate fluid intake. You can't drink enough while active to replace fluids as they're lost; so you must continue to drink during rest breaks and in the evening after the hunt.

Symptoms of heat exhaustion. Weakness and fatigue, irritability, headache, dizziness, and possibly vomiting accompany heat exhaustion. Opposed to heatstroke, in which the skin is hot, dry, and red, a victim's skin will be cool, clammy and pale, and his temperature will be normal.

First aid for heat exhaustion. A victim of heat exhaustion should be treated the same way as a shock victim (shock is covered later under First Aid). Lay him on his back in a cool place with his feet elevated 12 inches or so. Use wet cloths to keep him cool, and help him slowly drink lightly salted water. If he vomits, don't force him to drink. He should rest and stay out of the hot sun for at least a day after recovery.

A hunter can suffer heat exhaustion or heatstroke during warm early seasons, particularly in southern latitudes. If you're hunting hard, take time to rest and cool down to prevent excessive body-heat buildup.

DEHYDRATION

Dehydration underlies all body-heat injuries, because the bloodstream regulates body temperature, and thick, sluggish blood does a poor job of regulating. In hot weather the need for water is obvious. You feel thirsty. In cold weather the problem may be more subtle, but you can still become dehydrated, especially in the thin, dry air at high elevations where you lose body fluids rapidly through respiration.

Under normal conditions, you lose as much as 2 quarts of body fluid a day through sweating, urination, and respiration; so you must drink 2 quarts of liquids just to replace normal loss. During exercise you'll lose a lot more, and you must make up for the added loss. During hot weather, liquid demands may exceed a gallon each day. Diarrhea and vomiting also greatly increase your need for fluids.

Infrequent urination, or dark yellow or orange urine, are signs of dehydration. Fatigue, lethargy, and generally poor performance also accompany dehydration. If you notice these signs, drink more.

Plan for water needs. In some areas, potable water may be scarce; so carry water with you to camp. Allow at least 1 gallon a day for each hunter. For daily hunting, carry a bota bag or plastic bottle filled with water.

Beware of natural sources. Even seemingly pure waters can contain a parasite called Giardia lamblia that produces a malady called Giardiasis. Giardia are spread through the feces of mammals, and the parasite is particularly common among beavers (thus the common name "beaver fever.") Giardiasis causes acute diarrhea, stomach cramps, and vomiting that

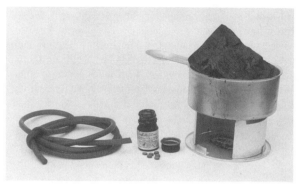

Don't be misled by the looks of water. It could be contaminated even in remote backcountry; so always go prepared to purify water in the field. You can syphon pure water directly from a spring with surgical tubing; purify water in a canteen with iodine tablets; and boil water with a small stove and cup.

With a desert still, you can collect pure water or purify contaminated water. There's a can in the hole to catch water (condensed water vapors) running down the underside of the plastic. One end of the rubber tubing at the right rests in the can, and you can suck out water through the tube.

Even in cold weather, especially at high altitudes, you can become dehydrated. Make provisions for water, and when you're pushing hard, drink regularly even if you don't feel thirsty.

can last for days. It not only causes great misery but can also produce severe dehydration, a serious problem if you're stuck for any time in the backcountry.

Many animals also spread other bacteria through their feces, and these can infect backcountry waters. Some of these bacteria can cause disorders similar to Giardiasis.

You're safest to treat all water before drinking. Boiling is the surest way to purify water. Most authorities recommend boiling for 5 minutes at sea level and adding 1 minute for every 1,000 feet of elevation. Thus, if you're at 10,000 feet elevation you should boil the water for 15 minutes.

You also can purify water chemically with iodine or chlorine. These chemicals are available in tablet form. If used according to directions on the container, they will destroy most contaminants.

In many areas springs are abundant, but they're often contaminated by livestock or wildlife. If you can tap water directly from the source, you have a better chance of getting pure water. One good way is to carry a 3-foot piece of surgical tubing. Insert one end directly into the spring and syphon water into a canteen or cup.

You also can collect water with a desert still. For this you need a 6-foot square of clear plastic, 5 feet of surgical tubing, and a can. Dig a hole about 3 feet across and 18 inches deep and put the can in the center of the hole. Place one end of the tubing in the can so that it touches the bottom and lead the other end out of the hole. Lay the plastic over the hole and anchor the edges with dirt. Then place a rock in the center of the plastic so that it stretches the plastic down until it almost touches the can. The rock should be hanging directly over the can. Make sure you seal off the edges of the plastic with dirt so that the still is air tight.

As hot sun shines onto the plastic, it evaporates moisture in the ground. This moisture condenses on the underside of the plastic and drips into the can. Suck water from the can through the tube. To increase efficiency, place moist, pulpy leaves or cacti inside the hole. You can also pour impure water into the hole. It will evaporate and run into the can as pure water. One still won't produce enough water to keep you alive in severe heat, so build several.

PROBLEMS AT HIGH ELEVATIONS

Deer hunting in the West, particularly in Colorado, can take you to elevations of 10,000 feet or more. For a person coming from sea level, the rapid change in elevation can cause problems. As mentioned above, one problem is dehydration. Even if you don't feel thirsty, drink several quarts of liquids each day.

Another altitude problem, lack of oxygen, produces high-altitude illnesses. The most common is acute mountain sickness. Anyone going from sea level to an altitude of 7,000 to 8,000 feet or higher probably will suffer symptoms. Dr. Charles S. Houston in *Going Higher,* an excellent book on all aspects of altitude, lists these symptoms: severe headache, nausea sometimes with vomiting, shortness of breath, disturbed sleep, and difficulty thinking.

A rapid ascent causes mountain sickness, but if you can acclimate gradually, you should have no problems. In going from low elevation to high, try to spend at least one night at mid-elevation, say 4,000 to 5,000 feet, and plan to spend a couple of easy days scouting before the season opens. With these precautions symptoms should be minimal.

A more serious malady is high-altitude pulmonary edema. Dr. Houston says that this problem normally occurs above 9,000 feet elevation and that symptoms take 36 hours or longer to develop. Pulmonary edema, in essence, means the lungs fill with liquid and the victim literally drowns in his own fluids. Again quoting Dr. Houston, symptoms include "shortness of breath, fatigue, cough, which sometimes produces bloody sputum, often a slight fever; may rapidly go on to unconsciousness and death."

In severe cases a victim may need hospitalization, but if symptoms are noticed early, the most effective treatment is simply getting to a lower altitude. The edema should clear up quickly. Dr. Houston goes on to say: ". . . altitude illness does not occur on the highest mountains only. In fact more people are affected between 8,000 and 12,000 feet than at higher altitudes. It is the innocent, the ignorant, or the overly bold who get into trouble and sometimes die."

BEARS, SNAKES, AND INSECTS

BEARS

Black bears. Though bears of all kinds can and do attack humans, black bears are more of a nuisance than a threat. Lynn Rogers, a biologist with the U.S. Forest Service in Minnesota, has studied black bears since 1967, and he has taken part in more than 1,000 bear captures.

"From my experience, I'd say most of this stuff about black bear attacks is greatly exaggerated," Rogers said. "Black bears just want to get away."

That doesn't mean bears never attack. Rogers has documented a number of bear-human encounters, and he breaks them into categories. Defensive attacks usually take place in national parks where people feed bears. "Veteran" bears used to handouts are relatively harmless, Rogers believes, but newcomers may not know how to act and occasionally attack.

Offensive attacks take place with no apparent provocation. In Ontario in 1978, for example, a black bear killed and ate three boys who were fishing. Rogers has records of 18 such attacks since 1906. He says most took place in backcountry, primarily in Canada, where the bears have had little or no contact with people. Apparently these were simply acts of predation. Rogers said unprovoked black bear attacks are very rare.

It's commonly thought that mother bears will aggressively defend their cubs, but Rogers doesn't agree. "Many times we've climbed trees to catch cubs. Even with all their bawling and screaming, no sow has ever attacked us. The sows woof and bluff charges, but 20 feet is about the closest they've ever come."

Bears are opportunists and will take a meal where they can get it, and if that happens to be in your camp, fine enough. To prevent bears from demolishing your food and gear, keep a clean camp. Burn food scraps thoroughly, and wash dishes and pans after every meal. Seal nonperishable foods in plastic bags and hang them out on a limb 10 feet off the ground. Seal perishables in coolers. If you're hunting in bear country and must leave a deer overnight in the field, hang it out of a bear's reach. If you encounter a black bear in camp or eating your deer, you may feel compelled to shoot it, but Rogers feels a hunter could chase it away easily enough. He says, "If there are several of you, just get in a group and start yelling and rush at the bear. I've never seen a black bear in my life that wouldn't run from that."

Remember though, Rogers knows black bears so well that he probably conveys dominance to any bear, and his "threat displays" are convincing to the bears. The average hunter may not always be as convincing.

Grizzly bears. Grizzly bears are another matter. In the Lower 48 states, grizzly range is limited. Deer hunters may encounter grizzlies in the Bob Marshall Wilderness just south of Glacier National Park, in the Cabinet Mountains in northwestern Montana, and in some remote ranges of northern Idaho. Grizzlies range throughout western Canada and Alaska. In grizzly country use extreme caution.

First learn to distinguish grizzlies from black bears. The grizzly generally has a square, blocky head with a dished-in nose compared to the sleeker, more pointed face and straight nose of the black bear. The grizzly has a distinct hump on its back above the front shoulders, in contrast to a fairly straight back on black bears.

You can distinguish the tracks too. Size is not a good criterion because a big black bear could have tracks equal to those of an average grizzly. But the toes of a grizzly tend to form a much straighter line across the print than they do on a black bear (see illustration for details). Also, a grizzly's front claws are much longer.

Steve Herrero, a professor at the University of Calgary in Alberta, has studied bears and other carnivores for 20 years and has published a book called *Bear Attacks—Causes and Deterrents.* Herrero says several circumstances could provoke a grizzly attack.

One is a sudden encounter. Unlike black bears, which will turn tail and run, a grizzly surprised at close quarters may attack. As a deer hunter, you may purposely slip quietly through the woods, but in grizzly country, particularly if you see fresh sign, avoid dense cover where bears could be resting. Be particularly cautious in berry patches and other good feed grounds.

As mentioned earlier, keep a clean camp. If a grizzly decides your camp makes a good diner, you may not be able to scare him away.

Herrero has documented eight cases in which hunters returning to retrieve game in the field have been attacked by grizzlies. Anytime you must leave a kill in grizzly country, assume a bear has found it, and use caution when you return. If you must leave game in the field, hang it at least 10 feet off the ground.

If a grizzly finds your deer, he'll claim it and possibly

HOW TO DISTINGUISH BLACKS FROM GRIZZLIES

Black bears are not always black. In western North America, black bears may be brown and even cinnamon in color, causing many people to mistake them for grizzlies. (Leonard Lee Rue III photo)

Grizzlies have a distinctive shoulder hump. Also notice how the broader forehead and dished face on this grizzly compares to the straighter facial profile of the black bear, shown at left. (Leonard Lee Rue III photo)

■ Grizzly range ■ Black-bear range

You can tell if you're dealing with a black bear or grizzly by the tracks. Notice the much longer claws on the grizzly and the straighter pattern of the toes. Size of the track is not a reliable distinction.

defend it. As you return to a kill site, Herrero suggests, go in noisily to avoid surprising a bear at close range. If a grizzly decides your deer is his and threatens as you approach, wish him a nice meal and leave.

What if a grizzly comes at you? One thing is for sure—you can't outrun him. Predators instinctively chase prey that runs away; so that is a bad move. Most authorities suggest speaking to the bear in firm tones and slowly backing away. Herrero suggests seeking shelter in a vehicle if you're close to one, and if you're not, climbing a tree. Grizzlies won't climb, but they can reach up 10 feet or higher—so climb high.

If a grizzly actually attacks, you may have to shoot it, but if you're not a crack shot, chances are you won't drop it in its tracks. Herrero believes your only real hope then is to play dead. Curl up in a ball to protect your stomach, and lock your hands behind your neck to protect your neck and head. Try not to move until the bear leaves. But the best advice is to avoid tangling with a grizzly in the first place.

SNAKES AND SNAKEBITES

An incident involving a bear may make a more sensational news item than a snakebite, but from the average deer hunter's point of view, snakes pose a greater threat. Nearly 7,000 cases of snakebite are reported each year in the United States. About a dozen of those victims die.

About 20 species of poisonous snakes live in North America. Two are coral snakes, and the rest—cottonmouths, copperheads, and rattlesnakes—are pit vi-

pers, named for the heat-sensing "pit" between the eye and nostril. Alaska, Hawaii, and Maine are the only states that have no poisonous snakes. In Canada various species of rattlesnakes inhabit the southern parts of British Columbia, Alberta, Saskatchewan, as well as scattered regions in Ontario. Snakebite cases are most common during the warm summer months, not during deer seasons, but while scouting or hunting during early fall, you may encounter snakes.

Rattlesnakes account for 60 percent of all the reported snakebites. All rattlers have lethal venom, and a victim should get antivenin treatments (antivenin is a serum that counteracts the effects of venom). Copperheads inhabit the eastern states, and within their range they account for the majority of snakebites. The bite causes extensive swelling, but it's not considered life threatening for healthy adults. Cottonmouths live in wet bottomlands of the southern states. They're fairly aggressive, but their bites normally are not deadly. However, cottonmouth bites should be treated with antivenin.

Defense against snakebites. The pit vipers have catlike, vertical pupils and broad, triangular heads. Learn to identify the specific snakes of your region and understand their habits. You can't count on snakes, even rattlers, to warn you before they strike.

Snakes can't tolerate sunbaked ground; so during hot summer days, they'll seek shade. On cooler fall days, they'll sun on open south slopes and lie over warm rocks. Watch where you're stepping, and before you step over logs or rocks, look on the other side. Snakes most commonly strike the foot or ankle, so high-topped boots afford some protection. Never poke your fingers into crevices or crannies, and as you're climbing, watch where you put your hands.

Note the distinctive heat-sensing pit between the nostril and eye on this timber rattler, as well as the vertical pupil. All pit vipers are poisonous. They include cottonmouths and copperheads as well as rattlers. (Leonard Lee Rue III photo)

VENOMOUS SNAKES

Four kinds of venomous snakes live in North America: rattlesnakes, copperheads, water moccasins, and coral snakes. Learn to recognize the species in your hunting territory. (Leonard Lee Rue III photos)

Coral snake

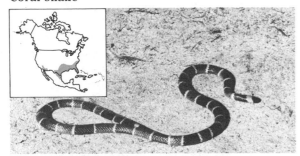

Cottonmouth

Copperhead

Timber rattler

Eastern diamondback rattler

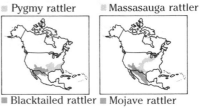

Canebrake rattler   Pygmy rattler   Massasauga rattler

Rock rattler   Blacktailed rattler   Mojave rattler

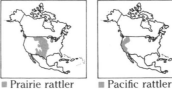

Prairie rattler   Pacific rattler   W. diamondback

Learn the habits of snakes to avoid being bitten. As you can see, blindly poking your fingers into cracks and crevices can be dangerous. Note the broad, triangular head on this Pacific rattlesnake.

Symptoms of snakebite. Dr. Findlay Russell, an authority on snakebites at the University of Southern California, has treated more than 650 cases of snakebite, and in more than 20 percent of the cases, no venom was injected. First aid can be far worse than the bite in such cases; so watch for symptoms to verify the need for first aid.

If venom from pit vipers has been injected, immediate symptoms are burning pain and swelling. The swelling normally starts at the bite within 5 minutes and spreads rapidly. If a person is bitten on the hand, his entire arm may swell within an hour.

Other early symptoms are numbness or tingling in the mouth and tongue. In severe cases these sensations may spread into the fingers and toes. Weakness, sweating, nausea, and other symptoms may occur with time.

First aid for snakebite. Antivenin treatment is prescribed for severe bites, but such treatments are administered only at hospitals. You can take steps in the field to minimize the effects of a bite.

First, place a constricting band above the bite. This can be a rubber band, shoe lace, belt, or strip of cloth

placed 2 to 3 inches above the bite (that is, between the bite and the heart). This is not a tourniquet and should be loose enough that you can slip a finger under it. It slows the spread of venom in the lymph system and shallow veins.

Second, using a razor blade or other sharp instrument (snakebite kits have a scalpel for this purpose) make slits through the fang marks about ¼-inch long and ⅛-inch deep. These should parallel the limb, not run cross grain.

Third, apply suction. Snakebite kits have suction cups for this purpose, but if these aren't available, use your mouth. There's no danger of poisoning yourself unless you have an open cut or sore in your mouth. This first-aid treatment reduces the volume of venom, and it may reduce a lethal bite to sublethal. Remember that the sooner you apply first aid, the more effective it will be. Dr. Russell suggests that it will do the most good if done within 15 minutes. If you delay more than 2 hours, it is probably best to just take the victim to a hospital.

Bob Jenni, who has studied snakes all his life and who has been bitten many times, recommends additional secondary care—alternating hot and cold packs. He recommends starting with a hot pack at about 125 degrees, which is tolerable but very hot to the touch. Leave this in place 3 to 5 minutes then apply a cold pack of about 34 degrees for 3 to 5 minutes. Ice wrapped in a towel or plastic bag is about right, but don't use straight ice, which could cause frostbite. Begin this treatment immediately, even as

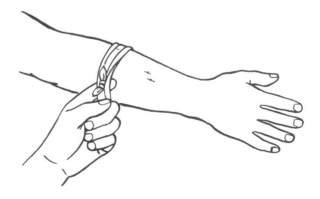

To give first aid for snakebite, first tie a constricting band above the bite—the band should be loose enough so that you can slip a finger under it. Then make shallow slits through the bite marks and suck venom from the wounds. Slits should only be made parallel with axis of the bitten limb.

you apply suction, and continue as long as swelling persists, up to 72 hours.

Jenni stresses the importance of alternating hot and cold. A detailed explanation would require an entire book, but put simply, snake venom is very complex, and some components work best at high temperatures, some at low. In essence alternating hot and cold confuses the venom to reduce its destructive power. Also, the cold slows circulation and the spread of venom, while the hot temporarily dilates blood vessels to bring in fresh blood and minimizes tissue damage.

Snakebite authorities agree on several points: Straight cold-pack treatments can produce great tissue damage and lead to amputation. Venom is highly complex, and the acute stage of a snakebite may not take place for three of four days. Seek medical treatment for all snakebites, even if you can't get to the doctor for several days. And if possible, kill the snake, without getting bitten again, and take it to the hospital with you, because the bites from some snakes must be treated differently from others.

It's also important to be tested for possible allergic reactions to antivenin, which is a horse serum. Allergic persons can die quickly from antivenin treatments. Jenni says you should call ahead on your way to the hospital. If the staff there knows what it's doing, someone will meet you in the emergency room, ready to administer a serum allergy test.

INSECT STINGS

Judging from statistics, insects may be the most dangerous creatures you face in the woods. In a recent representative year, 39 persons died from stings by bees, hornets, and wasps. They died from severe allergic reactions to insect venoms. The National Institute of Health estimates that four out of every 1,000 persons are hypersensitive to insect stings.

Among the stinging insects, yellow jackets are the most commonly troublesome to hunters. They swarm around a freshly killed deer, or invade camp to look for food. So in some areas, getting stung is almost an everyday part of hunting. If you're working on an animal during warm weather, keep your shirt cuffs tightly buttoned, and tie a string around your pants cuffs to keep out yellow jackets. And plug holes in your clothing. Yellow jackets have a habit of investigating holes, and it's common to have one fly in but not find his way out.

For most hunters getting stung is a painful nuisance, but for a person who's allergic, it may be deadly. If you've ever shown hypersensitivity to insect stings, consult your doctor. He can prescribe a kit that contains epinephrine and an antihistamine. These are used to counteract the effects of the insect's toxin, and you should always carry this kit ready for use.

NAVIGATION TECHNIQUES

Some hunters can find their way in the woods with ease while others seem to stumble around as though they are lost. The hunter who can find his way was not born with an instinct for backcountry navigation. Rather he has learned it. To put it another way, good pathfinders are made, not born.

Know your country. Search-and-rescue authorities say that many lost hunters and hikers just do not bother to learn enough about the area. Before ever setting foot afield, peruse maps, drive roads, and observe from vantage points to learn the lay of the land. If you know which direction rivers and streams run, where all roads and trails are located, and the position of peaks and ridges, you can tackle unfamiliar country with no fear of getting lost.

Learn to observe. The "sixth sense" of a good woods navigator could be defined more accurately as the power of observation. If you've ridden in a car with someone else through a city, you probably couldn't retrace your route because you paid no attention. Many persons hunt the same way. They make no mental notes as they travel.

Before heading into any new country, study maps to learn the lay of the land. Then carefully note landmarks as you hike and hunt.

As you hunt or hike, observe continually. Record the number of ridges and streams you cross and note your line of travel in relation to surrounding peaks. Watch for outstanding landmarks—big snags, meadows, cliffs, game trails, and so forth. Frequently look behind to see what terrain will look like on the return trip.

By using these techniques, you can probably find your way around most country with no additional help. Even so, you'll eventually run into situations where you'll need a map and compass, and you should always take them with you.

MAPS

Maps simply provide a bird's-eye view of the area they cover. Small-scale maps, such as state road maps, cover large areas and show little detail. Large-scale maps cover small areas and show a lot of detail.

The scale of a map is expressed as a ratio. For example, large-scale topographic maps published by the U.S. Geological Survey have a scale of 1:24,000. That means that every unit of measure, say an inch, on the map equals 24,000 inches on the ground. On 1:24,000 maps, 2 inches represents roughly one mile. On most road maps, 2 inches represents nearly 40 miles.

Maps also are classified according to plane. Those in one plane—that is, they show the earth as flat—are called planimetric maps. Road maps and U.S. Forest Service maps are planimetric. Those that show variations in terrain are called topographic maps. On these, contour lines represent specific elevations, and with practice you can read these lines to visualize clearly the mountains, valleys, and other landforms.

Grid lines. On all large-scale maps you'll find a grid of lines. Knowing what they mean could save your life. Most of the land in North America has been surveyed, and the lines on your maps were established by surveys.

The grid lines show townships, which are blocks of land 6 miles square. The north-south lines are called range lines, and the east-west lines are called township lines. Each township is numbered in relation to specific reference points—a base line that runs east-west, and a principal meridian that runs north-south. Thus, when numbers on the border of your map read T. 15 N. (Township 15 North), R. 5 W. (Range 5 West), you know that the township is number 15 north of the base line and number 5 west of the principal meridian.

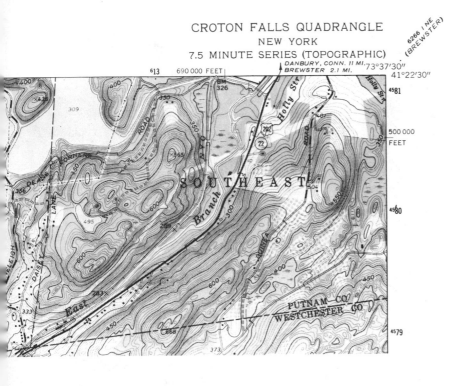

CROTON FALLS QUADRANGLE
NEW YORK
7.5 MINUTE SERIES (TOPOGRAPHIC)

Maps are classified according to scale and plane. This topographic map has a scale of 2 inches to the mile and shows terrain details in enough detail to meet the needs of most hunters. Such maps are available from the U.S. Geological Survey, as described in page 455.

In addition, each township is subdivided into sections, or square miles. These sections are numbered sequentially from 1 to 36, starting in the upper right corner and running back and forth. Sections are further broken down by quarter sections, such as northeast quarter, northwest quarter, and so forth.

During the survey process, surveyors mark the section lines. Commonly, you will find section-line markers in the field, and they tell your exact location. Each marker contains a metal tag or stake with a legal description of the location, including township, range, and section. From this information you can determine your exact location on a map.

Update your maps. You'll find that many topographic maps were made years ago, and although the topography shown remains accurate, the road and trail systems shown are obsolete. On the other hand, most maps published by public agencies such as the U.S. Forest Service and Bureau of Land Management are more recent. Before setting out, use the most recent maps to update topographic maps, and call land-management agencies to update further. Because logging and mining progress rapidly in many regions, even maps one or two years old are often inaccurate.

THE COMPASS

Flat country with heavy vegetation offers no vantage points from which to view your surroundings. On an overcast day you may need a compass just to maintain a straight line of travel. Or you may find yourself fogged in or blinded by falling snow. In these cases the only reliable recourse is a compass.

To buy a compass. Buying a compass is like buying tires—it pays to buy quality because your life may depend on it. You'll find a wide range of quality and styles on the market, but some kinds are easier to use and more reliable than others. Handy features include a liquid-filled capsule, which prevents the needle from oscillating, and a rectangular base, which helps when using the compass in conjunction with a map.

Another helpful feature is a rotating dial. On most compasses the dial is marked clockwise from zero to 360 degrees. Zero equals north, 90 east, 180 south, and 270 west. On some models, the 360-degree dial is marked counterclockwise. These are called forester's or cruiser's compasses. The two kinds work identically except for one point: on those with a clockwise dial you read compass direction at an index mark on the base of the compass; on those with a counterclockwise dial, you read compass direction at the north end of the magnetic needle.

Other handy compass features are a direction-of-travel-arrow; an orienting arrow on the dial; and meridian lines to help coordinate your compass with a map. A built-in mechanism to compensate for declination can also simplify compass use.

Declination. All compasses work the same way. Magnetic forces run through the earth and converge in Canada about 1,400 miles south of the North Pole,

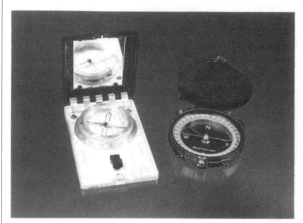

Compasses come in many styles. The sportsman compass at right is accurate for direction finding, but an Orienteering compass, such as the Silva Ranger at left is easier to use in conjunction with a map.

at what is called the magnetic North Pole. The needle on a compass always points toward magnetic north (unless it is influenced by magnetized objects or ore deposits), and from this one constant you can perform many other navigational functions.

True north and magnetic north generally are not the same, and the difference between the two, measured in degrees, is called declination. In North America, a line of zero declination—called the agonic line—runs from the North Pole down through Hudson Bay, Lake Michigan, and south to Florida. If you're on this line, your compass needle will point to both true north and magnetic north. But from anywhere to one side or the other, the needle points toward magnetic north, not true north.

Anytime you're working with true directions, you must compensate for declination. Consider, for example, that you want to head due north (not magnetic north). If you ignore declination, you'll be off 92 feet after one mile of travel for every degree of declination error. If declination in your area is 10 degrees, you'll be off 920 feet after the first mile, and more than a half mile after three miles of travel.

Topographic maps have a symbol on the bottom border that shows the declination. Many smaller-scale maps do not show declination, but you can get a chart from the U.S. Geological Survey that shows magnetic declinations for the entire United States.

The easiest way to adjust for declination is to buy a compass with a built-in compensator. This mechanism moves the orienting arrow in relation to the compass dial. If you're hunting west of the agonic line, declination is easterly. For example, if you're hunting in California where declination is 20 degrees east, then you move the orienting arrow until it points to a mark 20 degrees east of due north. With this done you can use your compass as normal without thinking about declination—until you move to a new location. If you're hunting east of the agonic line, where declination is westerly, you move the orienting arrow the appropriate number of degrees west of true north. If your compass does not have a built in compensator, you can simply add the correct number of degrees to each bearing.

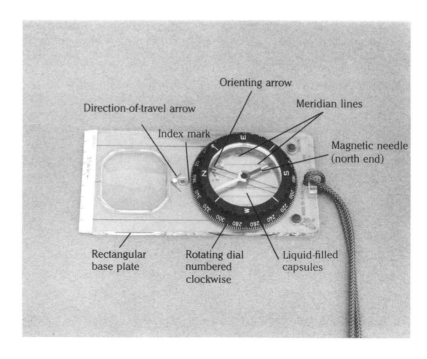

Helpful compass features include liquid-filled capsule to stop the magnetic needle from oscillating; meridian lines; orienting arrow; index mark; direction-of-travel arrow; rectangular baseplate for use with map; and a rotating dial that is numbered clockwise.

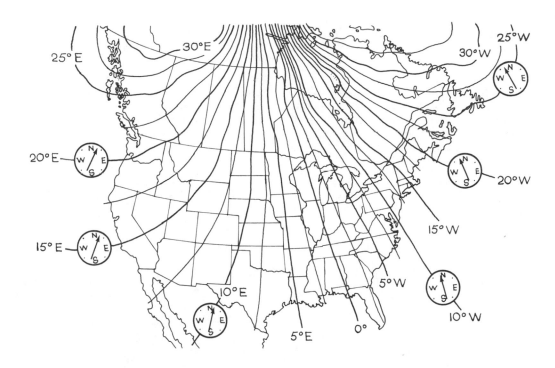

In most compass use, it's essential to compensate for declination—the difference in degrees between magnetic and true north. The heavy line running just west of Lake Michigan into the Gulf of Mexico west of Florida is called the agonic line, or line of zero declination. You can order a more detailed map from the U.S. Geological Survey, as noted on page 455. The map is updated every 5 years to reflect slight changes in the position of magnetic north.

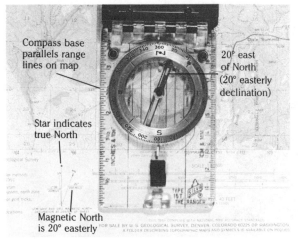

A symbol at the bottom of topographic maps gives the magnetic declination. In this case it's 20 degrees easterly. To orient a map, line the base of the compass up with range lines on the map, and then turn the map-compass unit until the magnetic needle points 20 degrees east of true north. The map is then oriented. This compass has a built-in declination compensator. With a screw adjustment, you can turn the orienting arrow the appropriate number of degrees east or west. Then when you line up the magnetic needle with the orienting arrow, the compass itself is pointing true north.

PUTTING THE COMPASS TO USE

To travel a straight line. The most fundamental use of a compass is to maintain a straight line of travel. If you get fogged in or caught out after dark, you could wander in a circle. To prevent that, aim the direction-of-travel arrow on your compass in the direction you want to walk and line up the magnetic needle with the orienting arrow. Pick out a tree or rock on your compass line and walk to it. Then take another compass sighting and pick out another landmark, and so forth. As long as the needle is lined up with the orienting arrow, the direction-of-travel arrow will point in your chosen direction.

To travel a known direction. Let's say you're sitting on top of Black Peak, and you can see on your map that Hidden Basin, a great place for big bucks, lies due north. Set zero (north) on your compass dial at the index mark, line up the needle with the orienting arrow, and walk in exactly the way in which the direction-of-travel arrow points. Remember, you must compensate for declination to hit your objective. Again, you'll maintain the most accurate line if you walk from one point to the next distant visible point, rather than looking at your compass constantly to stay on line.

To orient a map. You may be sitting on a knoll and want to identify surrounding landmarks by comparing them with your map, but you can't match up the map with the ground. To line up your map with the terrain, set the compass dial on true north (again, you must compensate for declination), lay the compass on the map with the straight edge of the base parallel with the north-south lines on the map, and turn the entire map-compass unit until the compass needle lines up with the orienting arrow (in other words, until the direction-of-travel arrow on the compass points due north.) The map is now oriented and you can compare features on the map with visible features on the ground.

HOW TO DETERMINE AN UNKNOWN DIRECTION

This three-photo sequence shows how to determine an unknown direction by using map and compass together. Notice that in the second and third photos the orienting arrow points 20 degrees east of north. That's because it has been set to compensate for a declination of 20 degrees easterly, required in California. **1.** *Using only a map and compass, you can determine the direction to your destination. Let's say you're at Little Squaw Spring and you want to reach Bear Spring, but you don't know which direction to walk. To find out, first place your compass on the map so the straight edge of the compass base bisects both your present location and your destination.* **2.** *Holding the compass in that position, turn the compass dial until the meridian lines in the dial parallel the north-south (range) lines on your map.* **3.** *Now pick up the compass and turn it until the north end of the magnetic needle lines up with the orienting arrow. Now the direction-of-travel arrow on the compass points directly toward Bear Spring, your destination. If you keep the magnetic needle and orienting arrow lined up and walk in the direction indicated by the direction-of-travel arrow, you will walk right to Bear Spring.*

1

You want to go to Bear Spring

You are here

2

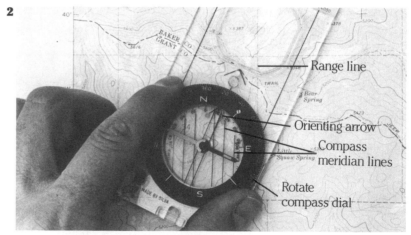

Range line

Orienting arrow

Compass meridian lines

Rotate compass dial

3

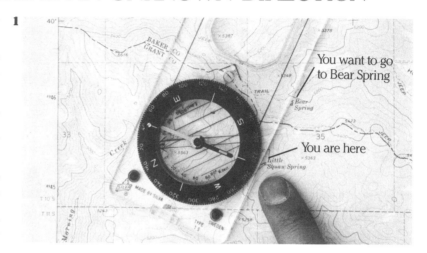

Direction-of-travel arrow

HOW TO FIND YOUR POSITION ON A MAP

If you can see known landmarks, you can find your position on a map with the process of triangulation; as follows: **1.** *Point the direction-of-travel arrow on your compass toward a known landmark, in this case Sharp Mountain, and turn the compass dial until the magnetic needle lines up with the orienting arrow. On this compass the orienting arrow has been set to compensate for 20 degrees easterly declination, needed in California.* **2.** *Bisect Sharp Mountain on your map with the edge of the compass. Swing the compass around until the meridian lines in the compass parallel range lines on the map. Without moving the compass, draw a line along the edge of the base. Now take a bearing on a second known landmark, in this case Wild Horse Mountain, and repeat the process. The point at which the lines meet marks your location.*

1

2

To determine an unknown direction. If you see a distant peak and want to know its direction from you, point the direction-of-travel arrow at the peak. Holding the compass in this position, rotate the dial until the orienting arrow lines up with the compass needle. Now you can read the direction of the peak at the index mark. If, for example, 90 degrees lines up with the index mark, you know the peak is due east.

You can do the same thing using only your map and compass. Say you're at Little Squaw Spring and want to walk to Bear Spring. Lay the edge of your compass on the map so it touches each point. Holding it in that position, turn the compass dial until the meridian lines parallel range lines on the map. Now pick up the compass and turn it until the compass needle lines up with the orienting arrow. The direction-of-travel arrow now points toward your destination. You

can read the direction at the index mark. Here again, compensate for declination.

To find your position on a map. If you don't know your exact position but can see known landmarks, you can "find" yourself by using your map and compass through the method of triangulation, as shown in accompanying photos.

These above basics serve as a foundation for backcountry navigation. The specifics will vary slightly, depending on the kind of compass you buy, the maps you're using, and the declination in your area, but the principles apply throughout North America. Practice these principles at home before you find yourself in an emergency in the field. Reading about map and compass use can be confusing, but practice makes use relatively simple.

SURVIVAL AND RESCUE

Prevention forms the real core of survival, but any hunter must face one reality: Accidents do happen. Consider a tragedy that involved two experienced hunters in the Pacific Northwest. The sequence of events is open to speculation, but rescue workers pieced together a plausible scenario from signs in the snow.

During late archery season, snow covered the ground and temperatures dropped close to zero during the nights. When the two hunters arrived in their hunting area, they set up a comfortable camp and then drove out to scout for game late in the afternoon. They parked their jeep and walked a few hundred yards over a ridge.

Apparently they just went out for a quick look around, because they wore only light jackets, and one had on canvas jungle boots. Somewhere along the line they lost their way, and they split to walk in separate directions. Each continued to circle, apparently trying to find his way back to the road. Four days later they were found dead about a mile apart. Each was lying on fir boughs under a tree.

"The really sad thing was that they had all the equipment they needed to survive," a rescue worker said later. "Matches, rain jackets, food, warm boots. But it was all in their car. They had left it behind."

PREPARE FOR THE WORST

These men violated the major survival principle—go prepared. Here's a rule of thumb: always carry adequate gear to spend at least 24 hours in the woods by yourself. That's true even if you're hunting the back 40. Who knows when you'll get hurt or fogged in? If you're hunting wilderness where you could get trapped alone by a blizzard, carry gear to sustain yourself for several days.

A pack must be light, comfortable, and convenient or you'll leave it behind half the time. For backcountry hunting, you'll probably carry game bags, warm clothing, extra socks, camera, and other gear; so you'll need a roomy rucksack or large fanny pack. Some hunters even carry both. More civilized surroundings call for less gear, and a small belt pack may do. Or you may just seal essential items in a small can or metal box (which doubles as a cup for boiling water) and slip them into the pocket of your hunting coat. Regardless, always carry survival gear.

A survival pack must be comfortable and convenient. For backcountry hunting, this man has chosen a roomy rucksack, but you might prefer a beltpack or small package you can slip in your coat pocket.

The following survival-gear list emphasizes the essentials for survival and rescue:

1. Map and compass. A map and compass can prevent the need for rescue operations.
2. Flashlight. A small light that uses two AA batteries is adequate in most cases. Turn one battery backwards so the light can't get switched on accidentally inside your pack, and always carry spare batteries and bulb.
3. Fire starter. A butane lighter, strike-anywhere matches, and flint and steel assure you of warmth under any conditions. (See the upcoming section on Fire for details.)
4. Shelter. Anywhere that rain or snow is a possibility, carry a lightweight square of plastic or a Space Blanket for emergency shelter.
5. Knife and sharpening steel. Any hunter will have a knife for cleaning game, and it is a must for fire or shelter building too. With a small steel or stone, you can keep the knife sharp. A saw blade proves handy for cutting branches.
6. Nylon twine or cord. Fifty feet of nylon twine can be used to hang meat, build shelter, tie splints into place, and so forth.
7. First-aid kit. Injury can strike anytime, and you can handle most emergencies with a simple kit.

The following items will serve you well in most emergency situations: **1.** *Map and compass;* **2.** *Flashlight with two spare batteries;* **3.** *Fire starters, including butane lighter, metal match, and commercial Heat Tabs;* **4.** *Space Blanket for emergency shelter;* **5.** *Knife with a saw blade, and small sharpening steel;* **6.** *50 feet of nylon cord;* **7.** *First aid kit;* **8.** *Metal cup;* **9.** *Iodine tablets for purifying water and 3 feet of surgical tubing for syphoning water;* **10.** *Metal police whistle for signaling;* **11.** *Signaling mirror;* **12.** *Roll of fluorescent tape for marking trail;* **13.** *Quick-energy food;* **14.** *Beltpack for carrying these items.*

8. Metal cup. In an area where water may be contaminated, you need a cup to gather water. It should be metal so you can boil water in it.
9. Water purification tablets and 3 feet of surgical tubing. With tablets you can purify water quickly, and with a length of surgical tubing, you can syphon pure water directly from a ground source.
10. Whistle. This lets you audibly signal.
11. Signal mirror. If hurt or lost, you can catch the attention of distant hunters or overhead planes. Many compasses contain mirrors that can double for this purpose.
12. Fluorescent flagging. You can mark a trail going into unknown country so that you can find your way back out, or you can mark your route for rescuers to follow.
13. High-energy food. Food isn't a high-priority item in most emergencies, but high-energy bars can give you a shot of energy when you need it most.

Additional items may be needed, depending on conditions: snakebite kit, raingear, sunscreen and sun glasses, spare eyeglasses, needle and thread, and so forth. Before setting out on any trip, assess the weather potential, your own health, danger from animals, and other conditions. Plan your gear accordingly.

FILE A TRIP PLAN

Search-and-rescue workers say one of their biggest headaches is trying to find someone who hasn't let anyone know his plans. They have no idea where to start looking. Before you set out, tell your spouse, a close relative, or friend where you're going. If that's not possible, leave word at a sheriff's office, or with a forest ranger or other authority.

Be specific with your information. First, when do you plan to return? If no one knows when you're due back, they can't know if you're overdue. Second, tell exactly where you plan to hunt. Search-and-rescue workers emphasize the need for specifics. If you simply say you'll be up in Jefferson County, precious hours or days may be lost in narrowing a search to your location. Tell which drainages you plan to hunt, and which roads and trails you'll follow to get in and out. A trip plan also should include a description of your car and license number, and a general picture of your equipment, such as the color of your tent, pack, and clothing.

One other thing: Stick to your plan or let someone know if you've changed it. Rescue workers get a little frustrated when they spend all night looking for a lost hunter who was sitting in a nearby bar all the time.

USE YOUR HEAD, NOT YOUR LEGS

Anytime you find yourself in a jam, your first reaction may be to do something—anything—fast! Panic is a natural reaction. Rescue authorities say that in many cases panic turns merely uncomfortable circumstances into tragedies.

Even embarrassment can produce these results. As one search-and-rescue veteran said, "Deer hunters are supposed to know their way around the woods. So when one gets lost he feels embarrassed and pushes on to the danger point. A person must admit he's fallible, or he'll force himself into real trouble."

Sit down and think. Before you do anything, sit down, rest and think. If the weather is cool, build a fire to kindle warmth and cheer, and then analyze your situation. If you're lost, and you've come prepared with a map and compass, as you should have, you may be able to figure out where you went wrong.

If you're injured, take time to apply the needed first aid measures. In particular beware of the effects of shock. Lie down and make yourself comfortable until your breathing and pulse rate are normal and strong. If your partner is injured, take the same precautions.

Possibly, if those two hunters who died in the snow, as described earlier, had followed this procedure, they would have lived. Panic may have distorted their reasoning. As one rescue worker said, "We can't figure out why they kept going. All they had to do was to follow their own tracks in the snow back to the road."

Stay together. With some thought, they would have stayed together too. Two heads are better than one, as the saying goes, and two persons often think of solutions that might escape one person. Just as important, two hunters who are lost together can offer each other moral support. They can also watch for warning signs of hypothermia, frostbite, and other dangerous conditions.

In addition, they can share their warmth. Two bodies huddling together can withstand cold much better than one alone. Unless one of your party is seriously injured and the other must go for help, stick together in an emergency.

To move or sit tight? As your thinking clears, you must make other decisions. First, should you stay where you are or head back to camp or your vehicle? If you're feeling good and know clearly how to find your way, or if you're not injured too badly, then heading back may be the wise choice.

In many situations, the only wise choice is to stay put. If you're caught in fog, blinding snow, or darkness, and you don't know your way back for certain, chances are good that by wandering you'll only make a bad situation worse. Veterans of search and rescue say that many people they find in predicaments would have done just fine if they'd only set up "camp" and stayed in one place until conditions improved or until rescue crews found them. Sleeping under a tree like an animal may seem foreign, almost perverse, but once you've decided to stay, you develop a new frame of mind and readily accept your situation.

FIRE

Once you've decided to stay put, major concerns become warmth and shelter. At the very least, fire can mean the difference between comfort and misery, and in many cases it means the difference between life and death. It will dry your clothes and warm your body, and it can provide psychological comfort too. Any

hunter knows that camp without a fire can be dank and lifeless, but with orange flames dancing it becomes homey and warm. Many rescue workers suggest that lost or injured persons should first build a fire. Home is where the fire is, so to speak, and the warmth and light of a fire provides a person in trauma with a sense of place and security.

You can also cook an emergency meal over fire, purify water, and not least of all, signal for help. When or wherever you're hunting, go prepared to build a fire.

FIRE STARTERS

Most survival books detail methods for starting fires with a fire bow or drill. The question is not whether these methods work, but whether the average hunter will take time to learn them. Most hunters follow the path of least resistance. Few will spend hours perfecting primitive methods when modern matches will do the job.

There's only one catch: Modern matches won't always do the job. First, they must be available. That's where the survival pack discussed above becomes important. Second, they must work under all conditions. A butane cigarette lighter serves as a handy, all-purpose fire starter. However, a lighter can malfunction or run out of fuel. In cold weather, butane doesn't burn well; so don't stake your life on a lighter.

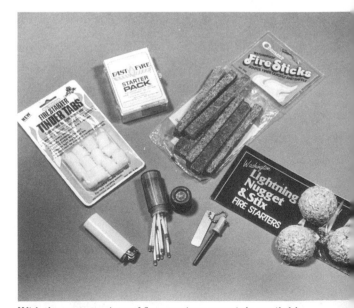

With the great variety of fire-starting materials available today, there's little excuse for getting caught shorthanded. A butane lighter, strike-anywhere matches, and flint-and-steel combined with one of the fire starters shown here, will give you a fire under the worst conditions.

For emergencies carry a good supply of strike-any-where matches. Don't depend on safety matches, because if the striker gets damp, you're sunk. And don't just roll the matches in a plastic bag, because the bag may get torn and let in moisture. Seal them in a plastic bottle or other watertight container. You can even dip the heads in melted paraffin to waterproof them further.

Along with a lighter or matches, carry a supplemental fire starter. You can make your own by soaking softboard used in ceilings (it's sometimes called Firtex) in paraffin, or you can soak sawdust with paint thinner and carry it in a sealed bottle. You also can buy commercial fire starters, such as Heat Tabs, Fire Stix, Lightning Nuggets, or Sterno. One excellent fire-starting kit contains matches, pitchy shavings, and small blocks of pitch wood. Once that pitch takes off, you're assured of a good fire under any conditions.

A flint-and-steel serves as a double backup. Commercial brands with a flint rod and steel striker produce a good spark. With these you need a "spark catcher," and 000 steel wool works well. When you strike a spark on it, the wool glows red hot, and by blowing on it you can intensify the heat enough to ignite dry tinder. You also can light commercial Heat Tabs with flint-and-steel.

To start a fire. "Prepare" is the secret word in fire starting. First pick a safe place. Even if you're freezing you don't want to start a forest fire. Never build a fire on thick duff or punky ground because the fire can creep down along roots and smoulder for days, despite your best efforts to put it out. Scrape out a fire ring at least 3 feet wide down to mineral soil, and if at all possible, build the fire near a creek or spring so that you can douse it later.

Find a spot protected from rain and snow and where heat will be reflected toward you. Don't build a fire ring, which only blocks heat, but rather build a rock semi-circle that will reflect heat toward you. Also, consider wind direction and build the fire where smoke won't suffocate you. If the ground is wet, lay a floor of dry rocks or limbs so your tinder won't soak up moisture and fizzle.

Once you've prepared a good base, gather tinder. Spruce and other dense conifers produce a shag of fine, dead twigs next to the trunk that make excellent tinder. If you rip the bark off blow downs or search

A flint-and-steel, commercial Heat Tab fire starter, and dry pine needles (left) will start a warming fire when you need it. Never get caught without reliable fire-building tools. Above right: Wood shavings or a fuzz stick—a stick of wood with shavings left attached—makes excellent tinder for quick fire starting. Dig around inside logs or under bark to look for dry tinder.

The key word in building a fire under tough conditions is "prepare." Gather armloads of wood graduated from the size of pencils up to the thickness of baseball bats before you strike the first match. Then stack the wood tepee style so that flames can spread rapidly from one twig to the next.

inside hollow logs or stumps you'll find dry wood that you can carve into shavings or fuzz sticks. (To make a fuzz stick, you leave splinters attached to the main piece of wood.) Dry lichens, grass, and leaves also make good tinder.

Store your tinder in a dry place and gather larger pieces of wood, starting with pencil-size twigs and branches and working up to substantial firewood. When you've got enough fuel to support a good fire, you're ready to light it. Never try to light a fire before you've done all of this, because you could end up wasting all your matches. And then you *will* have a problem.

Lay your tinder in a small heap, stand the pencil-size twigs over this like a small tepee, and stack successively larger pieces of wood over this. Organize the wood to allow enough air space so that the fire can breath, but compact it close enough so that the flames can creep rapidly from one piece to another. When you've built a guaranteed foundation, light the tinder on the upwind side so that the wind will blow flames into the wood. Then sit back and enjoy camp.

SHELTER

In many cases a fire may be all you need to dry your clothes and warm you up. Then you'll be on your way

hunting again. On the other hand, you may decide you're better off to hole up for a night or two. If that's the case, you have a second survival need. Shelter.

Often an overhanging cliff or small cave, the low-hanging branches of an evergreen tree, or a big fallen log may provide all the shelter you need. In other cases, you may need to build your own. Shelter designs are limited only by your creativity, but a couple of simple designs will serve in most short-term emergencies.

The A-frame. Probably the simplest design is the A-frame, and it can be erected in minutes. In many cases you can simply lay one end of a pole 8 to 10 feet long over a stump, large log, or low limb on a tree and set the other end on the ground to form a ridge line.

If you want it in the open you can make a quick tripod. For this you'll need three poles. Lay two 6-foot poles together and bind them near the top with a shear lashing. To make this knot, wrap cord around the two poles several times to bind them together. Then pull the cord between the poles and around the other wraps and tie it off with a square knot. Now stand the poles up and separate the bottoms to form an A. Set the ridge pole in the notch at the top. Now you have a stable frame for your shelter.

To build an A-frame shelter, lash two poles together by wrapping them tightly with cord and tying the cord in the middle. This knot is sometimes call a shear lashing.

Then separate the bottoms of the two poles and lash a third, longer pole over them to form a ridge line, and you have a solid tripod. You can cover this with plastic, as this hunter has done, or you can use bark, boughs or other natural materials to waterproof and insulate your shelter.

To complete the shelter, cover the sides. On any hunt you're wise to carry a small square of plastic for emergency shelter. A lightweight painter's drop cloth serves well for this purpose. Lay the plastic over the framework, anchor the edges with rocks, and you've got an instant weatherproof shelter.

If you don't have plastic, lay sticks against the ridge pole as ribs for additional support. Prop fir boughs, slabs of bark, or other dense foliage over this framework until the walls are thick enough to keep out water.

The thick walls on this shelter will also help preserve radiated body heat, and you can enhance this effect. The principle behind all insulation, whether in the walls of a house, sleeping bag, or warm jacket is the same—it traps dead air. To accomplish this it must be dry and fluffy. Keep this in mind as you insulate your shelter, and gather dry leaves or duff that will trap dead air around you.

Lean-to. You can build a lean-to almost as simply. Lay a pole between two large logs or tie it to adjacent tree trunks. Tie your plastic to this pole, stretch it down to the ground, and anchor it securely. If snow or wind poses problems, slope several straight limbs from the ridge pole to the ground to support the plastic.

You can also make a weatherproof roof on your lean-to with boughs or bark. Here again, use straight limbs to make several ribs to the ground from the ridge pole, and cover them with bark or boughs. You probably will want the roof high enough so you can sit up to enjoy your fire, but just as with the A-frame, the smaller the shelter, the easier it is to insulate and the better it holds in radiated heat.

A fire will provide warmth directly, but if you plan to sleep in your shelter you'll be more comfortable if you warm it with rocks. Most fires, especially those made with certain conifers, pop and shower you with sparks, and as the fire dies down, you have to restoke it. If you heat several large rocks and bury them under several inches of soil in your shelter, they'll radiate soothing heat throughout the night. If they are too hot to lie on, add another layer of dirt.

RESCUE

After a night or two in the woods, conditions may ease up and you may be able to get back to camp on your own. However, you may be hurt badly, may not know the way, or may have to buck waist-deep snow to get out. In such cases you must stay put until help arrives. Staying put saves energy, and for searchers, a stationary target is much easier to hit than a moving one. At this point you'll be glad you filed a trip plan.

The value of signals. Rarely during deer season are you all alone. Unless you're far in the backcountry, other hunters share the area with you, and your best hope for rescue is to attract their attention. If you've described your hunting plans to friends in camp—which should be standard operating procedure—your buddies will be looking for you if you don't return within a day.

Thus, most signals are aimed at attracting the attention of nearby hunters. Many survival books describe elaborate ground-to-air signal codes. But these are designed primarily for military and expedition personnel who may become stranded for days in vast stretches of wilderness. Harry Border, a veteran of

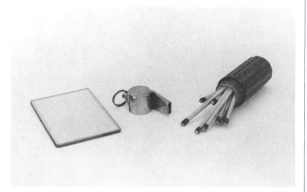

In case of emergency, you may need to signal for help. A mirror, loud whistle, and fire provide three of the most reliable signaling methods. The primary objective is not necessarily to convey a message but to attract attention.

search-and-rescue work in Illinois and Arizona, believes ground-to-air codes have much less value for deer hunters.

"Aircraft don't even get involved until a guy is reported lost, and in most cases he is found well before things get to that stage. During deer season, you just normally don't have the woods to yourself; so your biggest concern should be noise or some other method to attract people who are already on the ground."

Dick Suber, who has directed rescue work in Oregon for many years says, "When you try to add too much, people just get confused. Most people can't remember all those signals anyway. The best idea is to keep it simple."

The one signal code you should remember is "three." Anything repeated in a series of three—three whistle blasts, three fires, three flags—is considered a universal distress signal; so use this code when you need help. Conversely, if you hear or see someone signaling this way, never ignore it. Investigate. Someone might be calling for your help.

Signaling by sound. A series of three rifle shots may help if you're sure others know what you mean. Some parties set up their own signals, and if one member fires his rifle three times in rapid succession, it means he needs help. Either he's got game down, or he's hurt.

That method has its drawbacks, of course. It doesn't work for bowhunters, and during rifle seasons, hunters not privy to the code probably won't pay any attention. Others may fire three shots at deer.

Obviously, if you yell "Help!" the meaning will be clear. But if nobody is within earshot, you'll give yourself a sore throat to no avail. The signaling device prescribed by most search authorities is a shrill whistle, like that used by policemen and dog trainers. You can blow a whistle with little energy, your throat won't get raw, and the sound is foreign enough to attract attention in the woods. Repeatedly blow three-blast series.

Signaling by sight. A blazing fire in the woods will pique the curiosity of nearby hunters, and it will give hunters in your own party something to go by. If you've built a fire to attract attention during the day, throw green boughs or grass on it to create smoke. During the night, try to produce a big, bright blaze. If you think a search party has been contacted and aircraft might be used, build three small fires in the open where they can be seen from the air.

Reflected-sunlight emergency mirror signal: **1.** *Hold the mirror under your eye as a "back sight."* **2.** *Form a "V" with two fingers at arm's length, serving as the front sight.* **3.** *Move the mirror and the "V" so reflected sunlight passes through the "V" into the airplane cockpit.*

You also can signal with a mirror. Special signal mirrors with a hole in the middle are easiest to use. You sometimes can buy these at surplus stores, and instructions come with the mirror. Any small mirror, or even a shiny can lid, can serve as a substitute. When using a mirror without a sighting hole, you can roughly aim the mirror much as you do a rifle. Hold the mirror under your eye, and hold your other hand out at arm's length with two fingers forming a "V." Frame your target in the V and turn the mirror until it throws reflected sunlight onto the V. The flash should now hit your target. You can attract the attention of hunters on far hillsides or passing aircraft with a mirror. But a mirror has little value on cloudy days.

The amount of signaling material you carry in the field will be limited. Some books advise carrying smoke signals, flares, and small air horns in the field, but it's a rare person who'll hunt weighted down like a soldier going to war. The simple devices described here are adequate in most cases. The important point is to make yourself as obvious as possible. If you can move, get to an open hillside or on a peak where your signaling can be heard or seen from the greatest distances.

FIRST AID FOR DEER HUNTERS

A full course on first aid is not possible in a book of this type; so emphasis will be on injuries and illnesses most likely to strike deer hunters. First aid for physiological problems such as hypothermia, and for bites and stings, is included in earlier sections. Heart attacks and other serious medical complications require special training. Arrow and gunshot wounds usually require combinations of the steps listed below. Call the American National Red Cross or your local public health department for details on first aid and medical self-help courses.

LIFE-SAVING STEPS

For any serious injury, a set of rules or a list of priorities apply: Highest priority goes to aspects of the injury that most immediately threaten life. The order could change, depending on the nature of the injury, but the following list serves as a good starting point:

1. **Stop major bleeding.** Blood is life, and a person can die from loss of blood within minutes. If bright red blood spurts from a wound, you know a major artery has been cut and you must stop the bleeding fast. Apply hard, direct pressure to the wound.
2. **Restore breathing.** To do its job, blood must get fresh oxygen, and when a person stops breathing, oxygen is cut off. Make sure the victim's airway is clear and begin artificial respiration to restore breathing.
3. **Immobilize injuries.** Broken bones or other severely damaged parts of the body must be held stationary to prevent further damage and to reduce pain. Use splints and slings.
4. **Treat for shock.** You can assume an injured person will go into shock, which could be more serious than the injury itself. Always anticipate and treat for shock by keeping the victim calm, warm, and comfortable.
5. **Prevent infection.** If a wound gets dirty, germs can cause infection, which again can be more serious than the initial injury. Wash and dress wounds to keep them clean.

If you know nothing but these principles, you can deal with most medical emergencies in the field. Certain techniques help to carry out these principles, however. These, along with other miscellaneous first aid treatments, such as those for burns and choking, are discussed below.

STOP THE BLEEDING

Arteries carry blood from the heart to the extremities, and veins return blood from the extremities to the heart. If an artery is cut, bright red blood will spurt from the wound with each heartbeat. Any major bleeding is serious, of course, but arterial bleeding is especially so, and you must stop it quickly or the wounded person could die.

Direct pressure. Start with direct pressure. For severe injuries, don't take time to dig out bandages. Apply pressure immediately with your bare hand and maintain pressure until the bleeding stops. Push hard. One hospital emergency-room doctor who had seen accident victims bleed to death commented, "They would have lived if the person giving first aid had only pressed harder to stop the bleeding."

If time permits, apply a sterile dressing to the wound and press until blood stops flowing from the wound. Ideally this dressing should be a sterile gauze pad. If blood soaks the dressing, add another dressing over it because if you pull off the soaked one, bleeding could start all over again.

In the case of a severed artery, always see a doctor as soon as possible. The artery could reopen with deadly consequences. For smaller cuts direct pressure for a few minutes will allow the blood to clot and bleeding will stop. Then you can remove the bandages, wash up the wound, apply a clean dressing, and go on hunting.

Use a pressure bandage. If bleeding resumes when you let up, apply a pressure bandage and take the patient to a doctor. (Technically, you apply a dressing directly over a wound, and you hold the dressing in place with a bandage.)

To form a pressure bandage, apply several dressings. Then wrap them tightly with a gauze roll bandage or strips of your shirt, game bags, or other cloth. Pull this bandage tight enough to prevent further bleeding, but be careful not to cut off circulation. If fingers or toes below the bandage turn blue or white and begin to tingle or turn cold, or if you can't feel any pulse below the bandage, it's too tight. Loosen it enough to restore full circulation.

Avoid tourniquets. A tourniquet should be used only as a last resort to save a person's life. To form a tourniquet, you wrap a strip of cloth twice around

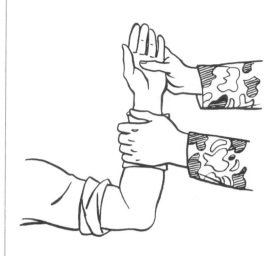

To stop bleeding, apply direct pressure to the wound. If time permits, lay a sterile pad over the wound, but if bleeding is severe, apply pressure immediately with your bare hand. Don't be afraid to press hard. In most cases direct pressure will be all that's needed, but if bleeding resumes when you release pressure, then apply a pressure bandage. Apply several dressings over the injury and wrap them tightly with a gauze bandage or strip of cloth. Caution: Be sure the bandage is not so tight that it cuts off circulation.

the arm or leg a few inches above the injury, place a stick in the outer wrap, and twist the stick to tighten the cloth. A tourniquet cuts off the flow of blood; so it should be used only when you must sacrifice a limb to save a life. If a limb is totally severed from the victim's body, a tourniquet may be needed. A tourniquet should be left in place and then removed only by a doctor.

Stitches. A deep laceration should be held closed to prevent further injury or contamination. Band-Aids or butterfly bandages made of adhesive tape make good sutures to pull a cut closed. If a cut is bad enough to require stitches, see a doctor.

Puncture wounds. A sharp stick, bullet, or arrow can cause a puncture wound. Puncture wounds normally don't bleed heavily, and major dangers are infection and tetanus. With a bullet wound, hidden damage could be extensive; so always see a doctor.

For minor punctures, say those caused by splinters, remove the object and promote bleeding by squeezing the sides of the wound. Wash it thoroughly and apply a clean dressing. Keep a close watch for infection (see below for treatment of infection).

If an object is imbedded deeply, don't try to remove it. Dress the wound to keep it as clean as possible and get medical help. With abdominal wounds, in-

ternal damage could be grave. Stop the bleeding and get the victim to a doctor quickly. If air is escaping from a chest wound, use a clean bandage to plug the air leak.

Blisters. You can prevent most blisters. Change socks often, and if you feel a hotspot developing on your foot, cover it with moleskin or a Band-Aid. You should have no further problems.

If a blister breaks, treat it as you would any open cut—wash it with soap and water and apply a sterile dressing. You may want to drain a large, unbroken blister to relieve pressure. To do that, sterilize a needle or knife blade by holding it in an open flame, and then use it to puncture the edge of the blister. Gently squeeze out the fluid, but leave the skin in place as a sterile covering. Protect the blister with a clean bandage.

RESTORE BREATHING

Electrical shock, chest injury, near-drowning, heart attack, carbon monoxide poisoning can halt breathing. Mouth-to-mouth artificial respiration generally is recognized as the best way to restore breathing.

First, lay the victim on his back and examine his mouth and throat for blockage. Use your fingers to clear the air passage. Then tilt the victim's head back by gently lifting the back of the neck and pushing the forehead down. The lower jaw should be jutting upward to open the throat for unrestricted air passage. Pinch the victim's nose closed and place your mouth fully over his.

Now blow in. When you see his chest rise, stop blowing and turn your head to listen for the sound of exhaling air. If his chest doesn't rise or air isn't exhaled, check again for obstructions in the mouth and throat. With an adult repeat the blowing and listening cycle about once every 5 seconds. With children blow more gently and repeat the cycle once every 3 seconds. Also, for children you can place your mouth over the nose and mouth, rather than pinching the nose closed.

Continue until the victim begins breathing again on his own. A victim of a near drowning should recover quickly. An electrocution or poisoning victim may recover slowly; so continue artificial respiration up to an hour.

Choking. Choking may seem far removed from deer hunting, but a feast of venison could become an instant tragedy if a piece of venison gets caught in someone's throat. Choking deaths are not uncommon. A survey in Florida showed that 50 of 51 deaths in restaurants were caused by choking (heart attack caused the other). If someone has a seizure while eating, assume he is choking.

ARTIFICIAL RESPIRATION

If a person has stopped breathing, administer artificial respiration.

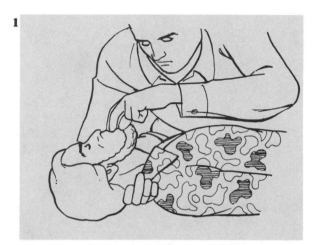

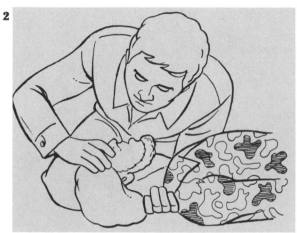

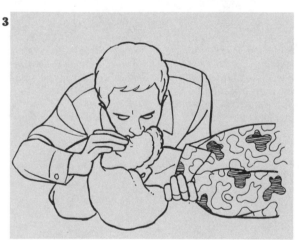

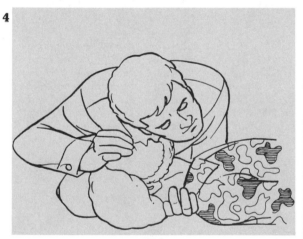

1. *Lay the victim on his back and check in his mouth to be sure the airway is clear.* **2.** *Tilt the victim's head back to open the airway. To do this lift his neck with one hand and press down gently on his forehead with the other until his chin juts upward.* **3.** *Pinch his nose closed, and place your mouth fully over his. Blow in until his chest rises.* **4.** *Turn your head and listen for air being expelled from the victim's lungs. Repeat steps 3 and 4 once every 5 seconds until the victim is breathing on his own.*

If he can breathe and cough, leave him alone. If he can't breathe, you must help him quickly. Start with the most obvious step: Ask him if he is choking. If you suspect choking open his mouth to see if you can see the obstruction. In many cases you can slip your finger down the side of the throat and hook out the object. Be careful not to push it farther down. If the person doesn't start breathing after you've cleared the throat, give artificial respiration.

If the person can't cough or breathe and you can't see the object, try other methods shown in drawings, next page.

IMMOBILIZE THE INJURY

Broken bones. Fractured bones must be held stable to prevent further injury and to reduce pain. Fractures are classified as closed (simple) and open (compound). With open fractures, a broken bone end protrudes through the skin to form an open wound. With open fractures, wrap the wound loosely with a clean bandage to prevent contamination, immobilize the break (as described below), and get the victim to a doctor. If that is not possible, bring medical aid to

CHOKING

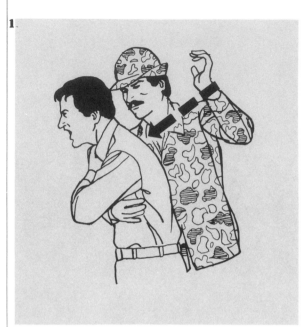

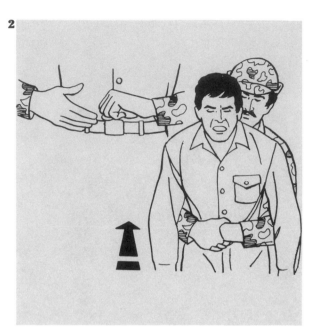

If one of your party has a seizure while eating, chances are good that he's choking. If he can't breathe or cough, follow the procedures below. **1.** *If the person is standing or sitting, support his chest with one hand and with the heel of your other hand, hit him forcefully four times between the shoulder blades.* **2.** *If that doesn't work, stand behind the victim and wrap your arms around his waist. Place your fist, thumb in, between his navel and rib cage. Grab that fist with your other hand and jerk in and up forcefully four times. Repeat 1 and 2 until you've dislodged the object from the victim's air passage and he can breathe again. If you dislodge the object and the victim doesn't start breathing, give artificial respiration.*

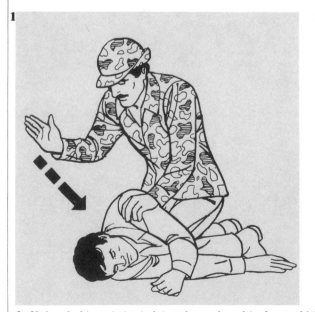

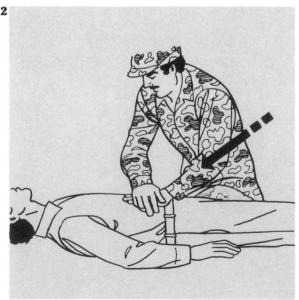

1. *If the choking victim is lying down, kneel in front of him with his chest braced against your knee, and with the heel of your hand, hit him forcefully four times between the shoulder blades.* **2.** *If that doesn't work, roll him onto his back and place your hands between his navel and rib cage. Thrust in and up forcefully four times. Repeat steps 1 and 2 until the airway is clear and the person resumes breathing. Again, you may need to apply artificial respiration.*

BROKEN ARM

If a broken arm is bent at the elbow, don't try to straighten it. Simply apply a splint and support the arm in a sling. If the arm is straight, don't try to bend it. Splint it and tie it snuggly to the person's body to keep it from swinging.

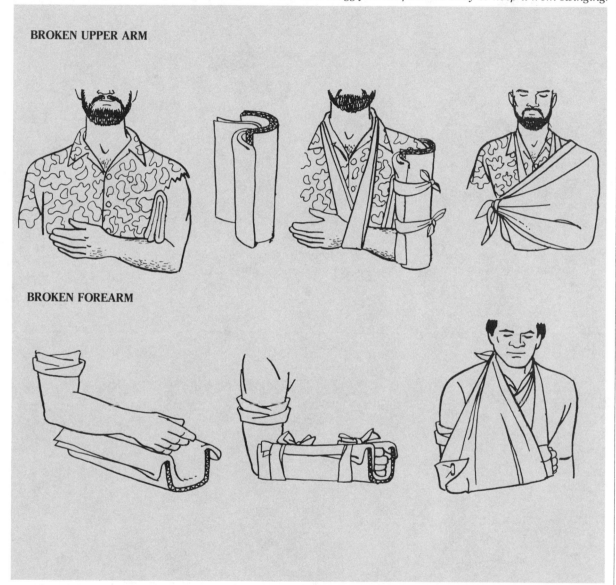

BROKEN UPPER ARM

BROKEN FOREARM

the victim. Don't try to wash the wound or push bones back into place.

A closed fracture may be harder to diagnose, but the following symptoms usually indicate broken bones: limb deformed, bent, or shorter than the opposing limb; intense pain or tenderness; swelling; blue or red color. In some cases, you may confuse fractures with sprains. If you have any doubt, treat a suspected sprain as a fracture.

Never try to reset a broken bone. You may have to apply mild traction to pull an arm or leg into line for splinting, but never go beyond that. Limbs from a tree, ski poles, pillows, rolled newspaper, clothing, and other handy materials make acceptable splints. Use clothing or other soft items to pad hard or rough splint materials.

For broken arms or legs, use straight splints, one on each side, and tie them in place with rope or strips of clothing. Tighten splints only enough to hold the bones stable, and check below the splint to make sure

BROKEN ANKLE

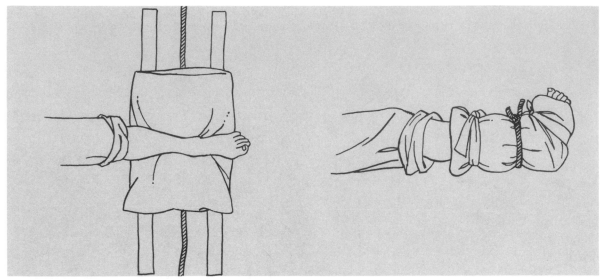

To splint a broken ankle, wrap it in a pillow or blanket and tie the splint in place with rope or strips of cloth. Never tie splints too tightly. Check the toes to make sure circulation is still good.

BROKEN LEG

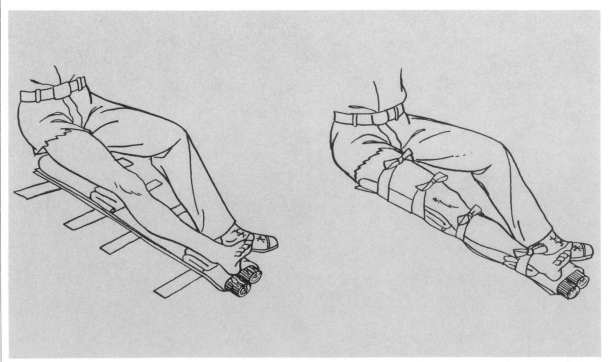

In splinting a broken leg, the splint must extend past joints above and below the break to prevent rotation of the leg. Use boards or tree limbs to splint the leg, and pad them to prevent rubbing. For added support, tie legs together.

circulation is good. If toes or fingers tingle, turn blue or white, or the pulse is weak, the splint is too tight. You can splint odd-shaped areas such as the ankle by wrapping a pillow around it and tying it snugly in place. You can close a broken hand around rolled socks or other soft round object. Tie it in place with a gauze bandage or strips of cloth.

The object in splinting is to prevent movement of fractured bone ends. To ensure that, you must splint past joints above and below the break. For example, to keep a broken lower leg from rotating, your splint must extend above the knee and below the ankle. For a broken thighbone, the splint must extend above the hip and below the knee. The splint on the outside of the leg should extend beyond the foot too, because the foot can rotate even if the knee is splinted. To give a broken leg extra support, tie it to the other leg.

If a broken arm is bent at the elbow, splint it and support the arm in a sling. To keep the arm from swinging out, wrap and tie a long cloth or rope around the chest and sling to hold the arm against the body. If the broken arm is straight, just splint it and tie it to the side of the body to prevent swinging. You can support a broken collarbone by placing the arm on the injured side in a sling and tying it against the body.

If you suspect a neck or back injury, don't move the person. Cover him, make him as comfortable as possible, and get medical help. Movement can damage the spinal cord and kill or permanently paralyze the victim. Use clothing or pillows to pad each side of the victim's head to keep it from rotating.

Symptoms of spinal injuries may be similar to those

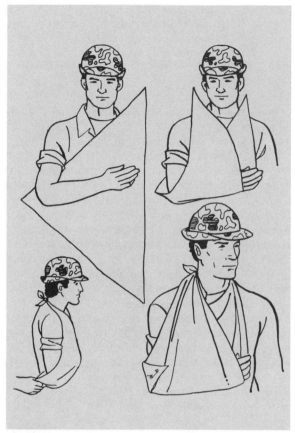

This sequence shows how to tie a sling. A sling is used to support a broken arm. Also, in case of a broken collarbone, support the arm on the broken side.

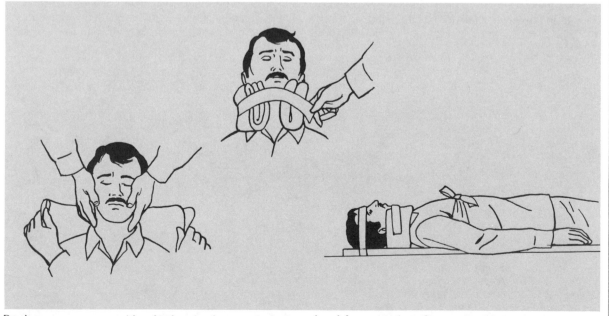

Don't move a person with a broken back or neck. Pad each side of the head in its present position to prevent *head from rotation. Get medical help. Any movement could damage the spinal cord and kill or paralyze.*

for other fractures: pain and tenderness at the break site; swelling; and redness. A vertebra may protrude noticeably. Pain radiating out from the injury, numbness or tingling, and partial paralysis also may accompany spinal injuries.

Dislocations. When a bone is pulled or twisted out of its joint, the injury is called a dislocation. Thumbs and shoulders are common dislocation sites. The joint may swell, appear deformed, hurt, and turn red. It may not move at all or may be painful when moved. Treat dislocations as fractures. Splint the joint to keep it from moving and get to a doctor. If you try to replace a dislocated bone, you may cause additional damage.

Sprains. When a joint is twisted so severely that ligaments—tissues that connect bones together—are stretched or torn, it's called a sprain. Ankles, knees, and wrists are commonly sprained. Sprains usually hurt, swell, and turn red or purple. Immediate first aid is designed to retard swelling.

First elevate the injury above heart level to reduce blood flow, and then apply cold packs, which constrict blood vessels and minimize swelling. After 24 hours, when the major threat of swelling has passed, you can apply warm packs to promote healing. To support the sprained joint, wrap it with an elastic bandage, or apply a pillow or blanket splint.

TREAT FOR SHOCK

Put simply, shock is a disabling reaction of the body to any kind of trauma. It's caused by loss of blood or body fluids, infection, lack of oxygen, pain, and anxiety or fear. It can be life threatening. Some common

symptoms are: pale or bluish and clammy skin; weakness and apathy; a weak, rapid heartbeat—faster than 100 beats per minute; shallow, rapid breathing; and nausea. Always anticipate shock following a serious injury and treat for it, even before the symptoms occur.

Treatment centers primarily on keeping the person warm and comfortable. Lay him on his back and if his face is pale, which indicates poor circulation there, elevate his feet 10 inches or so to increase blood flow to the head. If he has a head injury or breathing problems, elevate his head and upper body a few inches. If these elevated positions aren't comfortable, let him lie flat or assume the most comfortable position.

Cover the person with blankets or clothing to keep him comfortably warm. If circulation is poor, he may chill even if covered, and it helps for another person to lie close to share body heat with the victim. Above all, reassure the person and keep up his spirits. Keep him quiet and comfortable until all of his injuries are taken care of, and he has regained a strong, normal pulse rate.

PREVENT INFECTION

Infection is another serious aftereffect of injury. If an injury is so serious it requires a doctor's care, simply stop the bleeding, wrap the wound to prevent further contamination, and get medical help. If you decide to continue hunting, you must take steps to prevent infection. Even a tiny cut or blister can become infected and ruin a trip.

Cleanliness is the major preventive measure, and doctors recommend plain soap and clean water as the best means to clean a wound. After you've stopped the bleeding, wash the injury with soap to make sure

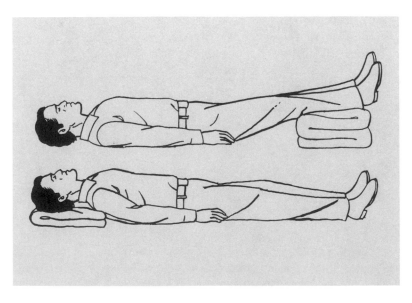

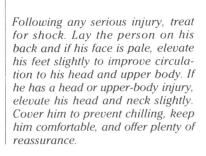

Following any serious injury, treat for shock. Lay the person on his back and if his face is pale, elevate his feet slightly to improve circulation to his head and upper body. If he has a head or upper-body injury, elevate his head and neck slightly. Cover him to prevent chilling, keep him comfortable, and offer plenty of reassurance.

you get out all dirt, and then apply a clean dressing and bandage. Most doctors do not recommend the use of iodine or other stinging disinfectants because these can kill skin tissue. However, an antibiotic that you apply directly onto the wound such as Neosporin or Polysporin can help. Continue to apply clean dressings until the injury has healed.

To treat infection. If infection sets in, the area around an injury will turn red, possibly become pussy, and become painful to the touch. Soak infections in hot, soapy, purified water several times a day. If the infection hasn't cleared up after a couple of days, see a doctor.

BURNS

Essentially, burn treatment involves four steps: (1) cool the burn as rapidly as possibly (without freezing it); (2) keep the burn clean; (3) treat for shock; (4) get to a doctor.

First-degree burns. Burns are classified by degrees, and first-degree burns are least serious because they affect only outer skin layers. The skin turns red and may be mildly swollen and painful, but no blisters develop. Moderate sunburn and fingers scalded by hot water or scorched by a hot pan are examples of first-degree burns. Immediately thrust burned areas into cold, running water until the pain subsides. First-degree burns require no further attention. A clean bandage wrapped around the burn will protect it from abrasions.

Second-degree burns. These go deeper into the skin and produce blisters and swelling. They are painful and may look moist and oozy. Immediately place the burns in cold water or apply cold, wet packs (not ice) until the pain subsides. Cover the burned area with clean bandages or cloth to prevent contamination and further injury. Do not break blisters. Elevate injured arms or legs above the level of the heart.

If more than 15 percent of the body has been burned—roughly one leg, both arms, or the chest or back—take the victim to a hospital immediately. Also, take the victim to a doctor immediately if burns affect the face, nose, or mouth. The respiratory tract could be seared, and swelling and fluid build-up could cause suffocation.

Third-degree burns. These involve charred skin, or muscle or organ tissue. The burned area may have a white, charred look. There may be less pain than with milder burns because nerves have been destroyed.

All third-degree burns require medical attention because of the serious threat of infection and the possible need for skin grafts. Immediately apply cool water or compresses (not ice). Don't try to pull away clothing that is stuck to the burn. Wrap burns with gauze or other clean, absorbent cloths. Blood serum and other body fluids seep into deep burn wounds and the predictable result is shock; so treat for shock in all cases involving serious burns. Then get medical help.

In treating burns don't apply ointments, creams or greases, and don't break blisters or try to remove charred skin or clothing. Simply cool the burn quickly, apply dressings to keep it clean, and treat for shock. Get medical help for second- and third-degree burns.

THE FIRST-AID KIT

A first-aid kit carried in a hunting pack must be small and light, yet complete. The following items will help deal with most emergencies: Band-Aids; sterile 3″ × 3″ gauze dressings; adhesive tape; gauze roll bandage; aspirin; moleskin for blisters; small bar of soap; Neosporin or other antibiotic.

For car or camp, a first-aid kit might also include: elastic bandages for sprains; cravats for slings; Dramamine or other medications to stop nausea and vomiting; antibiotic pills to fight infection; Kaopectate or other medications for diarrhea; medicines for heart problems, hypersensitivity to insect stings, or other special problems that could afflict members of your hunting gang.

PART 11
DEER WATCHING
& PHOTOGRAPHY

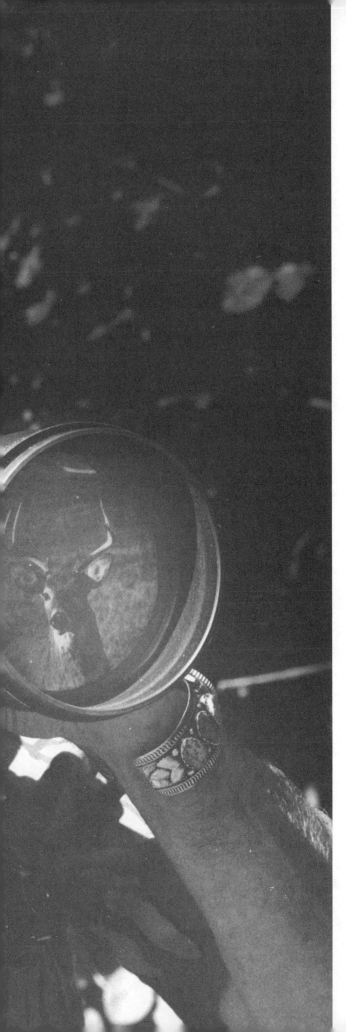

Photos by the author
unless otherwise credited

Many deer hunters make hunting itself just one of the many outdoor activities they enjoy year-round. For example, during the off-season, many outdoorsmen spend time tracking, watching, and photographing deer. Without question, these activities have practical applications during hunting season as well. The time a hunter spends watching and tracking deer teaches him a lot about how deer behave and what their favorite haunts are. It also helps him in scouting new spots for hunting during the next hunting season.

A hunter who enjoys deer watching doesn't have to know anything about photography, but the photographer who wants photos of deer must develop skill at tracking and stalking, and also have a general knowledge of deer behavior. A lot of deer hunters do have an interest in photography. Of course, some just take the occasional snapshot during a hunting trip, but many have more than "snapshot" interest in outdoor photography.

This part of the book is aimed at would-be deer photographers as well as deer watchers. It begins with deer watching and a detailed discussion of where the deer can be found and what their daily and monthly patterns of activity are. Then it covers some techniques the pros use to compose wildlife and hunting photos. This will be of interest to the amateur and serious outdoor photographer alike. The remainder of the pages cover the basics of photography and equipment—a must for anyone interested in pursuing deer photography and general wildlife photography.

RANGES OF DEER SPECIES

The deer that most North Americans see feeding in an open field or bounding into cover is the whitetail. Whitetail deer can be found most everywhere in the continental United States (except much of California, Nevada, Utah, and Colorado) and in the southern tier of the Canadian provinces. See range maps on pages 11 and 18.

While the whitetail deer population is clearly expanding, herds of another species of deer, the mule deer, are declining in the United States and Canada.

Len Rue Jr. photo

In areas such as Montana and Saskatchewan, whitetail herds are increasing as mule deer herds are shrinking. But muleys are not being forced out by whitetails. Instead, man has changed muley habitats in ways that are more favorable to whitetails.

The mule deer is changing some of its ways, however. It is not the inexperienced animal it was years ago, when it tended to be an easier prey for hunters. It has become more wary. Once found in more open country, canyon land, and rimrock areas, today's mule deer is just as likely to bed down in a brushy coulee.

The blacktail deer, a subspecies of mule deer, appears to be holding its own, though herds in California may be declining somewhat. Blacktails have always lived in closer proximity to man than the muley. Consequently, it has adapted better to man's changes of its habitat.

WHERE TO FIND DEER

So much for the generalities about where deer live. What most deer watchers and photographers want to know is where to find deer in their own immediate area. The key to finding deer is simple enough—find their feeding grounds. You can be reasonably sure that if there is food in a place that the deer know about, they will be back again.

In general, the type of feeding ground that is most likely to be frequented by deer is known in wildlife management lingo as "edge." Edge is nothing more than the transition zone between a forest and an open area, such as a field. Because there is more sunlight there (the tree canopy in a mature forest blocks out sunlight there), underbrush and small trees grow profusely in edge. This means more food for the deer to

A mature forest is an important feeding ground for deer when acorns or other nuts are dropping. Deer will also eat leaves as they fall.

browse and, more often than not, the type of foliage deer like best.

Everyone living in a rural area knows where deer cross the roads and where they can be seen feeding in the fields at certain times of the day. Most suburban areas also have these well-known locations. And any deer hunter who has done his homework knows these spots and many others, not visible from public roads, where deer feed. The one thing all of these locations have in common is that they are all open or comparatively clear areas in or near "edge." Generally, deer feed in such spots.

Hayfields, grainfields, roadside right of ways, power-line right of ways, orchards, produce farms, pastures, and rangeland, clear-cut timberland, burned-over forests, any area where the sun can get to the low-growing shrubs, are the places to observe deer, but only if such places are adjacent to brushy cover or woodlands.

Deer will feed in a transitional forest if there is brush growing there and will feed in a mature forest if acorns or other nuts are dropping or if leaves are falling from the trees. When food is available in forest areas where the deer bed, the deer will not go out into the fields to feed.

So deer and woodlands go together. Though deer cannot live in the middle of an extensive mature forest where small trees and underbrush do not grow, they

Deer are commonly seen in orchards because most fruits, particularly apples, are favored foods.

also do not live in places without at least some trees or other brushy cover. In flat terrain, such as that found throughout much of the Midwest, deer generally bed down in the densest cover they can find.

In farm country deer will live in a farm woodlot or brush row along the edge of cropland. The deer may actually seek cover in standing corn and may at times bed down in hay and grain fields. But if you remove the trees and the brush, you will drive out the deer as well. As a result, there are essentially no deer in intensively farmed areas of prairie states, where fields stretch to the horizon. Instead, deer live in the brushy river gorges, in the brush-covered coulees, gullies, and arroyos, and on the marginal land that can't be farmed.

In eastern and western areas of North America where the land is hilly or mountainous, deer usually prefer to spend the daytime hours bedded on tops of hills and ridges adjacent to their feeding areas. They lie on the southern side of the ridge in cold weather and on the northern side in warm weather. Thermals, created by the heat of the sun, carry the scent of any creature below up to the deer. From their vantage point on either side of the ridge, deer can monitor thermals coming up both sides.

In cold, windy weather mule deer will frequently lie up against a south-facing rock wall, which absorbs and then radiates the sun's warmth. But this position allows them to monitor only the thermal coming up the slope in front of them, and they have to depend on their hearing to detect anything on the rimrock above.

Deer can survive in extreme cold, but they cannot withstand cold in a strong wind. In northern states deer frequently "yard up" during a severe winter; that is, they collect in herds in swamps and hollows where there is less wind and thus less windchill. Yarded deer also maintain trails through deep snow in the yard, so that they can get to feeding areas. Snow deeper than 15 to 18 inches severely limits a deer's ability to move.

Unless you go to the yarding areas during a harsh winter, it is almost impossible to find any deer to photograph or observe. But by the time deer have been forced to yard up, most bucks have lost their antlers.

With all vestiges of browse consumed in the yarding area, this gaunt doe will probably starve to death by spring.

Bedding down in a field is not uncommon for deer in flatland areas. Deer will seek out hayfields, as here, or any other available cover.

This whitetail buck is bedded down in snow on the south side of a hill to take advantage of the sun's warmth and the thermals.

And does and fawns are in their worst condition because of the limited food supplies. So, unless your objective is to photographically record the death and destruction ever present in deer yards, it is advisable to stay out of them.

Deer in yards are usually starving because they have used and overbrowsed the yards year after year. Your intrusion into the yarding area will cause the deer to run, forcing them to waste precious energy. This is energy they need to survive and may mean the difference between life and death for them. In photographing or observing wildlife of any kind, you have a moral obligation to consider the welfare of that wildlife.

DAILY ACTIVITY CYCLES

Knowing when deer are likely to be feeding, or heading toward their feeding grounds, is every bit as important as knowing where they feed. Although deer are almost as individualistic as humans, they do tend to follow a fairly clear pattern of activity each day. The pattern revolves around their times of feeding and movement between places where they bed down and where they browse. By keeping these patterns in mind, photographers and deer watchers have much better luck in finding their quarry.

In general, deer are crepuscular animals; that is, their periods of greatest activity are at dawn and dusk. However, deer have become much more nocturnal than in centuries past because of pressure from man. This is important to remember because deer in completely protected areas are much more active in daytime. In fact, under normal circumstances, deer have five main periods of activity each day.

The accompanying "Deer Daily Activity" chart illustrates these periods graphically. Both the chart and the following comment are based on decades of close observation. Unless otherwise specified, patterns of activity are for deer that are not completely protected. These are deer the reader is most likely to encounter.

The chart shows deer activity periods (standard time, not daylight saving time) and the approximate duration of each. These should be taken only as rough guides and are appropriate for the period from late March through October. Horizontal straight lines in the "valleys" between activity peaks show the time deer spend in resting, sleeping, chewing their cuds, and moving to and from their feeding areas.

The times shown apply especially to does, fawns, and one- and two-year-old bucks. Mature bucks with large racks tend to appear at just about sunset, so that there is only half an hour of daylight left. In the morning the older bucks are heading for their beds at first light and are usually gone by sunrise 30 minutes later. During hunting season, the biggest trophy bucks tend to move only at night, unless they are forced from cover by hunters.

Most people know about the dawn and dusk feeding periods but are unaware of the other three active periods. The reason these three periods are so hard to detect is that activity is usually near the deer's bedding area. But deer are definitely moving around and feeding. This means that there are usually three additional opportunities to watch and photograph deer, once a bedding area has been located.

Deer activity is usually seen and photographed when deer are in open areas, such as orchards, fields, or open woodlands. But that does not guarantee the deer will always be in an open area during active periods shown on the chart. The distance that deer bed from feeding areas will determine when they show up. In addition, deer usually browse as they move to feeding areas. So, if the distance is over a half mile, it may take the deer a half hour to complete the journey.

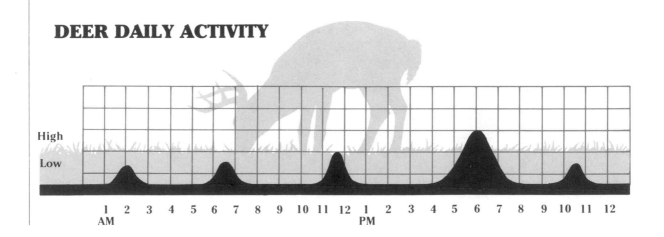

DEER DAILY ACTIVITY

High
Low

1 2 3 4 5 6 7 8 9 10 11 12 1 2 3 4 5 6 7 8 9 10 11 12
AM   PM

MONTHLY LOG OF ACTIVITY

Deer follow a pattern throughout the year, with each month being a little different from the previous month. Bucks have a different pattern from that of does. Because deer have periods when they are active only in the woods, where they are seldom seen, that will also be noted. The times given are for northwestern New Jersey and must be altered for your particular area.

January. By January, hunting seasons in most states are over. In states that allow an early January bow season, deer remain wary until the end of the month. Where the season ends in December, deer feed in fields until 8:00 A.M. Most bucks have lost their antlers, and so are indistinguishable from does at a distance. In the middle latitude states cold weather drives deer to the south-facing slopes, where the sun warms them and allows less snow buildup. In the afternoon the deer will be out about 5:00 P.M., but darkness settles in 30–45 minutes later. There is usually about a half hour of light before sunrise and after sunset.

February. This is usually the hardest month on deer. Food shortages force deer to spend more time feeding in the daytime. It is not unusual, at this time, to see deer feeding as late as 10:00 A.M. They may also be out in the afternoon as early as 4:00 P.M. In the northern tier of states deer will yard up if the snow is deep. This means they will not be seen at all, except in the yards.

March. March can go either way; some years temperatures are low, while in others the weather moderates and green sprouts appear along stream banks and on side-hills. Deer may stay in fields and open areas during midday because there is little pressure from humans. In all areas deer may be seen at any time of the day because food is still a scarce item. Even in the north, the snowmelt is usually sufficient to allow deer to leave yarding areas.

April. This month brings the first real warmth and the first real growth of vegetation. The deer are still ravenous and feed in the open till at least mid-morning and start again in the afternoon at about 3:00 P.M. The bucks' antlers start to grow about the middle of the month. This makes the bucks more reclusive, and they restrict their activities to the smallest possible area to avoid injuring their developing antlers.

Daylight saving time usually starts about the end of April so, although the deer don't change their times, we see them one hour later each morning. Sunrise now occurs about 5:45 A.M. and the sun sets about 8:15 P.M.

Most bucks shed their antlers in January. Here you can see the bloody pedicel from a shed antler. (Photo is by Irene Vandermolen)

In January and February deer feed more in the daytime hours to take advantage of what little warmth the sun provides.

In February the deer yard up in feeding areas and will be out as early as 4:00 P.M.

In April most deer start growing new antlers, which are then covered with a network of blood vessels called velvet. (Len Rue Jr. photo)

By the time the fawns are 20 minutes old, they are strong enough to stand.

Five to six times in a 24-hour period, a doe will come back to her fawns to nurse them.

By August the fawns are following after their mothers and, although still nursing, get much of their sustenance from the vegetation they eat.

The first of September finds the buck in his winter coat, and his antlers full grown and solidified. The velvet will soon dry and be peeled off. (Len Rue Jr. photo)

May. The deer are still in their winter coats and often stay in the shade to keep cool during warm days in May. Bucks continue to be inactive. But the middle of May to the middle of June is the peak of the birthing period; so the does and yearlings greatly increase their activity. The does may be seen at almost any time of the day. Prior to giving birth the does drive off or lose their yearlings. These frantic young are frequently seen, and often killed, on highways.

June. This is a poor month for deer observation and photography: "Summertime and the living is easy." Bucks are still in seclusion and are seldom seen. Does that have given birth become secretive. Yearling bucks move off on their own, and yearling does temporarily go off on their own and then rejoin the older does after the new fawns are about a week old. The sun rises about 5:30 A.M. and sets about 8:35 P.M., and from here on, the days will gradually become shorter. Deer shed the last of their winter hair early in June and are now in their red coats.

July. Deer observations pick up again in July. After the fawns are one week old they begin to follow the doe around. Yearling females now often rejoin their mothers. If they have also given birth they bring their young to join the female groupings, definitely a matriarchal society now. The weather is hot and deer will be out from about 5:30 A.M. until shortly after 7:00 A.M. Deer seek north-facing slopes in the daytime because it is cooler there. The bucks' antlers are almost full grown and the bucks become more active. None of the deer venture out in the afternoon until shadows stretch across the fields and the air becomes cooler.

August. This is the hottest month. Days are getting shorter: the sun rises about 6:15 A.M. and sets about 8:00 P.M. All midday activity takes place in the deepest woods, where it is too dark for photography, unless you are using the faster films. Most fawns lose their spots by the end of the month. Bucks' antlers are full grown and have solidified; so they no longer have to be careful about injuring them. Evenings may cool off and deer may go out to feed about 6:00 P.M.

September. This month brings warm days with cool nights, and all of the animals respond to the change. Deer can now be seen in the morning from sunrise at 6:00 A.M. until a little after 7:00 A.M. In the evening they feed from about 5:00 P.M. until dark. Between the fifth and the fifteenth, the bucks rub the velvet from their antlers and now "buck rubs" on saplings and small trees are increasingly common. Deer are active in daylight hours until the bowhunting season opens. When there is hunting pressure, deer feed later in the morning and earlier in the evening on Wednesday and Thursday nights. That is because weekends bring out hunters in the greatest numbers.

October. During the last week in September and the first two weeks in October all of the deer seem to virtually disappear. They abandon their regular haunts and trails; they stop feeding on corn, soybeans, and alfalfa, or in the orchards. That is because over most of North America, wherever oaks are found, the acorns are dropping. Deer feed on the acorns, particularly those of the white oak. In many states the gun-hunting season also opens and this increased pressure makes the deer generally more secretive. Where the gun season has not opened, most bowhunters have either gotten their deer or are hunting a lot less. Sunrise is now about 7:15 A.M. and sunset is about 5:15 P.M. At the end of the month daylight saving time is over. About the time the clocks change, so do the deer's activities.

November. The last week and a half in October, all of November, and the first two or three weeks in December are the rutting season, when bucks are most active. Their necks are now swollen, and the mating urge causes them to expand their range to 10 or 12 square miles. Except for the biggest, oldest, trophy bucks, bucks throw caution to the wind and may be seen at any time of the day. Small-game season opens in almost all states in November, and deer-hunting season starts in many. This pressure keeps does and their young out of sight during most of the daylight hours.

The breeding season peaks from the 10th to the 20th of November, although mating takes place for several weeks before, and up to a month and a half after, those dates. This is a very active time for does as well, because as their estrus approaches they become more active in order to attract bucks. If you are ever fortunate enough to photograph bucks fighting, it will probably be during this peak period.

December. This is usually a poor month to see deer and is even worse for photography. Days are the shortest of the year, with the sun rising about 7:15 A.M. and setting about 4:35 P.M. The deer population has been greatly reduced, with 20–30 percent having been harvested by hunters. Deer that haven't been shot have been shot at; so almost all deer activity now takes place under the cover of darkness.

FEEDING HABITS

A deer's life revolves around feeding. And as it happens, feeding time offers some of the best opportunities to watch and photograph them. Consequently, it is important to understand in some detail just how the deer feeds.

As mentioned earlier, deer are most often seen when they are browsing in an open field or near a

After peeling the velvet from their antlers, the bucks make many "rubs" as they ready themselves for the rut.

In most regions, the whitetail's breeding season occurs between late October and Christmas.

Deer feed less in the winter, not only because food is scarce but because their metabolism drops so that their body requires less food.

A whitetail doe feeds on the lush summer vegetation.

forest edge. But deer are at a serious disadvantage in this situation, because they are out in the open and because their senses are almost completely involved in gathering food. But evolution has provided deer with a compromise to this vulnerability that allows them to spend a comparatively short time (relative to their body weight) browsing in open areas. This unfortunately also limits the best opportunities to observe deer.

The compromise is a special stomach—deer are ruminants and have the ability to chew their cud the same way cattle, sheep, goats, and other animals of this type do. The reason this stomach is so important is that deer can strip off and swallow forage with very little chewing. This allows deer to take in large amounts of food rather quickly, when it is most exposed to danger.

The hastily swallowed forage (cud) is stored in the rumen, one of the four chambers ruminants have in their stomachs. Once the deer arrives at a safe place, it then regurgitates the cud from the rumen and chews it slowly and thoroughly. Then it reswallows the chewed cud for digestion in other parts of its stomach. Deer spend a total of 7 or 8 hours a day chewing their cud.

In winter deer eat much less food, not only because less food is available, but because they don't need as much food as in the summer months. As temperatures

drop in late autumn and winter, the deer's metabolism also slows down. As a result deer can survive in cold weather despite food shortages—up to a point. In fact, a deer in excellent condition in late autumn can go 60 days in the winter without food. This is another reason why deer may be hard to find in December and January, even though the weather is mild and yarding has not occurred. Hunting pressure has made them wary and they simply don't need to be out feeding in the expected places.

The best opportunities for observing deer will be in areas that offer good habitats. This means, of course, that protective cover is available and that food and water are nearby. The better the habitat, the more chances there will be to see deer, because the area will support a larger herd.

The presence of food in ample quantity is important. Every day during the spring, summer, and autumn, the average deer consumes 8 pounds of green forage for each 100 pounds of body weight. For good body and antler growth they need a diet that is 16–18 percent protein. They also need minerals and trace elements for bone and body development; they get them by going to natural mineral springs, licking certain types of rocks (natural licks), or by feeding in fertilized fields.

Browse, the tender tips of woody plants, is the deer's dietary staple throughout the year, but browse is usually all that is available in winter.

COMMON DEER FOODS

WINTER

Whitetail. Red maple, striped maple, witch hazel, sumac, blueberry, hemlock, willow, white pine, viburnums, yellow birch, ash, wintergreen, fir, white cedar, poplar, oaks, lespedeza, snowberry, blackgum, greenbrier, dogwood, swamp ironwood, live oak, persimmon, snakeweed, bearberry, wild rose, aspen, Oregon grape, spruce, white birch, sassafras, crabapple, Japanese honeysuckle, apple, coralberry, honey locust, lady's-tobacco, plantain, strawberry, speedwell, hawthorn, poison ivy, mints, goldenrod, pussytoes, aster, teaberry, acorns.

Mule deer. Creeping barberry, bearberry, snowberry, ceanothus, sagebrush, jack pine, Douglas fir, rabbitbrush, cedar, mountain mahogany, bitterbush, fendlera, sierra juniper, scrub oak, fescuegrass, sedge, wild oats, bromegrass, creek dogwood, mesquite, cliffrose, holly-leaf buckthorn, turbinella oak, mountain misery, stonecrop, elderberry, redberry, California buckeye, antelope brush, black oak, Pacific serviceberry, bitter cherry, western chokecherry, tesota, velvet elder, sunflower, cottonwood.

Blacktail. Douglas fir, trailing blackberry, red huckleberry, yew, madrone, salal, sword fern, vine maple, manzanita, chamise, red cedar, usnea, moss, bracken, yerba santa, scrub oak, buckbrush, toyon, chaparral pea, California laurel, live oak, coffeeberry, filaree, acorns, wavyleaf ceanothus.

SPRING

Whitetail. May hawthorn, clover, alfalfa, cinquefoil, crabapple, teaberry, trailing arbutus, greenbrier, dandelion, plantain, corn, wild strawberry, trefoils, lespedeza, aster, sunflower, pokeweed, jewelweed, poison ivy, New Jersey tea, bitterbush, serviceberry, red maple, Japanese honeysuckle, sassafras, willow, speedwell, blueberry, big and little bluestem, curly mesquite, tall dropseed, magnolia, yaupon holly, bigleaf gallberry.

Mule deer. Sunflower, fescuegrass, bluegrass, bromegrass, ragweed, kohleria, needlegrass, wheatgrass, ricegrass, goldeneye, mountain mahogany, silktassel, oak, manzanita, wild oats, dogwood.

Blacktail. Grasses, sedges, horsetail, bracken, trailing blackberry, fireweed, red elder, thimbleberry, salmonberry, salal, willow, cedar, deerbrush, chamise, live oak, scrub oak, mountain mahogany, Douglas fir.

SUMMER

Whitetail. Red maple, striped maple, blueberry, blackberry, greenbrier, alfalfa, corn, dogwood, swamp ironwood, ferns, wild rose, mushrooms, bluegrass, bearberry, wheatgrass, sassafras, wild grape, chestnut oak, pokeweed, sunflower, blackeyed susan, crabapple, soybean, wild hydrangea, elderberry, jewelweed, aster, sumac, cabbage palm.

Mule deer. Deerwitch, fescuegrass, pine, eriogonum, serviceberry, oak, bluegrass, kohleria, needlegrass, wheatgrass, ricegrass, wild cherry, mountain mahogany, silktassel, gramagrass, mushrooms, lupine, knotweed, thimbleberry, elderberry, dogwood, mesquite.

Blacktail. Salal, black raspberry, red alder leaves, willow, bracken, grasses, sedges, thimbleberry, vine maple, salmonberry, fireweed, red elder, sow thistle, figwort, mushrooms, trailing blackberry, huckleberry, plantain, clover, pearly everlasting, yarrow, rose, interior live oak, buckeye, chokecherry, chamise, honeysuckle, poison oak, foothill ash.

AUTUMN

Whitetail. Acorns, oxalis, plains lovegrass, whorled nodviolet, mat euphorbia, arrowleaf sida, maple, sweetfern, willow, wintergreen, grasses, oak, wild cherry, lespedeza, snowberry, greenbrier, blackgum, creeping blueberry, holly, live oak, persimmon, snakeweed, wheatgrass, honeysuckle, aster, goldenrod, pussytoes, palmetto berries, mushrooms, teaberry, sumac, blueberry, coralberry, sassafras, witch hazel, crabapple, dogwood, wild rose, wild grape, clover, elderberry, bittersweet, red raspberry.

Mule deer. Creeping barberry, bearberry, snowberry, snowbush, jack pine, sunflower, sagebrush, pine, cedar, mountain mahogany, cliffrose, poplar, needlegrass, gramagrass, paintbrush, bitterbush, rabbitbrush, wild cherry, fescuegrass, manzanita, eriogonum, quaking aspen, sedge, serviceberry, hackberry, arrowleaf sida, acorns.

Blacktail. Acorns, filaree, bromegrass, manzanita, chamise, scrub oak, deer brush, wavyleaf ceanothus, buckeye, wild grape, ferns, toyon, poison oak, western chokecherry, chaparral pea, wormwood, trailing blackberry, plantain, vine maple, annual agoseries, red alder, huckelberry, salmonberry, clover.

Douglas fir is a major western deer food.

Knowing what types of foods deer eat will help identify likely feeding grounds where they can be observed. The accompanying lists give the preferred foods for the three types of deer common to North America. Foods are presented by season, but are not listed by the deer's preference because these differ from one region to another. Also these lists cover deer ranges throughout the country; so some foods may not be found in your particular area.

WEATHER AND DEER ACTIVITY

All wild animals are extremely sensitive to changes in barometric pressure that occur before storms. They seem to be able to detect such changes before man-made devices do. During the spring, summer, and early fall, you can tell that rain is on the way when you see deer feeding much earlier in the afternoon than normal. It is not that deer want to stay out of the rain; rather, a rainy night means a dark night, and even deer need some light to see at night. So deer feed earlier in the day and for a longer period just before a storm. However, rain does not change a deer's activities during hunting season, because feeding habits have already been disrupted by man.

Deer don't like to get wet any more than man does. If the storm is a short, hard shower, deer will seek shelter beneath the tree canopy. If the storm is a protracted one, though, the deer will continue to feed in the rain.

During hot daytime weather in summer, or if the deer are heavily hunted, they will feed longer on moonlit nights. Otherwise, the deer's feeding activities are not affected by the moon.

THE HUNTING SEASON

Hunters often say that deer must have a calendar because, when the season opens, deer are not where they have been seen before. But prior to the hunting season, man's activity in and around the woodlands increases dramatically. First bowhunters scout the territory and then hunt it as the season opens. Small-game season follows: additional hunters tramp through the fields and woods, and most of them bring their dogs. This increased activity and noise makes the deer much more wary.

On opening day of gun season an army of hunters takes to the woods. Hundreds of automobile headlights pierce the predawn darkness on back roads, wood roads, and along the edge of fields where vehicular traffic is seldom seen. Car doors slam, voices crackle in the still morning air, and good natured banter and camaraderie prevail. Then, as this phalanx of men moves in from the roads, they push all the deer ahead of them, forcing the deer to seek safety in the most inaccessible regions available.

If the woodland is a small tract, it can be covered and the deer may be forced to move continuously. If the tract is a large one, some deer get so far from the roads that they may not be seen for the entire season. Usually, as darkness falls and the hunters leave, deer will start to drift back to their home range. But when they start from so far back, and so late in the evening, they usually will not be seen in their regular haunts.

The opening day's pressure is always the greatest on deer; the first week is usually intense; after that, as the season progresses, most of the pressure comes on weekends. Still, there is enough disruption by man to cause the deer to continue to be extremely wary throughout the rest of the hunting season and for at least a month afterward. Only then do the deer begin to resume their normal patterns and activities.

THE HUNTER AS PHOTOGRAPHER

Whether they are watching deer during the off-season or actually on a hunting trip, many hunters like to take snapshots as personal mementos and to show friends at home. Other hunters take their photography more seriously, and go after shots either as wildlife photography hobbyists or as an opportunity to get their photos published in sporting magazines. No matter what you intend to do with your hunting and wildlife photographs, the material in the following sections will help you take professional-quality shots. And, should you decide to try to get your work published, you will find detailed advice on what types of photos magazines look for and how to go about making a submission.

But it is important to remember that there is more to the relationship between hunting and photography than two hobbies that just happen to work together. Good deer hunters can become good photographers because the successful deer hunter knows deer, their habits, and their habitats. For those hunters who hunt during deer season and photograph deer for the rest of the year, the time spent in the field makes them more successful when they do carry a gun. There is no better way to thoroughly know deer than to spend countless hours watching, tracking, and photographing them.

While knowing how to get good shots of deer will not necessarily guarantee getting photographs published, magazines do buy pictures on merit, not the established reputation of the photographer. Although a pro's work may be looked at first because of his ability to produce good work consistently, a newcomer who happens to have precisely what an editor is looking for can almost count on being published. That is why it is virtually impossible for anyone to make a good living from the sale of still photographs of wildlife alone. But it also makes wildlife photography a profitable and enjoyable pastime for many hunters and outdoorsmen.

GRAB SHOTS

Many hunters carry a small 35mm camera with them when they go hunting. These tiny 35mm cameras are great for "grab shots," photos that are taken when nothing else is happening, after the kill has been made, or just around camp. You should remember, though, that to do the job right, you should either hunt or take pictures—not both.

Sometimes hunters plan to do wildlife photography while they hunt. But such plans are doomed to failure because, if hunting is the main objective, the hunter won't have the proper equipment to photograph wildlife. To do good photography, a lot of equipment is needed, and the hunter can't carry all that and a gun as well. Nor would any hunter in his right mind jeopardize his chance to take a trophy deer by photographing it first. So if photography is your second choice, your photos will probably show it—at least

A whitetail buck is here photographed slightly below his eye level. (Irene Vandermolen photo)

This mule deer was photographed from a low angle to silhouette him against the sky.

those taken while you are out in the field trying to bag a deer.

PHOTOGRAPHING DEER

If you are out photographing in the off-season, you will no doubt want to get shots of deer as they go through their daily cycle of activity. With hunting pressure eliminated, it should be possible to take photos of deer in nearby areas. But if you are really serious about photographing deer, you may want to work on public lands where deer are never hunted. This makes it easier to get close to them because they are less wary there.

There are a few things to remember when setting up shots of live deer. Photographs should be taken with the camera at the deer's eye level or lower. If possible, get below a deer on a hillside and shoot up at it. If you can get the deer on a ridge so that you can photograph it against the clear blue sky, you have the makings of a cover or calendar shot. Even on level ground, you may be able to silhouette the deer against the sky by shooting from ground level. And don't put your camera away when the sun starts to set. Position yourself so the deer is between you and the sun or the fading skylight, take a meter reading from the sky,

and take your photograph. This angle makes the deer a true, black silhouette.

It is very important, when possible, to get a catchlight, or highlight, in the deer's eye when you take the shot. The little dot of reflected light will breathe life into your photo. Some animals have overhanging eyebrows or hair that makes highlights all but impossible to obtain. But a deer's eyes protrude from the sides of its head so that the deer actually sees about 310 degrees of a circle. Those protruding eyes make it easy to get a highlight.

One other point is worth mentioning. When it comes to selling photos of live deer, the most salable shots are those in which the deer is alerted and holding its head up. You may find it necessary to make a slight sound to make it pick up its head.

COMPOSITION

Not everything you see makes a good photograph, but even the most commonplace item can be photographically enhanced—if you know the basics of composition and use a little imagination. That is because in a photograph you focus the viewer's attention on only what you want him to see.

Getting the viewer to focus on your subject is what

The catchlight, or highlight, in the eye of the buck at left brings the photo to life. The photo at right lacks life and interest because the shadows prevented a highlight in the buck's eye.

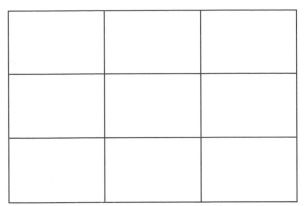

This grid divides photos into thirds horizontally and vertically, creating four points of greatest visual impact at grid intersections and illustrating the rule of thirds, as described in the text.

Strong horizontal lines, generally, should not split the photograph unless you need the strong horizontal to help create a special effect, such as a reflection.

good composition is all about, and there are two basic ways you put that attention where you want it. First, you include only a small part of a larger scene in the picture, thereby eliminating background detail that might distract attention from your subject. Second, you position the subject in a way that emphasizes it in the picture.

The fundamental rule of composition in regard to positioning a subject in a photograph is called the rule of thirds, or the four points of greatest visual impact. This is not to say that the strongest point of interest can never be positioned elsewhere successfully. It's just that in most cases this is where the viewers interest tends to be, whether the photographer plans it that way or not.

The accompanying photos show where these points of greatest visual impact are. The four points at which the horizontal and vertical lines cross mark the points of visual impact. Any one can be the main point of interest, but all four cannot be used at once. The accompanying photographs illustrate how to use points of impact to improve your shots.

There are other tricks you can use to emphasize, or even distort your subject. Many people are familiar with the trick of suspending a small fish on a string close to the camera, while having the "lucky" fisherman stand way back from the camera. In the photo the small fish becomes a creditable monster lunker.

You can do the same thing to enhance the antlers on your buck. Instead of sitting beside the deer and holding up its head, sit behind the deer's shoulders and lift up the head. That slight change in position, coupled with framing the hunter with the antlers, makes the trophy appear to be much larger. These photos may help sell your story, or at least impress your friends a bit. But they won't affect the official Boone and Crockett measurements. (The reason why the trick mentioned above works is simple. The cam-

Photographs can be framed, or cropped, either vertically or horizontally, depending on your need. In any case, a one-third line between the deer's eyes, rather than centering the eyes, improves the effect. (Irene Vander-molen photo)

Ellipses here hold your eye to the center of the photograph, adding to the impact of a feeding photo.

era records three dimensions as two—height and width. Depth can only be implied through proper camera techniques.)

If you have been fortunate enough to down a real trophy deer, then photograph the antlers to scale. One of the simplest ways to do this is by putting your rifle across the buck's rack. Everyone knows the approximate size of a rifle and that helps the viewer gauge the actual antler size. Or you can use any other familiar object to provide scale.

There are techniques for achieving emphasis in the finished photograph. As has already been mentioned, subject placement is important. Direction of the sub-

ject's motion is too, when it comes to action shots. For example, a broadside shot of a deer running full tilt often has far more impact than a shot of a deer running directly away from camera. Other ways of achieving emphasis in a photograph include lighting, shading, framing, simplifying, strengthening, perspective, scale, repetition, balance, form, and selective focusing.

KINDS OF PHOTOS THAT SELL

By luck alone, you may come up with a grab shot that an editor wants desperately for a coming issue. But more often than not you will have to begin thinking in terms of the types of shots that an outdoor magazine usually publishes. That does not mean you have to give up your chance at bagging a deer in order to get photos of someone else making the kill. But you will probably have to start taking more photographs than before during a hunting trip and also learn to keep your eye out for shots that will sell.

What sells? The easiest way to find this out is to check your favorite sporting magazines. Note the types of photos that illustrate other hunters' stories. You'll soon see that there are certain stock approaches to these photo stories—in fact, it's almost impossible to come up with a brand new approach. What makes the most published photos seem new is that they are of different hunters, with different deer, in different habitats. Once you get an idea of the standard approaches that editors look for in hunting photographs, then you will have to use some imagination to find

Triangles or wedge forms can create strong composition, as here, holding your attention on these fawns.

Backlighting can greatly enhance some photographs. This is also called rim-lighting. The deer form a triangle that helps the composition.

shots that tell your story without making it look just like the one in last month's issue.

The hunter who hopes to sell a story about a hunting trip cannot take too many photographs. Photographs of the living quarry are great if they can be gotten but, strange as this may sound, they are not the most important photos. It is the support photos that flesh out the bones of the basic story and make it different. Support photos are also the ones the editor can't buy; he can always get all the basic deer photos needed from the free-lance wildlife photographers. So you really can go out after deer—and do a photo story about the trip at the same time.

There are certain types of support photos you should look for to document your story properly. For instance, you need to take photos of your means of transportation to the hunting area. Did you drive, fly, canoe, or get in by horse? Don't show just the means of transportation, show the gear to be packed, the packing, any difficulties in packing, the unloading, and so on.

When you arrive at the hunting area or campsite, take lots of establishing photos of the terrain, habitat, and your companions. If you go to a hunting camp, take photos of the cook, food cooking, food being served, food being eaten, the sleeping quarters, and the fellows playing cards. Try to capture the warmth and the camaraderie that makes a hunting camp such a special place.

Close-up shots always enhance a story; take photographs of a hunter's hands sharpening his knife, loading his gun, or pointing to a big buck's tracks, to a buck rub, to a good trail crossing.

It's exceedingly difficult to take photos of a hunter actually shoting the deer unless you spend all of your

Support photos of a bowhunter's tent camp at mealtime can begin with an establishing shot like this.

Leave space in front of running deer so they don't appear to be leaving the picture. (Irene Vandermolen photo)

A follow-up to the establishing shot above might be breaded venison loin cooking and ready to eat.

Magazine editors tend to like shots with a hunter approaching a downed buck with his rifle at ready. (Irene Vandermolen photo)

A photo of dragging may help round out a photo story. (Irene Vandermolen photo)

An editor may want an entire skinning how-to series. (Irene Vandermolen photo)

time backing up the hunter for just that shot. What you can shoot easily is another hunter up in a tree stand, glassing for game with a binocular, sighting down his gun, or even eating his lunch while on his stand.

When a deer is bagged, take photographs of the hunter approaching the downed deer with his rifle at the ready. Stand beyond the deer and frame the advancing hunter, from a low angle, through the deer's antlers. If the story is about your buck get someone to take the same type picture of you. If you are alone, set up your camera on a small pocket tripod, set the shutter on self-timer, and hurry to the predetermined spot in the picture before the shutter clicks.

Take photos of tagging of the deer, field-dressing it, dragging or carrying it out of the woods, hanging it up, and so on. But be careful here. Today, blood offends many people and, most of the time, it doesn't have to be shown in photographs. If your deer died in a pool of blood, move the deer to a clean spot before taking the photographs. If there is blood on the snow, cover it up with fresh, clean snow. If the animal has blood on its muzzle or is bleeding from a wound, wipe the blood off with grass, snow, a paper towel or napkin. But wipe it off. After a deer has died the relaxing of the muscles allows the tongue to lengthen and hang out of the mouth. Push the tongue back in and close the mouth. Within 20 to 30 minutes of dying, the deer's eyes take on a green sheen. Close the deer's eyelids. Clean up your act! Clean up the deer before you take your picture.

If your deer is weighed on an outdoor beam scale, by all means photograph the weighing and take a close-up of the scale weight. Also, have photos taken as you skin out your deer. Just as there are "many ways to skin a cat," there are many ways to skin a deer. Perhaps your method will help some other hunters to do a better job. Such shots are difficult to do well because the body cavity is often filled with blood so that the photo may not show important anatomical parts clearly. For excellent examples of this type of how-to photography, refer to Part 7.

If you are proficient at butchering, have photographs taken of the entire processing of the meat. Every year this facet of deer hunting is covered in many sporting magazine photo spreads and some books. And as more and more hunters come from urban areas, the demand for this information increases. These hunters have to turn to photographic "how-to" stories because they have no one else to teach them. Perhaps it will be your photographs that will help do the job.

PHOTOGRAPHING DEER SIGN

Deer watchers sometimes take photos of tracks and signs for record purposes. But hunters who want to sell a photo story to a magazine should remember to include photos of this type with other supporting shots. Shots of a deer browse and tracks, trails, rubs, scrapes, droppings, beds, and other sign can help

flesh out the hunting story. And they can be instructive as well if, say, you want to give a slide presentation on hunting skills. The accompanying photographs show a few types of shots you may want to try.

SELLING YOUR PHOTOGRAPHS

Never ship your photographs to an editor without querying the editor first to see if he is interested in seeing them. If you ship your work without a query letter and don't enclose return postage, the editor is not obligated to return your photographs. If he has agreed to see them he will usually pay the return postage. The query is not only a courtesy, it's good business. Why send in photographs to someone who may not be interested in what you have to offer?

When submitting transparencies for consideration make sure you send the originals; do not send duplicate transparencies, commonly called dupes. Dupes never match the quality of originals. When you submit your work you are competing with many other wildlife photographers. It is in your interest to show the editor the best-quality photographs you have.

Shipping photographs. If you are shipping transparencies, put each slide in a separate Kimac plastic sleeve to protect them from dust and scratches. Then, to facilitate handling, 20 transparencies should be placed in a 9 × 11-inch plastic display sheet. That way an editor can look at a lot of transparencies in a short time. Your transparencies can be stored forever in the individual sleeves. Display sheets, if made of poly-

Take photographs of deer tracks with side lighting, above left, to create shadows and illustrate track depth. The deer tracks at right create an interesting picture. Note the effect of the S curve. Your eye starts at the bottom and goes right up the trail until it disappears.

This displays some of the more than 1,000 national covers that photographer Leonard Lee Rue III has sold.

All transparencies should be protected by Kimac sleeves at all times. These sleeves will not emit gases over time that damage transparencies. When submitting transparencies to photo editors, place them in 9×11-inch plastic sheets, as shown, for easy viewing by editors and for ease of tallying slides.

vinylchloride, can leach out gases harmful to transparencies over time. Ask about nonvolatile sheets at your camera dealer. Humidity also is harmful to transparencies.

Black-and-white prints should be protected from damage by sandwiching them between sheets of cardboard.

If you use shipping forms, you and the client know what the terms of your agreements are as to price, reproduction rights, usage, length of time the material can be kept, and so on. Keep one copy in your file and send two copies with the shipment. Your client should return one of these copies to you to acknowledge receipt. Many pros rely simply on letters itemizing the contents of the photo submission, and then send follow-up letters if there is a delay in acknowledgment of receipt.

Your shipment of color transparencies or black-and-white prints should then be sandwiched between sheets of heavy cardboard and placed in a box or stiff cardboard mailing envelope.

There is no way that you can insure your transparencies for their full potential value. The best protection you can give your photographs is to ship them only by one of the many services that offers a return receipt.

Photo fees. Although magazine and book publishers are dependent upon the photographers and writers for material, editors are in the driver's seat when it comes to pricing. Fees are based on a magazine's budget for photos, which is often based roughly on the magazine's circulation or on a book's press run.

Fees paid for photographs vary according to the way they are used. Advertising pays the highest rates; front covers of magazines are second; and calendars are third. The highest-circulation magazines tend to pay the best photo fees; so if your photos are top-notch it can pay to start at the top. This is one time when it doesn't pay to work your way up. Often the only right you have in negotiating prices with editors and publishers is the right of refusal.

Many photographers, when they are starting out, will practically give their work away just to see it published and their name in print. A few years later they wonder why they can't command much higher prices. It's simple. There are just so many other photographers out there willing to sell their photographs at whatever price is offered.

This is also the reason that most magazines do not send wildlife photographers out on assignment. Why pay someone, no matter how good he is, to go out to try to take the desired photographs? A general call to the professionals can result in a deluge of good photographs on just about any subject.

Photograph agents are taking on fewer photographers today because most of their files are glutted. But they will always take on a photographer who is doing exceptional work. Most agents today demand an exclusive contract with the photographers they handle.

Although some agents will split the fee 60/40, in favor of the client, most split it 50/50. While this may seem unfair to you after having put up the film, camera, trip expense, time, and experience, the agency has expenses too. These are in the form of salaries, office rent, overhead, time, experience, and *contacts*. Having an agent means that, while you are out shooting photographs, the agent may be selling enough of your work to allow you to be out in the field.

Editors prefer to receive 8 × 10-inch black-and-white photos processed by high-quality photo labs. Prints should have a ¼-inch white border for your identification and for the publisher's production notations.

This transparency is ready to be marketed. It is captioned and coded. It indicates restricted usage and copyright. And it has the photographer's name and address.

Where to sell photographs. You may not need these suggestions because you probably already read the magazines that you want to approach. The simplest way to find additional markets is to go to any well-stocked magazine rack and just study the magazines.

The best book on marketing photographs is *Photographer's Markets*, published by Writer's Digest Books.

If you become serious about wildlife photography, you will find a great deal of information and additional markets in the *Guilfoyle Report*, available from A. G. Editions, 142 Bank St., New York, NY 10014.

Copyright protection. The newest copyright laws protect you from the moment that you push the shutter on your camera. To inform the world that your work is copyrighted, it is necessary for you to stamp every slide and black-and-white photo with the © and your name and address. The © stamp gives you the needed protection and will be honored by almost everyone. In the case of litigation, you should then register your

© with the Library of Congress. But your work is copyrighted the moment you stamp the seal on it.

No photograph should ever be sent to a prospective client without a proper caption, a code number, the © stamp, your name and address, and the statement "One-time use only." A sample of a prepared slide is shown.

The rights to your photograph that you sell are becoming extremely complicated. Various publications buy first USA rights, or first North American rights, English-speaking world rights, entire world rights, ⅛, ¼, ½, ¾, full-page, and double-page rights, exclusive rights, first-time rights, one-time-use-only rights, etc.

It is illegal for an artist to reproduce one of your photographs in any art form so that it is recognizable as your work—even if the background has been changed—without your permission. Professional artists are aware of this, but most amateurs are not. Many artists will use a number of photographs as references and do a composite. This they can do legally. As a photographer, you can sell the artist the right to reproduce your photograph, hair for hair.

BASICS FOR PRO PHOTOGRAPHY

Any hunter can take decent grab shots with one of the many automated cameras that are available today. These cameras are designed to make all the critical adjustments for the photographer, and for the general public they work just fine. But to do serious wildlife photography, or to take hunting photos that are good enough to sell to magazines, the photographer must know much more about cameras than how to aim, focus, and trip the shutter. The following section provides a brief discussion of the workings of both camera and film, as well as some of the special concerns of hunting and wildlife photography.

THE CAMERA

The earliest cameras were nothing more than a closed box with a pinhole in one wall to admit light. The pinhole was kept covered until it was time to take the photograph. Then the hole was uncovered briefly and light entered the box, exposing the film mounted on the opposite wall inside the box. Pinhole cameras worked, but not well enough to be anything more than a curiosity.

Modern cameras are much more complex, having lenses, shutters, diaphragms, and the like. But they are all modeled on the basic principle of an enclosed box with a small light-admitting hole to expose the film inside.

The camera most commonly used by both amateur and professional outdoor photographers today is the 35mm camera. The 35mm designation indicates the size of the film used (a frame of film measured diagonally) in the camera. While film this size has some disadvantages, it nevertheless is the best compromise available for general outdoor work. There are many other film sizes and cameras designed to use them, of course, and these include 2¼ × 2¼-inch film for still cameras, 4 × 5-inch and 8 × 10-inch film sheets

The sizes of film available are shown here. Larger sized films do not need to be enlarged as much as the smaller films to make a print of a given size. But, finer-grain transparency film is available in only the two smaller sizes.

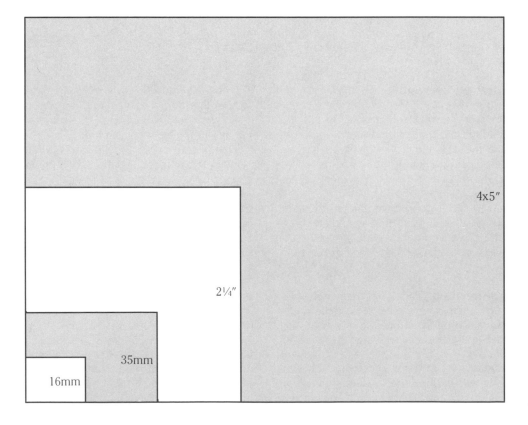

used in view cameras (for studio, scenic, and architectural work), and such movie camera film as 8mm and 16mm.

The camera consists of a camera body, a shutter, viewfinder, lens, and diaphragm. Each of these basic parts is discussed below. Light meters are covered later in this section.

THE CAMERA BODY

The camera body is really nothing more than a light-tight box that holds a piece of film in place for proper exposure. The camera body also serves as the mounting point for lenses, the viewfinder, and motor drive unit.

The camera body has a winding mechanism (if the camera is designed for roll film). This advances the film to the next frame, counts the number of exposures already made, and cocks the shutter for the next exposure. The frame of film that is in position for exposure is held flat and in place at a perfect right angle to the lens axis. Otherwise, parts of the film would be out of focus during an exposure.

THE SHUTTER

The shutter in most 35mm cameras is a built-in curtain with slits of various widths cut into it. The curtain is moved by spring tension. When the shutter button is pushed, the curtain moves and a slit passes in front of the film, allowing in light to expose the film. A few

cameras have a helical shutter that revolves. It allows light to pass through an opening as it turns. On some cameras the shutter is built into the lens and is a series of overlapping leaves. The center snaps open and then shuts again each time the shutter button is pushed.

The length of time that the shutter stays open, or the time it takes the curtain slit to move across the film, is known as the shutter speed. Some of the newer, still cameras can take photographs at $\frac{1}{4000}$ of a second, which is extremely fast.

Shutter speed can be changed on the camera, and a typical scale of speeds runs from $\frac{1}{1000}$ of a second on up to $\frac{1}{8}$, $\frac{1}{4}$, and $\frac{1}{2}$ second, and even 1 and 2 seconds. A "B" setting corresponds to "Bulb." Here the shutter stays open as long as the shutter button is held down. This feature is generally used for exposures of less than a minute.

For longer exposures the T (time) setting is used. With this setting the shutter opens when the shutter button or cable release activates the shutter. The shutter stays open, for hours if needed, until the release is activated again, closing the shutter.

Most focal plane shutters operate at top speeds of $\frac{1}{1000}$ of a second, some at $\frac{1}{2000}$, and at least one at $\frac{1}{4000}$. You can stop most motion of a running deer at $\frac{1}{500}$ of a second, but it takes a bright sunny day and a fast lens to allow you to use even that speed with the Kodachromes or Fujichrome professional slide (transparency) film.

The Viewfinder. Some sort of viewing system is needed to aim and focus the camera accurately. A twin lens camera has a top lens used for viewing and focusing while the bottom lens is actually used for

The movement of this deer was frozen with a shutter speed of $\frac{1}{1000th}$.

Most single-lens-reflex cameras (SLRs) use a mirror and a penta prism to allow you to see through the camera's lens for focusing.

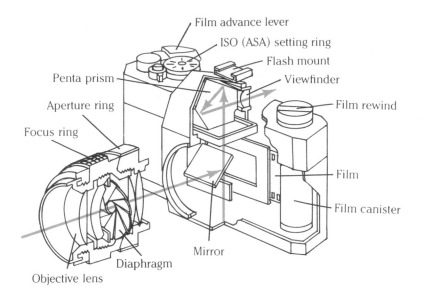

the photograph. Rangefinder cameras have a split image inside the viewer. The lens is turned until the two split fields are lined up perfectly. The camera is then focused. Usually, such viewfinders have etched lines on the ground glass to correspond to the focal length of the particular lens being used. If not, different viewfinders have to be used with different lenses.

About 95 percent of all cameras being used today are single lens reflexes, commonly called SLRs. These are preferred because you actually view your subject and thus focus through the lens that will take the photograph. This ensures the greatest accuracy in focusing.

In a single lens reflex, light entering the lens is bounced off a mirror and up to a penta prism. (The prism turns the image right side up.) The photographer focuses by looking at the image on a ground glass screen in the viewfinder. In most cameras, the screen can be changed. The different focusing screens are etched with various lines, circles, or surfaces to aid in focusing or composing according to the preference of the photographer.

Some screens incorporate a split image rangefinder with the ground glass focusing. A split image rangefinder can usually be focused faster under poor light conditions. The clear spot for the rangefinder is a drawback because it takes up the exact center of the ground glass and doesn't help you focus. Telephoto lenses usually work best with an overall fine-ground matte field.

For those who need them, prescription eyepieces can be gotten for the viewfinder so that you don't need to wear eyeglasses when looking through the viewfinder.

THE LENS

The lens is the very heart of the camera system and a single lens will often cost three to four times as much as the camera body. The better lenses have higher resolution, which means that more fine detail

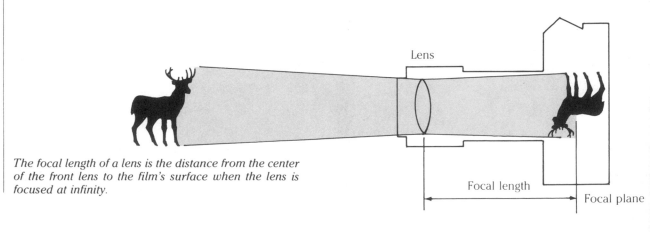

The focal length of a lens is the distance from the center of the front lens to the film's surface when the lens is focused at infinity.

can be recorded, and this is usually accomplished by using more glass elements. The speed of the lens (its light-gathering capability) is also extremely important to wildlife photographers because most wildlife subjects are photographed early in the morning, late in the afternoon, or under other less-than-ideal lighting conditions. To create "faster" lenses the front element must be made larger. This brings in more light to expose the film, but the large element means a heavier, more expensive lens.

A lens consists of a barrel to hold the glass elements in proper alignment, a diaphragm to control the amount of light entering the camera, and in some cases, a built-in shutter mechanism. A lens containing a shutter (not often used in 35mm cameras) is much more expensive than a similar lens without a shutter. Most lenses have from two to ten elements of precision glass inside the barrel.

THE DIAPHRAGM AND F/STOPS

The diaphragm inside the lens body consists of a circular arrangement of leaves that, when partly closed (or "stopped down") reduce the amount of light pass-

ing through the lens to the film during an exposure. Consequently, the diaphragm works in conjunction with the shutter to regulate the amount of light actually reaching the film. But changes in the diameter of the diaphragm opening affect the finished photograph in a different manner than shutter speed, as will be discussed later.

Diaphragm openings, or f/stops as they are called, are marked on the lens barrel. F/stops follow a mathematical progression and may range as follows: 1, 1.4, 2, 2.8, 4, 5.6, 8, 11, 16, 22, 32, 45, and 64. Though numbers in this progression range upward, a higher f/stop number indicates a smaller diaphragm opening (less light is admitted). That is because each higher number is multiplied by the square root of two. So f/8 lets in half as much light as f/5.6 and f/11 lets in one-fourth the light. Again, the higher the number, the less light; the lower the number, the more light.

Most lens barrels don't have the full range of f/stop numbers listed above. That is because the lowest f/stop possible on a given lens depends on the dimensions of that lens. In fact, the lowest f/stop (lens wide open) is calculated by dividing the focal length of the lens by the diameter of the front lens element (the largest element). So, take for example a 200mm lens, which has a focal length of 200mm (4 inches) from front lens to film plane. If the diameter of the

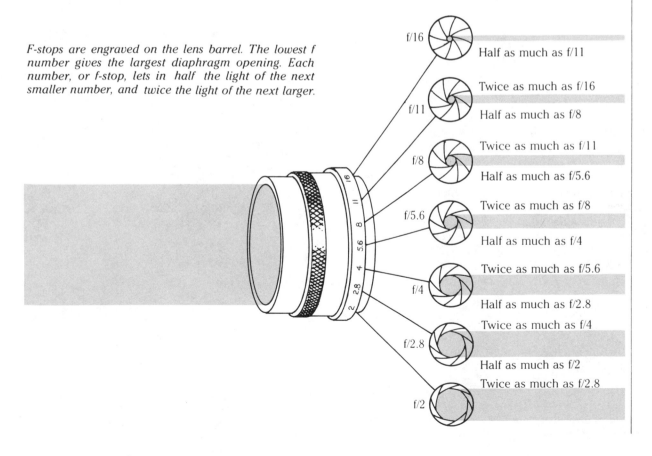

F-stops are engraved on the lens barrel. The lowest f number gives the largest diaphragm opening. Each number, or f-stop, lets in half the light of the next smaller number, and twice the light of the next larger.

f/16 — Half as much as f/11

f/11 — Twice as much as f/16 / Half as much as f/8

f/8 — Twice as much as f/11 / Half as much as f/5.6

f/5.6 — Twice as much as f/8 / Half as much as f/4

f/4 — Twice as much as f/5.6 / Half as much as f/2.8

f/2.8 — Twice as much as f/4 / Half as much as f/2

f/2 — Twice as much as f/2.8

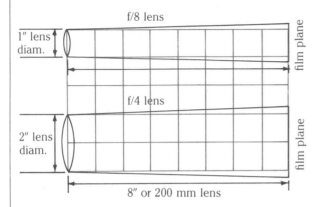

The speed of a lens is determined by dividing the focal length of the lens by the diameter of the lens. The top lens is an f/8 because its focal length is 8 times the lens diameter. The bottom lens is thus on f/4.

front element is 50mm, the first f/stop in the progression stamped on the barrel will be coincidentally 4. The next will be 5.6, 8, etc.

Often lenses will have f/stops that are not on the designated scale. The setting might be an f/3.6 or an f/4.5. These are one-half stops between the designated numbers. They mean that, for example, an f/3.6 lets in 50 percent more light than an f/4. And although the half stops may not be engraved on the lens barrel, most lenses can be set anywhere between the designated numbers that the light meter indicates will be the correct exposure.

Incidentally, the same f/stop used on any lens, of any focal length, on any format camera, will allow exactly the same amount of light to reach the film, given the same light conditions.

Full stops	1.4	2	2.8		4		5.6		8	11	16
Half stops				3.5		4.5		6.3			

Even though the ½ stops between standard f-stops are not engraved on your lens, your lens can be set between the regular stops as though the ½ stops were shown.

F/STOP AND SHUTTER SPEED

The two factors controlling the amount of light actually reaching the film, then, are the f/stop and the shutter speed. There is a constant relationship between these two factors. For example, all of the exposures listed below will be correct for the same light conditions (and the same type of film):

Shutter speed	**1/30**	**1/60**	**1/125**	**1/500**	**1/1000**
F/stops	f/16	f/11	f/5.6	f/4	f/2.8

A photograph can be taken with the same film at ⅟₆₀ at f/11 when depth of field is needed or at ⅟₅₀₀ at f/4 if action must be stopped.

There is in fact a direct relationship between the f/number and the depth of field in the finished photograph. The higher the f/stop number (diaphragm closed down more) the greater the depth of field. But by increasing the f/number beyond five f/stops to gain depth of field, you sacrifice some sharpness (critical focus) of the subject.

An optical law states that for any subject that is in critically sharp focus, the distance for one-third in front of the subject and two-thirds behind it will also be

This drawing shows the relationship of the shutter speed to the aperture setting for a given amount of light. Any one of the exposures allows the same total amount of light to strike the film. But the high shutter speed allows you to stop action with minimal depth of field. The low shutter speed ensures greater depth of field, but any movement of the camera or the subject will cause blur.

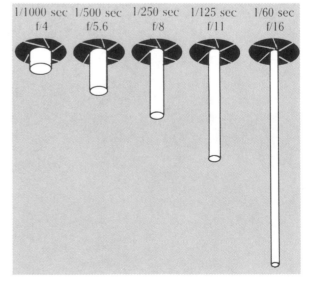

In the left-hand photo, the camera was focused on the picket noted, with the lens wide open at f/4 at ¹⁄₂₀₀₀ of a second. The result is a shallow depth of field. In the right-hand photo, the camera was focused on roughly the same picket indicated in the first photo, but with the lens closed down to f/22 at ¹⁄₁₂₅ of a second. Notice the tremendous depth of field achieved with the closed aperture.

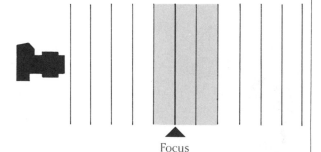

Focus

When a lens is focused on any given point, one-third of the distance in front of that point and two-thirds of the distance behind it will be the sharpest. The actual distance of sharpness is determined by the focal length of the lens and the distance the critical focusing point is from the lens.

sharp. (The exact distance is determined by the f/stop and the distance between the camera and the subject.) For this reason, the f/stop is a powerful working tool for controlling the amount of focus in the background of the photo. Using a faster shutter speed and lower f/stop will render a fuzzy, out-of-focus background that helps eliminate all background and thereby emphasize the subject.

Combinations of the f/stop and shutter speed usually must be set manually on most 35mm cameras. Some cameras are semi-automatic and are either aperture preferred or shutter preferred. On a camera with an aperture preferred setup, the photographer sets the desired aperture, and the camera automatically adjusts the shutter speed according to the available light. With a shutter preferred system, the photographer sets the shutter speed, and the camera selects the proper aperture setting, or f/stop. Lenses on Hasselblad cameras are cross-coupled. Once the photographer sets the proper f/stop/shutter speed, he can switch from ¹⁄₃₀ to ¹⁄₁₀₀₀ of a second and the f/stop changes automatically.

LENS CHARACTERISTICS

Lenses allow a circle of light to enter the camera, but the film itself is either a rectangle or a square. A "normal" lens produces a circle of light that will be as large as the square of the film's greatest diagonal. The 50mm lens is considered the normal lens for 35mm cameras, and the 80mm lens is the normal lens for the 2¼-inch square format.

A lens of any given focal length has only the magnification of that length, no matter what size film the image is being recorded on. A 200mm lens gives 4 times magnification for a 35mm film. A 200mm lens 8 gives times magnification for a 16mm film format. But the image size on the film would be identical with either film format, as shown on the next page. A standard, but false, rule is to divide the size of the normal length lens of a camera into the length of the telephoto lens being used to arrive at the magnification of the telephoto.

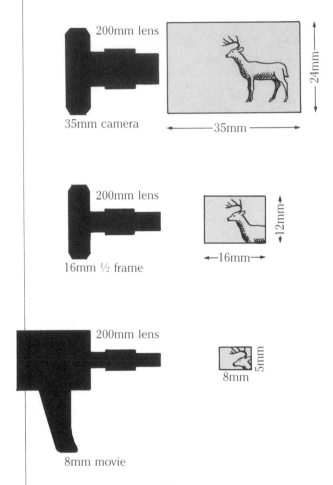

As this drawing shows, if the lens focal length and the distance to the subject are the same, the image size recorded on the film is the same. The difference is in the tighter crop that smaller film formats impose.

A lens is "fast" only in the relationship of the aperture to its focal length. A 600mm f/4 lens is considered exceedingly fast while a 50mm f/4 would be exceedingly slow.

An optical law states that a lens is at its sharpest when closed down three to five stops from its maximum aperture. This means that the faster telephoto lenses not only allow photographs to be taken under adverse light conditions, it also means under normal light conditions they are being used at their absolute sharpest.

WIDE ANGLE, TELEPHOTO, AND ZOOM LENSES

Any lens that has a shorter focal length than the camera's "normal" lens is considered a wide angle because the shorter the lens, the greater the angle of view it covers. The 35mm lens covers 62 degrees, the 28mm covers 74 degrees, and the 24mm covers 84 degrees. The 24mm is the favored lens because it encompasses just about the same angle of vision as the human eye, discounting peripheral vision. So this lens comes close to putting on film the scene that you are viewing. Wide angle lenses must be held perfectly horizontal to the ground or they will cause distortion of the vertical lines.

Medium telephoto lenses are the best for portraits of either wildlife or humans because they allow a large image of a nearby subject to be recorded without distortion of the facial features. The 85mm lens covers 28 degrees, the 105mm covers 23 degrees, the 135mm covers 18 degrees, and the 180mm covers 13 degrees.

Long telephotos are the ones most commonly used in wildlife photography because in most cases the subject cannot be approached closely. Also, some wildlife may be too dangerous to approach. The 400mm is the lens most commonly used by the pros.

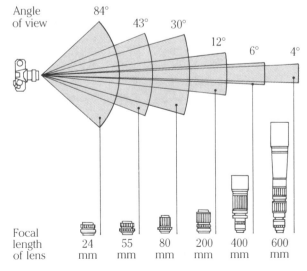

The angle of view of the area covered by a lens is determined by the focal length of that lens.

The 200mm lens covers 12 degrees, the 300mm covers 8 degrees, the 400mm covers 6 degrees, the 500mm covers 5 degrees, and the 600mm covers 4 degrees. There are longer telephotos available but they are seldom practical because of their size, weight, cost, and small apertures that require slow shutter speeds.

Telephoto lenses compress the scene being viewed, making subjects at different distances appear to be closer to one another than they actually are. This compression also multiplies the distortion created by heat thermals. Truly large telephotos cannot be used on hot days because the thermals cause vertical lines to bend.

Teleconverters, doublers or extenders, when they can be used, will effectively lengthen the focal length of the lens they are used on, the length depending on the multiplication factor of the converters. For the best results the converter should be made by the manufacturer of the lens it will be used on because it was designed for the lens. A drawback to converters is that they increase the need for additional light by the same factor by which they multiply the lens' focal length.

A great boon to all photographers has been the development of high quality zoom lenses, which incorporate different focal lengths in one lens. The early models were not sharp in all focal lengths, but most of the new lenses are extremely sharp in all modes. The zoom lenses offer the tremendous advantage of allowing the photographer to zoom from just the animal's head to include its entire body without having to change lenses with changing the distance to the subject. However, zoom lenses tend to be slower than their fixed focal length counterparts.

FILTERS

The only filter necessary in wildlife photography is a UV (ultraviolet) filter, which reduces haze and protects the front of the camera lens from scratches. Toning (colored) filters may be used for special effects, such as to darken and dramatize sky. Most camera dealers offer free leaflets published by filter makers that describe all the special effects obtainable with various filters.

MOTOR DRIVES

To the professional wildlife photographer the motor drive is as basic to the camera as the lens; it is seldom removed. The motor drive and the battery pack are expensive, and they often weigh more than the camera. The advantages, however, outweigh the disadvantages.

Only with a motor drive can you take sequence pictures of a running deer. You just can't hand crank a camera fast enough to do the job. Knowing the number of frames taken per second also allows you to time the speed of the deer. The motor drive can be used as a stopwatch and the exact distance a deer covered can be identified in the photographs.

Even if the deer is standing still, the motor drive will allow you to get a number of photos before it moves off.

The use of a motor drive allows you to maintain a consistent framing of the subject and also reduces camera shake because you do not have to move your hands to crank the winding lever.

The rewind feature of the motor drive is almost as much of an advantage as the fast advancing of the film. So much good action seems to take place the minute you have shot the last frame on the roll. The motor rewind lets you get the spent roll out of the camera in the shortest possible time and gets you back in action quickly. Some cameras pull juice out of the big motor drive battery to activate the exposure meter. This bypasses the small battery in the camera and makes it last much longer.

Only with a motor drive is it possible to capture a sequence of a deer running at full speed.

FILM

All films now come with a film-speed designation "ISO (ASA)," which is followed by a number. *ISO* is the acronym for International Standard Organization, the standard by which all films are now being formulated. *ASA* is the acronym for American Standard Association and is synonymous with ISO. The ASA notation will be phased out and lingers since the days when there were two systems used internationally—ASA and DIN.

All types of film have a clear acetate film base covered on one side by a light-sensitive layer. Black-and-white film has a layer of silver halide crystals that darken when exposed to light. Color film has layers of the primary colors. The thicker the layer of emulsion on the base, the higher the ISO(ASA) number, and the greater the latitude of the film, meaning there is more leeway in the proper exposure. The thinner the emulsion, the less latitude the film has, but the greater the sharpness of that particular film.

The larger grains of silver halide crystals in fast black-and-white film show up as a graininess in exposed film. The high-speed color films have dye clumpage that also results in graininess. These high-speed films can be used under adverse light conditions and are very tolerant of exposure error. But it is worthwhile to point out that high-speed films need special lab developing chemicals to minimize the graininess.

Color quality in a photo is a function of available light. When there is poor light there is little color brilliance. The resulting flat, muddy photos are color in name only and are hard to sell.

Black-and-white film. There is a market for black-and-white photographs although it is steadily shrinking. The payment for black-and-white photographs is usually about one-third that of color, even though it is much more expensive for the photographer to obtain a black-and-white print than it is to get a color transparency. But there are many times when the light conditions are such that only black and white can, or should, be used.

Very few professional wildlife photographers use the very finest Panatomic film, designated FX, put out by Kodak because of the low ISO(ASA) number. On an average sunny day, Kodak's Plus X or Plus X Pan Professional in the 120 size, ISO(ASA) 125, is the one used most frequently. This film has fine grain and a good range of tones from white to black. Kodak's Tri X film, with an ISO(ASA) of 320, can be used under low-light conditions, although many wildlife and even news photographers swear by this film as their all around black-and-white film.

All of the Kodak films can be developed in a higher speed developer, in effect "pushing" the films. Pushing increases their ISO(ASA) number, but does not adversely affect the grain (perceived graininess). When Plus X and Tri X are developed in Accufine, the ISO(ASA) numbers are increased to 320 and 1200 respectively. Developing time in Accufine is much shorter than in Kodak's own developer. This saves time and, because the film base is wet for a shorter period, it expands less. That helps to increase sharpness.

Ilford has a black-and-white film called XPI that is almost mistake proof. It has a variable ISO(ASA) number that ranges from 50 to 1600, although the best results are gotten with a rating around 800. It can be developed at home in the one-shot XPI chemicals or it can be run through the same commercial solution that Kodak has for processing negative film. Most photo stores now have these processors on the premises and can develop your film in 5 minutes.

Color negative film. Most amateurs prefer to shoot the negative (print) films so that they can have inexpensive prints made. With negative film, the negative is exposed and developed first. This is then used to make the color print in a separate operation. Negative, or print, film now represents about 90 percent of the general market sales for 35mm cameras. To accommodate this large market, manufacturers have made many more types of film.

The most commonly used are Kodak's VR films. The VR 100 has an ISO(ASA) guide number of 100. The VR 200 has an ISO(ASA) number of 200. Both of these films are good at rendering fine detail. VR 400 is a good general purpose film. VR 1000 can be used under very poor light conditions, and makes it possible to photograph deer early or late in the day with slower, less expensive lenses.

These films are now available in 12, 24, or 36 exposures, saving a lot of film if you want to have a dozen or two dozen frames processed quickly. The film can also be developed at home by using the C41 film developing kit.

There is also a Kodak professional print film, with an ISO(ASA) number of 160. It is designated as VPS 3. The main advantage to this film is that retouching can be done directly on the negative. But this film is adversely affected by the slightest heat.

Just about everything in photography is a trade-off. For the advantages of much higher film speeds and the ability to process the print films at home, there is a corresponding loss of sharpness. The print films are just not as sharp, nor can they render detail as finely as the positive (slide) films discussed below. If you are just photographing deer for your own pleasure and only want to show or to give prints to friends, use the negative films. However, if your goal is to eventually sell your photographs, then you should use the same film the pros use.

Color positive film. Color positive film, used for slides (transparencies), involves only one step in developing. Some of the most popular films for transparencies are the old standbys, Kodachrome 25 (KM) and Kodachrome 64 (KR) and, of late, Fujichrome 50 and 100. The slow Kodachrome 25 (ISO/ASA 25) is an exceedingly sharp film that is excellent for scenics and wildflowers, or generally for subjects that aren't going to get up and leave. Fujichrome 50 gives the same results with a faster speed.

Most professionals use either Kodachrome 64 (ISO/ASA 64) or Fujichrome Professional 100 (ISO/ASA 100). Both of these films have fine grain and a high contrast, which makes them better for projection (they have more impact). Most photographers underexpose both films slightly by alloting them the higher ISO(ASA) numbers of 80 and 125, respectively. This allows for more color saturation, resulting in richer colors. The Fujichrome film is not only faster than its Kodak counterparts, it also has finer grain.

Because it is faster, the Fujichrome 100 film can be used a half hour earlier in the morning and later in the afternoon than the Kodak film.

Kodachrome professional 64 and Fujichrome professional 100 are now available. These films are improved and properly aged so that there is no color shift as the film ages before being exposed. No color film should be used until after it has *less* than 12 months to go to the expiration date. Most color film is made to have a shelf life of 14 to 15 months. The film is usually, but not always, held by the manufacturer for at least two months before being released for sale.

Prints can be made from any of the Kodachrome or Fujichrome films by having an internegative made. This is much more expensive than having prints made from negative film.

Some of the Kodak Ektachrome films, and their ISO(ASA) speeds, are: EW 100, ED 200, EL 400, and EES 800. The 800 film can be pushed to 1000 or 3200. An advantage of the Ektachrome film is that it can be processed at home using the E6 film developing kit. And the Ektachromes are Kodak's only film for cameras larger than 35mm. A disadvantage is that in 35mm format publishers prefer Kodachromes or Fujichromes.

Fujichrome is making their 100 film available in 2¼ or 120 format. This film can also be processed at home in E6 solution and is much finer grained than the Ektachromes and Kodachromes. This means that photographers and editors will now be able to get subjects in a superior quality film in the much larger 2¼ format.

Buying film. The best buys on film can be found in the ads in the back of such magazines as *Modern Photography* and *Popular Photography*. This is usually referred to as the "gray market." The prices are the best around because all of the big photo dealers are competing with one another through their ads. You, the consumer, are the beneficiary. Kodak films sold on this market are usually shipped in from Canada or England, and the price includes a prepaid Kodak mailer. The film is of the highest quality.

Buy your film in as large a batch as you can afford; blocks of 20 or cases of 300 rolls. If you buy several cases, insist on getting the same emulsion batch number. Then, when you get your film, shoot a test roll. Every batch may have slight variations from another and you can tell only by testing a roll from the batch. Bulk purchases save on testing.

Film should always be kept cool and dry. When the film has only ten months left on it until expiration, refrigerate or freeze it. The cold will stop the aging process and the film can be kept for several years without changing its color tones and values. Make sure that the film has not been opened before cooling.

Remove film from either the refrigerator or freezer 24 hours before you plan to use it. Allow the film to come up to the ambient temperature slowly to prevent condensation. All moisture has usually evaporated in less than 24 hours, but allow at least that much time.

For best results, have your film processed as soon as you can after exposing it. Processed film should be kept in a temperature and humidity controlled environment to promote long life of the color dyes. With proper care, Kodachrome and Fujichrome transparencies will last over 30 years without fading.

EXPOSURE IS THE KEY

More miles of film have been ruined by improper exposure than by any other single mistake by photographers. Much of this is due to an increased dependency among photographers on automated cameras. Because of this many photographers have not learned how to calculate exposure correctly.

The automatic cameras are being produced for the general public to take family photos and outdoor photos of activities in good light and favorable conditions. What a camera of this type is built to do is to average out the reflected light and to set itself accordingly.

The cameras are in effect trying to do the photographer's thinking for him. But the camera can't think; so you as the photographer will have to. After you have had lots of experience at calculating exposure properly, it will become second nature to you. You will do it automatically because you will know what to look for and how to compensate. For example, where the subject contrasts with the background, the camera has no way of knowing what it is that you want to be correctly exposed. And if the contrast is high enough, such as a dark moose on snow or a white swan on dark water, the exposure will never be correct. Fortunately, a deer happens to have fairly neutral coloring that, under most circumstances, makes exposure much simpler.

Today, even the most advanced cameras used by the professionals have some automatic features. But professionals override the automatic features nearly all of the time.

Light meters. Most light meters, whether hand-held or installed in the camera, evaluate the light that is reflecting from the entire area being viewed. The meter then gives a reading that is an average of the lightest and darkest objects in the scene. Some of the more advanced cameras have meters that are center-weighted, allotting a higher value to the light reflecting from the center of the screen than to the periphery because that is where the subject being photographed is most likely to be.

CAMERA LIGHT METERS

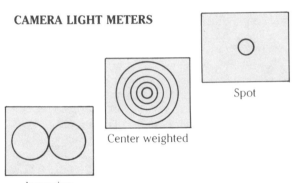

Spot

Center weighted

Averaging

Whether hand held or installed in the camera, some meters (left) average all of the light reflecting from the subject. Some meters (center) have center-weighted readings that give more value to the center of the scene. Spot meters read just a small area.

Deer, elk, antelope, and wild sheep all have coats that are shades of light tan or brown. After the leaves are off the trees, a deer's neutral coloring fits in very well with a meter that is reading an average grassy or woodland scene. At such times the automatic exposure features on the camera can be employed. It is a great convenience to be able to follow the action of your subject, whether it be in sunlight or in shadow, and be able to concentrate on just focusing and not have to worry about exposure. However, if the deer is on snow or contrasts greatly with its background, you will have to adjust the exposure manually.

Although it's more trouble to carry one, and takes more time to use it, one of the best ways to get an accurate meter reading is to use a photographic gray card. The average subject or scene reflects 18 percent of the light falling on it, the same as a tone of gray corresponding to that percentage. To obtain an ac-

A hand-held exposure meter is here used to take a reading from an 18 percent gray card. This provides an extremely accurate exposure reading. In a pinch you can take a reading directly from your hand. But because your hand reflects more light, you must open up the lens by one full f/stop over that indicated by the meter.

curate reading, the card must be held at the exact angle in relation to the sun and camera as is the subject to the sun and camera. You must also take care not to tilt the card backward or the sun will reflect off the surface creating both glare and an abnormally high reading. Conversely, the card should not be tipped forward enough to cast a shadow on itself.

A stopgap method that can be used instead of a gray card is to point your camera at the palm of your hand and take a reading. However, because the palm of your hand has a reflectance of about 40 percent it is much brighter than a gray card. So you must open up your lens one full stop over the meter reading.

The reflected-light meters discussed above measure the amount of light reflecting from a scene and are used at the camera and pointed at the subject. Incident-light meters are used at the camera and pointed at the sun with their light-measuring plastic sphere held or turned so that the sun falls on the sphere at the same angle that it is falling on the subject.

Incident-light meters are supposed to average light in the same way that a gray card reflects an average amount of light. Most reflected light meters can be converted to reading incident light by using a supplemental plastic sphere. Generally incident-light meters are used indoors with artificial light while the reflected-light meters give a more accurate reading out-of-doors. A new device being marketed is a filter that slips over your camera lens. It converts readings on the meter in your camera to incident-light readings when the camera lens is pointed at the sun.

Some wildlife photographers use a special spot meter. This meter allows you to take a pinpoint reading from the brightest and the darkest areas within the scene being viewed. You then average the reading to get the proper exposure settings. In using a spot meter on a deer, sheep or elk, you can take a reading directly from the animal's coat and, because the coat has a neutral color, the reading will fall into the average range of exposure. This fact holds true whether the deer is standing in snow or against a dark forest background. If there is sunlight bouncing off the snow, the

deer's coat will give a higher reading. If the scenic area is dark, there will be less light coming from the deer's coat.

One well-known wildlife photographer carries a piece of tanned deer skin with the hair on it. He meters this skin with whatever lens is on his camera, and the

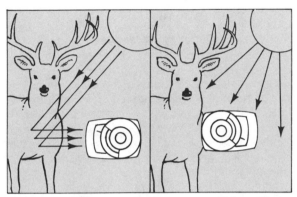

A reflected-light meter (left) measures light reflecting from the subject. An incident meter reads the amount of sunlight falling on the subject.

A reading taken from a deer hide with hair gives an accurate reading for deer, elk, sheep, and antelope. (Irene Vandermolen photo)

A one-degree-angle-of-view spot meter allows you to meter a precise area of the subject that is to be photographed. (Charlie Heidecker photo)

A 400mm lens has such a narrow area of coverage that your camera's meter works like a spot meter. (Irene Vandermolen photo)

exposure is perfect no matter what the background.

As noted earlier, the 400mm telephoto lens is the one most commonly used by professional wildlife photographers. Using this lens, in effect, makes the camera a spot meter. The 400mm reduces the angle of coverage (and area read by the internal meter) to 5.8 degrees. If a 1.4 extender or converter is used on the lens, it reduces the angle of coverage to 4 degrees. A doubler, making the 400mm lens an 800mm, reduces the angle of coverage to 2.34 degrees. With this setup, if the deer fills the viewfinder, the reading directly from the animal will be correct.

There are a couple of exceptions. The black bear and the wild turkey are the darkest subjects in the woods, darker even than rocks, tree trunks, or old stumps. If the deer photographer is using a 400mm telephoto and extenders to photograph a wild turkey (often found near deer), his meter reading will be way off. The turkey's feathers may be properly exposed at the f/stop indicated, but all the leaves in the forest will be so overexposed that the background will look almost as light as snow. In this type of situation, it is best to take your meter reading from the background leaves and vegetation, then swing back on the turkey or black bear and take the shot. Incidentally, metering the background is generally a good way of metering for deer unless there is snow on the ground.

If the deer is standing in snow at a distance too great to use your lens as a spot meter, then meter the snow itself. The high reflectiveness of the snow will give you an abnormally high meter reading. So you must compensate by opening up your camera's lens either 1½ or 2 full stops more than indicated by your meter. The difference in the results of the ½ stop is usually a matter of personal preference. When the sun is directly behind you (as you face your subject), opening 2 stops is preferred. If the sun is coming in from the side of the subject, opening 1½ stops is satisfactory.

SIGHTING-IN YOUR EQUIPMENT

No knowledgeable deer hunter would buy a new rifle and go hunting without first sighting-in the gun. The hunter has to know exactly where the bullet is going to hit. The same thing is true of the deer photographer. He must know how his camera, lens, and film combination will work together in the outdoor setting where he plans to take his shots.

Although all film of one kind from a particular manufacturer is supposed to give the same results when exposed properly, the truth is that there may be slight differences between each batch of film. And though all lenses are supposed to perform the same at their designated f/stops, the actual exposure may be plus or minus slightly. As a general rule, the serious photographer should have his camera cleaned, the pres-

In a snowscape where deer are only a part of the photograph, take your meter reading directly from the snow and then open your lens 2 or 1½ f-stops more than indicated. When photographing a dark subject, such as a wild turkey, take your meter reading from the neutral-hued leaves on the forest floor, not from the dark subject. (Deer photo by Irene Vandermolen)

For illustration purpose, this film strip was bracketed much more than necessary. The shutter speed was ¹/₂₅₀ of a second. Frame 2 was taken with the lens set at f/32; 3 at f/22; 4 at f/16; 5 at f/11; 6 at f/8; and 7 at f/5.6. Frame 2 is greatly underexposed (not enough light reached the film). Frame 7 is greatly overexposed; so much light hit the film that it completely burned out detail. Frame 5 is perfect, although a good print could be made from frame 4.

sure plate checked for scratches, and the shutter speeds checked at least once a year. And whenever new color slide film is purchased (all rolls from the same batch), one roll should be shot to test exposure settings. This is unnecessary for black-and-white film, because slight under or over exposures can be compensated for in the lab when prints are being made.

Sighting-in your camera is particularly important if you have a new camera, are using a new lens setup, are shooting outdoors for the first time, or plan to shoot in an unfamiliar locale (or during a different season). Take the camera, lens, and film you plan to use for photographing deer and shoot a roll on the type of background in which you intend to photograph the deer. If you have a mounted deer head or a tanned skin with the hair on it, put that in the scene too to test exposures on that.

Now set the exposure that you believe is correct and take the shot. Then "bracket" this exposure setting by first taking a series of shots consecutively at ⅓, ½, ⅔, and 1 stop above and below the estimated proper setting. Keep records of each shot, noting the f/stop and shutter speed. Have the film processed and check the results. Choose the exposure that, in your opinion, is perfect when viewed on a color-light table with color correction bulbs designed for the viewing of color transparencies. With your equipment sighted-in, you will be better able to judge the correct exposure under the varying light and background conditions encountered in the field.

Yet it is important to avoid relying too heavily on this system of bracketing for routine shots. Pro's use it as insurance, if subjects allow them the time to take several shots at various exposures. It often guarantees that they "come home with the bacon." But don't bracket because you have not learned to set exposures properly in the first place. Many times you simply will not have the time to bracket. Your first shot may be your only shot, so learn to expose it properly.

HOLDING THE CAMERA STEADY

The finest equipment in the world will not produce sharp photographs if the camera and lens are not held rock-steady when the shutter is tripped. Just as some hunters can hold their guns much more steadily than others, some photographers are much better at steadying their cameras. But no matter how young, or strong, or practiced you might be, it is to your advantage to brace the camera, the lens, and yourself with something solid whenever the opportunity presents itself.

A rule of thumb is that you should be able to hand-hold a lens of the same focal length as the shutter speed you are using. For example, if conditions are such that you have a shutter speed of ¹/₅₀₀ you, theoretically, could hand-hold a 500mm lens. But don't do it with a long telephoto lens. Lens shake becomes a factor and fuzzies up the result.

Whenever you are hand-holding a camera you should use your body properly to maximize steadiness. Brace your arms against your body. Use your camera strap for additional support whenever possible. Take a tip from the rifle shooter; hold your breath and then slowly squeeze the shutter release. *Don't jab at it.* The photos and captions on the next page cover these concerns in detail.

PROTECTING CAMERAS

When traveling by air (or other public conveyance), carry your camera gear in foam-lined backpacks or camera bags. That way you can give it maximum protection, and you will be sure to have it when you step off the plane. Jet planes can wreak havoc with cameras

HOLDING THE CAMERA STEADY

You can hold your camera steady while standing if you shorten the neck strap and wrap it around your hands as shown. Then brace your elbows against your body and brace your forehead against the camera. (Photo series on holding a camera by Charlie Heidecker)

Additional support for your camera can be gotten by bracing your elbows on the lens pockets of a Rue Photo Vest. This position is so steady you will not need to keep the neck strap around your hands.

Whenever possible, whether standing or kneeling—lean against a post or a tree to steady your camera.

Sitting, brace your elbows against your knees, whether cross-legged as shown, or with feet extended forward.

If it is possible to lie down, the basic prone position (left) is almost rock steady. You won't be able to take this position if the ground is wet or if the vegetation is too high. Photo right: you can improve on the basic prone position by resting your camera on a support.

because the engine vibration will loosen screws inside the equipment and cause them to fall out. When you must ship equipment as luggage, send it only in the rigid Pelican or Halliburton cases. *All* camera bags and cases should be spray painted in camo colors and scuffed up. Bright shiny cases are an invitaion to thieves.

If you are going to be around water, pack your gear in the Coleman Dry-Sac, Early Winters Super Sack, or L. L. Bean's River Duffle. Be particularly careful of salt water and its spray.

Do not carry your cameras from warm to cold conditions because condensation will form and could freeze. Keep your cameras as close to the ambient temperature as possible. At sub-zero temperatures most of the electronic cameras will fail while mechanical cameras, such as the Nikon FM2, will continue to work. You can carry your cameras under your jacket in extremely cold weather to prevent them from freezing, but not if you are perspiring. The moisture of perspiration will fog the cameras.

If you must take a cold camera into a warmer area, seal the camera and lenses in a plastic bag to prevent condensation. Then place the gear next to the door where some cold will filter under the sill. Or put the gear in the coolest spot in the house.

PROTECTING YOUR FILM

Film that is to be carried in the field should be kept in the canisters the filmmaker provides. This keeps out dust and moisture and will keep the film dry if it is dropped in snow or water. First though discard the

Cameras can be shipped as luggage if packed in foam-lined Pelican or Halliburton cases. You can carry basic lenses and camera in a Lowe-Pro sack (right) on the plane with you. The sack will fit under the seat.

When you are around water (especially salt water) keep your gear protected in a Coleman Dry-Sac.

maker's cardboard boxes because you won't have time to open boxes in the field when the action gets going. The Rue vest has two film pockets; so you can separate your color film from the black and white. Each pocket will hold 30 film canisters.

Under most conditions the film can be carried in the cardboard case in which it is shipped. Do not leave the case in the sun or in a locked vehicle in hot weather. In very hot weather such as in the desert, the film can be carried in a foam ice chest. Frozen ice packs can be used to keep it cool. Or, since temperatures usually plummet at night in the desert, open the ice chest lid at night to cool the film. Then close it at dawn before temperatures rise. Keep the chest in the shade during the daytime and cover it with a white sheet. The sheet reflects both the heat and light. With these precautions, ice packs are seldom needed.

In the tropics the problem is as much humidity as it is heat. Bags of silica gel can be kept in your film and camera cases to remove the excess moisture. They will have to be dried in the sun or in a toaster or oven to regain their efficiency.

In extremely cold weather you will have to warm up film in your pants pocket before you put it in your camera. Film can be as brittle as glass when it is cold.

INSURANCE

The most important protection you can give your equipment is to insure it as soon as you get it. Most insurance companies will either attach a rider to your homeowners policy or write you a special policy. The going rate for such insurance is $2 per $100 of the gear's insured valuation. If you are a member of the Outdoor Writers' Association of America or some of the larger camera groups, you can get this insurance for about $1 per $100.

GEAR FOR PRO PHOTOGRAPHY

The hunter who wants to take professional-quality photographs of deer and other wildlife will find he needs more than just his camera and lenses. Some of the gear discussed below, such as tripods, will be needed by just about any serious wildlife photographer. Other items, such as remote tripping devices for cameras, are clearly for special situations.

CAMERA GUNSTOCKS AND UNIPODS

The shoulder stock on a rifle makes the rifle shooter much more accurate than a shooter holding a pistol. The camera gunstock serves a similar function. Although the shoulder stock is superb for taking photographs of running deer, it is equally important for shots of deer that are standing still.

The stock allows you to brace the camera against your body more efficiently. If your camera is equipped with a motor drive it is even better. You hold the stock snug against your shoulder and trip the trigger release with one hand. Your head rests on the stock, bracing it further, while your free hand rests on the top of the stock to focus the lens. With a shoulder stock and these four points of contact, your camera almost becomes a part of your body.

Some photographers can hold a 400mm lens steady with just a gunstock, but most cannot. A 300mm lens can be held quite easily. The gunstock is ideal for the 70–210 zoom lens if you are following after deer that are relatively used to human proximity, such as some deer in national parks.

If you have the opportunity to brace yourself against a tree, the gunstock allows you to do a better job. In both the kneeling and the sitting position, the stock can rest against your knee. If you lie down, you can rest the stock on the ground.

But the most effective way to use a gunstock is to couple it with a unipod. This is not as steady as using a tripod but it comes close. The unipod, when not being used on the gunstock, makes an ideal walking stick and is of great help in negotiating a steep mountainside or crossing a swift stream. And, if need be, the unipod can be used as a protective weapon.

The use of a gyroscope on the gunstock will allow almost anyone to hold a 400mm rock steady. This is an excellent combination for photographing ducks and geese in flight. It does not work well with deer because the high pitched whine of the spinning gyroscope alarms deer and most other animals.

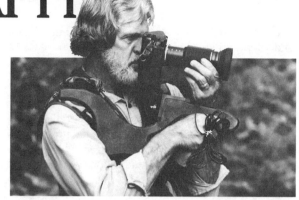

A shoulder stock is almost a must for holding lenses up to 300mm. You can hold a camera far more steadily with a stock than without. (Len Rue Jr. photo)

A gyroscope will allow you to hold even a 400mm lens easily. But the whine of the motor may alarm deer. (Charlie Heidecker photo)

A unipod fastened into the bottom of a Rue modified camera stock makes a very steady rest for your camera. (Len Rue Jr. photo)

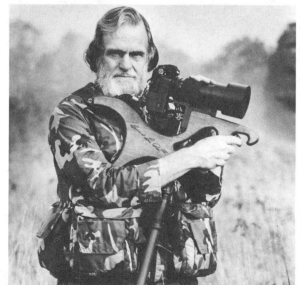

TRIPODS

The only reason to use a tripod is to hold your camera and telephoto lens steady, and you can't do that with many of the tripods offered for sale today. The lightweight, flimsy tripods are an abomination. To be steady, a tripod must be strong, and that usually means heavy, weighing from 6 to 12 pounds.

Most older photographers started taking photographs when the ASA number of Kodachrome was eight and almost all photographs were taken using a tripod. To these photographers tripods were a way of life and these photographers are still most likely to use the larger, heavier tripods. Many younger photographers have had access to the modern, high-speed films and so eschew the idea of using a tripod. They claim they can get into action faster by not using a tripod. Although these photographers may get into action quicker, their photographs cannot be as sharp as those taken with a tripod. It's just physically impossible to do so.

Most tripods are made so that different types of heads can be used on them. The finest heads in the world, and perhaps the fastest to get into action, are the larger monoballs. Instead of having two knobs to tighten to level a camera horizontally and vertically, the big monoballs do the job much better with a single large knob. With this head your tripod can be set down on uneven ground and no adjustments are needed on the legs; the monoball takes care of that problem with a single twist of the wrist.

Most tripods are not made with the wildlife photographer in mind—most are made of shiny chrome. And some wildlife photographers use them just like that, although the sun glinting on the chrome alerts, and perhaps alarms, all wildlife in the area. The Gitzo Safari model tripods, made in France, are done in an annodized army drab color, and the company plans to bring out all of their tripods in flat black. If you don't buy a tripod done in flat black, spray paint the tripod you have. Don't brush paint on it because this thick coat of paint won't allow the legs to telescope easily. A light coat of spray paint does the job.

When working in the field, carry your 400mm lens and camera on the tripod and have the legs fully extended. It may be more awkward to carry this way, but it does allow you to get into action fast. If you are working on a steep hill, shorten the uphill leg so that when you put the tripod down to take a photograph you won't have to adjust the leg. If you are carrying your camera in your pack, fasten the tripod (with legs shortened) to your pack in a vertical position. Carried horizontally it would catch on brush. And on steep hillsides, it could catch on an obstruction, tossing you off balance.

The sturdy Gitzo 320 tripod can be used in either the standing or sitting position and will hold lenses of 400mm, or larger, motionless. The large monoball used as a head requires just the twist of one knob to level your camera both horizontally and vertically. (Charlie Heidecker photo)

Where possible, carry your 400mm lens and camera on a tripod with legs extended. This will allow you to get into action fast. (Len Rue Jr. photo)

WINDOW PODS

Most animals have become so accustomed to motor vehicles that they have no fear of them. Many good photographs can be taken from your automobile or truck, if you are prepared. A Gitzo window pod, with a monoball head and a 400mm lens and camera mounted on it, can easily be carried on the seat.

When game is spotted, get as close as you can, roll down the window, drop the window pod over the glass and against the door and shoot. *Don't* attempt to get out of your vehicle. The deer that pay no attention to

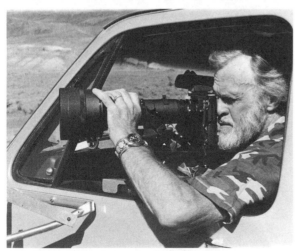

The Gitzo windowpod will hold your camera and big lenses as steady as a good tripod. Many animals can be easily photographed from a vehicle. (Len Rue Jr. photo)

your car will panic at the sight of a person stepping out. So, be prepared; carry your gear all assembled.

Make sure that you shut off the engine before you attempt to take the photograph because the vibrations of the motor will shake the camera. Be sure to get in the best position before you shut off the engine, for if you have to start your engine again, you will probably scare the deer off.

REMOTE TRIPPING DEVICES

Before the human population explosion, many photographers took deer pictures at night by setting trip wires across deer trails. Later, an electronic treadle trigger was buried in the trail; the deer set off the camera when they stepped on the device. Today there are so many people running all over the place that they would probably discover your gear before a deer passed by. A sad commentary on our times is that many people would probably take any gear left unguarded in the woods.

But this kind of setup can be used to good advantage if you watch, or trip it, from a distance. The camera can be fastened directly to a tree with a Rue's

The Rue camera tree bracket holds a camera for remote-control photography. The motor drive can be controlled by 150 feet of stereo wire or the Modulite, shown next page. (Len Rue Jr. photo)

The electronic Modulite Remote Control unit has two channels to trip two cameras independently from a distance. It works by flashing a beam of red light at the receivers. (Len Rue Jr. photo)

remote bracket. This bracket is light, strong, easy to carry, and can be put up in a few seconds. It is easy to camouflage both the bracket and camera. Or, you can mount your camera on a lowered tripod and camouflage the entire rig.

With any remote device, the deer will have to be in a precise spot and the camera will have to be preset. The deer can be baited to the spot; this can be a spot the deer is attracted to naturally, or a trail that the deer follow consistently. Such photography will be done at comparatively short ranges so that lenses in the lengths of 40mm to 80mm will best do the job. The camera shutter can be tripped in many ways, but there are four that are the most practical.

The simplest, and least expensive, way to trip the shutter is to employ an electronic cord that activates the motor drive. The cords that are supplied by the photo-accessory companies are usually only 6 to 12 feet in length. But you can cut this cord and splice in as much as 150 feet of lightweight stereo wire. The drawback to this rig is that you can't use much more than 150 feet of wire without using additional batteries to compensate for the drain on the batteries created by the wire.

Nikon offers a red-light camera-release activator. A battery-powered receiving unit is connected to the camera's triggering device. At a distance of up to 300 feet, you merely point a hand-held transmitter at the receiver and push a button when you want to take a picture. A pulse of red light from the transmitter is picked up by the receiver and the shutter is tripped.

The transmitter has two channels. You can mount a camera with color film next to one loaded with black-and-white film. Each camera is set for a different channel. Then, by merely flipping a switch on the transmitter, you can activate either of the two cameras. Caution: Intervening foliage will block the beam.

Radio controlled units are the most expensive, but they can be used at distances up to 1 mile—a far greater distance than necessary or practical.

The Dale Beam photographic tripper is a portable electric-eye transmitter and reflector system. It is activated when the deer breaks the beam going between the units. This one you won't have to activate yourself. But you'd be well advised to stay in the area to prevent its being stolen.

The Dale Beam photographic tripper is a portable electric eye that activates a camera when a deer breaks the beam between eye and reflector. (Len Rue Jr. photo)

FLASH UNITS

The remote units discussed above can only be used if your light is constant. Fluctuating cloud cover or the increasing or diminishing light of dawn and dusk makes exposure impossible to calculate unless the camera has an automatic exposure control. The only other choice is to use flash.

Flashbulbs pack a fantastic burst of light but are seldom, if ever, used today because you can get only one flash from each bulb. The smallest electronic flash is also useless because the batteries are not large enough to allow the unit to be turned on for the extended periods of time the remote work requires.

A powerful flash unit must be used to take photographs of deer at night because the dark surroundings absorb so much light.

Most of the regular electronic flash units, having thyristors (which automatically measure light reflected back to them) can be used if they can be set within 10 to 12 feet of the deer. Don't believe the high guide numbers that the manufacturers claim their lights are capable of delivering. The lights are tested in average-sized rooms having lots of reflecting surfaces. Test these lights outdoors where light is absorbed by all surfaces and you will discover that you are lucky to have ½ to ⅓ of the light advertised.

To do remote work requires a professional flash unit having a large battery power pack. Most of the big units can be left on for hours and will still deliver a lot of light when flashed. Most of these units have a light duration of about ⅕₀₀₀ of a second. This is more than fast enough to stop a running deer, but it will not freeze all the action of a bird in flight.

Most 35mm cameras having a focal plane shutter can only synchronize with electronic flash at ⅟₆₀ or ⅟₁₀₀ of a second. This will not be a problem unless you are taking flash pictures in bright sunshine when the slow shutter speed may record "ghost images."

CARRYING YOUR GEAR

Most professional wildlife photographers carry their 400mm lens on their tripod and their accessory lenses in a fannypack. Others carry accessory lenses in a small backpack. But the best way to carry lenses is in a pro photo vest. The advantage of a vest is that you have your normal lens, your extenders, and your 70–210 zoom lens at your fingertips in the front pockets where they can be gotten instantly. Large film pockets, holding 20 to 30 rolls each, means you don't have to hunt for your film. The additional pockets hold the indispensible small items, such as lens-cleaning material, a photographic screwdriver, toilet tissue, binoculars, exposure meter, pad, pens, a small ruler to lay next to small track to indicate scale, animal scents, insect repellent, close-up tubes, etc. The large rear pocket can hold the 400mm, if you want to carry it there, or it can be used to hold such items as a plastic garbage bag to cover your gear in case of storm, a length of light nylon cord, a few granola bars for energy, or a poncho. In the small inside pockets you should have silk gloves for warmth and camo gloves and a face mask for concealment.

That may sound like a lot of gear to carry, but it is all gear that is needed if you are going to do serious deer photography. If you are properly prepared you will get photos and not have to give excuses.

If a large zoom lens (50–300mm) on a camera mounted on a tripod is to be carried, then use a padded frameless backpack such as the Lowe-Pro or the North Face Internal Frame Pack, with the tripod and camera carried over your shoulder, ready for use. If you want to pack all of your equipment, including your tripod, to a distant location and you will not be doing photography enroute, then use the large frame packs, such as Coleman, Kelty, and Alpenlite, and strap the tripod to the pack frame. The main bag should have no dividers so that you can utilize the maximum depth of the bag.

CLOTHING FOR PHOTOGRAPHERS

Camouflage clothing should be worn whenever possible when doing wildlife photography. Basic browns and greens should be worn in spring and summer, mixed browns work well in autumn, and Trebark (tree bark) works best when the leaves are off the trees.

Camouflage should be worn because it minimizes the chances of your being seen by the deer or other wildlife. It also minimizes the chances of your being seen by anyone else, particularly competing photographers. Today, fortunately, camouflage clothing comes in every possible weight and can used in summer heat or winter cold.

The one exception to this rule of wearing camo clothes is during the hunting season. At such a time your safety is more important than any photograph;

WILDLIFE PHOTOGRAPHER'S VEST

The vest has mesh back and side panels for ventilation. The back mesh area can be covered during cold or wet weather. A back closure panel is carried in the large rear pocket, which is big enough to take a 400mm lens. (Len Rue Jr. photo)

The Rue Photo Vest has 19 pockets, padded shoulders, built-in camera carrying straps, and eliminates the need for a fannypack or small backpack for accessory lenses. The Rue Film Pouch is worn on the belt and is used for exposed film. (Len Rue Jr. photo)

Here the mesh panel of the photo vest is covered for cold or wet weather. The same closure panel can be fastened to the bottom of the rear of the vest to keep your bottom dry when sitting on wet logs or on the ground. (Charlie Heidecker photo)

When your camera and gunstock are fastened to the shoulder straps there is no drag on your neck because the weight is carried from the center of your back. When additional large lenses must be carried, a padded backpack is recommended. (Len Rue Jr. photos)

so blaze orange clothing should be worn. Camo clothing incorporating blaze orange swatches is available at sporting goods stores. Wearing blaze orange in some form is required of hunters in many states, and for good reason—some novice hunters will shoot at anything that moves.

Most people do not realize how much light is reflected off their hands and face. Lightweight mesh gloves and a face mask are very important for effective camouflage when photographing deer. In the summertime the mesh will keep the biting insects off you; in the winter a camo face mask will help to keep you warm.

Pants and upper body wear. Mosquitos and black flies are attracted to the color blue; so you should wear green or tan clothing if you are not wearing camouflage. Cotton jeans and a long-sleeved work shirt are fine for warm or hot weather for about six months out of the year. Never wear shorts because your bare legs will be scratched by brush and are an invitation to stinging, biting insects.

When the weather turns cooler, heavier denim will suffice. When it turns cold, wear long-john underwear (polypropylene and wool blend) under the denim to help keep you warm. Both of these materials will wick

moisture away from the body and both will provide warmth even when wet.

In cold weather lightweight or heavyweight wool pants should be used over the poly-wool underwear. In extremely cold weather, two pair of underwear are better, and the layer next to the body can be made of silk. Layering clothing is very important when the weather is cold. It is the dead air trapped between the layers that keeps you warm.

Wool shirts or Patagonia pile shirts will keep the upper torso warm. A bulky wool camo sweater can go over the shirt. If you are going to be in a windy or wet area, wear a nylon shell over your wool. A disadvantage to most shells is that they are hard surfaced and noisy, making rasping sounds if rubbed against branches. A Thinsulate or down vest is excellent.

Gloves. Light mesh gloves are fine for summer, cotton camo gloves can be used in cool weather. In cold weather silk gloves covered with wool wristlets are great. The wristlets cover the wrists to keep the blood in the arteries and veins warm. The silk is very warm and prevents your hands from sticking to metal equipment; yet it allows you enough manual dexterity to operate your camera and to change film. In extremely cold weather loose mittens should be worn

Silk gloves and wool wristlets, shown above and below, are one of the warmest combinations for the photographer. The silk is thin enough so that you can change film without taking off the gloves. (Len Rue Jr. photo)

over the above combination for maximum warmth. The mittens should be attached to strings so that while you shoot they can be taken off without your dropping or losing them.

Footwear. Shoes or boots should reach above the ankle to protect the ankle and foot, but should not be high enough to constrict the calf muscle. They should have a Vibram lug sole to provide the most secure footing. The extremely lightweight Gore-Tex boots are best for warm weather because the material breathes. Wear wick socks with these boots.

In cold weather insulated boots of Gore-Tex are good. If the terrain is wet or there is some snow on the ground, the rubber-bottomed, leather-topped hunting shoe will keep your feet dry. For very cold weather you can get these boots with a felt liner. But make sure both types of these boots have the lug soles.

In extremely cold weather or when you are going to be sitting in a blind for long periods of time get a pair of Army surplus arctic mukluks. These have canvas tops that come up to the knee and a leather bottom. Each boot has two layers of felt insoles in the bottom and two pairs of high felt boots inside. Wear them with ice creepers if the snow is crusted or icy.

To be able to sit for hours in a blind in cold weather, you need warm clothing such as this Orvis down overcoat and pants. (Len Rue Jr. photo)

A knitted hat will keep you warm but will allow perspiration and excess heat, caused by exertion, to escape. (Len Rue Jr. photo)

Gaiters are great for keeping dew, rain, snow, and dirt off your pants cuffs and boots. (Len Rue Jr. photo)

The real Eskimo camaks have a sealskin outer layer and several layers of wool duffle boots inside. These two types of boots are the warmest you can get.

In extremely cold weather you should wear a pair of silk socks, a pair of wick socks, and the best wool and nylon reinforced socks you can buy. While sitting in the blind keep flexing your toes to promote circulation. And avoid alcohol and tobacco in cold weather because they cause capillaries to constrict, making the extremities colder.

Hats. In the heat of summer a ventilated straw hat with a wide brim will prevent sunstroke. A ventilated tennis hat is also good. In cool weather the Trebark porkpie-type hat is ideal. In cold weather a knitted hat, such as the Winona Mills hat, is great.

As the saying goes, if you want to keep your feet warm, wear a hat. Forty percent of the body's heat can be lost through the head and neck. That is why, if you are moving, the knitted hat is recommended; it will act as a vent and allow the perspiration to escape. In windy conditions, or if you are sitting in a blind, then a down hat with ear flaps is good. A face mask of mesh or chamois, or a balaclava hat will keep your face warmer on cold, windy days. Do not wear a face

mask in the Arctic as your breath will freeze into ice inside the mask.

Special gear for cold or wet weather. When photographing from a blind in the bitterest cold, you should wear something like the Orvis down coat and zippered overpants. Do not wear these heavy clothes while going to your blind. Carry them so that you don't wet them with perspiration. When you get to the blind, cool off a bit before putting on your heavy clothing. In very cold weather, perspiring heavily in insulated clothing can lead to serious problems. Carry granola bars or other heat-producing food snacks and drink lots of liquid. Carry a large rain poncho with you at all times so that you can cover yourself and your gear when the unexpected shower shows up. A poncho is best if you are moving because it allows air to circulate underneath, carrying off sweat. A rainsuit is fine if your are going to be sitting.

Knee-high, lightweight gaiters are also a must if the vegetation is wet with dew or rain or if there is snow of any depth. Gaiters keep moisture off your clothing and boots, prevent stickers from adhering to your pants, prevent scratches from briars, and keep small stones and dirt from getting in your ankle-high boots.

BLIND SETUPS AND STALKING

No serious wildlife photographer can trust luck to produce consistent shots of deer in their natural habitat. Instead, he must either stalk deer to get close enough to photograph them or set up a blind in a likely spot and wait for the deer to approach.

Probably more wildlife photographs are taken from blinds than by all other methods combined. A blind can be any one of a variety of setups—fixed or portable—that camouflage the photographer. With a blind it is possible to get close-up shots without alarming the deer, and such intimate shots of deer in their natural habitat tend to sell.

POSITIONING THE BLIND

Fortunately, deer are predictable and reliable in their actions. So thorough knowledge of deer, their habits, and habitat makes photographing them from a blind relatively easy. In park areas, some deer are accustomed to human proximity and so can sometimes be stalked to ranges that allow telephoto shooting. Other animals are exceedingly wary and cannot be followed or stalked so that a blind must be used.

Because most wild animals are creatures of habit, blinds can be set up at dens, water holes, feeding areas, and along trails. Migratory animals are hard to work from a blind except as they are passing through the area. And they are soon gone. Some animals, such as members of the weasel family, move almost constantly on a seven- to ten-day cycle of their territory, so they are also hard to work from a blind.

There are a number of basic factors that must be considered when positioning and using a blind. The angle of light is of prime importance. Dramatic photographs can be taken against the light, but this lighting should be used for special effects, not for the bulk of your work. It is only with the sun behind or nearly behind you that the subject and background will be illuminated properly for good detail. So keep in mind the time of day when you expect to be using the blind. If you plan to use it from dawn to dusk, place it facing due north to give you the best possible lighting for the longest time.

The direction of the prevailing wind is also of great

A blind set up near a water hole, as at left, can produce good photos. With desert animals, water holes are more important than food. Your blind must be placed so that the prevailing wind does not carry your scent to deer.

importance and, on occasion, may take priority over the direction of light. Most birds have little or no sense of smell so that wind direction does not have to be considered in placing the blind to photograph them. Many of the smaller mammals, such as woodchucks, tree squirrels, and ground squirrels, pay little attention to scent; they depend on their eyesight for protection. However, when photographing members of the feline, canine, and deer families, wind direction is of paramount importance. These animals all live in a world of scent; the odors carried to them by the wind determines what they do. Where these animals are wary because they are hunted, your blind must be placed so that your scent does not betray your presence.

Scent, however, can also be used to your advantage to attract the deer to the spot where you want them to be. There are many commerical scents on the market, such as Hunter's Pro Pack, made from natural deer secretions or glands. Musk scents can be used throughout the year, as they are used primarily to allay the deer's fears and to arouse it's curiosity. Although deer do not claim territory, they all have their own particular home range and are used to odors of the other deer that share their range. The introduction of a new scent into their area does not alarm them in any way, but it does arouse their curiosity. They want to check out the stranger.

Sex scents are usually made from the female deer during her estrus, or heat, period. This odor is exceptionally attractive to the bucks during the rutting season. It is the odor they are searching for and is the reason bucks greatly expand their ranges during the rut.

These scents should not be used, or worn, on your person even though some scent companies are promoting foot packs and containers to be worn. *Don't do it!*

You can lay a trail of scent by dragging a cottonball saturated with these scents through the woods leading to the spot in front of your blind where you want to photograph the deer. Then the cottonball can be hung on a tree 6 to 7 feet above the ground. The deer will follow the trail to the spot and will often hold in the area trying to get at the cottonball. Do not bring the cottonball closer than 60 to 70 feet to your blind. At this distance the deer will pay little attention to the blind and the sound of your camera's shutter will be muffled sufficiently by the walls of the blind.

Food scents are also of great help and can be used in conjunction with existing natural foods when you are deciding where to set up a blind.

Where they are found, acorns are one of the most preferred of all deer foods. The white oak acorn is the most eagerly sought by deer. A blind placed in a stand of white oak trees in the latter part of September and the first part of October will produce deer photographs. Every deer knows the location of every white oak tree, and when the acorns are dropping, they search under the trees every day for the tasty morsels. Whether there is a good acorn crop or not is immaterial. White acorn scent poured on the ground will attract the deer like a magnet to the spot you have selected.

Apple orchards are also great places to put up a blind. Old abandoned orchards are even better than those under heavy cultivation. Although the deer will visit both, they will be out earlier in the abandoned orchard. You can bait the deer with drop apples if the crop is poor, or you can use apple concentrate scent. Using the scent is easier and actually cheaper in terms of time and money. The scent works well and a bottle of scent can be carried in your pocket.

If the deer have been feeding on corn in your area, you can put your blind in the corn field, or you can put out corn in the nearby woodlands. If you are going to use corn for bait, use shelled corn because it is easier to hide by scattering beneath the leaves. You don't want the corn to show in the photos you take of the deer. Corn without the cob is also much easier to carry.

Although photographs of deer feeding are good behavioral studies, they have a very limited sales value. Most editors want photos of alert, wary deer. Deer in areas where they are hunted are constantly wary so that all you have to do is wait until the deer picks its head up to look around for danger and then take your photo. Or you can make a slight sound to get the deer to pick its head up and look in the direction of the blind.

TYPES OF BLINDS

Many people in rural areas enjoy watching deer so they feed them close to their homes. If you feed deer or know someone who does by all means take advantage of the opportunity. Special care must be taken to eliminate all signs of man-made objects in the shot. Although some people advocate shooting through the windows, don't do it. Window glass will almost always cause distortion in your photographs. Open the window and stick your lens out. You can mask your activities by drawing the curtain across the window or by lowering the shade, although this also blocks your view. Ordinarily a deer pays no attention to people in a house, even when they are close to a window. A deer soon learns that the glass is a protective barrier.

If deer are accustomed to feeding or being fed in particular areas, permanent or semipermanent blinds can be erected and left there. The author has a blind that is made of wood and looks like the old-style outhouse. It has been in place for more than 16 years and is built into a fence on a private estate where the

This semipermanent blind is made in plywood sections that can be taken apart and moved to a new location.

deer have been fed for more than 30 years. Although the deer feed upon many natural foods, they still come to the estate to feed on the corn placed there.

Semipermanent blinds can be made in sections from plywood and can be moved to appropriate spots at different times of the year. On site they can be bolted together and their rigidity makes for a large, comfortable, absolutely stormproof blind that the deer soon come to accept. One of these blinds can be placed in an orchard in the fall, in an oak forest when the acorns are dropping, near a feeding station in the winter, at the edge of an alfalfa field in the spring, or near a pond in the summer.

VEHICLES AS BLINDS

Vehicles of all sorts can also be used for photography. Except for moving vehicles on roads where deer are crossing, many deer tend to regard vehicles as little threat and as a part of their natural habitat.

Many good photographs of deer feeding in adjacent fields can be taken from your car window. Cushion your camera and the telephoto lens on the windowsill by using a blanket or any other padded material.

However, the camera and lens will still have a tendency to rock. The Gitzo window pod, discussed earlier, gives the best support when photographing from a car window.

If you have a truck or a trailer that is not being used regularly, you can park it in a desired area and bait the deer to it. Deer soon accept a stationary vehicle as an integral part of their environment.

TREE STAND BLINDS

To get the most attractive photos possible, you should take photographs at the deer's eye level. Unless you are trying to show how the deer looks from the perspective of a hunter on a tree stand, do not take photos from a tree stand. If you want to take the hunting angle photos, you can use any of the many tree stands commercially made for hunters. (See Part 5 of this book for details on tree stands.) The accompanying photograph shows how a Baker tree stand can be modified to use a pipe as a camera tripod.

After getting yourself, the camera, and lens in position, you can cover yourself with a Pocket Blind. You are ready to start taking photos as soon as the deer shows up.

You have one real advantage in a tree blind. By being above the ground in the first place, your human scent is carried up and away if there is any warmth at all or if the wind is blowing. Overcast or drizzly days are not good for photography anyway, and those are the only conditions under which your scent would be carried to the ground.

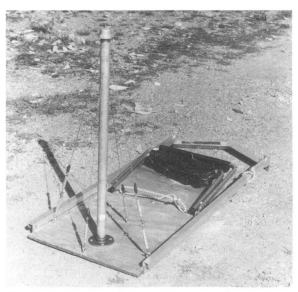

This is a Baker tree stand modified to support a camera at eye level when the photographer is seated. (Irene Vandermolen photo)

Draped with a Rue Pocket Blind, this photographer is ready in his tree stand. (Irene Vandermolen photo)

BLINDS FROM NATURAL MATERIAL

Many hunters make a screen out of native materials to conceal themselves from the sharp eyes of the deer. Blinds on private lands can be made of natural materials if you have the owner's permission. Blinds made of natural material are expressly prohibited on most public lands either by policy or by law. Indiscriminate cutting of vegetation would soon denude national parks and refuges.

Shocks of corn are not seen very often today because modern farming practices have changed and the corn is picked or chopped by a machine. However, corn shocks make good blinds. A hundred stalks of dried corn can be set up, tipi-fashioned, in a circle over a framework of poles and tied at the top·to make a blind that can be set up on most farm lands and particularly in and around cornfields.

Bales of hay can be set up in hayfields where deer feed on the alfalfa, clover, soybeans, buckwheat, etc. Bales should be stacked high enough so that you can sit inside comfortably. But make a roof on it using a few poles and some black plastic. Lay the poles across the bales and spread the plastic over them. Tie the plastic down. The roof contains your scent and, by darkening the inside of the blind, makes your movements hard to see.

In overgrown fields throughout a good part of the country, cedar trees are as common as weeds. Excellent blinds can be made by cutting a dozen or so (if permitted) and standing them on end tepee-style. The fragrance of the cedar trees will also help to mask your human odor.

You can take a trick from the duck hunter's book in making blinds. Use a roll of very lightweight, woven wire with a 4 × 4-inch neck for a framework. Thread marsh grass, timothy hay, or foxtail grasses back and forth through the mesh to form the covering and the roof. Then a couple of camera ports can be cut in the mesh.

Some photographers use pit blinds. However, in most areas they are too hard to dig, and if the soil is composed of clay, they hold water when it rains. Sandy soil requires some sort of a framework to prevent the walls from collapsing all the time.

Use caution whenever you are using a blind that has been put up and allowed to stand for some period of time. A blind offers shelter to many different forms of wildlife. Always check carefully before you enter a blind to make sure a snake hasn't crawled in there before you. In desert country watch out for scorpions.

Spiders may also take up residence in the blind. Paper wasps, white-faced hornets, and mud-dauber wasps find a blind an ideal spot to build their egg nests. Nuisance caterpillars, particularly the gypsy moth, seek out sheltered areas to shed their instar cases or to lay their egg masses. Most of these insect pests can be killed with wasp-killer sprays.

PORTABLE BLINDS

Of all the blinds in use, a portable blind is probably the one used most often because it is by nature so flexible. If you are photographing animals in a number of habitats or are traveling to areas some distance from your home, a portable blind is a must.

These blinds should be as compact as possible and simple enough to set up quickly. Complicated blinds, though portable, result in frustration, loss of time, and missed shots.

If possible, set up your portable blind a couple of times in advance of the day you plan to shoot. This way you can study the activity of animals in the area. And this lets them become used to the presence of your blind. Even without the opportunity for setting up in advance, this type of blind is exceedingly useful for getting good photographs of deer. The presence of the blind may cause them to be a bit more alert than usual, but that is fine because photographs of alert animals are the best sellers.

Rue's Pocket Blind is the most portable blind available. (Irene Vandermolen photo)

Get to the spot you have selected well ahead of the deer, and set up your blind and equipment so that you are settled before there is any chance that your intended animals will enter the area.

Because of the movement of wildlife in the area and the movement of the sun throughout the day, your blind should have several lens ports to allow you to make adjustments accordingly. A word of caution: Do not move your lens from one port to another if there is any chance that the animal will see or hear your movement. If so, your chances for photographs will be ruined.

This type of blind can be made of various materials but must be designed to blend into the environment more carefully than permanent or semipermanent blinds. That is because the animals will not have time to become accustomed to its presence before you use it. When you do set up a portable blind, be sure to nestle it into the area so that it is as inconspicuous as possible.

A portable blind is also an advantage for those occasions when you spot an animal headed for a particular area. By moving in a circuitous route, well ahead of the animal, you could have your blind and equipment set up well before the animal gets there. But you must be able to get your blind set up in a hurry.

There are several good blinds on the market de-

Rue's Ultimate Blind weighs 9½ pounds and can be carried over the shoulder. Set up, at right, the opened blind shows the work space. A comfortable stool with a back is a must. The stool should also have tubing between the legs to prevent its sinking into soft ground. (Photos by Len Rue Jr.)

Rue's Simplex Blind is 40 inches square and weighs 7½ pounds. (Len Rue Jr. photo)

signed for just these purposes. It would be well worth your time and effort to investigate some of them. Examples of these blinds are the Pocket, Ultimate, and Simplex blinds. When selecting your blind be sure to consider weight and ease of packing. A heavy or cumbersome blind, no matter how functional or well camouflaged, will seem to grow heavier the longer you have to carry it.

The Rue's Pocket Blind is the most portable blind available. It is made out of fitted and shaped camouflage material that rolls up into a 12 × 4-inch packet and can be carried in the pocket of your photo vest. If you plan to sit in a blind for quite a while a stool with a back is required. With the Pocket Blind, just select your location, set up your camera and tripod, sit down on your stool, slip on the Pocket Blind, and you are ready to take photographs.

The Rue's Ultimate and Simplex Blinds both have frames of spring steel rods that are an integral part of the blind. The Ultimate Blind is circular in shape, 60 inches in diameter and 56 inches high, and weighs only 9½ pounds. The Simplex Blind is 40 inches square, 56 inches high, and weighs 7½ pounds. When folded up, these blinds can be carried on one shoulder like a bandolier.

These blinds can be set up and ready for use in 30 seconds, a real plus in the field. When using the blind,

The mist and dew had softened the leaves, a close stalk to this buck chewing on a twig over his scrape. (Marilyn Maring photo)

you place your stool on the radiating rods to hold the blind firmly in place. The guylines are not needed unless the wind is blowing or the blind is to be left in position for several days. The blinds come in a mixed camouflage pattern of browns. Tie an old white cotton bedsheet over the top of the blind when you use it in the snow. The blinds are water resistant and come with a loose floor cloth for use on damp soil or in snow.

STALKING AND WALKING DEER

When you attempt to stalk a deer, *everything* is in the deer's favor. You cannot stalk a deer in extremely dry weather because every step you take makes the leaves sound like you are wading knee-deep in cornflakes. You cannot stalk on extremely cold snow because the edges of the snow crystals will be exceedingly sharp and will squeak when they are compressed under your feet. You should not attempt to stalk deer when it is very windy because at such times a deer is thoroughly panicked by the crashing of leaves and tree branches, and the eddying air currents.

Deer can be stalked after a hard rain has soaked and softened the leaves on the ground, in the early morning when the dew has done the same thing, or when a soft, fluffy snow has just fallen.

You have to rely on your knowledge of the deer's feeding areas so that you can locate the deer you want to stalk. If the deer have left the feeding areas, you must know where they are spending the day. Although light is important to the photographer, wind direction is of the greatest importance when stalking. The wild deer that smells you is gone.

Always remember that most deer escape detection by remaining in hiding and allowing people to walk by. Deer are cud-chewers so that they can remain motionless and hidden while watching for anything that moves. Also, a deer's eyes are designed to detect the slightest motion. This means that you will have to spend much more time looking closely for deer than you will walking widely for deer.

Your greatest chance of success is to start out very early in the morning to locate the deer before they have left their feeding areas. Then try to position yourself between the deer and their bedding areas so you can ambush them as they come by. When a deer is moving, more factors will be in your favor.

A favorite method is to locate the deer when they come out to feed and then, by taking advantage of the lay of the land and the wind, try to position yourself ahead of them, allowing them to feed to you. If the deer are habitual feeders in one particular spot, it is better to work from a blind than to attempt to stalk them.

In working on wild deer, you must avoid being seen. In working with deer in National Parks and refuges you have to expend almost as much energy to remain in their sight after you have located them. Nothing scares deer more than to have a person or an animal it has been watching disappear from sight. When you drop out of sight just to cross a gully or for some other

All deer, like this five-point muley buck, can hide in skimpy cover. (Irene Vandermolen photo)

reason, the deer then thinks it is being stalked by a predator. When you reappear the deer will probably disappear.

The best way to find deer in the parks and refuges is to ask the biologist or the rangers where the animals usually hang out at that time of the year. The next best way is to cruise the roads in your vehicle because you can cover far more ground. If it is possible to photograph the deer from your vehicle, don't get out.

If you have to get out to approach the deer, do it in a circuitous manner. Don't get out of the vehicle and dash directly at the animal or it will show you how fast it can run. Wind direction means little to the park animals; so you can disregard it too. Now, as you circle toward the animal, you can plan your approach so as to get the benefit of the sun. Don't hurry, and don't pay attention to the deer you want to photograph. Don't even look at it. Be casual and nonchalant, acting as if the deer was the last thing in the world in which you had any interest. It is the direct approach that alarms animals. Studied indifference will allow you to get close.

Everyone working with domestic animals talks to them. This lets the animal know where you are and the sound of a reassuring human voice soothes them. Do the same thing with any park deer you are attempting to photograph; talk to it. It doesn't really matter what you say, just talk to it. Stalking predators depend upon stealth; your noise tells the animal where you are at all times and will actually serve to identify you.

If the deer bounds off when you approach, follow it, but do so slowly. Try to keep the animal in sight and, if you can, follow as slowly and from as great a distance as possible until the animal calms down. If the animal was bedded when you first saw it, hold back until it beds down again. Then approach slowly so as not to push the animal into getting up. Perhaps you can sit down for a while in plain sight of the animal, but keep talking to it. Slowly work yourself closer. Then when the deer does get up of its own accord, it is very likely to accept your presence because you have proven that you are not a threat.

THE DEER AS A THREAT

Deer are easiest to photograph where they have become used to people. These same park deer can become a threat to you because, where they have become used to people, they have also lost their fear of man. One of the most dangerous creatures in North America is a captive whitetail buck.

Most deer photos are taken in the fall when the buck's antlers are hardened and the velvet has been stripped off. By the time the leaves have come off the

This whitetail buck is showing an extremely aggressive attitude. His ears are back, all of his body hair is standing on end, and he is walking with a stiff-legged gait and giving the photographer a "hard" look.

trees, allowing enough light to photograph deer in the woodlands, the rutting season is on. It is during the rut that any buck, captive, semi-tame, or wild, can be a threat. Bucks have antlers to fight for the breeding privileges of the does. But when they are crazed by hormones, they are also likely to turn those antlers on a man. Whitetail bucks are much more likely to do this than the mule or blacktail deer. But don't trust any buck during the rutting season.

The signs of aggression that a buck shows to a rival are the same he shows to a man. By knowing the signs and what they mean, you may avoid being hurt. The first sign of a probable attack is when the deer lays its ear back along its neck, tucks its chin in, and projects its antlers forward. It may paw the ground. It may flick its tongue out of its mouth. Then the buck advances with all of its body hair standing on end. This makes the buck look larger and is an effort to intimidate its opponent. The buck then advances with a stiff-legged gait, walking almost as if it were crippled. It either grunts or makes a high-pitched whine.

Long before these last signs, you had better be climbing a tree or seeking some protective shelter. When the charge comes, it happens so fast that you have little chance to run or to defend yourself. So at the first sign of danger, get out of the area. A man is no match for an angry buck in the rut. People die every year proving this point.

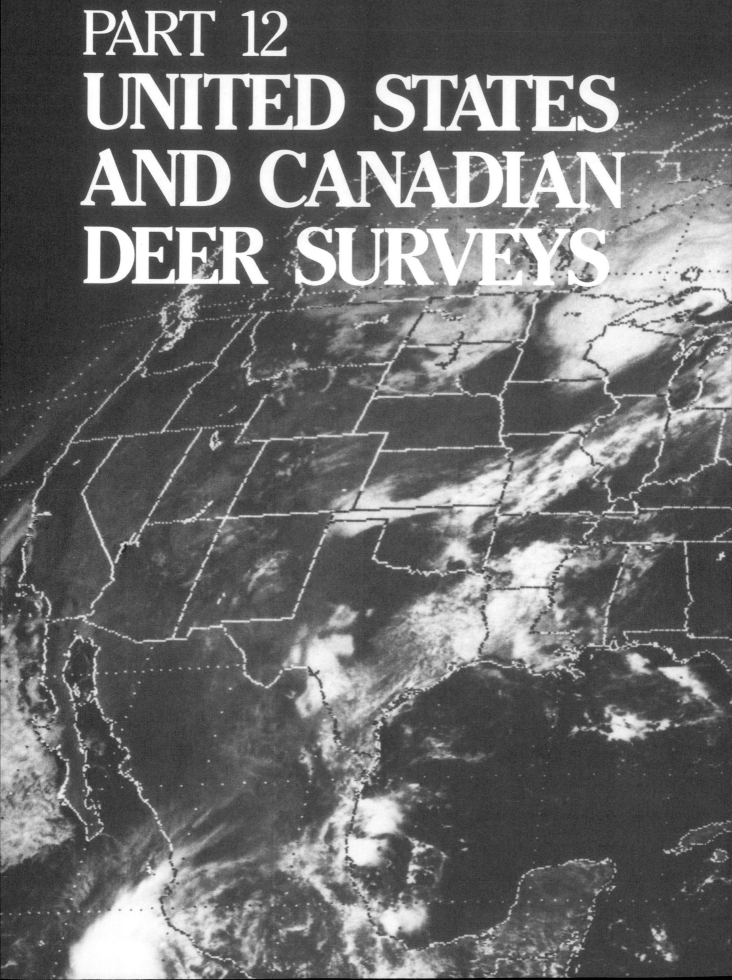

PART 12
UNITED STATES AND CANADIAN DEER SURVEYS

BY DWIGHT SCHUH
Maps by Manfred Milkuhn

At one time, hunters seemed more content to hunt their home territory. But with increased ease of travel, more free time, and more money, hunters now routinely look beyond home-state or provincial boundaries. It's not unusual for hunters to pursue deer in two, three, or even four states or provinces each season. Today's traveling hunter needs a broad-based guide for planning hunting trips, and this part of the encyclopedia should provide a good basis for planning. Even nontraveling hunters should find the surveys on states and provinces quite fascinating.

On upcoming pages, you will find a separate survey for each U.S. state and for the Canadian provinces that have deer in huntable numbers. Surveys on the states appear first and are, by state, in alphabetical order. Canadian provinces follow the states, also alphabetically.

None of the surveys is intended to serve as a guide to specific hunting hotspots, which can change from year to year. Again, the surveys are meant to be starting points for planning. Here you'll find which states have the most deer, the biggest deer, and usually the most liberal seasons, as well as places where you can normally take more than one deer a year. With this information, you can determine the states or provinces that appear to meet your hunting interests. Then you can begin to research specific hunting spots by consulting additional information sources.

For your convenience, each survey on a state or province is presented in a standardized format. Here is a brief look at what you will find:

Deer numbers. This first paragraph gives the area of the state or province in square miles, the amount of area that supports deer, and for most states, the estimated overall deer population (some wildlife departments refuse to make such estimates).

Hunters and harvest. This section lists the average number of hunters (firearms and bow), average yearly harvest, average hunter success, and other related statistics. From these figures you can assess the amount of competition and the quality of hunting. For example, in one state the annual harvest may be 100,000 deer with a hunter success rate of 15 percent and in another 30,000 deer with a success rate of 40 percent. Your chances for killing a deer might actually be better in the state with the 30,000 kill, because of the high success rate. Of course, record-keeping systems do vary greatly among states; so the data presented here is approximate and may vary from one state to the next.

Distribution. In every state there are certain areas that produce more deer than others. Also there are places that consistently produce large bucks. This section on distribution gives you a brief tour of the state to describe types of terrain and the quality of deer herds in each region.

Seasons. Most states have traditional seasons and bag limits. However, dates and other specifics change from year to year, so that information must be generalized. But from the general guidelines given, you can tell whether a state has a September or December season, whether seasons fall during the rut, whether the bag limit is generally one deer or three, and so forth.

Records. This section gives some idea of the size of deer taken in the state, and it lists the record antlers. From this you can gauge the trophy potential in each state. Again, not all states and provinces keep records, and completeness of the data presented here may vary from survey to survey.

The future. Habitat and deer numbers are never static. In some states conditions are improving, and in others they're declining. This section gives you some idea of what to expect into the 1990s.

Contact. The address of each state wildlife agency is given here to provide a starting point for further planning.

DEER HUNTING: AN OVERVIEW

Prospects for deer hunting at least into the 1990s, are excellent. With few exceptions, deer numbers in most states are at all-time highs and they're increasing. Deer hunters have never had better opportunities for quality hunting than they do at present.

Some rough figures will give you an idea of the magnitude of deer herds in North America. These are based on estimates from individual state and provincial game departments. Some departments refuse to estimate the numbers of their deer, so estimated populations for those states are here based on harvest figures. Commonly hunters harvest about one-fifth of the total deer herd annually, so populations for these states were estimated to be five times the average annual harvest.

The United States supports a total population of about 17.6 million whitetails, and the Canadian provinces have an additional 1.2 million for a total north of Mexico of nearly 19 million whitetails. Of this, an estimated 50,000 Coues whitetails live in Arizona and New Mexico. Mule deer number about 3.5 million in the United States and 270,000 in Canada for a total of about 3.8 million. The Pacific States maintain about 980,000 blacktails, and British Columbia has about 310,000 for a total of nearly 1.3 million blacktails. British Columbia estimates its Sitka blacktail population at 75,000, and Alaska says it has "several hundred thousand."

The long-term outlook, though, is not as bright. Throughout North America, certain logging practices, mining, housing development, land clearing for farming, and other changes are reducing deer habitats. At the same time, the human population is increasing steadily, and the interest in deer hunting continues to rise. So the deer resource will probably be spread more thinly among hunters each year. In many states, biologists don't see loss of habitat as a major problem. Instead it is competition among hunters for available deer and for hunting access to private lands.

Far West. Blacktail deer, which live in a coastal strip about 100 miles wide from Southern California to Alaska, have maintained fairly stable numbers for many years. Because their habitat has a temperate climate, blacktails rarely suffer major winter die-offs, and their brushy environment provides good refuge from hunters. In general, blacktails are at or near carrying capacity in most regions, and their numbers fluctuate little from year to year. Logging of dense old-growth timber has improved forage for blacktails from northern California through Washington, and overall populations have grown. The near future for blacktails appears to be secure.

A major exception can be seen in northern British Columbia and Alaska where Sitka blacktails depend on old-growth timber for shelter from deep snow during winter. Extensive clear-cutting has destroyed much of the deer's winter range, and Sitka deer populations probably will decline.

The Intermountain West. Mule deer are the prevalent species in the region from the Cascade Range of Washington and Oregon and the Sierra Nevada of California eastward to the Rocky Mountains. From low numbers in the early 1900s, mule deer populations exploded and provided great hunting through the 1950s and 1960s. Then in the late 1960s and early 1970s, mule deer numbers inexplicably sagged lower again. This decline occurred in all of the 11 western states except Washington.

In the late 1970s, mule deer herds rebounded, and by the 1980s, they were hitting record highs again. Rapid land development, particularly related to oil and gas exploration, logging to some extent, and rural subdivisions on critical winter range will reduce the quality and acreage of mule deer habitat, especially in the Rocky Mountains. Yet mule deer hunting should remain good into the 1990s.

Keep in mind, however, that mule deer populations can, and generally do, fluctuate rapidly. Unlike most eastern whitetails or Pacific blacktails that live year-round in small areas and generally in temperate climates, most mule deer summer at high elevations and migrate long distances to lower elevations for winter. Given mild winter weather, they do fine. But when a hard winter piles deep snow on winter ranges, deer frequently die by the thousands. This is common in Colorado and other mountainous states where winter ranges are limited in size. As a result, mule deer numbers are erratic, and can go from high densities to low in a single year. So it's always wise to check on the condition of herds from year to year. If the winter has been tough in your preferred spot, look for a new area where conditions have been more favorable.

While the range of mule deer has remained static or shrunk slightly since the 1960s, the range of Intermountain West whitetails has steadily expanded. These hardy animals seem to adapt to changing conditions better than mule deer, and they're constantly expanding into new range. For example, they're now abundant south of the Salmon River in Idaho and in southwestern Montana where they were rare or nonexistent in the late 1970s. They've spread throughout northeastern Oregon too. In southwestern New Mexico, Coues whitetails began expanding their range greatly in the 1980s.

The Plains States. The history of deer herds for every state from North Dakota south to Texas and east as far as Ohio reads almost identically. The deer, primarily whitetails but with some mule deer in the western fringes, were abundant in the colonial Americas, and they served as a major food source for explorers and pioneers. About 1850, as the westward movement intensified, both subsistence and market hunting for mining camps, railroad crews, and logging camps began to take a heavy toll on deer. In the open terrain of the Great Plains, these animals didn't have much chance in the face of unrestricted hunting. By 1900, deer herds either had been wiped out or severely threatened in the Plains States.

Then people began to realize the loss. So local governments adopted rudimentary game laws. In some states hunting was prohibited outright, and in others seasons were limited to certain months, and bag limits were imposed.

Under this protection, herds began to reappear and expand. At the same time some states began to stock deer in areas where none had been seen for years. With these efforts, primarily in the 1930s, new herds

Mule deer (Irene Vandermolen photo)

took root. They grew slowly at first, but in the 1950s, they began to explode. In general, deer populations and harvests hit record highs every year from the 1960s into the 1980s.

The harvest in Oklahoma is typical of these states. During the first open season in 1933, hunters killed 235 deer, and the harvest fluctuated between 300 and 800 through 1953. In 1954 all 77 counties in the state were opened to hunting for the first time, and the harvest hit a high of 1,487. From that point on it jumped virtually every year, exceeding 14,000 in the early 1980s.

In Kansas, deer were still considered extinct as late as 1933, and they were scarce until the 1960s. During the first open season in 1965, hunters killed 1,340 deer. By 1983, the harvest was up to over 13,000.

Most game officials agree that herds have just about reached their upper limits. Farm depredation and other complaints, such as deer-vehicle collisions, have become common. Landowners and other residents will tolerate only so many deer. In recent years, most Prairie States have liberalized seasons and bag limits, particularly for does, to stabilize or reduce the size of deer herds.

The South. The general pattern of decline, near extinction, and explosion holds for the South as well as for the Great Plains, but for slightly different reasons. Following the Civil War, virtually the entire South from Mississippi to the Atlantic Ocean and north to Virginia and Delaware, was cleared and planted with farm crops. The lack of woody cover, combined with unrestrained subsistence hunting, wiped out deer in the South. Relic herds survived in remote, forested bastions of the Appalachian Mountains and in inaccessible marshes along the coasts, but otherwise, the Deep South and the Appalachian Region had no deer.

In the early 1900s, with an economy changing from an agrarian to an industrial base, many families abandoned farms and moved to the cities. And where cotton once grew, trees and brush began to take over, with the result that many states were becoming reforested and even heavily timbered. For example, Georgia, which supported almost border-to-border cotton fields in the late 1800s, has become the No. 2 timber-producing state.

Now the southern states have the highest deer numbers found anywhere. Densities of 50 deer or more per square mile are not uncommon in Arkansas, Mississippi, Alabama, and other states of the Deep South. Harvest in Mississippi characterizes the pattern for this entire region: in 1970 hunters killed 40,000 deer; in the early 1980s, they were killing more than 200,000 deer each fall.

Herds continue to grow throughout the southern and Appalachian states, and in many places they now exceed carrying capacity and must be reduced. Multiple-deer bag limits, or no bag limits at all, are the rule in most southern states. Hunting clubs have a traditional place in southern hunting, and much of the best private land has been leased by private clubs, which severely restricts access from the general public.

The Appalachian Mountains present a major exception to the rule of high deer numbers in the South. In this subregion, heavy hardwood forests with little green forage have an inherently low carrying capacity for deer. That fact, coupled with continued subsistence hunting, commercial poaching, harassment of deer by dogs, has held deer populations at low levels.

New England. In New York and the southern New England states, deer herds have followed a pattern similar to states farther south. In Massachusetts, for example, the land was virtually denuded for farm crops in the early 1900s. Since then many farms have been abandoned, and now forests cover nearly 75 percent of the state. With the return of forests, deer populations have rebounded dramatically. In the 1960s the Massachusetts deer population was estimated at 6,000, and now it's over 30,000.

In other parts of new England, the pattern hasn't been as favorable. This far north, deer are at the mercy of winter conditions. In northern Vermont and New Hampshire, unfavorable logging practices have eliminated vast amounts of timber needed by deer for winter cover, and overall deer numbers are much lower now than in the early 1970s.

In northern Maine, forests that were logged in the early 1900s once provided ideal habitat for a large deer herd. But now they have grown into older stands with limited forage, and deer herds have declined in that area. In agricultural areas and hardwood forests of southern Maine, deer have thrived in recent years

and made up for some of the loss. But overall deer numbers have declined, and the harvest has dropped from an average of about 39,000 in the 1950s, to around 30,000 in the 1980s.

Canadian provinces. Some Canadian provinces—Yukon, Northwest Territories, Newfoundland, Prince Edward Island—have either few deer or none at all. Others, however, have large herds. In the western provinces—British Columbia and Alberta—mule deer generally have declined as a result of habitat loss, while whitetails have grown in both distribution and numbers.

In the prairie provinces—Saskatchewan, Manitoba, and Ontario—the history and present condition of herds differ greatly from neighboring states in the United States. Deer were never totally killed off in these provinces, and as logging opened up northern forests, and agriculture created a rich food supply on the prairies, whitetail deer flourished and reached all-time high numbers in the 1950s and 1960s. Since then, however, many of the northern forests have matured, which has reduced the quality and abundance of forage for deer. And continued clearing for agriculture in the prairie zones has eliminated vast amounts of valuable woody cover required to sustain high numbers of whitetails.

Under protective management, mule deer numbers have rebounded dramatically in Saskatchewan, but in general, whitetail herds have declined in the prairie provinces by 30 to 50 percent since the mid-1960s.

In the eastern provinces—Quebec, New Brunswick, and Nova Scotia—mild winters beginning about 1975 allowed deer numbers to build up dramatically, and this region generally had all-time high whitetail populations in the early 1980s. However, the spruce-fir forests that blanket most of this region are not generally productive deer range, and deer normally are forced onto small yarding grounds during tough winters. Given continued mild winter weather, herds probably will remain at high levels. But severe winters will create population "busts" and herds will have to start rebuilding again.

THE DECADE OF THE DEER

With minor exceptions deer numbers generally have risen steadily since about 1900, and they've grown explosively in many regions since the mid-1960s to reach all-time highs. The 1980s may truly be called the "Decade of the Deer." Deer hunters have never had it better, and may never have it as good again. It's time to go hunting.

ALABAMA

Deer numbers. Alabama has an area of 51,609 square miles, and whitetail deer are abundant in all counties. The average preseason population is estimated at 1.3 million deer.

Hunters and harvest. For the past several years, Alabama has attracted an average of a little over 200,000 resident and nonresident hunters combined. Of these, 50,000 are estimated to be archers. The average annual harvest has been 157,000 deer, and the record harvest, which took place in the 1981–82 season, was 202,000 deer.

Distribution. Generally speaking, the northern two-thirds of Alabama has a higher human population and lower deer densities. The southern third, roughly south of Montgomery, has fewer people, large tracts of privately owned land, and high deer numbers.

The Tennessee Valley **(No. 1)** in the northwest consists of flatlands planted in cotton, soybeans, and row crops intermixed with woodlots of hardwood trees. Deer numbers are low to moderate here.

The southern tip of the Appalachian Chain covers the northeast corner **(No. 2)**. Vegetation on the steep, rugged mountains here consists of oak and hickory hardwoods mixed with pines. Some small plateaus have been converted to pastureland. In general the soils are poor, and deer numbers are comparatively low.

Broken, steep ridges of the Piedmont Region **(No. 3)** aren't conducive to large clearing projects; so the region consists of small pastures and pine plantations. The clay soils aren't very fertile, and deer densities are moderate.

West-central Alabama **(No. 4)** is known as the peach capital of the world. Some fertile coastal plains soils extend north into this region, and many pine plantations exist here. However, the human population is high and land is broken into small privately owned lots, which prevents large-scale deer-management programs. As a result, overall deer numbers are only moderate in this region.

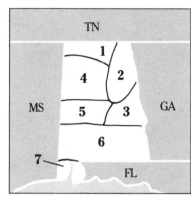

Zones created by author

The Black Belt Region **(No. 5)** has extensive areas of black, heavy soil. Small pastures and pine plantations are the primary land uses here. Deer numbers are considered good to excellent throughout the Black Belt.

The Coastal Plain **(No. 6)** generally has the highest deer densities in Alabama (except in Houston county in the extreme southeast, where intense peanut production has removed most wooded cover). Large timber companies own huge pine plantations here, and these are intermixed with truck and peanut farms.

The Delta Region **(No. 7)** consists of dunes along the shore bordered by marshlands where few deer exist. The upper delta north of Mobile has some cypress woodlands, but even this part of the delta remains wet most of the time, and deer numbers are low.

Alabama law requires hunters to obtain permission to hunt whether the land is posted or not. Some large timber companies allow public hunting for a modest few, but the trend on private land in Alabama has been toward large-scale hunting leases, and private clubs or commercial hunting operations now control much of the best hunting. But the state administers more than two doz-

en public wildlife management areas that contain 657,000 acres, and the U.S. Forest Service and other agencies own more than 500,000 acres that are open to the public.

Seasons. Many counties have seasons that allow the use of dogs for deer hunting from November into January, and these are followed by two weeks or more of stalk-hunting only (no dogs). Other counties have stalk-hunting only seasons from November through January. Seasons on state management areas generally are shorter than the statewide season to assure high-quality hunts. At least a few management areas are open at all times during the general season to guarantee public hunting.

Bow seasons are liberal in some counties, running from October through January.

The bag limit during all seasons is one buck per day, although some hunter's choice seasons allow the taking of one deer, either sex, per day.

Records. The largest whitetail deer on record weighed 275 pounds live weight. Alabama has produced only one Boone and Crockett buck which scored about 175.

The future. In 1940 Alabama's deer population was estimated at 18,000 animals, and by 1950 that number had shrunk to 3,000. Following extensive stocking programs and enactment of tight regulations, better enforcement, and habitat improvement work in the 1950s, deer numbers built rapidly. The present population is estimated at 1.3 million. Herds may continue to grow in the northern regions, but they've reached or exceeded carrying capacity in most of south Alabama and will be stabilized or reduced slightly there. The outlook is for good hunting at least into the 1990s.

Contact. Department of Conservation and Natural Resources, Administrative Division, Montgomery, AL 36130–1901.

ALASKA

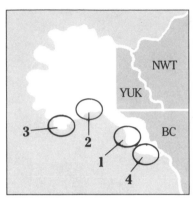

Zones created by author

Deer numbers. The Sitka blacktail is the only species of deer in Alaska. Its range covers about 25,000 square miles, or roughly 5 percent of the state's 586,000 square miles. In Alaska deer are overshadowed in importance by sheep, moose, caribou, and other big game. Thus little time and effort have gone into the survey and management of the state's Sitka blacktails. Biologists say the state contains "several hundred thousand" deer, but no specific estimates have been made.

Hunters and harvest. Deer don't get much publicity in Alaska, and most hunting pressure comes from locals hunting for meat. An average of 10,000 hunters kill from 10,000 to 15,000 Sitka blacktails each year. In better years, 13,000 hunters kill about 15,000 bucks and 5,000 does. No precise harvest statistics are kept, but biologists estimate that 60 percent of the hunters kill at least one deer each year. Some kill many more than that because the limit is four or five deer per year in some areas.

Distribution. Sitka blacktails are native to southeastern Alaska, but they have been transplanted and have become well established near Yakutat, on Prince William Sound southeast of Anchorage, on Kodiak Island, and on Afognak island. Their range generally coincides with coastal spruce and hemlock forests. There big trees keep most of the ground free of snow so that food is available throughout the winter. Where old growth forests do not occur naturally or where they've been cut, deer numbers generally are low. Kodiak Island presents one exception, and deer have thrived there in the absence of old-growth timber.

Some of the highest densities during the 1970s and early 1980s were found on Admiralty, Chichagof, and

Baranof islands **(No. 1)**; islands in Prince William Sound **(No. 2)**; and Kodiak and Afognak islands **(No. 3)**. Predators such as wolves and bears take some deer, but the loss is not significant, and winters have remained relatively mild.

During that same time, however, deer numbers dropped to very low levels on some islands and on the mainland in the southeast **(No. 4)**. Biologists attribute the severe decline primarily to extensive logging of critical winter habitat and to wolf predation. With low hunting pressure, the primary concern of Alaskan biologists is to maintain suitable winter habitat. If logging proceeds rapidly to eliminate old-growth forests, Sitka blacktails in Alaska do not face a bright future.

Early in the season, in August and September, the deer live relatively high in alpine terrain where they are fairly visible and the scenery is spectacular. After the first frosts, which nip feed in the high country, and the coming of snow, the deer descend to lower elevations. The majority of deer killed each year are taken in November at low elevations. During particularly hard winters, deer concentrate along the beaches.

Seasons. Seasons in several state hunting units run from early August through late December. The bag limit is four or five deer per year depending on the unit. In some cases both bucks and does can be taken legally. In other units where popula-

tions are low, however, the season either is closed or only limited buck hunting is allowed. Most of the harvest comes from units 2 and 4 (southeastern islands) and unit 8 (Kodiak and Afognak islands). Bowhunters and muzzleloaders may hunt throughout the general season, and have no special seasons.

Records. Biologists say that many deer in Alaska never see a hunter because much of the country is rough and remote, the weather can be nasty, and local hunters looking for meat can find easier pickings without venturing into outback trophy areas. Both the Boone and Crockett and Pope and Young clubs recognize Sitka blacktails as a separate category. For a hunter dedicated to putting a trophy in the record book, this deer offers wide-open opportunity. The typical antler conformation consists of only two branched points and a brow tine (that is, three points total on each side). The largest bucks score close to 130, although the average is much smaller. Sitka blacktails have a reputation of being tiny deer, but they can reach hefty proportions. The largest field-dressed buck on record weighed 209 pounds.

The future. Sitka deer rely on oldgrowth timber for shelter in winter. As clear-cutting removes massive blocks of mature timber in southeast Alaska, Sitka deer numbers will decline.

Contact. The Department of Fish and Game, PO Box 3-2000, Juneau, AK 99802.

ARIZONA

Deer numbers. Arizona has a total area of 113,956 square miles, and mule deer occupy 73,330 square miles, or 65 percent of the land. Coues deer (Arizona whitetails) occupy 11,000 square miles, or 19 percent. (Arizona contains several large Indian reservations, and the above figures don't include these.) The average preseason deer population is 130,000 mule deer and 40,000 Coues.

Hunters and harvest. The average total number of rifle hunters is 70,000, and of bowhunters, 8,000. Nonresidents account for less than 2 percent of that total. The average annual firearms harvest is 15,000, and 98 percent of the kills are bucks. In 1983, a high year, rifle hunters killed just under 17,000 deer. Hunter success for the past two decades has been about 20 percent. The high occurred in 1975 when hunters had a 23 percent success. The low of 16 percent was recorded in 1978.

The average archery harvest is 390 deer, and in 1979 archers took 620 deer. Average bowhunter success has been 4.7 percent.

Distribution. In Arizona you'll find three kinds of mule deer—Rocky Mountain, desert, and burro. Arizona is roughly divided into two sections by the Mogollon Rim, which runs diagonally from Flagstaff southeast to the New Mexico border. North of this plateau, the Rocky Mountain mule deer predominates. The North Kaibab **(No. 1)** lies on the north rim of Grand Canyon. Deer numbers in this legendary country have fluctuated drastically, but in recent years herds have been growing. With a growing population, the percentage of yearlings is high. But the North Kaibab has some remote country, and it produces large bucks. The east side of the North Kaibab is being managed—through a reduction in the number of tags—primarily as a trophy-buck area.

The extreme northwest corner of Arizona, adjacent to the North Kaibab, is commonly called The Strip **(No. 2)**, and it also is known for huge bucks, although deer are relatively scarce in this low-elevation

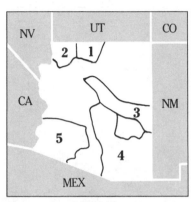

Zones created by author

country. Arizona has produced many record-book bucks, and most of these have come from the North Kaibab or The Strip.

The Mogollon Rim **(No. 3)** cuts across the center of Arizona, and this region contains a fair number of mule deer. South of the rim and throughout southeastern Arizona **(No. 4)**, the habitat changes to Sonoran Desert. Here Rocky Mountain mule deer give way to desert mule deer. These animals live at relatively low elevations, 3,000 to 5,500 feet. They're not as large on the average as their northern cousins, but many respectable desert mule deer come from southern Arizona. Mule deer live throughout the hot lowlands from Phoenix to Yuma **(No. 5)**, and many biologists classify these animals as burro deer. In this flat, brushy country deer are tough to find and present a unique hunting challenge.

Another inhabitant of southern Arizona **(No. 4)** is the Coues whitetail. This diminutive deer rubs shoulders with desert mule deer to some extent, but in any given range, they generally live at slightly higher elevations in oak grasslands and pine forests. Southeastern Arizona may be some of the most interesting country in North America. It consists of low, hot Sonoran desert interspersed with rugged mountain islands, such as the Santa Rita, Huachuca, Chiricahua, and Graham mountains, and

many others. These beautiful little mountain ranges harbor major herds of Coues deer.

Seasons. Most general rifle seasons take place in late October and November. Since 1971 all tags have been issued by drawing. Arizona has generous archery seasons, and the number of tags is not restricted. Some bow seasons are held in August and September, and many others occur in January. Many bowhunters like to combine javelina (desert pig) and deer hunting in January. In the southern deserts, both mule and Coues deer rut in January. Arizona also has special muzzleloader hunts.

Records. The average size of a field-dressed mule deer buck in Arizona is 100 pounds, and the weight of the heaviest mule deer on record is 309 pounds. For Coues bucks, average field-dressed weight is 70 pounds, and the record weight for Coues deer is 145.

When it comes to trophy size, the largest typical mule deer from Arizona scored 208⅝, and the largest nontypical, 316⅞. Arizona has produced good numbers of Boone and Crockett mule deer.

The world-record typical Coues deer, taken in Pima County in 1953, scored 143. The world-record nontypical came from Cochise County and scored 151⅛. By far the majority of Coues deer listed by Boone and Crockett have come from Arizona.

The future. Following a general decline in deer numbers in the early 1970s, herds have gradually returned to high levels. But pressure from Arizona's growing human population (it is a popular retirement state) has resulted in loss of habitat and increasing competition for available deer tags. However, most of Arizona's best deer range lies on public land where deer can be maintained at maximum numbers. So deer hunting prospects for the near future look good.

Contact. Arizona Game & Fish Department, 2222 W. Greenway Road, Phoenix, AZ 85023.

ARKANSAS

Deer numbers. Arkansas has a total land area of 53,103 square miles. An estimated population of 400,000 whitetail deer occupy 75 percent of that land area.

Hunters and harvest. Arkansas attracts about 260,000 resident and 10,000 nonresident hunters each year. The average firearms harvest has been about 47,000 deer (39,500 bucks and 7,500 does), with a high of 57,779 in 1983. Special muzzleloader hunts are held, and about 6,000 of the total harvest fall to muzzleloaders. Average success for modern firearms and muzzleloader hunters runs about 14 percent.

Bow and firearms licenses are not separated; so there are no accurate figures on the number of bowhunters. However, the average archery harvest has been about 1,500 (800 bucks and 700 does), and in 1983, one of the higher years, bowhunters took 2,469 deer. Bowhunters have a success rate of about 6 percent.

Distribution. The Ozark Mountains **(No. 1)** cover the northwestern quarter of Arkansas. These mountains range from about 300 feet in elevation to 2,800 feet, and much of the country is steep with many bluffs. Hardwood forests, primarily oak and hickory, blanket 75 percent of the Ozarks. Deer herds have been grown steadily here for several years, but they still have not reached the carrying capacity of the land, and numbers will continue to increase. In general the bucks are not large here, but some backcountry pockets receive little hunting pressure. There some bucks grow to maturity.

The Ouachita Mountain region **(No. 2)** is similar to the Ozarks although the mountains generally aren't as steep and bluffy, and hardwoods are interspersed with extensive pine forests. This region has the lowest deer densities in Arkansas, but herds are growing there, and biologists expect the kill to increase steadily. Some backcountry areas grow large bucks.

The Gulf Coastal Plain **(No. 3)** consists of flat or low, rolling terrain covered with extensive pine planta-

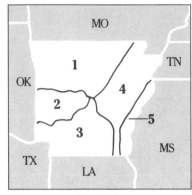

Zones created by author

tions owned by large timber companies. Deer numbers are very high throughout this region. The biggest problem here is an overabundance of deer, and liberal regulations have been in effect to reduce numbers. It's a high-production deer area, and big bucks are scarce.

The Delta region **(No. 4)**, consists largely of farmland where rice and soybeans are the major crops. Overall, deer numbers are low in this region, although animals are abundant along riverbottoms where woody plants provide adequate cover. Most land in the Delta is private and is posted against hunting. Some big bucks are taken along the lower Arkansas River.

The highest deer densities in Arkansas are found in a narrow strip along the wooded breaks of the Mississippi River **(No. 5)**. However, private clubs lease virtually all of the land here so that it's not available to the general public.

Compared to most states in the central United States, Arkansas offers a great deal of excellent public hunting. The Ozark and Ouachita National Forests **(Nos. 1** and **2)** comprise more than 2.5 million acres. Several blocks of wilderness lands in these national forests provide the potential for backcountry hunting. A number of national wild-

life refuges and state management areas assure public hunting on thousands of additional acres. Large timber companies own most of the land in the eastern and southern parts of Arkansas. Some of their lands are leased to clubs, and some companies charge a trespass fee, but much of the land also is open to the hunter who simply asks permission.

Seasons. Generally three rifle seasons are held during November and December, and season length varies from two to nine days with a bag limit of two deer. Season lengths and bag limits vary depending on current conditions.

Normally two muzzleloader seasons are held in October and December. Season length varies from 5 to 43 days, depending on the particular management zone. Some years a person can legally take as many as four deer.

Bow season runs from October through February with a bag limit of four deer.

Records. The average field-dressed weight of bucks in Arkansas is 100 pounds, and the heaviest buck on record weighed 245 pounds.

The state record typical whitetail was killed in Arkansas County in 1952 and scored 186⅞. Boone and Crockett lists about a dozen others but most of those were taken before 1960.

The record nontypical was taken near Boydell in 1959 and scored 206⅛. Boone and Crockett lists only a couple of others, and they were taken in the 1950s.

The future. The statewide deer population has been fairly stable in recent years, but it is increasing in the Ouachita and Ozark Mountain regions. Arkansas anticipates a legal harvest of 75,000 to 100,000 deer in the future, nearly double the recent average harvest.

Contact. Arkansas Game and Fish Commission, Game and Fish Building, Number 2 Natural Resources Drive, Little Rock, AR 72205.

CALIFORNIA

Deer numbers. California extends along the Pacific Coast for nearly 1,000 miles and covers 159,693 square miles. Mule deer occupy about 15 percent, or 25,000 square miles, primarily in the northeast corner and south along the east side of the Sierra Nevada to the Mojave Desert. Biologists estimate the total mule deer population at about 290,000. Blacktail deer occupy another 15 percent of the state. These deer are found primarily in the Coast Range from Los Angeles north to the Oregon border. Blacktail numbers are estimated at over 310,000.

Hunters and harvest. Over a 20-year period, residents have bought an average of 375,000 deer tags, and nonresidents have bought about 900. Traditionally, hunting antlerless deer has been taboo in California; so virtually the entire harvest consists of bucks. Long-term average harvest has been about 40,000 deer with a high in 1966 of 69,118. The average bow harvest has been 471 with a high in 1977 of 778. California has one of the lowest hunter success rates of any western state. The average is just under 12 percent success.

Distribution. California has two major mountain ranges, the Sierra Nevada and the Coast Range. In general, the major mule deer counties are Siskiyou, Modoc, Lassen, and Plumas **(No. 1)**, which occupy the high desert lands of the northeast corner. Mule deer extend down the east side of the Sierra **(No. 2)** to the Mojave Desert **(No. 3)**, where the predominant form is the burro deer, a subspecies of mule deer.

Mule deer are hunted heavily, and the percentage of bucks is low in many areas. However, to improve the quality of herds, the number of tags has been restricted in some units, such as in state hunting zones X5a and X5b in the northeast. In these the hunting success has been high and hunters have taken many trophy bucks. Competition for tags is high, but if you want to kill a truly good mule deer in California, one of the limited-permit zones is the place to do it.

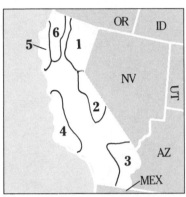

Zones created by author

Blacktails live throughout the Coast Range. From Los Angeles to San Francisco **(No. 4)**, the Coast Range is covered with dense chaparral that makes hunting difficult. The Los Padres and Angeles National Forests offer some public hunting, but a large percentage of the land in this region is private. You can pay to hunt some of this land, but much of it is leased by private hunting clubs. The deer here are numerous, but small.

North of San Francisco, the Coast Range splits into exterior and interior arms. The exterior arm extends along the coast **(No. 5)**, and the interior arm **(No. 6)** lies about 50 miles inland. The exterior arm has many deer, but virtually all of the land is private and is leased to hunting clubs.

The interior arm, in contrast, contains vast areas of public land. The Yolla Bolly-Middle Eel, Salmon-Trinity Alps, and Marble Mountains wilderness areas, and surrounding forest lands offer some of the best blacktail hunting in North America. Unlike much blacktail country, which is dense and hard to hunt, the interior Coast Range consists of relatively open forests and even some alpine country. Heavy chaparral has reduced deer numbers in places, but prescribed burning has opened up the brush and deer herds have flourished. Hunting pressure is fairly heavy, but the remote and rugged country provides excellent sanctuary.

Buck-doe ratios are good, as high as 40 bucks/100 does in some units.

Seasons. The archery season in the central and southern Coast Range **(No. 4)**, generally runs for two weeks in July, and the rifle season opens for five to six weeks in August and September.

In the northern coastal zones, the bow season runs from mid-August through early September. The rifle season extends from mid-September through October.

Most mule deer seasons in the northeast and the Sierras take place in October.

Records. California is probably not the place to go for mule deer. A nontypical buck taken in Mariposa County in 1972 scored 319⅛, but you have to look hard to find other mule deer from California listed in the Boone and Crockett records.

Blacktails are another story. Nearly 45 percent of the blacktails listed in *Records of North American Big Game* came from California. The top region is the crest of the interior Coast Range **(No. 6)** in Siskiyou, Trinity, and Mendocino counties. Some special late-season rifle and muzzleloader hunts in particular offer the potential to take a record-class blacktail.

The future. With an exploding human population, California deer hunting faces a shaky future. The Department of Game estimates that since 1949, California has lost 55 percent of its deer range. Deer numbers decreased sharply during the period but the decline bottomed out in 1974. Since then deer numbers have gradually increased. Much of the remaining deer habitat lies on large ranches and on public lands; so future loss of habitat may be slowed somewhat. California has developed a herd-by-herd management plan. This makes hunting regulations very complicated but has improved the overall quality of deer hunting.

Contact. Department of Fish & Game, 1416 Ninth St., Sacramento, CA 95814.

COLORADO

Deer numbers. Colorado has a total area of 104,247 square miles. Whitetails occupy about 5 percent of the state, and mule deer occupy about 99 percent. Preseason counts indicate populations of 5,000 to 8,000 whitetails and nearly 500,000 mule deer.

Hunters and harvest. On the average, 125,000 residents and 55,000 nonresidents hunt with firearms, and 15,000 residents and 5,000 nonresidents hunt with bow and arrow. The number of hunters allowed fluctuates drastically from year to year depending on the deer population which relates to winterkill.

The average annual harvest for 40 years, beginning in the 1930s, was about 73,000 (45,000 bucks and 28,000 antlerless deer). The highest harvest of 147,322 deer (65,292 bucks and 82,030 antlerless) took place in 1963. Average hunting success has been 53 percent. In 1957 hunters enjoyed a record high success of 89 percent. The record low of 26 percent occurred in 1975.

Average yearly archery harvest has been about 1,700 (1,200 bucks and 500 antlerless). In 1983 bowhunters killed a high of 4,473 deer (2,413 bucks and 2,060 antlerless). Average bowhunting success has been 16 percent, with a high in 1978 of 25 percent and a low in 1971 of 8 percent.

Distribution. The Continental Divide splits Colorado in two. East of Denver **(No. 1)** the country consists of farmlands, prairies, and badlands. Mule deer are scattered sparsely throughout this entire region, and whitetails live in the bottomlands of three major drainages—the Platte, Republican, and Arkansas rivers. Deer numbers are fairly low; so the number of permits is limited throughout the plains units.

With limited hunting pressure, the proportion of old bucks is high, particularly among whitetails. Whitetails comprise 90 percent of the deer population on the Colorado plains, but mule deer comprise nearly 90 percent of the kill. To increase whitetail harvest, some late hunts are held. Eastern Colorado offers good poten-

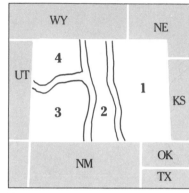

Zones created by author

tial for a trophy whitetail. Most of this region is private land and you must get permission to hunt. The Division of Wildlife owns some public hunting land.

In the Front Range **(No. 2)** west of Denver, mule deer are numerous, and some huge bucks can be found above timberline. South of Denver huge ranches extend far up into the mountains; so some of the best hunting lies on private land.

The West Slope—from the Continental Divide to the Utah border—contains the most famous, if not the best, mule deer hunting in North America. The southwest quarter **(No. 3)** has large deer herds and has produced more Boone and Crockett bucks than any other single region. The areas around Durango and Cortez, the Dolores river drainage, the Uncompahgre Plateau, and the Battlement and Grand mesas—all have many deer and big bucks.

Diversity of habitat in the southwest quarter **(No. 3)** probably accounts for the big bucks. In just a few miles, the terrain goes from jagged 14,000-foot peaks to alpine bowls at 11,000 feet, to sprawling aspen parks at 9,000 feet, to tangles of oak brush at 8,000 feet, to pinyon-juniper slopes at 7,000 feet. The region forms a kaleidoscope of intermixed elevations and habitats, and this diversity provides not only ideal habitat for mule deer, but an array of mixed hunting conditions as well. You can find easy hunting for average bucks, but if you're after a

whopper, expect to work for him.

The northwest quarter **(No. 4)** often has been described as Colorado's "deer factory." The Piceance Basin near Meeker is reputed to hold the largest single deer herd in North America. At one time as many as 60,000 deer wintered here, although the herd is much smaller now. This region consists of sagebrush plateaus at modest elevations (for Colorado) of 6,000-7,000 feet, and the slopes surrounding these contain dense oak brush and aspen.

Throughout the West Slope, National Forest and Bureau of Land Management (BLM) lands provide plenty of hunting, but big ranches take in some of the finest lands. Most of these ranches are either leased by outfitters, or ranchers charge a seasonal fee for hunting.

Seasons. Deer seasons generally take place in October and early November. In addition, occasional September seasons allow hunting in specified alpine areas. Bow and muzzleloader seasons in September provide excellent early-fall opportunities for big bucks.

Records. Colorado has produced some whitetails that score over 180 Boone and Crockett points, but the state is more famous for huge mule deer. The world-record typical mule deer, with a score of 225⅝ came from southwest Colorado. The largest nontypical scored 306⅞. Colorado has produced over one-third of all the mule deer listed in Boone and Crockett.

The future. Periodically, severe winters decimate deer herds in Colorado, but the herds quickly rebuild. This pattern of highs and lows will continue. Energy development has swept across the West Slope to alter much excellent deer country and has brought an influx of new residents. This development will no doubt have an adverse effect on the overall hunting quality. But Colorado contains so much excellent habitat that it will always provide some quality hunting.

Contact. Division of Wildlife, 6060 Broadway, Denver, CO 80216.

CONNECTICUT

Deer numbers. Connecticut has a total area of 5,009 square miles. About 4,000 square miles support an estimated 30,000 whitetail deer.

Hunters and harvest. In recent years, an average of 25,000 residents and 300 nonresidents have hunted with firearms each year. The average annual harvest has been 2,500 deer (1,500 bucks and 1,000 does) with a high in 1983 of 3,152 (1,789 bucks). Average firearms hunting success has been 10 percent, with a high in 1983 of almost 12 percent and a low in 1975 of about 6 percent.

The average number of bowhunters has been about 8,000, resident and nonresident. The average recent archery harvest has been about 3,000 (1,700 bucks and 1,300 does) with a high in 1983 of 3,791 (2,191 bucks). Average archery success has been just under 6 percent.

Distribution. The northwest corner **(No. 1)**, an extension of the Berkshire Hills in Massachusetts, holds the only mountainous country in Connecticut. Much of the land here exceeds 1,200 feet in elevation, and the highest point in Connecticut (2,380 feet) lies in the extreme northwest corner. Forests here consist of hemlock, white pine, and northern hardwoods—maple, beech, birch. Deer numbers may be as high as 30 deer per square mile, the highest densities in the state. Many farms are scattered throughout the region, and several large state forests offer public hunting.

Deer numbers aren't as high in the eastern half of the state **(No. 2)**, but they're still fairly high and growing as old-growth forests are opened up by logging and firewood cutting. This region has a number of public hunting areas. The north half of this region consists of rolling hills, and these slope southward into a flat, coastal plain. Oak and hickory forests, along with white pine in the northern hills, cover a high percentage of the area, and farm and pasturelands are scattered throughout.

The Connecticut River Valley and the southwest corner **(No. 3)** form a major population corridor. Woodlots and farmlands in this region support

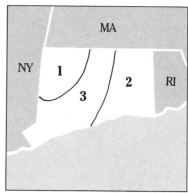

Zones created by author

deer, but a strong antihunting sentiment prevails, and much land is closed to hunting.

Connecticut has about two dozen deer management areas totaling more than 130,000 acres. During shotgun and muzzleloader seasons, a limited quota of permits is issued by lottery, but there is no quota during archery season. To hunt legally on private land, a hunter must have written permission on a "consent to hunt" form.

Seasons. In recent years the bow season has run from early October through mid-November. That has been followed by a muzzleloader season in late November, and then state and private-land shotgun seasons in December. Regulations may be changed in the future to ensure proper management and healthy herds. Archery tags are not limited, but permits for shotgun and muzzleloader seasons on state lands are limited and are issued by lottery. Landowners can issue only a set number of firearms permits, depending on acreage. In many cases the bag limits has been two deer per hunter for each season. By taking part in all season combinations, a hunter legally has been able to take as many as seven deer in one year.

Records. Yearling bucks have made up only about 14 percent of the harvest, and the average age of deer harvested is 2½ to 3½ years. Average field-dressed weight of bucks killed is 125 pounds. The state record buck weighed an estimated 264 pounds field-dressed and 321 pounds on the hoof.

The future. Connecticut's deer herd has been growing in recent years. Firewood cutting and logging for hardwood lumber have increased, and these land disturbances have improved habitat for deer. Antihunting sentiment is prevalent in the southwest, and many landowners refuse to allow hunting. Deer herds have built up to excessive numbers there. In general, the future for hunting looks good, and harvest figures will continue to rise if more private land can be opened to hunting. Liberal seasons will continue in some areas to reduce deer damage complaints, collisions between deer and cars, and other deer-human conflicts.

Contact. Department of Environmental Protection, Wildlife Bureau, 165 Capitol Ave., Hartford, CT 06106.

Whitetail (Leonard Lee Rue III photo)

DELAWARE

Deer numbers. Delaware has an area of 2,057 square miles. An estimated 10,000 deer occupy 100 percent of the undeveloped land in the state.

Hunters and harvest. Delaware allows hunting by three methods: shotgun, muzzleloader, and bow. Each year an average of 4,300 residents and 130 nonresidents hunt with muzzleloader, and 13,400 residents and 485 nonresidents hunt with shotguns. The total average firearms harvest has been about 2,000 deer (60 percent bucks) with a high in 1983 of 2,190. Average hunter success for muzzleloader has been about 3 percent, and for shotgun it has been 6 percent.

An average of 3,300 residents and 150 nonresidents have hunted during archery seasons in recent years. The average kill has been 25 deer (45 to 50 percent bucks), with a high in 1982 of 48 deer. Average bowhunter success has been about 1 percent.

Distribution. Delaware has only three counties—Newcastle, Kent, and Sussex. In Newcastle, the northernmost county, hunters take an average of 1.15 deer per square mile; in Kent, the central county, hunters take 1.27 deer per square mile; and in Sussex, the southern county, they harvest .85 deer per square mile.

Northern Newcastle County **(No. 1)** lies within the Piedmont ecological zone. Many large estates restrict hunting access here, and deer numbers may be above carrying capacity.

Tidal marsh along Delaware Bay and Delaware River **(No. 2)**, comprises 10 percent of the state's total area. Forest and croplands abut the marshes and some high ground with timber can be found in the marshes. Deer numbers are good throughout this marsh region.

The remainder of Delaware **(No. 3)** lies within the Coastal Plain ecological zone. The country is fairly flat and consists of mixed woodlands and crop fields. Corn and soybeans are major crops. In the south, 30 to 40 percent of the land is cultivated and the remainder supports loblolly and other southern pines along with

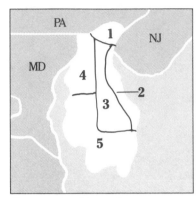

Zones created by author

mixed hardwoods. Farther north, croplands cover 60 percent of the land, and woodlots of mixed hardwoods are scattered among the fields.

Public lands—state and federal—make up 6 to 7 percent of the state. These provide some good hunting, but permits are limited and are issued by lottery. The idea of leasing lands for hunting isn't foreign to Delaware, because virtually all goose hunting is by lease. But that trend isn't as prevalent for deer hunting, and it is still possible to get permission to hunt private land.

Seasons. Recent seasons have provided as much as 133 total hunting days—113 for archery, 6 for muzzleloader, and 14 for shotgun. Bag limit has been two deer (at least one must be taken during archery or muzzleloader season) of either sex and any age.

Records. Because of the rich food source found in corn and soybean fields, Delaware grows some exceptionally heavy deer. Average field-dressed weights for bucks has been 121 pounds for yearlings; 143 pounds for 2½-year olds; and 175 for 3½-year olds. The heaviest buck on record field-dressed 244 pounds,

with an estimated live weight of 295 pounds.

Delaware produces healthy deer and many yearling bucks grow four- or six-point racks. However, few bucks in Delaware live long enough to make the record book.

The future. Delaware has a young, healthy herd of deer that is still expanding, and the harvest has steadily increased during the 1970s and early 1980s. Urban growth and clean farming are reducing habitat. But for the near future, the herd probably will continue to grow, and biologists anticipate an increasing harvest and good hunting into the 1990s.

Contact. Division of Fish & Wildlife, 89 Kings Highway, PO Box 1401, Dover, DE 19903.

Whitetail (Irene Vandermolen photo)

FLORIDA

Deer numbers. Florida has an area of 58,560 square miles. An estimated 650,000 whitetail deer occupy about 70 percent of the state.

Hunters and harvest. An average of 166,000 residents and 1,400 non-residents buy firearms deer licenses in Florida each year, and they buy an additional 22,000 archery licenses. The average total harvest for a recent 10-year period has been 62,000 deer (57,000 bucks and 5,000 does), and 1980 produced the highest recorded harvest of 75,000 deer. For record-keeping purposes, Florida doesn't distinguish between firearms and bow hunters.

The apparent hunter success appears to be about 37 percent, but because of liberal bag limits, some hunters harvest several deer each year. Overall hunting success probably is lower than 37 percent.

Distribution. Northwest Florida **(No. 1)** maintains the highest deer numbers. Pine and oak uplands and pine flatwoods are the two major habitat types here. The uplands consist of mildly rolling, well-drained hills covered with a mix of longleaf pines and one of several species of oaks. The flatwoods are low, flat, poorly drained country, and much of this land has been converted to a monoculture of commercial pines. In general the pine and oak uplands are more productive and support an average of one deer for every 20 to 25 acres. The flatwoods support about one deer per 50 acres. This is one of the least populated regions in Florida, so hunting pressure is not excessive.

Northeast Florida **(No. 2)** has a higher percentage of pine flatwoods, and much of the upland country has been converted to agriculture. As a result, the overall carrying capacity is lower than in the northwest. Still, this region has good deer numbers in some localities and is lightly hunted, by Florida standards.

The Central Region **(No. 3)** has a mixture of flatwoods and uplands, but much of the upland has been developed either for housing or for agriculture, such as oranges or row

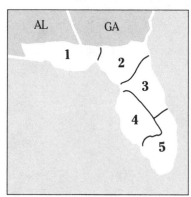

Zones created by author

crops like corn, and overall deer numbers on private land are low. Some remaining upland areas have high numbers of deer, and the Ocala National Forest supports a good herd.

The South Florida Region **(No. 4)** consists primarily of low pine flatwoods with a limited deer carrying capacity. Some private ranches are managed for wildlife and maintain good deer herds, but in general numbers in this region are fair at best. Human population is high, so hunting pressure is heavy on the few public lands.

The Everglades Region **(No. 5)** contains a mixture of poorly drained flatwoods and many thousands of acres of marshland. When water levels are low, deer disperse throughout the marshes. They have no problem living in 18 inches of water. But during high-water years, they're forced to concentrate on a limited number of small plots of high ground, where disease and overcrowding take a heavy toll. As a result, the total carrying capacity of the Everglades is low, about one deer for every 75 to 100 acres. Hunters must use air boats, half-tracks or other specialized vehicles to penetrate the marshes, and hunting this region is difficult at best.

Florida maintains more than 60 wildlife management areas covering

6 million acres that are all open to public hunting. Three national forests are included in this management-area program. Most private land in Florida is leased by clubs or commercial hunting operations. Chances of getting permission to hunt just by asking are slim.

Seasons. In the northwest region, the general gun season runs from about Thanksgiving through January. In the remainder of the state, it opens in early November and closes in early January.

The archery season opens in late September or early October and remains open for a month. Exact dates vary by region. An additional archery-muzzleloader season opens for two weeks or more in February.

Generally the bag limit is two bucks per day, three in possession with no season limit. The above regulations apply generally, but season dates and bag limits vary on state wildlife management areas.

Records. The overall average live weight of deer taken in Florida is 124 pounds. The heaviest deer on record, killed in 1966, weighed 306 pounds before field-dressing.

The state record typical whitetail antlers measured 168⅛ inches, and the record nontypical 163⅛, both well below Boone and Crockett minimums.

The future. Deer numbers have steadily increased for the past 30 years and now appear to be at or above carrying capacity over most of the state. The annual deer harvest should average about 60,000 in the future. It may increase slightly with greater emphasis on antlerless deer hunts, which are needed to reduce overpopulation in some areas and to improve the ratio of bucks to does. Urban development will take a heavy toll on deer habitat; so total deer numbers probably will decrease with time.

Contact. Game and Fresh Water Fish Commission, 620 S. Meridian St., Tallahassee, FL 32301.

GEORGIA

Deer numbers. Georgia has an area of 58,406 square miles and whitetail deer occupy roughly 98 percent of that area. Biologists estimate the deer population at 850,000.

Hunters and harvest. In Georgia an average of 250,000 residents and 10,000 nonresidents buy deer licenses each year. In addition, about 39,000 residents buy archery licenses, although many of these also hunt with a gun. No distinction is made between nonresident firearms and archery hunters.

Each year firearms hunters take about 100,000 deer (75 percent bucks) and archers kill an additional 4,000 (25 percent bucks). Overall hunting success is 21 percent.

Distribution. The Blue Ridge Mountains **(No. 1)** cover the northeast corner of Georgia. These mountains rise to elevations of 4,000 feet and higher. Forests of oak and hickory, along with some pine, hemlock, and other conifers blanket most of this region. Mast is the major deer food, and there is little green feed. So the mountains support only about 15 deer per square mile, which is low by Georgia standards.

The Ridge and Valley Region **(No. 2),** as the name implies, consists of alternating ridges and valleys. Soybeans, corn, and other crops are grown in the valleys, and the ridges support stands of hardwoods and pine. The limestone soils here are fertile, and the deer herds are growing. Densities are about 25 deer per square mile.

The Piedmont Region **(No. 3)** is characterized by low-elevation, rolling hills bisected by many creek drainages. Most of the region has been converted to pine plantations and pasturelands, although some hardwoods persist here. The Piedmont supports 35 to 40 deer per square mile. This is the richest deer region in Georgia. Fifty percent of the total kill each year comes from the Piedmont, and some large bucks are taken here.

The Upper Coastal Plain **(No. 4)** has rich soils but overall deer densities are lower than in the Piedmont

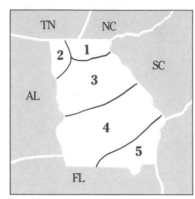

Zones created by author

because there is less cover. The region has many broad valleys, and agriculture is intense. The primary crops are peanuts, cotton, and soybeans. The region supports only about 25 deer per square mile, but some of the largest bucks taken in Georgia come from here.

The Lower Coastal Plain **(No. 5)** contains mostly lowlands with many swamps, pine flatwoods, and palmettos. Deer numbers are fairly high, from 25 per square mile in poorer areas up to 60 per square mile in others. But because the soils are relatively infertile, deer are smaller than they are in regions to the north. This area contains large land holdings, and the tradition of running deer with dogs remains strong.

Private-land hunting is fairly restricted for the general public in Georgia. Virtually all good private lands in the Piedmont and southern regions are leased by private clubs. Clubs are not as prevalent in the Blue Ridge, and Ridge and Valley regions. National forest land provides some public hunting, and the Oconee National Forest east of Atlanta is heavily hunted. The state maintains about 1 million acres for public hunting on a number of wildlife management areas, and several military bases offer public hunting.

Seasons. The general gun season opens in mid-October. In the northern zone it closes in early December, and in the southern zone it extends into early January. The general bag limit is three deer. Additional seasons and either-sex hunts are offered.

The archery season usually opens in mid-September and remains open through the Friday preceding the gun season. Usually, the bag limit is three of either sex.

Records. Average field-dressed weight for all deer taken in Georgia is 105 pounds. The heaviest buck on record field-dressed 355 pounds and so must have weighed well over 400 on the hoof.

The state record typical whitetail antlers scored 184 in the Boone and Crockett system, and the record nontypical 242. The Upper Coastal Plain and Piedmont regions have produced a number of large bucks, but few of these show up in the Boone and Crockett records.

The future. From Civil War times until the early 1900s, Georgia was blanketed with farms, and woody cover was scarce. That fact, coupled with uncontrolled subsistence hunting, eliminated deer from Georgia except in isolated mountain areas and some remote refuge areas along the coast. With exanding timber plantations, enforced hunting regulations, and an extensive stocking program in the 1950s, deer have rebounded to all-time highs. (Georgia now is second only to Oregon in timber production in the United States.) Biologists expect herds to remain at present levels through the 1990s. However, Georgia is one of the fastest growing states. Each year much habitat is lost to development, and with a growing interest in hunting and the trend toward leasing by private clubs, finding a place to hunt will become harder.

Contact. Department of Natural Resources, 270 Washington St., S.W., Atlanta, GA 30334.

HAWAII

Deer numbers. Hawaii, with a total area of 6,450 square miles, has an axis deer population of 10,000 to 15,000. The deer range over about 225 square miles on the islands of Lanai, Molokai, and Maui. On the island of Kauai, 400 to 500 blacktail deer live in an area of 50 square miles.

Hunters and harvest. About 2,500 resident and 100 nonresident firearms hunters kill an average of 500 bucks each year. In 1984 they enjoyed a record harvest of 777 deer (422 bucks and 355 does).

Archery hunters number about 150 residents and 10 nonresidents, and they take only a few deer each year.

These harvest statistics apply to public hunting areas only. They do not include private land.

Distribution. Hawaii has no native deer: so deer species found there were introduced. The axis deer came from India and Ceylon. On the island of Lanai **(No. 1)** the axis deer population stands at about 10,000 and is increasing. Hunter success there runs between 30 and 50 percent, depending on whether it's a bucks-only or either-sex season. The axis deer population on Molokai **(No. 2)** is down and the season is closed. On Maui **(No. 3)** the herd is increasing

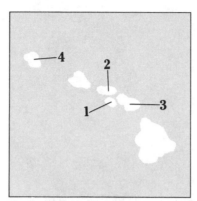

Zones created by author

slowly, but hunting has not been allowed there yet. Axis deer live primarily in open, parklike forests of the mesquite zone, but some herds also have been established in rain forests.

Blacktails were transplanted from Oregon to Hawaii in 1961. They're found only on the island of Kauai **(No. 4)**, and most of the 500 deer there inhabit the brushy, broken ridges west of Waimea Canyon, where dense cover is intermingled with open meadows and open ridgetops.

Seasons. No regulations govern hunting on private lands in Hawaii. Each island that contains deer has large public hunting areas, and the following regulations pertain to public areas. The bag limit for blacktails

is usually one buck deer per season per hunter, and hunting is usually allowed only on the five weekends preceding the last full weekend in October. Hunters are assigned hunting days by public drawing.

Hunting for axis deer is usually allowed only on weekends for nine weeks in March and April. The bag limit is one deer. Hunters are assigned hunting days by public drawing. Hawaii has liberal seasons and limits for wild goats and pigs, so that a combination hunt is possible.

Records. The average field-dressed weight of axis deer is 100 to 125 pounds; for blacktails, 120 to 150 pounds. No trophy antler records have been kept.

Contact. Division of Forestry & Wildlife, 1151 Punchbowl St., Honolulu, HI 96813.

IDAHO

Deer numbers. Deer range over about 85 percent of Idaho's 82,708 square miles. An estimated 50,000 whitetails occupy about 25 percent of the state, and about 275,000 mule deer inhabit nearly 75 percent.

Hunters and harvest. An average of 147,000 residents and 11,500 nonresidents hunt with firearms each year. About 17,000 archers hunt deer in Idaho. Over recent years firearms hunters have killed an average of 47,000 deer (about 34,000 bucks and 13,000 does). The highest year on record was 1968 when they took over 78,000 (46,000 of them bucks). Average hunting success is 34 percent, with a high in 1955 of 62 percent and a low in 1976 of 18 percent.

Archers have taken an average of 800 deer (450 bucks and 350 does) for the past few years, and 1983 marked a high year when bowhunters killed 1,200 deer (600 bucks and 600 does). Average bowhunting success has been 11 percent.

Distribution. The southwest quarter **(No. 1)** consists primarily of true desert on the north edge of the Great Basin. This is primarily juniper and sagebrush country, and the Owyhee, Bruneau, and Jarbidge river drainages contain vast areas of remote country broken by rims and deep gorges. This region has good numbers of mule deer and produces some large bucks.

The southeast corner **(No. 2)** consists of rugged mountain ranges covered with huge aspen parks and conifer forests. These ranges are separated by farmed river valleys. This region is second only to southwest Colorado for production of Boone-and-Crockett-class mule deer. Franklin, Bear Lake, and Caribou counties have yielded a number of record-class heads.

Central Idaho **(No. 3)** may contain more rugged wilderness than any other single region. The Church Wilderness on the Salmon River and the Selway-Bitterroot Wilderness just to

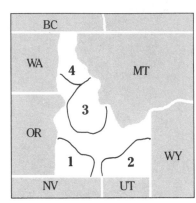

Zones created by author

the north total nearly 4 million acres. In the sanctuary of this roadless backcountry, many bucks grow to maturity and bragging size. Seasons run from mid-September through November here. During September you can hunt mule deer in higher, alpine country, but many hunters wait for late snows to push bucks into the more open breaks of the Salmon River and its tributaries. There the deer are more concentrated and visible. Unless you own horses, the most feasible way to hunt most of this backcountry is to hire an outfitter. Guides and outfitters work most of central Idaho.

Mule deer live throughout northern Idaho, but north of the Salmon River they're found primarily at higher elevations, and whitetails are far more abundant throughout the heavily forested country and bottomlands. Northern Idaho **(No. 4)**, from the Clearwater River drainage north to the Canadian border receives heavy rainfall, and the forests are damp and jungle-like. Whitetails are extremely numerous, and rifle seasons in some units take in most of November and run into December, an ideal time to hunt trophy whitetails during the rut.

Virtually all of the best deer hunting in Idaho takes place on public land, primarily national forest, so getting access to the better hunting is no problem.

Seasons. Idaho offers a diversity of seasons that vary greatly by region. In the panhandle at the north end, the general rifle season for whitetails traditionally falls in November and December. In wilderness units that cover the central state, most deer seasons run from mid-September through November and coincide with elk seasons. Many of the deer taken in this country are killed incidentally by those on outfitted elk hunts. In southern Idaho the general rifle season traditionally takes place during October and early November.

In addition to generous rifle seasons, Idaho offers excellent bowhunting opportunities. A general season in some units takes place in September, and both whitetail and trophy mule deer units are open for bowhunting in November and December. Idaho also offers special muzzleloader-only hunts.

Records. Although Idaho has an abundance of whitetails, they don't grow particularly large. The state record typical whitetail scored 181 and the record nontypical is 228⅛.

In terms of record-book heads, Idaho is far better known for mule deer. The state-record typical mule deer scored 214⅖ and the record nontypical scored 288⅛. Idaho ranks second only to Colorado for the number of mule deer in the Boone and Crockett record book. As mentioned above, a majority of these whoppers come from the extreme southeast corner.

The future. As in all western states, development has taken its toll on deer habitat in Idaho. However, the vast areas of public domain and wilderness make much of the deer habitat in the state immune to devastating development. Since 1975 deer numbers and harvest have generally increased. Except for fluctuations resulting from hard winters, authorities in Idaho expect no decrease in hunting quality within the foreseeable future.

Contact. Idaho Department of Fish and Game, 600 S. Walnut, PO Box 25, Boise, ID 83707.

ILLINOIS

Deer numbers. Illinois has a total area of 56,400 square miles. No deer population estimates are made, but if hunters take 20 percent of the total whitetails each year (being the average in states where official population estimates are made), then the population is somewhere between 120,000 and 150,000 animals. Deer inhabit all 102 counties in Illinois.

Hunters and harvest. Illinois has had an average of about 82,000 resident and 40 nonresident firearms hunters each year. The average annual harvest has been about 20,000 deer. It has steadily increased for many years and in 1984 reached nearly 29,000. Firearms success has ranged from 26 to 32 percent.

Illinois sells about 40,000 resident archery permits each year, and 100 or so nonresident archery permits. In 1983, one of the highest years on record, bowhunters killed 3,500 deer (2,310 bucks and 1,190 does). Archery success runs about 10 to 12 percent.

Distribution. The northwest corner **(No. 1)** contains unglaciated hills with rock outcroppings and fair amounts of timber. Traditionally, deer numbers have remained high in this region, and they have stabilized in recent years.

The western and central counties **(No. 2)** have shown the greatest increases in deer numbers in recent years. This country consists of rolling fields of corn and soybeans interspersed with woodlands along the many drainages feeding into the Mississippi River. Some of the highest harvests in the state are recorded in counties bordering the Mississippi.

The black prairie soil region of eastern Illinois **(No. 3)** is the least productive section. The area is intensively farmed with little cover for deer.

Southern Illinois **(No. 4)** contains rough, unglaciated hills similar to the northeast corner. Oak and hickory forests cover many of the hills here, and this region traditionally has produced high harvests. However, herds have pretty well stabilized at densities of about five deer

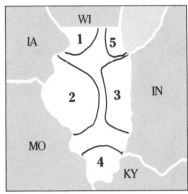

Zones created by author

per square mile. Private land covers most of Illinois except in this southern tip where the Shawnee National Forest provides more than a quarter-million acres of public hunting.

Counties surrounding Chicago **(No. 5)** have been closed to firearms hunting for a number of years.

Seasons. The firearms season traditionally has been open for two three-day weekends in November and December. Nonresidents can buy unused permits, but the number generally is small. Only shotguns and muzzleloaders are legal for use during the firearms season.

Ill. Dept. of Conservation photo

The bow season runs from early October through the end of December statewide, except that it closes during the firearms season in counties open to firearms hunting.

Records. Illinois with its rich farm crops grows some large bucks. The average yearling field-dresses 123 pounds, and deer of 4½ years average 185 pounds. The heaviest on record weighed 396 pounds, before field-dressing.

The record typical whitetail, killed near Peoria in 1965, measured 204⅛ points. It ranks No. 3 in Boone and Crockett and No. 1 in Pope and Young. The state record nontypical scored more than 260 points.

The future. As in most other midwestern states, deer were extinct in Illinois in the early 1900s. They returned gradually at first, but populations and harvest have increased steadily since initiation of any-deer hunting in 1957. Herds have stabilized in the wooded northern and southern sections, but they are still increasing in central and west-central Illinois. The outlook into the 1990s appears bright.

Contact. Department of Conservation, Lincoln Tower Plaza, 524 South Second St., Springfield, IL 62708.

INDIANA

Deer numbers. Indiana covers an area of 36,143 square miles. An estimated population of 150,000 whitetails is scattered throughout the state.

Hunters and harvest. Each year about 125,000 residents and 1,500 nonresidents hunt deer during the gun season. Average deer kill has been about 17,000 (13,000 bucks and 4,000 does). As in many midwestern states, 1983 produced a record harvest in Indiana, and that year hunters took just over 20,000 deer (over 15,000 of those were bucks). Average firearms hunting success has been 12 percent and fluctuates between a high of 15 percent and a low of 9 percent.

About 47,000 resident and 500 nonresident archers hunt deer annually in Indiana. The average harvest has been about 4,500 (2,500 bucks and 2,000 does). The highest year on record was 1983 with a harvest of 4,970. Average bowhunting success has been about 9 percent, with a high of slightly over 10 percent and a low of around 6 percent.

Distribution. North of Indianapolis **(No. 1)**, farmland dominates a fairly flat landscape. Primary crops here are corn and soybeans. Small woodlots of oak and hickory, as well as riparian cover along streams and rivers, provide most of the cover for deer here. Most plots of suitable woody cover support good numbers of deer, and hunting can be very good in this region. With the excellent feed provided by farm crops, bucks grow to trophy proportions in this country.

In general, the southern half of Indiana is hilly and wooded. The southwest corner **(No. 2)** contains many old coal strip mines that have created broken, rugged terrain that harbors good numbers of deer and some big bucks. The south-central section **(No. 3)** is the most popular deer hunting section of the state. Roughly 30 percent of the hunters take 35 to 40 percent of all the deer killed each year in Indiana from this region. Oak and hickory forests blanket nearly 80 percent of the rolling

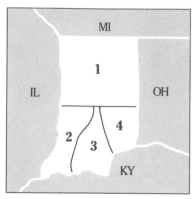

Zones created by author

hills here, and farms and pastures are scattered among the timber. The southeast corner **(No. 4)** has similar terrain to No. 3 except that the hills may be a little higher and more rugged. Again, good herds live throughout this corner.

More than 90 percent of Indiana is privately owned. The Hoosier National Forest assures public access to large tracts of land in the south-central portion **(No. 3)**, and some state wildlife management areas provide public hunting throughout the state. Some farmers will grant permission to hunt, although access to private land is getting tighter. Some clubs have leased the hunting rights to private land, although the trend hasn't been extensive.

Seasons. Hunting regulations are set every two years. Deer hunting is done only with shotguns, muzzleloaders, and archery tackle. No high-power rifles are allowed.

A general shotgun and muzzleloader season runs for 15 days in mid-November, and it's followed by a 9-day muzzleloader season in December.

The archery season opens in early October and closes the day before the gun season opens. It then opens again in early December and continues through December.

Records. Indiana grows some very large bucks. The average 3½-year-old buck field-dresses to about 155 pounds. No records have been kept on the heaviest deer.

The Indiana state record typical whitetail scored 197⅛ and the record nontypical, 254⅛. Boone and Crockett lists fewer than a half-dozen bucks from Indiana.

The future. For many years deer were extinct in Indiana. The last known deer was killed in 1893, and no deer were seen for four decades. During the 1930s and 1940s, 296 whitetails were stocked in the state, and herds have steadily increased to a healthy population of 150,000. Herds are still growing in some regions, but conflicts with landowners have become a problem in others. Usually more liberal harvests are then allowed. Urban development erodes habitat here as in all states. But at least into the 1990s, deer herds should remain stable or increase slightly.

Contact. Department of Natural Resources, Division of Fish & Wildlife, 607 State Office Building, Indianapolis, IN 46204.

Leonard Lee Rue III photo

I O W A

Deer numbers. Iowa covers an area of 56,000 square miles, and 100 percent of the state supports whitetail deer. The estimated preseason population is somewhere between 90,000 and 100,000 deer.

Hunters and harvest. Roughly 90,000 resident firearms hunters and 20,000 resident bowhunters pursue deer each year in Iowa. Nonresidents cannot hunt deer in Iowa. As in many of the midwestern states where deer herds and harvest have increased dramatically since the 1950s, it's hard to give an average harvest for Iowa because each successive year sets a record. In recent years the harvest with firearms has been about 20,000 deer (12,000 bucks and 8,000 does) annually, with an average success rate of 55 percent. The bow kill has been about 5,000 (3,350 bucks and 1,650 does), and the success rate has averaged about 25 percent.

Distribution. Iowa has a high percentage of agricultural land, and the major crops are corn and soybeans. During summer, corn "forests" provide good cover and feed for deer, but after harvest animals must retreat into other types of shelter. So deer numbers are limited by the extent of permanent cover.

Most of the land north of Interstate 80 **(No. 1)** is cropland. The only permanent cover is found along river bottoms, in small woodlots, and around wetlands (in the form of cattails and weed patches). Deer live throughout this region, but as can been expected, the overall number is not high.

The Loess Hills region **(No. 2)**, which takes in the southwest corner from Sioux City south to the Missouri line, has rugged hills covered with low-growing, shrubby timber. Farms are scattered throughout this region, but cover is more extensive than in the northern part of the state.

A strip across the southern part of the state holds Iowa's primary deer range **(No. 3)**. This region contains extensive timber, primarily oak and hickory, spread over rolling hills. The major activity here is livestock

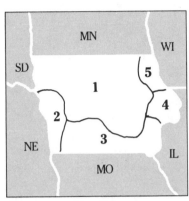

Zones created by author

farming; so pastures, along with some farmlands, are scattered throughout the forested region. Deer densities are particularly high in the southeast corner near the Mississippi River.

The east-central portion **(No. 4)**, from Cedar Rapids to Davenport to Dubuque, has lots of breaks and bluffs along the Mississippi River and its tributaries, and deer numbers are fairly high. The northeast corner **(No. 5)**, from Dubuque north along the Mississippi River, contains rough breaks, limestone bluffs, and good stands of maple, oak, hickory, and other timber. This regions supports some of the largest deer herds found in Iowa.

Seasons. Hunters using firearms are restricted to the use of shotguns and muzzleloaders. No hunting with high-power rifles is allowed, primarily because the state is flat and open and there are many farmhouses and other dwellings throughout hunting country. Again, nonresidents may not hunt.

The bow season generally runs from early October through November. The shotgun season is open for a few days in early December, and the muzzleloader season follows in mid-December. These vary according to management goals, growth of deer herds, and landowner tolerance.

Records. Iowa, with plentiful food in the form of corn and soybeans, grows some huge bucks. Average live weight of 2½-year-old bucks is 200 pounds, and many mature bucks weigh 250 pounds and more (live weight). The heaviest on record weighed 440 pounds.

Iowa deer grow equally impressive antlers. The state record typical whitetail antlers scored 199⅝, and the record nontypical, one of the largest taken anywhere, scored 282. Iowa is well represented throughout the Boone and Crockett whitetail listings.

Because of its trophy potential, many nonresidents have expressed interest in hunting Iowa, but until deer herds are large enough to meet the resident-hunting demand, hunting by nonresidents probably will not be allowed.

The future. Most states have two kinds of carrying capacity for deer—biological and economical. That's particularly true in intensively farmed Iowa. With all of its agriculture, the state has a virtually unlimited food base for animals, and the biological carrying capacity has not been reached. In some areas, herds are still growing.

However, landowners will tolerate only so many animals, and in many areas the deer population has been stabilized well below biological capacity of the land to minimize conflicts with landowners.

Overall, the deer population and harvest will continue to rise through the 1980s. Hunting should be excellent in Iowa, both in terms of hunter success and trophy-class deer.

Contact. Iowa Conservation Commission, Wallace State Office Building, Des Moines, IA 50319.

K A N S A S

Deer numbers. Deer are found throughout Kansas's 82,264 square miles. An estimated population of 100,000 whitetails occupy about 75 percent of the state, and 20,000 mule deer range over about 33 percent of it.

Hunters and harvest. In Kansas, hunting is open to residents only. In the early 1970s, about 15,000 permits were issued annually, but the number has increased to over 20,000. The average annual harvest was once about 7,000 (6,500 bucks and 1,500 does), but that number rose to a recent high of 13,640 (over 9,500 of those were bucks). Average hunting success with firearms has been 40 percent, with a high of 64 percent in 1983 and a low of 23 percent in 1969.

Archery licenses are not limited in number, and the number of archers has increased steadily. The recent average has been about 15,000 bowhunters annually. They've killed an average of about 2,200 deer (1,450 bucks and 750 does). Overall archery success has been a very respectable 20 percent with a high of 29 percent in 1983 and a low of 14 percent in 1971.

Distribution. The eastern edge of Kansas **(No. 1)** contains upland forests of oak and hickory interspersed with small farms raising corn, milo, and other crops. In terms of densities, this is the best whitetail land in Kansas because it's one of the few areas that contains any extensive woodlands.

Just to the west is a strip called the Flint Hills **(No. 2)**, which contains primarily tall-grass prairies. In this region, whitetails are confined primarily to groves of cottonwood, oak, walnut, and other trees and shrubs along streambeds.

A large block of land that takes in most of mid- and north-central Kan-

Zones created by author

sas **(No. 3)** contains grassland mixed with fields of winter wheat, corn, milo, soybeans, and alfalfa. Cover is limited and most deer live in the wooded areas along stream bottoms. Overall, the deer population (mostly whitetail) is low here, but the north-central section near the Nebraska border produces some of Kansas's largest whitetails.

Another area that has a relatively low deer population but produces high-quality whitetails with massive antlers is the south-central Red Hills region **(No. 4)** near the Oklahoma line. Eastern red cedar has invaded much of the pastureland to provide good cover here, and whitetails also live along the stream bottoms.

The southwestern corner **(No. 5)** contains a large amount of irrigated farmland and very limited bottomland cover. Some whitetails live in cornfields, and a fair number of mule deer inhabit what native prairie remains. In general, though, the deer herds are small in this region.

The northwest corner **(No. 6)** has extensive short grass prairies with large rolling hills and some canyons and breaks with plum thickets and other brushy cover. This is the best mule deer country in Kansas. Whitetails also live along the creek bottoms.

Seasons. Hunting in Kansas traditionally has been open to residents only. The season runs for about 10 days in early December. Rifle permits are issued by drawing.

Archery tags are not limited in number, but they also are available only to residents. The archery season is open through October and November, and again in late December. Kansas has considered issuing some nonresident archery permits.

Records. The average whitetail buck in Kansas weighs 130 pounds field-dressed, and the average mule deer weighs 115 pounds.

The Kansas state record typical whitetail antlers scored 200⅞ points, and the record nontypical 258⅝. In terms of total entries in Boone and Crockett Club records, Kansas may appear insignificant compared to major whitetail states. But when the state's relatively small annual harvest is taken into account, Kansas makes an excellent trophy-whitetail showing.

The state record typical mule deer scored 184⅔, well below the Boone and Crockett minimum. The record nontypical scored 260⅝, but that's one of very few outstanding mule deer taken in Kansas.

The future. Kansas deer have had a history similar to those in other prairie states. Historically Kansas had both mule deer and whitetails, but market hunters had ravaged the state's deer population by the turn of the century. From 1904 until 1933, deer were apparently extinct in Kansas. Deer subsequently began to come back, and by the 1950s, they were scattered across the state. Hunting was not permitted until 1965, however, and that first year 3,925 hunters took 1,340 deer. Since then both the growth of the deer population and harvest have accelerated. Now deer numbers have reached a point that must be restricted to reduce conflicts between deer and landowners, and populations probably will remain fairly stable.

Contact. Kansas Fish & Game, Box 54A, Rural Route 2, Pratt, KS 67124.

K E N T U C K Y

Deer numbers. Kentucky covers an area of 40,505 square miles. Ninety percent of the land supports an estimated population of 185,000 white-tails.

Hunters and harvest. Kentucky sells an average of 88,000 resident and 1,200 nonresident firearms licenses each year. The harvest has increased annually for many years with highs in the early 1980s of about 23,000 deer (19,000 bucks and 4,000 does). Overall hunting success (including archery) has been 13 percent, with a high of over 18 percent and a low of 10 percent.

On the average, 50,000 residents and 800 nonresidents bowhunt for deer in Kentucky each year. Here again, the annual harvest has increased steadily from year to year. In 1983 bowhunters enjoyed one of their best years by taking 4,619 deer (2,672 bucks and 1,947 does).

Distribution. The Jackson Purchase region **(No. 1)** takes in the area from Kentucky Lake west to the Mississippi River. The land along the northern border to Owensboro is similar. This region is flat with extensive soybean and cornfields broken up by scattered woodlots. Deer numbers here are moderate and growing.

The Pennyrile Region **(No. 2)** consists of extensively forested, rolling hills spotted here and there with soybean and cornfields, as well as some coal strip mines. This region contains some of the most expansive areas of rugged land in Kentucky. Deer habitat is excellent here, and this region produces Kentucky's largest deer harvest per square mile.

Pastureland, scattered woodlots, and rolling hills characterize south-central Kentucky **(No. 3)**. Deer numbers are fairly low throughout this region, but they're growing. Some of Kentucky's largest deer are taken here. The state record typical and nontypical bucks both came from Pulaski County south of Lexington.

The Blue Grass Hills-Knobs Region **(No. 4)** contains steeply rolling hills. The region is about 40 percent

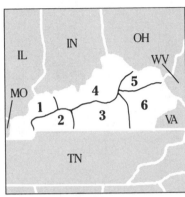

Zones created by author

pastureland and 60 percent cedar thickets and second-growth oak and hickory. Several large cities are located here so that this region is the most heavily hunted in Kentucky. Deer herds are close to carrying capacity throughout the region and may be reduced in specific localities to alleviate crop damage complaints.

The northeast region **(No. 5)** takes in the foothills of the Appalachians. The country is mountainous but not as high—up to 2,000 feet elevation—as the main Appalachians. About 80 percent of the region supports oak and hickory forests. It's not overly productive country, and it has a small but growing deer herd.

The southeast region **(No. 6)** consists primarily of the rugged Appalachian Mountains. Hardwood forests blanket most of this region. The major industry is coal mining. Soils are relatively infertile and aren't capable of supporting large numbers of deer. In addition, poaching and free-roaming dogs take a large toll on deer here. Despite repeated stocking efforts by the Department of Fish and Wildlife, deer numbers are low and may be declining.

Kentucky maintains 43 wildlife management areas, including four large military reservations, that assure some good public hunting. National forest lands also offer public hunting. However, the majority of Kentucky is privately owned and permission to hunt is required. Traditionally, landowners have granted permission to polite hunters, but hunting leases have begun to appear, and they undoubtedly will become more prevalent in the future.

Seasons. In counties with high deer numbers the firearms season runs for 10 days, and in poorer counties it's 3 days long. The bow seasons total 85 days, including all of October, the last two weeks of November, and all of December. The archery limit is one deer of either sex in most counties. Hunters are allowed one deer with bow and one with gun, although bag limits and either-sex hunting may be liberalized as deer numbers increase.

Records. The overall average weight for bucks is 150 pounds, field-dressed. The heaviest buck on record was 290 pounds field-dressed.

The state record typical whitetail antlers, taken in 1982, measured 187⅛. The record nontypical, also taken in 1982, scored 221⅞.

The future. Deer numbers and harvest increased steadily through the 1970s and early 1980s. These numbers are expected to increase through the 1980s and stabilize at about 400,000 deer with an annual harvest of about 60,000. In some areas deer have reached carrying capacity (or the tolerance level of landowners) and either-sex hunts will be liberalized to reduce the size of herds.

Contact. Division of Wildlife, Department of Fish and Wildlife Resources, #1 Game Farm Road, Frankfort, KY 40601.

LOUISIANA

Deer numbers. Louisiana has an area of 48,523 square miles. An estimated 450,000 whitetail deer occupy about 58 percent of the state.

Hunters and harvest. Louisiana sells an average of 200,000 resident and 1,500 nonresident firearms deer licenses each year. The average annual kill is about 100,000 deer (75,000 bucks and 25,000 does) with a high in 1984 of about 126,500. The firearms hunting success has been as high as 50 percent.

Louisiana also sells an average of 20,000 archery licenses each year, primarily to residents. The average recent kill has been 3,500 deer (55 percent bucks and 45 percent does) with a high kill in 1984 of 3,800. Archery success ranges from 25 to 30 percent.

Distribution. *The Louisiana Deer Story,* a booklet published by the Department of Wildlife and Fisheries, divides the state into five general ecological types. The Pine-Hardwood Hill Land covers most of west Louisiana **(No. 1)** and the Florida Parishes **(No. 2)**. The fertile hill country in the northwest supports more deer than the sand hills in the west-central area. These entire regions are forested with a mix of pine and hardwoods, and deer are abundant throughout. Large blocks of land in the western part of the state remain unposted so that public hunting access is good. As a result, the deer harvest is heavy.

The Upper Mississippi and Red River Bottomland **(No. 3)** takes in most of northeastern Louisiana, and a strip from Alexandria to Shreveport. The soil is fertile here, and when it was covered with hardwoods it supported more deer than anywhere else in Louisiana. Now much of it has been cleared and planted with cotton and soybeans, and the number of deer has been reduced significantly.

The Mississippi-Atchafalaya Delta **(No. 4)** comprises about 400,000 acres of swamp and timbered bottomland. Most of it is covered with water, and only low ridges and lowland fringes are cultivated. This re-

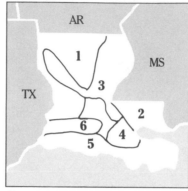

Zones created by author

gion contains one of the largest unspoiled swamps in the United States and supports large numbers of deer. However, pressure to drain much of the bottomland here will increase as demand for agricultural land intensifies. This region contains the most heavily posted land in Louisiana, and most of the land here is leased to private gun clubs.

The Coastal Marshes **(No. 5)** cover about 5 million acres of marshland, with timber growing only along natural levees and the northern fringe of the marshes. Deer are common throughout the marshes, and hunting pressure is fairly high here.

The Southwest Prairie Land **(No. 6)** contains Louisiana's only natural prairie land. This region now consists primarily of rice fields. Deer numbers are fairly high in patches of scattered timber along drainage bottoms, but overall, deer numbers are low.

The Department of Wildlife and Fisheries operates 35 wildlife management areas that cover nearly 1 million acres. These are all open to hunting and fishing and are heavily utilized.

Seasons. Usually, the firearms hunting is divided into three seasons.

The first opens early in November and extends to Thanksgiving. Still-hunting only (no dogs) is allowed. The second runs from Thanksgiving into early December and dogs are allowed. The third extends from late December into January and dogs are allowed. The total is 45 to 55 days, depending on the area. Bag limit is one per day and six per person per season. The six deer may be taken by all legal means (archery or firearms) during any open season.

The archery season opens in early October and runs through most of January statewide. Either sex of deer may be taken except during gun seasons when all hunters are restricted to bucks only.

Records. The average 2½-year-old buck weighs 100 pounds field-dressed. The heaviest buck on record field-dressed to 226 pounds.

The state record typical whitetail antlers measured 184⅜, and the record nontypical scored 218⅛. Boone and Crockett lists a scant handful of bucks from Louisiana.

The future. In the early 1900s, deer were scarce in Louisiana, and they lived only in isolated swamp regions where market hunters couldn't wipe them out. During the 1950s, many deer were live-trapped and then stocked throughout the state and herds began to grow. The legal harvest jumped from 5,000 deer in 1960 to 105,000 in 1980. Now deer are at or above carrying capacity on most ranges.

Habitat loss, due largely to drainage and clearing of bottomlands has been significant since the 1960s. The statewide herd has been stable recently, but numbers will decline as habitat is lost. About one-half of the state is leased by hunting clubs. This land is under-hunted and as a result is overpopulated with deer in poor condition. The remaining public-hunting lands are heavily hunted. Deer herds in Louisiana have peaked and will stabilize or decrease.

Contact. Department of Wildlife and Fisheries, PO Box 15570, Baton Rouge, LA 70895.

MAINE

Deer numbers. Maine has a total area of 31,885 square miles, and almost 28,000 square miles support whitetail deer. The deer population is estimated at 180,000 to 200,000.

Hunters and harvest. An average of 170,000 residents and 31,000 non-residents have hunted during Maine's deer firearms seasons in recent years. Average harvest during the late 1970s and early 1980s was about 31,000 (17,500 bucks and 13,500 does). Hunters took a recent of 37,115 (20,620 bucks) in 1980, although harvests exceeded 40,000 in the 1950s. Average firearms success during the 1980s was 15 percent with a high in 1980 of 19 percent and a low in 1982 of 14 percent.

An average of 4,000 resident and 700 nonresident archers have hunted deer in Maine each year. Average harvest has been about 110 deer (about 60 bucks). Bowhunting success has been 2.5 percent.

Distribution. Until the 1930s, the north half of the state supported nearly 75 percent of the deer in Maine, but since then deer have become more abundant in central and southern zones.

In the northern half of the state **(No. 1)**, spruce-fir forests dominate the landscape. In the northeast corner along the border of New Brunswick, spruce-fir forests are broken up by farmlands and some stands of hardwoods. Farms and woodlands are in fairly large tracts with little interspersion and edge cover. The northeast corner supports 7 to 12 deer per square mile, which is below the statewide average.

Spruce-fir forests cover two-thirds of the northwest quarter of the state. Farther south along the western border, spruce-fir gives way to equal amounts of maple, beech, and birch. Unbroken forests blanket most of the northwest and western areas, and severe winters here often take a heavy toll on deer. These regions support 3 to 6 deer per square mile, the lowest densities in the state.

The central region **(No. 2)** contains nearly equal amounts of spruce-fir, hardwoods, and white

Zones created by author

pine and hemlock. Farmland occupies about 6 percent of the region. Winter weather is moderately severe in this region. Reproduction is not especially high, but the deer grow to large size, and densities of 10 to 16 deer per square mile in the central and western portions of this region are above the state average. At the eastern end of this region, farmland is not prevalent. Here size and weight of deer is only average, and deer population density ranges from 5 to 9 deer per square mile.

Along the coast **(No. 3)** winters are mild to moderate so overall survival is better than farther north. Abandoned farms reverting to timber have provided ideal habitat for deer. On the eastern end of this region, roughly from Bangor east, spruce-fir forests blanket two-thirds of the country, and aspen and birch are also major forest species. Agricultural lands, primarily along the coast, occupy about 6 percent of this area. Deer population density ranges from 8 to 14 deer per square mile.

The central coast, roughly from Augusta to Bangor, supports the highest deer densities in Maine, from 14 to 24 deer per square mile. Forests consist of mixed hardwoods and conifers, and farmlands cover 13 percent of this area. Deer size and reproduction are the best in Maine.

The southwest coastal area also contains a good mix of young hardwoods among conifer forests, and farmland occupies about 10 percent of the region. Deer size and repro-

duction are above average. Deer density is 9 to 15 deer per square mile.

Road access is good in the south end of the state, but it is severely limited farther north. Much land is open to hunting, although posted lands are becoming more common.

Seasons. The statewide firearms season has been reduced over the years, but recently it has run for about a month from late October until about Thanksgiving. In some regions the bag limit is one deer of either sex, and in others it's bucks only. The statewide archery season generally has opened at the beginning of October and stayed open until late October.

Records. Average weight for all bucks taken in Maine is 148½ pounds field-dressed. The heaviest buck on record field-dressed to 355 pounds and weighed an estimated 461 pounds on the hoof.

The state record typical whitetail antlers measured 192⅞ and the record nontypical, 259. The Maine Antler and Skull Trophy Club lists dozens of racks that score over 150.

The future. In contrast to most other states, Maine's deer population is somewhat lower now than 25 to 30 years ago. Average deer harvest has dropped from 39,000 in the 1950s, to 35,000 in the 1960s, to 31,000 in the 1970s and 1980s. Habitat changes, excessive hunting, and predation are listed as reasons for the decrease.

Maine's hunting seasons traditionally have allowed harvest of does and bucks. Since the mid-1960s, season length has been reduced from six weeks to two or four weeks (depending on the area). Beginning in 1983, the department broke tradition and restricted harvest to antlered bucks only in about one-quarter of the state in an effort to bolster deer numbers. The department plans to institute a permit system to regulate harvest of does and to control hunting pressure.

Contact. Department of Inland Fisheries and Wildlife, 284 State St., Augusta, ME 04333.

MARYLAND

Deer numbers. Maryland has a total area of 10,577 square miles and an estimated deer population of 85,000 to 100,000.

Hunters and harvest. In recent years Maryland has sold an average of 100,000 firearms, 38,000 bow, and 12,000 muzzleloader deer licenses. Nonresidents buy about 2 percent of the total. The annual harvest has climbed steadily in recent years to about 15,000 (9,000 bucks and 6,000 does). Firearms hunters have averaged about 14 percent success.

Average bow harvest has been almost 2,000 (1,000 of those were bucks) with a success rate of about 5 percent. In a recent year, muzzleloaders killed 414 deer (122 bucks and 292 does) and had a success rate of 3.5 percent.

Distribution. The western region **(No. 1)**, which includes all of the country west of Frederick County, is mountainous and heavily wooded with hardwoods, such as maple and beech. Deer numbers are high in this region. State forest land, which is open to public hunting, covers nearly 20 percent of Garrett and Allegany counties (the westernmost counties). These forests provide most of the public hunting available in the state and hunting pressure during regular seasons is high. Private hunting clubs lease most of the private land in this western region.

The Piedmont Region **(No. 2)** takes in most of the land from Washington, D.C., north to the Pennsylvania border. The rural lands are heavily farmed for corn, soybeans, and small grains, and cover is restricted to small woodlots. This area has the highest human population in Maryland, and access to private land is very difficult.

The land south of Washington **(No. 3)** lies within the Coastal Plain ecological zone. Most of the uplands are planted in corn, soybeans, and other crops, but this is flat country with many swampy hardwood bottomlands. About 30 to 40 percent of the region is forested, and deer numbers are high. Public land is scarce, but in some cases it's possible to get

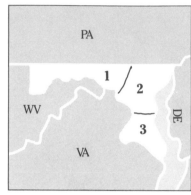

Zones created by author

permission to hunt by asking.

The Eastern Shore also consists of flat coastal plain. The north half **(No. 4)** is 25 percent wooded. This area holds the best deer habitat in the state, and deer numbers are high. Most of the land, however, is leased to private hunting clubs.

The south half of the Eastern Shore **(No. 5)**, is heavily wooded, primarily with loblolly pine. Deer numbers are as high here as in the north Eastern Shore, but average size of the deer is much smaller. This dense, swampy region presents tough hunting conditions. There is some public land, but it's better for waterfowl hunting than for deer. Sika deer are abundant in Dorchester County and on Assateague Island. Again, private clubs have leased the hunting rights on most private lands and access for the public is difficult.

Seasons. The archery season usually runs from mid-September through the first week in January. Firearms season usually opens the Saturday after Thanksgiving and remains open for seven hunting days (no hunting is allowed on Sunday). A special muzzleloader season is open for seven hunting days in mid-December. The bag limit is one deer during the archery season, one during a firearm season (maximum of two a year). The limit for Sika deer is three during each season, or nine total in one year.

Records. In the northern Eastern Shore, yearling whitetail bucks average 120 pounds field-dressed, but in the lower Eastern Shore they average only 90 to 95 pounds field-dressed. The state record buck unofficially weighed 383 pounds live weight. The state doesn't keep records of antler size.

The future. The history of Maryland's deer parallels that of surrounding states. By 1900 most of the land had been cleared for farming, but since then land has been abandoned, and as woodlands have increased, deer herds have grown dramatically. Deer harvests reached record highs in the early 1980s. Harvest probably will remain stable at 15,000 to 20,000 deer through the 1980s, but it probably will decline as urban development and rural housing reduce overall habitat.

Contact. Department of Natural Resources, Tawes State Office Building, Annapolis, MD 21401.

Sika bucks (Leonard Lee Rue III photo)

MASSACHUSETTS

Deer numbers. Massachusetts has a total area of 8,000 square miles. A herd of 25,000 to 30,000 whitetail deer live on about 6,200 square miles.

Hunters and harvest. An average of about 85,000 firearms hunters and 23,000 bowhunters pursue deer in this state each year (resident and nonresident). Many of these hunt with both firearms and bow. A recent four-year average firearms harvest was just over 3,500 deer (2,500 bucks and 1,000 does), with a high harvest in 1981 of 4,321 (3,081 bucks). Average bow kill has been about 375 deer. Overall average hunting success has been 10 percent. No separate records are kept for firearms and archery hunters.

Distribution. The rolling sand dunes that make up Nantucket Island and Martha's Vineyard **(No. 1)** historically had no trees or deer, but now the islands are covered with dense stands of pitch pine and scrub oak, and deer numbers are very high. Nantucket Island sustains a higher deer kill per square mile than any other area in Massachusetts. These islands offer a fair amount of public hunting.

The eastern end of the state **(No. 2)** contains the highest human population, and continued land development stands to shape the future of deer herds here. Cape Cod, the hook-shaped peninsula southeast of Boston, contains habitat and deer numbers similar to Nantucket Island. Historically, this is the only place where deer were not eliminated from Massachusetts during the late 1800s. But this region is undergoing tremendous development now, and deer hunting doesn't seem to have a great future there. The entire eastern end of the state, with Boston at the center, is undergoing heavy development. As a result deer numbers will be stabilized or reduced throughout this region. The northeast corner contains some large farms and estates with good deer habitat. But landowners there allow very little hunting so that overpopulation of deer has been a problem.

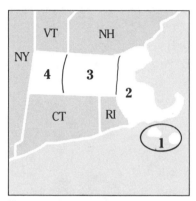

Zones created by author

The hilly central region **(No. 3)** consists of northern hardwoods mixed with spruce and pine along the northern border. Deer hunting is good in this area. Farther south, hardwoods and white pine forests predominate, but the area around Worcester is experiencing rapid growth and development. Regulations will be designed to reduce the size of herds there.

The best deer hunting in Massachusetts takes place west of the broad Connecticut River Valley, where rich soils grow potatoes, tobacco, and truck-farm crops. The western region **(No. 4)** contains the Holyoke Mountains, a narrow range covered with hardwoods, hemlock, and white pine. The more extensive Berkshire Mountains have some rugged peaks, and the hardwood and spruce forests there support good deer numbers. This region is the most popular among the state's deer hunters, and the kill per square mile in the Berkshires ranks second only to Nantucket Island. This region contains large expanses of undeveloped land, and public access is good.

More than 15 percent of Massachusetts is publicly owned, and hunters can hunt any land that isn't posted. For these reasons, public access is better than average for a heavily populated eastern state.

Seasons. The archery season usually lasts about three weeks from early to mid-November. The shotgun season usually runs from late November into early December. Length varies by zone. A short muzzleloader season is held in mid-December. The daily bag limit is one deer and the season limit is two.

Records. Bucks 4½ to 5½ years old weigh an average of 165 pounds field-dressed and 205 on the hoof. The heaviest deer on record field-dressed 265 pounds and had an estimated live weight of 310 pounds. No records on antler size have been kept.

The future. In the late 1800s, much of Massachusetts' timber was cleared for extensive farms, and deer herds nearly disappeared. Many farms have been abandoned, and now forests blanket nearly 75 percent of the state. In 1966 Massachusetts adopted a mandatory checking system for all deer killed, and biological data from check stations are used to assess herd condition and to set regulations. From an estimated 6,000 deer statewide in the mid-1960s, the herd has grown steadily to nearly 30,000 in the 1980s. Deer are now reported where no deer had been seen for decades. Using an antlerless permit system, deer herds will be held below carrying capacity to ensure adequate winter food. Herds in eastern zones will be reduced as deer range is lost to urbanization, and deer numbers there won't be allowed to grow further.

Contact. Division of Fisheries and Wildlife, Field Headquarters, Westboro, MA 01581.

MICHIGAN

Deer numbers. Michigan covers an area of 57,019 square miles. Roughly 95 percent of that area supports whitetails. And the deer population is estimated at about 1 million animals.

Hunters and harvest. Traditionally, Michigan has ranked third behind Texas and Pennsylvania in total hunting licenses sold. Over the past few years, an average of 745,000 residents and 10,000 nonresidents have hunted with firearms in Michigan each season. They've killed an average of 130,000 deer (100,000 bucks and 30,000 does) each year. In 1981, the highest year on record, firearms hunters bagged 173,120 deer (123,690 of those were bucks). Average firearms hunting success has been 17 percent.

Each year Michigan sells an average of over 200,000 resident and 4,000 nonresident archery licenses. Yearly average bow harvest in recent years has been 26,000 deer (11,500 bucks and 14,500 does). In 1982, the highest year on record, archers killed over 38,000 deer (about 17,000 of those were bucks). The average bowhunting success has been 10 percent, with a high in 1982 of 17 percent. The low of 2 percent was recorded in 1937. That was the first year of archery-only hunting, then allowed in two counties.

Distribution. The Upper Peninsula **(No. 1)** contains the most wild lands in Michigan. Most of it had been logged by the early 1900s, and then fires ravaged the country until the 1930s. Since then, fires have been suppressed, and now young timber blankets most of the area. These forestlands are broken by some stump lands and other breaks. Some farms are found in the southern and eastern section, but otherwise it's all forestland. The west end is hilly to mountainous, and the eastern section is rolling or flat. Deer densities are moderate throughout the region, although deer herds are growing in Iron and Dickinson counties. These counties offer some of the best hunting on the Upper Peninsula. State and national forests cover

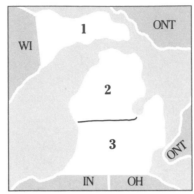

Zones created by author

a majority of the Upper Peninsula, and paper, timber, and mining companies, which generally allow hunting, own large tracts. So access is virtually unlimited here.

The northern Lower Peninsula **(No. 2)** contains the highest deer numbers and highest harvest in Michigan. Hunters kill an average of five deer per square mile each year from a band of counties extending from the southwest to northeast across this region. Medium-age forests similar to those on the Upper Peninsula spread across much of this area, although extensive farmlands, mostly fruit orchards, stretch along the northwest shoreline. According to the book *Hunting in Michigan* (published by the Department of Natural Resources), "The northeast part of this zone, particularly Montmorency, Oscoda, Alcona, and Alpena counties, is known as 'The Club Country' and is largely fenced, posted, privately owned land held by hunting clubs." Elsewhere in the northern Lower Peninsula, two national forests and six state forests assure good public access.

The southern Lower Peninsula **(No. 3)** consists largely of private farmlands, where permission to hunt is needed. However, many state game areas do offer public hunting, and the Department of Natural Re-

sources has leased the hunting rights to thousands of acres of private land. Hunters must buy a Public Access Stamp in order to get permission to hunt these leased private lands. The deer numbers are growing here, and the herd is slightly larger than on the Upper Peninsula.

The Department of Natural Resources publishes some excellent books for hunters as well as detailed maps, showing public access and good hunting areas.

Seasons. The general gun season takes place the last two weeks in November. High-power rifles are allowed in the Upper Peninsula and the northern Lower Peninsula. Only shotguns and muzzleloaders are allowed in the southern Lower Peninsula. The bag limit usually is one buck. A special muzzleloader season usually takes place the first 10 days of December.

The bow season usually runs from early October through mid-November, and opens again for December. The bag limit is usually one deer.

Records. The largest deer on record field-dressed to 354 pounds with an estimated live weight of 425 pounds.

The state record typical whitetail scored 181⅜ points, and the record nontypical scored 232⅝. *Records of North American Big Game* lists fewer than a dozen whitetails from Michigan, evenly divided between typicals and nontypicals. Given the large kill in Michigan, that does not give the trophy hunter good odds.

The future. During the 1970s, Michigan carried out a large-scale habitat development program to increase the deer herd. As a result the average total harvest is now nearly double what it was in the early 1970s. Deer numbers will be stabilized at about current levels, and the annual harvest through the 1980s should fall somewhere between 150,000 and 200,000 animals.

Contact. Department of Natural Resources, Box 30028, Lansing, MI 48909.

MINNESOTA

Deer numbers. Minnesota covers an area of 84,068 square miles and has an estimated population of 850,000 whitetails.

Hunters and harvest. Minnesota has an average of over 320,000 resident and 2,000 nonresident firearms hunters. The long-term average harvest has been 68,000 deer (41,000 bucks and 27,000 does), but in 1983 the harvest swelled to over 132,000. Average hunter success with firearms has been 21 percent, and the range has varied from about 11 percent in 1976 to 34 percent in 1983.

On average, 38,000 resident and over 500 nonresident hunters buy archery licenses each year. Since the early 1970s, bowhunters have killed an average of over 3,000 deer. During the early 1980s, the annual archery harvest hit a peak of about 5,500. Average bowhunting success has been between 8 and 9 percent, with a high in 1981 of about 11 percent and a low in 1976 of 5 percent.

Distribution. For management purposes the Department of Natural Resources divides Minnesota into four zones. Zone 1 **(No. 1)** covers the northeast quarter. Heavy forests of hardwoods, aspens, and conifers, such as spruce, balsam fir, and jack pine, blanket most of this flat to rolling country. The region also contains some large, flat bogs. Deer population densities are fairly high— 20 to 30 deer per square mile— throughout most of the forested zone, except in the Boundary Waters Canoe Area in the extreme northeast. Old-growth forests there support densities of only five deer per square mile or less. State and national forests assure good public hunting throughout the forested zone.

Zone 2 **(No. 2)** is a transition area between forests to the east and prairie farmlands to the west. This transition area consists of crop fields interspersed with forested riverbottoms and woodlots of oak and other hardwoods. Topography in this northern transition zone is level to rolling. With densities of 20 to 30 deer per square mile here, deer numbers are probably the highest in

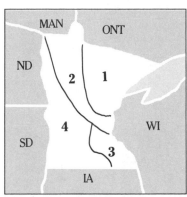

Zones created by author

the state. This country's mixed woodlands and farms grow some of the largest bucks. Public and private land are intermixed.

Zone 3 **(No. 3)** is considered a transition area similar to Zone 2 except that the unglaciated breaks along the Mississippi River and its tributaries contain more rugged, broken country than that found farther north. This country contains the only major relief found in Minnesota. The woodlands of oak, maple, and basswood contain high numbers of deer, and state forests assure some public access. This zone has produced a number of Boone and Crockett bucks.

Zone 4 **(No. 4)** historically was prairie and now consists primarily of farmland. The country is flat to gently rolling. Corn and soybeans are the major crops in the southern portion, and these are replaced by grain crops farther north. The goal is to maintain densities of five deer per square mile as an average throughout the zone, although densities are higher in isolated localities. Most deer in this region live near wooded riverbottoms, or near wetlands where they use cattails, high grass, and weeds for cover. Some public wildlife areas are scattered throughout the zone, but most of the land is private, and permission to hunt is required.

Seasons. General firearms seasons in Minnesota have varied in recent

years but take place in November. In the forested northeast section, the season usually runs longer than in the other zones—usually more than two weeks. In the transition zones, it may be only nine days. And in the western prairie zone, the season may be only a few days long. In most zones, limited numbers of antlerless permits are available. Only shotguns and muzzleloading guns are allowed in the southern half of the state. Hunters can use high-power firearms in the north half.

Special muzzleloader seasons are held during early December in specified areas.

Usually the statewide bow season runs from mid-September through November, and part of the state is open to bowhunting in December.

Records. Minnesota ranks among the top three or four trophy whitetail states. The state record typical scored 202, and the record nontypical 268⅝. More than three-dozen Minnesota typicals and two-dozen nontypicals—8 percent of the total in each category—are listed by Boone and Crockett, and significantly, half of those have been killed since 1970. Trophy bucks have been taken throughout the state, but generally the greatest numbers of large animals come from the central transition zones.

The future. In the western prairie country, deer were eliminated in the early 1900s. Under tight hunting regulations and with the help of stocking programs, deer numbers have increased greatly there and are at relatively high levels now. Deer numbers in the forest zone have fluctuated dramatically in response to logging, fire, and other influences. Since the mid-1970s antlerless permits have been limited in number, and since that time the deer herd in Minnesota has more than doubled. It should remain fairly stable into the 1990s.

Contact. Minnesota Department of Natural Resources, Division of Fish & Wildlife, 500 Lafayette Road, St. Paul, MN 55146.

MISSISSIPPI

Deer numbers. Whitetail deer occupy nearly 100 percent of Mississippi's total area of 47,296 square miles. The deer population is estimated at 1.7 to 2 million.

Hunters and harvest. Mississippi usually has about 190,000 firearms deer hunters and 37,000 bowhunters. No figures are available on the percentage of nonresidents. As in many states the harvest has increased steadily since 1970 so that average harvest figures mean little. During the 1982–83 seasons, firearms hunters killed a record 227,500 deer (181,400 bucks and 46,100 does). The total kill exceeds the number of hunters in the field, with an average success of 1.25 deer per hunter. That's because Mississippi has a multiple bag limit and many hunters killed more than one deer. The actual number of hunters who killed deer was 52 percent. The lowest per-hunter success rate occurred in 1970–71 and was 23 percent.

During the 1981–82 season, 37,000 archers killed about 17,000 deer (9,000 bucks and 8,000 does). Average bowhunter success has been about 25 percent, with a low in 1970 of 14 percent.

Distribution. The flat Mississippi Alluvial Plain **(No. 1)**—locally called the Delta—contains rich soils and is farmed heavily. Expansive fields of soybeans and cotton cover most of this region. Wooded lands are scarce here, and they exist primarily along river levees. While a high percentage of the region supports few deer, animals are plentiful in the remaining woodlands.

The Loess Bluffs **(No. 2)**, which stretch in a narrow band all the way from Tennessee to Louisiana, contain rugged hills covered with oak, hickory, and other hardwoods. The topography varies by as much as 200 feet in the form of steep, eroded breaks. The Bluffs are productive deer country, and a fair amount of public land, particularly toward the south end, assures public hunting.

The North-Central Hills **(No. 3)** contain the most extensive uplands in Mississippi. Some of the most rug-

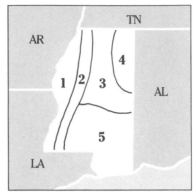

Zones created by author

ged hills in the entire Coastal Plain, which spans most of the southeastern states, are found at the south end of the North-Central Hills near Meridian. But rolling hills characterize most of the region, and forest cover is mostly pine mixed with stands of oak and hickory. Deer numbers are good throughout this region.

The northeast corner **(No. 4)** comprises several bands of varied topography that run in a crescent shape from the Tennessee border down to Alabama. Just east of the North-Central Hills is the Flatwoods, next comes the narrow Pontotoc Ridge, then the Black Prairie (a westward extension of Alabama's Black Belt), and in the extreme northeast, the Tennessee River Hills. Some of the larger bucks taken in Mississippi come from the Black Prairie region around Starkville. Deer numbers are good throughout the northeast except in part of the Tennessee River Hills where subsistence hunting continues to take a heavy toll.

The Pine Woods Region **(No. 5)** covers most of southeast Mississippi. Elevations here vary from 300 to 500 feet. In general, the topography is flat or rolling, with some modest ridges dividing stream drainages. As the name implies, the region consists of pine forests, and these are mixed with some oaks and other hardwoods. Commercial pine plantations are fairly common in this region. Deer densities are relatively high here, although soils aren't espe-

cially rich. So the deer are smaller in size than in the northeast and the western regions. Several blocks of national land assure public hunting here.

Mississippi contains more than 30 public wildlife management areas, including several national forests. It's possible to get permission to hunt private land by asking, but the major trend is toward hunting clubs and private leases.

Seasons. The archery season usually runs from the first Saturday in October through the Friday before Thanksgiving. The gun season with dogs runs from the Saturday before Thanksgiving through December. A primitive weapons-archery season follows for about two weeks. That is followed by a gun season without dogs in mid-December, and then a gun season with dogs for about a month after Christmas. Hunting with dogs remains a popular way to hunt in Mississippi.

The bag limit is usually one antlered buck per day, five per license year. During legal seasons for taking antlerless deer, it is usually one antlerless deer per day, three per license year.

Records. The state record typical whitetail antlers measured 183⅝, and the record nontypical 216⅜.

The future. Along with other southern states, most of Mississippi was cleared of timber by the early 1900s and deer herds nearly disappeared. Since then, forests have been restored. With major deer stocking programs and an increasing concern about game laws, deer have rebounded dramatically. Major growth took place during the 1970s, when the harvest jumped from 40,000 in 1970 to more than 200,000 in the early 1980s. Deer numbers continue to increase at a moderate rate. The major increase in recent years has taken place in the northeast section of the state.

Contact. Department of Wildlife Conservation, Southport Mall, PO Box 451, Jackson, MS 39205.

MISSOURI

Deer numbers. Missouri has a total area of 68,995 square miles, and 80 to 90 percent of that supports healthy whitetail herds. The Department of Conservation does not make a deer population estimate.

Hunters and harvest. On the average, 280,000 residents and 10,000 nonresidents hunt deer during firearms seasons in Missouri. Average firearms harvest in the early 1980s was 57,801 (45,000 bucks and 13,000 does), but the harvest has been steadily increasing in recent years. The average firearms success rate has remained fairly steady in the 17 to 20 percent range.

About 50,000 resident and 2,000 nonresident archers hunt deer in Missouri each year. In the early 1980s, they killed an average of 4,600 deer, but like the firearms harvest, the bow kill has steadily increased in recent years.

Distribution. The Missouri River cuts across the middle of Missouri and roughly divides the state in half. The north half is primarily agricultural, and the south half contains extensive forests. Missouri has gained a reputation for trophy-class bucks, and most of these have come from the north half. A strip about 20 miles wide along the Mississippi River in the northeast corner **(No. 1)** contains rough breaks, valleys with heavy woods, and oak and hickory forests throughout the uplands. Deer densities are high here.

The Green Hills region **(No. 2)** is a strip down the north-central part of the state from the Iowa border down through Columbia. It has rolling hills with generous stands of oak and hickory timber throughout. This section provides the best deer hunting in Missouri. Numbers of deer are fairly high, and a majority of the trophy bucks taken in Missouri have come from this section.

The flat country of northwest Missouri **(No. 3)** is virtually all farmland with only a scattering of woodland cover along the stream bottoms, and deer numbers are relatively low. There is some good hunting along

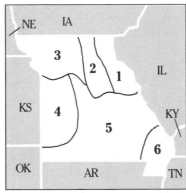

Zones created by author

the Missouri River near Kansas City, but hunting pressure is high there.

The west-central section **(No. 4)** runs west of a line drawn roughly from Joplin to Springfield and then north to the Missouri River, comprises native prairie and croplands. Farm crops are corn and soybeans and provide good feed for deer. Woody cover is restricted primarily to creek and riverbottoms. Deer herds are necessarily limited, but in some places the hunting is very good in this region.

The Ozarks **(No. 5)** cover most of the rest of Missouri. These are mostly rocky hills, 200 to 400 feet high. Some pastures are scattered throughout the Ozarks, and bottomlands are farmed, but oak and hickory forests cover a high percentage of the land here. With a lack of farmland, the Ozarks generally don't grow the huge bucks found north of the Missouri River. But the number of deer is fairly high and is growing, and the Ozarks provide good hunting.

The Boot Heel **(No. 6)** is east of Poplar Bluff. It is low, flat country with little cover, and deer are scarce here.

Missouri offers a surprising amount of public hunting. The Mark Twain National Forest (in **No. 5**) contains 1.5 million acres scattered

throughout the Missouri Ozarks, and the Department of Conservation administers nearly 600,000 acres for public hunting throughout the state. Much of this public land supports good deer herds. Still, nearly 90 percent of Missouri is privately owned, and getting permission to hunt can be tough. If you're coming from another state, you're wise to have a hunting spot lined up ahead of time. The leasing of hunting rights has become fairly prevalent.

Seasons. Normally, the general firearms season, with a limit of one buck, runs for nine days in mid-November. Special quota hunts for any deer are held in various management units.

Usually, the bow season runs from early October through the day preceding the rifle season. Following the general firearms season, the bow season reopens and lasts through December.

Records. The average field-dressed adult buck weighs 132 pounds. The heaviest field-dressed buck on record weighed 320 pounds.

The No. 2 Boone and Crockett typical whitetail, which scored 205, was taken in Randolph County **(No. 2)** in 1971. The world-record nontypical with a score of 333⅞ was picked up near St. Louis in 1981. Boone and Crockett lists many other typical and nontypical Missouri whitetails, and significantly, many have been taken since 1970. Missouri has excellent potential for trophy whitetails.

The future. As in most states, land development for housing and agriculture continues to eat away cover for deer. But most available habitat has not reached carrying capacity, and herds continue to grow. Biologists anticipate that the annual harvest may approach 100,000 deer, and they forecast excellent hunting.

Contact. Missouri Department of Conservation, PO Box 180, Jefferson City, MO 65102.

MONTANA

Deer numbers. Montana covers over 147,139 square miles. Roughly 90 percent of that supports mule deer, and 29 percent holds whitetails. The Department of Fish, Wildlife, & Parks does not estimate the number of animals.

Hunters and harvest. No long-term averages are available, but figures from 1982 provide a representative sampling. That year 125,000 residents and 20,000 nonresidents hunted deer. About 16,000 of the hunters used bow and arrow. Firearms hunters killed nearly 100,000 deer, including about 70,000 mule deer (about 53,000 bucks and 17,000 does) and almost 28,000 whitetails (some 21,000 bucks and 7,000 does). They enjoyed a 63 percent success rate. Bowhunters took 1,160 mule deer (687 bucks and 473 does) and 631 whitetails (429 bucks and 202 does) for 13 percent success on mule deer and 9 percent on whitetails.

Distribution. Montana offers great diversity. The western one-third consists of mountains and evergreen forests, and the eastern two-thirds consists of prairies, breaks, and badlands.

No. 1 takes in the northwest corner west of the Continental Divide. Steep, heavily forested mountain ranges are separated by river valleys. This is one of the best whitetail areas in North America. Numbers are highest in riverbottoms, but whitetails live throughout the forests, and the region grows exceptional trophy heads. Mule deer live in isolated pockets, primarily at the highest elevations in rocky, dry habitat. Much of the mule deer range is remote and good-size bucks are taken here.

West-central Montana **(No. 2)** is similar to No. 1 with a good mix of mule deer and whitetails. But some of the mountains, such as the Bitterroots, are drier and rockier, so mule deer are more widely distributed here.

No. 3, the southwest corner east to Yellowstone National Park, consists of classic mountain-foothill mule deer country. Rugged mountain

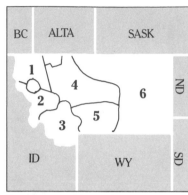

Zones created by author

ranges rise to elevations of 10,000 feet and more. Mule deer summer high and then winter in foothills surrounding the mountains. Because all herds here migrate, weather has a great bearing on hunting strategy. Some ranges have high numbers of mule deer, and remote areas grow excellent trophies. Whitetails are expanding throughout this region, but they live primarily in broad, cultivated river valleys.

No. 4 lies in north-central Montana east of the Continental Divide. The west side contains mountain-foothill mule deer country similar to **No. 3** but to the east the foothills give away to rugged breaks with pockets of pine along the Missouri River and its tributaries. The Missouri Breaks contain high numbers of mule deer and some large bucks. Farther east, mule deer and whitetails are found throughout the rolling prairies. Whitetails stick primarily to riparian habitat along stream courses.

No. 5 has extensive agriculture. Deer numbers—whitetails in the valleys and mule deer in scattered mountain ranges—are high, but getting access to private land is difficult.

No. 6 covers most of eastern Montana. In general, the Missouri River and its major tributaries provide excellent mule-deer hunting. Extensive prairies and grain country support plenty of mule deer and whitetails.

They're found side by side, but generally whitetails live along stream bottoms, and mule deer live in higher country with junipers and natural prairie grasses. Extensive badlands cover large blocks in the southeast. These provide excellent mule-deer hunting.

In eastern Montana most land is private, but in general landowners will allow hunting. Bureau of Land Management (BLM) lands are also scattered throughout the region. In western Montana most mountain ranges are National Forest land, but in some cases private landowners block access to public lands.

Seasons. The bow season usually runs for six weeks from early September through mid-October, and the rifle season follows from mid-October through November. Other special seasons are held, and frequently multiple licenses are issued for antlerless deer.

Records. The state record typical mule deer antlers scored 201⅛, and several others are listed in Boone and Crockett records. The largest nontypical scored 275⅛. Boone and Crockett lists about two dozen nontypical mule deer taken from various parts of Montana.

The state record typical whitetail scored 199⅜, and the record nontypical scored 252⅛. Many Montana whitetails are in the Boone and Crockett records. Again these come from scattered areas, but the northwest—Flathead, Lake, Missoula, and Lincoln counties—makes the strongest showing.

The future. The size of Montana's deer herds has ranged from extremes of high and low, and these cycles will continue. However, excellent habitat is extensive, and biologists predict thriving herds for the foreseeable future. Hunter-landowner conflicts have been a problem and could restrict overall hunting opportunity.

Contact. Department of Fish, Wildlife & Parks, 1420 E. Sixth Ave., Helena, MT 59620.

NEBRASKA

Deer numbers. With a total area of 77,227 square miles, Nebraska has a population of about 70,000 whitetails scattered across the entire state. Some 40,000 mule deer occupy about 60 percent of the state.

Hunters and harvest. On the average, 33,000 residents and 300 non-residents hunt deer with firearms each year in Nebraska. Since 1970, hunters have killed an average of 28,000 deer a year, with a low of 23,658 in 1978, and a high of 35,285 in 1983. Average hunter success since 1970 has been 55 percent, the low 43 percent, and the high 70 percent.

Archery harvest has steadily increased from just over 900 in 1970 to more than 3,000 annually in recent years. Overall bowhunter success has averaged 18 percent with a range from 13 percent to 26 percent. Whitetails make up about 80 percent of the bow harvest.

Distribution. Nebraska consists primarily of farm and pasture land, and in most cases the only major topographical relief occurs in the breaks along rivers and streams. Less than 2 percent of the state has timber cover. The average deer density overall is one-to-two deer per square mile, but it's much higher in pockets of good habitat. Most wooded stream courses support 10 to 20 deer per square mile. In some ideal refuge situations with woods, marshlands, and weedy cover, the density can be as high as 100 deer per square mile.

In the eastern half of Nebraska **(No. 1)**, whitetails are by far the most abundant species. This region consists largely of irrigated farmlands, but numerous tributaries to the Missouri River provide cover in the form of woodlands and broken terrain. Thousands of miles of shelter belts consisting of hardwoods, shrubs, and red cedar have been planted in this region, and deer frequently use these for protection.

In the western half of the state **(No. 2)**, mule deer are more abundant, and whitetails are limited primarily to bottomlands along drainages. This half of the state has

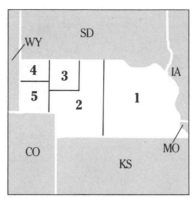

Zones created by author

some irrigated crops, but grazing lands are more widespread and drainages with good deer cover are less common than in the eastern half.

The Sand Hills region **(No. 3)** consists of grasslands covering topography that ranges from flat to rugged. Lakes and marshes provide some good cover for deer, and deer numbers are fairly high along the Niobrara River, but overall densities are low. Livestock grazing is the predominant agricultural activity in the Sand Hills.

The Pine Ridge region **(No. 4)** in the extreme northwest covers about 600 square miles, and about half of that consists of ponderosa pine forests where mule deer numbers are relatively high. Some ponderosa forests are found in the Wildcat Hills and Cheyenne Escarpment region south of Pine Ridge **(No. 5)**.

Ninety-seven percent of Nebraska is privately owned, but generally farmers will allow courteous hunters on their lands. Some landowners charge a modest trespass fee.

Seasons. Usually, the general firearms season runs for nine days beginning the second Saturday in November. All firearms permits are limited in number and are issued by drawing. Special late rifle and muzzleloader seasons also are available.

The bow season opens mid-September and closes the day preceding the rifle season. It then opens again

after the rifle season and continues through December. Bow licenses are not limited in number.

Records. The state record typical whitetail scored 196⅛, and nearly three dozen typical whitetails taken in Nebraska have been large enough to make the Boone and Crockett records. The record nontypical whitetail scored 279⅞. This buck, killed by Del Austin, ranks as the Pope and Young world record. Nebraska has produced more than two dozen other nontypical whitetails large enough to make Boone and Crockett. With its limited permit hunting, Nebraska has good trophy whitetail potential.

No typical mule deer have met the minimum Boone and Crockett score of 195. The largest nontypical mule deer scored 256⅞, but only one other nontypical mule deer has qualified for Boone and Crockett records.

The future. By the early 1980s, deer had reached all-time high numbers in Nebraska. However, each year 3 to 4 percent of the remaining woodlands in Nebraska are cleared for agriculture and other development, and as a result herds probably will decrease. In addition, increasing deer numbers have led to crop damage, and herds will be trimmed to reduce damage complaints.

Contact. Nebraska Game and Parks Commission, PO Box 30370, Lincoln, NE 68503.

Nebraska Game and Parks photo

NEVADA

Deer numbers. Nevada covers 110,000 square miles, and 35 to 40 percent of that range supports mule deer. The Department of Game estimates the preseason mule deer population at 130,000.

Hunters and harvest. Since 1975 hunter numbers have been restricted statewide. An annual average of 20,000 resident rifle, 1,250 resident archery, 2,000 nonresident rifle, and 250 nonresident archery tags have been issued since that time. The biggest harvest in recent years occurred in 1981 when hunters killed 13,595 bucks. The average annual harvest has been just over 11,000. Overall rifle-hunting success has averaged about 50 percent, but in many units hunter success runs to 60 or 70 percent with a high proportion of large deer taken. Bowhunter success runs about 25 percent.

Distribution. Virtually all good hunting in Nevada takes place on public lands owned either by the Bureau of Land Management (BLM) or the U.S. Forest Service. Nevada forms the heart of the Great Basin and presents classic basin-and-range country. Broad, sweeping valleys about 5,000 feet in elevation are interrupted by rugged, isolated mountain ranges, many of which rise to heights of 11,000 feet or more. Most mountain ranges higher than 6,000 feet elevation support deer herds, but the largest herds live in the major mountain chains.

Elko County **(No. 1)** in the northeast corner of the state consistently produces the most deer. The Jarbidge Mountains near the Idaho border and the Ruby Mountains just south of Elko support high deer numbers. Because both of these ranges contain large backcountry areas and rugged terrain, they offer good trophy potential.

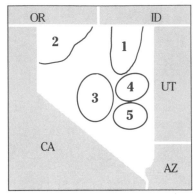

Zones created by author

In the northwest corner **(No. 2)**, the Santa Rosa, Pine Forest, and Bilk Creek ranges support thriving deer herds, and the Sheldon Antelope Range produces some huge bucks.

In central Nevada highest deer densities are found in the the Monitor, Toiyabe, and Shoshone ranges **(No. 3)**. Heavy deer populations are also found farther east in the White Pine and Schell Creek ranges **(No. 4)** near Ely. In some places the buck-doe ratio is as high as 40 bucks per 100 does, indicating excellent trophy potential.

Early in the season deer roam high, from 9,000 to 11,000 feet. So you must be in condition for high-elevation hunting to cope with conditions in Nevada. This high country consists of alpine basins, and open sage ridges broken by aspen parks, small forests of limber pine, and pockets of lush mountain shrubs.

With the first heavy snows, generally about mid-October, the deer descend to lower slopes covered with pinyon, juniper, mountain mahogany, and sagebrush. Deer live year-round at lower elevations where there is adequate water, even if it is in the form of stock tanks or small reservoirs. Some "marginal" country produces the biggest bucks. Lesser-known desert mountains in northern Lincoln and eastern Nye counties **(No. 5)** have produced some of Nevada's biggest bucks. Finding these bucks takes some scouting time, however.

Seasons. The general rifle season runs for about a month in October and November, and many rifle hunters go late in the season when snow has pushed the bigger bucks onto winter ranges where they're fairly accessible. Hunting tag numbers are limited for all seasons, and they're allotted through a drawing.

The general archery season opens in mid-August. This is an excellent time to hunt high because bucks with their velvet-covered antlers remain out in the open. The muzzleloader season (for residents only) follows in September.

Records. The state record typical mule deer scored 205⅜, and the record nontypical 299⅛. Nevada doesn't produce lots of Boone and Crockett bucks, but it offers perhaps a better opportunity to take a mature buck than any other state. The average buck-doe ratio for the entire state is about 25 bucks per 100 does, and in many areas it exceeds 35 per 100. This indicates a very high carry-over of bucks each year. In many units more than half the bucks taken are 4-points or larger, and bucks with 30-inch spreads are not uncommon.

The future. Despite Nevada's large land area, good deer habitat is limited; so hunting will be restricted as indicated on the map. As in all western states, herds fluctuate in response to winter weather conditions. However, under the limited-permit system, Nevada's deer herds have thrived and remained fairly stable. High-quality hunting has created a great deal of interest; so drawing a tag may be difficult. But if you do get one, your chances for taking a good buck are excellent. Outfitters work the major mountain ranges, but you can hunt this state on your own.

Contact. Department of Wildlife, PO Box 10678, Reno, NV 89520.

NEW HAMPSHIRE

Deer numbers. New Hampshire has a total area of about 9,000 square miles. An estimated 30,000 whitetail deer occupy about 90 percent of that area.

Hunters and harvest. An average of 80,000 residents and 6,000 nonresidents hunt with firearms each year. In the early 1980s, firearms hunters killed 3,000 to 4,500 deer annually (two-thirds bucks), but the highest annual harvest on record of 14,000 was recorded in 1968. Average firearms hunting success has been about 5 percent.

An average of 7,000 residents and 1,400 nonresidents hunt during New Hampshire's archery seasons. Average annual harvest has been about 125 deer (55 percent bucks), and hunting success has averaged less than 2 percent.

Distribution. The northern three counties of New Hampshire **(No. 1)** contain mountains with elevations of 1,500 to 2,000 feet. The primary vegetation here is spruce and fir. In the 1960s deer numbers were high here, but extensive cutting of balsam fir and red spruce, the primary lowland species required by deer for winter cover, has led to severe winterkill of deer. Aspen and other leafy plants that have taken the place of conifers provide unlimited forage, but lack of

Irene Vandermolen photo

Zones created by author

winter cover limits the potential for deer. Moose have become the predominant big-game species here. Large timber companies own most of this northern region, and they generally allow public access and hunting.

The White Mountain region **(No. 2)** contains very rugged mountains up to 6,000 feet elevation. The forests here consist primarily of northern hardwoods—beech, sugar maple, and birch. Logging has not been as extensive in this region as farther north. Higher elevations in these mountains support few deer, and most whitetails live below 2,500 feet elevation. The lowlands support fair numbers of deer, but they make up a small percentage of the total area. So the overall deer population per square mile is lower in the White Mountain region than anywhere else in the state.

From Lake Winnipesaukee south **(No. 3)** the primary forest species are white pine and red oak. A narrow band of mountains runs along the west side south to the Massachusetts border, but rolling hills predominate throughout this region. Deer densities in this region run from 6 to 10 per square mile, the best in New Hampshire. Highest deer numbers are found in the Connecticut and Merrimack river valleys. Dairy farming and growing of silage corn are the primary land uses in these valleys. This southern region is

undergoing some of the fastest human population growth and development in the East.

Forests cover nearly 85 percent of the state. Public access remains good throughout. Large blocks of national forest land cover the central part of the state, and timber companies generally allow hunting on their lands to the north. Lands in the south are broken into small, privately owned lots. But true to tradition in New England, hunters can trespass if the land is not posted, and fair amounts of land remain unposted.

Seasons. The firearms season traditionally has opened the first Wednesday in November and closed the first Sunday in December. The archery season opens in mid-September and lasts for about 95 days until mid-December. A muzzleloader season of about 10 days precedes the regular firearms season. The bag limit is one deer with bow, one with a firearm, and a maximum of two deer per hunter per season.

Records. The heaviest buck on record field-dressed to 265 pounds.

The future. Following several mild winters, deer numbers hit all-time highs in the 1960s. Since then several hard winters have periodically devastated deer herds. Clearcutting of large blocks of winter cover in the far north may prevent the recovery of herds there for some time, and rapid urban and industrial development in the south will reduce habitat.

Traditionally, hunters could kill deer of either sex in New Hampshire, but in 1983 the first bucks-only law was established. This has reduced the harvest of does. That change and several mild winters in the early 1980s have produced an upswing in deer numbers. Hunting should improve at least into the 1990s. However, herd size will continue to fluctuate in response to winter weather.

Contact. Fish and Game Department, 34 Bridge St., Concord, NH 03301.

NEW JERSEY

Deer numbers. New Jersey covers an area of 7,836 square miles. About 65 percent of that consists of undeveloped lands that support deer, and the estimated whitetail deer population is about 135,000 animals.

Hunters and harvest. Each year an average of 115,000 residents and 2,200 nonresidents hunt with firearms in New Jersey. Average annual harvest in the early 1980s was over 16,500 deer (10,500 of those were bucks). Average firearms hunting success has been 14 percent.

An average of 41,000 residents and 650 nonresidents hunt with bow and arrow each fall. Many of these also hunt during rifle seasons. Average archery harvest during the early 1980s was about 7,000 deer (3,000 bucks and 4,000 does), and average bowhunting success has been about 14 percent.

Distribution. The Outer Coastal Plain **(No. 1)** consists of poor, sandy soils and extensive pine forests. Pitch pine and scrub oak are most extensive, but these grade into pure oak forests in some places. Swamps and bottomlands comprise as much as 40 percent of the region. Deer densities range from 10 to 30 deer per square mile, which is only average for New Jersey. Average size of the deer is small. This region contains some extensive public hunting lands, and some of the private land remains unposted and open to hunting.

The Inner Coastal Plain **(No. 2)** has more fertile soil, and the average size of deer here is larger than in the pine country to the east. Deer that field-dress to 200 pounds aren't uncommon in this agricultural region. Corn, soybeans, and produce are the major crops raised here. The country is flat to hilly, and woody cover is relatively sparse. There are some hardwood forests and forested bottomlands. Overall this area has an average of fewer than 10 deer per square mile, but in the southern end, densities are as high as 30 to 40 per square mile. Virtually all land

Zones created by author

is private, and club leases are fairly common.

The hilly Piedmont **(No. 3)** is a fertile agricultural region that maintains the best hunting in New Jersey. Deer densities exceed 50 per square mile in many localities, and many large bucks are taken. About 50 percent of the land is forested, and the remainder has been cleared for hay production, vineyards, and other agriculture. Virtually all of the hunting takes place on private land, and it is tightly restricted.

The Highlands Region **(No. 4)** is hilly, heavily forested country with little agriculture except some dairy farms. Deer numbers are somewhat lower here than in the Piedmont, and public access to private lands is difficult.

The Ridge and Valley Region **(No. 5)** used to be major dairy country, but many farms have been abandoned to become overgrown with brush and forest. Deer numbers range from 10 per square mile to as high as 50, depending on the site. Public lands in the extreme northwest corner provide access to some good hunting.

Posting and leasing of hunting rights has been the rule on private lands in the northern and agricultural areas, and the trend has spread into southern New Jersey. About 80

percent of the deer harvest takes place on private land. However, a number of public hunting areas on state and federal lands and in city watersheds provide fairly extensive public access. Hunting pressure on public lands can vary from crowded during regular seasons to light during bow and muzzleloader seasons. New Jersey prints several guides to public hunting lands.

Seasons. Seasons vary from year to year and by management zone, but in general they follow this pattern: Fall bow season, all of October and into November; six-day firearm season, early December; shotgun permit season, one day in December; muzzleloader permit season, several days spread out in December; and winter bow season, about two weeks in January. In total, hunting a combination of all seasons, a hunter could take up to eight deer in one year.

Records. Overall, the average field-dressed weight of deer taken in New Jersey is 106 pounds. The heaviest buck on record field-dressed to 240 pounds (estimated 295 pounds live weight).

The state record typical whitetail measured 175⅝ points and the record nontypical, 214⅜.

The future. Habitat continues to shrink in New Jersey as human development expands. That's particularly true in the northeast in the Newark area, and around Camden in the southwest. Another major problem has been closure of land to hunting through local ordinances and establishment of parks. As a result, deer numbers rise to excessive levels, and then deer-vehicle collisions increase along with increasing crop damage. However, the long-term forecast, at least through the 1990s, is good. Deer numbers have grown to all-time highs in the 1980s, and excellent hunting is forecast.

Contact. Department of Environmental Protection, Division of Fish, Game and Wildlife, CN 400, Trenton, NJ 08625.

NEW MEXICO

Deer numbers. New Mexico has a land area of 121,666 square miles. Deer live on 63 percent of it. An estimated 260,000 mule deer live on 59 percent of the land; Texas whitetails on 5 percent; and Coues deer on 4 percent.

Hunters and harvest. About 90,000 resident and 10,000 nonresident firearms hunters, and 3,200 resident and over 350 nonresident archers hunt deer in New Mexico each year. The average yearly firearms harvest has been about 22,000 (20,000 bucks and 2,000 does). The highest year on record was 1970 when hunters killed 32,441 deer, which included 29,748 bucks. The average firearms hunting success has been 20 percent.

Bowhunters kill about 400 deer a year (240 bucks and 160 does), and their record high year was 1981 with a total of 735 deer. Average archery success has been 7 percent.

Distribution. Mule deer provide the bulk of hunting in New Mexico, and they live throughout the state except for large blocks of farmland and prairie in the northwest corner and along the eastern border. The north-central section **(No. 1)** has long held the reputation for growing huge mule deer. A number of record-book bucks have been taken near Chama, and during the 1960s the Jicarilla Apache Indian Reservation produced many huge mule deer. During the late 1960s, the deer population here dropped off sharply and has not recovered to former levels.

This country ranges in elevation from 9,000 to 14,000 feet, and it contains a mixture of expansive conifer forests, aspens, and alpine terrain. The Carson and Santa Fe National Forests provide extensive public hunting, but much of the best deer country lies on huge ranches that are not open to the general public.

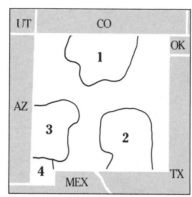

Zones created by author

Because of limited access and relatively light hunting pressure, this region has some large bucks and still holds the opportunity for a record-book mule deer.

The southeast corner **(No. 2)** is considered New Mexico's "deer factory." The Guadalupe and Sacramento mountains and other ranges in this section of the state produce 56 percent of the total deer kill in New Mexico. The average elevation of these mountains is 7,000 to 8,000 feet, and they contain oak and mountain mahogany cover, with some ponderosa pine and aspen at the highest elevations. Large blocks of public land assure good access. This region produces an occasional large buck, but it's managed primarily for a large number of deer, so the buck-doe ratio is low.

Texas whitetails also live in the Sacramento Mountains, the Mescalero Sands **(No. 2)**, and other isolated pockets, but they are not numerous. Only a handful are killed each year, incidental to mule deer hunting.

The Gila National Forest **(No. 3)** in the southwest grows some good-size desert mule deer. This national forest also has Coues whitetails. Coues deer also thrive in the Peloncillo and Animas mountains **(No. 4)** in the extreme southwest tip of the state. Coues deer seem to be spreading here, and some record-class bucks have been taken in recent years.

Seasons. For several years New Mexico utilized a stratified system with two or three separate seasons in each area. The north half of the state had three seasons in November, beginning with a two-day season, followed by a five-day season, and concluding with a seven-day season. Hunters had to choose one of those three seasons. However, with increasing demand for better hunting, New Mexico has considered limiting the number of permits for the entire state. Tags would be issued by drawing.

Records. In the past New Mexico has produced many record-class mule deer. The state record typical mule deer scored 212, and the record nontypical 306⅝. The majority of Boone and Crockett record-book mule deer have come from the Chama area **(No. 1)** near the Colorado border.

The state record typical Coues deer scored 119. No record-book nontypical Coues deer have been recorded from New Mexico.

The future. Like many other western states, New Mexico's deer population declined during the late 1960s. From 1970 to 1980, deer numbers and harvest remained stable at fairly low levels. Since then deer herds and harvest have improved gradually. Most of the best deer country lies either on public land or on huge ranches so that the land base for good deer herds seems relatively stable.

A major problem facing deer in New Mexico has been hunting pressure. To fine tune its regulations for optimum deer hunting, the Department of Game and Fish has developed a computer model to predict the effects of various factors on deer. Biologists believe this will help them better manage deer herds to provide a higher success rate. They predict excellent deer hunting in the future.

Contact. New Mexico Department of Game and Fish, State Capitol, Villagra Building, Santa Fe, NM 87503.

NEW YORK

Deer numbers. New York has an area of 47,377 square miles, and an estimated 600,000 whitetail deer occupy about 95 percent of that area.

Hunters and harvest. Each year an average of 755,000 residents and 25,000 nonresidents hunt with firearms for deer. Average firearms harvest for the early 1980s was about 150,000 deer (75,000 bucks). Average firearms hunting success has been about 10 percent.

An average of 105,000 archers hunt deer each year. During the early 1980s, archers harvested an average of 4,700 deer (about 50/50 bucks and does). Average bowhunter success has been about 5 percent.

Distribution. The Adirondack Region **(No. 1)** consists of extensive northern hardwood—maple, birch, beech—and spruce-fir forests. In the central Adirondacks, the lowland spruce-fir "yards" are especially important for winter cover. However, these areas don't offer an abundance of good feed. So the region's productivity is comparatively low. In the eastern Adirondack foothills, oak-hickory forests on south slopes are more prominent. Deer generally winter better there, and as a result deer populations remain a little higher. Overall the Adirondacks support about 15 deer per square mile, the lowest density in New York. This region consists of high mountains up to 5,300 feet near Lake Placid, and extensive backcountry where a hunter can find solitude.

Statewide, New York offers 4½ million acres of public land open to hunting, and 2½ million of those acres lie in the Adirondacks. Paper companies own vast amounts of land throughout this region, and private hunting clubs have leased hunting rights to much of this land.

The Great Lakes Plain **(No. 2)** has fertile soils and supports extensive agriculture, including fruit orchards, dairy, and truck farms. Only about 20 percent of the area has wooded cover, and much of this is in hardwood swamplands. Some woodlots of maple, beech, hickory, and other

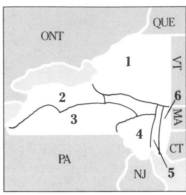

Zones created by author

hardwoods remain. Hunting regulations are fairly liberal here to hold deer numbers down and to reduce farm depredation. With its rich soils, this region produces some heavy deer and fairly good antler growth. Virtually all of the land is private, and about 50 percent of it is posted, although it is possible to obtain permission to hunt in many cases.

The Appalachian Plateau **(No. 3)** supports the overall highest deer densities in the state, but heavy hunting pressure results in a fast turnover of deer, and most bucks killed are yearlings. Average size is smaller than in the Great Lakes Plain, except in the Finger Lakes region where fertile soils produce some big bucks. This region had wall-to-wall farms in the 1800s, but since then many farms have been abandoned, and now vegetation consists of mixed hardwood forests and brush. The terrain ranges from broadly rolling to hilly with steep valleys. Some of the valleys and flat plateaus support dairies and truck farms. Vineyards are common around the Finger Lakes. Some state parks offer public hunting, and access to private lands is fairly good.

The Catskill Mountains **(No. 4)** contain peaks up to 4,000 feet. In these steep, heavily forested mountains, hunting pressure is much lighter than farther west; so the percentage of older bucks is much higher, and the chances of taking a wall-hanger are better. One-quarter million acres of state land assure

good public access in the Catskills.

The Hudson River Valley **(No. 5)** contains agricultural land mixed with residential areas. Deer numbers are fair.

The Taconic Highlands **(No. 6)** supports a good mix of openings, brushlands, and forest. Deer numbers are fairly high, although few large bucks are taken. Nearly all land near New York City is posted, but hunting opportunity is greater farther north.

Seasons. In the northern zone, archery season runs from late September through most of October; regular firearms season opens in late October and in early December. A special muzzleloader season also is held.

In the southern half of the state, the regular firearms season opens in mid- to late November and closes in early December. The archery season opens in mid-October. It closes just before the regular season and then opens for five days following the firearms season.

Records. Average weights vary greatly by region. The largest buck on record killed in New York field-dressed to 388 pounds and weighed an estimated 494 pounds on the hoof. The state record typical whitetail measured 198⅜ points, and the record nontypical 244⅔. Boone and Crockett lists several bucks from New York.

The future. In the northern zone, deer numbers ebb and flow in response to winter conditions. In general, overall deer numbers will remain fairly low and public hunting opportunity will remain extensive.

In the southern half of the state, populations are on the downswing after hitting record highs. Permits for antlerless deer have been increased to reduce deer damage complaints and prevent overbrowsing. Deer hunting prospects are good.

Contact. Department of Environmental Conservation, 50 Wolf Road, Albany, NY 12233–0001.

NORTH CAROLINA

Deer numbers. North Carolina covers an area of 49,317 square miles. An estimated 400,000 whitetails occupy over 60 percent of the land.

Harvest and hunters. Each year residents buy an average of 260,000 deer firearms licenses and 60,000 bowhunting licenses. In one recent high year the annual harvest was 47,855 deer (36,566 bucks and 11,289 does). That same year the archery harvest was 2,543 deer (1,298 bucks and 1,245 does). No official success statistics are available. Dividing the number of deer taken by the number of licenses sold, the firearms success rate appears to be about 18 percent, and archery success about 4 percent.

Distribution. North Carolina can be divided into three broad ecological regions. The flat Coastal Plain **(No. 1)** supports extensive agriculture. The lower Coastal Plain has large acreages of pine flatwoods, with hardwoods along some ridges and along major river drainages. Farther inland on the upper Coastal Plain, large fields of corn, soybeans, peanuts, cotton, and tobacco dominate the landscape. These fields are interspersed with hardwoods, primarily in the drainage bottomlands. Deer densities vary greatly in the Coastal Plain from extremely high to moderately low. Some places with the highest numbers have poor habitat. So deer quality in terms of body weight and antler size is poor in some localities.

The Piedmont Region **(No. 2)** consists of rolling hills. Many of the crop fields are smaller than on the Coastal Plain, and there are small pasturelands and dairy farms. The region has a number of small commercial pine plantations. Hardwood cover grows along the ridges and bottomlands. The northern Piedmont supports high densities of deer. In the central and southern portions, deer herds are below carrying capacity and are expanding. These areas produce some of North Carolina's heaviest deer and largest antlers.

The Mountain Region **(No. 3)** is

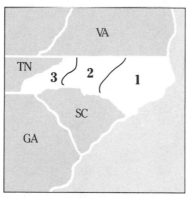

Zones created by author

heavily forested. Hardwoods predominate, but some commercial pine plantations, pastureland, and small-grain croplands are found in the foothills on the eastern side of this region. Spruce, fir, and other conifers grow at the highest elevations. North Carolina's Blue Ridge Mountains, which essentially form the southern end of the Appalachians, contain some of the highest and most rugged country in the East. Mount Mitchell northeast of Asheville, with an elevation of 6,684 feet, is the highest point east of the Mississippi. Deer numbers are fairly high in localized areas in the mountains. Overall this region is not as productive as the Piedmont, and deer numbers are relatively low.

The Wildlife Resources Commission manages for public hunting nearly 2 million acres of land, including national forest, timber company, military, and other lands. Competition among hunters is heavy in some public areas, but in certain mountain areas, access is poor and hunting pressure is relatively light. Overall, as in most other southern states, private land is tied up. Much of the better deer lands, particularly in the Piedmont and Coastal Plain regions, are leased to private hunting clubs.

Seasons. Seasons vary by region within the state. In general the bow season opens in early September and runs into October or November. That is followed by a muzzleloader season about one week long, and then comes the general gun season. The gun season varies from two weeks to 2½ months long, depending on the region.

In most cases the bag limit is two bucks per day, two in possession, four per season. Special antlerless and either-sex hunts also are held. Hunting with dogs is allowed during gun seasons. State law prohibits hunting on Sunday.

Records. The overall average live weight of deer in North Carolina is 120 pounds. The Wildlife Resources Commission keeps no records on antler sizes. And Boone and Crockett records don't list any deer from North Carolina.

The future. As in most southern states, North Carolina's deer became scarce in the late 1800s as a result of extensive land clearing and unregulated hunting. In the early 1900s, many small farmers migrated to the cities, and cotton fields reverted to timberland. Increased cover for deer, coupled with deer stocking programs and tightened game laws, led to a dramatic comeback of deer herds. Now deer occupy most of the suitable habitat and have reached carrying capacity in many areas, although numbers are still increasing slightly in the southern Piedmont and foothill counties. The near future of deer hunting in North Carolina looks good, although expanding human population and development continue to displace habitat and increase competition among hunters.

Contact. Wildlife Resources Commission, Archdale Building, 512 N. Salisbury St., Raleigh, NC 27611.

NORTH DAKOTA

Deer numbers. North Dakota covers 70,665 square miles. An estimated 135,000 whitetails occupy about 50 percent of the land, and 35,000 mule deer are found in 25 percent of the state.

Hunters and harvest. About 50,000 residents and 300 nonresidents hunt with firearms in North Dakota each year. Over a recent 10-year period, hunters each year killed an average of over 27,000 whitetails (about 16,000 bucks and 11,000 does) and 3,200 mule deer (2,000 bucks and 1,200 does). In 1983 they killed a record 36,009 whitetails and 4,238 mule deer. Overall success has averaged 60 percent with a high of 71 percent and a low of 35 percent.

About 8,000 resident and 200 nonresident archers hunt deer each year. The average harvest has been 1,050 whitetails (450 bucks and 600 does) and 200 mule deer (105 bucks and 95 does). In 1983, archers killed a record 1,135 whitetails and 200 mule deer. Average bowhunter success has been 14 percent and ranges from 8 percent to 17 percent.

Distribution. The Red River Valley **(No. 1)** along the eastern edge is intensively farmed. Some whitetails live throughout the farmland, but most live in wooded riverbottoms. Overall densities are not high. The Pembina Hills in the northeast corner are covered with oak, aspen, chokecherry, ash, and other trees. This is the closest North Dakota comes to having forests, and whitetail numbers are relatively high here. The Devil's Lake area, a small unit just west of the Red River Valley, is similar to the Pembina Hills.

The Sheyenne and James rivers region **(No. 2)** in the southeast supports high numbers of whitetails. Agriculture is extensive. Sunflowers are a major crop and whitetails have taken to the sunflower "forests." Large blocks of native prairie with patches of aspen, buck brush, and wild rose support good numbers of deer, and the stream bottoms with woody cover serve as the core for major deer herds.

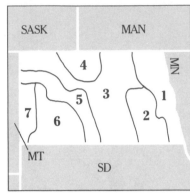

Zones created by author

The Coteau Hills **(No. 3)** takes in most of central North Dakota east of the Missouri River and north to the Canadian border. This region contains large grain fields mixed with prairies and marshes. Few major drainages provide bottomland cover here; so many of the deer live near sloughs and marshes that dot the region. Densities aren't high, but the Coteau Hills produces some good-size whitetail bucks.

The Souris (Mouse) River drainage **(No. 4)** in north-central North Dakota contains large waterfowl refuges. This is primarily an agricultural area, and most deer live in the cattails and other thick cover around marshes.

The Missouri River serves as a deer management unit in itself **(No. 5)**. At one time whitetail densities were as high here as anywhere in the United States with 25 to 30 deer per square mile. Huge reservoirs have flooded the best habitat, but many whitetails still live in the woody cover of adjacent bottomlands. A fair number of mule deer live in breaks west of the river.

The Slope Unit **(No. 6)** includes all drainages that flow into the Missouri River from the west. This area has extensive strip farming, and most deer live in the natural cover along river and creek bottoms, although they're scattered throughout most farmlands. A third of the deer here are mule deer, and two-thirds are whitetails.

The Badlands **(No. 7)** take in the southwest corner from the Missouri River to South Dakota. This is extremely broken, ragged, eroded country with pockets of pine and juniper. Hardwoods occur along the riverbottoms. Mule deer predominate in the Badlands, although whitetails thrive along the Little Missouri River and other creek bottoms.

The Badlands and Missouri River breaks contain fair amounts of public land, and some blocks of state land provide public hunting throughout the state. Otherwise, all of North Dakota is private. However, many landowners will give permission to hunt.

Seasons. Gun-season permits are limited in number throughout the state. No more than 1 percent of the gun licenses are issued to nonresidents. Generally two gun seasons are held, one in early November, the other in mid-November.

The bow season runs from early September until early November. It reopens in late November and remains open through December. The number of bow permits is not limited.

Records. The state record typical whitetail antlers scored 187⅝ points, and the record nontypical scored 248⅝. The Boone and Crockett Club lists several other North Dakota whitetails, but few have been taken in recent years. Few mule deer in North Dakota reach record-book size.

The future. Following several mild winters, deer herds reached all-time highs in the early 1980s. Conflicts between deer and landowners have become a problem. Oil exploration and coal mining have altered habitats in the western half of the state, and this will undoubtedly reduce deer numbers. Also, farmland is replacing native prairie country, a trend that adversely affects deer herds.

Contact. North Dakota Game and Fish Department, 2121 Lovett Ave., Bismark, ND 58505.

OHIO

Deer numbers. Ohio covers a total area of 40,982 square miles, and deer are found in varying densities throughout the state. The whitetail population is estimated at 120,000 animals.

Hunters and harvest. Ohio attracts an average of 224,000 resident and 2,600 nonresident gun hunters each fall. Since 1980, they've harvested an average of 40,000 deer (23,000 bucks and 17,000 does). In 1983, the highest year on record, they killed over 59,000 deer (31,000 of those were bucks). Average hunting success has been about 7 percent, with a high in 1981 of 21 percent and a low in 1965 of 3 percent. (These figures include bowhunting so that the gunhunting success rate is actually higher than the combined rate).

An average of 91,000 resident and 1,000 nonresident archers hunt deer in Ohio each year. They've taken an average in recent years of 3,800 deer (about 2,800 bucks and 1,000 does), and in 1982, the highest year on record, archers took over 4,200 deer (3,000 of those were bucks).

Distribution. The northwest quarter of Ohio **(No. 1)** contains the fewest deer. This region consists primarily of corn and soybean fields and other croplands. Cover for deer is limited to that along a few scattered stream bottoms. The estimated density is about two deer per square mile. Some wooded hills in the extreme northwestern corner have higher densities, but these are heavily hunted.

The southwest corner **(No. 2)** consists of rolling hills covered with mixed agricultural lands and forest. Some fairly large woodlands of beech and maple are found in the southern part of this region. But farther north good deer cover consists primarily of small woodlots and bottomland cover—cottonwoods, elm, maple—along tributaries that feed into the Ohio River. Deer numbers are considered low to medium in this region.

The extreme northeast corner **(No. 3)** contains rolling hills with fairly large blocks of woods. Some of this

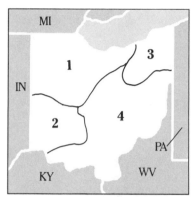

Zones created by author

country has medium-to-high deer densities, but Cleveland, Youngstown, and other spreading cities reduce the quality of hunting here.

The southeast third of the state **(No. 4)** contains the best all-around deer country. An estimated 80 percent of the deer in Ohio range over this section, and densities are as high as 10 to 15 deer per square mile. The poor soils here aren't ideal for raising crops, and many farms active in the 1940s have been abandoned. The weeds and shrubs overgrowing these old farms provide good deer habitat. The rolling hills found throughout this region support extensive forests of oak, hickory, ash, and other hardwoods that assure deer of good feed and cover.

The Wayne National Forest and several smaller state forests provide public access and fairly good hunting in the southeast corner of Ohio. However, the state is 97 percent private land. The idea of hunting clubs and private leases has not become widespread in Ohio. In many cases you can obtain permission to hunt by asking landowners.

Ohio has produced some huge bucks, and many of these have come from the north-central and east-central portions of the state. There a mix of corn and other crops interspersed with woodlots provide deer with ample feed and escape cover. Although the southeast corner has the most deer, bucks generally are smaller there.

Seasons. Firearms hunting is restricted to shotguns and muzzleloaders. No high-power rifles are allowed.

The gun season usually runs about six days in late November and early December. In most areas the limit is one buck, although some antlerless permits are issued too.

The bow season usually runs from early October through the end of January, except that it's closed during gun season. The limit is one deer of either sex.

Some special primitive-weapons hunts are also held in restricted areas.

Records. In some regions Ohio grows very large deer. Average field-dressed weight for all bucks is nearly 130 pounds, and 2½-year-old bucks average 165 to 185 pounds field-dressed. The state record weight is close to 350 pounds field-dressed.

The state record typical whitetail antlers scored 187⅝ points (Boone and Crockett), and the record non-typical scored 342⅜, which exceeds the standing world record. Boone and Crockett lists many typical and nontypical whitetails from Ohio, and a significant number of those have been taken in recent years. Ohio ranks among the top states for a potential trophy buck.

The future. Deer numbers and harvest have increased steadily from a harvest of 406 deer in 1965 to 59,812 in 1983. Biologically, Ohio could support even more deer, but conflicts between deer and landowners have called for a reduction in numbers. In the southeast where densities are highest, the number of deer may be reduced by as much as 50 percent. In other regions, herds will be allowed to expand. For the state as a whole, deer numbers will be stabilized at current levels or slightly below. Ohio's deer herds should continue to produce trophy bucks.

Contact. Department of Natural Resources, Division of Wildlife, Fountain Square, Columbus, OH 43224.

OKLAHOMA

Deer numbers. Oklahoma has a total land area of 69,919 square miles. A population of 100,000 to 150,000 whitetails range over that entire area. A small mule deer herd numbering just 500 to 1,000 occupies 13 percent of the land.

Hunters and harvest. Oklahoma attracts an average of 140,000 resident and 600 nonresident hunters using firearms. The average deer harvest in recent years has been about 13,700 (11,000 bucks and 2,700 does). In 1983, one of the best years, hunters using firearms killed 18,308 deer (15,155 of those were bucks). Average hunting success has been 9 percent.

Archery hunters number about 35,000. Only about 100 of those are nonresidents. The average harvest by bowhunters in recent years has been about 2,100 (1,200 bucks and 900 does). Average bowhunting success has been 3.5 percent.

The average age of buck deer harvested is 1½ to 2½ years old. Statewide, 69 percent of all the bucks harvested are yearlings.

Distribution. Whitetails live in all 77 of Oklahoma's counties, and mule deer live only in scattered herds in the northwestern and panhandle counties.

The northeast corner **(No. 1)** consists of mountainous terrain covered with oak-hickory forests, locally called Missouri Ozarks. Whitetail numbers are fairly high here despite hunting pressure. The southeast corner **(No. 2)** consists of oak-hickory forestland interspersed with pines. This country, too, is mountainous. Traditionally, hunting has been excellent here, but timber companies are replacing hardwood stands with pine plantations, and the overall quality of deer herds is declining. The region is heavily hunted, but the steep terrain and forest cover make hunting fairly tough.

Native tall-grass prairie covers several counties—Kay, Osage, Washington—in the north-central section **(No. 3)**. This is open country, and about the only deer habitat is found

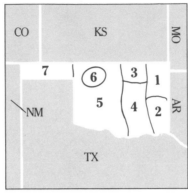

Zones created by author

along major drainages and around reservoirs. Good numbers of whitetails live in pockets that provide cover.

Most of central Oklahoma **(No. 4)** fits the ecological category called Cross Timbers, which consists of open prairie interspersed with post and blackjack oak woodlands. In the northern part of this region herds are growing and healthy, and densities are fairly high. In south-central Oklahoma, the herds have reached carrying capacity and may be decreasing.

Interstate Highway 35 forms a rough western boundary of the Cross Timbers zone, and from there west the country becomes primarily open, short-grass prairies **(No. 5)**. Woody cover here is restricted primarily to stream and river bottomlands, and this is where most of the deer are found. Whitetail herds are growing throughout western Oklahoma, and the deer are in good condition. Some of the biggest bucks each year come from Woods, Woodward, and Ellis **(No. 6)** counties in the northwest. The Panhandle **(No. 7)** contains open sand hills covered with prairie grasses and sage. The area produces a few mule deer along with whitetails that live along the creek bottoms.

Seasons. The general gun season usually runs from mid to late November. The bag limit is one antlered deer, although special bonus antlerless tags are offered in some units. The archery season normally is open for the entire month of October and again for all of December. The bag limit is two deer (one must be a buck). A special muzzleloader season is held in early November with a bag limit of one buck.

Records. The average weight of a field-dressed whitetail is 108 pounds; of a mule deer, 135 pounds. The heaviest mule deer on record is 237 pounds field-dressed.

The Oklahoma record typical whitetail antlers scored 174⅝, and the record nontypical scored 230⅞. The Oklahoma record nontypical mule deer scored 248⅛. Because of a high turnover of deer and overall young age, Oklahoma is not the place to look for Boone and Crockett bucks.

The future. In the early 1900s market hunting wiped out deer in Oklahoma. In 1916 the estimated whitetail population was 500, and deer hunting was outlawed. In 1933 the state held its first bucks-only season and 4,000 hunters killed 235 deer in the seven open counties. Deer numbers remained fairly static until the 1950s. In 1953 only 8 counties were open to deer hunting, but then in 1954, all 77 counties held deer seasons. Hunting has generally been statewide since, and the harvest has steadily increased. Hunting will probably level off. In traditional deer areas in the east, herds have stabilized or decreased as hardwood forests are being cut and replaced by pine, and as native prairie is tilled for crops. The central and western parts of the state have shown a steady increase in deer numbers and harvest. Drought conditions can temporarily reduce deer numbers.

Contact. Oklahoma Department of Wildlife Conservation, PO Box 53465, Oklahoma City, OK 73152.

OREGON

Deer numbers. About 80 percent of Oregon's 97,000 square miles supports deer. Whitetails occupy about 3 percent of the state, blacktails 28 percent, and mule deer 55 percent. The average populations are about 4–5,000 whitetails, 460,000 blacktails, and 250,000 mule deer for a total of over 700,000 adult deer.

Hunters and harvest. In recent years Oregon has annually sold about 300,000 resident rifle deer tags, 4,000 nonresident rifle tags, 20,000 resident archery tags, and 800 nonresident archery tags. The average harvest since 1960 has been about 80,000. Hunter success has averaged about 28 percent. Bowhunters take about 3,000 deer each year (75 percent bucks), and the average archery success rate is 15 percent.

Distribution. Oregon is divided into distinct segments—western and eastern—by the Cascade Range, which runs north and south from Washington to California. Western Oregon has fairly low but very steep-sided mountains. Rainstorms constantly come off the Pacific Ocean during winter and produce lush forests with dense, jungle-like undergrowth. This is the home of the blacktail deer. The McKenzie and Santiam units **(No. 1)** contain remote country at higher elevations along the Cascade crest, as well as private-land sanctuaries along the Willamette Valley. These areas maintain good populations of mature trophy bucks. Jackson County **(No. 2)** in southern Oregon also produces many deer and good-size blacktails.

Because of the mild climate, abundant feed, and dense cover in western Oregon, blacktail numbers remain high. Buck-doe ratios are often higher than 25 bucks per 100 does. Seasons are generous.

Most land adjacent to valley floors in western Oregon is private, but you can get permission to hunt in many places. In the foothills and higher into the Coast Range and Cascade Mountains, the Forest Service, Bureau of Land Management, and large timber companies own much of the land. Land access is good.

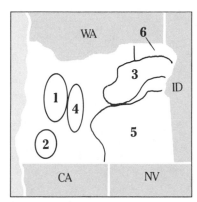

Zones created by author

Eastern Oregon lies in the rain shadow of the Cascade Range; so the eastern two-thirds of the state is dry with an average rainfall of less than 15 inches. The Blue and Wallowa Mountains **(No. 3)** are major ranges in eastern Oregon. Good numbers of mule deer live throughout the forests and alpine terrain.

Units throughout the central Cascades **(No. 4)** contain large blocks of backcountry and buck-doe ratios are higher than average here. This country is heavily timbered and can be difficult to hunt, but chances for taking a large buck are good.

The greater part of eastern Oregon **(No. 5)** comprises sagebrush desert and grasslands. Mule deer live throughout the desert at elevations of 6,000 feet and higher. The terrain here consists of rimrocks, plateaus, and deep canyons. It is wide-open sagebrush country with scattered pockets of aspen, mountain mahogany, and juniper. The region is heavily hunted because many hunters prefer the open vistas of mule deer country to the enclosed haunts of the blacktail. Permit numbers are limited on several desert units, such as Steens Mountain and Trout Creek Mountains, and trophy-hunting potential in these areas is good.

Deer herds fluctuate drastically with weather extremes in eastern Oregon; so season lengths vary greatly. Most of the best mule-deer hunting takes place on lands owned by the

Forest Service or Bureau of Land Management.

Whitetails occupy only about 3 percent of the land area in Oregon, and hunted populations are restricted to the extreme northeastern corner **(No. 6)** of the state in Wallowa, Union, and Umatilla counties. Whitetails aren't numerous, but some large bucks are taken. The Columbian whitetail also lives along the Columbia River between Portland and Astoria, and in the Umpqua Valley near Roseburg. Columbian whitetails are listed as endangered though and are not hunted.

Seasons. General firearms seasons for blacktail in western Oregon normally run for a month or longer in October and early November. In contrast, mule deer seasons on the east side of the Cascades fluctuate drastically in response to deer numbers. They range from five days up to three weeks.

The statewide early archery season provides several weeks of hunting in August and September. Late November seasons on the west side in several units provide good hunting for blacktails during the rut. Oregon has special muzzleloader seasons too.

Records. The state record typical mule deer antlers scored 209⅛, and the top nontypical scored 291⅛. However, very few other mule deer from Oregon are listed by the Boone and Crockett Club.

Blacktails are another matter. The state-record and former world-record buck scored 172⅜. The top five blacktails in the Boone and Crockett records came from Oregon.

The future. Blacktail herds have remained stable or increased recently, and their future looks secure for now. In eastern Oregon land development continues to eat away at critical winter range, and many mule deer herds are declining. Mule deer herds fluctuate drastically in response to weather conditions.

Contact. Oregon Department of Fish and Wildlife, PO Box 3503, Portland, OR 97208.

PENNSYLVANIA

Deer numbers. Pennsylvania contains 45,333 square miles and supports a whitetail deer population estimated at 750,000.

Hunters and harvest. Hunters buy an average of 950,000 firearms deer licenses each year. About 10 percent of those are bought by nonresidents. The average annual firearms harvest has been about 140,000 deer (50/50, bucks and does). Overall firearms success has been about 10 percent, and success for bucks only has been about 5 percent.

Pennsylvania also sells about 300,000 archery deer licenses each year. The bow harvest has averaged about 5,000 deer each year and average bowhunting success has been about 4 percent.

Pennsylvania holds a special muzzleloader season, and license sales have varied in recent years from 85,000 to 125,000 annually. During the brief season, muzzleloaders have averaged 2,900 deer, and the success rate has been 6 to 7 percent.

Distribution. The Northern Region **(No. 1)** takes in roughly all the land north of Interstate 80 and west of Scranton. This region is 60 percent forested with intermixed pastureland and strip mines. The older hardwood forests here do not produce a lot of productive deer forage, and deer numbers are lower in this northern tier than anywhere else in the state. Average deer densities are about 18 deer per square mile. However, this is a popular hunting region because it offers vast amounts of public hunting in state and national forests. Deer camps have been a popular tradition in this region. At one time, hunters could lease campsites in state forests. This program has been discontinued, although existing leases are allowed to continue until members of the original party have died. Most private lands in this region also are leased by clubs.

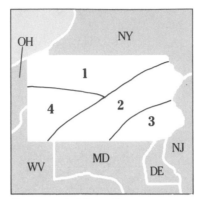

Zones created by author

The Ridge and Valley Region **(No. 2)** consists of relatively steep ridges forested with mixed oaks, and these ridges are separated by parallel valleys. The more fertile valleys are farmed or planted in fruit orchards, such as apple and peach. The less fertile valleys contain dairy farms. Deer numbers are somewhat higher in this region than in the northern forests. Land ownership is more broken up here so that club leases aren't as common. It's possible to get permission to hunt in some areas. Fair amounts of state forest, which provide public hunting, are found in this region.

The Southeast Region **(No. 3)** lies within the Coastal Plain physiographic zone. This relatively flat country is intensively farmed, with corn, oats, wheat, and soybeans as the major crops. Small woodlots are scattered throughout the croplands. This is the richest area for wildlife in Pennsylvania, and deer number as high as 40 per square mile here. Permission to use private land is difficult to obtain though.

The Southwest Region **(No. 4)** is wooded, and deer numbers are relatively high and growing. Houses have been built on small acreages throughout the region, and permission to hunt private land is difficult to obtain.

Overall, Pennsylvania contains about 4½ million acres of public land open to the general public for hunting. These lands are heavily hunted.

Seasons. The archery season traditionally has run from the first Saturday in October to the last Saturday in October, and then is open again for a few days after Christmas. The general firearms, bucks-only season usually runs for two weeks starting the Monday following Thanksgiving. This is followed by a two-day antlerless hunt. The four-day muzzleloader season is held in late December. The bag limit has usually been one deer per hunter per license year regardless of which seasons he hunts.

Records. Overall average weight of bucks killed in Pennyslvania is about 105 pounds.

The largest typical whitetail antlers from Pennsylvania listed in Boone and Crockett records measured 184⅝, and the largest nontypical, 207⅞. The record book lists over a dozen deer from this state. Measured against the high annual harvest, the percentage of trophy deer from Pennsylvania is very small.

The future. By the late 1800s, there were virtually no deer left in Pennyslvania, but 1900–1935 was a major timber-cutting period and deer populations exploded. Herds probably reached an all-time high of more than 1 million animals in the late 1930s. Since that time the population has stabilized at about 750,000 animals. The highest harvests on record have taken place during the 1970s and 1980s.

Urban growth is consuming deer range, but biologists believe that total deer numbers will remain high at least through the 1980s. A major concern has become access. Even though the deer are abundant, continued posting and leasing of lands has closed a high percentage of private land to the hunting public.

Contact. Game Commission, PO Box 1567, Harrisburg, PA 17120.

RHODE ISLAND

Deer numbers. Rhode Island has an area of 1,214 square miles. Roughly 30 percent of that supports an estimated population of 2,400 whitetail deer.

Hunters and harvest. In recent years, an annual average of 3,600 residents and 40 nonresidents have hunted with firearms in Rhode Island. The average firearms harvest has been about 120 deer (about 50/50, bucks and does) with a high in 1981 of 155 deer (77 bucks and 78 does).

The average number of archery hunters has been 1,100 residents and 90 nonresidents. Bowhunters have killed about 100 deer annually with a high in 1982 of 104 (about 50/50, bucks and does).

Distribution. Nearly 80 percent of the state is forested, but the percentage is decreasing with firewood cutting and development for housing. Rhode Island supports some farming, particularly in the south where potatoes and turf grass are major crops. Oak forests and some beech cover most of the state. In scattered wet lowlands, maple predominates. Basically, the topography is flat. Overall deer densities average from 10 to 20 per square mile, but on Prudence Island deer numbers are as high as 70 per square mile.

In a state only 30 miles wide and 50 long, with a human population of 1 million people, human population density necessarily limits hunting op-

Zones created by author

portunity. But Rhode Island does offer 38,000 acres of public hunting on state-owned lands. The Division of Fish and Wildlife plans to buy more lands to increase that acreage. Little private land in Rhode Island is leased for hunting, but law requires written permission from the owner. So hunters have to work at access to private lands.

Seasons. The archery season is usually open four months, from early October through January. The limit is one deer of either sex. The shotgun season has generally been open for nine days in mid-December with a limit of one deer. Hunting with

muzzleloaders was allowed for the first time in 1984. The season was split, half in November, half in late December. The limit was one deer.

In Rhode Island, a person can take one deer by each method—shotgun, archery, muzzleloader—totaling a yearly bag limit of three animals.

Records. Average field-dressed weight of yearling bucks is 126 pounds and of adult bucks, 158 pounds. No records on antler size have been kept.

The future. With ongoing development for housing, the total land base will continue to shrink. However, a surge in firewood cutting in recent years has opened up forests. This has improved browse for deer, and herds have remained stable or increased. This trend may continue, and biologists predict herds and hunting will remain stable into the 1980s.

Contact. Department of Environmental Management, 83 Park St., Providence, RI 02903.

Leonard Lee Rue III photo

SOUTH CAROLINA

Deer numbers. South Carolina has an area of 31,055 square miles. An estimated 300,000 whitetail deer occupy roughly 60 percent of that area.

Hunters and harvest. The recent average number of hunters has been 125,000 residents and 25,000 nonresidents. South Carolina doesn't record the firearms/bowhunter breakout. In 1983 hunters killed a high of 57,927 deer (41,732 were bucks).

Distribution. South Carolina covers three major physiographic regions. The Coastal Plain **(No. 1)** covers the eastern two-thirds of the state. With the exception of the 250,000-acre Francis Marion National Forest and scattered small state hunting areas, this entire region consists of private land. It's split about 50/50 between croplands and forest. Major farm crops are corn and soybeans, and much of the forestland consists of small commercial plots of loblolly pine. Bottomlands scattered throughout this region support stands of oak and other hardwoods. The Coastal Plain maintains the highest deer densities in South Carolina, but the average size of deer here is smaller than in other regions. Here a high percentage of private lands are leased by private hunting clubs. Hunting with dogs is allowed.

The Piedmont Region **(No. 2)** supports nearly as many deer per square mile as the Coastal Plain, but the deer have a heavier average weight and grow larger antlers, especially in the Western Piedmont. Intensively managed pine forests and hardwoods, primarily oak and hickory, cover most of the Piedmont's rolling topography, although some croplands are scattered throughout the region. The Piedmont offers good public hunting on 990,800 acres of public lands. Competition among hunters, particularly during rifle seasons, can be heavy. No special permits are required to hunt public lands. Hunting with dogs is not allowed in the Piedmont.

Zones created by author

The Foothills Region **(No. 3)** receives relatively light hunting pressure. This is scenic mountain country along the fringe of the Blue Ridge Mountains. The steep topography here supports extensive hardwood forests. Deer herds are growing here, but densities are lower than in other parts of South Carolina. The potential for high deer numbers is not as great here because the hardwood forests do not produce the leafy forage needed to maintain large herds. The mountains here contain some semi-wilderness territory, and this region offers good scenery and solitude. Public huntng lands in this region total 180,000 acres.

Statewide, 1.6 million acres of state-managed lands are open to public hunting.

Seasons. Seasons vary by management zone. The most generous run from mid-August through December in the Coastal Plain. In the Piedmont and Foothills regions, seasons run from early October through early January. These ranges of dates include archery, muzzleloader, and regular gun seasons. Multiple-deer bag limits are in effect throughout the state.

Regulations for public game management areas vary by area. Most have bow seasons in October and December with a three-deer limit. Gun hunts take place at different times throughout the fall with limits as high as five deer per hunter.

Records. Overall, deer in South Carolina have an average field-dressed weight of 105 pounds.

The state record typical whitetail antlers scored 166⅜, just below the Boone and Crockett minimum. The record nontypical scored 208⅝ points. That is the only deer from South Carolina listed in the Boone and Crockett records.

The future. As in all other southern states, deer were eliminated by the late 1800s. Since that time they've been stocked throughout the state. With enlightened management and a growing respect for game laws, deer herds grew rapidly through the 1970s. The deer herd continues to increase slowly now, although it has peaked in much of the eastern half of the state. The major threats to deer are urban and industrial growth, which eliminate deer habitat. It is predicted that the harvest will stabilize at 55,000 to 60,000 deer annually and will be sustained at that level at least into the 1990s.

Contact. Wildlife & Marine Resources Department, Rembert C. Dennis Building, PO Box 167, Columbia, SC 29202.

SOUTH DAKOTA

Deer numbers. South Dakota covers a land area of 77,047 square miles. About 80 percent of that supports a population of 150,000 whitetail deer, and 60 percent of the land is home to 80,000 mule deer.

Hunters and harvest. On the average, 63,000 resident and 10,000 nonresident firearms hunters take an average of 25,000 deer (18,000 bucks and 7,000 does) each year. In 1983, one of the best years, they killed 48,000 deer. Hunter success has been high, generally between 40 and 60 percent.

Roughly 3,000 resident and 500 nonresident archers hunt deer each year, and they take about 1,500 deer (500 bucks and 1,000 does). During one high year in the early 1980s, archers killed 3,000 deer.

Distribution. For management purposes, biologists break South Dakota into three segments—East River, West River, and Black Hills.

The East River portion **(No. 1)** includes all the country east of the Missouri River, which roughly splits South Dakota in half. This area is farmed intensively; so deer necessarily must be limited in number to prevent conflicts with landowners. Filling of impoundments on the Missouri River eliminated nearly 60 percent of the best whitetail habitat in this region, but many whitetails are still scattered throughout the farmlands. Small woodlots and belts of hardwood trees, dry marshes, and brushy cover along stream and river bottoms support most of the deer in eastern South Dakota.

West of the Missouri River **(No. 2)**, habitat varies greatly, and both whitetails and mule deer live throughout. Upland prairie consisting of grasslands and cultivated crops covers 80 percent of this region outside of the Black Hills. Throughout the prairie country, scattered islands of woody cover and brushy stream courses provide cover for moderate numbers of deer. The most densely populated areas are high bluffs and creek drainages adjacent to major rivers.

The northwest corner **(No. 3)**—

Zones created by author

Harding, Butte, Perkins, and Meade counties—contains expanses of sagebrush country with some ponderosa pine and hardwoods. Western Harding county in the extreme northwest also has some badlands that provide good mule deer hunting. Most of western South Dakota is less suitable to whitetails than mule deer. Whitetails are confined primarily to riparian zones along stream and riverbottoms.

The Black Hills **(No. 4)** form an island of excellent deer range about 100 miles long and 40 miles wide. Both mule deer and whitetails are abundant. The vegetation consists largely of ponderosa pine. The Black Hills contain the highest deer densitites found anywhere in South Dakota.

Eighty percent of the Black Hills is National Forest land so that access there is good. Otherwise, most of South Dakota is privately owned. Some farmers charge a trespass fee, but many let hunters on free if the hunters ask permission. Line up your hunting spot before the season.

Seasons. In the East River region, the season opens the Saturday after Thanksgiving and stays open for nine days. It traditionally has been closed to nonresidents, but with in-

creasing deer populations, that may change.

The West River prairies have a general season that opens the second weekend of November and runs for nine days. Some areas have a split season and special regulations. Permits are limited throughout this region, and only a small percent of those are allotted to nonresidents.

In the Black Hills, permits for bucks-only are unlimited to residents and nonresidents. The general buck season is open the entire month of November.

The bow season generally opens in early October and runs until the opening of firearms season. It's closed during firearms season, but then it reopens and runs through December. It's open statewide to residents and nonresidents, and the number of archer permits is not limited.

Records. South Dakota offers reasonable potential for taking a trophy buck. The largest typical whitetail scored 192 and the largest nontypical 249⅛. Nearly two dozen South Dakota whitetails are listed in Boone and Crockett records, about evenly divided between typicals and nontypicals.

Only one mule deer, killed in 1945, has made the book. It was a nontypical with a score of 249⅛. South Dakota's mule deer generally don't grow to record-class size.

The future. As in other prairie states, deer were eliminated from South Dakota in the early 1900s. Then populations began to rebuild in the 1950s and hit all-time highs in the early 1980s. The whitetail population should remain fairly stable at high levels. Continued conversion of prairie to croplands in the western half of the state will reduce mule deer herds, and encroachment·of ponderosa pine in the Black Hills, which reduces the quality of shrubs and other forage, probably will cut down overall deer populations there.

Contact. Division of Wildlife, Sigurd Anderson Building, 445 East Capitol, Pierre, SD 57501–3185.

TENNESSEE

Deer numbers. Tennessee covers 42,187 square miles. About 325,000 whitetails occupy 98 percent of the land.

Hunters and harvest. On average, about 177,000 residents and 3,500 nonresidents have hunted deer annually. About 160,000 hunt with firearms, and 44,000 hunt with bow and arrow. The deer population and harvest have grown dramatically each year since the 1960s; so the average harvest means little. In one recent year the firearms harvest was about 42,000 deer (35,000 bucks and 7,000 does). Firearms hunters enjoyed their highest success rate of 23 percent in 1983, and their lowest, 10 percent, in 1974.

Bowhunters have harvested as many as 6,700 deer (3,000 bucks and 3,700 does) in one year. The highest archery success on record has been 13 percent and the lowest, about 5 percent.

Distribution. The Smoky Mountain region along the state's extreme eastern edge **(No. 1)** consists of steep mountains covered with timber, primarily oak and hickory. Some conifers grow at the highest elevations. Soils in this region are relatively infertile, and there are few openings to grow forage for animals. Deer feed primarily on mast, an unreliable food source, and as a result deer numbers are low in this mountain region.

In the Ridge and Valley region **(No. 2)** low, steep ridges are bisected by river valleys. Pasturelands cover more than 50 percent of the region, and oak-hickory woodlots are interspersed. This area has the highest human population in Tennessee. Some localities have high numbers of deer, but in others deer are scarce.

The Cumberland Plateau **(No. 3)** is 75 percent forested with oak, hickory, and pine. The topography is fairly flat. Some areas have been cleared for pastureland and grain crops, but the shallow soils here are not ideal for agriculture. This is one of the most sparsely settled areas of

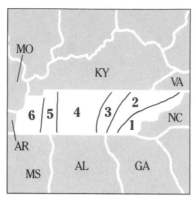

Zones created by author

Tennessee. Deer numbers here are moderate.

The Nashville Basin **(No. 4)** is largely rolling hills divided about 50/50 between agriculture, mostly soybeans and corn, and woodlands. Deer densities are good to excellent here, and herds continue to grow rapidly. Some counties have gone from closed seasons in the early 1970s to harvests exceeding 1,000 deer in recent years.

The Tennessee River zone **(No. 5)**, a strip extending about 30 miles on each side of the Tennessee River, has steep ridges and breaks adjoining the fertile river valley. The rocky breaks are wooded, and deer numbers are high in this zone.

The west Tennessee Coastal Plain **(No. 6)** contains very fertile farmlands, and soybean and cotton fields are intermixed with woodlots that provide good deer cover. Except in the extreme northwest corner where fields are large and woody cover is scarce, this region contains the highest deer densities in Tennessee. Some deer live along the wooded Mississippi River bottoms, but heavy flooding here limits the total number of deer.

About 5 percent of the land in Tennessee is federal or state owned, and these lands provide public hunting. In the past it has been fairly easy to get permission to hunt private lands, but the trend toward hunting leases has grown in recent years.

Seasons. The general gun season usually runs from the Saturday before Thanksgiving through the first weekend in December, and then opens again the third weekend in December and runs through the beginning of January. This is the broadest season structure, and it varies by unit.

The bow season usually opens the last Saturday in September and closes at the end of October. A muzzleloader season usually runs from the second weekend in December through the following Friday, although this may change from year to year.

Most areas have generous bag limits, ranging from one to four deer per hunter.

Records. The overall average weight of deer taken by hunters is 98 pounds, field-dressed. The heaviest buck on record field-dressed to 275 pounds, which is about 357 pounds live weight.

The state record typical whitetail scored 186⅛, and the record nontypical 196⅝. Boone and Crockett lists only a few animals from Tennessee.

The future. The story in Tennessee echoes the story in many surrounding states—rapidly growing deer herds. Biologists refuse to give any "average" harvest, because the harvest increased every year from the 1960s through the early 1980s. In 1952 hunters killed 550 deer in Tennessee. In 1979, they killed 28,540. Wildlife managers expect deer numbers and harvest to grow through the 1980s, and they expect a stable annual harvest of 50,000 animals in the 1990s. Deer hunting faces some problems in Tennessee. With growing interest in deer hunting, more and more private land is being leased by clubs or posted against hunting. Strip mining, clearing for soybean fields, urban expansion, and other developments also will continue to reduce overall habitat for deer.

Contact. Tennessee Wildlife Resources Agency, Ellington Agricultural Center, PO Box 40747, Nashville, TN 37204.

TEXAS

Deer numbers. In terms of sheer numbers, Texas stands out well above all other states. About 50 percent of the state's total land area of 267,338 square miles supports deer. An estimated 3.4 million whitetails live on about 42 percent of the land, and mule deer occupy another 12 percent. There is some overlap in range.

Hunters and harvest. Each year Texas has a turnout of about 500,000 resident and 13,000 nonresident hunters. The average annual harvest has been 302,000 (223,500 bucks and 73,500 does), and in 1973, one of the best years on record, hunters killed a total of 373,000 deer in Texas. The average hunter success remains fairly stable at about 50 percent.

The average archery harvest has been about 3,000 deer, evenly divided between bucks and does. Archers enjoyed a high year in 1983 with a kill of 5,000 deer. Average bowhunter success has remained fairly stable at about 10 percent.

Distribution. Virtually all land in Texas is privately owned, and hunting is on a fee basis. The quality of hunting in Texas varies from outstanding to poor, depending on how landowners manage their deer herds.

Biologists break Texas down into several ecological zones based on vegetation and terrain. The Pineywoods **(No. 1)** lies along the eastern edge adjacent to Louisiana. The rolling terrain of this area is covered with pine forests as well as hardwoods, but about one-third of it now has been opened up for farming. Two-thirds of this region supports whitetails, and hunting pressure is moderate to heavy.

Just to the west of the Pineywoods are the Post Oak Savannah and Cross Timbers and Prairies zones **(No. 2)**. These regions are characterized by fairly high hunting pressure and a high turnover of bucks. From 55 to 75 percent of the bucks taken are yearlings, and a very small

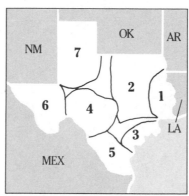

Zones created by author

percentage reach the age of 4½ years and older.

Overall kill in the Gulf Prairies **(No. 3)** is not high compared to some other regions, but deer densitites are very high in some localities.

Many states have traditional "deer factories," and in Texas, it's the Edwards Plateau **(No. 4)**, which roughly covers the west-central portion of the state. The total estimated whitetail population on the Edwards Plateau exceeds 1.6 million, or nearly 50 percent of the deer in Texas. The Edwards Plateau consists primarily of hill-country rangeland, but some of the valleys that have better soil are cultivated. The vegetation consists of a mixture of oaks, mesquite, and brushy plants that provide excellent forage for livestock and deer. Hunting pressure ranges from light to moderate, with the percentage of yearling bucks as low as 5 percent in some counties to about 40 percent in others. Many bucks live to maturity, but competition with livestock, and other deer in some areas, has resulted in small average size and poor trophy quality.

Texas has gained a reputation for producing trophy whitetails, and that reputation comes primarily from the south Texas plains zone **(No. 5)**, or as many hunters call it, the south Texas brush country. This 20-million-acre region extends from San Antonio south to the lower Rio Grande Valley and contains a variety of

shrubs, trees, forbs, and grasses that provide excellent forage for deer. Deer herds on many ranches here are managed to produce trophy bucks. Deer harvest is relatively light and herds contain a high percentage of older bucks. The average percentage of yearlings killed in south Texas ranges from 10 to 15 percent. From one-third to one-half the bucks taken are 4½ years old or older.

The Trans-Pecos region **(No. 6)** of Texas also takes in the extreme western corner south of New Mexico. Some whitetails are scattered throughout this arid region of mountains and basins, but mule deer are predominant. Throughout the plains country of the Texas Panhandle **(No. 7)**, deer are sparse.

Seasons. The general rifle season runs from mid-November through early January. The limit is three deer in many regions. In addition, an archery-only season runs for about one month, starting in early October.

Records. The average Texas buck weighs 80 pounds field-dressed, although some bucks from south Texas dress as heavy as 200 pounds. Texas whitetails, at least in some regions, do produce trophy antlers. Texas has ranked third in the percentage of whitetails listed in the Boone and Crockett records. The record typical scored 196⅛, and the record nontypical, which held the Boone and Crockett world-record position for many years, scored 286. Virtually all record-class bucks have come from the south Texas plains with Webb and Dimmit counties leading the list. Texas doesn't grow record-book mule deer.

The future. Texas has a fairly static deer population. Most ranges are up to capacity with deer, and the future depends on management of private lands by individuals.

Contact. Texas Parks & Wildlife Department, 4200 Smith School Road, Austin, TX 78744.

UTAH

Deer numbers. The total area of Utah is 84,916 square miles. There are no whitetails. Mule deer number 500,000 in the preseason.

Hunters and harvest. Since about 1970, Utah has supported an average of 171,000 resident and 17,500 non-resident firearms hunters, and 19,300 bowhunters. The average firearms harvest since then has been about 75,000 (62,000 bucks and 13,000 does). The highest harvest on record took place in 1972 when hunters killed 105,175 deer (about 70,000 of those were bucks). The long-term average hunting success has been 44 percent. The highest occurred in 1961 (when hunters could take either buck or doe) and was 60 percent. The lowest hunting success on record (when the bag limit was bucks only) took place in 1975 when hunters had only 23 percent success.

The average archery harvest has been about 2,500 bucks each year. Archers enjoyed their best season in 1973 when they killed 3,825 bucks. The average bowhunting success rate has been 15 percent.

Distribution. Typical basin-and-range topography of the Great Basin covers the western one-third of Utah **(No. 1)**. This arid desert country is interspersed with small, rugged mountain ranges that are covered with sage brush, pinyon-juniper, and mountain mahogany. Most of these ranges support modest deer herds that include some fairly large bucks.

The oakbrush, aspen, and sage country of northern Utah **(No. 2)** generally supports the highest deer numbers and produces quality bucks. Some of the best hunting country here lies on private land, and you must pay to hunt. Severe winters often ravage herds so that numbers fluctuate drastically. Some years the hunting is exceptional. Other years it's poor.

The Wasatch Range **(No. 3)** cuts down through the center of Utah just east of the major population centers of Ogden, Salt Lake City, and Provo. This range is productive, and remote backcountry areas produce some

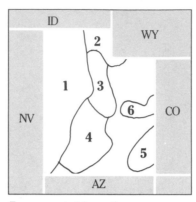

Zones created by author

huge bucks. Hunting the rugged Wasatch isn't for the faint of heart, but it can pay off if killing a big buck is your goal. Here again, rough winters can take a heavy toll on the deer.

Mountains in the south-central part of the state **(No. 4)** have thriving deer herds. The Escalante, Tushar, Pavant, Boulder, and other ranges and plateaus on the Fishlake and Dixie National Forests form a series of parallel ridges divided by river valleys. Many of the mountains exceed 10,000 feet elevation, and they're covered with grasslands, aspens, mountain mahogany, and pockets of dense evergreen trees. Severe winters occasionally decimate herds here, but generally weather is milder than at the north end of the state, and deer numbers don't fluctuate as drastically. This country is heavily hunted, but many canyons have no roads to them. Ample sanctuary assures that some bucks will grow to trophy size.

The La Sal Mountains near the Colorado border and Elk Ridge west of Monticello **(No. 5)** at one time produced many record-class mule deer. Due to low deer numbers, parts of this country were closed to all hunting in the early 1980s, and now only limited permits are issued for some areas. The potential for taking a big buck here is very good.

The Book Cliffs **(No. 6)**, which

parallel Interstate 70 in east-central Utah, have long been famous for mule deer. This country consists of plateaus interspersed with steep canyons that contain huge aspen parks, pockets of Douglas fir, and sagebrush meadows. Some roadless canyons produce large bucks, but the country is heavily hunted.

Except in northeast Utah, much of the best hunting in Utah takes place on public lands.

Seasons. Traditionally the rifle season has opened on the Saturday closest to October 20 and remained open for 11 days. The archery season generally opens on the third Saturday in August and continues through Labor Day. A general muzzleloader season usually lasts nine days, beginning the first Saturday in November.

Records. Utah has produced more than its share of Boone and Crockett mule deer. A sampling of typical mule deer shows scores of 212⅛, 210, 208, 205⅝, and 205⅝. Nontypicals have been equally impressive: 330⅛, 284⅜, 284, 283, and 276⅝. Unfortunately many of these were taken years ago, and Utah has fallen off as a trophy producer. However, some units have been closed to hunting, and permit numbers have been limited in others. So with these restrictions, Utah could again reach its trophy potential in some areas.

The future. Metro areas continually eat away winter range along the Wasatch Range. The Division of Wildlife Resources has a goal of buying 600,000 acres of winter range in key areas, but this has been a slow and expensive process. The potential for major oil shale and tar sands development poses a serious long-range threat. For the near future, however, Utah contains huge areas of public land. Except for fluctuations as a result of severe weather, hunting is expected to remain good into the 1990s.

Contact. Utah Division of Wildlife Resources, 1596 North Temple, Salt Lake City, UT 84116.

VERMONT

Deer numbers. Vermont covers a total area of 9,609 square miles. An estimated 80,000 to 90,000 whitetail deer live throughout 85 percent of that area.

Hunters and harvest. Each year Vermont sells an average of 100,000 firearms licenses to residents and 20,000 to nonresidents. Hunters killed a record high of 24,675 deer in 1980, but that included a large percentage of does. The highest buck harvest on record of 17,384 occurred in 1966. Overall average hunting success, including bucks and does, has been 27 percent, with a high in 1964 of 34 percent, and a low in 1982 of 21 percent.

An average of 12,000 residents and 5,000 nonresidents take part in the archery season each year. Average bow harvest, including bucks and does, has been about 1,300 deer, and in 1977 archers killed a record high of 2,094. Average archery success has been 5 percent.

Distribution. The western fringe of Vermont **(No. 1)** along the New York border can be divided into two sections. Roughly north of Highway 4 is considered the Lakes Plain region. The climate is relatively mild, and the flat terrain supports extensive agriculture for row crops and pastureland. Deer numbers are moderate here, but bucks in this region are heavier than average and grow heavy antlers. South of Highway 4, the Western Foothills maintain the highest deer densities in Vermont, although average size is small. Northern hardwoods—maple, beech—along with some oak-hickory forests and pine and hemlock blanket the rolling hills.

The Green Mountains **(No. 2)** extend the length of the state from north to south. The rugged, mountainous terrain attains elevations of 4,000 feet. Northern hardwoods and spruce-fir make up most of the forests here. Harsh winters and restricted winter range limit the number of deer in this region. Densities are fairly low, although the mountain region produces some very large bucks. The Green Mountains are hunted

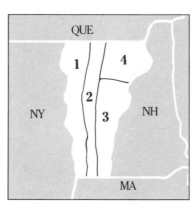

Zones created by author

fairly heavily because the region contains extensive public land, but rugged backcountry offers potential for escaping the crowds.

The Southeastern Region **(No. 3)** takes in all the land between the Green Mountains and the New Hampshire border roughly as far north as Montpelier. The southern two-thirds of this region consists of forested rolling hills intermixed with some dairy farms, alfalfa, and corn fields along with a number of abandoned farms and orchards. Deer numbers are high here per square mile, second only to those in the Western Foothills. Farther north in Orange and Washington counties, which essentially surround Montpelier, the climate is more severe, and deer numbers are lower. The area consists of fairly extensive forestland mixed with agriculture, and it's fairly heavily hunted.

In the Northeastern Region **(No. 4)** winters are very severe with cold temperatures and deep snow. In general, the terrain consists of rolling hills. Spruce-fir forests cover most of the land, along with pockets of northern hardwoods. At one time deer numbers were very high here, and body size was small. But severe winters have reduced herds greatly, and now this region has the sparsest herds in Vermont. With a decrease in numbers, average size of the deer has improved considerably, and the extreme northeast—Essex County— produces some of Vermont's largest

deer. As in northern New Hampshire, the spruce budworm has wrought havoc on forests here, and as a result large paper companies have clear-cut many forests that provided winter cover for deer. The overall result has been a reduced carrying capacity for deer in this harsh region.

About 90 percent of Vermont is private land, but access is fairly good. The Green Mountain National Forest and some state lands assure good public access in certain regions, and in Vermont tradition has it that if land is not posted, it's open for hunting. Posting has spread in recent years, but much private land can still be hunted. The tradition of hunting clubs hasn't spread into Vermont.

Seasons. The archery season traditionally has been open for 16 days, starting the second Saturday in October. The rifle season usually runs for 16 days, beginning 12 days prior to Thanksgiving.

Records. Average field-dressed weight of bucks is about 120 pounds. The heaviest bucks come from the mountain region and the northeastern corner. Deer numbers are highest in the southeast and southwest foothills, but average body weight is less. The heaviest buck on record field-dressed to 319 pounds and weighed an estimated 400 pounds on the hoof. No records of antler size are available.

The future. Vermont had bucks-only hunting until 1978, and under this law deer herds grew and exceeded carrying capacity in some regions. At its highest point, the deer herd was estimated at 200,000 animals. A severe winter in 1977–78 and antlerless deer seasons expressly designed to decrease the population have reduced overall numbers to about 80,000 deer. Biologists want to increase that to an optimum of about 120,000 deer statewide.

Contact. Agency of Environmental Conservation, Fish and Game Department, Montpelier, VT 05602.

VIRGINIA

Deer numbers. Virginia has a total area of 40,817 square miles and an estimated deer herd of 500,000 animals.

Hunters and harvest. Hunters have bought an average of 310,000 big game licenses each year. Average annual harvest from the mid-1970s into the 1980s was about 70,000 deer (43,000 bucks) taken annually, although the annual kill increased almost every year from about 41,000 in 1973, to a high of about 89,000 (60,000 bucks) in 1982. Hunting success has hovered close to 24 percent.

Average bow and arrow harvest has been about 1,100 deer annually, but that has increased steadily and hit a high in 1983 at 2,917. No breakdown was available on the number of bowhunters.

Distribution. Based on hunting regulations, Virginia breaks down into two regions—west of the Blue Ridge, and east of the Blue Ridge. In general, that country west of the Blue Ridge **(No. 1)** consists of mountains and ridge-and-valley terrain. Fertile soils in the valleys are farmed, but a majority of the uplands remain in hardwoods, interspersed with some pine, hemlock, and other species. In expansive hardwood forests, such as those in western Virginia, mast provides the major food source, and the carrying capacity for deer is relatively low. More than 20 percent of this region lies within the George Wash-

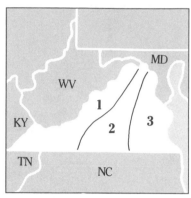

Zones created by author

ington and Jefferson National Forests. Access is good, and some remote areas offer the potential for uncrowded hunting.

The region east of the Blue Ridge can be broken into two major ecological zones. The Piedmont **(No. 2)** covers most of central Virginia. This is rolling country where farmlands are mixed with extensive timberlands. Pasturelands and cattle make up a major part of the agricultural scene here, but corn and small grains, soybeans, peanuts, and other crops are grown in the Piedmont. Some timberlands have been converted to commercial pine species, but hardwoods also are prevalent. Deer numbers are moderate to high in the Piedmont.

The Coastal Plain **(No. 3)**, called the Tidewater locally, supports many commercial pine plantations. Soybeans, small grains, and grasslands comprise much of the agricultural usage here. Deer numbers are moderate in the northern Tidewater, but the southern Tidewater supports the highest deer densities in Virginia. However, the deer are relatively small in size here.

Except for a few small, heavily hunted public areas, all of eastern Virginia is privately owned, and private hunting clubs lease large tracts of land. Unless you know the right person, you may have a hard time getting permission to hunt in eastern Virginia.

Seasons. Season lengths vary by county from 11 days to 1½ months long. Most of the longer seasons take place in eastern Virginia where extensive hunting clubs limit deer harvest. Hunting with dogs is allowed throughout most of eastern Virginia but not west of the Blue Ridge. Most seasons take place in November and some extend into January. In general, the bag limit is one buck per day, two per license year, and antlerless deer may be taken at specific times in some areas.

Special archery seasons also are held in October in most counties, and again in November into January in a few counties. In most areas the limit is two deer per license year.

Records. The largest typical whitetail antlers recorded by Boone and Crockett from Virginia scored 177⅞, and the largest nontypical scored 219⅞. Boone and Crockett lists only a half-dozen or so bucks from Virginia.

The future. The history of deer in Virginia parallels that of other southeastern states. Deer were nearly extinct in the early 1900s. But with improved habitat, extensive stocking, and law enforcement, deer herds grew rapidly after the 1930s. In 1947, for example, hunters harvested 4,011 deer in Virginia; in 1982 they harvested 88,745. Biologists predict the harvest will stabilize somewhere around 100,000 deer.

Barring any major land-use changes, that level should be maintained for many years. Primary problems will occur in the population corridor from Washington, D.C., south to Norfolk. There urban development is consuming most deer habitat. With increasing demand for good hunting, leasing will expand and access will be a greater problem for the average hunter.

Contact. Commission of Game and Inland Fisheries, PO Box 11104, Richmond, VA 23230–1104.

WASHINGTON

Deer numbers. Many states have good hunting for two kinds of deer, but Washington may offer the best hunting for three species. (Oregon also has three, but whitetail numbers are small.) In Washington, a state covering 66,570 square miles, some 69,000 whitetails occupy 20 percent of the state; 138,000 mule deer, about 50 percent; and 210,000 black-tails, about 35 percent.

Hunters and harvest. On the average 220,000 residents and 500 non-residents hunt deer in Washington each year. No distinction is made between bow and firearms hunters. For the first 48 years of record keeping, hunters killed an average of 50,000 deer (36,000 bucks and 14,000 does) each year. Roughly 47 percent of those have been black-tails, and the other 53 percent have been mule deer or whitetails from the state's East Side. The average success rate has been 25 percent. Seventy percent of all bucks killed in Washington have been yearlings.

Distribution. The Cascade Range, which runs north and south from Canada to the Oregon border, divides Washington into two sections. The West Side **(No. 1)** receives some of the highest rainfall in North America. As a result the vegetation, which consists of huge Douglas fir, cedar, spruce, ferns, and tangles of countless species of brush, is nearly impenetrable in many places. This country is heavily logged and many clear-cut patches are interspersed with pockets of old-growth timber. This is the home of the blacktail deer. Blacktails like fringes. They feed along the edges of clear-cuts or natural openings and bed in heavy timber. Nearly a quarter of the black-tails listed in the Boone and Crockett records come from the southwest corner of Washington, roughly from King County—where Seattle is located—southwest of the Columbia River.

Mule deer predominate east of the Cascades. The Okanogan Country **(No. 2)** in north-central Washington is generally considered Washington's "deer factory." Herds here are man-

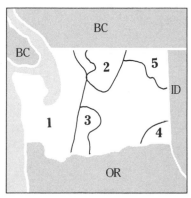

Zones created by author

aged for maximum production; so densities are high, but most deer killed are yearlings. However, the Cascade Range contains rugged country that provides good deer refuge. When heavy snow falls during hunting season, it pushes bucks from the remote mountains, and hunters take some huge bucks in the Okanogan.

The south end of the Cascades **(No. 3)** near Yakima is managed primarily for elk; so deer numbers are low. As a result, hunting pressure on deer is fairly light, and a high percentage of bucks live to maturity. This is not a place to see lots of deer, but the chances of taking a large buck are good.

Between the forested Cascades and the Idaho border, much of the land is rolling grainfields and open prairies. This country supports few deer. But the southeast corner **(No. 4)** in the Snake River drainage consists of deep canyons with timbered breaks, and this country has large numbers of mule deer and some whitetails. Much of this country is heavily hunted, and trophy bucks are scarce.

Some mule deer live in the northeast corner **(No. 5)** in the higher mountains north of Spokane, but whitetails predominate here. A late season held during the rut provides excellent prospects for taking a quality whitetail buck.

Washington contains a great deal of national forest land in the Cascades and in the northeast and southeast corners. But much of the land in the Okanogan Country and on the West Side is private; there you must obtain permission to hunt.

Seasons. Compared to many western states, Washington has a fairly high human population with a small land base. So excessive hunting pressure has presented problems there. Regulations restricting hunters to specific hunting methods—modern firearms, bow, or muzzleloader—and early or late season have been designed to reduce conflicts and restore quality. Timber companies and public agencies have also closed roads during hunting seasons to limit access and improve hunting quality.

Records. A number of whitetails from Washington are listed in the Boone and Crockett records. The state record typical whitetail scored 184⅝, and the record nontypical whitetail, 234⅛.

The state record mule deer scored 201⅝ and the nontypical 266⅛. Washington has produced very few Boone and Crockett record mule deer.

The potential for a record blacktail is fair to good. The world-record blacktail, with a score of 182⅝, was killed in Lewis County in 1953.

The future. Because of mild climate on the West Side, blacktail deer numbers remain fairly stable. Also, blacktails thrive on logged lands. Mule deer populations tend to fluctuate, but numbers have remained relatively high. Land development has taken a heavy toll on some East Side winter ranges. But barring drastic land-use changes, biologists predict that with streamlined hunting regulations adopted in 1984, deer herds will remain stable for many years.

Contact. Washington Department of Game, 600 N. Capitol Way, Olympia, WA 98504.

WEST VIRGINIA

Deer numbers. West Virginia has an area of 24,292 square miles. An estimated 600,000 whitetail deer occupy about 94 percent of the land area.

Hunters and harvest. In recent years, about 240,000 residents and 41,000 nonresidents have hunted each year with firearms. The harvest has averaged 63,000 (75 percent bucks, 25 percent does), and 1982 produced a record high harvest of 78,605 deer (56,774 bucks). Average firearms hunting success has been 13 percent.

West Virginia is a popular bow-hunting state and attracts about 80,000 resident and 15,000 nonresident archers annually. Average bow harvest has been about 9,000 (about 50/50, bucks and does). Again 1982 produced a record high harvest of 13,454 deer. Archers have averaged 10 percent success.

Distribution. West Virginia lies totally within the Appalachian Mountain region. Average elevation of this mountain state is 1,500 feet, the highest average elevation of any state east of the Mississippi.

The mountainous eastern portion **(No. 1)** along the Virginia border at one time yielded the heaviest harvest, but permits for antlerless deer have been increased there to reduce overall deer numbers and crop damage. In the panhandle, extensive cornfields and other grains are mixed with hardwood forests. Land is most heavily posted here, and because this section of West Virginia lies closest to major cities, much of the land has been tied up in private hunting leases and by clubs. The highest mountains in West Virginia lie south of the panhandle along the eastern border. The U.S. Forest Service administers much of this rugged, forested region.

Deer herds have grown dramatically in central and western areas **(No. 2)**. Much of this region consists of rolling country. Strip mining is fairly widespread, and the Ohio River Valley and its major tributaries support active farms, primarily corn. How-

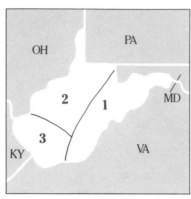

Zones created by author

ever, much of this region consists of abandoned farms grown up into brush, with good hardwood and pine cover, and these areas are ideal deer habitat. The average harvest ranges from four to five deer per square mile, but it's much higher in some localities. In Lewis County, for example, during the 1984 season hunters killed an average of 16 deer per square mile. Some of the largest bucks taken in West Virginia also come from this region.

The south end of the state **(No. 3)** has the poorest deer herds. Coal mining has been the major industry in this steep, rough country. The country has been cut over and burned extensively, but biologists believe it could support many more deer than are now present. Free-roaming dogs take a heavy toll on deer, and poaching is a common practice. So herds scarcely have a chance to build up in this region. As a result of the poor herd conditions, four counties here on occasion have been closed to firearms hunting. Game managers hope that increased education and law enforcement will allow herds in this region to rise to their potential.

More than 90 percent of West Virginia is privately owned. However three national forests provide more than 1 million acres of public hunt-

ing, and state management areas offer another 250,000 acres of public hunting. Except in the northeast corner, and to a lesser extent the western counties, clubs and leases have not become prevalent. A hunter can still get permission by asking.

Seasons. The general bucks-only firearms season usually runs for about two weeks in late November. An antlerless season is usually open only to residents.

The bow season usually runs from mid-October through December, and hunters can take a deer of either sex (except during bucks-only gun seasons). A special muzzleloader season also is held.

In some cases, by participating in various seasons, hunters have been able to take from three to five deer per year.

Records. Average field-dressed weight for all deer taken in West Virginia is 114 pounds.

The state record typical whitetail, killed in 1976 in Braxton County (in **No. 2**), measured 182⅜, and the record nontypical, taken in Mason County on the western border (also **No. 2**) in 1966, measured 207⅞.

The future. Unrestricted logging and market hunting pushed deer herds in West Virginia to the brink in the late 1800s. In 1910 the deer population was estimated at 1,000 animals. The first regulations were enacted in 1909 when a season was set for October and November and a "buck law" was initiated. Deer herds were improving noticeably by 1920. Extensive stocking through the 1940s and improved law enforcement led to dramatic growth of deer herds. Even into the 1980s, deer numbers continue to increase in the central, western, and southern regions. Antlerless seasons have slowed or stabilized herd growth in some eastern and western counties. The outlook for deer hunting is excellent.

Contact. Department of Natural Resources, 1800 Washington St., East, Charleston, WV 25305.

WISCONSIN

Deer numbers. Wisconsin has a total of area of 56,154 square miles. An estimated population of 850,000 whitetails occupy 60 percent of the state.

Hunters and harvest. Each year about 620,000 residents and 14,000 nonresidents hunt with firearms, and they kill an average of 150,000 deer (90,000 bucks and 60,000 does). During 1984, one of the highest years on record, hunters using firearms took 255,000 deer, roughly half of them bucks. Average firearms hunting success has been 20 percent, with a high in 1983 of 30 percent, and a low in 1971 of 14 percent.

Wisconsin is one of the major bowhunting states, and an average of 180,000 resident and 6,000 nonresident archers hunt deer in the state each year. The average harvest with bow and arrow has been 25,000 deer (10,000 bucks and 15,000 does). In 1983, with one of the highest kills on record, archers took 33,000 deer (15,000 bucks and 18,000 does). Bowhunters have an average success rate of 10 percent, with a high of 17 percent and a low of 7 percent.

Distribution. The northern one-third of Wisconsin is called the Northern Forest region **(No. 1)**. This rolling, hilly country contains many lakes, streams, and swamps. Small blocks of agricultural land are scattered across the region, but extensive forests dominate the landscape.

Deer densities vary according to local habitat types. Sandy soil areas, characterized by jack pine, scrub oak, and aspen, hold the highest numbers of deer, and this kind of habitat covers roughly half the region. Second-growth forests consisting of maple, white pine, and hemlock support much lower densities of deer. Severe winters also can take a heavy toll on deer in this northern region; so deer numbers fluctuate more than they do farther south.

National, state, and county forests assure vast public hunting grounds.

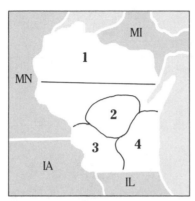

Zones created by author

Along the Minnesota border and near Lake Superior, hunters can find large roadless blocks of land that offer backcountry hunting opportunities. These areas with poor road access offer some good hunting for trophy-class bucks.

The Central Forest Region **(No. 2)** is flat country covered with jack pine, scrub oak, and aspen. This ideal habitat supports high numbers of deer, and this region does not suffer the severe winters that plague the northern forests; so deer numbers are relatively stable. Throughout this region, state and county forests assure good public access. Given the good numbers of deer and good public access, this region is popular with hunters.

The southwest corner **(No. 3)** consists of rough breaks and deep valleys associated with the Mississippi River and its tributaries. Farmlands occupy the hilltops and valley bottoms, and oak-hickory forests cover the steep hillsides. This mixture of farm and woodland provides ideal habitat for whitetails, and densities are as high as 70 deer per square mile in this area. Most of the land is private, but many landowners will grant permission to hunt.

The southeast corner **(No. 4)** is the most intensively farmed section of Wisconsin. Deer numbers are moderate, and because of the high human population in the region, hunting opportunity is more restricted here than elsewhere in the state.

Seasons. Generally the firearms season runs in mid-November (length varies by units), and the limit is usually one deer. In some units hunters can take either sex of deer.

The bow season is usually open statewide from mid-September until mid-November. It closes during the firearms season, but opens again during December.

Records. Average field-dressed weight of mature bucks is 120 pounds, and the heaviest buck on record field-dressed to 321 pounds (406 pounds live weight).

Wisconsin traditionally has ranked among the top three trophy whitetail states and provinces. Many of the bigger bucks come from the northern forest region, where hunting pressure is lightest, and from the productive southwest corner. The world-record whitetail (206⅛) was killed in northwest Wisconsin close to the Minnesota border in 1914. Boone and Crockett lists more than 30 typical whitetails from Wisconsin, and about 10 percent of those have been killed since 1970.

The state record nontypical buck scored 245. More than 30 nontypicals are listed in Boone and Crockett, and about 20 percent of those have been taken since 1970.

The future. Deer numbers have increased greatly in recent years and are causing excessive crop damage. Hunting regulations are designed to reduce numbers of deer in some areas, but hunting prospects will remain excellent into the 1990s. Over the long term, deer numbers may be reduced in the Central Forest Region because much woodland there may be converted to farmlands. At the same time, deer numbers should increase in the Northern Forest Region as logging opens up older stands of timber and creates better deer habitat.

Contact. Department of Natural Resources, Bureau of Wildlife Management, Box 7921, Madison, WI 53707.

WYOMING

Deer numbers. Wyoming covers an area of 97,914 square miles. An estimated 60,000 whitetails occupy about 25 percent of that area, and roughly 400,000 mule deer live on 95 percent of the land.

Hunters and harvest. Wyoming sells an average of 80,000 resident and 35,000 nonresident deer licenses. With an average harvest of about 75,000 deer, the success rate is about 60 percent, which is the highest in the West with the possible exception of Nevada. Some years the average success rate has even been higher than 70 percent. On the average, 5,400 bowhunters (5,000 resident and 400 nonresident) kill 800 deer for a 15 percent success rate.

Distribution. Wyoming has excellent hunting for good-size whitetails, particularly in the Black Hills in the northeast corner **(No. 1)**. National forest land provides good hunting here. Hunter success on whitetails is close to 60 percent. The foothills of the Bighorn Mountains also hold plenty of whitetails, but getting permission to hunt private land here can be a problem.

The Bighorn Mountains **(No. 2)** is considered one of Wyoming's "deer factories." Mule deer numbers are high throughout the range and national forest land assures good access. Deep, rugged canyons provide good sanctuary for large bucks.

The east-central portion between Gillette and Douglas **(No. 3)** is open prairie land with many breaks, arroyos, and brush and timber pockets. It's a high-density mule deer area with high rate of hunter success. Most of the land is private, and most landowners charge a trespass fee.

The southeast corner **(No. 4)** contains several mountain ranges in the Medicine Bow National Forest. Mule deer are fairly numerous here. The Sierra Madre provides excellent deer habitat ranging from alpine to desert. The Snowy Range has dense timber and can be tough to hunt.

The central portion **(No. 5)** from the Bighorns south to Rawlins consists of isolated mountain ranges and badlands. The Rattlesnake Hills,

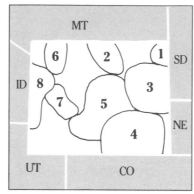

Zones created by author

Shirley Mountains, and other ranges have some timber and support high numbers of mule deer. Deer are scattered throughout the prairies and badlands, and small pockets of good habitat hold sizable herds of deer. Much of this is Bureau of Land Management (BLM) land, so public access is good.

The rugged, high mountains west of Cody **(No. 6)** grow some big bucks, but much of this country is remote wilderness and largely inaccessible to the hunter on foot. Horses are required to hunt much of the territory. Many bucks probably die of old age here.

At one time the Wind River Range **(No. 7)** produced many fine bucks. But after the 1960s it became poor, and biologists believe lack of good winter range may be the problem.

The Wyoming Range **(No. 8)**, which includes the mountain complex extending from Kemmerer north to Afton, supports an estimated 30,000 mule deer and may provide Wyoming's best deer hunting. Several Boone and Crockett bucks have been taken here. This range contains classic mountain hunting with pockets of forest land interspersed with open parks, meadows, and brushlands. Large roadless blocks of land provide sanctuary for big bucks. Exploration for oil and gas in this region has disrupted hunting to some extent. The deer are still there but man's activities has made them harder to hunt.

The Gros Ventre Range **(No. 8)** just to the north offers good hunting for record-class bucks too. The west side of the Teton Range, which is rocky country with scattered timber, has a large deer population and some big bucks. Extensive public land assures entry into most of the better hunting areas in this region.

Seasons. The season in most whitetail areas in the northeastern quarter falls in November to provide excellent rut hunting. In general most mule deer seasons open in early October and run for two to three weeks, although there are many exceptions. Bow seasons precede most rifle seasons and usually run for two weeks.

Records. The largest Wyoming whitetail recorded in Boone and Crockett was a nontypical that scored 224⅛, and the largest typical 177⅛. Few record-class heads show up in the book and this means Wyoming is not the place to pursue a Boone and Crockett whitetail.

Mule deer are another story. For all-time records, Wyoming is among the top six states for Boone and Crockett mule deer, and since 1970 it has ranked in the top three. The No. 2 typical, with a score of 217, came from Hoback Canyon near Jackson **(No. 8)**. The largest nontypical scored 292⅝. Most record-book heads have come from mountains along the western border.

The future. Oil and gas exploration and coal mining have changed the complexion of Wyoming since the 1970s and have brought in many new residents. However, Game and Fish biologists think the land base for deer herds is fairly stable. Regulations will change periodically to redistribute hunting pressure, but biologists see no major reduction in deer numbers. Much work is needed to restore winter ranges that have grown past their prime for deer food in some mountain regions.

Contact. Wyoming Game & Fish Department, 5400 Bishop Boulevard, Cheyenne, WY 82002.

ALBERTA

Deer numbers. Alberta covers 255,285 square miles. An estimated 142,000 whitetail deer occupy about 60 percent of that area, and about 97,000 mule deer range over nearly 80 percent of the land. Nearly 80 percent of the province supports either species or both.

Hunters and harvest. Each year Alberta sells about 75,000 whitetail licenses and 60,000 mule deer licenses to an estimated 90,000 resident deer hunters. Few nonresidents venture to Alberta strictly to hunt deer. The average has been about 400 a year. Firearms hunters kill about 24,000 deer each year—a success rate of about 20 percent.

An estimated 6,000 bowhunters kill about 600 deer each year.

Distribution. Zone **No. 1** includes the Rocky Mountains from alpine country at 10,000 feet and higher down to foothills covered with dense conifer forests. Some of the lowlands support a few whitetails, but this is primarily mule deer country. Deer numbers are good but not outstanding throughout the mountain zones. Much of this land is government owned, which assures good public access.

Moving eastward from the foothills into zone **No. 2,** you find mixed woodlands of aspen and conifers. In the southeast corner of the province **(No. 3)**—a big-game zone in the hunting regulations—the country consists primarily of pure prairie grasslands and open grain country. There deer cover is restricted to softwood groves along creek and riverbottoms. North of the prairies along the eastern border and north to Edmonton **(No. 4)**, the country switch-

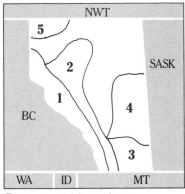

Zones created by author

es from open prairies to aspen parklands. This region is flat, except for some rolling hills and rocky bluffs. The vegetation consists primarily of aspen mixed with open grasslands. Whitetails predominate throughout eastern Alberta **(Nos. 3 and 4)**, and they're found in good numbers around any suitable cover. Most of the land in southern and eastern Alberta is privately owned.

The range of whitetails extends as far north as the Peace River **(No. 5)**, and some mule deer live in the higher areas at the north end of the province. Most of the northern one-third of Alberta consists of flat spruce country along with muskeg, which isn't good habitat for deer. In general, Alberta's best deer range lies south of Edmonton.

Seasons. In mountain zones along the western boundary and in northern zones, deer seasons usually run from late September through November. In the foothills, parklands, and grasslands, the season generally runs throughout November. Antlerless permits are issued in many units, particularly for whitetails. A bow season of 10 days to three weeks usually precedes the firearms season throughout the province. Nonresidents must be accompanied by a licensed guide to hunt big game.

Records. The world-record nontypical mule deer, with a score of 355⅝, was killed in 1926 near Chip Lake, Alberta. However, only a half-dozen other mule deer from the province have qualified for the record book, and all but one of those were killed before 1950. So it would appear that Alberta is not the place to go for trophy mule deer.

The province's largest typical whitetail antlers listed in Boone and Crockett records scored 188⅛, and the largest nontypical scored 230⅝. About 5 percent of the typical whitetails and 3 percent of nontypicals have come from Alberta. Numerically those figures may not appear outstanding, but considering that most of those record deer have been killed since 1970, and given a growing whitetail population, Alberta shows promise for trophy whitetails.

The future. In the 1950s Alberta had an estimated 175,000 mule deer. Lately the total is between 75,000 and 90,000. The decline in southern and central Alberta has resulted primarily from the clearing of land for farming and subdivisions. The Fish and Wildlife Division, through habitat improvements on critical ranges, plans to increase the total to 100,000 mule deer. Special efforts will be aimed at high-demand areas and regions where mule deer were found historically. It appears that mule deer are slowly repopulating some prairie lands.

During the 1940s the whitetail population was estimated at 60,000. The population is now close to 140,000. The same change—land clearing for farming—that has reduced mule deer numbers has contributed to the increase of whitetails. Whitetails eat farm crops and live comfortably in proximity to man. The Fish and Wildlife Division plans to maintain a population of 125,000 whitetails.

Contact. Energy & Natural Resources, Fish and Wildlife Division, Main Floor, North Tower, Petroleum Plaza, 9945–108 St., Edmonton, AB, Canada T5K 2G6.

BRITISH COLUMBIA

Deer numbers. Roughly 75 percent of British Columbia's 366,200 square miles supports at least one of four subspecies of deer. An estimated population of 119,000 mule deer are spread across 60 percent of the province. Whitetails number about 31,000 and occupy 15 percent. An estimated 310,000 blacktail deer are found in about 20 percent of the province, and 75,000 Sitka deer live on about 5 percent of the land.

Hunters and harvest. British Columbia has about 130,000 resident hunters, and 2,800 of those hunt with bow and arrow. An average of 850 nonresidents hunt deer in British Columbia. No records are kept on nonresident archers.

The average harvest is about 25,000 bucks and 5,000 does. In 1980 hunters killed a record high of 36,079. Average hunting success has been 37 percent. Highest success rates are about 40 percent and the lowest about 30 percent.

In an average year, bowhunters kill 185 deer total and have a success rate of about 12 percent.

Distribution. Whitetails are most abundant in the southeast corner **(No. 1)** in the thick bottomlands along the Columbia, Kootenay, and Kettle rivers. They live throughout the southern interior in scattered pockets of suitable habitat. A separate population also lives along the Peace River near the border of Alberta.

Blacktails, which numericaly are most abundant (among whitetails, mule deer, and Sitka deer), live in the dense rain forests along the coast from the U.S. border to Smith Sound **(No. 2)**. They're numerous throughout Vancouver Island, which has an estimated 200,000 blacktails. Deer distribution is uninterrupted north along the coast, but north of Smith Sound **(No. 3)** the animals are considered Sitka blacktails. Sitka deer live on all of the islands along the northern coast of British Columbia including the Queen Charlotte Islands.

Mule deer are the most widely dis-

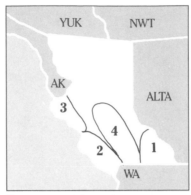

Zones created by author

tributed deer in the province. They live throughout the southern interior from the border of Alberta west to the Coast Range. They range as far north in the Fraser River drainage as Prince George. The Kootenay, Okanagan, and Thompson districts **(No. 4)** have the most mule deer. Some mule deer are scattered through the entire southern two-thirds of the province and along the eastern side as far north as Fort Nelson. The northwestern quarter and the extreme north end of British Columbia do not have any deer.

Seasons. In general, coastal seasons open the first Saturday after Labor Day and close in early December. The basic bag limit is two deer. Inland seasons open in September and run through November or into December. The bag limit is one for more interior areas, although a hunter can take one mule deer and one whitetail in the southeast corner. Nonresidents must be accompanied by a licensed British Columbia guide to hunt any big game in the province.

Records. British Columbia does not appear to be the place to go for trophy deer. A huge nontypical whitetail with a score of 245⅞ was taken in 1905, but in all only a half-dozen whitetails taken in British Columbia are listed by Boone and Crockett. Mule deer don't show much better.

The province produced a nontypical of 265⅜ and a typical of 197⅞, but fewer than 10 mule deer total appear in the record book. The province's record blacktail scored 152⅛, but only 4 percent of the blacktails listed in the record book come from British Columbia. Most of those are at the low end of the listings.

Mule deer (Len Rue Jr. photo)

The future. Deer probably reached peak numbers in the late 1950s and early 1960s, and they dipped to lows in the 1970s. In recent years clearcut logging, large reservoirs, and urban expansion have eliminated much valuable habitat for deer. Mule deer and blacktail populations generally are stable or declining, while the whitetail herd is apparently increasing.

Contact. Ministry of Environment, Fish and Wildlife Branch, Parliament Buildings, Victoria, BC, Canada V8V 1X5.

MANITOBA

Deer numbers. Manitoba has a total area of 251,000 square miles, but only 27 percent of that supports deer. Whitetail deer are estimated to number about 150,000, and mule deer are scarce to nonexistent.

Hunters and harvest. An average of 44,000 residents and about 300 nonresidents have hunted with firearms in Manitoba in recent years. The average kill has been about 26,000 deer (57 percent bucks). The highest recorded kill of 31,000 took place in 1951, and the highest recent harvest was 27,709 (50 percent bucks) in 1981. Average firearms hunting success has been 55 percent, with a high of 65 percent and a low of 36 percent.

The average number of archers has been about 2,000, although this figure increases each year as interest in bowhunting grows. The average bow kill has been about 200 deer each year (bucks and does combined) with a high kill in 1982 of 291. Average bowhunting success has been 13 percent with a high in 1981 of about 17 percent and a low in 1979 of just over 5 percent (when archers were restricted to bucks only).

Distribution. Most of Manitoba's deer live in the agricultural southern one-quarter of the province. In southeast Manitoba **(No. 1)**, wide expanses of hardwood and coniferous forests are interspersed with farm fields. Deer numbers are relatively high in localities with adequate woody cover.

The southwestern area **(No. 2)** consists of rugged river valleys with sand dunes supporting broad expanses of grass mixed with groves of hardwoods. Clumps of aspen, sloughs bordered with willows, and farmlands are extensive throughout this region. This is the most popular deer hunting region in Manitoba.

Zones created by author

The Interlake Region **(No. 3)** contains interspersed ridges and low marshy areas. Aspen parklands provide cover among sedge meadows and numerous farm fields.

In the northwestern part of Manitoba's farm belt **(No. 4)**, deer live in extensive forests of the Riding, Duck, and Porcupine mountains. They also inhabit the large marshes around Lake Manitoba, Lake Winnepeg, and other major bodies of water.

Throughout the northern, interlake, and southeastern regions, 60 percent of the land is privately owned. In the southwest, 85 percent is private. In the northern region, deer densities are very low. Throughout the three southern regions, numbers are considered light overall. In specific localities in the southeast, southwest, and near Lake Manitoba, whitetail densities are medium to heavy. In places where 50 percent or more of the land remains forested, densities may be as high as 50 deer per square mile. Where cover is limited, deer number fewer than 10 per square mile.

Seasons. Firearms seasons vary by area. In the south and southwest, the season usually runs for about two weeks in mid-November. In the north and the extreme east, where more public land and extensive cover exists, the season opens a week earlier than in the north and west. It usually remains open for three weeks.

Archery seasons open in early September and continue into November. Nonresident aliens must hire a guide to hunt legally in Manitoba. Seasons for nonresidents differ from those for residents in some cases.

Records. Manitoba's record typical whitetail, killed in 1980, measured 187⅞. The record nontypical, taken in 1973, measured 256⅝.

The future. Prior to 1900, mule deer were the only deer found in Manitoba. As a result of settlement, land clearing, and other changes, mule deer numbers have declined to zero in the province.

Whitetails were first reported about 1880, but did not become common until the early 1900s. Rapid development of farmlands from 1900 to 1950 created ideal conditions for whitetails. Their numbers hit an all-time high around 1950 of about 200,000. In 1950, hunters killed 20,000 bucks, and the following year during an any-deer season, they harvested 31,000 animals. Since that time, continued clearing for agriculture, heavy hunting, and severe winters, have reduced numbers drastically. The population in 1974 was estimated at 30,000 deer. The deer season was closed for three years, from 1975 through 1977, and deer numbers jumped to about 90,000.

Herds have remained fairly stable, but land clearing continues to destroy more habitat. During a 20-year period starting in the mid-1960s, more than 40 percent of Manitoba's whitetail range was lost to clearing, reservoirs, and other development. Deer hunting will remain good for the near future, but the long-range forecast is not as bright.

Contact. Department of Natural Resources, Box 22, 1495 St. James Street, Winnipeg, Manitoba, Canada R3H 0W9.

NEW BRUNSWICK

Deer numbers. New Brunswick has an area of 27,985 square miles. An estimated 120,000 to 150,000 whitetail deer occupy nearly 100 percent of that area.

Hunters and harvest. An average of 110,000 residents and 3,000 nonresidents hunt deer during firearms seasons each year. Hunters killed a record high of 27,119 deer (12,727 bucks and 14,392 does) in 1983. Average hunter success has been about 23 percent.

New Brunswick held its first special archery season in 1982. In 1983 1,000 residents and 250 nonresidents hunted with bow and arrow and killed 46 deer.

Distribution. The south part of New Brunswick and the St. John River Valley north to Grand Falls **(No. 1)** is glaciated, hilly country with a number of rock outcroppings. Timber dominates the landscape, but this region also has a patchwork of farmlands. This region supports the most deer and highest deer kill in the province. The highest percentage of private land in New Brunswick is centered in this southern region. In general, access to private land is good. Some big timber companies throughout the province put gates on their roads to prevent vehicle traffic, but hunters can still walk in.

The northern two-thirds **(No. 2)** has elevations as high as 2,600 feet, but the mountains are glaciated and tend to be rolling rather than rugged. Spruce-fir forests predominate throughout this region, with some sugar maple, birch, and other species of soft and hardwoods. Whitetail densities are fairly low. Generally this can be considered better moose than deer country.

Seasons. The general firearms season runs for about a month from late October until late November. In

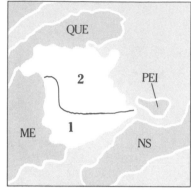

Zones created by author

some units it's a week or so shorter. A special bow season is open for about three weeks in early to mid-October. The bag limit is one deer of either sex. Nonresidents (Canadian and alien) are required to hunt with a guide.

Records. Average field-dressed weight of deer 4½ years old and older is 205 pounds. The heaviest buck on record field-dressed to 307 pounds. No records of antler measurements are available.

The future. Following several mild winters beginning in the mid-1970s, the herd sizes increased through the early 1980s. Some valuable yard areas have been cut, but generally cooperation between landowners and the Fish and Wildlife Branch has been good, and winter ranges have been protected or enhanced. Barring severe winter conditions, good deer populations are expected into the 1990s. Winter weather is the chief limiting factor for deer in New Brunswick.

Contact. Department of Natural Resources, Fish and Wildlife Branch, PO Box 6000, Fredericton, NB, Canada E3B 5H1.

New Brunswick piebald whitetail (R. Moller photo)

NOVA SCOTIA

Deer numbers. Nova Scotia has a total area of 21,425 square miles. An estimated 150,000 whitetail deer live on about 83 percent of that area.

Hunters and harvest. During the late 1970s and early 1980s, an average of 79,000 residents and 750 nonresidents hunted deer each year. Average harvest for that same period was 33,000 deer (20,000 bucks and 13,000 does) with a high in 1983 of 44,500 deer (27,000 bucks). Average firearms success has been 39 percent, with a high of 52 percent in 1982 and a low in 1971 of 28 percent. No separate records are available for archers.

Distribution. On the north peninsula **(No. 1)** the Cobequid Hills, with elevations up to 900 feet and some fairly steep slopes toward the Bay of Fundy, run along the south side of this peninsula. They slope gradually into a flatter plain on the north side. In recent years, this region has been the most productive for deer and has maintained the highest harvest in the province.

On the south peninsula **(No. 2)**, a narrow band of mountains called South Mountain, which has elevations of 600 and 700 feet and fairly gentle slopes, runs along the north side of the peninsula and slopes gradually southward toward the At-

Leonard Lee Rue III photo

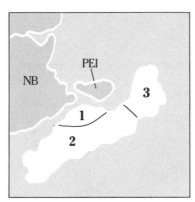

Zones created by author

lantic Ocean. The west end of the south peninsula has fairly rugged land and unproductive, rocky soils. And deer numbers are low. The southern half of the south peninsula, roughly from Halifax eastward to Cape Breton Island, contains the most productive deer country in this region. The deer kill is high here, second only to the north peninsula.

Cape Breton Island **(No. 3)** contains the highest elevations in Nova Scotia. The Highlands on the northern tip rise to elevations of 1,400 feet directly from the ocean. Forests throughout this region have been infected with spruce budworm, and as a result much of the highlands have been clear-cut. Topography on the

south half of Cape Breton is hilly to flat. At one time Cape Breton Island was Nova Scotia's most popular deer hunting ground. But in recent years, increases in deer numbers have not kept pace with other areas of the province, and heaviest hunting pressure has shifted from the island to the mainland.

There is some fruit growing in the Annapolis Valley on the south peninsula, but, in general, agriculture is a minor land use. Nova Scotia is covered primarily with spruce-fir forests, along with some mixed stands of sugar maple, birch, and other hardwoods. Two-thirds of the land is privately owned, but about the only place hunters can't hunt without restriction is on cultivated land.

Seasons. The general season opens the last Friday in October and closes the first Saturday in December. The bag limit is one deer of either sex. One area on the north peninsula has been set aside for bowhunting-only during the regular season, but there are no special bow seasons. Nonresidents are required to hire a guide.

Records. The average weight of 2½-year-old bucks is 160 pounds. No further records have been kept on weight or antler measurements.

The future. Deer numbers have mushroomed since 1975. Extensive clear-cutting for pulpwood has created openings in many forests, and firewood cutting has opened up hardwood stands. Forage growing in these openings has contributed to increasing deer numbers. However, the major factor has been mild winters, during which deer have not even been forced into traditional winter yarding areas. Severe winter weather can take a heavy toll.

Contact. Department of Lands and Forests, PO Box 698, Halifax, NS Canada B3J 2T9.

ONTARIO

Deer numbers. Ontario covers a total of 412,582 square miles. Only a small portion of this, primarily along the southern edge, supports deer. The whitetail deer herd is estimated at 150,000 animals.

Hunters and harvest. In 1983 Ontario had over 12,000 deer hunters who harvested 2,201 deer (65 percent bucks). About 79 percent hunted with rifles and had a success rate of 18 percent; 20 percent hunted with shotguns and had a 16 percent success; 10 percent hunted with bows and had a 7 percent success; and 1 percent hunted with muzzleloaders and had an 18 percent success.

Distribution. Despite its large size, Ontario has a fairly restricted deer range. This range can be divided into three general sections.

The southern agricultural zone **(No. 1)** lies south of the Canadian

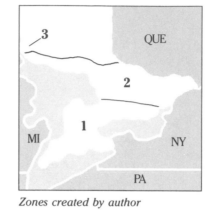

Zones created by author

Shield. This is the most fertile agricultural region in Ontario, and the landscape consists primarily of croplands interspersed with small woodlots and wooded bottomlands along streams and rivers. This region supports the highest deer numbers in Ontario. The eastern end of this zone north of Lake Ontario has a good amount of untilled land with plenty of leafy plants, edge, and second-growth timber to maintain good populations of deer. In the southwestern corner, farmland is more fertile, and 80 percent of Ontario's human population is centered here. Intensified farming and expanding urban areas have reduced good habitat here. Some good deer habitat remains, however, and with mild weather in recent years, deer have become overabundant in specific localities.

The central zone **(No. 2)** covers the southern end of the Canadian shield. The shallow soils here generally are unsuitable for agriculture. The landscape is irregular, rough, and hilly with broad areas of exposed bedrock. Vegetation consists primarily of hardwoods, such as sugar maple and oak trees, along with white pine, hemlock, and other conifers. Deer are common throughout the central zone, but they're not generally as abundant as they are throughout the southern agricultural zone. In the mid-1900s, deer were more numerous in the central zone,

but aging timber stands have reduced high-quality forage.

The northwestern zone **(No. 3)** extends westward from the Nipigon River along the U.S. border. The northern portion of this zone consists of broken hills characteristic of the Canadian Shield. The southern portion is flatter and provides some fertile agricultural land, particularly around Rainy River on the U.S. border. Highest deer numbers live around croplands in this zone.

Seasons. Regulations vary greatly from one management unit to the next. In general, gun seasons are held in October and November, and some units have long bow seasons ranging from October into December. The use of dogs is legal during some seasons. Some units do not allow hunting by nonresidents, and nonresidents are required to hire guides in some areas.

Records. Boone and Crockett records list only one buck from Ontario, a typical whitetail that scored 171⅜.

The future. Deer have a varied history in Ontario. In the early 1900s, market hunters made such inroads on herds in the open southern end that deer became scarce there. At the same time, however, logging, mining, and railroad construction were opening up many of the northern forests, and whitetails became abundant as far north as James Bay. From 1900 until about 1950, Ontario had higher overall deer numbers than at any other time in history. Since 1950, northern forests have grown into older timber, and deer have declined drastically. Even though deer in the southern and central zones have rebounded well, the overall deer population diminished by about two-thirds between 1955 and 1980. Recent management programs have begun to reverse this trend in the southern zones, and deer are increasing there again.

Contact. Ministry of Natural Resources, Toronto, Ontario, Canada, M7A 1W3.

Irene Vandermolen photo

QUEBEC

Deer numbers. Quebec has a total area of 594,860 square miles. An estimated 70,000 whitetail deer live on less than 7 percent of that area.

Hunters and harvest. On the average, 96,000 residents and 2,000 nonresidents hunt during the firearms season. Average harvest for the mainland has been about 4,000 deer (all bucks). In 1983, hunters killed a total of 11,213 deer in Quebec; 4,503 bucks were taken on the mainland, and 6,470 bucks and does were killed on Anticosti Island. Average firearms success has been 5 percent, with a high of 15 percent, and a low of 2 percent. Bowhunters take a few hundred deer annually.

Distribution. The Canadian Shield **(No. 1)** covers most of Quebec north of the St. Lawrence River. Boreal forests, which consist primarily of spruce and balsam fir, blanket this region. Harsh winters severely limit the range of deer. Only small isolated populations are scattered throughout the southern fringe of the Canadian Shield. Predation by wolves also limits deer numbers.

In the St. Lawrence Lowlands **(No. 2)**, roughly south of a line from Quebec City due west to the Ottawa River, agriculture is a predominant land use. There farmlands, especially dairies and hay crops, as well as extensive cornfields, are mixed with timberlands. Near Montreal, as much as 90 percent of the land is farmed, but farther away from the St. Lawrence River, the percentage of woodland is much higher. This region produces the most deer on the Quebec mainland. Most of the land in this area is privately owned. Access

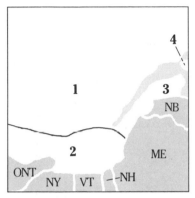

Zones created by author

has not been a major problem north of the St. Lawrence River. South of the river along the U.S. border, private hunting clubs lease the hunting rights to most of the best deer lands.

The Gaspé Peninsula **(No. 3)** supports very little farming. This entire region is heavily timbered, and toward the eastern end, mountains rise to elevations as high as 4,000 feet. At higher elevations, unproductive boreal forests support good numbers of moose but very few deer. Most of the whitetails on the Gaspé live in river valleys that drain to the south, where spruce-fir forests are replaced by balsam fir mixed with birch and maple. Within the range of whitetails in Quebec, the Gaspé sustains the lowest deer harvest per square mile.

Anticosti Island **(No. 4)** is a story unto itself. Deer were introduced to the island in 1896, and the population exploded to highs in the 1930s. Then the population crashed and has gradually rebuilt with only minor fluctuations in recent years. Boreal forests on the island provide very poor habitat, yet deer numbers remain very high. The average harvest rate is 2.5 deer per square mile, and the average kill is 1.5 to 1.7 deer per hunter (the bag limit is two deer). Biologists attribute the overabundance of deer—despite poor habitat—to a complete lack of predators, relatively mild maritime winters, and a lack of poaching. Very few people live on Anticosti.

Seasons. The archery season throughout whitetail range usually runs for two weeks in October. The limit is one deer of either sex. The firearms season on Anticosti Island usually opens in early September and closes in early December. The bag limit is two deer of either sex. On the Gaspé Peninsula, the firearms season runs for a couple weeks in November. In most agricultural zones, it's open for fewer days in November. The bag limit during mainland firearms seasons is one buck. Nonresident deer hunters aren't required to hire a guide.

Records. About 50 percent of the deer harvested are yearlings. On the mainland yearlings field-dress to an average weight of 120 pounds, and a number of deer in the 200-to-250-pound class are taken. On Anticosti Island, they average about 20 percent less.

The future. Deer numbers have increased by two to three times since 1974 when a bucks-only law was adopted. Mild winters have also contributed to the increase, and in the early 1980s, overpopulation appeared to be a problem in some localities. To a large extent, year-to-year deer numbers depend on winter weather, and severe winters will reduce the size of herds drastically. As in northern New Hampshire and Vermont, the spruce budworm has killed vast acreages of timber, and trees needed for cover in winter deer yards have been cut extensively. However, land agencies have worked well with the wildlife agency, and the future looks fairly bright for Quebec's whitetails.

Contact. Wildlife Management Division, Fish and Game Branch, Place de la Capitale 150 East, St-Cyrille Blvd., Quebec City, Quebec, Canada G1R 4Y1.

SASKATCHEWAN

Deer numbers. This province contains 251,700 square miles. An estimated 300,000 to 400,000 whitetails occupy about 60 percent of that territory, and 50,000 to 60,000 mule deer live in about 30 percent.

Hunters and harvest. On the average, 58,000 residents and 1,000 nonresidents hunt deer each year. The recent average annual harvest has been about 38,000 (25,000 bucks and 13,000 does), with a high in 1969 of 49,075 (32,389 bucks). Firearms success has averaged 65 percent, with a low in 1982 of 47 percent.

About 2,000 bowhunters pursue deer in Saskatchewan each fall. Few statistics have been kept on archery harvest, but it appears archers have a success rate of about 9 percent.

Distribution. The terrain throughout Saskatchewan can be described as low relief, which means it varies from flat to rolling hills. That holds true throughout primary deer range.

For management purposes, biologists divide the province into six ecological zones. About 50 percent of the land in the Grasslands Zone **(No. 1)** remains in native short-grass prairie, and the other half is planted in wheat and other grains. The region has little tree cover except in the ravines and bottomlands. Mule deer are the predominant deer species. Crown lands cover nearly 40 percent of the region, and these are largely open to hunting.

About 80 percent of the Farmland Zone **(No. 2)** is under cultivation. The major crop is wheat. The other 20 percent of the land is evenly divided between aspen and native grasslands.

In the Parklands Zone **(No. 3)**, cultivated croplands are mixed with extensive groves of aspen. The aspen provides good winter cover; so deer here generally survive tough winters much better than they do in the southern two zones. This is the prime area for whitetails, and about 40 percent of all the whitetails killed in Saskatchewan come from the Parklands. About 80 percent of the

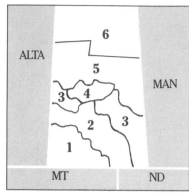

Zones created by author

land in the Farmland and Parklands zones is private, but access to the land remains good among those who ask permission.

The Forest Fringe Zone **(No. 4)** consists of some agricultural land interspersed with mixed woodlands of spruce, aspen, and poplar. Deer numbers are much lower than in the parklands. This is a transition region between prairies and forests.

The Forest Zone **(No. 5)** consists of expansive conifer forests. Hunting pressure remains light because most residents of Saskatchewan prefer hunting farm and parklands to dense forest. As a result, the limit is usually two deer in much of this region. Most whitetails here live in riparian bottomlands containing aspen, willow, poplar, and other leafy browse. As one biologist said, "This is where whitetails and winter meet head on. Following mild winters, deer do well and numbers go up rapidly, but a tough winter wipes out many deer, and then the herds have to rebuild." La Ronge is effectively the northern limit of deer range. All of this zone is Crown land and is open to public hunting.

The Northern Shield **(No. 6)** supports very few deer.

The trophy whitetails for which Saskatchewan is so famous come from throughout the three southern zones. These are open only to Canadian residents. Nonresidents can hunt deer in the Forest Zone. No guide is required.

Seasons. Special archery seasons are held throughout most of the province in September, and rifle seasons take place in early October, but these are open to Saskatchewan residents only. Additional general seasons in November allow residents from other Canadian provinces to hunt in the southern zones. Nonresidents are allowed to hunt deer only in the forest zones during seasons held in November and December. Unfortunately, most of the trophy whitetails in Saskatchewan come from the southern agricultural zones.

Records. The record whitetail, taken in 1983, scored 204⅝ points, and the record nontypical whitetail, also killed in 1983, scored 254. The province record typical mule deer scored 199⅔, and the record nontypical mule deer, 282⅔.

Without question, Saskatchewan leads the way for trophy whitetails. It has nearly 12 percent of the total listings in the Boone and Crockett record book. Unfortunately, nonresident alien hunters are not allowed to hunt agricultural zones where most of the whoppers live.

The future. Prior to 1920, mule deer were dominant, but with the expansion of agriculture, mule deer were virtually eliminated and whitetails became more prevalent. Whitetails thrived and reached a peak of more than 500,000 animals in the 1960s. With continued land clearing, however, whitetail numbers have declined. With poor economic conditions in the 1980s, land clearing for more crops is expected to slow, and whitetail numbers probably will stabilize.

As whitetail numbers have gone down recently, mule deer, under protective regulations, have exploded in the southwestern grasslands. Generous antlerless hunts have been needed to reduce some herds.

Contact. Saskatchewan Parks and Renewable Resources, 3211 Albert St., Regina, SK, Canada S4S 5W6.

BIBLIOGRAPHY

This section of the *Encyclopedia* lists books that the authors recommend, rather than just the books the authors used for research. Each listing includes a brief review followed by the initials of the reviewer, as follows: John Madson (*JM*), George H. Haas (*GHH*), Chuck Adams (*CA*), Dwight Schuh (*DS*), Leonard Lee Rue III (*LLR*), and Neil Soderstrom (*NS*).

Many books in this bibliography can be obtained by consulting *Books in Print* at any bookstore or by writing the publisher. For out-of-print books, your options include libraries; used-book stores; and book dealers that specialize in hunting, firearms, and general sporting books. The dealers offer catalogs for fees that tend to reflect the detail of listings and the costs for publication and postage. Some dealers also conduct book searches; that is, they hunt up the book you want for a fee, which may be modest to considerable, depending on the book's availability and condition. Rare books may be worth hundreds of dollars.

Book dealers

- *Judith Bowman Books*, Pound Ridge Rd., Bedford, NY 10506. Hunting, fishing, natural history. Will search.
- *Henderson and Park*, Fifth and Main, Greenwood, MO 64034. Hunting and fishing. Will search.
- *Pisces & Capricorn Books*, 514 Linden Ave., Albion, MI 49224. Hunting and fishing. Will search.
- *Ray Riling Arms Books Co.*, 6844 Gorsten St., Philadelphia, PA 19119. Hunting, weapons, and related subjects.
- *Rutgers Book Center*, 127 Raritan Ave., Highland Park, NJ 08904. Mainly guns, some hunting.
- *Henry Siegel*, Angler's and Shooter's Bookshelf, Goshen, CT 06756. Will search (regular clients).

PARTS 1 & 2
THE DEER FAMILY and DEER MANAGEMENT

Allen, Durward. *Our Wildlife Legacy.* New York: Funk & Wagnalls Company, 1954. A thorough, professional, and extremely well-written summary of American wildlife conservation and management. One of the classics of conservation, examining such management devices as predator control, hunting, transplanting and restocking, fish and game limits, and carrying capacity, all through the eyes of a deeply experienced wildlife scientist who happens to be an excellent writer.—*JM*

Cahalane, Victor H. *Mammals of North America.* New York: The Macmillan Co., 1961. An invaluable reference for professionals and nonprofessionals, this is a collection of brief but authoritative summaries of the life histories of mammals. Simple, disciplined writing by a veteran wildlife biologist.—*JM*

Davis, John W., Lars H. Karstad and Daniel O. Trainer, editors. *Infectious Diseases of Wild Mammals.* Second edition. Ames: The Iowa State University Press, 1981. A useful and long-needed summary of the infectious diseases, both endemic and introduced, occurring among wild North American mammals. Technical. Extremely well documented and indexed.—*JM*

Hall, E. Raymond. *The Mammals of North America.* Second edition, two volumes. New York: John Wiley & Sons, 1981. This superb reference not only contains identification keys, measurements, and general descriptions of every wild mammal in North America, but also includes detailed range maps for each. It is *the* authoritative source of such range maps and a valuable addition to the serious outdoors library.—*JM*

Halls, Lowell K., editor. *White-Tailed Deer: Ecology and Management.* A Wildlife Management Institute Book. Published in Harrisburg, Pennsylvania by Stackpole Books, 1984. The finest recent summary of the life and times of the whitetail. An exhaustive treatment that includes biology, ecology, research, population management, populations, and habitats, in all American regions. A comprehensive authority of 870 large-format pages.—*JM*

Honacki, James H., Kenneth E. Kinman and James W. Koeppl. *Mammal Species of the World: A Taxonomic and Geographic Reference.* Lawrence, Kansas, published jointly by the Allen Press, Inc., and The Association of Systematics Collections, 1982. This checklist of the world's mammal species provides the latest in scientific species names as well as the geographic ranges of all species. Intended primarily for the researcher, it contains no illustrations nor life history material.—*JM*

Leopold, Aldo. *Game Management.* New York: Charles Scribner's Sons, 1933. This is the keystone of modern American wildlife management and conservation writings. No outdoors library is complete without it.—*JM*

Leopold, Aldo. *A Sand County Almanac.* New York: Oxford University Press, 1949. An American classic, and essential reading for anyone who loves the outdoors. Some of these essays are brief gems of natural history as seen through the eyes of our most eminent modern naturalist-philosopher; some are concise but profound statements of our relationships to land and wildlife as perceived by Leopold, the "father of American game management." A superb collection of graceful, often beautiful essays. Illustrated with drawings by Charles Schwartz.—*JM*

McSpadden, J. Walker, managing editor. *Animals of the World.* Garden City, NY: Garden City Publishing Co., 1947. Consisting of two parts: "Animals of America" and "Animals of Other Lands." This is an interesting bridge between the technical and the popular, and although it was obviously written for the general public it contains letters, records, and life history notes that would be of use and interest to the professional wildlifer and serious hunter.—*JM*

Madson, John. *Game, Gunners, and Biology: The Scientific Approach To Wildlife Management.* Conservation Department, Winchester-Western Division, Olin Corporation. East Alton, Illinois, 1971. A brief summary of the history, problems and successes of professional wildlife management in the United States. Illustrated with cartoons by Oscar Warbach. 48 pages.—*NS*

Madson, John. *The White-tailed Deer.* Conservation Department, Olin Mathieson Chemical Corporation, East Alton, Illinois, 1961. A concise summary of the biology, management, hunting, and future of the whitetail. Illustrated with photos, and drawings by Charles Schwartz. Paperback, 108 pages.—*NS*

Rue, Leonard Lee, III. *Complete Guide to Game Animals: A Field Book of North American Species.* Second edition. New York: Outdoor Life Books, Times Mirror Magazines Inc., 1981. In this small-format but comprehensive 638-page volume, the author has included just about everything the average outdoorsman would want to know about our American game animals, large and small. Life histories, physical descriptions, ranges, predators, and status. Another must for the outdoors library.—*JM*

Rue, Leonard Lee, III. *The Deer of North America.* New York: Outdoor Life Books, Times Mirror Magazines, Inc., 1978. An excellent expansion of his earlier work on whitetails, this book includes material on blacktails and mule deer as well. In three parts: The Animal and Its Behavior, How the Year Goes, and Toward Sound Deer Management.—*JM*

Schmidt, John L. and Douglas L. Gilbert, editors. *Big Game of North America.* A Wildlife Management Institute Book. Published in Harrisburg, Pennsylvania, by Stackpole Books, 1978. The first in WMI's trilogy on big game, this is the most authoritative and comprehensive work on the subject. Includes the 14 North American big-game species and also introduced big game. Following the specific summaries are excellent sections on early management, behavior, populations, nutrition, habitat changes, predators, and hunting management. Illustrated with excellent drawings and photos, 494 pages.—*JM*

Schwartz, Charles W. and Elizabeth R. Schwartz. *The Wild Mammals of Missouri.* Columbia: University of Missouri Press and Missouri Dept. of Conservation, 1981. Written and illustrated by a widely acclaimed husband-and-wife team of biologists, this excellent book bridges the gap between specialized scientific studies and popular handbooks. Contains nearly 500 drawings (66 of which are full page) by Charles Schwartz, one of America's most distinguished wildlife artists. The text is equally impressive: accurate, thorough and readable.—*JM*

Seton, Ernest Thompson. *Lives of Game Animals,* Vol. 3. New York: Literary Guild of America, Inc. 1937. This is the final edition of Seton's great four-volume classic on American game animals, including all species of American deer. An excellent example of the classic naturalist's writings, with anecdotes and examples gathered during a lifetime of observation. Although some of the material is questionable in light of subsequent research, this is a valuable addition to any library. The original volumes are long out of print, and expensive.—*JM*

Taylor, Walter P., editor. *The Deer of North America.* The Stackpole Company, Harrisburg, Pennsylvania, and the Wildlife Management Institute, Washington, D.C., 1956. At the time of publication, and years afterward, this was the authoritative book on the biology, distribution, and management of whitetails, mule deer, and blacktails. This is an excellent summary, and although some of it is now dated, it still stands as a notable reference.—*JM*

Thorne, E. Tom, Newton Kinston, William R. Jolley, and Robert C. Bergstrom, editors. *Diseases of Wildlife in Wyoming.* Second edition. Cheyenne: Wyoming Game and Fish Department, 1962. A thorough account of the viruses, bacteria, protozoa, parasites, and toxic plants affecting major species of Wyoming wildlife. Includes starvation in wild ruminants, lead poisoning, and field collection and preservation of specimens. Technical, but clearly illustrated and written. A bargain in paperback.—*JM*

Trefethen, James B. *An American Crusade for Wildlife.* Published by Winchester Press and the Boone and Crockett Club, 1975. Probably the finest and most complete summary of the North American conservation movement ever published. With the efforts of the Boone and Crockett Club as a unifying element, this excellent work traces the development of conservation from the late 1800s to the 1970s.—*JM*

Trippensee, Reuben E. *Wildlife Management: Upland Game and General Principles.* New York: McGraw-Hill Book Company, Inc., 1948. One of the earliest textbooks of modern game management, this includes three sections on farm, forest and wilderness wildlife. The distribution, life history, mortality and management of the most important large and small game species is summarized. A landmark in literature of North American wildlife and its management.—*JM*

Wallmo, Olof C., editor. *Mule and Black-tailed Deer of North America.* A Wildlife Management Institute Book. Lincoln: University of Nebraska Press, 1981. The immediate predecessor of the Institute's book on whitetails, this exhaustive treatment of the western deer touches all bases: distribution, habitats, biology, nutrition, management. Heavily illustrated, it is 605 pages of the best and most recent technical information on the subject.—*JM*

Walker, Ernest P. *Mammals of the World.* Fourth edition, two volumes. Baltimore: Johns Hopkins University Press, 1983. Since the 1964 first publication, this has been the standard reference on the world's mammals. Illustrated with photographs, each entry notes the range, measurements, and coloration of the mammal, and usually includes interesting comment on life history. 1,500 pages.—*JM*

Wildlife Conservation: Principles and Practices. The Wildlife Society. Washington, D.C. 1979. A summary of modern wildlife conservation subjects written by top professionals. Originally meant as a manual for the Game and Fish Management Short Course begun at Colorado State University for citizen conservationists, fish and game commissioners, etc., it has also been widely adopted as a college text. Includes nearly 50 chapters of fish and game management problems, methods, and public relations.—*JM*

PART 3

FIREARMS AND SHOOTING

Barnes, Frank C., *Cartridges of the World.* Fourth edition. Northbrook, IL: DBI Books Inc., 1984. Describes rifle, handgun, shotgun, and muzzleloader cartridges in detail. Gives history of each cartridge, dimensions and, very often, reloading data. Exhaustive treatment of the entire subject. Illustrations of each cartridge and numerous dimensional drawings. Ballistic tables. Softcover. 384 large-format pages.—*GHH*

Bridges, Toby. *Advanced Muzzleloader's Guide.* South Hackensack, NJ: Stoeger Publishing Co., 1985. Starts where the Ned Roberts book (see below) leaves off with a chapter on modern replica muzzleloaders. Goes on to describe their use with great emphasis on safety. Especially good when discussing varied methods of loading. Title is misleading. This book was written with the beginner in mind but it does include much material for the "advanced" shooter. Well illustrated; softcover in large format. 256 pages.—*GHH*

Carmichel, Jim. *Do-it-Yourself Gunsmithing.* New York: Outdoor Life Books, Times Mirror Magazines Inc., 1977. A profusely illustrated, step-by-step description of gunsmithing projects within the capabilities of home craftsmen with limited tools. Includes a wealth of information on how to do the work efficiently without great expense. 372 pages.—*GHH*

Carmichel, Jim. *Jim Carmichel's Book of the Rifle.* New York: Outdoor Life Books, Times Mirror Magazines Inc., 1985. Comprehensive discussion of hunting rifles, including .22 rimfires. It includes much on how the arms

were developed and designed, how to use these firearms, and a great deal on ballistics. Information is authoritative but is presented in easy-to-absorb style with unfailing wit. 608 pages; profusely illustrated.—*GHH*

Dunlap, Roy. *Gun Owner's Book of Care, Repair and Improvement.* New York: Popular Science/Outdoor Life Books, Times Mirror Magazines Inc., 1974. A gunsmith describes care and alteration of rifles, handguns, shotguns, muzzleloaders, and airguns with special emphasis on the home workshop. Concentrates on workshop methods rather than work on specific models. Illustrated. 336 pages.—*GHH*

Frankonia Jagd (chain of West German retail stores that caters to hunters and shooters). *Ratgeber für den Jäger und Schützen* (Counsellor for Hunters and Shooters), published annually in German. Munich, West Germany. In many ways, this is the equivalent of *Gun Digest* or *Shooter's Bible.* Contains much useful information on firearms currently available in Germany, including many made in Czechoslovakia, Yugoslavia, and the Soviet Union. Excellent metric ballistic tables. Includes accessories and clothing for the hunt. Profusely illustrated; 400 pages or more. Softcover.—*GHH*

Hogg, Ivan. *The Complete Illustrated Encyclopedia of the World's Firearms.* New York: A&W Publishers, Inc., originally published in Britain by Quarto Publishing Limited, 1978. Fourteen chapters provide a good overall review of firearms history from earliest times. The main body of the work consists of A to Z entries. Authoritative specifications. Includes rifles, automatic weapons, handguns, some light artillery. Very little on shotguns. Profusely illustrated. 320 large-format pages.—*GHH*

Jarrett, William S., editor. *Shooter's Bible* (published annually). South Hackensack, New Jersey: Stoeger Publishing Co., 1985. In many ways, competitive with *Gun Digest* (see below). Includes feature articles and detailed specifications on current firearms and ammunition. More material on ammunition, ballistics, and reloading than in *Gun Digest.* Excellent "Gunfinder" index. Both publications should be consulted if you want to buy any specialized firearm. Profusely illustrated; softcover; 575 pages.—*GHH*

Keith, Elmer. *Sixguns by Keith.* Harrisburg, Pennsylvania: The Stackpole Co., 1955. No one who wishes to understand American revolvers should be without this classic book. Especially informative about early attempts to develop modern magnum revolvers. Many tips on handloading heavy revolver cartridges. Includes much colorful and humorous anecdotal material. Well illustrated. 308 pages.—*GHH*

Nonte, George C., Jr. *Firearms Encyclopedia.* New York: Outdoor Life Books, Times Mirror Magazines Inc., 1973. Terse, clear definitions of firearms terminology and nomenclature, though some entries are lengthy and explain complex subjects. An excellent book for reference when reading in a new firearms field. Well illustrated, 342 pages.—*GHH*

O'Connor, Jack. *The Rifle Book.* Revised edition. New York: Alfred A. Knopf, 1964. *The* classic American book on hunting rifles and how to use them. Though much of the specific data has been outmoded, O'Connor's remarks on how to shoot, told with candor and humor, will remain useful and interesting as long as firearms are used to hunt. The illustrations are inadequate but the text is superb. 332 pages.—*GHH*

Reid, William. *The Lore of Arms: A Concise History of Weaponry.* New York: Facts on File, Inc., 1984. A concise study of the development of all forms of weapons from the earliest times. It is especially useful on the relationship between hand-held firearms and the crossbow, edged weapons, and other devices. Includes artillery. Concentrates on military arms, but, in doing so, gives a broad picture of arms throughout the world. Charming period art. Lack of chapter titles and subject index is annoying. Pocket size; 256 pages.—*GHH*

Roberts, Ned H. *The Muzzle-Loading Cap Lock Rifle.* Harrisburg, Pennsylvania: The Military Service Publishing Company (Stackpole), 1947. The most-influential book on this form of firearm. The author discusses target rifles and hunting rifles. A virtue is that he describes the original muzzleloaders as used by authentic old-time shooters of previous generations. In this way, the reader obtains a thorough-going understanding of these guns that applies to the use of modern replica muzzleloaders. Fascinating photographs of a great variety of rifles, all originals. 308 pages.—*GHH*

Page, Warren. *The Accurate Rifle.* New York: Winchester Press, 1973. One of the best-known gun writers describes how to tune a rifle to obtain the best-possible accuracy and how to select or handload the most-accurate ammunition. Though some material is dated, this book remains the best on squeezing ultimate accuracy out of a rifle. Illustrated. 238 pages.—*GHH*

Ramage, C. Kenneth., editor. *Lyman Shotshell Handbook.* Third edition. Middlefield, Connecticut: Lyman Products Corp., 1984. Comprehensive discussion of shotshell reloading followed by detailed reloading data on components for almost any conceivable cartridge. Includes procedures and data for rifled-slug and buckshot loads. Softcover; profusely illustrated. 312 pages.—*GHH*

Ramage, C. Kenneth, editor. *Lyman Reloading Handbook.* 46th Edition. Middlefield, Connecticut: Lyman Products Corp., 1982. Generally describes rifle and handgun ammunition and then provides detailed reloading data for a comprehensive list of rifle and handgun cartridges. Excellent ballistic data. Softcover; profusely illustrated. 464 pages.—*GHH*

Ramage, C. Kenneth, editor. *Lyman Cast Bullet Handbook.* Third edition. Middlefield, Connecticut: Lyman Products Corp., 1980. Explains in detail how to cast lead bullets and load them into a comprehensive series of cartridge cases. Much of the information on casting applies to shotgun slugs as well as rifle and handgun projectiles. Excellent ballistic tables. Softcover; profusely illustrated. 416 pages.—*GHH*

Smith, W.H.B. *Book of Rifles.* Harrisburg, Pennsylvania: The Stackpole Company, 1960. Second edition. After a brief history of firearms development, the author describes the military rifles of each country in some detail, up to and including the semi-automatics of World War II. Also included are briefer descriptions of sporting arms. Chief virtue is that detailed text and good sectional and cutaway drawings really tell the reader how rifles function down to the last detail. Well illustrated. 576 pages.—*GHH*

Wallack, L.R. *American Pistol and Revolver Design and Performance.* New York: Winchester Press, 1978. A theoretical and practical discussion of handguns and how to use them. Much information on handgun ammunition. Well illustrated; 234 pages.—*GHH*

Warner, Ken, editor. *Gun Digest* (published annually). Northbrook, Illinois: DBI Books Inc. Includes feature articles and various aspects of firearms but the majority of the work is devoted to specifications of currently available U.S. and imported firearms and accessories. Heavily concentrates on firearms rather than ammunition and ballistics. Includes an excellent Directory of the Arms Trade. Softcover; over 400 pages.—*GHH*

Wood, J.B. *Gun Care, Cleaning and Refinishing* (two volumes). Northbrook, IL: DBI Books Inc., 1985. Up-to-date and almost too detailed on some subjects. If you have a gun, any gun, and want to care for it properly and perhaps improve it through modifications, this softcover set will be useful. Profusely illustrated. 320 pages total for both volumes.—*GHH*

PARTS 4–8

BOWHUNTING, HUNTING GEAR & METHODS, AFTER THE DEER IS DOWN, TAXIDERMY & TANNING

Acerrano, Anthony J. *The Outdoorsman's Emergency Manual.* South Hackensack, NJ: Stoeger Publishing Co., 1981. This 337-page manual covers virtually every emergency a hunter is apt to encounter, from poison oak to snakebite to broken legs. Includes survival tips for hunters lost or hurt afield, practical first aid, and identification of edible plants. A handy and complete guide to coping with the entire spectrum of trouble in the woods.—*CA*

Adams, Chuck. *ABC's of Bowhunting.* North Palm Beach: Archery Manufacturers Organization, 1978. This basic introduction to modern bowhunting equipment and technique lays a solid groundwork for more extensive research on the subject. Heavily illustrated to clearly show shooting techniques, equipment preparation, and other essential bowhunting skills.—*NS*

Adams, Chuck. *Bowhunter's Digest.* Northfield, IL: DBI Books, Inc., 1981. This 288-page, heavily illustrated book details the latest in bow-shooting gear, shooting technique, and archery hunting methods used by North American bowhunters. Includes a complete photo how-to sequence of bow-shooting basics plus information on bow tuning, archery safety afield, and special trophy-hunting methods.—*NS*

Adams, Chuck. *The Complete Book of Bowhunting.* New York: Winchester Press, 1978. This fine book is exactly what its name implies, beginning with tips on selecting basic bow-shooting equipment, discussing in depth how to use this equipment, and then explaining how to set up close-range shots with bow-and-arrow tackle. An excellent general reference with plenty of lively anecdotes.—*NS*

Adams, Chuck. *The Complete Guide to Bowhunting Deer.* Northfield, IL: DBI Books, Inc., 1983. This informative, A-to-Z instruction book on bowhunting discusses particulars of equipment selection and use, deer-hunting technique, trailing and tracking methods, and field care of trophies. It also includes unique, well-illustrated sections on how to tune a bow for accuracy and how to vary bow-shooting style to improve accuracy. Very heavily illustrated with black-and-white photos. —*NS*

Bear, Fred. *Fred Bear's World of Archery.* Garden City, NY: Doubleday and Co. Inc., 1979. This unique book by the dean of American bowhunters includes chapters on the history of archery, archery organizations in North America, Olympic competition, and the mental aspects of hitting a target. Good reading for anyone interested in trends in target and hunting archery.—*CA*

Brister, Bob. *Shotgunning—the Art and the Science.* New York: Winchester Press, 1976. A detailed look at how to select scatterguns and what makes them work. Sections on choke selection and patterning are especially informative for deer hunters, with dozens of cause and effect photographs.—*CA*

Gillelan, G. Howard. *The Complete Book of Bow & Arrow.* Harrisburg, PA: Stackpole Books, 1977. A general how-to book on all phases of target archery, bowhunting, and bowfishing. Includes special sections on how to make archery a career and what the future of archery is likely to be.—*CA*

Grantz, Gerald J. *Home Book of Taxidermy and Tanning.* Harrisburg, PA: Stackpole Books, 1969. How any novice can become a semi-professional taxidermist at home. Includes chapters on mounting trophy deer heads. The chapter on novelty taxidermy is especially informative

and useful for the average deer hunter.—*CA*

Helgeland, Glenn. *Complete Guide to Bowhunting.* Englewood Cliffs, NJ: Prentice-Hall, Inc., 1975. This 262-page volume takes a close look at bows and arrows for big game hunting, methods for taking deer and other large animals, and special methods for dropping trophy game. Small-game hunting and bowfishing also covered in detail.—*CA*

Latham, Sid. *Knives and Knifemakers.* New York: Winchester Press, 1976. A well-researched book on custom knife design. The sections on knife steel and knife care are of special interest to any serious deer hunter. Very well illustrated.—*CA*

McFall, Waddy F. *Taxidermy Step by Step.* New York: Winchester Press, 1975. A book designed to help train the aspiring professional taxidermist. Details all equipment necessary to mount birds, small game, and big game, and illustrates such complex procedures as making manikins and ear liners, making fur rugs, and making artificial teeth, tongues, and eyes. Has an extensive section on taxidermy formulas.—*CA*

Sparano, Vin T. *Complete Outdoors Encyclopedia.* New York: Times Mirror Magazines, Inc., 1986. Second edition. Exactly what its title implies, this 607-page reference volume covers every phase of the outdoors from hunting and shooting to game birds and animals, camping, boating, hunting dogs, and first aid. A veritable storehouse of knowledge anyone can benefit by. Heavily illustrated.—*CA*

Thornberry, Russell. *Trophy Deer of Alberta.* Rocky Mountain House: Greenhorn Publishing Ltd., 1982. A heavily illustrated compilation of magnum-sized whitetail deer and mule deer taken in Alberta by gunners and archers. Includes a unique new antler-scoring system and excellent discussions of deer habits and habitat.—*CA*

Warner, Ken. *The Practical Book of Knives.* New York: Winchester Press, 1976. A sportsman's view of knife selection, use, and care. Chapters on knife terminology and pocket knives are especially complete and informative. Very well illustrated.—*CA*

Weiss, John. *Venison: From Field to Table.* New York: Outdoor Life Books, Times Mirror Magazines Inc., 1984. The most complete deer-care guide available to hunters. Over 360 pages, with sections on judging deer meat on the hoof, transporting deer, camp care of meat, taxidermy tips, and butchering at home. Over 200 venison recipes included.—*CA*

Zumbo, Jim. *Hunting America's Mule Deer.* Tulsa: Winchester Press, 1981. An intricate look at hunting America's largest-racked species of deer. The author guides you through facts on mule-deer distribution, basic hunting technique, specialized deer-bagging methods, and carcass care from field to freezer. Good basic reading for beginners and experts alike.—*CA*

PART 9
TROPHY RECORDS

Coziah, Calvin. *Bucks, Bows, and Campfires.* Soda Springs, Idaho, Coziah Enterprises, 1981. This self-published book was written by one of the best bowhunters of modern times. Coziah's ideas and lore on hunting trophy mule deer make this book worthwile for all serious deer hunters.—*DS*

Darner, Kirt. *How to Find Giant Bucks.* Montrose, Colorado, Kirt Darner, 1983. This self-publisher may be the most successful hunter of all time for big mule deer. He shares his techniques and his knowledge of places to find trophy mule deer. A well-written book with lots of interesting anecdotes. The trophy mule deer hunter's bible. 283 pages.—*DS*

Fitz, Grancel. *How to Measure and Score Big-Game Trophies.* Fort Wayne, IN: Blue-J Inc., Publishers, revised 1977. The authoritative guide to measuring big-game heads and antlers. The late Grancel Fitz was the primary force behind the present scoring system, and he presented here all the facts any trophy hunter needs to score his own animals. The book includes score charts for North American big game. 135 pages.—*DS*

Pope and Young Club. *Bowhunting Big Game Records of North America.* Moscow, ID: Pope and Young Club. Revised periodically. This official record book for big-game bowhunting in North America contains all of the latest record heads. The book also contains history of the Pope and Young Club, as well as chapters on hunting technique and stories behind world-record heads. An excellent guide for bowhunters planning a big-game hunt. Over 250 pages.—*DS*

Boone and Crockett Club. *Records of North American Big Game.* Alexandria, VA: Boone and Crockett Club, revised periodically. When most hunters refer to *the* record book, this is it. It lists all of the largest big-game heads ever recorded, and can thus serve as a primary reference for anyone planning a trophy deer hunt. Also included are the history of the Boone and Crockett Club, stories behind the record heads, and more. Over 400 pages.—*DS*

Reneau, Jack and Susan. *Colorado's Biggest Bucks and Bulls.* Colorado Springs, CO: Colorado Big Game Trophy Records, Inc., 1983. Basically a collection of photos and stories about many huge deer and elk taken in Colorado. Because Colorado is far and away the premier state for trophy mule deer, this book offers valuable insights for trophy hunters. 275 pages.—*DS*

Rhothhaar, Roger. *In Pursuit of Trophy Whitetails.* Fort Wayne, IN: Blue-J Inc., Publishers, 1982. Essentially a collection of articles published in *Bowhunter* magazine, this paperback book doesn't have a lot of continuity, but it does offer great tips on hunting for oversized whitetails. The author hunts with bow and arrow, but his observations also apply to firearm hunting. 112 pages, softcover.—*DS*

Wootters, John. *Hunting Trophy Deer.* New York, Winchester Press, 1977. This book could more accurately be called "Hunting Trophy Texas Whitetails." Nevertheless, it's a fine book with excellent lore on deer hunting that applies anywhere. It has especially good information on judging trophy deer and on management programs required to produce big bucks. It's beautifully illustrated with many photos. The photos alone are worth the book price. 251 pages.—*DS*

PART 10
SAFETY, SURVIVAL, AND FIRST AID

American Medical Association. *The American Medical Association's Handbook of First Aid and Emergency Care.* New York: Random House, 1980. This presents first aid for most common emergency diseases and injuries. It's organized alphabetically and has many cross-references for quick access. Drawings clearly show most procedures. 235 pages.—*DS*

Boswell, John, editor. *The U.S. Armed Forces Survival Manual.* New York: Rawson, Wade Publishers, Inc., 1980. An overview of survival techniques under emergency conditions around the world, from arctic to equatorial. Because the book covers so much ground, discussion are often brief. Over 300 pages.—*DS*

Breyfogle, Newell D. *The Common Sense Medical Guide and Outdoor Reference.* New York: McGraw-Hill, Inc., 1981. More than half of this book deals with first aid. Discussions are fairly complete. The book also offers some tips on weather, rescue, shelters, path finding and other aspects of survival. Small enough to slip in glove compartment of car. 410 pages.—*DS*

Brown, Tom, Jr., with Brandt Morgan. *Tom Brown's Field Guide to Wilderness Survival.* New York: A Berkley Book, 1983. Written by a primitive-survival expert, this book contains lore that would serve you in living off the land. Emphasizes building fires with primitive methods, constructing shelter with natural materials, eating wild plants and animals. 287 pages.—*DS*

Elias, Thomas S., and Peter A. Dykeman. *Field Guide to North American Edible Wild Plants.* New York: Outdoor Life Books, Times Mirror Magazines Inc., 1982. A complete look at edible wild plants across the United States. Color photos show plants in detail. For the person who wants to eat wild fare. 285 pages.—*DS*

Fry, Alan. *Wilderness Survival Handbook: A Practical, All-season Guide to Short-trip Preparation and Survival Techniques for Hikers, Skiers, Backpackers, Canoeists, Travelers in Light Aircraft—and Anyone Stranded in the Bush.* New York: St. Martin's Press, 1981. The subtitle tells it all. Illustrated with drawings, the book gives a rounded view of techniques that will keep you alive during outdoors emergencies. 285 pages.—*DS*

Houston, Charles S. *Going Higher: The Story of Man and Altitude.* Burlington, Vermont: Charles S. Houston, 1983. Explores problems of high-mountain travel in extreme detail. The information on high-altitude problems makes the book worthwhile for any hunter, particularly in the western mountains. But the book also explains physiological concepts that make it valuable for all outdoorsmen. Excellent book. 273 pages.—*DS*

Kals, W.S. *Land Navigation Handbook: The Sierra Club Guide to Map and Compass.* San Francisco: Sierra Club Books, 1983. A thorough guide to choosing a compass and using map and compass to find your way in the outdoors. Also gives many other tips on pathfinding, such as using natural signs. In softcover, it's small enough to fit into a pack. 230 pages.—*DS*

Levy, Charles K. *A Field Guide to Poisonous Plants and Mushrooms of North America.* Brattleboro, VT: The Stephen Greene Press, 1984. This book emerges as an obvious companion and supplement to *Field Guide to North American Edible Wild Plants.* It details most of the significant dangerous and bothersome plants of North America. Well illustrated with photos and line drawings. 178 pages.—*DS*

Levy, Charles K. *A Field Guide to Dangerous Animals of North America.* Brattleboro, VT: The Stephen Greene Press, 1983. A complete rundown of poisonous or vicious animals, from insects to snakes, fishes to mammals. Illustrated with color photos and drawings. It tells how to avoid problems and how to treat bites, stings, and wounds inflicted by animals.—*DS*

Schuh, Dwight R. *Modern Outdoor Survival: Outdoor Gear and Savvy to Bring You Back Alive.* New York: Arco Publishing, 1983. Emphasizes prevention and preparation rather than knowledge of primitive survival skills. Gives the basics for gear and common-sense knowledge safe, trouble-free outings. 182 pages.—*NS*

Simer, Peter, and John Sullivan. *The National Outdoor Leadership School's Wilderness Guide.* New York, Simon & Schuster, 1983. More than another guide to wilderness survival, this book presents backcountry camping techniques that will keep you safe and comfortable. It serves as a survival manual and as a wilderness camping guide with tips for backpack selection, lightweight stoves and food. 344 pages.—*DS*

PART 11
DEER WATCHING AND PHOTOGRAPHY

Angel, Heather. *The Book of Nature Photography.* New York: Knopf, 1982. Written by one of the most talented wildlife photographers, this 222-page book covers every aspect of photography and is well grounded in the basics. The mammal section will be of great help in photographing deer.—*LLR*

Barley, Adrian and Adrian Holloway. *The Book of Color Photography.* New York: Knopf, 1979. The 216 large-format pages contain a complete course in photography.—*LLR*

Bauer, Erwin. *Erwin Bauer's Deer in Their World.* New York: Outdoor Life Books, Times Mirror Magazines Inc., 1983. Great deer photos, by a truly great deer photographer—and advice on how you, too, can take similar photos. Deer in their world, through the seasons and throughout the world. 256 pages, mainly in full color.—*LLR*

Bauer, Erwin A. *Hunting With a Camera.* New York: Winchester Press, 1974. The author has been everywhere, seen everything, and photographed it. Although sections of this 324-page book describe other countries, the emphasis is on the United States, and hoofed animals.—*LLR*

Bauer, Erwin and Peggy. *Photographing the West: A State-by-State Guide.* Flagstaff, Arizona: Northland Press, 1980. "Must" information for anyone seeking to photograph wildlife in the western half of the United States. 204 pages.—*LLR*

Freeman, Michael. *The Complete Book of Wildlife and Nature Photography.* New York: Simon & Schuster, 1981. An exceedingly good mix of photographs, drawings, and text, giving a complete course in outdoor photography.—*LLR*

Rue, Leonard Lee III. *How I Photograph Wildlife and Nature.* New York: W. W. Norton, 1984. A distillation of the experience of the most widely published wildlife photographer. No punches pulled. The facts and secrets are here to help everyone take better photos of deer, for which the author is famed, as well as all other wildlife. This is *the* handbook on wildlife photography.—*NS*

Shaw, John. *The Nature Photographer's Complete Guide to Professional Field Techniques.* New York: Amphoto, 1984. In these 144 large-format pages you will see why Shaw has become such an acclaimed photographer. His artistic touch is seen in every photo, and he tells you how you can do it too.—*LLR*

Wootters, John and Jerry T. Smith. *Wildlife Images: A Complete Guide to Outdoor Photography.* Los Angeles: Petersen Publishing Company, 1981. Wootters is as well known for his deer articles as Smith is for his deer photographs. In 180 large-format pages, these men share their knowledge of deer and how to photograph them.—*LLR*